ISSUES IN GLOBAL BUSINESS

Sara Miller McCune founded SAGE Publishing in 1965 to support the dissemination of usable knowledge and educate a global community. SAGE publishes more than 1000 journals and over 800 new books each year, spanning a wide range of subject areas. Our growing selection of library products includes archives, data, case studies and video. SAGE remains majority owned by our founder and after her lifetime will become owned by a charitable trust that secures the company's continued independence.

Los Angeles | London | New Delhi | Singapore | Washington DC | Melbourne

ISSUES IN GLOBAL BUSINESS

SELECTIONS FROM *SAGE BUSINESS RESEARCHER*

Introduction by Mamoun Benmamoun, Ph.D.

SAGE reference

Los Angeles | London | New Delhi | Singapore | Washington DC | Melbourne

SAGE

FOR INFORMATION:

SAGE Publications, Inc.
2455 Teller Road
Thousand Oaks, California 91320
E-mail: order@sagepub.com

SAGE Publications Ltd.
1 Oliver's Yard
55 City Road
London, EC1Y 1SP
United Kingdom

SAGE Publications India Pvt. Ltd.
B 1/I 1 Mohan Cooperative Industrial Area
Mathura Road, New Delhi 110 044
India

SAGE Publications Asia-Pacific Pte. Ltd.
18 Cross Street #10-10/11/12
China Square Central
Singapore 048423

Printed in the United States of America

Library of Congress Control Number: 2021930994

This book is printed on acid-free paper.

Senior Acquisitions Editor: Andrew Boney
Assistant Editor: Tamara Tanso
Production Editor: Astha Jaiswal
Copy Editor: QuADS Prepress Pvt. Ltd
Typesetter: Hurix Digital
Proofreader: Ellen Brink
Cover Designer: Candice Harman
Marketing Manager: Brianna Griffith

21 22 23 24 25 10 9 8 7 6 5 4 3 2 1

BRIEF CONTENTS

DETAILED CONTENTS

ABOUT THE AUTHORS

Matthew Benjamin is a freelance journalist in Washington following economic and trade policy. He is also an editorial consultant at the World Bank and the International Monetary Fund.

Mamoun Benmamoun (Ben), Ph.D. is currently an assistant professor of international business at the Boeing Institute of International Business at the Richard Chaifetz School of Business, Saint Louis University. His research interests center on international e-business strategies, foreign entry modes, and the political economy of international trade and finance. His practical experience includes global market intelligence, data analytics, and localization and cultural customization of digital content.

Jonathan Broder is a Washington-based reporter and editor. He was a senior writer for Newsweek, a senior editor at Congressional Quarterly and served as a foreign correspondent in the Middle East, South Asia and the Far East for the Chicago Tribune. Broder's writing also has appeared in The New York Times Magazine, The Washington Post, Smithsonian and the World Policy Journal, among other publications.

Marcia Clemmitt is a veteran social policy reporter who previously served as editor-in-chief of Medicine & Health and staff writer for The Scientist. She has also been a high school math and physics teacher. She holds a liberal arts and sciences degree from St. John's College in Annapolis, Md., and a master's degree in English from Georgetown University. Her recent reports for CQ Researcher, an imprint of SAGE, include "Humanities Education" and "Government Spending."

Vickie Elmer works as a business journalist and creativity and careers coach. Her articles appear in The Washington Post and Crain's Detroit Business among others. She and a group of artists and entrepreneurs launched a startup nonprofit called Mint Artists Guild in Detroit that helps high school artists develop skills and opportunities to sell their work, including jewelry and fashion items. She buys most of her "fashion clothing" at art fairs or vintage and resale shops.

Born in Caracas, Venezuela, in the midst of the 1970s oil boom, **Ángel González** has dedicated a big part of his journalism career to covering the energy industry. He was the bureau chief for Dow Jones in Houston until 2013. He wrote about oil companies, OPEC and the death of Hugo Chavez for Dow Jones Newswires and The Wall Street Journal. He lives in the Seattle area.

After graduating from The George Washington University, **Heather Kerrigan** started her journalism career at Governing magazine, reporting on state and local politics and policy, with a focus on public workforce, environment, health care, education and technology issues. Since co-founding River Horse Communications, Heather has offered freelance editorial services and blogs for two government-focused publications. She is the author of the book "Retire Rich with Your 401(k) Plan."

Patrick Marshall is a freelance writer in Seattle who writes about public policy and technology issues. He is a technology columnist for The Seattle Times and Government Computer News. He holds a B.A. in anthropology from the University of California, Santa Cruz, and a master's degree in international studies from the Fletcher School of Law and Diplomacy, a program of Harvard and Tufts universities.

Micheline Maynard is a veteran business journalist who has worked for The New York Times and NPR (National Public Radio). She is the creator of the Culinary Woman Newsletter and podcast, and the crowdfunded journalism site Curbing Cars, which looks at the future of transportation. She writes on food topics for Forbes.com and The Takeout and writes about American politics for ABC Australia. Maynard has taught at the University of Michigan, Arizona State University and Central Michigan University.

Andy McSmith is a veteran British journalist who has worked for many years as a top political correspondent and political editor for major newspapers in the United Kingdom, including The Independent, The Observer and the Daily Telegraph. He has written books about Great Britain in the Margaret Thatcher era, the British Labour Party and its leaders, and a history of Soviet artists during Stalin's reign.

Julie Morse is a freelance journalist and researcher based in San Francisco and Mexico City. She focuses on immigration, health care and the prison system. She has previously written for The Atlantic, Vice News and Pacific Standard.

Matt Mossman is a global economics journalist and consultant based in Washington. He focuses on developing countries in Africa, the Middle East and Southeast Asia, and topics including resources, infrastructure and finance.

Sharon O'Malley, an instructor at the Philip Merrill College of Journalism at the University of Maryland, is a freelance writer, editor, consultant and trainer who has published articles in dozens of newspapers and magazines, including USA Today, Ladies' Home Journal, Working Woman and American Demographics.

Suzanne Sataline is a freelance writer and former national correspondent for The Wall Street Journal, where she covered religion, politics and health care. She also has worked for the Boston Globe, the New York Daily News and The South China Morning Post in Hong Kong. She was a Nieman fellow at Harvard University. Her writing has been published by The New York Times, The New Yorker, The Economist, The Guardian, The Washington Post, Popular Science and National Geographic.

Scott Sowers is a freelance writer and independent film producer based in Washington, D.C. He writes and creates content about architecture, design, real estate, energy, technology, travel and the automotive industry. His work has appeared in The Washington Post, The New York Times, Home & Design and Hemispheres Magazine. His first novel, "Life and Death at the Dog Park," is available through Big Gorilla Press. In 2014, he accepted an invitation from the Foreign Press Center/Japan to travel through post-Fukushima Japan.

Charles Wallace was a foreign correspondent for 35 years, working for United Press International, the Los Angeles Times and Time magazine on virtually every continent. He won the Business Journalist of the Year award in 1999 for economic reporting on Europe.

Pat Wechsler is a veteran journalist who has held senior editing and writing positions at Businessweek, Bloomberg, Newsday and New York magazine. She served as a senior vice president at FleishmanHillard, where she created and ran an award-winning online thought-leadership magazine focused on the intersection of communications, marketing and media.

INTRODUCTION

The State of Global Business

Mamoun Benmamoun, Ph.D.
Boeing Institute of International Business
Saint Louis University
Richard A. Chaifetz School of Business

The latest trends in the global business environment are altering the pattern of international trade and investment. Businesses are dealing with myriad new disruptive trends that present both opportunities and considerable risks. The severe crisis caused by the COVID-19 pandemic, the political shift toward economic nationalism, the deepening of China's economic slowdown, the evolving role of disruptive technologies and automation, Brexit, and other economic, social, and political trends have prompted firms to rethink their business strategies. They must manage these trends effectively to exploit opportunities and mitigate risks.

COVID-19 PANDEMIC: IMPLICATIONS FOR INTERNATIONAL BUSINESS

While the economic impact of the coronavirus pandemic is ambiguous and varies from country to country, many have seen their rate of economic growth trending downward. Virtually no country has been immune to the economic impact of the pandemic. The World Bank estimates that advanced economies and emerging market and developing economies would shrink by 7.2 percent and 2.5 percent, respectively.[1] The International Monetary Fund is also projecting "a deeper recession in 2020 and a slower recovery in 2021."[2] In the words of Ceyla Pazarbasioglu, World Bank Group vice president, "This is a deeply sobering outlook, with the crisis likely to leave long-lasting scars and pose major global challenges."

Against this backdrop, China, the country at the heart of the coronavirus, has defied expectations and managed to recover, albeit modestly. After a record contraction during the first wave of the pandemic, China's economy was forecasted to grow by 2.5 percent in April 2020.[3]

Beyond its human toll, the COVID-19 pandemic and the mitigation measures to contain it are devastating businesses globally, except for a fortunate few that serve the pandemic economy and have benefited from prompt virtualization and dramatic swings in consumer behavior. For instance, Amazon.com Inc. reported that revenue rose 26 percent to $75.5 billion in the first three months of the year, as the pandemic has triggered massive shopping online.[4] The revenue of Zoom, the video-conferencing service provider, has soared 169 percent to $328 million for the three months ending in April 2020.[5]

The impact on the retail sector has been mixed, depending on whether the retail items are essential or non-essential.[6] While non-essential retail businesses were ordered to close their physical stores for specific times, essential retail businesses remained open during the

Global Growth

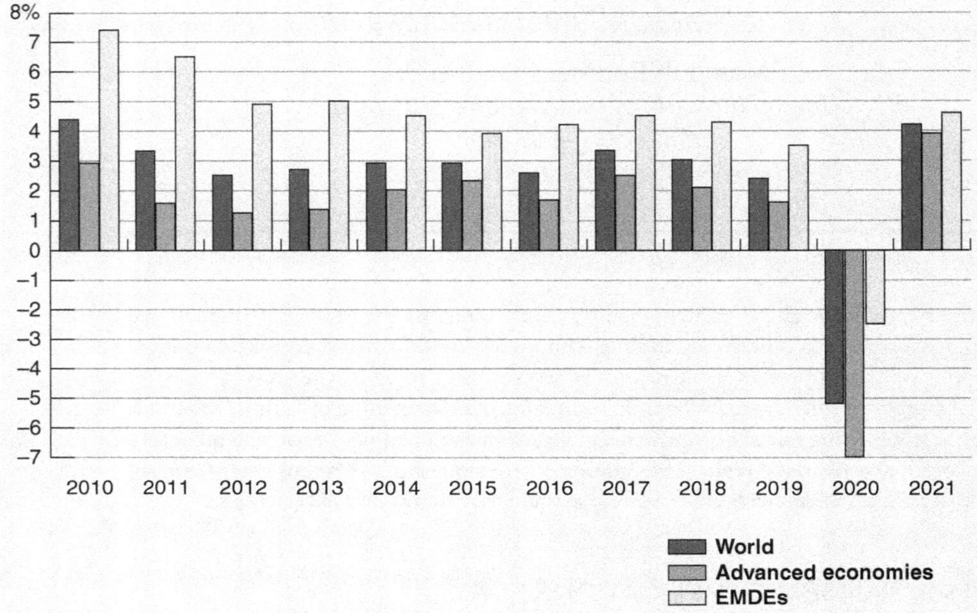

Note: EMDEs = emerging market and developing economies. The shaded area indicates forecasts. Data for 2019 are estimates. Aggregate growth rates are calculated using GDP weights at 2010 prices and market exchange rates.

Source: World Bank, "Global Economic Prospects, June 2020," https://tinyurl.com/yyfyr24m.

pandemic and experienced large spikes in demand for certain products such as groceries, paper towels and cleaning materials. Essential retail stores even faced shortages because of panic buying and hoarding, and disruptions in the supply chain. As a result, the shares of essential retail businesses such as Kroger, Costco, and Walmart have performed better than the industrial average. On the other hand, the sale of non-essential retail items has seen a massive decline. In some instances, retailers removed non-essential items from aisles to limit in-person sales.

The impact of the pandemic was especially severe for small-business owners. Forty-one worldwide surveys on the impact of COVID-19 on small and medium-sized enterprises (SMEs) found that "more than half of SMEs face severe losses in revenues. One third of SMEs fear to be out of business without further support within one month, and up to 50 percent within three months."[7] In the United States, Goldman Sachs offered a sobering prediction that approximately 75 percent of small businesses might close permanently within 90 days because of the drop-off in sales.[8]

However, multinational enterprises are also not immune to the coronavirus-induced recession. An updated estimate from the United Nations Conference on Trade and Development shows that the top 5,000 multinational corporations have reduced their 2020 earnings estimates by 30 percent, and the downward trend is likely to continue.[9] The industries hit hard are the energy and basic materials industries, airlines, and the automotive industry, which have seen a downward revision of their 2020 earnings by –208 percent, –116 percent, and –47 percent, respectively.[10] It is easy to comprehend the scale of damage to the energy industry when one also considers the harm from the recent drop in oil prices and the 2020 Saudi-Russia oil price war. Many companies in the airline industry declared or flirted with bankruptcy as flights and travel demands plummeted and governments imposed travel bans. The automotive industry has seen its production drop significantly because of disruption in supply and manufacturing and the initial plant-closing regulations.

The devastating results of the pandemic have forced governments in many countries to provide large-scale financial assistance measures and stimulus packages. Some of these governmental rescue measures have far exceeded those enacted during the 2008–2009 global financial crisis.[11]

RISE OF TRADE-RESTRICTIVE MEASURES: THE GHOST OF DEPRESSION-ERA TRADE POLICIES

According to the World Trade Organization (WTO), members implemented trade-restrictive measures at historically high levels, with trade coverage of import-restrictive measures at $746.9 billion between mid-October 2018 and mid-October 2019.[12] This is the highest

Trade Coverage of New Import-Restrictive Measures

USD billions

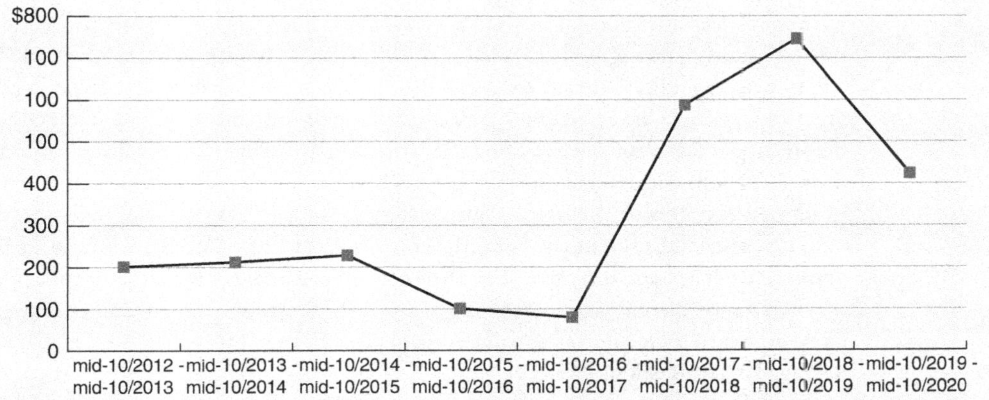

Note: These figures are estimates and represent the trade coverage of the measures introduced during each reporting period, and not the cumulative impact of the trade measures. COVID-19 trade and trade-related measures are not included.

Source: WTO Secretariat, "WTO Report Shows Members Moving to Facilitate Imports Even As Trade Restrictions Remain High," https://tinyurl.com/yydk7u5s.

recorded figure since October 2012.[13] The trade-restrictive measures targeted mainly mineral and fuel oils (17.7 percent), machinery and mechanical appliances (13 percent), electrical machinery and parts thereof (11.7 percent) and precious metals (6 percent).[14]

As a result, world merchandise trade registered a slight decline in 2019 of −0.1 percent in volume terms and 3 percent in dollar value.[15] In contrast, world commercial services trade expanded in 2019, albeit at a slower pace than in 2018.[16]

While there is hope for the easing of trade tensions between major economies, there is a growing concern that protectionism "has become ingrained in trade relations."[17] Although some domestic companies and other stakeholders might welcome these protectionist measures, for many others, this trend could be troubling. The implementation of trade barriers by a country will likely lead to retaliation, forcing companies to reconsider their foreign trade and investment strategies. Also, countries that remain dependent on exports would be severely affected if the protectionist trend continues.

For instance, since early 2018, U.S. President Donald Trump has started imposing a round of tariffs affecting goods from major trading partners—namely, China, Canada, Mexico and the European Union (EU). A few domestic companies welcomed these policies, such as U.S. steel, aluminum, lumber, home appliances, and solar manufacturers.[18] The likes of Century Aluminum and United States Steel have long accused foreign rivals of dumping their products on the U.S. market, along with other unfair trade practices. Hence, they have often lobbied for import duties and quota. In response, the U.S. instituted 25 percent tariffs on imported steel and 10 percent tariffs on aluminum in March 2018. Not surprisingly, and almost immediately, the targeted countries, such as China, pledged retaliatory measures by imposing their own tariffs on the United States' most valuable goods, such as U.S. agricultural exports. Consequently, U.S. agricultural exports to China dropped substantially, and China's industrial production recorded the worst growth in 17 years.[19]

Despite the numerous advantages of free trade, governments occasionally turn to protectionist measures (as Matthew Benjamin discusses in Chapter 9). Governments impose trade restrictions to achieve economic, social or political objectives, such as fighting unemployment, protecting infant industries, maintaining essential industries, preserving national culture or coercing other countries to amend their political, military or social practices (e.g., U.S. sanctions against Cuba and Iran).[20] Recently, as political and economic uncertainty have become more prevalent since the financial crisis of 2007–2008 and the European sovereign debt crisis, right-wing and nationalist agendas have gained momentum and a growing appeal in advanced economies. A common feature of these agendas is the anti-free trade sentiment.

The pandemic risks intensifying the move toward protectionism in the near term as affected countries would try to mitigate the economic damage from the pandemic. Deborah Elms, executive director at the consultancy Asian Trade Centre, posited that governments are likely to turn to protectionism in an attempt to protect the industries and sectors that stand to lose most in terms of jobs.[21]

However, many trade analysts and economists, such as Nobel laureates Alvin Roth and Richard Thaler, have questioned the rationale for protectionism. They argue that protectionism can do more harm than good—like the adverse outcomes of the last big trade war in 1930, triggered by the Smoot-Hawley Act.

DEEPENING OF CHINA'S ECONOMIC SLOWDOWN

China, the world's second-largest economy, reported that its first-quarter GDP contracted by 6.8 percent in 2020. This figure represents the worst contraction of the Chinese economy in decades. While this contraction is attributed to the disruption caused by the COVID-19 pandemic, the Chinese economy has been stagnating since the 2008 global financial crisis and is expected to drop to 5.5 percent in 2024.[22]

Factors contributing to China's economic slowdown include staggering debt (at 300 percent of China's GDP in the first quarter of 2019), weaker consumer spending in the face of rising personal debt, and the growing trade tension between China and the U.S. (see Chapter 3 for a detailed analysis).

Several analysts have warned that these factors, namely the credit surge, could trigger a financial crisis in China if underlying issues are not addressed. Indeed, China is so deeply ingrained in the global economy that its economic or financial crisis would be devastating to international business. China has provided the impetus for economic growth over the past three decades and remains very much at the center of the global economy. Still, the sharp slowdown risks hurting an already vulnerable global business environment and could cause further global slowdown.

GLOBAL TECHNOLOGY RACE

Besides the trade war between major economies, another major battle is playing out now in the technology sector, namely in the fifth-generation (5G) telecoms infrastructure. Security fears over the Chinese telecom giant Huawei Technologies Co., the world's largest provider of telecommunications equipment, are at the center of the battle over 5G. The U.S. and the U.K. are leading the efforts in banning Huawei from their 5G networks over spying concerns. The EU took a milder stance but made recommendations to member countries to restrict the supply of sensitive 5G technology if they pose a threat to national security.[23]

5G is becoming a geopolitical issue because it has the potential to transform strategic military and commercial sectors and profoundly change economies. It is characterized by ultra-fast speed of data transfer, nearly 100 times faster than 4G; massive capacity; and low latency (time for data to travel from the point of origin to the target point), which is virtually zero. According to the U.S. Senate Republican Policy Committee, "The country that leads the world in the adoption of 5G technology will have a distinct technological, economic, and national security advantage over other countries."[24] So far, it does appear that China has claimed the lead as a global 5G supplier. However, the ban on Huawei by the U.S. and its allies has given non-Chinese suppliers, namely Sweden's Ericsson and Finland's Nokia, an excellent opportunity to take the lead.

The battle over 5G has extended to relevant sectors, specifically artificial intelligence (AI). In 2017, China set the goal of allocating $150 billion to become the world leader in AI by 2030. However, China's commitment to dominating the AI race is raising concern in the United States. Attorney General William Barr echoed this feeling by saying that "whichever nation emerges as the global leader in AI will be best positioned to unlock not only its considerable economic potential, but a range of military applications." Barr added that China "plans to dominate the world's digital infrastructure." While there are several countries with significant stakes in AI, the U.S. and China remain the front-runners with a robust technology ecosystem and considerable AI funding.

The AI geopolitical competition has led to a sweeping funding increase for AI development. AI start-up funding worldwide has increased 10-fold from 2013 to 2019, with the U.S. and Chinese companies getting the lion's share.[25]

POST-BREXIT TRADE NEGOTIATION: DEAL OR NO DEAL?

The EU has seen its economy fall into a period of long-term stagnation, deepened by the eurozone and refugee crisis, which created profound social and political scars. Even major economies like Germany's, which has largely performed better than other EU members, face serious challenges that threaten the future of European integration.

The EU's challenges include a rapidly declining working-age population, a continental drift toward nationalism and populism, and a growing discontent with EU institutions (as Charles Wallace discusses in Chapter 7). A clear manifestation of these ills is the exit of the United Kingdom, the second-largest economy in Europe, from the EU (aka Brexit). Brexit became official on Jan. 31, 2020, and the U.K. and the EU are now in an 11-month transition while they negotiate a long-term post-Brexit deal (see Chapter 2 for a detailed analysis of Brexit). The trading rules between the two will remain temporarily the same during the transition period.

While it is encouraging that the two parties are willing to settle for a free-trade agreement on the trade negotiations, the devil will be really in the details. Several free-trade deal alternatives have been speculated for the EU-U.K. relationship, such as the EU's agreement with Canada (the Comprehensive Economic and Trade Agreement), favored by the U.K.; some form of bilateral agreement with limited access to the EU; or the WTO option, under which the U.K. would adopt WTO rules for trade with the EU. The latter is equivalent to no deal. At the time of writing, the negotiation is seemingly at a dead end, raising the prospect of no deal.

Whatever trade deal the U.K. would secure with the EU, the impact of Brexit has been keenly felt by companies and consumers in the U.K. and the EU. Those operating in the U.K. would lose some of the benefits and preferential arrangements they enjoyed under the EU. Hence, it is not surprising that several financial institutions in the United Kingdom have relocated to other countries in Europe.

REGIONAL TRENDS AND PROSPECTS

Since the collapse of the Soviet Union, nations within the same geographic proximity have increasingly joined forces to cooperate, at least in the form of lower trade barriers to the international flow of goods and services. They established reciprocal preferential trade agreements between two or more nations, or what is known as regional trade agreements (RTAs). As of Jun. 1, 2020, there were 303 RTAs, with some of them dating back to the 1940s.[26] Some of the world's main RTAs are the EU, the North American Free Trade Agreement (NAFTA), The European Free Trade Association (EFTA), the Southern Common Market (MERCOSUR), the ASEAN (Association of Southeast Asian Nations) Free Trade Area (AFTA), and the Gulf Cooperation Council (GCC). While the primary goals of these agreements are to increase trade and investment among members, expand the market size, and remain competitive with other regional blocs, they might also be driven by geopolitical motivations and ambitions. For instance, European integration started shortly after World War II with the key objective of maintaining peace in war-torn Europe.

However, the rise of protectionism, regional conflicts, and the growing discontent with the movement of labor and loss of national sovereignty are challenging the progress of regional integration, particularly in Europe and North America. In Europe, Brexit has set a precedent that threatens the future of the EU. In North America, the Trump administration fulfilled its pledge to tear up NAFTA and replace it with a new deal: the US-Mexico-Canada Agreement (USMCA). Trump also pulled the United States out of the Trans-Pacific Partnership (TPP) on his first day in office in January 2017, and has shown little interest in the Transatlantic Trade and Investment Partnership (TTIP) with the EU. In the Middle East, internal rifts, notably the blockade of Qatar, have seriously undermined the six Arab Gulf states' political and economic union known as the GCC.

Despite these challenges, RTAs remain on the rise, including a notable increase in plurilateral trade agreements.[27] The most noteworthy of these agreements is the Comprehensive and Progressive Agreement for Trans-Pacific Partnership (CPTPP) among 11 countries in the Asia-Pacific region. It is a free-trade agreement that emerged from the ashes of the TPP after the U.S. withdrew from the deal in 2017. Even with the U.S. absence, the CPTPP is significant as the remaining parties involved represent 14 percent of the world GDP. Other recent RTAs include the EU-MERCOSUR Agreement and the African Continental Free Trade Agreement (AfCFTA). Even USMCA is considered a positive development as it "provides certainty for business groups and farmers who feared Trump would rip up NAFTA without having a new deal in place."[28]

INTERNATIONAL BUSINESS OUTLOOK: GLIMMERS OF HOPE

Unquestionably, most businesses are caught up in challenging times, compounded by the disruptive power of the COVID-19 pandemic. However, the trends in the global business environment, such as those illustrated in this chapter, invariably affect firms' competitiveness.

While the data paint a bleak picture of the devastating impact the coronavirus pandemic and other trade policies have had on international business, there are some glimmers of hope. The stimulus packages, the relaxation of coronavirus lockdowns, and the reopening of foreign markets have already shown some encouraging results.

Hopeful signs emerged in the services industry in China, the labor market in the U.S., industrial production in Japan, and retail sales in some European countries. Although the rebounds remain, in general, timid and beyond pre-pandemic rates, they offer reason for optimism when combined with the news of the arrival of a vaccine against COVID-19.

With that in mind, we have designed a book that describes the contemporary issues shaping international business. Each chapter of this book delves into an important aspect of international business, such as the emergence of shared and on-demand economies, the evolving role of social media, the implications of Brexit and the economic developments in Japan and China. As this book demonstrates, the ongoing business trends and rapid global changes and events call for businesses, policymakers and students of international business to stay adequately up-to-date on the breadth of development in this truly global business environment.

1 BITCOIN

Are cryptocurrencies just another asset bubble?

Pat Wechsler

From *SAGE Business Researcher*, March 12, 2018

EXECUTIVE SUMMARY

Transformative technology? Asset bubble about to pop? Garden-variety fraud? Bitcoin and other cryptocurrencies have no shortage of fans and detractors, and there is no lack of opinions about how real the phenomenon is—but they have caught the world's attention, at least for the moment. Bitcoin was invented by libertarians who wanted to circumvent governments and financial institutions by creating a currency that was anonymous and untraceable. But the speculative frenzy that surrounded it, of a kind once reserved for hot tech IPOs, took off in earnest in 2017: Bitcoin's price shot up to more than $19,700 in December, then fell in January almost as steeply as it had risen. Bitcoin uses a technology called blockchain, a public digital ledger run by computers that promises to be both transparent and unhackable. Even bitcoin critics call blockchain an innovative technology that could have wide applications in many areas of the economy.

Some key takeaways:

- Bitcoin's rise has spawned more than 1,300 rival cryptocurrencies, some of which seek a competitive edge against it by offering greater anonymity or faster processing speeds.
- While free from government and its regulation, cryptocurrencies offer no investor protection on investments that have been subject to great market volatility.
- Cryptocurrencies are not widely held and attract a criminal element because of their offer of anonymity, making the market potentially vulnerable to manipulation.

OVERVIEW

Bitcoin fans knew the cryptocurrency had finally arrived in September 2017, when JPMorgan Chase CEO Jamie Dimon said he would fire any employee caught trading in it. He went on to call it a fraud fit only for drug dealers, murderers—or North Korea.[1]

Obviously, bitcoin was on his radar, and that of many executives and government officials, after its stunning gains in value over the prior 12 months. But Dimon's unbridled animosity revealed the financial elite's anxiety about the sudden rise of unregulated cryptocurrencies and the implications for the wider economy if they grow more popular and prove to be—as many suspect—a speculative bubble.

Dan Kitwood/Getty Images

Bitcoin is the oldest and best-known cryptocurrency.

What is a cryptocurrency? In essence, it is digital money that uses encryption techniques and coding rather than a central bank to regulate its supply and verify transactions. The virtual currency exists outside the traditional financial framework, without the safeguards consumers and investors have come to expect. As the first and best known of more than 1,300 cryptocurrencies available today, bitcoin has been the primary target of attacks by a raft of financial heavyweights like Dimon over the past year.[2] As bitcoin's price shot up—topping out at $19,783.21 on Dec. 17, almost doubling in less than a month—the level and ferocity of criticism rose with it.[3]

New York University economist Nouriel Roubini, also known as Dr. Doom for his prescient forecast of the 2008 global financial collapse, has been among its most vocal critics. In early February, just weeks after bitcoin's price had peaked and then dropped as fast as it went up, Roubini called it "the mother of all [asset] bubbles" reserved for "charlatans and swindlers."[4] He predicted its price would fall "all the way down to zero" in the near future because fundamentally it has no real value.

The chairman of the Royal Bank of Scotland, Sir Howard Davies, invoked Dante's vision of hell to warn investors against buying bitcoin: "Abandon hope all ye who enter here," he suggested regulators tell potential investors.[5] Nobel Prize-winning economist Joseph Stiglitz called for cryptocurrencies to be outlawed.[6] In January, at the 2018 World Economic Forum conference in Davos, Switzerland, the consensus among central bankers, corporate executives and economists was that while bitcoin might be a plausible if volatile investment, it most certainly should not be considered a currency.[7] And billionaire investment guru Warren Buffett said simply, "I can say almost with certainty that they [cryptocurrencies] will come to a bad ending."[8]

Why does the idea of bitcoin and other cryptocurrencies rattle the global economic elite so much?

To answer that question, it is necessary to understand how bitcoin works and why it and other cryptocurrencies even exist. At their foundation, they represent a rejection of government-guaranteed money and bank-controlled payments. Cryptocurrencies were created over the past two decades by a group of libertarian computer scientists, fighting foremost, they would say, for individual privacy through the extensive use of encryption techniques.[9] The vision behind bitcoin was to create a globally accepted means of payment outside the purview of any state or financial institution—free from their restrictions, but also without their protections. That bitcoin transactions are largely untraceable, anonymous and unregulated is not merely a random by-product of this maverick technology-driven currency but its raison d'être.

It also is no coincidence that bitcoin emerged out of the despair of a financial crisis that caused the banking system to implode. While bitcoin was on the drawing board long before the 2007–2009 recession, its creator, known as Satoshi Nakamoto—a pseudonym for the person or persons responsible for developing bitcoin and its technology—decided to unveil the new currency in 2009 at the nadir of a global economic plunge brought on by corporate avarice.

"Nakamoto was very clearly motivated in this effort by the fallout from the 2008 financial crisis," Maria Bustillos, a journalist who covers cultural trends, wrote in a 2013 New Yorker article. And with people's trust in financial institutions at its lowest, the bitcoin mastermind released the first 50 bitcoins with a line of text in the data that made the cryptocurrency's juxtaposition to the state of the global economy clear: "The Times 03/Jan/2009 Chancellor [of the Exchequer] on brink of second bailout for banks."[10]

"More and more, we are losing faith in humans and depending instead on machines," wrote Tim Wu, a Columbia University law professor and the author of "The Attention Merchants: The Epic Struggle to Get Inside Our Heads."[11] "We trust in computers to fly airplanes, help surgeons cut into our bodies, and simplify daily tasks, like finding our way home. In this respect, finance is actually behind: Where we no longer feel we can trust people, we let computer code take over."

"Institutions do not let go of their influence easily."

In the case of bitcoin, that computer code is a sophisticated, artificial intelligence-based technology known as blockchain—a public digital ledger run on a programming algorithm that monitors and verifies all bitcoin transactions. Unlike the dollar and other so-called fiat currencies—money that a government has declared to be legal tender and guarantees but is not backed by a tangible commodity such as gold—blockchain allows cryptocurrencies to exist without that government endorsement of their worth or a designated authority to make sure the system runs smoothly. Instead of central bankers, a network of powerful computers runs bitcoin operations, following the protocol of the blockchain's governing algorithm.[12] Cryptocurrencies place their trust in code, not in God, and certainly not in the state.

Blockchain's "key innovation is how it reduces the need for central third-party institutions to serve as central authorities of trust—banks, courts, large corporations, stock markets and even governments," wrote Marc-David L. Seidel, a professor of entrepreneurship at the University of British Columbia, in a World Economic Forum report. "It can distribute power away from centralized institutions to those that traditionally have less power. . . . Institutions do not let go of their influence easily."[13]

And that potential reallocation helps explain the virulence of attacks by the elite. No doubt, many feel at least a bit threatened by currencies that do not fall under the authority of the state and desire to make the state and banking system irrelevant over time.

"It's worth thinking through some of the implications if something like Bitcoin . . . were to wholly or even partially supplant central bank fiat currency," wrote Tony Yates, an economics professor at the U.K.'s University of Birmingham and a former Bank of England economist. "Not least because central banks themselves are thinking about it out loud, and wondering what they might do to avoid being usurped in this way."[14]

How Do Bitcoins Work?

While bitcoin clearly annoys the financial establishment, its blockchain technology seems to delight it with its potential application beyond bitcoin. Many view blockchain as the skeleton for a new internet—a way of communicating that allows digital information to

Bitcoin units are generated and regulated using encryption techniques and then can be obtained and exchanged digitally by businesses and individuals like conventional currencies.

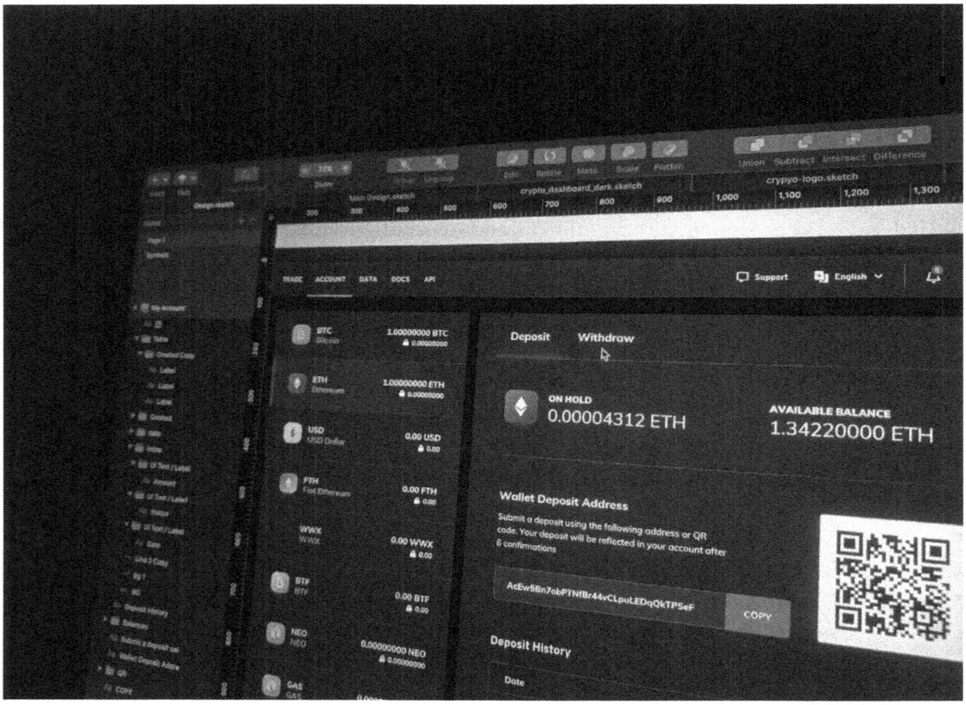

Source: Photo by Eftakher Alam on Unsplash

be distributed but not copied, making the system less vulnerable to hackers.[15] Even while he argued that bitcoin purchases were more akin to gambling than investing, the governor of the Bank of Canada, Stephen Poloz, praised the blockchain technology upon which bitcoin is built as "a true piece of genius" that "will be applied to many, many areas in the economy."[16] The Bank of Canada currently has a project, codenamed Jasper, investigating potential uses for blockchain.[17]

"I'm impressed with the technology, but it seems to me that it's technology for something else," Nobel Prize-winning economist Robert Shiller told a panel at Davos. "I tend to think of bitcoin as an interesting experiment . . . not a permanent feature of our lives."[18]

As a system, blockchain operates like a spreadsheet that is duplicated thousands of times across its decentralized network of volunteer-run computers.[19] The network is constantly updated and reconciled, as the computers verify transactions and compile them into "blocks." Since no central bank is running the show, the computers are responsible for releasing new bitcoins. This process is known as mining, an allusion to the creator's intent to make bitcoin an asset similar to gold.[20]

One of the most important jobs "miners" do is to ensure that a holder does not attempt to spend the same bitcoin twice. They do this by adding the data from transactions as they are completed to bitcoin blocks that have available capacity, according to the algorithm. To find blocks with this capacity, miners must solve complex computational equations. The requirement to do calculations is intended to prevent miners from adding blocks willy-nilly and deviating from the algorithm.

"Only once about every ten minutes will a miner somewhere succeed and thus add a new block to the blockchain," according to Bitcoin Magazine, the oldest publication covering cryptocurrency and blockchain news.[21] With the discovery of every new block, miners are rewarded with the release of new bitcoins.

Miners also charge transaction fees for their work maintaining the blockchain, and those fees have been described as substantial. Based on uncorroborated reports, the fees can be as much as 15 percent to 40 percent of the total transaction.[22] According to BitInfoCharts, a repository of statistics on cryptocurrencies, the average transaction fee in December 2017 was $28.[23] There is also a suggestion that a coin holder could get faster processing by paying a higher fee, just as an online shopper can choose pricey overnight delivery.

Based on Nakamoto's algorithm, a finite number of bitcoins are in circulation at any time, and a finite number can ever be released, again mimicking the finite supply of gold. In December 2017, there were 16.78 million bitcoins in circulation.[24] According to digital forensics firm Chainalysis, somewhere between 2.78 million and 3.79 million of them have been "lost" because holders have misplaced the identifying keys for the coins or have forgotten they once bought them. The maximum number that can ever be mined is 21 million, which will be reached when the final block is added to the blockchain, based on limits set by the algorithm.[25]

The blockchain database, hosted simultaneously by millions of computers, is open to the public and transparent, with no single entity controlling it. Its invulnerability to hacking—because of its complete transparency and because the information is held simultaneously by more than one million computers—is a key attribute that has made the technology of interest to many industries, from the obvious beneficiaries in tech and banking to health care, supply chain management, music streaming and real estate.[26]

IBM, for instance, began building cloud-based custom blockchains for corporate customers in 2017.[27] That same year, Barclays performed the first blockchain-enabled trade finance deal, reducing a process that once took between seven and 10 days to less than four hours by exploiting the speed of computer-to-computer communication.[28] In health care, blockchain may prove invaluable in allowing hospitals and other providers to share electronic medical records securely. Among other major corporations developing blockchain: Microsoft, Walmart, Airbus, Overstock.com, American Express, Accenture, Intel, Visa and Nasdaq.[29]

If blockchain is the leading positive byproduct of bitcoin, cryptocurrencies also come with some troubling realities, including their close association with criminal activities.

The current speculative frenzy aside, bitcoin has been best known since its inception as the payment method of choice for drug dealers, arms traders, terrorists, hackers and blackmailers. It is used most often on marketplaces on the Dark Web, a shadowy corner of the internet where people go when they have things to hide and want to operate anonymously. Although nothing about bitcoin and other cryptocurrencies is inherently illegal, their ability to mask the identity of the holder too often has made them tools of criminals and terrorists.

In May 2017, a "ransomware" attack known as WannaCry incapacitated tens of thousands of computers around the globe, including the network running Britain's National Health Service. The hackers demanded the equivalent of $300 to $600 to release each computer and the data being held hostage and required that the ransom be paid in bitcoin.[30] The U.S. National Security Agency (NSA) and several cybersecurity firms have since identified the perpetrators as a state-sponsored team from North Korea.

To be paid, the hackers provided addresses to "bitcoin wallets" where the victims could send the ransom. Bitcoin wallets are software programs that hold the identifying private keys to bitcoins, and, according to the MIT Technology Review, the addresses look something like this: 15VjRaDX9zpbA8LVnbrCAFzrVzN7ixHNsC.[31]

Months later, the hackers emptied three wallets of bitcoin worth at the time close to $150,000 and then "laundered" the ill-gotten gains.[32] If the hackers had kept their bitcoins into 2018, the value would have been more than three times what it was in late July and early August 2017 when the wallets were emptied, even taking into account the recent plunge in bitcoin price. If the hackers had sold the bitcoins in December, at the cryptocurrency's peak, the ransom would have been worth seven times more than when it was withdrawn.

State-sponsored North Korean hackers, affiliated with the team responsible for the WannaCry attack and cyberattacks on Sony Pictures in 2014, have also been linked to a spree of bitcoin robberies from South Korean cryptocurrency exchanges, according to several

Bitcoin's Value Spiked in 2017

Bitcoin price index, 2016–18

Bitcoin's price fell in the first month of 2018 after skyrocketing in the latter part of 2017.

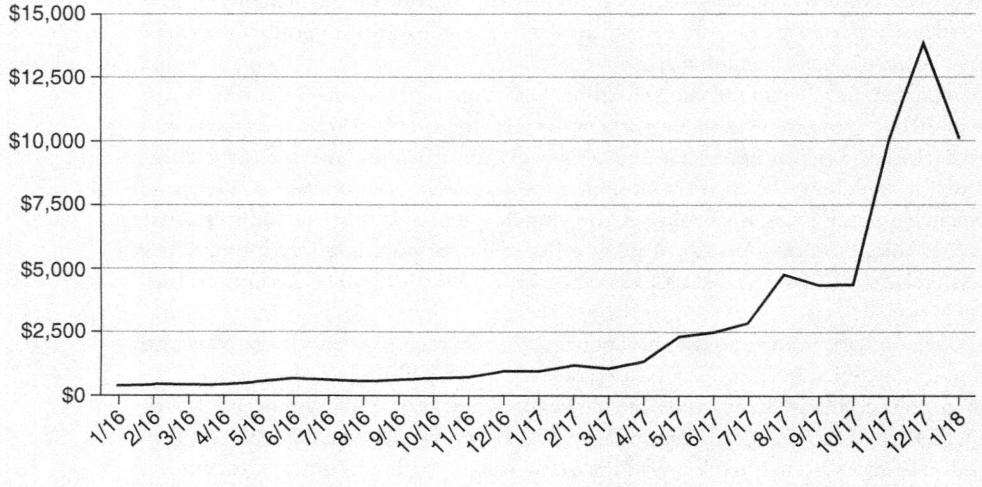

Source: "Bitcoin Price Index From January 2016 to January 2018 (in U.S. Dollars)," Statista/CoinDesk, February 2018, https://tinyurl.com/ybhdmymy.

cybersecurity firms. As the prices for cybercurrencies have skyrocketed, cyber experts say North Korea, hampered by international trade sanctions imposed because of its nuclear weapons program, has been stealing cryptocurrencies outright from the exchanges as well as mining them.[33]

The high prices of cryptocurrencies are also attracting terrorists. In December, around the peak of the bitcoin price rise, a woman from Long Island, New York, was indicted on charges of defrauding financial institutions of $85,000. Authorities said she laundered the cash by buying bitcoin and other cryptocurrencies and transferred the money to the Islamic terrorist group ISIS. The woman was arrested as she tried to leave the United States for Syria.[34]

The ability to mask ownership and launder funds is one reason cryptocurrencies do not sit well with the authorities. In January, Treasury Secretary Steven Mnuchin said the United States was working closely with other G-20 nations to ensure that cryptocurrencies do not become the modern version of Swiss numbered bank accounts, referring to past Swiss bank secrecy that deterred investigations into criminal activities and tax evasion. (In recent years, Switzerland has begun cooperating with such investigations.)[35] "We want to make sure that bad people cannot use these currencies to do bad things," Mnuchin said.[36]

In fact, bitcoin may not be private enough anymore for those seeking anonymity since law enforcement and cybersecurity firms have developed software tools to track bitcoin transactions and monitor users. Over the past year, Dark Web denizens have been switching to other more hyper-anonymized cryptocurrencies, such as monero, z-cash and dash.[37] Thanks to the new demand, monero grew more in value than any other major cryptocurrency in 2016 and was up another 2,596 percent in 2017, which was almost double bitcoin's rise.[38] Although cryptocurrency developers deny there was ever any conscious connection to the Dark Web, consider this: The original name for the dash cryptocurrency was darkcoin.[39]

Bitcoin also suffers from limitations on its technology that are giving its rivals—even in the traditional financial system—the upper hand. For instance, one disadvantage is the length of time it takes to process bitcoin transactions compared to newer maverick currencies. According to Blockchain.com, a company that helps organizations understand how to use blockchain, it took 78 minutes to process the average bitcoin transaction in December, when the system was overwhelmed with speculative excess.[40]

But even under normal volume, it faces problems. Of the six largest cryptocurrencies by market cap, bitcoin's transaction speeds were by far the slowest, according to research by data firm HowMuch.net. While bitcoin theoretically can process only seven transactions per second, Ripple's XRP processes 1,500; litecoin, 56; and Ethereum's ether, 20.[41] By comparison, VisaNet, the electronic network behind the Visa credit card, processed an average of 150 million transactions per day, or around 1,667 transactions per second, on average in 2016.[42]

Slow transaction speeds are the consequence of bitcoin's scalability problem, one shared by all blockchains. Where traditional database systems such as VisaNet can add more computer power with more servers to meet increased demand, blockchain is a prisoner of its algorithm, which has set the size and frequency for blocks being added. For bitcoin, that size is one megabyte per block, and that defines how many transactions the system can process.[43]

Proposed solutions to the scalability problem all involve changing the size of the blocks. Among those that have been considered: Bitcoin Unlimited, which would remove the block size limit altogether, and Segregated Witness, which proposes doubling it to two megabytes.[44] But both solutions have had trouble mustering a majority of support from bitcoin holders and miners.

Block size changes are called hard forks and soft forks, which are either accomplished through consensus among miners and holders or when a group of miners decides to break off from the blockchain. With a hard fork, the blockchain splits and a second currency is created. In August 2017, one such newcomer, called bitcoin cash, was created after a hard fork.[45] The new cryptocurrency's blockchain has blocks of eight megabytes each—eight times the original bitcoin blocks—allowing bitcoin cash to process at almost 62 transactions per second.[46]

A soft fork keeps the blockchain together; only the programming algorithm changes to accommodate growth. But can even those changes keep up with a market growing so rapidly? On the day CME, the largest global futures exchange, announced it was planning to launch a bitcoin futures contract, 100,000 users signed up for an account on the bitcoin exchange Coinbase.[47]

Scalability deals with more than just transaction speeds. The longer transactions take, the higher the transaction fee. Logically, an elevated fee and slower processing should result in a less competitive cryptocurrency, and its rivals are growing faster than bitcoin, albeit from smaller bases.

But bitcoin has the advantage of name recognition and wider usage. "Ultimately, the lowest fee for a transaction wins, and as cryptocurrencies attempt to unclog congestion in their blockchains, the ones with the most innovative [technology] and lower fees have an advantage," said Charles Hayter, chief executive of the cryptocurrency comparison site Crypto Compare. But he added that "the more established the crypto, the more likely someone will accept it due to the lower volatility and conversion risk."[48]

Indeed, bitcoin remains the most established of the cryptocurrencies with the broadest infrastructure of exchanges and companies that will accept it. Among the most popular exchanges for trading bitcoin and other altcoins are San Francisco-based Coinbase, the biggest trading venue with more than 13 million customers in December 2017, and Bitstamp, a Slovenia- and Luxembourg-based operation that boasts one of the top trading volumes and is ranked the third-largest exchange.[49]

From a Coinbase account, a client can store, spend and buy bitcoin. The exchange's easy-to-maneuver setup is made for beginners. The exchange does not hold dollars or other currencies in accounts, requiring customers to link Coinbase accounts with traditional banking accounts. Besides bitcoin, Coinbase sells ether and litecoin, two other popular cryptocurrencies.[50] After the hard fork in August created bitcoin cash, the exchange said it would support it.[51] Operating in 18 countries, Coinbase also acts as a bitcoin processor for such companies as Expedia, Dell and Overstock.com, among the handful accepting it for purchases.[52]

By contrast, Bitstamp facilitates conversion from bitcoin to dollars or other fiat currencies back to bitcoin. Bitstamp trades in the top five cryptocurrencies based on market cap: bitcoin, litecoin, ether, bitcoin cash and XRP. Its greater user complexity makes it more geared for professional and institutional traders than Coinbase.[53]

Bitcoin Has Plenty of Competition

Cryptocurrencies Rise in Value but Also Volatility

Bitcoin has generated a host of crypto-competitors, and many outperformed it during 2017's turbulent trading. Some observers say the environment reminds them of the high-tech boom of the late 1990s.

While 2017 may have been the year of the bitcoin, it was also a time of explosive growth for many rival cryptocurrencies.

As the total market capitalization for cryptocurrencies soared from $18 billion to $600 billion over the course of the year, bitcoin's share of it fell from 85 percent to 43 percent.[54] While bitcoin's price increased 1,300 percent in 2017, that only put it in 14th place among the best-performing of these digital assets. Although lesser known than bitcoin, cryptocurrencies such as ripple, dash, ether and litecoin all managed to outperform it.[55]

So far, cryptocurrencies have been on a roller coaster in 2018—and market pundits are having trouble figuring out what will happen next. While Saxo Bank analyst Kay Van-Petersen told CNBC in January that she "wouldn't be surprised" if the value of a bitcoin peaked at between $50,000 and $100,000 this year, Vitalik Buterin, founder of the ether currency, had a more sobering message for his Twitter followers: "Reminder: Cryptocurrencies are still a new and hyper-volatile asset class, and could drop to near-zero at any time."[56]

Many observers liken the explosion of cryptocurrencies to the high-tech boom of the late 1990s. And some have suggested it will end the same way: with wholesale investor carnage.

Back then, a few people had a new, potentially transformative idea: to use the internet as the primary tool for communication and commerce. Hordes of venture capitalists and techies followed, creating thousands of Web-based businesses. Investors raced to pull their savings out of old-line industries and pour them into the hot new things that were generating hundreds of millions of dollars in initial public offerings.

Then came the crash, when the Nasdaq index fell from a high of 5,132 in March 2000 to just 1,470 a few months later.[57] Every tech stock was affected. But while stocks such as Kozmo.com—an online bicycle-courier service in which Amazon invested $60 million and Starbucks partnered—suffered ignominious deaths, Amazon itself went on to become one of the most valuable equities on the market today.[58]

The cryptocurrency market resembles tech's heady, pre-crash days, albeit on a much smaller scale and involving far fewer investors. In 2017, initial coin offerings—campaigns that initiate new digital assets called tokens—exceeded $4 billion.[59] Billionaires were quickly made and unmade as prices gyrated. Worried regulators looked for places to restrain the enthusiasm, but found it hard to contain.

Here are five of the best-known cryptocurrencies other than bitcoin:

Ethereum's ether (trading symbol ETH)

Ether is the currency created by an organization known as Ethereum, started by Buterin, a 24-year-old Russian-born, Canadian-educated programmer.[60] Ethereum is also the name of the organization's decentralized platform that runs so-called smart contracts on a custom-built blockchain. According to Ethereum's website, smart contracts are "applications that run exactly as programmed without any possibility of downtime, censorship, fraud or third-party interference."[61] Launched in 2015, Ethereum wants to use its blockchain for more than just creating a virtual currency, bitcoin's essential mission. It is considered one of bitcoin's biggest competitors.[62] The price of one ether coin was around $867 in early March.[63]

Litecoin (LTC)

Charlie Lee, a Massachusetts Institute of Technology graduate and former Google coder, created litecoin in 2011. Like bitcoin, it is blockchain-based and it strives to be used in commerce. Considered the silver to bitcoin's gold, litecoin was created with the goal of providing faster transactional speed, so it plans to put a total of 84 million coins into circulation, four times more than bitcoin's upper limit.[64] The greater number and size of litecoin's blocks will help keep its transaction speeds up and fees down. One litecoin was worth about $208 at the end of February 2018, compared to one bitcoin at $10,670.[65]

Ripple (XRP)

In contrast to bitcoin, Ripple was developed for use by banks and international businesses. It is the name of a real-time payment settling, currency exchange and remittance

(*Continued*)

(Continued)

system that offers instant, certain and low-cost international payments.[66] The cryptocurrency Ripple trades in is XRP. The company behind ripple, called OpenCoin (now Ripple Labs), strives to keep money flowing freely, unencumbered by transaction fees, charges for currency exchanges and processing delays.[67] This cryptocurrency is among the fastest to process transactions. Its website says that the cryptocurrency seeks to do "for money what the internet did for all other forms of information." At the end of February, one ripple coin was worth a little under $1 and its market cap was over $35 billion.[68]

Dash (DASH)

Dash seeks to make transactions untraceable, hence its popularity among Dark Web users; it was originally known as darkcoin but rebranded in an attempt to dissociate itself from the Dark Web. The goal of its creator, a software developer named Evan Duffield, is to keep transactions fast, cheap and private.[69] It functions much like bitcoin, and like bitcoin its primary use so far has been as an investment. When new coins are released, 10 percent is reserved to invest in the payment ecosystem. For instance, Dash has said it would invest up to $1.2 million in Alt Thirty Six, which makes point-of-sale payment software aimed at the legal marijuana industry.[70] In 2017 Dash, based in Scottsdale, Arizona, also announced a partnership with Arizona State University to research blockchain and provide scholarships.[71] Dash rose faster in price than bitcoin, ether and litecoin in 2017, up 9,265 percent.[72] It ended February worth just short of $600 per coin.[73]

Monero (XMR)

Like dash, monero strives for complete privacy by using a special technique called "ring signatures," a type of digital signature that can be performed by any member of a group of users who have keys.[74] And like dash, it is popular with black-market shoppers. It was created in 2014 as a "fork," or split-off, of another cryptocurrency. Where a bitcoin user has to provide his "address" to anyone who wants to send money, a monero user does not, making it essentially untraceable.[75] One monero was worth just under $300 at the end of February.[76] At the beginning of 2017, it was worth about $10 per monero.[77]

—*Pat Wechsler*

As in all closely held markets, the possibility of manipulation exists with bitcoin and all cryptocurrencies. The bitcoin market is essentially controlled by 1,000 investors, known as whales, who hold as much as 40 percent of the worldwide supply, according to Bloomberg Businessweek.[78]

Bitcoin has made and unmade billionaires: for instance, the Winklevoss twins, Cameron and Tyler. Known best as the two Harvard graduates and Olympic rowers who lost a battle with Mark Zuckerberg for control of Facebook, the brothers took their $65 million settlement from Zuckerberg and bought bitcoin in 2013.[79] By December 2017, as the price of the currency soared, their holding climbed to $1.3 billion. But by January, as the currency plunged to below $8,000, the value of their holdings fell by almost $1 billion.[80]

The twins say they are committed to developing bitcoin as an investment asset and have petitioned the Securities and Exchange Commission (SEC), so far unsuccessfully, to create an exchange-traded fund in bitcoin. The SEC may reconsider the petition.[81]

Michael Novogratz, a former Goldman Sachs trader and ex-hedge fund manager, is another bitcoin whale. On Dec. 15, 2017, two days before bitcoin hit its peak, Novogratz shelved plans to create a cryptocurrency hedge fund, citing market conditions. He predicted that the cryptocurrency would sink to $8,000, which it did a month later.[82] Of course, that eventual decline was at least partially a self-fulfilling prophecy, as Novogratz said he expected to liquidate part of his position.

The bitcoin market is essentially controlled by 1,000 investors, known as whales.

Bitcoin clearly is a speculative investment asset, but is it a currency? Most economists have concluded it is not because of its exchange rate volatility, which makes it unlikely anyone would choose to purchase anything with it for fear of missing out on a spike.

But some businesses are accepting it. In 2016, CNET, the media purveyor of news related to consumer technology breakthroughs and digital innovation, wrote about "28 things you didn't know you could buy with Bitcoin." These included Subway sandwiches in Allentown, Pa.; plastic surgery at a clinic in New York City; funerals in St. Paul, Minn.; certain hotel rooms in Las Vegas; and a cab ride in Argentina or Hungary.[83]

On the website 99bitcoins.com, 90 companies are listed that accept bitcoin; they range from Microsoft, Overstock.com, and Bloomberg to The Pink Cow, a diner in Toyko; Helen's Pizza in Jersey City, N.J.; and Grass Hill Alpacas, a farm in Haydensville, Mass.[84] Some require a shopper to use a physical or electronic gift card to make a purchase with bitcoin. But volume is light; Overstock.com said earlier this year that cryptocurrencies accounted for just 0.25 percent of its revenue.[85]

Bitcoin Has Highest Market Cap

Top 10 cryptocurrencies by market capitalization

Bitcoin's market cap is more than twice the size of its next-biggest competitor among cryptocurrencies, Ethereum.

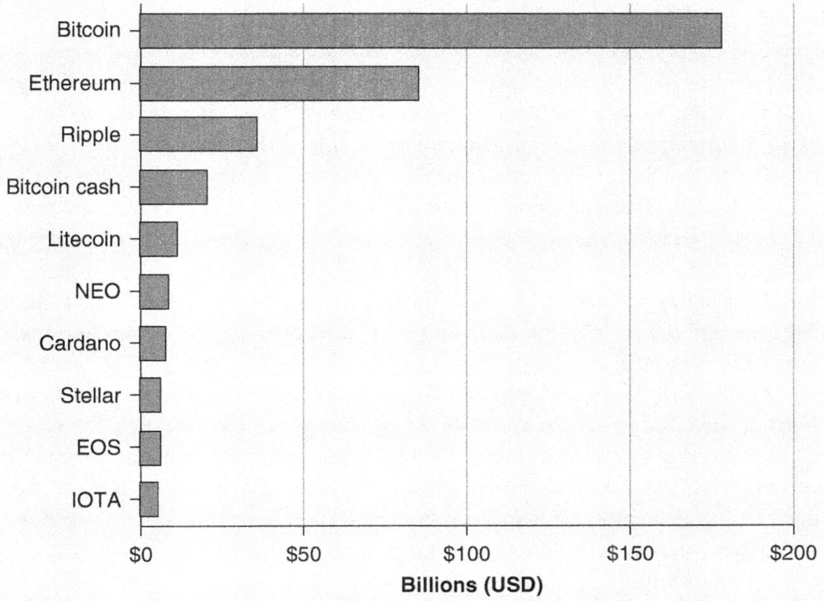

Note: Market capitalization data as of Feb. 28, 2018.

Sources: "Cryptocurrency Market Capitalization," CoinMarketCap, last accessed Feb. 28, 2018, https://tinyurl.com/hqxs3dw.

And why would consumers use bitcoin, given its price swings? A shopper who used bitcoin to buy a $500 coat on Feb. 11, 2018, when bitcoin was around $8,100, would have used 0.06 bitcoins for the transaction. If the shopper had waited until Feb. 17, the $500 coat would have cost only 0.045 bitcoins because the currency's price had risen. So the consumer who bought with bitcoin on Feb. 11 would feel that the coat had become one-third more expensive six days later. The phenomenon is similar to what consumers experience in countries suffering from hyperinflation or deflation.

Take, for instance, the most famous early bitcoin purchase: In 2010, when the currency was worth a fraction of a penny, software programmer Laszlo Hanyecz bought two Papa John pizzas for 10,000 bitcoins. If Hanyecz had held on to those 10,000 bitcoins, they would have been worth about $100 million at the end of February. Those were two expensive pizzas.[86]

Then there is the question of taxes. The Internal Revenue Service considers bitcoin to be property rather than currency. Therefore, when a bitcoin owner cashes in the cryptocurrency to buy something, he or she must pay capital gains tax, assuming the bitcoin has appreciated in value.[87] Of course, if it has lost value, there may be a tax benefit to using it for a purchase and taking a loss. Let's just say, shopping with bitcoin requires consumers to bring along a calculator and perhaps an accountant.

Still, despite a mixed picture of success, the financial establishment does not like to miss out on a potentially money-making invention. Wall Street and institutional investors are starting to get into the speculative bitcoin game where the cryptocurrency has shown itself to be resilient enough to ride the market's highs and lows.

At the end of 2017, as bitcoin soared in value, Goldman Sachs said it would set up a cryptocurrency trading desk, likening bitcoin to the digital version of gold, the same comparison Nakamoto and bitcoin supporters made nine years earlier.[88] In a report issued in January, the investment bank's economists concluded that emerging markets may find a role for bitcoin as currency, although in the developed world it was unlikely to replace the dollar or euro any time soon.[89] Even JPMorgan's Dimon retracted his comment that bitcoin was a fraud. He added that while he is still not an enthusiast, his bank has been investigating the possibilities of blockchain.[90]

Almost inevitably, as market gyrations rocked cryptocurrencies, governments also have begun to step in to protect investors and bring some stability to the market, lest the frenzy spill over into the conventional economy.

One of the swiftest to act was China. As early as January 2017, its central bank, the People's Bank of China, moved to tighten oversight of China's three cryptocurrency exchanges, known as "The Big Three."[91] In September that tightening led to a shutdown of initial coin offerings (ICOs) of new cryptocurrencies and eventually a ban on bitcoin exchange trading.[92] In January 2018, China closed bitcoin mining operations in the country.[93] In February, China moved to close down all cryptocurrency trading by banning trading on foreign crypto exchanges.[94]

China is not alone. South Korea, another hotbed of cryptocurrency trading, also has sought to rein in activities. At one point the government contemplated a ban on all trading, but eventually settled for barring trading through anonymous bank accounts.[95] Tax regulators also have said they would investigate the Bithumb exchange, where bitcoin and other cryptocurrencies are traded. Regardless, as the economic divide between young and old widens based on spiraling property values that benefit older Koreans, young South Koreans have embraced cryptocurrencies as an investment path to wealth and are protesting the crackdown.[96]

In the United States, regulators have sought to intervene when they suspect fraud, as the SEC did in three initial coin offerings last year, but regulators have generally not maintained a consistent position or made a broad statement about the role it feels cryptocurrencies should play in the economy.[97]

On the one hand, the SEC turned down the first request for an exchange-traded fund; on the other, the Commodities Futures Trading Commission, which regulates futures markets, allowed the CME (Chicago Mercantile Exchange) and CBOE (Chicago Board Options Exchange) to launch bitcoin futures contracts.[98] As the trading volume in cryptocurrencies has increased, even their critics are encouraging U.S. regulators to get more involved to "reduce shenanigans in the market," as Georgetown University finance professor James Angel puts it.

"I am now of the opinion that the best way to clamp down on the illegal uses is to strictly regulate the entry and exit points" through exchanges and traded instruments, Angel says. Given that much bitcoin trading happens on poorly regulated exchanges, he says, "it is more likely that a properly regulated financial sector will apply anti-money laundering and know-your-customer rules, making it easier to track the bad guys. It should also bring in increasing liquidity that will help reduce volatility."

Bitcoin does have its enthusiasts among nation-states. Switzerland, with its legacy of bank secrecy, seems ready to embrace cryptocurrencies. In January, Economics Minister Johann Schneider-Ammann made the case for Switzerland to become a "crypto-nation" at a crypto finance conference in the alpine resort town of St. Moritz, where bitcoin can be used to buy lift tickets on the ski slopes.[99]

Already, Switzerland is becoming the country of choice for initial coin offerings: Of the 10 biggest ICOs, four have used Switzerland as a base, according to accounting firm PricewaterhouseCoopers.[100]

Venezuela is another nation that thinks it has a future with cryptocurrencies. On Feb. 20, it launched its own cryptocurrency, known as the petro, which many say the nation plans to use to skirt U.S. trade sanctions.[101] Unlike other cryptocurrencies, the petro is backed by physical assets, the nation's substantial oil reserves. Venezuela is using the new cryptocurrency to help raise money to bail out its faltering economy, which has contracted by one-third in the past five years. Inflation is projected to hit 13,000 percent this year, according to the International Monetary Fund. Vice President Tareck El Aissami said it was resorting to the cryptocurrency to try to overcome the "economic sabotage" inflicted by the United States.[102]

Among the other countries considered bitcoin-friendly: Denmark, Estonia, the Netherlands, Sweden, Australia, Canada, Finland and the United Kingdom.[103] Most recently, Russia—which had been hostile to cryptocurrencies—said it too may consider its own digital currency to help avoid international sanctions. Sergei Glazyev, an aide to Russian President Vladimir Putin, confirmed recently that his nation was contemplating a crypto-ruble that would allow Russia to "settle payments with our business partners all over the world regardless of sanctions."[104]

In the end, is bitcoin a bubble, as Roubini claims, one worse than the Netherlands' tulip mania of 1634 to 1637 when the price of a bulb at times exceeded the annual income of a skilled worker? Or is it a transformative innovation, a technological advance that will redefine commerce? While many economists lean in the direction of calling it a bubble, only a few are as definitive as Roubini.

But there is agreement that bitcoin has changed the world, if only because of its blockchain technology. Despite its speculative extremes, bitcoin relies on a "durable technology that is likely to continue to evolve and strengthen," Viktor Shvets, head of global and Asia-Pacific equity strategy for Australian investment banking firm Macquarie, told investors last year.[105]

Bitcoin may turn out to be the Netscape of cryptocurrency: an adventurous pioneer that changed the landscape but then lost momentum to faster-reacting and innovative competitors. In other words, there is no guarantee it will be around to witness all of the commercial and industrial disruption its technology is apt to spawn.

"Blockchain is the killer app, but most of the billions being invested in blockchain have nothing to do with bitcoin or cryptocurrencies," says Georgetown's Angel. "Bitcoin has enough defects that I expect it will fade into obscurity eventually. I see it being bypassed by many of the newer blockchain applications like ethereum and ripple that have much better long-term prospects."

Chronology

1980–2008	**Pioneers lay groundwork for cryptocurrencies.**
Mid 1980s	Cryptographer David Chaum invents the blind signature for untraceable payments, which lays the groundwork for digitalized currency transactions. He later creates eCash, a precursor to cryptocurrencies.
1993	Eric Hughes, an American mathematician and computer programmer, publishes "A Cypherpunk's Manifesto" and helps create the cypherpunk movement of privacy advocates who develop and support privacy-enhancing technologies such as cryptocurrencies as a means to social and political change.
1998	Computer scientist Wei Dai proposes the creation of a cryptocurrency, known as b-money, and outlines the basic properties underlying all cryptocurrencies today.
2008	A person or persons using the pseudonym Satoshi Nakamoto propose bitcoin, a peer-to-peer version of electronic cash that would send online payments without going through a financial institution.
2009–2015	**Bitcoin and its imitators take off.**
2009	Bitcoin software is released to the public, and the peer-to-peer, distributed-ledger technology by which bitcoins are created and transactions are recorded and verified, known as blockchain, goes live.
2010	One of the first legal bitcoin-based transactions is completed: 10,000 bitcoins for two pizzas. At the bitcoin price of around $10,000 prevailing in late February 2018, the buyer would have paid $100 million for the pies.

2011	Litecoin, a bitcoin clone that clears transactions four times faster, hits the cryptocurrency market, followed over the next few years by more than 1,300 other rivals.
2012	Coinbase, a digital-currency exchange that brokers transactions of cryptocurrencies—bitcoin, ethereum, bitcoin cash and litecoin—opens in San Francisco. It currently has more than 13 million customers
2013	The price of a bitcoin crosses the $1,000 threshold.
2014	Mt. Gox, the biggest bitcoin exchange at the time, collapses after the theft of 850,000 bitcoins, most likely by hackers who increasingly have been targeting bitcoin and cryptocurrency sites after prices rise.
2015	Ethereum initiates its live blockchain. It becomes the second most valuable cryptocurrency as it gains popularity against bitcoin.
2017–Present	**Bitcoin market becomes highly volatile.**
2017	The U.S. Securities and Exchange Commission rejects a proposal by bitcoin investors Cameron and Tyler Winklevoss for a bitcoin exchange-traded fund (ETF). . . . Hackers, allegedly from North Korea, demand ransom in bitcoin from hundreds of thousands of computer users in 150 countries to release their systems and keep their data confidential. . . . The Swiss municipality of Chiasso says it will let residents pay their taxes in bitcoin. . . . The price of bitcoin hits $10,000 in late November. . . . On Dec. 17, the price of bitcoin peaks at $19,783.21. . . . The Commodity Futures Trading Commission, which regulates futures markets, approves bitcoin futures contracts on the CBOE (Chicago Board Options Exchange) and CME (Chicago Mercantile Exchange).
2018	Bitcoin loses 40 percent of its value in January as the entire cryptocurrency market plummets. . . . The International Monetary Fund calls for global coordination on regulating bitcoin and other cryptocurrencies. . . . South Korea, home to one of the world's most popular bitcoin markets, bans the use of anonymous banking accounts when trading cryptocurrencies.

Discussion Questions

Here are some questions to discuss regarding cryptocurrencies:

- What were the goals that motivated bitcoin's creator or creators? Have they been fulfilled?
- Why do law enforcement authorities dislike bitcoin?
- Why are many critics of bitcoin nonetheless intrigued by the blockchain technology that undergirds it?
- In what ways do bitcoin and other cryptocurrencies resemble classic asset bubbles?
- If you were looking for an attractive investment opportunity, would you put money into a cryptocurrency? Why or why not?

UPDATE IN 2020

After spiking to a record-high value in 2017, bitcoin went on a roller-coaster ride during 2019 and 2020 that caused it to lose three-quarters of its value.[106]

Just as bitcoin's value was beginning to climb again in 2020, economic fears over the COVID-19 pandemic sent it plunging, and the currency's up-and-down path continued once more. While it did not achieve its record level, investors were watching closely to see if bitcoin could hold a value of $12,000 or more, a level briefly touched in August.[107]

The pandemic brought a flood of young investors into the market, according to analysts at J.P. Morgan. By contrast, their older counterparts were attracted more by gold.[108] "The two cohorts show divergence in their preference for 'alternative' currencies," wrote a team of analysts led by Nikolaos Panigirtzoglou.

Meanwhile, John Todaro, director of digital currency research for TradeBlock, said the new high could reflect the shifting preferences of institutional buyers. "As institutional investors grow in the space, and increase their appetite for bitcoin, demand will easily outstrip supply." For instance, 36 percent of small- to medium-sized businesses were accepting bitcoin in 2020, including big ones like Burger King, Norwegian Air and ExpressVPN.[109] That market demand could result in upward movement of the digital currency's price, Todaro said.

The report also stated that COVID-19 could reveal vulnerabilities in cash-based transactions and markets, highlighting outdated technology. Because of that, the U.S. Federal Reserve, which up until now has not delved into the crypto market, could reconsider issuing a digital currency, it predicted.[110]

However, in a 32-page research paper published in June 2020, the Federal Reserve of Philadelphia warned that there could be consequences in an economic emergency should the central bank create a crypto competitor.[111]

"If the competition from commercial banks is impaired (for example, through some fiscal subsidization of central bank deposits), the central bank has to be careful in its choices to avoid creating havoc with maturity transformation," the paper said.

—Micheline Maynard

2

BREXIT

Can the EU and U.K. survive a breakup?

Andy McSmith

From *SAGE Business Researcher*, August 15, 2016

EXECUTIVE SUMMARY

The United Kingdom's vote to leave the European Union is the worst setback Europe's leaders have suffered during more than half a century of painstaking efforts to bind that continent together economically and politically. It was wholly unforeseen and ran counter to the bulk of expert advice, which warned that a British exit would badly hurt the U.K. economy. But foes of the EU dismissed the warnings as overblown, argued that "Brexit" is essential to regain control of immigration and said the U.K. can compensate for a loss of trade with Europe by negotiating deals with other parts of the world. As the new government of Prime Minister Theresa May ponders what to do in the aftermath of the Brexit vote, leaders across Europe are wrestling with their own crisis—how to hold the Union together and protect the continent's fragile economy. Among the issues under debate: Can the EU survive without Britain? Will the U.K. prosper outside the European Union? Can London retain its place as a global financial center?

Christopher Furlong/Getty Images

A Brexit advocate at a rally in Bolton, England, one month before voters approved a withdrawal from the EU. Some analysts saw the vote as the latest manifestation of a growing reaction against global integration.

OVERVIEW

When David Cameron appeared outside 10 Downing Street on the morning of June 24, he was decidedly downcast. With his wife, Samantha, at his side and close to tears, the United Kingdom's prime minister since 2010 announced he was leaving office. He suggested he might stay on until October, but his party decided that he would leave much sooner.

This was the man who had pulled the Conservative Party together after 13 years out of office, who had cut a figure on the world stage for six years. But now, at the age of 49, he was going to become Great

Britain's youngest ex-prime minister since 1895. This announcement did not cause so much as a ripple of surprise. It was not even at the top of that day's news bulletins. His career had been washed away by something much, much bigger.

The previous day, nearly 34 million Britons, out of a potential electorate of 46.5 million, had turned out to vote in a referendum whose effects will reverberate for decades. Against the advice of the great majority of expert and authoritative opinion, they voted by 17.4 million to 16.1 million to leave the European Union, 43 years after the U.K. joined its forerunner.

The vote for "Brexit" was the worst setback for European unity since Europe was torn apart by war in the 1940s, and it set off political and economic shock waves near and far. Stock markets around the world plummeted in the immediate days after the vote, before recovering much of the lost ground. Brexit called into question the continued global dominance of London's financial sector, which accounts for almost 10 percent of the country's national output, and the status of nearly 3 million immigrants from other EU countries. It also raised questions about the EU's viability—and, ironically, whether the United Kingdom itself could hold together.

Amid all these uncertainties, the International Monetary Fund (IMF) predicted that Brexit would lower worldwide economic growth by at least 0.1 percent both this year and next, and said it would reduce U.K. growth by 0.9 percent next year.[1]

Some analysts discerned a broader message. They saw the vote as the latest manifestation of a growing popular reaction against the forces of global integration, a turn away from the trends of freer movement of goods, capital and people that seemed so dominant in recent years. To these observers, the Brexit vote, the rise of U.S presidential candidate Donald J. Trump and the growing support for anti-immigrant parties in France, Austria and other European countries are all of a piece.[2]

At ground zero, in the U.K., more immediate concerns predominated. The value of the pound fell to its lowest level in more than 30 years, and Britain's top 250 companies saw their stock values drop in one day by 25 billion pounds (about $33 billion)—three times the U.K.'s net annual contribution to the EU budget. Britain's main political parties were in turmoil. In places, it appeared that the vote had given legitimacy to racism, with abuse directed at EU migrants and non-whites, including the British-born broadcaster Trish Adudu, a familiar face on radio and television for nearly 20 years, who said a passerby shouted a racially derogatory term and told her to "go home."[3]

A few of those who voted for Brexit admitted to having regrets about the instability and social tensions it has spawned. "I would go back to the polling station and vote to stay, simply because this morning the reality is kicking in," a student named Mandy Suthi told ITV News.[4] Ayesha Vardag, a lawyer who specialized, rather appropriately, in divorce law, wrote: "I'm sorry I voted out, given how it has transpired. I am so sorry so many people I care about are upset about the referendum result. I feel guilty."[5]

Pro-Brexit voters cannot say they were not warned. The leaders of all but one of the political parties represented in the British Parliament, most business leaders, the main trade unions and the vast majority of those who spoke with authority on economic or security issues were for remaining in the EU, as were the heads of all the other 27 EU member states.

Even the nation's best-loved former soccer heroes, Gary Lineker and David Beckham, were for Remain.

The warnings were so frequent and dire that the Remain campaign acquired the nickname "Project Fear." The U.K. Treasury set the tone with a 200-page analysis published on April 18, setting out the various possibilities open to the country if it chose Brexit. It concluded: "None of the alternatives come close to matching the net economic benefits to the U.K. of EU membership. . . . The U.K. economy is 6.2 percent larger in the EU, British families are 4,300 pounds better off in the EU, and the U.K.'s [tax] receipts are 36 billion pounds healthier in the EU."[6]

On April 22, President Obama was in London, urging a Remain vote and giving notice that when it came to a trade deal with the United States, a post-Brexit Britain would be at the "back of the queue." Five days later, the Organisation for Economic Co-operation and Development warned the U.K. that leaving the European Union would harm its economy. "By 2020, GDP would be over 3 percent smaller than . . . with continued EU membership . . . , equivalent to a cost per household of 2,200 pounds," it said in a report. By 2030, "GDP would be over 5 percent lower than otherwise."[7]

When the Bank of England, the country's central bank, produced its quarterly report on May 12, its governor, Mark Carney, said Brexit could lead to a recession.[8]

In the final week of the referendum campaign, the IMF, headed by the French politician Christine Lagarde, inserted a warning that if the U.K. left the Union and was not able to secure a free trade deal without protracted negotiations, its GDP could plunge by 5.6 percent by 2019.[9]

Retired heads of the security services also stressed the importance of EU-wide cooperation in the fight against terrorism. In one speech, Cameron even appeared to say that if the EU broke up, another major European war was possible. "Can we be so sure peace and stability on our continent are assured?" he asked.[10]

The peak of Project Fear was then-Chancellor of the Exchequer George Osborne's "austerity budget" of June 15—not a real budget, but an "illustrative" one in which he said a vote for Brexit could lead to tax increases amounting to 15 billion pounds a year, as well as corresponding annual spending cuts.

The Leave campaign's response to this tidal wave of calamity was succinctly summed up by the pro-Brexit Cabinet minister Michael Gove: "People in this country have had enough of experts."[11]

Gove and other Brexit supporters said that their adversaries were exaggerating the ill effects of leaving, and that the economic costs would be more than offset by being freed from EU regulations and the U.K.'s financial contribution to the EU. They argued that any loss of trade within Europe would be balanced by increases with other parts of the world.

The pro-Brexit campaign was a disparate group that encompassed right-wing Conservative politicians; the U.K. Independence Party (UKIP), led by former commodities trader Nigel Farage; and a small number of Labour parliamentarians and supporters of the ultra-left. The campaign's best-known front man was former London Mayor Boris Johnson, a Conservative whose ambition to succeed Cameron was undisguised but ultimately unsuccessful.

These groups entered the campaign so bitterly divided that Farage, the best-known "outer" after Johnson, was never part of the official Vote Leave campaign. Farage gave notice

Going Bananas

Euromyths from A to Z

The European Union's extensive regulatory regime has spawned numerous examples of bureaucratic overreach. But some of the juiciest stories don't stand up to scrutiny.

One of the lighter moments of the Brexit referendum campaign occurred the day Boris Johnson went bananas. Standing in a town center in the West Midlands, the Brexit advocate and future foreign secretary denounced the European Union bureaucracy for its absurd regulations.

"It is absurd that you cannot sell bananas in bunches of more than two or three," he declared on May 17. "You cannot sell bananas with abnormal curvature of the fingers. Why should they tell us? Why should they tell us how powerful our vacuum cleaners should be? Why should they tell us how powerful our hair dryers should be?"[12]

The British public has been fed stories like these for years. Johnson made his reputation as a journalist based in Brussels for The Daily Telegraph newspaper supplying his news desk with wild stories about EU regulations, some of which had a kernel of truth.

Anyone visiting a grocer or supermarket in the EU can see that no regulation bans large bunches of bananas. Nor does any EU law ban the sale of straight ones. But to avoid disputes among cultivators, wholesalers and retailers, the EU did produce a directive distinguishing between class 1 and class 2 bananas. The ones with abnormal curvature are class 2.

Johnson was closer to being right about electrical goods, if a little behind the news. The EU did intend to ban high-powered vacuum cleaners, kettles and hair dryers on environmental grounds, but it abandoned the idea in February—because of the British reaction.

There are so many such stories that the European Commission, the EU's governing body, has produced an A–Z of "Euromyths," with entries under every letter of the alphabet except U and X.[13] Among its entries:

- In 2006, a story surfaced in The Sun and the Daily Mirror newspapers that the EU was on the point of calling for a renaming of a favorite snack, "Bombay Mix," because it was a reminder of Mumbai's colonial days and might offend Indian sensibilities. A journalist who checked out the story discovered that it had been invented by "a small regional news agency in the south of England"—he declined to give its name—and sold to the newspapers without verification.[14]
- In 2001, The Sun newspaper reported that the traditional British sausage "was under threat from Brussels chiefs" who wanted to reduce the amount of meat that a pork sausage had to contain before it could be sold as such. Actually, the EU proposed to improve the labeling of sausages by making manufacturers specify how much of the meat in a sausage was "mechanically recovered" by sucking it out of bones.[15]
- In 2006, the Sunday Mirror reported that the EU was going to order that yogurt should be sold as Fermented Milk Pudding.[16] In 2003, the EU had considered whether to draw up a standardized definition of yogurt but decided not to.
- In 1996, The Independent reported that the EU had "given new meaning to what it means to be a member" with a directive imposing a minimum length of 170 millimeters on condoms, 10 millimeters longer than the U.K. minimum.[17] Actually, this was a decision of the European Committee for Standardization, a separate organization to which 33 European states are voluntary members.
- In 2005, the EU produced a draft Optical Radiation directive aimed at protecting employees from skin cancer by compelling employers to ensure that they were either covered or protected by sun cream. It did not mention barmaids, but the British tabloids chose to interpret this as an assault on male revellers who liked an eyeful of barmaids' cleavage.[18] The directive was amended before it was passed, so that it applied to lasers and other sources of artificial radiation but not to sunlight, and therefore in no way affected customers who like to ogle barmaids.

—*Andy McSmith*

in 2015 that he intended immigration to be the referendum's "defining issue."[19] On June 16, he released a poster depicting thousands of refugees trying to enter the EU to escape conflict in Syria with the stark slogan "Breaking Point." Johnson said he was "profoundly unhappy" with the poster. Others denounced it in much blunter language; the head of one of the country's biggest trade unions called it a "blatant attempt to incite racial hatred."[20]

Immigration wasn't initially a concern for the "Euroskeptic" Conservatives who had advocated leaving the EU since the early 1990s; they instead said the Union's large bureaucracy and reams of rules stunted economic growth and harmed British sovereignty. Immigration did not become an issue until after eight former communist states, including Poland—the so-called EU8—became members of the Union in 2004, giving their nationals the right to seek work in any EU state. By 2014 more than 3 million EU nationals were in the U.K.; 1.3 million of them were from the EU8, making up 2.1 percent of the population.[21] In the heat of the campaign, even old-style Conservatives saw that migration was a very strong selling point, and pushed the message that leaving the EU would be "the only way to take back control of immigration."

Immigration to the U.K.

By British, EU and non-EU citizenship, 2015

In 2015, citizens from European Union nations accounted for 43 percent of all immigration into the United Kingdom, while citizens from outside the EU made up 44 percent—the largest group.

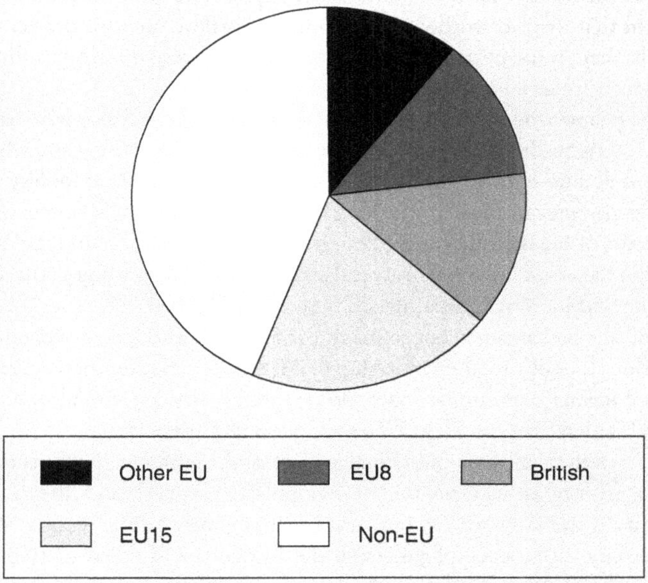

Notes: Data are for long-term immigration, defined as a person who is in residence for at least 12 months. British immigrants may include citizens who were born abroad or returned to the United Kingdom after living abroad. The EU8 are the former Soviet-bloc countries that joined the EU in 2004: Czech Republic, Estonia, Hungary, Latvia, Lithuania, Poland, Slovakia and Slovenia. EU15 refers to the countries that were in the EU before the 2004 expansion: Austria, Belgium, Denmark, Finland, France, Germany, Greece, Ireland, Italy, Luxembourg, Netherlands, Portugal, Spain, Sweden and United Kingdom.

Source: Long-Term International Migration Estimates, Office for National Statistics (ONS), http://tinyurl.com/zxh8hf8.

By the morning of June 24, as Cameron stood in front of 10 Downing Street to announce his resignation, two things were clear. The first was that the late polls and betting houses had got it wrong, and the voters had opted for Brexit. The second was that leaving the EU was a contingency for which the leaders who had urged this outcome—as well as their rivals—were wholly unprepared.

It falls to Cameron's successor, Theresa May, to decide when to invoke Article 50 of the 2007 Lisbon Treaty on European Union, which will commit the U.K. to leave within two years, and then to square the circle of trying to negotiate a free-trade deal with the EU while satisfying voters' demands for restrictions on immigration.

As politicians, business leaders and economists ponder what comes next, these are among the issues under debate:

WEIGHING THE ISSUES

Can the EU Survive without Britain?

Speaking about the EU on BBC radio a few days before the referendum, UKIP leader Farage declared that, with or without Great Britain, "believe me, this project is doomed."[22] After the result, there could be no dispute that the EU was facing the greatest threat to its existence since its forerunner was created in the 1950s.

Most of the people who want the EU to fall apart and believe that it will can be found on Europe's political right. But there are those who wanted the U.K. to stay and who nonetheless fear that the whole ship may be sinking. Ed Conway, economic editor for Sky, a major U.K. television network, forecast that "in the long run, the EU is probably doomed"—but, referring to the demise of the British Empire, he argued that the British should stay in because "no other country in the world has more historical experience of dismantling a crumbling political institution from within, relatively painlessly, than the U.K."[23]

The root of this pessimism is not so much the EU itself as the ever-expanding eurozone, the 19 EU nations (out of a total membership of 28) that use the common currency, the euro. Another six, all former communist states, do not yet qualify but intend to join. The U.K., Denmark and Sweden have chosen to keep their national currencies.

The single currency prevents individual states from reacting to shocks such as the 2008 global banking crisis by either devaluing or manipulating interest rates. Brexit supporters say that this rigidity is to blame for the rampant unemployment in the weaker southern economies. In February 2016, unemployment in the eurozone had fallen to 10.3 percent, held down, as ever, by Germany, where it was 4.3 percent, and by the U.K., where it was 5 percent. In Greece it was 24 percent, in Spain 20.4 percent.[24] Youth unemployment in those two countries was at 49 percent and 45 percent respectively.[25] The figures for the eastern part of the EU were better, because of the greater willingness of their young to head to richer parts in search of work. In that same month, by comparison, Canada's jobless rate was 7.3 percent, the highest in almost three years.

Neither Greece nor Spain is seeking to leave the EU. The Greek government's strategy is to try to extract more-favorable terms within the system. In Spain's general election, held three days after the Brexit referendum, the main winner was the conservative People's Party, which has no interest in breaking with the EU.

Highs and Lows of European Migration

European Union Nations with the Highest and Lowest Net Migration in 2014

The United Kingdom was among five European Union nations with the highest net migration in 2014. The country reported a positive net migration of 312,905, second only to Germany's 560,672. EU nations with negative net migration included Portugal, Romania, Poland, Greece and Spain. Download the Excel file above for data on all EU nations between 2003 and 2014.

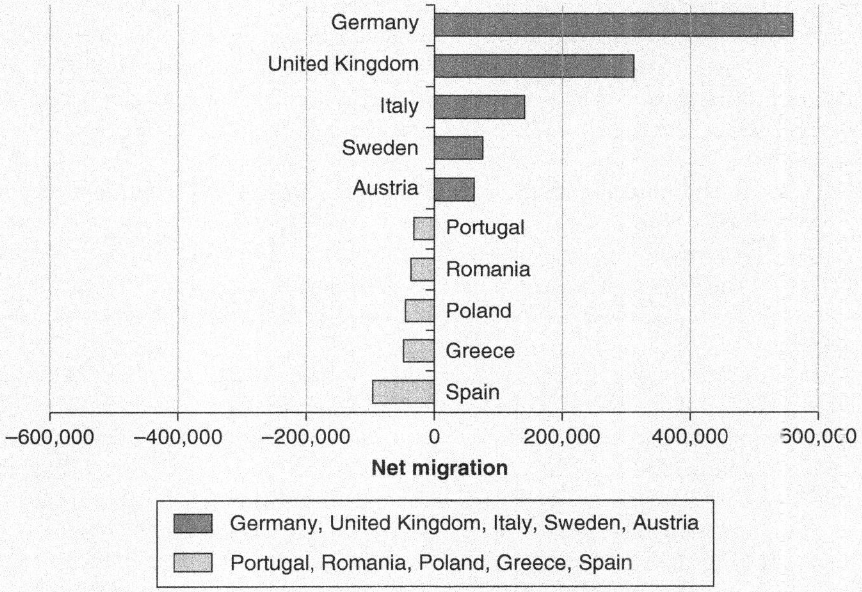

Source: Eurostat, "Immigration," http://tinyurl.com/z3nt27y, and "Emigration," http://tinyurl.com/znyw5v5.

The greater risk is in the north and east, where Brexit could cause "referendum fever." The day after the Brexit result was announced, Slovakia's far right People's Party demanded a referendum like the U.K.'s.[26] The leader of France's National Front, Marine le Pen, the Dutch anti-immigration politician Geert Wilders and Italy's Northern League made similar calls.[27] The German finance ministry raised the possibility that France, the Netherlands, Austria, Finland and Hungary might all follow the British example.[28]

The U.K.'s departure will leave Denmark and Sweden as the only wealthy EU countries outside the eurozone. Even if the Remain camp had prevailed, there would have been continuing tension over what is known in British political circles as "two-speed Europe," with those countries in the eurozone becoming ever more closely integrated and those outside asserting their national sovereignty. Without the U.K., the outer zone would seem to be seriously weakened.

According to the IMF, Great Britain's departure will weaken the eurozone's economy but won't throw it into recession. The Fund forecasts eurozone growth of 1.4 percent next year, 0.2 percent lower than its pre-Brexit vote estimate.[29] And, of course, once Brexit is completed, the EU will have to make do without the U.K.'s annual financial contribution to its coffers.

Whether the EU survives is less a matter of economics than politics and, for now, European leaders express a willingness to hold the project together. Attachment is strongest in Germany, the EU's economic powerhouse, where there are no significant voices calling for the country to extricate itself from the EU, although there is fear for the future. Chancellor Angela Merkel assured the Bundestag on June 28: "The European Union is strong enough to withstand the United Kingdom leaving. It is strong enough to move ahead with 27 member states. And it is strong enough in the future too to stand up for its interests in the world."[30]

Michelle Trimborn, communications officer of the Leipzig-based European Centre for Press & Media Freedom, who has monitored press reports and commentary across the EU, says: "In most EU states, Brexit is seen as a threat to the whole EU project. I have seen a lot of headlines comparing it to the 2008 financial crisis. It was never foreseen that a member could leave the Union. No one knows what is going to happen, so people are afraid."

After Brexit, there was no immediate indication that the EU was about to disintegrate, as financier/philanthropist George Soros and others forecast, if only because all the mainstream political parties are committed to its survival. Besides Merkel, leaders such as European Commission President Jean-Claude Juncker and European Council President Donald Tusk have asserted that the EU will survive without Britain; they believe that other states wealthy enough to be net contributors to the EU budget, such as Denmark and the Netherlands, will think the benefits of membership are worth the price.[31] There is little risk that the poorer EU states in the south and east that rely on German largesse will want to leave.

However, there is a danger that the EU's fundamental purpose could be subverted from within by former communist states such as Poland and Hungary, whose current governments are engaged in "democratic backsliding," according to Adam Twardowski, a researcher at the Center for a New American Security in Washington. By accepting the economic benefits of membership while breaching EU rules on free speech and the rule of law, these governments may provide a model for Euroskeptic parties in other countries, Twardowski wrote.[32]

And the possibility exists that the anti-establishment, anti-politician mood now so contagious across the Western world could lead another nation to defy expert advice, hold a referendum and vote to get out, with others following. Farage has cheerfully forecast such a cascade: "There will be big pressure for a referendum in Denmark, so we could get Dexit. I think there is chance of a referendum in the Netherlands, so we could get Nexit. And, who knows, if we go for Sweden there could be Sexit."[33] A future in which the EU consists only of Germany and a clutch of dependent satellites would raise the question of whether the whole experiment should be judged as a grand failure.

Will the U.K. Prosper Outside the European Union?

Brexit supporters contend that the Remain side exaggerated the economic risks of coming out of the European Union. It helped their case that few people actually felt the economic consequences in its immediate aftermath, except perhaps for those who had planned holidays abroad and had not taken the precaution of buying their foreign currency before the referendum. Nothing more was heard of then-Chancellor of the Exchequer Osborne's threat of an emergency budget. The FTSE 100 stock index in London soon recovered from its initial drop, largely because multinational firms benefited from the fall of the pound. A lower pound makes British manufactured goods cheaper internationally and thus easier to export. Some of the thousands of steel workers who had been warned before the referendum that they would face layoffs may find their jobs have been saved.

However, the pound's initial fall to its lowest level since 1985 and subsequent signs of economic weakness were serious enough for the Bank of England on Aug. 4 to loosen its monetary policy by lowering the benchmark interest rate to 0.25 percent from 0.5 percent.[34] Kenneth Clarke, a former chancellor of the exchequer and the most experienced MP in Parliament, believes the economy may fall into recession. The initial impact of the Brexit vote on economic drivers such as retail sales, employment and industrial production aren't yet clear, and the longer-term impact will take years to be felt. In the meantime, it is clear where those who supported Brexit believe the U.K. can reap benefits.

During the campaign, Brexit leaders traveled the country in a bus on that was emblazoned with the message: "We send the EU £350 million a week: let's fund our NHS [National Health Service] instead." There is no cause more likely to attract votes in a U.K. election than promising more money for the NHS; it is much-loved, but because it is free, demand is limitless, and the NHS exists in a state of chronic financial stress. However, Brexit opponents accused advocates of deliberately misleading voters by using a gross and not a net figure. In 2015, the U.K.'s total contribution to EU funds was 17.8 billion pounds, of which 9.3 billion was returned through a rebate, grants and subsidies, making a net contribution of 8.5 billion, or 163 million pounds a week.[35] (The EU's biggest expenditure is for agricultural subsidies, followed by grants that mainly transfer wealth from richer to poorer regions; the EU also has hefty administrative costs.)

One of the few clear commitments to come out of the Brexit campaign was in a letter jointly signed by Johnson, Gove and other Cabinet ministers, who vouchsafed that "there is more than enough money to ensure that those who now get funding from the EU—including universities, scientists, family farmers, regional funds, cultural organizations and others—will continue to do so."[36] But if the U.K. government is to continue paying the grants now funded by the EU, the maximum that would in theory be left over for the NHS would be that 163 million pounds a week. When Gove began his ill-fated campaign to be prime minister, the offer dropped to 100 million a week.[37] May, the incoming prime minister, is in the advantageous position that, not having supported Brexit, she has made no commitment to any extra investment in the NHS.

Another economic boost that Brexit supporters forecast for the country are savings accruing to businesses relieved of the burden of EU regulation. The London-based think tank

U.K. Running a Deficit with EU

U.K.'s operating budgetary balance, 2001–15

The U.K. has contributed more to the European Union than it has received for the past 14 years. The last year the European Commission recorded a positive budgetary balance for the U.K. was 2001. In 2015, the negative balance peaked at 11,521 million euros.

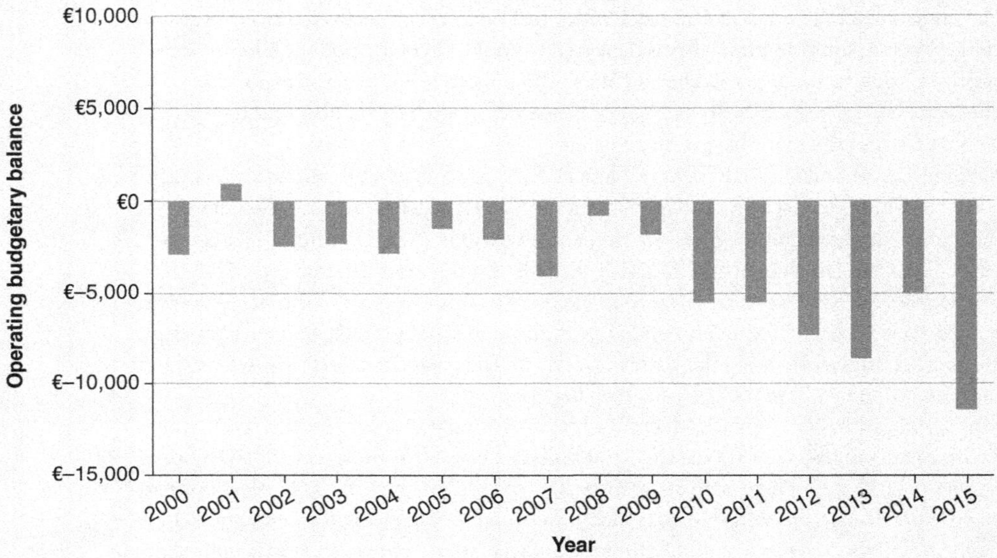

Note: Values are in millions of euros. The operating budgetary balance is derived by totaling the difference between what a member state contributes to the EU budget and what it gets back in the form of subsidies and other aid.

Source: European Commission, "EU Expenditure and Revenue 2014–2020," http://tinyurl.com/adltkux.

Open Europe estimated in March that the 100 most burdensome EU regulations were costing the U.K. 33.3 billion pounds a year. No one can know, until trade negotiations are completed, how many of those regulations will remain in force in the U.K. Open Europe has calculated that the maximum feasible reduction would be 12.8 billion pounds a year.[38]

But if the country were to choose a relationship with the EU similar to Norway's, which might be the best way to protect trading relations with the continent, the savings would be less than two billion pounds. Under this scenario, the U.K. would retain access to the European Economic Area, the internal market that encompasses the EU and several associated states; continue to contribute to the EU budget; remain subject to many EU regulations; and accept free movement of labor.

These promises of gains rely on an assumption that the British economy will not tank, and that the government will not have to raise taxes and cut spending, as Osborne threatened. There are threats of jobs being moved from the U.K. to the continent, with London's highly lucrative financial services sector being potentially one of the worst affected; but Brexit supporters were confident that the U.K. can make trade deals with economies outside Europe, such as India and China, to compensate for any fall in trade with Europe.

Doubtless, for many years economic commentators will compare the U.K.'s economic performance with a counterfactual estimate of how it would have progressed within the EU. It is unlikely that Brexit is going to be so traumatic as to send the country into economic decline, given its residual economic strength; it is the fifth-largest economy in the world and second largest in Europe, and its growth rate last year was the strongest of the Group of Seven major industrialized nations. Its unemployment rate has fallen steadily over the past four years, reaching 4.9 percent in the three months ending in May, the last period for which data have been reported. Major sectors include financial services, aerospace, pharmaceuticals and energy production.[39]

"Economic growth [has consistently been] near the top among major advanced economies, the employment rate has risen to a record high, the fiscal deficit has been reduced, and major financial sector reforms have been adopted," the IMF wrote in an assessment of the U.K. economy issued just before the Brexit referendum.[40]

Nonetheless, the Conservatives had a commitment to end the government deficit and achieve a surplus, which they had to abandon post-Brexit, and the IMF has forecast since the referendum that the U.K. economy will grow by just 1.3 percent in 2017, 0.9 percent lower than when it produced its World Economic Outlook in April.[41] Even before the Brexit vote, the IMF identified as potential risk factors persistently low productivity, a record current accounts deficit and potential weakness in the housing market.[42]

Others are convinced that the U.K. will enjoy a surge of prosperity once freed from the EU cage. Daniel Hannan, a Conservative member of the European Parliament and the author of several books arguing that the U.K. should get out of the EU, predicted that "five years from now, Britain will be flourishing as never before and people will look back and wonder why we didn't do this long before."[43] Clarke, who opposed Brexit, is skeptical; he was caught on camera describing certain unnamed Conservative colleagues as a "tiny band of lunatics who think we can have a sort of glorious economic future outside the Single Market."[44]

Can London Retain Its Place as a Global Financial Center?

It would be hard to overstate the value of London's financial district to the U.K. economy, or to global trade. In 2014, financial and insurance services contributed 126.9 billion pounds in Gross Added Value (GVA) to the U.K.'s economy, more than half of it in London; that represented 8 percent of the country's total GVA.[45] There are 251 foreign banks with subsidiaries based in London; 588 overseas companies are quoted on London markets; 62 percent of dealings in Chinese currency outside China and Hong Kong take place in London; it is home to 80 percent of the world's nonferrous metal trading; and some 3,800 companies employing 1.2 million people around the world are backed by equity funds managed in the U.K.[46]

Since 2000, the British government has been nervous that Germany would try to make Frankfurt Europe's greatest financial trading center at London's expense. One significant threat to London's supremacy was that the EU would introduce rules making it disadvantageous to deal in euros outside the eurozone. London, however, was protected by the "passporting" regime enshrined in the 2007 Lisbon Treaty. This allows banks with their headquarters in the United Kingdom, non-EU banks with a subsidiary in the United Kingdom and asset managers and other investment firms based in the U.K. to operate freely across the European Economic Area while continuing to be regulated by the U.K. authorities.

Before Cameron announced the referendum, the House of Commons Treasury Select Committee wrote to two major U.S. banks seeking their views on the value of the U.K.'s membership in the EU. JPMorgan Chase replied: "We value the flexibility London offers as a platform for access to the Single Market in a variety of formats. Our trading activity in London benefits from an EU passport across the EU."

Germany Sees Record Number of Asylum Seekers

EU nations reporting highest number of asylum seekers, 2015

Germany, Hungary, Sweden and Austria had the highest number of asylum applications in 2015. Indeed, asylum applications more than doubled in those four nations between 2014 and 2015. During that same period, asylum applications in Italy increased by 20,000. In comparison, the United Kingdom reported 38,800 asylum applications, less than half of Italy's total in 2015.

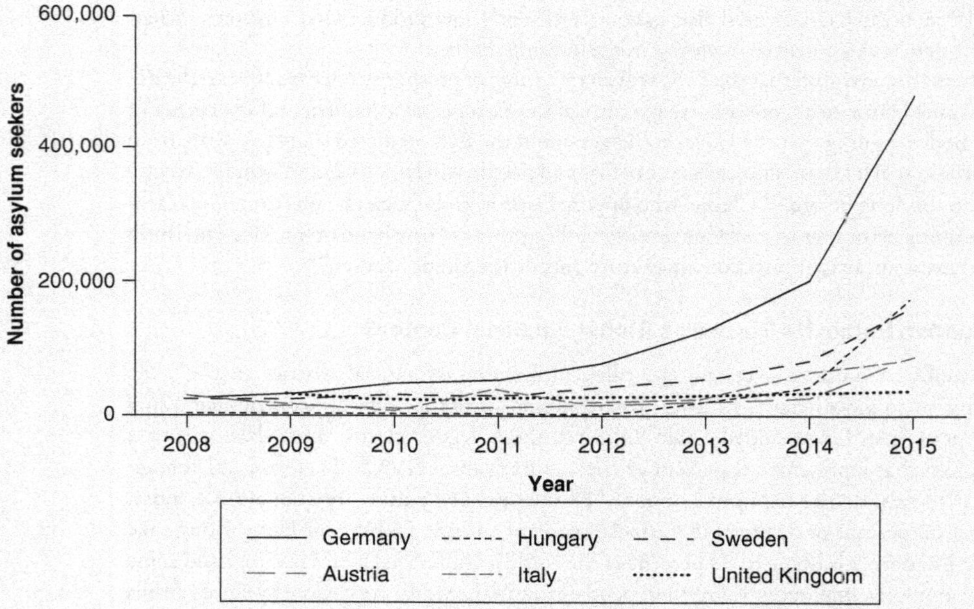

Note: Data represent the total number of asylum seekers, including first-time applicants, reported by EU nations.

Source: Eurostat, http://tinyurl.com/z97n5lx.

Goldman Sachs was more specific: "Our ability to provide services to clients and engage in investment activities throughout Europe is dependent on the passport that London-based firms enjoy to operate on a cross-border basis within the Union. If the U.K. leaves, it is likely that the passport will no longer be available, thereby forcing firms that wish to access EU markets to move their operations to within those markets."[47]

On the day after the referendum result became known, the head of France's central bank, Francois Villeroy de Galhau, spelled out the threat to the passporting regime: "If tomorrow Britain is not part of the Single Market, the city cannot keep this European passport, and clearing houses cannot be located in London either."[48]

The threat to London appears to be real: Jamie Dimon, chief executive of New York-based JPMorgan Chase, warned before the vote that his bank might shift 4,000 jobs out of the U.K., and London-based HSBC Bank said it might move 1,000 jobs to Paris.[49] After the vote, the Boston Consulting Group surveyed 360 bankers and calculated that a fifth of the jobs in London's financial industry—around 80,000—could shift abroad, with Frankfurt the main beneficiary.[50]

This exodus will not happen at once because Britain will remain an EU member, protected by the passporting arrangements, for at least two years. Andrea Leadsom, who was the Conservatives' unsuccessful candidate for the party leadership, and who worked in the banking sector for 25 years, believes that it will not happen at all. "The U.K. is a massive global financial services center," she told the BBC. "Just Canary Wharf, one tiny bit of it, is bigger than the entire Frankfurt financial district. Outside of London, we have masses of financial services centers. . . . This is a huge, vast industry. It's not going anywhere."[51]

There is one certain way to save the passporting regime, and that is for the U.K. to take the "Norway option" and negotiate its way into the European Economic Area. But because that would mean continuing to contribute to the EU budget, being subject to the bulk of EU regulations and accepting free movement of labor, the 17 million people who voted for Brexit would likely feel betrayed.

Brexit Befuddles British Pollsters

Are Telephone or Online Surveys More Accurate?

British polling firms are picking through the rubble of their reputations for clues on why most mistakenly forecast a win for the Remain camp.

The embarrassment that followed the United Kingdom's vote for Brexit was not confined to those who had campaigned to remain in the European Union: The pollsters did not cover themselves in glory, either. The betting shops and online betting companies, who do a brisk trade in the U.K. taking wagers on elections and other political events, also took a hit because, after reading the polls, they had offered generous odds to anyone wanting to place a late bet on Brexit winning.

Two out of the 10 main polling companies called it right, even if their predictions were off target. The final internet polls conducted by Opinium and TNS both predicted Leave to win 51 percent, with Remain at 49 percent. Since the actual result was Leave 51.9 percent, Remain 48.1 percent, those polls were within the margin of error of 2 percentage points. YouGov conducted its last poll a few days earlier and also called the result roughly right.

(Continued)

(Continued)

Meanwhile, one pollster, Populus, gave Remain a 10-percentage-point lead; another, ComRes, put Remain 8 points ahead. Every poll conducted in the last few days underestimated the Leave vote. Averaging out the result to produce a "poll of polls" put Remain at 52 percent and Leave at 48 percent. The numbers, oddly, were right, but they were the wrong way round.

The reason polling companies do political polls is not because they are particularly lucrative, but because of the free publicity they attract, which helps establish the pollsters' brands. However, they need to be able to reassure their commercial clients that they can measure public reactions accurately, so it is not good for business when they very publicly get it wrong.

In all, it was an embarrassing reminder of how, in the run-up to the U.K.'s 2015 general election, the polls consistently underestimated the Conservative vote and overestimated Labour's. One argument during the campaign was over the relative reliability of telephone versus internet surveys. In the final slew of polls, those conducted by telephone gave Remain a 6-point lead on average, while online polls put Remain a mere 2 points ahead.

Both approaches have drawbacks. Online polls are weak because they have difficulty drawing in people who are too uninterested in politics to take part, and affluent, socially liberal professionals who don't have the time to spare. The weakness of telephone polling is the low rate of replies: Reaching 2,000 respondents can require dialing 28,000 randomly generated numbers. There is also the problem of "social satisficing," which makes people inclined to express the opinion they believe to be socially acceptable, rather than the one they actually hold, when talking to someone on the phone. Pollsters believe this is less of a problem in online surveys, which are more anonymous.

One of the U.K.'s best known political pollsters was Peter Kellner, a former journalist whose wife, Cathy Ashton, was the EU's first foreign minister. Having recently retired, he was able to give a detached view. He acknowledged that "satisficing" might tempt people who proposed to vote Leave to tell telephone pollsters that they were supporting Remain, because that was the "establishment" view, but he said that telephone polls were nonetheless more reliable than online polls.[52]

This was also the view reached in a paper published in March by two analysts from Populus.[53]

Kellner had several reasons for drawing this conclusion, not least that in the United States, telephone polls had measured Donald J. Trump's support in Republican presidential primaries more accurately than online polls.[54] This led Kellner to the embarrassing prediction that Remain would win by 8 points.

The pollsters have barely begun the painful process of working out why they got it so wrong. One obvious trap was that the turnout, at 72 percent, was higher than for almost any election since 1992. In adjusting their samples, pollsters always allow for the fact that not everyone votes. Thus, in the last week, the fieldwork by the ORB International polling firm and TNS produced identical results—Remain 49, Leave 51. The previous week, TNS had eliminated all but those certain to vote, giving Remain an 8-point lead. In the last week, TNS changed course and stayed with its original figures, to its great relief. ORB stuck to the policy of eliminating those uncertain to vote and—like Kellner—forecast an 8-point win for Remain.

After the result, Andrew Hawkins, the chairman of the ComRes polling firm—which had had a good run in recent elections but got the referendum badly wrong—issued a statement in which he suggested that two factors had led their pollsters astray.[55] One was the pollsters' standard excuse that people changed their minds at the last minute. The more interesting proposition was that pollsters may need to take more account of regional disparities. "We will need to find a way to manage this new dynamic," Hawkins wrote.

The evidence can be founded in the voter turnout data released by the U.K.'s Electoral Commission. Turnout was below 70 percent in each of the three areas—London, Scotland and Northern Ireland—that voted Remain, and above 70 percent in every other region except for the north-east of England, where it was 69.3 percent.[56]

By contrast, in the 2015 general election, Scotland was the only region of the U.K. where turnout was above 70 percent.[57] In the East Midlands, to take one example, turnout was 63.3 percent in 2015 and 74.2 percent a year later, and "Leave" won by 1.5 million votes to 1 million. In all, 3 million people voted in the Brexit referendum who had not voted in the previous year's general election.

The statistical evidence is that the Brexit campaign won by turning out people in the poorer parts of the country, who had perhaps never voted before. It was a localized phenomenon that the pollsters simply failed to see.

—Andy McSmith

BACKGROUND

Coal and Steel

The war in Europe that lasted from 1939 to 1945 left a continent in ruins. More than 36 million Europeans were dead. The economic damage was so great, it defied accurate calculation. One indication is that in 1939, France's railway system had 12,000 trains operating; by 1945, it had 2,800. The Netherlands was reckoned to have lost 60 percent of its transport infrastructure. In Germany, 20 million people were homeless.[58] The political institutions of almost every combatant nation—the U.K. and the Soviet Union being the notable exceptions—had been shattered by foreign occupation.

In these circumstances, few opposed using the state to stimulate economic regeneration. And in a Europe divided between hostile communist and capitalist camps, the victors were not tempted to inflict the kind of revenge that was visited upon a defeated Germany in 1918 at the close of World War I. West Germany had to be allowed to reinvent itself as a prospering democracy, assisted by U.S. aid through the Marshall Plan.

However, a German revival raised the prospect of economic rivalry between Germany and France, two countries that had been at war three times in 75 years. French statesmen proposed to create a High Authority that would regulate coal and steel, the main suppliers of war machines. The High Authority barely functioned as an economic regulator: Its actual purpose was to enable the French and West German economies to grow in harmony.

Six nations—France, West Germany, Italy, Belgium, the Netherlands and Luxembourg—signed the April 1951 Paris Treaty that created the European Coal and Steel Community. All had recent experience of living under foreign occupation, and so were not exercised by the issue of sovereignty that was at the root of the United Kingdom's refusal to take part. When the Belgians and Dutch called a conference at Messina, Italy, in June 1955 to discuss a more general trading agreement, the only dissenter was a low-ranking observer from the U.K. British leaders recoiled at the idea of surrendering authority to a supranational body. "If you open that Pandora's box," Labour Foreign Secretary Ernest Bevin observed, "you never know what Trojan horses might jump out." The 1957 Treaty of Rome, which created the European Economic Community (EEC), or Common Market, was signed only by the same six nations.

France dominated the early years of the EEC, under its strong-willed president, Charles de Gaulle. Strasbourg, France, was designated the official seat of the European Parliament, under the 1965 Merger Treaty, and its members (MEPs) are obliged to meet there at least 12 times a year, though they and the European Commission have their offices in Brussels. The primary purpose of the Common Agricultural Policy, created in 1962, was to shift the burden of subsidizing France's farmers onto the EEC. By fixing prices, it denied efficient Dutch farms their competitive advantage and made all EEC produce too expensive for the world market. To cope with overproduction, the EEC bought produce and exported it at a loss.

Enter Great Britain

The U.K. liked to think of itself after World War II as the world's third superpower, but its economy floundered in the war's immediate aftermath. The fighting had drained its gold reserves, the end of the British Empire curtailed trade, and austerity became a necessity in the face of government debt that in 1945 was 225 percent of GDP and rising.[59] In 1967, the government accepted the inevitable and applied to join the EEC. De Gaulle, however, blocked it in what the British saw as petulant revenge for imagined slights the general had suffered during the war, although there were genuine problems involving the favored trading status the U.K. gave to former colonies such as New Zealand.

In 1970, after de Gaulle's resignation from the presidency, negotiations were restarted and completed over the opposition of the Labour Party. The U.K., Denmark and the Irish Republic all joined at the start of 1973. Two years later, when Labour was in office, the U.K. held the first nationwide referendum in its history, instigated by Labour politicians hoping that the nation would vote to leave. They were disappointed; the vote was 17.3 million to 8.4 million in favor of staying.

From 1973 to '86, the European Community underwent what has been described as a "sequence of irregular big bangs."[60] The first direct elections to the European Parliament were held in 1979, exciting little interest and a low turnout. In 1985, the Single European Act was adopted by EEC members. British Prime Minister Margaret Thatcher approved it, despite the clause that committed member states to "making concrete progress towards European unity," because it created a single internal market in goods and labor. It also improved the decision-making process by introducing "qualified majority voting," which ended the cumbersome rule that required decisions to be agreed by all 10 member states. That, however, meant that EEC law could be introduced over the opposition of national governments. The loss of the British veto was a factor in the opposition in the U.K. to EU membership.

An issue that would come to feature yet more prominently in the U.K. referendum campaign arose from the so-called Schengen agreement, signed in June 1985, under which five nations initially—Germany, France and the "Benelux" countries—dismantled their common frontiers, meaning that anyone inside the Schengen area could travel from the East German border to the Pyrenees without going through passport control. Five more states joined the Schengen area during the 1990s. Since 2000, it has expanded to take in 22 states that are members of the EU—which formally came into existence in 1993—plus Iceland, Norway, Switzerland and Liechtenstein. The U.K. and Ireland opted out.

Right-wing dictatorships in Greece, Portugal and Spain collapsed in 1974 and 1975, creating three emerging democracies, all aspiring to EEC membership. Greece was admitted relatively quickly, in 1981, because it threatened no one's interests, although Greece's inclusion created a huge disparity of wealth within the community. Average income in Denmark was nearly three times that in Greece.

Spain and Portugal were forced to spend nine years negotiating entry because of the threat that they might put French farmers and wine producers out of business; the new members accepted restrictions on their ability to regulate their agricultural sector. Their accession in 1986 set off rapid growth in the system of European regional subsidies, the "Structural" and "Cohesion" Funds, which in the current century have accounted for around 35 percent of all EU expenditures. The Treaty of Rome authorized only one agency to disperse cash, the European Investment Bank. In 1975, the EEC created the European Regional Development Fund, which eventually came to support the economies of most of Greece and Portugal, large parts of Spain and Italy, most of Ireland and even portions of the U.K. In dispersing these subsidies, the Commission, in Brussels, dealt directly with the regions, bypassing national governments.

The Maastricht Treaty

Communism's collapse reunited Germany in 1990, setting off anxiety in other European capitals at the prospect of an EEC under German domination. This provided the impetus for the Maastricht Treaty, signed in February 1992, under which the EEC became the European Community (EC), and it was agreed that the national currencies of the member states would be subsumed in a single currency.

The single currency was anathema to the British. Even tying the pound to other EU currencies through the Exchange Rate Mechanism (ERM), precursor to the single currency, set off a political crisis that culminated in Thatcher's fall from power after 11 years as prime minister. The government did agree to enter the ERM, which required that it keep the pound within a certain band in relation to other European currencies, but it proved unable to do so in the face of a massive sell-off by speculators. In September 1992, the U.K. was forced to withdraw from the ERM, and never returned.

During the Maastricht negotiations, the U.K. and Denmark both secured opt-outs. Even so, the treaty was rejected in a referendum in Denmark in June 1992—but approved a year later—and in the U.K. it threatened the stability of the Conservative government of Prime Minister John Major, who had replaced Thatcher.

The treaty laid the path to creating the European Union in 1993, with its three "pillars": the European Communities, which took in the Single Market, plus the older agreements about coal, steel and atomic energy; the common foreign and security policy; and police and judicial cooperation. British opponents saw this as a plot to create a centralized European state. In 1996, a right-wing Conservative MP, Tony Marlow, told Parliament that the U.K. was being "consumed by something that we now look upon as called a country called Europe."[61] The same phrase, "a country called Europe," was deployed by Brexit advocate Johnson 20 years later.[62]

Progress toward a single currency proceeded rapidly, without the British and Danes. In October 1993, Frankfurt was designated the headquarters of the forerunner of the European Central Bank (ECB), which was founded in June 1998. In December 1995, EU members agreed the new common currency would be called the euro.

The Maastricht Treaty laid down five macroeconomic indicators that member states had to meet before joining the euro. In May 1998, it was agreed that 11 EU members met the Maastricht criteria. Only Greece failed. On Jan. 1, 1999, the mark, franc, lira and other long-established European currencies disappeared as the 11 states entered the new eurozone.

EU Grows

The biggest territorial expansion of the EU in its history began in May 2004, when the Union admitted 10 countries, including eight former communist states. Bulgaria and Romania joined in 2007, and Croatia in 2013, bringing the total to 28. These accessions increased the EU's population by more than 25 percent, from 384 million to 508 million, but there was no proportionate increase in the overall GDP. In 2014, the average GDP in the pre-2004 EU was almost three times that of the accession states: the equivalent of $42,157 per capita in the former and $14,233 in the latter.[63]

Enlargement created a vast movement of labor from east to west. By 2012, there were as many EU citizens moving within the EU in search of work as there were migrants from outside. Germany was the preferred destination for a third of all Eastern European migrants. The highest number of migrants per capita were in Switzerland and Norway, which had joined the Schengen agreement without being EU members.[64] For example, Norway by 2015 was home to 91,000 Polish immigrants, or 1.8 percent of its total population. The U.K. had 826,000 Poles in 2014 and Germany had 670,000, which represented 1.3 percent and 0.8 percent, respectively, of those nations' populations.[65] All told, by 2015 Germany was home to 4 million immigrants from other EU states.[66]

The conflicted attitudes of U.K. voters on immigration were reflected in a poll taken shortly after the Brexit referendum. Two-thirds of those who voted Leave said EU immigration needed to be reduced regardless of the consequences for access to the Single Market. However, 48 percent of all those surveyed favored keeping Single-Market access, while 37 percent said limiting immigration was more important.[67]

Concerns over immigration may have intersected with fears about terrorism after the attacks in Paris in November. One of the Paris killers, a man who may have posed as a Syrian refugee, had entered Greece from Syria a month earlier, and once within the Schengen area could travel unchecked back to Paris. However, the U.K. has never been part of the Schengen agreement, and EU membership does not prevent the U.K. from barring non-EU citizens from entering the country.

Greece was belatedly admitted to the eurozone in January 2001, after a debt swap from dollars and yen to euros using a historical exchange rate that critics said made the country's debt look about 2 percent smaller than it actually was.[68] The upshot was a demonstration of the perils of bringing a weak economy into the eurozone.

Greece's GDP per capita grew on borrowed money from $136 billion in 2001 to $345.5 billion in 2008, by which time government debt was 273 billion euros, an increase of almost 68 billion euros in three years. This success was wiped out with shocking rapidity in 2009, in the wake of the global financial crisis, by which time national debt was 262 billion euros, an increase of 94 billion in five years. The EU granted a 110 billion euro aid package in May 2010 to prevent economic collapse, but the markets judged that it was not enough, and the EU approved a second 130 billion euro bailout in February 2012.[69]

By then, Greece's per capita GDP had fallen back to the 2001 level. In 2013, youth unemployment peaked at 58.3 percent and overall joblessness was almost 28 percent.[70] The struggle to get Greece's debts under control provoked civil unrest and the rise of political movements on the radical right and left. In January 2015, the left-wing coalition, Syriza, swept into power on a promise to end austerity, begin economic recovery and stay in the euro. These aims proved to be incompatible. The first two had to be abandoned when the government negotiated yet another bailout involving welfare cuts and tax increases; yet, despite widespread predictions that Greece would be forced out of the euro, it is still in. German Chancellor Merkel is one of many who have said the country should never have been allowed to join.[71]

CURRENT SITUATION

"Brexit Means Brexit"

The United Kingdom is still a member of the EU. The procedure for leaving, laid down in Article 50 of the 2007 Lisbon Treaty, has not been started. (The procedure is triggered when a member state notifies the EU of its intention to leave. The EU and the departing nation then begin negotiations on a withdrawal agreement, but if no such accord is reached within two years of the date of notification, the state ceases to be a member anyway.) In theory, it need never be, because a referendum has no constitutional force. After the initial shock of the result, many hoped there might be a way to prevent it from happening. A petition on a British government website calling for a second referendum attracted more than 4 million signatures within two weeks of the June 23 vote.[72]

May quashed those hopes, speaking on July 11, a few hours before she knew for certain that she would be prime minister, when she declared: "Brexit means Brexit, and we're going to make a success of it."[73]

It is in May's power to decide when to invoke Article 50. Other EU leaders had urged the U.K. to get on with it, but she has said the government needs time to work out its negotiating position.

One critical question is whether she can keep the United Kingdom united. The majority of Scots voted to remain in the EU. This raises the distinct possibility that as Britain departs the Union, Scotland will stage a second referendum on leaving the United Kingdom with a view to reapplying for EU membership. (Scots voted down independence from the U.K. in a 2014 referendum by about 55 percent to 45 percent.) That prospect alarms some other EU governments, notably the Spanish, who fear that Catalonia might follow the Scottish example. May has said she is determined to keep the U.K. together but has not said how she proposes to reconcile the Scots to being dragged out of the EU because the English and Welsh voted to leave.[74]

A more immediate problem is deciding what Brexit means. The Leave side never produced a manifesto, and could not have agreed among themselves if they had tried. They were irreconcilably divided before the referendum, and afterward did not show much appetite for assuming the responsibility of negotiating the exit. Farage, the best known of the Brexiteers after Johnson, resigned the leadership of the U.K. Independent Party. Three days after the referendum result, Johnson published an article in which he promised "a new and better relationship with the EU, based on free trade," while adding: "Yes—the government will be able to take back democratic control of immigration policy."[75]

The intellectual muddle Johnson displayed contributed to the sudden collapse of his political support in his bid to become prime minister; in less than a week, he went from the favorite to succeed Cameron to being forced to withdraw from the contest. Leadsom and Gove also fell short in their bids to win the leadership.

As she took the helm, May appointed three Leave supporters to prominent Cabinet posts: Johnson as foreign secretary, David Davis in the newly created position of secretary for exiting the EU and Liam Fox as international trade minister. She sacked Osborne as chancellor of the exchequer and replaced him with Philip Hammond, who, like May, had backed Remain.

It will be for May to decide whether Brexit means entering into a free-trade agreement with the truncated European Union. The EU regards free movement of labor as a basic principle of the Single Market, and the early indication from the heads of other EU states is that they do not intend to compromise this principle for the U.K.'s sake. Belgian Prime Minister Charles Michel said that if the U.K. were allowed special treatment, "other European countries can hope, can think that it is possible to have the advantages but not the disadvantages. It's not possible." British politicians such as Johnson who think it is "are dreaming," he said.[76]

Fall of the British Pound

Pound's value weakens against the dollar after Brexit

The value of the pound dropped dramatically after the Brexit vote in late June. The HM Revenue & Customs office in the U.K. estimates the exchange rate between the dollar and pound in August will be $1.32, a drop of more than 10 percent from July's exchange rate of $1.47.

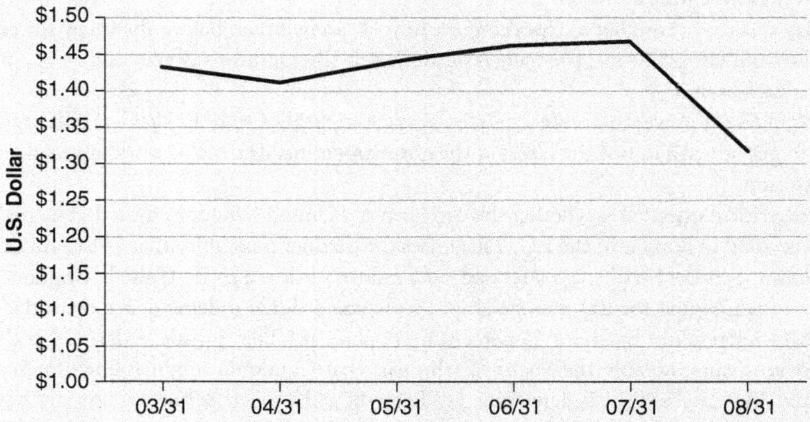

Source: HM Revenue & Customs, "HMRC Exchange Rates for 2016: Monthly," http://tinyurl.com/zwrxnhu.

For middle-class Britons, the arrival of 1.3 million immigrants from the 15 states that have joined the EU since 2003 has produced all manner of benefits. The managers of medium-sized businesses have had an enlarged pool of labor from which to hire. At home, the affluent could employ cleaners, baby sitters or gardeners, who worked for low wages and contributed more in taxes than they cost the public services.

But for the working class, the presence of so many migrants has meant competition for jobs, housing and access to public services, and created a sense of unsettling change. This explains the striking class difference in the referendum result: The affluent generally voted to stay in the EU, the less well-heeled voted to leave.[77] Politically, it will be extremely difficult for the new prime minister to ignore the expectations of those who voted Brexit thinking that it comes with a promise of fewer foreigners in their neighborhood. If the U.K. will not compromise on free movement of labor, it could be excluded not just from the EU but from the looser European Economic Area, to which Norway belongs, and the European Free Trade Association, which includes Switzerland. The U.K. will then need to regularize its position with the World Trade Organization, because none of the U.K.'s existing trade treaties and tariffs have ever needed to be approved by the WTO, which treats the EU as a single member. This could take years.[78]

For other EU leaders, the main priority is to hold the project together and do nothing to encourage separatism in the remaining member states. "I'm firmly convinced the European Union is strong enough to absorb this break," Merkel said at a reception for diplomats near Berlin in July, adding that the U.K. will have to clarify its relationship with the EU 'quickly.'"[79]

LOOKING AHEAD

"A Protracted Process"

Brexit was so unexpected and its consequences are so unpredictable that it takes a lot of guesswork to suggest how the United Kingdom and the EU will be coping in 10 months, let alone 10 years. In 2015, Gregor Irwin, former chief economist at the U.K. Foreign Office, warned that Brexit would be "a protracted process, lasting around 10 years."[80] When Obama visited the U.K. early in the referendum campaign, the president said that a new trade deal with the United States could take up to 10 years.[81]

Most of the U.K.'s political leaders expect the shape of the country's new relationship with the EU to become clear much sooner than that, and when it does, clarity in relations with the rest of the world may follow swiftly. In this field, there is no greater optimist than Davis, the Cabinet minister now in charge of Brexit negotiations. He believes that, freed from the cumbersome business of finding a deal acceptable to 28 governments, the U.K. will be able to broker new bilateral agreements at great speed.[82] His opening bid is that the EU needs free trade with the U.K. so badly that it will have to give British business unrestricted access to the Single Market while accepting that the U.K. is not going to permit free movement of labor. "Once the European nations realize we will not budge on control of our borders, they will want to talk," he said.[83]

Others are far less sanguine. An analysis by four economists at the London School of Economics' Centre for Economic Performance concluded that even under the most optimistic scenario—a Norway-style free trade deal with the EU—the U.K.'s trade with the rest of Europe would still decline, and this loss would far outweigh the savings from no longer contributing to the EU budget.[84]

The net outcome, under this optimistic scenario, would be a 0.98 percent reduction in U.K. per capita income, they concluded. And under a more pessimistic scenario in which no U.K.-EU free trade accord is reached, the loss in per capita income would be 2.29 percent.

"The economic consequences of leaving the EU will depend on what policies the U.K. adopts following Brexit," the LSE economists wrote. "But lower trade due to reduced integration with EU countries is likely to cost the U.K. economy far more than is gained from lower contributions to the EU budget."[85]

One issue not publicly discussed by officials or most politicians in the U.K. post-referendum is the prospect of recession. It is as if the British public is being allowed to think that all those warnings from the Treasury and so many others were all false alarms. This is because of the fear that to talk about recession would be self-fulfilling.

However, speaking on a condition of anonymity, one British official who was previously at the center of the country's relations with the EU forecasts that an economic crisis will force May to compromise with the EU very quickly. "Nobody wants to be the prime minister who presided over a recession," this official says. "I think that Theresa May will come to a quick agreement with Angela Merkel, because the two of them will get on very well. Then she will call a general election, which she will win, and she will use that as a mandate to impose the new agreement."

Asked what that agreement might be, the official reckons it would include some restriction on free movement of labor, for the sake of U.K. domestic opinion, but not on the scale many of those who voted Brexit are expecting, while leaving most of the current trading arrangements intact. Having packed a decade's worth of political upheaval into one year, most Britons may feel that is enough, so that whatever settlement May negotiates is likely to last for a decade.

Chronology

1945–69	**From the ashes of war, the European Union's forerunner is created.**
1945	World War II ends with Europe in ruins, more than 36 million dead and 20 million homeless in Germany alone.
1951	West Germany, France, Italy, Belgium, Luxembourg and the Netherlands form the European Coal and Steel Community.
1957	Treaty of Rome creates the European Economic Community (EEC), or Common Market.
1962	The Common Agricultural Policy is passed to push up food prices to protect farmers.
1967	French President Charles de Gaulle blocks the United Kingdom's first application to join the EEC.
1969	De Gaulle is forced out of office after failing to win voter approval for his proposed constitutional reforms.
1970–98	**The U.K. enters the EEC, but later partially opts out.**
1970	U.K. voters back a Conservative government headed by Edward Heath, an enthusiast for EEC membership.
1973	The U.K., Denmark and Ireland join the EEC.
1974	The U.K. elects a Labour government, many of whose senior members oppose EEC membership.
1975	The first U.K. referendum produces a 2 to 1 majority in favor of remaining in the EEC.
1979	First direct elections to the European Parliament in Strasbourg, France, draw few voters.
1981	Greece is admitted to the EEC, creating an unprecedented gap between its richest and poorest members.
1985	The Schengen agreement abolishes internal passport controls, initially in five EU states. The U.K. obtains an opt-out as Schengen expands.

1986	Spain and Portugal are admitted to the EEC. Their arrival, along with Greece's, produces a rapid increase in regional grants administered by staff in Brussels, bypassing national governments.
1990	Margaret Thatcher, who became increasingly hostile to the EEC during her tenure in office, is forced out as U.K. prime minister.
1992	The Maastricht Treaty paves the way for the creation of a single currency, with the U.K. and Denmark opting out.
1993	The European Union formally comes into existence.
1997	Election of a Labour government in the U.K., led by pro-EU Tony Blair, temporarily halts the perennial conflict between Britain and the rest of the EU.
1999–2014	**Integration and enlargement**
1999	Eleven EU states abandon their national currencies and adopt the euro.
2001	Greece adopts the euro. German Chancellor Angela Merkel, among many others, comes to regard Greece's admission to the eurozone as a mistake.
2004	Ten new states, eight of them formerly under communist rule, join the EU, increasing its population by a quarter.
2007	The Treaty of Lisbon, reluctantly signed by the U.K., leads to further EU integration, including the appointment of a president of the European Council and an EU high representative, or foreign minister.
2010	Greece is granted the first of a series of emergency aid packages to prevent it from falling out of the eurozone. The U.K.'s newly elected coalition government declines to contribute.
2015–Present	**The road to Brexit**
2015	The Conservatives, running on a manifesto that includes a promise to hold a referendum on EU membership, are returned to office with a parliamentary majority in the U.K. general election.
2016	The U.K. referendum on June 23 results in an unexpected victory for Brexit advocates. Three weeks later, Theresa May replaces David Cameron as prime minister; she promises to negotiate Britain's withdrawal from the EU. . . . The Bank of England on Aug. 4 announces that it will cut its main interest rate to a historic low in an effort to boost the U.K. economy in the Brexit aftermath.

PERSPECTIVE

Pro/Con: John Longworth on Brexit

YES

DID THE U.K. ELECTORATE MAKE THE RIGHT DECISION?

John Longworth

Former Director General of the British Chambers of Commerce

Written for *SAGE Business Researcher*, August 2016

The market reaction to Brexit was more than it needed to be. Markets always overreact anyway, but when they have the government telling the entire world that it was going to be a disaster, that is a self-fulfilling prophecy.

The government should not have positioned itself as a campaigning organization. When [then-Prime Minister] David Cameron came back from the negotiations [with the European Union] with practically nothing, he decided to campaign for Remain, and having decided that, went way over the top. The Treasury report warning of the consequences of Brexit was widely seen as flawed because it did not consider the upsides.

If the U.K. government does certain things, we will reap the full benefits economically. The government will need to get on and do them quickly. It will need to abandon what we have done before.

The potential benefits will be, first, a more than 1 percent boost in GDP per annum. That is a considerable gain. It is derived from ending the contribution to the EU, and a 12.5 billion-pound-a-year saving from reduced regulations.

That is not an unreasonable figure. The Treasury itself has estimated the cost of EU regulation to the U.K. economy to be 125 billion pounds a year, and if we shave 10 percent off that, we save 12.5 billion pounds. That is one thing the U.K. government can do, and the quicker it does it, the more benefit we will receive.

Second, we can remove EU tariffs. On foodstuffs they average 20 percent to 50 percent on some—on clothing 10 percent. That is a tax burden on working families. Removing them would benefit the economy.

Also, we have to stop loving the Single Market. People confuse Single Market membership with Single Market access. Access means you have got a deal that allows free trade with the EU.

It is only a Single Market in goods and manufacturing. Manufacturing is less than 10 percent of the U.K. economy, and manufacturers have difficulty accessing the Single Market because of all sorts of clever barriers that the Germans and French erect.

What the government ought to do is leave, and wait—and within the blink of an eye, the German automobile manufacturers will want access to their biggest market.

The benefits are not all economic. Migration was a major issue in the referendum, and one thing I think the metropolitan elite have missed is how, if you go around the country, an awful lot of people mention control of our own affairs, and democracy.

PERSPECTIVE

Pro/Con: Stewart Hosie on Brexit

NO **DID THE U.K. ELECTORATE MAKE THE RIGHT DECISION?**

Stewart Hosie

Deputy leader of the Scottish Nationalist Party

Extract from speech to the House of Commons, Jun. 29, 2016

Brexit poses huge and real risks to the economy, to jobs and to prosperity. Those risks were brought about in part by the decision to hold the referendum, but much more importantly by the failure of those advocating Brexit to have any plan if they won. What the Brexit leaders Michael Gove and Boris Johnson had prepared was a few scribbled notes on the back of Nigel Farage's cigarette packet. It really was not good enough.

The FTSE 100 [stock index] dropped by 8.4 percent on the morning of June 24, which meant that 137 billion pounds was wiped off U.K. blue chip stocks within minutes of the markets' opening. On June 27 the downward trend continued. By late afternoon, the FTSE was down another 2.5 percent. Banks, house builders and others were the biggest fallers. The FTSE 250 index, which has more businesses in it that are exposed to the domestic market, fell even further—by 7.2 percent, or 1,200 points. Those were extraordinary falls in both markets.

It was not simply stock prices that were affected. The value of the pound against the dollar fell by almost 8 percent on June 24. By Monday, it fell another 2 percent, to $1.32, a three-decade low, because of the actions taken by the Brexit campaign, which failed to have a plan. The value of the pound against the euro fell almost 6 percent on Friday, June 24, and it fell again on Monday.

Most alarming was that the U.K. lost its triple-A credit rating from Standard & Poor's, who said that the referendum result could lead to a deterioration of the U.K.'s economic performance, including its large financial services sector. It was the first time that Standard & Poor's had downgraded a triple A-rated sovereign by two notches in one go.

On Friday, June 24, Moody's cut the credit outlook from stable to negative, saying the result could lead to a prolonged period of uncertainty. It has warned that the U.K.'s Aa1 rating is also at risk of being lowered, and with that, obviously, comes the risk of higher borrowing costs. And that is before we get to the real world and job security. The Institute of Directors [an organization for company directors] surveyed 1,000 of its members. It found that a quarter plan to freeze recruitment. Two-thirds said the vote was negative for their business.

This is a Brexit campaign without a plan, leading to the chaos and potential difficulties in the economy for many, many years to come.

UPDATE IN 2020

At 11 p.m. local time on Jan. 31, 2020, Britain ceased to be a member of the European Union (EU). A light show illuminated 10 Downing Street, headquarters of British Prime Minister Boris Johnson, while a countdown clock lit up the White Cliffs of Dover.

In a video message, Johnson said Brexit represented an "astonishing moment of hope," although he acknowledged the anxiety that many Britons felt over the separation.[86] Hundreds of Brexit supporters thronged Trafalgar Square in London, where Brexit Party leader Nigel Farage proclaimed that Brexit was the "greatest moment in the modern history of our great nation."

Others disagreed.

"The UK will leave the most successful experiment in multi-national collaboration the world has ever seen," said commentator Martin Fletcher.

Brexit Day came almost a year after the scheduled exit of Britain from the EU in March 2019. British Prime Minister Teresa May was voted out of her job for moving too slowly, and replaced by Johnson in December 2019.

A key sticking point that remained was the fate of Ireland and Northern Ireland. Because Northern Ireland was part of the United Kingdom, the exit—in theory—would require Britain to re-erect a border with Ireland, which remained part of the EU. However, doing so would violate the Good Friday Accords, reached in 1998, which removed physical and trade barriers between the two regions.[87]

Meanwhile, Scottish separatists, led by First Minister Nicola Sturgeon, called for another vote on leaving the U.K. The first effort failed in 2014, and Johnson declared he would not support a second ballot.[88]

In October 2019, the EU and Britain reached a withdrawal agreement that established an 11-month transition for Britain's departure.[89]

There was plenty to address, such as air transportation, aviation safety, civil nuclear energy, and international security cooperation. They needed to reach a free-trade agreement, with the bargainers aiming for a zero-quota, zero-tariff deal similar to the EU's recent agreement with Canada.[90]

Both sides published draft documents, and negotiations commenced.[91] But then came the coronavirus pandemic, which triggered extraordinary lockdown measures across the EU and Britain during late winter and spring in 2020.

By summer, the negotiations seemed deadlocked over issues such as British fishing boats in EU waters and unfair business subsidies.

Without any kind of Brexit agreement by the end of 2020, Britain and the EU could be headed for significant changes. EU citizens would no longer have the right to move to the U.K. to work and settle, while Britain plans to institute new immigration policies in 2021. There would be new restrictions concerning travel, while customs formalities and regulatory controls will be introduced.

By fall, doubts were increasing that a deal could get done by year end.

"Given the COVID-19 pandemic, it is increasingly likely the government will need to extend this timeline, or risk additional economic shocks," predicted Amanda Sloat of the Brookings Institution.[92]

—Micheline Maynard

3 CHINA'S SLOWDOWN

Can its leaders navigate a soft landing?

Suzanne Sataline

From *SAGE Business Researcher*, October 10, 2016

EXECUTIVE SUMMARY

China's headlong leap into the ranks of the world's largest economies has slowed since the severe global recession of 2008, with real gross domestic product growth falling from 10.6 percent in 2010 to an estimated 6.6 percent this year. Chinese leaders are struggling to cope with the lower growth, along with rising debt, a loss of jobs to lower-wage countries and the need to institute more market-oriented reforms. The country's difficulties have generated economic shock waves throughout the world, from financial markets in New York and London to commodity exporters in Brazil, Australia and Central Africa. As China and other nations try to handle the situation, here are the key takeaways:

- The years of China's 10-percent-plus annual growth are over, and Chinese leaders must manage lower growth without creating serious disruption, internally or globally.
- President Xi faces conflicting impulses to reduce state control of the economy while preserving government and Communist Party authority.
- How China resolves these issues will reverberate from Australia to Latin America to Africa; one study estimates China will contribute almost 39 percent of total global GDP growth this year.

OVERVIEW

On Sunday afternoons in Dongguan, a city in southern China, a factory worker named Yu finds herself nearly alone. A line worker at a clothing factory, she and more than 2,000 workers bunked in the nearby dormitory last year. Now, only about 100 employees remain after the owner sent most production to Southeast Asian countries such as Vietnam, where labor costs are cheaper.

The city was once the epicenter of China's export manufacturing boom, making iPhones, Nike sneakers and other products for Western brands. Those workers are gone. Yu is considering moving back to Chongqing, in central China, a place she left 20 years ago.

"This is the worst time ever," said Yu, who asked a journalist to use only her family name to avoid trouble with the authorities. "The factories hurt by the 2008 financial crisis were the smaller ones, but this time the big ones are affected."[1]

Workers install scaffolding at an offshore oil platform in Shandong province. China's yearly growth rate has slowed from 10.6 percent in 2010 to 6.6 percent this year.

China, the country synonymous with cheap goods, cheap labor and phenomenal economic growth, is struggling with growing pains. And the country's difficult passage has sent shock waves rippling across markets throughout the world, from equity values in New York and London to commodity prices in Brazil, Australia and central Africa.

The nation of nearly 1.4 billion people has leapt onto the list of the world's fastest-growing economies, with real gross domestic product (GDP) growth averaging nearly 10 percent annually from 1979, the year after it started market reforms, through 2014.[2] In recent years, China has emerged as the world's second-largest economy, behind just the United States, and ranked No. 1 in manufacturing, merchandise trades and foreign exchange reserves. In three decades the government's policies helped pull 225 million households into the middle class (defined as those with annual incomes equivalent to $11,500 to $43,000) and fostered a wealthy elite who crave luxury goods.[3]

But China's economy slowed sharply after the global recession began in 2008. The nation injected $586 billion to stimulate growth and loosened monetary policies, which created a mound of corporate debt as compared with its GDP.[4] The country's exports, imports and foreign direct investment slowed. Real GDP growth fell from 10.6 percent in 2010 to an estimated 6.6 percent in 2016, according to the International Monetary Fund (IMF).[5]

Some economists, such as those at Fathom Consulting in London, which studies "hidden unemployment" in China, are convinced that millions of Chinese workers lost their jobs.[6] (Such numbers are hard to come by from the opaque Chinese government.) Demand for the nation's low-cost goods, such as shoes and household items, plunged, while pressure from workers for better pay and benefits induced companies to ship their production overseas to nations such as Vietnam with cheaper workers.[7]

How bad is the slowdown? Economists agree it's troubling, but differ as to how dire the situation is. David Dollar, a senior fellow at the Brookings Institution's John L. Thornton China Center, points out that the economy is still growing, at more than 6 percent, a far greater rate than in Europe or the United States.

China has a cushion: Its corporations and households sock away enormous savings. "As long as there are oceans of money that they're floating on, you can go along. You have a lot of leeway," says Arthur R. Kroeber, founding partner at Gavekal Dragonomics, a research firm in Beijing. "I don't believe China is going to face a dramatic financial crisis in the coming years."

Some economists, such as Derek Scissors, a resident scholar at the American Enterprise Institute (AEI), a Washington think tank, say that the staggering debt on China's books cannot be paid off. "China's in the process of stagnating," Scissors says. "This is not a slowdown; it's a stop. It's a stop in progress."

While there are numerous causes for the debt, overinvestment in, and overproduction by, China's corporations and low spending by its cautious citizens loom large, says Howard Shatz, a Washington-based senior economist for the RAND Corp., a research organization headquartered in Santa Monica, Calif.

When it embarked on its market reforms, the government followed the lead of other Asian nations such as Japan and South Korea that quickly created great wealth. China's government urged state-owned banks to lend capital. And China started to build, Dollar says. Companies built factories, housing, dams and infrastructure. Warehouses filled with unsold goods. Cities replaced housing blocks and airports that weren't very old, and sometimes new apartment buildings sat unoccupied. Recently, he said, companies built airports in cities that had just a few flights a day. "Their growth was rapid, probably too rapid," says. "China is at this dilemma."

Debt is the issue that concerns much of the world. To keep the economy functioning, the government allowed Chinese companies to continue borrowing from government banks. The country's debt load reached $26.6 trillion in 2015—five times greater than a decade earlier, and an amount that's more than two and a half times the country's entire economy.[8]

With that much owed, companies must pay with money that might go toward expanding or diversifying businesses. Less spending on investing and hiring hurts the overall economy, hitting corporate bottom lines and making it even harder for companies to pay off debt.

Chinese Economic Growth Slows

China's GDP growth rate by year, 1996–2016

China's annual growth rate has slowed to 6.7 percent after peaking in 2007.

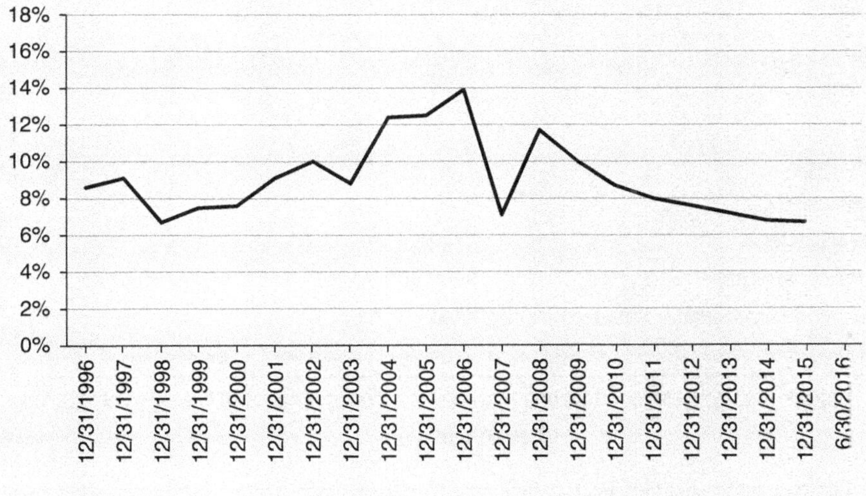

Source: "China GDP Annual Growth Rate," Trading Economics, July 2016, http://tinyurl.com/pzthrrq

As bad loans rise, banks freeze lending, and confidence in the financial system can be shaken. With memories of 2008 fresh in economists' minds, many worry that China is heading for a banking crisis.[9]

"If China were a small country it wouldn't make that big a difference," says Scott Kennedy, a director at the Center for Strategic and International Studies (CSIS), a think tank in Washington. "But it's so huge, whatever it does is a big challenge for everybody."

These problems have triggered concern in other nations. In the summer of 2015, and again earlier this year, global stock markets tumbled. The worry started when investors sold off stock

China and U.S. Compete for Highest GDP

GDP by country, 2015

China's gross domestic product, at just under $11 trillion, was second only to the United States' $17.9 trillion in 2015.

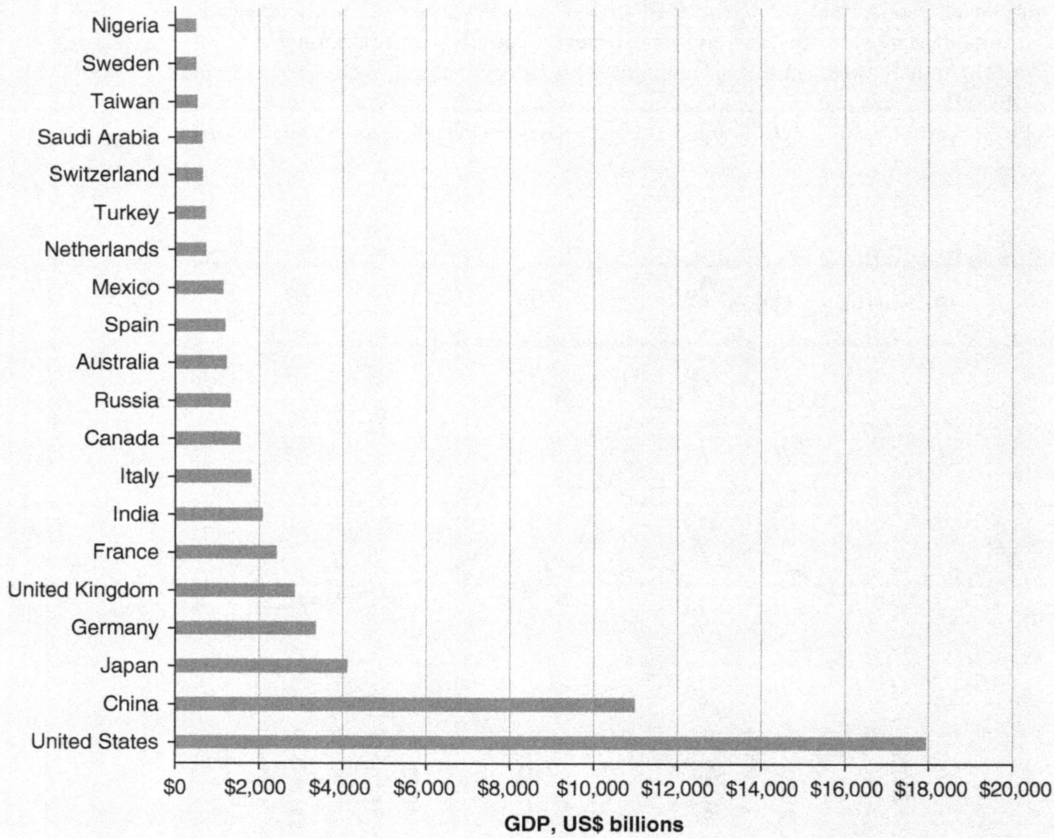

Source: IMF, World Economic Outlook Database, April 2016, https://www.imf.org/external/pubs/ft/weo/2016/01/weodata/index.aspx.

on the Shanghai exchange, and China slightly devalued its currency, which is officially known as the renminbi and whose unit of denomination is the yuan.[10]

For more than a year, global prices of iron ore, coal, oil and other commodities sank, partly because of the slowing China demand and partly because of a glut created by mining companies that hoped China's hunger for raw materials would keep growing. This badly hurt emerging economies such as Brazil, Venezuela and Zambia that rely on resource exports. [1]

China's leaders haven't been willing to close many inefficient, or unneeded, companies. Officials announced plans this year to cut steel production. But that creates a social problem: Each steel plant employs many people, and closing one raises unemployment. China's plan would throw an estimated 1.8 million coal miners and steelworkers, or 15 percent of the total, out of work and could create social unrest that worries the Communist government.[12]

What's more, economists are unsure whether the numbers they're crunching are accurate. Many experts are skeptical about the veracity of Chinese data, particularly the GDP numbers.[13] The IMF said in August that China's statistics continue to have gaps that hamper surveillance.[14]

China's economic issues worry many U.S. policymakers, as well as the two major-party presidential nominees, Democrat Hillary Clinton and Republican Donald J. Trump. They and other Americans have complained that China has used unfair trade practices—such as an undervalued currency and subsidies to home-grown companies—to flood U.S. markets with low-cost goods. At the same time, the government imposes high tariffs and restrictions on U.S. companies that hope to sell in China.[15] Both Clinton and Trump say they intend to renegotiate trade treaties that are fairer.[16]

The nation's economic rise has also created an environmental problem. China emits more greenhouse gases than any other country, having exceeded the United States in that category nine years ago.[17] In January 2013, Beijing experienced a prolonged bout of smog so severe that citizens dubbed it an "airpocalypse," with hazardous particles surpassing international safety levels.[18]

China Pays Price for Rapid Economic Expansion

Pollution Fuels Citizens' Health Ills, Global Climate Change

China's swift rise to become the world's second-largest economy has exacted a toll on the quality of its air and water and made the country a major emitter of greenhouse gases. The government's cleanup targets will not be easy to achieve. Here's the key takeaway: Chinese leaders must decide whether they will sacrifice some economic growth to curb rampant pollution.

In September, Presidents Obama and Xi Jinping signed the Paris climate agreement, vowing that the world's No. 1 and No. 2 carbon polluters would cut emissions to reduce global temperatures. In joining nearly 200 nations that had already ratified the accord, China said it will allow its emissions to peak around 2030, and the United States has said it would cut greenhouse gases by at least 26 percent by 2025.[19]

The signing happened nine months after Beijing issued a "red alert," an environmental emergency that led officials to close schools, ban traffic and temporarily halt factory production. Observers said the city was cloaked in a "soupy, metallic haze."[20]

China has paid a heavy price for its rapid industrialization, stoking dangerous environmental problems that plague its nearly 1.4 billion people. As the country retools its economy, many observers wonder if China's leaders are willing to sacrifice some growth, even as China's economy slows, to sharply curb pollution—and whether officials

(Continued)

(Continued)

have the will to alter the political and legal system to cleanse the land and address its citizens' health problems.

What's more, China's pollution becomes the world's problem. Its toxic chemicals go airborne, contributing to altered weather patterns and warmer temperatures worldwide.[21] During China's economic boom of the last 30 years, air particles have contributed to denser clouds, and storms in the Northwest Pacific have become about 10 percent stronger, NASA researchers have found.[22]

The list of China's environmental problems is lengthy. The air in major cities routinely fails to meet international health standards. Pollution has shortened life expectancy in some regions, increased asthma rates, contaminated water, destroyed land, and is linked to the rise of certain diseases. Even as the economy sputters, leaders in Beijing have taken steps to prevent further damage and to make the country greener.[23] Fears of environmental damage are discussed on China's online chat platforms and have sparked large protests in several cities.[24]

Levels of the fine particulate matter that's considered most dangerous to human health—called PM 2.5—were 10 times higher in China than in the United States in January 2016. One study concluded that people living in Northern China lived an average of 5.5 years less because of the sooty air.[25]

The situation frustrates Chinese citizens. In 2015, an online documentary by a former state television journalist called "Under the Dome" surveyed the extent of China's air problems. In days the film was viewed hundreds of millions of times before state censors ordered websites to delete it.[26]

A major contributor to the problem is coal. China is the world's largest coal producer and accounts for about half of global consumption.[27]

Between 2000 and 2007 coal consumption doubled, and then doubled again in the next seven years, says Jennifer Turner, director of the China Environment Forum at the Woodrow Wilson International Center for Scholars, a Washington research organization. "They're urbanizing at a rate unseen in the world," she says. "It's getting people out of poverty. But they have been dependent on coal. And also increasingly on gas. The coal/car combo gives you the toxic mix that you see over Chinese cities."

There are reasons to doubt that China can meet its commitment to cleanup accords, such as the one signed with Obama.

In the first half of 2015, the capacity of China's coal power plants jumped by 55 percent, the state approved 155 new coal-fired plants and it acknowledged that it had understated the annual level of coal use since 2000.[28]

"They're are using less coal as a consequence of the economic slowdown, but they're still building coal-fired plants," says Debra Knopman, an environmental engineering professor at the Pardee RAND Graduate School in Santa Monica, Calif. "That's the cheapest form of electricity they have available."

The other big problem is a direct consequence of China's newly created wealth—cars. Auto ownership soared to 154 million in 2014, up from roughly 27 million in 2004.[29] (Americans owned about 240 million cars as of 2010.)[30]

China does not lack for strong environmental laws, says Knopman. The nation has rigorous regulations—but they're applied unevenly, or not at all. Safety standards often can take a back seat to the goal of expanding the economy, she says.

The economic reforms of paramount leader Deng Xiaoping from 1978 to 1989 encouraged local governments to spur manufacturing production, but local officials seldom monitored environmental standards. Today, state-owned enterprises such as steel smelters and cement factories can employ tens of thousands of people in one city, "and it can be hard for a local environmental protection bureau to stand up to what is a very powerful economic force in that area. They have a hard time enforcing the laws on the books," Knopman says.

Water comes from industrial discharges that haven't been properly treated. In Shandong province, officials don't know the source of water pollution, she says, because individual factories and pipes don't always have permits.

The nation has sometimes had trouble harnessing alternative-energy sources. China has installed dams for hydropower, but they have choked off rivers running to lakes, destroying ecosystems, Turner says. Attempts to harness wind power have been spotty, because the country has installed lower-quality machines that haven't performed well, Bloomberg News reported this year.[31] Large protests have erupted in some cities where residents worry about nuclear facilities, especially after Japan's Fukushima disaster in 2011.[32]

Xi has issued stern warnings to pollution violators. In 2013, he told government officials that anyone who approves a project that damages the environment will face lifelong sanctions.[33]

Such steps, as well as signing the Paris climate agreement, encourage many scholars. Enforcement of the accords will be meted out through worldwide monitoring—including the public's attention—on nations that don't uphold their commitments.[34]

Much will depend in China on the will of Xi's government, but a clearly agitated populace can pressure the government. The country, says Turner, doesn't have much choice but to act. "They are on the razor's edge," she says. "It matters for China's political stability and it matters for the world."

—Suzanne Sataline

Some observers wonder if China is entering a crisis like Japan's "lost decade" of the 1990s. In that country, in the late 1980s, inexpensive credit fueled overseas investment. When the stock market crashed, corporations were left valued at a fraction of what they had been years earlier, Kroeber says, and the government's efforts at stimulus failed. Kroeber says land and stock prices in China don't approach that level of bloated value. Still, if China doesn't make major reforms, the country will run into a debt crisis, Shatz says.

Not just financial change is needed. Economists say China must alter its politics, laws and social policies to strengthen the economy. Reform won't be easy. China's leaders know they need to foster innovation and depend less on exports and construction. But its bureaucratic-authoritarian system means the Communist Party orchestrates policy, while local governments wield great power in controlling local enterprises and jobs. In short: A centralized, one-party state presides over a decentralized economy.[35]

Trusting the markets has not come easily. When traders in 2015 and earlier this year dumped lots of stock on China's markets, the government stepped in to prevent a rout.[36] In December, China said it needed to cut stockpiles of industrial goods and unsold homes, lower costs for businesses, and mitigate financial risks, according to China's official Xinhua News Agency. Economists say they are still waiting for those fixes.[37]

Beijing's Air Pollution Remains Dangerous

Highest monthly measurements of PM2.5 in 2015

Beijing's air pollution last year was highest in April and lowest in August. But in all months, it was unhealthy or worse, according to measurements of PM2.5, a fine particulate matter. PM2.5 is especially hazardous to humans because its micro size allows it to easily penetrate the lungs and bloodstream. The graphic represents the highest measurement of PM2.5 for each month in 2015.

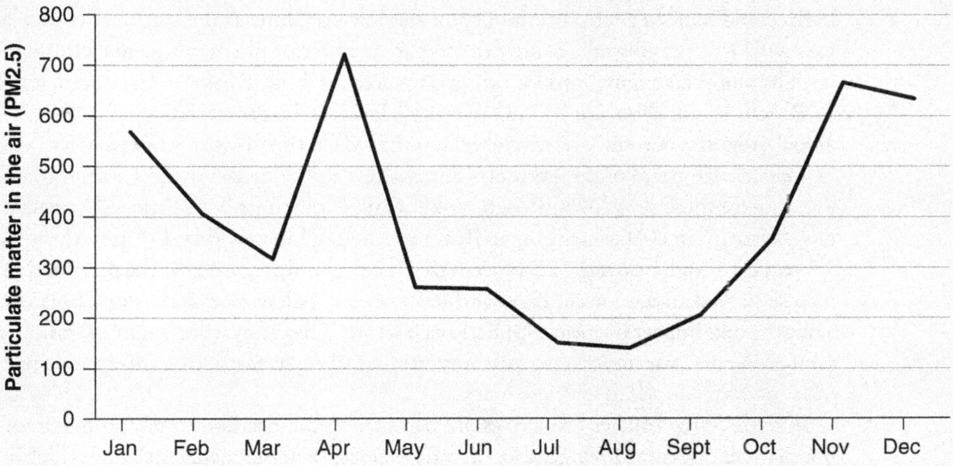

Note: Anything greater than 200 is considered very unhealthy; greater than 300 is hazardous; and greater than 500 is beyond the index.

Source: U.S. Department of State, Beijing Embassy, http://www.stateair.net/web/post/1/1.html.

Some observers worry that President Xi Jinping has been so intent on rooting out corruption and consolidating his power, in preparation for next year's Politburo meeting, that no reforms will be imminent. "Right now I don't think anybody has any courage to do anything regarding the economy," says Ho-Fung Hung, professor of sociology at Johns Hopkins University. "When they feel secure enough, they might do something."

As policymakers, economists and business officials ponder China's future and its impact on the global economy, here are the issues under discussion:

WEIGHING THE ISSUES

Will China's Economic Slowdown Harm Other Countries?

When China stopped building highways, airports and apartment towers, it badly hurt emerging economies that relied on exporting resources and technical goods. Brazil, for one, with its stores of iron ore, is struggling through its worst crisis since the Great Depression.[38] The slowdown hurt manufacturers in rich countries such as Japan, South Korea and Taiwan, which sell goods to China. Its impact on American trading partners will dampen U.S. growth, according to economists with the Dallas Federal Reserve.[39]

Economists and researchers debate the extent to which a slower, less hungry China will harm other countries.

AEI's Scissors is convinced the threat is real. The over-reliance on exports to China helped to hollow out the economies of Venezuela and South Sudan, he says. Those countries "were too busy making money" to see that China's economy was overheated, he says. Commodities producers from Australia to Zambia were harmed when Beijing no longer needed so much iron ore.

"Countries in every habitable climate were incredibly shortsighted," Scissors says. Such harm could happen again if certain countries rely on China as the source of money for whatever will be its next big area of growth, perhaps health care or environmental cleanup, he says.

The world economy has a lot riding on whether China keeps decelerating, wrote Stephen S. Roach, senior fellow at Yale University's Jackson Institute of Global Affairs.[40] Because global growth is currently relatively weak—the IMF estimates it at 3.1 percent this year, below its longer-term trend of 3.6 percent—there is less ability by the world's economies to absorb a lasting Chinese slowdown, Roach wrote. China will contribute almost 39 percent of total global growth in 2016, according to Roach; without China, world GDP growth would be just 1.9 percent—well below the 2.5 percent that is commonly regarded as the threshold of a global recession. And an economic "hard landing"—a rapid halt or recession—for China would have a devastating impact on global GDP, Roach wrote. The effect will remain harmful, he said, if Chinese leaders continue to restrain domestic spending by restricting what goods and services other nations can sell to Chinese markets.[41]

Indeed, some smaller economies are bemoaning the decision to rely so much on China's boom times. "We are looking at a lost decade, where growth stagnates, inflation is high and, most sadly, a decade where you've learned nothing," said Marcos Troyjo, a former Brazilian diplomat who co-directs BRICLab at Columbia University, a center that studies emerging markets.[42]

Economist Michael Pettis, professor of finance at Peking University's Guanghua School of Management, said he's not convinced that China's growth rate has that much effect on worldwide GDP. China's annual growth rate, once 10 percent, has sunk below 7 percent and will likely settle at half that. "China is not the world's growth engine and never has been," he wrote. "It is simply the largest arithmetical component of growth, which is a very different thing."[43]

Pessimists such as billionaire investor George Soros said they fear a banking crisis could be worse than the commodities glut.[44]

Pettis is not convinced. "Insolvency doesn't necessarily lead to crisis, as countries like Spain have made clear," he wrote. "It takes a collapse in liquidity to create a crisis, and if insolvent borrowers remain liquid, we are likely instead to see a long, difficult period of slow growth. . . . As long as Beijing implicitly or explicitly guarantees deposits, and as long as Beijing's credibility with Chinese households is solid, and I believe it is, I think we are more likely to see many years of Japanese-style 'zombie banks' [banks with bad debts] than a banking crisis."[45]

Much will depend on Beijing's efforts to rebalance its economy away from a reliance on exports and foster more services and consumer spending, Pettis said. "My best guess is that Beijing will drive an orderly rebalancing of the Chinese economy, even as it drives growth rates down to levels that most analysts would find unexpectedly low, and this will be net positive for the global economy."[46]

CSIS's Kennedy sees China's global impact slightly differently. "It could maintain a moderately fast growth rate without hurting other countries," he says. "But it depends on how China approaches achieving growth." If China continues with its current path of intervention—providing stimulus to the economy, targeted spending on high technology and protection of domestic industries through tariffs and other barriers—that creates obstacles to outside investment. And it builds debt.

Kennedy thinks China will affect other economies in new sectors. The government continues to be protectionist about its technology. As its workers move beyond assembling digital goods to making more sophisticated products, they will pose a competitive threat to other countries that make computer components, such as South Korea and Taiwan, he says. If China overproduces, it will prompt prices to fall. That will dampen inflation and potentially lead to deflation, or the contraction of the pool of money in an economy. If enough companies are affected, that will pressure financial markets.

Is China Still an Important Market for U.S. Companies?

American businesses and foreign governments want to believe that the world's largest marketplace will continue to be a profitable place to do business. But an annual survey of members of the American Chamber of Commerce in China in 2016 found that the business environment has worsened.[47]

More than half (57 percent) of the 496 companies that responded said their top challenges were unsold goods, inconsistent regulatory practices and skilled labor shortages. One in 10 companies said it planned to move or had sent part of its business outside of China because of government obstacles. More companies said they felt less welcome than a year ago, with technology, industrial and resource companies citing the greatest displeasure. And 44 percent of technology companies said they were pessimistic about the future regulatory environment. Other complaints included risks of data breaches, internet censorship and online controls, and rising labor costs; according to the Oxford Economics research firm, unit labor costs in China are now just 4 percent lower than in the United States, a sharp increase since 2003.[48]

"Some of the policies which are being considered or have already been enacted are fundamentally leading China in the wrong direction," Lester Ross, the chamber's vice chairman, said.[49]

Many businesses have complained for years that heavy regulation and internet filters restrict access to products of foreign tech companies. Some American companies like Uber have spent heavily to try to make it in China, only to wind up selling a substantial stake to a Chinese brand.[50] Uber joined Google and eBay, which were unable to capitalize on early endeavors in China. EBay could not combat the size and popularity of e-commerce competitor Alibaba, while Google left the country after executives said it was the target of government-sponsored cyberattacks, and after taking criticism over its initial decision to comply with government censorship.[51]

Some critics of China say they're concerned about corruption and intellectual property theft, which means a company's proprietary products could end up being marketed by a Chinese firm. The government makes demands of foreign companies that some find overly intrusive. For instance, the state is reviewing foreign software development companies' encryption and data storage.[52] Local operations of global companies have become less profitable as domestic competition spiked. Many multinational companies have closed offices and factories in China, including Microsoft, Adobe, Panasonic, Yahoo and Adidas.[53]

Corruption Ranks High as Chinese Business Problem

Tax rates seen as most problematic factor

Corruption ranked second among the most problematic factors for doing business in China, below tax rates and above inadequate supply of infrastructure, according to a survey of business leaders.

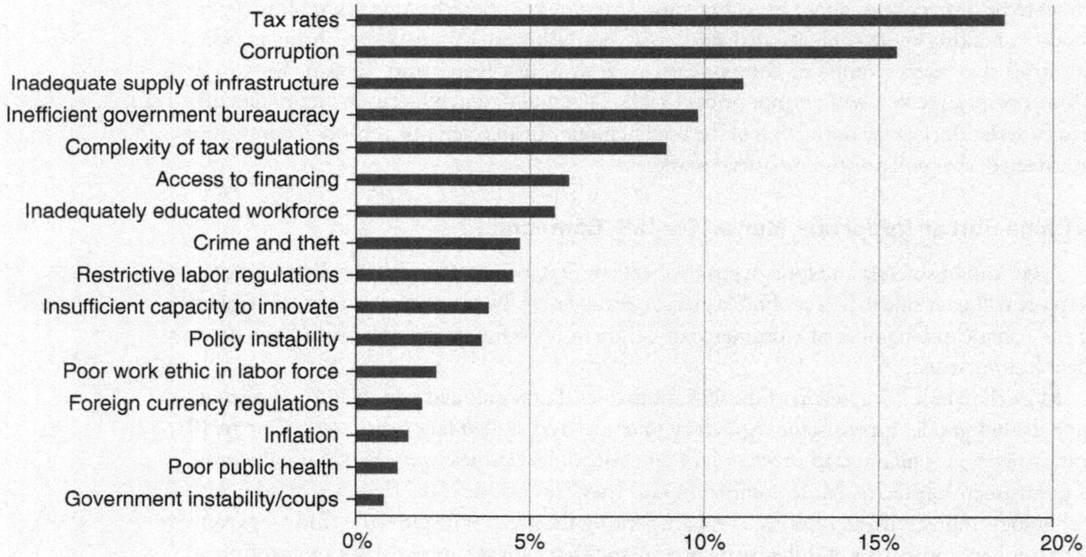

Note: More than 14,000 business leaders globally were asked to select the five most problematic aspects of doing business in China and to rank them between 1 (most problematic) and 5. The bars in the graphic show the responses weighted according to their rankings.

Source: "The Global Competitiveness Report 2015–2016," World Economic Forum, http://tinyurl.com/q976g9x.

Manufacturers say they can work more easily in Vietnam, Thailand and Malaysia with less government hassle and lower wages (one study found that the total cost of labor in Vietnam was less than half of that in China).[54]

"Multinationals' China operations have become less and less profitable as domestic competition has intensified. The Chinese government, of course, has aided this process by systematically discriminating against foreign companies, enforcing laws and regulations with regards to multinationals while looking the other way when a domestic company commits a violation," wrote Noah Smith, a former assistant professor of finance at Stony Brook University.[55]

Despite the challenges, many economists are bullish on the ability of American companies to work in and do business with China. "If China continues to grow or adapt, there's lot of job opportunities for people in business," says Kennedy of the Center for Strategic and International Studies. Health care, education and consumer products are all growth sectors. Several hundred thousand multinational firms operate in China, and Chinese companies are hiring lots of people outside China.

China's expanding middle class continues to be an attractive market for products ranging from consumer goods—mobile phones, electronics and autos—to financial services and money-market funds, Kroeber says.

"In terms of employment prospects, I'd still go long on China," Kennedy says. "As a growth area for work and attention, China is going to continue to be important and require a disproportionate amount of global attention, whether in business, public policy, the media, NGOs."

Shatz of RAND agrees. "They are not going to close themselves off to the world, or going to collapse," he says. "The one pitfall that foreign business people have, is China becoming a more difficult environment for foreign businesses?" He's not dissuaded. "I think it's still worth learning Chinese."

Will President Xi Foster a True Market-Based Economy Centered on Innovation?

In November 2013, China's president pledged to give market forces a "decisive" role in China's economy. At the same time, Xi said state-owned enterprises would remain "dominant," a sign that his government would still meddle.[56]

Even the state-owned news agency Xinhua detected the inherent conflict in those statements. "Even after the reform and opening up in 1978, the country had struggled to define the market and some dogmatists still questioned whether socialism could accommodate the market economy," the paper wrote.[57]

The stakes riding on how this dilemma is resolved are high. A Chinese economy that retools to become more market-based would be more likely to ease trade conflicts and imbalances, end protectionist practices and create or expand markets in other countries, according to many economists.

China's transition toward a market economy has been piecemeal—some might say messy—mixing doses of government regulation, state enterprise and a growing private sector.

For example, in August 2015, Beijing made changes to the value of the renminbi, to make it more market-oriented. At the same time, the government slightly devalued the currency: (China allows the renminbi to trade within a certain range against the dollar, rather than

China's Leader Battles Pervasive Corruption

Deals, Payoffs Power Nation's Vast Economic Machine

Chinese President Xi Jinping began his tenure by launching a concerted drive to root out the corruption that has penetrated to the heart of his country's massive economy. While some observers say Xi's hand was forced, others fear that the campaign has become a witch hunt. Here's the key takeaway: A drive to curb corruption risks creating unintended consequences, such as local government paralysis.

Xi Jinping, the Communist Party's general secretary, was about to ascend to China's presidency and he had a message for the party's top disciplinary committee.

In a speech delivered in January 2013, Xi promised to stop powerful leaders and lowly bureaucrats alike from conducting business using favors, kickbacks and other deceitful transactions. In doing so, he seemed to acknowledge that the scandals that had snared several powerful leaders, and the petty fraud and inefficiency of everyday civic life, had fueled massive discontent.

"We must uphold the fighting of tigers and flies at the same time, resolutely investigating lawbreaking cases of leading officials and also earnestly resolving the unhealthy tendencies and corruption problems which happen all around people," Xi said. He vowed to take down both tigers, or powerful officials, and flies, lowly bureaucrats.[58]

That speech ignited a major government crackdown against officials low and high that's still reverberating. The government prosecuted nearly 300,000 officials in 2015, including 82,000 who were severely punished and demoted.[59] Included were the nation's former chief of domestic security, a retired general and the highest-ranking military official. Many top officials were sentenced to life in prison.[60]

As Xi promised, not just party bigwigs have been targeted; in fact, the people responsible for rooting out graft were disciplined, including several police officials, judges and prosecutors.[61]

Corruption has burrowed into every aspect of China's economic life, especially since reforms were introduced in the late 1970s, according to those familiar with the country, such as Arthur R. Kroeber, founding partner at the Beijing research firm Gavekal Dragonomics.[62] From prices to smuggling, from land deals to bank loans, China's vast economic machine motors along through backroom deals and under-the-table transactions. The corruption persists, observers say, because it is perversely efficient, providing a way around a sclerotic bureaucracy that delays projects with unnecessary steps and prevents businesses from taking off.

In China, government officials are entrepreneurs. The Communist Party has allowed local officials to compete for investments, which gives them enormous sway, and has prompted some officials to demand bribes and offer favors.[63] Construction and infrastructure sectors have been riddled with corruption, according to protesting citizens, and the results have at times proven deadly.[64] Shoddy construction of dorms and schools was partly to blame for the deaths of more than 69,000 people during the 2008 Sichuan earthquake.[65]

Studies by the Clean Governance Research Center at Beijing's Beihang University found that up to a third of party leaders ranked at the minister level or above took bribes and commissions or assisted close relatives or friends in commercial deals.[66]

The new quasi-market economy that has evolved since the 1980s created more wealth and a competition for services that were often hard to obtain. That spawned a marketplace for graft, says Liao Ran, a senior program coordinator of the Asia and Pacific department at Transparency International, a Berlin-based international corruption monitoring group.

For instance, in the 1980s, when an entrepreneur submitted a government application to obtain a license, one might need a few hundred departments to stamp documents papers, he says. The process could take weeks, if not months. Someone with enough money could pay for those stamp marks and obtain the necessary approvals in one day.

"There's a perfect state for corruption," Liao says. "There's a huge demand in the market. As a [hypothetical] government official, I have huge power. I can trade my power and get back cash. Now with cash in China, there's an open market price for everything, from a job to a title." The government eliminated some graft, he says, when it partially abolished some of its onerous bureaucracy.

But the vast effort to control government officials and stop graft has led to complaints that Xi is on a witch hunt, attacking party members with a zeal that hasn't been seen since Mao Zedong, who ruled China from 1949 to 1976.[67]

Xi had no choice but to clean up the government; at the close of predecessor Xu Jintao's presidency in 2013, corruption was "out of control and everyone in government was stealing right and left," Kroeber says. There is, however, some merit to the concern that Xi is using the corruption campaign to banish enemies. "There's no question that the anti-corruption campaign is being used to get rid of rival political networks, and tighten his authority," he says.

And that has helped dampen future government initiatives, Kroeber says. "The anti-corruption campaign is so pervasive and so draconian, it has really eliminated incentives for local government officials to do anything interesting and innovative or approve a project," he says. Government officials worry, "'If I do, they'll accuse me of getting a kickback.' The easiest thing is to do nothing. . . . It has really had a chilling effect on all kind of economic activity and government innovation."

Kroeber says corruption in China is systemic, and that unless the government institutes some judicial or institutional reforms that raise the cost of graft and introduce a cleaner government, the state probably will not be able to end corruption in the long run.

The campaign's targets included some civil society groups that were deemed potential threats to the party, such as nonprofit human rights law centers and labor organizers, says Scott Kennedy, a director at the Center for Strategic and International Studies, a Washington-based research group.

"That central tightening and clampdown have made it easier for Xi Jinping to announce policies," he said. "It's made it harder to implement these policies successfully, and harder when they make mistakes to adapt. The higher centralization has contributed to them making more mistakes."

—*Suzanne Sataline*

freely.) Traders assumed that devaluation was the goal and started a selloff, until the national bank intervened and spent down its foreign-currency reserves to prop up the renminbi's value.[68] When there was another selloff in December, again the state bank jumped in.[69]

Xi's promises of market reforms would require that the state, or the party, stop its interventions and micro-management, wrote Guy de Jonquières, a senior fellow at the European Centre for International Political Economy. China must develop sound institutions that vigorously regulate market function, a colossal task, he wrote.[70]

At times it seems as if Xi's government is trying to pull off the impossible: maintain growth, full employment, innovation and tight control, and keep the economy from plunging into the "middle income trap." That's the chasm in which developing economies struggle to compete with lower-cost competitors, but don't have the capacity or resources to leap into the richest tier.[71]

"In China today, property rights are still ill-defined; the rule of law is applied unevenly; the courts are subject to political control; market regulation is haphazard and subject to political manipulation; and crucially, every institution is constitutionally subordinated to the will of the party, whose decision-making is opaque, unaccountable and often unpredictable," de Jonquières wrote. "Even if Beijing is committed to changing all those things—itself a highly questionable assumption—they will not be changed quickly."[72]

To avoid triggering massive unemployment, and prompting calls for political freedoms, Xi and his coterie must correctly time domestic reforms with currency conversion, he wrote. Xi's clampdown on the political sphere as he ponders economic reforms signals that he's "optimistic that the tension can be managed," de Jonquieres wrote.[73]

Some economists have said that they're encouraged by China's shift to new engines of growth, such as the service sector and high tech.[74] The government is pouring money into start-up incubators and offers grants to some private businesses. Having the government involved, though, raises similar concerns as with state-owned enterprises, such as favoritism and waste. "The question is: in an effort to promote the private sector, is that creating so much debt and inefficiency that it's going to bring the system down?" CSIS's Kennedy said. "Or will it shift the adjustment cost to everyone else?"

One view among China-watchers is that Xi is waiting for the next party congress to conclude in autumn 2017, and that once the president installs his people in key positions, he'll shift to making aggressive economic reforms. Ryan Rutkowski of Matthews Asia, an investment fund focused on Asia, is encouraged that China announced a plan in 2015 that would move electricity prices to a market system, showing that the government will push past resistance from central regulators, power grid companies and local officials. "This is a comforting reminder that even in a slowing economy, the Chinese government is still looking for opportunities to make long-term reforms," he wrote.[75]

There are reasons to doubt that Xi's government is committed to market-oriented reforms, because these would require an "unacceptable dilution of Communist Party power," Kroeber of Gavekal Dragonomics wrote.[76] Most of the reforms outlined in 2013 have not been implemented, he says in an interview, including changes to the state-owned enterprise system. Other ideas, such as allowing private companies to invest in state companies, haven't happened, either, he says.

China, he says, is trying to pull off something no other country has managed: to move up the technological innovation consumer society ladder while bolstering the authoritarian single-party's role in society. Many people are skeptical that the government can achieve both of those aims.

"I think it's possible for the next five years or longer China can enjoy pretty rapid economic growth—5 percent a year, impressive—and do it in the context of tightening control by the Communist Party," Kroeber says. "In the short term they can have it both ways, but the longer that goes on, the harder it is for that act to be sustained."

George Magnus, an independent economist and former chief economist at UBS, wrote that much of the talk about reforms "has run aground, been diluted or faced opposition from vested interests."[77] Under Xi, he said, rigorous suppression of journalists, rights activists and critics proves that the government does not welcome alternative views. And state internet censors, referred to as the Great Firewall, are dogged, suppressing unwelcome news such as Hong Kong's democracy protest in 2014 and even news from the recent G-20 summit.[78]

"Quite how the authorities plan to build an economy in the information age without permitting the free flow of information is a question no one in authority is prepared to answer," Magnus wrote.[79]

BACKGROUND

The Chinese Republic

The last emperor abdicated in 1912, ending centuries of Qing dynasty rule. National finances were in tatters. The state was deeply in debt to several foreign governments, a legacy of agreements made after the Qing lost the 19th century Opium Wars and were forced into treaties that gave foreign enterprises access to Chinese markets.[80] Great Britain and Japan owned stakes in China's railways, shipping, public utilities, mills, refineries and more. (America's stake was much smaller.)

Members of the newly formed Chinese Communist Party joined protests against foreign factory owners.[81] Mill workers—with few workplace rights, harassed by gang leaders and foremen—were attracted to the Communist credo.[82] When police opened fire on striking factory workers in 1925, killing some, anger mounted against foreigners.[83]

In 1927 the Nationalist, or Guomindang, party, headed by Chiang Kai-Shek, sought to unify the country.[84] Chiang's government was deeply in debt and tried to survive by heavily taxing industries and rebuilding. That led to bankruptcies and inflation.[85] Urban centers flourished, but rural residents were still plagued by corrupt landlords, crop failures and almost no security.[86]

The sprouting of new industry halted when Japan invaded China in 1937, igniting more than a decade of foreign occupation and war. Industry spread in Japanese-occupied Manchuria, and Japan shifted production at Shanghai firms from consumer goods to machinery and armaments.[87] That resulted in the post-war government's control of 90 percent of iron and steel production, and a hefty portion of the electricity and cement.[88] The budding state-run economy was set in place when the Communists took over in 1949.

Two separate Guomindang's alliances with the Communists frayed, and Communist Party members went into hiding. With rural residents plagued by corrupt landlords, crop failures and almost no help from the government, Mao Zedong and his Communist comrades capitalized on the peasants' mounting frustrations.[89] Once the Japanese were routed after World War II, the Communists were able to regroup and attack Chiang's exhausted troops, forcing the Guomindang into exile on the offshore island of Taiwan in 1949.[90]

Mao, 1949 and the Creation of the Centralized Economy

After Mao and the Chinese Communist Party founded the People's Republic of China in 1949, the new government propelled the Chinese economy into a new direction. They set out to develop a massive socialist system orchestrated by the state, modeled on the Soviet Union. The Communists aimed to pull China into modernity by developing an industrialized economy. But the government adopted and abandoned plans and policies quickly, leading to periods of great productivity followed by years of stagnation.[91]

During Mao's rule, which ran from 1949 to 1976, the Communist Party systematically abolished private property.[92] The government owned all big factories, transport and communication. In the countryside, collectives assumed ownership of the land and managed farms.[93] Work was centralized and state planners set productivity targets, such as in the First Five Year Plan (1953 to 1957).[94] The state planning commission allocated raw materials and production items—coal, timber, cement, steel, and lathes—to state enterprises to meet the output targets.[95]

Markets were structured by the state. Most farming was controlled by state communes, which delivered crops to a state commission for sale.[96] Most farmers were permitted to grow extra food only for their family's consumption.[97] The government requisitioned grain supplies, and most vital consumables—grains, vegetable oil, cotton cloth and bicycles—were rationed in urban areas.[98] Factories and government offices issued coupons to employees that were used with cash to buy goods from state stores.[99]

The government controlled the system of prices and didn't factor in market conditions. As a result, factory goods were expensive and farm goods were cheap. Any surplus became a source of government revenue. With prices distorted, the state-owned enterprises were very profitable and served as wealth producers for the economy.[100]

To keep the system working, the state exercised strict control of materials, credit, personnel and career paths and workers' movements. Typical state-owned enterprises had little authority and could not retain profits or hire as it needed. Workers stayed in their jobs for life, sometimes passing on their jobs to their children.[101]

Mao's economic and social movements further disrupted the economy. From 1958 to 1961 Mao instituted the Great Leap Forward, an industrial and social campaign to create a full communist society in a few years. Resources were transferred from agriculture to industry, and the state demanded that even more grain be sent to the state. With less food produced and more taken by the government, famine spread in 1960 and killed some 30 million people.[102]

The government addressed the crisis by importing goods and opening the markets so peasants could provide more food. Mao then set out on a "Third Front" in 1964 to create an industrial base that would free China from dependence on and pressure from its Cold War rivals, the United States and the Soviet Union.[103]

Soon after, Mao launched the Cultural Revolution (1966–76), in which he encouraged students organized as Red Guards to overthrow party leadership, resulting in attacks and murders of party officials, teachers and perceived enemies. Seventeen million city students left school and were sent to the countryside to learn from the farmers. By the end, the People's Liberation Army clamped down on political divisions and was managing industrial centers.[104]

Deng, Reform and Opening

With Mao's death in 1976, and his fiercest supporters imprisoned, his successors focused on strengthening the economy. At the Third Party Plenum—or meeting of all members—in 1978, Deng Xiaoping, the new paramount leader, forged a plan for a new command economy.[105] China decided that its priority must be economic growth. Leaders were especially aware that grain policies had paid little to farmers, and there was concern that they would drop their production. The initial plans mostly concerned allowing rural residents to earn money in private businesses. That ushered in competition and the privatization of the 1990s.[106]

In time, Deng and the fragmented leadership realized they needed to free more of the economy from the Soviet-style planning model and gradually introduce a host of free-market principles. "Reform and opening" allowed for private businesses, free trade and investment with the West, with the goal of growing the economy and raising living standards.

The government selected four areas on the coast to be special economic zones. The aim was to lure foreign investment, increase exports and import technology goods. The state gave economic control of many enterprises to provincial and local governments, which were freed from state planning and urged to compete on the free market. In 1980, the southern city of Shenzhen became the first special economic zone to experiment with flexible market policies. A fishing center bordering what was then the British crown colony of Hong Kong, Shenzhen was allowed to invite in foreign partners to start building an industrial core.[107]

The government eased restrictions on movement, dropping lifetime job assignments in the mid-1980s.[108] The state encouraged citizens to start their own businesses and to experiment with free-market reforms and tax and trade incentives to lure foreign investment. In time, those four open cities grew to 14.[109] The first wave of reforms fostered a generation of entrepreneurs in the 1980s.[110] For help, they often tied themselves to local officials, creating subsidiaries of government enterprises or agencies. These newest enterprises were all dependent, in varying degrees, on the Communist Party's approval.[111]

Trade liberalization was also a key to China's economic success. Removing some trade barriers encouraged greater competition and attracted foreign investment. China's gradual execution of economic reforms sought to weigh and choose which policies produced favorable economic outcomes and which failed, so the successes could be deployed elsewhere in the country.[112]

Low-interest bank lending for projects began.[113] This created personal patronage networks in which bankers could choose to lend to certain people.

But certain things didn't change. Rural residents were not permitted to move permanently to cities. And state enterprises were still protected.

Creation of Great Wealth

Managing China's growing wealth, and capitalizing on it, became a focus in the 1990s.

In 1990, the Shanghai Stock Exchange opened, the first ever such market in Communist China.[114]

Starting in 1992, the government shifted its emphasis to ensure a well-regulated, competitive market.[115] Laws dictated the corporate structure of state-owned enterprises, a nearly uniform value-added tax, foreign exchange rates, and a well-run banking system. The currency became convertible in 1996, which allowed the free flow of money for imports and exports.

The era also marked the rise of private business in China. In 1995, the state began extensively shrinking state enterprises. Thirty million employees—nearly two-fifths of the total workforce at such enterprises—lost their jobs as companies closed or were placed in private hands.[116] In 2002, the state ended the system of job assignments for college graduates. Companies were allowed to keep part of their profits, and more wage flexibility took hold. Private-sector employment grew, from 73 million in 1990 to nearly 282 million in 2010.[117] Still, the labor force wasn't fully market-led; the state still controlled where people could live.

Foreign direct investment ballooned from $4.4 billion in 1992 to $53 billion in 2002. Ethnic Chinese business families in Hong Kong, Macao and Taiwan invested in infrastructure, ports, railways, highways, commercial buildings, residential areas, department stores, luxury hotels and utilities. Taiwanese investment helped to develop high-tech zones in coastal cities.[118] That ushered in non-native investors. In 1992, Toyota established its first joint venture on the mainland and Japanese electronics firms such as Panasonic and Sony began pouring in money.[119] A few American companies followed. The more successful established zones became, the more other cities wanted in, creating a "zone fever." By 2004, China had 6,399 special zones.[120]

A crop of internet and mobile technology entrepreneurs took root, including Alibaba, Tencent and Baidu, becoming some of the nation's more profitable companies. Many entrepreneurs delved into other sectors of the economy: energy, health care, financial services, consumer and retail.[121]

Companies View Business Climate Positively

Returns on investments in China are strong, 2015 survey finds

More than three in four companies in China reported positive or very positive returns on investments since entering the country. Only 8 percent reported negative or very negative returns on investments.

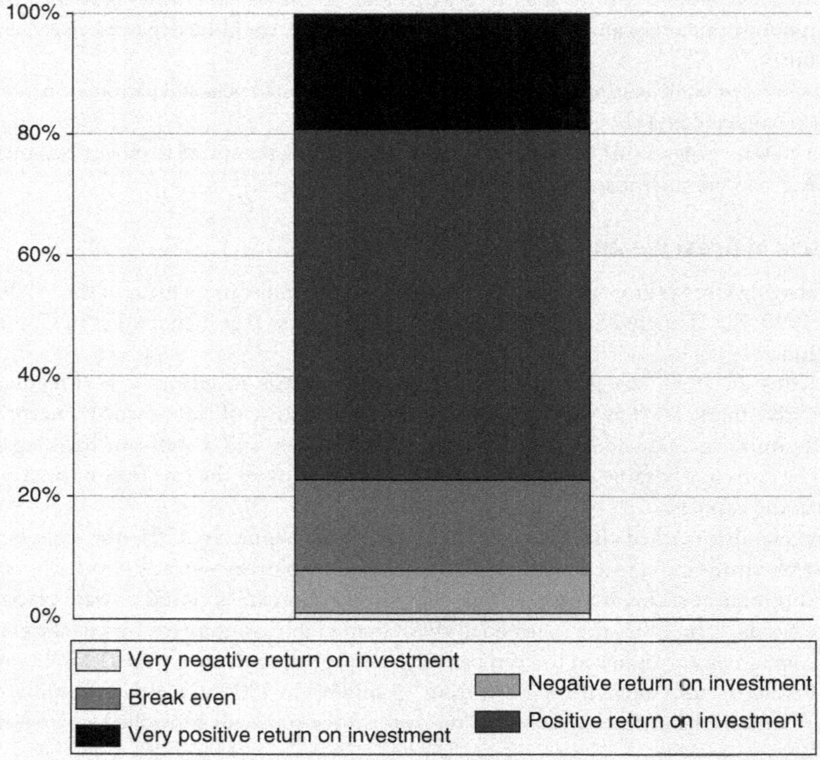

Note: The American Chamber of Commerce in the People's Republic of China concucted the survey in 2015; 532 member companies out of 961 partially or fully completed the survey (a 55 percent response rate).

Source: "2016 China Business Climate Support Survey Report," American Chamber of Commerce in the People's Republic of China, p. 13, http://tinyurl.com/hugwrop.

In 1997, Great Britain returned control of Hong Kong to China. The territory had been a British colony since 1842, when China relinquished it after losing the Opium Wars. In the handover, Britain tried to ensure Hong Kong's financial and social stability by crafting a constitution that guarantees its finances, elections and legal system will remain independent from Beijing for 50 years.[122]

The handover allowed China's government to set up ministry corporations in Hong Kong, which provided financing to clients in favor, notably the "princelings" or children of top party leaders. Government officials received bonuses for fulfilling targets.[123]

All of these changes helped push China into the global economy. In 2001, the nation became a member of the World Trade Organization (WTO), which governs international trade. While there were expectations that WTO membership would lead China to curtail trade barriers in many industries and end entrenched monopolies, it was clear from the start that the government would still be allowed to prop up favored companies.[124]

In 2007, for the first time in its history, China gave private property owners protection. But the law's application became contentious when many local governments sought to sell occupied land for massive redevelopment projects. Some farmers fought a sweeping government plan to move 250 million rural residents to cities by 2025. Homeowners who delayed said they were forced from their land. China's laws did not require just compensation for government seizures. The problem was called "Nail House" syndrome, referring to homeowners who defy eviction notices and "stick out like nails."[125]

By 2013, the economy was 25 times heftier than in 1978, and the nation's share of global GDP had more than quadrupled, rising from 3 percent to 12 percent.[126] By abandoning Mao's policies, China became the world's largest trading economy.

After assuming the presidency in 2013, Xi announced policy changes designed to turn the nation into a high-income country. The 12th Five-Year Plan (2011–2015) and the newly approved 13th Five-Year Plan (2016–2020) set goals to lower pollution, increase energy efficiency, expand access to education and health care, and end labor camps. The government vowed to achieve a "moderately prosperous society" by 2020.[127]

CURRENT SITUATION

International Business and Trade

China is the United States' second-largest trading partner (after Canada), but there is inequity. The U.S. imports nearly $252 billion of goods from China, but exports just $60 billion.[128]

Both major-party U.S. presidential candidates this year mention China frequently. They say they want the nation to abide by trade rules and accuse it of dumping products such as steel on American markets. Democratic nominee Clinton says she will confront countries that keep their goods artificially cheap by manipulating their currencies, and respond with duties, tariffs and other measures. Clinton says she objects to China's requests that it be recognized by the WTO as a market economy, saying such a designation would weaken anti-dumping laws.[129] Her Republican opponent asserts that since China's inclusion in the WTO, the U.S. has closed 50,000 factories and lost tens of millions of jobs. Trump says he intends to renegotiate treaties so American goods can access the Chinese market and to formally declare that China's currency is manipulated, imposing extra duties on imported goods.[130]

The country's attempts to address its slowdown and to shift from making low-cost goods to more items that are value-added in a consumer economy are expected to create challenges and also opportunities for other countries. It will likely lead to more growth slowdown in the immediate future, as wasteful investment is slowed. China's appetite for minerals and

U.S. Trade Deficit with China Keeps Growing

Deficit reached record in 2015

The U.S. trade deficit with China has risen every year but two between 1985 and 2015. It now stands at more than $367 billion.

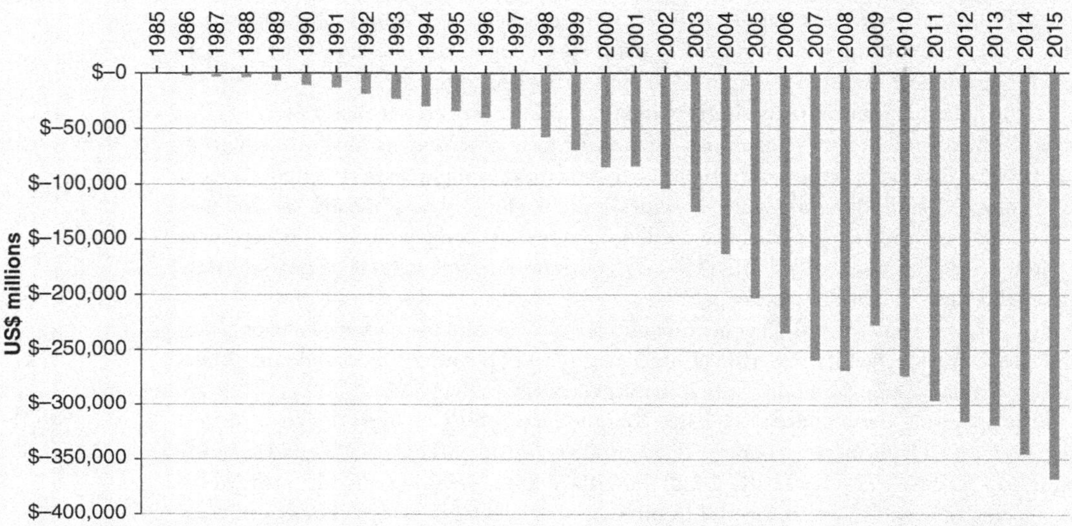

Source: U.S. Census Bureau, Foreign Trade, https://www.census.gov/foreign-trade/balance/c5700.html.

energy—iron ore, coal and crude oil—is likely to slow. Economists also expect softer commodity prices for energy and materials.[131]

Changes have hit hard in Brazil, an exporter of iron ore. Troyjo, the head of Columbia's BRICLab, said the nation faces stagnating growth and high inflation.[132]

China's slowdown has bruised its neighbors the most. Singapore's economy relies on exporting petroleum and integrated circuits to China.[133] Mongolia has fallen into an economic crisis, as China is not importing as much copper.[134] China is a major trading partner of many other countries, including Japan and South Korea, and developing nations such as Kyrgyzstan and Myanmar.[135] Taiwan's technology makers, especially those that produce mobile phone components, are facing more competition from mainland rivals as the island struggles from weaker demand from China, its biggest market, for its electronics and metals.[136]

CSIS's Kennedy says he expects China's slowdown, and the rising cost of labor, to prod the nation to shift production to cheaper countries and move from low value-added products (much of the clothing and shoe production has moved elsewhere) to higher-value items such as full electronics production. The United States and Europe, with their diverse economies, would be expected to weather a Chinese slowdown well. As China moves from assembling products such as iPhones to making high-tech components, that will put more competitive pressure on South Korea and Taiwan, leaders in that field.

Fostering Entrepreneurs

Today, China is awash in start-up companies that have made it big: electronics maker Xiaomi, Uber rival Didi Chuxing, China Internet Plus (a product of the recent merger of Meituan and Dianping) and drone producer DJI. In addition, there's Baidu, Alibaba and Tencent, which all operate internet businesses. China's Ministry of Science and Technology counts 115 university science parks and more than 1,600 technology business incubators in the country providing mentorship, legal advice and office space to dreamers and aspiring entrepreneurs.[137] One of the government incubators, Dream Town, offers subsidies to pay equipment and staff.[138]

And the world can likely expect more. In spring 2016, Premier Li Keqiang called for "mass entrepreneurship and innovation" and made it the leading agenda item of China's national economic strategy.[139] In March at the National People's Congress, Li crowed that 12,000 companies were founded each day in 2015.[140] Across the country, officials are creating investment funds, providing cash subsidies and building incubators.

These companies got a big push two decades ago when the government started to wall off its internet from the world—a kind of virtual protectionism to foster growth. U.S.-based companies that tried to enter China could not compete with local brands. And so in China there's a Baidu search engine, but no Google. WeChat prevailed over Facebook. Alibaba surpassed Amazon.

Some tech watchers say China leads the way in creating apps. Already in China, more people use their mobile devices to pay their bills, order services, watch videos and find dates than anywhere else in the world, the New York Times reported in August. Mobile payments in the country last year surpassed those in the United States.[141]

China's government is betting on its creative class and spending lots of money to foster the start-up culture. One city, Suzhou, near Shanghai, says it will open 300 incubators by 2020 that will host 30,000 start-ups.[142]

"Without these kinds of subsidies, you only rely on private money, and you wouldn't see so many technology start-ups happening today," said Ning Tao, a partner at Innovation Works, a venture capital fund in Beijing. "Without quantity, you cannot have quality."[143]

Big state spending on incubators and start-ups concerns some economists who say China is further inflating its lending bubble. Along with the government funds, venture capital money is flooding the country. Deals worth roughly $49 billion were signed last year, putting China second to only the United States, according to the accounting firm Ernst & Young. Some economists and entrepreneurs worry that the government's start-up zeal might lead to too many business failures, which will waste money.[144]

The other concern with the state getting involved is that governments don't necessarily recognize where the biggest demand lies and which new thing might be the next tech breakout. The state is keeping an element of control in certain sectors, discouraging innovation in health care, the management of chronic diseases and elder care, and making innovation there hard, says Kroeber. "There are several sectors like that that need more deregulation, reduction of state roles, and the government is not moving very fast to make that happen," he says. "A lot of people who study technology are skeptical that you can get the same kind of innovation when you dictate it from top down."

LOOKING AHEAD

Are Political Reforms Likely?

Numerous global institutions, such as the IMF, as well as economists say that China must institute political as well as market reforms if China's economy is to stabilize and grow.

Economists such as Magnus point out that changes to China's civil society—such as an independent judiciary, and the removal of the online censorship called the Great Firewall—would boost trust and, therefore, the health of the economy. Party cadres drive many important decisions and replace CEOs of the large companies as they please.[145]

Several economists say China must allow full mobility of its citizens to go where they can find work. China's *hukou* system keeps about 60 percent of the population registered as rural residents, and it is difficult for them to modify their address.[146] If they can't register in cities, residents don't have access to health, social and education benefits. "If you allowed people to move more freely, tons of people would be pouring into Shanghai, Guangzhou, Shenzhen," Scissors of AEI says. One reason that's not being done: Those cities can't absorb the number of people who might come seeking work, perhaps creating a breeding ground for instability.

Magnus said change is the last thing China's leadership wants before the end of 2017 and the 19th Party Congress. Xi will want to fill top-level government vacancies with his own supporters. "His case will not be advanced if the economy falls on harder times," Magnus said.[147]

RAND's Shatz says he'll "bet on continued market reforms." But he says political reforms won't be considered. Xi will lead China through 2021, the 100th anniversary of the Communist Party of China. "One of his missions is to restore it to its ideological purity and glory," Shatz says. "Therefore, I think there will be few if any reforms toward liberalization, and perhaps even more tightening."

Ho-Fung Hung, the sociologist, says that if anything the country will continue to become more tightly controlled. He points out that under Xi, China has embarked on a crackdown on nongovernment organizations, labor activists, human-rights workers and lawyers, detaining and convicting them.[148] "I don't think it's on the table," Hung says. "It's the last thing they think of. If anything, it moves in opposite direction, becomes more and more draconian. . . . I don't see any incentive."

Some economists and scholars speculate that China is heading for an economic meltdown similar to the one that crippled Japan during the 1990s, a period called the "Lost Decade." (Some people think it lasted even longer.) In Japan, in the late 1980s, loans and cheap credit increased overseas investment, but also prompted many bad loans and poor business decisions. In 1990, the Japanese stock market tanked and companies were suddenly valued at a fraction of what they believed they were worth, Kroeber says. Many declared bankruptcy, some banks failed, and taxpayers bailed out others.

Hung says he sees many similarities to the collapse in Japan. "The nature of the problem is quite similar," he says. "There's a long period of debt-financed growth, investment-driven growth, and they're now living with the hangover of this crazy expansion of investment financed by bank loans." As with Japan, he thinks China "will perpetuate a whole system of zombies," companies that produce but aren't profitable and are kept alive by the government.

In China's case, Kroeber says, land and stock prices don't approach Japan's level of bloated value. What's more, China has a pool of government, corporate and consumer savings, about 45 percent of GDP.

Pettis, though, argued that insolvency doesn't necessarily lead to crisis: "As long as Beijing implicitly or explicitly guarantees deposits, and as long as Beijing's credibility with Chinese households is solid," the country can motor on with banks that need bailouts.[149]

Even economists who are the most critical of China's handling of the economy say that despite the downturn, there will be at least some growth. More credit is being offered solely so borrowers can service their debt, according to Magnus. "But no credit boom can go on forever," he wrote. "Given the buildup of bad debt and . . . absent a change in policy," he expects a crisis in three to four years. "China may have a couple of years before it deals with its looming financial instability, which will usher in a protracted period of low growth."[150]

Chronology

1911–49	**From republic to People's Republic**
1911	Republic of China is born, ending centuries of Qing dynasty rule.
1921	Communist Party is founded.
1945–49	Civil war between the Communists and Nationalists ends with defeat of the latter's leader, Chiang Kai-shek. He and his followers flee to Taiwan.
1949	Mao Zedong declares the founding of the People's Republic of China, led by the Chinese Communist Party.
1949–78	**From Maoism to Deng's opening**
1954–56	Agriculture is collectivized.
1956	Private enterprise is abolished.
1958–61	Mao calls for the Great Leap Forward, an industrial and social campaign to modernize the economy. The resulting famine kills an estimated 30 million people.
1966–76	The Great Proletarian Cultural Revolution unfolds, with Communists attacking perceived enemies, including people accused of acts of capitalism.
1972	U.S. President Richard M. Nixon visits Beijing, meets Mao, and rapprochement between the nations begins.
1976	Mao dies; his most fervent supporters, known as the Gang of Four, are imprisoned.

(Continued)

(Continued)

1978	New leader Deng Xiaoping adopts economic reforms, opening China to the outside world. He declares certain cities special economic zones for market-oriented trade.
Late 20th Century	**Era of economic reforms**
1979	To control explosive population growth, the government mandates a policy of one child per couple for most citizens.
1979–82	The government dismantles collective agricultural production.
1980	Southern city of Shenzhen becomes the first special economic zone to experiment with flexible market policies. It balloons from a fishing village to a manufacturing and shipping hub.
1985	Private enterprise is permitted in urban areas.
Late 1980s	Restrictions on migration to cities collapse, allowing people to move and seek work.
1989	More than 1 million protesters gather in public squares nationwide as governments in other Communist countries crumble. Chinese participants demand liberal reforms and an end to corruption. Soldiers kill hundreds, perhaps thousands, around Beijing's Tiananmen Square. Economic sanctions meted out by the U.S. and other nations slow China's growth.
1990	The Shanghai Stock Exchange, the first ever stock market in Communist China, opens.
1996	The yuan becomes convertible, allowing the free flow of money for imports and exports.
1997	Britain relinquishes colony of Hong Kong to China. Hong Kong is allowed to preserve its civil and legal rights and relative autonomy in a system called one-country, two-systems.
2000–Present	**China on the rise**
2001	China is accepted into the World Trade Organization after relaxing tariffs, quotas and other trade barriers.
2005	China outpaces Great Britain, France and Italy to become the world's fourth-largest economy. It will go on to become the second biggest.
2008	Beijing hosts successful Summer Olympic Games, announcing China's arrival on the world stage.
2012	Party General Secretary Xi Jinping takes control of the state and the presidency. He soon begins a drive to stamp out state corruption.
2013	Xi announces a plan for greater market reforms. He also proposes "One Belt-One Road," a sweeping modern Silk Road investment and trade corridor linking 60 countries in Asia, Europe, East Africa and Oceana with China.
2015	The government ends one-child policy to offset the rise in elderly citizens.

Discussion Questions

Here are some questions for discussion on the implications of the Chinese economic slowdown for China and the global economy:

- If you were involved in a business that relied on sales to China for some part of its revenue, would you advocate decreasing or increasing your exposure to China? What factor or factors would shape your advice?
- Why do you think U.S. companies such as Uber, Google and eBay have had such difficulty penetrating the Chinese market?
- If the current trend continues, China will pass the United States as the world's largest economy within a few decades. Do you think this will happen, or will the trend line change? Why? What are the implications if this does take place?
- What is the relationship, if any, between political governance and economic performance in China? Is the doubtful outlook for political reform an impediment to putting the economy on a firmer foundation, or is it irrelevant?

PERSPECTIVE

Q&A: Arthur R. Kroeber on China

"IT'S A GOOD PLACE TO DO BUSINESS, BUT YOU HAVE TO ROLL UP YOUR SLEEVES"

Arthur R. Kroeber

Arthur R. Kroeber is founding partner at Gavekal Dragonomics, a research firm in Beijing, and editor in chief of China Economic Quarterly. He is a fellow of the Brookings-Tsinghua Center in Beijing and the author of "China's Economy: What Everyone Needs to Know" (Oxford University Press, 2016). The following interview with SAGE Business Researcher freelance correspondent Suzanne Sataline was condensed for space.

What must China do to avoid getting stuck in an era of low growth, when it's unable to become a wealthy country?

The growth of the future is consumer spending. China's more affluent urban consumer class is buying goods and services that are more modern, and companies are responding to that changing demand.

One thing China needs to do is give space to private companies. That's basically happening. I think there are certain areas which continue to be very controlled by the state. There's more demand for sophisticated health care, chronic disease treatment, elder care. And the government is not moving very fast to make that [reform] happen.

Why not?

The government thinks state-owned enterprise [SOE] is the big way by which it controls society. A large SOE is crucial to the longevity of the [Communist] Party and crucial to social stability. They're concerned about lost employment. And lots of state enterprises are controlled by local governments. The national government has very little ability to compel or sell off these enterprises.

Will the state create a market-based system where innovation can flourish?

For China to be successful for the next 10, 20 years, they definitely need more space for innovation and domestic technology development. The government is trying to do that with a set of top-down policies, making funds available. A lot of people who study technology are skeptical.

The Communist Party is clear about this. Their vision is that the party needs to have control over all institutions in society—judiciary, internet, media, civil society, education—all these things guided by the party. There's an increased effort to get party cells into NGOs [non-government organizations], or educational institutions, or private companies, the idea that the party needs to be everywhere.

China is trying to pull off something no other country has done: to move up this technology innovation consumer society ladder while at the same time strengthening the role of the authoritarian single-party aspect in all society. A lot of people are skeptical that they can achieve both of those aims.

Because?

Ultimately, private companies are not going to invest in an economy where they don't have confidence in the sustainability of the political and societal arrangements.

Does China's slowdown resemble Japan's?

A lot of people will say, there's going to be a traumatic financial crisis. Banks are sitting on all these loans. They can't be paid. I don't believe that is the most likely scenario. China has this pool of national savings. If you add the savings of the government, companies and households, that winds up as 45 percent of GDP. I don't believe China is going to face a dramatic financial crisis in the coming years.

The big difference between China and Japan in 1990 is that Japan had specific circumstances, a gigantic asset bubble in the late '80s, and a combination of stock prices and land prices that rose to stratospheric levels.

China doesn't have that problem. They have overbuilt real estate, and there's just no way that land prices or stock prices in China are anywhere near that level of bloat.

Is President Xi committed to reforms? If so, when?

If you look at the public statements of Xi, half the time he says, "Yes, yes, press ahead [with reforms]." [Then it's,] "No, we must uphold the role of the state sector and the principles of Marxist economics." No one knows where he stands.

The next Party Congress is in October or November 2017. Once he puts people in key positions, he'll shift to aggressive economic reforms.

Can China maintain lower growth without harming other countries?

If China continues to grow 5-plus percent a year, driven by consumer demand, there are potentially a lot of benefits for other countries. For example, with Chinese tourism. If you host tours like France or Italy, you're getting a lot more dollars.

Is China still a good place to do business?

It's complicated. It's the world's second-biggest economy, and it's growing much [faster] than anywhere else. It's an interesting place to be. It's changing very rapidly. But it's not easy, and it's highly competitive. It's a good place to do business, but you have to roll up your sleeves.

UPDATE IN 2020

Although economists have been watching for an economic slowdown in China for years, its gross domestic product (GDP) continued to increase through the late 2010s, as information from the Economic Data Research Center of the Federal Reserve of St. Louis showed.[151]

China's GDP, which stood at $12.3 trillion in 2017, had climbed to $14.3 trillion in 2019. That same year, President Xi Jinping used the 70th anniversary of the founding of the Peoples' Republic to declare that nothing could stop China from moving forward. With the centenary of the Chinese Communist Party looming in 2021, analysts said Xi wanted to make the party more resilient to global challenges.[152]

Then COVID-19, which was first detected in the city of Wuhan in China in late December 2019, struck with full force in the first quarter of 2020, prompting airlines to curb flights, while global brands including Starbucks and General Motors closed Chinese outlets.

The government eventually imposed strict lockdowns to contain the virus, but China's economy took an immediate hit, as its GDP fell by 6.8 percent—the first quarterly decline since 1992, according to government records.[153] The outbreak even dampened China's famous smog, long a symbol of its environmental issues,[154] and further heightened fears that the decline signaled the end of the Chinese economic boom.

Yet the economic decline only lasted one quarter, as did the clear skies. By the second quarter of 2020, China's GDP rose 3.2 percent and the smog returned, with the latter surpassing pre-lockdown levels.[155]

As it turned out, Chinese consumers embraced home shopping for luxury goods, due to both the pandemic and the Hong Kong protests, which kept them from getting to the stores, and so factory output began rising again.[156]

Another key statistic not only revealed the impact of the coronavirus but also reflected the trade tensions between the U.S. and China.

Throughout the 2010s, U.S. imports of Chinese goods resembled a cardiogram: rising and falling consistently by quarters, according to seasonal demand. In November 2018, the figure peaked at $46.4 billion. After a seasonal plunge to $31.7 billion in March 2019, it rebounded to only $40.1 billion. In March 2020, U.S. imports plummeted to $22.8 billion, the lowest level in 15 years, and rose back to $37 billion in June 2020.[157]

In 2018, President Donald Trump began using tariffs to punish China for what he called unfair trading practices and intellectual property theft. He imposed four rounds of tariffs in 2018 and another in 2019, for a total of $360 billion in levies on Chinese goods.

China responded with its own tariffs of $110 billion, saying the U.S. was actually trying to curb its rise as a competing global economic power.[158] The pair signed a "phase one" trade deal that included a commitment by China to purchase an additional $200 million in U.S. goods by 2021.

A study by the Brookings Institution contended that the trade war may have hurt the U.S. more than China, however.

"Despite Trump's claim that 'trade wars are good, and easy to win,' the ultimate results of the phase one trade deal between China and the United States—and the trade war that preceded it—have significantly hurt the American economy without solving the underlying economic concerns that the trade war was meant to resolve," wrote Brookings' Ryan Hass and Abraham Denmark.[159]

Regardless, the trade battle did not dampen economists' outlook for China through 2021. The International Monetary Fund's (IMF) World Economic Outlook predicted that China would grow 1 percent in 2020 and 8.2 percent in 2021.

While the 1 percent forecast was weak by historic terms, the IMF was predicting downturns of 8 percent and 12 percent for the U.S. and the European Union, respectively.[160]

The IMF also noted China's economic stimulus package as a key factor. The government is focused on supporting small- and medium-sized companies by delaying loan repayments and making bank loans available, while expanding the social security net for under-pressure households.

But the IMF remained cautious in its forecast, saying there was uncertainty over the duration of the pandemic, the extent of the lockdowns, unemployment rates, and the global supply chain reconfiguration, among other factors.[161]

—Micheline Maynard

4 COMMODITIES SUPERCYCLES

Will China drive the next boom?

Jonathan Broder

From *SAGE Business Researcher*, February 12, 2018

EXECUTIVE SUMMARY

Just a few years after the last great global commodities supercycle ended, economists and investors are watching relatively obscure metals such as vanadium, cobalt and lithium as possible harbingers of another commodities boom. The metals are key components of batteries used in electric vehicles, which are growing in popularity. The last supercycle—an extended period of steadily rising commodities prices—was driven primarily by China's explosive economic growth and its appetite for raw materials and agricultural products to fuel that growth. As the Chinese economy decelerated starting in 2013, a wide range of commodities prices tumbled, and exporting nations bore the brunt. Now, China's heavy investment in the manufacture of electric-vehicle batteries may cause another turnaround.

Some key takeaways:

- Commodities supercycles can be a mixed blessing for exporters, creating a roller-coaster effect and leading to considerable human misery.
- Many exporting nations have been able to navigate the most recent downside of the cycle because they created rainy-day sovereign wealth funds during the price run-up.
- The falloff in global oil prices that began in 2014 was caused in part by the development of new techniques for extracting oil from shale rock formations, commonly known as fracking.

OVERVIEW

With the stock market swinging wildly and oil stabilizing above $60 per barrel, most investors have not been paying much attention to vanadium. But prices for the obscure metal, which is used in steel production, have been rising steadily—and it's not the only mover.[1]

Over the past two years, cobalt has more than tripled to about $80,000 per ton on the London Metal Exchange as of early February, and commodities analysts predict it will double again by 2020. Lithium prices have nearly doubled since 2014, reaching $9,100 per metric ton by the end of 2017, according to metals brokers. Both metals are used in electric-car batteries.[2]

Share prices and investment in several Canadian and Australian companies that are poised to extract these metals have soared as well, even though some have not even started digging.[3]

Junior Kannah/AFP/Getty Images

A child breaks rocks extracted from a cobalt mine in the Democratic Republic of the Congo. Most cobalt comes from that country, which has been accused of using laborers as young as 7.

The metals fever has spread to nickel and copper, whose per-ton prices on the London exchange of $13,790 and $7,066 respectively on Feb. 2 were their highest in two years. Analysts predicted demand for vanadium and other metals used to strengthen steel alloys would only grow in the coming years.[4]

What does this rally mean? Some analysts say it is driven by the global turn to electric vehicles and investors' eagerness to get in early on a disruptive technology that could spark a major metals boom.[5] Some of these analysts, such as Nariman Behravesh, chief economist for IHS Markit, a global economic research and consulting firm, say it could even usher in the next commodities "supercycle": an extended period in which prices climb steadily thanks to a rare confluence of technological change, shortages of the commodities needed to fuel it and huge investments to create new supply. But others, including Edward L. Morse, global head of commodities research at Citigroup, worry about the potential downside: that countries dependent on commodities exports will be flattened by the boom-bust roller coaster, just as they have been hurt in previous gyrations.

"It's like having all the planets align in one straight line as they rotate around the sun."

Economics scholars say examples of supercycles include the years between the Second Industrial Revolution of 1870 and the financial panic of 1907, and the post-World War II economic expansion that ended with the 1973 Arab oil boycott and an ensuing recession. The most recent was an especially intense and broadly based rally that began in the mid-2000s and ran for a decade, lifting prices for a wide array of commodities ranging from oil to metals to agricultural products.

"A supercycle occurs rarely, when all of the commodities are in the same position at the bottom of the [investment] cycle," says Morse. "It's like having all the planets align in one straight line as they rotate around the sun."

Some investors are betting that China will spark the next metals boom as it pushes to become a major producer of electric-car batteries.[6] Investors also are counting on a new Chinese regulation that takes effect this year, requiring both domestic and foreign automakers to meet escalating requirements for energy-efficient vehicles. These vehicles also require the use of lighter metals, such as copper and nickel.[7]

In addition to the enormous weight that China brings to a potential metals boom, India aims to sell only electric vehicles by 2030, and Britain and France plan to phase out gasoline and diesel-powered vehicles by 2040. In the United States, automakers are sinking billions of dollars into the development of electric vehicles.[8] California has provided additional incentives to both U.S. and foreign automakers with a program that calls for putting 1.5 million zero-emission electrical vehicles on the state's roads by 2025.[9]

Morse cautions that it is still too early to say whether the current surge in metals prices augurs a supercycle. Despite the popularity of battery-powered Tesla automobiles among celebrities, he says there simply are not enough electric cars on the streets yet to determine how much of the market they will capture. Besides, he adds, gasoline remains relatively cheap, internal combustion engines are becoming ever more fuel-efficient and electric charging stations are still scarce.

Michel Andre Robe, a derivatives trading professor at the University of Illinois at Urbana-Champaign, adds that even if the move to electric vehicles sparks a major metals boom, other commodities wouldn't be affected equally, reducing the likelihood of an across-the-board supercycle. For example, while the prices of cobalt and lithium likely would continue to rise with the popularity of electric vehicles, oil would decline, he says. So would prices for some precious metals, such as palladium, which is used in the catalytic converters of gasoline engines.

Robe, who works as a consultant for the U.S. Commodities Futures Trading Commission, which regulates futures markets, adds that any metals boom would be "essentially irrelevant" to most agricultural prices. Nevertheless, he says, a boom could indirectly undercut prices for sugarcane, corn and sweet sorghum, all used in the production of ethanol, a gasoline additive.

Cobalt Price Has Tripled Since 2016

Prices on London Metal Exchange, 2016–2018

The price of cobalt, a metal used in the production of electric-car batteries, has increased by 239 percent since the beginning of 2016.

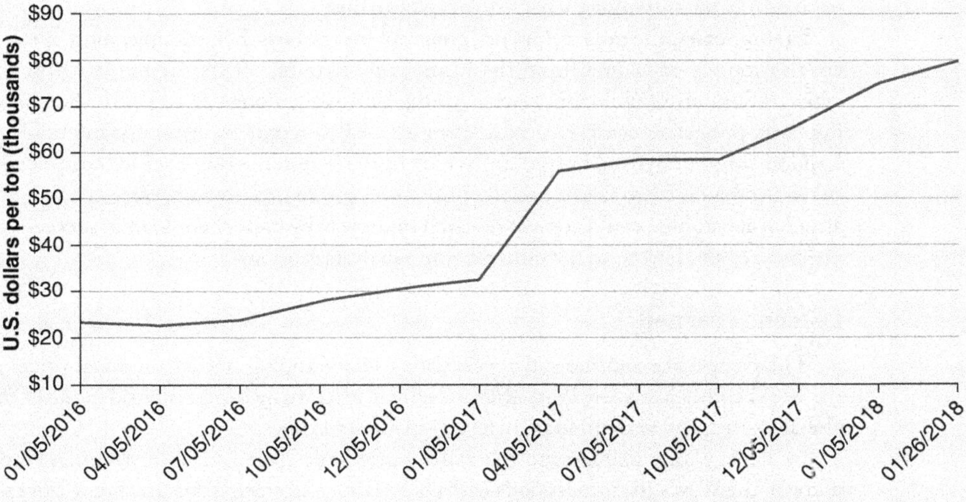

Source: "LME COBALT, Historical Prices Graph," The London Metal Exchange, Jan. 26, 2018, https://tinyurl.com/yco5v627.

In any event, investment forecasters predict automakers will soon claim a bigger share of the metals market. According to Citigroup projections, automotive demand for lithium is set to increase by 35 percent annually through 2021.[10] Morgan Stanley predicts that cobalt used in electric vehicles will increase by roughly 450 percent by 2025. And a JPMorgan Chase & Co. forecast has demand for nickel increasing nearly 10-fold by the same year, with electric vehicles becoming the second largest user of the metal. The forecast shows demand for copper growing steadily, too.[11]

In Canada, the share price for First Cobalt Corp., which has yet to begin drilling for cobalt in an abandoned open-pit silver mine 300 miles north of Toronto, jumped 215 percent last year to 1.23 Canadian dollars (about $1 U.S.).[12] In Australia, the market capitalization of the mining firm Pilbara Minerals rose from 25 million Australian dollars (about $20 million) in 2015 to AU$1.5 billion last year as the rising price of battery-grade lithium made it worthwhile to extract it from Australia's spodumene mineral deposits.[13] Another Australian company, Clean TeQ, increased in value by 240 percent to AU$838 million last year, based on its plans to produce nickel and cobalt sulfates, both key materials for lithium-ion battery cathodes.[14]

"It's going from that niche space to something that's kind of inevitable at this point," said Jay Jacobs, referring to the transition to electric vehicles. Jacobs is director of research at Global X Funds, which offers the Lithium and Battery Technology exchange-traded fund. The fund increased in value by more than 55 percent in 2017. "I just can't say we've really seen something recently that stacks up to this," he said.[15]

Whether such projections turn out to be the beginning of another commodities supercycle remains to be seen. If the forecasters are right, it will mean happy days for the countries that export these metals. But past supercycles also have proven to be something of a devil's bargain for these countries. The riches they earn during the boom times give way to scarcity and a good deal of human misery when these cycles go bust.

In some cases, the misery does not even wait for the bust. For example, most of the world's cobalt supply today comes from the Democratic Republic of the Congo in Central Africa, where thousands of children, some as young as 7, work alongside adults in the mines, lacking basic protective equipment, according to a 2016 report by Amnesty International, the London-based human rights group.[16] Much of the investor enthusiasm for cobalt companies stems from a desire to find a socially responsible alternative to Congolese cobalt.[17] Looking ahead, a cobalt bust could come if research underway by battery companies succeeds in finding cheaper alternatives to the mineral, some analysts caution.[18]

Lessons Learned

The prospect of another supercycle with a wide-ranging impact on metal prices around the world comes just a few years after the end of what many experts consider one of the most globally disruptive and unique supercycles in modern times.

In 1993, China roared onto the world's economic stage as it built factories to produce many of the West's consumer goods with cheap labor and erected dozens of new cities to house its burgeoning middle class. With China's economy rapidly expanding, Brazil, Russia, India and Argentina became major economic players as they met China's demands for energy, raw materials and food. Prices surged, generating windfalls for the world's commodity producers.

In addition to oil workers and U.S. farmers, emerging economies in Latin America and Africa and petro-states profited.

But from 2013 to 2015, China struggled with overcapacity and excessive debt, and Beijing's central planners recognized the need to shift their investment-led economy to a more consumer-based model. As China's demand for commodities tumbled, so did global prices. Meanwhile, the development of technology that enabled the extraction of shale oil and gas through hydraulic fracturing of rock, or fracking, along with Saudi Arabia's decision to maintain peak production levels, severely undercut oil prices. Just as several economic factors had aligned to create the boom, they realigned to set the stage for the bust.

Yet when commodities prices fell, experts say, the result was not the enduring, across-the-board busts of previous commodity supercycles. To be sure, the twin blows of reduced exports to China and lower commodity prices pummeled several emerging economies, especially in Latin America and Africa.[19]

But for many other commodity-exporting countries, the fallout from the price crash turned out to be manageable, according to experts—in large part because their governments had taken steps during the boom times to make their economies more resilient to recessionary headwinds. Since then, another, more modest type of convergence has occurred. Commodity prices have climbed back to at least 50 percent of their highest levels, sparking some measure

Crude Oil Plunged After 2014 Run-Up

Brent crude oil spot prices, 2008–2017

The price of Brent crude oil fell 66 percent between mid-2014 and the end of 2015 before beginning to rebound.

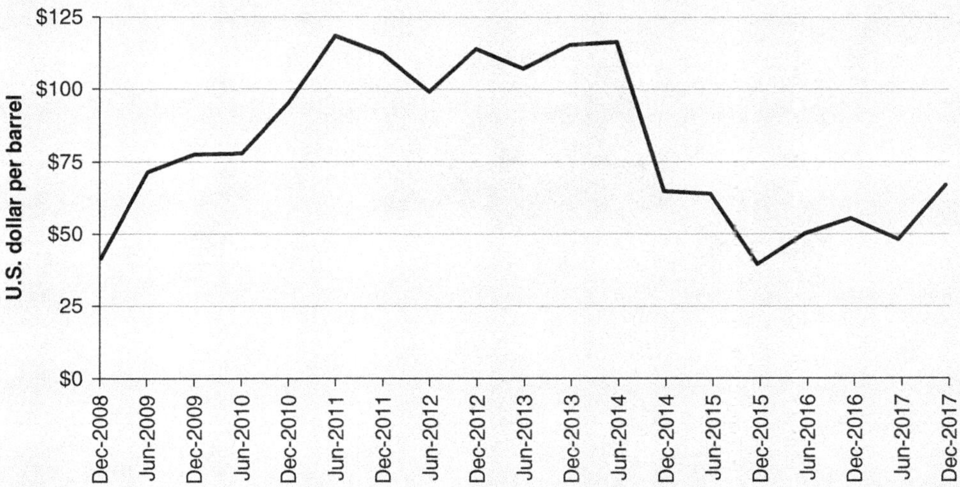

Source: "Europe Brent Spot Price FOB," U.S. Energy Information Administration, Jan. 31, 2018, http://tinyurl.com/y95a88ye.

of recovery. Meanwhile, the drop in oil prices has stabilized Europe's economy and prevented Russia from becoming an energy superpower, among other broader geopolitical consequences, according to Robert D. Kaplan, a senior fellow at the Center for a New American Security, a Washington think tank.[20]

Economists agree one of the steps that helped many commodity-exporting countries weather the price crash was their creation of state-owned sovereign wealth funds, which provided a cushion against the loss of revenue to their national treasuries.

Norway, with the world's largest fund of $1 trillion, easily absorbed losses from its oil exports, as did Saudi Arabia, Kuwait, the United Arab Emirates and other oil-producing

Texas Led Nation in Energy Exports

Petroleum and coal products exports by state, 2016

Texas topped the nation in petroleum and coal products exports in 2016, followed by Louisiana and California.

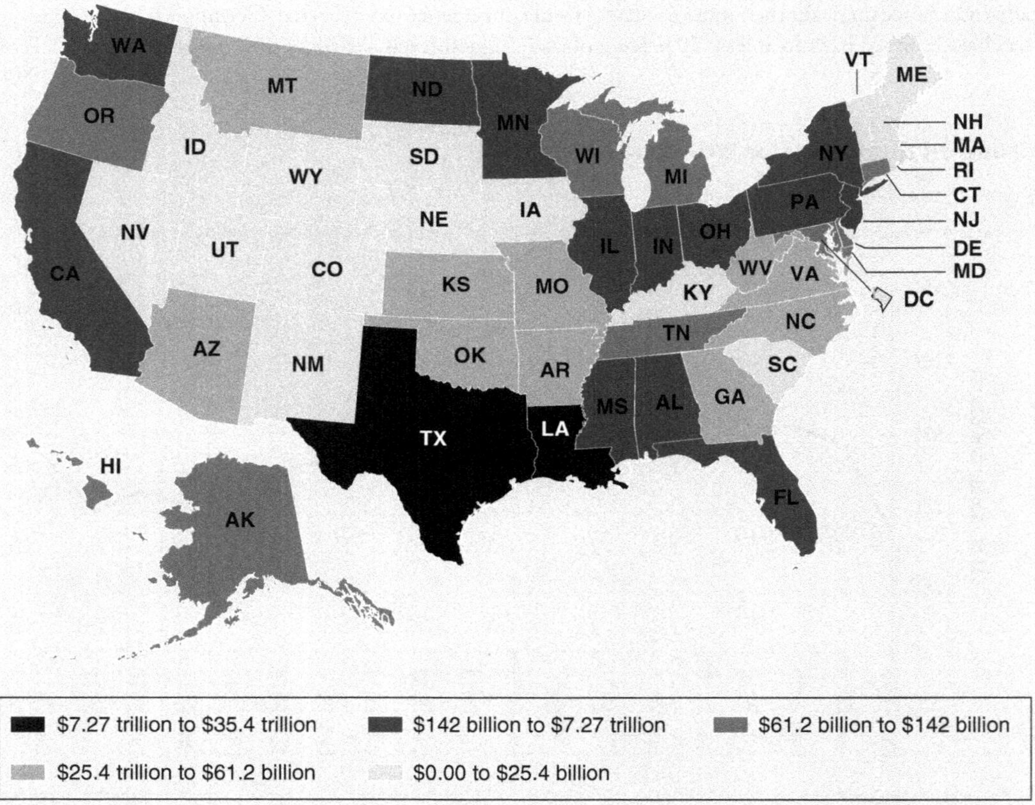

Source: "Petroleum and Coal Products Exports (State)," SAGE Stats, September 2017, https://tinyurl.com/y8gm32qa.

states, all of whom have well-stocked funds. Economists including Morse and Robe say Australia, Canada, Chile and several African countries, as well as several U.S. oil-producing states, also were able to fall back on their rainy-day reserves. North Dakota, where the boom from shale oil production had created as many as 2,000 millionaires in 2012 alone, sank into recession as a result of the commodities crash.[21] But with a cushion of more than $4 billion in its Legacy Fund in 2016, the state was able to weather the worst.[22] As oil prices have risen more recently, economists say, North Dakota has begun to regain its financial footing.

Argentina, one of the world's largest exporters of soybeans, stands out as a country whose leaders failed to recognize the importance of a rainy-day fund, economists say. The country not only never created one, but when commodity prices crashed, the government compounded the problem with ill-advised protectionist trade policies, oppressive regulations and a spending spree. The result, analysts say, was a recession that was far more painful than it had to be. In 2015, the country rejected the old ruling party and elected as president Mauricio Macri, who has since instituted more orthodox fiscal and monetary policies aimed at reversing a decade of economic damage.[23]

Russia, however, could not rely solely on its $75 billion sovereign wealth fund to cushion the country from the double blow of falling oil prices and Western sanctions imposed over its 2014 annexation of Crimea, economists say. With the economy struggling and the ruble losing a third of its value since the beginning of 2014, Moscow took what some economists regarded as a dangerous step: In November of that year, Russia's central bank allowed the currency to float freely, resulting in a 40 percent depreciation. At the time, observers spoke of the potential for social unrest as buying power declined and warned that the country's financial stability was at risk.[24]

But Citigroup's Morse says the 40 percent drop in oil prices by June 2015 and the ruble's fall by a similar percentage meant that the same amount of oil produced roughly the same amount of rubles that it had a year earlier. He says the move significantly reduced Russia's production costs. Moreover, Morse adds, in the wake of the oil price collapse in the fall of 2014, many analysts had predicted Russia's oil production would fall by 1 million barrels a day. But because of the ruble's depreciation, Morse says, the Russian economy adjusted faster, and production grew.

"Russia was by far the most dramatically successful adjustment to the lower-priced world," says Morse, an energy economist who served in senior positions at the State Department in both the Carter and Reagan administrations. "Yes, they did have a sovereign fund, and yes, they did draw it down, but now they're building it up again because oil is $60 a barrel and their break-even price is about $40 a barrel. Now they're now running a current account surplus, and they're putting cash into their sovereign fund."

The other principal measure that some commodity-exporting countries took to help cushion them from the pain of the price collapse was economic diversification, economists say. Saudi Arabia, totally dependent on its oil and gas exports, has developed a blueprint to diversify its economy by 2030, although many experts question whether the plan's architect, 32-year-old Crown Prince Mohammed bin Salman, can successfully carry out the required economic and social reforms without destabilizing the kingdom.[25] No other Arab oil state has a similar plan, and all are drawing down their sovereign wealth funds, the University of Illinois' Robe says. Australia and Canada, both exporters of metals and minerals, were able to fall back on their manufacturing and agricultural sectors to get through the bust more easily than other nations, Robe says.

Russia and Brazil have begun to emerge from the recessions they suffered after the collapse in commodities prices. But Brazil's economy, which the International Monetary Fund (IMF) expects will increase by only 1.5 percent in 2018, is projected to average 2 percent growth over the next five years because it exports iron ore and soybeans in addition to energy, economists say.[26] In addition, Brazil's Embraer SA, regarded as a crown jewel of Brazilian industry, exports high-quality civilian and military aircraft. The company is in talks with Boeing Co., which wants to buy the aircraft manufacturer in a bid to enter the market for smaller passenger jets. The Brazilian government, which has veto power over the sale, is reluctant to relinquish control over Embraer to a foreign company.[27]

By comparison, the IMF forecasts an equally sluggish 1.6 percent growth rate for Russia in 2018 and an average of only 1.5 percent growth through 2022.[28] Economists say that despite the country's highly educated workforce, Russia has failed to diversify its petroleum-dependent economy by creating a high-tech sector. "To sustain a higher rate of growth, the Russian economy needs a significantly higher level of diversification," says Morse. "But there is nobody in Russia that has a well-planned approach for diversifying the economy."

While China's economic slowdown was a major factor in the price crash of commodities other than oil, energy experts say the sharp decline in oil prices was brought on by the immense economic pressure that $100-per-barrel oil placed on developed nations at the height of the commodities boom. That burden, they say, in turn spurred the development of fracking technology. And that breakthrough, together with the Saudi decision to maintain maximum production, flooded the market with oil and lowered its price, while also carrying far-reaching geopolitical ramifications.

In a 2017 book, Meghan L. O'Sullivan, a Harvard University international affairs professor and former aide to President George W. Bush, wrote that the shale oil revolution transformed the United States from "the world's thirstiest consumer of overseas oil to a position of greater self-sufficiency."[29]

Besides helping stabilize Europe, the price drop lowered Japan's energy costs after the 2011 Fukushima nuclear disaster and helped China build its "Silk Road" trade routes across Eurasia, said Kaplan, the Center for a New American Security fellow. Losers from the energy price crash included undiversified petro-states such as Venezuela and those in the Middle East, as well as oil-rich sub-Saharan African countries such as Nigeria and Angola, who found their prospects suddenly weakened by their reduced oil earnings, Kaplan said.[30]

Another China-Driven Boom?

Even amid the rally in metals prices and investor excitement over electric vehicles, one of the biggest looming questions is what role China will play in the global marketplace over the next five years. During that time, the IMF forecasts, China will continue to grow, but at slower pace of 5.8 percent annually, as opposed to the double-digit rates the country clocked in the 2000s.[31]

"In terms of China's locomotive power, especially for the emerging world, 5 percent is massive," says IHS Markit's Behravesh. "So China can still exert massive power on the global economy in terms of growth rates. To the extent that it's importing commodities from other countries, it can be a major engine of growth."

Investors says China's plans to manufacture batteries for electric vehicles already have spurred a number of agreements by Chinese companies to secure lithium supplies that are reminiscent of the deals Beijing struck back in the early 2000s, when it needed dependable supplies of iron ore and other raw materials to build up the country's infrastructure.

Recent deals include investments by Chinese carmaker Great Wall Motors and mining company Pengxin International in several Australian lithium mines, as well as agreements to buy the production of others.[32] These investments, along with the boom in metals, are attracting the attention of other mining companies from around the world. The multinational mining giant Rio Tinto was recently rumored to be considering a bid to take over SQM, Chile's biggest lithium producer.[33]

Moreover, investment analysts say future demand for batteries will not be restricted to the electric vehicle industry. As the world moves toward renewable energy, Morse says, it is going to need a clean-energy source that cannot be cut off by the weather or darkness. "Hydro energy is interruptible by droughts; solar energy is interruptible by nighttime; and wind energy is interrupted when the wind stops blowing," he says. "So you need significantly large battery power, both for electric vehicles and for the movement to distribute energy."

But Behravesh and other economists also worry about China's debt, which exploded from about 120 percent of GDP to 260 percent in the 10-year period ending in 2016.[34] "No country has ever gone through that without something bad happening," Behravesh says. "The question is, what is that something bad?"

Many economists rule out a financial meltdown because of China's huge sovereign wealth fund, which reached $900 billion last August.[35] They add that most of China's debt is domestic, and because the government effectively owns the banks, it can pay off the debt on its own schedule. What is likely, they predict, is a repeat of Japan's "lost decade" in the 1990s—a decade or two of subpar growth as Beijing tries to unload its excess capacity and lower its debt levels.

But Robe and other experts say even that scenario leaves room for a targeted drive by China to make the batteries that will meet growing worldwide demand for electric vehicles and a clean, uninterruptible energy source. "I do not necessarily see an inherent contradiction between seeking to foster new technologies and dealing with current economic issues," Robe says.

Ralph Aldis, director of research and a fund manager at U.S. Global Investors, said he has added several lithium producers to the firm's World's Precious Minerals Fund, which contains a portfolio of mid-sized mining companies. "I just know that's the direction that the world seems to be going," he said, "and I'm not going to fight it."[36]

Chronology

1870–1907	**The Second Industrial Revolution**
1870s	Demand for iron ore spikes as new technological processes lead to mass production of cheap, durable steel, enabling construction of larger bridges, the first skyscrapers, railroads, ships and more powerful military weapons.
1877	London Metal Exchange is established at a coffee house where metal merchants gather to sell ores and concentrates imported from as far away as Chile and Malaya.
1882	New York's Butter and Cheese Exchange changes its name to the New York Mercantile Exchange, which is destined to become the world's largest trading platform for energy and metals.
1907	A failed attempt by Otto Heinze, brother of the owner of the United Copper Company, to corner the market on copper precipitates a financial panic, which leads to collapse of the commodities markets. Financial historians cite this as the end of the first modern commodities supercycle.
1929–44	**Fixing the price of gold**
1929–34	Stock market crash leads to widespread gold hoarding by the public, jeopardizing the government's gold reserves. President Franklin D. Roosevelt in 1933 orders all citizens holding gold to return it to banks or face imprisonment and fines. The Gold Reserve Act authorizes the government to fix gold prices at $35 per ounce.
1944	Bretton Woods System establishes an international monetary regime that ties currency exchange rates to the U.S. dollar, which is indexed to gold.
1946–74	**Post-war boom and bust**
1946	The post-war period becomes one of the greatest eras of economic expansion in history. Raw materials and other commodities that had been diverted to the war effort now fuel economic development in the United States, Western Europe and Japan. Cheap oil drives rapid growth of the automotive industry, while agricultural commodities exports grow with development of new chemical fertilizers, pesticides and high-yield seeds.
1947	General Agreement on Tariffs and Trade (GATT) aims to reduce commodity tariffs among member countries.
1961	To defend the fixed price of gold and the Bretton Woods System of fixed-rate convertible currencies, the United States and seven European central banks combine their gold reserves to form the London Gold Pool.
1968–71	After runs on gold, the U.S. dollar and the British pound, France withdraws from the London Gold Pool, precipitating its collapse.
1971	An effort to keep gold prices low with a two-tiered system of official exchange and open-market transactions collapses when President Richard Nixon announces the end of government regulation of gold prices, ushering in the current monetary system of floating exchange rates.

1973–74	Petroleum-producing Arab states impose oil embargo on the United States and a handful of other Western countries, including the Netherlands, Portugal and South Africa, as punishment for their support for Israel during the 1973 Arab-Israeli war. Additional production cuts by the Organization of the Petroleum Exporting Countries (OPEC) quadruple the price of oil to $12 per barrel by 1974, triggering a recession that causes a bust in all commodity prices.
1995–2017	**The China-led supercycle and its aftermath**
1995	China launches a massive state-run drive to build factories and housing, sparking a worldwide commodities boom as countries boost production and exports to fuel China's growth.
2008–2012	Commodity-exporting countries register unprecedented levels of growth as worldwide demand escalates and supplies tighten, triggering high prices. Oil prices hit $100 per barrel for the first time, sending billions of dollars to Russia and the Middle East.
2013–2015	China's economy cools as the country confronts overcapacity and mounting debt. Exporters suffer as world commodity prices plummet. Oil prices fall further because of the hydraulic fracking revolution and Saudi Arabia's decision to maximize its oil production.
2017	Commodities prices rebound to 50 percent of boom-time highs.

Discussion Questions

Here are some questions to discuss regarding commodities supercycles:

- What was the main driving force behind the last global commodities supercycle?
- What factors were responsible for ending that supercycle?
- What were the geopolitical effects of the end of the supercycle? Which countries suffered the greatest consequences?
- How can exporters protect themselves against gyrating commodities prices?
- Why are relatively obscure metals such as vanadium and lithium attracting increased attention?

PERSPECTIVE

Q&A: Edward L. Morse on Supercycles

"IT'S A PERFECT STORM, AND IT TAKES PEOPLE BY SURPRISE"

Edward L. Morse

Edward L. Morse is the global head of commodities research at Citigroup in New York. He served as deputy assistant secretary of state for international energy policy in the Carter and Reagan administrations. After leaving government service, he served in senior positions at Phillips Petroleum, Hess Energy Trading Company, PFC Energy, Lehman Brothers and Credit Suisse before joining Citigroup in 2011. He spoke with SAGE Business Researcher freelance correspondent Jonathan Broder. The interview was edited for clarity and space.

How would you define a commodities supercycle?

A commodities supercycle is a period of time when all major commodities are lined up in terms of an investment cycle. It starts when commercial stocks of metals, oil and gas, coal and iron ore, even agricultural commodities have run out, and there's no new capacity to produce significant additional amounts. That's exactly what happened in the 1990s into the middle of this [current] decade. The agricultural commodities had run out of stock, and then all of the commodities aligned at the same point at the same time. It's a perfect storm, and it takes people by surprise because they've been luxuriating in seeing their past investments come to fruition. And then all of a sudden, there's a very radical turning point.

Which countries and U.S. states have prospered most during the supercycle boom years?

The commodity-rich countries benefited a great deal, such as Russia, Canada, Australia, Brazil and of course all of the petro-states. On the bulk commodities side, in Brazil and Australia, new coal and iron ore supplies were found in abundance, and the price structures went up a lot, to give a signal to invest. But the new supplies were so abundant it caused a price collapse. For example, in 2014, iron ore prices around the world were averaging about $145 per ton, and now they're around half of that. Similarly, coal prices went up a lot; discoveries were made, and now coal prices are roughly half of what they were [in 2014].

Why did oil prices collapse?

On the oil side, a combination of factors unfolded. On one hand, exporting countries benefited as prices went up. But on the other hand, public expectations in the petro states also grew. Over time, people in these states started to challenge their governments. In Libya, Nigeria, Iraq, Iran and Venezuela, people started making demands that those governments couldn't meet. We had unrest, and in some places, revolutions. Supplies began to suffer radically, starting with Libya, where 1.5 million barrels a day were disrupted.

Then something dramatic occurred. High prices led to technological innovations that allowed exploitation of supplies that had never before been commercially available. Shale oil was one, oil sands was another and deep water was a third. There was virtually no production from any of these sources when the century began. But by 2014, Brazil, the U.S. and Canada had a combined production growth of 2.3 million barrels a day. That production overwhelmed demand and led to the oil price collapse of 2015.

It also led to the restructuring of global oil markets. Because the U.S., Canada and Brazil were all in the Western Hemisphere, the Atlantic Basin now had a permanent supply of oil, leaving only the Pacific Basin without enough supplies. And this has led to competition for market share in that part of the world. The competition from the U.S. has been revolutionary in its impact. In 2017, the U.S. became the largest exporter of petroleum products in the world. Seven years before, the U.S. was the largest importer of petroleum products in the world. Also, the U.S. now exports more liquefied petroleum gases, like propane and butane, than all Middle Eastern countries combined. The U.S. is also now a big exporter of crude oil and natural gas. And one of the largest buyers of U.S. crude oil and natural gas is China.

Some analysts have said the bust after the last supercycle that ended in 2015 was more manageable for most countries and didn't last as long. Was this because they had diversified their economies and had built up sovereign wealth funds during the boom times to cushion their economies during the bust times?

There was a hope that there was going to be a softer landing with the growth of sovereign funds. Norway, with the world's largest sovereign wealth fund, had a cushion, and they used it for the very rainy-day purpose for which it was created. Other countries that have been well-cushioned include the United Arab Emirates, Kuwait and Saudi Arabia, all of whom had a very large amount of cash available.

The countries that export metals suffered, but most have adjusted. Chile has a well-managed economy and has been able to adjust. Brazil had negative growth [in 2016] but is finally coming out of the dog days of the bust part of the cycle. Fortunately, the metals-producing countries like Brazil, Canada and Australia are highly diversified.

I think the most dramatically successful adjustment to the lower priced world was in Russia. That was a function of several factors, the most important of which was their allowing the [ruble] exchange rate to float, which significantly brought down the costs of production. In the fall/winter of 2014–15, many analysts predicted Russian production would fall by 1 million barrels a day by 2017 if prices remained at a low level. But, in fact, because of the radical 50 percent depreciation of the Russian ruble, the Russian economy adjusted faster, and Russian production grew, rather than fell.

There's lots being written lately about a growing demand for a wide range of metals—lithium, cobalt, nickel, copper and several minor metals—caused by the boom in electric vehicles. Does this herald the start of a major metals boom, or perhaps the beginning of another commodities supercycle?

It's too early to tell. We don't know what the penetration of electric vehicles is going to be. So projecting future need for lithium, cobalt and other commodities is difficult. But these batteries are not just for electric vehicles. They are going to be needed for uninterrupted power generation around the world. It's just not clear where and when the supply bottlenecks will be.

UPDATE IN 2020

In April 2020, market watchers couldn't believe their eyes—the price of U.S. crude oil for May delivery actually turned negative for the first time in history, clocking in at minus $37.83. Sellers of crude oil would have to pay buyers to take the commodity off their hands.

The negative stay was brief, as by late summer, the price of crude oil futures was back to the low $40-per-barrel range. Yet the oil industry was experiencing the worst recession in recent memory.[37]

Prices for nearly every type of commodity fell from the start of 2020, including platinum, coal, natural rubber, base metals and silver. Cobalt continued its downward trend, a stark contrast to the high it had been experiencing until March 2018.

Why were the prices of precious metals and materials falling so much, even before COVID-19? For one thing, analysts had been too optimistic about the speed with which consumers would embrace electric vehicles, especially in the U.S.

While the percentage increases in sales seemed dramatic, the actual numbers were dwarfed by conventional vehicles. For instance, there were 1.3 million electric vehicles in use in the U.S. in 2019, out of a total fleet of 284.5 million.[38]

Outside the U.S., the use of electric vehicles seemed likely to grow in the coming years and decades. Countries including France, Britain, and the U.K. planned bans on vehicles with conventional engines, but they were still more than a decade away.

The exception to the declines in commodities was gold.[39]

Analysts at Citibank said it was possible that gold, which was trading for around $1,940 in September, would pass the $2,000-per-ounce mark.[40] The investment bank said trade tensions, geopolitical rifts and the uncertainty around the U.S. election all were potential positives, "given that it is seen as a safe haven asset that is typically uncorrelated with other financial assets in times of market stress or turmoil."

But an eventual U.S.-China trade agreement and a surge in manufacturing activity might take away some of gold's attractiveness, Citibank remarked.

While some investors felt that commodities might be a better bet than volatile stock markets, it was difficult for some analysts to recommend one over the other.

"To answer definitively as to which is safer . . . right now is impossible," wrote Hollie Tomlinson in Investment U. "Proper precautions and strategic investment selection can still lead to success in a volatile stock market."[41]

But analyst Eric Fry, the global macro-specialist at InvestorPlace, was confident the world was in for a "second electric revolution" once bans on conventional vehicles eventually took place. "The base metals boom is here and so is a brand-new commodity supercycle," he said.[42]

—Micheline Maynard

5 DATA SECURITY

Can the cybercrime threat be contained?

Pat Wechsler

From *SAGE Business Researcher*, September 18, 2017

EXECUTIVE SUMMARY

In an increasingly digital world, a daily battle is being waged over the safety of internet users' data. The 3.9 billion people who use the Web to shop, invest, communicate with friends or interact with healthcare providers are constantly providing personal information that can offer entry points to their financial assets, health histories and credit records. The cyberthieves working to steal this data are increasing in number and sophistication, as recent online attacks demonstrate. Some hackers offer their stolen wares for sale on the so-called Dark Web; others seek to extort money from victims by, in effect, making them buy back their own data. "Cybercriminals are evolving and pushing the boundaries," one analyst said. In response, companies are strengthening security measures and governments at all levels are imposing new rules to contain the threat.

Here are some key takeaways:

- Hacking has morphed from a lone-wolf activity to a full-blown corporate enterprise.
- The average cost of a data breach to an individual company is $3.62 million, and the global cost of cybercrime is projected to reach $6 trillion by 2021.
- Banking and healthcare are among the favorite targets of cybercriminals because these industries gather so much valuable personal information.

OVERVIEW

To some people, the Dark Overlord of the Universe is a villain from the surrealist Marvel comic series and cult film "Howard the Duck." To the Peachtree Orthopedic Clinic in Atlanta and the Tampa Bay Surgery Center in Florida, the Dark Overlord is anything but fictional.

Both healthcare providers fell victim to a cyber rampage by what is believed to be a hacking collective using the name of Howard's archrival as its calling card. Both had hundreds of thousands of personal medical records stolen and were then threatened with their sale, or exposure, if they failed to pay a ransom.[1] In Peachtree's case, where more than a half million files were taken, the Overlord also threatened to make public the personal information of several professional athletes who used the clinic.[2]

The Overlord has a standard M.O. First, the hacker takes over the healthcare clinics' computer systems, then makes the personal data inaccessible to the clinic by encrypting it and offers it for sale on illegal websites. But the primary aim is not to sell records, but rather to extort money from the providers to buy the data back.[3]

The hacker even exploits the media to increase the pressure by granting interviews. According to Milpitas, California-based cybersecurity experts FireEye, the Dark Overlord used this extortion technique on at least a dozen healthcare facilities between June 2016 and June 2017, not to mention random financial, manufacturing and entertainment firms.[4] One of the hacker's more famous exploits was stealing and then leaking episodes of the Netflix series "Orange Is the New Black" despite a $50,000 ransom being paid.[5] FireEye intelligence also suggested that there are likely co-conspirators using the Overlord persona, expressed on the Web as "thedarkoverlord."

And the ransom threats are real, as the Tampa Bay facility discovered after the Overlord released more than 140,000 of its files. "This clinic didn't do anything wrong except annoy us," the Dark Overlord wrote in a Twitter post that seemed a warning to other potential victims who fail to pay the ransom.[6] At the time, Dr. Jay L. Rosen, the chief executive of the clinic, said simply: "The country is under siege."[7]

In that period, the hacker also put up for sale close to 10 million patient records, the bulk of which were lifted from a health insurer's server. The price was demanded in bitcoin, an unregulated, almost untraceable virtual currency: The hacker sought 1,280 bitcoins, at the time the equivalent of $820,000.[8] (Because the value of bitcoin has soared in recent months, as of early September that ransom would be worth more than $5 million.[9]) The venue for the sale: TheRealDeal, a black market site found in the recesses of the internet known as the Dark Web that is used by people engaged in illegal activities or who want to keep their identities secret.

The Dark Overlord is hardly alone. Whoever is behind it is among the countless hackers who have made it their full-time business to steal digitized personal data for financial gain. The scariest consideration: Cyber experts such as FireEye do not think of the Overlord as particularly technologically advanced. "Based on our observations, it is likely thedarkoverlord uses relatively unsophisticated tactics, techniques and procedures (TPP) and publicly available open-source tools," FireEye wrote in a recent Threat Actor Profile on the Overlord.[10] What then can be expected from a cyberthief the experts consider top-notch?

In a world that has become progressively digitized, thanks to both business strategy and customer choice, a battle is being waged daily to protect the sanctity of personal data. Every day, every hour—in the course of shopping, handling finances, investing, taking care of health, choosing entertainment and communicating with friends and relatives—the 3.9 billion consumers using the internet are providing numbers, dates, addresses and telephone numbers online. This data, known as personally identifiable information or PII, can unlock doors to their assets, health histories, credit cards and bank accounts, among other things.[11]

With attacks by criminals and rogue states rising in frequency, daring and sophistication, and people spending more and more time online, those data—along with protected health information—have become increasingly vulnerable, despite the best efforts of business and government to protect the information. Just consider these numbers: In 2017, the average cost of a data breach is about $3.62 million, and the odds of a company experiencing one have risen to one in four, the Ponemon Institute, a Michigan-based research firm, and IBM Security reported.[12] The cost is based on the number of records lost, but there are indirect costs as well, such as executives losing their jobs, stock prices falling, and business deals being canceled.

Between 2015 and 2021, the cost of global cybercrime is expected to double, rising to $6 trillion from $3 trillion, according to the cybersecurity research and market intelligence firm Cybersecurity Ventures.[13] IBM X-Force, the research arm of IBM's security division, reported in its 2017 Threat Intelligence Index that the number of compromised records grew a historic 566 percent to more than 4 billion in 2016 from 600 million the year before, exceeding the combined total of the two previous years.[14]

"Companies—large, midsized and small—have been incorporating cybersecurity practices into their regular operations, but cybercriminals are evolving and pushing the boundaries," says David Mainor, principal threat intelligence analyst at FireEye. "What continues to surprise me is the professionalization of the e-crime marketplace. We've got individuals and groups of actors who operate more like Fortune 500 companies, not just in the way they conduct their businesses but even in the way they market and work with affiliates to distribute their malware and bolster the operational effectiveness of their efforts."

Hacking has evolved from a largely lone-wolf enterprise of computer geeks living in their parents' basements or skulking around university laboratories to a full-scale corporate enterprise with some hackers working in offices, clocking in and clocking out and even taking a salary. While cyber criminals once sought to make their mark by creating diabolical viruses and demonstrating their technological prowess, today many simply buy ready-made virus components that execute malicious activities off the Dark Web or even outsource aspects of their operation to other hackers, Mainor says.

"We're in trouble if we don't understand that cybercriminals evolve quickly and constantly," says Alan Brill, a senior cybersecurity expert at the corporate investigations and risk consulting firm Kroll Inc. "They use information from things like Wikileaks [a site that publishes leaked information] where national security methodologies are being exposed and they at least collectively know more about the technology than anybody.

"There's a lot more collaboration and specialization these days," Brill adds. "It's a maturing industry."

Most importantly, attacker tactics, techniques and procedures shift as corporations throw up defenses, Mainor points out. Organizations cannot afford to implement a static solution and then think their work is done; adversaries and threats evolve.

"Black-Hats are ahead of White-Hats" say Adam Segal, the director of digital and cyberspace policy program at the Council on Foreign Relations, a New York-based think tank, using the vernacular for hackers and those trying to defend data. "That is symptomatic of the larger problem in cybersecurity that offense still has the edge over defense. The defender has to worry about millions of lines of code, thousands of devices, thousands of networks. The attacker only has to be right once."

Top Targets for Hackers

Two industries that have become favorite targets of the hacker community are financial services and healthcare—primarily because companies and organizations in those sectors are the repositories of so much of the most personal, difficult to attain, and hence valuable information. It's like the oft-quoted line about robbing banks because that's where the money is.

That certainly was the case when hackers broke into the computers of credit monitoring firm Equifax earlier this year, potentially giving them access to data on 143 million U.S. consumers, including their Social Security and driver's license numbers, birth dates and addresses. This one breach affected more than four out of every 10 people living in the country.[15]

The hackers also took more than 200,000 credit card numbers. It was the third breach for Equifax in recent years; in the other two, hackers took W-2 tax data.[16] After the hack was discovered but before it was made public, three senior executives, including Equifax's chief financial officer, made a sale of company stock—not previously planned—worth $1.8 million.[17]

Banking and healthcare are also industries that have been in the process of digital transformations. In the case of financial services, it has been the transition to online and mobile banking. In the case of healthcare, it has been the move from paper to digits in the industry's record keeping and operations.

"Increasing online and mobile banking became a question of keeping up with the competition in financial services," Brill explains. "Healthcare has been pushed to digitize by regulation, and inadvertently, that opened up doctors and hospitals to getting hacked. While the government has provided incentives to move to electronic medical records, it didn't necessarily give money to make sure the industry used the best cybersecurity tools and techniques."

Healthcare ranked No. 1 among industry targets in 2015, when more than 100 million personal accounts were violated in hacks of insurers Anthem BlueCross BlueShield, Premera BlueCross BlueShield and Excellus BlueCross BlueShield.[18] The industry dropped a bit in the rankings in 2016 because hackers went after smaller healthcare targets and ended up harvesting fewer records. Still, by one estimate from TrapX Labs, a cybersecurity defense company, hackers attacked the U.S. healthcare sector 63 percent more often in 2016 than the year before.[18] While the volume of records stolen fell, the frequency of the attacks rose significantly.

Besides healthcare's digitization, new targets within the industry are opening up—for instance, the loosely regulated medical device arena. These devices are part of the Internet of Things (IoT), the interconnection via the internet of computing devices embedded in everyday objects that enable them to send and receive data. Medical devices connect to an array of sensors and monitors, making them potential entry points to larger hospital networks and vulnerable to ransomware attacks that hold vital systems hostage until administrators pay up. For instance, if such a system were hacked, the attackers could threaten to administer fatal doses to patients on insulin pumps.

With the threat to medical devices, "the entire extortion landscape has changed," Ed Cabrera, chief cybersecurity officer at the threat research firm Trend Micro, told Wired magazine in an article discussing medical device vulnerability. "You do get into this life or death situation potentially."

And there are a lot of these wireless devices to target. According to IoT security firm Zingbox, U.S. hospitals currently average 10–15 connected devices per bed. Multiply that by about 900,000—the number of hospital beds in the United States based on a 2015 survey by the American Hospital Association—and the magnitude of the threat can be appreciated.[19]

Experts have been warning of the risk inherent in these wireless products for years. The threat was so real that doctors disabled the wireless capability of former Vice President Dick Cheney's pacemaker in 2013 for fear of a life-threatening hack.[20] Johnson & Johnson warned its patients in 2016 that its insulin pump may be vulnerable.[21] In 2015, the U.S. Food & Drug

Business, Healthcare Suffered Most from Data Breaches

Total number hit all-time high in 2016

The business and healthcare sectors of the U.S. economy suffered the vast majority of cyberattacks in 2016. The total number of data breaches reached an all-time high, according to research from the Identity Theft Resource Center and CyberScout.

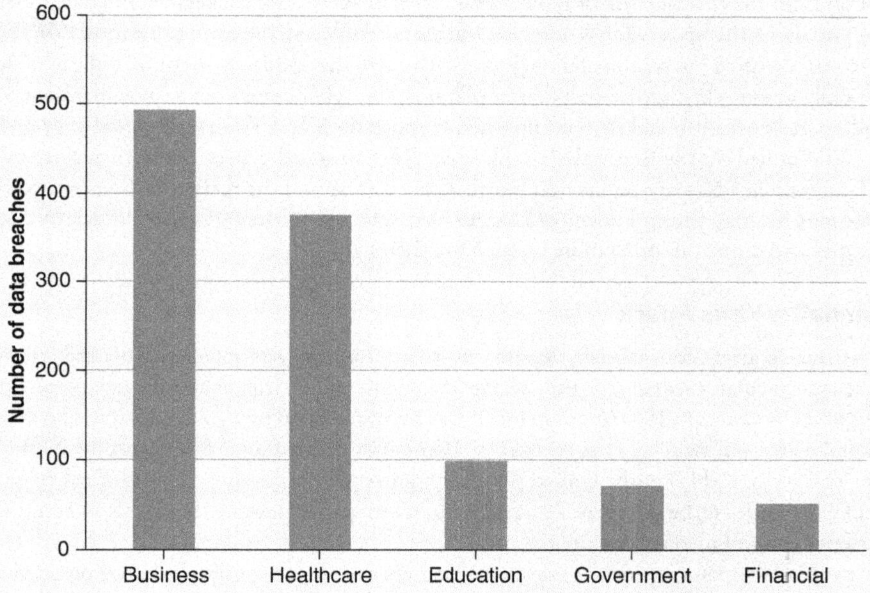

Source: Rajiv Leventhal, "Report: Healthcare Sector Hit Hard in 2016 by Data Breaches," Healthcare Informatics, Jan. 24, 2017, http://tinyurl.com/yc27eukq.

Administration (FDA) told hospitals not to use Hospira's Symbiq infusion pumps because of a vulnerability that could allow the pump to be accessed through a hospital network.

That fear was finally realized in the spring of 2017 when Windows-based devices of German pharmaceutical and chemical giant Bayer were infected by a virus at several U.S. hospitals.[22] Bayer confirmed the hack and said it would be sending out a Microsoft patch for its Windows-based devices "soon." But, in a way, Pandora's box had already been opened.

How lucrative for hackers is medical data? Where a Social Security number might fetch only a dollar and credit card data up to $20, medical information may garner as much as $50.[23] Packages of data on an individual might be sold for as much as $500 to $1,300 each.

Banks and other financial services companies are frequent targets for the same reason: Their data are valuable. According to IBM X-Force research, the financial services sector experienced 29 percent more attacks in 2016 than the year before, with the average financial services company experiencing 65 percent more attacks than the average company in any other sector.[24] Two-thirds of financial organizations faced at least one cybersecurity attack in the last year. And the cost to consumers was dear—more than 8 billion U.K. pounds, according to one estimate, or almost $9.9 billion in 2016, using the conversion rate at the end of the year of $1.235 to 1 pound.[25]

One daring assault took place in February 2016 when hackers sought to steal close to $1 billion from the central bank of Bangladesh. To gain access, the hackers obtained legitimate credentials for the Society for Worldwide Interbank Financial Telecommunication (SWIFT) network, a trusted international money transfer system that banks use to move billions of dollars daily among themselves. In a matter of hours, the cyber crooks got away with about $81 million, but were ultimately tripped up when a typo in the SWIFT messages raised concerns.[26]

Who pulled off the Bangladesh bank heist? Russian-based cybersecurity firm Kaspersky Lab asserted in a 58-page report that North Korea was behind the theft and also operated the infamous hacking group known as Lazarus that was tied to the 2014 hack attack on Sony Pictures and numerous other more recent bank thefts.[27]

WannaCry Virus Attack

A month after the Kaspersky report was issued, Lazarus was apparently behind an even more spectacular cybercrime: unleashing the WannaCry virus that infected more than 300,000 computers in 150 nations before it was finally stopped by a young analyst who found an embedded kill switch in the malware.[28] WannaCry created total disarray at the National Health Service (NHS) in the United Kingdom, preventing access to patient medical records, forcing surgeries to be postponed and sending many patients home. It was also behind the hack of the Bayer medical device.

In this WannaCry attack, Lazarus utilized encrypting ransomware, based on a cyberweapon stolen from the U.S. National Security Agency (NSA) in 2013. Eternal Blue, the tool developed by the NSA, targeted a vulnerability in Microsoft's Windows program.[29]

Microsoft issued a patch in March for its current versions of Windows, after the NSA cyberweapon first appeared on the Dark Web.[30] While the repair would have protected against WannaCry, thousands of computers, including some at the NHS, had not had the patch installed.

"I wish I could say that's unusual," Kroll's Brill says. "But sadly, that's one of the most common reasons we hear from companies about why their computer systems have been compromised. They simply neglected to install updates."

Additionally, about 5 percent of the NHS computers were running Windows XP, a version of the popular software too old to be supported by Microsoft with repairs.[31] After the attack, Microsoft took the unusual step of issuing a patch for the XP version in an attempt to halt the global spread of WannaCry. An estimated 70 million computers worldwide still run the XP version.[32]

But as spectacular as WannaCry seemed when it was launched, it turned out that its creators actually made many "amateur mistakes," according to Wired magazine—especially including the kill switch. What's more, despite its scope, high profile and destructive nature, the hack ended up earning very little ransom—just over $55,000, according to Wired.[33]

And that matters to the North Koreans, who in recent months have begun to look at their hacking capabilities as not only an important weapon but as a potential profit center.[34]

According to a report by the Financial Security Institute in South Korea, the North Korean hackers now seem more likely to target places where they can steal cash, not government secrets. In addition to the Bangladesh bank attack, North Korean hackers also tried to breach banks in Poland and other countries and steal bank card data in order to withdraw cash from accounts.

The institute, which is backed by the South Korean government, asserted that the North has trained as many as 1,700 young hackers whose instruction began when they were teenagers. The report said the cash is used to finance the country's nuclear weapons program and the luxurious lifestyle of the nation's leaders.

Not all cyber experts agree with Kaspersky that Lazarus works for North Korea. Flashpoint, a U.S.-based firm, issued a report pointing a finger at China based on the translations of the ransom notes.[35]

Healthcare Data Theft Will Affect 25 Million

Many will suffer identity theft, out-of-pocket costs

More than 25 million patients will have their medical information stolen through online data breaches between 2015 and 2019, according to projections by the consulting firm Accenture. More than 6 million people over that period will become victims of medical identity theft and more than 4 million will incur out-of-pocket medical expenses related to identity theft.

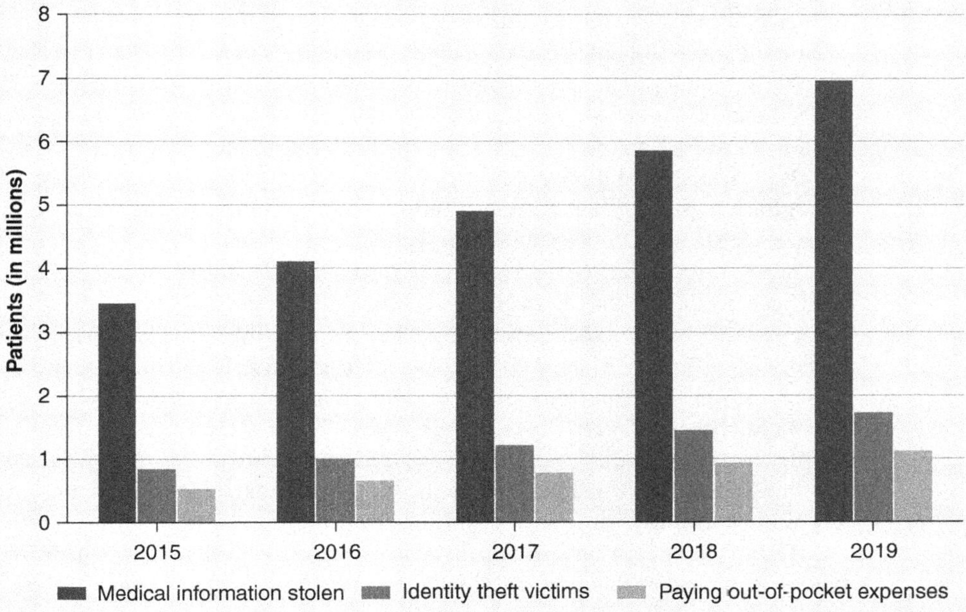

Source: "The $300 Billion Attack: The Revenue Risk and Human Impact of Healthcare Provider Cyber Security Inaction," Accenture, 2015, https://tinyurl.com/y7dbwzn7.

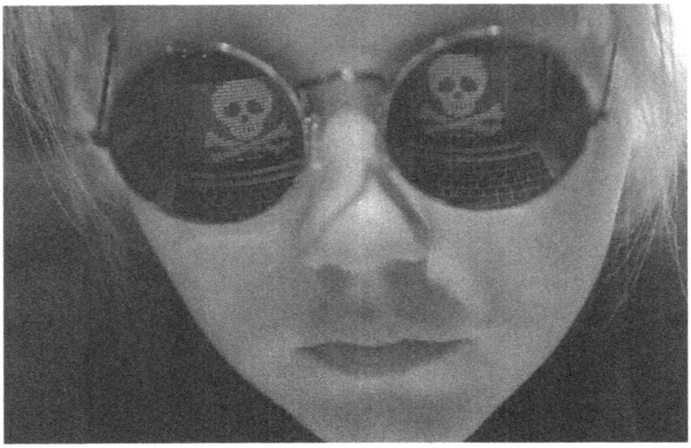

Donat Sorokin/TASS via Getty Images

A computer attacked by the Petya virus is reflected in a user's glasses. The hack paralyzed Ukraine's central bank.

The first half of 2017 proved an inordinately busy period for hackers, primarily based on the cyberweapons stolen from the NSA that were being slowly sold or dumped on the Dark Web. Only a month after the WannaCry attack in May, a more skillfully executed assault paralyzed the National Bank of Ukraine, as well as that nation's electrical grid and much of its infrastructure. The virus then attacked large multinationals, including Danish shipping company Maersk and pharmaceutical giant Merck.[36] This attack, known by many different names—Petya, NotPetya and Golden Eye—also involved encrypting malware connected to the dump of NSA exploits. It was designed to look like ransomware, but wasn't and was far more sophisticated and destructive.

To experts, the goal of the June attack did not appear to be about making money, but rather causing damage and chaos—particularly within Ukraine, where ATMs stopped working and workers at the decommissioned Chernobyl nuclear power plant were forced to test for radiation manually.[37] Given the target, many cyber experts suspected Russia might be behind the attack, although Russian computers were also infected. Cyberattacks on Ukraine are not uncommon, and most Ukrainians presume Russia is behind most of them.[38] Russia and Ukraine have been fighting on and off since 2014, when pro-Russian Ukrainian President Viktor Yanukovych was driven from power and Russia seized the Crimea, a region of Ukraine mostly populated by ethnic Russians.

Unlike WannaCry, the Petya/NotPetya attack only masqueraded as a ransomware attack.[39] The malware irretrievably destroyed files, and the ransom was almost impossible to pay. So far, there has been no definitive verdict on who was behind the attack.

That is not the case with the theft of the cyberweapons from the NSA, the inspiration for the malware used in most of the recent attacks. Here, the cyberthief was a hacking group known as the Shadow Brokers, which suddenly appeared in August 2016 and has been intermittently dumping stolen NSA exploits ever since, according to Bruce Schneier, chief technology officer of IBM Resilient Systems Inc., which advises clients on cyberattack protection and response. The material they are selling or leaking comes from material stolen from the NSA in 2013, and the hacking tools provided have compromised Cisco routers and Linux mail servers as well as Microsoft Windows.[40]

"They have publicly embarrassed the NSA and damaged its intelligence-gathering capabilities, while at the same time [they] have put sophisticated cyberweapons in the hands of anyone who wants them," Schneier wrote. While Schneier said the group could be connected to Russia, he said they also may have gotten the NSA trove through a disaffected insider.[41]

Over the past decade, the war against hackers has been waged on two fronts—the first led somewhat reluctantly by businesses as they beef up their defenses against penetration, and the second by governments, on all levels, as they look to ensure the physical and financial safety of citizens and their personal data. Thanks to the relentless efforts of hackers, including Russian attempts to influence elections in the United States and France, new rules are proliferating at an exponential pace—globally, in the United States in spite of the Trump administration's otherwise strong opposition to business regulation and at the state level.

The biggest thing on the horizon for European companies and those doing business in Europe is the European Union's General Data Protection Regulation (GDPR), which includes comprehensive data security, management and transparency requirements. Passed in 2016, the regulation intends to give citizens more control over how companies use their personal data and bring a certain standardization across the region about how data are handled. The EU gave organizations two years to comply, but the implementation deadline is approaching next May. Organizations that fail to meet it will face substantial fines.[42]

In Japan and Brazil, similar regulations on the use of personal data are also in the process of being implemented. And in the United States, it is hard to find an agency not working on beefing up protection of personal data.

On May 11, President Trump issued an executive order on cybersecurity that called for beefing up the cyber defenses of government agencies, the nation's infrastructure and ultimately the personal data of private citizens. Since the executive order, which took months to produce, progress has been unclear, according to experts. Members of both parties in Washington and cyber experts have told the president that the country cannot afford to drag its feet, given the scale of the attacks this spring.[43]

One source of doubt about Trump's commitment to the issue is the president's skepticism about the conclusion by U.S. intelligence agencies that Russian hacking, under the direction of President Vladimir Putin, interfered with the 2016 U.S. presidential election. At one point, Trump even suggested that the United States join forces with Russia to combat hacking. Secretary of State Rex Tillerson and Treasury Secretary Steven Mnuchin touted the cooperation agreement as one of the key wins from Trump's meeting with Putin during the G20 summit in Hamburg this year.[44]

The Russia pact encountered widespread opposition—Republican Senator Lindsey Graham of South Carolina called it close to "the dumbest idea I've ever heard"—and Trump rapidly ditched it.[45]

Meanwhile, the rest of the federal government, particularly financial service regulators, has been pushing forward on numerous fronts to protect personal data. The Federal Deposit Insurance Corporation, the Comptroller of the Currency and the Federal Reserve are working to finalize cybersecurity guidance for financial institutions with consolidated assets of $50 billion or more.[46] Proposed rules include establishing board-approved cyber risk governance processes, implementing formal policies to manage workforce and supply chain risks and adopting new standards to ensure that covered entities can effectively plan for, respond to and recover from cyber incidents.

The Securities and Exchange Commission is also calling on public companies to conduct more active oversight of company cybersecurity practices. So is the Commodity Futures Trading Commission, which approved a set of rules that will require frequent testing of information technology at U.S. commodities and derivatives firms, including exchanges and clearinghouses. Key elements of the rules include specified cybersecurity testing, minimum testing frequency, use of independent contractors, testing scope, and internal reporting, review and remediation.

The state of New York has outpaced the federal efforts. The state Department of Financial Services put into place on March 1 a first-in-the-nation cybersecurity regulation to protect New York's financial services industry and consumers from the threat of cyberattacks.[47] The regulation requires banks, insurance companies and other financial services institutions to establish and maintain a cybersecurity program designed to protect consumers' private data and ensure the safety and soundness of New York's financial services industry. It also addresses what some consider the soft underbelly of cybersecurity—third-party vendors—by applying regularity requirements to them as well. IBM, a leader in cybersecurity, has for years enforced rigorous standards on its vendors, pointing to the fact that many hackers breached retailers through their supply chains.

One of the standout features of the new regulations, the toughest in the nation, is that it holds senior company leadership accountable for compliance by requiring the filing of an annual certificate attesting to an institution's adherence to the regulation.[48] The New York state regulation also has implications for healthcare insurers, requiring that they maintain state-approved plans to protect their businesses, information systems and their customers' personal information.[49]

But as is frequently the case when regulations are left to the states to draft, a patchwork quilt of rules is developing. Without umbrella regulation, companies doing business in multiple states—as most do now thanks to the internet—have to figure out how they can stay on the right side of the law in all of them.

In the healthcare arena, the Centers for Medicare & Medicaid Services, which administers the Medicare program, is issuing new Medicare cards to all beneficiaries. The replacement cards are needed because current Medicare numbers are based on Social Security numbers with a few letters or numbers added. So the theft of a Medicare number also gives access to a person's Social Security number. The change was mandated by a 2015 law, and the first new cards are expected out next year.[50]

The federal Department of Health and Human Services (HHS) also is working to stop cybercrime with some tough enforcement actions against health facilities. For instance, in February, Memorial Healthcare System agreed to pay $5.5 million for violations of the Health Insurance Portability and Accountability Act (HIPAA) Privacy and Security Rules.[51] Memorial, which operates hospitals, nursing homes and clinics, said it would correct what HHS called weak internal controls that permitted employees to improperly access more than 100,000 patient records.

The biggest ongoing struggle is how to fight this security threat, given that hackers seem to uncover new holes in defense systems as soon as they get installed. Even the suggestion to use biometric verification—using biologically identifiable traits to confirm people's identities, such as fingerprints, iris scans, DNA and earlobe geometry—has encountered pushback from experts, particularly if that is the sole identifier.

"Fingerprint patterns can be reproduced—sometimes even from a photograph," Kroll's Brill says. "I can always change my password, but what happens if someone steals my fingerprint. Then I've got problems."

Chronology

20th Century	**Early efforts to create safeguards**
1981	European countries ratify the "Convention for the Protection of Individuals with Regard to Automatic Processing of Personal Data," a Council of Europe treaty designed to protect individuals' privacy rights.
1992	Beth Givens, a University of San Diego student, forms the nonprofit Privacy Rights Clearinghouse to make consumers more aware of technology's impact on privacy.
1998	The U.S. Health Insurance Portability and Accountability Act takes effect, setting national standards for protecting certain health data held or transferred electronically.
1999	President Bill Clinton signs the Financial Services Modernization Act, which requires financial services companies to safeguard sensitive data.
2000–Present	**Growing stakes, growing threats**
2005	The Privacy Rights Clearinghouse creates the Chronology of Data Breaches database to track a rapidly escalating number of personal data breaches affecting people in the United States. As of Aug. 30, 2017, the organization had tracked 7,645 breaches involving more than 927 million records.
2006	Heartland Payment Systems, a credit and payroll services company in Washington, is targeted by hackers who are not discovered until 2008—by which time they have stolen more than 130 million credit and debit card numbers.
2014	Hackers hit financial services giant JPMorgan Chase, stealing sensitive financial and personal information on 76 million households and 7 million small businesses.
2015	Security experts dub it the "Year of the Healthcare Hack" as more than 120 million health care records are breached nationwide, according to the U.S. Department of Health and Human Services, including 80 million patient and employee records stolen from insurer Anthem.
2016	Hackers steal $81 million from a Bangladesh bank using the SWIFT message system, which handles trillions of dollars in banking wire transfers every day. . . . President Barack Obama unveils the Cybersecurity National Action Plan, a long-term strategy to enhance cybersecurity awareness and digital security in the United States.
2017	WannaCry ransomware infects more than 200,000 computers in more than 150 nations and creates havoc for the U.K. National Health System, which is using old computers and software because of underfunding. . . . A Petya/NotPetya ransomware attack hits Ukraine's central bank and several other international banks.

Discussion Questions

Here are some issues to consider regarding the security of digital data:

- What is the key difference between a ransomware attack and other forms of data theft? Which do you think is harder to prevent, or to stop once it occurs?
- How have the operations of cybercriminals evolved in recent years? How have their goals changed, and why?
- Why are the banking and healthcare industries such prominent targets of cyberattacks? What other industries are most at risk?
- How has the growth of the Internet of Things (IoT) created a new target of opportunity for online thieves?
- What can companies do to further protect themselves and their customers' information? Should companies be legally liable for damages stemming from data breaches?
- What opportunities exist to create new businesses that would address the vulnerability of cyberdata?

UPDATE IN 2020

Although data security is often thought of in relation to hackers, government agencies were also scrutinizing corporate technology centers for invading customers' privacy.

When the COVID-19 pandemic began spreading across the United States, millions of Americans were sent to work from home. That left the door open for a spike in cybercrime. According to the FBI's Internet Crime Complaint Center (IC3), the number of cybersecurity complaints in the spring of 2020 leapt to over 3,000 per day. That contrasted with about 1,000 complaints per day that IC3 received pre-pandemic.[52]

Similarly, Google reported a huge jump in malicious email messages in the same period. In one week in April, Google said it blocked an average of 18 million messages daily, and more than 240 million spam messages related to COVID-19. It said the hackers were impersonating agencies such as the World Health Organization and were capitalizing on less-secure remote work settings. Through April, Americans lost nearly $12 million to scammers trying to take advantage of the pandemic.[53]

The situation was compounded by the increased use of mobile devices. In its 2020 Data Attack Surface Report, Cybersecurity Ventures estimated that more than 5 billion people access and store data on their devices and in internet clouds. By 2030, it estimated that 7.5 billion people would be doing so, and that 50 percent of all data would be stored in clouds.[54]

"To underestimate the amount of data, which is earth's new natural resource, is to underestimate our need to protect it from cybercrime," said Steve Morgan, founder of Cybersecurity Ventures and editor-in-chief of Cybercrime Magazine.[55] The magazine also estimated that a business or consumer would be the subject of a ransomware attack every five seconds in 2020.[56]

In Europe, however, the issue of data security was less focused on hackers and more on companies' invasion of consumers' privacy.

In 2018, the European Union (EU) implemented the General Data Protection Regulation (GDPR), which was meant to promote a common privacy culture and threatened stiff fines if companies did not comply.

That sparked a widespread effort to monitor data protection, with some 500,000 organizations reporting that they had data protection officers. In 2019, the EU began assessing fines. At the top: British Airways, at 204.6 million Euro, followed by Marriott International, at 110.4 million Euro. Google's operations in France and Sweden were also fined.[57]

In the U.S., the California Consumer Privacy Act (CCPA) was signed into law in June 2018 and went into effect in January 2020.[58] New York followed suit with its Stop Hacks and Improve Electronic Data Security (SHIELD) Act in July 2019, and a handful of other states are also looking into passing similar laws, though a universal data privacy law is yet to fully materialize at the federal level.[59]

—Micheline Maynard

6 DOING BUSINESS WITH JAPAN

Can Abenomics and a "third opening" revive the economy?

Scott Sowers

From *SAGE Business Researcher,* October 12, 2015

EXECUTIVE SUMMARY

Since the late 1980s, Japan's economy has struggled to overcome years of recession and punishing price deflation, plus a declining population and aging citizenry. Among the forces pushing against these head winds: a small but growing group of entrepreneurs who are trying to bring creativity and energy to the economy, and the government of Prime Minister Shinzo Abe, which is attempting to spark growth through "Abenomics" and a "third opening" consisting of free trade. Reviews of these efforts are mixed, but many experts agree Abenomics is comprehensive and ambitious. Many also agree Japan's fate is tied to implementation of the trade pact known as the Trans-Pacific Partnership and to the nation's ability to solve its demographic crisis. As Japan attempts to rebuild its economy, economists and policymakers are debating a number of crucial questions. Will an aging population, falling birth rate and restricted immigration doom the Japanese economy? Should Japan restart its nuclear plants? Is Abenomics working?

Toru Yamanaka/AFP/Getty Images

Shinzo Abe, Japan's prime minister, walks past a campaign poster of himself after his December 2014 reelection. He championed a multipart program to attempt to pull the nation out of its long economic slump.

OVERVIEW

Satoshi Sugie was working as an engineer at Nissan designing headlights when he decided to strike out on his own. "The Japanese are sometimes too conservative and don't want to take a risk," he says. "In 2010, I met a wheelchair user who told me he had stopped going to the store because he didn't want to be seen as weak, and I realized that wheelchair design hadn't changed in 50 years."

So Sugie poached other engineers from Sony and Toyota and started working on a prototype for what would become the Whill, a four-wheel drive, personal mobility device that can be controlled via a smartphone app and looks like something that came out of Apple's lab. He leveraged the prototype to raise $13 million, opened a sales and marketing office in San Francisco and began taking orders for his invention, which sells for $13,995 and is available in both Japan and the United States.[1]

His venture is one small sign of change in Japan, where entrepreneurship is gaining strength and the government under Prime Minister Shinzo Abe is attempting to lift the world's third-largest economy out of its doldrums by pursuing a sweeping reform program he calls Abenomics and a "third opening" built around the Trans-Pacific Partnership (TPP) and free trade.[2] Reviews are mixed—some statistics indicate Japan's economy is improving; others don't—but most experts agree Abenomics is comprehensive and ambitious.

Japan, an Asian nation of 127 million, has historically been wary of opening its markets to competitors. What's regarded as the first opening occurred in 1853 when the gunboats of U.S. Commodore Matthew Perry forced Japan to begin trading with other nations. The second opening was after World War II, during the U.S. occupation.[3] Japan has also been lukewarm to entrepreneurs. Its business history is defined by rigid traditions of the diligent salary man and lifetime employment, with different companies locked together in the keiretsu system, networks of business relationships that foster close collaboration between companies but limit innovation and shield domestic markets from imported products. It also is defined by a sometimes too-close relationship between the public and private sectors.

Since the late 1980s, the economy has struggled, including years of recession and punishing price deflation. Additionally, for the last few years, Japan has imported more goods than it has exported, posting record trade deficits.[4] Imports are mostly oil, natural gas and coal. The only items on the top 10 list of imports that aren't energy related are computers, medicine, iron ore, phones and broadcasting equipment.[5]

Because of high tariffs and policies that discourage imports, U.S. businesses interested in the Japanese market face a formidable challenge. The United States shipped $65.1 billion worth of goods to Japan in 2013, the most current official data available from the Office of the United States Trade Representative, down 6.9 percent from the year before.[6] American businesses have long complained about Japan's policies. In 2013, for instance, the American Automotive Policy Council, which represents Detroit's Big Three automakers, said that the Japanese government manipulates its currency to favor exports and block foreign competition.[7]

Abe, who briefly served as Japan's prime minister in 2006–2007, was elected again in 2012. The ambitious economic program he calls Abenomics seeks to correct the nation's trade imbalance and end two decades of deflation, as well as address serious demographic issues. The plan's three prongs, or "arrows," include monetary easing, fiscal expansion and structural reform.

Abe's first arrow is loose monetary policy. Because Japan's benchmark interest rate has been at zero for years, that involves what is known as quantitative easing. Japan's central bank,

Japan's Decades of Weak Growth

GDP growth rate, United States and Japan, 1985–2017

The Japanese economy is projected to grow at an anemic average rate of 1.3 percent from 2015 to 2017, roughly half the projected rate for the United States. Japan's economic output soared during the 1980s, driven by its thriving auto industry, but plunged after its stock market crashed in late 1990. During the 1990s and 2000s, known as the Lost Decades, growth mostly hovered below 2 percent. The country's economy expanded by nearly 5 percent in 2010 after shrinking for two years during the worldwide recession, but has since grown little.

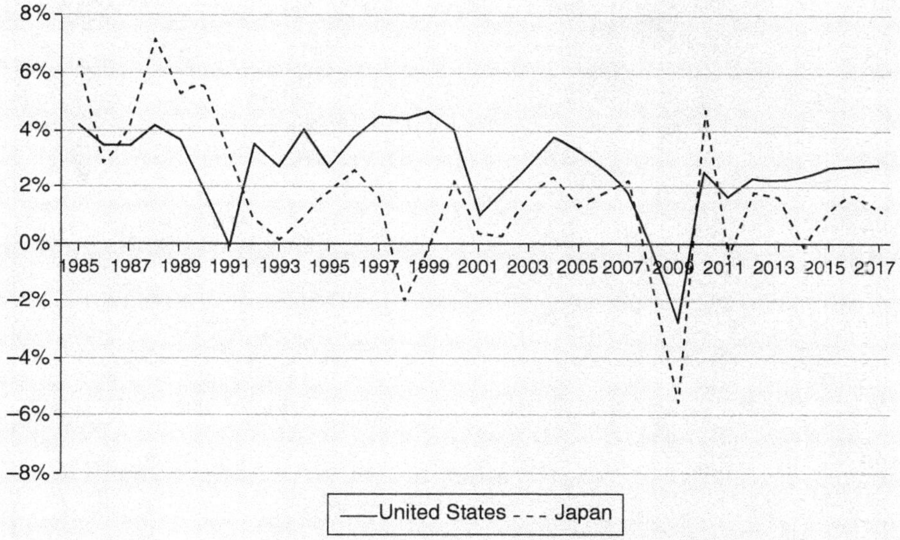

Note: Figures for 2015–17 are projections.

Sources: Data for 1985–2014 downloaded from the World Bank, http://tinyurl.com/o3z46zw; estimates for 2015–17 downloaded from the World Bank, http://tinyurl.com/nvbuzwo.

the Bank of Japan, is buying government securities to pump more money into the economy and thus raise consumer spending and bring about inflation—years of deflation battered the Japanese economy. The bank has gone through two rounds of bond buying, but it has been unable to raise inflation to 2 percent.[8]

The second arrow, expansive fiscal policy, involved $116 billion worth of government spending, including for infrastructure projects designed to repair damage from the catastrophic Great East Japan earthquake of 2011.[9] Other government spending goals included expanding foreign trade, investing in renewable energy, promoting research and development, supporting small businesses, improving access to health care and expanding tourism.[10]

Map: Major Earthquakes in Japan

Japan's location atop four shifting tectonic plates has made the country vulnerable to destructive earthquakes. The largest one on record, a 9.0-magnitude quake off the Tohoku coast of Honshu island in March 2011, killed nearly 16,000 people and caused an estimated $300 billion in damage. Six of Japan's largest recorded earthquakes occurred during the last 100 years, although others killed hundreds of thousands of people during the 18th and 19th centuries.

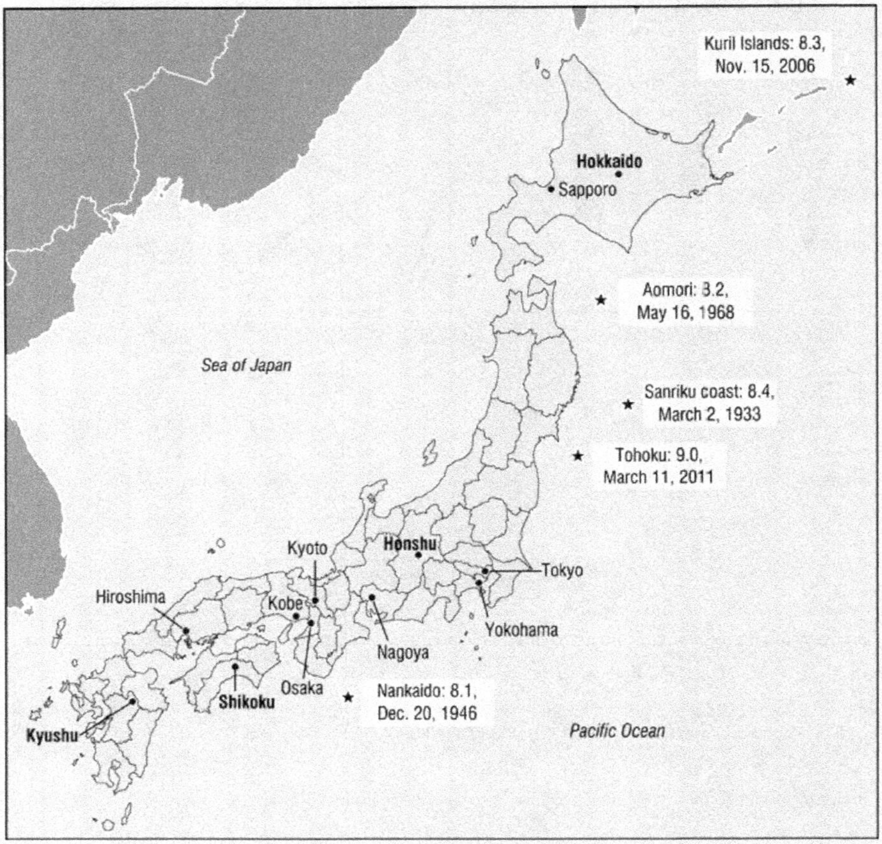

Note: Points on maps are approximations based on U.S. Geological Survey mapping data

Sources: "Japan's Biggest Earthquakes," Live Science, Apr. 8, 2011, http://tinyurl.com/oxcgu5z; "Earthquake Archives" map tool, U.S. Geological Survey, accessed Sep. 25, 2015, http://tinyurl.com/m4ksz7h.

The last arrow involves a broad range of adjustments to the economic and financial structure, including opening up labor markets (possibly to foreign workers) and making farming more efficient. Abe also is pursuing structural change by cutting corporate taxes; tinkering with regulations on energy, the environment and health care; and incentivizing career opportunities for women. Getting more women in the workforce would expand Japan's labor force, which has dropped 6 percent in the past 10 years, largely because of an aging and decreasing population.[11]

To foster new small businesses, Abe is supporting the Kakehashi Project, an incubator funded by the Japanese government to encourage Japanese start-ups to launch in Silicon Valley.[12] Incubators in hubs such as Samurai Startup Island have also sprouted.[13] Going independent remains challenging in Japan, though. In a survey conducted by the Global Entrepreneurship Monitor, only 6 percent of the Japanese surveyed believed there were opportunities to start a business in their country.[14]

Key parts of Abe's strategy are interwoven in what real estate development firm Mitsui Fudosan calls "Kashiwa-no-ha," or the Smart City, in Chiba prefecture. Its concept centers on creating a regionalized, energy-efficient planned city where residents can work, play and shop in a small-town environment that is still connected to a major metropolitan area, in this case, by rail to Tokyo about 28 miles away. Construction on the Smart City began in 2005; according to Kiyoko Hama, a representative of Mitsui Fudosan, 5,000 people now live there.[15]

The development is geared to saving energy, promoting a healthy lifestyle and providing an environment that encourages job creation through entrepreneurship. The community's major buildings are all adjacent to the train station, and the town is walkable.

Energy needs are controlled by a community-wide "energy management system." Its smart grid system includes large banks of batteries to store power. On a smaller scale, residents are encouraged to reduce their carbon footprints by turning off appliances and using the fleet of community vehicles.

Improving access to health care is another principle of Abenomics. The Japanese telecom giant Nippon Telegraph and Telephone (NTT) is using optical-fiber broadband information and communication technology to bring new health care initiatives to the 600 residents of Hinoemata, a tourist destination in Fukushima prefecture known primarily for its buckwheat soba noodles and kabuki theater productions.[16] The technology takes the form of a landline-based telephone with a video screen and large, easy-to-read number buttons.

Hinoemata Mayor Mitsuyoshi Hoshi says, "In 2011, NTT contacted us and said they wanted to distribute step counters to the villagers so they could register their steps, track their blood pressure, body weight, and send all that data to a regional health center. All the households would also be supplied with an Internet connection."

The closest hospital to the village is two hours away by twisting mountain roads. The villagers are encouraged to send their vital signs to the local health clinic using electronic blood pressure cuffs, blood sugar measuring devices and electronic scales.

The data is sent via a videophone, designed and sold by NTT, that gives the patient face-to-face contact with doctors and nurses. "The younger generation already uses the Internet, but if we can make a simpler product for the older people, there's a lot of possibility there," says Hideki Ishida, an executive with NTT East.

Abe also is pushing structural change in Japan's agriculture system, which, through tariffs, restricts imports and protects a farm workforce of aging part-timers.[17]

After World War II, reform laws redistributed farmland from large landlords to tenant farmers. The average size of the smaller parcels was 7.4 acres. The government assumed the small farmers would eventually sell out to larger farmers, but soaring land prices kept the system intact as the smaller farmers chose not to sell.

For the past 60 years, Japanese agriculture has been dominated by JA-Zenchu, or JA, known in English as the Central Union of Agricultural Co-operatives. The group is an independent lobbying organization that maintains strong control over Japanese agriculture. Change under Abenomics is coming down to fights over the JA's power, the fees that farmers pay to the JA and the high tariffs on pork and beef.[18]

Japan's farmers are old—their average age in 2010 was 70. Most young people are not interested in farming as a career: Of Japan's 1.5 million farmers, only 420,000 work full time. The JA, which is tightly linked with Abe's Liberal Democratic Party (LDP), employs 240,000 people.[19]

Non-Japanese food companies back the Trans-Pacific Partnership—an agreement among 12 countries, including the United States, Japan, Vietnam and Australia, that would phase out tariffs between the members and lead to increased trade—because the pact might open the door to a Japanese market hungry for lower food prices. The TPP remains politically controversial in some would-be member countries, including the United States.[20]

Japan would also like to export more food and has set a goal of doubling food exports by 2020. Since Abe relaxed price supports for rice, prices for the Japanese diet staple have fallen to their lowest level since 2006. "The TPP is pushing for all that, but we don't know where it's going yet," says Shihoko Goto, an associate with the Wilson Center, a foreign policy think tank in Washington, D.C. "Part of the base of Abe's political party is agriculture."

As Japan proceeds with its third opening and seeks to revitalize its economy, here are some of the questions under debate.

WEIGHING THE ISSUES

Will an Aging Population, Falling Birthrate and Restricted Immigration Doom the Japanese Economy?

Demographic factors present some of the largest impediments to putting the Japanese economy back on track. The country's population, which started falling in 2004, is aging more quickly than that of any other nation. More than 22 percent of the population is already over 65, and a government report indicates that by 2060 the population will fall from 127 million to 87 million—and nearly 40 percent of them will be over 65.[21] Council on Foreign Relations senior fellow Sheila Smith said, "Many of [Abe's] reforms call for significant adjustments in the norms of Japanese society. It's a huge agenda, and there is no one silver bullet."[22]

Abe is looking at ways to increase birthrates, including taking some unusual measures, such as assigning lifelong gynecologists to women and providing financial help to singles looking for partners. Another way to raise birthrates is to get more women in the workplace: "Evidence shows that workforces with a higher female participation rate also have higher birthrates," said Kathy Matsui, chief Japan equity strategist at Goldman Sachs in Tokyo.[23]

While a falling population means smaller markets, an aging population does present business opportunities—especially in health care. By 2020, more adult diapers will likely be sold in Japan than those made for children. Telemedicine systems, similar to the system NTT is

Working-Age Japanese Population Declining

Percentage distribution of Japan's population, 2015, 2030 and 2050

Japan's population is projected to age significantly in the next 35 years. The share of Japanese age 65 and older will grow from 26 percent of the population in 2015 to 31 percent in 2030 and 36 percent in 2050, according to United Nations projections. The share of 35- to 49-year-olds, meanwhile, will shrink from 21 percent of the population in 2015 to 16 percent in 2050, while the share of 15- to 34-year-olds will drop from 21 percent to 18 percent.

Distribution by age group, 2015

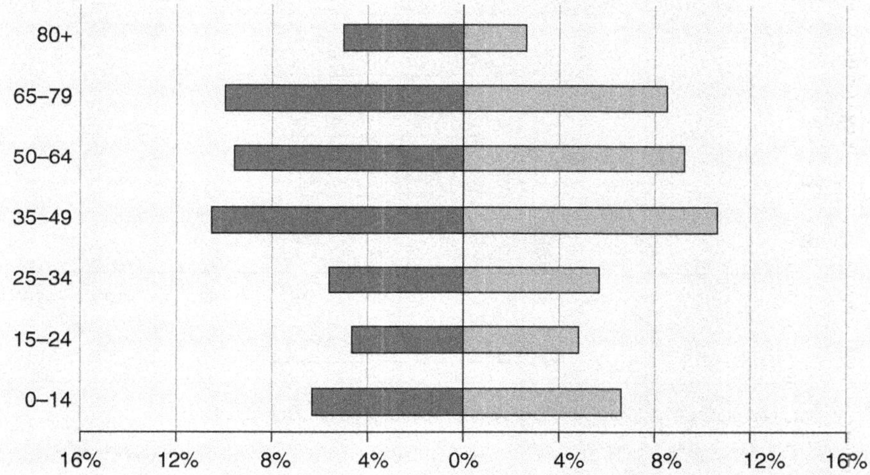

Distribution by age group, 2030

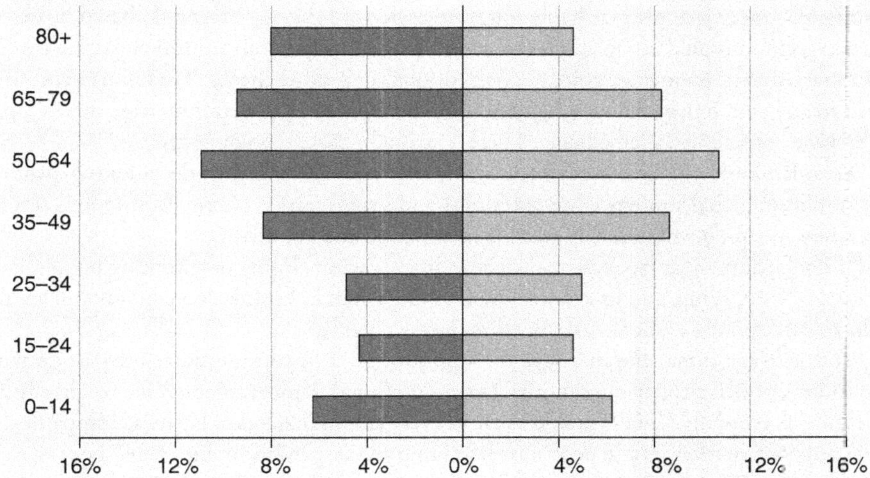

(Continued)

(Continued)

Distribution by age group, 2050

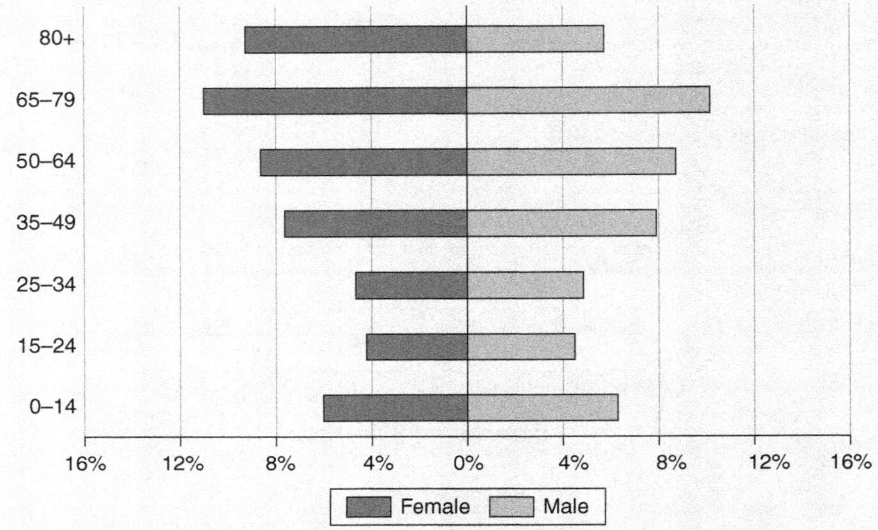

Note: Data calculated from projections for the total population for each listed year.

Source: Data downloaded from "World Population Prospects, the 2015 Revision," United Nations Population Division, 2015, http://tinyurl.com/nwxctxy.

testing in Hinoemata, also are being put into service in Japan by Biotronik, based in Berlin. "If you go to a hospital in Japan, it's not uncommon for a doctor to see 100 outpatients a day. Of these patients, [many] are going for prescriptions or routine checks. They don't necessarily need to go," said Jeffrey Annis, president of Biotronik. "How to better manage this as Japan ages? One option is . . . telemedicine. There is no doubt that [it] is going to grow."[24]

Yoko Ishikura, a professor emeritus at Hitotsubashi University, works as an independent consultant in global strategy competitiveness and says Japan's economy is in serious trouble because of the problems posed by an aging population and low birthrate.

"I don't think most Japanese realize how quickly we are losing our working population," she says. "We're aging, and unless we do something about it, I think the economy will go into a downward spiral if we don't take measures pretty quickly."

Toshio Nagashima, the manager for Vegi Dream, a Toyota subsidiary that is growing 1,000 tons of bell peppers a year, says Japan's profound demographic problems already are affecting its economy. "These problems are the very reason that lots of Japanese companies are targeting foreign markets and people are hesitating about spending money here," he says. As of midsummer 2015, household spending had dropped in 14 of the previous 15 months.[25]

William H. Saito, an entrepreneur who is an adviser to Abe, doesn't buy into the gloom: "Assuming things like the Second Machine Age and Industry 4.0 are happening, a shrinking and aging population, which the rest of the world will soon experience, will be a positive."

Saito is referencing thinking defined in "The Second Machine Age: Work, Progress, and Prosperity in a Time of Brilliant Technologies," a 2014 book by Erik Brynjolfsson and Andrew McAfee. These Massachusetts Institute of Technology educators point to transformational technological advances, including self-driving cars and IBM's Watson computer, as examples of why humans should be optimistic about the future.[26]

Industry 4.0 is a term for the transformational forces at work in the business world resulting from the increased use of data analytics, cybersecurity solutions, cloud-based technology, robots and interconnectivity.[27]

"The key building blocks are already in place for digital technologies to be as important and transformational to society and the economy as the steam engine," Brynjolfsson and McAfee wrote. "In short, we're at an inflection point—a point where the curve starts to bend a lot—because of computers. We are entering a second machine age."[28]

Saito believes technology will save us all, and that a smaller population won't be a problem for Japan because machines will help humans do more with less. Goto at the Wilson Center agrees. "It's really about can we make lemonade out of the lemons?" Goto asks.

Yet reversing a falling birthrate is difficult. Japan's fertility rate is 8.4 children per 1,000 inhabitants; only Germany's is lower, at 8.2 per 1,000.[29] One-quarter of the population is 65 or older.[30] The Pew Foundation rates Japan as No. 1 in its old-age dependency ratio, a comparison of the number of people 65 and over with the number of working age people. Its ratio is 72—twice as high as in the United States.[31]

Although government can't do much about birthrates or aging, it can do something about immigration policy—which in Japan remains controversial and problematic. In February 2014, the government prepared a report recommending that the country accept 200,000 new permanent residents while also stressing that it was not changing immigration policy.[32] Abe has issued temporary visas for construction workers on the condition that the workers return home once projects are completed. Many of the construction workers are helping Tokyo prepare for the 2020 Olympics. But even with the temps figured in, the government projects a total labor shortage of 150,000 workers.[33]

"The subject of immigration used to be such a taboo, [but] now we are at least talking about it, which is a good step," says Ishikura of Hitotsubashi University. She points to South Korean and Chinese immigrants working in 7-Elevens—the Japanese-owned convenience store chain has 17,000 outlets in Japan, more than twice as many as in the much larger United States.[34] The convenience store workers are often students who don't become permanent residents.[35]

Less than 2 percent of Japan's working population is foreign born, one of the lowest rates in the world. Abe is allowing some health care workers from Indonesia, the Philippines and Vietnam to come to Japan and work toward long-term residency. However, their formal training often is not recognized in Japan and they must learn Japanese within three to four years or they are sent home. As a result, the program has never reached its goal.[36]

Should Japan Restart Its Nuclear Plants?

In March 2011 a major earthquake shook Japan, spawning a tsunami. Almost 16,000 people died; damage was estimated at $300 billion.[37] The disasters cut off power and cooling to three nuclear reactors in Fukushima prefecture in northern Japan.[38] Before the accident, nuclear accounted for 30 percent of Japan's energy output and plans were in place to raise that to 50 percent.[39] In the wake of the meltdown, all 54 Japanese reactors were taken offline as a precaution. To replace the offline reactors, Japan began running generators off fossil fuels. Its oil imports rose 4 percent between 2010 and 2012 while imports of liquefied natural gas went up 24 percent. The costs of power generation jumped 41 percent.[40]

Shutting down all the reactors after the accident "has increased our dependence on fossil fuels," said Japanese energy official Toshikazu Okuya. "Money has flowed out of the country and electricity prices have risen."[41]

Of the country's 54 reactors, 42 are operable and 7 are expected to be restarted over the next two years.[42] As of early October 2015, one reactor is currently operating while a second is scheduled to start by mid-October.[43]

Environmentalists want the reactors left off, but the business community generally wants them turned back on.

Converting to renewables is not yet a viable option, according to analysts. "For utilities, there is no economic incentive to add clean energy," said Ali Izadi-Najafabadi, an analyst at Bloomberg New Energy Finance in Tokyo. "In the long term, it hurts the country, including manufacturers."[44]

Public sentiment about nuclear power is mixed, and legal battles have erupted as the process of turning the reactors back on moves from the stress-test stage to active. In April 2015, a Japanese court in the Kagoshima district rejected an injunction filed by residents to leave the local plant turned off.[45]

In the meantime, "Japan's nuclear village"—a widely used term that includes the pro-nuclear forces consisting of academics, utility providers, the financial sector, the government and the media—urges both restarting the reactors and developing renewables.[46] "The most important thing is to optimize different power sources such as nuclear, thermal and renewables," said Hajimu Yamana, a professor at the Kyoto University Research Reactor Institute.[47]

Nagashima, who gets the power to run his Vegi Dream pepper farm from a natural gas cogeneration plant, opposes restarting the reactors. "Lots of Japanese people believe in the potential of alternatives such as solar, geothermal heat, etcetera," he says. "I think the problem constricting the alternatives' development is too much regulatory and administrative policies."

Businesses responded to the loss of a reliable power source by developing large-scale backup battery systems, alternative-energy sources and smart grids for their factories and plants. The same Toyota Motor East facility where Vegi Dream operates lost power for several days after the earthquake. The company worked with the government and the local utility provider to install a natural gas-fired generator and a smart grid system that connects the main factory with nine other surrounding manufacturing plants—also owned by Toyota—and the village town hall a few miles away.

Ichiro Suzuki, spokesman for Toyota Motor East, says, "We expected the supply-demand balance for electricity would be very tight because of the long-term shutdown of nuclear reactors caused by the East Japan earthquake. The biggest challenge was the deregulation needed to supply electricity to the other factories." Similar backup battery systems and smart grids also are in use at the Smart City project and at a complex of test houses being built by Honda in Saitama.

Junichi Takeuchi is the CEO of Fasotec, a Chiba technology company that is pioneering the use of 3-D printers to produce realistic models of human organs used to train surgeons. He's accepted that, despite problems, nuclear power will be part of Japan's energy makeup for years to come.

"We as a people in Japan have understood the great risks of nuclear and gained major distrust," he says. "On the other hand, we do not have many feasible options. The best option, of course, is to find alternative energy resources as soon as possible while buying time by operating a part of the nuclear plants with extra care."

Jun Yamadera, a graduate of the Samurai Startup Island program, runs the technology firm Eyes Japan. It's located about a three-hour drive from the crippled nuclear plant. Living and working that close to the danger zone has given him mixed feelings about the future of nuclear energy in Japan. "Oh, boy. I really don't know," he says. "I have studied nuclear so hard after the accident—since I live in Fukushima. But as I learn, I realize there's more I don't know. I am not pro-nuclear or anti-nuclear. But I am pro-data and pro-science. However, I do believe humans always invent things like the wing by jumping from the cliff."

Is "Abenomics" Working?

Shinzo Abe, now three years into his second term, has loosened monetary policy and poured money into Japan's infrastructure. Some early verdicts are coming in, and they are mixed. Although the Nikkei stock index has been rising since he was elected, Japan's GDP fell 1.2 percent in the second quarter of 2015. Price deflation is still an issue as the core Consumer Price Index dropped 1 percent, not including food prices. Overall, GDP has been going up since Abe's election, but slowly: It has increased only 2.3 percent since the start of 2013.[48]

Although most sources give him kudos for trying new medicine on old problems, Abe has his critics. Reforming the agriculture system will dilute power from the JA, the face of the farm lobby and a political powerhouse with strong ties to Abe's party. Health care companies also are complaining about changes to the centralized health system that could increase the availability of foreign-made drugs and medical devices.

"We have to protect the universal health insurance system to which everyone belongs," said Takashi Hanyuda, a member of Abe's political party and vice president of the Japan Medical Association, a powerful doctors' lobby. "If the system starts to break down a little, it will turn into a flood and it would be extremely hard to halt the trend."[49]

Some critics also raise the specter of hyperinflation because of all the cash being pumped into the monetary system, but so far there's not much evidence to support this fear.[50] Japan's record high debt-to-GDP ratio of more than 200 percent also garners lots of dire warnings. That the debt is held domestically and at low interest rates is often lost amid the gloom. Most of the debt is held by entities of the Japanese government, including the Bank of Japan, and when that is calculated in, the debt numbers fall to a less distressing figure of below 140 percent.[51]

Japan Carries World's Highest Debt-to-GDP Ratio

Government debt as a percentage of GDP, by country, 2013

The Japanese government's debt equaled 239 percent of the nation's gross domestic product in 2013, well above second-ranked Greece (180 percent) and third-ranked Italy (143 percent). By comparison, the United States' debt-to-GDP ratio was 123 percent, while Germany and South Korea had ratios of 82 percent and 51 percent, respectively.

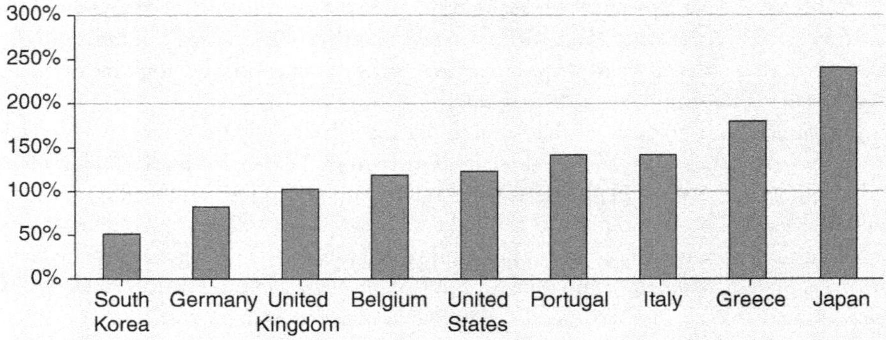

Source: "General Government Debt," Organisation for Economic Co-operation and Development, accessed Sep. 21, 2015, http://tinyurl.com/pk86w59.

People going through their daily lives have a more specific complaint: Some say Abenomics is not helping them. "I am in Fukushima and I don't feel it," says Yamadera, the tech entrepreneur. "But maybe some people in big cities may be getting an advantage."

Takeuchi at Fasotec shares the belief that Abenomics and the soaring stock market help only rich urbanites. "Statistics say that the lower-income citizens have yet to gain benefit from the economic policy. It has dramatically vitalized the economy and changed the nation's mood into a cheerful one. Our nation needs to make wide investments on equipment and increase salary to have a well-balanced and stable economic growth so people of lower income also gain benefits from Abenomics."

The prime minister raised the consumption tax rate from 5 percent to 8 percent in 2014. The economy retracted, and opponents pounced. "It's quite striking that despite the massive scale of monetary loosening, that even just a fairly small tax increase is enough to plunge the economy into recession," said Jonathan Buss, an economist at Oxford Economics, a British firm that provides economic forecasts.[52]

At the same time, other financial experts said taxes had to be raised and will need to be raised again to reduce the national debt. "The consumption tax hike certainly weakened the economy, but it was also an unavoidable step for Japan. It was just a question of when to hike taxes," said Bill Adams, senior international economist at PNC Financial Services Group.[53]

Abe's popularity has fallen somewhat since he won a snap reelection in December 2014 with a mandate to continue his economic program: His approval rating was 41 percent in June, down 2.5 points from the previous month, but he still has a strong parliamentary advantage.[54] Abe's party re-elected him as its leader in September.[55]

Ishikura, a frequent speaker at international business management conferences, remains a believer in Abe's reforms. "Abenomics has done good things," she says. "His fiscal and monetary policy has worked to some extent, and companies are showing good earnings, but structural reform is slower and will take time. Much remains to be seen."

Since it became clear in October 2012 that Abe was a lock to win that year's election, the Nikkei stock index has doubled; however, real wages have been flat for more than two years.[56]

Goto of the Wilson Center also remains bullish about Abenomics. "You can talk about the stock market, which has boomed. People are encouraged to invest in stocks again, which has pushed up the GDP," she says. "Abe has also brought back political stability by coming up with a strategic plan. For a while we had a revolving door of prime ministers, and it was kind of a joke."

BACKGROUND

Shoguns and Samurai

Kenichi Komatsu, a journalist at Mainichi Shimbun, one of Japan's major newspapers, says, "There is a long tradition in Japan, which we call, 'import and modify.'" Japan imported a written language from China, then changed it. Its imperial army was modeled on Prussia's. The Big Three U.S. automakers all had factories in Japan until they were forced out before World War II and Japan began making its own cars. It's not unusual to see Christmas trees in Japan, even though the nation is overwhelmingly Shinto and Buddhist. The Japanese way of doing business is often portrayed as stubborn acceptance followed by total assimilation.

During the Kamakura period, which lasted from around 1185 to 1333, the military moved into the seats of power, which would influence Japanese politics, business and society for centuries to come. Minamoto no Yoritomo became Japan's first shogun, marking the establishment of the samurai system.[57] Shoguns, which means "military leaders," were regional warlords sanctioned by the emperor; they employed private armies of samurai—armor clad, sword-bearing warriors.

Under the shoguns, Japan remained an isolated and closed society until Commodore Perry arrived in Tokyo Bay in 1853. With this voyage, Perry literally defined the term "gunboat diplomacy," as his mission included forcing the Japanese to engage in trade. The United States wanted an agreement with Japan to safeguard shipwrecked sailors, and to open a port in Japan for taking on supplies and refueling. Perry's letter of introduction addressed to the emperor of Japan displayed the West's ignorance about Japan, as the real power resided with the shoguns.[58]

After Perry's visit, Japan began a modernization drive that would become known as the "Meiji Restoration." The process started with a reshuffling of the shoguns that eventually restored power to the emperor, who ruled under the name Meiji. Meiji's official rule began in 1868.

Under Meiji, a modern army was created through a national draft as feudal domains were abolished. He established an education system and a land tax. A constitution was created in 1889. The days of samurai and shoguns were over, as Japan moved quickly into its own version of modern imperialism.[59]

World Wars

Borrowing Perry's tactics, Japan forced Korea, which was rich in coal and iron, to open its ports for trade. Japan also wanted Korea to declare itself independent from China.[60]

China and Japan had been meddling in Korean affairs for years, and the two sides fought a war in 1894–95 over who would control Korea. Although experts predicted a quick victory for China, Meiji's military modernization gave Japan a decisive victory. The peace treaty recognized Korea's independence and granted Japan trading privileges in China. The treaty also handed over Taiwan, the Pescadores Islands and the Liaodong Peninsula in Manchuria to Japan, along with a cash settlement.[61]

However, just after the treaty was signed, the Russians enlisted support from Germany and France to take over the Liaodong Peninsula, an arrangement that would become known as the "Triple Intervention."[62]

Years of disputes between Russia and Japan over control of the area led to a 1904 Japanese attack on the Russian fleet at Port Arthur, a warm-water port at the peninsula's tip. Japan declared war on Russia, and the fighting proved costly for both sides. U.S. President Theodore Roosevelt in 1905 brokered a treaty that gave Japan control of Korea, much of southern Manchuria and half of Sakhalin Island. The Russians weren't interested in Korea and focused their energy on maintaining a presence on Sakhalin and on avoiding paying the Japanese any kind of indemnity. Roosevelt helped foster an arrangement where no money changed hands and the Russians kept the northern half of Sakhalin. He won the Nobel Peace Prize for his efforts, and Japan was now a major power in the Pacific.[63]

"The war with Russia marked the first time an Asian country had defeated a country from the West," says Goto of the Wilson Center. In 1910 Japan annexed Korea. Although legal questions swirled, the arrangement remained in place until after World War II.[64]

Imperial Japan was not driven by ideology or religion as much as it was by economics. Japan is not rich in natural resources. The war with Russia was all about access to ports, while the first conflict with China centered on control of Korea's coal and iron.[65]

When World War I started in 1914, Britain called on the Japanese to honor the 1902 Anglo-Japan Alliance. Japan complied by declaring war on Germany. Although not a major player in the fighting, Japan took advantage of being on the winning side of World War I to issue 21 demands that gave it even greater control over China and mineral-rich Manchuria.[66]

The buildup to World War II saw Japan invade Manchuria in 1931 after the "Mukden Incident," which raised suspicions that Japan blew up a railroad bridge as a pretext to send in its army.[67] In 1937, Japan went after China again in an attempt to overthrow the Nationalist government of Chiang Kai-shek.[68] In 1940 Japan attacked French Indochina to cut off China's supply route; on Dec. 7, 1941, it bombed the U.S. Pacific fleet at Pearl Harbor, drawing the United States into World War II. The war in Asia ended with Japan surrendering after the United States dropped nuclear bombs on Hiroshima and Nagasaki in August 1945.

Rise to Economic Power

U.S. General Douglas MacArthur was put in charge of the punishment and eventual rebuilding of Japan after the war. The occupation produced a democratic constitution that moved political power from the emperor to a new parliament called the Diet. By 1947, concerns about Japanese militarism had been replaced with fears of a Chinese communist-controlled Asia.[69]

During the seven-year occupation, MacArthur attempted to break up the zaibatsu, or "financial clique," system of interlocking businesses that dated back to the 1500s. The original 10 cliques or groups included Mitsubishi, still a major player in the auto industry. The groups were usually formed between a merchant needing capital to expand his business and a shogun or government leader who could benefit from an alliance with the merchant. If the group prospered it would add other businesses to strengthen the organization.[70]

Lessons from the Road

Rise of Japan's Auto Industry Traces to 1930s

The emergence of Japan's auto industry was a long time coming. The seeds of its dominance were planted in the aftermath of World War II as it overcame not only damage from the fighting but also the earlier supremacy of American manufacturers. Its growth illustrates how Japan became a manufacturing power.

U.S. automakers once dominated Japan: Before World War II, Ford sold 75 percent of the cars on Japanese roads.[71] But that's ancient history. For decades, the Japanese auto industry has been a global titan, perhaps the business that best illustrates how an economic power arose from the rubble of the war. From humble beginnings, Japanese automakers established a foothold in the United States, the world's largest car market, and never stopped moving forward.

In the buildup to World War II, as Japan became more hostile to foreign influence, its 1936 Automobile Manufacturing Industry law required companies to have an official license from the government to build cars there. Only two licenses were initially granted, one for Toyota and one for Nissan.[72] By 1939, the Japanese had kicked out Ford and General Motors and closed their plants.[73]

During the war, the Japanese car builders and other large manufacturing firms produced only war material. Mitsubishi, which started in 1870 as a steamship carrier, built nearly 4,000 Zeros, the planes used to bomb Pearl Harbor in 1941. Nakajima Aircraft produced more than 6,000 Zeros, but after the war, it morphed into Fuji Heavy Industries, which now makes Subarus.[74]

During the Allied occupation, Japanese manufacturers switched to producing cars and trucks for consumers. The occupying forces required them to submit applications outlining what they intended to build and also to agree to dissolve the business arrangements known as zaibatsu, imperial-era conglomerates that were the predecessors to the modern networks of interlocking business relationships called keiretsu.

The occupying forces were suspicious of the zaibatsu and attempted to dismantle them.[75] Toyota was targeted; the company complied by splitting itself and shedding some plants.[76] Japan's major automakers would eventually all become charter members of the same keiretsu.[77]

The Japanese companies specialized in producing small, inexpensive cars. These became more popular globally, including in the United States, when the oil embargos of the 1970s sent gasoline prices soaring. In 1982, Honda moved beyond exporting cars to the United States, building an automotive plant in Marysville, Ohio, to crank out the Accord, its popular sedan, a move that put the factory closer to the sales market.[78]

Honda broke a lot of industry practices by moving auto painting, welding and assembly under one roof and bypassing the powerful United Autoworkers Union to hire locals with no experience in building cars, a move skeptics questioned.[79]

More skepticism arose when the Japanese pioneered the use of robots in auto plants. But this gamble also paid off: Figures from the past few years indicate that Japan is the second-largest market for robot sales and has the highest number of industrial robots in operation, more than 300,000.[80] Other car manufacturers followed Japan's lead, automating their assembly lines. In 2012, auto industry sources estimated that 78,000 robot units were sold to car builders, worth an estimated $15 billion, with an estimated 60 percent of those coming from Japanese firms, including Fanuc, Yaskawa Electric and Nachi-Fujikoshi.[81]

Innovations in car manufacturing eventually led to new forms of car propulsion. Toyota helped pave the way for a mass-produced electric hybrid vehicle with the Prius, unveiled in 1997 and selling worldwide in 2000. As of September 2014, cumulative sales exceeded 7 million units.[82] (The brightest days of the world's

(Continued)

(Continued)

best-selling hybrid may be coming to an end, as recent figures indicate Prius sales fell by 11.5 percent in 2014.)[83]

The Japanese have also pioneered all-electric vehicles, the Nissan Leaf and Mitsubishi i-MiEV.

And Toyota has taken a step toward bringing the first hydrogen fuel cell car to market, the Mirai. "Automaking has been the backbone of the Japanese economy for the last 30 years," says Masato Otaka, spokesman for the Embassy of Japan in Washington. "But the car factories are actually moving out of the country, and two-thirds of the cars sold by Japan are now made in the U.S. because it's closer to the market. We are making less and less cars in Japan, which is why we have to diversify."

—*Scott Sowers*

As the occupation ended in 1952, Japanese business interests teamed up with the government and concentrated on building an economy based on steel production, electronics, shipbuilding and eventually cars.

Financing and enlarging the newly repurposed firms fell back to the zaibatsu, except the structure and makeup of the groups had changed slightly and they were now known as keiretsu, which means "business association." The keiretsu system gained strength and legitimacy in 1953 after the Diet changed the anti-monopoly laws put in place by the United States during the occupation.[84]

During World War II, 11 automakers produced trucks for Japan's war effort. Ten of those companies survived the war, including Toyota, Nissan and Isuzu. Along with a new company called Honda, they turned to making consumer goods.[85]

The new arrangements of the old zaibatsu alliances began to reorganize themselves horizontally, which brought companies from different industries together, and vertically, which linked different companies in the same business. The new groups formed around key banks as opposed to the government. The original six horizontal keiretsus included Mitsui, Mitsubishi, Sumitomo, Fuyo, Sanwa and the DKB group. The vertical group of electronics firms included Hitachi, Toshiba, Sanyo, Matsushita (Panasonic) and Sony. The vertical automotive group included Toyota, Nissan, Honda, Isuzu and Daihatsu.[86]

Holding companies shielded owners and reduced risk; insurance firms and other related industries joined the mix, with stock ownership shared by all the players. Critics of the system say it encouraged monopolies, discouraged competitive pricing, limited innovation and overprotected domestic markets from imported products.

Proponents say it reduced risk, improved stability and allowed firms in different industries to share R&D efforts. "It still exists in Japan, and many Asian countries have the same kind of system," Goto says. "Some say it stifles creativity, but . . . when one company is not doing so well, another one can prop it up. If an employee is struggling at one company, they may move him to a different position within a different company in the organization."

The oil crises in the 1970s boosted Japan's economy because the nation's automotive industry began specializing in affordable, fuel-efficient vehicles that sold widely in the United States and elsewhere. Japan became an economic powerhouse, and its symbolic dominance peaked in 1989, when Mitsubishi bought a 51 percent interest in Rockefeller Center in New York City for $846 million in cash.[87] The same year, Sony purchased Columbia Pictures for $3.4 billion. Japanese automakers added car factories in the United States staffed by younger and nonunion employees. Lower labor costs meant these factories could produce cars more cheaply than unionized ones—one estimate put it at $500 to $800 less per car.[88]

In the late 1980s, money and credit were cheap in Japan, which boosted overseas investment but also prompted a lot of bad loans and poor business decisions. Soon, it all started crashing down.

The "Lost Decade"

At the end of 1990, the Japanese stock market nosedived as businesses went bankrupt, banks closed and capital losses reached $2 trillion. Taxpayers bailed out the banks, corporations were restructured and trade with longtime nemesis China increased. All of this eventually edged the country out of crisis but fell far short of a full recovery.[89]

The actual parameters of what became known as the Lost Decade are imprecise. Some experts reference two Lost Decades, when economic growth stagnated and financial markets teetered. The Nikkei 225 stock market index peaked in December 1989 at 38,916, and bottomed out in March 2003 at less than 8,000. By June 2007, the index was back up to 17,000 but then took another hit in February 2009 when it fell to 7,568. It started a steady ascent late in 2012, heading over 20,000 in summer 2015. As of early October 2015, the index is over 18,000.[90]

Another financial blow landed in 1997. Thailand's central bank floated the value of the baht, its national currency, against the U.S. dollar in an attempt to spur its economy, beginning what has become known as the Asian banking crisis. Unpegged from a stabilized exchange rate, the baht immediately lost as much as 20 percent of its value. Thailand then brought lending rates up 2 percentage points to 12.5 percent.[91]

As the value of its currency continued to fall, Thailand asked the International Monetary Fund (IMF) for an emergency loan to stabilize the economy. Countries with investments in Thailand, including Japan, were hurt by the falling value of assets as loans were compromised. Two months later, the U.S. Dow Jones industrial average dropped 554 points, and two of Japan's largest financial institutions collapsed, with losses exceeding $3 billion. Problems spread globally, including to South Korea, Russia and Indonesia. In June 1998, Japan announced it was in a recession for the first time in 23 years.[92] GDP increased slowly over the next 10 years, but the growth rate trailed many other advanced countries, including the United States and Germany.[93]

Abe's first term as prime minister began in September 2006 and lasted a year and a day. He had served in the Diet, the Japanese parliament, since 1993 and came from a politically active family. Scandals rocked his administration; four of his Cabinet members resigned and another committed suicide. Abe resigned in 2007.[94] The economy seemed to be on the road to recovery from the tumult of the 1990s, but then fell back into recession along with much of the world in 2008–2009.[95]

In 2009, Japan's flirtation with immigration come to an ugly end. When the economy was still booming in 1990, Japan issued work visas to the South American descendants of Japanese who had emigrated in the early 1900s to work on coffee plantations.[96] By 2009, more than 300,000 Brazilians and Peruvians lived in Japan. With the economy mired in recession, Japan asked the foreign workers to leave, offering them cash settlements to fly to South America and promise not to return.[97] More than 20,000 South American workers took the offer.[98]

The deadly March 2011 earthquake and tsunami, which killed nearly 16,000 people and left a quarter-million homeless, also dealt Japan another economic blow.[99] In 2012, Abe was again elected as prime minister after promising to turn the country's economic fortunes around—a tall order. Japan was still carrying the highest debt-to-GDP ratio in the world, at 240 percent. For comparison, Greece's ratio currently hovers around 175 percent.[100] Experts continue to debate the seriousness of the problem, how the ratio is calculated and what anybody could or should be doing about it.[101]

CURRENT SITUATION

Free Trade and the TPP

Assessing Japan's business environment begins with a status check of the various negotiations swirling around the Trans-Pacific Partnership. Although recent events have moved the TPP to the front of geopolitical and commercial discourse, the roots of the agreement stretch back to a free trade agreement signed by New Zealand, Chile, Singapore and Brunei in 2005. The United States entered the negotiations in 2008 due to an interest in expanding financial services and investment opportunities.[102]

Japanese Vehicle Production Rose in 2014

Number of motor vehicles produced in Japan, in millions, by type, 2005–14

Automakers manufactured nearly 9.8 million cars, trucks and buses in Japan in 2014, an increase in all three categories from 2013. Motor vehicle production in Japan climbed from 2005 to 2008 before falling by nearly one-third in 2009 during the recession. Production fell again to 8.4 million vehicles in 2011, but rose in 2012 and has since fluctuated between 9.6 million and 9.9 million vehicles.

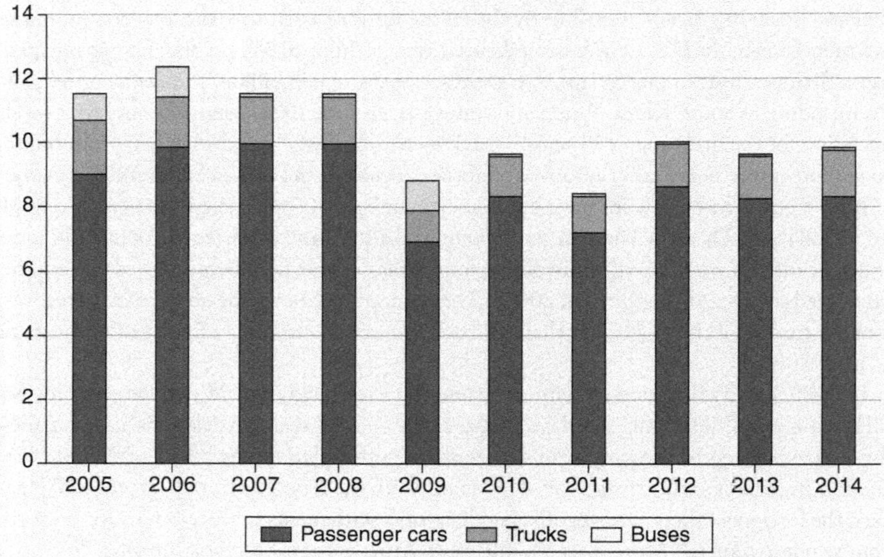

Source: "The Motor Industry of Japan 2015," Japanese Automobile Manufacturers Association, May 2015, p. 5, http://tinyurl.com/qyyr3lq; data downloaded from http://tinyurl.com/p27y4on.

In July 2013, Japan became the 12th and final member to join talks.[103] Abe is especially interested in implementing the TPP because it represents a chance to expand automobile exports and restructure Japan's agriculture industry. "Japan must remain at the center of the Asian-Pacific century," he said in 2013. "If Japan alone continues to look inward, we will have no hope for growth. This is our last chance. If we don't seize it, Japan will be left out."[104]

On Oct. 5, 2015, the 12 TPP members reached final agreement on the trade accord, and experts say Japan will be a big winner if member legislatures approve the accord. Exports of Japanese cars, textiles and chemicals are expected to go way up.[105]

"The TPP could be a huge boost for our economy because we have never had a free trade agreement with the United States," says Masato Otaka, spokesman for the Japanese Embassy

Japanese Imports Overtake Exports

Imports and exports as percentage of GDP

Japan's economy has long been export-oriented. Exports as a percentage of gross domestic product fell sharply in 2009 amid a worldwide recession. Since 2011, after the catastrophic earthquake and tsunami that caused the Fukushima nuclear disaster, imports have outstripped exports to create a growing trade deficit.

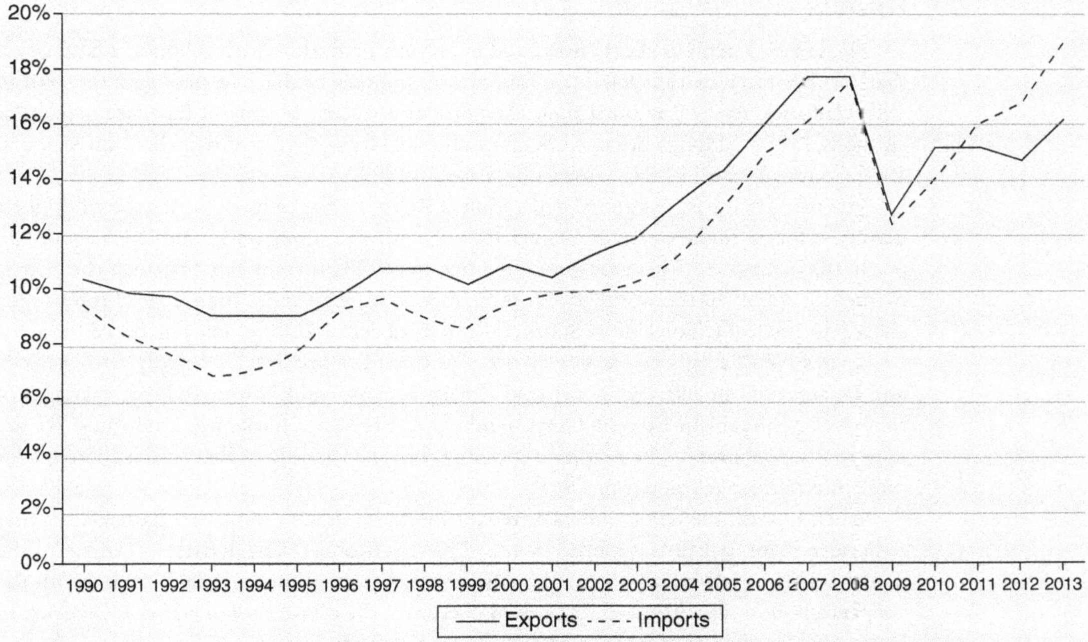

Notes: Fiscal year ends March 31. The reporting period for national accounts data is the current year. Imports and exports of goods and services represent the value of all goods and other market services received by or provided to the rest of the world. They include the value of merchandise, freight, insurance, transport, travel, royalties, license fees and other services, such as communication, construction, financial, information, business, personal and government services. They exclude compensation of employees and investment income (formerly called factor services) and transfer payments.

Source: "World DataBank: Japan," World Bank, http://data.worldbank.org/country/japan.

in Washington, D.C. "A tariff reduction would override all other trade agreements and make it all about the competition."

The trade pact is "definitely on our radar," said Geoffrey Pazzanese of Federated Investors, a financial services company in Pittsburgh that has more than $350 billion in assets under management. "To me the biggest winner, country-wise, will be Japan."[106]

The U.S. food and agriculture community and other businesses interested in exporting products to Japan wanted provisions that would gradually remove all tariffs on trade between member states. According to Bernard K. Gordon, a professor emeritus of political science at the University of New Hampshire who has written about trade and the TPP, opening up free trade with Japan would add $60 billion to the U.S. export market.[107]

From 1980 to 2010, Japan recorded a trade surplus every year. That changed when Fukushima melted down and the country shuttered its nuclear power plants. Imports of oil and natural gas shot up, resulting in trade deficits, the worst in 2014. Japan still had trade surpluses with the United States, Hong Kong, South Korea, Taiwan and Singapore but ran deficits with Australia, Russia, the United Arab Emirates, Malaysia, China and Saudi Arabia.[108] Japan's exports rose steadily from the 1960s until the 2008–2009 recession, when they fell precipitously. They have still not returned to their pre-recession peak.[109]

Robotics

The Japanese remain keenly interested in everything dealing with robotics, a fascination that can be traced to the "karakuri," automated puppets of the Edo period of the 17th to 19th centuries. Astro Boy burst onto the pop culture scene by way of Japanese manga, or cartoons, in 1952. Honda began work on a humanoid robot that eventually became Asimo in 1986; Sony unleashed its mechanical dog, Aibo, in 1999.

According to the International Federation of Robotics, the country has the second-highest density of robots in the world, at 323 per 10,000 workers, trailing only South Korea with 437 per 10,000 workers.[110] The same group said that in 2013 China unseated Japan as the biggest market for robots in the world. Japan came in second, with more than 25,000 robots purchased domestically. The United States came in third with 23,700 robots purchased.[111]

Japan's No. 2 status has some worried. "Automation in China is rapidly taking place, and Japan could be left out in the cold if it is careless," said Norio Kodaira, manager of robotics in Mitsubishi Electric Corp.'s Industrial Products Marketing Division. "We are now at a critical point. The market is growing, but the flip side of that is that there is a lot more international competition."[112]

When Fukushima failed, robots were sent inside the reactor to inspect damage; the first responders were PackBots, supplied by the U.S. firm iRobot. "The disaster . . . triggered the need to create a system to utilize robots in emergency situations," Kodaira said. "With the cooperation of universities and robot manufacturers, the disaster robot center is expected to have a pool of robots ready whenever they may be necessary."[113]

Abe is keen to expand the country's research in robotics, which is leading Japan down some unusual roads in the form of "muscle suits," mechanically assisted exoskeletons being developed at the National Institute of Technology and Evaluation (NITE) by educators and scientists such as Hiroshi Kobayashi, whose intention is to "release man from hard labor."

An engineer by training, Kobayashi began his research in an attempt to help people with gait disorders learn to walk again. "We wanted to make people's lives more comfortable and raise the quality of life," he says. As the research moved forward, the suits were imagined for use on farms, manufacturing plants and eventually in health care where caretakers are frequently tasked with lifting the elderly into beds and bathtubs.

"In the past when workers lifted people, they had to really exert themselves, which also had the effect of causing anxiety among the elderly people they were caring for," Kobayashi said. "The muscle suit makes lifting so much easier, and the people being cared for don't have to worry about being dropped."[114]

Japanese technology firm Cyberdyne, which shares a name with the fictional maker of Hollywood's evil Terminator robot—according to a company spokesman, this was purely unintentional—is melding human and machine with the introduction of several products designed to assist the elderly and disabled. Those include its HAL system, which stands for "hybrid assistive limb."[115] (Incidentally, the computer-gone-amok in "2001: A Space Odyssey" is named HAL.) According to a study by the Yano Research Institute, the robotics care industry will be worth $300 million by the end of the decade.[116]

Robots also are moving into the travel and tourism industry, as seen at the Huis Ten Bosch theme park in Nagasaki, where 10 robots will serve as staff members at the Henn-na Hotel. Huis Ten Bosch Co. President Hideo Sawada told a news conference, "In the future, we'd like to have more than 90 percent of hotel services operated by robots."[117]

Tourism and the Olympics

Japan's tourism industry has been improving, mostly due to a weaker yen, which is making the country more affordable to international visitors. Japan is a long plane ride from the United States and Europe; it also remains relatively expensive and language can be a barrier even in large cities.[118] Most of the 13 million visitors who came in 2014 were from South Korea, Taiwan and other neighboring countries, especially China. The Japanese government's goal is for tourism to grow to 20 million visitors by 2020—the year that the Olympics return to Japan.[119]

Japan is scurrying to be ready for the Summer Games, with major construction projects including a national stadium, gymnasium, swimming pools, tennis courts and a baseball field. Transportation systems are being upgraded, and roads, apartments and hotels are being built. The numbers associated with the upgrades are staggering: The government is pouring $22 billion into infrastructure improvements, creating 200,000 jobs.[120]

Loosening immigration to fill all those jobs and bolster Japan's falling population remains a touchy issue. "Many think accepting more immigrants would be a quick fix, but when it was tried before with the Latin Americans it didn't go so well," Goto says.

"They can talk about immigration all they want, but real economic growth is not going to happen unless we get more productivity out of our service industries and our white-collar sectors," Ishikura of Hitotsubashi University says.

"We don't really have the infrastructure to accept a lot of immigrants," embassy spokesman Otaka says. "We're not used to it, but I do think we will be seeing more in terms of nursing and care workers. It will be looked at industry by industry."

LOOKING AHEAD

Women-omics

From Abe on down, everybody seems to agree that the savior of the Japanese business world will probably be female. "With our shrinking workforce we need to make the best of the resources we have," Ishikura of Hitotsubashi University says. "Our women are very well educated, and if we had the same ratio of women in the workplace as other developed countries, our GDP will go up."

He adds, "The Abe administration has empowered women by declaring it as a pillar of the third arrow. The city of Yokohama has been doing things like getting private companies to help pay for day care so that women can stay in the workforce."

Traditionally, Japanese women are seldom promoted from low-level jobs, and they drop out of the workforce when they marry and have children. Abe's proposed goals include filling 30 percent of Japanese leadership posts with women by 2020.[121]

In the United States, women hold 14 percent of the executive jobs; in Japan they hold 1.1 percent. In January, 20,000 Japanese children were on waiting lists for nursery school, and Abe's administration was weighing tax incentives that would encourage more women to work full time and allow more foreign laborers into the country to work as housekeepers.[122]

Although questions remain about whether men will accept more women in the workplace and whether women will want to stay on the job, lower wages and higher expenses render the question moot for many families. "It's already happening out of economic necessity," says Goto of the Wilson Center. "Many people have no choice and have had to become a two-income family."

Ishikura looks forward to seeing Japanese business initiate changes that might help draw more women into the workplace and keep them there. "I'm hoping the time of long workdays and evaluation based on tenure and seniority are disappearing," she says. The salary-man lifestyle of long days and drinking with the boss doesn't hold the same appeal for many women.

Says Ikuko Shirota, a finance ministry official, "Being a mother and family obligations prevent us from experiencing essential posts for career advancement; we must work dramatically less. The essential point of [the government's] . . . proposal is to change all of 'kasumigaseki' [Japanese bureaucracy] to streamline work and lessen overtime hours."[123]

Because of the shrinking population, technology entrepreneur Yamadera says, Japanese business needs to change its focus, despite Japan's reputation as a gifted exporter. "Most of Japanese business focus on the domestic market, like Germany does," he says. "But we are a shrinking economy. How are we going to survive like that? The domestic markets in places like Korea and most of Nordic countries are so small, that's why they design their products for global market first. I think the biggest advantage in most of Japanese companies doing business in Japan is they can speak fluent Japanese. That's all. I don't think we have such high technical advantage anymore."

Fostering Entrepreneurs

As part of the government's drive to increase entrepreneurship, Yoshiaki Ishii, director of the New Business Policy Office in the Ministry of Economy, Trade and Industry (METI), is on the lookout for promising start-ups to support with government resources. He was instrumental in revising Japanese business regulations in 2006 to allow the formation of limited liability corporations and limited liability partnerships. Changes to the law simplified regulations and reduced start-up registration costs from $30,000 to pennies. The even-higher cost of incorporating was cut from about $100,000 to practically nothing. Business registrations the following year increased from 80,000 to 101,000.[124]

Taking a Bow: Etiquette in Japan

For Westerners, Acting Politely Can Be Challenging

Visiting business executives, beware: Being polite in Japanese society presents a number of etiquette traps for the Westerner. Even the bow is no simple thing.

Westerners visiting Japan can spend a lot of time worrying about the Japanese equivalent of the handshake, which is the bow. When to bow? How low, how long, how many times?

And things can get even more complicated than that—mastering the nuances of Japanese society is actually not realistic for most visitors. "The biggest etiquette mistake Westerners make when they come to Japan is thinking they're going to get it right," says Shihoko Goto, an associate with the Wilson Center, a foreign policy think tank in Washington. "You should be prepared to be humbled."

First things first, though. If you're going inside a home, school, country inn or certain restaurants, you should take your shoes off. Put them on the rack facing the same direction as everybody else's. If slippers are provided, use them. When you leave, use the shoehorn to put footwear back on. Loafers tend to simplify things—just like at the airport.

Then comes the bow. While some Japanese say the importance of the bow is diminishing, a first meeting with Japanese adults in their home country will usually begin with a bow as opposed to a handshake. The correct posture is hands at your sides, take the bow and straighten back up. Don't go too low or stay down too long and don't repeat; just move on to the next ritual, which in a business setting is the exchange of cards.

In Japan, business cards are offered after the bow and presented with both hands, as if you are handing over an important letter. Say your name as you hand over your card and look the receiver in the eye. When your counterpart presents his or her card, use both hands to take the card, read it, even if it's in Japanese; maybe make another shallow head bow and make it look like you are receiving very important information—which you are.

"Sometimes, visitors are not careful with how they treat the name card, which is very rude in a Japanese business meeting," says Jun Yamadera, CEO of Eyes, Japan, a technology company in Fukushima prefecture.

Speaking of eyes, watch your eye contact. Too much makes the Japanese uncomfortable. It's OK to look someone in the eye, but don't linger.

After the greeting and card exchange you may be asked to sit down for a PowerPoint presentation, which are popular in Japan, just as they are in the United States. Although all Japanese are required to take six years of English in school, many struggle with speaking or understanding the language because they don't get a lot of practice, so you may need to arrange translation. Hot green tea is often served as a liquid refreshment greeting for guests, usually minus any cream or sugar. Nobody will be insulted if you don't drink it.

If your business dealings include a meal, be advised that large restaurants and hotels that are accustomed to tourists will have signs and menus written in somewhat fractured English. The backup plan is pointing at pictures. If you are going to a smaller, local place, having somebody with you who speaks both languages is helpful.

Seafood is popular, even for breakfast, but sushi is considered a treat as opposed to a staple. "Most Japanese eat sushi only on special occasions," says Megumi Kikuchi, a coordinator for the Japan International Cooperation Center, a business outreach group based in Tokyo. "It's very expensive here and we can't afford to eat it all the time." Noodles in the form of ramen, soba or udon in hot broth are a staple and a favorite at a business lunch or any other kind of meal. Bringing the bowl to your lips and slurping loudly is encouraged.

Besides tea, beer is popular; sake is distilled in villages all over the country. Some brands of sake are expensive and smooth-tasting; others are less expensive and harsh.

(*Continued*)

(Continued)

"Lots of people like the smooth brands, which can be almost like drinking French cognac," Yamadera says. "But I like mine to have a bit of a bite in the taste."

In the United States, sake is often served in small clay vessels, either hot or cold, and then poured into small handle-less cups. In Japan, don't be surprised if your sake is pulled out of a cooler and arrives in a clear glass about the size of a juice glass. If you are a favored guest in an establishment, the glass will be filled to overflowing and will sit in a shallow dish that is also swimming in sake. "This is a sign of hospitality and welcome in Japan," explains Yamadera. It's perfectly acceptable to lower your lips to the glass, slurp some out, remove the glass, down the liquid in the bowl and then return to working on the glass.

Physical contact with Japanese people should be approached with caution. "The Japanese are much more used to Western ways than we used to be," says Masato Otaka, spokesman for the Embassy of Japan, who is stationed in Washington. "We are doing more handshaking, less bowing, but some people want to hug the second time you meet them"—a Western approach that makes many in Japan uncomfortable.

So avoid the hugs and don't be late—another big sign of rudeness. Otaka says, "Punctuality is very important in Japan."

—*Scott Sowers*

"Venture businesses innovate, and young companies create jobs," Ishii said. "Older, established companies hire a lot of people, but they're not making new jobs. We have to find a way to support" new ventures. The odds are formidable. In the United States and Britain, one out of 10 companies is a start-up. In Japan, it's one out of 20, a ratio that Abe wants to double.[125]

Ishii puts part of the blame on Japanese society's view of risk-taking, which is generally not favorable. "The fact is, even if a guy wants to start his own company, it's often their wife, their mother or their wife's mother who stops them," Ishii said. "They'll say it's too risky to quit their job. Somehow, we have to get them to think that not taking a risk is also a risk."

Despite forces resisting entrepreneurship, efforts continue at the incubators and within Japan's formal educational system. Waseda University, a highly ranked private school in Tokyo, began an Incubation Promotion Office in 2001. By 2014, the program had hatched 73 ventures, a relatively small number. Of the school's 50,000 undergraduate and graduate students, only 300 a year embark on the entrepreneurial track. The program is run by Tadashi Takiguchi, who has taken his students on field trips to Silicon Valley and Israel while remaining keenly aware that he's up against an entrenched culture.

Talking about the difference in the mindset of the Japanese business student as compared to their U.S. counterparts, he said, "At Stanford or Harvard, the No. 1 goal is becoming entrepreneurs." In Japan, "it's totally different."[126]

Chronology

1853–1946	**Japan enters an imperial period by going to war with China and Russia, siding with Britain in World War I and joining the Axis powers in World War II.**
1853	Commodore Matthew Perry arrives in Tokyo Bay with four armed ships and forces the shogun to begin trading with the United States.
1874	One of the original business conglomerates known as zaibatsu forms around government contacts and a shipping company called Mitsubishi; this company later makes automobiles.
1868	Emperor Meiji puts Japan on course for modernization by establishing the "Meiji Restoration," a time of economic revival as new international connections begin opening.
1910	Hitachi is founded by Namihei Odaira; the new company builds a 5-horsepower electric motor for Kuhara Mining, which had been Odaira's employer.
1922	Ford Motor Co. builds an assembly plant in Yokohama, Japan, to sell cars to the Asian automotive market.
1937	Toyota Motor is founded by Sakichi Toyoda, the inventor of a wooden hand loom.
1939	Toshiba is formed when two firms, Shibaura Engineering Works and Tokyo Electric Co., join forces; it grows into an electronics giant.
1941	Japan bombs Pearl Harbor. The United States enters World War II by declaring war on Japan.
1945	The United States drops nuclear bombs on Hiroshima and Nagasaki, killing more than 120,000 people and ending World War II. . . . The U.S. occupies Japan, as General Douglas MacArthur attempts to untangle the zaibatsu system from the Japanese business world.
1946	Sochiro Honda mounts a small engine on a bicycle and founds what would become the Honda Motor Co.
1947–Present	**Japan rebuilds its economy after World War II to become an economic powerhouse.**
1947	A new constitution gives every citizen the right to vote and establishes a parliamentary system.
1952	The U.S. occupation of Japan ends.
1955	Tokyo Telecommunications Engineering Corp. begins selling transistor radios in the United States under the brand name Sony.
1973	The OPEC oil embargo cuts Japan's energy supplies. The world's attention begins to turn to fuel-efficient cars.

(Continued)

(Continued)

1982	Honda opens its first auto factory in the United States in Marysville, Ohio.
1989	Sony takes over Columbia Pictures and enters the feature film industry.
1991	The "Lost Decade" begins when bad loans made to major corporations cripple the Japanese economy and the stock market crashes. Some experts say this bad economy actually lasted two decades.
1997	The Asian financial crisis starts in Thailand and harms the Japanese economy; it spreads in coming months to Russia and Brazil.
2000	Toyota Prius goes on sale worldwide as hybrid auto technology moves into the mainstream.
2007	Toyota surpasses General Motors in total sales to become the world's largest automaker.
2011	A severe earthquake rocks Japan and causes a tsunami. The nuclear reactor in Fukushima melts down and leaks radiation into the atmosphere and the sea. All the country's nuclear reactors are taken offline.
2012	Shinzo Abe makes an unlikely political comeback by winning the election for prime minister and launching "Abenomics," promising to reboot the country's economy.
2013	Toyota surpasses General Motors again as the world's largest automaker after GM retook the title in 2011. Japan announces its interest in entering the Trans-Pacific Partnership.
2015	Mitsubishi, Kawasaki, Hitachi and Toshiba move into arms sales as Abe lifts the ban on exporting military hardware. . . . Nikkei stock index reaches an 18-year high, but the value of the yen falls 50 percent against the U.S. dollar. . . . The first nuclear reactor returns to operation.

PERSPECTIVE

Pro/Con: Richard S. Grossman on Abenomics

YES WILL JAPAN'S ECONOMY REBOUND UNDER ABENOMICS AND RESUME ITS GROWTH?

Richard S. Grossman

Professor of economics at Wesleyan University and visiting scholar at Harvard University's Institute for Quantitative Social Science

Written for *SAGE Business Researcher*, October 2015

Japan's economy has performed abysmally during the past two decades. From world-beating average annual gross domestic product (GDP) growth rates during the quarter century following World War II to respectable—if not spectacular—growth after the oil shocks of the 1970s, the Japanese economy has slowed almost to a snail's pace since its economic implosion in the early 1990s. Can it recover its former glory?

Although it is unlikely that Japan—or any other industrialized economy—will ever duplicate its astonishing 1960s growth, there is good reason to believe that Japan will emerge from its funk and achieve growth rates similar to those of its counterparts in the developed world. The prospects for success will depend upon the effectiveness of the aggressive economic policies proposed—and partially implemented—by Prime Minister Shinzo Abe since his election at the end of 2012. Abe's policies consist of "three arrows": (1) expansionary monetary policy, (2) expansionary fiscal policy and (3) structural reforms.

An important drag on the Japanese economy for the past two decades has been unrelenting deflationary pressure. Deflation increases real interest rates and reduces the incentive for consumers to spend and for firms to invest in plant and equipment. After taking office in 2012, Abe nominated Haruhiko Kuroda as the new governor of the Bank of Japan. Kuroda doubled the bank's inflation target to 2 percent and strengthened Japan's quantitative easing program. An important byproduct of Kuroda's approach has been a substantial depreciation of the yen, which has boosted the crucial Japanese export sector.

The second arrow of Abe's policy is fiscal stimulus. His 2013 spending package, focusing on infrastructure, amounted to 10.3 trillion yen ($116 billion). It was followed by a 5.5 trillion yen ($54 billion) stimulus in April 2014, and a 3.5 trillion yen ($29.2 billion) package at the beginning of 2015, targeted at boosting small business. These stimuli were dampened somewhat by a hike in the sales tax; nonetheless, the government predicts that the stimulus will boost GDP by 0.7 percent in 2016.

Abe's third arrow is structural reform, which is clearly the most important of the three components for Japan's long-term prospects—and the one that will be the trickiest to enact. The structural reform package announced last year includes changes to Japan's corporate tax, agriculture and labor policies. The success of these policies—particularly those that enhance the participation of Japanese women in the labor force—holds the key to Japan's economic comeback.

PERSPECTIVE

Pro/Con: Derek M. Scissors on Abenomics

NO

WILL JAPAN'S ECONOMY REBOUND UNDER ABENOMICS AND RESUME ITS GROWTH?

Derek M. Scissors

Resident scholar at the American Enterprise Institute, focusing on Asian economies and U.S. economic relations with Asia; author of the China Global Investment Tracker; and adjunct professor at George Washington University, where he teaches about the Chinese economy.

Written for *SAGE Business Researcher*, October 2015

If Abenomics means the economic policies that have actually been adopted under Prime Minister Shinzo Abe, it will not be enough to revitalize Japan's economy. These policies are entirely inadequate to meet the severe challenges that Japan faces.

The best-known challenge is demographic. Japan has a shrinking and aging population, unprecedented in some ways. An obvious response is immigration, but there has never been political support for this. Creating a dynamic economy in the face of a labor force that is becoming less capable as a whole is very difficult in itself.

Unfortunately, there is another world-leading problem: debt. For those unsure if "quadrillion" is a proper numeric term, it is, as Japan's national government debt exceeds 1 quadrillion yen. Debt is related to and has similar economic effects as aging, encouraging stagnation or even contraction.

To add insult to injury, Japan lacks natural resources. So there is no shale boom, or anything similar, to come to the rescue.

The most courageous policies would be tested by such obstacles. And Abenomics sounds much more courageous than it is.

On government debt, the prime minister called in 2015 for a balanced budget. However, this only refers to what is termed the "primary" budget. While there has been reform, the bulk of Japanese national government spending remains outside the primary budget in "special" budget accounts. Primary budget balance translates to continued debt accumulation.

Taking immigration off the table leaves few meaningful options to offset a shrinking labor force. The government has offered only minor tweaks, such as the treatment of overtime, to the sharply divided system of lifetime employment supplemented by contract workers. Instead, firing must be made easier and pension plans should immediately be made fully portable, even though both of these would be initially disruptive.

Japan could use both land and labor more productively if it opened to agriculture imports by embracing a strong Trans-Pacific Partnership agreement. Instead, the prime minister has promised to protect sacred farm products, again foregoing the economic actions needed to achieve and sustain growth.

Stripped of its sound and lights, Abenomics effectively boils down to loose money and credit. Loose monetary policy has an impact on the domestic economy for about a year (the impact can be longer on trade depending on conditions in partner countries). The rest of what has been said and done in the name of Abenomics falls far short of what is necessary to move Japan forward again.

UPDATE IN 2020

Japanese citizens ushered out the 2010s with a unique occurrence: a new emperor.

On May 1, 2019, Emperor Naruhito succeeded his father, Akihito, who stepped aside after 30 years on the Chrysanthemum Throne. He became the first emperor to abdicate in more than two centuries.[127]

And in 2020, Japan also got a new prime minister, after the surprise resignation of Shinzo Abe, who cited poor health. He was the longest-serving prime minister in Japanese history, holding his position for eight years, after a one-year stint in 2007.[128]

The year 2020 was supposed to be a year of celebration for Japan. It was scheduled to host the Summer Olympic Games, which were expected to draw athletes and tourists from around the world, and by the start of the year, Japan had invested $12 billion to get ready. Abe had hoped the games would boost Japan's economy, and give the nation a boost in tourism and consumer spending. Japan had lined up $3 billion in domestic sponsors.

But by late March 2020, the pandemic forced Abe and International Olympic Committee President Thomas Bach to announce that the games were being postponed for a year—the first time an Olympics had been postponed for something other than war.

And if the games ultimately were not held, it was likely Japan would miss its turn at becoming an Olympic host.[129]

The COVID-19 pandemic interrupted several years of Abe's efforts to reduce Japan's debt-to-GDP ratio. In June 2019, it stood at 253 percent, the highest among the industrialized nations, a position it had held for years, according to the World Population Review. The next highest was that of Greece at 181.1 percent.[130]

Abe's departure prompted a review of whether his heralded economic plan, Abenomics, had actually worked. Reviews found that it had mixed success. On the plus side, Abenomics caused an employment boom, with 5.5 million jobs added from 2013 to 2019.

Japanese employment rose during the Abe years, in part because Japan became more welcoming to immigrants. The employment of Japanese women also rose, with 78.5 percent holding jobs in 2020 versus 74 percent of American women.[131] Yet Abe's goal of increasing the percentage of women in leadership positions to 30 percent by 2020 was deemed "impossible," and so the Japanese government is looking to push back the deadline by up to a decade.[132]

Companies were also criticized for hoarding too much cash during the Abe years, although that helped some withstand the impact of the coronavirus.

Internationally, Abe may be best remembered for his concerted efforts to cultivate a personal relationship with Donald Trump. By January 2020, the men had met 20 times, played five rounds of golf, and exchanged 32 phone calls, at times speaking twice a week.[133] In a newsletter published by the Center for Strategic & International Studies, analyst Ayumi Teraoka maintained that the personal relationship helped blunt Trump's rhetoric toward Japan, at a time when he was regularly critical of traditional American allies in Europe and North America.

In October 2019, the U.S. and Japan signed the U.S.-Japan Trade Agreement and the U.S.-Japan Digital Trade Agreement, both of which took effect in 2020. The U.S.-Japan Trade agreement eliminates or reduces tariffs on approximately $7.2 billion in U.S. agricultural exports.[134]

However, in January 2020, the U.S. extended tariffs on Japanese steel and aluminum imports, despite waivers given to a group of other countries, including Canada and Australia.[135] While the tariffs were relatively small, compared with those that Trump had imposed on goods from Japan, the action seemed to violate the same trade agreement the countries had signed just a few months earlier.

"While Trump's tariffs certainly seem against the spirit of the deal, Japanese Prime Minister Shinzo Abe apparently decided it was not worth throwing away the entire agreement for $61 million of Japanese exports subject to new tariffs," wrote Chad P. Brown at the Peterson Institute for International Economics, an economic and financial affairs think tank.[136]

There were fears, meanwhile, that tensions between Japan and China might be escalating in a dispute over waters near the Senkaku and Diaoyu Islands. Although not a violation of international law, the constant presence of Chinese ships was viewed as a deliberate irritant to Japan.[137]

—Micheline Maynard

7

EU AT THE CROSSROADS

Can European unity handle a populist challenge?

Charles Wallace

From *SAGE Business Researcher*, August 20, 2018

EXECUTIVE SUMMARY

Dan Kitwood/Getty Images

Demonstrators outside the Houses of Parliament in London call for a reconsideration of the United Kingdom's vote to leave the European Union.

The European Union (EU) is facing one of its gravest challenges since it was founded as a coal and steel community in 1951. Great Britain's decision to leave the EU in March 2019 is causing consternation as governments and businesses scramble to prepare for "Brexit," unsure of its terms or even whether a formal agreement will be reached beforehand by London and Brussels. The EU also is coping with a trade dispute with the United States growing out of President Trump's imposition of tariffs on imported steel and aluminum and his threat to add duties to European car imports. It is unclear whether a tentative truce worked out in July will hold. In addition, the EU is facing internal strains caused by nationalist and populist political parties pressing for greater limits on immigration, particularly for those seeking asylum. While European leaders reached a temporary accord on strengthening their external borders, they have yet to win agreement about where asylum centers will be established to screen migrants or how to stop refugees from taking to the seas to gain entry into the EU.

Key takeaways include:

- One-third of all financial institutions in the United Kingdom are planning or considering relocating some operations to other European cities because of Brexit
- The International Monetary Fund has cut its growth projections for the 19 countries that use the euro currency because of uncertainty over the EU's future.
- A political backlash against migrants has weakened the authority of German Chancellor Angela Merkel, a leading voice supporting the liberal international order.

OVERVIEW

Sanaz Zaimi is moving from London to Paris early next year. It's no ordinary transfer.

As head of global fixed income, currencies and commodities, Zaimi is one of Bank of America Merrill Lynch's most senior executives. She and two other executives are leaving London to ensure their firm can continue to operate next year in the European Union (EU) after "Brexit"—the United Kingdom's departure from the EU. Their departure is a sign of things to come.[1]

According to the business consulting firm EY, 75 of 222 financial institutions in the United Kingdom—34 percent—have confirmed they are relocating or considering relocating some operations to other cities in Europe, with Dublin and Frankfurt the leading destinations. EY said it expected 10,000 financial services employees to leave the United Kingdom before Brexit occurs.[2]

These departures are a clear setback for London, one of the world's most important financial centers. But it also shows the potential impact Brexit could have on the rest of Europe, which had come to rely on Great Britain as the continent's primary marketplace for banking, asset management and currency exchange. Economists say Brexit will hold back economic growth not only in the United Kingdom but in several other European nations that have strong trade links with Great Britain, even though some countries will gain from the relocations.

The British exit from the EU, scheduled to occur on March 29, 2019, is just one of the many economic difficulties now facing the European Union.

The EU and Great Britain still have not reached a final agreement on their impending divorce, which could lead to an abrupt Brexit without a formal deal. In addition, the rise of

Financial Firms Leaving Britain

Number of U.K.-based companies considering or planning moves

One-third of major financial services firms in the United Kingdom are considering or planning to move operations or staff elsewhere in Europe, a 2-percentage-point increase from March, according to the global professional services firm EY.

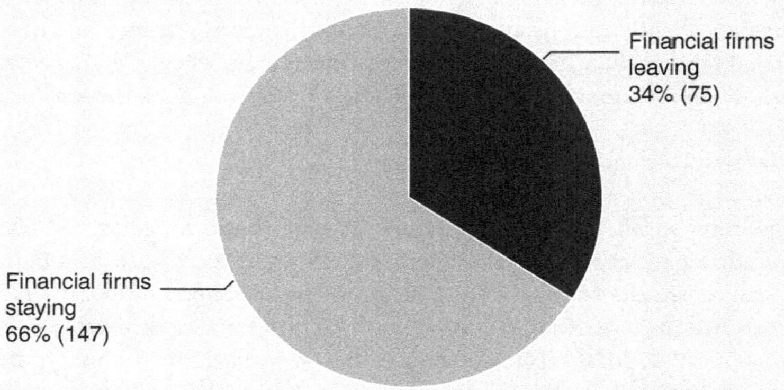

Source: Sarah Graham, "EY Financial Services Brexit Tracker: Firms Forge Ahead with Contingency Plans Despite Transition Agreement," Ernst & Young Global Limited, Jun. 25, 2018, https://tinyurl.com/yayogssw.

populist political parties in Europe has led to growing disputes within the EU over migration policy, which threatens to divide the organization and delay agreement on key economic reforms. At the same time, the prospect of a trade war with the United States, while temporarily on hold, has nonetheless begun to dampen the EU's economic outlook.

The confluence of these challenges, according to many experts and policymakers, has created one of the gravest crises the 28-member bloc has faced since it was founded as the European Coal and Steel Community in 1951.

Taking these diverse factors into account, the International Monetary Fund (IMF) said in its July World Economic Outlook that it expects growth in the 19 countries that use the euro currency to slow from 2.4 percent in 2017 to 2.2 percent this year and 1.9 percent in 2019.[3]

"Political uncertainty has risen in Europe, where the European Union faces fundamental political challenges regarding migration policy, fiscal governance, norms concerning the rule of law and the euro area institutional architecture," said Maurice Obstfeld, the IMF's chief economist.[4]

The IMF has concluded that the United Kingdom was already paying an economic price for its 2016 referendum vote to leave the EU, even before it has departed. "Despite a strong recovery in global growth and supportive macroeconomic policies, the impact of the decision to exit the European Union has weighed on private domestic demand," the fund said in a statement.[5]

Economic growth in Great Britain slowed to just 0.2 percent in the first quarter of 2018, down from 0.4 percent in the previous quarter. Business investment fell by 0.4 percent.[6]

One reason for the slowdown widely cited by purchasing managers in the service industry was uncertainty about the exact terms of the U.K. departure.[7] By July, the British government still had not reached agreement with the EU on a wide range of outstanding issues, such as how Brexit would affect the border between the Republic of Ireland and the British province of Northern Ireland and under what terms trade between the United Kingdom and the EU would be conducted.

EU and U.K. leaders hope to have a final deal in place in time for an EU summit meeting in October, to give both sides time to pass enacting legislation. They have already agreed to a transition period lasting until December 2020 to allow businesses to prepare for Brexit's final terms.[8] During the proposed transition, the United Kingdom would allow goods and EU citizens to move freely in and out of the country, but it would be free to reach separate trade agreements with other nations. As part of the deal, the United Kingdom has agreed to pay the EU $47 billion for outstanding expenses and prior financial commitments.[9]

Hoping to unite pro- and anti-Brexit politicians in her Cabinet, British Prime Minister Theresa May presented a compromise proposal in July that called for continuing to apply EU regulations for goods and agriculture after Brexit and keeping her country in an arrangement described as "a combined customs territory with the EU." Under the plan, Great Britain would collect tariffs on behalf of the European Union for any goods that arrive in the country destined for the EU, and the EU would do the same for Great Britain. But the services sector, which includes the country's important financial services, would have less access to EU nations than before Brexit.[10]

EU officials rejected May's proposal, saying her plan to have Britain collect customs duties for the EU was unacceptable.[11] Nonetheless, they called it a step in the right direction. "Relative to where the U.K. was before, the official position has softened significantly," says Holger Schmieding, chief economist for Berenberg Bank in London.

Auto Industry Would Suffer Most from Hard Brexit

Potential impact on U.K. exports to EU, by sector

A "hard Brexit," in which the United Kingdom would relinquish full access to the customs union with the European Union and the single market, could cost its largest export sectors almost 17 billion pounds (about $20 billion) annually in revenue. The automotive sector would be hit hardest, followed by consumer goods, according to a 2017 report by an international law firm.

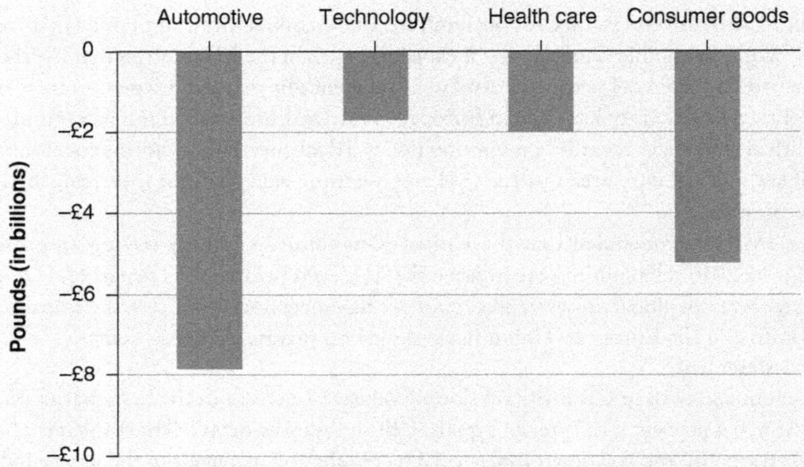

Source: Emily Franca and Elora Glucksman, "Hard Brexit to Create £17 Billion Fall in Annual EU Export Revenues Across UK's Key Manufacturing Sectors," Baker McKenzie, Oct. 2, 2017, https://tinyurl.com/yaz7z3or.

May's proposal attempted to finesse the biggest stumbling block to a deal—the issue of the border between Ireland, an EU member, and Northern Ireland—by eliminating the need for a border or customs checks between the two.[12] But proponents of a "hard Brexit," who argued that Great Britain would be better off severing most of its ties with the EU, said they were upset with May's compromise. Foreign Minister Boris Johnson and David Davis, the minister responsible for Brexit negotiations, resigned in protest. Johnson said May's proposals would leave Britain in a "miserable permanent limbo" and would create "a democratic disaster of ongoing harmonization with no way out and no say for the U.K."[13]

The lack of unity in May's government has raised concerns that Great Britain may not be able to reach a final agreement with the EU and might simply fall out of the European Union next March without any arrangements in place.[14]

That possibility has caused alarm among major businesses with a presence in Great Britain, with automakers BMW and Jaguar Land Rover and aircraft maker Airbus warning that they may have to rethink their investment plans.[15] Airbus, which employs 14,000 people at 25 U.K. factories and supports another 100,000 workers at British suppliers, said a departure from the EU's customs union—where goods pass freely from country to country without border checks or import duties—without a transition agreement would cause "severe disruption and interruption of U.K. production."[16]

The mounting concerns about possible Brexit chaos led a number of British politicians, including former Prime Minister Tony Blair, to call for a second referendum on withdrawal.[17] Financier George Soros said he is helping finance the campaign for a new vote. "The EU is in an existential crisis," Soros said. "Everything that could go wrong has gone wrong."[18]

While it is difficult to gauge the economic fallout of Brexit in the absence of a finished deal, the impact will likely be felt not only in the United Kingdom but in surrounding countries.

A study of regional trade linkages by researchers at Erasmus University in Rotterdam, Holland, estimated that Brexit's impact on trade could cost the United Kingdom 10 percent to 17 percent of economic growth depending on the affected region; parts of neighboring Ireland had a risk exposure of 10 percent of GDP. But the study also found significant economic effects in regions of Germany, the Netherlands, Belgium and France.[19]

"Everything that could go wrong has gone wrong."

Elwin de Groot, chief macroeconomist at Holland's Rabobank, says his models also showed that the effects could reach far beyond Great Britain. "In addition to the effect on British growth, Brexit—especially a hard Brexit—will have quite a significant impact on European growth, especially for those countries that have strong links with the U.K., such as the Netherland and Germany," de Groot says.

"Hard Brexit" Carries Costs

If a hard Brexit does take place, the costs for the 27 remaining EU members could reach $40 billion in annual bureaucratic expenses for tariffs and non-tariff expenses and hit British exporters with $35 billion in additional costs, according to Oliver Wyman, a New York-based business consulting firm.[20]

For example, the French port of Calais, which is linked by ferry and the Eurotunnel with Great Britain, has purchased 42 acres for use as a customs facility if one is required after Brexit. French officials estimate that a customs delay of just two minutes could cause the line of trucks waiting to enter the Eurotunnel to stretch 34 miles on both sides. "The way things are going, we are going to be left standing staring at each other like strangers. It's madness, pure utter madness," said Xavier Bertrand, president of Hauts-de-France, the region around Calais.[21]

Adding to concern about possible economic harm from Brexit were trade tensions between the United States and Europe. While the two sides agreed in late July to negotiate a solution to end all tariffs and non-tariff barriers on industrial goods, economists warned the talks could fail, as they had previously when the administration of President Barack Obama attempted to negotiate a sweeping free-trade deal with the EU called the Transatlantic Trade and Investment Partnership.[22]

"The lack of specifics in today's U.S.-EU announcement raises the possibility that the negotiations could falter at a later stage, as U.S.-China negotiations did earlier this year," investment bank Goldman Sachs said in a note to clients.[23]

The trade tensions came to a head when President Trump, invoking national security concerns, on June 1 imposed tariffs of 25 percent on imported steel and 10 percent on imported aluminum from the EU, Canada and Mexico.[24] U.S. steel and aluminum imports from the EU totaled around $7.5 billion in 2017.[25]

Trump lashed out at Europe for its large trade surplus with the United States, which reached $151.3 billion in 2017, according to the U.S. Census Bureau.[26] "I think the European

Many Europeans Call Refugees a Burden

Percentage who say migrants help or hurt economy

Many Europeans believe that refugees are a burden on their country, taking jobs and social benefits, with the strongest negative opinion in Hungary, Poland and Greece, according to a 2016 Pew Research Center survey.

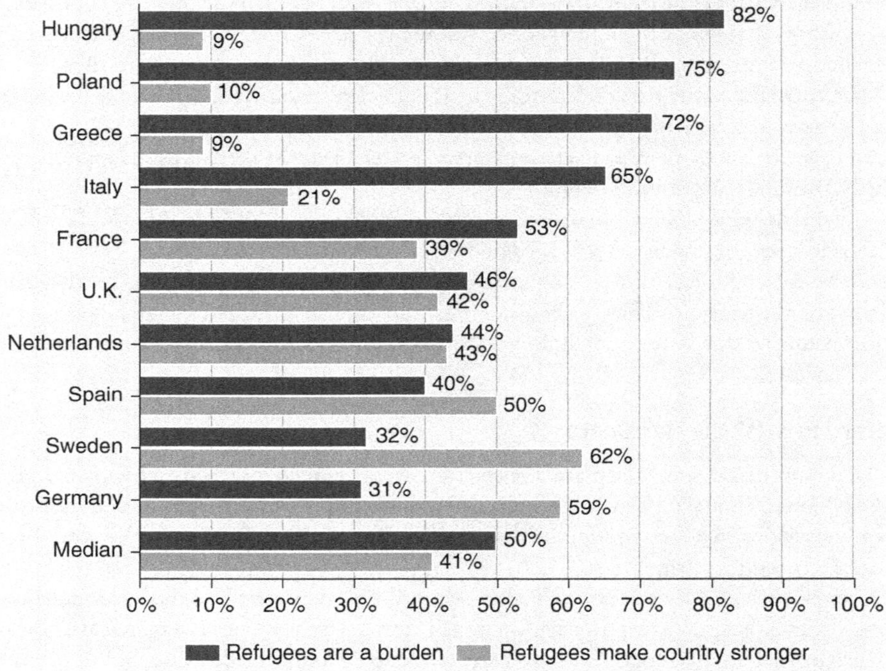

Source: Richard Wike, Bruce Stokes and Katie Simmons, "Negative Views of Minorities, Refugees Common in EU," Pew Research Center, Jul. 11, 2016, https://tinyurl.com/zvhb3cn.

Union is a foe, what they do to us in trade," Trump told an interviewer. In explaining his rationale for imposing tariffs, Trump told a political rally that the EU "was set up to take advantage of the United States, to attack our piggy bank."[27]

On June 22, the European Union announced retaliatory 25 percent import duties on $3.2 billion worth of U.S. imports, including 180 products ranging from orange juice to pleasure boats and motorcycles.[28]

One of the first to be hit was Harley-Davidson, the iconic U.S. motorcycle manufacturer, which announced that it was moving some of its production out of the United States to escape the additional $2,200 tax on each of its motorcycles in Europe, its second largest market.[29]

Trump in late June ratcheted up the dispute with the EU, threatening to impose 20 percent tariffs on imports of European cars and auto parts. He said he was angered that the Europeans put 10 percent duties on imported U.S. cars, while the United States charges only

2.5 percent tariffs for European autos.[30] The United States, Trump said, would impose "tremendous retribution" on the European Union if it did not agree to lower import duties on cars.[31]

After a July 25 meeting at the White House with Jean-Claude Juncker, the president of the European Commission, the EU's executive body, Trump said the two sides had entered a new phase, with the EU agreeing to increase purchases of U.S. soybeans and liquefied natural gas. Trump's threat to tax auto imports was put on hold while negotiating teams met to work out a detailed plan to end tariffs and non-tariff trade barriers on industrial goods. But the duties on steel and aluminum remained in place, as did the EU's retaliatory tariffs.[32]

While the EU recorded a trade surplus in goods with the United States, the U.S. had a $51 billion surplus in services with the EU.[33] The ifo Center for International Economics, a Munich-based think tank, said that when goods, services and corporate profit flows were combined, the United States enjoyed a current account surplus of $14 billion with the EU in 2017.[34]

With 516 million people and an annual GDP in excess of $17 trillion, the European economy is a powerful rival to the United States, as well as its largest trading partner. As the tensions with Washington increased, the EU signed a free-trade deal with Japan on July 17, eliminating most bilateral tariffs. "We are sending a clear message that we stand together against protectionism," European Council President Donald Tusk said at a press conference.[35]

Economists said it was too early to assess the damage that a trade war with the United States could cause. The IMF estimated it might reduce global growth by 0.5 percent, and Rabobank's de Groot says it might eventually reduce European output by 2 percent of GDP.[36]

Josef Joffe, publisher-editor of the German newspaper Die Zeit, says that by focusing on such things as who has a trade deficit and who has a surplus, Trump is trying to "demolish the very foundation of the liberal world order by replacing its non-zero sum game, where we both win, with zero sum, where your losses are my gains."

Joffe says the EU is now the last bastion of that liberal order, with open borders for goods, capital and people. "Not even the authoritarians want to tear down this structure," he says.

Former Enemies Unite

The tensions between the United States and the EU stand in sharp contrast to the atmosphere immediately after World War II, when the idea of a "United States of Europe" was proposed by British Prime Minister Winston Churchill as an antidote to the nationalism that tore the continent apart in the war and President Harry S. Truman agreed to provide U.S. financial support for European reconstruction.[37]

The EU has its origins in a 1951 plan conceived primarily as a way to bring former foes France and West Germany closer together economically in what was called the European Coal and Steel Community. The six founding members became the European Economic Community in 1957 and expanded to include Denmark, Ireland and Great Britain in 1973. The idea was to reduce national frictions by increasing commerce among the members, leading to the elimination of inter-European tariffs and borders, with European nationals free to live and work in other member countries thanks to the so-called Schengen agreement of 1985.

After the collapse of the Soviet bloc in 1989 and then the Soviet Union itself in 1991, the group expanded to include what had been East Germany when it became part of a reunited

Germany. Another major enlargement occurred in 2004 that included many of the former Soviet-bloc states of Eastern Europe. With the United Kingdom's departure, the EU will stand at 27 countries.

Joffe acknowledges that in addition to the tensions between Europe and the United States over issues such as defense and trade, pressure is increasing in Europe—thanks to the electoral success of nationalist and populist politicians—to secure the EU's external borders against illegal immigration.

In fact, disputes over those borders and the treatment of refugees trying to cross them has erupted into open conflict between EU leaders. After Germany agreed to receive more than 800,000 Syrian, Afghan and African refugees in 2015, populist parties garnered increasing support in a number of European countries by vocally opposing immigration. German Chancellor Angela Merkel, who had opened her country to the tide of refugees and became the leading voice promoting the liberal world order, emerged from national elections in 2017 greatly weakened because of the rise of an anti-immigrant party called the Alternative for Germany.[38]

In defiance of an EU agreement on migration, Eastern European countries refused to take in asylum seekers, and the EU Commission began legal action to force them to comply.[39]

The issue came to a head following the March election of a populist government in Italy that had campaigned against illegal migration.[40] Italian Interior Minister Matteo Salvini turned away a ship carrying more than 600 migrants rescued from the Mediterranean and said Italy had had enough. "Rescuing lives is a duty," Salvini said. "Transforming Italy into an enormous refugee camp is not."[41]

The migration dispute had economic side effects as well. At an EU summit at the end of June, Italy forced a postponement of decisions on pressing economic matters such as fiscal integration and EU-wide bank deposit insurance until the leaders agreed to take steps to limit illegal immigration.[42]

The summit agreed to a vaguely worded plan to set up EU-funded reception centers in Mediterranean countries such as Italy and Greece where refugees can be screened; beefing up the EU's border agency by 10,000 agents to increase patrols; and trying to set up "disembarkation platforms" in Africa where refugees can be screened away from European territory and quickly sent home if they fail to get refugee status.[43]

"Rescuing lives is a duty. Transforming Italy into a refugee camp is not."

Despite the summit agreement, efforts to reduce illegal migration are likely to remain at the top of the EU agenda in the second half of the year. Sebastian Kurz, a conservative, took over as Austria's chancellor in December by forming a coalition government that included the far-right Freedom Party. He has called progress on curbing illegal immigration essential.[44] "Protecting the European people has to be our top priority," he said in July as Austria assumed the rotating presidency of the European Council. "That is why we need a paradigm shift in our migration policy. We need to focus more on the safeguarding of our external borders as the prerequisite for a common border-free Europe."[45]

Kurz, like other leaders whose countries are net contributors to the EU's finances, also opposes increasing the EU budget at a time when the United Kingdom will no longer be contributing its annual dues of $13 billion.[46] The European Commission had proposed a long-term budget for the years 2021–27 that increases spending to $1.48 trillion, or 1.17 percent of European economic output, up from 1 percent in the last budget.[47]

While the proposed budget calls for greater spending on border security and digital research, it will cut farm subsidies under the Common Agricultural Policy to $438 billion, a reduction of 5 percent.[48] So-called cohesion spending, which finances roads and other projects mainly in former Soviet-bloc states in Eastern Europe, is to be reduced by 7 percent.

France, the largest recipient of EU farm subsidies, said such a "drastic" cut was unthinkable. "It poses an unprecedented risk to farms' viability by seriously impacting farmers' incomes, for whom direct aid is an essential safety net," said Stephane Travert, France's agriculture and food minister.[49]

At the same time, France hinted that future cohesion aid might be made contingent on countries abiding by the rule of law, after governments in Poland and Hungary took steps to restrict press freedom and the independence of the judiciary. "There is a double betrayal," said French President Emmanuel Macron. "They decide to abandon EU principles, turn their back on Europe and have a cynical approach to the union which gives them money, without respecting its values."[50]

While European policymakers are currently focused on migration issues, the populist governments could also challenge EU policy on financial matters such as continued membership in the euro or the 1992 Maastricht Treaty's requirement that EU governments keep annual fiscal deficits below 3 percent of the budget.

Italy's new administration, combining the leftist Five-Star Movement with the far-right League into what Italian newspaper La Stampa described as Europe's first populist government, quickly dropped an earlier suggestion that it might abandon the euro after financial markets sent interest rates on Italian government bonds soaring.[51]

But the government of Prime Minister Giuseppe Conte is forging ahead with plans for higher spending and tax cuts totaling around $116 billion, including partial reversal of a recent pension reform, skipping a value-added tax increase scheduled for next January, introduction of a flat income tax and a guaranteed income for all. With Italy running a public debt equal to 130 percent of its GDP, markets worry about Italy's ability to repay its lenders and stay within the 3 percent EU limit on budget deficits.[52]

"The large debt overhang will continue to cast its shadow on medium- to long-term prospects given its fragile sustainability," said Silvia Dall'Angelo, a senior economist at Hermes Investment Management in London.[53]

Economists say that despite the potential damage caused by Brexit, a trade war with the United States and populist unease with EU budget restraints, the EU is in much better economic shape now than it was in 2010, when a debt crisis caused interest rates to soar on sovereign bonds in Greece, Ireland, Portugal, Italy and Spain.[54] The debt crisis eased only in 2012 when Mario Draghi, president of the European Central Bank, vowed to "do whatever it takes to preserve the euro" and began buying the bonds of distressed countries.[55]

Nicolas Véron, a French economist at the Bruegel think tank in Brussels, says he doubts that the EU's existence is more threatened now because it has managed to mature as an organization, has grown economically and has put in place more safeguards to protect it from downside shocks than it had during the debt problem in 2010. He cited the fact that EU leaders have agreed to expand the mandate of the European Stability Mechanism, which was originally created in 2012 to provide financial assistance to struggling governments, to include making loans to European banks in danger of failing.[56]

"I think it's fair to say that the EU was born from the transatlantic alliance after the war and now the alliance is challenged and it's not clear if it's here to stay," Véron says. "But that doesn't mean the EU faces an existential challenge. In the 70 years that it has been around, the EU has acquired an identity and a strength of its own. I think it is much less critically dependent on American support and the transatlantic alliance now than it was at the outset."

Chronology

1951–93	**Former enemies forge a partnership.**
1951	The European Coal and Steel Community is established by Belgium, France, West Germany, the Netherlands, Luxembourg and Italy to regulate industrial production in war-devastated Europe.
1957	The same six nations form the European Economic Community (EEC) under the Treaty of Rome to promote integration of their economies. They also create a European Atomic Energy Community.
1965	The six members sign a treaty merging the EEC, European Steel and Coal Community and the European Atomic Energy Community. The merger goes into force in 1967.
1973	The United Kingdom joins the EEC.
1975	The United Kingdom holds its first nationwide referendum on the question of whether to remain in the EEC. More than 67 percent of voters back remaining in the community.
1984	British Prime Minister Margaret Thatcher gets West Germany and France to agree to give the United Kingdom a 66 percent "rebate" on its financial contribution to the EEC.
1985	The Schengen Agreement is signed, removing border controls among most EEC members. The United Kingdom and the Republic of Ireland opt out.
1993	The European Union is formally established when the Maastricht Treaty goes into force. The signatories agree to have a common foreign and security policy and to cooperate in areas of justice and home affairs. The treaty also lays the groundwork for the creation of the euro currency.
2000–Present	**Crises over debt, migration test the union.**
2002	A common currency is established as 12 countries introduce euro banknotes and coins. The United Kingdom, Denmark and Sweden stay with their own national currencies.
2004	Ten additional countries join the European Union, raising fears that investment will flow out of the founding members and that poor citizens of the new member countries will migrate to the richer nations.
2009	The Lisbon Treaty changes the EU's legal structure and creates the post of permanent president of the European Council.

2010	A debt crisis hits Greece, Portugal, Ireland, Spain and Cyprus when their governments are unable to repay or refinance their sovereign debt and interest rates spike. Greece nearly exits from the euro currency to save its economy, a plan labeled Grexit, but the crisis is resolved in 2012 when the European Central Bank vows to do "whatever necessary" to preserve the euro and begins buying the government bonds of the indebted nations.
2015	An immigration crisis erupts in the European Union when 1.2 million refugees from the Middle East and Africa attempt to enter by crossing the Mediterranean from Africa or making their way through Turkey. Eastern European countries such as Hungary erect fences to keep out refugees.
2016	British Prime Minister David Cameron calls a referendum on EU membership. The Leave vote wins by 51.9 percent to 48.1 percent. Cameron resigns and is succeeded by Theresa May, who begins negotiating her country's departure from the EU.
2017	Angered by increased immigration, populist parties opposed to migration win seats in parliament in Germany and Austria. Tensions escalate between the EU and Hungary and Poland over resettling refugees.
2018	Disputes erupt between the European Union and the United States over trade and defense spending, with President Trump imposing tariffs on imports of EU steel and aluminum and the EU retaliating against U.S. exports. . . . German Chancellor Angela Merkel's coalition government narrowly averts collapse when Merkel agrees to allow border checks of asylum seekers along the frontier with Austria, a humiliating retreat for Europe's leading liberal voice.

Discussion Questions

Here are some issues to discuss regarding the future of the European Union (EU):

- Why are London-based financial institutions transferring employees and operations to other European cities in advance of "Brexit," the United Kingdom's departure from the EU?
- What effect will Brexit have on economic growth in Great Britain, according to economists? On growth in Europe generally?
- Why did President Trump impose tariffs on European steel and aluminum exports to the United States? How did the EU respond?
- Which EU countries have been most affected by the stream of refugees seeking to reach Europe? How have those countries reacted?
- If you were an executive at a company that was considering investing or starting operations in Europe, how would the challenges confronting the EU affect your thinking?
- If you worked for a company based in the United Kingdom, would the uncertainties about Brexit and the EU's future lead you to find a job in another country?

PERSPECTIVE

Q&A: Nicolas Véron on the EU's Future

"THE EU HAS DEMONSTRATED AN ABILITY FOR SURVIVAL"

Nicolas Véron

Nicolas Véron is a French economist and a senior fellow at the Bruegel think tank in Brussels and the Peterson Institute for International Economics in Washington. He spoke with SAGE Business Researcher freelance correspondent Charles Wallace about the European Union's challenges and prospects. The transcript has been edited for space and clarity.

With the European Union facing Brexit, a possible trade war with the United States and divisions over migration policy, what do you see as the EU's prospects?

There's no denying the seriousness of the challenges, but there's a feeling in the EU, which I think is justified, that the EU has demonstrated an ability for survival and so that creates a form of self-confidence. There is a tendency to repeat the headlines we had at the peak of the euro crisis that this is an existential moment for the EU, but it no longer is.

The EU was a product of the liberal world order that emerged after World War II, at least in the West. With so many people now questioning that order, will that hurt the EU's chances of survival?

It's fair to say that EU was born from the transatlantic alliance after the war and now the alliance is challenged and it's not clear if it's here to stay. But that doesn't mean the EU faces an existential challenge. In the 70 years that it has been around, the EU has acquired an identity and a strength of its own. I think it is much less critically dependent on American support and the transatlantic alliance now than it was at the outset.

Even if the transatlantic alliance survives, what about the demise of the so-called liberal world order? How will that affect the EU?

There is no simple equation between withdrawal of the United States, which is certainly happening, and the unraveling of the whole international order. What's happening is that President Trump is making the EU more active in terms of promoting free trade and openness in the economy. I think there's a tendency in the U.S. to say that because America no longer supports the international order, the international order is dead. But outside of the U.S., things are more nuanced. It may be that the international order needs an anchor and that's been the U.S. for the last 70 years. But the question is: Can there be another anchor? Or can the liberal world order be sustained for a couple of years without an anchor?

What are the prospects now for reform of the European Union as envisaged by French President Emmanuel Macron on things like fiscal policy?

It's difficult to reform the euro zone, especially when you're not forced to by an immediate crisis. There's a lot of inertia, but I think there's been enormous progress in the last few years. For example, the last EU summit [in June 2018] didn't make as much progress as some would have wished, but given the political circumstances—Brexit, disputes about migration, a new government in Italy—it did make some important progress, and that is actually quite remarkable.

What in your view are the implications of an apparent rollback in democratic freedoms in Eastern European members of the European Union, such as clampdowns on freedom of the press and restricting the independence of the judiciary?

It's certainly a new phase. There had been a feeling there would be a convergence not only economically but also politically. Central and Eastern European countries would become what were called normal countries. That was kind of a patronizing way of saying all Western countries abide by this model and so they should convert to the Western model. There is no longer the same certainty about the existence of the Western model. I also think these countries need to develop a political identity of their own. Because they're in the European Union, that political identity has to be based on compliance with the rules of the game, and that means specific things in terms of the independence of the judiciary and all that. Unlike in Turkey, where it's pretty clear that the regime has passed a point of no return, the Central and Eastern European countries are not yet there. They haven't passed that point of no return. Maybe they are on their way in that direction but perhaps not.

UPDATE IN 2020

It took over three years, but Britain left the European Union (EU) at 11 p.m. Greenwich Mean Time on Jan. 31, 2020.[57]

Implementing Brexit did not mean immediate changes for the U.K. The action launched a transition period in which free trade and free travel were supposed to continue until the end of 2020 while negotiations took place to reach a free-trade deal.

However, the COVID-19 shutdowns across the U.K. and European nations interrupted the flow of people and goods, and brought about the first illustration of European unity post-Brexit.

Meanwhile, the United States and the EU clashed regularly during U.S. President Donald Trump's administration. Trump repeatedly threatened to impose duties on European car imports, despite the presence of European car plants in the American South.

Among the steps taken: The U.S. approved steel and aluminum tariffs on the EU in 2018; opened an investigation into European plans to impose a tax on digital giants; and slapped 25 percent levies on certain EU goods in return for previous state subsidies to Airbus.[58]

But in the summer of 2020, there was a tiny thaw. The European Commission agreed to end tariffs on imports of U.S. frozen and fresh lobster for the next five years. "We intend for this package of tariff reductions to mark just the beginning of a process that will lead to additional agreements that create more free, fair, and reciprocal transatlantic trade," the two chief negotiators, U.S. Trade Representative Robert Lighthizer and EU Trade Commissioner Phil Hogan, said in a joint statement.[59]

The unresolved issue of immigration still faced the EU in the fall of 2020. Devastating fires at Greece's Moria refugee camp prompted a series of migration reforms, but there was no agreement among the 27 nations over the direction those should take.[60]

Meanwhile, analysts said it was becoming clear that Germany would play a dominant role in determining the future direction of the EU. One reason was that it was Germany's turn on a rotating calendar to take charge of the body. But another was that Angela Merkel was providing strong leadership in her country, which could extend to the EU as a whole.

"Usually, German power in Brussels is the political equivalent of dark matter: invisible, difficult to measure and yet everywhere. Now the Germans are stars, shining so bright as to be impossible to ignore," wrote the anonymous columnist Charlemagne in The Economist.[61]

—Micheline Maynard

8

FASHION INDUSTRY

Can it adapt to changing times?

Vickie Elmer

From *SAGE Business Researcher*, January 16, 2017

EXECUTIVE SUMMARY

The global fashion business is going through a period of intense change and competition, with disruption coming in many colors: global online marketplaces, slower growth, more startups and consumers who now seem bored by what once excited them. Many U.S. shoppers have grown tired of buying Prada and Chanel suits and prefer to spend their money on experiences rather than clothes. Questions about fashion companies' labor and environmental practices are leading to new policies, although some critics remain unconvinced. Fashion still relies on creativity, innovation and consumer attention, some of which comes from technology and some from celebrities.

Here are some key takeaways:

- High-fashion brands must now compete with "fast fashion," apparel sold on eBay and vintage sites.
- Risk factors for fashion companies include China's growth slowdown, reduced global trade, Brexit, terrorist attacks and erratic commodity prices.
- Plus-size women are a growing segment of the market, yet critics say designers are ignoring them.

OVERVIEW

José Neves launched Farfetch during the global economic crisis of 2008, drawing more on his background in IT and software than a love of fashion. His idea: Allow small designers and fashion shops to sell their wares worldwide on a single online marketplace. The site will "fetch" fashion from far-off places.

Despite having no investment backing until 2010, Farfetch has grown dramatically. It employs more than 1,000 people in 10 offices and has secured six rounds of investments. More than 400 boutiques sell on the site.[1]

Farfetch relies on creative exclusivity and fashion brands like Dolce & Gabbana and Alexander McQueen. It carries an eclectic mix of new and vintage items, jewelry, bags, iPhone cases, $150 candles, art and fashion books.

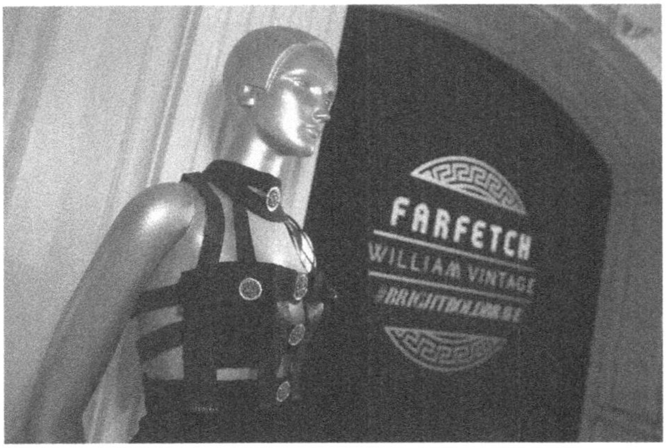

Rachel Murray/Getty Images for Farfetch

In 2017, Farfetch collaborated with U.K.-based William Vintage and debuted the William Vintage x Gianni Versace collection, which features about 500 Versace-designed pieces.

"The flavor, the fuel of the brand is a boutique feel. It's all about uniqueness of expression, of individual taste," said Neves. "But I don't think that's incompatible with big numbers."[2]

Farfetch has 410,000 Instagram followers and 2016 revenue of more than $800 million, up from around $500 million in 2015.[3]

It's a bright spot in a fashion industry fraught with change, challenges and criticism—over "fast fashion" ending up in landfills, the treatment of apparel workers, the exclusive nature of fashion that leaves many feeling left out and the accusation that fashion snubs or marginalizes larger women.

Fashion lines are easier to start and harder to sustain than ever before. Innovation is upending expectations: Companies employ 3-D printers to create running shoes and recycle salmon skins into wallets and accessories. Fashion, along with the rest of the luxury-goods sector, is contending with what the consulting firm Deloitte dubbed "the decade of change": new digital channels and platforms, China's growing middle class and the rise of Millennial buyers.[4]

With fast fashion from H&M, Zara and others hustling new merchandise to market many times a year, the fashion sector has sped up its production cycle—with a see now, buy now approach to runway shows that worries many designers. "Fashion is recognizing the changing desires and rhythms of consumers and figuring how to respond to that," says Robin Givhan, The Washington Post's fashion critic, who won a Pulitzer Prize in 2006.

Yet parts of the global fashion industry are slow to adapt to new consumer trends and digital selling. Some experts say fashion has fallen out of fashion in some cities and demographics. Consumers today may skip shopping for an Italian suit in favor of a trip to Italy or an Italian film festival. They are spending less on fashion in developed countries and more in emerging nations such as Vietnam and India.[5]

Fashion is a labor-intensive business that is moving to online sales, fittings and previews. High-fashion brands such as Giorgio Armani, Christian Dior and Chanel must compete with apparel sold on eBay and vintage sites such as LuxuryGarageSale.com. Questions persist about whether people will wear the same clothing in different countries. And yet the sector continues to serve as a cultural connector to our past and our identities, a way to show status and a way to fit in with our peers at work.

Disruption has been rumbling through the fashion sector, and its cousin the retail chains, for years, as online sales take a larger share and startups create new products or services.

"The fashion industry is suffering because it's not listening to the consumer," says Pamela Danziger, author of several books on luxury markets and consumers, who leads the luxury consultancy Unity Marketing. She cites "very deep and structural problems," ranging from ignoring women over 40 and the "experience economy"—consumers' increasing preference for spending on experiences—to simply making too many clothes. "We're just drowning in all this [low-quality] apparel," she says.

Nike Leads U.S. Apparel Brands in Revenue

Ralph Lauren, Old Navy trail by more than $20 billion

Nike is the undisputed leader of American apparel brands, bringing in well over $20 billion, more than second- and third-place fashion companies Ralph Lauren and Old Navy. Activewear brand Under Armour raked in $3.1 billion and solidified its status as the fastest-growing brand in that category.

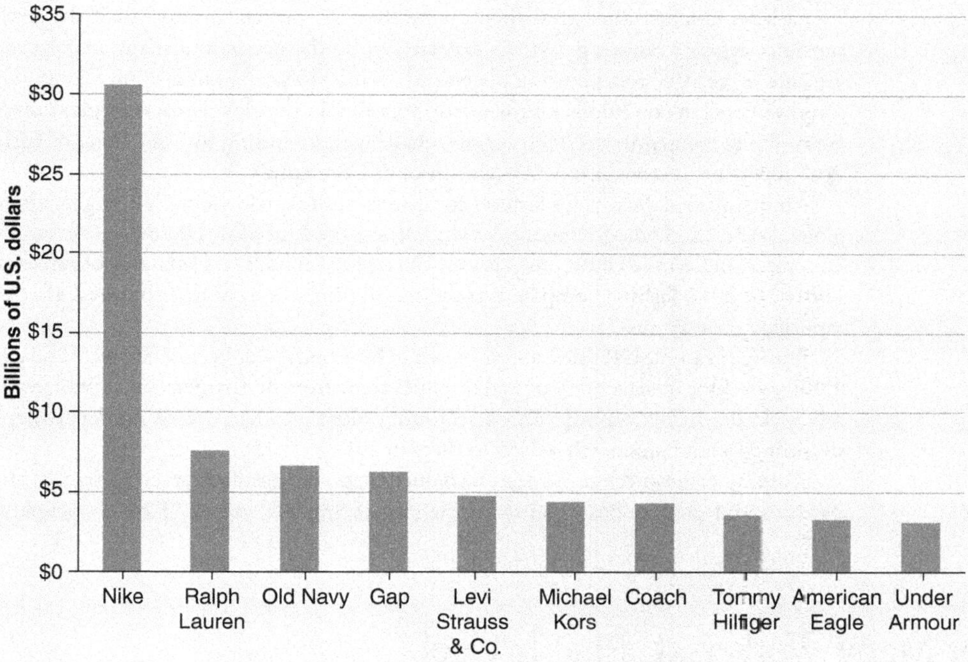

Source: Dhani Mau, "The 10 Biggest U.S. Apparel Companies," Fashionista, Jul. 2, 2016, http://tinyurl.com/zvhkgwy.

U.S. clothing and accessories stores sold around $254 billion in 2016, about the same as in 2015, according to the U.S. Census Bureau.[6] (The numbers don't count fashion sales by department stores, which have declined for years.) Globally, fashion generated $1.69 trillion in revenue, and that is expected to increase to $1.73 trillion in 2017, according to the market research firm Euromonitor International. Despite growth in many developing countries, that's essentially unchanged from the $1.7 trillion rung up in 2012.[7]

Most urban consumers will spend more on clothing and fashion by 2020, but will allocate a larger share of their budgets to other items such as leisure.[8]

Fashion includes many styles and price points. At the top is haute couture, typified by Chanel, Christian Dior, Prada and other brands whose prices and focus appeal to wealthy consumers or rising stars. Couture is a half step lower in the hierarchy, followed by "bridge," a fast-disappearing category that is fine fashion but not as elegant and pricey as couture. Ready-to-wear clothing is sold at discounters and department stores for the masses. The newest category is "athleisure," athletic apparel that may be worn to a pub or the office.

Fashion also refers to an array of accessories including belts, scarves, coats and swim suits. It encompasses formal or evening wear, sports and athletic attire, and often includes jewelry and shoes.

Fashion industry sales grew by no more than 2.5 percent in 2016, half the level of the previous decade.[9] Slower growth is expected to be the norm, and many major companies are cutting costs or restructuring operations. While 40 percent of fashion executives expect improvements in conditions for the sector, volatility in the global economy plus competition from online companies are their biggest challenges, according to "The State of Fashion," a 2016 report by the consulting firm McKinsey & Company.[10]

Among the risk factors for fashion companies are a slowdown in China's growth, reduced global trade, the United Kingdom's vote to leave the European Union, the threat of terrorist attacks and erratic commodity prices, the report found.[11] "As volatility becomes the new normal in 2017, fashion companies could see all dimensions of their business affected," the report's authors wrote.

A prime example is Ralph Lauren, which in June said it would close 50 stores and eliminate 1,000 jobs. One quarter of its annual revenues come from department stores, which are themselves closing many locations and discounting more merchandise. With department stores declining Ralph Lauren will sell less to them in 2017.[12]

Keeping fashion relevant may be trickier than ever amid divergent interests, shopping patterns and choices based on consumers' ages and life stages. "Fashion people are out

For Many Workers, Casual Is Cool

"We Have Turned Far Away from . . . Rigid Dress Codes"

Fashion in the modern workplace means being able to dress comfortably, but there are numerous holdouts, especially outside the United States. A key takeaway: 40 percent of workers worldwide dress casually.

Much of the workaday world, it seems, from JPMorgan Chase bond traders to Silicon Valley code jockeys, is wearing casual clothes to the office.

Dress-down days used to be the exception, occurring once a week or month. Now, in the United States at least, they've stretched so far that wearing comfortable clothing has taken over even conservative workplaces such as banks and some law firms. Suits, if they're worn, may be stretchy jersey or other easy-to-wear fabrics.

The rise of casual attire has sparked debate about whether the trend boosts business productivity. For casual's admirers, comfortable workers are productive workers; others say that to be professional, you need to dress professionally.

Defenders of the old are plentiful in countries such as Hungary and Mexico, where 40 percent of workers wear uniforms to work, or Turkey and South Korea, where nearly half wear business or "smart dress" to their job, an Ipsos Poll of workers in 24 countries found. Some 40 percent worldwide dress casually for work, varying from a low of 22 percent in Australia, India and Saudi Arabia to a high of 58 percent in Russia.[13]

Men's suits are not disappearing, but they are becoming softer, without shoulder pads or rigidly constructed jackets, and more likely to be subtle grays or blue or worn with a sweater or turtleneck under them.[14]

"People expect comfort," Caroline Belhumeur, creative director for the Club Monaco apparel label, told The

Wall Street Journal. "It's not like in the '80s when people were stuffing themselves into blazers and stilettos and hobbling around."[15]

The change is driven partly by Millennials and partly by the need to recruit people by providing a more relaxed, informal workplace. "Employers are having to be more appealing to the current workforce" and future hires, said Brandi Britton, Los Angeles district president for the staffing agency OfficeTeam.[16] Workers in their 20s and 30s are especially insistent about being able to wear comfortable clothes for work, and companies started by young entrepreneurs are creating lines that they want to wear. "We have turned far away from the rigid dress codes that we once had," said Christina Binkley, a Wall Street Journal editor who covers style.[17]

There are fewer ties in offices and more fashion sweatshirts or hoodies. One reason: The workday flows into the evening, and life and work are more combined because of technology and flexible work arrangements.

The trend may have started around or just after World War II when Hawaiians began wearing casual local shirts.[18] Honolulu city and county allowed workers to wear sports shirts in place of dress shirts and ties from June through October. The intent was to support locally made "aloha" shirts.[19] It took wing in 1966, when Wilson P. Cannon Jr., president of the Bank of Hawaii, decided to wear aloha shirts to work and allowed his staff to wear them on what became Aloha Fridays.[20]

When the idea spread to the rest of the United States in the late 1980s and early 1990s, it was dubbed Casual Friday or Dress-Down Friday. Silicon Valley companies adopted black turtlenecks (Apple CEO Steve Jobs made it his signature look) and jeans; more recently, startup founders don hoodies to signal they're ready to code all night. They used the casual attire as an indicator of their fun corporate culture, or a way to appeal to recent college graduates who were not eager to adopt the pinstriped or black suits required by many consulting and financial firms.

By 1999 and 2000, as dot-com companies proliferated, Goldman Sachs, Credit Suisse and other financial firms developed full-time casual dress policies, although the idea of what "dressing down" or "business casual" meant varied considerably. In some multinational firms in 2000, the decision on what to wear required phoning ahead to see whether the client would wear a suit, khakis or something in between.[21]

Opinions vary as to whether the move into leggings and hoodies has affected worker productivity and morale.

Many workers believe casual clothes increase productivity, camaraderie and office morale. About 45 percent of those in the Ipsos global survey said casual dress may improve productivity, although only 30 percent or fewer of workers in France and Mexico said they believe it. Yet 44 percent of human resources executives reported more tardiness and absenteeism after their company instituted a casual dress policy, and others say productivity declined.[22]

Dressing up for work—think suit or blazer—could increase productivity, improve the perception of success and even raise an employee's confidence level, some analysts say. Clothes that demonstrate high social status may project an air of dominance and raise performance in high-stakes competitive tasks such as negotiating, Yale University assistant professor Michael W. Kraus found.[23]

Other researchers say it may facilitate thinking big. "When you need to think creatively, about the bigger picture, that's when dressing formally will increase your productivity," Michael L. Slepian, an adjunct assistant professor at Columbia Business School said.[24]

—*Vickie Elmer*

of touch," says Danziger, adding that jeans and jackets are fine for most of her business meetings.

Yet discounting seems the norm, and consumers expect virtually everything to go on sale. "Luxury shoppers used to be embarrassed to compare price or ask about price, and it's commonplace today," said Robert Burke, a fashion and retail consultant.[25]

Now, when consumers look online to compare prices, they see the Jimmy Choo shoe that interests them—and a variety of knockoffs. This helps to erode brand loyalty. "When was the last time brand was important, really? It might have been right before the recession when aspirational luxury was on the rise," said Gabriella Santaniello, analyst with the retail research firm A Line Partners.[26]

U.S. consumers spend on average 3.1 percent of their budgets on clothing, though those age 34 and younger spend much more, according to federal data.[27] Clothing remains the No. 1 purchase for holiday gifts, but its share has been stagnant at around 50 percent since 2011, while jewelry, liquor and food steadily rise, a Deloitte study found.[28]

In the experience economy, people spend more on wine and travel or an evening out with friends than on clothing, experts said.

"On the whole, conditions have never been more challenging for luxury brands," said Fflur Roberts, a Euromonitor analyst, noting consumers' "massive push" toward luxury experiences at restaurants and hotels. Roberts expects China to overtake the United States shortly as the largest market for luxury goods, which includes cars, travel and fashion.[29]

For many decades, the fashion sector has offered up the style or styles for a particular year. "Most brands are in the business of telling people what it is they desire before they know," Givhan says. But in recent years, consumers have become more independent and less likely to swoon and buy whatever the latest style is from Paris or New York. "People used to ask, 'What's going on with hemlines?' Now the hemline is whatever hemline is flattering to you," says Givhan.

For those who want to inject change in their wardrobe, a growing number of companies will rent work attire or VIP celebration duds. Rent the Runway offered an early version of the sharing economy with fancy gowns and dresses, then in 2016 added a women's work wardrobe with an "Unlimited" plan. Similar to Netflix, it allows women to borrow three items at a time for as long as they want for $139 a month.[30]

Some travelers prefer to rent a suit or running shoes. This "bag-free, hassle-free" trend is fueled by hotel chains and a handful of Uber-like startups that provide a suitcase of clothing to travelers when they arrive.[31]

With the average American woman now wearing a size 16 to 18, plus-size women are increasing their clothing budgets faster than women wearing size 6 or 8.[32] "Many designers, dripping with disdain, lacking imagination or simply too cowardly to take a risk—still refuse to make clothes for them," wrote Tim Gunn, co-host of the TV show "Project Runway" and former chief creative officer for Liz Claiborne. He called the problem the mythology of "glamour and thinness" and said designers must create clothes for women in a variety of shapes and sizes.[33]

A few fashion companies are starting to expand their offerings, and one Virginia woman started ResellXL in 2016 to sell denim sportswear, designer evening gowns and the St. John's Knits brand in larger sizes.[34]

"Fashion is really about passion and creativity, just like music or dance or poetry," First Lady Michelle Obama said in welcoming design students to the White House in 2014. "For so many people across the country, it is a calling; it is a career. It's the way they feed their families."[35]

Millions of jobs have been created in the textiles, clothing, leather and footwear industries, mostly in developing countries and mainly for women. At the same time, around 80 percent of apparel jobs have disappeared in the United States from 1990 to 2011.[36] Four countries benefited most from shifts to low-cost production centers: China, India, Brazil and Indonesia. In 2010, China became the largest exporter of clothing and textiles, accounting for more than one-third of worldwide production and 11.2 million jobs.[37]

Women hold more than two-thirds of jobs in global apparel manufacturing, according to the International Labour Organization, which notes that pay remains low; in several countries they earn only $75 to $300 a month despite working long hours. And workers still face hazardous conditions in apparel factories, long after a 2012 fire in a Bangladeshi garment factory killed more than 100 workers.[38]

Despite low factory wages, many in the fashion business do well. Profit margins for luxury apparel and accessories average 24.8 percent of sales, higher than high-end cars or jets or hotel companies, according to Deloitte data. So apparel and accessories companies remain tempting targets for financial and buyout firms to acquire.[39]

Farfetch is among those buying, including the purchase of British fashion retailer Browns in 2015. In November of last year, Browns unveiled modern branding and a revised website to showcase its support of new fashion designers and the addition of 68 brands.[40]

The company's website focuses on luxury fashion—and speed. It adds about 1,000 new listings a week. Most items are photographed on a model, to help customers better see draping, fit and scale. At Farfetch's Los Angeles studio, the goal is for a model to wear clothing for four minutes at most. Purchases average $700 and the company's sales in 2016 were expected to grow 56 percent from the previous year.[41]

In late 2016, Farfetch was "firmly on track to become profitable" and founder Neves expected an initial public offering in two or three years.[42]

As the fashion industry tries to adjust to all these new realities, here are the issues under consideration.

WEIGHING THE ISSUES

Is the Fashion Industry Going Out of Fashion?

Helen Boxall, a teaching assistant in a small English city, has a degree in fashion design. She loves fashion, yet she's taking a year off from buying any clothing.

Her reasons are simple: She agreed to stop clothes shopping as part of a crowdfunding campaign to raise money for the anti-poverty group Oxfam—and she's appalled at all the fashion that ends up in landfills or lost in the backs of closets. "Fast fashion is killing the planet, and we as consumers are voting for it," she said.[43]

She's part of a global minimalism movement of people who focus on paying off debts and sharing experiences, time or castoff items instead of gifts.[44] Another version of this shows up as fashion video bloggers who swap clothing or mend it. They also head to charity or vintage shops for their "haulternative" to the malls or boutiques.[45]

People who used to buy at high-end department stores now order their clothing from Target.com or Farfetch, or browse vintage or independent shops. They seek classic clothing, some made with a flair or a twist, say Katiti Kirondé, a designer and former model who has worked for fashion companies for 30 years.

Even though Instagram or social media make it easier to find new clothing or shoes, some consumers are less interested in acquiring them, some experts said. Those who buy luxury goods are more interested in "more meaningful luxury experiences," Euromonitor said,

Macy's Remains Dominant Force Among Department Stores

Struggling anchor store J.C. Penney brought in less than half of Macy's sales

Macy's is leading the department store pack, bringing in more than twice the sales of Sears and J.C. Penney. Despite having almost 400 fewer U.S. locations than Kohl's, Macy's took in about $7 billion more than the second-place retailer.

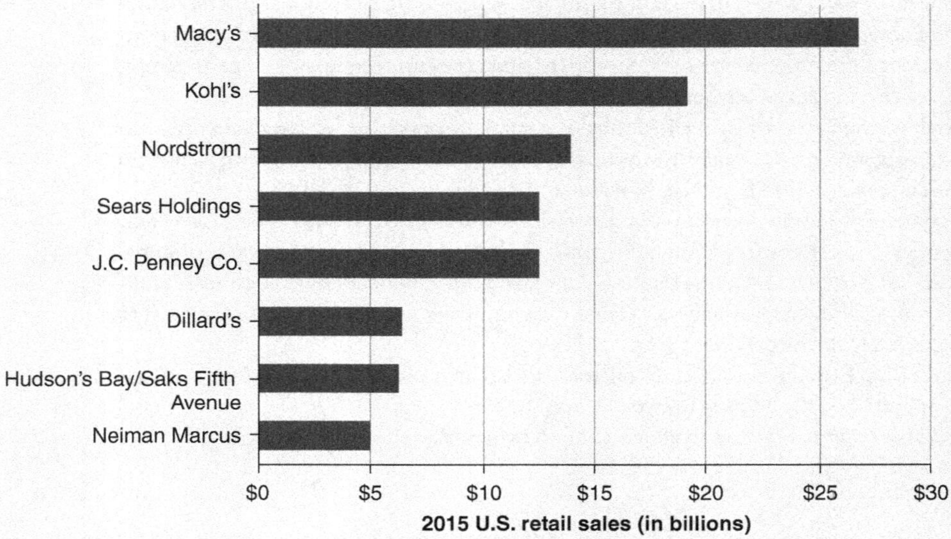

Source: "Top 100 Retailers 2016," National Retail Federation, Jun. 30, 2016, http://tinyurl.com/zaman6e.

though they may be less inclined to travel to potential terrorist targets such as Paris to experience them.[46]

Others are trading their fashionable suits for more comfortable and casual work clothing. The divide between weekday work and weekend leisure attire is lessening, and there's lots more stretch and give to fabrics.[47]

"Peoples' relationships with fashion are changing," says critic Givhan. "People are more interested in technology and experiences and all those other things. But it won't necessarily put the fashion industry out of business."

Consultant Danziger isn't so sure. "Materialism is falling out of favor," she says, and fashion brands are used to telling consumers what to wear. Now, she says, consumers want to choose—and they want a relationship with brands. "Fashion has lost its relevance to the consumer," says Danziger.

Even when they buy a handbag, designer logos are losing their allure. "Consumers are becoming less focused on image and more focused on individuality—especially the younger generations," said Marshal Cohen, chief industry analyst for market researcher NPD Group.[48]

Luxury Fashion Brands Had Mixed Year

Half rose, half fell in 2016, Savigny Luxury Index found

Luxury fashion brand Moncler had the largest estimated sales growth in 2016, according to the Savigny Luxury Index. Prada and Ralph Lauren were on the lower end of the scale, with decreased sales of about 10 percent.

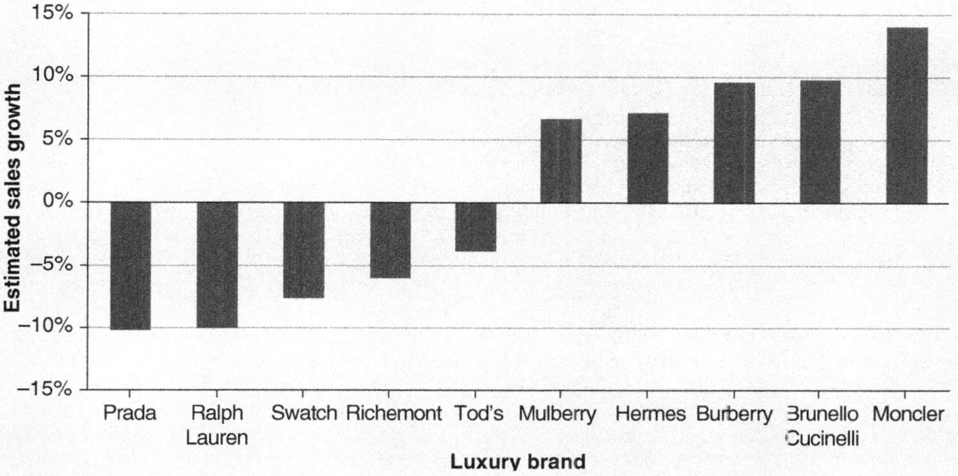

Note: Estimates are for 2016 and are as of Dec. 30, 2016.

Source: Savigny Luxury Index (SLI), Reuters, http://tinyurl.com/her7pol.

In the United States, low- and middle-income households have altered their spending patterns since 1984. They spend less on clothing and more on housing and health care, in part because the relative costs of clothing have declined while health care rose.[49]

Fashion "has lost its magic a little for Millennials," who instead are focused on food, Javier Seara, partner of Boston Consulting Group, said.[50]

Fashion brands are fighting back by personalizing the shopping experience, including opening restaurants based on their brand.

Burberry store employees sometimes organize birthday parties and art visits for shoppers who spend liberally, pouring a glass of champagne or even flying them to its London fashion show. Cultivating strong relationships with well-heeled customers, using a mix of big data and personal attention, is important to high-end brands.[51]

So is serving coffee, fresh juice or macarons. Gucci operates three artisanal food cafés in Florence, Tokyo and Shanghai, where the first one opened in July 2015. Giorgio Armani, Roberto Cavalli and Versace followed Ralph Lauren's lead into restaurants. "The more experiential you can make your shopping destination, the longer they stay and the more money they spend," said Dave Moore, president of retail at Irvine Co., a Newport Beach, Calif.-based real estate developer.[52]

Instagram and other social media—plus celebrities who love to show up wearing something glittery or new—bring fashion to more people than ever before. "Social media has intensified celebrity influence and helped stars be more involved in fashion," said designer Zaid Affas, who began his eponymous clothing line in 2014.[53]

"Michelle Markup" Shows Celebrity Impact

Millennials Especially Swayed by Endorsements

From first ladies to movie stars and pop divas, celebrities can amp up the appeal of a fashion brand by lending their aura—for love or money. A key takeaway: Millennials are more likely than Gen X-ers or Baby Boomers to be influenced by celebrity endorsements, especially for clothes.

When First Lady Michelle Obama showed up at a state dinner wearing a stunning dress from designers Versace or Jason Wu, her choice drew the attention of fashion bloggers, social media and the American consumer.

Wall Street also paid attention—so much that New York University Professor David Yermack dubbed the effect on share prices the "Michelle Markup."[54] The unexpected rise in stock values for fashion companies whose clothes were worn by Mrs. Obama totaled $8.3 billion within two days of the first lady's appearance in a particular fashion piece in 2009, and gains may have continued for weeks. Boosts were bestowed on mass brands, including J. Crew and Target, and more elite ones: Givenchy (owned by LVMH) and Ralph Lauren.[55]

"Few models or celebrities make the kind of impact on company stock price that Michelle Obama does," Yermack told Harvard Business Review. "The first lady's astonishing influence may be tied to the fact that consumers know she's not paid to wear what she does." Her influence comes from her genuine interest in fashion, her role as first lady, and the power of social media to spread news and allow consumers to buy some of her dresses or accessories immediately, according to Yermack.[56]

Though Obama's impact is huge and measurable, for decades well-attired celebrities have sashayed down red carpets, off Air Force One or onto the stage. First Lady Jacqueline Kennedy wore French and American designers in 1960. Pop superstar Madonna popularized the cone bra in her 1990 Blond Ambition tour, and Dolce and Gabbana put the bras on models in 2010 fashion shows.[57]

Celebrities may show up in fashion in many ways. Some, like Obama, genuinely enjoy dressing well, and choose and pay for their fashion statements. Others, such as Ivanka Trump, daughter of incoming President Donald Trump, wear clothing created by their own companies. And celebrities such as actresses Whoopi Goldberg and Sandra Bullock are paid to wear and promote a brand of jewelry, shoes or evening gowns, either for a specific event or an ongoing campaign. Actresses may pick up $100,000 to $250,000 to wear a designer dress to the Oscars, stylist Jessica Paster told Business Insider.[58]

About 70 percent of commercials in South Korea and Japan feature a celebrity, while in the United States it's about one in four and lower still in Europe. A famous person may lend credibility to a brand and draw consumer interest, but it's difficult to measure the impact.[59]

If the celebrity is attractive or if the character being played matches that of the brand being endorsed, the campaign may be more persuasive, researchers have found. Millennials are twice as likely as Gen Xers and four times as likely as Baby Boomers to be swayed by celebrity endorsements, and this is especially true for apparel and luxury goods.[60]

"Having a well-liked and familiar celebrity is as important as liking or being familiar with the advertised brand," Retail Merchandising Assistant Professor Karla McCormick of Florida State University concluded.[61]

A growing number of performers and artists—Eva Longoria, Jennifer Lopez (JLo) and P. Diddy (Sean John Combs)—have created their own lines of clothing or perfume, handbags or jewelry. And Hollywood agents and licensing companies keep searching to "cook up fashion deals for celebrities and professional athletes," wrote Teri Agins, author of "Hijacking the Runway: How Celebrities Are Stealing the Spotlight from Fashion Designers." She believes the trend will continue with new lines by pop music superstar Beyoncé and others with name recognition and millions of followers on Instagram and Twitter.[62]

Jessica Simpson established one of the big successes in celebrity fashion, a brand of women's clothing sold in Macy's, Dillard's and elsewhere. Starting with shoes, the brand's sales now top $1 billion. "Here's to the next billion," said Simpson, an all-American singer-mom known for "The Dukes of Hazzard" movie remake. (Her line is owned by Sequential Brands, which wants to double or triple sales.)[63]

The trend started decades ago. Marilyn Monroe wore sultry evening gowns to parties and donned a white pleated halter dress that became famous in the New York subway grate scene from "The Seven Year Itch."[64] Copies of that white dress "flew off the racks every summer for years, and new modified versions continued to appear every couple of seasons," wrote authors Christopher Nickens and George Zeno.[65]

Yet for every best-seller like Marilyn's dress or Elizabeth Taylor's White Diamonds perfume are a number of fashion and accessory lines backed by celebrities that fail or barely sell. Brands backed by celebrities with superstar status and a commitment to market the products tend to do better, experts said.[66]

Celebrities may draw the attention of many consumers, but are not effective with affluent buyers. "For people who have status, it's a turn-off and not a turn-on" to have a celebrity promoting apparel or shoes, says Pamela Danziger, author of several books on consumer behavior and luxury marketing.

Those celebrity brands create fewer opportunities for graduates of Parsons and other fashion design schools, who "are sadly up against these instant designers," says Katiti Kirondé, a fashion designer and former model. With celebrity fashion lines, "there's always somebody new and more fascinating coming along."

With a reality television star in the White House, it's possible that celebrity fashion could gain more prominence. Ivanka Trump's eponymous line of clothing for working women registered big increases in sales and followers during her dad's presidential run, although some women were turned off and launched a boycott under the hashtag #GrabYourWallet.[67]

"I'm very very proud of this company that I've built. We're doing hundreds of millions of dollars in retail sales," she told Fortune magazine at its Most Powerful Women Summit in 2016.[68]

Incoming First Lady Melania Trump, a former model, has thus far been lower-key than Michelle Obama. And while a few fashion designers are reluctant to dress Melania Trump because of her husband's political stances, plenty will be glad to see her glide off Air Force One wearing their suit or shoes.[69]

—Vickie Elmer

Fashion magazines also are reinventing themselves, with several launching e-commerce sites and even connecting their brand's to the hit animated comedy movie "The Minions." Vogue and its parent Condé Nast, which owns GQ, Allure and other titles, plans to produce 2,500 videos, bringing the editorial off the page and onto the screen. A series called "Inside the Wardrobe" is devoted to uncovering the secret styles of actress Suki Waterhouse, singer Lilly Allen and reality TV performer Olivia Palermo.[70]

Fashion is in a "time of disruption," says Kirondé, with robotics and technology influencing the way clothing looks and feels. "It's a time of incredible experimentation."

Is the Fashion Industry Really Global?

Latin American retailers buy plenty of fashion clothing made in Italy, China and elsewhere. Increasingly they offer local designers found at the growing number of South and Central American fashion weeks in Honduras, Peru, Chile and Argentina. "There's kind of been an awakening . . . that you can create amazing products [here] and people will want them," said Karla Martinez, editor-in-chief of Vogue Mexico and Vogue Latin America.[71]

The global fashion business—clothing designed in Los Angeles or Paris, sewn in Spain or Vietnam and sold in New York, Beijing and Brasilia—continues to develop international supply chains. And increasingly, it seeks out local makers and designers whose work reflects the cultures and interests of one city or one group, whether they're Zambians or U.S. Latinas.

"Some people want that uniqueness and the connection to the producer," says Givhan. She cited The Row, created by actresses Mary-Kate and Ashley Olsen, as a brand that proudly embraces its made-in-the-U.S. approach. "The more expensive it is, the easier it is to produce here," she says, though the United States lacks the infrastructure and machinery to produce shoes or fine knits.

Fashion houses may be huge multinationals such as Gucci and Chanel, but more likely they are small companies with only a dozen or so staffers. That is particularly true in Europe, where the average clothing company employs 10 workers. (Yet Italy's clothing and textile industries employ almost as many workers as its U.S. counterparts, both close to 400,000.)[72]

Through crowdfunding, it's easy to launch a fashion line based on a product with a focused appeal. One crowdfunding site, Before the Label, focuses exclusively on fashion startups, and donors receive the apparel or accessory they back.[73]

Danziger, the luxury fashion and retail expert, expects the buy-local movement that has changed the food and restaurant business, to take hold in the fashion world too. "People want to buy items made close to home, made with authentic materials," she says.

Regional tastes in work attire still vary considerably across the United States and the globe. What works in Washington, D.C., may not in Seattle, never mind in a business meeting in Shenzhen. McKinsey explores the projected differences in fashion spending in 2025 and concludes that "growth is also granular and varies by category and city. . . . What it takes to win in one category in one city is not necessarily the same as what it will take in a different category in the same city, or . . . in a neighboring city."[74]

"Cultivating a local clientele can help global fashion players deal with volatility, as they can intensify their focus on one geography during a prosperous time and shift to another when the first hits a low," wrote the McKinsey analysts. This means creating limited edition and specialized products based partly on predictive analytics.[75]

Fashion clothing is traded globally and accounted for $483 billion in exports in 2014. In a few countries, including Bangladesh, Haiti and El Salvador, more than one-third of all exports are apparel and fashion items. In China, clothing accounted for 8 percent of all exports in 2014 and worldwide, it's 2.6 percent.[76]

LVMH, owner of Louis Vuitton, Fendi leather goods and TAG Heuer watches, demonstrated the power of global reach serving as a buffer when business is bad in one region. It reported strong third-quarter 2016 sales in Asia even as they slid in parts of Europe.[77]

Smart brands are adopting a "glocal" strategy that uses their global experience, then tailoring products and services to local markets. So Louis Vuitton sells its bags and purses from stands in shopping centers in Hong Kong, the United Arab Emirates and Romania, but will not use this approach in most of Europe or the United Kingdom, where such a sales channel would damage its status.[78]

Gucci and Zara are both focused on global growth, with room for local adaptation to reflect tastes and incomes of different cities in China and elsewhere. Gucci offers a tiered approach to product assortment, so in Chinese cities with less affluent residents, more affordable leather goods and accessories largely fill the shops, but in Beijing and Shanghai, the higher end items dominate.[79]

International travel and the internet both will make fashion a global experience, even for those who stay in one city. The consulting firm Bain & Company and others point to the growth of e-commerce in luxury goods and fashion. By 2020, 940 million online shoppers are expected to spend almost $1 trillion in cross-border e-commerce purchases, including fashion, electronics, food and much more, according to the McKinsey Global Institute.[80]

Those well-heeled consumers will buy many items while traveling, with tourists accounting for almost half of luxury shopping in 2016, according to the Bain Luxury Report. High-end tourists buy fashions, accessories, jewelry, art and more, driven partly by currency fluctuations. So the higher value of the yen has led Japanese and Chinese tourists to visit and spend in Hawaii and California, rather than Tokyo, and travel to many parts of Europe is curtailed because of fears of terrorism.[81]

Yet the Chinese soon may want to bypass the United States. President-elect Donald Trump has talked of levying tariffs as high as 35 percent on imports from China and other countries—even though some Trump-brand clothing is made in China.[82] His choice for U.S. trade representative, Robert Lighthizer, has accused China of engaging in unfair trade and advocated the use of tariffs to promote American industry.[83]

The fashion and retail industries are cautiously waiting to see how or whether Trump's comments will turn into new policies. Some industry representatives say if they are enacted, the cost of tariffs could be passed on to consumers in higher prices.[84]

Is the Fashion Business Failing at Sustainability?

For anyone who tours the fashion recycling plant in Wolfen, Germany, the size and scope of fast fashion, and the willingness to buy and discard clothing, looks very clear.

The gargantuan I: CO plant, located about 85 miles southwest of Berlin, operates around the clock. It processes apparel dropped off at recycling banks from H&M stores across Europe and also from Levi's, Timberland and Nike. About 50 workers per shift sort through the 350 to 400 tons of clothing that arrive daily, mostly in yellow wire cubicles weighing 1 ton apiece. Denim is among the most popular materials coming through, and also one of the easiest to recycle.[85]

Yet recycling, even on such a massive scale, will not solve the global problem of disposable fashions. It clogs landfills in many U.S. cities and floods Kenya and Rwanda and elsewhere with cheap used clothing. Recycling techniques currently in use won't work on newer fibers or clothing made of two or more fibers. Many recycled fabrics may not be turned into clothing again, but must be mashed up and turned into insulation or other industrial products.

The real solution: "Fashion brands need to urgently rethink the throwaway business model and produce clothing that's durable, repairable and fit for re-use," said Kirsten Brodde, head of the environmental group Greenpeace's Detox My Fashion campaign. The project works with dozens of apparel brands to reduce their environmental footprint.[86]

Yet with the global growth of fast fashion and buyers' love of bargain clothing, a change in business models won't come easily. "Sustainability is important to some designers, but not all," says Givhan, adding that consumers bear some culpability in the growth of fashion throwaways.

Price, quality and recommendations from family or friends are more important in purchasing decisions than environmental or fair trade practices, according to a Euromonitor poll.[87]

U.S. Exports of Used Clothing Increase

Value rose by $97 million since 2011

More than $700 million worth of used clothing was exported from the United States to other countries in 2015. The value of such exports has grown by more than $97 million since 2011.

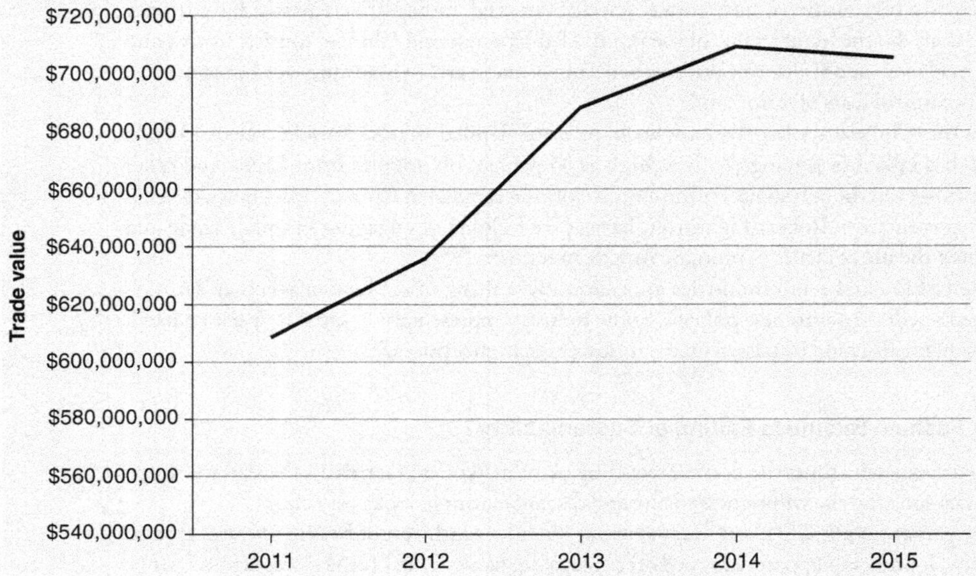

Note: Data represent trade value for worn clothing and other worn articles.

Source: DESA/UNSD, United Nations Comtrade database, http://tinyurl.com/hnl867l.

A recent Newsweek article detailed the limits of reusing and recycling fashions. It reported that only 0.1 percent of clothing that is reclaimed by retailers or donated to charities is turned into new textile fiber. Far more of it is thrown into landfills or incinerators—about 80 pounds per American each year, or double what it was 20 years ago. This has created what the magazine called an "environmental crisis," with leached chemicals getting into groundwater and ripped-up textile industries in several African countries.[88]

The global clothing recycling industry may not be able to keep up with the new castoffs; inventories are piling up and some recyclers have gone out of business in the United Kingdom and elsewhere.[89]

Consumers are buying more clothing and wearing them less. British women wear clothes only three to seven times, and then may throw them away, survey shows.[90] In the United States, the average person bought 67.9 garments in 2015, and 7.8 pair of shoes, according to the American Apparel and Footwear Association, up from 64 garments in 2013.[91]

Still, Greenpeace's Detox Fashion campaign has nudged mainstream fashion to more sustainable practices around water and other areas, Euromonitor said. "Greenwashing"—an insincere or superficial interest in environmental measures—is still commonplace even as more companies look for ways to reduce their environmental impact.[92]

Some smaller companies make eco-friendly fabric from bamboo, eucalyptus and other wood. and major fashion houses are slowly changing raw materials and processes. They want to become part of the "circular economy" in which nothing is wasted and everything is repaired or recycled or reused. This has led startups to develop platforms to resell clothing, among them The RealReal, Poshmark and Tradesy.[93]

Fashion companies, working in organizations such as the Sustainable Apparel Coalition, are sharing resources and creating goals to reduce their environmental footprints and improve working conditions, and to be transparent about their progress. A number have pledged to cut water and chemical usage.[94]

Yet it's complicated, because the fashion industry relies on many suppliers, and often, the new, more environmentally friendly methods are more costly—at least initially. "We are not an NGO specializing in sustainability. We are a corporation, and through our creativity we have to find economically viable solutions," said Francois-Henri Pinault, CEO of Kering, the fashion giant that owns Saint Laurent.[95]

Luxury brands are joining the green fashion initiatives, though often quietly. In June 2015, Kering released its first environmental profit and loss report, measuring water consumption, greenhouse gas emissions and air pollution. Producing its luxury goods cost the environment $838 million—half of it from the production of raw materials, such as greenhouse gases from cattle ranching. Yet neither Kering nor other couture brands "weave sustainability into the mysterious magic" of their brand's marketing, wrote Givhan in the Washington Post.[96]

Greenpeace, in a rating of fashion and retail brands called Detox the Catwalk, said many high-fashion brands "avoid tackling the problem with the seriousness it deserves." It singled out for praise H&M, Benetton and Inditex, owner of Zara.[97]

Progress continues even as discarded clothing piles up. So SOEX Group, which owns the huge 700-worker recycling plant in Wolfen, will build another one in the United Arab Emirates sometime in 2017.[98] It will employ around 400 people to sort and repackage clothing for export to Africa, the Middle East and elsewhere.[99]

BACKGROUND

A Tale of Three Women

When Gabrielle Chanel began making hats around 1905, she was a kept woman, a mistress whose restless energy required a creative outlet. Her ideas contradicted most of the fashion world as she created simple headwear followed years later by almost austere dresses and suits.

Her target customers were modern women like herself, those who wanted pockets and clothing that didn't demand corsets and frills and lace. Some were courtesans, others countesses or wealthy wives. "Coco" Chanel was a dressmaker who sewed together creativity, ambition and business sense, and a willingness to cultivate a mystique about herself and her background of poverty.

She became one of the best-known women in the fashion industry, then and now. By the 1930s, she was reportedly the wealthiest woman in France and her success drew poets and writers and painters to her. More than 85 books have been written about her.[100]

The history of the fashion industry is closely woven into the stories of some of its best-known designers from Linda Allard, a woman from Akron, Ohio, who was hired as a designer for $60 a week and went on to create the Ellen Tracy line; to Sonia Rykiel, who started out making maternity clothes for herself and became the queen of knitwear from her Paris studios. It is a story of entrepreneurship and risk-taking, of dropping out and coming back, as Chanel's ins and outs demonstrate.

Born in 1883 to an impoverished unmarried mother, Chanel grew up in small French towns. When her mother died, she, her sisters and brother were sent to live in a Catholic orphanage and school. It is said the nuns taught her to sew.

A dark, slender beauty, Chanel worked at a tailor's shop and also for a time as a music-hall singer in Paris, where she collected her nickname Coco because it figured in the refrain of one of her most popular songs. "She would become the muse, patron, collaborator or mistress of a number of remarkable men, including some of the most celebrated artists of modern times," such as Picasso, Cocteau, Dali and Diaghilev, wrote biographer Lisa Chaney.[101]

She made hats for noble women and courtesans. In 1913 she opened a hat shop in Paris, backed by a wealthy English lover. Chanel considered Arthur Capel, the rich British man who bankrolled her first business ventures, as her true love. Some believe the entwined CC in Chanel's logo stand for Chanel and Capel. (Others say they represent Coco Chanel.)[102]

When she was 30, Chanel designed and sold a comfortable knit suit that she first made for herself. The simple suit, similar to a school girl's uniform, became a staple of women's wardrobes.[103]

Her shop flourished and she soon started making custom clothing—for sport, for evening wear and for ladies' lunches. Many of her designs were intended to be worn without a corset, and gave women more freedom of movement, whether they worked in a department store or attended high society events.

Yet Chanel was not the first fashion designer to understand that women wanted clothing that suited their lives, perspectives and adventures.

Starting around 1850, a number of suffragettes started wearing "bloomers"—also called "Turkish trousers"—as a way to declare their independence or to exercise and build good health. (Fashionable young women in Europe wore them for recreation and exercise, and to masquerade balls and for informal portraits.[104]) Bloomers became closely associated with and took their name from Amelia Jenks Bloomer, a women's rights activist and editor of The Lily newspaper. She wrote about the pants and wore them to rallies, which encouraged other women to don them as well. Yet some wearing bloomers were scorned in person and in articles and cartoons, and it took decades for more women to adopt them as bicycling attire.[105]

Women's hemlines did not change during the 1800s, but the shape of their skirts certainly did, going from very narrow to wider and bell-like. The introduction of hoops reduced the need for layers of petticoats. The bustle—shaped and draped cloth added to the back of a woman's dress or suit—grew bigger or smaller in the late 1880s.[106]

During that time, John Redfern, an English designer, began to create tailor-made jackets and skirts for women who golfed or went yachting. Redfern, the son of a tailor, grew up on the Isle of Wight in England. Each year, European aristocrats and Americans would flock there for the Cowes Regatta. Redfern's fashionable deck-side dresses made of serge, jersey and silk became very popular and his reputation as a ladies' tailor soared.[107]

In 1876, Redfern & Sons opened a shop in London, and expanded to Paris in 1881 and Fifth Avenue in New York City in 1884.[108] Some fashion experts say his styles previewed the more relaxed women's clothing styles of the 20th century.[109]

In Paris, Chanel created style trends and previewed others. Her short hair prompted many women to adopt the boyish style. She was a strong, forceful manager who planned ahead for new products and embellishments to her fashions.[110]

Around 1924, she became one of the first fashion designers to create a perfume bearing her name. It was Chanel No. 5, the five because a fortune teller said it was her lucky number.[111] To bring Chanel No. 5 to market successfully, she partnered with two brothers named Wertheimer, who ran a major cosmetic company in France. They made, bottled and distributed her perfume and received 70 percent of its receipts; the owner of Galeries Lafayette, one of the major Paris department stores, received 20 percent for serving as connector and Chanel kept 10 percent. "The spectacular success of the scent cemented her fortune," wrote biographer Anka Muhlstein in the New York Review of Books.[112]

The Wertheimer family has held a controlling interest in Chanel's company since 1924, despite Chanel's efforts to unseat them in the 1930s.[113]

Then, three weeks after France and Britain declared war on Germany in 1939, Chanel closed her couture house and laid off most of her workers, with only her boutique at 31 rue Cambon remaining open selling perfumes and jewelry. Public opinion turned against her and trade unions and government begged her to reopen. She refused. "I had the feeling that we had reached the end of an era. And that no one would ever make [couture] dresses again," she said.[114]

While Chanel's business and reputation grew in the 1930s, Anne Elisabeth Jane Claiborne, another advocate for working women's clothing, was growing up in and around Brussels. Her father, a banker, wanted her to become a painter, so he took her to museums around Europe. Her mother, a fine seamstress, taught her to sew.[115]

She came from a prominent Louisiana family, yet her sensibility came from her early years in Belgium: "The look of things is as important as their function." When the Nazis started their European conquests, she moved to New Orleans in 1939 and decided to look to the fashion world for employment.[116]

She moved to New York, where she won a Harper's Bazaar design contest, and in 1950 landed a job as a sketcher for a Seventh Avenue sportswear designer.[117] Claiborne spent most of her career as a working mother; she had one son and two stepchildren from her second marriage to Arthur Ortenberg, who had hired her in that design job. In 1960, Claiborne was hired as the chief designer for the Jonathan Logan junior dress division. She spent years trying to convince senior management of the need for comfortable career clothing for women who worked.[118]

A New Start

In Paris, after the war, Chanel, bored without work, decided to restart her fashion house, and developed a line of clothing shown in a 1954 fashion show. It was largely panned by fashion writers for failing to adapt to the styles set by Christian Dior's more rich, feminine look.[119]

Yet she persevered, and in 1955 debuted the 2.55 handbag, quilted with a gold chain and leather shoulder strap. Strong and light, it allowed the woman's hands to remain free.[120] It initially sold for about $220; today they run closer to $4,900.[121]

Chanel very much liked wearing pants, even though a French law forbade women from wearing two-legged apparel except when riding bicycles or horses. The law stayed on the books until 2013.[122]

In the 1960s and 1970s, the fashion world took its cues from the women's rights movements. In 1960, 37.7 percent of U.S. women were working or looking for work: By 1980, that increased to 51.5 percent, and the labor force participation rate for women ages 25 to 34 nearly doubled in that span.[123] As women landed jobs as accountants, lawyers, professors and journalists, they needed professional wardrobes—and a new group of designers, many of them women, stepped up to outfit them.

In 1976, Claiborne, Ortenberg and a business partner established Liz Claiborne Inc. with a goal of offering a collection of fashions, displayed in one place so customers could mix and match pieces, and aimed at the array of women entering the workforce. "The clothes became an instant hit, and the company went public in 1981," said Givhan, The Post's fashion writer.[124]

Claiborne's wearable blouses and pants were less sophisticated than those of other 1980s designers such as Donna Karan and "Yuppie" designer Ralph Lauren, but they were brightly colored, professional and sold well. "I wanted to dress busy and active women like myself, women who dress in a rush and who weren't perfect," Claiborne said in 1989. "And I tried to bring good taste to a mass level."[125]

By 1985, Claiborne's company became the first Fortune 500 enterprise to be founded by a woman. And by the late 1980s, her clothing carpeted the major department store brands: Macy's, May Company, The Broadway and others. "I would go into Dayton's Department Store in Minneapolis, Minnesota, and marvel at how much acreage was devoted to the Liz Claiborne apparel," wrote Walter Loeb, an influential retail analyst. "Liz Claiborne was everywhere."[126]

That ubiquitousness worked against her, as department stores decided to create their own house brands or exclusive relationships with designers. Claiborne's company had acquired other brands such as Dana Buchman and Lucky jeans; the company's new management focused on them. Shoppers no longer connected to Claiborne, whose fashions felt dated.[127]

Miuccia Prada, born in 1949 in Milan, creates fashion that many say is intelligent and international. Yet she lives in the same building where she grew up, the granddaughter of the great fashion designer Mario Prada, who founded Prada in 1913. In the mid-1970s, she went to work for the family's fashion leather house, after receiving a doctorate in politics. She was a Communist, and hated the rigid tastes of that decade defined by designer brands.[128]

The youngest daughter, known to her family as Miu Miu, she launched the Miu Miu brand in 1993 to be more colorful and avant-garde than the rest of the fashion house.[129]

"Ugly Chic"

In the 1990s, she introduced Prada's take on "ugly chic"—attire that defies conventional views on what's attractive—and changed direction every season, a slap against Milan's consistency of style and silhouette. "There is a key point that people keep underestimating about me:

I am a very trendy person! I mean, my job is more complicated, but basically I am interested in what's next. Since I was 16, I wanted to be the first one," Prada told Harper's Bazaar.[130]

Like Chanel, she has championed the arts and funded filmmakers and an array of other creative endeavors. Some fashion writers say she is the closest thing to Chanel today, with a cultural recognition that extends far beyond the fashion world.[131]

Prada's talents as a designer spring from her intense curiosity and an understanding that fashion is both artistic and commercial—and that selling matters. "If people take money out of their pockets, it means that what you are doing is relevant to them. . . . To sell is to prove that what you are doing makes sense. I'm completely against the idea that we do fashion for an elite—that would be too easy, in a way," Prada said in 2013.[132]

Today, Forbes magazine ranks Prada as the 79th most powerful woman in the world.[133] The fashion house is a $3.96 billion company that must contend with volatility in currency markets and a slow move to online sales.[134] The Chanel brand, with headquarters in Paris and $5.2 billion in sales, is worth $7.2 billion.[135] And Liz Claiborne's brand was sold to J.C. Penney for $308 million in 2011 after posting losses since 2006. The decision forced the company to seek a new name: initially Fifth & Pacific Cos. Inc., then in 2014 Kate Spade & Co.[136]

CURRENT SITUATION

Speeding Up and Selling Online

Online sales now represent a growing share of all fashion merchandise sales. Independent fashion designers and boutiques must grab attention or find a niche or they will close, designer Kirondé and others say. And with "see now, buy now" becoming the norm, speed matters—even if designers must work long hours on incredibly tight deadlines

A Zara designer and pattern maker in Spain spent five days creating a loose-fitting winter coat based on a store manager's description of what women in New York and elsewhere wanted. After 20 more days of sewing and finishing, 8,000 of the coats—ironed, tagged and quality inspected—were flown from Barcelona to Zara's Fifth Avenue store in New York, priced at $189 each. Other clothing goes from idea to stores in only two weeks. "Think of Zara not as a brand but as a very speedy chameleon that adapts instantly to fashion trends," said Anne Critchlow, an analyst for the French bank Société Générale. By offering new designs that others do not yet have, Zara may charge more than its competitors.[137]

"See now, buy now" means the new clothing shown at Fashion Weeks are almost immediately available to consumers who used to have to wait six months or longer.

Prada sees no sense in the see now, buy now trend. "It's less creative and less interesting," and for quality brands, they may have to pretend that something is fresh and brand new when it was created months ago, she told WWD.[138]

The idea is to avoid consumer fatigue or boredom with styles, which show up on fashion blogs, in Instagram feeds and more for months before they're even in stores. Yet Givhan, the Washington Post critic, suggests that what's being shown on the runway and on Instagram is "not that great to begin with." Previews should increase the appeal, she says, noting that movie trailers are around for months and often whet the public's appetite to see the film.

Female Consumers Dominate Apparel Spending

Expenditures reach peak between ages 35 and 44

Women of all age groups consistently outspent their male counterparts on apparel in 2015. The average annual expenditures peaked for both groups in the 35–44 age range, with women spending $1,581 and men spending $961.

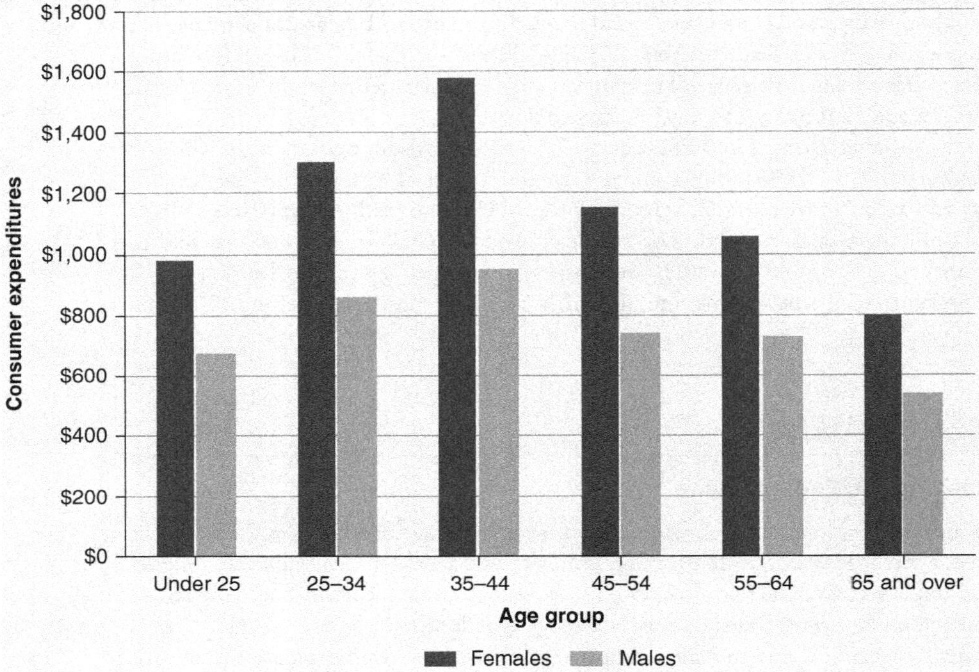

Source: "Singles by Age of Reference Person," Consumer Expenditure Survey, U.S. Bureau of Labor Statistics, Aug. 2016, https://www.bls.gov/cex/tables.htm#crosstab.

Amazon previewed its fashion and apparel aspirations in 2016 when it launched seven in-house brands of apparel and accessories for women, men and children. The labels, including Lark & Ro and Franklin Tailored, give no clue they are controlled by Amazon. The online marketplace started into apparel in 2009 with the purchase of Zappos, an online shoe site.[139]

Automation Spreading

The pace of change has accelerated in other ways too: with technology and innovations in fabric, new ways to share fashion digitally, and a growing use of robots or computerized sewing machines.

More than 80 percent of garment and footwear workers in Vietnam and Cambodia could lose their jobs to automation, according to the International Labour Organization.[140]

Reprogrammable robots could churn out new fashions and "shorten supply chains and lessen . . . lead times," Jonathan Zornow, founder of Sewbo, a garment robot startup, told Quartz.[141]

Garment workers in Bangladesh, Cambodia and elsewhere have attempted to unionize and staged several strikes over low wages and poor working conditions. In some cases wages increased, although they often remained below their government's living wage measures.[142]

Burnout among designers may be another problem. "The fashion cycle: Does it cause designers to burn out? Brands were producing two or four or six collections in a year, some of these brands are producing like 12, and it's kind of crazy," says Givhan.

Yet companies that develop systems and expectations for speed may have an advantage. "Since the beginning, the idea has been to understand what the customer wants first and then have an integrated manufacturing and logistics system to be able to deliver it to them quickly," Pablo Isla, chairman and chief executive of Zara parent Inditex, said.[143]

Some say "slow fashion"—where stages and players in the production are carefully considered and documented—may be an antidote to the burnout and environmental worries. It's intended to be ethical and mindful.[144]

Fashion boutiques that continue to develop fresh, interesting designers will find a following online on Farfetch or one of its competitors. "They sell things that nobody has,

Athletic Wear Scored Strongest Sales Growth Last Year

Luxury sector was weakest performer in 2016

Sales in the athletic wear sector of the fashion industry grew by 8.5 percent in 2016 over the previous year, more than double that of any other category. Sales in the luxury sector increased by only 1 percent, while the total global industry grew by 2.5 percent.

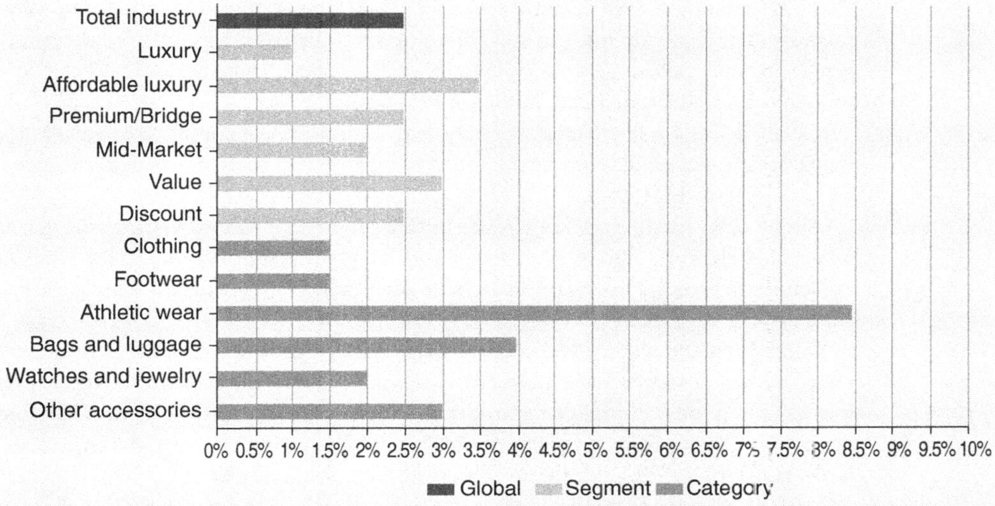

Note: "The State of Fashion 2020" is available at https://tinyurl.com/y73rteuz.

Source: Imran Amed et al., "The State of Fashion 2017," McKinsey & Company, Dec. 2016, http://tinyurl.com/zevx5gj.

incredibly different, fabulous things. You won't find them elsewhere," says Kirondé, who in 2011 launched a fashion line based on creating a better white shirt for women. Those that stick with old ways or offer up fashions that are widely available will die, she says.

More fashion and beauty brands—and in particular sneaker companies—use "the drop," a carefully timed release to sell limited edition items quickly. Kanye West's Yeezy line for Adidas and several designers' collaborations on limited edition lines for Target and H&M sell out quickly, online or in shops—and then often are resold at twice the price on various reseller sites. Individuals share their score, then post and resell them on DePop and other sites.[145]

Yet they are not heading out to shop. Kenneth Cole will shut all 63 outlet stores to focus on online sales.[146] Other apparel retailers are facing what is known as "the Amazon effect"—sales lost to lower-cost, easy-to-shop online marketplace: American Eagle, Macy's and others all are closing many stores.[147]

Online shopping and promotion contribute to a flood of counterfeit fashion items sold on Amazon, eBay and in pop-up stores and less scrupulous retailers. In the European Union the cost of counterfeit fashion apparel—from coats and skirts to shoes—is 26.3 billion euros ($27.7 billion as of early January), or 9.7 percent of total sales, and at least 363,000 jobs lost. Organized crime syndicates from China or Morocco set up factories in Italy and elsewhere and use social media to sell the fake shoes or capes.[148]

Some brands are fighting back. Alexander Wang won a $90 million judgment in 2016 after suing the owners of 459 websites believed to be selling counterfeit clothing, handbags and shoes. The court transferred their domain names to the fashion designer.[149]

The fashion industry is growing into niches, offering growth prospects and opportunities to those catering to new buyers who have fewer choices or more cash.

"Kinky Boots," a 1999 documentary turned 2005 movie, told of a Northamptonshire shoe manufacturer that moved from tired designs to creating sparkling boots and shoes for transgender men. Today, an array of companies create lingerie, shoes and suits for the up to 3.2 million transgender individuals in the United States.[150]

LBGTQ fashion has a longer history, but "Single's Day" and androgynous fashions—jackets, shirts, jeans and suits that may be worn by men or women or men becoming women—are two fast-growing trends.

Single's Day has turned into China's busiest online shopping day of the year. The online retailer Alibaba sells billions, and the tally for all e-retailers was $55 billion. It could take hold in Denmark, France, Finland or Australia, among the countries with at least one-sixth of their adult population single.[151]

Single men and women and couples may buy into genderless clothing, which focuses on jeans, shirts and jackets for all. Despite issues about fitting both men and women, they are increasingly trendy and marketed under such labels as ungendered, gender-fluid and gender-neutral. "It's a tricky, complicated thing" to fit hips and legs to men and women simultaneously, said Tim Kaeding, Mother Denim designer and co-founder.[152]

Fashion brands and retailers also are starting to catch on to the myriad ways that consumers want to shop. It varies considerably by age and life stage, and also by their interests and the "channels and retailers that each generation grew up with," reported NPD Group and Wharton. Yet all generations want one-stop or convenient shopping, value and leisure and entertainment as they shop.[153]

Generation X, those ages 34 to 44, shop more at department stores than other age groups, while Baby Boomers favor warehouse clubs for apparel and accessories as well as groceries and gas, The NPD Group report found. And across all age cohorts, the largest share of online dollars was spent on travel, apparel, electronics and home and kitchen.

While buying online continues to be a major influence for fashion brands, becoming the next big thing has proved more difficult—especially if you're not named Kardashian or Trump. Only rarely does Project Runway, the U.S. reality TV show depicting designers creating, really launch a major brand.[154]

By failing to bring about a huge success, Givhan wrote, the show "offered a nuanced tale about what success means in today's fashion industry, why it is so difficult and why it mostly has nothing to do with having one's name up in lights."[155]

LOOKING AHEAD

Smart Clothing

Before long, your clothing may be an eclectic mix of fabric made of vegetable or organic matter and tech tags that log onto the internet and provide invitations to VIP events.

Perhaps a sensor in the pocket of your jacket will alert you when you are within 100 feet of someone who attended your university or is part of your social circle, creating opportunities to connect and converse.[156]

A new coat will be embedded with sensors that serve up tickets to an event by the apparel manufacturer or instructions on washing that will be transmitted directly to the wearer's washing machine. Avery Dennison, the company that makes care labels for clothing, is working with designers on such internet-connected clothing and has a goal of 10 billion connected pieces.[157]

The Janela "smart products" platform will allow buyers to check the authenticity or manufacturing history of the pants purchased, see exclusive smartphone content, order other products and participate in loyalty programs. "Products are able to be born digital," Cisco CEO Niall Murphy said.[158]

Technological and other advances will weave their way into 3-D printed clothing and smart fabrics. Augmented reality and "magic mirrors" with high definition cameras will transport shoppers to catwalks or advise them on possible purchases.[159]

Fashion will be much more personalized for a consumer's taste and size, The Post's Givhan and others say.

Within a decade, an array of "open source" fashion items may be available to download and print on home 3-D printers, futurist Ray Kurzweil predicted. New forms of printers and printing materials will overcome the stiff, synthetic quality that makes printing fabric difficult now. And fashion brands will follow the music and media sectors in adapting to the reduced control over manufacturing, execution and other factors, Kurzweil said.[160]

Expect more performance clothing to help swimmers, runners and other athletes compete better. Already a British company has created a triathlon suit and other tools with performance enhancements carefully measured by the founders.[161]

One such advance is a fabric created by Stanford University professors that will allow heat to pass through it and also wick away sweat. Its aim is to cool people off during warmer weather; it could be ready for commercial use by 2018.[162]

Fashion brands will adopt new technologies to meet social and environmental concerns. A company is developing DNA-based technology to prevent counterfeiting, clarify the origin and avoid cotton apparel produced with slave labor.[163] Researchers at Birmingham City University in England are developing connected clothing that will contact charity shops or eBay and put themselves up for sale if they are not worn for a long time—after first tweeting or chatting with the owner, reminding that they are being neglected. Researchers hope to address overconsumption of clothing and the related environmental damage.[164]

At the Massachusetts Institute of Technology, a team of design, engineering and occupational therapy students adjust their prototype design of a shirt. As their summer ends at the Open Style Lab program, they may have created clothing that will help an autistic girl named Eliza Mury concentrate better and learn more in school. The Open Style Lab has turned into an incubator for functional fashion that serves a niche of people with disabilities or other needs. Though each design is personalized for one client's needs, it also is intended to be adapted for a wider audience.[165]

Having clothing that collects data and transmits and collects it via the cloud raises privacy concerns. Could your new jacket track your whereabouts? Data protection and consumer trust must be sewn into the future clothing, Cisco's Murphy said.[166]

Another trend will turn recycled food, from banana leaves to salmon skins, into clothing and shoes. One Madrid-based company named Ecoalf uses old coffee grounds and discarded plastic bottles to create insulated vests, purses and shoes.[167]

And for those who want something more fashionable, Apichet "Madaew'" Atirattana, a transgender designer from Thailand, uses cabbage leaves and foliage, chicken wire and other found objects in his attire. Atirattana, whom Time magazine called one of the world's "Next Generation Leaders," is already partnering with a major Thai artist and maker—at 17.[168]

Chronology

1860s–1940s	**Fashion brands and designers rise—and so do knockoffs.**
1860	The Englishwoman's Domestic Magazine sells mail-order paper dress patterns. The magazine catered to middle-class women and was inexpensive.
1873	Levi Strauss and Jacob Davis invent blue jeans with their patent for "improvement in fastening pocket-openings"—rivets. The Levi 501 jeans would evolve from the working man's uniform to 1950s fashion must-have.
1892	Arthur Baldwin Turnure creates Vogue as a weekly magazine for the social elite.
1900s	Paris rises as the haute couture capital with the designs of Coco Chanel, Jeanne Lanvin and Paul Poiret.
1912	Simpson Crawford Co., a U.S. manufacturer, advertises its American adaption of a $485 Parisian Drecoll gown. Simpson's version sold for $24.75. It was part of a wave of American manufacturers copying French fashion.

1919	Value of the U.S. ready-to-wear industry rises to $1.2 billion, accounting for one of the country's largest manufacturing sectors behind food, and iron and steel manufacturing.
1929	With the U.S. stock market crash, fashion prices drop and the comparison-price shopper emerges.
1932	The "Letty Lynton" dress, worn by film star Joan Crawford and designed by Gilbert Adrian, sells more than 50,000 copies at Macy's.
1939	Nylon debuts at the New York World's Fair as a replacement for silk stockings, but the material was removed from the U.S. civilian market during World War II to go for military parachute manufacturing.
1947	Christian Dior makes fashion history with his "New Look" collection debut. Emphasizing the feminine look, Dior's collection took advantage of the end of fabric rationing.
1950s–1960s	**Consumerism expands, teenagers emerge as a market.**
1953	Black designer Ann Lowe, already known for her dressmaking in debutante circles, crafts Jacqueline Bouvier's wedding dress for her marriage to John F. Kennedy. Ann Lowe Originals Inc. would open in the 1960s on New York's Madison Avenue.
1954	Audrey Hepburn wears her first design by Hubert de Givenchy in the movie "Sabrina." . . . Coco Chanel, who closed her couture house at the start of World War II, stages her comeback fashion show and reopens her Paris shop.
1960	John Fairchild, the new editor of Women's Wear Daily, criticizes future first lady Jacqueline Kennedy for wearing French haute couture and not supporting American designers.
1966	The miniskirt, whose origins are credited to London designer Mary Quant and others, becomes mainstream U.S. fashion.
1968	Katiti Kirondé, a Harvard undergrad, becomes the first African-American woman on the cover of a fashion magazine, appearing in the August issue of Glamour.
1970s–1990s	**Power suits become popular for both genders in the workforce.**
1971	Vivienne Westwood brings punk to London with her shop Let it Rock and promotes her own designs via the punk rock band Sex Pistols in 1976.
1974	Designer Diane von Furstenberg creates the wrap dress to great success, and in 1976 she lands on the cover of Newsweek wearing her iconic creation.
1982	Amid a national recession, the unemployment rate for apparel workers hits 14.1 percent.
1983	J.C. Penney seals an exclusive deal with American designer Halston for the Halston III dress line. Luxury department store Bergdorf Goodman drops Halston over the discount line, which had dresses retailing at $100, one-tenth of Halston's high-end prices.
1984	"Dynasty," the hit ABC prime-time soap opera, obtains licensing rights to make upscale products, the first time a clothing line is inspired by its characters.

(Continued)

(Continued)

1992	Donna Karan previews her spring collection with the ad campaign "In Women We Trust." Model Rosemary McGrotha wears Karan's tailored looks in ads showing her being sworn into political office, which some speculate was the presidency.
2000s–Present	**Fashion goes online and up- and down-market.**
2000	Luxury meets the internet with Natalie Massenet's Net-a-Porter website catering to high-fashion taste.
2004	Hermès International stops taking names for its two-and-half-year waiting list for the Hermès Birkin bag, which has a starting price of $6,000. . . . Chanel designer Karl Lagerfeld announces his ready-to-wear collection exclusively available through fast-fashion retailer H&M.
2008	A severe economic contraction helps coin new phrases in the fashion industry: "Recession Chic," or "Recessionista." Anna Wintour, editor of American Vogue, reinforces the terms with the December issue, focusing on style for a tough economy.
2010	Burberry live-streams in 2-D and 3-D its fall show from London, becoming the first major fashion brand to utilize this technology. As part of the live stream, Burberry offers direct-from-runway ordering; costumers could place an order within seven days on about 20 garments and all the bags worn during the show.
2011	Greenpeace begins its Detox Fashion campaign, challenging sportswear makers to commit to a toxic-free future. . . Designer-shoe maker Christian Louboutin sues Yves Saint Laurent over trademark infringement involving the former's red sole. The New York Court of Appeals would rule in favor of Yves Saint Laurent in 2012, holding that Louboutin's red sole was protected except when the shoe itself is red.
2016	Christie's sells the most expensive handbag ever sold at auction: a $300,168 Hermès Birkin bag made of white matte Himalaya crocodile leather with 18-karat white gold and diamond hardware.

—Rivan Stinson

Discussion Questions

Here are some questions for discussion on the fashion industry and the changes that are buffeting it:

- Why do you think the fashion industry, according to its critics, has been reluctant to design clothes for plus-size women, even though they are a growing segment of the market?
- Is there a difference between Millennials and other generations in the way they shop for clothes?
- If you were trying to get a fashion brand off the ground, what or whom would you seek out as an effective influencer? Who or what exerts the biggest influence on you when you buy clothes?
- Do you think the move toward more casual clothes in the workplace has improved or damaged productivity?

PERSPECTIVE

Q&A: Matthew Mueller on Industry Trends

"WHEN SOMEONE SAYS THE FASHION INDUSTRY IS GOING OUT OF FASHION, THEY'RE WRONG"

Matthew Mueller

A large number of men tend to be like Matthew Mueller was, dreading shopping and preferring to pick up a suit off the rack—until 2010, when he and John Ballay started Knot Standard. The company is a menswear online retailer, which allows shoppers to customize suits from their computers with the help of stylists and a speedy supply chain. In an interview with SAGE Business Researcher editorial assistant Anika Reed, he discusses modern disruptions in the fashion industry and his company's take on luxury. The interview has been edited for clarity and length.

How did you get started in fashion?

Part of our DNA and why we have succeeded where other people haven't is in our origins. My fashion background actually began with a custom-suit gift voucher that my wife bought me while we were living in Dubai. I ended up going down the rabbit hole of an entire industry and an entire supply chain. And I think that's a pretty good parallel for most American male consumers: Go to the department store, buy something that you like.

We started by making suits and selling them online; we were really kind of the second company to do an online custom suit maker store. My co-founder, [who was] living in Dubai at the time, comes from a finance background, and I come from an IT background, and I was basically over there building hospitals in the Middle East. It's a very different industry. But coming into fashion and learning about fabric mills and learning the way these things are manufactured and how antiquated the entire process was, it blew my mind. Our supposition was that there was a better way.

Is the fashion industry going out of fashion?

From a very macro perspective, when someone says the fashion industry is going out of fashion, they're wrong. Until natural selection ceases to exist, there will be fashion. Clothes will be part of fashion. Your social media profile is fashion. What's in your garage, believe it or not, is fashion. If you don't think you're picking the interior fabrics and leather for your car for a reason, you're crazy. As long as there is a measuring stick as simple and as global as what you wear, fashion will be around.

What you're seeing now is traditional retail, where you come up with collections, you launch the collections and then you see how it sells over months or even years—that's what's dying. It's dying because of speed. It's not dying because looking good is out of fashion or going to a store to buy clothes is necessarily out of fashion, it's dying because [between] the time you bought that sweater and went home, three of your friends have already had it delivered and posted on a social media profile.

Speed and convenience are not killing fashion; they're changing it. The only thing I see as universal here and permanent is competition—competition to be the most fashionable. The game will change and the tools will change, but being the most fashionable, being the best dressed, or looking like you're successful is never going to stop being important until someone figures out how to kill natural selection.

What challenges have occurred that you didn't expect?

The first thing that kind of surprised us was how it would work when you want to get a client to try something new. You see the look on their face when they get something that they were really worried about for three or four weeks, a stylist or something they read online pushed them out of their comfort zone, [and] that therefore becomes their new best in their closet.

You get something that's a little bit tighter than something you would normally wear or [has] a slightly bolder liner or a highlighted thread, and it all of a sudden becomes the thing you're most proud of. We've actually centered our corporate culture on creating pride. Because, as cheesy as it sounds, that is literally what we do. The guys will stand up a little bit straighter, feel a little bit more confident and know that they look good. We've shifted their thinking; we've educated them a little bit. What's really surprised me is the level to which guys are willing to be educated.

What are the best ways to get started in fashion, especially for recent college graduates?

Well, getting a job is similar to a product in that you can work in a job that already exists and be better, faster [and] cheaper. Or you can create something new that disrupts the industry a little bit, and that's being an entrepreneur versus being an employee.

There are two different ways to going about it. I do not know a single venture capitalist or angel investor who thinks

(*Continued*)

(Continued)

being an entrepreneur is a good idea. Everybody loves the entrepreneurs, but it is a tough, tough thing to do. You need to find out that thing that you spike in. Everyone is going to be really, really good at a few things, especially by the time you've been in school for almost 20 years. You're going to know something better than the people around you, and you're going to be faster and better at it. And you may not even know what that is or have a good understanding of it until you get into the workforce and get pressure tested. The very first thing that people should do is get pressure tested. Do something you don't think you're necessarily good at. If you turn out to be good at it, learn from it. If you find out that you truly aren't good at it, what parts did you do well? What parts did you not do well? And now figure out what you want to do with this skill set.

What are Knot Standard's growth plans?

I'll address the most popular question first, which is, "Do you make clothes for women?" We can do it, but it's beholden to the same economics as any other brand would be beholden to. Just because we can do it doesn't mean we can instantly launch a line for women. That would take some expansion, and there's so much growth on the men's side that I think we need to focus on that first, and that's similar to children's to an extent.

The same rules apply for international. We started in Dubai, so we're an international company by nature. We do order processing in two global locations; we buy our fabrics from England and Belgium and Italy; we manufacture in multiple locations, from Asia to Brooklyn to LA. We're probably one of the most multicultural fashion companies out there. We will be doing our first new international showrooms [in 2017] both in Canada and the U.K. It's simply a question of management and doing a good job. We don't do disappointment.

How are you tailoring your business to reach out to people who typically wouldn't know much about custom suits?

We only outreach to people whom we haven't worked with before, and for the most part it's with people who haven't had custom suits before. The next year, the first thing we're doing is something we've just launched. We have this wonderful virtual reality technology, and we have stylists assigned to every single client. Why not let the designer, every month, similar to a subscription service, design outfits for you? Deliver them to you in virtual reality in an email, all customized, and made from scratch for you, and do that monthly. Since we don't have a warehouse, we make it [the email service] free.

That for us is the next frontier and turning [our customers] into [saying], "I have now seen more things that would look good on me in three emails over three months than I have seen in my entire life browsing through Sunday newspaper ads."

UPDATE IN 2020

In 2020, the prevailing atmosphere in the fashion industry was one of fear. Up and down the supply chain, manufacturers and retailers were fearful of the permanent impact that COVID-19 would have on their goods and employees.

Even before the pandemic hit, retailing experts were feeling little optimism about the outlook for the industry.

In the United States, figures from the Bureau of Labor Statistics showed that spending on apparel was lagging. It rose 1.8 percent in 2018 compared with 2017, but was up only 0.9 percent in 2019 from the year before.

While some analysts predicted American consumers would shift spending instead to entertainment, that did not seem to play out. Entertainment spending rose only 0.7 percent in 2018 compared with the previous year, and fell 4.2 percent in 2019.[169]

In 2019, U.S. President Trump launched a trade dispute with China, threatening to impose a 15 percent tariff on imports of $350 billion in Chinese goods, including the first levies on apparel. The two countries subsequently signed a trade agreement that cut the tariff in half, but it still affected about $250 billion of imports, including $3.7 billion in textile imports.[170]

The trade war only helped accelerate a shift by manufacturers out of China and into neighboring Asian countries. Since the start of Trump's presidency, a variety of fashion companies, such as Uniqlo, Levi's and Crocs, had moved operations out of China. "There is a real sense of panic," said Sean Coxall, the president of solutions at Hong Kong-based supply chain manager Li & Fung.[171]

In the beginning of 2020, consulting firm McKinsey & Co. predicted that global fashion retailers would grow 3 percent to 4 percent during the year, blaming cautiousness in consumers, the threat of further trade wars that could cut off the supply of goods from Asia and political upheaval.[172]

It forecast that Asia was best suited to withstand any weakness in the fashion industry since sales were still growing, while Europe was suffering from a wider malaise and uncertainty about Brexit. American consumers, it said, were uncertain about spending as the 2020 presidential election approached.

As it turned out, that view was far too optimistic.

In the immediate wake of the pandemic, retail sales in the U.S. fell a record 14.7 percent in April 2020, on top of an 8.2 percent decline in March. The Boston Consulting Group estimated that fashion retail sales fell as much as 80 percent in April.[173]

Retail sales in China fell 8.6 percent in the first eight months of 2020, stalled by shutdown orders and a slow return by businesses. But they began to recover in August, as consumers and producers began to recover from the pandemic.[174]

In the fall, American retailers including Amazon decided to stage sales well before the Christmas holidays, hoping to entice consumers to spend more. Still, significant damage was done to the global retail environment, as big-name department store chains and fashion houses sought bankruptcy protection.[175]

On April 1, Germany's biggest retailer, Galeria Karstadt Kaufhof, filed for insolvency after losing $90 million in revenue per week. On April 6, Britain's Debenham's announced it would appoint an administrator, the British equivalent of Chapter 11. On May 4, the United States' J. Crew filed for bankruptcy protection, while the Neiman-Marcus department store chain followed on May 7. J.C. Penney, Pier 1 Imports and Tuesday Morning followed within days.[176]

In March 2020, 46,000 employees in the U.S. retail sector lost their jobs. Vogue Business estimated that millions of workers in factories across Asia were affected when factories that produced garments for the world's retailers closed.

Meanwhile, in Europe, the retail fairs and fashion weeks that were so crucial to showing off designers' wares were shifted to fall dates.

Designer Giorgio Armani, in an unusual statement, pleaded for his fellow designers to shift away from the "fast fashion" that had dominated the retail environment during the first 20 years of the 21st century.[177] Instead, Armani said the industry would be better served by reverting to "slow fashion"—well-made goods that consumers could keep for years.

"Luxury cannot and must not be fast," he said. "A careful and intelligent slowdown is the only way out, a road that will finally bring value back to our work, and that will make final customers perceive its true importance and value."

His plea echoed a growing movement among environmentalists, who were urging consumers to restyle their clothes or purchase from second-hand stores, rather than buy all-new garments.

Some fashion experts predicted that a focus on sustainability could be the key to the industry's rebound. Despite the plunge during the spring, the Boston Consulting Group forecast that the industry might wind up with a sales decline of only 10 percent to 15 percent for 2020, if it could shift quickly enough.

"This should be used as the blueprint for how we come out of the crisis and how we make sustainability relevant within our companies, if perhaps they had not been previously," said Kate Heiny, the director of corporate responsibility at online retailer Zalando. "Now is the time for a clear sustainability strategy and ambitious goals."[178]

—*Micheline Maynard*

9 FREE TRADE

Is its age of expansion at an end?

Matthew Benjamin

From *SAGE Business Researcher*, March 13, 2017

EXECUTIVE SUMMARY

Is the era of trade liberalization that began in 1945 over? The collapse of world trade talks in 2008, Great Britain's shocking vote last year to leave the European Union and the election of President Trump on an anti-globalization platform suggest that it might be. The gains from trade for both advanced and emerging economies are hotly debated. While economic globalization lifted hundreds of millions from poverty, developing countries have balked at further trade talks dominated by rich nations. Workers in industrialized countries have begun to doubt that free trade is a net positive for them, and politicians have responded with an about-face on new agreements. For supporters of global economic integration, the way forward is unclear.

Among the key takeaways:

- World trade fell precipitously during the Great Recession of 2007–2009, and dropped again in 2015 by nearly 14 percent.
- A trade war—possibly sparked by new U.S. policies, followed by retaliatory tariffs by China and other trade partners—could result in massive job losses in the United States and elsewhere and trigger a recession.
- Further trade liberalization looks unlikely in the near term; merely maintaining current levels of integration may require new strategies and policies.

OVERVIEW

Joe Del Signore Jr. runs a catering business in Johnstown, Pa., and has voted for Democrats his entire life. Until last November, that is, when the 60-year old pulled the lever for Donald Trump in the presidential election, because "we needed a change in the way the country was being run."

One of Del Signore's biggest concerns was jobs, especially those lost to deindustrialization in this part of Western Pennsylvania. "We lost thousands of jobs in the last 15 years in coal, steel and railroads," says Del Signore. "Free trade had gone too far. We were being taken advantage of in so many areas."

Del Signore's vote, along with those of more than 2.9 million other Pennsylvanians, handed the swing state and its 20 electoral votes to Trump, who campaigned on promises to upend U.S. trade and immigration policies.

Largely because of people like Del Signore, the growth of international free trade is at a potential inflection point, as voters in the United States and around the world turn against global integration and politicians follow their lead. The costs of a global trade contraction could be significant in terms of economic growth and geopolitical stability; yet a path forward even to maintain the current level of trade is difficult and may require more compromise and political courage than politicians can muster in the near term.

The depth of this challenge can be gauged on different levels: the hard data of trade flows and the more subjective attitudes of policy makers and their constituents.

Global trade expanded at a rapid pace for six decades following World War II. It was particularly brisk from 1985 to 2007, a period that "witnessed substantial globalization and rapid economic growth," when trade grew twice as fast as global gross domestic product (GDP), according to the International Monetary Fund.[1]

The Great Recession of 2007–2009 interrupted that trend and sent trade volumes plummeting. They recovered by 2011, but not robustly. The volume of world trade, both goods and services, has grown around 3 percent a year since 2012, less than half the average rate of the previous three decades.[2] The slowdown is largely due to weaker economic growth in advanced and emerging economies.

These figures concern many economists, who believe the growth of trade has significantly contributed to the overall welfare of people in advanced and emerging economies alike.[3]

But a thornier problem is now emerging for proponents of growing free trade. The appetite for economic integration—the free movement of people, investment or goods across borders—is waning in both poor and rich nations.

The former expressed their discontent about trade liberalization in the first decade of this century when they collectively put a halt to the latest round of World Trade Organization (WTO) negotiations, in the belief that rich countries were not treating them fairly.[4] The latter found their voice in recent anti-globalization votes in Great Britain and the United States, as well as the rise of anti-immigrant and anti-trade political parties in many European nations.

Pedro Pardo/AFP/Getty Images

The Trans-Pacific Partnership and other trade deals have sparked opposition in many nations, including Mexico, where this woman demonstrated in 2016.

As a result, additional trade liberalization through the WTO is, for the moment at least, completely off the table. Free-trade deals that have been in the works for years, including the Trans-Pacific Partnership (TPP) and the U.S.-EU Transatlantic Trade and Investment Partnership (TTIP), have been abandoned by the United States, which may ultimately doom them. Meanwhile, the pace of new treaties globally has slowed significantly, and existing ones, including the North American Free Trade Agreement (NAFTA), may be scaled back. Barriers to trade are suddenly being erected at an alarming pace, according to the WTO.[5] These developments portend not just a halt to greater levels of trade, but a possible contraction.

"At this point in time what we don't need is the slamming of the door on trade," Roberto Azevêdo, the WTO's director-general, told the Financial Times in June. "Quite the contrary, we need to get trade going."[6]

But there is a growing chorus of voices that disagree vehemently with that conclusion. "Right now we are at the delegitimization stage of the Free Trade 101 folks," says Michael Stumo, chief executive officer of the Coalition for a Prosperous America, a Washington-based think tank that advocates a more restrictive kind of trade policy.

Stumo and like-minded opponents of the current global trade system don't dispute the assertion that free trade has lifted hundreds of millions from poverty in recent decades. But they point out that the vast majority of those people reside in developing nations, particularly in Asia, while advanced economies may have paid the price for it.

"Globalization, the way it's been implemented, has delivered a very bad, unhappy situation for millions of people in the top 20 countries of the world," says Stumo's colleague, Jeff Ferry, who serves as the organization's research director.

According to research done by former World Bank economist Branko Milanovic, workers in developing countries—predominantly China, India, Thailand, Vietnam and Indonesia—have reaped substantial benefits from globalization that occurred between 1988 and 2008.[7] Rich citizens of advanced economies—call them the elites—also benefited. Who did not? The lower middle class in the rich world, says Milanovic. And more and more residents of those economies are coming to believe that the much-touted gains from trade have evaded them and that it is time to do something about it.

Yet there is considerable evidence that residents of wealthier nations have indeed benefited from trade. The Obama administration, which pushed but failed to finalize the TPP accord before it left office in January, enumerated those benefits in a May 2015 document assembled by the White House's Council of Economic Advisers.[8] The document said that:

- Trade agreements lower foreign barriers to U.S. exports
- Exporting firms pay higher wages to U.S. workers than non-exporting firms
- The lower prices on imported goods that trade allows have significantly boosted the purchasing power, and thus the real wages, of middle-class Americans
- Trade increases the productivity of businesses and the broader economy
- Trade has produced significant benefits for U.S. agriculture and services firms

All of that equals faster economic growth, trade enthusiasts say. One well-known 2008 study by economists Romain Wacziarg and Karen Horn Welch found that countries that liberalized their trade regimes grew faster by about 1.5 percentage points than they did before liberalization.[9] And there are a host of similar studies.[10]

A major problem for free trade, proponents argue, is one of optics: The gains from it are diffuse—low prices at Wal-Mart, for example—while the harmful effects are concentrated and highly visible in terms of displaced workers, shuttered factories and lower incomes. Making a better argument for trade is a big part of the solution, trade supporters say, as is compensating the losers from trade through programs such as the U.S. Trade Adjustment Assistance program, which offers retraining, job search aid and income subsidies.

Disruptions from trade, as with any economic change, cause some jobs to vanish and others to emerge. This kind of churn is healthy and normal in an economy. Yet it is much

American Support for Free Trade Declining

Most still believe free-trade deals are good for the U.S.

Although a plurality thinks free-trade agreements have benefited the United States, the percentage of Americans who believe free trade is a bad deal has risen 12 points since 2014.

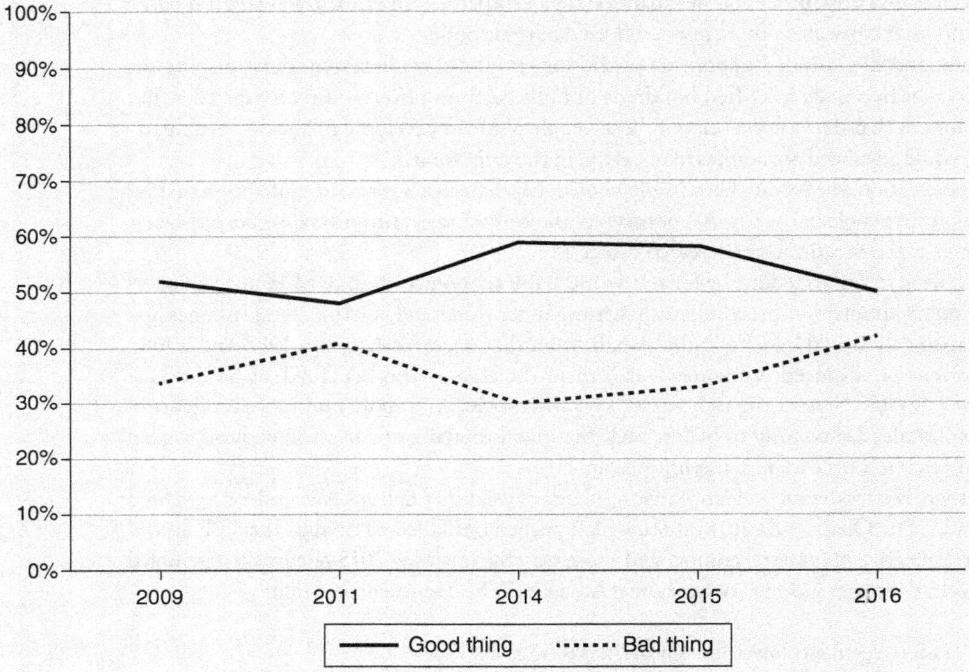

Source: Katie Simmons and Bruce Stokes, "Populism and Global Engagement: Europe, North America and Emerging Economies," Pew Research Center, Dec. 15, 2016, http://tinyurl.com/z9kupuj.

more difficult to deal with when a nation has a weak social safety net, as does the United States, says economic historian William Bernstein. "You can't have free trade without a generous social safety net, especially healthcare coverage," says Bernstein. Consider, he says, that the loss of a manufacturing job in the United States can mean the loss of that worker's healthcare insurance, a limited period of unemployment insurance compensation (26 weeks in most states) and often a lower-paying replacement job in retail or healthcare. The United States spends far less than other advanced economies on programs to help workers dislocated by trade, according to a study by the Brookings Institution, a centrist Washington-based think tank.[11]

Another problem, free-trade advocates say, is that, while advanced economies are gaining from free trade, the gains are not evenly distributed. While trade went gangbusters in recent decades, the real incomes of some two-thirds of households in 25 rich nations were stagnant or fell from 2005 to 2014, according to a July 2016 report by the McKinsey Global Institute.[12] A survey in the study found that those workers whose incomes did not rise had negative views of trade and immigration.

A better safety net would smooth the rough edges of free trade by helping those displaced by it regain their footing, improving education so more workers can benefit from trade and even redistributing more of the gains through the tax code, according to Matthew Slaughter, dean of the Tuck School of Business at Dartmouth College and former economic adviser to President George W. Bush. "There are decades of research that says first best policies are to continue to be connected to the global economy and use the fiscal regime of taxes, transfers and other policies to create and adequately fund a social safety net to those who aren't being directly helped by trade," says Slaughter.

Opponents of the current global system say this is off the mark. They maintain that so-called free trade has actually been rigged trade. The underlying idea of free trade, 19th century British political economist David Ricardo's theory of comparative advantage, held that residents of all countries could benefit by focusing on producing things they were best at. But that system also assumed a world in which all nations played by the same rules. And that, say critics, has not been the case over the last 70 years.

"The premise of our trade negotiations since 1950, whether we were negotiating with the European Union, Korea, Japan, or whoever, is that we're all playing the same game," says Clyde Prestowitz, president of the Economic Strategy Institute, a Washington-based think tank. "That premise is wrong. We're playing tennis and they're playing football."

He points to non-tariff measures used by U.S. trading partners that give unfair advantages to companies manufacturing within their borders. These range from interventions to keep their currencies artificially low (which benefits exporters) to industrial subsidies, state-owned companies and national champions, intellectual property theft and more.

"There are lots of ways outside of tariffs to preference your own companies," says Stumo. "Our trade partners are using all of them, and we are not."

Even though the United States and European nations continue to maintain protectionist trade policies in agriculture, Stumo's argument is gaining traction among citizens of advanced economies. And it has become intertwined with concerns about immigration, whether those concerns stem from resentment about competition for jobs, strains on social safety nets or fears about terrorism.

As economists, policy makers and ordinary citizens debate the merits of free trade, here are some of the main issues under discussion.

WEIGHING THE ISSUES

Is Globalized Trade the Main Reason for Manufacturing Job Losses in the United States and Other Developed Countries?

Economic truth, like beauty, is frequently in the eye of the beholder. There are many quality studies and reports on the topic of job loss, and they often tell different tales.

There is widespread agreement that while manufacturing output has continued to grow in recent decades, manufacturing employment has not. Manufacturing provided a quarter of all U.S. jobs in the early 1970s, and that has fallen to less than 9 percent today.[13]

An often-cited 2015 Ball State University study found that while productivity, trade and domestic demand all affected U.S. employment in the 2000–2010 period, almost 88 percent of manufacturing job losses over that decade was due to the growth of productivity—that is, fewer workers were needed to produce the same output because of automation, computerization and robots. It found that trade deficits (net exports have been negative since 1980) were responsible for only about 13 percent of job losses during the period.[14] (There is some overlap between the effects of trade and productivity, so the numbers slightly exceed 100 percent.)

If the United States had remained at 2000 levels of productivity through 2010, the Ball State study found, 20.9 million manufacturing workers would have been employed. Instead, there were 12.1 million that year. "Manufacturing production remains robust. Productivity growth is the largest contributor to job displacement over the past several decades," the study said.

NAFTA Unpopular in the U.S.

44 percent think agreement has been bad for the economy

Americans are skeptical about the benefits of the North American Free Trade Agreement (NAFTA) for the U.S. economy. In 2016, 44 percent thought the free-trade pact has been bad for the U.S. economy, 29 percent thought it was positive and 27 percent were unsure.

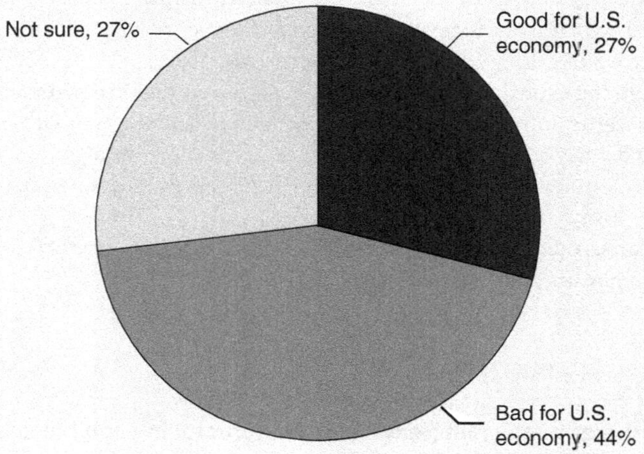

Source: "Bloomberg Politics National Poll," Bloomberg, Mar. 19–22, 2016, p. 12, http://tinyurl.com/zqf3yox.

And yet recent, well-respected research by economist Susan Houseman of the W.E. Upjohn Institute for Employment Research has called into question those and similar findings.[15] The underlying data on productivity and trade are not reliable, Houseman found, as national statistical systems were not designed to measure many of the transactions occurring in today's global economy. She also doubts statistics on the growth of manufacturing output, pointing to questionable ways it is measured in national accounts.

"The reason for manufacturing's anemic performance is that U.S. consumers and businesses are buying more imported products, and American exports have not risen commensurately," Houseman said in an October 2016 interview with the Washington Post. "Instead of manufacturing their products in the United States and exporting them to foreign markets, U.S. multinational companies now often locate production overseas to take advantage of lower labor costs and taxes, among other factors."[16]

One widely cited 2015 economic paper estimates that rising competition from Chinese imports in the 1999–2011 period resulted in U.S. job losses of between 2 million and 2.4 million. Total manufacturing employment fell by 5.8 million jobs during that period.[17]

"Trade deficits, even in times of strong growth, have negative, concentrated impacts on the quantity and quality of jobs in parts of the country where manufacturing employment diminishes," says Jared Bernstein, a former Obama White House economic adviser who is now a senior fellow at the Center on Budget and Policy Priorities, a liberal Washington-based think tank.

China Is Top U.S. Trading Partner

China accounted for 15.9 percent of total trade in goods in 2016

China accounted for 15.9 percent of U.S. total trade in goods in 2016, followed closely by Canada at 15 percent and Mexico with 14.4 percent.

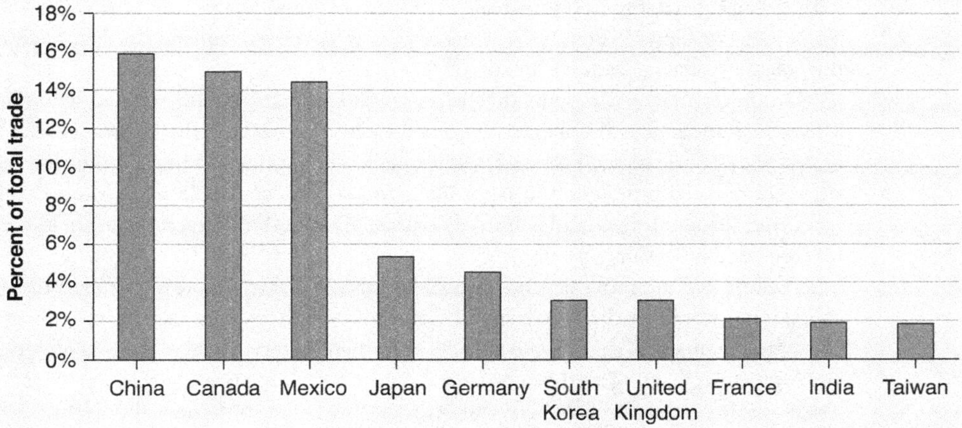

Note: Data reflect goods only.

Source: U.S. Census Bureau, "Foreign Trade," http://tinyurl.com/hd7kfno.

U.S. Trade Gap Is Largest with China

Deficit in trade of goods was $347 billion in 2016

The U.S. trade deficit in goods with China in 2016 was five times greater than its deficit with Japan, which ranked second.

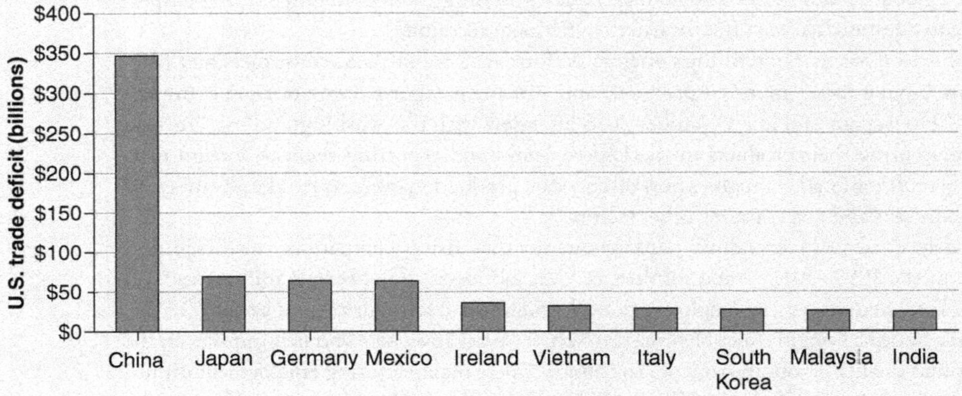

Note: Data reflect goods only.

Source: U.S. Census Bureau, "Foreign Trade," http://tinyurl.com/hd7kfno.

And trade with low-wage nations has hurt pay levels, too, according to a 2013 study by the Economic Policy Institute, a left-leaning Washington research group. Growing trade with emerging economies lowered the average wage for a typical U.S. blue collar worker by 5.5 percent, or about $1,800, in 2011, according to the report, and one-third of that effect was due solely to growing trade with China.[18]

The paper makes the point that while trade increases overall national income, it also affects how income is distributed *within* a nation. And because the United States has integrated with poorer global economies, it has increased production in capital-intensive industries and reduced production in labor-intensive industries. This leads to lower demand for labor, and so lower wages, and increased demand for capital services, resulting in higher wages for those in that sector.

The loss of American manufacturing jobs was inevitable, according to Brad DeLong, an economic historian at the University of California, Berkeley. It is just the latest in a number of employment shifts that have occurred in human history, such as the loss of agricultural employment as farming methods became more efficient and people left the fields for factories. Trade accords such as TPP, NAFTA and China's 2001 entry into the WTO "are not a big part of the long-run decline in the manufacturing job share," DeLong wrote.[19]

But even if this is true, "the move from agriculture employment to manufacturing employment was a good thing," says Ferry of the Coalition for a Prosperous America, "because the latter paid better. But manufacturing to services, especially to retail and healthcare, is not a good thing, because those pay worse."

Manufacturing Jobs Decline in Rust Belt

Employment fell in five states between 1995 and 2009

Manufacturing jobs declined steadily between 1995 and 2009 in the Rust Belt states of Indiana, Illinois, Michigan, Ohio and Pennsylvania. Between 2009 and 2015, manufacturing employment rose in Indiana, Michigan and Ohio, but plateaued in Illinois and Pennsylvania.

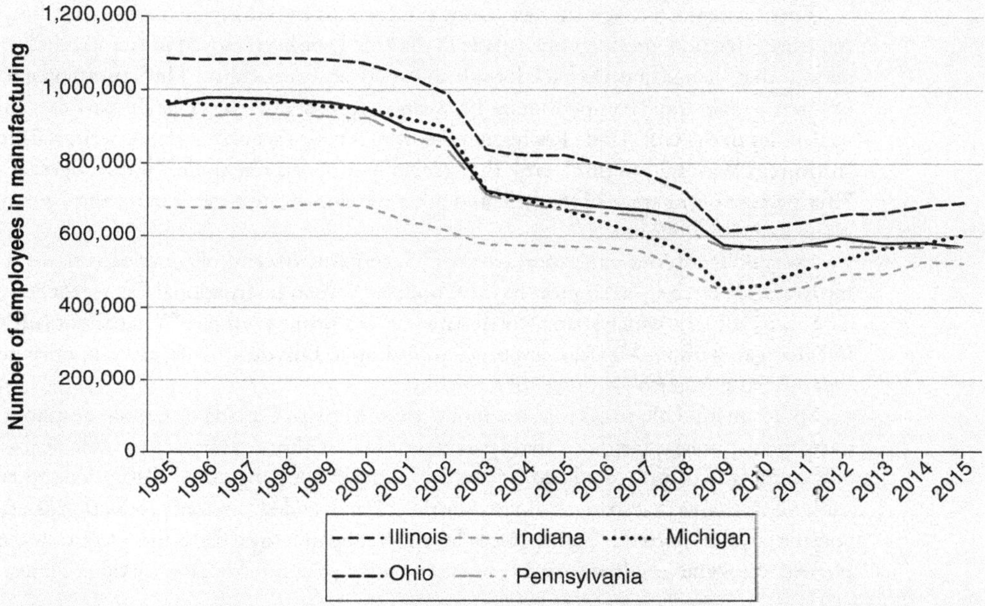

Note: Data reflect seasonally adjusted preliminary estimates.

Source: Generated from SAGE Stats database, http://tinyurl.com/gssmycc.

Either way, it is becoming clear that U.S. industries more exposed to import competition have been hardest hit, according to a 2016 study by economists David Autor, David Dorn and Gordon Hanson.[20] And employment in the local labor markets in which those industries are concentrated has also suffered. Labor immobility—geographical or skill-based barriers to workers moving between jobs—and other frictions in the U.S. economy mean that entire communities and regions have been devastated by trade and unable to adjust for years.

Can Globalized Trade Be Reversed?

Many Americans need look no further than the phone they're holding in their hand to understand the state of much of modern manufacturing.

Apple designs the iPhone at its headquarters in Cupertino, Calif., and then farms out the manufacturing of the phone's many parts to dozens of companies around the world. The touchscreen controller and flash memory are manufactured in the United States, and various other parts are made in Italy, Germany, Taiwan, Japan and South Korea. At the end of the process, the phone is assembled in a factory in Shenzhen, China, by Foxconn, a Taiwanese firm.[21]

The iPhone and many other products in daily use are truly global. And global supply chains (sometimes called global value chains) account for as much as 80 percent of global trade, according to a 2015 report by London's Standard Chartered Bank. Intermediate goods, those that will go into other final goods, are about 60 percent of global trade.[22]

These statistics weaken the case—one put forward by Trump advisers—that, because of trade liberalization, products once made in the U.S. have been moved to factories in low-wage nations that then ship them back for sale to American consumers. "The Trump people think of international trade competition as between end products," says Claude Barfield, a former consultant to the U.S. Trade Representative, who is now a scholar at the American Enterprise Institute, a Washington think tank that generally supports free trade. "It no longer largely is. Fifty percent of the trade of the U.S. and other developed countries is parts and components, it's no longer final products."

Every dollar of Mexican exports to the U.S. contains 40 cents of American output, according to a study by the Washington-based Woodrow Wilson International Center for Scholars.[23] The auto industry, which spans North America, is a prime example. "You cannot run a plant in Michigan without Mexican imports," according to Luis de la Calle, an economist and former official at Mexico's Ministry of Economy.[24]

So, for many U.S. firms that use inputs from Mexico, Canada or China, or manufacture parts there, punitive tariffs on trade partners or U.S. withdrawal from free trade deals—both advocated by Trump—could mean suddenly higher sourcing costs, disruptions to complicated value chains that span multiple countries, even stranded or seized production assets.[25] For consumers, that portends higher prices for shoes, apparel, toys, furniture, electronics, mobile phones, autos and hundreds of other products whose prices are kept low by value chains.

Developed World Absorbs "China Shock"

Transformation Upends Economists' Models

China's integration into the global economy, especially since its accession to the World Trade Organization (WTO) in 2001, has helped turn the country into an exporting giant and generated steady economic growth. It has also sparked fierce debate about whether China's emergence has been positive or negative for developed nations. A key takeaway: The WTO granted exceptions that allowed China to join even though its economy was heavily state-controlled and labor and industry associations lacked independence.

China's growth since the 1980s, when it began the transition from a centrally planned and largely agricultural economy to a market-oriented export powerhouse, has been nothing short of miraculous. From 1991 to 2012 China's share of world manufacturing rose from 4.1 percent to 24 percent, transforming it into a "global factory" that has lifted hundreds of millions of Chinese out of poverty.[26]

But the impact of China's emergence on the world's advanced economies continues to inspire heated debate. China's exports surged after its 2001 entry into the World Trade Organization (WTO), partly because of WTO rules, according to a 2016 paper by economists David Autor, David Dorn and Gordon Hanson.[27] WTO provisions forced a reallocation of Chinese capital and labor from small, unproductive state-owned companies to privately owned factories, raising productivity and output and driving exports, according to the paper.

Theoretically, China's integration into the world economy should have created a giant consumer market for other countries to exploit, as well as a manufacturing and exporting giant. In addition, most theoretical models say that workers in the United States and other rich nations who were displaced by Chinese imports should have been able to find equally good or better jobs in exporting industries that were growing as a result of increasing trade.

But this did not occur nearly to the extent that economic theory predicted it should have. Consider that China's average surplus in its current account (a broad measure of a nation's trade balance) rose from 1.7 percent of gross domestic product in the 1990s to 4.8 percent in the 2000s, while the U.S. current account *deficit* rose from 1.6 percent to 4.4 percent over the same period.[28] Mirror images.

The rules for China were not always the same as for other WTO members, many trade analysts say. China's economy did not conform to the economic forms envisioned under WTO rules, since large sectors were state-controlled and labor and industry associations lacked independence, so provisions and exceptions were made to allow the country to accede to the WTO on its own terms.[29]

"China was allowed to enter the WTO on more emerging-market terms than your typical advanced economy," says Brad Setser, an expert on geoeconomic studies at the Council on Foreign Relations in New York. In addition, the Chinese government has many levers it can—and does—pull, through state-owned enterprises and banks, among others, to make it very difficult for foreign firms to compete in China if they're not producing in China, Setser adds.

Multinational firms didn't seem to mind this, and U.S. and European firms benefited a great deal from producing their goods in China—through both market access and low labor costs—despite the consequences for manufacturing employment in their home countries. "The interests of U.S. firms and U.S. labor were not always aligned," Setser says.

And labor markets, especially in the United States, were not nearly as flexible and fluid as once thought, with displaced workers struggling to move to new areas and industries. As a result, competition from imports inflicted long-term damage on some workers and communities. For example, entire towns surrounding furniture factories in Tennessee were devastated by Chinese competition in the early years of this century, affecting both manufacturing and non-manufacturing workers, and they still have not fully recovered.[30]

Essentially, things did not work out the way the textbooks said they would. "The advance of China," wrote Autor, Dorn and Hanson, "has also toppled much of the received empirical wisdom about the impact of trade on labor markets."[31]

And even before President Trump emerged on the American political scene, there was a political backlash. Politicians in both parties called for the Treasury Department to officially label China a currency manipulator, asserting that Beijing kept the yuan undervalued to make its exports cheaper. WTO disputes initiated by major economic powers became almost exclusively focused on China in recent years.[32] Yet before Trump, U.S. presidents of both political parties continued to pursue multilateral trade agreements and avoided naming China as a manipulator.

A dollar that was overvalued relative to other currencies, making U.S. exports more expensive, was also a problem, argues Setser. The United States, he says, adhered to a strong-dollar policy in the early 2000s, even when it began weighing heavily on U.S. exports and the economy. It was, says Setser, the wrong policy.

The flood of emerging-economy imports to the United States and other advanced economies would have occurred with or without China's WTO accession, argues Harvard University economist Larry Summers, who served as Treasury secretary in the Clinton administration: "The reason for the rise in U.S. imports is not reduced trade barriers. Rather it is that emerging markets are indeed emerging. They are growing in their economic potential because of successful economic reforms and greater global integration."[33]

Either way, the so-called China Shock may have run its course, according to Autor, Dorn and Hanson. China's period of economic "catch-up" with advanced economies is coming to an end, and China is now becoming a middle-income nation, with rapidly rising wages that are quickly shrinking its pool of cheap labor and its comparative advantage with it.

Yet even as that happens, other Asian nations are stepping in to provide cheap labor. Wages in Vietnam and Indonesia are a third or less of those in China, which may mean ongoing misery for workers in advanced nations.[34]

—Matthew Benjamin

"Even if no [U.S.-China] trade war occurs, protectionist tariffs will severely disrupt global value chains of not only U.S. and Chinese firms, but thousands of foreign subsidiaries that have embedded themselves in cross-border production networks," according to global trade scholar and adviser Alex Capri of the National University of Singapore Business School. "If Trumpian policies disrupt these value chains, it's likely that many U.S. firms and U.S.-based foreign subsidiaries will relocate their activities elsewhere, creating the exact opposite outcome intended."

Trump trade adviser and former University of California economics professor Peter Navarro says he would like the United States to unwind and repatriate global supply chains so that more, or even most, components of final goods assembled in the U.S. are also made here. Too much of American manufacturing, he says, is merely assembling parts produced in other nations.[35]

Of course, bringing global supply chains back to the United States would cause disruptions, according to Greg Autry, a professor at the University of Southern California and co-author with Navarro of "Death by China: Confronting the Dragon—a Global Call to Action." "We moved our supply chain to Asia in about two decades," he told The New York Times in December. "You certainly can do it in the U.S. a whole lot faster. It's going to take a few years, but it's going to be a much better America."[36]

That may sound like a good idea to some, but replicating the production that goes on in factories in China and elsewhere would be a massive, costly, long-term effort. Even U.S. companies that compete with imported goods use imported components themselves to produce their own final products. The share of imported components in American manufactured goods rose to 34 percent from 24 percent between 1998 and 2006, according to a 2010 study by the federal government's Bureau of Labor Statistics.[37] So disrupting supply chains or taxing imports would drive up the prices of imported goods—as well as the prices of many goods that carry the label "Made in the USA."

Would Eliminating or Reducing the Trade Deficit Boost U.S. Economic Growth?

Trump's economic and trade advisers call persistent U.S. trade deficits—especially those with China, Germany, Japan, Mexico and South Korea—a major drag on economic growth. They state unequivocally that reducing the U.S.'s overall $500 billion trade deficit, by increasing exports and decreasing imports, would increase growth.[38]

And there's a certain elemental truth to that statement. Consider the formula for GDP:

$$GDP = \textit{Consumer Spending} + \textit{Business Investment} + \textit{Government Spending} + (\textit{Exports} - \textit{Imports})$$

So rising imports naturally subtract from GDP. If they fall, and exports rise, GDP is greater.

And it's pretty clear that reducing the trade deficit would increase manufacturing employment, though by how much is a matter of great debate. Nobel economics laureate and New York Times columnist Paul Krugman estimates that completely eliminating the trade gap in manufactured goods (the U.S. runs a surplus in services) would add 2 million manufacturing jobs.[39]

When an economy is going full tilt, a trade deficit can be a good thing, as supply-side factors such as limits on available labor can restrict how much is produced domestically, so consumers turn to imports to meet their consumption needs. That helps hold inflation in check, among other things. But in an economy not at full capacity, which is the situation now with many U.S. workers still unemployed or underemployed and a falling labor participation rate, a trade deficit can be a drag on demand.

Also, the United States is borrowing from abroad to finance its persistent trade deficits. As Gary Hufbauer, a senior fellow at the Washington-based Peterson Institute for International Economics, points out, if net foreign claims on the United States, now about $7.3 trillion, become a very high fraction of U.S. GDP, the burden of paying interest and dividends on the debt could become a significant drain on the economy.[40]

So getting closer to a balance on trade is a good idea, yet how to do it remains an open question. "Ideally, the deficit would be eliminated by a combination of rising U.S. exports stemming from a more equitable global trading environment," says Prestowitz. "In that case, eliminating the trade deficit would indeed stimulate growth."

But the evolving Trump trade doctrine seems to be to deal with deficits on a country-by-country, or bilateral, basis, renegotiating each deal to ensure that it "must increase the GDP growth rate, decrease the trade deficit, and strengthen the U.S. manufacturing base," as advisers Navarro and Wilbur Ross, Trump's new Commerce secretary, wrote last year.[41]

This idea, most economists say, is unworkable. "If you reduce the deficit with one country, it doesn't stand to reason that the U.S. is the next cheapest producer of the goods that you're not importing from that country. The next cheapest producer is likely some other foreign country. So you'll just shift U.S. imports . . . from, say, Mexico to Brazil," says Hufbauer.

Tariffs that reduce imports and invite retaliation from trade partners are also a flawed solution. "If we reduce our imports and other countries retaliate by reducing the amount they import from us, then the net result is less growth," says Brad Setser, an expert on geoeconomic studies at the Council on Foreign Relations in New York. "If you just slap a tariff on all goods and it's a big enough one, and we don't immediately start producing those goods in the U.S., in the short run you have to pay more for the same set of goods, that's less money to spend on other things. And that is contractionary."

Also, it's important to remember that multiple factors create trade deficits, including Americans' propensity to spend too much and save too little and the ability of many nations to produce the goods we buy more cheaply than the United States can. So a good start might be to encourage Americans to balance their budgets.

Reducing the relative value of the dollar would also help, although it's complicated by the fact that it is the world's reserve currency—that is, many nations use dollars and dollar-denominated assets to make international payments or to defend the value of their own currency, or just for a rainy day, which boosts demand for the U.S. currency.

The current "strong dollar" policy, adopted in 1995 by then-Treasury Secretary Robert Rubin, maintains that a robust dollar exchange rate is always in the best interests of the nation. But economists are beginning to question that assumption, as the policy has at times made U.S. exports more expensive on world markets. Trump may have already signaled the beginning of the end of that policy in an interview with The Wall Street Journal shortly before taking office: "Our companies can't compete with them now because our currency is too strong. And it's killing us."[42]

Convincing U.S. trade partners to swear off practices that keep their own currencies artificially cheap against the dollar would help too, most economists agree. "We should make sure, as best we can, that the dollar is relatively fairly valued in international markets," says Jared Bernstein, "and then let the competition rip."

BACKGROUND

"An Irreducible and Intrinsic Impulse"

Humans, wrote economic philosopher Adam Smith, have a natural propensity to "truck, barter, and exchange one thing for another."[43] That propensity, arguably, has driven world history.

The Silk Routes—bringing fabrics, spices and gunpowder west in exchange for furs, metals, dyes and other items going east—first connected ancient empires in Rome, China and India. Muslim traders were largely responsible for the spread of their new faith west to Spain and east to Indonesia. The quest for pepper, cinnamon and other Asian spices drove exploration of the globe by Vasco da Gama, Christopher Columbus and other Europeans. Trade also spread bubonic plague from Himalayan rodents to the Middle East, Europe and China, devastating entire populations and economies.

Trade created empires—and destroyed them. Historians link the fall of Rome to the depletion of its gold and silver reserves, exchanged over centuries for Eastern luxury goods. The establishment of the Dutch and English East India companies, which drove world trade for two centuries, helped pave the way for Western dominance of the world economy and the vast disparities in the wealth of nations that remain in place today.

Trade, writes William Bernstein, the economic historian, "is an irreducible and intrinsic impulse" that "has profoundly affected the trajectory of the human species."[44]

In the modern era, technologies such as the steam engine and steelmaking entwined nations much more tightly through trade. Yet the path to the current global system has never been straight or seamless, and reversals, though usually temporary, have come as often as advances.

Perhaps the founding argument for modern free trade was the theory of comparative advantage, put forward in 1817 by political economist Ricardo. It challenged the popular mercantilist view that accumulating gold via a national trade surplus was the true purpose of trade. Instead, said Ricardo, all nations can benefit through trade if they concentrate on making products in which their advantage is relatively greatest. Essentially, he said, trade is not a zero-sum game, but instead can benefit all who partake in it.

Within a few decades, the free trade views of Ricardo, Smith and others gained traction in Great Britain and the rest of Europe, leading to the repeal in 1846 of England's draconian Corn Laws, which held down grain imports, and subsequently the Cobden-Chevalier Treaty of 1860, which slashed tariffs between Great Britain and France and led to tariff-cutting throughout Europe. Much lower trade barriers, together with rapidly falling prices for transportation and communication, ushered in an era of free trade in the second half of the 19th century.

That was not, however, the end of world economic history. Exploration, colonialism and trade had created vibrant agricultural producers in the New World and elsewhere. As their economies grew and shipping costs continued to drop, the United States, Canada, Argentina,

Australia and Russia began to flood Europe with grain imports in the last two decades of the 19th century, hurting farmers there and leading to a new era of anti-trade sentiment and rising import tariffs. The fall in shipping costs, however, also helped keep international trading volumes robust.

In a major blow to free trade, in the 1920s Republicans in the United States pushed for higher tariffs, partly because of a resurgence of isolationist ideas after the First World War and partly to appeal politically to farmers, who, unlike those in other sectors of the American economy, did not prosper in the Jazz Age.[45] Several new tariffs were enacted, and European and Latin American nations retaliated. The infamous Smoot-Hawley Tariff of 1930 helped push up the average tax on imports to nearly 50 percent. Its name has since become synonymous with protectionism.[46]

"While economic historians do not believe that the Smoot-Hawley tariff caused the Depression, the high tariffs contributed to the downward spiral of trade as other countries retaliated against the United States," wrote Dartmouth economist Douglas Irwin in "Free Trade under Fire."[47]

Were Smoot-Hawley and its aftereffects a major cause of the Second World War? Historians disagree on the issue, but it is clear that the tariffs increased economic isolationism and nationalism around the world, conditions often conducive to conflict. Historian Bernstein thinks they did more than that. "Smoot-Hawley and retaliatory tariffs were absolutely a contributing factor to World War II," he says. "Because of them, Germany couldn't export and so couldn't pay reparations imposed on them after the first war."

The U.S. State Department of the time seemed to agree. Cordell Hull, President Franklin D. Roosevelt's secretary of state, was a firm believer that free trade promoted prosperity and peace.[48] And in the aftermath of World War II, a famous 1945 State Department document, "Proposals for Expansion of World Trade and Employment," made the case that a system of international free trade could help avoid another global catastrophe. Unless countries act together, the document stated, "they will act at cross purposes and may well do serious damage to each other. But if they do act together, there is every possibility that the peoples of the world may enjoy, in our lifetime, a higher degree of prosperity and welfare than they have ever had before."[49]

Blueprint for a New Era

Using the document as a blueprint, 23 nations met in Geneva in 1947 and hammered out an agreement unprecedented in human history, the General Agreement on Tariffs and Trade, or GATT, the first multilateral trade agreement and the one that launched a new era of trade and globalization.[50]

Some economists and historians contend, however, that a fundamental mistake was made at the beginning of this era, the effects of which would only materialize decades later. At the seminal 1944 economic conference held in Bretton Woods, N.H., delegates from 44 nations met and designed the postwar economic and trade system.[51] British economist John Maynard Keynes, a principal architect of that system, advocated for a system of balanced trade, in which nations with chronic trade deficits would be helped and those with chronic surpluses would be given incentives to return to balance. The United States, which then enjoyed the world's largest trade surplus, vetoed this system in order to preserve its trade advantages.[52]

(The U.S. balance of trade went negative in the 1970s and now runs a deficit of about $500 billion a year.[53])

That sowed the seeds of "a persistent global structure in which a handful of countries now make up two-thirds of the global current account deficit, and another handful combine for two-thirds of the surplus," says Prestowitz. (The current account is a broader measure of trade that includes the balance of trade plus smaller components, including interest and income from assets held abroad.)

Still, for multiple decades, the GATT pushed free trade forward at a dizzying pace. Seven negotiating rounds largely demolished tariffs among member countries. "The reduction in trade barriers and the stability of tariff policy in most countries in the decades after 1947 have permitted the expansion of world trade to proceed unchecked," Irwin wrote.[54]

The GATT was succeeded in 1995 by the World Trade Organization, which coordinates and regulates trade among member countries and resolves disputes. Whether or not the WTO has been effective, however, is a matter of debate.[55]

Other developments advanced economic globalization. Not least among them was Malcolm McLean's 1956 invention of the intermodal shipping container, which dramatically reduced shipping and port costs because it could be used to move freight from ship to rail to truck.

In addition to multinational GATT—and later WTO—talks, nations pursued broad trading blocs in the 1990s, averaging nearly 30 signed accords a year during that decade.[56] Two of the largest were NAFTA, signed in 1992 by the United States, Mexico and Canada, and Mercosur, a 1991 treaty encompassing Argentina, Brazil, Paraguay, Uruguay and Venezuela. A monumental development was the economic integration of Europe, begun in 1951 with the Treaty of Paris, which established the European Coal and Steel Community. The immediate idea behind the trading bloc was to create a single coal and steel industry by removing barriers to trade on those goods within continental Europe. The larger underlying idea was to remove those commodities most necessary for war from the control of national governments, thereby preventing another devastating conflagration like the one that had ended just six years earlier with much of the continent in ruins.[57]

That agreement was the forerunner to the European Union (EU), established in the 1992 Maastricht Treaty, which put in place a single market with free movement of people and goods, eventually among 28 nations. Seven years later, a monetary union was established, with 11 EU states adopting the euro currency, and eight others joining later. Since then, the euro has become the world's second largest reserve currency behind the dollar. Not all EU member countries have adopted the euro, for various political and economic reasons.

The EU Under Scrutiny

The economic success of the EU is under debate. Certainly there have been hiccups, many of them due to the fact that there is a monetary union among 19 nations but no fiscal or political union.[58] This created major problems during the global financial crisis of 2008–2009. More recently, refugees from conflicts in the Middle East have tested the EU's commitment to free movement of people across borders.

Still, the noneconomic gains may outweigh all of that, says historian Bernstein: "Since time immemorial, since the reign of Charlemagne, the major European powers have been at war with each other. And now, because of the EU, the idea of a shooting war between Western European powers is incomprehensible."

However, opponents of freewheeling free trade call China's WTO entry in 2001 a turning point, especially for the United States. Allowing China into the WTO "was the worst political and economic mistake in American history in the last 100 years," according to Navarro.[59] He and many other economists and trade analysts say China didn't—and doesn't—play by global free trade rules. They argue that while China may technically adhere to the lower tariffs negotiated by the GATT and WTO, it engages in a host of other unfair trade practices, including currency manipulation, illegal export subsidies and intellectual property theft, among others. And China is not the only nation accused of gaming the free trade system. Nations such as

U.S. International Trade Deficit Rises

Both exports and imports decreased in 2016

The U.S. international trade deficit hit $502.3 billion in 2016, an increase of about $2 billion from 2015 and the highest the deficit for trading in goods and services has been since 2012, when it was nearly $537 billion.

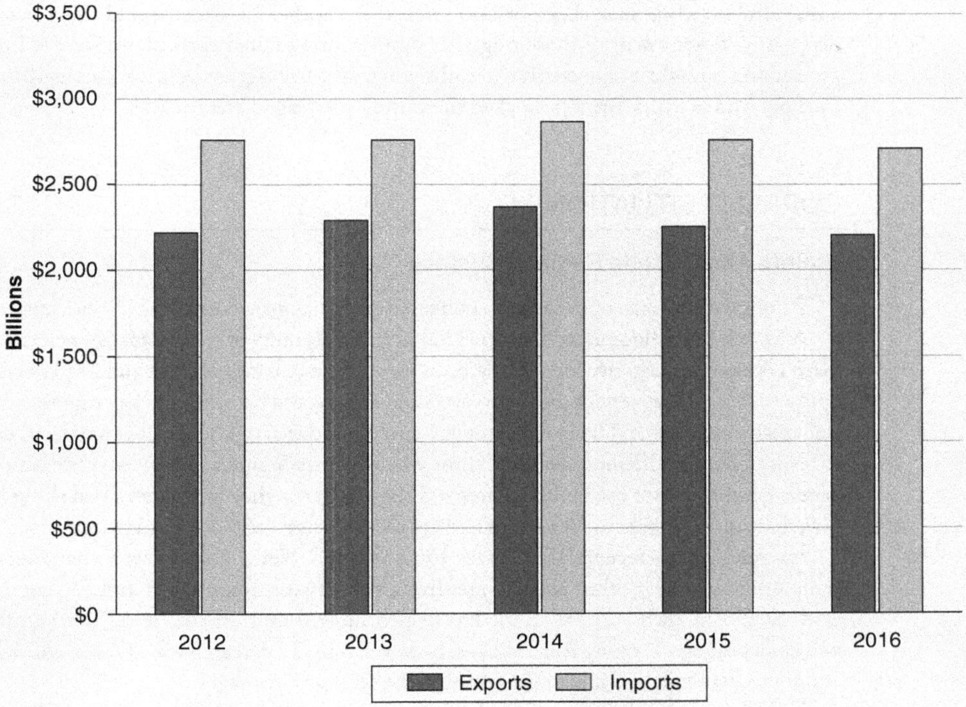

Source: "U.S. International Trade in Goods and Services: December 2016," U.S. Bureau of Economic Analysis, U.S. Census Bureau, Feb. 7, 2017, http://tinyurl.com/lb6vwpk.

Japan, South Korea, Taiwan, Singapore and even Germany have done so, critics assert, often through interventions to keep their currencies undervalued and thus their exports artificially strong. (Germany is taking advantage of a "grossly undervalued" euro to exploit the United States, Navarro said in January.[60])

Many developing nations also oppose the post-World War II free-trade regime, which, they say, has been unfair to them, largely because it has not reduced or eliminated rich countries' agricultural subsidies and import barriers. Citing those inequities, developing nations, many of whom rely on farm exports, collectively derailed the latest round of WTO trade talks, the so-called Doha Development Round. As a result, these developing nations expected "that developed countries would open their markets completely to developing countries, which would not have to do anything in return," according to Irwin.[61] Negotiations collapsed in 2008 and have not been revived.

And then came the financial crisis and Great Recession of 2007–2009. Falling demand sent world trade volumes plummeting. Trade recovered by 2011, but real damage had been done, especially in the EU, where resentments from the center (mainly Germany) about helping the periphery (Portugal, Italy, Greece and Spain) boiled over and continue to simmer.

Worse, strife in the Middle East, particularly in Syria beginning in 2011, flooded Europe with refugees who, once they got into Greece or another EU state, could move across borders easily. Resentment of those migrants significantly diluted enthusiasm for the European project and brought a rejuvenation of right-wing, anti-immigrant political parties throughout Europe. And in 2016, Britain shocked the world by voting to exit the EU.

CURRENT SITUATION

Doubts About Trade Begin to Surface

By many measures, opposition to increased trade has grown among U.S. citizens, too.

A March 2016 Bloomberg News poll found that a plurality of Americans (44 percent) believe NAFTA has been negative for the U.S. economy (29 percent said positive and 27 percent had no opinion). And 82 percent of those surveyed said they would be willing to pay more for domestically made products.[62] The Pew Research Center found that, while Americans overall continue to favor trade, the difference between those who think trade agreements with other nations have been a good thing for the United States and those who say they have been a bad thing has narrowed, from 59 percent to 30 percent in 2014 to 51 percent to 39 percent a year ago.[63]

Interestingly, a recent Wall Street Journal/NBC News Poll showed that ideas about trade—like so many other issues—are diverging between Republican and Democratic voters.[64] Democrats who say free trade has helped more than hurt rose to 57 percent, from 34 percent a year ago. Among Republicans, however, only 27 percent viewed free trade favorably, and more than half said it hurt the country, the same as a year ago.

Today, among politicians, anti-trade sentiment spans the political spectrum. Republican Donald Trump and democratic socialist Bernie Sanders both railed against NAFTA and other trade deals on the campaign trail in 2016. Democratic presidential nominee Hillary Clinton, who supported TPP while she was secretary of state, abruptly reversed her position and opposed it during the election.

A New Administration

In his inaugural address, Trump erased all doubts that protectionism will be central to his agenda: "We must protect our borders from the ravages of other countries making our products, stealing our companies and destroying our jobs. Protection will lead to great prosperity and strength."

The first month of his administration is proving that Trump's campaign promises and speeches were not empty rhetoric. He appointed Navarro, a prominent China critic, to lead his newly created National Trade Council, and Robert Lighthizer, another China critic, as his chief trade negotiator. Ross, a billionaire financier who has called for pro-American trade policies, is Trump's Commerce secretary.

In a September 2016 paper, Navarro and Ross spelled out Trump's trade policy.[65] They laid blame for U.S. economic woes such as slow growth, deindustrialization and wage stagnation largely on a trade imbalance with China and five other nations: Canada, Germany, Japan, Mexico and South Korea. And they called for a rebalancing of those trade relationships through renegotiation of existing trade deals, as well as defending against other nations' "trade cheating" by all available means, including punitive tariffs.

On the Monday after his inauguration, Trump officially withdrew the United States from the TPP and his advisers have declared the EU-U.S. negotiations on TTIP dead. In addition, the White House has taken initial steps toward renegotiating NAFTA, which the president has called "the single worst trade deal ever approved in this country."

The new administration says it plans to eschew multilateral trade pacts in favor of bilateral deals with the United Kingdom, Japan, New Zealand, Malaysia, Thailand and Australia. The idea, says trade scholar Barfield, is to take advantage of American economic muscle in one-on-one negotiations. "They hope that the market power of the U.S. would force whatever country we're dealing with to bow to our will, and we'll get all the things we want and not have to give anything up," he says. "It's something they couldn't accomplish in multilateral negotiations."

Navarro seems to agree with that assessment. "The problem with multilateral deals is we reduce our bargaining power, we surrender our sovereignty," he told Fox News on Jan. 29. Yet it is far from clear that the Trump administration can secure better terms through bilateral trade agreements than previous negotiators got through multilateral deals.

In a trade policy statement on March 1, the White House asserted that American voters have rejected the current framework for international trade, that the status quo is unacceptable, and that these facts mandate a new approach.[66] It said the United States will use "all possible sources of leverage" to ensure fair market access for U.S. goods and services, including strict enforcement of U.S. laws, changes to current trade agreements and "reciprocity"—meaning that barriers to U.S. products in other nations will prompt similar restrictions on entry to the U.S. market. The White House also expressed discontent with major existing trade agreements and said it did not regard WTO rulings as necessarily binding on the United States: "The Trump administration will aggressively defend American sovereignty over matters of trade policy."

Nor is the new president shying away from using the bully pulpit—or bully Twitter account—to keep U.S. jobs from going abroad. Trump has already leaned on several companies, including Carrier, a unit of United Technologies, and Ford Motor Co., to abandon or alter plans to build factories abroad.

More worrisome to large manufacturers, perhaps, are Navarro's comments about taking measures to unwind and repatriate international supply chains.[67] Toward that goal, the White House is pushing for a new corporate tax code that would tax imports and exempt exports, a so-called border adjustment levy. The objectives of the move, which congressional Republicans have advocated for some time, are twofold: raise revenue on imports to compensate for a lower overall corporate tax rate and make off-shoring of production less attractive to U.S. firms.

Supporters of the change, which would be the linchpin of a long-hoped-for overhaul of the corporate tax code, say it would merely implement in the United States a scheme similar to the value-added tax (VAT) that other nations use. (A VAT, common in the EU, imposes a tax at each point that value is added in the production process of a good, including at final sale.) Opponents say the border adjustment levy looks like an export subsidy with a protectionist structure and would hurt retailers, who import much of what they sell. Others say the dollar would strengthen due to the tax, moderating import prices, but there is little consensus among economists exactly what the border tax would do to the economy.

It is not yet clear how the plan will be implemented, if at all, but if it strays far from an ordinary VAT it will begin to resemble an import tax and export subsidy, and will invite retaliation from trading partners, says Chad Bown, a senior fellow and trade expert at the Peterson Institute. "If so, the best-case scenario has them trying to work it out through negotiations or through a formal WTO dispute," says Bown. "The worst-case scenario has them acting unilaterally with retaliation."

And by driving up prices of imported goods at Wal-Mart and other retailers, the border tax also may be bad politics. "I'm not sure the people of the Congress should be thinking in terms of responding to white rural middle-class anger by doing a corporate tax cut to raise consumer prices," Peterson Institute President Adam Posen said at a recent event focused on the border tax proposal.

International Issues

Meanwhile, as U.K. Prime Minister Theresa May begins to navigate her nation's difficult departure from the European Union, movements to exit the alliance are growing in other nations, including the Netherlands, France, Italy, Austria and Sweden.[68] Even if some of the nationalist parties pushing for an exit are small and unlikely to achieve referendums, their growth and message cannot be ignored.

"In the wake of anti-establishment referendum votes in the U.K. and Italy [where voters in December rejected constitutional changes], Europe's leaders have yet to find convincing answers to the wave of political disaffection sweeping the continent," says Iain Begg, a fellow at the London School of Economics.

And financial markets, initially buoyed by what they considered to be pro-growth Trump policies, are beginning to worry. Protectionism was named the top threat to U.S. growth by over half of respondents to a January CNBC survey of economists, fund managers and strategists, the first time in the survey's history that a majority agreed on a single concern.[69]

"Trashing the Mexican economy with tariffs and other bad policies is like throwing rocks through your neighbors' windows, thereby reducing the value of YOUR home," Robert Fry, chief economist at Robert Fry Economics, told the survey.

Next Free-Trade Era May Not Be Made in America

U.S. Ceding Leadership under Trump's "America-First" Policy

The U.S. withdrawal from the Trans-Pacific Partnership under President Trump signals a broad retreat from the leading role that the United States has played in shaping the post-World War II global economic order. A key takeaway: The U.S. pullback creates an opening for other nations to exert leadership—and China is already moving to do so.

The 20th century was the American Century, Time magazine publisher Henry Luce famously proclaimed in 1941—and the post-World War II global trade agenda was designed and led by the United States.

Yet just days after taking office in January, President Trump withdrew the United States from the Trans-Pacific Partnership (TPP). Not only would TPP have been the largest regional trade deal in history, with a dozen member countries that account for some 40 percent of the global economy, but U.S. negotiators hoped it would allow the United States to define trading standards and set the rules for the world's most dynamic economic region.

The withdrawal is a lot bigger than that, geopolitical analysts say. "The real meaning of Trump's announcement is almost certainly not limited to TPP," says Michael Pettis, a professor of finance at Peking University's Guanghua School of Management and a scholar at the Washington-based Carnegie Endowment for International Peace. "It represents a rejection of the central role played by the United States in the governance of the global trading system." Trump trade advisers Peter Navarro and Wilbur Ross have also expressed disdain for World Trade Organization rules and have hinted that the United States could withdraw from that organization as well.[70]

So what happens now? Claude Barfield, a trade scholar at Washington's American Enterprise Institute, thinks the rest of the world should push on without the United States, or until another administration changes U.S. policy. The other TPP members would be wise to pursue a modified pact without Washington, he says. Such a TPP accord would still be significant, encompassing almost 14 percent of global gross domestic product and 13 percent of world trade. Offering South Korea membership would increase that power substantially. "Recreating the TPP is by far the best course for the eleven remaining TPP members," says Barfield.

But forging ahead may be too difficult without U.S. leadership and market power. Japanese Prime Minister Shinzo Abe said in November that TPP has "no meaning" without the United States.[71]

Either way, China, the world's second-largest economy, sees an opening to take the lead on trade and integration in the Asia-Pacific region, if not more broadly. China was excluded from the TPP negotiations because it cannot yet meet the pact's labor and environmental standards, although some trade watchers such as Financial Times commentator David Pilling say TPP was designed to be an "anyone but China" club to punish that nation for flaunting international trade and investment rules.[72]

China is pushing two trade blocs, the Free Trade Area of the Asia-Pacific and the Regional Comprehensive Economic Partnership. Both would give Beijing considerable power to set the regional and, to a lesser extent, the global trade agenda.[73]

"China believes we should set a new and very practical working plan," Vice Foreign Minister Li Baodong said in September, "and sustain momentum and establish a free trade area in Asia-Pacific at an early date." Chinese President Xi Jinping made official visits to Ecuador, Chile and Peru in November in an attempt to solidify ties in Latin America and, commentators such as foreign policy writer Frida Ghitis believe, to attempt to replace the United States as the country with the most influence there.[74]

"China has a regional strategy for the Asia-Pacific," former U.S. Trade Representative Michael Froman said in January 2016. "And they're executing on that strategy. And that positions them in a very powerful way to—in the region—to be able to call the shots."[75]

That may have implications far beyond tariff levels or favorable trade conditions for the United States or China. The current American-led global trade system worked well for many decades despite its many flaws, integrating the world, preventing conflict and helping hundreds of millions emerge from poverty.

"By withdrawing from the TPP and pursuing an isolationist, 'America First' foreign policy, Trump seems intent on throwing that system in the trash," wrote former U.S. trade official John Brinkley. "This will give China an opening to run rough-shod over East Asia and Russia to do the same in Europe."[76]

—*Matthew Benjamin*

LOOKING AHEAD

Uncertain Times

With new economic and trade policy being set daily, it's far from clear what international trade will look six months from now, let alone five years down the road. Predictions of the future, therefore, range from rosy scenarios to disaster.

The Trump administration foresees a U.S. economy that looks very different from today's, with an American manufacturing renaissance at the heart of it.

"We envision a more German-style economy, where 20 percent of our workforce is in manufacturing," Navarro recently told CNBC. (About 9 percent of American workers are currently in that sector.) "And we're not talking about banging tin in the back room. We're talking about high technology across the board, whether it's computer chips or cars or anything in between."[77]

Navarro dismisses the idea that increasing automation will continue to thin out factory floors, saying there is room for both robots and humans in this new economy. He also predicts a "robust domestic supply chain that will spur job and wage growth."[78]

And trade will continue to flow, say other critics of the current system. Prestowitz predicts separate bilateral U.S. trade deals with the United Kingdom and Japan, as well as a new NAFTA "which might actually turn out to be good for both Mexico and the U.S." In fact, Japan, the United Kingdom and Korea might all become part of a loose free trade and customs area, he says.

Others are less sanguine. If multi-country supply chains are disrupted or if a renegotiation of NAFTA is bungled, it could hurt U.S. auto workers and consumers, according to New York Times economic columnist Neil Irwin.[79]

But it would take a great deal of misguided effort to undo 60 years of trade and investment liberalization, says Barfield. "The Trump people at their worst probably couldn't roll that back more than a bit," he says.

Setser of the Council on Foreign Relations disagrees, saying that utter chaos is certainly within the realm of possibility: "The worst-case scenario in the short run for the global economy is that the U.S. does something big and broad to punish China for cheating and China responds by weakening their currency, and then the U.S. responds with another round of tariffs." That would lead to a currency war, he says, with all countries that compete with China facing pressure to depreciate alongside of China, "with a lot of collateral damage."

And some economists fear that Trump's immigration and trade policies could send the United States, Mexico and China into recession. According to an economic model Moody's Analytics prepared for The Washington Post, up to 4 million U.S. jobs would be lost, and another 3 million potential jobs not created, if the Trump administration starts a trade war and U.S. trade partners retaliate.[80]

Europe could face its own meltdown, says Begg. "With two of the EU's largest members, France and Germany, facing general elections in 2017 and the Dutch populist party led by Geert Wilders ahead in the polls for the election due in March, further electoral earthquakes may be on the horizon."

It's also possible, however, that the importance attached to manufacturing goods may subside as services—such as information technology services, business services, education and entertainment—become more productive, unbundled, and tradeable due to the internet and other communications technologies.[81] Increased trade in services could be a solution to the current war over trade—or the next battlefield.

Chronology

1810s–1870s	**Falling barriers, better transportation ramp up international trade.**
1817	British economist David Ricardo's "On the Principles of Political Economy and Taxation" sets forth the comparative advantage theory of free trade, which holds that nations can benefit through trade if they concentrate on making those products in which their advantage is relatively greatest and purchase products for which their advantage is smaller.
1846	Great Britain's Corn Laws are repealed, eliminating the last of hundreds of regulations and tariffs imposed over two centuries on English grain and grain imports.
1860	Cobden-Chevalier Treaty, an Anglo-French free trade agreement, slashes tariffs in the two nations. Other nations and cities join and tariffs throughout Europe fall. By 1875 nearly all of Europe is a low-tariff zone and an era of free trade ensues, accelerated by lower transportation and communication costs.
1880s–1930s	**Protectionism rises around the world.**
1885–1900	Cheap grain from the United States, Canada, Argentina, Australia and Russia begins to flood Europe, leading to a new era of anti-trade sentiment and rising tariffs.
1922	Protectionist Fordney-McCumber Tariff increases U.S. import duties to 40 percent or higher.
1930	Smoot-Hawley Tariff Act raises nearly 900 U.S. import duties further; Europe responds with retaliatory tariffs, leading to intensified nationalism globally.
1939	World War II begins; many historians cite economic protectionism and isolationism as contributing factors.
1940s–1990s	**Golden era of free trade begins, led by United States.**
1945	The U.S. State Department lays out a plan for countries "to harmonize their policies with respect to international trade and employment" in its Proposals for Expansion of Trade and Employment.
1947	The General Agreement on Tariffs and Trade (GATT) is signed by 23 nations, beginning a new era of increased trade and globalization. The first GATT round (Geneva) reduces 45,000 tariffs covering one-fifth of world trade.
1951	The Treaty of Paris establishes the European Coal and Steel Community, the first supranational international organization

(Continued)

(Continued)

1986–1993	GATT Uruguay Round leads to major tariff and subsidy reductions and introduces three new issues: trade in services, intellectual property rights and investment.
1992	Maastricht Treaty is signed, creating the European Union (EU), a single market with free movement of people and goods.
1994	North American Free Trade Agreement (NAFTA) takes force, creating a giant trade bloc encompassing the United States, Canada and Mexico.
1995	World Trade Organization is established in the Marrakesh Agreement and eventually grows to 164 members.
1999	Eurozone monetary union established among 19 EU nations. Initially an accounting currency, the euro becomes the world's second-largest reserve currency, after the U.S. dollar. Coins and notes enter circulation in 2002.
2000s–Present	**Multilateral talks founder and protectionism rises again.**
2000s	In a strategy of "competitive liberalization," the United States signs multiple bilateral and multilateral trade agreements, including accords with Jordan, Singapore, Chile, Australia, Morocco, five Central American nations, Peru and South Korea. This creates what some trade experts call a "spaghetti bowl" of rules and preferences that may undermine the multilateral trading system.
2001	WTO Doha Round launched, but eventually falters over agricultural tariffs, as well as diverging views of emerging and advanced economies. Talks fail at a 2003 WTO ministerial meeting in Cancun, Mexico, and collapse completely by 2008.
2008	Negotiations begin for a trade agreement among 12 nations called the Trans-Pacific Partnership (TPP), which would be the largest regional trade pact in history.
2015	TPP negotiations conclude with the signing of the agreement.
2016	The United Kingdom votes in a referendum to withdraw from the European Union, a move known as Brexit (June). The vote brings down Prime Minister David Cameron's government and sends the British pound to a 31-year low. . . . Donald Trump is elected U.S. president on a platform of economic nationalism and anti-immigration (November). His campaign trade positions include renegotiating NAFTA, labeling China a currency manipulator and bringing trade cases against China to halt its "illegal activities."
2017	Trump withdraws the United States from the Trans-Pacific Partnership and schedules meetings with Canadian and Mexican leaders to open NAFTA for renegotiation. New taxes on imports, aimed at promoting U.S. exports, are mulled in Washington.

Discussion Questions

Here are some questions for discussion regarding the future of free trade:

- Why have developing nations balked at further steps to liberalize global trade? Why do voters in more advanced countries question the wisdom of free trade?
- Why would China benefit from a U.S. withdrawal from the Trans-Pacific Partnership trade deal?
- To what extent is the decline of U.S. manufacturing jobs attributable to the North American Free Trade Agreement and other trade pacts? To what extent is it the result of automation and greater economic productivity?
- What are the tradeoffs that would be involved in a policy that seeks to promote U.S. exports and curb imports through tariffs and/or tax code changes? Who would be the winners from such an approach, and who would lose?
- Is it feasible to reverse the advance of global economic integration in an era of worldwide supply chains?

PERSPECTIVE

Q&A: Matthew Slaughter and Jeff Ferry on Trade

"THE BENEFITS HAVE BEEN UNEVENLY DISTRIBUTED"

Matthew J. Slaughter and Jeff Ferry

Matthew J. Slaughter is the Paul Danos dean and the Earl C. Daum 1924 professor of international business at the Tuck School of Business at Dartmouth College. He is also a research associate at the National Bureau of Economic Research. He served on the White House Council of Economic Advisers from 2005 to 2007; he held the international portfolio, advising President George W. Bush and his Cabinet on issues that included international trade.

Jeff Ferry is research director at the Coalition for a Prosperous America, a Washington-based think tank, and a former journalist and technology entrepreneur. His first book, "The British Renaissance" (Hutchinson, 1994), focused on the strategies and culture of six world-class British companies that emerged from the Thatcher era. He worked in the technology industry for 15 years, and during that time served on an industry advisory committee at the U.S. Department of Commerce. Slaughter and Ferry responded to questions from SAGE Business Researcher freelance correspondent Matthew Benjamin.

What do you see as the fundamental issue with trade and globalization?

Ferry: Globalization is a license for those countries that are willing to abuse trade rules to drive their export-led growth so aggressively that it causes a hollowing out and a deindustrialization of formerly prosperous countries.

Globalization, the way it's been implemented, is a mistake for the top 20 countries in the world. It has delivered a very bad, unhappy situation for millions of people in those countries.

Yes, many elites and well-educated people in these countries have benefited from globalization. But if you have an ever-shrinking population of very prosperous people in the U.S. and other advanced economies, even if they're willing to vote for redistribution, the country will ultimately get poorer. You will end up like medieval France with an aristocracy that owns all of agriculture and a very large, underpaid, underemployed, discontented peasant class. You just can't generate enough wealth that way.

Slaughter: Globalization has boosted productivity and wealth in the U.S. and much of the world, but within many countries the benefits have been unevenly distributed. What is new in the past decade in many advanced countries is that income growth for a majority of workers and households has stopped. Income pressures have been spreading in the U.S. and many other countries, and there is a perception that trade is increasing those pressures, so people want less of it, not more.

We as a country have not been doing nearly enough to address the legitimate concerns of dislocation and opportunity pressures for blue-collar and increasingly white-collar workers as well.

What should we do about it?

Slaughter: An industrial policy to favor manufacturing is not a good answer. There's a host of empirical evidence that says governments are very poor at picking winners and losers.

U.S. policymakers need to recognize and address the causes of opposition to freer trade and investment. And the solutions proposed in the past—more education and trade adjustment assistance for dislocated workers—are not sufficient.

We need a much better funded, better designed, modern social safety net to address the dynamism of the labor market of the 21st century, not the 20th century. And we need policies that link engagement with the world economy to a more progressive tax code that serves to share globalization's gains more widely.

Ferry: To say that the problem of globalization is that it increases inequality in prosperous countries, and that redistribution through the tax code is the answer, is an argument that doesn't go far enough.

The U.S. needs a new economic policy based on balanced trade, restoring manufacturing to health, and export-led growth. The ultimate answer is to create conditions for the success of the industries that will put a large number of people to work in jobs that pay well. We're against mercantilism and in favor of strengthening manufacturing and exports, reducing imports, balancing trade and putting people to work in well-paying jobs that deliver consistent improvements in pay and productivity.

UPDATE IN 2020

U.S. President Donald Trump based his 2016 presidential campaign in part on denouncing other countries for unfair trade practices. And in the first years of his administration, Trump launched trade skirmishes with China, the European Union and even Canada, America's biggest trading partner.

Yet in early 2020, more Americans had a favorable view of international trade than at any time in the past quarter century, according to The Gallup Organization. Seventy-nine percent of those who took part in a survey said foreign trade was "an opportunity for economic growth through increased U.S. exports."[82]

Further, only 18 percent of those surveyed saw a "threat to the economy from foreign imports." This was down nearly half from 2016, when 34 percent held that view. During the 2008 recession, 52 percent of Americans perceived a threat, the highest since Gallup began measuring responses in 1992.

What caused the significant shift in attitude? Said Gallup, "As the economy improved and unemployment declined to historical lows, so too have perceptions of trade as an economic threat."

But soon after the survey, the coronavirus pandemic forced the highest unemployment rate in the United States since the Great Depression, as well as a slump in the economy.

The World Trade Organization (WTO) predicted that the volume of merchandise trade would fall between 13 percent, on an optimistic basis, and 32 percent, on a pessimistic one. However, by the middle of the year, trade volume seemed likely to be down 18.5 percent for 2020.[83]

"The fall in trade we are now seeing is historically large—in fact, it would be the steepest on record. But there is an important silver lining here: It could have been much worse," said WTO Director-General Roberto Azevêdo.

The WTO credited two key moves for moderating the impact on trade. First, the swift lockdowns implemented by Asian and European governments, as well as actions taken by individual American states, initially helped limit the spread of COVID-19. It also cited restrictions on border crossings and a near halt to international air traffic.

For their part, the United States and Canada were locked in a roller-coaster relationship. On Jul. 1, 2020, the U.S.-Mexico-Canada (USMCA) Free Trade Agreement took effect. It was an updated version of the North American Free Trade Agreement, which Trump denounced during his presidential campaign as a "nightmare." He hailed the new agreement as "a tremendous victory for American workers, farmers, manufacturers, and businesses alike," although it was fundamentally the same as the pact it replaced.[84]

Only a month after the agreement took effect, however, Trump resumed a tariff skirmish with Canada over steel and aluminum imports.[85]

In 2018, the U.S. imposed a 25 percent duty on steel and a 10 percent duty on aluminum. Canada responded with tariffs on hundreds of U.S. products, such as ketchup, coffee, strawberry jam and whisky. Those efforts were dropped as negotiations intensified on the USMCA deal.

However, Trump reimposed the aluminum duty in August 2020, alleging there had been a surge in Canadian exports. "Canada was taking advantage of us, as usual," Trump said during a speech in Ohio.[86]

Industry figures showed that while aluminum exports from Canada rose sharply in February and March, they fell steeply in April and May, as federal and state governments in both countries instituted stay-at-home orders.[87]

Canada said it would match the U.S. tariffs "dollar for dollar" and said it was considering duties on a range of items, such as golf clubs, bicycles, refrigerators, washing machines, tripods, sports equipment like bats and hockey sticks, and embossed aluminum cans for beverages. In a tweet, Canadian Prime Minister Justin Trudeau said, "We will always stand up for our aluminum workers. We did so in 2018, and we will stand up for them again now."

—Micheline Maynard

10 GLOBAL MANUFACTURING

Are companies reconsidering their worldwide strategies?

Micheline Maynard

From *SAGE Business Researcher*, September 28, 2015

EXECUTIVE SUMMARY

Corporations rushed to expand their global operations over the last three decades, motivated in part by China's aggressive policies seeking foreign investment. Industries including automobiles, clothing manufacturing and technology opened factories there and in other parts of the developing world, with the United States losing jobs from the shift: In 1979, a record 19.5 million Americans worked in factories; now, around 12.3 million do so, and China has replaced the United States as the No. 1 manufacturing nation. But the complexity of operating overseas, rising labor costs in China and rapidly changing consumer tastes are causing some companies to reconsider their global manufacturing strategies. A growing number view Mexico as a closer-to-home low-wage alternative, and a few corporations are bringing work back to their home countries in a process known as "re-shoring." The challenges of global manufacturing raise a number of questions. Can China keep its manufacturing lead? Will low wages continue to drive global manufacturing? Is re-shoring real?

OVERVIEW

Throughout May and into June, a heat wave enveloped Western Europe. Temperatures soared in Spain, Portugal and France, prompting government warnings, especially for small children and the elderly, about the heat.[1]

Such hot weather might have caught some retailers off guard, as they waited for shipments of summer clothes to arrive. But for Zara, the Spanish mega-retailer, the heat wave represented an opportunity.

With more than half its production in Spain, which is also where it sells 20 percent of its merchandise, Zara quickly adjusted its "fast fashion" lineup.

That meant the company changed its production mix and shipped lightweight summer garments to its stores in the hottest zones weeks before they normally would have received them.

The strategy worked: Spring 2015 sales for Zara's parent company, Inditex, jumped 13.5 percent from February 1 to June 7, while competitors such as Sweden's Hennes & Mauritz (H&M), which produces more than half its garments in Asia, could not respond as quickly.[2]

Zara's nimble response illustrates how manufacturing is changing in the 21st century. Speed is essential, as is flexibility—the ability to meet rapidly changing market conditions.

"If they own the factory, they exert more control," says Amit Khandelwal, a professor of business at Columbia University. He explains that Zara essentially operates two sets of factories: one in low-cost Asian countries to produce basics like T-shirts and jeans, the other in Europe, where it produces limited-edition on-trend clothes that frequently fly out of stores within days of being put on the sales floor.

Apple is another company that has to move fast to satisfy its demanding customers. As soon as the technology company introduces its latest products, "early intenders" place their orders online and line up outside Apple stores to be the first to own them. That puts pressure on Apple's global production network, directed by its lead contractor in Taiwan, to get phones and watches out the door fast.

This pressure to be both fast and efficient illustrates a second change in manufacturing: Globalization and the quest for cheap labor no longer work the way they did in the 1990s, because a far-flung operation can pose major headaches for managers, while the advantage of lower labor costs, which drew so many companies to China, is vanishing.

Manufacturing Role in Economy Varies by Nation

Gross value added by manufacturing as a percentage of national GDP, 2013

Manufacturing accounted for 31 percent of South Korea's economy in 2013, 30 percent of China's, 24 percent of Indonesia's and 22 percent of Germany's. The United States, by comparison, generated 12 percent of its economic output from manufacturing.

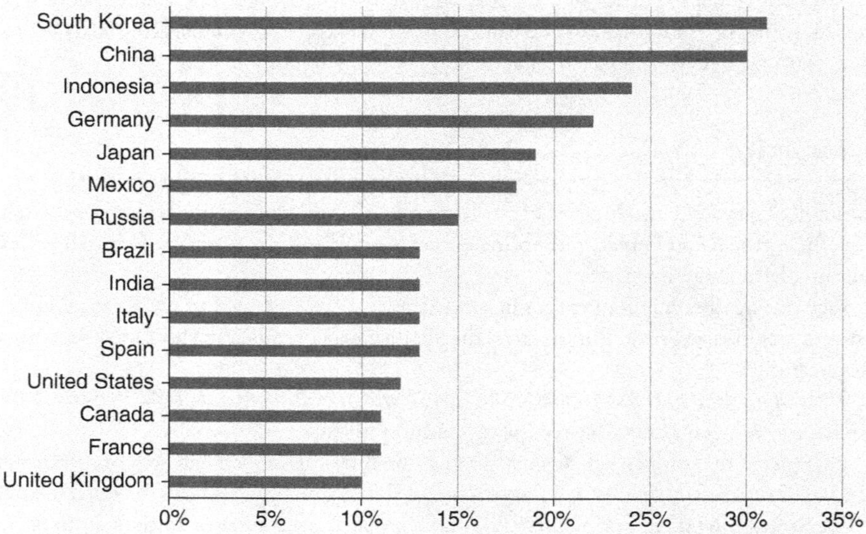

Note: Based on value added in each country's national currency. Figures represent the total value of each country's economic output minus the value of any goods and services used in production.

Source: "National Accounts Statistics: Analysis of Main Aggregates, 2013," Department of Economic and Social Affairs, United Nations, 2014, pp. 88-135, http://tinyurl.com/o688uar.

In the final decades of the 20th century, many CEOs and academics hailed globalization as the future, with corporations believing that opening factories overseas was the best way to thrive in an increasingly competitive world.

One proponent was Harvard University economist Theodore Levitt, who in 1983 predicted a new commercial reality: "the emergence of global markets for standardized consumer products on a previously unimagined scale of magnitude." Instead of operating as multinational companies, with disparate operations planted in various parts of the world, corporations would operate seamlessly in this new global environment, Levitt wrote in the Harvard Business Review.[3]

Wang Chun/VCG via Getty Images

Rows of shipping containers wait at Lianyungang port in China's Jiangsu province; managers of global manufacturing firms must continually assess the efficiency of shipping from China to distant markets.

Executives at all manner of companies defended their growing overseas investments, citing lower labor costs, the incentives offered by countries to open new factories and the chance to sell more goods abroad.

Also fueling their determination to go global was China's huge potential as a market as well as a place to invest. And the opening up of Eastern Europe and the former Soviet Union after the fall of the Berlin Wall led to additional opportunities. "It was kind of a no-brainer," said Jack Smith, the former chief executive of GM.[4] "One of the things that stood out right away was that China had a GDP per capita that was very similar to what was happening in Central and Eastern Europe," where GM had invested after the Berlin Wall came down.

As companies took advantage of a plentiful workforce and, until recently, low labor costs, they shifted millions of jobs and entire industries, especially in textiles and electronics, from the United States, Europe and elsewhere to China, as well as parts of South Asia and Mexico. Companies especially rushed to invest in China after it joined the World Trade Organization in 2001. Its membership created tens of millions of manufacturing jobs in China, and later led to the displacing of the United States as the world's biggest manufacturer.

But such success eventually resulted in higher labor costs in China, and some U.S. manufacturers now see Mexico as a closer-to-home low-wage alternative, thanks to the infrastructure developed there since the North American Free Trade Agreement (NAFTA) was adopted in 1994, and a few companies are even bringing work back to the United States.

Foster Finley, a managing director at the consulting firm AlixPartners in Southfield, Mich., does not expect any sort of wholesale departure from overseas markets, or a return to the glory days of 1979, when 19.5 million people worked in American manufacturing. That figure is now around 12.3 million, according to the Bureau of Labor Statistics.[5]

The Decline of U.S. Manufacturing Jobs

Number of U.S. manufacturing employees, in millions, 1939–2015

The number of manufacturing workers in the United States rebounded slightly to 12.3 million after it had fallen to a 75-year low of 11.5 million in late 2009. Manufacturing employment climbed steadily after World War II, peaking at 19.6 million in June 1979. The number fell over the next three decades, dropping most rapidly during recessions in the early 1980s and early and late 2000s.

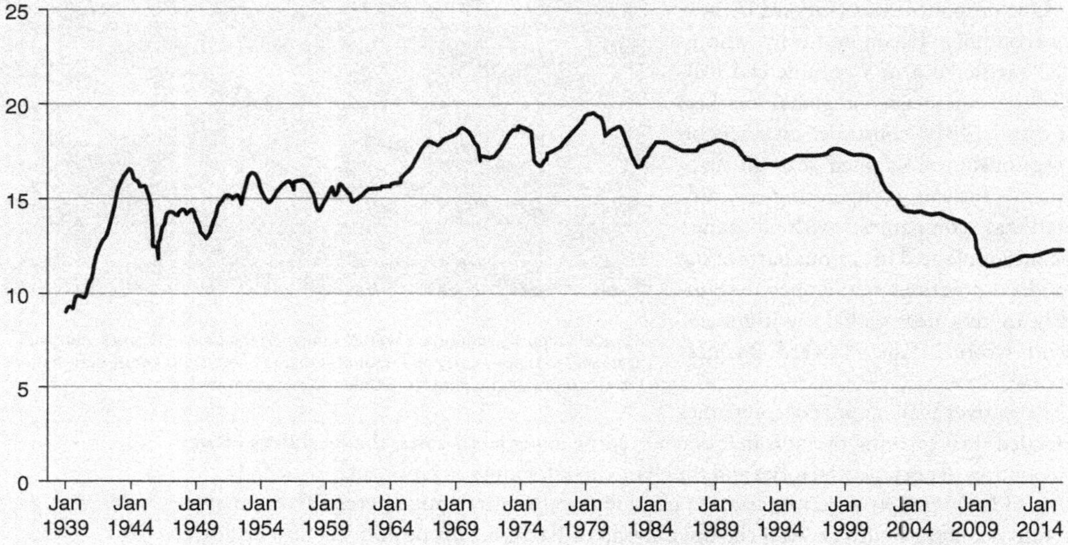

Source: U.S. Bureau of Labor Statistics, accessed Sep. 14, 2015, http://tinyurl.com/42x5ru3.

He's skeptical about the idea of "insourcing," which some global companies such as General Electric have touted, even as they maintain broad networks of factories overseas.

Finley uses another term: "near-shoring," or shifting production to Western Hemisphere nations such as Mexico, where U.S. companies can still save on labor costs but manage operations more easily than if executives are a 15-hour plane ride away.

The reason isn't patriotism, Finley says. "It's very much an effort to produce better business results for the company."

Ian Bremmer, a political scientist and consultant, has a different term for the changes occurring: "guarded globalization." He noted the emergence of a "very different flavor of globalization [in developing nations]—slow-moving, selective and with a heavy dash of nationalism and regionalism."[6]

Haste and scattered global operations can lead to mistakes, as one glaring example shows: In 2010, Toyota CEO Akio Toyoda sat uncomfortably before a congressional committee in Washington, D.C., explaining why millions of his company's cars had to be recalled for defective gas pedals that sometimes led to the autos accelerating out of drivers' control. The issue led to as many as 89 deaths worldwide.

A big reason for the defect, he and others at the carmaker acknowledged then and afterward, was Toyota's push over the past 25 years to become a global manufacturer.[7] As Toyota grew, its internal communication process did not change, despite all the modern tools that technology offered. Toyota remained a Japanese-focused company, with decisions centered there and information not shared fast enough with the rest of the world. In the aftermath of the crisis, Toyota abandoned the idea that it should expand production wherever it could, no matter the stress on its operations.

Justin Rose, a partner and managing director with The Boston Consulting Group, says Toyota's crisis coincided with twin developments in China, where wages were rising and the government was focusing on attracting technology centers and developing an internal culture of innovation.

"The era of super-cheap, highly accessible labor in China is quickly passing or is already over," Rose says. "The next frontier is to transform those workers into more highly skilled laborers and move up the food chain into increasingly value-added activities"—those tasks that are more sophisticated than simple assembly-line ones. That includes devising new manufacturing methods and assembling an entire product, rather than just attaching a part as a device moves down the line.

But, as Zara showed during the heat wave, too much caution and China's new approach could clash with consumers' expectations, honed by a quarter century of seeing the marketplace change with lightning speed.

As the World Wide Web became widely available in the 1990s, and as social media grew this past decade, consumers demanded new products much more quickly than factory output could adjust, especially in industries such as technology and fashion.

Celebrities didn't want to wait for runway fashions to be available during the following season: They wanted the gowns to wear to awards shows *now*. Millions of people who followed the apparel of movie stars and the Duchess of Cambridge also wanted to order those clothes, too, whether or not faraway factories had yet ramped up to produce and ship them.

As economists, business executives and others debate the outlook for manufacturing, here are some of the questions they are asking.

WEIGHING THE ISSUES

Can China Maintain Its Manufacturing Lead?

Over the past 35 years, China made a dedicated push to dominate global manufacturing. But with its economy faltering and labor costs rising, China wants to compete with industrialized countries such as Germany and the United States and to create advanced engineering development centers. That could be tougher to accomplish than simply making the economy bigger.

China's domination of global manufacturing resulted from its government-controlled industrial policy and helped lead to years of extraordinary economic growth.

Growth of China's Role in Global Manufacturing

Percentage value added by country to the global manufacturing economy, 2005 and 2014

China's importance to global manufacturing can be measured by "manufacturing value added"—the share of global gross domestic product generated from manufacturing. It contributed 18 percent of the global manufacturing economy in 2014, far more than in 2005 and well over the 11 percent added by Japan, formerly the second-largest contributor. South Korea and India also increased their share of the global manufacturing economy's value between 2005 and 2014. The contribution of most other countries shrank, including that of the United States.

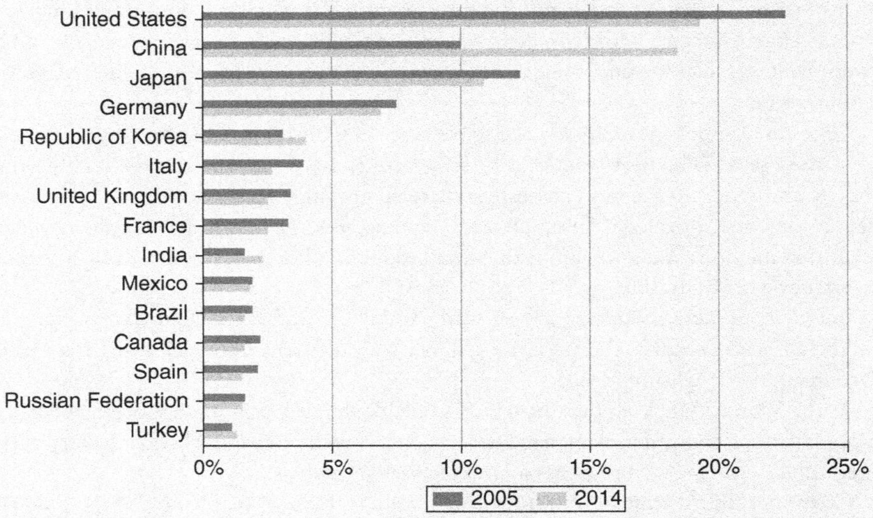

Note: 2014 figures are estimates.

Source: "Leading Manufacturing Economies Share in World MVA," United Nations Industrial Development Organization, June 2015, http://tinyurl.com/pdr3mvo.

Into 2015, China achieved an increase in its gross domestic product (GDP) of at least 7 percent annually for a quarter century. It accompanied its rapid expansion with an industrial policy that called for investments in infrastructure, including roads, high-speed rail and ports. It developed an industrial corridor along its southeastern coast, which is home to about 60 percent of the nation's manufacturing output. To fulfill its goals, 150 million people left villages and towns over three decades to work in cities and factories, in the largest rural-to-urban migration in history.[8]

China's major industries remain state owned. Unlike the United States, China has not put a premium on innovation, although the government wants that to change as the country encourages the development of technology centers. In 2015, it began "Made in China 2025," a plan to "comprehensively upgrade Chinese industry," according to the Center for Strategic and International Studies.

China wants to create 15 innovation centers by 2020 and 40 by 2025, serving 10 priority market sectors. They include advanced information technology, machine tools and robotics, aeronautics and biopharmaceuticals.[9]

China's long-held advantage as a low-cost producer is eroding, as the workers from villages who flocked to cities to work in factories return home, having saved up enough money to live more comfortable lives. New opportunities have arisen for some outside factories, and China's formerly strict one-child policy has limited their replacements.

Now, with China changing its focus from mass-market production to a more sophisticated manufacturing approach, experts question whether it will maintain its manufacturing lead. China continues to grow, meeting its 7 percent target in the first half of 2015, but the crash of the Chinese stock market in mid-2015 raised questions about the world's confidence in the nation's economy, which some investors fear could be an unsustainable bubble.

In July 2015, China's auto dealer group said the nation could see its first decline in auto sales in more than 17 years, amid fears that consumers would avoid major purchases in the wake of the stock market's decline.[10]

Certainly, wage growth has caused some manufacturers to look elsewhere. "If you make textile products, labor is a relatively large part of the cost structure," says Rose. These companies tend to pick the lowest-cost locations, and those now include Vietnam, Bangladesh and North African countries, he says. In 2006, Chinese workers' annual wages averaged about $3,000 (in 2015 dollars), according to figures compiled by TradingEconomics.com. By 2014, that had almost tripled to about $8,200 (in 2015 dollars).[11] In comparison, annual wages for workers in Mexico averaged $5,600 per year, the website estimated.

A trio of analysts at The Boston Consulting Group saw the rise coming in a 2011 research report. "For many goods, when transportation, duties, supply chain risks, industrial real estate, and other costs are fully accounted for, the cost savings of manufacturing in China rather than in some U.S. states will become minimal within the next five years," Harold L. Sirkin, Michael Zinser and Douglas Hohner wrote.[12]

But other experts say too much is at stake for China to abandon the cornerstone of its economic growth.

"You really have to think of China as three pieces," says Finley at AlixPartners. There is coastal China, where manufacturing operations were first established; inland China, which Beijing is touting to manufacturers unhappy with the costs of doing business in the industrial area; and the agriculture-focused hinterlands, areas not yet ready for foreign investment

Finley says his company's clients have been put off by China's efforts to get them to invest inland. "People are not overly thrilled," he says. "You can tap into a China with a much lower wage rate, but the workers are less skilled, less sophisticated; it's a less-infrastructure supported part of China, and you'll have all the commensurate problems."

Despite decades of economic growth, China still does not offer manufacturers the local market for their products that many companies hoped it would. About 70 percent of goods are still exported, Finley says, just the opposite of the United States, where 70 percent of domestic production is purchased by American companies and consumers.

Exports to Asia by State

In $U.S. trillions

With the exception of 2009 and 2012, California's exports to Asia have increased each year since 2005. Exports from Washington have grown since 2009 and surpassed Texas's exports in 2014.

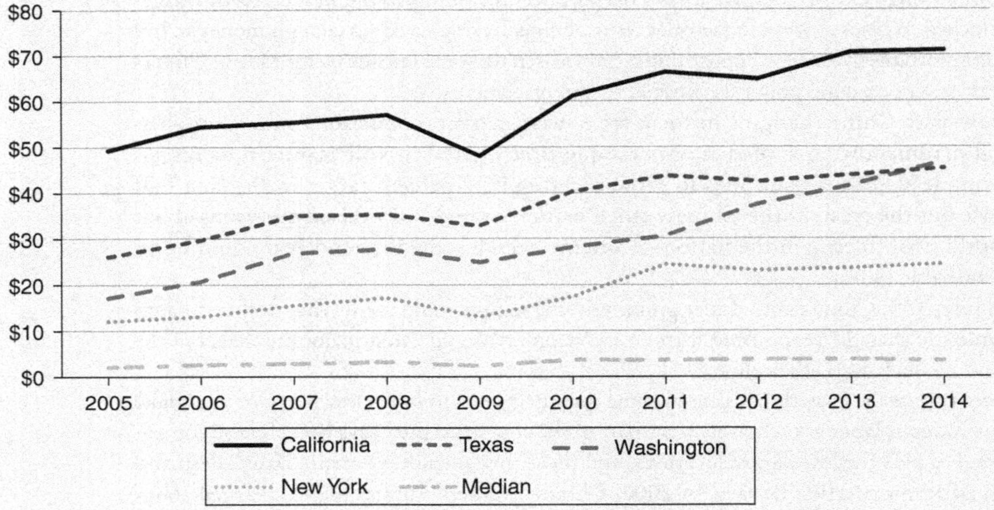

Note: Data are subject to nonsampling errors. Median value gives the value for the "average" state for this metric—the 50th percentile of all states reporting data.

Source: "Exports to Asia (State)," SAGE Stats (website), CQ Press, 2015, http://data.sagepub.com/sagestats/document.php?id=14281#.

He does not write off China's chances for continued global leadership, however. "China has a lot of resources, a lot of people and a lot of ambition," Finley says. "China has plans for expansion and control that are not what the U.S. wants."

Will Low Wages Continue to Drive Global Manufacturing?

The global push of the past 30 years has meant tremendous upheaval for American labor. The days of well-paying working-class jobs with attractive benefits and requiring minimal training are long over.

Union leaders blame globalization, and it's easy to see why. Manufacturing jobs in the United States have plummeted by about 7 million since 1980, even though there has been a slight rebound since the depth of the recession in 2008. At the same time, the number of manufacturing jobs in China has multiplied five times, to around 68 million.[13]

"When you're in the U.S. and talk to trade union folks, they will all say that globalization is bad for labor," says Stephen J. Silvia, a professor at the School of International Service at American University.

For instance, unions have fought hard against the Trans-Pacific Partnership (TPP) treaty, a sprawling agreement that would involve a dozen nations, including the United States, Canada, Australia, Japan, Malaysia and Singapore. The Obama administration vows to protect jobs under TPP. But the AFL-CIO calls the deal "deeply flawed," and says the United States is pushing to grant favored trade status to some countries "with deeply troubling records of human and labor rights violations."[14]

But take the conversation outside the United States, however, and the attitude changes. Employees at companies in developed countries may, or may not, have been hurt by globalization. It depends on the country, the company and the industry, Silvia says.

He contends that the push overseas has not hurt skilled workers in Germany, Japan and, to some extent, the United States.

At the lower end of the scale, the quintupling of manufacturing jobs in China and the growth of jobs in countries such as Mexico, Cambodia and Indonesia has benefited their workers and raised their standard of living, even though their wages are less than in the United States.

Economic experts divide industrial jobs into three categories. The first, entry-level jobs, require few skills and can be performed by pretty much anyone with basic literacy skills. The second, midlevel jobs, may require some training but not formal education. Finally, skilled jobs, with technology components, require intensive training for industrial workers.

The first two categories have grown the most as companies invested in China—and they are the most threatened in any economy, if the sole determinant is low-wage levels, says manufacturing efficiency expert James P. Womack. He describes this practice as "labor arbitrage," in which companies locate investments based entirely on pay rates.

"Once the Cold War was over and the Soviet Union fell apart, it was off to the races in terms of finding cheap labor," he says.

Textiles aside, Womack contends labor arbitrage may be coming to an end in China and elsewhere for some industries, simply because of consumer demand. "The easy part is over for China," he says. "The large part of what could be moved has been moved."

Two things are colliding to limit Chinese job growth, Silvia says. One is demographics. China's one-child policy means that fewer young people will be filing into factories in coming years.

The second is China's own shift away from mass production to advanced technology and innovation. Khandelwal, at Columbia, says it isn't a detriment to China that wages are rising.

"The fact that China is no longer a cheap place to produce means the country has developed quite a bit," he says. "So, what's going to be your next move? It's not going to be assembling components. It's going to be creating value added."

Given the depth and breadth of China's manufacturing economy, Khandelwal believes that companies will not abandon it simply for lower-wage countries. For one thing, China may have been a historic anomaly.

For years, his native India has been talking about expanding its economy, only to fail to develop the kind of working class that has emerged in China.

"Can India, or Brazil or African countries industrialize?" he asks. "It's a really deep question and important for policy, too. Can you leapfrog, or do you need a transition period?" The answer, he says, is not yet evident.

Is Re-Shoring Real?

Over the past 30 years, American manufacturing was awash in "outsourcing," or moving work to production sites outside the United States.

In recent years, there has been anecdotal evidence of "insourcing," or moving production back to the United States, a practice that some also call re-shoring.

The Organization for International Investment, a trade group representing foreign companies in the United States, says these firms have created 5.8 million U.S. jobs, or about 5 percent of private-sector employment. That includes 2.2 million manufacturing jobs, the group says. There has been direct foreign investment in all 50 states, in industries ranging from automobiles to food and beverage products to chemicals.[15]

Japanese Lead in U.S. Manufacturing Jobs

Number of workers in the United States employed in foreign-owned factories, by country, 2012

Japanese manufacturers employed more than 326,000 American workers in 2012. Together, Japanese, German (293,300), British (258,300) and Swiss (191,600) companies provided almost half of the nearly 2.2 million foreign manufacturing positions in the United States.

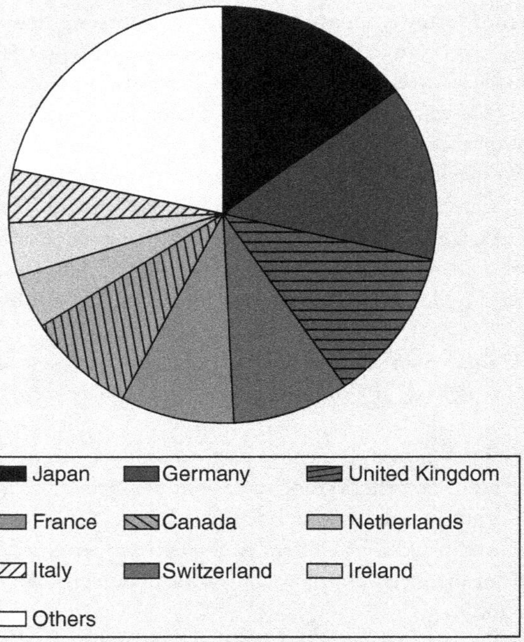

Source: "Insourcing Benefits U.S. Manufacturing," Organization for International Investment, January 2015, p. 2, http://tinyurl.com/p9c282n.

But beyond foreign companies doing business in the United States, the data about U.S. companies moving work home are sketchy. Individual companies have trumpeted the things they are doing to bring back work. For instance, General Electric outsourced about 80 percent of its IT work to India and other countries in the 1990s but has since reduced that outsourcing to some 70 percent.[16]

In a 2014 study, the accounting firm Deloitte found that technological advances such as cloud computing and online business processes were allowing companies to keep work overseas. Eighty-nine percent of survey respondents said they would continue outsourcing, until there was legislation blocking them from doing so.[17]

But there is evidence of a growing interest in near-shoring, or moving work closer to the United States. For a number of companies, that means Mexico.[18] Finley of AlixPartners says such a shift is a far more likely prospect than wholesale returns of factories and products.

More than 40 percent of respondents to an AlixPartners survey said they would consider moving production if it meant their companies could better meet U.S. demand. And 86 percent said they have shifted production already, or plan to do so in the next two to three years.[19]

Saravanan Kesavan, associate professor of operations at the Kenan-Flagler Business School at the University of North Carolina, Chapel Hill, says near-shoring has become tempting for companies that want to escape long supply chains. "Manufacturers set up shop where costs were low," he says, "but when you're sourcing from the other side of the world, you might be placing orders six to nine months in advance. Who knows what's actually going to sell six months in advance?"

Finley and others say Mexico's maturing supply network, or base, has finally made it a viable alternative to Asian production for many industries, especially those producing more expensive goods such as automobiles and electronics.

"In the case of Mexico, the supply base in the past few years has become drastically well developed," says Osamu "Simon" Nagata, executive vice president of Toyota North America and the veteran purchasing director at Toyota.

Between 2002 and 2012, Mexico's automotive exports increased 152 percent, to $70.3 billion, and electronics exports grew by 73 percent, to $74 billion, according to Stratfor, a global consulting firm.[20]

Mexico's emergence has come not only because of the North American Free Trade Agreement, now 20 years old, but also because of free trade pacts it has signed with other regions, such as Europe and Latin America.[21]

"Firms want to be located in countries where they can freely export to any market," says Donald Grimes, an economist at the University of Michigan.

But Mexico still has its ups and downs because of competition and the weaknesses in its labor force. For one thing, foreign direct investment fell in 2014, to $22.6 billion, well short of the record $42.1 billion in 2013. (A major investment by Anheuser-Busch InBev, the international beverage company, in Mexican beverage giant Groupo Modelo helped boost the 2013 figure.)[22]

Increasingly, it is losing its textile business, lured from the Northeast and Southern United States, to Asian manufacturers who produce in high volumes that Mexican plants can't match.

Some companies, analysts note, are put off by the activities of Mexican drug lords, who are profiting from the growth in foreign investment by tightening their grip on industries they can control, such as mining and logging.[23]

Finley, however, says that American businesses in general feel more comfortable working with their Mexican neighbors than with the Chinese government. "People view China with some wariness and skepticism. I don't come across a lot of people who worry about the Mexicans because they'll take us over someday," he says.

BACKGROUND

Trade's Deep Roots

Manufacturing has been an international industry for hundreds of years, with the concept of global trade at its heart. In the 1600s, English and Dutch traders crossed the Atlantic seeking business opportunities.

English entrepreneurs in 1607 founded Virginia's Jamestown colony, where they manufactured soap, pitch, glass and lumber—some of the first American-made products to be exported.[24]

At the beginning of the industrial age in the late 18th century, English factories began exporting goods. In the 19th century, the American South expanded its economy by exporting raw materials, primarily cotton, to foreign countries, where they were made into finished products, in contrast to the North, where industries developed to supply local markets.

After President Abraham Lincoln ordered the blockade of Southern ports during the Civil War, smugglers brought in goods from Bermuda, the Bahamas and Cuba, scooping up illegal shipments of tobacco and cotton to supply factories overseas.[25]

By the 20th century, companies considered global production as soon as they reached significant scale. Henry Ford, who founded his eponymous car company in 1903, declared he wanted Ford Motor to produce vehicles abroad as soon as possible. He made good on his promise, building his first cars in Canada and England starting in 1911, two years before he perfected the automatic assembly line.

Two world wars interrupted the flow of global manufacturing and trade. German companies, in particular, were stymied in efforts to produce abroad immediately after World War I, leading them to focus on their internal markets. British and Japanese companies actually opened their first car assembly factories in the United States before World War II, just as American companies including GM and Ford opened production facilities in Japan.[26]

Growth after World War II

As the world economy regrouped after World War II, manufacturing became the key step in moving a country from an agrarian society to a wealthier, industrialized one. In 1970, manufacturing employment accounted for just under 300 million jobs worldwide, or about 25 percent of global employment, according to the United Nations Industrial Development Organization (UNIDO). In 2009, manufacturing accounted for roughly 500 million jobs worldwide, or about 16 percent of global jobs, UNIDO says.[27]

Now, manufacturing accounts for roughly 500 million jobs worldwide, or about 16 percent of global jobs, UNIDO says.

Manufacturing employment has been rising in developing countries and falling in developed ones, where service jobs have made up for some of the lost factory jobs. Manufacturing as a share of GDP has declined from 16.4 percent in 1990 in industrialized countries to 15 percent in 2010, said UNIDO. In industrializing countries, or those still making the transition from agriculture, manufacturing as a share of GDP has risen from 16.5 percent to 21.3 percent.

Worldwide, 64.1 percent of global manufacturing output takes place in industrialized countries, compared with 67.7 percent in 2010, according to UNIDO.

The United States is one of the nations most affected by the recent global shift. According to the Bureau of Labor Statistics, the nation had 19.3 million manufacturing jobs at the beginning of 1980. Manufacturing fell to a low of 11.5 million jobs at the beginning of 2010, after the depth of the recession. By mid-2015, U.S. manufacturing employment had rebounded to 12.3 million jobs.[28]

Some of the positions, including those at union-represented U.S. auto factories, were restored at lower pay than before the recession. For instance, veteran workers at factories represented by

California Manufacturing Payroll at $70 Billion

Annual manufacturing employee payrolls and wages of production workers, 2013, in $U.S. billions

In 2013, California establishments had the highest annual payroll for manufacturing employees in the country. Wages for production workers accounted for a little less than half of that total. However, in other manufacturing states such as Ohio and Michigan, annual wages for production workers exceeded 50 percent of the annual payroll for manufacturing employees.

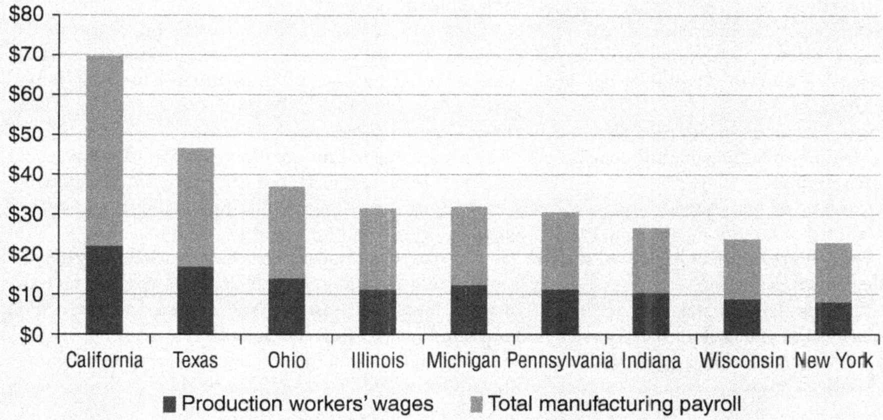

Notes: Employees above the supervisor level are excluded from the annual wages of production workers. "Payroll" includes gross earnings of all employees on the payrolls of operating manufacturing establishments paid in the calendar year, including production workers. It also includes salaries, wages, commissions, dismissal pay, bonuses, vacation and sick-leave pay, as well as compensation in kind, before such deductions as employees' Social Security contributions, withholding taxes, group insurance, union dues and savings bonds.

Sources: "Annual Payroll in Manufacturing (State)," SAGE Stats (website), CQ Press, 2015, http://data.sagepub.com/sagestats/document.php?id=12630; "Production Workers Annual Wages in Manufacturing (State)," SAGE Stats (website), CQ Press, 2015, http://data.sagepub.com/sagestats/document.php?id=12921#.

the United Auto Workers earned about $28 an hour in wages during their most recent contract (which expires in fall 2015). But starting pay for newer workers, under a two-tier wage system implemented in the wake of the 2009 auto bailout, was about $19 per hour. Those workers do not have the opportunity to "grow" to full pay during the life of the contract.[29]

Foreign companies in a variety of industries, including automotive, appliances, food and beverages, are one of the major sources of manufacturing investment in the United States. Manufacturing investment by foreign companies in 2013, the most recent year for which information is available, was $65.9 billion, according to the Commerce Department.[30]

These jobs tend to be more stable than those at U.S.-based companies, because investments were made recently and companies want to be able to fully amortize them. During the 2007–2009 recession, manufacturing jobs at U.S. companies fell by 33 percent, but by just 6 percent at U.S. plants of foreign companies, Commerce said.

U.S. Milliner Hangs His Hat on Quality, Innovation

Manufacturer Thrives by Staying Small

When Aretha Franklin bought a gray felt hat in 2009, business soared for Mr. Song Millinery. The Detroit hat maker could have gone to China or partnered with other fashion houses to make its stylish toppers. It chose not to do so.

For its first quarter century, Mr. Song Millinery was a small but beloved hat shop in Detroit, owned by Korean-American immigrants.

Members of the Song family designed, produced and sold hats mainly for a clientele of fashionable and religious women of all ethnic backgrounds.

Six women made the hats in a small workshop on the premises, part of a "dead art," as Luke Song, the shop's lead designer, put it.[31] He estimates there are only a dozen such custom milliners in the United States.

But when Aretha Franklin chose a gray felt Mr. Song hat with a large rhinestone-trimmed box for her appearance at the 2009 presidential inauguration, the shop's business exploded. In the weeks after President Obama's inauguration, Song received 5,000 orders for the Aretha hat alone (a version remains in his lineup, at a retail price of $179).

Before the inauguration, Moza Inc., the hat firm's parent company, did $1 million in annual business. By the following year, the company had $7 million to $8 million in orders, a sales volume that it has maintained, although the business has changed significantly since then. The staff grew from 11 to as many as 27, and Mr. Song Millinery moved out of Detroit to much larger quarters in suburban Southfield, Mich.

But with the notoriety and additional business came the pressures of trying to manufacture a specialty product in the United States.

Song says he was offered numerous opportunities to partner with fashion houses, and to expand his core business by producing some of his lineup in China and other parts of Asia. He refused. "By producing in the U.S., I can control inventory and quality," he says.

It's one thing to produce iPhones or car parts overseas, he says. If he simply produced the same hats, season after season, Song says, "then global production might make sense."

The hat business, like the fashion business in general, is constantly changing, he explains, and dealing with an overseas supplier or maintaining his own factories could keep him from creating new designs.

Song offers a fresh lineup each fall and spring, supplying hats for attendees at the Kentucky Derby, Royal Ascot in England, the Gold Cup in Melbourne, Australia, and for numerous celebrities. In the post-Franklin years, he has retired many of the line's more traditional large-brimmed hats and shifted to producing fascinators, which are small hats that are attached to the head with a hair comb, rather than sitting squarely on the head.

Elaborate fascinators are favorites of the Duchess of Cambridge (the former Kate Middleton) and other young British socialites, causing demand for them to soar as fans look for "RepliKates."

Fascinators and their slightly larger cousins, which Song calls "hatinators," retail from $75 to $350. Unlike bigger hats, whose bases can be built on a frame and produced in multiples, each fascinator essentially must be handcrafted. The trim on them is especially noticeable because the hat is so small. That means Song, and other custom hat designers, must use unusual and expensive material like stiffened ribbons, feathers and netting.

Here, Song has run into one of the challenges of trying to guide a domestic company in an era of global manufacturing.

He says he is unable to find U.S. sources of the décor he wants to use on these hats and must import the trimmings from China and elsewhere. "Raw materials are very hard to find," he says. "I'm still importing raw materials."

Along with changing his line, Song also has shifted his sales from his family's brick-and-mortar store to selling completely online.

By the time he closed the shop in 2015, internet sales were outnumbering individual purchases by 10 to 1, and it did not make sense to pay rent on a retail space or employ sales staff. It was a bittersweet decision, Song says. "I miss the interaction with clients."

His internet sales plus his U.S. location have allowed Song to avoid one of the biggest pitfalls of global production: missing deadlines. Because he can simply walk into his workroom, he knows whether his production is on track. In fact, says Song, "I often turn away clients if we are overwhelmed with orders. Only when I know we have plenty of available time for the design will I take an order."

Song, whose background was in biochemistry, says he is constantly wrestling with the practical side of production versus the styles he wants to make.

"My analytical side always attempts to create less labor-intensive designs. But my fashion side always wins that argument."

—*Micheline Maynard*

China's Rise

Outside the United States, China by far has led the expansion of manufacturing employment. In 1970, it had 14.2 million manufacturing jobs, placing third behind the United States with 18.2 million and the Soviet Union with 27.1 million, according to UNIDO.

By 1990, China had 42.4 million manufacturing jobs, dwarfing the Soviet Union (which was about to disintegrate) and the United States. In 2010, China had 68.8 million manufacturing jobs, leading the United States and the new third player, India. By 2012, 50 percent of all manufactured goods in the world were produced in China.

In the last decade, Vietnam grew almost as quickly as China. Between 2005 and 2010, Vietnam's manufacturing sector rose by an average of 9 percent a year, according to McKinsey & Co. The growth was fueled by Vietnam's 2007 entry in the World Trade Organization, and it was balanced between the industrial and services sectors, with each accounting for about 40 percent of Vietnam's annual output.[32]

Vietnam has a thriving retail market of its own. Its retail sales have risen from $42.3 billion in 2008 to $75.6 billion in 2014, and the forecasting group Economist Intelligence Unit predicts sales could soar to $109 billion by 2017. Ho Chi Minh City and Hanoi both have fast-growing retail markets, with new shopping centers featuring global brand names such as Hermès, Banana Republic and Topshop.[33]

Bangladesh, now the world's third-largest exporter of clothing among developing countries, has become an Asian center for garment manufacturing. It nearly doubled its garment exports between 2004 and 2009, according to The New York Times, and that industry employs 3 million people, more than any other in a nation of 160 million whose economy is largely based on agriculture.[34]

Bangladesh has nearly 70 million people of working age, and it could easily absorb some of China's 20 million garment industry jobs, should companies choose to move them. But Bangladesh has a literacy rate of only 55 percent, compared with 92 percent for China. And regular blackouts lasting several hours a day beset the country.

Trade Wars

Two major trade confrontations in the 1980s between the United States and Asian countries had a significant impact on U.S. industry. One was the Voluntary Restraint Agreement negotiated between the United States and Japan over automobile manufacturing, after Japanese imports captured more than 30 percent of U.S. auto sales. The agreement limited Japanese imports to 2 million vehicles; to sell more vehicles in the United States, the companies had to produce them at domestic plants.

Union leaders thought that if the Japanese built plants here, they would quickly be unionized, Womack says. They miscalculated: The Japanese, German and Korean manufacturers built an entire nonunion industry, largely in the American South.

Meanwhile, China focused on developing a steel industry that is now the world's biggest, capturing about half of global market share. A key reason it wanted its own steel industry was to attract auto companies, which invested more money in China in 2014 than in any other global market.[35]

China produces more than four times as much steel as the U.S. industry did at its peak in the 1970s.[36] The industry is largely government owned. In recent years, it has focused more on exports, leading to charges in the United States and Europe that China is dumping steel at prices lower than other manufacturers can afford.

Chinese policies have allowed foreign manufacturers to depart from the past practice of sourcing parts locally and then exporting finished goods. Apple's iPhone is a good example of how things have changed.

The iPhone is designed in the United States and assembled in China (as well as at one production site in Brazil), but Apple sources the components from suppliers in 30 countries, according to the company.[37]

Andrew Rassweiler, senior director of materials and cost benchmarking at IHS Technology, told the public radio program Marketplace that a U.S.-built iPhone could cost as much as $2,000 at retail, if all U.S.-sourced materials were used. The parts alone, he estimated, would cost $600, and Apple could be expected to add a substantial markup.[38]

The Supply Chain

The iPhone is but one example of the evolution of supply chains in global manufacturing, both in China and the United States. Supply chains refer to the flow of components to a factory, and the flow of finished goods to the end user. Until the 1990s, American manufacturers typically kept days' and even weeks' worth of parts on hand. But that meant they had cash tied up in inventory they were not using.

As the 1990 book "The Machine That Changed the World" explained, Japanese manufacturers embraced the practice of just-in-time inventory, or keeping as little inventory on hand as possible and relying on frequent shipments of parts ordered as needed.

For one thing, they did not have the money to tie up in inventory during their rebuilding years after World War II. For another, their factories tended to be smaller than sprawling U.S. facilities, meaning they didn't have space to store the parts.

Now, just-in-time is a standard practice across the world's manufacturers, made possible by developments in shipping, including air freight and the standardization of containers, says Womack, co-author of the 1990 book.

Before World War II, goods were shipped in all kinds of packages and sizes. But the need to ship materials around the world for wartime led to the development of a global standard for shipping containers. In 1955, the first standardized container that could be loaded directly onto a ship, train or truck was developed.[39]

Freighters are now built to hold standard-sized shipping containers, which can be loaded at a factory and taken by rail or truck to a nearby port, for transportation around the world.

Technology Revolution

Beyond the ability to move goods, communications technology allowed manufacturers to monitor their operations in real time, and to communicate with suppliers from different parts of the globe. As computers began to appear on desktops during the 1980s, and companies were linked by telephone and then high-speed modems, managers found it easier to share information about their operations.

Depending on the company, this information was available to different departments within a corporation and sometimes shared with suppliers, and was easily viewable on a computer screen.

Bob Shanks, chief financial officer at Ford, says computer technology has helped shift Ford from a company with flags planted in different markets, mainly the United States and Europe, to one operating seamlessly worldwide. About 50 percent of its manufacturing footprint is outside the United States, and he expects that to grow.

"We are very much a global company—global in terms of our investment, global in driving a consistent strategy across the region, global in terms of product," Shanks says.

He reached for his tablet computer to demonstrate how he could see Ford's operations in real time. Each region regularly submits data on cost, revenue and manufacturing output. Rather than wait for information to arrive by email, Shanks need only bring up the region of a business unit he wants to review, then click on various data and compare regions with each other in real time.

"Before you had separate area rugs," he says. "Now, it's a tapestry, and it's all woven into one fabric."

Technology links are only a tool for executives, however, says Shanks. They still face significant challenges in managing their factories around the world.

CURRENT SITUATION

The Zara Model

The spring 2015 heat wave only enhanced the global manufacturing reputation of the Spanish fashion retailer Zara.

It is a presence in American shopping malls, on high streets across Europe and in countries from Azerbaijan to Venezuela. Zara sells clothing for men, women and children, with a home-goods business offering tableware, fragrances and bedding. Whether you speak English or Greek, Spanish or French, Zara's website can adjust to your preference.

"If you go to Zara every week, you see something new," says Khandelwal, the Columbia University business professor.

Zara is inextricably linked with its Spanish base, yet it taps production sources around the world. Khandelwal says many experts point to Zara as the company that most successfully manipulates its supply chain, the flow of goods to its factories and the distribution of finished products afterward.

"Envision it as literally a thread from retailers to manufacturers," says Kesavan of the University of North Carolina. "It used to be a smaller thread. Now, it literally wraps around the world."

Basics like T-shirts are made in cheap-labor countries such as Indonesia, but Zara also offers limited-edition products, often featuring international designers, which it aims to sell at close to the retail price, without deep discounts.

When those products sell out, they are not restocked. The healthy margins on these items are meant to offset the slimmer margins on cheaper goods, Khandelwal explains. Zara's flexibility has allowed it to avoid the long lead times that plague other fashion companies, which are often stuck with too much inventory of goods that don't take off with consumers.

Because of its size, Zara has the flexibility to own its own factories, or to contract out the work, Khandelwal says. All these decisions are made at its headquarters in Arteixo, Spain, called The Cube, home to its 200 designers, who keep its eight labels fresh.

Communication Issues

Even though a company can operate globally and control its supply chain, manufacturing is far from a trouble-free proposition. Language barriers, time differences and human nature interfere with the best of intentions.

Toyota in 2015 is a much different company from the Toyota that began this decade. CEO Akio Toyoda is now an experienced chief executive, known for his love of racing as much as his company leadership.

Then, he was only months in the job, despite his status as the grandson of Toyota's owner, and he faced one of the biggest crises at Toyota since his grandfather had to restart the company after World War II.

In 2009 and 2010, the company recalled millions of its cars worldwide for problems with unintended acceleration, which caused drivers to have trouble keeping their cars under control.

As it turned out, the problem was discovered first in Europe, and repairs swiftly ordered, but information on how to fix the cars was not shared across Toyota's operations.[40] That meant Americans waited longer for repairs, even though Toyota knew how to make the fixes.

"We were like a tree that grew too rapidly, that as a result was not able to form a strong enough trunk to protect it from the elements," Toyoda said, looking back on the situation in March 2014.[41]

Toyota's recalls in Japan, Europe, the United States and elsewhere were a wake-up call that the company had to evolve from a Japan-focused company to a global one that could act quickly, no matter where a problem occurred.

After the recall crisis, Toyota established a global executive in charge of quality and delegated responsibility for addressing quality issues to each of its major regions.

The company opened up its top management ranks to non-Japanese executives, naming an American, Julie Hamp, as its global communications chief and a Frenchman, Didier LeRoy, as one of six executive vice presidents. (Hamp resigned in 2015 after her arrest on charges of illegally importing prescription drugs from California to Japan.)[42]

And it put a three-year hold on building more factories. That, in part, enabled Germany's Volkswagen to eclipse Toyota in the first half of 2015 as the world's biggest carmaker.

The hold lifted in 2015, when Toyota announced plans to build a factory in Mexico. It will mark the first time in North America that Toyota will have an established supply chain to feed the plant, says Nagata, the company's longtime purchasing executive.

After "the Learning Period" at Toyota

Automaker Embraces Sustainable, and Smarter, Growth

A deadly mistake that caused some of its cars to unexpectedly accelerate led Toyota to assess its worldwide operations and a corporate culture that stressed growth over safety. The result: Toyota adopted a new approach the company calls sustainable growth.

In 2002, Toyota, the largest Japanese automaker, quietly introduced a set of goals it wanted to achieve by 2010. The most striking was its ambition to become the world's largest auto manufacturer, with 15 percent of the global car market.

At that time, the No. 1 manufacturer held just 14 percent of the market: General Motors, long the world's leading carmaker. Toyota itself had only 10 percent of the market.

Analysts were skeptical, given that Toyota at the time ranked fourth in U.S. sales and was only beginning to build its sales in other markets.

But Toyota embarked on an aggressive plan to open factories everywhere, from France to China to Canada and the United States. By 2008, as GM fell into a spiral that would lead to bankruptcy, Toyota had achieved dominance of the global car market with 14.2 percent of the recession-hit market.[43]

Then came what is euphemistically known inside the company as "the learning period" and what any other company might consider an existential crisis. Toyota recalled millions of cars worldwide, due to a defect involving unintended acceleration, in which the car could surge out of the driver's control. The issue ultimately resulted in as many as 89 deaths worldwide.

The carmaker knew of the problem first in Europe and ordered repairs there but did not share the information with other parts of its global operations. The lag led to millions of recalls worldwide, a congressional investigation and a U.S. government probe.

Toyota reached a then-record $1.2 billion settlement with the U.S. Justice Department, and admitted that it lied twice about the problem. "Toyota put sales over safety and profit over principle," said George Venizelos, assistant director of the FBI.[44] The company voluntarily halted its global expansion and took a years-long look at itself.

Osamu "Simon" Nagata, who had led the company's purchasing operations throughout its global push, was tapped by the CEO, Akio Toyoda, to thoroughly review Toyota's production network.

Toyoda asked Nagata to devise preventive measures so a mistake on such a grand scale could never occur again. In the process, Nagata says, Toyota shifted from simply expanding production wherever it could, no matter the stress on its operations, to the idea of sustainable growth, which it could more easily manage. In the process, the company gave more authority to executives around the world, and vowed to share information faster and more widely.

"Sustainable growth," Nagata explains, "may be different from simple growth, in quantity, or in market share, or the amount of profit. Our management team has been re-identifying, redefining what kind of growth Toyota should have."

(Continued)

(Continued)

Nagata says two global auto companies build more than 10 million units a year: Toyota and Volkswagen, which passed Toyota to become the world's biggest carmaker in the first half of 2015.

"Do we want to be a 20 million-unit carmaker? Is that our goal? Is that what we should look for? Bigger is better? Or more is better?" he says, with a skeptical tone, clearly indicating he does not think that will be the case.

Although it wants its sales to expand, Nagata says, Toyota realizes that transportation now means more than automobiles. The key word has become "mobility," which can be everything from car sharing to public transit to self-driving vehicles, as well as the fuel-efficient and electric vehicles the company has been developing.

"If there are more customers who are happy with our product, we're happy, too. Toyota would like to be a leading company in the future of mobility. That may be one of the goals we need to realize instead of market share or sales," Nagata says.

In 2015, Toyota lifted a self-imposed three-year ban on building new factories. In April, it announced a $1 billion investment in Mexico to manufacture the Corolla, and Nagata will oversee the project.[45]

The decision is striking for two reasons. For the first time in building a factory, Nagata says, Toyota will tap a well-developed network of automotive parts suppliers, in contrast to the empty landscape that Toyota encountered when it opened its first plants in North America.

Back then, the company had to persuade Japanese and other suppliers to build satellite factories nearby, he says, but now that won't be necessary because the Mexican market is well established and because Toyota has a network in the United States.

Second, Toyota plans to use its Mexico plant to institute a more streamlined approach than in its big U.S. plants. Under the Toyota New Global Architecture, plants will have shorter assembly lines and will be able to produce vehicles from more than one platform, or the underpinnings of a car.

Although factories have been able to produce multiple types of automobiles, the assembly lines were configured for individual platforms.

All this requires strong collaboration with Toyota's suppliers so Toyota does not anger or endanger its customers again.

Says Nagata: "We should be capable enough to do several things—immediate communication. After learning that quality problems happened in the manufacturing process, we should immediately understand what kind of problems suppliers made, or Toyota made. We need to quickly make a judgment, and inform our customers."

—*Micheline Maynard*

Supply Chain Problems

Toyota was able to find solutions to the problems that led to its recalls. But ensuring quality across the supply chain has been a major headache for some global manufacturers.

Take the recall of airbags made by the Japanese company Takata, a supplier to Toyota, Honda and a dozen other global carmakers.

The airbags were installed in more than 30 million cars worldwide, but have been exploding with more force than intended. Takata doesn't know how to fix the problem, although it is making replacements, and the U.S. government can't say whether the replacement airbags will be free of defects. The issue is likely to drag on for years, until a solution is found and the cars can be repaired.

Meanwhile, the flooring giant Lumber Liquidators, once a darling of Wall Street, is struggling. It became the subject of an investigation by "60 Minutes" alleging that laminated flooring products imported from China had higher levels of formaldehyde than were allowed by California law.

Lumber Liquidators' CEO resigned, and its shares fell to new lows in summer 2015.[46] The complexities of the supply chain and the jobs that have been lost to global competition have prompted warnings from Democrats and trade groups that companies should be cautious about expanding further.

And yet, one of the most aggressive trade pacts ever is now the subject of sweeping negotiations. The Trans-Pacific Partnership, involving a dozen Pacific Rim countries including the United States, would cover nearly 40 percent of the global economy.

In the United States, the TPP has become the 21st century version of NAFTA, in terms of the political debate that it has raised. Support for the treaty has been generated by the U.S. Coalition for TPP, a group of companies and associations ranging from farming to publishing to retailing. They say the agreement will open up markets for farmers and manufacturers and create U.S. jobs.[47]

Foes have run television ads opposing it, and a variety of websites denounce it, especially because details of the agreement are being kept secret until a final draft is ready.

Nonetheless, President Obama, a Democrat, has continued to push for the pact. In June 2015, Congress gave him "fast track" authorization to proceed on the agreement, meant to lower tariffs and create new regulations for everything from global banking to agriculture and the pharmaceutical industry.[48]

Obama insists that the TPP will not threaten American jobs. "We should level the playing field so that our workers have the chance to compete and win," he said.[49]

But others say that globalization harms the American industrial workforce. "In terms of the future, American manufacturing workers will be the big losers, with significant downward pressure on their wages and benefits, and increased job insecurity," says Gary Chaison, professor of industrial relations at Clark University.

Negotiators failed to reach a deal this summer, but talks were set to continue in fall 2015.

LOOKING AHEAD

Automation Threat

Experts say two factors will determine what happens to global manufacturing. One is innovation: Who can find creative ways to compete in a rapidly changing global economy? And the second is technology: How much work will be performed by industrial workers, and how much by machines?

"The big thing I'm keeping an eye on is automation," says Khandelwal of Columbia University. "The same trends that have hit the U.S. in manufacturing are now hitting China. It's allowing firms to increase value added without extra workers."

Rose, the managing director at The Boston Consulting Group, believes the swell of manufacturing employment in China is over.

"Companies have learned from going to China and other places that there are penalties in productivity that [come] with low-wage labor, and they have become more sophisticated in looking at productivity-adjusted wages," Rose says.

As in the United States, Kandelwal sees a difficult period in China as automation displaces vast numbers of workers.

"That's going to be a painful adjustment process," he says, "but it's not necessarily a bad thing."

A drop in manufacturing employment could free up workers for other industries, such as the technology centers that China is encouraging employers to create, Khandelwal says.

It also could help overcome a possible worker shortage resulting from China's one-child policy of the late 20th century.

Khandelwal says automation could allow other emerging countries, perhaps those in the Middle East or Africa, to catch up faster because they would bypass what has historically been the first step—opening factories with human-operated assembly lines. That step requires creating thousands or even millions of manufacturing jobs and training workers to fill them.

These factories would require fewer employees for the same amount of production, but those overseeing production would need to be better educated to make the best use of the technology. That is a challenge, even in industrialized countries, where skilled production workers are in demand. "Can India or Brazil or African countries actually industrialize? Some people think not," Khandelwal says. "Others say that China will be the last country to experience [massive job growth] because of automation."

Innovating Globally

To succeed, global manufacturing investments also require innovation. Where will the best ideas come from? And, equally important, can innovation translate to other markets?

In this area, the manufacturing world is paying close attention to Elon Musk, the billionaire CEO of Tesla Motors and SpaceX.

Musk is a modern-day Henry Ford for the disruptive effect he is having on the automobile and space aviation industries.

Before Tesla, electric vehicles were considered curiosities with limited appeal. GM, for instance, killed its EV1 electric vehicle in 1999 when it failed to sell (and spawned a popular documentary, "Who Killed the Electric Car?").

But Musk's approach has been to sell directly to consumers, with whom the company has constant contact.

Starting with a limited-edition $100,000 electric car, Musk has since added a $70,000 Model S. He also is developing the Model X sport utility and a far-cheaper small electric vehicle due by the end of the decade. All are or will be produced in the United States, according to Tesla.

Eventually, the vehicles will be powered by electric battery packs produced by Musk's gigafactories, the first of which is under construction near Reno, Nev. The battery packs would be built in conjunction with Panasonic, and assure Musk of a supply that cannot be guaranteed from Japan and elsewhere.

The 5 million-square-foot gigafactory, which is being built in partnership with Panasonic of Japan, also will produce home batteries called Powerwall that can be used to supplement solar panels and as a backup electrical power source.

Musk decided to build the giant factory, which is more than twice the size of a typical automotive assembly plant, because he did not want to risk an interruption in the battery supply chain for his vehicles. "The way we're approaching the gigafactory is really like a product," Musk said during a news event in May 2015. "What we're designing is a giant machine."[50]

At the same event, Musk said he could envision "many gigafactories in the future. Many companies will need to build gigafactory-class plants of their own."

Where those factories will be located—and indeed, where other manufacturing operations of all kinds will be set—is a question that could take the rest of this century to answer.

Chronology

1870s–1920s	**Companies in the United States, Japan and Europe begin opening offices and factories in other parts of the world as manufacturing spreads.**
1887	England-based Lever and Co. purchases a site near Liverpool for a huge soap factory.
1903	Henry Ford founds the Ford Motor Co.; a year later he opens Ford of Canada.
1905	The Swiss-owned Nestlé merges with the American-owned Anglo-Swiss Condensed Milk Co.; the merger gives the new company factories in the United States, Britain, Germany and Spain.
1908	William Durant creates General Motors and soon owns 11 companies, including Chevrolet and Oldsmobile.
1913	Ford Motor develops the automatic assembly line, speeding the expansion of global production.
1917	Ford opens its first factory outside North America in Ireland, followed by plants in England and France.
1919	The United States emerges as the world's dominant manufacturer, accounting for 40 percent of all output and 60 percent of the world's steel.
1920s	Beset by hyperinflation after World War I, Germany eclipses England as Europe's dominant manufacturing power, in part because it cannot spend money on its military under the Treaty of Versailles.
1930s–1940s	**The Great Depression and World War II dampen global expansion.**
1932	Stock market prices plummet after the 1929 crash and manufacturing output drops to half its 1929 level.
1941	With the United States entering World War II, the aviation and automobile industries convert their operations to armament production, which they will do until the war ends in 1945.
1947	The General Agreement on Tariffs and Trade (GATT) is negotiated, with 23 nations participating. The agreement, in place until 1994, marks an effort to set global trade rules and combat protectionism. . . . The Cold War shuts off Russia and much of Eastern Europe to global manufacturing, causing international companies to focus on the Western Hemisphere.
1950s–1960s	**New ways to transport and manufacture goods sweep global companies.**
1955	North Carolina trucking entrepreneur Malcolm McLean introduces "intermodalism," which allows shipping containers to be moved seamlessly between trucks, trains and ships. . . . The European Economic Community (now the European Union) is formed.

(Continued)

(Continued)

1958	Toyota sells its first car in the United States, the Toyopet. The poor reception causes Toyota to stop selling the vehicle and return with a more powerful model in 1959.
1959	The first industrial robot is developed by inventors George Devol and Joseph Engelberger. Two years later, an industrial robot is installed at GM's Trenton, N.J., plant.
1960	International standards for containers are set.
1964	Mexico establishes the maquiladora program, allowing foreign companies to open manufacturing operations for export, rather than be required to serve the Mexican market.
1966	The first international container ship sets sail.
1970s–1990s	**Communist China invites investment, and trade agreements are negotiated.**
1979	China opens its economy to foreign investment. . . . U.S. manufacturing employment peaks at 19.6 million.
1981	With the U.S. economy declining, Japan becomes a dominant global manufacturing power, exporting electronic products, automobiles and other consumer goods. . . . The United States and Japan negotiate the Voluntary Restraint Agreement (VRA), setting limits on imports of Japanese vehicles. The VRA prompts Japanese automakers to undertake joint ventures, and they subsequently open their own American factories.
1994	The North American Free Trade Agreement goes into effect, allowing for the easier flow of goods between the United States, Canada and Mexico.
1995	The World Trade Organization replaces GATT; more than 160 nations are now members.
2000s–Present	**Manufacturing booms in China, but companies begin to reassess expansion.**
2007	Apple introduces the iPhone. Manufacturing initially is overseen by Foxconn, a contractor based in Taiwan, which assembles about 40 percent of consumer electronics sold around the world.
2008–2009	After a Wall Street meltdown, the Bush and Obama administrations restructure General Motors and Chrysler, part of an $82 billion bailout of the U.S. automobile industry. Italy's Fiat takes control of Chrysler's management.
2010	China becomes the world's biggest car producer.
2014	Mexican car production sets a record, with further expansion expected due to new plants from Toyota, Audi and Ford.
2015	China's economy stumbles amid its stock market meltdown.

PERSPECTIVE

Q&A: James P. Womack on Global Manufacturing

"ALWAYS, YOU'VE GOT TO HAVE GOOD PRODUCT"

James P. Womack

James P. Womack helped create one of the most commonly quoted phrases of the 1990s: lean manufacturing. He was co-author of the landmark 1990 book "The Machine That Changed the World: The Story of Lean Production," which resulted from a five-year, 14-country study by the Massachusetts Institute of Technology on the future of the automobile industry.

Lean manufacturing referred to practices, primarily by Japanese automakers, that were designed to assemble products with maximum efficiency and as little waste as possible, both in terms of material and worker hours. The book led to the creation in 1997 of the Lean Enterprise Institute (LEI), an education, research and consulting organization led by Womack that is aimed at making companies and clients more efficient.

Womack spoke with SAGE Business Researcher reporter Micheline Maynard about global manufacturing. This is an edited transcript of their conversation.

What are some of the trends you've seen in the past few decades?

The way the world worked when I came on the scene [in the 1970s], companies like General Motors and Ford were required by politics to create local subsidiaries if they wanted to manufacture somewhere. By the 1980s, Mexico was the next stop. But there was no local supply base, so you had to ship parts to Mexico. That led to a fantastic boom in maquiladoras [manufacturing production in free trade zones that could be exported as finished goods].

As the Cold War came to an end, and the Soviet Union collapsed, companies were off to the races to get cheap labor. China was a combination of labor discipline driven by a dictatorship. The amount of infrastructure that was put in place in the past 35 years is absolutely mind-boggling.

Where does automation fit into global production?

Always in the background was another strain of thinking: Why don't we just automate it? At one time, the robots were going to beat humans. That was a complete fantasy; it never happened and isn't going to happen. Automation is always coming as the thing that's going to change everything. It changes some things, but not everything.

How do you explain the big push by U.S. companies to manufacture in China, versus overhauling their American plants?

Going to China was a lot easier. You didn't have to worry about changing management strategies and dug-in practices. You could just go and get very, very cheap labor. And, thanks to containerization, the transport cost per unit turned out to be a big, big reduction in the '70s, '80s and '90s. These behemoths are so difficult to change, and you can see the attraction to management of saying "Let's get the hell out of here."

It seems in a correctly run world, everybody would have embraced lean, and there would have been a lot less cross regional movement of products. It's not surprising that everybody went to China.

How does your "lean" philosophy help these manufacturers?

The real future is the total flow of value. Somebody has got to make a product. What I find the most interesting is how to get from the factory to the customer. What is our relationship? What is the use of the product, going forward? Are people at a point where they want more brilliant objects, or do more people want ways to get problems solved?

What we were trying to do was put those two things together—the product and the problem-solving.

(*Continued*)

(Continued)

Now there's talk about Mexico as the next major production center. How do you see its future?

[Mexican government officials] called me in 1990, '91. My thinking at the time was that a lot of automotive would move to Mexico. I was just wrong by 25 years. The future of the auto industry will be Mexico. There's now coming into place a big and pretty good supply base.

What will be the secret to successful production in a global environment?

Always, you've got to have good product. There are two pieces to this. First, the whole space between product planner visionary and the user—how you get in touch at the front end to give people what they want. Second, there's the use end of it. How do you want to get in touch with customers? Are the current maintenance systems the way you want to deal with them?

The interesting thinking is not going on in manufacturing in terms of the output of factories and all that, but in the use space. How are manufacturers going to use factories to solve their problems? No matter what you think of Elon Musk, the most interesting thing is not the [Tesla] car but in how he's dealing directly with his customers. Most companies are better at designing objects than they are at dealing with customer issues.

What about your customers? Are companies still interested in improving their factories?

LEI continues to be successful. One-third of our business comes from health care, one-third from financial services and from things that are transactional and in the office space. We don't get calls from manufacturing people.

UPDATE IN 2020

China overtook the U.S. as the world's largest manufacturing nation in 2010. In the last half of the decade, its lead has only widened.

In 2018, the latest year for which statistics were available, China accounted for 28.4 percent of global manufacturing output, according to the United Nations Statistics Division.[51] The U.S. trailed by nearly a dozen percentage points, coming in at 16.6 percent of global output. (In terms of U.S. gross domestic product, manufacturing in 2019 ranked at the lowest percentage of the economy in the past 72 years.[52])

Globally, however, the U.S. and China were the only two countries with double-digit shares of manufacturing output. In third place was Japan, long a global manufacturing power, at 7.2 percent.

For the past 40 years, the story of China's rise in manufacturing has been a global focus. Given its wide lead, it's unlikely that any country can challenge its supremacy.

That doesn't mean politicians are sanguine about the situation. Throughout his presidential campaign as well as his presidency, Donald Trump has been vocally critical of China, and has vowed that the U.S. would take back some of its lost market share.

Likewise, Trump repeatedly vowed that manufacturing would return to the United States from abroad, a key tenet of his "Make America Great Again" slogan.

However, The New York Times reported that Trump's effort had limited results. Foreign investment grew at a slower pace in the first two years of his administration than during the Obama presidency, according to Commerce Department data.[53]

In Trump's first two years in office, companies announced plans to relocate 145,000 jobs from overseas locations. But more than half of those job announcements were made before a sweeping package of tax cuts that was meant to stimulate job relocation.[54]

Growth in manufacturing was put on hold in 2020 by the COVID-19 outbreak, however. Shutdowns in China, Italy and other nations caused first-quarter output to fall by 6 percent, according to the United Nations.[55]

It caused some analysts to question whether the long-time manufacturing practice called "just-in-time" (JIT) inventory was still viable. Under JIT, manufacturers kept only enough parts on hand for a short period of time, choosing instead to receive regular shipments. That could easily get disrupted if manufacturing at a supplier was halted. As a buffer against interruptions, companies could keep larger supplies of essential components on hand, a concept nicknamed "just in case," even though that could lead to great expense.[56]

However, economist Susan Helper at Case Western Reserve University says that the idea of excess inventory will run afoul of the cost-cutting drives that are already under way in many major companies. "Purchasing managers are intensely measured on how low their costs are. So that doesn't leave a lot of room to spend extra money because there might be some contingency in which everything falls apart," Helper says.[57]

Rather than set aside the entire concept, Helper says some manufacturers might look for suppliers closer to their home markets that can substitute for those based in China.

That's exactly what Canadian Prime Minister Justin Trudeau ordered when his nation experienced shortage of personal protective equipment (PPE) needed by hospitals and nursing homes when COVID-19 cases spiked. By June 2020, however, Trudeau told a news conference that his nation had become almost self-sufficient in producing those items. Given that, Trudeau said Canada hoped to begin sharing PPE items with the rest of the world.[58]

—Micheline Maynard

11

GLOBAL OIL AND GAS INDUSTRY

What are the important choices in an age of abundance?

Ángel González

From *SAGE Business Researcher*, March 2, 2015

EXECUTIVE SUMMARY

The world is experiencing a new age of energy abundance, largely because the United States, the largest energy consumer, is also increasingly a producer. In addition, Brazil and Canada, among others, are emerging as oil powers. Hydraulic fracturing, or fracking in which high-pressure streams of water and chemicals are injected into shale rock formations, is unlocking vast supplies of oil and natural gas. Increased energy production is helping the U.S. balance of trade with other countries, lowering energy bills nationwide and reigniting hopes of regaining lost manufacturing jobs. The shifts may also give the United States new flexibility in foreign policy. But the boom comes with a price: Many worry about what fracking is doing to drinking water and other aspects of the environment. Moreover, after accidents involving oil-carrying trains, critics are concerned about the safety of the nation's energy-transportation system.

OVERVIEW

For years, Seattleites viewed oil, pumped in Alaska and sent by ship to refineries along the Washington coast, as a faraway concern: sometimes cause for alarm, such as when the Exxon Valdez spilled millions of gallons of oil a few thousand miles away, but generally invisible

Now, as the United States has overtaken Russia and Saudi Arabia as the world's largest producer of oil and natural gas, the eco-conscious city has become part of one of the busiest crude transportation corridors, one that might one day tie oil fields in the Midwest to markets across the Pacific.[1] Two 100-car trains loaded with crude extracted in North Dakota pass through its downtown every day—blocking traffic at busy intersections, slowly chugging past packed stadiums and rolling through a tunnel beneath Pike Place, the city's famous landmark market. A few minor derailments, coupled with news of catastrophic oil train explosions in Canada, North Dakota and elsewhere, have disturbed residents. City council members wrote the U.S. secretary of Transportation asking that he forbid the shipping of oil via rail until all train cars are replaced with newer, safer models, and in late 2014, protesters were arrested after trying to block tracks north of the city.[2]

Seattle's newfound role in the energy industry surprised the city—but it is indicative of how profoundly an oil and gas boom triggered by unconventional drilling techniques is redrawing the economy and geography of the United States, as the country moves rapidly toward energy self-sufficiency. Domestic energy has eliminated the need to buy natural gas abroad and is already lowering oil imports, thus reducing America's dependence on the Middle East, in addition to creating more jobs and profit.

Seattle's reaction also underscores how the new landscape is not always comfortable: Regions that hitherto were peripheral to the energy industry—from upstate New York to rural North Dakota—are now oil production centers. In some places, boomtowns are struggling with inflation, housing shortages and escalating drug-related crime.[3]

For the Pacific Northwest, long drawn to renewable sources of energy, "it almost raises a cultural identity question about what this region is," says Eric de Place, policy director at the Sightline Institute, an environmental advocacy think tank in Seattle. "Is it a major fossil fuel transit center or a green utopia in the corner of the continent?"

America's energy renaissance is one of the great economic stories of the 21st century, and many see it as a bright spot in a country still recovering from recession. More than 3 million barrels of oil per day, nearly as much crude as Iran pumps out, has been unlocked by injecting high-pressure jets of water and chemicals into shale rock formations, a process known as hydraulic fracturing, or fracking.[4] Natural gas from shale has reached more than 35 billion cubic feet per day, nearly half of total U.S. production.[5] The abundance of crude has helped usher in a big drop in prices—as of Jan. 13, the price for the U.S. benchmark crude contract, at $45.89 per barrel, was less than half what it had been in July.[6]

International Monetary Fund economists have predicted that the fuel price plunge will boost global gross domestic product by between 0.3 percent and 0.7 percent in 2015.[7]

Some experts think it's the beginning of a long era of cheap crude that will affect geopolitics, as oil-producing countries such as Russia, Iran and Venezuela see their wealth wither.[8]

Cheap crude and the need to import less of it is strengthening the U.S. trade balance, lowering energy bills nationwide and reigniting hopes of regaining lost manufacturing jobs in industries such as petrochemicals and steel that rely on cheap energy.[9] The U.S. deployment of unconventional drilling techniques "in just 10 years completely redefined the energy landscape," says Robert Clarke, manager for unconventional oil and gas at Wood Mackenzie, a global energy consulting firm. The boom comes with a price: Many worry about what fracking is doing to drinking water supplies in populated areas where energy production is relatively new. Moreover, safety concerns about how to move all that energy are on the rise, in the wake of major accidents with oil-carrying trains.

The changes in U.S. production also are upsetting the traditional power balance of the energy industry, dominated for decades by a few integrated oil companies such as BP and Exxon Mobil and by the humongous national oil companies of countries belonging to the Organization of the Petroleum Exporting Countries (OPEC). Traditional oil powers "are scared, absolutely scared," says Fadel Gheit, a prominent analyst with Oppenheimer & Co. who has followed the industry for decades. The fall in the price of crude that began in late 2014 was triggered in part by OPEC's decision not to cut production—a move seen by experts as a sign of Saudi Arabia's desire to make U.S. oil producers lose money.[10]

Now the field is open to a whole range of new players—from Wall Street money seeking high yields in pipeline companies to wildcatter-minded independents such as Chesapeake

Oil Imports on the Decline

Annual U.S. imports of crude oil and other petroleum products, 1981–2014 (in billions of barrels)

U.S. imports of crude oil and other petroleum products fell 28 percent from a 25-year peak of 5 billion barrels in 2005 to 3.6 billion in 2013, and continued to fall in 2014.

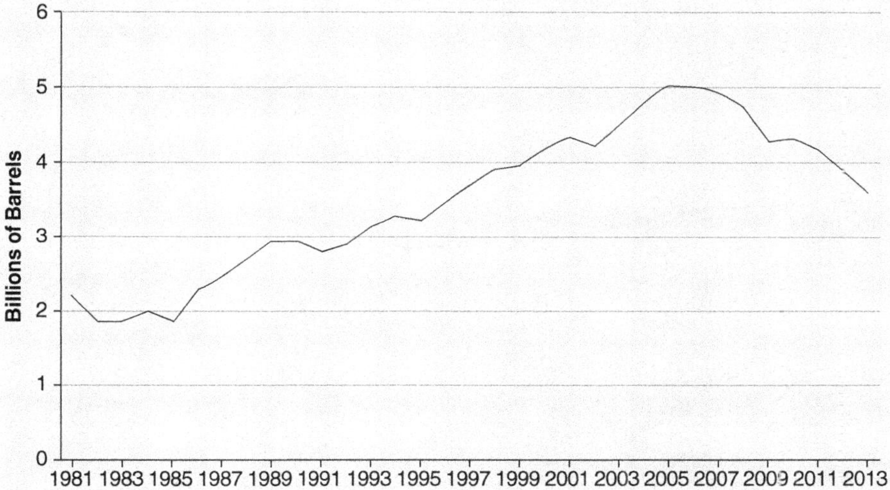

Note: 2014 total is a full-year estimate based on amount imported in the first 10 months of the year.

Source: "U.S. Imports of Crude Oil and Petroleum Products," U.S. Energy Information Administration, Dec. 30, 2014, http://tinyurl.com/nxqborb; 2014 estimate based on *SAGE Business Researcher* calculations.

Energy Corp., which in less than two decades became one of the biggest domestic producers after applying hydraulic fracturing techniques on oil-and-gas-rich rocks previously thought too hard to crack. Because much of the new oil unlocked by fracking is in out-of-the-way places with little pipeline capacity, such as North Dakota, railway companies including BNSF, the Berkshire Hathaway railroad giant, have played an unexpected, and profitable, role.[11]

Even as the U.S. economy wobbled in the aftermath of the 2008 global financial crisis, cities in energy-rich areas of North Dakota and Texas boomed. Houston, home to much of the intellectual capital of the energy industry, has become, in the words of the Dallas Morning News, a "middle-class magnet" thanks to its abundance of high-paying jobs and relatively low cost of living. Employment there grew by nearly a quarter between 2000 and 2013, vs. 15 percent for Washington, D.C., and 4 percent for New York City.[12] That boom is now endangered by falling crude prices—but it helped a wide swath of the United States recover.

The average American household also wins—with cheap natural gas cutting heating and air conditioning bills by hundreds of dollars a year and gasoline expenditures expected to drop this year to the lowest level in 11 years, according to the U.S. Energy Information Administration.[13] Consulting firm IHS estimates unconventional oil and gas will boost disposable income by $2,700 per household in 2020 compared with what it would have been otherwise.[14]

Annual Average of Daily Crude Oil Production by State, 1999 to 2013

Daily production of crude oil in the United States was on a slow decline from 1999 to 2008, led by declines in the second- and third-largest oil-producing states, Alaska and California. But from 2009 through 2013, the tide turned. The rising tide of daily crude oil was driven by the long-time No. 1 producer, Texas, and by North Dakota, which accelerated from the No. 8 state with less than 100,000 barrels per day in 1999 to overtake Alaska and California in 2012 and reach 860,014 barrels per day by 2013. The increase in just Texas and North Dakota from 2008 to 2013 was nearly 2.14 million barrels, accounting for the lion's share of the 2.5 million barrel increase in the national total between 2008 and 2013. However, increases in other states like New Mexico (+113,864 barrels per day) and Oklahoma (+137,195 barrels per day) were necessary to offset the continued decline in Alaska and California.

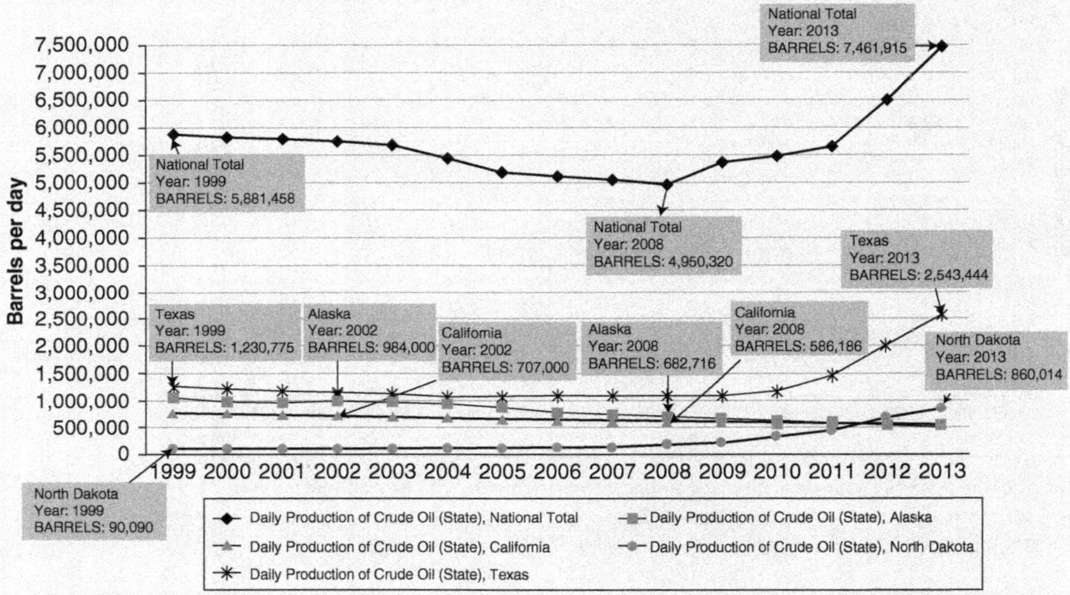

Note: National total includes federal offshore production. Figures for Alaska, California, Louisiana and Texas include state offshore production. Production numbers not included for states with less than 500 barrels per day.

Source: "Daily Production of Crude Oil (State)." In SAGE Stats (website) Washington, DC: CQ Press, 2014, http://data.sagepub.com/sagestats/2226. Calculated from U.S. Department of Energy, Energy Information Administration, "Petroleum Supply Annual [Year], Volume 1," http://tinyurl.com/32brj22. In earlier years, the report was labeled "Production of Crude Oil by PAD District and State."

Despite the economic benefits, environmentalists, officials and residents of newly energy-rich areas are concerned about the negative effects of the boom. One worry is that widespread drilling might be contaminating water resources, even though the oil industry contends that the fracking process is not responsible for any water pollution. Deborah Nardone, director of the Sierra Club's Beyond Natural Gas campaign, says the energy revolution "is coming with significant public health and environmental concerns" due to the oil industry's resistance to state and federal environmental regulation. In December, New

Percentage of U.S. Total Crude Oil Production by State, 2008 and 2013

U.S. petroleum production is usually associated in the public imagination with Texas and Alaska, but it is time to revise that perception. In just five years, North Dakota has vaulted above Alaska and California as the second-largest oil-producing state. On the other hand, the Texas share of the U.S. total has ballooned from 22.0 percent to 34.1 percent. Alaska, seeing its production fall from 1,049,858 barrels per day in 1999 to 514,825 barrels per day in 2013, passed a law in 2013 called the "More Alaska Production Act" that eliminated progressive taxes on increased production. It took effect on Jan. 1, 2014, but it may take several years for companies to build capacity to take advantage of the new regime, whereas the effects on government revenue will happen more quickly (http://tinyurl.com/mgo546d).

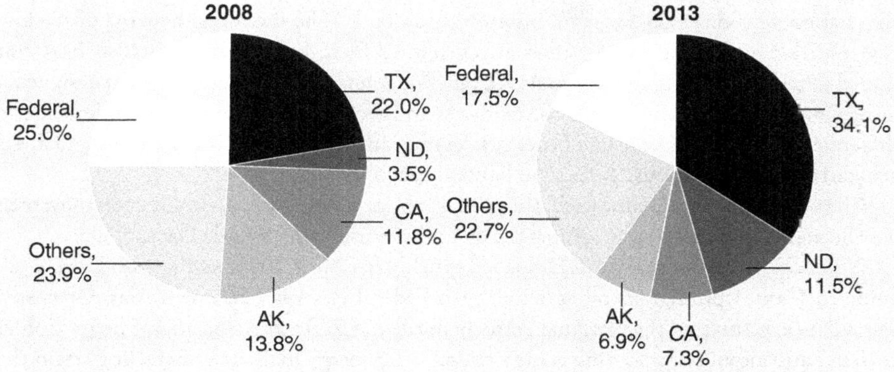

Note: Federal is primarily federal offshore production. Figures for Alaska, California, Louisiana and Texas include state offshore production.

Source: "Daily Production of Crude Oil (State)." In SAGE Stats (website) Washington, DC: CQ Press, 2014, http://data.sagepub.com/sagestats/2226. Calculated from U.S. Department of Energy, Energy Information Administration, "Petroleum Supply Annual [Year], Volume 1," http://tinyurl.com/32brj22. In earlier years, the report was labeled "Production of Crude Oil by PAD District and State."

York State banned hydraulic fracturing due to health concerns.[15]

Some communities are uncomfortable that energy is being produced in them or transported through them, and the use of railroads to haul crude has generated bottlenecks in other shipments, such as grain and automobiles.[16] Derailments and explosions, especially a catastrophic blast in Quebec in July 2013, have stoked fear. And the urge to tap the deeply buried oil riches of the U.S. Gulf of Mexico caused a major disaster in the form of the Deepwater Horizon oil spill of 2010. That spill, the largest offshore oil leak in U.S. history, for several months put the brakes on exploration and production in the

Bryan Thomas/Getty Images

Demonstrators protest against fracking in New York in 2014. Environmentalists contend that drilling techniques threaten water supplies. In December 2014, the state banned fracking.

area and nearly crippled BP, the U.K.-based company that owned the ill-fated well that blew out and killed 11 people.[17]

Others worry that a lot of America's new energy wealth is going to end up feeding hungry global markets as fuel is exported at higher prices than it might bring domestically—thus erasing some of the advantages of having cheap energy at home.

There's also the question of whether the boom will last. While oil companies have gained a reasonably good understanding of natural gas fracking, they're still in the early stages of figuring out how oil fracking works, says Guy Caruso, a former administrator of the U.S. Energy Information Administration (EIA) who is now a fellow at the Center for Strategic and International Studies (CSIS), a Washington think tank. The economic benefits of fracking have muffled once-loud calls for alternatives to fossil fuels. But environmentalists have continued to resist extending the Keystone XL pipeline, a huge transportation system designed to bring Canadian oil sands crude to the Midwest and the Gulf of Mexico. The crude is heavier than most varieties. It takes a lot of energy to extract and then convert into gasoline and diesel, generating more greenhouse gases than lighter types of crude.

More than just the pipeline itself, the issue is "about whether the environmental movement has the political strength to go against the oil industry and win," says de Place.

America's energy turnaround happened quickly. In April 2005, as the world was awakening to China's prodigious oil appetite, then-Federal Reserve Chairman Alan Greenspan warned oil executives at the National Petrochemical and Refiners Association Energy Conference in San Antonio of a coming energy crisis.[18] The energy markets were feeling strain that had not been "experienced for a generation," he said, bringing "feared shortfalls" in the world's ability to produce enough crude oil to sate the thirst of emerging economies.[19]

Greenspan advocated expensive new facilities to import liquefied natural gas (LNG) to check soaring prices for the commodity, crucial to Sun Belt air conditioning and power generation. He mentioned the need to harvest Arctic gas in Alaska and Canada's northern territories, which experts later estimated would cost more than $30 billion.[20]

At the time, the United States was buying nearly 70 percent of its crude from overseas. Today, that proportion has dropped to less than half.[21] The surge in production of relatively cheap domestic crude has enabled the United States to become a net gasoline exporter for the first time in 60 years.[22] It also has emboldened companies to find ways to evade a longstanding ban on shipping unrefined oil overseas, a law that Congress passed after the Arab oil embargo and the price spikes of the 1970s.[23] As for those LNG import terminals that Greenspan encouraged, they ended up idle—huge, newly tapped natural gas reserves rendered them unneeded.[24] Some of those that were built, at the cost of billions, are now being readied to ship out U.S. natural gas to markets in Europe and Asia instead, where it can fetch higher prices—although that prospect has prompted some concern among industrial users that unfettered exports may raise the price of gas in the United States. The first exports are scheduled to hit the global market in 2015.

Meanwhile, plans to ship the gas overseas have replaced an expensive project to bring Alaskan natural gas to the lower 48 states.[25]

"Six years ago I'd be telling an audience how dependent the U.S. was going to be on [liquefied natural gas] from Qatar," says CSIS's Caruso, who headed the EIA under President George W. Bush. "Now I'm saying we're going to be an exporter. It's just so remarkable, the change that has taken place in just six years."

This transformation was born of several factors, starting with the ingenuity of wildcatters such as George Mitchell, who discovered that an old technique, hydraulic fracturing, could be commercially viable in Texas's gas-rich Barnett Shale. Caruso adds that energy-friendly regulations aided fracking's spread, and when natural gas prices spiked after hurricanes Katrina and Rita in 2005, the technique became truly profitable in many other natural-gas-rich formations. Success in natural gas drilling and high prices for crude stemming from China's oil hunger enabled companies to apply fracking to revitalize old oil fields such as West Texas's Permian Basin and new fields such as North Dakota's Bakken Shale. "It all had to come together, and it did," Caruso says.

As businesses, environmentalists, consumers and policymakers adapt to the new world of energy abundance, here are some of the questions they are debating.

WEIGHING THE ISSUES

Is Big Oil Obsolete?

For decades, the oil industry was dominated by vertically integrated behemoths that combined the ownership of oil fields, refineries and gasoline stations, mostly based in the United States and Western Europe. These companies traditionally have been known as Big Oil.[26] Analysts now question whether scrappy U.S. players and large national oil companies in oil-rich countries are challenging their supremacy.

OPEC's rise challenged Big Oil's dominance in the 1970s. Many OPEC nations nationalized oil fields operated by Western companies, creating state-owned firms such as Saudi Aramco and Petróleos de Venezuela S.A. that copied the integrated model.[27]

A drastic fall in oil prices in the mid- and late 1980s and most of the 1990s led to more cracks in the model, and to a series of mergers that resulted in even larger companies.[28] Exxon Mobil, Chevron, BP, Royal Dutch Shell, ConocoPhillips and France's Total S.A. produced as much crude as many oil-producing countries, making them worth hundreds of billions of dollars in market capitalization. With prices low, some oil-rich OPEC nations such as Venezuela opened their doors once again to Western oil giants, giving them a temporary boost.

But at the beginning of the 21st century, when Asia's energy appetite seemed unquenchable and analysts fretted about scarce oil supplies, countries from Russia to Venezuela once again began closing doors to multinationals.[29] This pushed the multinationals to seek new sources—from digging wells a mile beneath the ocean's surface to unlocking remote natural gas reservoirs buried under the Alaskan permafrost.

Significant growth—enough new production to move the needle—became a challenge, as costs and risks skyrocketed.[30] For Chevron, America's second-largest oil giant after Exxon Mobil, the average cost of producing a barrel of oil and natural gas rose to \$17.10 in 2013 from \$4.12 in 1998.[31]

Investors criticized Big Oil companies for sluggish growth. Some companies faced scandals. For example, Shell acknowledged in 2004 that it had been improperly accounting for its reserves, misleading investors into thinking it had more energy reserves than it actually did.[32]

Meanwhile, in the United States, a cast of relatively minor players—the so-called independents, because they produced oil without engaging in refining operations—figured out how to squeeze natural gas and oil out of shale rock. That provided energy investors with something they had been starved for—production growth. Oklahoma City-based Chesapeake

Energy, one of the pioneers of fracking, produced 670,000 barrels a day of oil and gas in 2013, five and a half times the volume it had produced 10 years prior.[33] In comparison, Exxon Mobil production declined to 4.12 million barrels of oil equivalent, from 4.2 million barrels of oil equivalent in the same period.[34]

The supermajors were late to shale—and paid high prices to enter partnerships with independents such as Chesapeake Energy, or for outright acquisitions, such as Exxon Mobil's purchase of XTO Energy in 2010.

Some investors began to sour on the integrated model.[35] Smaller integrated companies spun off refining operations that Wall Street deemed lackluster, so they could better devote their resources to shale.[36] Marathon Oil and ConocoPhillips sold their refineries in 2011 and 2012, respectively. "The market greeted these [spinoffs] with tremendous enthusiasm," says Gheit, the Oppenheimer oil analyst. "It sent a very clear message to the integrated oil companies that they are a thing of the past."

Nonetheless, the bigger majors, such as Exxon Mobil and Chevron, have reiterated their support for the integrated model. It brings a hedging advantage in what's long been a cyclical business: When low prices, such as those that the markets starting seeing in the fall of 2014, challenge earnings from crude oil and natural gas sales, refineries that benefit from these same low prices help profits.

"We do think our refineries are very competitive and are a source of value creation for us," Chevron CEO John Watson told analysts in March 2013. Watson added that it would be hard to replace the $4 billion a year in profit derived from its refining and petrochemical business.[37]

Some oil executives see operational advantages to vertical integration. In a presentation to analysts in March 2012, Exxon Mobil CEO Rex Tillerson said integration allows the managers of different segments, by talking to each other, to get a better grasp of a very complicated industry. "There's no doubt in my mind that the integrated model adds incremental value to just about everything we do," he said.[38]

Despite criticism from some investors and analysts, and despite being somewhat late to the North American energy renaissance, integrated oil companies remain adept at deploying large amounts of capital and know-how to extract oil and gas from hard-to-access places. That is showcased by deals such as Exxon Mobil's partnership with Russia's Rosneft to scour that country's Arctic Ocean for oil and gas, a project that spans decades going forward and could cost hundreds of billions of dollars.

The ability to manage complex projects can open doors to resource-rich countries. "Scope and reach are no longer the advantages they once were. Having a range of specialisms, however, is becoming critical," BP Group Chief of Staff and Executive Vice President Dev Sanyal said in a speech at the Oxford Energy Seminar in 2012. "The super-major of the past was essentially defined by the scale of its operations. I believe the super-major of the future will be defined by the quality of its operations."[39]

And in a business characterized historically by booms and busts, integrated oil companies offer investors some stability due to their huge cash flow and strong dividends, says Allen Good, an analyst with Morningstar Inc. "They do provide a sense of being in the commodity space with relative safety," he says. Especially in low-oil-price environments, "larger companies are better positioned" to withstand a few lean years, he says.

It's hard to predict whether the current low oil prices will last, but the stock market reflects the resilience of the integrated companies—and the fragility of the independents—in a bear market for crude. As of Jan. 19, Exxon shares had fallen about 12.7 percent since late July. In comparison, shares for Continental Resources, a successful driller in North Dakota's Bakken Shale, fell by 47.8 percent in the same period.

Does the Shifting Energy Balance Give U.S. Foreign Policy More Flexibility?

Because the Middle East holds some of the world's biggest oil reserves, it has been at the forefront of the world's geopolitical agenda—and in the eyes of many, that has put the United States in some tight situations.

America's need for crude has buttressed strong military and diplomatic alliances with autocratic states such as Saudi Arabia and the Persian Gulf countries despite their general hostility to another key U.S. ally in the region, Israel. Critics have blamed American oil interests for two wars in oil-rich Iraq; an entire naval fleet, the U.S. 5th Fleet, is dedicated to protecting the critical Persian Gulf gateway. The United States spends $50 billion a year protecting oil shipments.[40]

U.S. politicians and commentators of various ideologies have long called for breaking those ties. President George W. Bush, in his 2006 State of the Union address, highlighted a domestic problem: "America is addicted to oil, which is often imported from unstable parts of the world." By moving beyond petroleum, the U.S. could "make our dependence on Middle Eastern oil a thing of the past," Bush said.[41]

But now America's reliance on Middle Eastern oil is waning, as crude from North Dakota, Texas and Canada increasingly replace imports. The United States imported about 2.1 million barrels a day of crude from Persian Gulf OPEC nations in 2012. By 2020, that amount will be only 900,000 barrels a day, the Energy Information Administration predicts.[42]

Foreign policy experts are debating whether America's rapid progress toward self-sufficiency will reduce U.S. ties to the Middle East.

From a pure access-to-supplies perspective, the answer appears to be yes. As a high-ranking State Department official told The Wall Street Journal in 2011, "Whereas at one point there were real and serious concerns about the ability to maintain sustainable access of supplies to the United States if there were disruptions in the Middle East, that has changed."[43]

Caruso, the former EIA administrator, says America's oil bounty has emboldened it—allowing it to become more aggressive than it might have been otherwise in dealing with Iran's nuclear ambitions or with Russia's aggression against Ukraine.

The recent fall in oil prices partly spurred by America's energy boom also threatens the stability of some of Washington's bêtes noires—Russia, Iran, and Venezuela.[44]

But the United States is not immune to volatility in the price of a fungible commodity, as long as it imports even a small amount of crude. If Persian Gulf crude flows are interrupted, prices will rise everywhere as China, Europe and those U.S. refineries that don't have access to domestically produced crude scramble to compete for fewer barrels available in the global market.[45]

Analysts and policymakers say the United States, as the world's foremost superpower, has an outsized role in protecting the stability of global trade lanes. "The U.S. will still have to worry about what an oil cutoff would mean for its allies and trading partners," Amy Myers Jaffe, executive director for energy and sustainability at the Institute of Transportation Studies in the University of California, Davis, told a congressional committee in May 2013.[46]

U.S., China Lead in Oil Imports

Net daily oil imports, 2013 (in millions of barrels)

The United States was the world's largest net oil importer in 2013 at 6.6 million barrels per day, followed by China at 6.2 million barrels and Japan at 4.4 million barrels. China is expected to surpass the United States in 2014 as its rapidly growing demand for petroleum outpaces production growth.

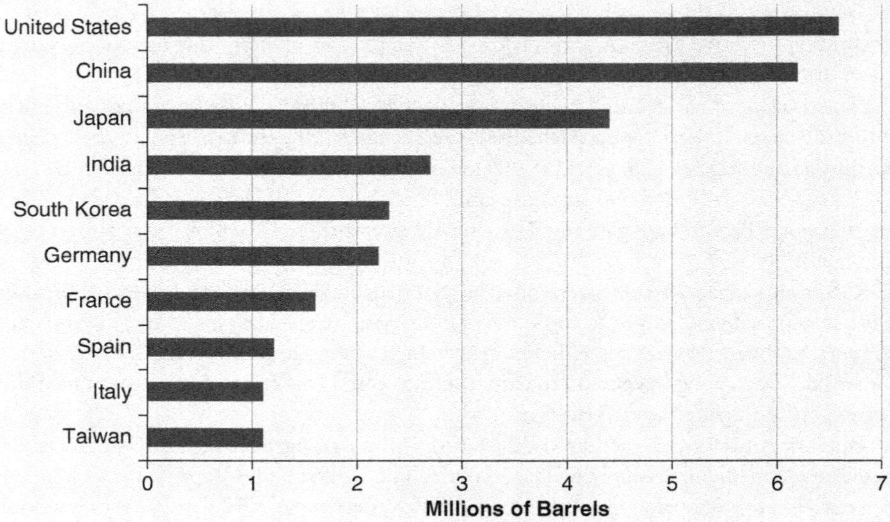

Note: Net imports are total imports of petroleum and other liquid fuels minus exports of petroleum and other liquid fuels.

Source: U.S. Energy Information Administration, http://tinyurl.com/q2wowx6 and http://tinyurl.com/ohrrrlb.

That responsibility is generating tensions with China, an emerging superpower that has become the biggest importer of Middle Eastern oil and an important factor in the U.S. economy. Chinese officials have asked the United States to reaffirm its commitment to protecting choke points in the Persian Gulf, arguing China doesn't have the ships to project its military power there, according to The Wall Street Journal; but Americans complain of footing the bill and not getting Chinese support in key Mideast security initiatives.[47]

America's new energy wealth does, however, give the global oil market a breather, reducing price and supply volatility. At the same time this wealth provides the United States with options in counterbalancing the geopolitical moves of other energy-rich countries. Venezuela, a longtime supplier of oil to the United States and a former Latin American ally turned bitter rival, has seen its U.S. exports drop to about 700,000 barrels a day in June 2014 from a peak of 1.4 million in 2004.[48] In fact, because Venezuela's refineries are in poor repair, the country has become dependent on U.S. refined products.[49]

According to Caruso, the United States has added more oil-producing capacity in the last three years than Iran produces annually. That production buffer has also minimized the oil price impact of the Syrian civil war, which has spilled into Iraq, a huge producing nation, he says.

The U.S. natural gas bounty also offers Europe an alternative to Russia by lowering the price of shipborne liquefied natural gas, Caruso says. Overall, the shale boom strengthens America's hand vis-à-vis China, its main creditor, by strengthening the domestic economy, Jaffe said in her testimony.

In an interview, Jaffe points out that the shale boom buttresses the U.S. strategic advantage regarding China. "They have to be conscious of how much more dependent they are in the Middle East than we are going to be," she says.

Should the U.S. Government Allow More Energy Exports?

Now that the United States has become a major energy source, producers are arguing that the government should lift restrictions on exports of energy, which is considered a strategic national asset. Industries that have profited from cheap energy, however, oppose a change.

The International Energy Agency (IEA)—which provides advice on energy matters to its 29 members, all developed oil-importing countries—projects that the United States is close to overtaking Saudi Arabia as a producer of crude oil and petroleum liquids.[50] By 2013, the United States had already surpassed Russia as the world's largest producer of oil and natural gas combined.[51] The surge has exceeded expectations; as recently as 2012, the IEA projected that the United States wouldn't overtake Saudi Arabia until the end of the decade.[52]

The United States, long the world's biggest energy hog, has already become an energy exporter, in some ways. In 2011, for the first time in six decades, the country became a net exporter of refined products such as gasoline and diesel.[53]

Exports of refined products and the reduction of crude oil imports have improved the nation's balance of trade: Between January and November 2014, the U.S. deficit in petroleum products shrank to $174 billion from $217 billion during the same period the previous year, according to the Commerce Department.[54] With U.S. oil and natural production growing, and with Asia becoming the driver of global demand for energy, many think it's natural—and profitable—to sell energy abroad.[55]

Regulatory and technical barriers prevent the United States from becoming a full-fledged exporter of oil and natural gas. Under federal law, with only a few exceptions including for consumption in Canada, domestically produced crude oil can't legally be exported.[56]

Natural gas must be chilled to become liquid so it can be loaded onto giant vessels, and that requires expensive coastal facilities, dozens of which have been proposed.[57]

But so far, as of January 2015, only four facilities have obtained key approval from the Federal Energy Regulatory Commission (FERC) to export so-called liquefied natural gas, including Cheniere Energy's Sabine Pass terminal and Sempra Energy's Cameron LNG export project, both in Louisiana.[58] The Department of Energy must also weigh in on whether it's in the public interest for each project to sell gas to countries that haven't signed free-trade agreements with the United States—which include some of the biggest markets for the gas, such as China and Japan.

Energy companies and many U.S. officials, particularly in oil-and-gas producing states, favor energy exports, on the grounds that it is good for the country's pocketbook, encourages further development of energy resources and offers a diplomatic edge.

Then-Sen. Mary Landrieu, D-La., said at a Senate hearing in March 2014 that "LNG exports will not only drive continued investment in domestic production and create jobs, they are also a powerful geopolitical tool" that can offset the influence of gas-rich Russia.[59]

Sen. Lisa Murkowski, R-Alaska, the ranking member on the Senate's Energy and Natural Resources Committee, said at an energy industry conference in March 2014 that the ban on crude oil exports should end. "Lifting the oil export ban will send a powerful message that America has the resources and the resolve to be the preeminent power in the world," she said.[60]

Shell CEO Ben van Beurden said in a speech in September 2014 at Columbia University that U.S. "oil and gas exports would reinforce the long-term future of North American energy production, significantly improve the [U.S.] balance of trade and help to make the global energy system more stable."[61]

Allowing exports has generated opposition, however, as relatively cheap domestic oil and gas have benefited refiners and energy-intensive industries.

Some independent refiners such as Alon USA Energy and PBF Energy, which don't produce crude oil but instead buy it and turn it into fuel, oppose the idea of crude exports, which might wipe out the discounts they get from domestically produced fuel.[62] "We have concerns because we buy crude oil and independent refiners have a competitive advantage" in the current situation, says Bill Day, a spokesman for San Antonio-based Valero Energy, one of the nation's largest independent refiners and a big exporter of refined products.

Dow Chemical, a petrochemical giant that has benefited from a drop in the price of natural gas to boost its U.S. manufacturing and its profit, said that the fracking boom has led global companies to rush to invest in the United States, "helping grow our economy and create jobs." But, the company said, "by shipping our own energy resources abroad and without fully understanding the implications of domestic manufacturing, this renaissance and our economic growth could be potentially threatened."

The company also asked the Department of Energy to take a "pause in the LNG export approval process" until it figures out the long-term implications of exports. Dow is part of an anti-LNG export coalition that includes Alcoa, the aluminum manufacturer, and Huntsman, a specialized chemical maker.[63]

Ken Cohen, vice president of public and government affairs at Exxon Mobil, both a huge refiner and the largest U.S. natural gas producer, said opponents are missing the fact that shale is so rich that it represents a "paradigm shift." In his company's blog, ExxonMobil Perspectives, he argued that exports will spur domestic producers to extract more natural gas, nullifying any increase in price.

"Trade expands the pie," he wrote. "That wisdom is well understood when it comes to our major exports of chemicals, cars and agricultural products—and so it should be with energy as well."[64]

BACKGROUND

Oil seeped out of the ground in ancient Mesopotamia, and Daniel Yergin, author of "The Prize," the most authoritative story of the oil industry, says this seepage may have inspired fire worship.[65] In Venezuela, which was to become a major oil producer in the 20th century and a founding member of OPEC, the natives knew of oil and used it for medicinal purposes.

Spanish conquistadors wrote about it as early as the 16th century; a portion of Venezuelan "rock oil" was shipped in galleons to Spain to alleviate the gout of Charles V, king of Spain and Holy Roman emperor.[66]

But oil didn't become a modern industry until the mid-1800s, when entrepreneurs in rural Pennsylvania pioneered drilling techniques. They were seeking to secure a steady supply of lighting fuel to replace expensive whale oil and candles, as more and more people congregated in industrializing cities. The first well was drilled in Titusville, Pa., in 1859; soon, oil was abundant and cheap.[67]

American inventor Samuel Kier built the first small refinery to convert crude oil into flammable kerosene in Pittsburgh in the 1850s.[68] The entire industry would enter a boom-and-bust cycle as oil drilling spread and refineries opened in numerous American cities; fortunes were made and lost.

A Cleveland businessman, John D. Rockefeller, began buying refineries under Standard Oil, which he founded in 1870.[69] He quickly dominated the U.S. refining industry, and he later branched out into buying the oil wells themselves, starting the race toward vertical integration that was to define the energy industry for the next century and beyond. Standard Oil, broken up in 1911 by the U.S. government because it was a monopoly, is the ancestor of modern-day Exxon Mobil and Chevron Corp.[70]

Autos and Battleships

The nascent oil industry got another boost from a late 19th-century innovation, the internal combustion engine, and its main application, the automobile. Until then, gasoline was used mostly as a solvent. Henry Ford popularized cars in the United States; the first Model T was assembled in 1908.[71] Standard Oil built the first modern service station, in Seattle, in 1907.[72]

World War I underscored oil's value. On the eve of the war Winston Churchill, then in charge of the British navy, had succeeded in pushing the navy to switch from coal to oil, arguing it would give battleships more flexibility and range.[73] As the war progressed, oil helped taxis carry French troops to the defense of Paris, fueled the tanks that helped break the stalemate of trench warfare and propelled dogfighting airplanes. A French senator called oil "the blood of victory."[74]

At the end of the war, the dissolution of the Turkish Empire led to the partitioning of the Middle East into self-ruling protectorates under heavy British and French influence. British oil interests, in the form of the Anglo-Persian Oil Co. and Royal Dutch Shell, were preeminent in tapping the region's riches. Even though the United States produced most of the world's oil thanks to the discovery of rich fields in Texas, California and the Midwest, U.S. and U.K. oil companies began scouring the globe for prospects, giving birth to prospering industries in Mexico and Venezuela.[75] Russia, which along with the United States was one of the birthplaces of the modern oil industry, became a major player under the Soviet regime.[76]

The Seven Sisters and Nationalization

With few exceptions, a cartel of Anglo-Saxon oil companies dominated the industry: It drilled for oil, processed it in refineries and distributed the resulting products. In the 1950s, Enrico Mattei, the founder of Italian energy monopoly ENI, dubbed this group "the Seven Sisters."[77] ENI and the other national monopolies that arose after World War II also adopted the integrated model.

The rise of nationalism in oil-producing countries in the 1960s challenged the Sisters' dominance. There had been precedents—in 1938, Mexico under President Lázaro Cárdenas nationalized its oil industry and created a state oil monopoly. Administrations in Venezuela increased their taxes on oil production in the 1940s. In the early 1950s, nationalist Iranian Prime Minister Mohammed Mossadegh took control of the oil industry from the British, but he was ousted in a CIA-backed coup, and reforms were reversed.[78]

Eventually, several oil-producing countries, dependent on petroleum for their development, became concerned about falling prices. In September 1960, Saudi Arabia, Venezuela, Kuwait, Iraq and Iran formed OPEC, which focused on regulating oil production to keep prices high, inspired by the example of the Texas Railroad Commission, which had done the same for Texas producers decades earlier.[79] OPEC eventually had a huge impact.

The Energy Crisis

By 1973, rapid economic growth had brought oil demand to par with supply. OPEC countries felt emboldened to take oil production into their own hands; as Israel and the Arab world went to war, Arab countries sharply decreased production quotas, sending oil prices to shocking heights and triggering panic in oil-consuming countries.[80] Gas lines were common in the 1970s; soaring gas prices stoked inflation. The economic crisis compounded the political malaise that had been haunting the United States and many European countries and ended the long period of prosperity that followed World War II.[81]

The price spike also led to a huge transfer of wealth from developed countries to oil-exporting developing nations. These billions emboldened leaders such as Venezuela's Carlos Andrés Pérez, Iraq's Saddam Hussein and Iran's Shah Mohammad Reza Pahlavi to pursue major industrialization projects and to seek leadership roles among developing nations.[82] The money also paid for the nationalization of oil assets by Libya in 1973, Saudi Arabia in 1975 and Venezuela in 1976. A second oil shock occurred in 1978, when Iranian revolutionaries deposed the shah and replaced him with an anti-U.S. theocracy. Oil-rich nations prospered, but the bounty was short-lived.[83]

The Oil Crash

The high price of crude, while enriching OPEC, prompted importing countries to become more efficient in their energy use and non-OPEC countries to search for petroleum in areas that earlier had not been considered commercially viable. Mexico discovered Cantarell, one of the greatest oil fields ever, in the shallow waters of the Gulf of Mexico, in the 1970s. Norway and the United Kingdom opened rich oil and gas fields in the North Sea. A surge in oil production, combined with a weak global economy, led to a rapid fall in the price of crude in the mid-1980s.[84]

That dashed the dreams of rapid development of many oil-rich countries. Economic pressure destabilized democracy in Venezuela, undermined the oil-dependent Mexican economy and helped prod Saddam Hussein to invade Kuwait to conquer the emirate's oil wealth. It also led to political liberalization in Eastern Europe, as the cash-strapped Soviet regime couldn't afford to keep subsidizing communism.[85]

Oil Prices Tied to World Events

What U.S. refiners pay for crude oil, 1968–2013 (in 2013 $US)

Oil prices jumped in 1973, due to an embargo by Arab oil-producing countries, and in 1979, during the Iranian Revolution. Prices fell rapidly in the early 1980s because of an abundance of global reserves, and then remained between $20 and $40 per barrel for almost two decades. Prices rose after the 2003 U.S. invasion of Iraq, then tumbled in the recession following the 2008 global financial crisis. Prices peaked in 2011 and have since fallen.

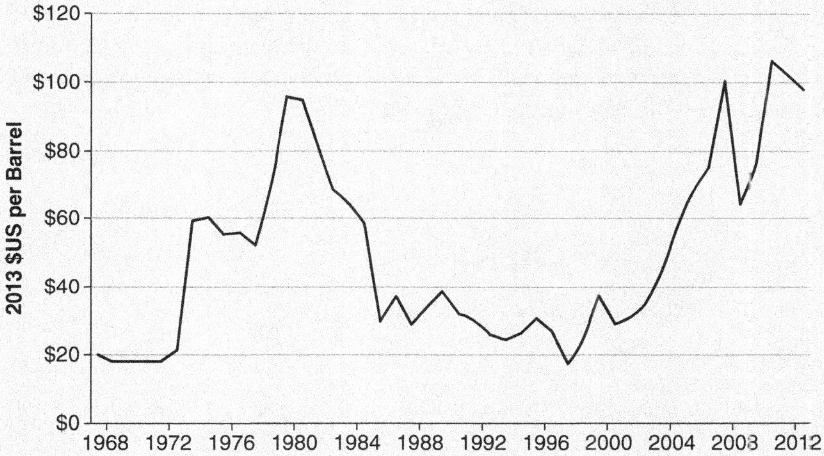

Source: Data from 1968–2013 from "U.S. Crude Oil Imported Acquisition Cost by Refiners," U.S. Energy Information Administration, updated Oct. 1, 2014, http://tinyurl.com/m7nytrd; adjusted for inflation using "CPI Inflation Calculator," U.S. Bureau of Labor Statistics, undated, http://tinyurl.com/68gks8.

The big Western oil companies suffered, too. Hundreds of thousands of oil engineers were laid off. These firings planted the seed of future problems, as oil companies later found it hard to hire enough experienced midlevel experts, and many youngsters were discouraged from entering the field.[86] Poor profits and trouble opening new reserves led to consolidation in the late 1990s and early 2000s among the biggest oil companies—BP gobbled up Amoco, Chevron bought Texaco, Exxon merged with Mobil, Conoco partnered with Phillips, and France's Total bought out Belgian integrated oil company Petrofina and local rival Elf Aquitaine.

Tech Revolution

Years of low oil prices led to underinvestment in exploration, even as a booming American economy in the 1990s increased sales of gas-guzzling sport utility vehicles and China's economic liberalization led to the rise of its middle class, a trend that revolutionized energy markets.[87]

The growing appetite of emerging nations for fuel boosted prices beginning in 2003. The rapid rise—which peaked at about $145 per barrel of benchmark U.S. crude in the summer of 2008—led to predictions of a crushing energy crisis, as producers seemed unable to catch up to demand. Russia and OPEC nations tightened their grip on their resources. Asian national oil companies began scouring the globe for oil and gas to feed fast-growing economies in China, India and South Korea, jostling with more established Western giants.[88]

The rise in prices made previously uneconomical sources of energy suddenly profitable: Big Oil flocked to the oil sands of Alberta, first tapped in the 1960s, where petroleum-soaked sand had to be mined and crushed to extract heavy oil. Deep-water drilling increased in the U.S. Gulf of Mexico, off the Brazilian coast and in West Africa, where Angola became first a major oil producer and then an OPEC member. Arctic drilling began to be seriously considered, with Royal Dutch Shell investing billions in securing permits to drill in remote locations off Alaska. Houston oilman George Mitchell perfected the combination of hydraulic fracturing, a decades-old technique, with horizontal drilling in North Texas to squeeze commercially viable energy out of shale rock throughout the United States.[89]

Brazil Taps Its Deep-Water Oil Riches

"An Enviable Position in the Global Energy System"

Brazil, South America's largest nation and its biggest energy consumer, has emerged as an oil power—an unlikely, technology-driven evolution for a country long reliant on expensive foreign crude.

In 1980, the country produced just 182,000 barrels of crude oil per day, enough to cover about one-sixth of its needs.[90] At the time, Brazil's military government had embarked on an ambitious program to replace gasoline and diesel with ethanol produced from domestic sugarcane.[91]

But the energy crisis of the 1970s, which wrecked the emerging power's economy, also pushed the state oil monopoly, Petroleo Brasileiro S.A., known as Petrobras, to scout for oil offshore and in places such as Iraq and the U.S. Gulf of Mexico, says Jeremy Martin, director of the energy program at the Institute of the Americas at the University of California, San Diego.

In 1974, Petrobras struck oil in the Campos Basin, just offshore of Rio de Janeiro. After that, "Petrobras was setting deep-water drilling records in the 1980s and 1990s," Martin says.

That pioneering effort faced problems, however. In 2001, a Petrobras platform, the P-36, exploded and sank, killing 11 and foreshadowing the disaster that destroyed BP's Deepwater Horizon platform in the Gulf of Mexico nearly a decade later.[92] But its drilling work gave Petrobras expertise that many large integrated oil companies lacked, opening the door to deep-water opportunities even beyond Brazil: It was the first company, in 2012, to bring to the U.S. Gulf of Mexico a floating production storage and offloading system, which is basically a deep-water platform based on a vessel so it doesn't require pipelines.[93]

Brazil's own domestic deep-water foray also got a big boost from a 1998 law that opened the door to foreign companies such as Royal Dutch Shell, Chevron and Exxon Mobil. But the biggest triumph came when Petrobras discovered rich deposits of crude under thick domes of salt buried deep beneath the sea. Even though hard to extract, the deposits led President Luiz Inácio Lula da Silva to proclaim in 2008 that Brazil got a "lottery ticket."[94]

It was not an overstatement, says Martin: The oil riches beneath the Atlantic are "Saudi Arabia-style," he says. Now the country produces more than 2 million barrels of crude a day. Brazil in 2009 dethroned long-reigning Venezuela as South America's largest producer of liquid fuels, according to data from the U.S. Energy Information Administration (EIA).[95]

Brazil has had to "look harder for resources than most other oil-rich countries," according to a report from the Paris-based International Energy Agency (IEA). But even though the process has taken time, the offshore discoveries "have confirmed Brazil's status as one of the world's foremost oil and gas provinces."[96]

But these riches also led the Brazilian government to devise a hybrid legal system that gave foreign investment a secondary role in many Brazilian oil fields.[97]

That led to a big slowdown in foreign investment and the discovery of less oil, says Martin. He adds that Petrobras also "wildly miscalculated" how quickly it could develop these resources, and how much money it would cost. "It was way too optimistic," Martin says.

According to its latest 10-year energy plan, Brazil seeks to produce more than 5 million barrels a day by 2021.[98] That's more than double its current production capacity—but it's also less than the 6 million barrels a day it had projected producing in a previous plan, according to the EIA. The goal is to export more than 2.25 million barrels a day.

Numerous other problems have beset Petrobras, including a scandal that implicated company officials in a kickback scheme involving contractors and politicians.[99]

It also has soaring debt because of the amount of cash it needs to finance expensive deep-water exploration, and because of what some say was overpayment for a 50 percent interest in a Houston refinery at the peak of its global expansions.[100] Not only has the company been unable to build enough refining capacity, but it also is grappling with strong government rules mandating the use of costly local suppliers.[101]

Nevertheless, when taking into account the combination of its oil riches and its strong portfolio of renewable energy—from ethanol to hydropower-generated electricity—Brazil has successfully tackled challenges that still befuddle other countries. "Brazil occupies, in many ways, an enviable position in the global energy system," the IEA said. "Its endowment of energy resources is vast, varied, and more than sufficient to meet the country's needs."[102]

—*Ángel González*

The rush for fossil fuel resources coincided with growing awareness about their impact on climate change, nurturing a parallel effort to develop sustainable and environmentally friendly sources of energy. Giant biodiesel facilities were built in coastal Washington state and Texas; ethanol plants, making fuel from corn, popped up all over the Midwest, and the fuel became a widely used additive in gasoline thanks to federal fuel mandates. Solar and wind generation facilities also proliferated as government mandates and the rising price of natural gas helped make these expensive methods more competitive.

Oil-related disasters, from the massive Exxon Valdez oil spill in Alaska in 1989 to the refinery explosion in Texas City that killed 15 in 2005, brought home the environmental and human cost of fossil fuel energy.

Crisis and Recovery

The global financial crisis of 2008 brought oil prices back to below $40 per barrel, creating concerns about the economics of hard-to-develop areas such as Alberta's oil sands. But the tumble was brief: After several months, benchmark crude was back above $60 per barrel, as China, which had become the world's second-largest importer of crude, remained economically robust. Prices for that benchmark product, West Texas Intermediate, rose above $100 per barrel again in 2011.[103]

Alternative fuels such as biodiesel lost momentum, as technological breakthroughs that would have made them a cheaper alternative to fossil motor fuels failed to become commercially viable.[104] Also, the U.S. government's zeal to replace fossil fuels was muted because the energy industry was generating jobs in the midst of the recession.[105]

In the midst of the bonanza, however, catastrophe struck. On April 20, 2010, two days before Earth Day, the Deepwater Horizon, a rig that BP leased to drill a well in the U.S. Gulf of Mexico, exploded and sank, killing 11 people and unleashing the worst marine spill in the nation's history. The spill led to a moratorium on drilling in the Gulf, but the pause was lifted several months later, and deep-water drilling continued after a safety overhaul by oil companies. A U.S. court, however, in 2014 found BP guilty of gross negligence in the Deepwater Horizon tragedy, a ruling that could carry a price tag of $13 billion, highlighting the risks of pushing the frontiers of oil exploration.[106]

In early 2015, oil producers were facing another challenge: a significant drop in oil prices, which have fallen by more than half since July 2014.[107] The drop is due in large part to the new abundance of oil, but also to an economic slowdown in Europe and Asia. Some experts argue this is the beginning of a new era of relatively low oil prices, similar to the bust seen in 1980s—but others say the fact that shale producers can cheaply and quickly change the amount of crude they extract could help them avoid economic catastrophe.[108]

CURRENT SITUATION

Dangerous Haul

Few aspects of America's oil wealth are generating more controversy than the railroad issue. When oil producers began shipping crude out of North Dakota's Bakken Shale via rail, many thought it would be a temporary arrangement. But now it seems a more permanent solution, because refiners like the flexibility. North Dakota rose from a relatively small oil producer to dethrone Alaska as the nation's second largest, behind Texas. Railroads moved 407,761 carloads of crude in 2013, up from 9,500 in 2008.[109]

Critics, however, say railroads are more accident-prone than pipelines. A series of explosions, starting in 2013 with a blast in Lac-Mégantic, Quebec, that killed 47 people, underlined these fears.[110] In July 2014, the U.S. Department of Transportation concluded that Bakken crude is more volatile than other types of oil and therefore poses a special safety risk, a risk magnified by the increasing volume being shipped throughout the country in trips averaging 1,000 miles. It has proposed replacing old tank cars known as DOT 111 with cars built with tougher hulls, as well as beefing up braking controls and speed restrictions.[111] The Association of American Railroads responded that the rule is a "much-needed pathway," and that the industry has already voluntarily implemented many of the proposed safeguards.[112]

More recently, a train carrying Bakken crude from North Dakota to Virginia derailed in West Virginia on Feb. 16, bursting into flames and causing the evacuation of two towns.[113]

Railroad capacity is also an issue. In the winter of 2013–14, farmers in North Dakota and elsewhere in the Midwest encountered delays in shipping grain, the result, according to many, of the transport strain the oil boom has created.[114] Congress has been pressing the railroad industry to fix the problem. At a Senate hearing in September 2014, railroad association President Edward Hamberger acknowledged the challenges, which he said were compounded by bad weather, but said railroads are investing record amounts to meet demand.[115]

Trouble in Russia

The reemergence of Russia as a geopolitical rival is sending shock waves through the world of energy, especially in the wake of President Vladimir Putin's aggressive 2014 annexation of Crimea from Ukraine.

Western oil companies have long been on shaky ground in Russia, one of the world's largest energy producers, but before the Ukraine standoff things were looking up.

Throughout the first decade of the 2000s, BP had trouble dealing with its Russian partners and the country's government in what's known as the TNK-BP joint venture, which, when launched in 2003, was the largest foreign investment in Russia and produced nearly a third of BP's crude.[116] But in 2013, BP sold its stake in TNK-BP to Russian oil giant Rosneft and acquired an 18.5 percent stake in that company, which gives it access to the Russian Arctic, a key potential source of wealth.[117] Exxon Mobil, which at the turn of the century had unsuccessfully tried to buy Russian oil giant Yukos, in 2012 struck a $500 billion deal with Rosneft for joint Arctic offshore exploration.[118]

However, Western sanctions against Russia over Ukraine threaten these ambitious joint ventures. The sanctions ban U.S. and European oil companies from partnering with five top Russian energy firms.[119] If prolonged, the sanctions could delay Arctic oil exploration, which is key to Russia retaining its role as a major energy player, and could endanger Exxon Mobil's relationship with Russia, crucial to its growth plans.[120]

It remains to be seen, however, whether the havoc wrought on Russia's economy by the fall in oil prices will deflate Putin's geopolitical ambitions. Amid a weakening ruble, lower government revenue and the continuing effect of sanctions, experts forecast a recession this year.[121]

Canadian Hurdles

The energy industry views the planned Keystone XL pipeline, designed to move 830,000 barrels of crude a day from Alberta to the Midwest and the U.S. Gulf Coast, as integral to both the U.S. national interest and to the profitable development of some of the world's largest reserves of crude.[122] TransCanada, the Canadian company behind the project, expected the U.S. government to approve construction in 2013, which would have led to operations starting in 2015.[123] In early 2015, a decision by the U.S. government was still pending amid stiff opposition from environmentalists and some Democratic officials over concerns about how shipping oil sands crude through the line could result in toxic spills in U.S. soil and contribute to climate change (more greenhouse gases are produced extracting and refining this type of crude than lighter forms of oil).[124] The Republican-controlled Congress in February passed a bill authorizing the pipeline, but President Obama vetoed it. It was just the third veto during his six years in office. The State Department, which has a say in the project because it crosses an international border, continues to evaluate the pipeline.[125]

The delay has prompted Alberta premier David Hancock to say that he was "disappointed," given that the project provides "energy security, jobs and a dependable energy source from an environmentally responsible and democratic friend and ally."[126]

For Canada, Keystone is an important outlet: So much oil is stuck in Alberta, it sells significantly below global prices; in mid-September, crude sold in Alberta was $13.50 below the price of U.S. crude.[127] As the price of Canadian crude plummeted toward $40 per barrel in December, experts said that the drop in prices threatened the viability of new oil sands projects, which are expensive to launch.[128]

For that country to fully develop its oil sands, which contain some of the largest deposits of oil on earth but are expensive to exploit, that crude needs an outlet to more buyers willing to pay higher prices. Greg Stringham, vice president of markets and oil sands at the Canadian Association of Petroleum Producers, says the delays with Keystone have been a "wake-up call" for Canada to find reliable buyers for its bounty beyond the United States.

Calgary-based Enbridge, another pipeline company, has proposed shipping oil through the Pacific to Asia; last June, Canada's government approved Enbridge's bid for the so-called Northern Gateway pipeline to bring crude from Alberta to British Columbia, where it would be put on ships.[129] But such a move would draw hundreds of tankers a year to British Columbia's pristine shores and has triggered opposition from First Nations, as Canadians refer to native tribes. Enbridge's projected schedule of completing the pipeline by 2018 faces numerous regulatory hurdles.[130]

LOOKING AHEAD

Diverse Future

An irony of America's energy revolution is that it coincides with declining demand for gasoline. The IEA and other experts estimate that even as the thirst for fuel grows in developing countries, demand in developed nations, including the United States, peaked in 2007.[131] That's partly due to the recession—lower industrial demand and fewer people commuting to jobs.

But a longer-term transformation also is in the works, as engine efficiency improves. Federal automotive fuel standards will require an average of 49 miles per gallon in 2025, vs. 33 mpg in 2012, and that will continue to reduce gasoline consumption, the U.S. Energy Information Administration says.[132]

Electric vehicles, which are becoming common in the United States, also are helping to reduce gasoline use. The IEA estimates that in 2012, 180,000 electric vehicles were on the road worldwide, and sales doubled compared with 2011.[133] Jaffe, from the University of California, Davis, energy program, says the combination of better fuel efficiency, more electric cars and the surging popularity of natural gas as an alternative to oil means more stability for the global economy, and fewer energy shocks in the future.

"We're not all on one fuel, so when you have one shock in one of the sources of energy, people switch," she says. It's also likely to make energy cheaper. "Demand destruction and unexpected substitutions will affect the whole industry."

Natural gas burns more cleanly than coal, so the vast amounts unlocked from shale have prompted scientists and policymakers to consider it as an ideal "bridge fuel" to temporarily replace dirtier sources of power generation until the world figures out how to take advantage of true renewables like solar and wind.[134]

But natural gas is so abundant, some are thinking about the fossil fuel as an inexhaustible source, available for centuries. Exxon Mobil, America's largest natural gas producer, says the world has about 200 years of recoverable natural gas at current production levels.[135] The IEA said the world is entering a "golden age of gas" but that it will require countries outside North America to develop their shale potential—and lots of continued investment. That might be difficult, as there's steadfast opposition to fracking in many shale-rich countries, such as France.[136]

Around the World, Fracking Faces Political, Technical Barriers

Shale Gas "Being Found Almost Everywhere"

Fracking has transformed the energy industry in the United States and Canada. Shale rock rich in oil and gas is also present in France, Poland, Germany, China and elsewhere. However, in many countries fracking—short for hydraulic fracturing, which uses high-pressure water and chemicals to release fuel from rock—faces political and technical challenges.

Fracking has transformed the U.S. energy industry and, to a lesser extent, that of Canada. But oil-and-gas-rich shale rock is present not only in North America but also around the world, from the soil beneath Paris to the deserts of Algeria.

In many countries, though, fracking—short for hydraulic fracturing, which uses high-pressure water and chemicals to release fuel from rock—faces political and technical challenges.

"Within 10 years we don't see a country having the type of unconventional production that the U.S. does," says Robert Clarke, head of unconventional oil and gas for energy consultancy Wood Mackenzie. "There's a difference between technical potential and actual commercial projects."

Financial and geopolitical incentives to tap shale abound. It would make gas cheaper in the global market. For Europe, which has rich shale deposits in France, Poland and Germany, fracking could loosen the embrace of the Russian bear. For financially harried Argentina, the technology could provide a huge boost to its oil industry and its trade balance. Developing gas-rich shale deposits in northern China would greatly increase that country's domestic security, currently endangered by growing reliance on Middle Eastern oil.

China has the largest recoverable shale gas resources in the world, nearly twice the amount estimated to be held by the United States, and the third-largest shale oil resources after Russia and the United States.[137]

However, factors that helped fracking take off in the United States—relatively laissez-faire regulations and private-property laws that give land owners control of the resources beneath their property and, therefore, an incentive to develop those resources—are lacking in most other countries.

For instance, in France, which holds the second-largest European shale reserves after Poland, fracking is banned due to regulators' environmental concerns.[138]

There are also technical problems. In China's gas-rich Sichuan province, critics fear fracking might contaminate scarce clean water supplies.[139] In 2012, Exxon Mobil pulled out of Poland, one of the countries with the largest shale gas reserves, because it was unable to figure out how to make extraction commercially viable.[140] In Argentina, home to the promising Vaca Muerta shale formation, price controls, export tariffs and political instability retard rapid development, even though exploitation of that resource could lead Argentina to energy self-sufficiency.[141]

Nonetheless, shale's allure persists. Algeria, which according to the U.S. Energy Information Administration has the third-largest recoverable shale gas resources, surpassing those of the United States, has announced plans to drill shale gas wells, even though locations are remote and water resources precious.[142]

Russia sees its huge shale oil potential as key to maintaining its status as an oil superpower; in 2012, it extended its Arctic oil deal with Exxon Mobil to include the prospecting of western Siberia shale.[143]

(Continued)

(Continued)

In Germany, which began phasing out nuclear energy after Japan's 2011 Fukushima catastrophe, when an earthquake and tsunami caused the meltdown of three nuclear reactors, authorities are leaning toward allowing fracking despite steadfast opposition from environmentalists.[144] And Britain's government is easing the way for increased fracking by readying proposals that would allow producers to drill deep wells horizontally without requesting the consent of each landowner above.[145] In China, where pollution is a political headache, the government has a strong incentive to develop cleaner-burning shale to feed natural-gas-powered trucks, says Amy Jaffe, executive director of energy and sustainability at the University of California, Davis.

Argentina's Vaca Muerta shale has "really high-quality rock"—meaning that it's rich in oil and gas and responds well to fracking techniques, says Wood Mackenzie's Clarke. He adds, however, that Argentina is unlikely to replicate the success of projects such as Texas's Eagle Ford shale, where production ballooned from practically nothing to 1 million barrels a day in three years, because the oil field services industry in that country is less mature and the regulatory environment a bit riskier than in Texas.

Whatever the obstacles, management consulting firm KPMG has estimated that "shale gas has the potential to turn the world's energy industry on its head." It's abundant, cheap, burns cleaner than other fossil fuels, and "it's being found almost everywhere."[146]

—*Ángel González*

Some fear that the natural gas bounty may undermine a true long-term solution, the development of renewable alternatives. "I don't see how you put the genie back in the bottle with natural gas," says de Place, policy director at the Sightline Institute, the Seattle environmental group. "Gas is taking over the world right now."

Global Warming

The fight against climate change gained momentum right before the financial crisis, with even oil titans such as Exxon Mobil formally acknowledging the challenge.[147] But then the public's attention shifted to the economy, and the U.S. oil industry emphasized domestic energy's role in job creation.

Some say the world soon will regain its sense of urgency about climate change. The Sierra Club's Nardone says U.S. public opinion is already shifting. "I'm beginning to see important leaders back away from the notion" that climate change is not a top priority, she says, referring to recent steps such as the Environmental Protection Agency's move in June 2014 to force states to reduce carbon pollution from power plants.

Jaffe says climate change increasingly will become an issue as consequences become visible, notably in China. "There are lots of provinces in China where climate change is having a big effect," she says. "In five years, environmental impact is going to change global politics."

Chronology

1850s–1870s	**Oil drilling begins.**
1859	Edwin Drake drills the first modern well in Titusville, Pa.
1870	John D. Rockefeller creates Standard Oil, which would eventually dominate the global oil industry.
1871	First wells drilled in Russia.
1900s–1930s	**Automobiles create demand for oil.**
1901	A drilling crew strikes oil at the Spindletop well, near Beaumont, Texas. The discovery would spawn Texaco, which later merged with Chevron. Spindletop is now quiet, but more than a century later, Texas still dominates the U.S. energy industry.
1908	Ford Motor's first Model T is assembled in Michigan, giving the automobile era—and the oil industry—a major boost.
1910–19	American prospectors develop the Mexican oil industry.
1920s	American prospectors shift to Venezuela, which offered friendlier terms to foreign companies.
1931	Oversupply of crude causes financial crisis for producers in the U.S. market. The Texas Railroad Commission, a state regulatory agency, gets the power to set production quotas.
1932	Standard Oil of California, Chevron's precursor, strikes oil in Bahrain, launching the Arab world's rise in the oil industry. Kuwait and Saudi Arabia follow in 1938.
1938	Mexican President Lazaro Cardenas expels foreign oil companies, making Mexico the first developing country to nationalize oil.
1940s–1960s	**New sources discovered.**
1941	The U.S. cuts off supplies of crude to Japan, before Japan's attack on Pearl Harbor.
1947	Kerr-McGee, an Oklahoma independent producer, strikes oil in the Gulf of Mexico.
Late 1940s	Oil-rich nations from Saudi Arabia to Venezuela demand bigger cuts from the oil extracted by foreign companies.
1953	A CIA-backed coup overthrows Iranian Prime Minister Mohammed Mossadegh, who wanted to wrest control of the oil industry away from foreign companies.
1960	Several oil-exporting countries in the developing world form the Organization of the Petroleum Exporting Countries (OPEC), dedicated to maintaining a fair price for the commodity.
1967	Oil is discovered in Alaska's Prudhoe Bay.

(Continued)

(Continued)

1970s	**OPEC embargo wreaks economic havoc.**
1973	Between 1970 and 1973, price of crude doubles due to rising demand. While OPEC countries negotiate with Western companies for a bigger share of profits, Egypt attacks Israel. After the attack, Persian Gulf countries unilaterally hike oil prices. Later they announce supply cuts to countries backing Israel. Prices spike further.
1973	Libya begins to nationalize oil assets owned by foreign companies; Kuwait in 1974 and Venezuela in 1976 follow suit.
1978	The overthrow of the Shah of Iran triggers another energy shock. Price reaches a then-astounding $34 a barrel.
1980s–1990s	**Supply and demand shift.**
1982	New supplies in Alaska, Mexico and the North Sea, combined with a recession and conservation measures, lead to a slump in oil prices that would last nearly a decade.
1990	Saddam Hussein's invasion of Kuwait triggers a short-lived spike in the price of crude.
1997	After years of tinkering, a well drilled by George Mitchell's company in North Texas shows that hydraulic fracturing, known as fracking, is economically viable.
Late 1990s	Enabled by new technology, oil companies begin tapping sizable reservoirs in the deep-water U.S. Gulf of Mexico.
2004–Present	**Fracking becomes a force.**
2004	Oil prices rise, as Chinese demand begins eating away at the world's spare crude production capacity.
2005	Hurricanes Katrina and Rita severely curtail U.S. Gulf of Mexico energy production, sending oil and natural gas prices soaring.
2008	Price of a barrel of oil reaches a record $145, right before the global financial crisis. It soon drops below $40 per barrel.
2009	Prices for oil quickly recover due to strong demand in China and other emerging countries, but those for natural gas stay low as a bounty of supply unlocked by fracking floods the market.
2010	Oil rig Deepwater Horizon explodes in the Gulf of Mexico, killing 11 people, injuring others and spilling hundreds of millions of barrels of oil.
2010–14	Oil companies apply fracking techniques to oil-rich formations, triggering supply booms in North Dakota's Bakken Shale and in South Texas's Eagle Ford Shale.
2014	Oil prices tumble as OPEC decides not to cut production despite growing crude production worldwide.
2015	Oil prices continue to slide, with crude prices at about $45 per barrel and gasoline prices close to $2 per gallon in mid-January.

PERSPECTIVE

Pro/Con: John Felmy on Fracking

YES ARE THE ECONOMIC BENEFITS FROM HYDRAULIC FRACTURING WORTH THE POTENTIAL ENVIRONMENTAL AND SOCIAL IMPACTS?

John Felmy

Chief Economist, American Petroleum Institute

Written for *SAGE Business Researcher*, January 2015

Hydraulic fracturing has brought significant economic benefits to communities across the nation. In North Dakota, oil and natural gas production has transformed the economy, lifting the state's per capita income 114 percent since 2000 (raising the state from 39th in personal income to fifth) and shrinking its unemployment rate to 2.67 percent—the lowest in the nation.

Nationwide, shale energy developed through hydraulic fracturing coupled with horizontal drilling has spurred job creation and economic benefits on a massive scale. According to a study by consulting firm IHS, energy development from shale and other tight-rock formations supported 2.1 million jobs in 2012, and that figure could grow to 3.3 million by 2020. Greater access to affordable domestic natural gas reduces operating costs for manufacturers, leading to a manufacturing renaissance. By 2015, nearly 400,000 manufacturing jobs, or 3.2 percent of all U.S. manufacturing jobs, will be supported by unconventional oil and natural gas—rising to more than 500,000 (4.2 percent) in 2025. Shale energy helps Americans save on costs of heating, electricity and everyday items, which increased disposable income for American households by an average of $1,200 in 2012 and saves state and local governments an estimated $720 million annually in taxpayer money.

Due to hydraulic fracturing, the United States now leads the world in natural gas production, and we've also reduced our total carbon emissions more than any other country on Earth. The availability of clean-burning natural gas is a key factor in reducing emissions to near 20-year lows, and Department of Energy calculations indicate that exporting a portion of our plentiful liquefied natural gas (LNG) resources could reduce emissions by 42 percent overseas, as well. Multiple studies confirm that increasing exports of LNG and crude oil could generate billions of dollars in consumer savings and economic growth, reduce the trade deficit, create hundreds of thousands of jobs, exert downward pressure on gasoline prices and enhance our positive geopolitical influence.

Although hydraulic fracturing has been used safely and successfully for more than 65 years, recent innovations make it even more effective and have raised the technology's profile—leading to misconceptions. However, current and former heads of the Interior and Energy departments, the Bureau of Land Management and the Environmental Protection Agency (EPA) have all affirmed the technology's safety—with former EPA Administrator Lisa Jackson stating in congressional testimony that she was "not aware of any proven case where the fracking process itself has affected water." Robust industry standards, coupled with strong state and federal oversight, continue to keep hydraulic fracturing safe.

By safely unlocking previously inaccessible energy resources, hydraulic fracturing has helped change America's energy outlook from scarcity to abundance, and—with the right policies—the benefits of shale energy will extend to more and more American households.

PERSPECTIVE

Pro/Con: Wenonah Hauter on Fracking

NO ARE THE ECONOMIC BENEFITS FROM HYDRAULIC FRACTURING WORTH THE POTENTIAL ENVIRONMENTAL AND SOCIAL IMPACTS?

Wenonah Hauter
Executive Director, Food and Water Watch

Written for *SAGE Business Researcher*, January 2015

Fracking, or hydraulic fracturing, is a process used to extract natural gas and oil from rock deep underground. A well is drilled and millions of gallons of toxic fracking fluid—a mix of water, sand and harsh chemicals—are injected at a high enough pressure to fracture the rock and release the oil or gas. The process has major environmental, health and socioeconomic issues associated with it, yet the purported economic benefits are often overhyped.

Fracking is known to produce massive amounts of toxic and radioactive waste, which contaminates the air and water near fracking operations and is hazardous to the more than 15 million Americans who live within one mile of a well drilled after the year 2000.[148] Fracking uses hundreds of dangerous chemicals known to cause life-threatening illnesses, including cancer. Quantifying exactly how much of these pollutants enter the air and leach into water resources is difficult, because much of the data available are given voluntarily by the industry, rather than through mandatory reporting.[149]

Fracking is also exempt from major environmental laws, including the Safe Drinking Water Act. Spills and accidents are far too common, with several thousand such incidents reported each year, including more than 7,500 in 2013.[150]

Not only do these incidents threaten the health of surrounding communities, but fracking also leads to a number of other consequences, including earthquakes, damage to public roads, declines in property value, increased crime and a rising demand on emergency services. These effects, and the low quality, dangerous jobs brought to communities by fracking, discredit the industry's claims of economic prosperity.

Additionally, fracking touches billions globally who are affected by climate change. The primary hydrocarbon in natural gas is methane, a potent greenhouse gas that, over a 20-year time frame, traps 87 times more heat than carbon dioxide, pound for pound.[151]

The environmental, health, climate and socioeconomic blunders caused by fracking are enough to outweigh any claimed benefits, but as it turns out, these purported benefits do more harm than good.

UPDATE IN 2020

The oil and gas industry finds itself in one of the most turbulent periods in recent memory.

While U.S. oil and gas imports rose slightly during the latter part of the 2010s, by 2019, imports had fallen to 3.3 billion barrels—nearly two billion barrels fewer than in 2005.[152] That was consistent with a prediction by the U.S. Energy Information Administration (EIA) that imports were likely to fall.

A key reason was fracking. By 2017, the U.S. led countries worldwide in producing oil from natural gas sources. Its closest rival was Russia, and the pair each produced roughly three times more oil from fracking than third-place Iran.[153]

It was clear that the industry was long past its peak of oil imports. Of what remained, Canada was clearly the biggest beneficiary. In 2019, 56 percent of U.S. crude oil imports came from Canada, while about 60 percent of crude oil imports came from four countries—Canada, Mexico, Saudi Arabia and Venezuela, according to the EIA.[154] Canadian imports were more than seven times greater than those from Saudi Arabia and six times greater than those from Mexico.[155]

A smaller factor was consumers' interest in sustainable energy. About 77 percent of Americans surveyed by the Pew Research Center said it was important to develop alternative sources to fossil fuels, such as solar and wind power.

But those sources are yet to be a meaningful threat to fossil fuels. In 2018, they constituted only 4 percent of Americans' energy use.[156]

Meanwhile, the Institute for Energy Research, a think tank focusing on energy analysis, maintained that the U.S. was energy independent in 2019 for the first time since 1957. In other words, U.S. energy production was higher than its consumption.[157]

In 1957, fossil fuels represented 93 percent of U.S. production and consumption. By 2019, fossil fuels represented 80 percent. The biggest difference came in the use of energy produced by coal. In 1957, coal-derived fuel represented 30 percent of production and consumption. By 2019, it had fallen by more than half to 14 percent, due to the advent of nuclear energy and other production methods.[158]

Coal's decline was a constant focus for U.S. President Donald Trump. He vowed throughout the 2016 presidential campaign and during his administration to protect the coal industry and restore coal jobs.

However, data showed that there were 1,000 fewer jobs in the coal industry in 2019 than when Trump took office.[159]

A far bigger problem for the energy industry occurred in 2020 in the wake of the COVID-19 pandemic. During spring and summer, fuel demand fell about 30 percent, as countries and governors ordered citizens to stay home.

Just as demand plummeted, Saudi Arabia and Russia launched a price war that temporarily sent the price of unleaded gasoline as low as $1 a gallon in parts of the United States. At one point, oil prices fell into negative territory, closing in April 2020 at minus $38 a barrel, before rebounding.[160]

In June 2020, Chesapeake Energy Corporation, a pioneer in fracking, filed for Chapter 11 bankruptcy protection in Texas, saying production was not profitable enough to cover a heavy debt load. Chesapeake, based in Oklahoma City, is one of the largest oil and gas exploration and production companies in the United States.[161]

Texas, long the nation's center of energy production, stood to suffer worse. Even before the COVID-19 emergency took hold in early 2020, the Federal Reserve of Dallas estimated there would be 8,100 job losses in Texas. But after the state shut down production in March, drilling companies and refineries cut more than 51,000 jobs, according to an estimate by BW Research Partnership. In April, BW Research Vice President Philip Jordan told Bloomberg News, "We're looking at anywhere between five and seven years of job growth wiped out in a month."[162]

By early July 2020, energy companies abandoned their efforts to build the 600-mile Atlantic Coast Pipeline, a natural gas facility that would have traversed the Appalachian Trail on its way from West Virginia to North Carolina. Virginia-based Dominion Energy and North Carolina-based Duke Energy said the project had become too costly, and the regulatory environment was too uncertain to continue.[163]

—Micheline Maynard

12

HONG KONG'S ECONOMY

Can it regain its luster?

Suzanne Sataline

From *SAGE Business Researcher*, January 15, 2018

EXECUTIVE SUMMARY

Hong Kong provided much of the economic muscle that has transformed China into a global financial powerhouse over the past three decades. The city of 7.3 million, which has been a special administrative region of China since the United Kingdom relinquished control in 1997, is increasingly intertwined with the mainland. But while Hong Kong remains relatively prosperous and is still a regional financial center, its recent growth rate is well below that of the People's Republic. The territory has failed to diversify to mitigate its reliance on trade services and finance and faces a host of problems that will be difficult to overcome, according to economic experts. "Hong Kong has gone sideways," says one.

Key takeaways include:

- Hong Kong's economic growth rate has fallen from more than 7 percent in the 1980s to about half of that late last year, while China has expanded to become the world's second-largest economy.
- China now accounts for more than half of Hong Kong's goods exports and 40 percent of its service exports.
- Hong Kong was the world's busiest port in 2004; it has since slipped to number five while Shanghai has moved into the top spot.

OVERVIEW

Long before Great Britain lowered the Union Jack on its colony of Hong Kong in 1997, the city was already entwined with China's emerging market-based economy. The ruling Chinese Communist Party had decided in the late 1970s to use capitalism as the vehicle to overhaul its underdeveloped economy, and it welcomed Hong Kong tycoons as they moved their operations to the mainland.[1]

Manufacturers that once spit out radios, umbrellas and housewares in post-World War II Hong Kong began in the 1980s to make clothing, shoes and electronics in China's nearby Guangdong province, where land was plentiful and labor was cheap.[2] Goods trucked to Hong Kong for export worldwide made the city one of the world's busiest ports and a global center for banking, finance and trade support.[3] If Chinese manufacturing powered the nation's growth, Hong Kong was the turbine of money and ideas.

A destroyer cruises past the Hong Kong skyline, part of a Chinese naval task force that visited the city on the 20th anniversary of the British handover.

Three decades later, Hong Kong's boom times may be over. The city of 7.3 million, situated on a group of peninsulas and islands in the South China Sea, depends heavily on China's economy, a nation where GDP rocketed from $962 billion in 1997 to $11 trillion in 2016.[4] That represents more than 18 percent of the world's economy.[5]

Yet there is little evidence of that growth in Hong Kong, which became a "special administrative region" of the People's Republic after the British handover in 1997. The modern neon-bathed city that enjoyed annual average GDP growth of 9 percent in the 1970s and 7.4 percent in the 1980s has floundered under China's leadership.[6] For example, in the third quarter of 2017, the territory's economy grew just 3.6 percent year-on-year.[7]

Hong Kong's economy is hardly in danger of failing—and some knowledgeable economists argue that it is fundamentally sound and well-positioned for growth. "It's always going to be the financial hub and the gateway. You're never going to get rid of it," said Stephen Innes, the Singapore-based head of trading for Asia Pacific with Oanda Corp., a foreign exchange firm.[8] Nonetheless, the city's financial picture is marred by problems that may take a long while to fix. After years of complaints by analysts, even Hong Kong cheerleaders acknowledge that the city's free-market system relied too much and for too long on trade services, banking and finance, and failed to diversify and join the digital revolution, according to economic experts.

Democracy advocates fault a government that has favored stability and obedience to Beijing over moves that would make the city fairer and ultimately more prosperous for all. These pessimists assert that Hong Kong has lost its innovative edge through a combination of missed chances, crony capitalism, constrained competition and government mismanagement and mistrust.

"Hong Kong is stuck, with remarkably little change to show for the last two decades," wrote Simon Cartledge, former editor-in-chief for Asia of the Economist Intelligence Unit, a research and consulting firm in London. "It's not a place that has failed, but it is one of lost opportunity, of diminished expectations and modest ambition. Despite living on the doorstep of the world's most dynamic economy of the last two decades, and despite having played a role in that economy's initial opening and development, Hong Kong has gone sideways."[9]

Ties That Bind to China

In 1978, when China's paramount leader, Deng Xiaoping, set out to rebuild an economy that had been devastated by Mao Zedong, Deng took advantage of Hong Kong's openness to the world. The city, originally built up by the British as a trading center for opium in the 19th century, had open markets and a transparent court system based on legal precedents. These assets provided a path for Communist officials to rebuild a nation broken by decades of war and poverty.[10]

To convince the world's markets that Hong Kong would remain stable after Britain relinquished control, Chinese leaders created a governance system called "one country, two systems" that guaranteed that capitalism and Hong Kong's "way of life" would remain until 2047.[11] That political and economic arrangement preserved Hong Kong's markets and legal system while working with China's partially market-based, partially state-controlled economy.

Hong Kong's Economic Growth Slowed in 2016

Hong Kong GDP, 2007–16

Hong Kong's gross domestic product (GDP) rose 3.7 percent in 2016 over the previous year. That was the smallest yearly increase since the territory's economy began growing again in 2010.

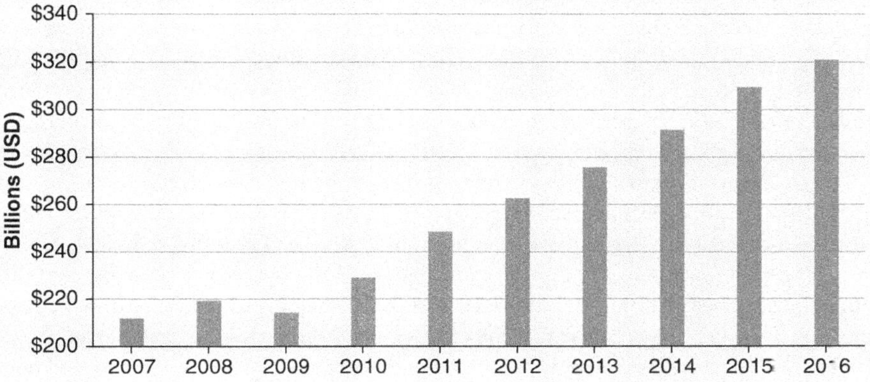

Source: "Hong Kong GDP," Trading Economics/World Bank, https://tinyurl.com/ydaus53e.

The marriage has worked for many. Some of the British and U.S. firms established there more than a century earlier to service the opium trade mushroomed into giant trading and financial services corporations, while many other global companies opened offices there.[12] Those companies include a major U.K. overseas bank, HSBC, and U.S. financial service companies Merrill Lynch, Citibank, Goldman Sachs and JPMorgan Chase.

By establishing a reliable banking industry, Hong Kong developed in the second half of the 20th century into a growing financial center that serviced trade in East Asia and assisted China's growth through loans to individuals or syndicates, wrote historian Steve Tsang.[13]

The capital provided by these bankers helped to finance shipbuilding, cement making and houseware manufacturing in Hong Kong, until Hong Kong entrepreneurs decided to invest in the special economic zone in Shenzhen, created in 1980 as China's first step in opening its economy. These owners closed factories in Hong Kong and poured their resources into mainland endeavors, maneuvering through a quasi-command economy "where bureaucratic corruption and the party machine distorted the market forces," Tsang wrote. "Their successes, which attracted more attention than those who failed, encouraged others to invest."[14]

By the time of the handover in 1997, those Hong Kong companies employed 5 million people, and Hong Kong was the mainland's "key trading partner, middleman, financier and facilitator," according to Tsang.[15]

That relationship has deepened in the years since. "Hong Kong doesn't really exist anymore as a separate state," says Andrew Clarke, director of trading at the Hong Kong brokerage firm Mirabaud Asia Ltd. "Hong Kong is part of China, whether you like it or not. It's done."

> ***"Hong Kong is part of China, whether you like it or not. It's done."***

China accounts for more than 50 percent of Hong Kong's goods exports, 40 percent of its service exports and 75 percent of its tourists, according to Moody's Investors Service.[16] New programs connecting the Shanghai and Hong Kong stock markets aim to bring more liquidity, but also more risk of "contagion" between the financial markets in the mainland and the city, Moody's said.[17]

Amid these ever-tighter connections with the mainland's economy, Hong Kong still relies on trade services and finance. Its departed manufacturing sector was never fully replaced. Once the world's busiest port, Hong Kong lost that title to Singapore in 2005 and soon after slipped behind Shanghai, then Shenzhen and even Ningbo-Zhoushan in Zhejiang province.[18] While Hong Kong's total port tonnage rose a scant 11 percent from 2001 to 2016, Shanghai's increased fivefold during the same period.[19]

The government's unwillingness to address long-standing problems has contributed significantly to the port's decline, according to Greg Knowler, a senior journalist specializing in maritime and trade with the market research firm IHS Markit. Those problems include insufficient land at the terminals, the high cost and delays of bringing containers across the border from mainland factories and the container lines' unwillingness to reduce terminal charges, which has made using the port costlier than alternatives in Shenzhen, Knowler wrote.[20]

China, which has blocked many Western digital technology platforms, has created homegrown start-ups that mimic Amazon, Twitter, Google and WhatsApp: Tencent, Sina Weibo, Baidu and WeChat have become some of the world's biggest technology companies.[21] Yet Hong Kong has been slow to join the digital boom.[22] Some residents, business owners and business school professors complain that Hong Kong's government has not provided benefits or capital to entrepreneurs or immigrants that would enable them to start businesses.[23]

Carrie Lam, who became the city's chief executive in 2017, is trying to address some of these complaints by rolling out an innovation plan.[24] Some officials, such as lawmaker Charles Mok, who represents the technology sector, criticized the plan for failing to include a broader array of digital enterprise, such as ride-hailing services and a system to alleviate traffic congestion.[25] And one of Lam's proposals, for an updated identity card that would allow the government to mine and store more information about individuals, may worry people concerned with personal freedom as the Chinese government amasses ever more data on its citizens.[26]

Hong Kong's dependence on the mainland economy left it vulnerable to the Chinese economic slowdown that began in 2015, when the annual pace of expansion slackened to the weakest in a quarter century.[27] Experts, even Chinese officials, blamed growing debt (total indebtedness, including government, business and household, in 2016 equaled 250 percent of annual GDP) and an abundance of housing and property investment.[28] Tactics the government had employed previously to boost the economy, such as spending on infrastructure, easing credit and pushing exports, had not worked.[29]

Beijing has struggled with a choice: cut interest rates and risk capital flowing out of the country, or raise interest rates, which might force more debt-laden companies to fail, driving joblessness.[30]

The slowdown had many causes. China's working-age population peaked in 2012 and investment reached its height at 49 percent of GDP, a level seen by few countries.[31] The nation narrowed its technology gap, which means there now are fewer new consumers to bring on board.[32]

Chinese Government Debt Reaches Record High

China's government debt-to-GDP ratio, 2007–16

China's government debt, measured as a percentage of the nation's GDP, reached an all-time high of 46.2 percent in 2016.

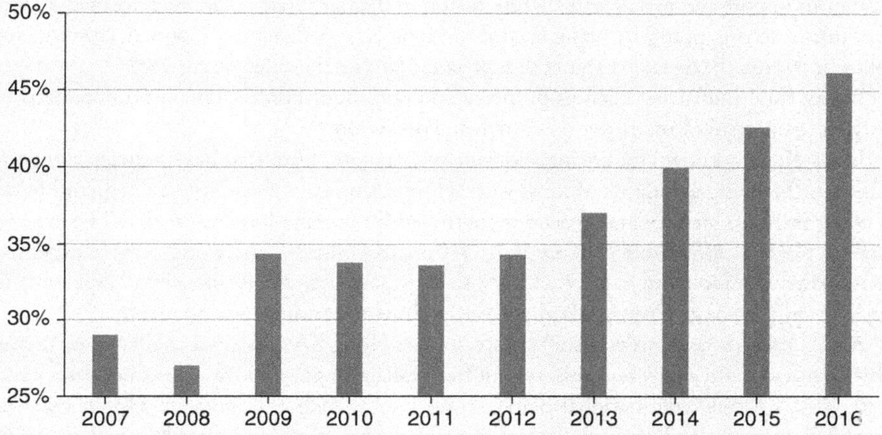

Source: "China Government Debt to GDP," Trading Economics/IMF, https://tinyurl.com/ydc3xccj.

Its tactics for growth help explain the slowdown: Easy credit spawned a major boom to rebuild ancient cities into modern ones through construction of new housing, shopping malls, highways, high-speed rail lines and airports.[33] Chinese state investments fueled overcapacity and rising debt; government debt alone was estimated to be 46 percent of GDP in 2016.[34] Chinese manufacturers that once flourished by enjoying relatively inexpensive labor costs have been moving operations to places that pay even cheaper wages, such as Vietnam.[35] The impact of that exports drop hit Hong Kong, as well. Growth in 2017 was dependent on private consumption and government spending.[36]

Structure of Hong Kong Economy

When it took control of Hong Kong from the British, China made sure that the city's wealthy and elite would remain in power. That arrangement warps Hong Kong's politics to this day and influences its economy, according to analysts such as former government official Leo Goodstadt and former property development professional Alice Poon.[37] They assert that while Hong Kong is often called one of the world's most liberal economies, it is actually controlled by a few wealthy families and companies that stifle competition. Poon wrote that major property companies wield a virtual monopoly in private housing and commercial property, and have bought up gas, electricity, telecommunications, grocery stores and building management companies that homeowners must hire.[38]

As they prepared for the handover, officials from the People's Republic recognized the need to work with and assuage Hong Kong's leading Chinese businessmen. When Chinese leaders set up a committee to draft Hong Kong's constitution, most of those named were from the business class whose investments were important to China. The selection was "a sufficiently large representation of Hong Kong residents to give it a democratic façade, but not large enough to oppose the PRC's will," wrote historian Tsang.[39] The elites were ensured a long-term role in setting policy by being named to Hong Kong's Executive Council, the city's top policy body, and the de facto cabinet that privately advises the chief executive.[40]

Today, vital industries, such as property and communications, remain monopolized by cartels and oligopolies and thrive on cronyism, Poon wrote.[41]

Hong Kong is known for having a low income tax rate.[42] But that has not been enough to maintain the living standards of most workers. Housing costs have skyrocketed, and prices of many utilities, services and groceries controlled by monopolies are rising.[43] The city has become the least affordable of more than 370 metropolises in the world—more expensive than Sydney, London and San Jose, Calif., the costliest U.S. city for housing.[44] Apartments, tiny even by New York City standards, cost 18.5 times the annual median income.[45]

As a consequence, entrepreneurs complain that Hong Kong poses a challenge to anyone who wishes to build a new business, recruit fresh talent, or grow a loyal consumer base, wrote Peter Guy, a former international banker there.[46] One such entrepreneur, Horan Fu, who started an internet lending firm, set up an office on the mainland after he was rejected by Hong Kong government-backed programs that aimed to nurture start-ups.[47]

According to UBS, six cities around the world are ripe for a housing bubble—high prices fueled by demand, limited supply and speculation—and Hong Kong is one of them.[48] Demand has been fed by a combination of tight government regulations on development, low interest rates, and a stable currency as the supply of land, controlled by the government, continues to shrink.[49] Borrowing costs have been nearly the lowest in the city's history, driving more sales.

Prices zoomed northward after the 2008 Western financial crisis, as global capital shifted to emerging economies. To discourage foreign ownership and speculation, the Hong Kong government imposed sharp fees on home purchases; the fees rose to 15 percent of the price in late 2016.[50] That did not discourage Chinese developers, who have outbid Hong Kong companies for land set at record prices.[51]

Unable to continue to pour cash into local mainland government property, Chinese developers bought $4.9 billion of land from the Hong Kong government in the first half of 2017, or 96 percent of all such transactions by value, compared with 39 percent of the total in all of 2016.[52]

The developers' exuberance has drawn parallels to the 1997 Asian financial crisis, a moment when Hong Kong's crucial and fraught ties to Asia's economies and the American stock markets became clear.

In that year, just days after Hong Kong was turned over to China, Thailand's government devalued its currency. Hong Kong's dollar came under speculative attack.[53] To defend the currency, Hong Kong's government raised interest rates, which caused Hong Kong stocks to sink further as investors left the equity markets to buy high-yielding bonds. The stock market index fell by about 60 percent from its height. Some observers worry that Hong Kong's inflated housing market could trigger a similar cataclysm today.[54]

Hong Kong No Longer World's Busiest Port

Ranking of top container ports, 2001–16

Hong Kong was the world's fifth-busiest container port in 2016, down from No. 1 in 2004. Shanghai, meanwhile, has maintained its top ranking since 2010.

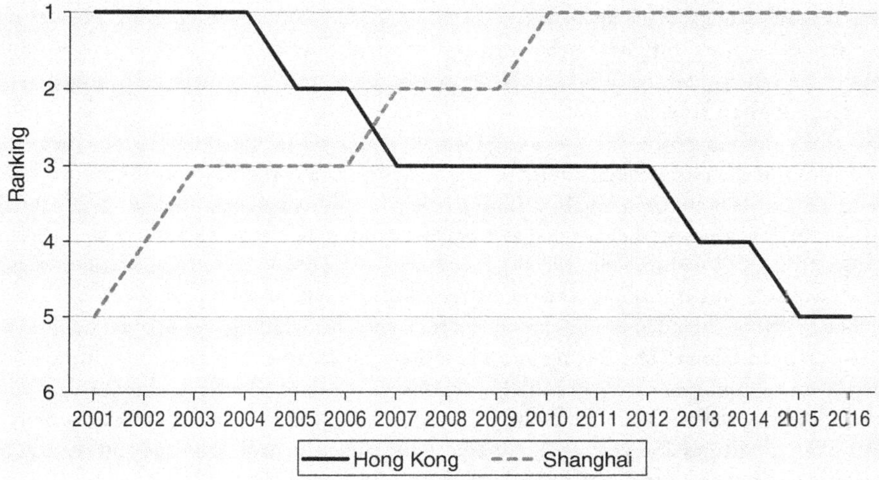

Source: "Ranking of Container Ports of the World," Marine Department, Government of the Hong Kong Special Administrative Region, https://tinyurl.com/yd2ddcf3.

This situation has placed enormous strains on Hong Kong residents, who privately complain bitterly about the cost of living. Fearing they will be priced out of the market altogether, buyers deplete all of their assets and borrow on their parents' existing homes to put money down on tiny flats.[55] Existing home prices climbed to a record in early 2017.[56] In April, new 430-square-foot flats on the eastern edge of Hong Kong island, a congested suburban stretch a half-hour train commute from the city center, sold for at least $1.33 million.[57]

Many cannot save enough to buy. About a third of the city's 2.5 million households live in public housing.[58] Thousands live in units subsidized by the government.[59] Demand is heavy; by the end of September, the city had received about 152,700 applications for public housing, about 127,400 from single adults of working age. The average waiting time for applicants has been 4.6 years.[60]

Meanwhile, income growth has stagnated. The median monthly wage of the city's workers was HK$16,200 (about US $2,075) in 2016.[61] In real dollars, that was an increase of HK$700 from 2015.[62] But since the handover, income growth has nearly stopped for people in the lower third of wage earners.[63] Income has risen for just the top 30 percent of residents.[64] One-fifth of the city's residents live below the poverty line—deemed to be less than half of the median monthly household income—with the elderly most vulnerable.[65]

Officials realize that the situation is becoming a crisis for even middle-class residents. In her first policy address in July, Chief Executive Lam announced that some developers will be required to pursue mixed-income developments and some homes will be priced for first-time buyers.[66]

Political Discontent

Politicians, economists and journalists agree that Hong Kong's government must address these challenges to avoid losing its richest, smartest residents through migration. The city has been mired for years in fights to change its governance, reforms that proponents say would allow the electorate and the camp that favors democracy a greater say in Hong Kong's policies and its economic future.

China's announcement three years ago that it would permit elections for the chief executive but limit the number and choice of candidates touched off a nearly three-month street occupation with more than a half million participants at its height. Dubbed the Umbrella Revolution, for the use of the rain gear as protection from police pepper spray, the revolt ended in December 2014 without winning any concessions. As a result, the city legislature rejected what it called "fake democracy," and the current elections system remains in place.[67]

The resulting anger fed even more radical movements, including one that demands independence from China. The Beijing and Hong Kong governments responded with a crackdown. After an unusual ruling from Beijing's national legislature in November 2016, a judge expelled six Legislative Council members who backed democracy, opposed massive development of rural villages and favored a mandatory pension scheme.[68] Students and opposition figures are being prosecuted, and several have been imprisoned.[69]

Chinese President Xi Jinping's government has moved swiftly to tamp down talk of secession and made clear that Beijing controls Hong Kong. When he visited in July for the first time as president, he warned that opposing China would be "impermissible."[70] Pro-democracy activists, such as the League of Social Democrats, and Anson Chan, once the second-highest official in the Hong Kong government before and after the handover, say they expect that economic strains and limits on residents' protests will feed anger and instability.[71] Many more residents talk about leaving the city.[72] All of those factors could create problems for the economy.

Slow Going Ahead?

Some economists say that important economic indicators show Hong Kong doing well. Wage growth, consumer price trends, GDP, tourist arrivals and even betting turnover on horse racing are all positive, according to Asianomics Group, a Hong Kong-based economic research firm. Some analysts, such as Innes of Oanda, say the city will continue to thrive because of its necessary role as a financial service provider.[73]

Jim Walker, an economist and managing director of Asianomics, says Hong Kong enhances China's finances, while China has aided property investment and rising consumption that feeds wage growth and low unemployment. He says he is not worried about China's large debt or its cooling growth rate.

"Every headline about China this year has been about an impending financial collapse, the growth of economic slowing, monetary policy tightening. I'm afraid none of it is true," Walker says. While the Chinese economy softened in 2015–16, since then it has picked up, he says, and when the national economy grows, Hong Kong's does, as well.

Some economists and analysts say it is likely that Hong Kong will continue to motor along as long as China's economy grows. But that is not certain. In May, Moody's downgraded China and Hong Kong's credit ratings.[74] The ratings firm said that "any erosion in China's credit profile" affects Hong Kong's.[75]

"I would say there's a lot of uncertainty around the Chinese economy. The most likely scenario is it slows down gradually in 2018," says David Dollar, senior fellow at the John L. Thornton China Center at the Brookings Institution, a Washington think tank. China is trying to slow credit growth to address the debt that has risen faster than GDP, Dollar says.

"This tighter financial condition should lead to slower investment and slower growth. . . . Any kind of slowdown should have some effect on Hong Kong," Dollar says. "But a gradual slowing should have a minor effect."

Chronology

1841–1945	**Hong Kong becomes a British dependency.**
1841	Two years after Britain began a war with China over the right to sell opium, the Crown claims sovereignty over Hong Kong island. Days later, British officer Charles Elliot declares Hong Kong a free port.
1842	Treaty of Nanking cedes Hong Kong to Britain "in perpetuity."
1865	The Hong Kong and Shanghai Banking Corporation—later known as HSBC—is founded.
1898	With the Convention of Peking, Hong Kong's New Territories—a mainland stretch of wetlands and mountains south of the Sham Chun River—are leased to Britain for 99 years.
1937	Japan invades China. Refugees pour into Hong Kong.
1941	After bombing Pearl Harbor, Japanese forces invade and occupy Hong Kong.
1947-1997	**The economy and unrest both grow.**
1947-49	During the civil war between Chinese Communist and Nationalist forces, Shanghai firms move their operations to Hong Kong. . . . With the Communist victory in 1949, Mao Zedong declares the founding of the People's Republic of China. Nationalists flee to Taiwan. The next year, Hong Kong's government limits immigration from China.
1953	A squatter fire in Hong Kong's Kowloon region leaves more than 58,000 homeless. The government undertakes housing, health and education changes.
1960s	Low taxes, lenient employment laws, absence of government debt and free trade spur Hong Kong's economic development. But social unrest leads Hong Kong to devote public money to welfare programs.

(Continued)

(Continued)

1967	A labor dispute turns into riots led by city leftists, who use bombs and gunfire against the colonial police force.
1978	Chinese paramount leader Deng Xiaoping announces a new economic plan to open his country to the outside world. Hong Kong becomes China's main provider of capital and, soon, commercial and financial services.
1980	Chinese city of Shenzhen, bordering Hong Kong, becomes the nation's first economic zone to experiment with market policies. The fishing village balloons into a manufacturing and shipping hub with financing help from Hong Kong tycoons. Hong Kong companies start to transfer work to the mainland to take advantage of cheaper wages, and Hong Kong moves toward a service economy.
1983	Deng announces unilaterally that China will assume sovereignty over Hong Kong in 1997. China and U.K. Prime Minister Margaret Thatcher formalize the move one year later with the Sino-British Joint Declaration. . . . Hong Kong pegs its currency to the U.S. dollar to stop a currency crisis.
1989	More than a million protesters throughout China demand democratic changes and an end to corruption. Soldiers kill hundreds, perhaps thousands, around Beijing's central Tiananmen Square. More than a million people protest in Hong Kong and two members of its constitutional drafting committee resign in protest.
1991	China approves Hong Kong's Basic Law, which gives the territory's residents unprecedented rights and freedoms. The document also permits China's legislature, after the handover, to amend any Hong Kong law and issue opinions on legal cases before the territory's courts.
1997	Britain relinquishes control of Hong Kong to China. The territory is governed by its own constitution that protects civil and legal rights and provides for relative autonomy in a system under "one country, two systems." Shortly after the handover, an Asian financial crisis begins after Thailand devalues its currency.
2000–Present	**China rises and takes control.**
2003	A viral disease called SARS strikes Hong Kong, killing nearly 300 people. . . . After a recession pushes up unemployment, China seeks to stimulate the economy by allowing mainland citizens to travel individually to Hong Kong, spurring migration to the territory.
2004	China's legislature rules that changes to Hong Kong's election laws require Beijing's approval.
2005	China becomes the world's fourth-largest economy. It will later become the second biggest.
2012	Party General Secretary Xi Jinping assumes control of the state and the presidency.

2014	Students launch a nearly three-month protest joined by tens of thousands of residents to demand changes to the city's election system. No concessions result.
2015	Some Hong Kong residents demand the government limit the number of mainland Chinese moving to the city. . . . Four men linked to a company that sells books critical of China's elite go missing; one resurfaces and tells the press that Chinese state security kidnapped them.
2016	Hong Kong's economy contracts. Some Hong Kong activists demand that Hong Kong become independent of China. Beijing officials label them separatists and order that such talk cease.
2017	Xi visits Hong Kong for the 20th anniversary of the handover and warns that challenges to Beijing's authority will not be allowed. Hong Kong chief executive Carrie Lam signals that the city will join China's trade and development initiative called "One Belt, One Road."

Discussion Questions

Here are some issues to consider regarding Hong Kong's economic evolution:

- What role has Hong Kong played in China's economic expansion over recent decades?
- Why has Hong Kong slipped behind the mainland in economic growth?
- What are the key characteristics of China's "one country, two systems" approach to governing Hong Kong?
- What economic and political issues have Hong Kong's leaders failed to address, according to critics?
- If you were starting a business that wanted a presence in East Asia, would you want it to be involved in Hong Kong? Why or why not?

PERSPECTIVE

Q&A: Ho-Fung Hung on Red Capital

"HONG KONG IS A FIRST DESTINATION"

Ho-Fung Hung

Ho-Fung Hung, an associate professor of political economy at Johns Hopkins University in Baltimore, studies the global economy, protest, nation-state formation and social theory with a focus on East Asia. He is the author of a forthcoming book chapter on Chinese state capital in Hong Kong, otherwise known as "red capital." He discovered that 60 percent of China's foreign investment was channeled to Hong Kong by the end of 2015, an amount that totaled $656 billion USD. Hung spoke with *SAGE Business Researcher* freelance correspondent Suzanne Sataline. This transcript has been edited for space and clarity.

Why is Chinese money being invested in Hong Kong?

All these rich people and wealthy and resourceful companies have a huge incentive to move [their money] out of China to keep it in a safer place. So, Hong Kong is a first destination because it's easier for them to move to Hong Kong than to California or Canada.

Politically, there's a risk. If your money and all your wealth is kept in China, and if your protector or you yourself get into some political trouble, you can see all your wealth vanish and be confiscated.

Second: Property [rights] in China are not guaranteed. China still maintains a system that even if you buy an apartment or a piece of land, the ultimate ownership is still with the state. You only have the use rights. The state can take it at any time. Wealthy people and companies won't see the money totally as theirs unless they move it to where private property is absolutely protected. Moving it to Hong Kong is the easiest way. The financial border between China and Hong Kong is really porous, with a lot of mainland companies having branches and operations in Hong Kong.

What are the implications of all that money flowing into Hong Kong?

It drives up property prices. Property prices in Hong Kong will not go down anytime soon because of this money. Even when the Chinese economy is in a bit of trouble, property prices in Hong Kong will go up, because the more troubled the Chinese economy is, the more incentive people have to move the money out of China and to Hong Kong. It creates a social problem—the inequality. Even local Hong Kong [residents] like Li Ka-shing [a billionaire and one of Asia's wealthiest men] and Gordon Wu [chairman of the property firm Hopewell Holdings Ltd.] are crowded out by this Chinese money. They are selling their property mostly to Chinese companies and moving out of Hong Kong. In the end, this trend will enhance the capability and incentive of Beijing to exert direct rule on Hong Kong.

Why?

Since the 1980s, China cannot exert direct rule over Hong Kong because the old families and old wealthy people like Li Ka-shing and Gordon Wu are very powerful. Beijing has to collaborate with them to govern Hong Kong because they control the economy. Now they [the old elite] are moving out or being crowded out and Chinese capital is the king of the economy. This old elite network became much weakened. Beijing no longer needs to be concerned about their opinion or ideas.

Is there a housing bubble?

Definitely. The huge amount of Chinese investors have a strong incentive to buy property in Hong Kong. Definitely they are the backbone of the housing bubble. And the Hong Kong housing bubble won't pop anytime soon.

After the 2015 financial trouble in China [when the Chinese stock market plunged and government efforts to halt trading did not stop the fall], that housing bubble in Hong Kong redoubled. The more troubled the Chinese economy is, the more people desperately want to get money to Hong Kong. And there's no way for the Chinese government to stem it. They will find some way or other to smuggle money out.

How might red capital shape Hong Kong politics?

From the top elite level to the middle-class professional level all the way to the lower-class level, there's a displacement of local Hong Kong people by the newcomers. It's one of the reasons why this kind of localist [political] sentiment has been brewing among the local Hong Kong youngsters.

On the surface, the [new elite] must be very much in line with the center of [the Chinese Communist Party] and Beijing. In the long run, I suspect there might be some differences emerging between these people and mainland Chinese people established in Hong Kong. When "one country, two systems" formally runs out in 2047, there should be a kind of discussion or negotiation [about] what Hong Kong becomes after that. When that discussion comes up, it will be interesting to see the new Hong Kongers' orientation. I suspect their interests will drive them to perpetuate the status quo, to protect their property.

In the end, it may be the new Chinese migrants who ask for the independence of Hong Kong. And they have the means to do it. Maybe it's fantasy. These rich mainland Chinese may eventually feel they are not that safe in Hong Kong. Of course, they will see Hong Kong as a springboard to somewhere else, like Canada, the U.S. and Australia.

UPDATE IN 2020

The 2014 Umbrella Revolution, in retrospect, was a three-month warm-up for the protests that would envelop Hong Kong in 2019 and 2020, interrupted only by the outbreak of COVID-19.

The protests centered on legislation introduced in April 2019 that would have allowed criminal suspects to be extradited to mainland China under certain circumstances. Critics said that would have subjected Hong Kong residents to unfair trials and violent treatment, and could strengthen China's influence over Hong Kong, which was supposed to maintain its independence until 2047.[76]

Protests began erupting in June 2019, and continued until fall, when Hong Kong Governor Carrie Lam withdrew the legislation. Despite her action, the demonstrations turned violent in the fall, resulting in the shooting of at least two protestors and the temporary shutdown of the Hong Kong airport and its subway.[77]

By November 2019, economists declared that Hong Kong had entered a recession for the first time in a decade, based on government data. The downturn was blamed on the protests, as well as U.S.-China trade tensions. "They're getting hit on two fronts. The protests are impacting retail sales. It is impacting tourism. Added to that, of course, you've got the U.S.-China trade war, which is impacting exports," said Sian Fenner, lead Asia economist at Oxford Economics.[78]

Then in 2020, an economic shutdown prompted by the coronavirus pandemic caused a further contraction. Hong Kong experienced two waves of the pandemic, one during winter, which brought protests to a halt, and a second outbreak in mid-summer, which prompted the government to tighten social-distancing restrictions.

After the first outbreak, Hong Kong's official government forecast called for a 4 percent to 7 percent decline in GDP for the year. But by late summer, that had been revised to 6 percent to 8 percent.[79]

Amid all this, China did not remain quiet. On June 30, the government implemented a new security law, which included vague clauses that criminalized language urging subversion, secession and collusion with foreign forces. Violations could result in jail sentences for life.

That prompted some Hong Kong residents to delete Facebook posts critical of the Chinese government. Books by pro-democracy figures were removed from public libraries, while activists were warned not to raise anti-government slogans.[80]

British Prime Minister Boris Johnson said he would implement new rules that would make it easier for Hong Kong citizens to emigrate to the U.K. The new security law "constitutes a clear and serious breach" of the 1997 agreement between Britain and China, which was meant to ensure Hong Kong's independence, said Johnson.[81]

Meanwhile, the U.S. issued a declaration that Hong Kong was no longer considered an autonomous region but was now part of China. U.S. President Donald Trump said Hong Kong residents and businesses would now be treated the same as their Chinese counterparts. He ordered a series of moves that would cancel cooperation between U.S. entities and Hong Kong.[82]

Given the turmoil throughout 2020, the Hong Kong government warned that the outlook for the economy was pessimistic. "Looking ahead, the continued spread of COVID-19 in various parts of the world is still a key threat to the global economic outlook," said an official government press release. "The increasingly tense China-US relations have also added to the uncertainties. In face of a challenging external environment, Hong Kong's merchandise export performance will likely remain constrained in the near term. The government will continue to monitor the situation closely."[83]

The main question for many multinational firms and investment banks was whether Hong Kong could still function as an effective hub for global business. Many had seen Hong Kong, which has 150 licensed banks and 1,600 asset managers, as a well-located jumping-off point for activities in South Asia, versus Seoul and Tokyo to the north. "I am thinking about it a great deal," said Heribert Dieter, an expert at the Berlin-based German Institute for International and Security Affairs.[84]

—Micheline Maynard

13 MINIMUM WAGE

Do increases help economies or hurt businesses?

Marcia Clemmitt

From *SAGE Business Researcher*, March 1, 2015

EXECUTIVE SUMMARY

In the United States and around the world, public concern has grown that the lowest-paid workers are falling behind as national economies recover from the global recession. Most Americans support raising the minimum wage to assist low-paid workers, and lawmakers in some U.S. states and cities have done so. As of January 2015, a total of 29 states had set their own hourly minimum wages higher than the federal minimum, $7.25 an hour since 2009. Politicians in many countries besides the United States also have pushed their minimum wages higher. Washington remains sharply divided on the issue, however. President Obama backs a Democratic proposal to raise the federal minimum to $10.10 an hour, phased in over a little more than two years. Raising the minimum wage would boost the economy by increasing consumer demand and ease taxpayers' burden by removing some workers from Medicaid and food stamp rolls, advocates say. Congressional Republicans, however, who control both houses of Congress following the November 2014 elections, join many businesses in opposing a wage hike. Increasing the wage wouldn't help the poor, most of whom are not in the workforce, and would make it harder for the lowest skilled to find employment, opponents say. Congress seems unlikely to enact a wage increase in the near future, but public concern over unequal incomes is certain to continue, political analysts say.

OVERVIEW

The McDonald's restaurant chain got unwelcome attention in the summer of 2013, when media outlets reported on a sample budget for minimum wage workers that the company posted on its employee-assistance website.

Quickly ridiculed as unrealistic, the budget estimated a monthly heating bill at $0 and a health insurance premium at $20. Moreover, it entirely omitted groceries and gasoline from the list of predictable expenses. But the most damaging gaffe was a summary of a hypothetical worker's wages. To pay for even the minimal expenses the website named, it listed one full-time minimum-wage salary—presumably from a job at McDonald's—supplemented with another nearly full-time minimum-wage salary from a second job.[1]

A McDonald's spokesperson said the budget samples were "generic examples" intended only "to help provide a general outline of what an individual budget may look like."[2]

Carl D. Walsh/Portland Press Herald/Getty Images

Union members protest in Portland, Maine, in September 2014 to call for an increase in the $7.25 per hour U.S. federal minimum wage.

"By positing two jobs for this fictional worker," McDonald's "has tacitly admitted that its employees can't live off the wages it pays," observed Forbes finance blogger Laura Shin.[3]

Public concern is growing that the lowest-paid workers are falling behind as the global economy recovers from a steep and prolonged recession. With that concern comes increased scrutiny of minimum wage rates, both in the United States and internationally. The U.S. minimum has remained $7.25 an hour since 2009. Minimum wages in other countries span a huge range, from well under 50 cents an hour in countries such as Bangladesh, in South Asia, and Botswana, in Southern Africa, to nearly $17 an hour in Australia.

In a January 2014 poll of U.S. respondents by the nonpartisan Pew Research Center for the People & the Press, 65 percent said inequality between rich and poor has grown over the past decade. Sixty-nine percent said the government should do "some" or "a lot" to reduce that gap, and 73 percent—90 percent of Democrats and 53 percent of Republicans—said they favored raising the minimum wage to $10.10 an hour.[4]

Public opinion in many countries tends to support having a minimum wage and increasing it annually, at least moderately. An October 2013 poll of Germans found that 83 percent supported instituting the country's first national minimum wage.[5] In a January 2014 poll in the United Kingdom, 66 percent of respondents supported a "substantial increase" in the U.K.'s minimum wage, while only 19 percent favored no increase.[6]

But many business groups in the United States and elsewhere contend that raising the minimum wage increases employers' cost of doing business in an unsteady post-recession economy and does little or nothing to help the most vulnerable citizens.

In his 2014 State of the Union address, President Obama announced support for a Democratic proposal to raise the federal minimum to $10.10 in three increments of 95 cents each, spread over a two-year and three-month period. That proposal was part of the Fair Minimum Wage Act of 2013, sponsored by Sen. Tom Harkin, D-Iowa, and Rep. George Miller, D-Calif., both now retired from Congress. The proposal, which would ultimately raise the wage automatically each year based on the inflation rate, has not yet been introduced for the 114th Congress but is still believed to have substantial Democratic support.[7]

Determined congressional opposition, mostly from Republicans, has stalled the measure for the past two years. In January 2015, a handful of centrist Democratic and Republican senators proposed potential deals they said might be struck to gain bipartisan support for

States Split on Minimum Wage

Seventeen U.S. states and territories match the federal minimum wage of $7.25 per hour, vs. 29 states and the District of Columbia that have a higher minimum wage. Georgia and Wyoming set a minimum lower than the federal rate.

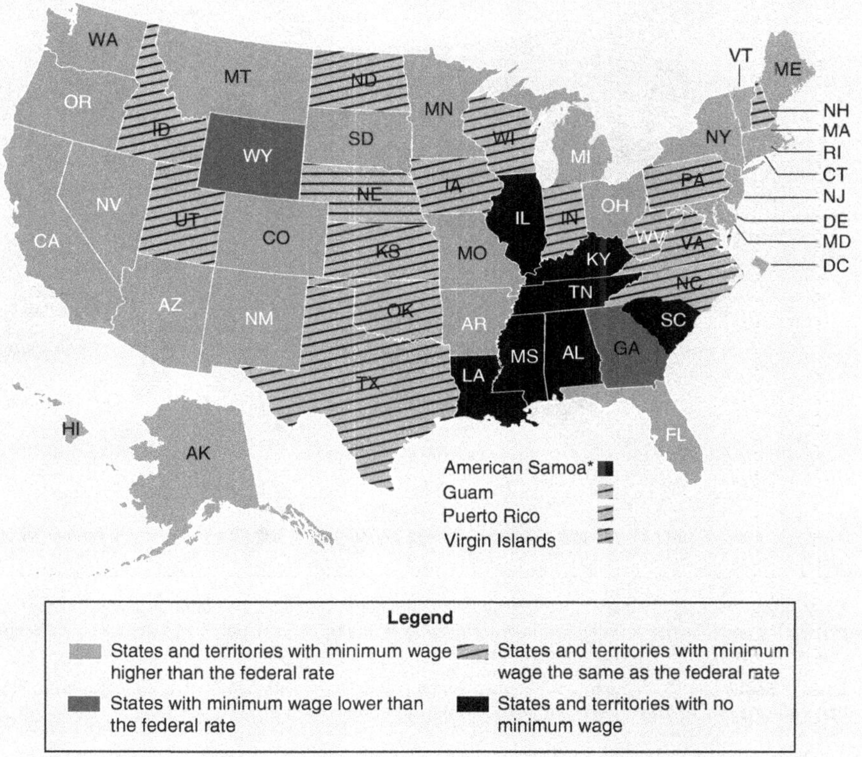

Note: American Samoa sets minimum wage rates for specific industries.

Source: "Minimum Wage Laws in the States," U.S. Department of Labor Wage and Hour Division, Jan. 1, 2015, http://tinyurl.com/yh6mqwz.

a minimum-wage hike. Sen. Heidi Heldkamp, D.-N.D., suggested that Democrats offer to support construction of the Keystone XL oil pipeline in exchange for Republican support for a minimum-wage increase. Sen. Susan Collins, R-Maine, proposed a minimum-wage measure she said might win Republican votes—raising the wage over three years to $9 an hour.[8]

Last year, with Congress stalemated over the minimum wage, Obama used his executive powers to address the issue in one of the few ways available to him. A February 2014 executive order required companies that contract with the federal government to raise their minimum from $7.25 an hour to $10.10.[9]

State Minimum Wage Rates (2015)

States can set their minimum wage rate higher than the federal minimum wage of $7.25. The highest rates are found in the Northeast and the Northwest, and the lowest rates are found in the South, but there are some interesting exceptions such as Illinois and Florida.

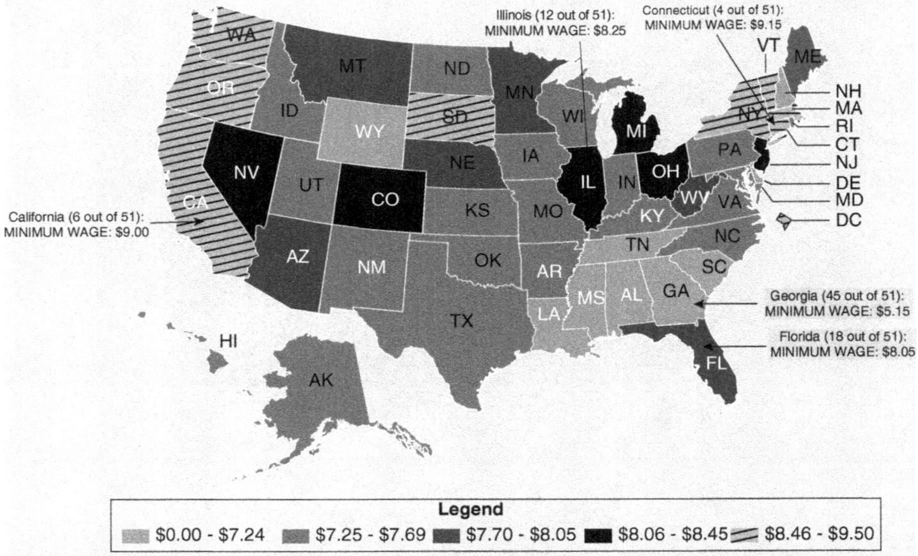

Note: As of Jan. 1, 2015. State minimum wage rates lower than the federal minimum wage are for those employers and jobs not covered by the federal rules. Alabama, Louisiana, Mississippi, South Carolina and Tennessee have no state minimum wage.

Source: Based on U.S. Department of Labor, Employment Standards Administration, "Minimum Wage Laws in the States," http://www.dol.gov/esa/minwage/america.htm.

Lawmakers around the world also are under pressure to raise their nations' minimum wages:

- In the U.K., a nonpartisan commission that sets the nation's annual minimum wage increases announced a 3 percent wage rise in 2014 to 6.5 British pounds per hour, or about $9.87. The uptick exceeded the inflation rate for the first time in six years. Even conservative politicians applauded, saying it was time to boost Britons' living standards after the recession led to stagnant wages and the loss of tens of thousands of U.K. jobs. The hike will likely be "the start of a new phase of bigger increases," said Low Pay Commission Chair David Norgrove, a businessman who was private secretary to conservative Prime Minister Margaret Thatcher in the 1980s.[10]
- In Germany, nationwide collective bargaining set wages for various industrial sectors until January 2015, when the country implemented its first government-set multi-industry, national minimum wage of 8.50 euros per hour—around $9.85.[11] To secure

a parliamentary majority in 2013, Chancellor Angela Merkel and her center-right Christian Democratic Union (CDU) formed a coalition government with liberal Social Democrats, who demanded the national minimum as their price for sealing the deal.[12] German conservatives argue that raising payroll costs may cost jobs. The CDU particularly fears a nationwide wage could hurt Germany's economically weaker eastern regions, said Merkel, vowing to "try everything to prevent the loss of jobs from this measure."[13]

- With a huge population of more than 1.35 billion, China sets minimum wages province by province. Recently, the ruling Communist Party has urged all provinces to implement large minimum wage hikes. It's part of a strategy to encourage low-wage manufacturing industries to leave the country and shift China toward a higher-wage, more service-focused economy. The minimum wage for workers in Guangdong province rose by 13 percent in 2014, for example, and by 15.6 percent in Jiangsu province.[14]
- South Africa has set minimum wages only for some especially low-paid business sectors that don't have unions, such as farm work, housecleaning, janitorial work and taxi driving. But labor leaders and the country's ruling African National Congress (ANC) party have warmed to the idea of creating a more inclusive minimum wage to combat racial wage disparities.[15] Two decades after apartheid's end, the average white South African worker earns six times more than the average black South African worker, says the party. In hopes of remedying the inequity, the ANC plans to institute a national minimum wage in the next several years.[16]

In the United States, pressure on government leaders has translated into minimum wage hikes in Democratic-led states such as Washington and Connecticut and cities such as Washington, D.C., and San Francisco.

Supporters of a wage hike argue that raising the pay floor would help millions of low-paid Americans keep their heads above water while boosting consumer demand in the economy, thereby helping all businesses. Opponents contend that it's unfair to expect businesses rather than taxpayers to shoulder the cost of assisting low-income people and that businesses with many low-skilled workers would have to lay off employees.

In highly industrialized nations such as the United States, the U.K. and European Union countries, minimum wage workers cluster in a handful of job categories, mainly food service, sales, office support, transportation and personal care.[17]

Relatively few Americans—about 1.6 million, or 2 percent of hourly workers—earned the federal minimum of $7.25 in 2012. If the wage were raised to $10.10, however, many more than those 1.6 million minimum wage earners would see their wages rise, say analysts at the Economic Policy Institute (EPI), a liberal think tank in Washington. The nearly 17 million workers who earn between $7.25 and $10.10 per hour would get an automatic raise, and some 11 million others who earn just over $10.10 an hour would also see a bump-up, as employers adjust their pay scales upward, says EPI.[18]

The U.S. minimum wage hasn't kept up with the basic costs of living, leaving many low-paid workers struggling, notes an article on the website of the National Conference of State Legislatures, a bipartisan nongovernmental clearinghouse and communications center for state lawmakers. Minimum wage earners had to work nearly twice as long in 2012 as in 1968

States Vary in Share of Workers at 150% of Minimum

More than 32 percent of workers in 16 states earn 150 percent or less of their state's minimum wage. A smaller share of workers in other states earn within that range. Workers earning within 150 percent of minimum are most likely to earn more in the event of a minimum wage increase, according to the Brookings Institution.

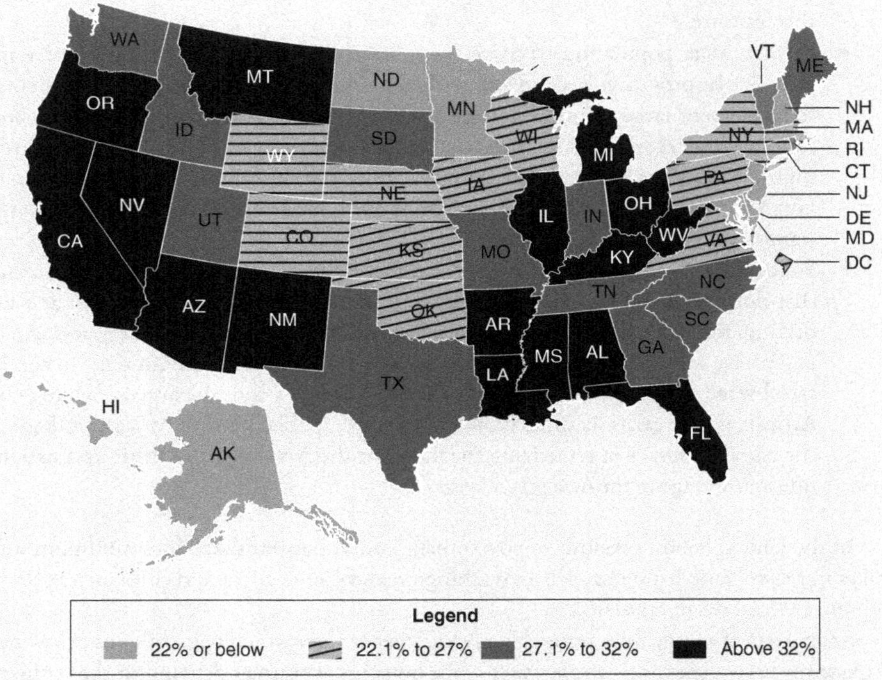

Source: Benjamin Harris and Melissa Kearney, "The 'Ripple Effect' of a Minimum Wage Increase on American Workers," Brookings Institution, Jan. 10, 2014, http://tinyurl.com/leuuf4q.

to buy a loaf of bread, for example. In 1968, a loaf cost 22 cents—14 percent of the hourly federal minimum of $1.60. By 2012, the price was $1.88—26 percent of the $7.25 minimum.[19]

Many businesses argue, however, that raising the wage would harm workers most in need of assistance and would hurt employers as well.

Keeping the minimum wage low is important to ensure that entry-level jobs remain available, even to the lowest-skilled people, says James Sherk, a senior policy analyst at the conservative Heritage Foundation think tank. "Employers need to be able to find out whether you come to work on time, work well with your boss, can learn skills," without busting a business's budget. Entry-level jobs are where this happens, he says. If the minimum wage is set too high, employers will be loath to use the jobs as tryouts for the youngest and lowest-skilled applicants, and "you'll leave some people stuck at the bottom with no way to learn basic workplace skills."

Moreover, raising consumer prices to pay for a minimum wage hike would be devastating to many businesses, some executives say. Since the recession, consumers remain super-sensitive to costs, said Jamie Richardson, vice president of the Columbus, Ohio-based White Castle chain of 415 hamburger restaurants. "Our customers are real resistant to paying more."[20]

Minimum wage increases have a cost that hurts someone—customers, business owners or workers themselves, said Scott DeFife, executive vice president for government affairs at the National Restaurant Association. "Prices might be increased, operations might be cut big, different food choices might be offered, hours of operation might be diminished," he said.[21]

WEIGHING THE ISSUES

Does Raising the Minimum Wage Mean Businesses Will Lay Off Workers?

"If you raise the minimum wage, the inevitable effect will be, number one, young people will lose their jobs or will not be able to get their first jobs," said Sen. Ted Cruz, R-Texas.[22]

It's the most frequently heard argument among opponents of raising the minimum wage. The reasons, they say, are clear: According to basic economic theory, as the price of low-skilled labor rises, demand for it will drop. Furthermore, they say, empirical research dating back several decades verifies the theory.

Advocates of a minimum wage increase say, however, that a more recent body of empirical evidence and the more complex economic theory that applies to labor markets back a different conclusion: that a wage hike at the level most current federal and state bills propose increases unemployment minimally or not at all.

"All the evidence says that there's at most a modest effect on unemployment," following a minimum wage hike, says Dale Belman, an economist at Michigan State University's School of Labor and Industrial Relations and co-author of a 2014 book that analyzes about 200 English-language studies published since 2000 on the effects of minimum wage increases[23]

The U.K. Low Pay Commission, an advisory body, wrote in its 2014 report that "there remains little evidence of significant adverse effects of the minimum wage on employment, whether analyzing aggregate employment; individual employment probabilities; relative employment shares of low-paying sectors; or regional employment differences."[24]

In 2014, as Germany geared up for its first-ever national minimum wage, some employers said that it might not mean significant layoffs, as many businesses had argued initially.

"There may be job losses in the low-wage sector, but those will be limited," said Stephan Johannes Reinhold, managing director of the Munich plant of photo-printing company CeWe Stiftung & Co.[25]

Businesses in economically weaker eastern Germany are expected to have the most difficulty adjusting to the national wage. Nevertheless, at least some large employers of low-skilled worker say they don't plan layoffs. For example, although the facilities-management company Piepenbrock Unternehmensgruppe GmbH employs 3,581 janitorial workers in eastern Germany who earn less than the proposed minimum wage, the company won't be laying any of them off, said managing partner Arnulf Piepenbrock. That's in large part because the proposed German wage would give companies such as his, which already operate under negotiated wage agreements, two years to adjust to the new wage, Piepenbrock said.[35]

Luxembourg, Netherlands Pay Highest Minimum Wages

Annual minimum wage, in 2013 $U.S. adjusted to reflect purchasing power

Minimum wage workers in Luxembourg earn more than $22,000 annually, slightly more than those in the Netherlands and Belgium, who make about $21,000 per year. Minimum wage workers in the United States, by comparison, earn about $15,000 annually.

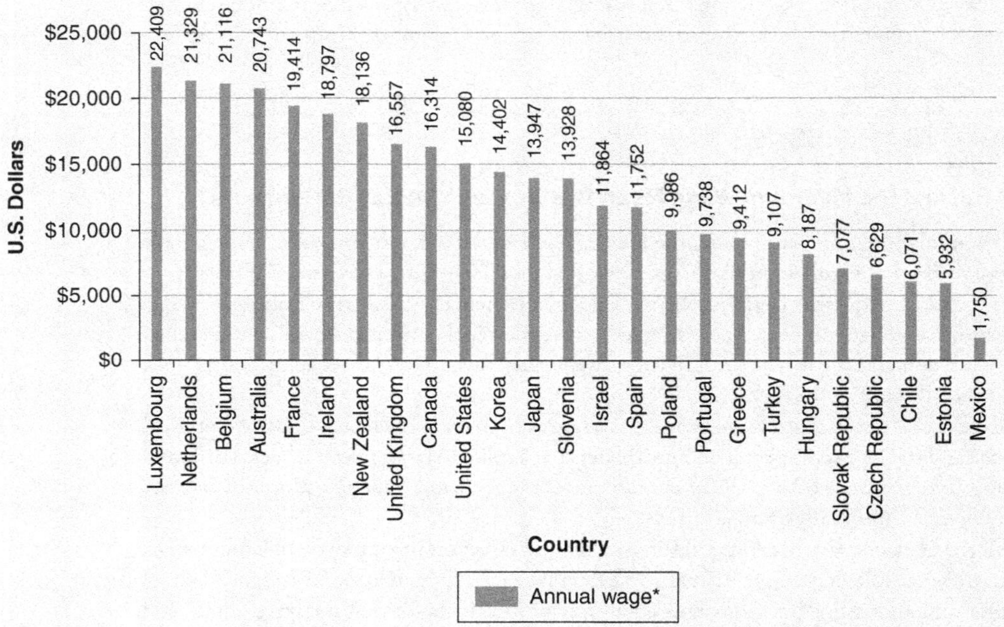

Note: Wages are expressed in a common currency—U.S. dollars—and adjusted to reflect inflation and the dollar's relative consumer purchasing power in each nation.

Source: "OECD State Extracts," Organisation for Economic Co-Operation and Development, http://tinyurl.com/79gmw4x.

For most kinds of businesses, a minimum wage increase doesn't raise costs more drastically than many other marketplace changes may do, some economists say. Moreover, they say, businesses have many more ways to adjust to a labor cost increase than by trimming the workforce.

"For most employers, a 10 or 20 percent increase in the minimum wage" doesn't change the business' costs so much "that it would be worth rearranging your whole operation" to the degree that employee layoffs often require, says Belman. "When you're in business, things like supply costs are moving on you all the time, things are always shifting."

Scholars Engage in "Data War" on Minimum Wage

Studies of Job-Loss Effects Produce Conflicting Results

Citing hundreds of studies, some economists say that raising the minimum wage causes little if any increase in unemployment. Other economists maintain that any wage increase will also increase unemployment.

The long-held consensus among economists that a minimum wage increase will raise unemployment may be shifting.

In February 2014, the nonpartisan Congressional Budget Office (CBO) assessed the employment effects of a $10.10 minimum wage, and its report showed how wide a range of conclusions researchers have drawn.

Based on a survey of existing studies, "there is about a two-thirds chance that the effect of the $10.10 [wage] would be in the range between a very slight decrease in employment and a decrease of 1.0 million workers," and a "one-third chance that the effect would be either above or below that range," CBO said.[26]

From the 1950s into the 1980s, studies of the minimum wage's employment effects were relatively few and generally found that raising the wage by 10 percent increased teenage unemployment by up to about 1.5 percent.[27]

Beginning in the mid-1980s, though, a number of states began to set their own minimum wages, giving economists a larger pool of data on minimum wage changes to study.

To isolate the impact of the minimum wage on employment, researchers must decide how to control for other variables that affect employment rates, such as underlying employment trends and economic conditions. Along with the new data came both new ideas about how to conduct such analyses and, increasingly, cracks in the old consensus.[28]

Reasoning that older studies had introduced errors by failing to take into account individual states' minimum wage histories, David Neumark, an economist at the University of California, Irvine, and William Wascher, an economist at the Federal Reserve, incorporated that information into a 1992 study. Nevertheless, their analysis confirmed previous findings that a 10 percent minimum wage increase raises teen unemployment by 1 percent to 2 percent.[29]

At about the same time, Princeton economists David Card and Alan Krueger hit on the idea of conducting a "natural" experiment. In 1992 New Jersey had just raised its minimum wage, from $4.25 an hour to $5.05, while neighboring Pennsylvania had not. To test the notion that when the wage floor goes up employment goes down, the economists used New Jersey as the experimental case and Pennsylvania as the control. The idea was that regional economic differences that might have skewed previous national research would disappear when comparing areas so close together and, presumably, economically alike.

For nearly a year, Card and Krueger surveyed employment levels at 410 fast-food outlets on both sides of the state line. To the surprise of many, they found "no indication that the rise in the minimum wage reduced employment."[30]

Neumark and Wascher criticized Card and Krueger's study for basing conclusions on too little data. In 1998, though, Card and Krueger performed the same analysis on a large set of randomized data from the federal Bureau of Labor Statistics and again found that the New Jersey wage hike had not increased unemployment.[31]

The 2000s saw many new studies, using a variety of methods, in the United States and elsewhere. Some of the best known apply a modified Card/Krueger approach to large numbers of cases.

In a 2010 study, economists Arindrajit Dube of the University of Massachusetts; T. William Lester of the University of North Carolina, Chapel Hill; and Michael Reich of the University of California, Berkeley, examined wage and employment data from all pairs of contiguous U.S. counties that lie on opposite sides of a state border. Counties that share a border should be enough alike to make good comparison pairs, they reasoned. In an analysis encompassing 16 and a half years of minimum wage changes, they "found no adverse employment effects."[32]

In 2009, an Australian and an American economist teamed up to perform a meta-analysis of 64 individual studies conducted between 1972 and 2007. Meta-analysis uses standardized statistical techniques to pool the results of many studies to identify patterns. What they found could

(Continued)

(Continued)

lead to one of two conclusions, the researchers wrote: "First, minimum wages may simply have no effect on employment. . . . Second, minimum-wage effects might exist, but they may be too difficult to detect and/or are very small."[33]

Dale Belman, a Michigan State University economist, and Paul Wolfson, a senior statistical research associate at Dartmouth College's Tuck School of Business, are the authors of "What Does the Minimum Wage Do?"—a 2014 book that closely analyzes about 200 English-language studies on the effects of minimum wage increases published since 2000.

Combining studies from the United States, Canada, Australia and New Zealand, plus a smaller number from Spain, Portugal and the United Kingdom, "we could find a negative effect on employment that was small. It wasn't enough to get your pants tied in knots over, but we could detect it," says Wolfson. U.S. studies analyzed alone, however, showed a "tiny" unemployment effect, "but it was not statistically significant." (Results are not statistically significant if there is a high probability that they occurred by chance.)

But UC's Neumark, whose studies have consistently found unemployment increases from minimum wage hikes, is giving no ground in the data war.

"It's simply a misstatement of the research evidence to say that most studies point to no effects of minimum wages on unemployment," he told the PBS NewsHour. Only "a few" recent studies find no or very minimal employment effects, and there have been some such studies in every era. No consensus backs them, he contended.

"There are costs to raising the minimum wage. There are some benefits to raising the minimum wage. We should be having an informed policy discussion about . . . how we trade them off against each other," Neumark said.[34]

—Marcia Clemmitt

"If you doubled the minimum wage, then people really would rearrange things," he says. "But a 20 percent increase in something that's only 20 percent of your total costs"—amounting to a 4 percent change—is relatively minor, Belman says. "Your producer of hot dog buns could do that to you without even trying." That being the case, a minimum wage hike of that magnitude "is unlikely" to cause most owners to lay off workers, because layoffs often require businesses to rethink and reorganize many work processes—no easy task, Belman argues.

There are many ways besides cutting staff to adjust to higher labor costs, said John Schmitt, a senior economist at the liberal Center for Economic and Policy Research, in Washington. These include raising consumer prices, reducing nonwage benefits such as retirement plans, accepting lower profits, setting higher performance standards to improve worker productivity, reorganizing the workplace to increase efficiency and seeking more-skilled workers to fill future minimum-wage positions, Schmitt wrote.[36]

Some studies and employment data also suggest that many employers may respond to minimum wage increases by reining in wage increases for more experienced employees, Schmitt said.[37]

But many employers say they would cut hiring or lay off workers if the minimum wage were to rise. And opponents of a minimum wage increase say there's plenty of research to indicate that a higher wage would lead to higher unemployment.

Raising the wage to $10.10 would tighten the job market in the retail, service and manufacturing sectors, according to the sponsors of a long-running survey of chief financial officers. In the March 2014 edition of a quarterly survey conducted by Duke University's

Fuqua School of Business and CFO magazine, 82 percent of retail chief financial officers said they would curtail hiring if the wage rose to $10.10.[38]

In fact, one 2014 study finds that one particular minimum wage increase—the federal three-step minimum wage increase in 2007, 2008 and 2009, just when the country was entering a severe recession—cost the nation a million jobs. That wage hike, from $5.15 an hour to $7.25, depressed the labor market most in states that had significantly lower wages than the new federal minimum, according to study authors Michael Wither, a Ph.D. candidate in economics, and Jeffrey Clemens, an assistant professor of economics, both at the University of California, San Diego.[39]

Today's retail environment is so competitive that companies are more likely to lay off workers than to raise prices, said Brooks Holtom, a management professor at Georgetown University's McDonough School of Business. Raising consumer prices to pay for a wage hike "is not an option because of the strong consumer preference for low prices," he argued.[40]

As South Africa's ruling ANC gears up to institute the nation's first national minimum wage within the next few years, some analysts are warning that minimum wages implemented in several particularly low-wage sectors of the South African economy historically have cut employment in those sectors. When minimum wages were introduced for farm labor, for example, farm employment fell from 2.1 million to 660,000, a "cataclysmic decline," said Loane Sharp, a labor analyst and economist at Adcorp, a South African workforce- and business process-management company.[41]

"One reason that you don't always see a jobs effect in studies is because so few people actually make the minimum wage" and thus its effects are hard to tease out statistically, says the Heritage Foundation's Sherk. But the $10.10 proposal Obama backs "covers 14 to 15 percent of the workforce, and that means we'll see real effects," he says.

In fact, some unemployment effects of minimum wage increases show up before—not after—a wage hike, another reason why studies of the effects of minimum wage increases may miss them, Sherk says. Business owners often trim their workforces in expectation of a minimum wage increase that lawmakers are debating but haven't yet enacted, Sherk says—a trend, he says, that is in evidence today as restaurant chains such as Applebee's and Chili's implement automated ordering of drinks and desserts.

Chili's and Applebee's deny that installing tablet computers at tables is a step toward cutting staff. "In no way are we looking at this as a replacement for servers," said Krista Gibson, a senior vice president at Chili's parent company, Dallas-based Brinker International.[42] "This really isn't a labor play," Julia Stewart, CEO of Applebee's parent company, Glendale, Calif.-based DineEquity, told CNBC.[43]

Is Raising the Minimum Wage the Best Way to Help Low-Paid Workers?

Economists generally agree that raising the minimum wage does not substantially dent the poverty rate. "Most people living near the poverty line are only lightly attached to the employment market," working few if any hours, so the effect of a minimum wage increase on their lives is minimal, says Michigan State's Belman.

Whether minimum wage increases are the best way to help the lowest-wage workers remains a hotly debated question, however.

Advocates of a higher minimum say increases help many working adults avoid bankruptcy or poverty. A higher minimum also reduces the amounts governments pay in welfare-type benefits because families are able to support themselves rather than rely on public assistance, advocates contend.

But wage-hike critics point out that a significant number of minimum wage earners, such as teenagers, live in middle-class families and don't rely on government assistance or otherwise live at or near the poverty level. Means-tested government programs, in which tax credits or food assistance is disbursed based on family income, more efficiently target workers who truly need help, they argue.

The Obama proposal to raise the minimum to $10.10 an hour would help a wide range of workers in need, including those making just over that amount, because employers would adjust their wage ladders to take the higher bottom into account, says David Cooper, an economic analyst at the Economic Policy Institute, a liberal think tank in Washington. By the time the wage reached $10.10, nearly 2.8 million Americans could see pay increases, he estimated.[44]

Among those getting raises, only 12.5 percent would be teenagers, Cooper wrote. Half would be 30 or older, and more than a third 40 or older. More than half would be working 35 or more hours a week, and nearly one-fourth would have annual family incomes below $20,000. On average, most workers who would see a raise would be bringing home half of their household's total income, he said.[45]

Democracy requires a citizenry that can support itself through its own work, contends Jerold Waltman, a professor of political science at Baylor University in Waco, Texas. "A vital requirement for full democratic citizenship is having independence of mind," he says. "If you're working, but your job doesn't earn you the minimal conditions for life, it's hard to feel that you have a full stake in society."

A recent analysis commissioned by the liberal Washington-based think tank Center for American Progress estimates that a hike to $10.10 would move between 3.3 million and 3.8 million workers off food stamps, saving taxpayers as much as $4.6 billion annually—about 6 percent of the program's total cost.[46]

In fact, such taxpayer-funded benefits aren't so much subsidies for the lowest-paid workers as "massive taxpayer subsidies for private companies" that don't need the help, argued Barry Ritholtz, a Bloomberg News columnist and the chairman of the New York City-based investment firm Ritholtz Wealth Management. "The system was set up long ago in ways that failed to imagine" that employers would be content to allow tax-funded programs to pay their workers' living expenses, and "the simplest solution is to raise the minimum wage," he asserted.[47]

"While corporate profits break records, the share of national income going to workers' wages has reached record lows," making more people income-eligible for public assistance, said a 2013 report by the Democratic staff of the House Committee on Education and the Workforce. Wisconsin Medicaid records, for example, show that just one 300-worker Walmart Supercenter may cost federal and state taxpayers more than $900,000 per year in Medicaid coverage of its low-income workers.[48]

In the U.K., the minimum wage "has raised the wages of those at the bottom of the [earnings] distribution relative to those higher up," wrote economists from Great Britain's

Three in Four Americans Favor Minimum Wage Increase

Nearly three-fourths of Americans responding to a 2014 Pew Research Center poll said they approve of increasing the federal minimum wage to $10.10 an hour. Fifty-three percent of Republicans favor such a move, compared with 90 percent of Democrats and 71 percent of Independents.

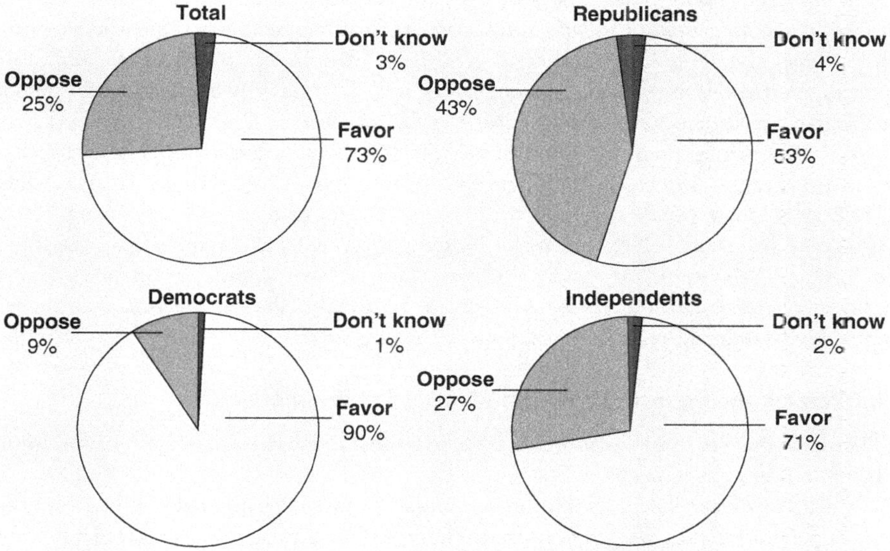

Note: Figures may not add to 100 percent because of rounding.

Source: Pew Research Center for the People & the Press, "Most See Inequality Growing, but Partisans Differ over Solutions," Jan. 23, 2014, http://tinyurl.com/luw6v7t.

University of Sussex and National Institute of Economic and Social Research in a study commissioned by the U.K. Low Pay Commission. "This has resulted in a fall in inequality in the bottom half of the wage distribution."[49]

However, opponents of raising the minimum argue that doing so fails to help—and perhaps even harms—some of the most vulnerable.

"Do we really care if a low-wage teenager in a middle-class family makes an extra dollar an hour?" asked Harvard University economist Gregory Mankiw, who served as chairman of the Council of Economic Advisers in the administration of Republican President George W. Bush. If the wage were increased from $7.25 to $8.25, for example, only 21.3 percent of workers who got the raise would live in families earning below-poverty-level incomes—the Americans who are truly in need of help, Mankiw said.[50]

In the Canadian province of Ontario, which raised its minimum wage in 2014 to $11 (Canadian) per hour, the highest in the country, 81.5 percent of workers earning minimum wage live in households with incomes above the national poverty level, said Charles Lamman, resident scholar in economic policy at the Fraser Institute, a Vancouver, British Columbia-based conservative/libertarian think tank. That makes a minimum wage hike ineffective in helping the Canadians who most need assistance, Lamman said[51] ($11 Canadian is equivalent to $9.20 U.S.).

The most vulnerable job applicants are the most likely to be left out in the cold when the minimum wage goes up, Sherk says. With the minimum set high, employers are likely to forgo hiring the poorest people, those who didn't graduate from high school or those who have been incarcerated, and opt to hire a middle-class college student instead, hoping to minimize the chances that the new hire won't work out, Sherk says. That unfairly disadvantages "the very people that advocates of a higher wage mean to help," he says.

Advocates of a minimum wage hike likely prefer it to public assistance programs such as tax credits because it's "less politically palatable" to take "money directly out of federal coffers" to help low-income people, wrote Kevin Hassett, director of economic policy studies, and Michael Strain, a research fellow, at the conservative American Enterprise Institute. But a minimum wage boost unfairly sends the entire bill for the low-income assistance to businesses and their customers, who will face higher prices. That makes the wage increase "a dishonest approach that hides the true cost of the policy," they argued.[52]

Will Raising the Federal Minimum Wage Harm Businesses?

Business owners in some labor-intensive, low-wage industries face serious uncertainties when minimum wages rise.

When New Jersey hiked its minimum from $7.25 to $8.25 in January 2014, child-care center operator Dolores Riley of Cinnaminson, near Philadelphia, knew she faced a substantial cost increase. Wages constitute 80 percent of the center's operating costs, she told The New York Times. "I hope we don't have to close."[53]

Her situation is typical of what many low-wage employers experience when the minimum wage goes up, some business analysts say. Others argue, however, that in most industries a minimum wage increase is not substantial enough to cause serious disruption.

At retail giant Walmart even a minimum wage hike to a hefty $12 an hour—increasing annual payroll costs by $3.21 billion—would add only 46 cents per shopping trip to the average customer's bill, according to an analysis by economists from the University of California, Berkeley, and the City University of New York.[54]

Furthermore, some economists argue that paying a higher wage can actually improve a business's bottom line over time. A comparison of Walmart's low-paying big-box retailing arm, Sam's Club, with high-paying chain Costco showed that higher wages can save companies substantial sums, argued Wayne Cascio, a management professor at the University of Colorado, Denver, in a 2006 article. Costco paid an average $17 an hour while Sam's Club/Walmart paid an average $10.11, he said.

Costco saw lower employee turnover—17 percent annually, compared with 44 percent for Walmart—as well as minimal employee theft and improved productivity, said Cascio. The drop in turnover alone saved substantial cash because replacing a worker typically costs 1.5 to 2.5 times an employee's annual salary. One Costco hourly worker generated an average annual U.S. operating profit of $21,805, compared with $11,615 for a Walmart worker, Cascio wrote.[55]

Labor economics differ from the economics of goods because "what you pay for an orange doesn't change the flavor of the orange, but what you pay a worker absolutely affects how that person works," says Paul Wolfson, senior statistical research associate at Dartmouth College's Tuck School of Business.

Raising wages for clerical and maintenance workers and other assistant-level employees at her company cut absenteeism rates, reported illnesses and other problems such as workers suffering fatigue from holding down two jobs, says Carmen Ortiz Larsen, president of the Montgomery County, Md.-based technical consultancy and staffing company Aquas.

At Charmington's Café, in Baltimore, "I don't have to run the counter or be on the floor, because the staff is dedicated and they handle it; I can do cost analysis and marketing to build the business," says Amanda Rothschild, managing partner of the coffeehouse, whose 13 employees get a starting wage of $8 an hour, 75 cents more than minimum, and qualify for health insurance and paid time off. Investing in workers sustains a business for the long haul, she argues.

In Germany, the lack of a mandated minimum wage has stymied some companies that have wanted to raise their wages and even has led to labor shortages in some industries, such as security services, where the prevailing wages are deemed so low for the task that workers don't want to take available jobs, said Martin Hildebrandt, deputy managing director of the Federation of Economic Security (BDSW), a membership organization that represents the interests of companies in the German security industry.

"Bottom-of-the-barrel wages are widespread in our sector," forcing all German security companies to compete on price, Hildebrandt said. "We don't have any problem" with a minimum wage of 8.50 euros, he said. Having a national minimum, he added, will create a level playing field that will no longer disadvantage companies that have wanted to pay their workers more.[56]

Raising wages for millions of U.S. workers would provide an economic stimulus that all businesses need in the sluggish economy, some advocates say.

Raising the minimum wage to just $9 an hour would increase workers' incomes by $30 billion the first year and boost consumer demand, wrote Daniel Aronson, director of microeconomic research, and Erik French, senior economist, at the Federal Reserve Bank of Chicago. A hike to $9 would provide a one-shot economic stimulus of $48 billion, because many workers would supplement the cash with loans to buy durable goods such as cars, they wrote.[57]

"Just about everyone agrees that what the economy most suffers from at present is lack of consumer demand. But workers and consumers are not two different species, so if wages stagnate so that they keep losing purchasing power, you can't be surprised that consumer demand is less," says Holly Sklar, director of Business for a Fair Minimum Wage, an advocacy group whose members include owners of small and large businesses who support a higher minimum wage.

But other business analysts say advocates of minimum wage hikes overlook the potentially drastic consequences for employers, especially small businesses.

Most fast-food establishments are owned by local franchisees, not large profitable corporations such as McDonald's, said Michael Saltsman, research director of the Washington-based Employment Policies Institute, a business-backed information and analysis group. Labor costs for a franchisee typically amount to about 31 percent of sales revenue while profit typically is only about 5 percent of sales, making any substantial labor-cost increase potentially devastating, he said.[58]

Also overlooked is that a minimum wage increase "tends to inflate wages up and down the scale," which would be devastating to many small businesses, said Jack Mozloom, regional Northeast manager for the Nashville-based small business association National Federation of Independent Business (NFIB). Most small businesses simply don't have the revenue to afford wage hikes across the spectrum.[59]

"There are businesses that operate on thin margins, who will struggle with any increase to the minimum wage," said Mike Cherry, national policy chairman of Great Britain's Federation of Small Businesses, explaining his group's objection to the 2014 increase in Britain's wage floor.[60]

Minimum wage increases that seem appropriate to lawmakers living in high-cost cities can sink businesses in poorer areas, some legislators say. A proposed state wage hike to $10.10 an hour in Maryland, for example, could be "devastating" to businesses in rural counties still struggling to emerge from the recession, said Republican state Sen. Richard Colburn.[61]

If the federal government sets a minimum at all, "it should be the appropriate wage for the lowest cost-of-living, lowest-paid part of the country" to avoid driving businesses over the brink, says Heritage's Sherk. Beyond that, "we should leave it up to the states—or counties—to raise wages if they want. I would leave the federal wage unchanged for a long while until it reaches that level."

BACKGROUND

Early Wage Setting

The idea that fairness demands that working people earn enough to live free from poverty is an old one. "It is but equity . . . that they who feed, clothe, and lodge the whole body of the people, should have such a share of the produce of their own labor as to be themselves tolerably well fed, clothed, and lodged," Scotsman Adam Smith, who almost singlehandedly invented the modern discipline of economics, wrote in his 1776 book, "The Wealth of Nations."[62]

How to achieve such equity has long been debated. Classical economics argues that proper wages are set in free markets, where workers sell and employers buy labor after haggling over its price. In the 19th century, though, concerns grew that in a rapidly industrializing world many workers might not have the clout to bargain for adequate pay.[63]

The first government wage-setting agencies were established in the 1890s. In 1894, New Zealand gave regional labor arbitration boards authority to set minimum wages. In 1896, the Australian state of Victoria established an independent agency to set minimum wages in six low-paying trades, including baking and apparel-making. Established at least in part to keep workers from China and the Pacific Islands from depressing wages for white males by accepting rock-bottom pay, the Victoria office set wages by 1904 for 150 industries.[64]

In the United States in the 1890s, the National Consumers League (NCL), a nonprofit advocacy and education group concerned with marketplace issues, tried to rouse moral outrage to fight poor treatment of women and children working in factories. The league urged consumers to buy only products that carried its white label, indicating that they were manufactured in fair labor conditions.

"To buy means to have power, to have power means to have responsibility," declared NCL General Secretary Florence Kelley.[65]

In 1909, the British Parliament implemented trade boards to set minimum wages for industries, such as garment making, that were organized as sweatshops.

The term "sweating" labor was coined in the early 19th century to describe a system in which large businesses subcontracted with middlemen to hire and manage industrial workers. "Sweaters" profit by employing workers in small, substandard facilities and paying low wages. Isolated in small groups, away from the business that actually sells the goods, sweatshop workers could not effectively organize, unionize or bargain. Thus, they warranted government protection, British trade board supporters reasoned.[66]

Most early U.S. minimum wage laws were state laws and applied only to women and children. The Massachusetts Legislature passed the first, in 1912, and within a decade 14 other states and Puerto Rico had passed their own laws. In 1918, Congress enacted a minimum wage for the District of Columbia.

At first, U.S. unions—like most unions everywhere—opposed legally set minimum wages. "They argued that if the government stepped in to ensure wage levels, people wouldn't join unions" and the tradition of collective bargaining would weaken, says Alan Manning, an economist at the London School of Economics (LSE).

The laws drew strong support from some other quarters, however.

"When a mercantile establishment pays its labor less than labor can live on . . . it is showing a profit it has not honorably earned," wrote journalist Walter Lippmann in 1915.[67]

By the end of the 1920s, though, U.S. courts had declared seven of the original state laws unconstitutional, and the rest had been repealed or were enforced minimally or not at all.[68]

The first reversal came in 1923, when the U.S. Supreme Court struck down the District of Columbia wage law, in a 5-3 vote.[69] The law violated employers' and workers' constitutional right to enter contracts without government interference, established by the Fifth Amendment's due process clause, the majority said.

Fifteen years earlier, the court had upheld an Oregon law stipulating that a woman could be required to work no more than 10 hours in a day. But the majority in the 1923 ruling argued that so much progress toward gender equality had occurred in the interim—with women gaining the vote in 1920—that women's need for special protections had "now come almost, if not quite, to the vanishing point."[70]

Fair Labor Standards

The Supreme Court also nixed Democratic President Franklin D. Roosevelt's first attempt to provide minimum wage protections during the Great Depression of the 1930s. With both prices and wages at disastrous lows, the 1933 National Industrial Recovery Act proposed to boost the economy by suspending antitrust laws. Businesses could work together to set prices as long as they also forged agreements to pay high minimum wages and improve working conditions. In May 1935, the Supreme Court declared the law an unconstitutional handover of governmental powers to private interests.[71]

In March 1937, though, as the Great Depression lingered, the justices reversed themselves. In West Coast Hotel Co. v. Parrish, the Supreme Court upheld the constitutionality of Washington State's long-standing minimum wage law in a 5-4 vote. "The exploitation of a class of workers who are in an unequal position with respect to bargaining power . . . is not only detrimental to their health and well-being but casts a direct burden for their support upon the community," wrote Chief Justice Charles Evans Hughes.[72]

Roosevelt quickly turned his attention to enacting a minimum wage law, dogged by bitter disputes every step of the way. An initial draft applied to both sexes and set a 40 cent-per-hour minimum, a 40-hour maximum workweek and a minimum working age of 16; a five-member board would be authorized to set higher pay and shorter hours after holding public hearings.

But many business leaders condemned the measure. The bill was "a step in the direction of communism, Bolshevism, and Nazism," said the National Association of Manufacturers.

Not until June 1938—after many controversies and setbacks—did Congress approve the Fair Labor Standards Act (FLSA), signed into law by Roosevelt on June 25.

To calm objections from businesses and from Southern lawmakers who argued that employers in their states couldn't afford a 40-cent wage, the first year's wage floor was set at 25 cents an hour, scheduled to rise to 40 cents in 1945. The law covered only workers who produced goods and services sold across state lines, in a limited number of industries such as public utilities. In all, the FLSA applied to about one-fifth of the labor force and gave a wage boost to about 300,000 people.

(A 25-cent hourly wage in 1938 would be equivalent to $4.19 today, and 40 cents in 1945 would be worth $5.25 now, using the Consumer Price Index to adjust for inflation.)

In the decades following World War II, more countries adopted minimum wages. In 1948, in India's first year of independence, its Parliament gave the country's central and state governments authority to set minimum wages. In 1950, France enacted a legally binding national minimum for all occupations. Japan adopted a minimum wage in 1959, and Spain in 1963.[73]

In the United States, a postwar economic boom and strong unions combined to raise wages for most workers, while the minimum wage and its buying power lagged behind.

In 1950, Congress raised the wage to 75 cents and in 1956 to $1. In 1961, the minimum wage was set at $1.15 for workers in categories previously eligible for it and $1 for workers in businesses newly covered by the law, such as large retailers.[74] In 1968, the wage rose to $1.60 an hour, the historical peak of its buying power, equivalent to either $8.41 or $10.86 in today's dollars, depending on which of two commonly used measures of price inflation is used.[75]

The Modern Wage

By the time Democratic President Jimmy Carter took office in 1977, the minimum wage had been repeatedly frozen for three to five years at a stretch throughout its 40-year existence. As a result, increases had sometimes been hefty. In 1950 the wage was hiked 87.5 percent, from 40 cents to 75 cents; in 1974, it rose 25 percent to $2.

To provide security for workers and predictability for business, Carter proposed that future increases be indexed so that the minimum wage would always equal half the average manufacturing wage. "But his proposal got shot down," says Baylor's Waltman.

The wage increase that Congress enacted for 1978—hiking the then-$2.30 wage in four steps to $3.35 by 1981—was the last enacted before the longest minimum wage freeze in U.S. history. The wage remained at $3.35 from 1981 to 1990, due to staunch opposition by Republican President Ronald Reagan and many congressional Republicans, as well as a lack of active support of wage increases by congressional Democrats. Democrats did not begin a strong push to raise the wage until 1987.

"If we had had our druthers, we would have eliminated [the minimum wage]," said Murray Weidenbaum, chairman of Reagan's first Council of Economic Advisers.[76]

Republicans in Washington were not the minimum wage's only foe in the 1980s. Conservative British Prime Minister Thatcher shared the Reagan administration's view that only when businesses were free from government regulatory actions—such as wage-setting—could they perform at their best and build the economy. Thatcher drastically weakened the trade councils that had long established wage floors for U.K. industries. In 1993 her successor, Conservative Prime Minister John Major, abolished the boards.[77]

In the United States, with the federal wage frozen, some states began anew to establish their own minimum wages. Ten states enacted minimums higher than the federal rate. When the federal wage was raised to $4.25 in 1991, though, only Alaska, Oregon and Rhode Island still had higher wage floors.[78]

As the federal minimum continued to rise sporadically in the 1990s and 2000s, more states set wage floors that remained higher than the federal rate even after a federal wage increase. As of January 2015, 29 states and the District of Columbia had minimum wages higher than the federal wage.[79]

The level of national minimum wages varies widely: Mexico's annual minimum was a bit over $1,200 in 2013, while Australia's was nearly $30,000, for example. Nevertheless, worldwide the practice of setting minimum wages for regions, industries or entire nations by law—or by industry-wide or even nationwide collective bargaining—has spread relatively unabated over the past 30 years.[80]

In some countries, mass collective bargaining between trade unions and business—rather than the legislature or a public agency—sets minimum wages. In Belgium and Greece, collective bargaining sets the wage for large geographical regions. In Sweden and Finland, among others, collective bargaining sets wages for whole industries or economic sectors.

Countries including Australia and Mexico appoint expert groups to set their minimum wages. Elsewhere, governments set them. In Japan and the United Kingdom, lawmakers set wages in consultation with an expert body. In Israel and Spain, the government must consult with labor and business representatives before setting a minimum wage. The United States is one of a relatively few countries—which include Canada, Brazil, Chile and Nigeria—in which lawmakers have no obligation to consult with experts or stakeholders before setting a minimum wage.[81]

CURRENT SITUATION

U.S. Federal Wage

Like Democratic presidents before him, President Obama repeatedly calls for increasing the minimum wage, which has remained at $7.25 since 2009. On Jan. 1, for example, an executive order raising the minimum wage to $10.10 for new federal construction and service contracts took effect. Obama signed the order in February 2014.[82] Also in 2014, Obama traveled the country, sometimes accompanied by Democratic governors who also support the wage increase, to talk up the $10.10 wage.[83]

The November 2014 election put Republicans in charge of both houses of Congress, however, and most congressional Republicans have stood strong against a federal wage increase.

"If we are interested in social justice, and we want to honor work instead of getting a welfare check," a better plan would be to increase the earned income tax credit, which reduces federal taxes owed by, or provides a tax refund for, low- to moderate-income workers, said Sen. Lamar Alexander, R-Tenn. By seeking a minimum wage increase instead, "what we're doing is coming up with the big idea and sending the bill to the employer," Alexander said.

Asked by Sen. Bernie Sanders, I-Vt., whether one of his comments meant that he would prefer to actually "abolish the minimum wage," Alexander replied: "Correct."[84]

In November, American voters proved to be of two minds about the wage issue. Measures to raise the state minimum wage passed in four states: Alaska, Arkansas, Nebraska and South Dakota. At the same time, though, Republican candidates won most offices in those states, although many of the winning candidates expressed either skepticism about or opposition to minimum-wage increases. In Arkansas, voters approved—by a 66-34 margin—a minimum wage increase from $6.25 to $8.50 but tossed out of office U.S. Sen. Mark Pryor, a Democrat who campaigned actively for the wage increase.[85]

Also in November, Illinois voters, by a 68-32 margin, approved a measure advising state legislators to raise the state's minimum wage from $8.25 to $10 per hour.[86] As governor, though, Illinois elected Republican Bruce Rauner, who had initially opposed a minimum wage hike then said he would support it only in a package that included pro-business tax and liability changes.[87] In January, Rauner canceled an executive order signed by ex-Gov. Pat Quinn, a Democrat, that would have required state vendors to raise their workers' minimum wages from $8.25 to $10.[88]

States and Cities

As of January 2015, 29 states and the District of Columbia had minimum wages higher than the federal level.[89] Legislatures in Connecticut, Delaware, Hawaii, Maryland, Massachusetts, Michigan, Minnesota, Rhode Island, Vermont, West Virginia and the District of Columbia approved increases during their 2014 sessions.[90]

In March 2014, Connecticut's Legislature became the first to approve a minimum wage hike to $10.10 by 2017, from a previous wage of $8.70.[91] Signed into law by Democratic Gov. Dannel Malloy, the bill passed without Republican support. The state praises small businesses as "our heroes," said Connecticut House Minority Leader Lawrence F. Cafero Jr., a Republican. "Then we keep . . . punching them in the gut."[92]

Controversy simmers over some current wage hikes.

In April 2014, Maryland lawmakers approved raising the state wage to $10.10 by 2018, but the proposal's trip through the Legislature was anything but smooth. Among other controversies was an ultimately rejected plan to allow all counties to set their own minimum wages either above or below the state level. The $10.10 wage "just doesn't make sense" for Maryland's rural, border counties, whose businesses must compete for customers with bordering states that use the lower, federal minimum wage, said Republican State Delegate Neil Parrott.[93]

In February 2014, commissioners of Santa Fe County, N. M., voted unanimously to raise the county minimum wage to $10.65 in 60 days, to match the wage in the county's central city, Santa Fe. Santa Fe City passed legislation in 2003 and 2007 raising the wage and indexing annual increases to inflation, a move that Mayor David Cross praises as a key part of Santa Fe's "economy that works for everyone."

Furthermore, the city has had consistently lower unemployment than elsewhere in the state, the mayor has pointed out.[94] As of January 2014, the unemployment rate in Santa Fe was 5.6 percent, compared with 6.6 percent in Farmington, 7.1 percent in Albuquerque and 7.8 percent in Las Cruces.[95]

For Santa Fe County, though, the 2014 hike constitutes a whopping 42 percent increase over the previous $7.50 an hour, and even some locals who say they support a higher minimum worry that raising the floor so high so quickly will make it too hard for businesses to adjust. Kenny Kalfin, president of Santa Fe Tortilla Co., a food manufacturer, branded it a "foolish" move that could require an increase in consumer prices so large it might drive him out of business.[96]

Much support for large minimum wage increases has been concentrated in Democratic-dominated large cities. In 2014, for example, city councils in both San Francisco and Seattle voted to raise their minimums in steps to $15 an hour, a national high. Seattle's $15 wage would apply to some businesses beginning in 2017 and to all businesses by 2021.[97] San Francisco's wage is set to rise to $15 an hour by 2018, with subsequent increases tied to inflation rates.[98]

The push for substantial minimum-wage increases is bringing some cities into conflict with their state legislatures, many of which are dominated by Republican opponents of the wage hikes. Laws—some old, some new—that bar cities from enacting their own minimum wage measures are on the books in 15 states.[99]

Last year, the Oklahoma Legislature approved a ban on locally enacted minimum-wage changes just as Oklahoma City, the state's capital and its largest city, was debating a plan to raise its local minimum wage to $10.10 an hour.

"To have fractured standards across the state is not a strong economic model," said state Sen. Dan Newberry, R, who sponsored the preemption bill.[100]

Apparel Company Cut from a Different Cloth

"We're Hoping to Prove That Doing Good Can Be Good Business"

The Alta Gracia brand of licensed collegiate and professional-sports apparel is manufactured by "the only apparel company in the developing world paying a living wage to all of its employees," the company boasts. The Alta Gracia factory in the Dominican Republic is part of an experiment by U.S. clothing company Knights Apparel to determine whether socially conscious manufacturing can be both ethical and profitable.

Browsing the website Shop.NHL.com in search of sweatshirts bearing the logo of their hometown professional hockey teams, customers find one line of shirts that carries an extra message.

The Alta Gracia brand of licensed collegiate and professional-sports apparel is manufactured by "the only apparel company in the developing world paying a living wage to all of its employees," say website descriptions. "Proceeds from the purchase . . . provide each employee wages and benefits to cover the cost of meeting a family's needs for all of life's necessities."[101]

(Continued)

(Continued)

The Alta Gracia factory in the Dominican Republic, in the Caribbean, is an audacious experiment in paying a livable wage to workers in one of the most globalized, lowest-wage industries on the planet. It's a small part of Spartanburg, S.C.-based Knights Apparel, a large, privately held company making college- and pro sports-logo clothing, and a passion project for Knights Apparel founder and CEO Joseph Bozich.

Opened in 2010, the factory pays about $3 an hour, or about three times the Dominican Republic's prevailing minimum wage, based on studies establishing that the $3 wage covers the cost of living for a family with children.[102]

"We're hoping to prove that doing good can be good business, that they're not mutually exclusive," said Bozich. Knights Apparel is the nation's top supplier to universities of college-logo clothing, and Bozich hatched the idea of a fair wage factory partly in response to requests from some universities and student activists to supply clothing not produced in sweatshop conditions.[103]

It's a tough assignment. The Alta Gracia wage raises production costs by 20 percent to 30 percent, and even with the Dominican Republic's lower minimum wage standard, the country has lost most of its garment industry to even lower-wage international competitors.

Alta Gracia clothing is priced the same as premium brands such as Nike that also produce college-logo apparel and have strong brand identities.

Bozich is trying to build Alta Gracia's specific brand identity as a socially conscious manufacturer in order to compete, says John Kline, a professor of international business diplomacy at the Georgetown University School of Foreign Service, who has been studying Alta Gracia.

In 2014, the small Alta Gracia factory was still getting up to speed but was on track to break even for the year, as production volume and customer numbers were increasing, Bozich said. In 2015, Bozich expects to turn a profit. "It is working," he said.[104]

The collegiate sector may be the best place to find out whether a brand identity as an ethical company can help a manufacturer turn a profit, Kline says. Universities "want to cut back on the number of licenses" they award to produce logo items, and many have expressed at least some level of interest in choosing companies as suppliers that don't mistreat or underpay employees, Kline says. Georgetown's agreement with licensees now stipulates that companies must demonstrate "ethical standards" that include, among other things, "respect for the intrinsic value of each human being" and report to the university "annually on their efforts to achieve a living wage," Kline notes.[105]

If enough universities actually follow through on such declarations, "that could send a signal to the market that [ensuring workers get a livable wage] is desirable," Kline says.

In studies, at least 30 percent of consumers say they'll pay a nondiscounted price for ethically produced goods, "but we don't have good follow-up of whether they actually will," Kline says.

Some apparel-industry experts are skeptical. "There are consumers who really care and will buy this apparel at a premium price, and then there are those who say they care but then just want value," said Andrew Jassin, managing director of the New York City-based apparel-industry consultancy Jassin Consulting Group.[106]

Whether any business model in the global garment industry will support paying a living wage is unclear. The international garment industry "is not a free market" for labor but what economists call an "oligopsony"—a market in which "you have many, many producers for every one big buyer, so the buyer can always set the price," says Kline.

That situation has led to a "race to the bottom" on wages, perpetuating poverty conditions in many countries even as companies whose garments are manufactured there score big profits, wrote Jason Hickel, a lecturer in anthropology at the London School of Economics. For policymakers in developing nations, one way to attract foreign dollars and boost gross domestic product (GDP) is by setting an attractively low minimum wage and turning a blind eye to poor working conditions, Hickel noted.[107]

"Having a garment factory in town is a first rung on the ladder of development," says Rachel Heath, an assistant professor of economics at the University of Washington, in Seattle. "Despite the wages being really low, women are happy to have the jobs. You see houses with concrete [rather than dirt] floors, and the level of girls' education has gone up a lot because supervisors need to be literate."

But when lawmakers in a developing nation contemplate taking the next step in development—seeking higher wages and better working conditions to move citizens out of poverty and create a middle class—the economic realities of the garment trade hit home, said Hickel. "If we improve labor standards in one poor country . . . , then companies . . . move somewhere else, wiping out local jobs and slashing much-needed GDP."

"If we're going to have a global labor market . . . , we need a global system of labor standards, something that will put a floor on the race to the bottom," Hickel argued.[108]

—*Marcia Clemmitt*

LOOKING AHEAD

Slow Change

With Republicans controlling both houses of the 114th Congress and many business groups continuing their long-standing opposition, U.S. federal minimum wage proposals seem to have little chance of passage in the near future. Nevertheless, some political analysts say that national governments worldwide will likely face increased pressure to raise their minimum wages in the coming years, as public uneasiness about income inequality grows.

In Congress this year, Republican Sen. Collins of Maine has said that she will continue to seek Republican and Democratic support for a compromise plan she put forward in 2014 to raise the federal wage to $9 over three years while exempting tipped workers from the increase. (Tipped workers' minimum wage has stood at $2.13 since 1991.) Collins' plan also would not link subsequent wage hikes to inflation, as many Democrats prefer.[109]

A handful of Democratic senators have expressed interest in crafting a bipartisan deal that would include Collins' proposal. Sen. Heidi Heitkamp of North Dakota suggested that Democrats might offer votes to authorize the Keystone XL oil pipeline in return for Republican votes on Collins' wage-hike measure. The pipeline is a priority for Republicans and some Democrats, including Heitkamp, who expect their home states to benefit economically from the project.[110]

"I think we definitely have to raise the minimum wage," said Sen. Barbara Mikulski, D-Md. "How we achieve it on a bipartisan basis is subject to negotiations, and Senator Collins would be a great person to do the talking."[111]

Even in 2014, when Democrats still controlled the Senate, lobbying groups on both sides of the question essentially had ceased trying to persuade Washington policymakers. Many conservative and liberal advocates considered the odds that Congress would vote on a minimum wage measure too low to be worth their lobbying effort, according to a report by Bloomberg Businessweek. Instead, lobbyists view the minimum wage fight as a years-long battle whose locus is likely to be states and cities for the time being.[112]

When it comes to the federal minimum wage, "people favor it, but it's not a passionate issue so it needs something—usually some public figure—to crystallize it," says Baylor's Waltman.

"In the wake of the financial crash, we're in a period of great conflict" economically, says Lowell Turner, a professor of international and comparative labor at Cornell University. For example, labor unions worldwide are broadening their agendas to push for items such as minimum wages that benefit all workers, not just union members, he says. "It's going to be a battle for a long time."

Internationally, some of the last few holdouts against enacting a national minimum wage may not resist much longer. "It's the combination of inequality and growing democracy" around the world that will drive the phenomenon, says the London School of Economics' Manning. "There are many places where it's coming up."

Chronology

1890s–1920s	**Several countries and U.S. states establish minimum wages, which apply only to women.**
1894	New Zealand enacts world's first minimum wage law.
1896	Australian state of Victoria creates a board to set minimum wages for low-paying industries, including furniture-making, baking and garment- and boot-making. By 1904, wage board covers 150 industries.
1905	U.S. Supreme Court voids a New York state law setting maximum working hours for male bakers (Lochner v. New York).
1908	U.S. Supreme Court upholds Oregon law regulating women's working hours, setting the stage for minimum wage laws for women (Muller v. Oregon).
1909	Britain's Parliament establishes a minimum wage-setting board.
1912	Massachusetts becomes first U.S. state to enact a minimum wage for women; others quickly follow.
1918	Canadian provinces British Columbia and Manitoba enact minimum wages for women.
1923	U.S. Supreme Court strikes down the District of Columbia's minimum wage law, arguing that women no longer need protection when entering work contracts (Adkins v. Children's Hospital).
1930s–1940s	**During the Great Depression, Supreme Court upholds minimum wage for women; Congress and states cover more workers.**
1938	Democratic President Franklin D. Roosevelt signs Fair Labor Standards Act establishing a minimum wage of 40 cents an hour by 1945 for male and female workers but covering only about one-fifth of the labor force.
1948	In first year after India's independence, Parliament gives the central government and state governments authority to set minimum wages.
1949	In compromise with pro-business legislators, Congress raises the minimum wage to 75 cents an hour while covering fewer workers.
1950s–1970s	**More countries enact minimum wages, and Congress repeatedly raises the U.S. wage despite business opposition.**
1950	France enacts minimum wage law.
1955	Republican President Dwight D. Eisenhower recommends raising the minimum wage to $1 an hour; Congress complies.
1959	Japan adopts minimum wage.
1963	Spain adopts minimum wage
1966	Democratic President Lyndon B. Johnson persuades Congress to raise the minimum to $1.60 and cover 9.1 million more workers.

1971	Turkey enacts minimum wage.
1977	Under Democratic President Jimmy Carter, Congress increases the minimum to $3.35 but rejects Carter's proposal to index it to the average manufacturing wage.
1981–Present	**Federal minimum wage does not rise under two-term Republican President Ronald Reagan, leading some states to adopt wages higher than the federal minimum. In the 1990s, the federal wage resumes sporadic increases.**
1998	United Kingdom enacts its first minimum wage.
2004	China's Ministry of Human Resources and Social Security establishes minimum wages for full-time and part-time workers.
2007	Thirty states and the District of Columbia have minimum wage levels above the $5.15 federal minimum. . . . Congress raises the minimum wage to $7.25 by July 2009 as part of a bill providing small-business tax breaks.
2013	Two congressional Democrats introduce legislation to raise the minimum in three stages to $10.10. . . . German Chancellor Angela Merkel announces that Germany will soon adopt its first minimum wage law.
2014	As of Jan. 1, a total of 21 states and the District of Columbia have wage floors above the federal minimum. . . . Connecticut becomes first state to raise its minimum to $10.10 by 2017; Maryland lawmakers approve raising the wage to $10.10 by 2018. . . . City councils in Seattle and San Francisco approve raising their local minimum wages to $15 over the next several years. . . . Voters in Alaska, Arkansas, Nebraska and South Dakota vote to raise their state minimum wages.
2015	As of Jan. 1, 29 states and the District of Columbia have wage floors about the federal minimum.

PERSPECTIVE

Pro/Con: Michael Saltsman on Wage Increases

YES

ARE MINIMUM WAGE INCREASES BAD FOR SMALL BUSINESS?

Michael Saltsman
Research Director, Employment Policies Institute

Written for *SAGE Business Researcher*, January 2015

President Obama has proposed raising the federal minimum wage to $10.10, with the stated goal of alleviating poverty. Unfortunately, the evidence suggests that this nearly 40 percent wage hike will reduce employment for less-skilled job seekers rather than reduce hardship. Small businesses and the young people they employ will be hit hardest.

It's a lesson that state legislators learned the hard way. Between 2003 and 2007, 28 states voted to increase their minimum wage, hoping to make progress against poverty. But a careful review of Census Bureau data from economists at Cornell University and American University produced less-than-encouraging results: These states saw no associated reduction in poverty rates.

One reason for this disappointing result was poor targeting. The Census Bureau says nearly 60 percent of individuals living in poverty don't have a job and thus can't receive a "raise" when the minimum wage increases. Instead, they just become more expensive to employ.

That's problematic for the service-industry employers who hire people at the minimum wage, where single-digit profit margins are the norm. When labor costs are forced higher, these businesses can't simply absorb the difference. (That's especially the case for small businesses with fewer than 100 employees, which represent nearly half of the group affected by a $10.10 minimum wage.)

Raising prices isn't typically an option, because higher prices can cause a drop in sales. Instead, businesses are forced to provide the same product at a lower cost. That means less customer service and more self-service. If you've bagged your own groceries recently or even pumped your own gas, you've experienced this transition firsthand.

The evidence backs up the intuition: Economists from the University of California, Irvine, and the Federal Reserve Board report that 85 percent of the best studies since the early 1990s detect job loss after a minimum wage increase. And research out of the University of Georgia finds a 4 percent to 9 percent decline in teen employment at small businesses for each 10 percent wage hike.

With an unemployment rate for young adults that's already been above 20 percent for more than five years, another steep drop in opportunities would be devastating. Yet a recent business survey from a national staffing agency suggests that's exactly what will happen if the minimum wage is hiked to $10.10. The survey found that 38 percent of employers affected by the higher minimum wage hike would be forced to reduce staffing levels.

PERSPECTIVE

Pro/Con: John Arensmeyer on Wage Increases

NO ARE MINIMUM WAGE INCREASES BAD FOR SMALL BUSINESS?

John Arensmeyer

Founder & CEO, Small Business Majority

Written for *SAGE Business Researcher*, January 2015

Small-business owners say, "Raise the wage." Small businesses are often at the center of political debates, and the issue of raising the minimum wage is no exception. But what do real small businesses think about raising the wage?

Small Business Majority polled a random sample of entrepreneurs from across the country with up to 100 employees and found 57 percent support increasing the federal minimum wage to $10.10 and indexing it to the cost of living.

Some claim that raising the minimum wage would strain small firms because they wouldn't be able to afford to pay their workers more. However, more than half of small-business owners agree increasing the minimum wage would not only help the economy; it would make low-income consumers more likely to spend money, driving up demand for goods and services at small businesses. Additionally, a striking 82 percent of small businesses say they already pay their workers more than the minimum wage.

An analysis conducted by the Economic Policy Institute found that raising the minimum wage to $10.10 would boost the economy by $22 billion during the initial phase-in period, creating 85,000 jobs.

Small Business Majority's poll also found six in 10 small-business owners in the retail/restaurant industries support increasing the minimum wage to $10.10. This support is in stark contrast to those who say retailers and restaurateurs, in particular, would go under if the minimum wage were increased.

Small employers believe it's not right that people working full time earn just $15,080 a year at the minimum wage. What's more, 54 percent of respondents said increasing the minimum wage would help decrease pressure on taxpayer-financed government assistance that's needed to make up for low wages, as it would help people afford basic necessities that might otherwise be out of reach.

While this issue has ncited considerable partisan debate, it finds broad support among small employers across a range of industries and political persuasions. The respondents were predominately Republican—with 47 percent identifying as Republican, 35 percent as Democrat and 18 percent as independent.

Consumer demand is small-business owners' No. 1 concern, and they see a raise in the minimum wage as a way to stoke that demand. An increase would help entrepreneurs create jobs, which strengthens the economy—creating an economic domino effect. Small-business owners are the nation's biggest job creators. Politicians should listen to what they're saying and act accordingly.

UPDATE IN 2020

In 2020, the national minimum wage was $7.25 an hour, the same level where it had been since Jul. 24, 2009.[113] Just as was reported in 2015, 29 states and the District of Columbia continue to pay a higher rate.

In 2020, there were 21 states that increased their minimum wage, according to the National Conference on State Legislatures.[114] Of those, seven automatically increased their rate according to the cost of living, while 14 states instituted higher payments because of previously implemented increases, or ballot initiatives.

The minimum-wage discussion was regularly in the news the past five years, in part due to a series of strikes across the country by fast-food workers. The collective protests were part of the Fight for $15, a movement that began in 2014 and gained steam through support from the Service Employees International Union.

In June 2019, the issue came up at a Democratic debate, with all but one of the 20 Democrats saying they supported raising the federal minimum wage to $15 an hour. The lone holdout was Andrew Yang, an attorney and entrepreneur, who favored universal guaranteed income, which would have paid $1,000 a month to each American adult.[115]

By contrast, the official Republican Party stance was that states and localities should continue to decide on the matter.[116]

In July 2019, the U.S. House voted to raise the federal minimum wage to $15 by 2025. The measure also would institute a process called "indexing," which ties the minimum wage to the rate of inflation.[117]

It was the first action taken by Congress in more than 10 years. However, the U.S. Senate did not take up the legislation during the 2019–20 session. "Research shows that hiking the minimum wage to $15 would kill jobs and depress the economy at a time when it's thriving for the American people," Senate Majority Leader Mitch McConnell said in a tweet.[118]

In recent years, the discussion of the minimum wage increasingly has been accompanied by the idea of a "living wage." Although there are numerous definitions, the most frequently used one reflects what someone would have to earn to clear the poverty line in their community or state. It includes food, child care, health care, including insurance premiums and typical costs, housing, transportation and other necessities.[119]

It is in effect in the U.K., where the living wage, which is slightly higher than the minimum wage, applies to workers 25 years and older. The minimum wage applies to workers of ages 16 to 24 years.[120] Both are adjusted each April.

However, a number of American municipalities, including Baltimore, Md.; New York City; and Ann Arbor, Mich., have required that vendors doing business with that city pay their employees a locally calculated living wage.

Amid the COVID-19 pandemic in the spring of 2020, a series of major retail chains temporarily increased wages for hourly workers, although some, including Kroger, rolled back the increases as the pandemic subsided.

However, in June, 2020, Target announced it would raise its minimum wage to $15, from $13, for about 250,000 workers. It said a number of front-line and distribution center workers would receive a one-time $200 bonus.[121]

In Canada, meanwhile, the federal minimum wage was set to rise in October 2020 to $11.45. Canada boosted its minimum wage to $11 in 2014, and the wage rises automatically each Oct. 1.[122]

However, all but one of Canada's provinces pay more than that. The highest minimum wage in Canada is $15, in Alberta; the lowest is in Saskatchewan, which pays the federal minimum wage.

Across Asia, minimum wage rates have risen or are scheduled to rise in countries such as Indonesia, Malaysia, Cambodia, Thailand and Vietnam. But the rates remain far lower than those in Western countries.[123]

—Micheline Maynard

14

PAID LEAVE

Should companies offer better policies?

Sharon O'Malley

From *SAGE Business Researcher*, May 8, 2017

EXECUTIVE SUMMARY

The United States is the only industrialized nation that does not require companies to offer paid leave to its workers to care for a baby, a sick relative or themselves. That is changing slowly, economists say, as more companies recognize that it makes business sense to provide paid leave to their employers. Silicon Valley, which is in a recruiting war with its tech rivals for the best talent, has taken the lead in offering more-generous time-off policies. But outside of the technology sector, many businesses—especially small ones—find it impractical or too expensive to offer paid leave. As few as 6 percent of low-wage earners can take paid maternity leave, and more than 40 percent of U.S. employees have no paid sick days.

Among the key takeaways:

- In the absence of federal guidance on the issue, talent-hungry corporations are writing their own rules in an effort to recruit and retain skilled young employees.
- President Trump during the 2016 campaign became the first Republican nominee to endorse paid maternity leave, but he has not pushed to enact such a policy.
- One survey found that 45 percent of firms with fewer than 100 employees would support a mandatory leave policy funded through employer and employee payroll contributions.

OVERVIEW

When Facebook Chief Operating Officer Sheryl Sandberg announced an upgrade to the tech giant's package of paid leave policies in February, she framed the issue in vividly personal terms, recalling how much her children needed her when her husband died unexpectedly in 2015.

And then Sandberg issued a stark challenge to other businesses to "step-up and lead" by adopting similar policies facilitating family leave.

"Making it easier for more Americans to be the workers and family members they want to be will make our economy and country stronger," Sandberg wrote in a Facebook post announcing the new policy. "Companies that stand by the people who work for them do the right thing and the smart thing—it helps them serve their mission, live their values, and improve their bottom line by increasing the loyalty and performance of their workforce."[1]

Jerod Harris/Getty Images

Facebook COO Sheryl Sandberg is urging businesses to improve their family leave policies. Facebook is offering employees up to 20 paid days off to grieve the death of an immediate family member.

Facebook is offering its 17,000 employees up to 20 paid days off to grieve the death of an immediate family member and 10 days for the loss of an extended family member; it already offers four months of paid parental leave to new mothers and fathers. Employees of the social media company also have a newly minted six weeks of paid time to care for a seriously ill relative and three days to spend with a family member suffering from a short-term illness.[2]

Few corporations outside of Silicon Valley have adopted such robust paid leave policies; in fact, just 12 percent of U.S. private-sector workers have access to paid family leave through their employers, according to the Department of Labor.[3] As few as 6 percent of low-wage earners may take paid maternity leave.[4] More than 40 percent of U.S. employees have no paid sick days.[5]

But Facebook is just the latest in a string of high-profile technology businesses to up their game when it comes to paying employees for the time they take off to care for a baby, a sick relative or themselves. Adobe in 2015 expanded its paid parental leave program to 26 weeks for new moms; Amazon excuses pregnant employees, with pay, for four weeks before they give birth and 10 weeks after.

Similarly, Apple lets expectant mothers take off four weeks before a birth and 14 weeks after, and fathers and adoptive or foster parents get six weeks of paid family leave.[6] Birth mothers who work for Google and Squarespace can take 18 weeks of fully paid leave.[7] And Netflix outdid all of its competitors with a 2015 parental leave policy that pays new mothers and fathers their regular salaries for up to a year after childbirth or an adoption.[8]

In addition, a handful of companies, including General Electric, Grubhub, Netflix and LinkedIn, offer some employees unlimited time off for illness, vacations and family matters.

More Companies Offering Unlimited Time Off

"People Won't Necessarily Take It, but If You Offer It, You Can Attract People into Your Company"

Analysts say unlimited vacation time is a hot trend among those companies seeking to recruit quality employees. A key takeaway: The benefit has to be clearly defined so it is not abused.

At payroll and benefits company Gusto, employees decide how much paid vacation time they take every year—with no limit. It's rare for anyone to misuse the perk, said CEO Joshua Reeves.

The unlimited benefit "helps build an ownership mentality," Reeves said. "We want our employees to think like owners and consider what's best for both themselves and the company. Letting them figure out their own vacation time shows that we trust and respect them, which in turn strengthens their commitment to the company."[9]

The five-year-old company, with a workforce of 300 and offices in San Francisco and Denver, is one of a growing number of businesses that don't restrict employees' vacation days. Many of those companies have found that, instead of taking too many days, most committed employees don't take enough.

Corinne Jones, president of CJC Human Resource Services in New York, calls unlimited vacation time, which she said "started popping up" around 2013, "a really hot trend."

"The thought is: People won't necessarily take it, but if you offer it, you can attract people into your company that you otherwise wouldn't have attracted," she says.

Some businesses confirm that employees with unlimited vacation time take no more days off than they did when their vacation time was defined.

In fact, marketing automation company Salesfusion said some of its 72 employees started taking fewer vacation days after the firm introduced unlimited vacations three years ago. CEO Carol O'Kelley said workers were unsure how much time off was too much, so the company wrote guidelines suggesting that two weeks would be enough to take at one time. "It really did help to provide folks something in writing they could review," O'Kelley said.[10]

To encourage employees to take vacation days, marketing software company HubSpot in Cambridge, Mass., adopted a "two weeks to infinity" policy in 2010. The message: Workers are expected to take at least two weeks off every year. Managers must report employees who refuse to take any time off.[11]

In 2012, contact management firm FullContact in Denver noticed that workers weren't taking any days off, despite the company's offer of unlimited vacation time. So it began paying up to $7,500 to help finance employee trips.[12] Use of vacation time soared, said CEO Bart Lorang.

A 2016 report from the Society for Human Resource Management estimates that only about 1 percent of companies offer unlimited vacation time. Working Mother magazine's 2016 list of the 100 Best Companies to Work For featured three firms with the benefit.[13]

Anecdotally, the practice began in the technology sector—Netflix, Hubspot and Evernote were early adopters—and is slowly spreading beyond Silicon Valley. Advertising firm PaperG in San Francisco and financial companies MarketWatch in Washington, D.C., ZestFinance in Los Angeles and SoFi in San Francisco also offer the benefit.[14]

Lawyers and executives who advocate unlimited vacation time have this advice for businesses considering the policy:

- **Make expectations clear.** If managers expect employees to schedule vacations around co-workers' plans, or they want to avoid absences during busy seasons, workers need to know that. Require a minimum advance notice so employees don't make a habit of waking up on sunny days and deciding to play 18 holes instead of working eight hours.
- **Define "unlimited."** Companies that offer unlimited vacation time should tell employees what's an acceptable range of days off. "Even if your time off is technically 'unlimited,'" Reeves said, "your manager obviously doesn't expect that you'll take off 75 percent of the time."[15]

  Derek Winn, lead consultant for Business Benefits Group in Fairfax, Va., says unlimited-vacation policies "create a murky scenario for employers when it comes down to extended leave: At what point to do you terminate an employee if they don't show up for work?"

  He says it's critical to hire workers who won't abuse the policy, and to understand how the policy will affect a company's finances.

  Unlimited vacation time works best at companies "that can be disrupted," Winn says. At companies working on federal contracts, he says, "if people aren't showing up for a month of a time, they can't fulfill the contract."
- **Honor the terms of past leave policies.** Companies that switch to an unlimited-vacation policy must still eventually compensate workers who leave the company for any time off that accrued before the new policy took effect, says attorney Michael Wahlander of Seyfarth Shaw in San Francisco.
- **Check with an attorney.** A few states make unlimited vacation time available only to salaried workers. In those states, vacation

(Continued)

(Continued)

time for hourly workers is part of their compensation. Human resources lawyers also advise businesses to clearly separate vacation policies from parental leave.[16]

- **Make performance a condition.** Before offering unlimited vacation time, set performance goals and identify the consequences of not reaching them. Employees who know they must meet defined deadlines probably won't take so many days off that they can't fulfill those requirements.

—Sharon O'Malley

Outside of the tech industry, a few financial and personal services firms like Deloitte; hospitality chains like Hilton; retailers like Starbucks; and energy companies like Duke Energy in North Carolina have improved their paid parental leave policies over the past few years.

Many smaller businesses, on the other hand, work informally with their employees to accommodate family and medical absences on a case-by-case basis rather than writing formal policies, says Aparna Mathur, resident scholar in economic policy studies for the conservative think tank American Enterprise Institute in Washington, D.C. "Small businesses can work something out with employees if they take leave," she says. "They feel much more responsibility in some ways toward their employees because there are so few of them."

"The big picture is that companies are recognizing that it makes business sense to provide paid . . . leave," says Sarah Fleisch Fink, director of workplace policy and senior counsel for the nonprofit National Partnership for Women & Families, an advocacy organization focusing on work and family, workplace fairness and women's health. "They recognize it because it improves employee morale; it can increase productivity and reduce turnover; it can help them compete for talent. Otherwise, we wouldn't see—almost weekly—companies coming out with these policies."

Although the 24-year-old federal Family and Medical Leave Act requires companies with more than 50 employees to allow staff members to miss up to 12 weeks of work for childbirth, a long sickness or a loved one's serious illness—and to guarantee that their jobs or something comparable will be waiting for them when they get back—the United States is the only industrialized nation without a policy to pay them for it.[17]

In the absence of federal guidance on the issue, talent-hungry corporations and state governments are writing their own rules in an effort to recruit and retain skilled young employees.

"They're going above and beyond the law," says Corinne Jones, president of consulting firm CJC Human Resource Services in New York. "As their HR advisers, we're saying, 'Here's what you need to do to retain the best employees.'"

From California to Boston, competition for qualified employees, especially in technical and other high-skill fields, has become fierce as the U.S. economy continues to improve and the labor market tightens.[18] Millennials, many of whom have delayed marriage and children, are slowly beginning to start their families and are shopping for employers offering family-friendly benefits.[19]

"Millennial employees like tech," says Kenneth Matos, vice president of research for the Park Ridge, Ill., consulting firm Life Meets Work. "So Amazon, Netflix, American Express, they're rethinking their parental leave policies to try to expand them to deal with the attractive people. Their jobs used to be their priority. But now they want to become parents."

Employees Average 10 Paid Vacation Days

About two-thirds receive between 5 and 14 days

The majority of private industry workers receive between five and 14 paid vacation days after one year of employment with their company. The average number of paid days was 10 among private-sector employees; only 2 percent received more than 24 days of paid vacation.

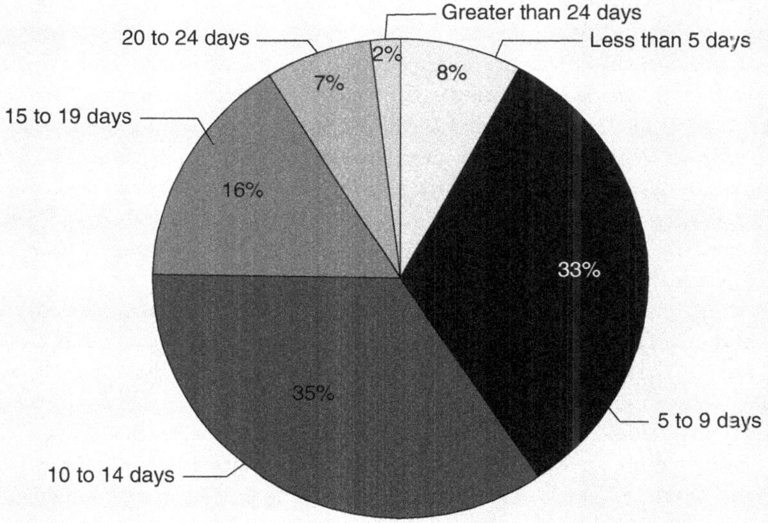

Note: Employees either are granted a specific number of days after completion of the indicated length of service or accrue days during the next 12-month period. Employees eligible for paid vacations but who have not fulfilled the minimum service requirement are listed as receiving 0 days.

Source: "Table 38. Paid vacations: Number of annual days by service requirement, private industry workers, March 2016," Bureau of Labor Statistics, U.S. Department of Labor, March 2016, http://tinyurl.com/lz2pxuv.

As early as 2015, the professional services firm Ernst & Young found in a study that 74 percent of Millennials consider paid parental leave "important."[20]

So, apparently, does President Trump, who, during his 2016 campaign, became the first Republican presidential nominee to endorse paid maternity leave.[21] During his January address to Congress, the president proposed that mothers get six weeks of paid, post-childbirth leave. The plan has come under fire by advocates of paternity leave, who cite the importance of fathers in shaping the culture of a new family.

An April Gallup Poll showed that 81 percent of Americans—both Republicans and Democrats—support federal legislation for paid maternity leave.[22]

But Trump has not made the effort a major policy emphasis. Part of the holdup, says Fink, is the difficulty in finding a way to pay for the benefit.

In most countries with mandates for paid parental leave and sick days, the national government foots the bill. Federal lawmakers, especially Republicans, are not keen on doing that in the United States.

"We've realized that parental leave has tentacles," says Rose Stanley, a senior practice leader at human resources trade association WorldatWork, "which is probably why organizations and even the government are going, 'What do we do with this?' . . . How are organizations paying? Should they have to pay? How are they able to pay? . . . We want to know."

For small businesses, Stanley says, "it's obviously financially going to be an issue."

In a memo to state legislators before they adopted New York's paid family leave law, which will take effect next January, Frank Kerbein of the Center for Human Resources of the Business Council of New York State. The law, he wrote, will burden small businesses with the cost of replacing employees while they are on extended leaves. Plus, he said business owners—not the government—should determine employment policies for their companies.[23]

In fact, the 1993 federal Family and Medical Leave Act exempts businesses with fewer than 50 employees from having to allow even unpaid leave for extended absences. But most state proposals would apply to all companies, regardless of the size of their workforces.

Still, a survey by the advocacy group Small Business Majority found that 45 percent of firms with fewer than 100 employees would support a mandatory leave policy that is paid for through employer and employee payroll contributions.[24]

Mathur confirms that most businesses, even small ones, agree that employees are entitled to paid time off to care for family. "Neither employers nor employees are opposing the policies," she says. "They know the larger problem is not having access to paid leave when you need it."

Studies by economists and family advocates generally have reached the same conclusion: Offering paid time off for childbirth, family medical emergencies, annual vacations and even the sniffles retains female employees, makes working parents more productive on the job, improves families' financial security and lowers young mothers' dependence on government assistance. Plus, it boosts a business's bottom line because it saves employers from having to recruit, hire and train replacements for moms who decide not to return to work after childbirth.[25]

"Organizations as a whole want to give, and they want to get back," says Stanley. "They know that the way they get back productivity, innovation and creativity is by treating their employees in a way that works well for both of them. But a lot of organizations don't have that mindset.

"They are beginning to."

As businesses, legislators, family advocates and employees weigh in on the pros and cons of employer- and government-paid leave, here are some of the issues being debated.

WEIGHING THE ISSUES

Is Paying for Leave Good for Businesses?

When Google increased its paid maternity leave from 12 to 18 weeks in 2007, it cut in half the number of new mothers who quit their jobs.[26]

"It may sound counterintuitive, but the research—and Google's own experience—shows a generous paid maternity leave actually increases retention," Susan Wojcicki, CEO of Google subsidiary YouTube, wrote in the The Huffington Post. "When women are given a short leave, or they're pressured to be on call, some decide it's just not worth it to return."[27]

Wojcicki's point: Technology firms, which spend enormous time and money recruiting and training female employees, can stop the ones they already have from leaving when they want to spend more time bonding with their babies.

Companies that offer substantial paid family leave to employees agree.

"Paid parental leave will help us recruit and retain the next generation of highly skilled workers," Melissa Anderson, chief human resources officer for Charlotte, N.C.-based Duke Energy, said of the firm's decision to offer the benefit for the first time this year.[28]

The electric utility had little choice, as it recruits from the same talent pool as a handful of other large, Charlotte-based companies that already offer paid family leave.

The same is true for any company in a competitive field. A year ago, Ernst & Young boasted that its new policy to provide 16 weeks of parental leave at full pay for new mothers and fathers in its U.S. offices "blows our competitors' benefits out of the water." EY also added policies to offer up to $25,000 for fertility, surrogacy, adoption and egg-freezing services.[29]

Five months later, competitor Deloitte splashed back, with an announcement the firm called "a first of its kind for professional services," matching EY's 16 weeks of paid leave, but offering it to any caregiver-employee, including those with sick relatives and elderly parents.[30]

Those generous benefits are aimed at potential employees, who apparently are taking notice. In a November–December 2016 survey of 5,934 adults who took or wanted to take paid family or medical leave, that benefit was cited more than any other as the most helpful, according to the nonpartisan Pew Research Center.[31]

The employer also benefits, according to various studies: New mothers who take paid leave typically return to work within nine to 12 months of childbirth, and first-time moms who use the benefit are more likely to return to the same employer than those who do not take it, according to the National Partnership for Women & Families.[32] In addition, Congress' Joint Economic Committee has found that businesses gain from retaining workers—especially those who are highly skilled—that they might lose without a paid leave benefit. And they save on the "sizable costs" of recruiting, hiring and training replacement employees.[33]

Evidence of that can be found in California, the first of four states to enact paid maternity leave laws for all businesses. The state, which passed its milestone program in 2002, uses employee and employer payroll taxes to pay new mothers and fathers 55 percent of their salaries, up to $1,173 per week, for six weeks to bond with a new child.[34] Employees who care for seriously ill family members may also use the benefit.

Similarly, many of the private-sector companies that offer paid maternity leave funnel the benefit through their group disability plans, according to Derek Winn, lead consultant with Business Benefits Group, a Fairfax, Va.-based benefits broker. New fathers, however, do not qualify for disability benefits, he says.

A Labor Department study found in 2014 that adding the California benefit increased the amount of time new mothers are absent from work by about two and a half weeks. But researchers concluded that the cost to cover their duties during their leaves might be offset by mothers who take the leave rather than quit their jobs. A separate study found that California's law "had either a positive effect or no effect on productivity, profit, morale and costs." In that study, California businesses owners said the paid leave policy did not affect their firms' performance or profit margins.[35]

More Californians Taking Advantage of Paid Leave

Total claims increased by 86,000 over 10 years

Almost 2.2 million California employees claimed paid family leave between fiscal 2004–05 and fiscal 2014–15. The total number of leave claims increased by 86,000 over the 10-year period.

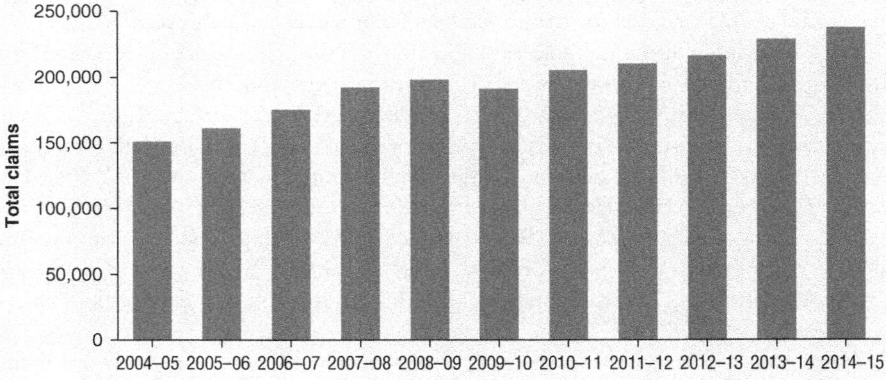

Source: "Paid Family Leave Market Research," Employment Development Department, State of California, Jul. 13, 2015, p. 28, http://tinyurl.com/ms9h5we.

While businesses reap best-in-class recruitment and retention status from a paid parental leave benefit, so does the economy, the Labor Department said. New mothers who are earning while on leave are less likely to tap public assistance benefits, the department said. The department has found that because paid maternity leave makes it easier for women to continue working after they have children, it contributes to female labor force participation.[36]

Some small-business owners, however, say these results don't apply to them. Jeb Breithaupt, owner of an 11-employee remodeling firm in Shreveport, La., says each member of his small staff has a skills-specific job. Anyone's extended absence, he says, would substantially slow business down.

Like others, Breithaupt says a government-enforced paid leave benefit would burden his company more than it would a corporation.

Like-minded business owners pushed hard—unsuccessfully—against a District of Columbia proposal to create a fund to pay private-sector employees up to 90 percent of their wages for a family or medical leave of eight weeks.

"You can't treat a mom-and-pop operation the same as a national chain; [they] operate on a much smaller profit margin," D.C. council member Nathan Ackerman explained. He called for an exception for businesses with fewer than 50 employees.[37]

Should the Federal Government Mandate Paid Time Off for Public- and Private-Sector Employees?

Whether Congress will enact a national law requiring paid leave for new parents after the birth of a child has—fairly suddenly—become a conversation about "when" rather than "if."

During the 2016 presidential campaign, Trump endorsed such a law, reportedly at the urging of his daughter, Ivanka, the mother of two sons and a daughter.[38] The break with conservative tradition has given hope to advocates of a federal family and medical leave law that provides for at least some wage replacement for new parents and for other employees who may miss work to care for a seriously ill loved one.

Still, neither Trump nor the Republican-controlled Congress has made paid leave a priority, at least for this year, says attorney Joan C. Williams, chair and director of the Center for WorkLife Law at the University of California's Hastings College of Law. "The good news is that Ivanka Trump is interested in paid leave," she says. "The bad news continues to be that the House is not, and now the Senate presumably isn't, either."

Trump's support came at a time when a fair number of conservatives, including those at the American Action Forum, a center-right think tank, and the American Enterprise Institute, were already tossing around ideas for establishing a federal paid-leave benefit.

A pre-election proposal from the American Action Forum promoted a paid leave benefit for employees with incomes lower than $28,000. The proposal called for low-income workers to take home up to $3,500 over 12 weeks.[39] And Republican Sen. Deb Fisher of Nebraska reintroduced her Strong Families Act, which would create a tax incentive for businesses to offer two weeks of paid family leave a year. Fisher introduced the bill in 2014 and 2015 without success.[40]

Advocates from both political parties have suggested that this might be a better year for such proposals, thanks partly to Trump's embrace of a paid leave law, coupled with a renewed attention to women's issues brought about, in part, by half a million participants in a women's march on Washington and around the country the day after the president's inauguration.[41]

Trump has not offered many details of what he might propose, only that he would like to offer new mothers six weeks of paid leave after childbirth. After criticism from advocates of paternity leave, he indicated he might be willing to allow paid leave for new fathers as well.[42]

Mathur of the American Enterprise Institute says a reluctance to pass a federal paid leave law remains among members of Congress—and it is driven by politics.

"We traditionally have few policies that are considered anti-business," she says. "Some people phrase it as a mandate on businesses to provide this leave, and businesses have to figure out how to pay for it. . . . [They believe] this is not something the government needs to do. Businesses need to do it on their own at whatever cost is comfortable to them. It's more the politics of it that has prevented the U.S. from passing this legislation."

WorldatWork's Stanley agrees.

"I don't know if America wants to run that way," she says. "What's unique in the U.S. is that companies take it upon themselves to figure out how we become more competitive, how that competitiveness helps build up our brand, our profitability, our shareholder value. It is sort of what America is known for."

As is true with so many legislative efforts, competing proposals are making their way through Congress.

Trump's original plan, which has not yet been introduced in Congress, would reserve wage replacement to working birth mothers. Most advocates support a broader law that covers adoptive and foster parents as well as any employee who misses work to care for a seriously ill relative.[43]

Matos of Life Meets Work is one of them. Limiting paid leave to birth mothers, he says, could "re-create the gender divide that creates the same problems for women in terms of career advancement and opportunity. . . . Even if we supported getting this maternity leave through, it would make any [proposals] in the future even harder for a broader, less gender approach to parental leave."

Still, Matos says, "The current political climate is very volatile. It could really go in more directions than I can understand."

Congressional Democrats have issued their own version of paid leave in the Family and Medical Insurance Leave (FAMILY) Act, which would pay for wage reimbursement with a 0.2 percent surtax on wages paid by both employers and employees.[44] The proposal calls for 12 weeks of paid leave at 66 percent of monthly wages for employees who give birth or adopt a new child, fall seriously ill or need to care for an immediate family member with a long-term health condition.[45]

Democrats offered up this bill, without success, in 2013 and 2015. Sen. Kirsten Gillibrand, D-N.Y., and Rep. Rosa DeLauro, D-Conn., modeled it on statewide paid leave laws in California, New Jersey, Rhode Island and New York, which pay employees on leave from self-sustaining funds dispersed by the state governments.[46]

It failed, in part, because critics—including many Republicans and some businesses—objected to imposing additional government regulations on companies, despite evidence

Most Small Businesses Support Paid Family Leave

Almost 50 percent strongly favor establishment of a national paid leave program

Seventy percent of small businesses showed some level of support for creating a national paid leave program, the Family and Medical Insurance Leave (FAMILY) Act. While 47 percent said they strongly favored the newly introduced legislation, which would be funded through employee and employer contributions and ensure up to 12 weeks of partial income, a quarter of respondents opposed the measure.

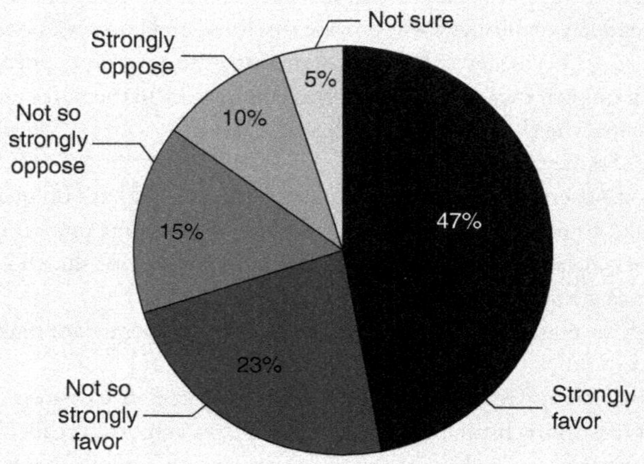

Source: "Small Businesses Support Paid Family Leave Programs," Small Business Majority, Center for American Progress, Mar. 30, 2017, http://tinyurl.com/k9bstug.

that the California law on which it was modeled has reported a neutral effect on the state's businesses.[47]

Its fate this year is anyone's guess, says Fink of the National Partnership for Women & Families. "There appears to be a recognition that there is a problem with not having paid family leave, on both sides of the aisle. . . . It's progress."

Can Employees Take Paid Leave without Damaging Their Careers?

In Singapore, a universal Employment Act guarantees employees with six or more months on the job 14 paid sick days each year and 60 days of paid hospital leave. But Singapore Airlines employees have accused their company of retaliating against those who take advantage of that legal right by denying them promotions.

The airline has a more generous leave policy than the national law requires: It offers 28 days of paid medical leave and six months off, with pay, for a hospital stay brought on by a chronic or prolonged illness. It bases promotions, in part, on points that employees earn each year for their service. Workers have claimed that the firm deducts points for each medical absence.

The airline has denied those claims.[48]

In the United States, no federal mandate requires employers to pay workers for sick days, parental leave or vacations. Yet studies show that employees who work for firms that voluntarily offer them often are reluctant to use the benefits for fear of derailing their careers.

The travel company Expedia's 2016 Vacation Deprivation report, for instance, revealed that Americans left an average of three paid vacation days apiece unclaimed last year.[49] That added up to 375 million unused paid days off.

In the survey of 9,424 working adults in 28 countries, 9 percent of Americans said they worried that their absence from work would "be perceived negatively," according to Expedia. About 14 percent reported feeling guilty for taking time off, the survey found. In fact, 6 percent said they felt so guilty that they did not take any time off in 2016.[50]

Yet 21 percent of Americans in the survey ranked additional vacation as their "second most-prized work incentive," trailing flexible work hours by just 1 percent.[51]

That practice isn't new. Project: Time Off, an advocacy group that promotes a cultural shift toward embracing time off from work as essential to success and good health, found that Americans' use of vacation days has dipped during most years since 2000.[52]

And the practice is not limited to vacations. Although the number of employers offering paid family leave policies is expanding, their use by new mothers is not, according to research by Ohio State University economist Jay Zagorsky.[53]

In an interview, Zagorsky said some women blame their choice to eschew paid leave on a perception that they will stall their career progress. But more likely, he says, the women cannot afford to take the leave because the income replacement their employers offer is rarely 100 percent.

For example, in California—the first state to adopt a policy for paid maternity leave, and later, for paternity leave for all public- and private-sector employees—those taking paid family leave qualify for reimbursement of 55 percent of their weekly wages for up to six weeks.[54] "Not everyone can afford to take half pay or no pay," Zagorsky says. "If you live paycheck to paycheck and you have the possibility of taking off two months, but of taking off those two months without any [or full] pay, it might not be financially feasible."

The result: The number of women taking maternity leave in 2015 was about the same as it was in 1994, an average of 273,000 per month, Zagorsky's research showed. The use of an extended leave after childbirth is static, he says, even though four states and the District of Columbia have added paid leave policies since 1994 and the economy has grown by 66 percent.[55]

Zagorsky calls the statistics "surprising and troubling."

The American Enterprise Institute's Mathur says the think tank's studies have shown that California mothers would have taken longer maternity leaves if their wage replacement were greater than 55 percent. "Paid leave is definitely an improvement over unpaid leave," Mathur says, "but how you design the paid leave policy is important."

Mathur points to the latest National Compensation Survey from the Bureau of Labor Statistics (BLS), which reports that 13 percent of private-sector workers in the United States have access to paid family leave.[56] But the 2012 BLS American Time Use Survey shows that fewer than 10 percent of employees who took paid or unpaid leave for any reason used it to care for children or sick family members.[57]

The use of paid leave by new fathers across the United States, on the other hand, increased from 5,800 men a month in 1994 to 22,000 a month in 2015, Zagorsky's research revealed.[58]

And while 47.5 percent of women who took maternity leave in 2015 were paid something during their absence from work, 70.7 percent of men on leave were, according to Zagorsky's report.[59]

Matos observes that men who take time off to bond with a newborn or care for a sick family member are more likely than women to be embraced when they return to the office.

"People will say, 'He's a father now; he needs this job,'" says Matos. But for women who take extended leaves, he says, "people will not be giving her assignments back."

Matos says many women and men "feel afraid to offer information to their bosses about taking time off for maternity and family." He says he looks forward to the day when executives and managers will say, "I know this is a tumultuous time. Let's figure something out that works for both of us."

Until then, Matos says, new mothers who would like to work while raising their families will quit their jobs in larger numbers than necessary. And bosses, he says, "will wish they would have told them [what they needed] before they quit."

BACKGROUND

European Head Start

America has no national law guaranteeing working mothers will continue to earn all or part of their salaries while they are on maternity leave. Four states—California, New Jersey, New York and Rhode Island, plus the District of Columbia—have statewide laws that provide pay to new parents on leave.

California's landmark 2002 law came 119 years after the world's first paid leave law, which Germany enacted countrywide in 1883.[60]

The Europeans pioneered both unpaid and paid maternity leaves. Switzerland was the first country in the world to offer working mothers time off to give birth, when it adopted a law in 1877 providing for eight weeks of unpaid leave for use before and after childbirth. That law forbade factory workers from returning to work for six weeks after delivery.

Bulgaria's Maternity Leave Most Generous

The Eastern European country offers 58.6 weeks

Bulgaria offers its mothers 58.6 weeks of paid maternity leave, the most of any developed country. The United States is the only developed country that does not offer mothers any governmental paid maternity leave, while the country average for Organisation for Economic Co-operation and Development (OECD) members is 17.7 weeks of paid leave.

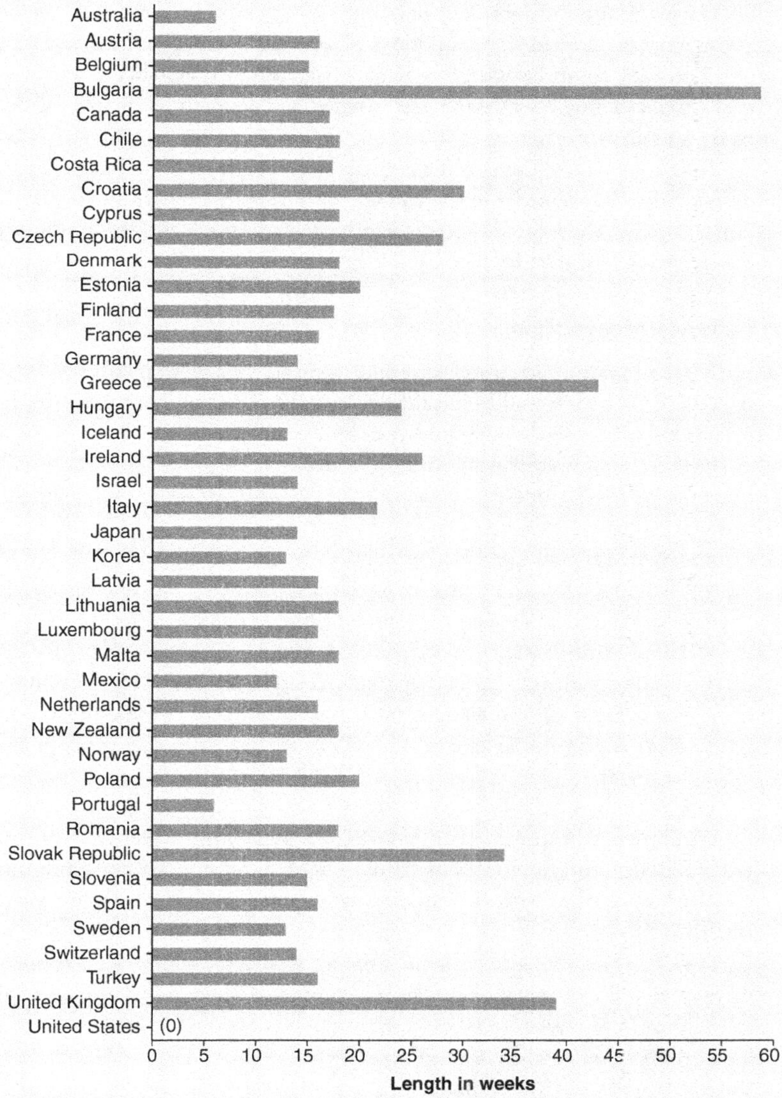

Source: "OECD Family Database," Organisation for Economic Co-operation and Development, Mar. 15, 2017, p. 3, http://tinyurl.com/mclgdbw.

A year later, Germany enacted a three-week leave law, also unpaid. In 1883, Germany amended its policy to legislate paid leave for three weeks after a birth for women who had insurance. Austria-Hungary did the same; both laws left the amount of the payment up to the women's insurance companies.[61]

Over the next 30 years, Great Britain, Portugal, Norway, Sweden, Holland and Belgium passed national laws providing unpaid time off from work for childbirth. In 1911, Sweden opened maternity and convalescent homes, where working women and their babies could stay as the moms recovered from childbirth. Two years later, France joined Switzerland as one of two European countries that allowed maternity leave to begin before a baby was born. And by then, Luxembourg, Switzerland and Sweden had adopted Germany and Austria-Hungary's paid maternity leave model.[62]

Today, the United States is the only developed country without a paid parental leave mandate. Of the 193 countries in the United Nations, only a handful have no national paid leave policy; besides the United States, the others are Papua New Guinea, Suriname and several South Pacific Island nations.[63]

Federal Intervention

Work and family advocates were able to garner bipartisan political support in Congress to pass the 1993 Family and Medical Leave Act (FMLA), but not until the legislation had been proposed—and failed—nine times over nine years.[64]

FMLA requires employers with 50 or more employees to allow them 12 weeks a year of unpaid leave for the following reasons:

- To deliver and care for the employee's newborn baby;
- To adopt or accept a child for foster care;
- To take care of a seriously ill spouse, child or parent;
- To take medical leave when the employee is seriously ill and unable to work;
- To deal with any urgent demands created by the status of an employee's next of kin as an active duty or reserve member of the military. The law allows 26 weeks of unpaid leave for an immediate family member to care for a seriously injured or ill military member.

Employees who use FMLA leave have jobs waiting when they return. However, the law does not require employers to offer returning workers their original jobs; they are entitled to positions with the same pay and benefits as the ones they had before they took the leave.[65]

FMLA is not intended as a stand-in for sick days, which 56 percent of small-business employees and 79 percent of employees at larger companies had access to in 2016, according to the Bureau of Labor Statistics.[66] Sick days—as opposed to family and medical leave—are for employees to use when they wake up with the flu or a migraine headache and need to miss a day or two of work, for example.

The Labor Department's Wage and Hour Division amended its interpretation of the FMLA in 2015 to update its definition of "spouse" to include eligible employees in same-sex marriages. The change brought the law into compliance with a 2013 U.S. Supreme Court

Low Employee Contributions Fund Paid Leave Programs

Payroll tax rate in California, New Jersey and Rhode Island is less than 2 percent

Employees in California, New Jersey and Rhode Island finance all or part of their state's paid-leave programs through payroll contributions. The payroll tax rate for family- and medical-leave programs is less than 2 percent in each state, and Rhode Island has the highest approximate annual cost to workers at $384 per year. New Jersey has the lowest.

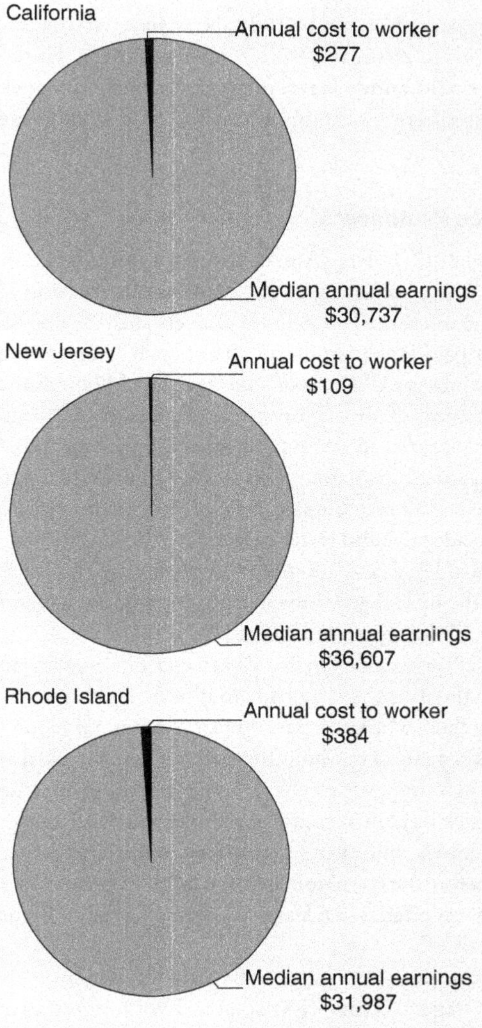

Note: Median annual earnings surpass New Jersey's taxable wage base of $32,000, so total contributions are based on wage base, not $38,607.

Source: "Paid Leave in Four States: Lessons for Montana Policymakers and Advocates," Montana Budget & Policy Center, December 2015, p. 5, http://tinyurl.com/mbztdt5.

decision that overturned the 1996 Defense of Marriage Act. That act held that "marriage" and "spouse" referred only to a union between a man and a woman.[67]

The FMLA applies to public- and private-sector employees in all states. It does not, however, restrict states or private businesses from voluntarily offering more-generous medical and family leave benefits to their employees. It also does not prohibit companies with fewer than 50 employees—those exempt from FMLA—from offering their own family and medical leave benefit.

After California enacted its law in 2002, New Jersey followed in 2008, Rhode Island in 2013 and New York in 2016. In 2007, Washington Gov. Christine O'Grady Gregoire signed a state law for paid family leave, but it never took effect because of a lack of funding. In 2017, the District of Columbia adopted a paid family leave law, which will take effect in 2020.[68]

Paid Leave Policies Proliferate

Between 2015 and 2017, 71 large American companies adopted their own versions of paid family and medical leave, according to the National Partnership for Women & Families. Aside from tech companies, the list includes retailers such as Nordstrom, which offers birth mothers 12 weeks of paid leave; restaurant chains such as Starbucks, where working moms who do not work in stores get 18 weeks of paid leave for childbirth and store employees get six weeks of paid and 12 weeks of unpaid leave; and financial firms, including American Express, whose new policy allows up to 28 weeks for its working parents.[69]

Some of the companies offer a few weeks of paid leave and an optional allotment of additional unpaid weeks; others include paid time off to care for sick relatives; and many offer lengthy paid leaves to adoptive and foster parents.

Family and medical leave laws are more comprehensive than state and corporate policies for sick days. While the federal government does not require that employees receive paid sick leave, nearly 40 state and local governments do.[70]

San Francisco in 2006 became the first city to enact its own law requiring local businesses to pay employees for the days they miss due to illness. The law requires employers to pay all employees, including those who work part time or in temporary jobs, for sick days. Employees accrue their sick days at a rate of one hour for every 30 hours worked after 90 days on the job.[71]

Between 2007, when the law took effect, and 2009, the proportion of San Francisco businesses offering paid sick days increased from 73 percent to 91 percent, mostly at firms with fewer than 100 employees, indicating that many of the city's larger firms were voluntarily offering the benefit before the law required it. By 2009, 99 percent of San Francisco firms with more than 20 employees offered sick leave, according to research published in the American Journal of Public Health.[72]

Connecticut became the first state to enact a paid sick day law in 2012. Since then, California, Massachusetts, Oregon, Vermont, Arizona and Washington have adopted laws requiring employers to offer paid sick days to employees.[73] Connecticut's law is for employees who have worked at least 680 hours, and the leave is accrued.[74]

In addition, 30 cities and two counties—Montgomery County, Md., and Cook County, Ill.—have sick day laws.[75] In a handful of other states, paid sick days legislation is working its way through legislatures.

The proposed federal Healthy Families Act would require businesses with 15 or more employees to offer each employee up to seven paid sick days per year to recover from illness, visit doctors, care for ill family members or attend school meetings about a child's health condition or disability.[76]

WorldatWork has estimated that organizations offer an average of seven to 11 days of sick time off each year.[77]

For the past decade, companies have drifted away from the traditional model for sick days, which allows employees to accrue hours every pay period to be used for sick days later. In a 2016 WorldatWork survey, a growing number of human resources professionals in most industries said they prefer to offer sick and vacation days in a single bucket, called a Paid Time Off, or PTO, bank.

For example, 42 percent of HR managers in publicly traded companies said they use paid time off banks; 51 percent of privately held firms prefer PTO banks; and 44 percent of nonprofits and private-sector companies use them.[78]

The Quirky and Just Plain Strange

Fighting Burnout? Just Got a Puppy? Some Leave Policies Can Help.

In 2015, 55 percent of working Americans ended the year without taking all their vacation days. Some companies are getting creative to change that. A key takeaway: Regional customs and other factors have prompted some businesses to fashion vacation policies that meet their particular needs.

The first day of deer-hunting season in New York used to paralyze the production line at Pall Trinity Micro.

For decades, dozens of employees at the high-tech filtration company in Cortland would skip work without notice and slip into forests upstate. The decision to play hooky put them at risk for disciplinary action, but that was fine with the workers as long they didn't have to use precious vacation time.

To fix the problem, Pall decided around 1990 to make the first day of deer season and turkey season sanctioned days off—without pay. That allows the company to plan for absences and keep the production line running smoothly. Hunters can miss work on either day—sometimes both days—without cutting into their two to five weeks of vacation time or their six to seven days of personal/sick leave.

"Now we have a much better ability to manage who's going to be at work as opposed to leaving it up in the air and hoping enough people would show up," says Jeff Wooten, Pall's senior vice president of human resources.

Regional customs, seasonal celebrations and other factors have prompted some businesses in the United States and abroad to fashion—or at least consider—vacation policies that meet their particular needs.

Along with standard maternity and paternity leave, a Scottish brewery offers a perk that may be unique: Employees get a week of paid time off when they bring home a new puppy or rescue dog.

The benefit can "take the stress out of" getting a new dog settled, BrewDog co-founder James Watt explained.[79]

In Egypt, a long-standing law grants Muslims a month of paid vacation to travel to Mecca on an Islamic pilgrimage known as the Hajj. In February, the country's Supreme Constitutional Court, saying the benefit was unconstitutional as long as it applied only to Muslims, extended it to include Christians wishing to visit Jerusalem at Christmas or any other time of year.[80]

In Britain, several employers allow workers to give last-minute notice to take a "well-being day"—equivalent to a "mental-health day" in the United States—when

(*Continued*)

(Continued)

they feel too stressed to show up for work. The left-wing Institute for Public Policy Research in Britain has proposed that all companies adopt the practice.[81]

Joe Dromey, the think tank's director, said so-called "Fit Pay" days help "employees who develop a health or mental health problem to manage their condition and stay in touch with work."[82]

In the United States, advocates for paid time off have a few unconventional ideas as well.

Meghann Foye, author of the 2016 novel "Meternity," has suggested that new mothers aren't the only women who need an extended break from work. She advocates a "meternity" leave for any employee—male or female—suffering from burnout.

Women, in particular, would benefit, Foye said. "Women—moms and non-moms alike—feel overloaded by the roles they have to take on at work and at home," she said.[83]

In 2015, 55 percent of working Americans ended the year without taking all their vacation days. There were 658 million of those days, with a total value of about $61.4 billion.[84]

A handful of companies, hoping to stem a chronic trend of workers skipping their vacations, pay employees extra to take paid leave.

Software company FullContact in Denver offers $7,500 to employees who take vacation time and disconnect from the office. Entertainment firm Travelzoo in Mountain View, Calif., offers $1,500 to employees who not only stay away from work but take a trip—defined as a hotel stay, a vacation package, a cruise or a flight. RAND Corp. in Santa Monica adds 5 percent to the annual salaries of employees who use all 20 of their vacation days.[85]

Rob Whalen, once a workaholic employee at Cisco Systems based in San Jose, Calif., has devised a system that lets workers trade their unused vacation and sick days for plane tickets and hotel rooms. His company, PTO Exchange, bases the trades on how much employers estimate the unused time is worth. Employees also may cash in unused paid leave for contributions to 401(k) plans and health savings accounts.[86]

Smart companies choose benefits packages that reflect workplace culture, are appreciated by workers and help achieve the company's goals, said Justin Held, a research analyst at the International Foundation of Employee Benefit plans. To that end, he said, "Organizations and their benefit departments have proven very creative in their offerings."[87]

—*Sharon O'Malley*

CURRENT SITUATION

A Double Edge

Netflix reaped positive publicity last August when it announced that it would begin allowing new mothers and fathers to take as much leave as they wanted with full pay during the first year after a child's birth or adoption. Virgin, which owns the airline Virgin Atlantic, was likewise praised when it announced in 2015 that it would offer up to 52 weeks of leave, paid at 100 percent of the new parents' salary, to biological and adoptive parents.

In both cases, it turned out, the policies came with a catch: Netflix's paid leave offer applied only to salaried employees who work in the entertainment company's digital operations, and not to those working in DVD distribution centers. That left at least 450 of its 3,500 workers without the benefit.[88] And at Virgin, which employs more than 50,000, just 140 qualified for paid parental leave.[89]

The benefits "rang hollow," says Matos of Life Meets Work. The announcements, he says, were deliberately sketchy on details so they would reap the greatest public relations value. But they reflected a practice not uncommon among businesses vying for a limited number of highly skilled technical workers such as engineers and IT professionals: The most valued employees are offered the best benefits, he says.

Still, both companies caught flak from the media and the public. One Netflix fan collected almost 8,000 signatures urging the movie streaming and DVD distribution company to make warehouse workers, including hourly employees, eligible. "It's wrong for Netflix to create two classes of employees," the fan, Shannon Murphy, wrote in a blog on Coworker.org. "Already, there's a divide between higher income earners (especially in the tech industry) and low-wage workers in terms of access to important benefits like parental leave."[90]

In response, Netflix created a paid leave policy for hourly employees in its streaming, DVD distribution and customer service divisions, but the benefits differ. Hourly workers in the streaming operation get 16 weeks of fully paid maternity, paternity or adoption leave; customer service employees get 14 weeks; and DVD-side workers get 12 weeks.[91]

More criticism followed over the two-track policy.[92] "I hate to see a pattern where some workers have access to important benefits and others don't," Katie Bethell, a member of the Working Families Party, who helped collect 100,000 signatures on petitions her group delivered to Netflix headquarters. "Tech companies aren't considering this as a fundamental thing for the health of their employees, they're looking at [paid leave] as a way to attract employees."[93]

But a Netflix spokeswoman defended the company's decision: "Across Netflix, we compare salary and benefits to those of employees at businesses performing similar work," Anne Marie Squeo wrote in an email. "Those comparisons show we provide all of our employees with comparable or better pay and benefits than at other companies."[94]

Mattos says that practice is business as usual among companies with a workforce divided between highly prized, highly skilled workers and those whose jobs require little training and are easier to fill.

At Walmart, the largest U.S. private employer, only salaried employees are eligible for parental leave: 90 days for new mothers and 14 days for dads. More than 40 percent of its workers are paid hourly and do not qualify for the benefit.[95]

In fact, approximately 40 million American employees do not have access to paid sick days; just 20 percent of low-wage workers have that benefit, according to the White House Council of Economic Advisers.[96] The Labor Department has estimated that about four out of 10 workers do not have access to paid leave of any type.[97]

Like Netflix, however, some others are beginning to level the playing field, although Virgin has stuck to its limited benefit. The National Partnership for Women & Families counted 89 companies that expanded their paid family leave policies between 2015 and 2017 to make them at least somewhat more inclusive.[98] Late last year, for example, Hilton Hotels and Resorts began offering 10 weeks of paid parental leave to all of its 40,000 U.S. employees, from C-suite executives to housekeepers and waiters.[99]

Matt Schulyer, chief human resources officer for Hilton Worldwide, said Millennials, who make up half of the hospitality chain's workforce, spurred the decision, which was about "being able to attract and retain the workforce of today and the workforce of tomorrow."[100]

LOOKING AHEAD

Maybe Next Year

Advocates of paid leave remain dubious about the chances that the United States will enact a law to pay employees for time off from work—at least not soon.

They predict that at large companies—and not just those in technology fields—the benefits divide between the haves and have-nots will keep expanding unless Congress acts by passing a universal, national law that provides pay to all working parents with new children; to employees who are caregivers to sick children and elderly parents; and to anyone who has to miss work, even for a day, because of a personal illness.

And the advocates don't anticipate that is about to happen. Even though Trump's interest in paid leave has amplified the national conversation about the lack of such a law, the chance that Congress will adopt one is slim as long as Republicans and Democrats disagree about which employees to cover and how to pay for it.

That's the conclusion of Williams, the Center for Worklife Law attorney, who says the lack of a federal law is what has driven the decision by Netflix and others who deem employees with hard-to-recruit skills more worthy of paid leave benefits than those in unskilled, hourly positions.

"This is the drawback of handling parental leave at an enterprise [business] level, which, by the way, no other industrialized economy does," she told NPR. "If you handle parental leave at the enterprise level, the incentives for the enterprise are to give a rich benefits package to

Benefits Boost Employee Morale

More than 70 percent of employers said retention and loyalty were significantly affected

In a 2016 survey, about three-quarters of employers said company benefits had a significant impact on employee retention and loyalty. A majority also said benefits help a company maintain its competitive advantage.

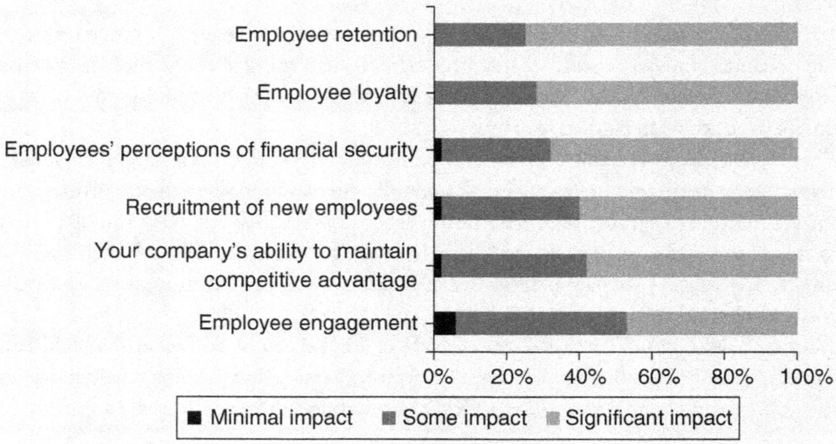

Note: The survey question asked, "To what extent have the benefits you offer had an impact on each of the following?"

Source: "Commitment to the Future: 10 Years of the Principal 10 Best Companies," Harvard Business Review Analytic Services, Apr. 24, 2016, p. 6, http://tinyurl.com/knybwpf.

highly valued, high human-capital workers and not give it to hourly workers. . . . That's just a structural reality."[101]

In an interview with SBR, Williams suggested that Congress adopt an imperfect bill just to get one on the books. "It's going to be so difficult to pass anything that they should package it anyway they can pass it," she says.

Mathur of the American Enterprise Institute agrees: Lawmakers, she says, "are serious about having a policy . . . at least a minimum policy."

But even paid leave advocates don't agree what that policy should look like. Attorney Fink of the National Partnership for Women & Families says Trump's idea for a mothers-only benefit "isn't a sufficient proposal. . . . It's progress that there's a recognition that there's a public policy problem," she says, but "it would be harmful to pass a bill that only provides paid leave to mothers. . . . It could lead to sex discrimination in hiring, and in promotions."

That split could perpetuate the status quo, the advocates say. "There's no simple answer," Zagorsky, the Ohio State University researcher, says.

Chronology

1877–1928	**Europe adopts world's first maternity leave laws.**
1877	Switzerland becomes the first country to adopt an unpaid maternity leave law; a year later, Germany becomes the second European nation to do so.
1883	Germany and Austria-Hungary adopt paid maternity leaves of three weeks after delivery for insured women.
1960s–1970s	**Temporary disability insurance laws pave way for maternity leave.**
1960s	California, Hawaii, New Jersey, New York and Rhode Island enact temporary disability insurance laws to protect employees from income loss in the case of a short-term medical disability. New mothers eventually are covered under these laws.
1978	The Pregnancy Discrimination Act requires companies that offer temporary disability programs to cover pregnancy. The act also prevents employers from firing women solely on the basis of pregnancy.
1980s–1990s	**Unpaid family leave becomes law.**
1984	Congressional Democrats introduce the Family and Medical Leave Act, which would allow employees to take up to 12 weeks of unpaid leave from work after the birth of a child or to care for a seriously ill family member. The bill is reintroduced every year until 1993, when it becomes law.
1987	A California court rules that most employers have to allow pregnant women four months of unpaid disability leave and guarantee them their jobs when they return to work.
2000–2009	**First paid family leave and sick-days laws take effect.**
2002	California becomes the first state to create a paid family leave program to provide income replacement to new mothers and to employees with caregiving duties for seriously ill family members.

(Continued)

2006	The city of San Francisco becomes the first U.S. jurisdiction to enact a paid sick-day law.
2007	Washington State's governor signs a paid family leave law; however, the law never takes effect because of a lack of funding.
2008	New Jersey enacts the country's second state paid family leave law. . . . Washington becomes the second U.S. city to adopt a paid sick-day law.
2010–2017	**Cities and local jurisdictions pass paid sick-day laws.**
2011	Seattle enacts a paid sick-day law.
2012	Connecticut becomes the first state to require employers to offer paid sick days. The law covers only nonexempt, hourly workers in service-sector firms of more than 50 employees.
2013	The Rhode Island Legislature passes the country's third state paid family leave law. . . . New York City enacts a paid sick-day law and expands it in 2014. . . . Eight municipal governments in New Jersey pass sick-day laws.
2014	California expands the definition of "family member" in its paid family leave program to include seriously ill siblings, grandparents, grandchildren and parents-in-law. The original program covered only parents, children, spouses and registered domestic partners.
2015	The U.S. Department of Labor's Wage and Hour Division amends the definition of "spouse" in the 1993 Family and Medical Leave Act to include eligible employees in legal, same-sex marriages.
2016	New York passes a statewide paid family leave law, the fourth such law in America. . . . Presidential candidates Hillary Clinton, a Democrat, and Donald Trump, a Republican, publicly support paid family leave. . . . Paid sick-day statutes pass in nine jurisdictions, from Spokane, Wash., to Elizabeth, N.J.
2017	The District of Columbia enacts a paid family leave law, which will take effect in July 2020.

Discussion Questions

Here are some questions for discussion on paid leave:

- Which nations offer the most-generous paid leave benefits to their workers? Why does the United States lag behind other industrialized nations?
- Is offering generous time off policies practical outside of Silicon Valley? How could a small business make it work?
- For a corporation, what are the arguments in favor of time off for workers dealing with personal issues? Should it embrace some of the more creative ideas out there for helping employees, such as giving days off to those who are overly stressed? Or is it better for a business to run a tighter ship?
- Should the federal government mandate national standards on paid leave—why or why not?

PERSPECTIVE

Q&A: Jeb Breithaupt on Paid Leave

"IF SOMEBODY'S NOT HERE, THERE'S A HOLE; YOU'VE GOT A FUNCTION THAT'S NOT BEING DONE"

Jeb Breithaupt

Jeb Breithaupt is the owner of JEB Design/Build, a remodeling firm in Shreveport, La., with 11 employees. In an interview with *SAGE Business Researcher* freelance correspondent Sharon O'Malley, he explains why he opposes any government requirement that would allow small-business employees to take extended leaves, even if insurance or taxes cover their salaries. His objection: He says he can't afford to hire temporary workers to cover for employees who are absent.

How do you feel about the possibility that federal law could require you to offer your employees paid parental leave?

I'm not a big, fat corporation. If someone is out for six weeks, I would lose thousands of dollars.

Some advocates of paid parental leave say small businesses can cross-train employees to cover for each other during extended leaves.

In a big corporation, some people could probably cover for others, but small business doesn't work that way. I've got people in super-specific positions. If somebody's not here, there's a hole; you've got a function that's not being done. We can't start a remodeling job if our only drafter is out for six weeks. We're not going to get jobs drawn, so we won't sell any jobs. I can't outsource that. If my production manager was out for six weeks, I'd be able to cover to a certain extent, but I'm the owner. I'm out selling.

Do you offer any paid leave?

Full-time employees have six paid holidays per year, and we have a vacation policy: one week after the first year, and two weeks after the second. [His company offers five paid sick days a year. Employees who use them, though, have to produce a doctor's note.]

What happens when someone has a baby?

That hasn't come up. We did have a salesperson who took maternity leave, but she was paid solely on commission, so she doesn't get paid when she doesn't sell anything.

Does your limited paid leave policy hurt you when it comes to recruiting employees?

I had an opening for a bookkeeper, and I got 773 résumés.

What happens if an employee needs to take time off beyond the vacation and sick days that you offer?

We try to be flexible about stuff. I have nine full-time employees and two hourly employees. Some of them have to be here from 8 a.m. to 6 p.m., Monday through Friday. But for others, like my bookkeeper, how much we need them is job-driven. In construction, you have light weeks and heavy weeks. If we're in between jobs or if it's a light week and someone wants to work four days instead of five, that's allowed—but they forfeit their pay for the day they take off. I think that flexibility is a draw. But my drafter, I need you here Monday through Friday.

What advice would you give to legislators considering a mandate to require all businesses, including small ones, to allow employees to take extended leave for childbirth and personal or family illnesses?

Government is like a big business. They have a big-government mindset. They think there's this big pot of money and you just turn on the faucet, and there's more money. Small businesses are not like that.

How will small businesses react if Congress passes a law requiring paid parental leave?

The market will adjust. Duh: They won't hire young women. The government thinks people aren't going to change when they pass these laws. It's frustrating.

UPDATE IN 2020

In his 2020 State of the Union address, U.S. President Trump became the first Republican president to call for paid family leave.[102]

The topic came up frequently during the 2016 presidential campaign, when he vowed to pursue the idea. In 2018, the U.S. remained the only country among 41 industrialized nations that did not offer paid family leave, according to the Organisation for Economic Co-operation and Development.[103]

But the bipartisan bill that Trump endorsed in January 2020 was not the equivalent of the family assistance that most advocates called for. It would enable new parents to collect a portion of their future child tax credits ahead of time and receive a smaller credit for the next 10 to 15 years, but did not provide a new source of funding for parents. It did not cover medical care for sick parents, nor did it provide job protection when taking the leave.[104]

However, paid leave provisions were included in the COVID-19 assistance legislation signed into law by Trump in March 2020, providing two weeks of paid sick leave as well as 12 weeks of paid family leave and reimbursing employers for it with tax credits.[105]

The legislation allowed states to set more expansive paid leave standards, which were in effect in California, Connecticut, District of Columbia, Hawaii, Maine, Minnesota, New Jersey, Oregon, Rhode Island, Vermont, Washington and Wisconsin.[106]

Although the pandemic prompted historic numbers of layoffs, several companies also implemented an expanded paid time off or paid sick time policy. A report from Alight Solutions, a business process outsourcing company, said 47 percent of 246 employers surveyed had done so and another 11 percent said they planned to do so.[107]

By contrast, the European Union (EU) issued a directive stating that by 2022, EU member states had to offer a minimum of 10 days' paid paternity leave and four months' paid parental leave for each parent, of which two months are non-transferable.

In late September 2020, France decided to double paid paternity leave from 14 days to 28, inching closer to Sweden's 90 days and Finland's 54 days.[108] Meanwhile, Switzerland—considered one of the European countries lagging on policies relating to gender equality—held a referendum, with voters approving the passing of a law on paid paternity leave, allowing 10 days of paid leave for new fathers instead of a single day.[109]

—*Micheline Maynard*

15 SUPPLY CHAINS AND PROTECTIONISM

Will tariffs shrink global production networks?

Matt Mossman

From *SAGE Business Researcher*, June 25, 2018

EXECUTIVE SUMMARY

Global supply chains arose and flourished in an era of falling tariffs—an era that may now be coming to an end amid an upsurge in protectionism. President Trump and other political leaders' plans to boost tariffs or overhaul free-trade agreements could increase costs and pose new risks for multinational companies that have built extensive worldwide networks of subsidiaries and supplier partnerships. However, experience suggests that in most economic sectors, supply chains do not need to change substantially in the face of protectionism. Small adjustments should be enough to allow most companies to preserve operations and avoid significant increases in the cost of their goods.

Key takeaways include:

- Global supply chains have multiple variable costs, and research shows that when some of those costs rise, suppliers often choose to absorb them and remain in the supply chain.
- In cases where companies pass on higher costs to retail customers, the strong global economy could help consumers absorb small price increases caused by increased tariffs.
- In the longer term, companies worried about protectionism may prioritize risk management over cost savings by focusing on regional rather than global supply strategies.

Qilai Shen/Corbis via Getty Images

The spread of globalized supply chains has helped turn Shanghai into the world's busiest port.

OVERVIEW

When President Trump announced new tariffs in March 2018 aimed at punishing China for intellectual property theft and China retaliated with its own tariffs, including ones targeting U.S. aircraft, Boeing was caught in the crossfire.[1] The airplane maker's share price plunged 5.2 percent on Mar. 22, the third time since the start of the year that the prospect of a trade war had sunk Boeing stock by 5 percent or more in a single day.[2]

The falloff wasn't solely attributable to fears about the prospect of canceled orders. Investors were also acutely aware that Boeing's planes include millions of parts, more than half of them sourced from upwards of 5,400 outside suppliers worldwide.[3] This intricate network of contracts and processes was designed to thrive in a world of open borders and low tariffs, not one of trade conflicts.

But after that March selloff, Boeing's share price rebounded—partly because investors suspect the company's global supply chain is not as fragile as they had first feared—before dipping again in mid-June as the United States and China announced new tariffs against each other.[4] For the year, Boeing shares were up 20.4 percent as of June 18, compared with a 3.7 percent gain in the same period for the Standard & Poor's 500 and a drop of almost 1 percent for the Dow Jones Industrial Average.[5]

Boeing's stock price yo-yo is just one example of how the far-flung and highly integrated global supply chains that multinational companies have built are now facing their first real test from protectionist politics. Experience suggests they will be able to survive increased tariffs for now, although the degree of resilience may vary by product, geographic location or economic sector, and long-term decision making could be altered. "In the short run it's going to be very hard for them to change their supply chains, but ultimately there will be an effect," says University of Wisconsin economics professor Charles Engel.

Open borders, easy logistics and the principle of comparative advantage—the idea that instead of trying to produce everything they need, countries should focus on goods they can make more cheaply than most and then trade with each other—led multinationals to expand their supply chains worldwide in recent decades. The process accelerated after global trade negotiations in 1986 in Punta Del Este, Uruguay. What is now known as the Uruguay Round led to a broad commitment by 123 countries to open borders and lower tariffs and to creation of the World Trade Organization (WTO) in 1994 to settle trade disputes.[6]

Once all these moves were implemented, the average tariff rate applied to imports by the WTO's 164 members plunged by 15 percent, to a rate just below 9 percent, where it has remained since, according to the World Trade Organization Statistics Database and World Tariff Profiles.[7]

Multinationals responded to these governmental commitments to lower trade barriers by picking the cheapest places for specific functions, or sometimes ones where operations could be done fastest. In textiles, for example, supply chains developed in Asia to produce at the lowest cost, and in Western countries to produce at top speed to handle trendy items expected to sell for just a few months before seasons and fashions change. The impact on global trade was substantial; its total value rose from $5 trillion in 1996 to $19 trillion in 2013, according to WTO data.[8]

Once companies had found new spots to locate or to contract with suppliers, they next sought to boost productivity, and for manufacturing sectors in countries that participated, the results were clear. A study by World Bank economists found that a 10 percent increase in participation in global supply chains led to an average productivity gain of 1.7 percent.[9]

Tariffs Declined in Past Two Decades

Average rate of tariffs on imports by WTO members, 1996–2016

The average percentage rate of tariffs on imports imposed by World Trade Organization members has generally declined since 1996, with a slight rise in 2015 and 2016.

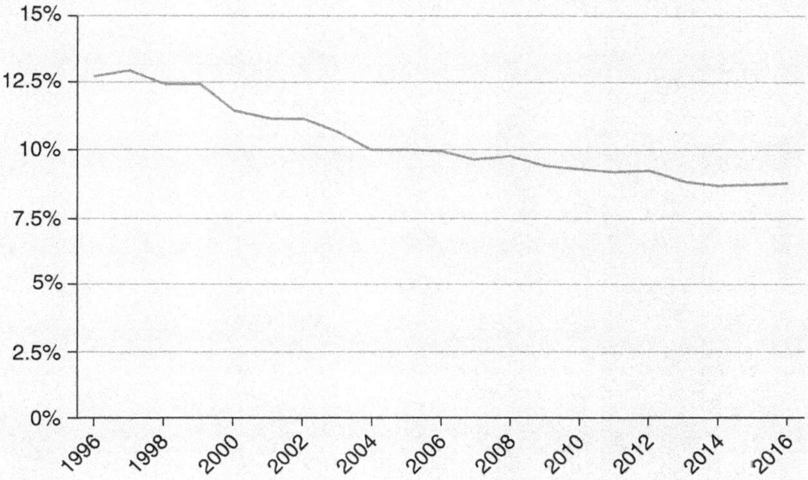

Source: Values are sums based on filings made to the Federal Emergency Management Agency (FEMA).

The World Bank's economists focused exclusively on manufacturing for their study, and defined participation in a global supply chain as using imported materials to make something destined for export. But global supply chains can also include services, such as when a company uses call centers in one country to handle customer service in another. Supply chains can also be flexible, with raw materials or partially finished goods such as auto parts coming from multiple suppliers worldwide. The decision to source them from various suppliers could be made according to which supplier has the lowest cost of production, for example, or the fastest shipping time.

In recent years, the political currents on trade have been flowing in the opposite direction. The so-called Doha Round of talks, aimed at further lowering trade barriers, foundered over disputes about agricultural subsidies.[10] Growing voter discontent over jobs lost because of trade liberalization helped propel Trump into the White House, and he has lived up to his protectionist campaign rhetoric. Since taking office in 2017, he has pulled the United States out of an emerging trans-Pacific trade deal, demanded that Canada and Mexico renegotiate the North American Free Trade Agreement (NAFTA), slapped tariffs on steel and aluminum imports from the European Union, Mexico and Canada, and threatened to impose additional tariffs on Chinese-made products. The targets of these U.S. tariffs have retaliated in kind, or promised to do so.[11]

Trade Expanded in Past Two Decades

Global imports, 1996–2016

The overall direction of global trade volume has been upward over the past two decades, although it dipped in 2015–16.

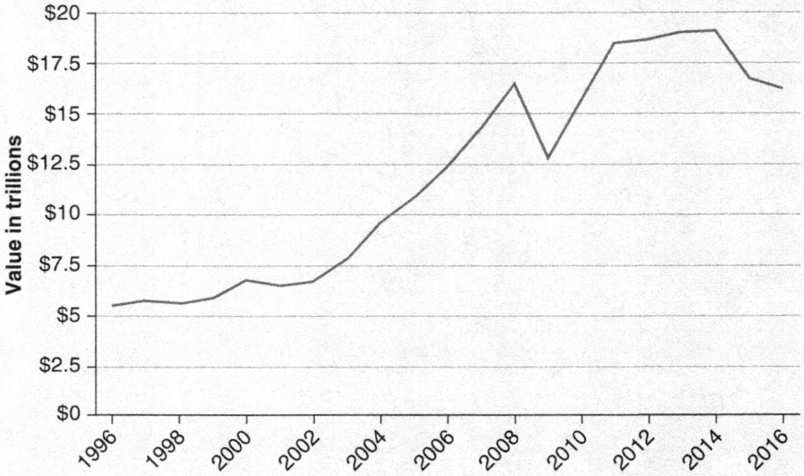

Source: "Trade and Tariffs: Trade Grows As Tariffs Decline," World Trade Organization, last updated Aug. 8, 2017, https://tinyurl.com/y8pu7d6q.

The dispute isolated Trump from the other six heads of state attending the Group of 7 summit of developed nations on June 8–9 in Charlevoix, Quebec, with the U.S. president ultimately disowning an agreement to sign a communique in which leaders agreed that all trade deals should be complementary to multilateral commitments to free and fair trade.[12]

Even before this backlash against free trade, the pace of geographical expansion of supply chains had slowed, as companies have finished the process of globalizing their processes or begun to consider priorities other than cost cutting. Participation in global supply chains has been flat since 2011, and in some situations has declined, according to World Bank data.[13] The numbers show the link between trade, productivity and global supply chains: World trade grew at an annual average of 7 percent from 1994 to 2008, then slowed to 3 percent from 2012 to 2016. Annual productivity growth was 2 percent in the same period, before the 2007–2009 financial crisis, and 1 percent after it.[14]

Before the onset of today's protectionism, the main risk of going global was complexity. Car makers, for example, decided to save on warehousing costs through just-in-time inventory management, in which parts are delivered precisely when needed. Ordering them from another country therefore required knowing what to expect in moving goods across borders. General Motors' Detroit/Hamtramck Assembly Plant, for example, would order one of more than 162 combinations of seats from a supplier just across the Detroit River in Windsor, Canada, and expect them to show up five hours later, when they needed to be installed.

This suddenly became almost impossible in the days and weeks after the Sep. 11, 2001, terrorist attacks, because heightened security at border crossings led to traffic jams miles long. The plant would have had to shut down temporarily were it not for customs officers and the privately owned Detroit-Windsor Truck Ferry working together with Cadillac to get its Canadian supplier's trucks across the river in time, according to a letter of thanks sent by the plant manager to U.S. Customs.

Supply-chain managers can adjust more readily to changing costs, in part because there are multiple factors built into the final price of the product.

The variables that ultimately determine costs come in three categories, says Steven Bowen, chairman and CEO of Maine Pointe, a global supply-chains and operations consultancy based in Boston: procurement, or buying the raw materials and semi-finished goods required; operations, which means labor and productivity factors; and, finally, logistics—shipping and storage. For most types of global supply chains, each of these categories holds opportunities to lower costs and offset the increased tax bills that could come from protectionist moves.

Currency exchange rates are an example of a common and manageable variable, according to research from the University of Wisconsin's Engel. His scholarship has shown that when foreign currencies rise against the U.S. dollar, multinationals have shifted the burden of higher costs to their suppliers in foreign countries, and that those suppliers have tended to absorb the loss rather than quit the larger company's supply chain.[15]

At the operations stage, rising labor costs often lead to supply-chain changes. For textiles producers, this is easy: "Just pack the sewing machines into a shipping container and move to the next place," says Shay Scott, a University of Tennessee business professor and the managing director of its Global Supply Chain Institute. For capital-intensive and technologically complex processes, this is harder to do and therefore less common. "Companies like Samsung have built multibillion-dollar wafer fabrication plants in Asia," Scott says. "Those aren't moving."

Supply chains can also be adjusted without moving operations, largely by pursuing productivity gains. In China in 2016, the price of apparel destined for the U.S. market fell by as much as 4.9 percent despite wages rising 6.3 percent.[16]

Supply chains can also be flexible in how they convert raw materials to finished goods. U.S. retailers in 2017 responded to protectionism by boosting geographical diversity in their purchasing patterns: Imports came from 150 countries during the year. The Herfindahl-Hirschman Index, which measures market concentration, fell from 0.17 in 2010 to 0.15 in 2017, indicating a greater diversity in supply.[17]

Supplier diversity is also useful in other economic sectors even if there is far less competition, such as in steel, a capital-intensive and complex manufacturing process. "There aren't a lot of U.S. firms that could ramp up production and meet the demand," economist Engel says. "For certain types you just have to buy it on the world market." That is what appears to have happened in April, when Chinese steel exports to the United States rose despite the Trump administration's application of a 25 percent import duty as of Mar. 23. The president also announced a 10 percent duty on imported aluminum, but imports of that metal from China also rose in April.[18]

But having a handful of overseas suppliers in different countries gives a company the option to adjust its mix to at least lower its tariff burden. "You want a few different buying options balanced across domestic and international suppliers," Bowen, the Maine Pointe CEO, says.

China, United States Are Top Global Traders

Top 10 merchandise exporters and importers, 2017

The United States and China are the world's leading importers and exporters of merchandise, with Germany a close third on exports.

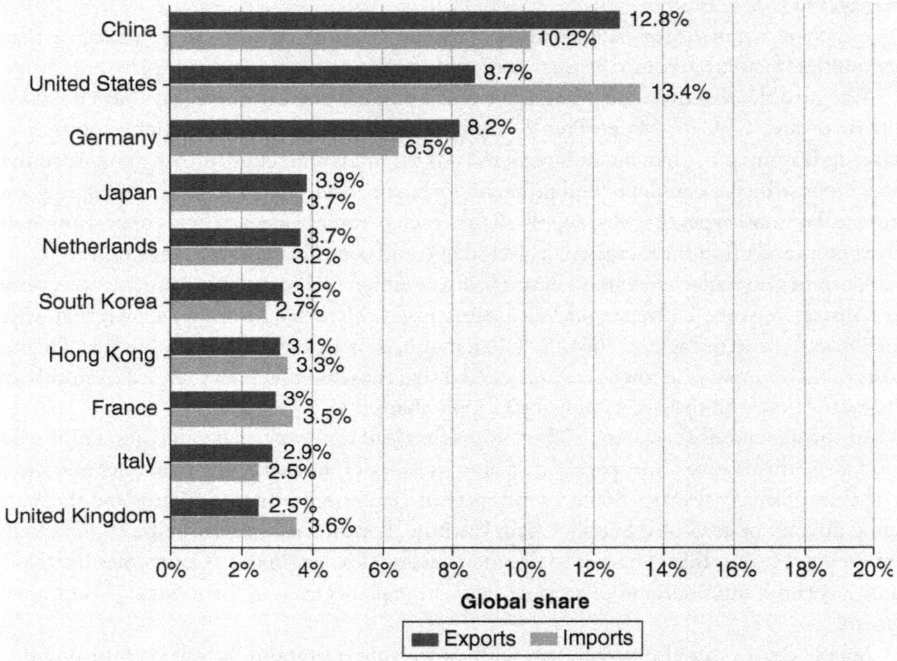

Source: "Strong Trade Growth in 2018 Rests on Policy Choices," Appendix Table 3, World Trade Organization, Apr. 12, 2018, https://tinyurl.com/ycjds4j4.

Steel could be an exception to the expectations of supply-chain resilience if protectionism is here to stay. According to Joseph Galimberti, president of the Canadian Steel Producers Association, producers have regional supply chains that would not be able to absorb higher costs. "We would have a hard time anticipating where domestic supply could increase fast enough to meet demand," he says.

Room for Price Increases

Passing along the costs to consumers is easier for companies that know their competitors are in the same situation, and that makes their supply chains more resilient for now. Car makers are a good example. "They are thinking about prices relative to their competitors, and there is a widespread expectation that everyone will do the same thing," Engel says. Economists say consumers can handle that, at least for now: "The economy is strong and nearing full employment," says Gary Hufbauer, a senior fellow at the Peterson Institute for International

Economics, a pro-trade think tank in Washington. "Wages are likely to rise, so there's room to pass some costs to consumers."

When the steel and aluminum tariffs were announced on Mar. 1, the Beer Institute, a U.S. trade association, suggested it would amount to a $347.7 million cost increase for aluminum cans, making it a tax on beer drinkers. But total amount looks different at the consumer's level. Cans cost about 10 cents to make, according The New York Times, so the average six-pack would rise in price by a maximum of 6 cents—an unlikely disincentive for beer drinkers.[19]

The same logic applies to Boeing, according to the securities analysts of investment banking firm J.P. Morgan. According to an investor note, aluminum can account for up to 70 percent of the weight of a plane, and materials account for about 30 percent of the cost of building it. Based on those figures, a 10 percent tariff would boost the cost of planes by less than 2 percent.[20]

At the third stage of supply-chain cost cutting, logistics, companies can lower costs with the right mix of transportation modes, Bowen says. In the United States there is a shortage of truck drivers, for example, which was estimated at 50,000 people at the end of 2017.[21] Trucks accounted for 71 percent of freight delivery in the United States as measured by weight, and driver salaries and benefits are rising to fill the gap.[22] Companies should use other modes of transport where possible, Bowen says. "If you can find a way to ship by container and then switch to rail, you can protect yourself from the driver shortage and lower your costs by using the roads just for local delivery," he says.

As companies respond to supply-chain cost variables in procurement, operations and logistics, economists and supply-chain specialists debate the long-term question: Can global supply chains stay resilient if protectionism is here to stay, or even develop further and trigger more growth and productivity gains? "Some people think supply chains have reached a natural limit, but it's more likely they've reached a political limit," Hufbauer says. The result could be more supply-chain decisions based on risk mitigation than on cost cutting or productivity gains.

For now, politics could certainly keep companies from investing in supply-chain reforms, because these are decisions with impacts measured in decades. "Why would a business invest tens or hundreds of millions of dollars into creating supply chain links in another country if there is a possibility it will have to pay tariffs on goods crossing the border with that country in a year or two?" wrote Mike Wilder, a vice president at Livingston International, a customs brokerage and trade-consulting firm.[23]

Another conclusion is that because companies invest based on a decades-long outlook, they are not likely to change their plans unless convinced that the current wave of protectionism will last beyond the current leadership pushing it. "Companies have long capital cycles. They're not thinking about investing $10 billion based on what's going to happen in the next few years," says Emily Sanchez, director of economics and data analytics for the American Chemistry Council, an industry trade group. "They're looking much farther down the line."

"Companies have long capital cycles. They're looking much farther down the line."

NAFTA Sunset Clause?

In its current negotiations with Canada and Mexico to revise NAFTA, the U.S. government is seeking a stipulation that could extend that sense of uncertainty and embed protectionism after the Trump administration: a clause that would allow each country to opt out every five years. If certainty about NAFTA's future is capped at five years, multinationals could decide to site North American operations in the United States just to be sure they won't lose access to that market, Wilder wrote, accepting higher costs and less competition in the process.[24] Canadian Prime Minister Justin Trudeau said he told U.S. Vice President Mike Pence that he would not agree to the opt-out clause and canceled a meeting with U.S. officials to discuss the NAFTA renegotiation.[25]

With location-based cost cutting more difficult for companies for multiple reasons, supply-chain executives could instead focus on other concerns. "Companies are starting to realize that having a very long global supply chain comes with more risks, and protectionism may be an extra shove back to a regional approach," Scott, the Tennessee professor, says. But Bowen says there is still room to cut costs at the logistics stage. James Bovenzi, a General Motors supply-chain executive, said at an automotive logistics conference in 2016 that GM is looking for new ideas in that area: "We spend as much on logistics as we do developing cars and trucks," he said.[26]

Scott thinks data organization and analysis is the next big evolution for supply chains. In a white paper on the topic, he and his colleagues recently cited IBM survey results on digitizing supply chains. The survey found that 87 percent of supply-chain executives said it is difficult to anticipate problems and that 80 percent of the data generated by those supply chains are not organized into databases for analysis.[27] Boeing in late 2017 said it had multiple divisions using their own unique tracking systems, rather than a harmonized system that can gather up data for faster and better decision making. It announced an overhaul of its supply chain, in part to improve how data are used to track supplies, spot problems, evaluate suppliers and determine what types of work should be outsourced.[28]

While companies are looking to such solutions to safeguard their supply chains against present-day threats and improve them by using new tools, what is clear at this point is that these systems still work and can be adjusted for market variables and political risks such as protectionism. As Boeing's share price recovery demonstrates, it appears that markets are gaining confidence in the companies, their global networks of suppliers and factories and their ability to adjust on the fly.

"It's a far reach to think there are going to be massive shifts in consumer pricing because of protectionism," Bowen says. "Just in some pockets here and there."

Chronology

1920–1950	**A protectionist period ends.**
1930	United States enacts the Tariff Act of 1930, commonly known as the Smoot-Hawley Tariff, in an effort to protect domestic manufacturers at the start of the Great Depression. Most economic historians now regard Smoot-Hawley as a counterproductive measure that worsened the Depression.
1934	Passage of the Reciprocal Trade Agreements Act begins a U.S. policy shift to trade liberalization.

1944	In the Bretton Woods Agreement, the United States and other nations negotiate a global monetary system to facilitate economic cooperation and avoid the harmful policy competition of previous decades. The new system features currency values set according to a country's gold reserves, creation of the International Monetary Fund as a lender of last resort for countries and the International Bank for Reconstruction and Development, which becomes the World Bank.
1947	Working through the United Nations, 23 countries accounting for 70 percent of global trade sign the General Agreement on Tariffs and Trade (GATT) to reduce trade barriers.
1980–2000	**A new era for world trade.**
1986	Global leaders gather in Punta Del Este, Uruguay, and agree on what would later be called the biggest reforms to global trade since the end of World War II. All 123 participating countries agree to implement a global trade system with lower tariffs and to create what would become the World Trade Organization (WTO), as a successor to GATT, to enforce the agreement and help resolve future disputes. GATT had addressed trade in goods; the WTO would expand global trade rules by covering services and intellectual property.
1994	The North American Free Trade Agreement (NAFTA) takes effect, eliminating tariffs and quotas among the United States, Canada and Mexico, with exemptions for some agricultural products. . . . World trade begins growing at an average rate of 7 percent a year, partly because open borders have made global supply chains easier and less costly to create. Productivity growth averages 2 percent per year.
1995	Uruguay Round trade negotiations wrap up and related reforms take effect, including beginning of operations of the WTO.
2001	China joins the WTO after 15 years of negotiations produce an agreement that requires Beijing to enact market reforms opening its economy to investment.
2011	Growth in participation in global supply chains declines and then levels off.
2012–Present	**Growth in world trade slows.**
2012–2016	As supply chains mature, the rate of growth in world trade slows to an average of 3 percent per year and productivity growth drops to 1 percent annually.
2017	President Trump withdraws the United States from the 12-country Trans-Pacific Partnership free-trade agreement. . . . U.S. Trade Representative Robert Lighthizer tells Congress the United States will formally seek renegotiation of NAFTA.
2018	Trump announces tariffs on steel (25 percent) and aluminum (10 percent) imported from Mexico, Canada, Japan, the European Union and other countries, angering U.S. allies. Mexico retaliates by imposing about $3 billion worth of tariffs on U.S. pork, steel, cheese and other goods (March). . . . Trump announces tariffs worth about $50 billion on Chinese imports, saying they are designed to protect U.S. companies from intellectual-property theft. China immediately responds by announcing $3 billion in tariffs on U.S. goods, including pork and steel pipes. (March

Discussion Questions

Here are some issues to discuss regarding global supply chains and the rise of protectionism:

- What conditions allowed global supply chains to develop and expand?
- What advantages do companies gain from participating in global supply chains?
- Why do experts believe these supply chains may be able to survive in an era of increased protectionism? How can they adapt to such an environment?
- What obstacles exist for expanding supply chains, apart from higher tariffs and other trade barriers?
- If you were starting a business in the current economic and political climate, would you source your products from a global supply chain, or from a more localized network of suppliers? What factors would go into your decision?

PERSPECTIVE

Q&A: Steven Bowen on Logistical Challenges

"START BY CONSIDERING ALL MODES OF TRANSPORTATION"

Steven Bowen

Steven Bowen is chairman and CEO of Maine Pointe, a supply-chains and business-operations consultancy. He spoke with *SAGE Business Researcher* freelance correspondent Matt Mossman about how companies can use logistics to improve global supply chains. This transcript has been edited for length and clarity.

What kinds of companies risk high logistics costs?

A lot of companies look at their freight cost as a ratio of product cost. A lot of products that have a high ratio are basic commodities, like salt, potash or coal, or chemicals like acids. Often, the cost to produce it is less than the cost of transporting it.

Beyond those basic commodities, you next have to think about how much air you are shipping. That means things that are light and have low value, like cereal. You can load a truck full of cereal boxes that might not weigh 10,000 pounds, but they're on a truck that could carry 50,000 pounds. That's not efficient.

Another thing we all consume lots of is water and soda. If you're shipping the empty bottles, you're basically paying to ship air. Bigger companies can blow up the plastic into bottles at the factory, but smaller specialty companies are often shipping the empty bottles.

How can companies improve their logistics?

The most common mistake is the mode of transportation a company chooses. They often default to thinking they must ship by truck. Maybe that's the way they have been doing it for 10 or 20 years, but it's possible they are missing out on opportunities.

What can companies do to address logistics costs?

They should start by considering all modes of transportation. There could be a railroad or another intermodal station [a transportation hub with more than one transit option available] close by. Companies at a higher level of maturity talk to their customers about the different ways they can receive the product. And they should ask their customers if they can hold more in inventory. If you're not worried about speed, you can save on transportation costs by holding a little bit more inventory.

President Trump has talked about the need to modernize American infrastructure. Can the government play a role in lowering logistics costs through investments in this area?

If you think our roads need investment, imagine what the railroads need. If you consider [that] the railroads are efficient compared to using barges on the rivers, then picture how things could improve with investments in locks and dams. There's a lot that could be done to speed up transportation, and time is money.

With trucking carrying most of the load now, and a driver shortage pushing up prices, what can be done?

Companies can no longer ship by trucks alone because demand is outstripping supply. The opportunity for railroads is tremendous, but they have been doing well in recent years by taking trains out of service and saving on their own costs. Driverless trucks are a technology we are hearing about, but we need it sooner rather than later.

UPDATE IN 2020

At its outset, the coronavirus pandemic turned into a nightmare for global supply chains.

Nations all over the world faced shortages of personal protection equipment (PPE), setting off a competition between countries to find scarce supplies.

Border closures wreaked havoc with just-in-time (JIT) inventory systems, in which manufacturers received goods just before they were needed on assembly lines. There were disruptions in the supply of groceries and paper goods, prompted in part by shoppers racing to stock up in advance of stay-at-home orders.

In April 2020, the United Nations launched the UN COVID-19 Supply Chain Task Force, coordinated by the World Health Organization and the World Food Programme. It oversaw the collective efforts of the World Bank, the UN Children's Fund, the UN's High Commissioner for Refugees and others.[29] "We're trying to bring some kind of order to a very fragmented, duplicative, and competitive procurement process," said Paul Molinaro, chief of the World Health Organization's Operations Support & Logistics.[30]

Meanwhile, COVID-19 accelerated several companies' move out of China, where the virus originated in late 2019. But this was only one factor.

A survey of 260 companies by Gartner Supply Chain Practice, a consulting firm, found that 33 percent had moved sourcing or manufacturing activities out of China or planned to do so within two to three years.[31] "Global supply chains were being disrupted long before COVID-19 emerged," said Kamal Rman, senior director analyst with Gartner.

In 2018 and 2019, the trade war between the U.S. and China made supply chain officials aware of the potential weakness of locating operations in China, he said. Gartner's survey found that more than 40 percent of organizations had supply chain costs go up by 10 percent or more.

As a result, manufacturers were looking at shifting sources to Mexico, Vietnam and India.

In Canada, Prime Minister Justin Trudeau pushed to find new sources of PPE beyond the U.S. and China, and said he wanted the nation to rely on Canadian manufacturers as much as possible going forward. (Indeed, Canadian sources were supplying nearly 50 percent of PPE by September 2020, as opposed to a low 0.2 percent back in March.)[32]

In a research report, Barclay's predicted the pandemic would lead to less focus on globalization and the use of JIT inventory systems, less reliance on travel and hypermobility, and a demand for greener policies.

"Health fears over close human contact and global travel, combined with concerns about the secure supply of essential goods and services, are likely to change the way people, businesses and economies behave," the report stated.[33]

—*Micheline Maynard*

16 THE BORDER ECONOMY

Will redrawing NAFTA disrupt Mexican-U.S. ties?

Julie Morse

From *SAGE Business Researcher*, May 29, 2017

EXECUTIVE SUMMARY

President Trump's bid to renegotiate the North American Free Trade Agreement (NAFTA) may have a pronounced impact on the strong economic relationship between Mexico and the United States that has developed in the 23 years since the accord took effect. During this time, U.S. trade with Mexico has increased more than 500 percent as tariffs and other restrictions disappeared. The relationship is especially close in cities along the U.S.-Mexican border, such as El Paso, Texas, and Ciudad Juarez just across the Rio Grande. These binational links are so strong that many experts say they can survive a redrawing of the trade agreement.

Among the key takeaways:

- While U.S. exports to Mexico have more than tripled under NAFTA, the U.S. trade balance with that country has swung from a $1.6 billion surplus to a $63.2 billion deficit.
- A substantial wage gap persists; the average wage in the United States is more than three times greater than in Mexico.
- Trump has moved from threatening to withdraw from NAFTA to calling for a renegotiation of the accord, which encompasses Canada as well as the United States and Mexico.

OVERVIEW

Miguel Fernandez believes he has glimpsed the economic future along the U.S.-Mexican border, and it is a bright one—regardless of the rhetoric emanating from Washington.

Telecom executive Fernandez has created a seed investment fund called Saba that has attracted more than 50 investors who are committed to grow the tech sector in border states. Saba looks for emerging startups that utilize both countries to develop resources, and Fernandez says there is plenty of fertile ground to be plowed, especially along the Texas-Mexico border.

"El Paso and Ciudad Juarez are really just one big city," says Fernandez, chief executive officer of Transtelco, a company based in both cities that facilitates internet exchanges between the two countries. Fernandez says he sees "big opportunities for companies to develop projects on either side of these two nations."

Ivan Pierre Aguirre for The Washington Post via Getty ImagesKitwood/Getty Images

This MFI International plant in El Paso produces fabric that is then sewn into mattress covers across the Mexican-U.S. border in Ciudad Juarez.

Fernandez remains upbeat despite the pall of uncertainty created by President Trump over the future of the North American Free Trade Agreement (NAFTA) that links Mexico, Canada and the United States. Trump last month called for a renegotiation of NAFTA, after hinting that he would unilaterally withdraw from the accord.[1] No one knows for sure how this will affect the open U.S.-Mexican market that has developed to both countries' benefit in the 23 years since the trade deal took effect.

The agreement eliminated tariffs on nearly all products exchanged among the United States, Mexico and Canada, creating the world's biggest freetrade arena. As a result, the United States and Mexico now share, in addition to a 2,000-mile border, extensive commercial production.[2] "We're not just selling things to each other; now we're producing things jointly," Jaime Serra Puche, Mexico's chief negotiator on the trade deal, said in 2014.[3]

NAFTA created a $1.1 trillion market among the three countries. It also imposed higher standards for protection of patents, trademarks and copyrights, and eliminated import substitution rules, local sourcing standards and other requirements. The United States has become the largest source of Mexico's foreign direct investment (FDI). U.S. FDI in Mexico rose from $17 billion in 1994, the year NAFTA took effect, to $92.8 billion in 2015.[4]

Before NAFTA, the average tariff for goods coming into the United States from Mexico was around 19 percent. Mexico, in turn, required import licenses for 230 products imported from the United States, which included about 60 percent of U.S. agricultural imports. Tariffs were gradually removed under NAFTA, and the impact was almost immediate: From 1994 to 1996, exports went from representing 12 percent of Mexico's gross domestic product to 24 percent.[5]

Since the agreement was enacted, U.S. trade with Mexico has increased more than 500 percent, from $88 billion in 1993 to $531 billion in 2015.[6] U.S. exports to Mexico have shot up from $68 billion in 1994 to $235 billion in 2016. A 2011 report by a Dutch research organization found that Mexican industries purchased $140 billion in U.S. products that year, and U.S. industries acquired $111 billion in Mexican goods.[7]

While trade has grown, its balance has changed. The year before NAFTA took effect, the United States had a $1.6 billion trade goods surplus with Mexico. That changed to a $15.8 billion deficit in 1995. The deficit peaked at $74.8 billion in 2007 and was $63.2 billion last year.[8]

This increased trade has not eliminated a substantial wage gap between the two countries. According to the Organisation for Economic Co-operation and Development (OECD), in 2014 the average wage was $12,850 in Mexico and $57,139 in the United States.[9] That was the case even though Mexicans that year worked an average of 2,246 hours, the highest of all 34 OECD countries, while the U.S. average was 1,790 hours.[10]

"The wage disparity is by far the biggest incentive for companies to come down" to Mexico, says Laura Carlsen, director of the Americas Program at the Center for International Policy, a Washington-based global-relations think tank. "The pay for jobs is a little better than what is paid in the national economy, but there's a tremendous amount of abuse that takes place as well. The payment that people receive is still barely at or slightly below a living wage, or what we would refer to as a living wage, and there tends to be no upward mobility."

In fact, income inequality in Mexico has become a pervasive issue since NAFTA took effect. Taking inflation into account, the minimum wage in Mexico actually fell 26.3 percent between 1994 and 2012, according to a 2014 study by the Center for Economic and Policy Research, a Washington think tank.[11] The national poverty rate showed no change over that period. Per capita GDP increased just 18.6 percent between 1994 and 2014, after almost doubling between 1960 and 1980, the study found.[12]

Despite these problems, Mexico has become "a middle-class society," and a primary reason is the "elimination of barriers to investment and commerce" as a result of NAFTA, according to a 2012 study done for the Woodrow Wilson International Center for Scholars by Mexican economists Luis de la Calle and Luis Rubio.[13]

Somewhat perversely, NAFTA may have helped expand the ranks of Mexico's superwealthy because of what the agreement didn't cover—specifically, telecommunications.[14] In hindsight, this was a mistake, says de la Calle, who helped negotiate the accord.[15]

For example, Mexico's richest man, telecom mogul Carlos Slim, owes much of his success to this aspect of NAFTA.[16] His fortune grew from $6.6 billion in 1994 to more than $62 billion today.[17] His companies control 70 percent of cell service and 80 percent of landlines in Mexico.[18]

Slim seems largely unperturbed by Trump's move to renegotiate NAFTA. "Trump is not Terminator. He is a negotiator," Slim said at a news conference in January.[19] Slim's equanimity could be due to the fact that if NAFTA is revised, broadband isn't likely to be integrated, says Fernandez, the Transtelco CEO.

Fernandez's company straddles the border and facilitates the exchange of internet between the two countries. The United States serves as the major hub for Latin America internet connectivity. Mexico City is the third-biggest consumer of bandwidth in the region, after Buenos Aires and São Paolo. Mexico is the second top international internet route in Latin America, and most of the country's connectivity is generated by a hub in Dallas. That means Mexico's estimated $35 billion telecommunication industry wouldn't be able to function without its connection to the United States.[20]

The internet is just one of many integral resources and services that the United States and Mexico share. Mexico sends about 80 percent of its export products to the United States and receives 47 percent of the U.S.'s imports.[21] There is a great deal of collaboration that goes into creating products. In fact, 40 percent of the content of goods shipped from Mexico to the United States contain content that originated in the U.S.[22]

For example, automotive assembly involves shipping parts back and forth across the border. NAFTA eliminates any tariffs on car imports from Mexico, allowing Mexico to be the largest export market of auto parts for the United States.[23] The automobile industry has become a massive facet of the binational economy. For example, there was $89.6 billion in automobile and auto parts imports from Mexico to the United States in the first 10 months of 2016.[24]

Marina v. N. Whitman, a former General Motors executive who is now a business administration and public policy professor at the University of Michigan, remembers the implementation of NAFTA as an exciting moment for the company.

"General Motors very much savored tying together the North American product market," she says. "We were already integrated with Canada, because there was a U.S.-Canadian auto agreement that preceded NAFTA. The notion of extending it to Mexico and having an integrated market was clearly very attractive, because it could increase the efficiency and competitiveness of North American production. The production of relatively low-value parts which could be produced by low-skill people moved to Mexico in a big way, and that of course enabled U.S. companies to be much more competitive."

Trump has criticized GM and other U.S. carmakers for producing vehicles in Mexico and shipping them northward. In January, General Motors announced it would move 7,000 jobs to the United States and invest $1 billion in its U.S. factories.[25] However, the company said it doesn't plan on decreasing its presence in Mexico. Ford has said it is going ahead with plans to expand two Mexican plants, investing $2.5 billion and hiring 3,800 workers.[26]

The Mexican presence in U.S. commerce extends well beyond the auto industry:

- Constellation Brands, the third largest U.S. beer producer, has manufacturing facilities in Coahuila.[27] Constellation markets Mexican brands Corona Extra and Modelo Especial, the two top-selling international beers in the U.S. in 2016.[28]
- Cemex, the Mexican cement company, has nearly 400 plants and 77 aggregate quarries in the U.S.[29] According to the Financial Times, Trump's call for a border wall, along with a weakened peso, helped push Cemex's share price to its highest level since 2009.[30]
- The Mexican conglomerate Grupo Bimbo owns many popular U.S.-based bread and pastry brands, such as Thomas English Muffins, Sara Lee and Mrs. Baird's.
- U.S. companies occupy a prominent place in Mexico's pharmaceutical industry. Johnson & Johnson, Pfizer and Gilead have manufacturing facilities there. Some 37.3 percent of medicines made in the United States are shipped to Mexico and 59.7 percent of pharmaceuticals manufactured in Mexico are sent north to the United States.[31]
- The U.S. firearm industry registered $127.2 million in sales to Mexico between 2010 and 2012, according to a study by the University of San Diego's Trans-Border Institute.[32] In 2015, the New Hampshire-based firearms manufacturer Sig Sauer, Inc. sold rifles and pistols to the Mexican military and police forces worth about $266 million.[33]

The Texas-Mexico border is the epicenter of this binational economy. Some companies have operated on both sides of the Rio Grande for many years. SEISA, a medical device company founded in 1984, is headquartered in Ciudad Juarez and takes care of assembling and shipping in El Paso. Tecma, started in 1985, provides services to companies that want to establish manufacturing facilities in Mexico; it has operations in El Paso, San Diego, Tijuana, Coahuila and Juarez.

Binational funding organizations such as the Hub of Human Innovation, an incubator for growing tech businesses, and the Medical Center of the Americas Foundation, a center for biomedical research and health care education along the border, help support the growth of tech startups in the area. According to Joe Wardy, the Hub of Human Innovation's CEO, 20 percent of the Hub's members are creating projects that involve leveraging resources and labor in both countries, and that figure is around 30 percent for prospective members.

U.S. Trade Deficit with Mexico Grows

Balance turned negative after NAFTA implemented

The U.S. trade deficit with Mexico, which was $63.2 billion in 2016, has trended upwards in most years following implementation of the North American Free Trade Agreement in 1994. And the deficit for the first three months of 2017 was higher than in the comparable period in 2016, signaling a continuation of the increase in the past three years.

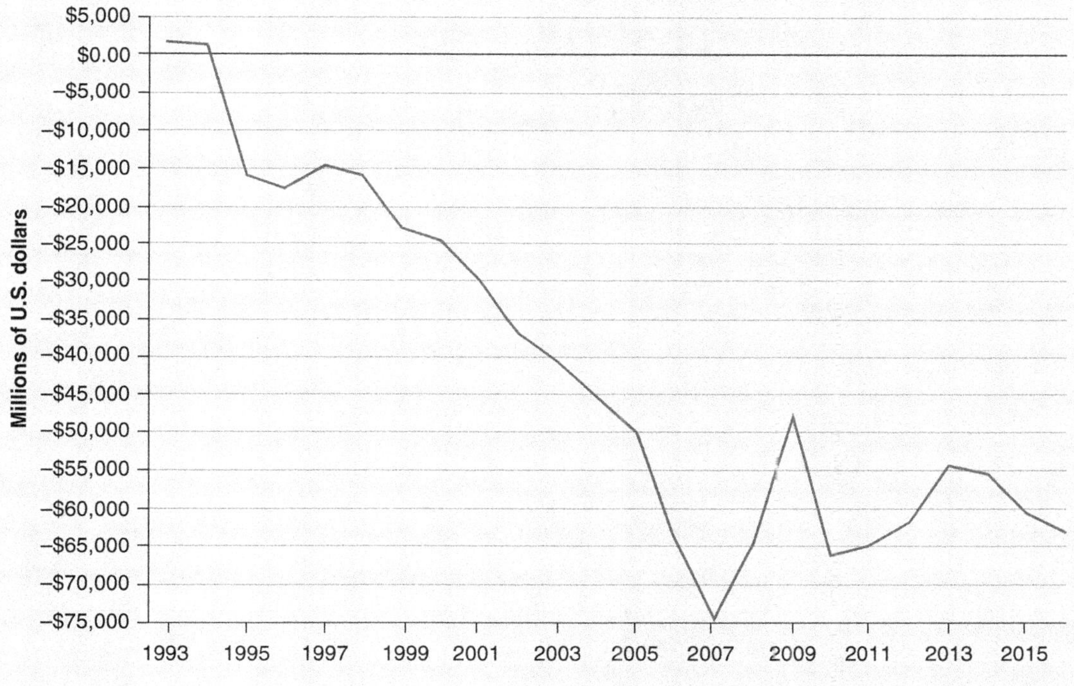

Source: "Trade in Goods with Mexico," United States Census Bureau, http://tinyurl.com/lzzv67q.

Ricardo Mora, the founder of Technology Hub, a business accelerator and startup incubator based in Ciudad Juarez that collaborates with the Hub of Human Innovation, calls his city a "place that has never been mined before for entrepreneurship and innovation." He says that since 2014 he's noticed a technology network develop on both sides of the border, complete with venture funds, co-working spaces and incubator resources.

This interest in developing binational business operations continues to grow, despite Trump's determination to create distance between the two countries. Fernandez says that until March, he noticed investors holding back on project decisions in Mexico. When the administration's first attempt to repeal and replace the Affordable Care Act failed in Congress, investors took it as a sign that Trump would struggle to enact his policy agenda, and therefore confidence levels to invest in the region have risen, he said.

Mexican Beer Brands Dominate U.S. Import Sales

Corona Extra, Modelo Especial are top sellers

Two Mexican beer brands, Corona Extra and Modelo Especial, had the highest sales of any imported brand in the United States in 2016. Each company brought in more than $1 billion in U.S. sales that year.

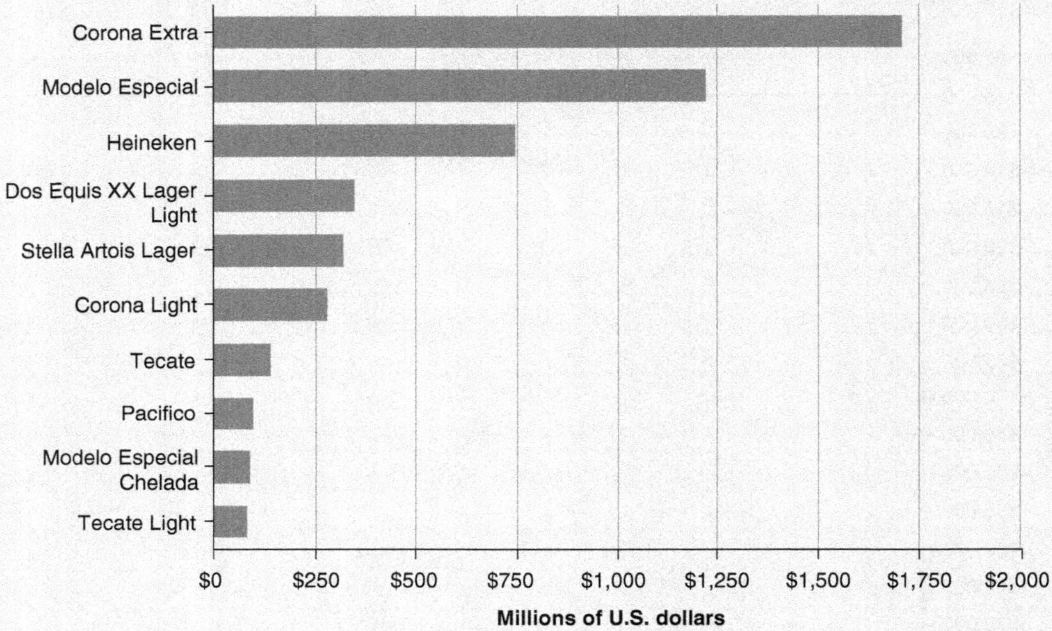

Source: "Sales of the Leading Imported Beer Brands of the United States in 2016 (in Million U.S. Dollars)," Statista, 2016, http://tinyurl.com/kcmub4s.

Since the Trump administration announced in early April that it will implement more stringent vetting measures for companies requesting H-1B visas for highly skilled employees, multinational tech companies are considering increasing their workforce in Mexico.[34] According to the Financial Times, the Indian IT firm Tech Mahindra says it will double its staff in Mexico City and Querétaro if U.S. H-1B regulations become more challenging.

However, Trump's attitude toward Mexico might be hurting other sectors. According to Transtelco Vice President of Sales and Development Alejandro Guzmán, small, family-owned manufacturing companies based in the Midwest are reluctant to invest in Mexican plants until they can confidently gage Trump's intentions for the industry. "My perspective is that those small manufacturing companies are the ones that are going to hold their final decision until they know what's going to happen," Guzmán says.

Mexican officials say they are ready to engage with Trump. "Mexico is ready to renegotiate NAFTA and we have extraordinary trade negotiators who are ready with a clear vision of what we want," Mexican Foreign Affairs Secretary Luis Videgaray said on April 19.[35]

Chronology

1930s–1993	**Nationalism gives way to NAFTA.**
1930s	Mexico establishes an import substitution policy that implements rigid restrictions on foreign investment.
1982	Mexico's debt crisis is ignited when the government can't pay back its $80 billion debt to U.S. banks and creditors. Mexico responds to the crisis by deciding to begin to open its markets through trade liberalization.
1987	Canada and the United States sign a bilateral freetrade agreement.
1992	The United States, Mexico, and Canada sign the North American Free Trade Agreement (NAFTA). Mexico hopes the agreement will help stabilize its economy and help it recover from the debt crisis.
1993	President Bill Clinton signs NAFTA into law after the U.S. Congress approves it.
1998–Present	**NAFTA is implemented, Trump calls for changes.**
1998	Tariffs on goods sold and delivered between the United States and Canada are eliminated, per the Canada-U.S. free trade agreement.
2003	Following a rolling timetable set forth in NAFTA, tariffs on all goods exchanged between the U.S. and Mexico are lifted except for some agriculture products.
2008	All remaining tariffs on agricultural goods are eliminated.
2013	U.S. President Barack Obama and Mexican President Enrique Peña Nieto establish the High Level Economic Dialogue (HLED), co-chaired by Vice President Joe Biden and Mexico's Secretary of Finance and Public Credit, Luis Videgaray, that aims to find ways to enhance the binational economy.
2016	Donald Trump runs for president on a platform of renegotiating or terminating NAFTA and threatens to impose a 35 percent tax on Ford cars that are built in Mexico and sold in the United States. The peso takes its deepest plunge in 20 years when Trump is elected.
2017	Trump calls for renegotiating NAFTA after first hinting that he might unilaterally withdraw the United States from it.

Discussion Questions

Here are some questions to discuss regarding U.S.-Mexican economic links:

- Which country has benefited the most under the North American Free Trade Agreement?
- Do you agree with President Trump's reasons for renegotiating the trade deal? Why or why not?
- Which industries and businesses have been most affected by the elimination of trade barriers under the accord?
- Why have the ranks of Mexico's super-wealthy expanded during the life of the trade agreement?

UPDATE IN 2020

In November 2018, the leaders of Canada, Mexico and the United States signed a new trade agreement to replace the North American Free Trade Agreement. Although it had a new name—the U.S.-Mexico-Canada Agreement (USMCA)—it was informally called NAFTA 2.0.[36]

The new agreement had been a signature campaign pledge for U.S. President Donald Trump, who had repeatedly criticized NAFTA as "the worst trade deal ever made."

Highlights of the USMCA included a provision that said automobiles produced in any of the three countries had to contain 75 percent North American components to be free of tariffs, up from the original 62.5 percent.[37] Moreover, 40 percent to 45 percent of auto parts had to be produced by workers earning at least $16 an hour by 2023.

There were also provisions meant to give U.S. dairy farmers greater access to the Canadian market, and an extension of copyright protections.

Although there were proposals to limit USMCA to just five years, Canada successfully argued in favor of a 16-year time frame, with a review of the treaty after six years.

Critics weren't happy with the minimum-wage requirements, however, saying that they resulted in government-managed trade.[38]

In June 2019, Mexico became the first country to ratify the deal. But congressional Democrats, who took control of the U.S. House after the original agreement was reached, insisted on stronger provisions to protect labor unions and the environment.

They formed a task force to negotiate with the Trump administration. In December 2019, the two sides reached agreement on a key provision called a rapid-response mechanism. It provided for a three-person panel to make sure that Mexico abides by union rules.

Congress subsequently approved the revised edition, and it was ratified by Canada in March 2020. Trump signed it on Jan. 29, 2020, and the agreement went into effect on Jul. 1, 2020.[39]

In the meantime, North America wrestled with the impact of the coronavirus pandemic. Instead of seeing an immediate wave of investments by large and small companies in Mexico, several firms announced job cuts because of the drop in consumer demand.

However, Stanley Black and Decker announced plans for a new $40 million manufacturing plant near Monterrey, around 140 miles south of Laredo, Tex. Karen Barraza, who will manage the new plant, said the site was chosen because of its proximity to the United States and the ease of serving customers there and in Canada.[40]

But with the Canadian border closed to all but essential travel since March 2020, economic activity between the U.S. and Canada slid, and Canada's GDP was projected to fall by 7 percent in 2020.[41]

Still, despite his frequent criticism of Mexico, including the building of part of a border wall promised during the 2016 campaign, Trump maintained the relationship with Mexico had "never been closer."[42]

—Micheline Maynard

17 THE ON-DEMAND ECONOMY

Will legacy businesses catch up with agile competitors?

Heather Kerrigan

From *SAGE Business Researcher*, January 8, 2018

EXECUTIVE SUMMARY

The on-demand economy—a digital marketplace offering immediate access to goods and services often delivered by contract, or gig, workers—continues to grow and to expand into new industries. The emergence of on-demand services, particularly in the transportation, retail, lodging, dining and grocery businesses, is built on mobile technologies that are especially attractive to middle-income Millennials. The sector's future is clouded, however, as some on-demand companies battle state and federal regulators and lawsuits. The ability of businesses to remain viable in the competitive, fast-paced world of the on-demand economy appears to rest on whether startups can compete against—or partner with—large, established corporations to secure and expand their customer base, attract investors and work with policymakers to develop supportive regulatory structures.

Some key takeaways:

- The rise of the on-demand economy is changing consumer habits, supply chains, regulations, competition and investment.
- Traditional businesses are grappling with how to respond to shifting consumer expectations and searching for ways to improve their supply chains to deliver goods and services more quickly.
- The on-demand economy's future may include drones or robots handling deliveries and consumers receiving goods even before they realize they need them, based on their buying history.

OVERVIEW

If any company typifies the legacy economy, it would be General Motors, the century-old automaker that once reigned supreme in Detroit and still outsells all U.S. rivals.

Yet GM's current leaders are positioning the company to survive in an on-demand economy dominated by consumers who expect rapid satisfaction of their desires. GM owns 9 percent of ride-sharing service Lyft, is talking with Uber about partnering on autonomous vehicles and has started a subscription service that delivers a Cadillac on request and lets users exchange it up to 18 times a year.[1]

Frazer Harrison/Getty Images for Airbnb

Jeremiah Owyang of Catalyst Companies discusses the on-demand economy at a 2016 event. He says change is so rapid that one-day delivery may soon be outdated.

GM is hardly alone in traveling this path. Companies of all sizes are adapting—or building from scratch—production and delivery models to meet consumer demand as close to the point of consumption as possible, which lowers inventory and cost and improves cash flow. This change in mindset and associated explosion in the on-demand economy—a digital marketplace of businesses seeking to improve the customer experience by offering immediate access to goods and services—has led to hundreds of new startups looking to upset traditional business models.

While established corporations are playing catch-up, those startups are not focused on the here and now. Instead, adapting to an ever-changing market is causing businesses to think big. Soon, says Jeremiah Owyang, founder of Catalyst Companies, an innovation council of large companies seeking new business models for the on-demand economy, "shopping carts and one-day delivery will be an anachronism. The modern retailer will deliver goods to a consumer's house or home before they even need it," based on their past purchasing patterns.

While the on-demand sector is still a relatively small part of the total U.S. economy, it has high growth potential, according to Charles Colby and Kelly Bell of Rockbridge Associates, a market research firm in suburban Washington.[2] And as consumer expectations continue to evolve, new and existing companies are stepping up to meet the need. But consumers' growing ability to immediately access goods and services, specifically those delivered by contract workers, invites a number of unanswered questions about how businesses will survive in this new environment and how regulators will respond to the monumental shift in traditional lines of service.

(Terms such as the sharing and gig economy are sometimes used interchangeably with on-demand. The sharing economy relates to digital platforms that facilitate the exchange of material assets between individuals, while the gig economy is the labor market of contract workers. Gig economy members often provide services in the on-demand economy, and some sharing-economy companies also are considered a part of the on-demand economy.)

The On-Demand Evolution

Two factors, in particular, have powered the on-demand economy in the past decade: consumer desire for time-saving ways to procure goods and services, particularly those that are curated and personalized, and innovations in digital app-based matching technology and electronic payment methods.

This economy is shifting power away from businesses large and small and giving it to consumers, who now expect to receive what they want, when they want it. No longer does the consumer need to rely on traditional supply chains or broken business models. They can instead look to each other—and their smartphones—to fulfill virtually any need.

"The change going on today . . . feels like 1995 when the internet first began to transfer from seller to buyer the greatest source of power since the dawn of time: information," said Alan Amling, vice president of global logistics and marketing at UPS, in a 2015 TED talk.[3]

"Information, the birth of the information superhighway, has changed our lives," Amling said. "Think about how it's changed your purchasing habits. It used to be that it was the car dealer and the retailer with their point-of-sale information that controlled all the cards. Now you're in the driver's seat."

"[T]he birth of the information superhighway has changed our lives." —Alan Amling/UPS

The result of this ongoing "rising expectation of consumers," he said, is a collision with "industrial-age manufacturing and transportation practices. As a result, rules are beginning to change. And when rules change, the impossible becomes possible."[4]

This emerging expectation of instant access has allowed companies such as home-sharing service Airbnb, ride-sharers Uber and Lyft, used-goods marketplace Yerdle Recommerce and food services Grubhub, HelloFresh and Instacart to quickly build brand loyalty and reduce consumer dependence on traditional corporations and slower lines of service. The expansion of the on-demand economy has introduced niche and luxury goods to a broader market, according to high-end automaker Porsche.[5] It also reaches underserved regions, such as city neighborhoods lacking fresh produce.

Consider the numbers that dramatize the on-demand economy's growth:

- More than 280 companies now provide on-demand goods and services across 16 industries, up from 76 companies in six industries offering such services in 2014.[6]
- More than 22 million Americans are spending nearly $58 billion per year in the on-demand economy. This spending is not limited to the highest income earners: 46 percent of on-demand consumers have an annual household income below $50,000.[7]
- An estimated one-third of the American workforce is engaged in contract or on-demand work.[8]
- Fueling the growth of the on-demand market is e-commerce, which also is expanding. By 2020, global e-commerce spending will total $4 trillion, or 14.6 percent of all consumer spending, up from an estimated $2 trillion in 2016.[9]
- By the end of 2017, more than 2 billion people worldwide were using their mobile devices to make a purchase.[10]
- In the United States, approximately 27 percent of all dollars spent in retail e-commerce transactions will be done via mobile devices by the end of 2018.[11]

Despite its rapid rise and the significant investments made, some warn the on-demand economy is a bubble waiting to burst. In an article for Quartz Media, entrepreneur/writer Sunil Rajaraman argued that on-demand consumers lack brand loyalty and make infrequent purchases, and that on-demand businesses have "precarious business models."[12]

Another skeptic, Howard Hartenbaum, general partner at Silicon Valley venture capital firm August Capital, said on-demand companies that cannot attract enough venture capital will not be able to hold a customer base because "mainstream customers are not willing to bear the cost for most on-demand services."[13] New York Times business columnist Farhad Manjoo agreed, saying that the inability of new startups to find a profitable long-term pricing model has led to "the end of the on-demand dream."[14]

Millennials Dominate On-Demand Market

On-demand consumers by age group

Millennials make up the largest generational slice of on-demand consumers, at 49 percent, followed by Generation-Xers at 29 percent and Baby Boomers at 22 percent, according to the 2015 National Technology Readiness Survey.

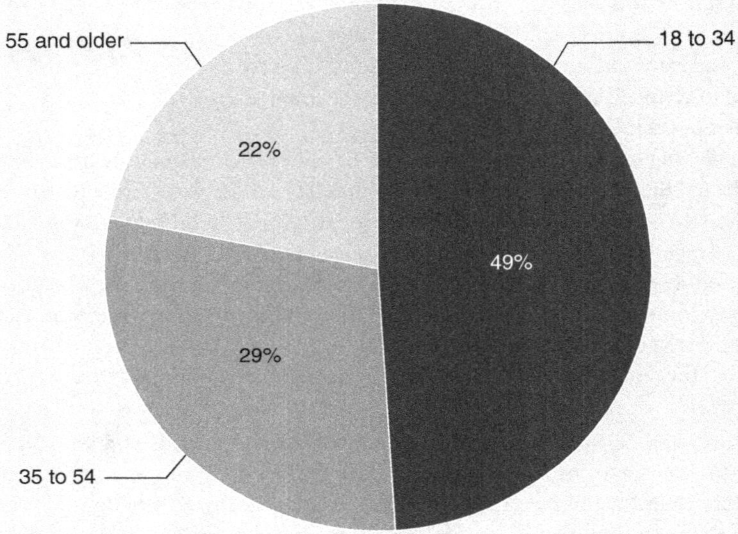

Source: Charles Colby and Kelly Bell, "The On-Demand Economy Is Growing, and Not Just for the Young and Wealthy," Harvard Business Review, Apr. 14, 2016, https://tinyurl.com/h9v4bqr.

London-based Edison Investment Research believes that costly labor in the markets where on-demand companies pop up also has a negative impact. "The initial phase of hype and euphoria is properly over and the shake-out has already begun," wrote Richard Windsor, an Edison analyst in a recent report. "Only the strongest with the most money are likely to survive and will do so by buying up the competition or waiting for them to wither on their own. For the rest, the unicorn disguises are already slipping, revealing the true colours of the donkeys underneath."[15]

Nonetheless, many middle-class consumers continue to flock to the on-demand economy, attracted partly by the ability to find deals quickly or to compare prices; but the growth also is closely linked to age, according to Nathan Resnick, CEO of Sourcify, an online manufacturing marketplace.[16] Millennials—now the nation's largest generation—are the driving force behind market growth and, as digital natives, are more likely to look to their social networks or individual, non-mainstream producers for a product or service they need.[17]

According to the University of Maryland's National Technology Readiness Survey, 49 percent of customers who purchase on-demand goods and services are ages 18 to 34, while 29 percent are between the ages of 35 and 54.[18] Analysts say Millennials will likely continue to be the catalyst for change in the economy.

The on-demand economy's focus on *fast* has left companies beholden to consumer "micro-moments" in which a shopper thinks of a need and then immediately tries to fulfill it as quickly as possible, typically through a digital transaction. According to Google, those using a smartphone are 50 percent more likely to expect to be able to purchase something in real time.[19] Google mobile searches for the term "same-day shipping" grew 120 percent from 2015 to 2017, while searches for phrases like "flights today" and "hotels tonight" have grown 150 percent.[20]

It is often here where traditional businesses struggle to fulfill customer needs, especially when they have a more conventional supply chain that is based on producing a high quantity of the same thing and then transporting these products through a network built to consolidate thousands of orders. Such a supply chain is "misaligned with the new retail formats that continue to be invented," wrote Karl Siebrecht, CEO of online warehouse marketplace Flexe. "Customers today have a taste for fast, low-cost delivery and there's no going back. It's no longer optional, but essential, to cater to the on-demand expectations of the modern economy."[21]

To compete in an on-demand world, Siebrecht argued that companies need to do a better job of forecasting customer demand, rethink distribution and use the vast amounts of customer data that can be collected in the e-commerce world to customize consumer experience. According to industry analyst Brian Solis, this is difficult because you have companies with "people who don't want to change and are clinging to the way things are and they're getting in their own way."

Effectively using consumer data is key for a company that wants to become less linear and more nimble. Traditional companies that are working to find their place in the on-demand world are looking to retail giant Amazon, which has revolutionized the customer experience, especially in its delivery concept. Amazon has partnered with major shipping companies and leases jets to get its packages where they need to be quickly and is offering two-day and, in some metropolitan areas, one-hour delivery. Fast, efficient shipping has been made possible by a huge warehousing network with products stocked in locations where they are most frequently purchased, based on customer data.

Similarly, Zara, a clothing store based in Europe, revolutionized its supply chain more than three decades ago by relying on consumer data to track preferences and trends, and then provided its producers with limited fabric options to increase the speed at which on-trend clothes hit stores.[22] Zara is able to put new clothes into its stores within 15 days, instead of the industry average six months.[23]

Challenges to Continued Growth and Sustainability

The growth of the on-demand economy has not been free of obstacles. A number of companies have faced lawsuits, tightening regulations or consolidation. "There have been layoffs, shuttered companies, dwindling funding for [venture capital]-backed startups, and a sobering realization among founders that they need to push for profitability to survive," wrote tech journalist Maya Kosoff for Vanity Fair.[24]

Others have closed because they lack the capital or customer base to stay afloat. For example, Homejoy, a housecleaning service, shuttered after five years because of legal battles with independent contractors and customers who were unhappy with inconsistent cleaning quality. Only 15 percent to 20 percent of customers booked a second visit with Homejoy within a month, according to former employees interviewed by Forbes.[25]

BlackJet, the Uber for the jet set, lasted less than four years before the high cost of its private jets and inconvenient scheduling led customers to abandon it. The company closed in

2016.[26] Take Eat Easy and Ordr.in (later OrdrX) raised enough capital to last a few years, but were ultimately pushed aside by other restaurant delivery apps.[27] Similarly, Tripda, SideCar and RideJoy could not compete with Uber and Lyft and failed to secure adequate funding.[28]

Others, like Vatler and Zirx, both valet companies, ran up against regulators and traditional companies, and without the resources of larger on-demand companies, were shuttered.[29] These examples indicate that to attract customers and investors, startups must deliver value and have a specific draw to differentiate themselves in already flooded markets. "A lot of these companies will be in trouble that haven't built a pathway to profitability," Matt Wong, a senior analyst at CB Insights, a venture capital research firm, told CNET.[30] It remains to be seen whether startups entering the market today can succeed in niche markets where customer demand is evolving, or whether regulatory hurdles and increased competition from larger rivals will lead to their demise.

Government at every level is grappling with the rise of on-demand companies and how to treat them. Many on-demand companies do not collect state and local sales and use taxes, arguing in many cases that they are simply digital platforms connecting users to individual service providers and should therefore not be liable for tax collection. In other instances, regulators are questioning employment practices such as companies labeling their workers as contractors who do not become eligible for health insurance or other benefits.

To make itself more palatable to local taxing authorities, Airbnb, for example, offers to collect sales taxes typically applied to traditional hotel lodging. As of December 2017, the company estimated that it was collecting state or local taxes in 38 states and Washington, D.C.[31]

Companies such as Uber and Lyft, in contrast, argue that their transportation services do not fall under the taxing jurisdiction of areas in which they operate because the legislation as written does not apply to them. Less than a dozen states currently apply gross or sales taxes to taxi or other similar hired rides, partly because at the time these tax laws were written, tracking consumer use of such services was difficult.[32]

That is starting to change. In Rhode Island, the state began levying sales tax on taxi fares in 2012, but both Lyft and Uber said that the law was too ambiguous to apply to their companies. In 2016, the state Legislature passed a law clarifying that Uber, Lyft and other digitally connected businesses would have to collect sales taxes.[33] Georgia's House passed similar legislation in March 2017; the bill is awaiting action in the state Senate.[34]

Policymakers also are questioning how on-demand companies fit into other regulations, such as zoning and rental ordinances. In October 2016, New York Gov. Andrew Cuomo signed a law banning the listing of unoccupied apartments as short-term rentals on sites such as Airbnb, FlipKey and HomeAway in violation of New York City's rental rules.[35] Airbnb sued the state but dropped the suit after the parties agreed that New York City—not the state—would be responsible for enforcing the law and that the platform itself would not be found liable for any infractions; instead, the host renting out a space would be subject to penalty.[36]

Overseas, the European Union's highest court weighed in with a ruling in late December 2017 that Uber was a transportation business, not merely a digital platform, and therefore subject to licensing and other regulations that apply to taxi companies.[37]

Labor law is of particular concern to legislators and the contract workers who provide services to on-demand companies. These individuals enjoy little job security or protection under current labor law, often receive low wages and have little recourse for demanding higher pay.

Some states have begun amending laws to define who qualifies as an employee rather than an independent contractor, including what are called "presumptive employee status" laws. These laws assume all workers are employees afforded the rights and benefits of full employment, and they leave the burden of proof on the employer to prove otherwise. Such classification has led to litigation against some of the most high-profile on-demand companies. In February 2017, a Florida state appellate court ruled that Uber drivers were independent contractors and therefore ineligible for unemployment benefits.[38] Such findings are beneficial for the companies but harm the employees they rely on. One on-demand worker said she made $6,000 on the freelance site TaskRabbit the previous year, "but even if I doubled that, that's still poverty—$12,000 a year. And there are no benefits," she said.[39]

As more legislative efforts and legal proceedings define who is an employee, on-demand companies may become liable for providing costly benefits to their workforce, something that could push some businesses to their breaking point. According to a report by Virginia's Joint Legislative Audit and Review Commission, companies that misclassify their workers as contractors instead of employees save anywhere from 10 percent to 40 percent on overall payroll costs.[40] "If you had the liability that we're talking about . . . it would shut a lot of these companies down," said Shelby Clark, the founder of car sharing service Turo.[41]

But for some companies, taking on higher payroll costs is worth it to build customer and worker loyalty and avoid costly lawsuits. For example, by providing training to ensure all staff deliver the expected level of service, Hello Alfred, a home management service, has built customer loyalty and trust resulting in higher use of the service and positive customer feedback. Similarly, Mulberrys Garment Care, which offers on-demand laundry and dry-cleaning services, hires full-time staff despite the extra cost. "Because of the fact that you have a more knowledgeable and more productive staff, you end up being able to deliver a better product at a competitive wage," said CEO Dan Miller. "It's a long-term play. . . . It's not the cheap, quick answer."[42]

U.S. Sen. Mark Warner, D-Va., is seeking ways for independent workers to receive unemployment insurance and other benefits such as 401(k)s and workers' compensation. In May, Warner and Rep. Suzan DelBene, D-Wash., introduced legislation to establish a $20 million grant fund within the U.S. Labor Department to encourage states, communities and nonprofit organizations to experiment with portable benefit models for independent workers.

"As more and more Americans engage in part-time, contract or other alternative worker arrangements," Warner said, "it's increasingly important that we provide them with an ability to access more flexible, portable benefits that they can carry with them to multiple jobs across a day, a year, and even a career."[43]

Future Trends

Market analysis indicates the on-demand economy has plenty of room to grow. BIA/Kelsey, a marketing and research firm based in suburban Washington, estimates that in 2017, local on-demand service made up only 7 percent of the U.S. market.[44] Startups that enter the market will face hurdles—as did their predecessors—in establishing themselves as viable investments for large investors. That problem will potentially limit the number and variety of companies offering on-demand services. In fact, venture funding for on-demand startups fell

On-Demand Spending Generated $57.6 Billion

U.S. consumer expenditures in on-demand economy, 2015

The on-demand economy generated $57.6 billion in spending in 2015, with the largest amount spent in online marketplaces such as eBay and Etsy, according to the National Technology Readiness Survey.

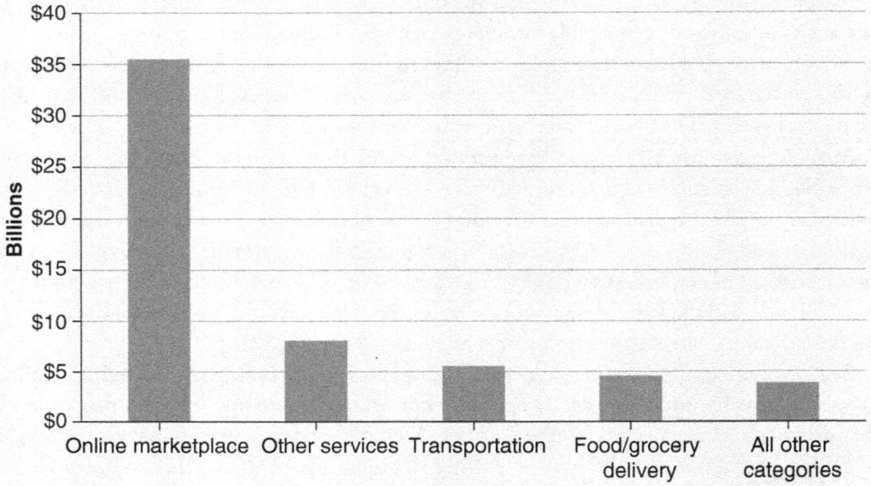

Source: Charles Colby and Kelly Bell, "The On-Demand Economy Is Growing, and Not Just for the Young and Wealthy," Harvard Business Review, Apr. 14, 2016, https://tinyurl.com/h9v4bqr.

by 35 percent in 2016.[45] This decline comes after venture capitalists invested $12.5 billion in 230 on-demand companies from 2000 to 2015, according to Accenture, the global management consultant firm.[46]

The disruption caused by the on-demand economy is forcing many traditional businesses to scramble to keep up. Accenture found that the transportation/automotive sector received the highest investment from venture capitalists between 2000 and 2015.[47] But, cautions Arun Sundararajan, a professor at New York University's Stern School of Business, all industries are vulnerable to disruption and should be evaluating their business models and considering how to respond to the on-demand threat. "No matter how far away your industry seems to be from digital, there's a digital disruption on the horizon," he says.

Established corporations seeking to retain their relevancy in an on-demand world have three choices: build, buy or partner. Businesses must identify their shortcomings in the on-demand world, develop new offerings geared toward their current and future customer bases, embrace digital technology—specifically seamless payment systems and services based on a customer's location—and reimagine their business models to provide the experience and level of service today's consumer expects.

Existing businesses willing to embrace this new consumer landscape can benefit from established loyalty and trust with their consumers, something startups must—and at times struggle to—quickly develop, but only if they can evolve to become more customer-experience oriented.[48] Amazon, for example, has positioned itself to compete with delivery companies such as Postmates by expanding its two-day Prime shipping service to one- and two-hour Amazon Prime Now in certain metropolitan areas.[49]

Short of finding ways in-house to meet on-demand consumer expectations, established companies must look to startups for help, as GM has done with Lyft. Partnerships between large, established corporations and startups are already becoming the norm in the grocery and restaurant industries, with companies including McDonald's, Costco, Target and 7-Eleven partnering with delivery services such as Instacart to make their products more readily accessible.

NYU's Sundararajan is closely monitoring those economic sectors that are testing the on-demand waters, specifically local retail and health care. Companies such as DoorDash and Postmates that traditionally offer restaurant meals are now looking to other goods—hardware, for example—so that they can deliver to consumers any item within minutes to an hour.

In health care, Sundararajan sees changes coming both in consultations with a doctor and access to certified health care providers for simple needs such as colds or stitches that would bypass the long wait times and inefficiencies at emergency rooms or urgent-care locations. There's "no tech revolution here," Sundararajan says. "The challenge here is building up the supply to get businesses up and running," he says, because most doctors are currently tied to certain health institutions for insurance purposes. The UBERDOC app, while not yet ready for widespread use, is paving the way, offering near real-time access to a specialist without a referral for the fixed price of $300.

Amazon Prime Subscribers Steadily Growing

U.S. subscribers, 2013–17

Amazon Prime subscribers in the United States have grown steadily, from 25 million at the end of 2013 to 80 million in March 2017.

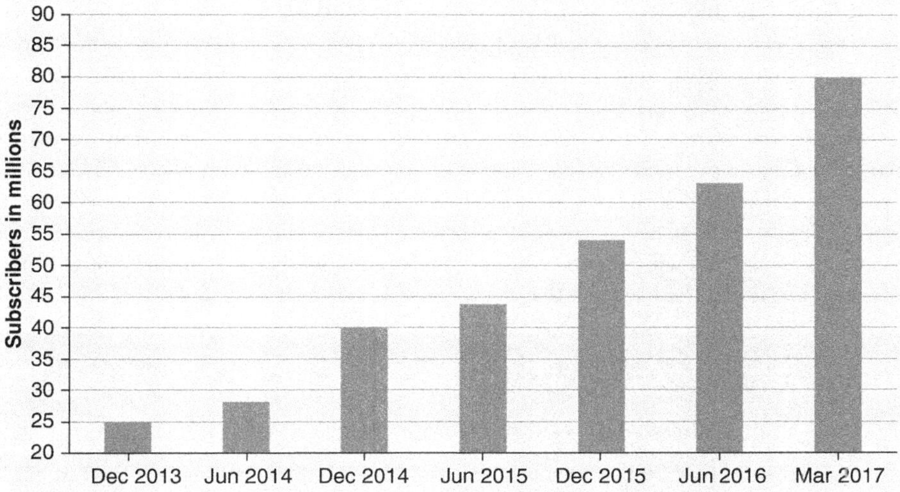

Source: "About 32% of U.S. e-Commerce customers subscribe to Amazon Prime," Slideshare, Consumer Intelligence Research Partners, Statista Digital Marketing Outlook, Apr. 26, 2017, http://tinyurl.com/y72hgcgy.

Owyang of Catalyst Companies believes that some technology companies provide a model for the on-demand economy. The IBMs, Apples, Googles and Microsofts of the world are offering on-demand products, providing platforms that allow independent developers to build new products and giving their customers online space to support one another. "But this same model shouldn't be limited to software companies alone," Owyang wrote.[50]

While success in the new economy will depend on established companies' ability to re-invent their supply chains to offer instant access to their goods and services, another shift is in the offing. According to Owyang, in the not-so-distant future, drones, robots and self-driving cars will likely replace humans as the primary mode of delivery. Already, companies are experimenting with robot and drone delivery for takeout and packages.

And there is talk of the ultra-high-speed transportation company Hyperloop One not only revolutionizing human transit, but changing how freight is moved to better fit into the micro-moment, on-demand expectation of consumers.[51] Such an agglomeration could increase competition, availability, and specialization of limitless goods and services to consumers, no matter where they are located.

Even that, Owyang says, could become outmoded, and consumers may one day find their homes prestocked with items they use, based on historical behavior and preferences, billed on a pay-for-use system.

As Amazon has found, however, the evolution of shipping speed and consumer convenience is costly, and the hit its earnings have taken may not be sustainable for everyone. "There's a lot of things that we're doing to shorten the time to delivery," Amazon CFO Brian Olsavsky told reporters in late 2016. "We acknowledge that's expensive, but it's certainly a great part of our value proposition, and customers love it, so we take it as a given and then we work very hard to bring down our costs through greater efficiency."[52]

The difficulty in making the moves necessary to reach this autonomous world—or even one that can just respond to consumer demands faster—is difficult for startups and traditional companies alike. "Agreeing on strategic actions while not being able to agree on what the consumer product landscape will likely look like in five years is challenging in itself; concurrently moving rapidly with thoroughgoing actions is even more difficult," a 2015 report by Deloitte Insights concluded.[53]

Whether the future involves self-driving rideshares or automatic delivery of groceries, the biggest issue for startups and established corporations will be resilience, says Owyang. Consumers have been empowered, and they are unlikely to turn back to older ways. Companies that can remain relevant are those that will not only be prepared to fulfill immediate needs with the right goods and services, but will prioritize customer service and continue to adapt and change alongside consumer needs. "It's inevitable that change is going to happen," says Solis.

Chronology

1979–99	**New technologies enable changing retail models.**
1979	First online shopping system is demonstrated by British inventor Michael Aldrich in the United Kingdom. Customers are hand-delivered goods and pay in cash upon delivery.
1984	Electronic Mall, created by CompuServe, begins operating in the United States and Canada as the first online shopping center where consumers could purchase goods from a number of retailers.

1991	The World Wide Web becomes publicly available on the internet.
1992	IBM releases the first smartphone, the Simon Personal Communicator, which could be used for calls and to receive faxes and emails; it also featured applications including a calendar, clock, scheduler, address book and note taker. An estimated 50,000 units were sold between August 1994 and February 1995.
1994	The Netscape Navigator browser is released by the Mosaic Corp., making internet access and e-commerce more widely available. . . . Jeff Bezos founds Amazon; one year later, Pierre Omidyar develops AuctionWeb, the precursor to eBay. Both websites begin to change consumers' mindset regarding how and where purchases are made.
1997	Mobile commerce is launched in Helsinki when two Coca-Cola vending machines are installed that accept payment via text message.
1999	SeamlessWeb (later Seamless) debuts in New York to provide a Web-based restaurant ordering system to companies; access to consumer diners begins in 2005 (Seamless will merge with Grubhub in 2013). . . . Apple adds a Wi-Fi option on its iBook computer and NTT DoCoMo in Japan begins offering mobile-optimized full internet service on its cellphones.
2000–Present	**The on-demand economy takes off.**
2004	Grubhub starts food delivery in Chicago. By 2017, the company says, it offers service in more than 1,300 U.S. cities and London.
2005	Amazon inaugurates Amazon Prime, an annual membership offering two-day shipping on millions of items.
2007	Apple CEO Steve Jobs unveils the iPhone in January; the first models are available for sale five months later. Labeled a "breakthrough internet communications device," the iPhone revolutionizes how the world communicates and receives information.
2008	Airbnb debuts under the name AirBed & Breakfast in San Francisco. The company changes its name to Airbnb in 2009.
2010	Uber begins offering service in San Francisco under the name UberCab; the name is shortened to Uber in 2011. In 2012, Lyft, which will become Uber's strongest competitor, begins service in the same city.
2013	UPS begins offering 3D printing at some of its locations, intended for retail customers, small businesses, and startups. Customers can print items such as personal accessories, functional prototypes, manufacturing jigs and fixtures and architectural models. Staples begins offering a similar service in 2014.
2014	Amazon introduces Prime Now in parts of New York City, offering delivery of certain products in an hour or less.
2016	An attempt by Uber to settle class-action lawsuits brought by drivers in California and Massachusetts who want to be classified as employees instead of independent contractors, which would have required the company to pay up to $100 million, is rejected by a federal judge. Additional lawsuits follow against Uber and similar companies. Analysts begin to question whether such litigation will spell the demise of the on-demand economy. . . . Amazon begins testing its Prime Air delivery in the United Kingdom, with packages delivered by unmanned drone.

(Continued)

(Continued)

2017	Starship Technologies in partnership with Postmates begins using the United States' first delivery robots in Washington. Postmates app users are able to order items from a convenience store or restaurant that are then delivered by a GPS-guided device (March). . . . The U.S. National Labor Relations Board (NLRB) issues a complaint against Handy Technologies, Inc., an on-demand service for hiring cleaners, alleging that its workers are employees and not independent contractors and therefore are covered by federal labor law (August). . . . The European Union's highest court rules that Uber is a transportation business subject to licensing and other rules governing taxi companies (December).

Discussion Questions

Here are some questions to discuss about the on-demand economy:

- What key factors are driving the on-demand economy's growth?
- Why do some observers call the on-demand economy a bubble ready to burst? Do you agree?
- Why do you think on-demand is especially popular with Millennials?
- How has the growth of on-demand businesses affected supply chains?
- How are governments seeking to regulate on-demand businesses? How does this differ from regulation of traditional businesses?
- How likely do you think it is that consumers will embrace delivery of products before they order them, based on their buying history? Is this a realistic future, or a step too far?

PERSPECTIVE

Q&A: Brian Solis on the On-Demand Economy

"IT'S GOING TO PENETRATE . . . MULTIPLE INDUSTRIES"

Brian Solis

Brian Solis is an industry analyst, author and speaker who has closely studied the impact and evolution of new technologies on business and society. In an interview with SAGE Business Researcher freelance correspondent Heather Kerrigan, he discusses the challenges facing businesses as they try to navigate changing consumer expectations that place a premium on speed and flexibility. The interview has been edited for space and clarity.

To whom is the on-demand economy most attractive?

The on-demand economy applies to what I call Generation C, where C stands for connected. The people who use mobile phones, use Facebook, those who live a digital lifestyle, that's who the on-demand economy appealed to initially. It's not just Millennials. People who are 25 and people who are 55 exhibit the same behavior once they enter the digital lifestyle.

What changes will companies need to make to remain viable in the on-demand economy and how are they working toward that?

Regardless of what business you are in, you are competing against any service in the on-demand economy. You'll hear it as the Uberization of something. Once you taste a modern convenience and an integrated service, that changes your behavior. It becomes the standard for what engagement is and what the expectation is.

Generation C isn't going to differentiate between a car service and a dentist. They just simply want that great, integrated, transparent experience across their entire lifestyle. Unfortunately, most companies are still assuming what people want. They'll ask, "If people like Uber, how do we become the Uber of our industry?" But they don't really understand how Uber has changed the behavior, expectations, preferences and value for a customer. They assume it as, let's build an app, let's get mobile, let's not change what we do, let's put something on the front end that seems more Uber-like.

You have all this money being applied to modernizing digital customer experiences, but only 34 percent of companies have studied what people expect in digital, what they value. It's not going digital and mobile that's the challenge—it's shifting essentially 60 years of how we've done business to be more competitive in an on-demand era.

Where most businesses are failing is because it's not something they've had to do before. It's challenging convention and management and mindsets. You can't just go digital, you have to go native and gain empathy to see how your marketplace is different than how you see it.

Where do you see the on-demand economy heading?

It's going to penetrate services across multiple industries. There's going to be this rivalry between traditional and evolved businesses where on-demand permeates not just mobile devices and the online world but also physical spaces. You're starting to see it in little pockets here and there. For example, Amazon Go began to experiment with an on-demand service in the store. You go in, you take things off a shelf, the app rings it up, and you just walk out. That experience is starting to be replicated in stores in Japan. Every aspect of life will become some on-demand experience to the point where you don't even have to ask for it; it will just come to you.

What is standing in the way of growth in the on-demand economy?

Older, traditional, conventional mindsets and perspectives. To get people to see things differently is difficult because those who don't want to change are clinging to the way that things are, and they're getting in their own way. While you're digging in and trying to go backwards, the world is progressing. You have to see that things are different in order to see things differently. Any story of innovation starts with personal innovation.

UPDATE IN 2020

Participation in the on-demand economy continues to boom—with COVID-19 only hastening its growth.

Just from 2018 to 2019, Americans' spending via on-demand services grew by another 18.5 percent to a record $110 billion, according to the National Technology Readiness Survey, which studies the spending habits of more than 1,000 individual consumers.[54]

The biggest chunk of that spending, about $29.2 billion, took place in online marketplaces, like Amazon and Walmart. Next came food delivery, followed by transportation, retail delivery and housing.

The survey found that on-demand economy users initially tended to be younger, better educated and concentrated in urban areas. However, as the on-demand economy became more accessible in different parts of the U.S., the demographics were shifting to look more like the rest of the consumers.

When COVID-19 brought about shutdown orders, consumers globally flocked to utilize contactless delivery and pick-up services for groceries and carry-out meals.[55] Two of Europe's most popular delivery companies, Deliveroo and Glovo, shifted to a drop-off option.[56] Lyft partnered with Grubhub—a food delivery service—as it recognized the demand for such services.[57]

In Asia, the Middle East and elsewhere, Delivery Hero began instituting sanitary and other COVID-19-related measures in its 44 markets in January, as soon as the first word of the pandemic surfaced. Singapore-based Grab, which started in ride-sharing and soon expanded to on-demand services across Southeast Asia, also saw a dip in ride-hailing but saw increased demand for delivery services.[58] It expanded such services, from food to groceries and packages, though it was unable to avoid laying off over 300 employees.[59]

Overwhelmingly, consumers said they wanted those services to continue, according to a survey by Medallia Zingle, a technology company that specializes in text messaging platforms.

Its May 2020 survey found that 87 percent of consumers wanted restaurants and other retailers to continue offering carry-out services and other processes that could limit contact.[60] Twenty-five percent of the people who took part in the survey said they had used delivery or pick-up services exclusively during the pandemic.

Online merchants also reported increased orders, especially during the early stages of the pandemic.

Amazon Founder and CEO Jeff Bezos described the pandemic as "the hardest time we've ever faced," though the company had a master plan in reserve in case of such an emergency. Bezos met daily with senior management, eventually authorizing the hiring of 175,000 additional employees to meet customer demand.[61]

Similarly, Walmart said it was hiring 235,000 additional employees to keep up with the demand in stores and online. It reported a 74 percent increase in online transactions during the first quarter of 2020, though it was costly to keep up: Walmart spent an additional $900 million in temporary pay increases and bonuses for employees.[62]

Yet the demand for goods was not translating to demand by investors. WeWork withdrew its plans for an IPO (initial public offering), while the shares of Uber in October 2020 were $5 lower than its introductory price in 2019. Lyft shares were down by two-thirds from their peak in 2019.

With millions of independent contractors unemployed due to the pandemic, the federal COVID-19 assistance package enacted in March 2020 allowed them to file for unemployment insurance, usually not available to gig workers. About 13 million people collected benefits through fall 2020.[63]

Companies large and small were learning that on-demand sales were critical in times of crisis. What they have yet to find out, however, is how much the interest in on-demand services would continue to grow once consumers felt confident enough to move about freely again.

One big test of the on-demand economy is coming in an unexpected place: higher education. Over the past couple of decades, remote learning has evolved to become an alternative to in-person learning.

But until the pandemic, many universities worldwide considered in-person learning their first choice. However, shutdown orders forced them to quickly shift to an on-demand format for all or some of their students.

One example was Bowdoin College, a private school in Maine. Only first-year students and those participating in special seminars were allowed on campus. Students in residence on campus would pay $33,935 for the fall semester, while those who were learning remotely would pay $27,911 in tuition.[64] The university thought about combining the two types of learning, but "in general, having a single model of delivery for the entire faculty gives us the best chance to deliver on our goal of achieving excellence," Bowdoin's president, Clayton Rose, said in a message to the college community.

—Micheline Maynard

18 THE SHARING ECONOMY

Is it really different from traditional business?

Patrick Marshall

From *SAGE Business Researcher*, August 3, 2015

EXECUTIVE SUMMARY

What's called the sharing economy—peer-to-peer transactions conducted via the internet and smartphones—has changed how people arrange car rides, find vacation lodging and more. Revenue is projected to soar in the coming years, although profitability remains untested. But as businesses such as Uber, Lyft and Airbnb flourish, regulation and collection of taxes, primarily by state and local authorities, have become more difficult to enforce. Traditional businesses such as taxis and hotels complain that these newcomers are gaining an unfair advantage by ducking oversight that's meant to protect consumers. Additionally, debate has grown over whether service providers in the sharing economy are independent contractors or employees. Some of the key issues under debate: Is the sharing economy more efficient than traditional markets? Should regulators treat the sharing economy the same way as conventional competitors? Are sharing-economy companies platforms for independent contractors, or are they employers?

Justin Sullivan/Getty Images

A Lyft car, marked with a bright pink mustache, lines up next to a traditional taxi in San Francisco traffic. Ride-hailing services such as Lyft are among the most visible players in the sharing economy. The taxi industry charges that these new firms compete unfairly.

OVERVIEW

The "sharing economy"—in which consumers connect with service providers using internet applications instead of relying on traditional providers—is booming. On a typical day, an estimated 247,000 items are sold on Etsy, 140,000 people rent accommodations through Airbnb and 1 million people ride with Uber.[1]

Because very few sharing-economy companies are publicly traded, it's unknown whether they are profitable. But many sharing-economy companies are attracting major investments and have quickly become players in the economy. Based on venture capital funds raised, The Wall Street Journal estimated Uber's value at more than $40 billion and Airbnb's at $25 billion.[2]

In fact, according to the Federal Trade Commission, sharing-economy transactions totaled about $26 billion globally in 2013.[3] And PricewaterhouseCoopers (PwC), an auditing and consulting firm, estimates that in 10 years, the biggest sectors of the sharing economy could see $335 billion in global revenue. PwC projects that by 2025, sharing-economy companies will account for about half of the business in their market sectors, up from only 6.25 percent in 2013.[4]

What's more, sharing-economy companies are emerging in numerous niche markets. It's not, in short, just about renting apartments and hailing cars. There is a platform that cities can use to share heavy equipment (MuniRent), a platform that skiers and bicycle and surfboard owners can use to rent their recreational equipment (Spinlister), and a platform that musicians can use to share their equipment (GearLode). There is also a robust group of platforms that connect investors to individuals and small businesses seeking funding (Funding Circle, LendingClub, Prosper, TransferWise).

Sharing Economy to Match Rental Revenue by 2025

Projected revenue for rental services, by sector, in $U.S. billions, 2013 and 2025

Internet-based sharing businesses will generate an estimated $335 billion in revenue by 2025, the same amount projected for five traditional rental sectors (equipment rental, B&B and hostels, car rental, book rental and DVD rental).

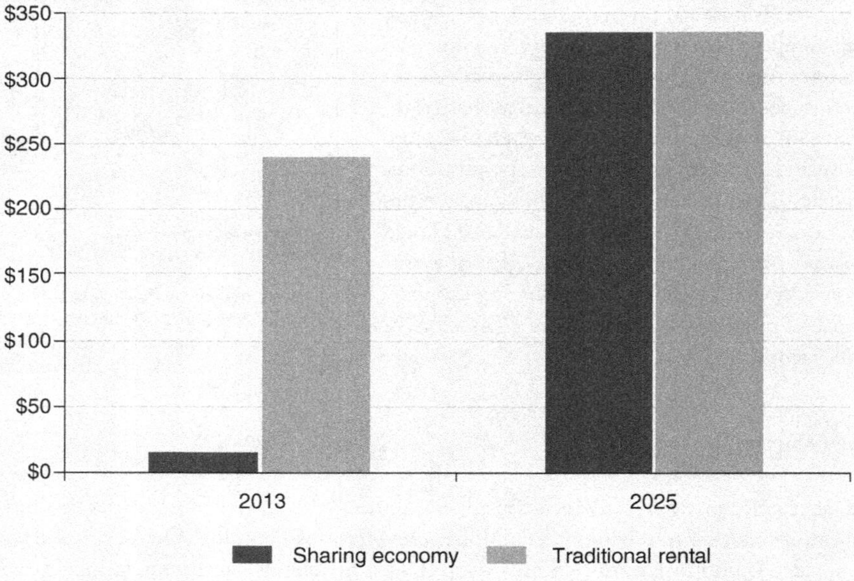

Note: 2025 estimates based on historical data and projected growth rates and economic outcomes for 10 industry sectors.

Source: "The Sharing Economy—Sizing the Revenue Opportunity," PricewaterhouseCoopers, 2014, http://tinyurl.com/ophtwcf.

Niche Markets Offer Big Potential

Entrepreneurs Find Success by Seeking Out the Underserved

From Makers Row (small businesses and start-ups) to GearLode (musicians), entrepreneurs are connecting geographically disparate people who share an interest—no matter how small the group. These niche markets are potentially efficient and profitable, analysts say.

If the measure of a sharing-economy company's success is use of underutilized resources, then the ranks of the successful extend well beyond the Ubers of the world.

Smart sharing-economy entrepreneurs realize that the ability of the internet to connect geographically disparate people who share an interest—whether it's monster truck rallies or stamp collecting—applies just as much to those who could benefit from sharing goods and services. And the more narrowly defined the community, the more efficient that market can be. As a result, sharing-economy entrepreneurs are increasingly targeting niche markets.

Of course, making more efficient use of resources doesn't always mean making money. In some cases, in fact, sharing-economy platforms are nonprofit enterprises, aimed primarily at providing for the needs of a user community. In other cases, the platform takes a small fee from each transaction to cover costs or, in some cases, to earn profit. Because very few sharing-economy companies are publicly held, however, information on actual financial results is scarce.

Take Alan Mond, CEO of 1000 Tools, a sharing-economy platform that allows users to rent tools to each other. In late 2013, he was looking for another community to serve. "After interviewing 30 municipalities in the southeastern Michigan region, we discovered an incredible gap," Mond told a congressional hearing. "Large municipalities have expensive equipment that is underutilized, and small municipalities tend to rent at a high premium rate instead of purchasing equipment."[5]

So Mond's team retooled the company's technology to cater to municipalities. The result is MuniRent, which launched in late 2013 and allows different levels of local government to rent equipment to each other.

Similarly, Zimride—a long-distance, ride-matching platform begun by Lyft founders John Zimmer and Logan Green in 2007—began serving only corporate and university subscribers after its recent sale to Enterprise.

"Folks are trying to do the right thing and find others who are headed the same direction that they are," says Chuck Welek, corporate Zimride manager. "Unlike Uber, we want people to take full advantage of filling the seats of vehicles that are already available on campus."

Because Zimride is simply a matching platform—and by limiting its "community" to individual campuses and companies—Welek says it doesn't face the liability issues that a company like Uber faces, nor does it have to pay for background checks.

On the app provided to end users, potential riders can check the profile of drivers offering rides. And for the subscribing company or university Zimride offers a dashboard that shows the impact of the service, including how many ride-matches have been made, how many cars have been taken off the roads and how much carbon dioxide has been reduced.

According to Welek, Zimride currently has more than 300,000 users in more than 130 networks.

The low cost of entering the sharing economy—which in some cases may be little more than the cost of starting a website—means that new niche businesses are emerging on a daily basis.

Among the more interesting recent additions:

- **GearLode:** Most musicians have their own instruments. But GearLode is aimed at those who need something more, such as a band playing an out-of-town gig who don't want to haul their own sound system and lighting equipment. In addition to sound and lighting equipment, the platform offers instrument and rehearsal spaces.
- **JustPark.com:** JustPark allows people to offer their driveways or other private parking spots for short-term or long-term rental. According to the company, the most sought-after spots, and those that can command the highest rental fees, are those near popular venues—nightclubs, zoos, amusement parks, train stations.
- **Kidizen.com:** Recognizing that children often outgrow perfectly good clothes, Kidizen offers style-conscious parents a platform for buying and selling children's clothing.
- **Maker's Row:** Maker's Row's target audience is start-ups and small businesses that need temporary factory space and equipment to create products, such as clothing or furniture. Beyond simply leasing space and equipment, Maker's Row also provides a forum for members to help each other with product development.

- **Spinlister:** Spinlister provides a platform for those with bicycles, surfboards and ski equipment to offer the equipment for rental. It markets its services to renters as a way to travel light but still have access to recreational equipment at destinations.
- **Trashswag.com:** Trashswag is a crowdsourced map that shares postings of reusable materials found outside, including abandoned building materials, old wood, doors and windows and furniture. According to the site, which so far is limited to parts of Canada, "the purpose of Trashswag is to promote creativity through reuse. Post salvageable materials and furniture. Architectural salvage could include old wood, windows, doors, radiators, bathtubs, sheet material or metal." Users simply post photos to the map as they come across items and, once approved by an administrator, the item will appear on the map. Users help keep the map up to date by notifying the site when the items are no longer there.

—*Patrick Marshall*

"It's clear that consumers are embracing it," says John Breyault, vice president of public policy at the National Consumers League, a consumer advocacy group in Washington, D.C.

Of course, the sharing economy—which has also been described as a peer-to-peer economy—is not actually new.

"Peer-to-peer businesses were around long before the internet," Philip Auerswald, associate professor of public policy at George Mason University, told a House hearing on the sharing economy last year. "Indeed, there was a time in this country and elsewhere in the world (roughly until the end of the 19th century) when the peer-to-peer economy *was* the economy. Large corporations providing consumer services simply did not exist. Regulation governing consumer services was minimal. People provided services on a personal basis to other people who were very much like them."[6]

While peer-to-peer transactions may not be new, analysts say, how those transactions occur is. The internet and smartphones have allowed transactions to take place around the block or around the globe, almost instantaneously. "It's these different technologies that are making things easier," says Dean Baker, an economist and the cofounder of the Center for Economic and Policy Research, a Washington, D.C., think tank.

Indeed, the internet has fundamentally changed the nature of peer-to-peer transactions. Where previously those dealings involved only the buyer and seller of goods or services, now they are mediated through a software platform, which is owned by a company or, in some cases, a nonprofit organization. That change has led to two developments. First, regulation and collection of taxes, primarily by state and local authorities, have become more difficult to enforce. Second, there is growing debate over whether service providers in the sharing economy are really independent contractors or employees.

The stakes involved are high. If regulators require sharing-economy companies to conform to laws governing employers' treatment of employees, the prices of their goods and services will likely rise and their competitive advantage against traditional companies will be reduced.

Corporate involvement in the sharing economy, some analysts say, means that much of this economy has little or nothing to do with sharing. "Make no mistake about it, today's sharing economy is big business, involving lots and lots of money and all kinds of players motivated powerfully by financial gain," said Nancy Koehn, a professor at Harvard Business School.[7]

Although the internet has enabled the sharing economy to blossom, other factors also have contributed. "While some of these sharing models might have resulted from a need for frugal spending after the global economic recession of 2008," wrote entrepreneurship professors Boyd Cohen and Jan Kietzmann, "their success was also driven by a growing environmental consciousness combined with the ubiquity of internet and associated information and communication technologies which make sharing possible at scale."[8]

Koehn speculated that deeper aspects of consumer psychology may explain the booming popularity of many sharing-economy companies. "There is a directness about calling a limo ride yourself on Uber or Lyft and then rating the driver and car after you get to your destination that is both empowering and seemingly more transparent than calling a car service or hailing a taxi," she said. "Individuals from all walks of life, particularly younger consumers, simply do not have much trust in established business, governmental, and other large-scale organizations. Against this backdrop, many consumers—and sellers—find peer-to-peer buying and selling to be more appealing because it is not so closely associated with a big business that may (or may not) have a mixed track record in their minds."[9]

The relatively new technologies that power the sharing economy have put many transactions outside the purview of regulators. While cities issue taxi medallions to a limited number of service providers, they have little control over the drivers who connect to passengers using Uber, Lyft or Sidecar. And while cities license and tax hotels, they haven't yet developed a way to manage and monitor homeowners and companies renting through sharing-economy companies such as Airbnb.

As a result, although consumers generally seem happy with the savings and convenience delivered by sharing-economy companies, many of those companies are beginning to feel pressure from several directions. Those include their contractors (or employees) unsatisfied with wages and the lack of benefits, government agencies and competing businesses that claim sharing-economy companies are dodging needed regulation, municipalities that accuse service providers of failing to pay taxes, and consumer groups that say some companies are underserving certain groups of people.

Not surprisingly, the greatest amount of attention has focused on the most successful sharing-economy companies: Uber and Airbnb.

"The growth of illegal hotels is rapidly becoming one of the biggest obstacles in the struggle to protect and expand New York City's stock of affordable housing," Democratic New York State Sen. Liz Krueger told the Federal Trade Commission in May. "Online platforms like Airbnb lure individuals into breaking the law with promises of more income from operating illegal hotels, leaving residents with an increasingly scarce supply of affordable housing."[10]

Krueger also charged that the lack of effective regulation over Airbnb exposes consumers to drawbacks of which they may not be aware. "Most illegal hotels fail to meet federal, state and city accessibility requirements for people with disabilities," she said. "Far from being a harmless service that promotes 'sharing,' companies like Airbnb threaten public safety and make it more difficult for everyday New Yorkers to find an affordable place to live."

Airbnb did not to respond to repeated requests for comment. In a blog post in 2013, however, CEO Brian Chesky argued that the company actually helps New Yorkers stay in their homes. "In New York, our 15,000 hosts are regular people from all five boroughs. Eighty-seven percent of them rent the homes in which they live," wrote Chesky. "On average, they are at the median income level and more than half of them depend on Airbnb to help them stay in their home."[11]

Ride-sharing companies have drawn even greater criticism from competitors and regulators. "The thing with Uber and Lyft, what they're doing is they are cutting corners on safety and responsibility under the guise of the sharing economy," says Dave Sutton, a spokesman for the Taxicab, Limousine & Paratransit Association, which represents 1,100 taxicab companies. "Their insurance has gaps, which has come to light, and more and more will be revealed. Their background checks are not conducted by law enforcement and don't involve fingerprinting. And those are truly undercutting public safety."

Uber declined requests for interviews and responded to questions only by providing links to materials on the company's website. The materials do not indicate that Uber's background checks include fingerprints and reviews by law enforcement agencies.

The reaction to Uber by taxi drivers in some other countries has been even more dramatic. In early July, for example, Uber was forced to suspend its UberPop service in France after taxi drivers violently protested.[12]

Because sharing-economy companies are using new technologies that transform the way business is conducted, analysts say, a period of adjustment is inevitably needed to balance the competing interests of companies, regulators and consumers. "It is no surprise that Uber, Airbnb and other new companies find themselves operating in an area where the application of existing laws is potentially unclear," said Koehn. "It is also not surprising that these companies are fighting efforts by regulators to apply government rules and standards to their growing market."[13]

As the market presence of the biggest sharing-market companies has surged, friction with regulators—particularly at the state and local levels—has grown more pronounced in recent months.

For example, in the wake of an October report by the New York State Office of the Attorney General, which found that 72 percent of units booked via Airbnb in New York City appeared to violate state and local laws, city officials have begun filing suit and imposing fines on property owners.[14] The day after the report was released, the New York Daily News learned that New York City had filed suit against two property owners.[15]

In fact, many cities have long banned rentals of fewer than 30 days for properties that have not been inspected and licensed. And several cities have successfully pressed Airbnb to collect appropriate taxes from hosts for payment to the cities.

For its part, Uber has been banned by several communities and airports and has been sued by drivers who say that the company should be treating them as employees rather than independent contractors. In June, in a ruling that could be portentous, the California Labor Commissioner's Office determined that an Uber driver should be classified as an employee, not an independent contractor. Uber was ordered to reimburse the driver, Barbara Ann Berwick, $4,152.20 in expenses and other costs for the eight weeks she worked as an Uber driver. While the ruling applies only to Berwick and Uber is appealing it, the case could significantly affect Uber's competitive pricing if other courts agree that drivers are employees.[16]

"The explosion of sharing or on-demand services like Uber and Airbnb is the beginning of an economic upheaval every bit as significant as the Industrial Revolution," warned Frank Shafroth, director of the Center for State and Local Government Leadership at George Mason University. "The on-demand economy promises to radically reshape the cost of services and change the face of the workforce. These upheavals, in turn, are altering state and local government policies—imposing unforeseen fiscal risks."[17]

Specifically, Shafroth wrote, in addition to the challenges of recovering lost tax revenue and ensuring public safety, policymakers will have to deal with an upsurge in the number of temporary or part-time workers in the economy. "These workers are providing on-demand services at rock bottom prices. They are not working in downtown or suburban office buildings or for traditional employers, nor are they eligible for traditional health-care or pension benefits," he said. "Leaders will need to be part of a discussion about changing rules for 'contract workers,' and of an even larger federalism and governance discussion about how pensions and health-care benefits are delivered in the future."

Number of Part-Time Workers Peaked During Recession

Number of Americans working part time, ages 16 and older, in millions, 2005–15

About 6.5 million Americans work part time for economic reasons, even though they say they would prefer to work full time, a number that experts say could rise with a growing sharing economy. The number of these part-time workers jumped from 4.3 million in October 2007 to 9.1 million by March 2009 during the recession, hovering there for about two years before gradually declining.

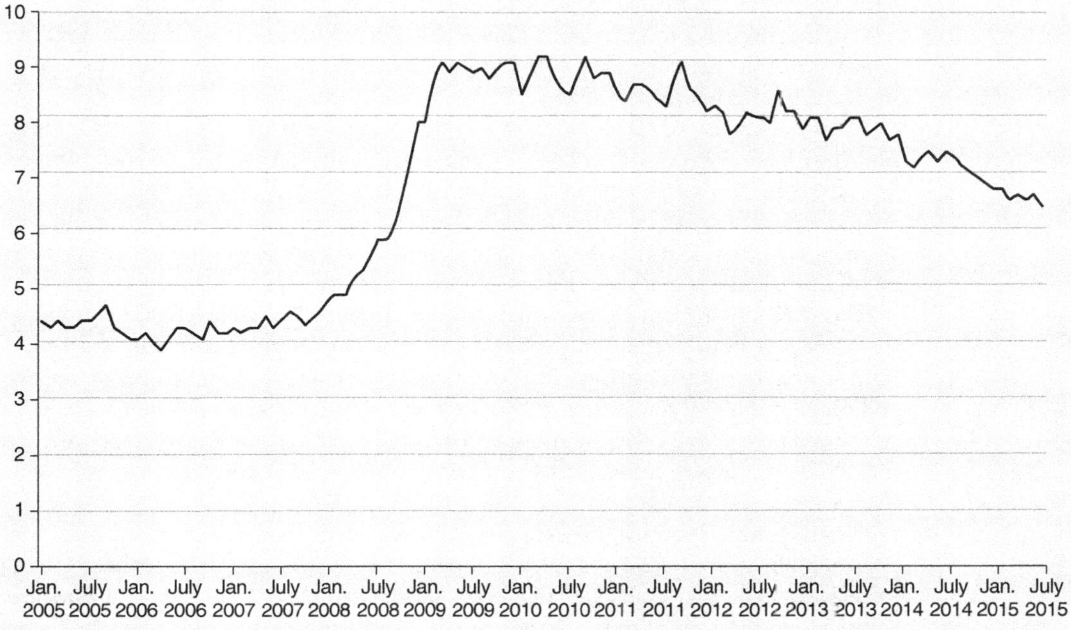

Note: Part-time workers are those who indicated they would like to work full time but were working 1 to 34 hours per week for economic reasons, such as being unable to find full-time jobs.

Source: "Labor Force Statistics from the Current Population Survey," U.S. Bureau of Labor Statistics, downloaded Jul. 20, 2015, http://tinyurl.com/m6996nd.

Additionally, the expansion of the sharing economy may have a lasting impact on other industries, such as automobile manufacturing. As consumers come to rely increasingly on sharing-economy transportation services, car ownership could decline. Indeed, a 2012 report by the U.S. Public Interest Research Group and the Frontier Group found that between 2001 and 2009, the average annual number of vehicle-miles of driving by young people (16- to 34-year-olds) decreased from 10,300 miles to 7,900 miles per capita—a drop of 23 percent. The report cites the rise of services such as Zipcar as a major factor in the trend.[18]

Shafroth said, "It's not for nothing that the on-demand economy is simultaneously dubbed the disruptive economy."[19]

As the controversy around the sharing economy grows, here are some of the questions being debated.

WEIGHING THE ISSUES

Is the Sharing Economy More Efficient Than Traditional Markets?

Sharing-economy supporters say that the companies and the platforms they offer are using technology not only to offer savings and convenience to consumers but also to make more efficient use of resources and to expand income opportunities for service providers.

The sharing economy, the staff of the House Committee on Small Business wrote in a January 2014 memo, more efficiently allocates "resources which in turn results in new consumption leading to new production."[20]

"Peer-to-peer marketplaces can have very different roles in an existing service industry," explains Chiara Farronato, an economist who is researching peer-to-peer internet platforms. "They can actually take a thin local market and make it 'thick' and very global." She cites eBay's creation of global markets for goods that previously were difficult to sell locally. "And you can create new markets," she says. "For example, Instacart delivery options are creating a new [grocery] market that was not previously available."

Even Airbnb, which may divert some customers from traditional hotels, has expanded the market, especially in locations where the supply of hotel rooms is constrained by either regulations or geography, Farronato says. "In San Francisco, for example, there is a limit to expansion and demand is high," she continues. "So the entry of Airbnb has actually not led to people substituting away from hotels. It's possible for more people to come to San Francisco to visit the city." Farronato says her research has shown that hotels didn't experience a large reduction in mean price and occupancy.

Similarly, while Uber has no doubt diverted some riders—and drivers—from other transportation providers, at least one study has found that the company has expanded jobs and ridership overall. "The availability of modern technology, like the Uber app, provides many advantages and lower prices for consumers compared with the traditional taxicab dispatch system, and this has boosted demand for ride services, which, in turn, has increased total demand for workers with the requisite skills to work as for-hire drivers, potentially raising earnings for all workers with such skills," write Princeton economist Alan B. Krueger and Jonathan V. Hall, head of policy research at Uber Technologies.[21]

Peer-to-Peer Markets Growing More Quickly Than Traditional Sectors

Projected growth of sharing economy and traditional rental sectors, 2013 and 2025

Sharing-economy sectors are expected to grow rapidly from 2013 to 2025, with the largest revenue growth in peer-to-peer lending/crowdfunding (up 63 percent) and online staffing services (up 37 percent). Forecasters project marginal or negative revenue growth for comparable traditional rental sectors.

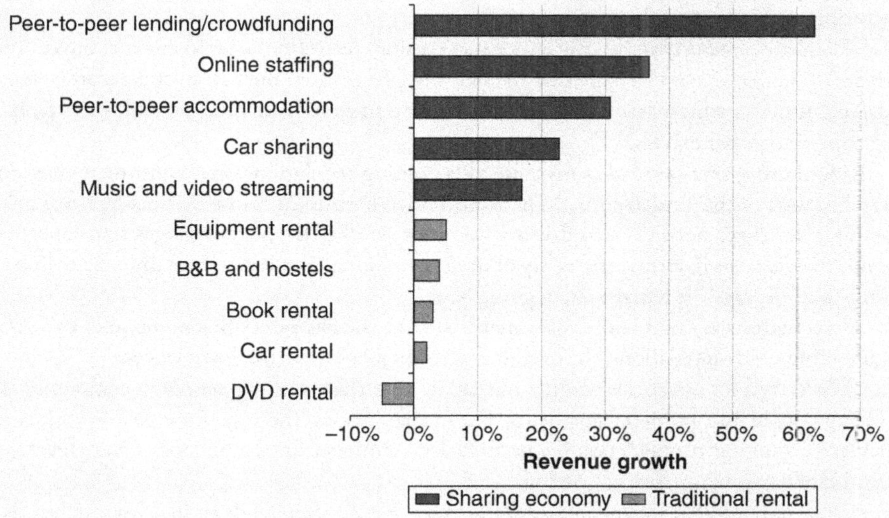

Note: Growth estimates based on historical data and projected economic outcomes for industry sectors.

Source: "The Sharing Economy—Sizing the Revenue Opportunity," PricewaterhouseCoopers, 2014, http://tinyurl.com/ophtwcf.

The study has been questioned by some economists, who note that it is based on selected Uber data. "Krueger's study looks at gross income for Uber drivers and compares it with ostensibly net income for cab drivers in the same cities," Baker of the Center for Economic and Policy Research says, "The reason he doesn't have an estimate of the net for Uber drivers is that he doesn't know how many miles those Uber drivers drove. Uber has that data. They just chose not to give it to him."

Sarah Cannon, Google Capital manager, and Lawrence H. Summers, former U.S. Treasury secretary, defend the sharing economy. "These firms bring significant economic, environmental, and entrepreneurial benefits, including an increase in employment," they argued in a Harvard Business Review article. They added that car-sharing services should reduce carbon dioxide emissions, benefiting the environment.[22]

Some analysts have estimated that for every shared vehicle, between nine and 13 private vehicles are removed from the roads, either by members selling a personal vehicle or postponing a planned purchase.[23] According to Susan Shaheen, an expert in innovative mobility research at the University of California, Berkeley, car sharers report reducing the vehicle miles traveled by 44 percent.[24]

While acknowledging that sharing-economy companies have had positive effects on markets, some analysts—as well as competitors—say that in some cases sharing-economy companies simply move jobs from existing industries to the new companies. They charge that these companies gain their competitive advantage by evading taxes, regulations and the cost of providing employee benefits.

"There are obviously some efficiencies there, using the technologies to connect buyers and sellers," Baker says. "And I'm sure there is some net job creation. But I suspect that for the most part it is displacement, that you have lost jobs in the traditional cab industry, and you're replacing them with Uber drivers."

Ride-sharing services, Baker says, are also evading regulations, and consumers may not even be aware of the hidden costs. "There are hidden costs in the sense that people are maybe getting a car that's not safe, or a driver who is not safe." Baker acknowledges that Uber has begun to take steps to ensure the safety of drivers and cars. "But they originally were trying to evade that," he says. "It remains an ongoing issue."

Some analysts say that while consumers may like the low prices that companies can offer by avoiding costly regulations, the overall impact on jobs is to drive down wages.

"There are a lot of articles coming out saying that these sharing-economy companies are turning people into mini-entrepreneurs, but in many cases, the way some people look at it, they are exploiting people," says Giana Eckhardt, professor in the School of Management, Royal Holloway, University of London.

Eckhardt notes that independent contractors not only often work for lower wages but also don't receive benefits, such as health insurance and sick leave. What's more, independent contractors must make their own payments for Social Security and Medicare, costs that are normally paid by a worker's employer.

Of the growing chorus of complaints by Uber drivers, Joseph De Wolf Sandoval, an Uber driver and the president of the California App-Based Drivers Association, told a reporter, "It's not just a small group of disgruntled or unprofessional drivers, as Uber would like to cast us. It's a nationwide feeling of general unhappiness and unease with policies and programs that are being promulgated by Uber without the drivers' input whatsoever."[25]

When Uber lowered fares in July, some drivers took exception. "Since Uber implemented the 20 percent off discount on all Uber rides, I've been losing $200 a week," Oris Fortuna, an Uber driver, said. "To make up for it, you have to work 20 percent more. That means more mileage and more gas. An $8 trip is not worth it."[26]

Should Regulators Treat the Sharing Economy the Same Way as Conventional Competitors?

Sharing-market companies, along with free market advocates, argue that the new platforms driving the sharing economy have features that make the old regulatory frameworks unnecessary.

"While some regulators are tempted to regulate sharing economy companies like their competitors, to do so would be a mistake that betrays a misunderstanding of how the sharing economy works," wrote Matthew Feeney, a policy analyst at the Cato Institute, a libertarian think tank.[27]

According to Feeney, the online customer ratings that sharing-economy companies such as Uber and Airbnb have made a central part of their business models are more effective than regulations at stopping misbehavior. "Badly behaved providers and consumers in the sharing economy do not last long, and the lack of anonymity means that anyone who does commit a crime is unlikely to escape justice," Feeney said.

As for dealing with bad actors, Arun Sundararajan, professor of information, operations and management sciences at New York University's Stern School of Business, says that the platforms can deal with them more efficiently than can regulators. "The interests of the platforms are well aligned with facilitating safe and profitable peer-to-peer trade (since their revenues are directly linked to the volume and continued growth of such trade)," Sundararajan told a House hearing in written testimony in January 2014. "The platforms are also better positioned to 'take action' against infringing entrepreneurs and consumers (for example, by simply disconnecting them from the platform)."[28]

Even in the absence of formal regulation, the review tools offered by sharing-economy platforms are not the only options for keeping bad actors in check.

"We have to remember there are always civil and criminal protections that will keep people safe," says Christopher Koopman, a research fellow at the Mercatus Center at George Mason University. "Just a few mistakes by these firms could sink one of these companies before they really have a chance to take off."

Other analysts point out the review system poses several problems, starting with the possibility that sharing-economy companies can manipulate the process.

Asked what assurance consumers have about the integrity of companies' review systems, economist Farronato says simply, "It's their word." She notes that historically 15 percent of reviews on Yelp proved to be fake. "The peer-to-peer platforms are very different in how they handle fake reviews," she says. "Some are working much harder than others. My take is that large companies are probably doing a very good job of weeding out the fake reviews."

Koopman says, in fact, that companies have a vested interest in earning consumers' trust. "If people are not trusting the rating systems, they're no longer trusting the companies," he says. "If they are no longer trusting the companies, they're not going to want to do business with them anymore."

A second problem, some analysts say, is that a negative consumer review doesn't appear until after something bad has happened.

"Unfortunately it takes a tragedy and then people become aware," says Sutton of the Taxicab, Limousine & Paratransit Association.

Ideally, advocates of regulation argue, regulators require behaviors that prevent abuses from happening in the first place.

Uber has begun running background checks on drivers, which Baker calls "wonderful." But unless there's a regulatory framework that requires those checks, he adds, "there's no guarantee they will always be doing it."

Baker says the need for regulations is just as great for hostelry services like Airbnb. "With hotels we have a set of regulatory structures that ensure they're not fire traps, that they are not a nuisance to their neighbors," he says.

And regulations often go beyond simple safety issues to require companies to meet societal goals. "There are important services that we expect people to have access to, and that means all people," says Baker. He notes that because of the Americans with Disabilities Act, cab companies must have a certain number of handicapped-accessible cabs. "That is a totally legitimate public purpose," he says. "But Uber is not bound by that and as long as we have the two systems side by side, Uber is essentially dumping off the cost on the traditional cab companies."

Free market advocates say the problem is regulation itself—and that the solution is to remove the regulations that apply to traditional companies. "Rather than pursue legislation that seeks to regulate sharing economy companies like their traditional competitors," Feeney wrote, "lawmakers ought to deregulate these competitors in order to make the regulatory playing field as level as possible while allowing for innovative disruptors to enter markets."[29]

Are Sharing-Economy Companies Platforms for Independent Contractors, or Are They Employers?

Sharing-economy companies that connect service providers with customers say they are simply providing a convenient platform to help the two parties connect. An Uber spokesperson, talking on background, described Uber as a technology company that matches riders with drivers. The company classifies drivers as "partners," not employees.

As long as service providers are considered independent contractors, companies aren't bound by minimum wage and overtime laws, nor do they incur expenses for such things as unemployment insurance, workers' compensation and health insurance.

However, service providers have sued some sharing-economy companies—including Uber and Lyft—saying they are really employees and should receive benefits. Those lawsuits are pending, and neither company responded to requests to discuss them.

The initial indications are that the companies may face a tough sell of their argument that the companies are just platforms and not transportation companies with driver employees. Judge Edward Chen of the federal District Court in San Francisco called that argument "fatally flawed," noting, "It is clear that Uber is most certainly a transportation company, albeit a technologically sophisticated one."[30]

As for the argument that the drivers are independent contractors and not employees, Chen said that the issue will have to be decided at trial under California law.

The California Labor Commission's determination in early June that at least one Uber driver was, in fact, an employee, will likely be taken into consideration.

"Defendants hold themselves out as nothing more than a neutral technological platform, designed simply to enable drivers and passengers to transact the business of transportation," the Labor Commissioner's Office wrote in its decision. "The reality, however, is that defendants are involved in every aspect of the operation."[31]

While several other states—including Georgia and Texas—have ruled Uber drivers to be contractors, Florida authorities decided in May that a former Uber driver had been an employee for purposes of claiming unemployment benefits. Uber is appealing that decision.

There is no federal law defining the difference between independent contractors and employees, nor have states been consistent in defining the terms. But, according to Kai Falkenberg, former editorial counsel for Forbes magazine and currently a visiting professor at Cardozo School of Law, there are a number factors the courts tend to consider in making such determinations, including the amount of control the company exerts over the service provider's activities.

For its part, the Internal Revenue Service applies "the usual common law rules" in determining employee status for tax purposes. This involves determining the extent to which the company exerts behavioral control and financial control over the service provider, as well as factors such as contract obligations, if any, and provision of benefits, such as health insurance.[32]

"One of the reasons that Uber drivers might be considered as employees is the degree of control that the companies are exerting," Falkenberg says. "And one of the manifestations of that is, interestingly, through the rating system. That seems to be a significant degree of control."

Falkenberg explains that Uber relies on its customer review system to cultivate trust in the service. If drivers get bad reviews from customers, they are likely to be let go.

"The companies really want to provide the best caliber service, and they want the people using the service to trust them," she says. "There's a tension between providing a high level of service but without changing your status from basically being a platform that provides a matchmaking service to a company that is actually employing people who are providing a service."

"For all practical purposes they are employees and if we're just going to play a semantic game here then there is no point in the regulations in the first place," Baker says of Uber drivers. "Obviously if you have the option to define someone as an independent contractor rather than an employee, and evade all of the regulations, then you've given companies enormous incentive to classify people as independent contractors."

Some analysts say the real problem is with the way important benefits are tied to employed positions vs. independent contractors.

"The sharing economy in a lot of ways is putting a spotlight on weak spots in public policy," says Koopman. "One of those is why we continue to insist on tying health insurance to employment."

Sundararajan of the Stern School of Business agreed. "The dichotomy of employees and independent contractors is out of date," he wrote. Sundararajan called for labor laws to "be updated to provide a social safety net to people whose chosen form of work is something other than full-time employment. Health coverage, insurance against workplace injuries, paid vacations and maternity leave: these have long been universal entitlements in many economies. They should not become exclusive perks for a dwindling band of salaried employees."[33]

BACKGROUND

Out of the Shadows

Before the development of effective monetary systems, nearly all economic activity took place within sharing economies that relied upon either barter or gifting to exchange goods and services. After the Industrial Revolution and the rapid spread of capitalism in the mid-1700s, the exchange modes of the sharing economy were relegated to an unofficial shadow economy in industrialized countries.

Some sources point to Harvard Law Professor Yochai Benkler as the first person to articulate the modern concept of the "sharing economy." Benkler coined the term "commons-based peer production" to describe activities in which numbers of people work together, primarily over the internet, to create value. Benkler further developed the concept in his 2004 paper, “Sharing Nicely: On Shareable Goods and the Emergence of Sharing as a Modality of Economic Production.”[34]

Benkler was describing a trend that had been developing for several years. Increasingly, individuals and companies were taking advantage of the emerging capabilities of the internet to connect people to information, products and each other. As early as 1995, when a person had something to sell, she could simply post it on eBay or Craigslist and instantly reach thousands of people instead of having to take out a relatively expensive ad in the local newspaper that might reach a small number of people.

Not surprisingly, different sectors of the sharing economy developed independently and at different times as new technologies enabled more complex interactions.

The earliest companies in the modern sharing economy were those focused on connecting individual buyers of products and services with individual sellers.

Person-to-Person (P2P) Markets

“It’s hard to believe now, but until 1991, commercial enterprise on the internet was strictly prohibited. Even then, the rules favored public institutions and forbade ‘extensive use for private or personal business,’” wrote Wired executive editor Keven Kelly.[35] In the eyes of the National Science Foundation (NSF), which at the time was the primary authority governing internet activity, “the internet was funded for research, not commerce,” he said.

The NSF didn’t officially lift its prohibition on commercial activity until 1995.[36] Even before then, however, e-commerce had begun. In 1992, Book Stacks Unlimited in Cleveland opened one of the first commercial sales websites that supported credit card processing. Only two years later, what would become a dominant e-commerce site—Amazon.com—was founded.[37]

Book Stacks Unlimited and Amazon were, of course, e-commerce sites rather than sharing-economy platforms. But they pioneered the technologies that would drive the emergence of online services that allowed consumers to share products through the Web.

And in 1995, two companies that would evolve into two of the largest drivers of the sharing economy appeared.

In early 1995, Craig Newmark began an email distribution list to inform his community of internet developers in the San Francisco area about local events. The service proved popular—especially for its job listings and listings of items for sale—and as the mailing list grew others began to contribute items. By 1996, Newmark converted the mailing list to a website, craigslist.org.[38]

EBay, also founded in 1995, was intended from the start by its founder Pierre Omidyar to be a commercial site for selling goods and services. Unlike Amazon, however, eBay aimed at connecting individual sellers with individual buyers through online auctions.[39]

In 2008, Shelby Clark, then a graduate student at Harvard Business School, realized that the P2P model didn’t have to be limited to individuals buying and selling products. It could also be used for sharing things like personal cars. On Thanksgiving Day in Boston that year, Clark wanted to visit his cousins but he didn’t have a car. “It was a frickin awful winter day in Boston,” he recalled in an interview. “It was snowing and the freezing wind was coming from every direction and I’m biking through the snow and sleet to get this damned car. Meanwhile,

I'm passing all these cars that are covered in snow. They clearly hadn't been driven in weeks."[40] That's when he got the idea to develop a platform on which car owners could offer their vehicles for rent.

Clark couldn't find any such service online, but he did discover the major hurdle he had to clear: insurance. Existing policies didn't cover car rentals between individuals. It took Clark 18 months to arrange appropriate coverage, after which he started RelayRides.

Also in 2008, Joe Gebbia and Brian Chesky were inspired to apply the model to another underused resource: living space.

"Joe Gebbia and Brian Chesky were two jobless friends living together when they received a terrifying letter from the landlord," wrote Alex Stephany, author and CEO of a European sharing company called JustPark.[41] The letter informed them that their rent was increasing by 25 percent. Chesky didn't have the money. "He had days to find a solution when the two noticed all the unused space in their living room," wrote Stephany. "What if someone would pay to sleep there? Gebbia had just been camping and had an airbed. They blew it up . . . and came up with the concept of 'airbed and breakfast': cheap accommodation on your beds with a no-frills breakfast of Pop-Tarts."

Two days later, www.airbedandbreakfast—later to be known as Airbnb—was born. The company grew so quickly that, in 2015, it has 1.2 million listings in 190 countries.[42]

But the power of the internet-powered sharing economy isn't just about big markets. It also allows smaller communities to connect across great distances.

Poshmark, a platform founded in 2011 that runs on a mobile application, connects women who want to buy and sell used clothes with each other. Sellers take photos of their items to offer for sale. When an item is sold, the Poshmark app emails the seller a shipping label addressed to the buyer.[43]

Product Sharing and Renting

While P2P markets connect individual buyers to individual sellers, Robin Chase's idea in 1999 was to provide a platform and products that individuals could easily share.

She had met a friend at a café in Cambridge, Mass., Chase recalled. The friend had just returned from a vacation in Germany and mentioned that she had come across a car being rented to people by the hour or by the day. Chase, who would become a cofounder of Zipcar, wondered if that idea might work in Cambridge.

"My husband drove our car out to his suburban office every morning, where it would sit in the parking lot all day," Chase wrote. "And while I definitely needed a car sometimes, there was absolutely no way I wanted to buy another, park it on the street in our city neighborhood, maintain it, and shovel it out after snowstorms."[44]

Zipcar began with an initial investment of $50,000. "Four months later, Zipcar had $68 in its bank account and three days before going live," Chase said. "The plan was to place four cars in four reserved parking spaces, one near each of four consecutive subway stops in Cambridge and Boston."[45]

According to Chase, the company's goal was to make renting a car "as easy and convenient as getting cash from an ATM."[46] Chase and her team accomplished this by creating a website for making reservations, then placing devices in the cars that could read members' cards for unlocking, enabling the ignition and tracking distances.

At the same time as major sharing-economy companies were launching, so too were scores of nonprofit grassroots efforts that, collectively, have greatly affected the economy and communities' use of resources.

In May 2003, for example, Deron Beal started the Freecycle Network to connect his friends and a few nonprofits in Tucson, Ariz., so that they could exchange goods they no longer needed without charge. Freecycle Network now has 5,000-plus groups and more than 7 million members worldwide.[47] It's a grassroots and entirely nonprofit movement of people who are giving (and getting) stuff for free in their own towns and keeping good things out of landfills.

Peer-to-Peer Loans

As companies were helping people share goods and services, some companies turned to the internet to allow people to loan each other money instead of going through banks and other financial institutions, which generally charge higher rates of interest.

The first such peer-to-peer lending service was Zopa, begun in Great Britain in 2005. Since then, Zopa has made more than $1.4 billion in loans with reserves pooled from more than 51,000 people.[48]

The next year, the first peer-to-peer lending company in the United States—Prosper Marketplace—launched in San Francisco.

According to a Federal Deposit Insurance Corp. report, however, early peer-to-peer lending platforms had few qualifications for borrowers, which led to defaults and high loss rates. The report noted that the major peer-to-peer services have tightened borrower requirements.[49]

Some platforms gave a twist to the peer-to-peer lending model by combining it with features of eBay-like auctions to create "crowdfunding." The best-known of these platforms—Kickstarter—was founded in 2009. Kickstarter provides a structured means for individuals or companies to pitch their products and services in order to enlist contributions. As of July 27, Kickstarter says it has funded 89,000 projects since 2009, with 9.1 million contributors pledging $1.8 billion.[50]

Fee-for-Service Markets

The preeminent example of fee-for-service firms are transportation network companies (TNCs), including Uber, Lyft and Sidecar. With TNCs—which offer rides to consumers, booked via websites or mobile apps—the vehicles aren't actually shared or rented. Instead, drivers with their own vehicles share the TNC platform to offer their services to consumers.

While car-renting companies such as Zipcar and car-sharing companies such as RelayRides had established themselves years earlier, TNCs, which deliver services on a moment's demand, had to await the development and ubiquity of smartphones and the apps that run on them.

That technological hurdle was cleared by 2009 when Uber was founded as "UberCab" by Travis Kalanick and Garrett Camp.

The Beginnings of Regulation

Regulators have struggled to find ways not only to regulate the various types of sharing-economy companies but also to monitor their activities and collect appropriate taxes. For the most part, such efforts have taken place at the local level.

The TNCs have drawn the greatest attention, because they compete in an industry that has long been heavily regulated for public safety reasons and because governments want to control their effects on communities and public facilities, such as airports. This process of fitting TNCs into the existing regulatory frameworks has been a challenge that has resulted in a patchwork of requirements.

In June 2014, Colorado became the first state to pass legislation creating a statewide regulatory framework for TNCs.[51] The legislation specifies necessary levels of insurance and details requirements for regular background checks. The state Public Utilities Commission is empowered to revoke or suspend a company's permit, but penalties against drivers are prohibited. Other measures include yearly safety inspections of drivers' vehicles and exterior markings signifying them as vehicles for hire. In addition, the TNC cannot discriminate against riders based on their location or destination, nor can it charge additional fees for passengers with disabilities.

CURRENT SITUATION

Regulatory Pressure Grows

The sharing economy is filled with companies that have as many differences as similarities. In fact, the only thing they have in common is that customers access goods or services through the internet.

Most of these businesses—such as Etsy, MuniRent and Zimride (a ride-sharing service for companies and universities)—pose few, if any, problems for consumers or regulators. That's because they simply connect providers to consumers and are not engaged in the types of activities that require safety regulations to protect the public. Most sharing-economy companies are also generally free of controversy because they are not directly competing with traditional companies. And most don't rely extensively, if at all, on service providers who might press claims for employee benefits.

Other companies—most notably, Uber, Lyft and Airbnb—are facing increasing pressure from regulators, employees and competitors.

In the last five months alone, legislatures, city councils, regulators and others have been active on numerous fronts:

- In early March, the Vermont Department of Financial Regulation issued a consumer alert, "Be aware before you share." The alert warned residents wanting to drive that participation in sharing-economy businesses could expose them to major liabilities if they lack appropriate insurance. The state labor commissioner announced she was investigating Uber in Vermont to determine whether its drivers are employees or independent contractors.[52]
- On April 21, the Portland, Ore., City Council voted 3-2 to end a prohibition on ride-sharing companies by allowing them to operate under a 120-day pilot program. The two dissenting council members indicated that they still have concerns about minimum insurance coverage and Uber's business practices.[53]
- On May 4, California Democratic State Sen. Mike McGuire introduced legislation that would require companies such as Airbnb to adhere to local laws with regard to

vacation rentals, including paying occupancy taxes. The legislation also calls for data reporting on room rates and the number of nights stayed by renters.[54]

- On May 5, Uber announced that it was ceasing operations in Kansas after the state Legislature overrode the governor's veto to pass legislation with stricter insurance requirements and background checks for drivers.[55]
- On May 12, the Santa Monica, Calif., City Council adopted a home-sharing ordinance that prohibits the rental of an entire unit for less than 30 days. The ordinance also requires hosts to obtain a business license and to pay a 14 percent hotel tax. Proceeds from the tax will help pay for enforcement officers and staff to search online for illegal rentals.[56]
- On May 26, San Francisco International Airport and the San Francisco Municipal Transportation Agency petitioned the California Public Utilities Commission to impose tighter regulations on ride-sharing companies. Specifically, the agencies called for mandated vehicle inspections, a limit of 375,000 miles on vehicles, the use of permanent "trade dress" markers on vehicles and training for drivers.[57]

Bike-Sharing on a Roll

Number of cities worldwide with bike-sharing systems

Bicycle-sharing systems have become popular in big cities and other densely populated areas with heavy traffic. This chart shows the growth of bike-sharing systems in cities around the world between 2001 and 2014. A notable increase in cities with such systems occurred between 2006 and 2008, with a jump from 24 to 131 cities. The number of cities has steadily increased since then, with 855 cities offering bike-sharing systems as of the end of 2014.

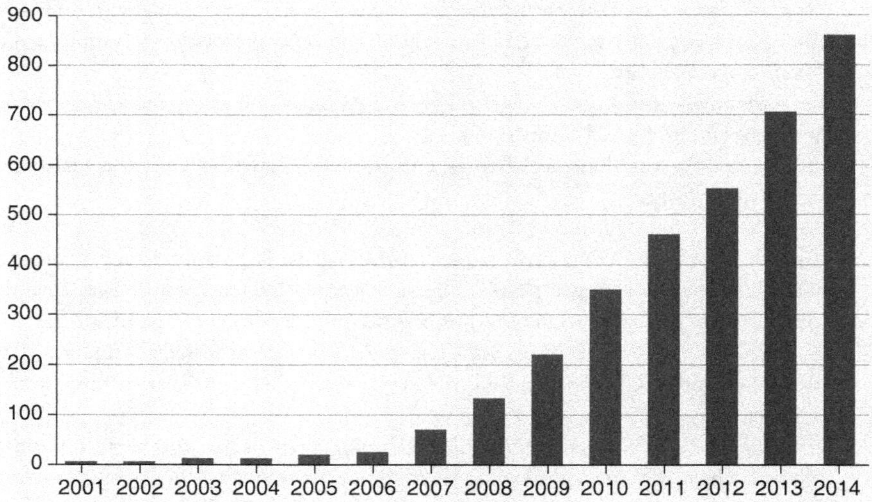

Source: Russell Meddin, "The Bike Sharing World—2014—Year End Data," The Bike-Sharing Blog, MetroBike, Jun. 30, 2015, http://tinyurl.com/pva8ddt.

- On May 29, Republican Nevada Gov. Brian Sandoval signed legislation providing a regulatory framework for ride-sharing services in the state. The framework includes a 3 percent tax on fares.[58]
- On June 18, Lyft agreed to pay the state of New York $300,000 to settle claims that it was in violation of state and municipal laws. The agreement also placed tighter requirements on insurance for Lyft drivers, and required the company to comply with state and local laws covering for-hire car services.[59]

Companies Responding

One of the major challenges facing sharing-economy companies is that to do business nationally, they must conform to not just one regulatory authority but potentially hundreds of state, municipal and port authorities.

"It's a problem for the companies," says John Browning, a Southern Methodist University adjunct law professor who also works with tech start-ups. "They have lobbyists going to 50 different state legislatures."

Browning says federal legislation could simplify things, although no bill has been introduced. "Are there companies, particularly in the tech sector, that have an interest in getting some sort of federal legislation? Absolutely," he says. "That would give companies some measure of predictability, reliability and, to a certain extent, protection."

Perhaps in anticipation of, or to fend off, regulation, many of the larger sharing-economy companies, in addition to stepping up lobbying efforts, have been introducing or increasing their own insurance coverage and taking other steps, such as performing background checks for relevant service providers.

"Generally, these companies want to at least have the appearance that they are in line with consumer expectations," says Breyault of the National Consumers League. "By and large, I think they are implementing these because they want to avoid more onerous regulations that could harm their business model."

Uber, for example, instituted background checks for drivers in 2014 that cover:

- County courthouse records going back seven years for every county of residence.
- Federal courthouse records going back seven years.
- The multistate criminal database going back seven years.
- A National Sex Offender Registry screen.
- A Social Security trace, which ensures the number is valid and confirms names and addresses.
- Checks of existing motor vehicle records, as well as regular future checks.[60]

Critics, however, charge that the background checks aren't thorough enough because they do not include fingerprinting and processing through law enforcement agencies.

In July 2014, Uber also announced it had obtained a commercial insurance policy to provide $1 million of liability coverage per incident, as well as contingent comprehensive and collision insurance.[61] The new coverage applies to Uber's most widely used service, called UberX. (Commercial insurance already covered the company's other more specialized services such as black-car limo rides.)

In March 2015, Uber and the Property Casualty Insurers Association of America (PCI) announced model legislation for consideration by states that they jointly developed; 18 states have already passed laws that mirror the model, according to Robert Passmore, PCI's senior director for personal lines.

"Auto insurance is based on years and years of track records and loss history," says Passmore. "We don't have a lot of loss history behind these folks." Thus, says Passmore, it's especially important to have clear rules about what kinds of coverage are required.

Airbnb, too, has moved to provide insurance. As of January 2015, the company's Host Protection Insurance provides up to $1 million in coverage in the event a guest is injured on a host's property during a stay. The insurance applies only in the United States.[62]

Airbnb has also made agreements with some localities—including the District of Columbia, San Francisco, Phoenix, Portland, Ore., San Jose and Chicago—to collect taxes owed by hosts and pay them directly to the local government. While Airbnb did not respond to requests for comment, its website notes that these agreements make "the tax collection process easier for all parties involved."

"In many cases, these taxes were designed for hotels and folks with teams of lawyers and accountants, and the reality is that the person who's renting out his basement in Cleveland Park [in D.C.] once a month probably doesn't have tax experts on payroll," Nick Papas, an Airbnb spokesman, told a Washington Post reporter. "You shouldn't need a lawyer and a tax specialist if you want to rent out your house."[63]

According to Stephen Cordi, the deputy chief financial officer in the Office of Tax and Revenue in D.C., it was Airbnb that approached the city about making the arrangement to pay taxes.

"It's undoubtedly true that people particularly at the bottom end of this probably didn't know what to do," Cordi told The Washington Post. While individual Airbnb hosts should have been registering with the city and paying the taxes all along, he said, "this will eliminate the need for them to do that."

Still, according to Norton Francis, senior research associate at the Tax Policy Center, which provides research on taxes for the Urban Institute and the Brookings Institution, cities and states are "losing tax revenue because of these new forms" of services in the sharing economy. "The product isn't any different; it's the delivery," he said. "States are one step behind commerce in an effort to try to maintain their tax bases."[64]

Advice for the Sharing Economy

Experts Say Regulation Brings Opportunities as Well as Perils

Sharing-economy companies can thrive in a more heavily regulated market by following six maxims, experts say, including reaching out to government and offering to work with regulators on developing commonsense rules.

Despite the pleas of free-market advocates, most analysts expect that regulatory oversight of sharing-economy companies will increase. But that doesn't have to mean the end of the business model.

"There is very little historical evidence that the presence of government oversight shuts down productive economic activity," Harvard Business School professor Nancy Koehn said. "Rather, the enterprises that succeed and endure are those that understand how to compete effectively within the framework of government regulation because these players understand what is really at stake in the specific lawmaking."[65]

All the same, wrote Google Capital Manager Sarah Cannon and former U.S. Treasury Secretary Lawrence H. Summers, "regulation is often the most significant barrier to future growth for sharing-economy firms."[66]

So how can a company thrive in a more regulated sharing economy?

Cannon and Summers advise companies to be "more cooperative with regulators." Specifically, they advise sharing-economy companies to follow six maxims:

- **Go on the offensive (rather than defensive) with regulators.** "The sharing economy is a new concept and many city regulators are unfamiliar with the business model. As a result they are often skeptical and assume sharing economy firms are trying to make a profit by skirting the regulations 'traditional' industries (i.e., taxis) face. It makes far more sense to be proactive and explain your business to regulators."
- **Be responsive to regulators' legitimate concerns.** "Where regulators' concerns are legitimate companies should respond, both because it is the right thing to do and because it will build credibility with the authorities. In making their case, companies should make arguments they would believe if they were regulators."
- **Use state-of-the-art approaches to reach out to government.** "Best practices in approaching government include forming coalitions and industry associations to represent a shared point of view rather than each company approaching regulators independently and only in times of crisis. Further, sharing-economy firms should seek outside validators."
- **Share your data.** "Data need not be made public in order to share it with government, and can help your case by reducing regulator concerns."
- **Make a well-researched case for the value provided by your firm.** "Rather than relying on maxims about the usefulness of the sharing economy, it helps to have concrete data, especially in the face of skeptical regulators."
- **Find the best regulations out there and share them with the government.** "City governments are often under-resourced and many existing rules are simply outdated and are not relevant given the business model of sharing economy firms. There's no reason firms themselves cannot find the best rules out there and propose them to the mayor's office."

Other analysts add that it's critical for those considering launching a sharing-economy business to consider carefully the sector and the product or service they will offer. "I encourage people to think about the sharing economy as being two things—on the one hand providing genuine efficiencies, and on the other hand of evading regulations. I would say if you focus on the first you won't go wrong," says economist Dean Baker.

Economist Chiarra Farronato stresses the importance of gaining and retaining consumer trust by getting ahead of problems that will inevitably arise. "One thing that peer-to-peer platforms are really working hard on is their review and reputation systems, and on setting up insurance policies on their own," she says. "The system seems to be working fine."

Business professor Giana Eckhardt of the School of Management, Royal Holloway, University of London, urges entrepreneurs to take care in selecting their product area. "Make sure that it's something where people feel comfortable being in close contact with other people," she says. "There are some product categories where it seems like a sharing-economy model is never going to work. These tend to be ones where you need high levels of trust."

And, while Eckhardt points out that the regulatory uncertainty in many areas of the sharing economy hasn't seemed to deter investment, she recommends that entrepreneurs "make sure that the regulatory environment has been sorted out."

Zipcar cofounder Robin Chase said that the most important thing for sharing-economy entrepreneurs is to leave the old economic models behind. "Those old barriers to entry—large privately held assets and closed intellectual property—no longer result in the greatest value," she wrote. "They are dated strategies, unable to match the potential that exists in shared assets, which will always deliver better returns and empower multitudes who represent infinitely larger intellectual pools."[67]

—Patrick Marshall

LOOKING AHEAD

Rivals Need to Adapt

The technologies that define the sharing economy—the internet-enabled applications that allow consumers to connect directly to service providers—are clearly not going to disappear.

"I think this is the beginning of the second-order issues of the sharing economy," says Koopman of the Mercatus Center. "The first-order issues were whether the sharing economy should exist at all. That debate is settled. The sharing economy is here to stay. Now comes the second wave of issues for sharing economy firms: How are the regulators going to treat them?"

Because the technologies driving the sharing economy are new, the old regulatory frameworks are no longer appropriate, most analysts agree. Even those who maintain the need for strong regulatory structures acknowledge that in some areas changes are warranted. "You can make plenty of arguments, and there some truth to them, that a lot of the regulations that we have in place are excessive," says Baker of the Center for Economic and Policy Research.

"Do you apply old regulations to new innovations or try to adapt and evolve the regulations to fit the market over time?" Koopman asks. "I think when you try to apply the old laws and the old rules to new innovation and new entrepreneurship, you end up hamstringing innovation. This should be an opportunity for everyone to critically reevaluate the regulations on the books."

In the meantime, say some analysts, it's time for traditional companies to adapt to the new technology environment. "The entry of these new platforms has put pressure on existing suppliers," economist Farronato says. "From the point of view of innovation, it is pressure for the better." She adds that as traditional companies adopt the new technologies—such as online review—old regulatory frameworks may no longer be needed. "It might be the case that the industry will actually evolve in a way that the regulatory environment will be more lax," she says.

While free market advocates worry about regulators stifling innovation, former Clinton administration Labor Secretary Robert Reich warns about the ramifications of an unfettered sharing economy.

"In effect, on-demand work is a reversion to the piece work of the nineteenth century—when workers had no power and no legal rights, took all the risks, and worked all hours for almost nothing," Reich wrote in an article on his website. "Uber drivers use their own cars, take out their own insurance, work as many hours as they want or can—and pay Uber a fat percent. Worker safety? Social Security? Uber says it's not the employer so it's not responsible."[68]

Of course, how consumers and investors will respond to higher costs caused by increased regulation of the sharing economy is unknown.

With respect to investors, they seem undeterred so far. "There have been very high investment levels within these areas where regulation hasn't been settled," says Eckhardt of the University of London.

Consumers' response, she says, may be more problematic. "When you start to see that competitive advantage eroding away, and prices rise, consumers may perceive [the companies] to be gouging," she says. "These so-called sharing-economy companies are, in a way, responsible for this because the way they tend to position themselves as, 'Oh, we're doing better for the world. We're somehow different than all of these regular companies.'"

Chronology

1990s	**Technologies that will power the sharing economy appear, and pioneer e-commerce companies take advantage.**
1991	The National Science Foundation (NSF), which controlled the internet backbone, allows commercial access to the formerly government and academic network.
1992	E-commerce begins when Book Stacks Unlimited in Cleveland opens a website that supports credit card processing.
1994	Amazon is founded and would soon grow into a dominant e-commerce site.
1995	Craig Newmark launches an email distribution list that will be converted the next year into a website that allows people to buy and sell goods and to find jobs: craigslist.org. . . . eBay is founded as an online platform to connect individual sellers with individual buyers through online auctions. . . . NSF formally lifts its prohibition on commercial activity on the Web.
1999	Zipcar—an online car rental service—appears, with four cars stationed near subway stops in Cambridge and Boston, Mass.
2000–2007	**Early sharing-economy companies are founded.**
2003	The Freecycle Network goes online, allowing individuals and nonprofits to exchange goods they no longer need.
2004	Yochai Benkler, a Harvard law professor, publishes "Sharing Nicely: On Shareable Goods and the Emergence of Sharing as a Modality of Economic Production," the first analysis of the modern sharing economy.
2005	Zopa, the world's first online peer-to-peer lending platform, debuts in London.
2007	Zimride, which became Lyft, begins offering on-demand rides; its drivers are independent contractors who own their own cars.
2008–Present	**Recession spurs growth of the sharing economy as regulators begin to take action.**
2008	Harvard Business School graduate student Shelby Clark launches RelayRides, a service that allows individuals to rent their personal cars to others. . . . Joe Gebbia and Brian Chesky, needing money to pay their rent, offer their living room online as a place for someone to sleep. A few days later, they launch www.airbedandbreakfast.com, which will soon become known as Airbnb.
2009	Kickstarter, a crowd-sourced platform for funding projects, opens. . . . UberCab, which will soon change its name to Uber, is founded in San Francisco.
2014	Colorado becomes the first state to pass legislation creating a statewide regulatory framework for "transportation network companies," such as Uber and Lyft. . . . In June, the California Labor Commissioner's Office rules that an Uber driver should be classified as an employee, not an independent contractor. . . . In October, the New York State Office of the Attorney General releases a report that finds that 72 percent of units booked over Airbnb in the state appeared to violate state and local laws. Within days, New York City files suit against two property owners.

2015	On May 5, Uber announces it is ceasing operations in Kansas after that state passes legislation with stricter insurance requirements and background checks for drivers. . . . On May 12, the Santa Monica, Calif., City Council adopts a home-sharing ordinance that prohibits the rental of an entire unit for less than 30 days. The ordinance also requires hosts to obtain a business license and to pay a 14 percent hotel tax. . . . On May 26, San Francisco International Airport and the San Francisco Municipal Transportation Agency petition the California Public Utilities Commission to impose tighter regulations on ride-sharing companies. . . . On May 29, Nevada Gov. Brian Sandoval announces passage of a regulatory framework for ride-sharing services in the state; the framework includes a 3 percent tax on fares. . . . On June 18, Lyft agrees to pay the state of New York $300,000 to settle claims that it was in violation of state and municipal laws. The agreement also places tighter requirements on insurance for Lyft drivers, and requires the company to comply with state and local laws covering for-hire car services.

PERSPECTIVE

Pro/Con: Dean Baker on Regulating the Sharing Economy

YES

SHOULD SHARING-ECONOMY COMPANIES BE BROUGHT INTO THE SAME REGULATORY FRAMEWORKS AS THEIR COMPETITORS?

Dean Baker

Economist, Cofounder of the Center for Economic and Policy Research

Written for SAGE Business Researcher, August 2015

Over many decades we have developed a long series of regulations that apply to taxi companies, hotels and other businesses that compete with upstart sharing-economy companies. These regulations cover a wide range of areas, including consumer protection, safety, worker protection and restrictions on discrimination based on race, gender and disability.

In some cases, these regulations are excessive, imposing unnecessary costs on business, which are in turn largely passed on to consumers. Some of the regulations were designed to protect the incumbents in the industry, most notably restrictions on the number of cabs that can be on the road. But most of these regulations do serve a public purpose. For this reason, it does not make sense to give the sharing-economy companies a pass, even if people order their service over the internet.

In the case of Uber, there should be guarantees that Uber's cars are safe, that passengers are covered by insurance in the event of an accident, that the drivers have good driving records, and that the drivers are not dangerous criminals who pose a threat to their passengers. This may not require the same sort of strict rules that are imposed on the traditional cab industry in most cities, but it does mean a mechanism should be in place to ensure that Uber meets basic standards.

Similarly, Uber drivers need the same sort of protections as other workers. This means they should be covered by minimum wage laws, overtime rules, workers' compensation and be insured not only when they have a rider in the car but also on their way to and from cab pick-ups. If this is too complicated for Uber to deal with, then they can be replaced by companies that are more computer-savvy.

Uber should be required to have a certain percentage of its cars handicap-accessible; the company also needs to either develop a mechanism for payment by customers without access to credit cards or to pay a fee to ensure that such people have access to taxi service.

Similarly, Airbnb facilities should not be fire traps and should comply with building and neighborhood rental codes. Airbnb must also take responsibility for ensuring that people have access to facilities it rents regardless of their race and ethnicity. We expect this of traditional hotels; Airbnb should be held to similar standards.

PERSPECTIVE

Pro/Con: Christopher Koopman, Matthew Mitchell and Adam Thierer on Regulating the Sharing Economy

NO

SHOULD SHARING-ECONOMY COMPANIES BE BROUGHT INTO THE SAME REGULATORY FRAMEWORKS AS THEIR COMPETITORS?

Christopher Koopman, Matthew Mitchell and Adam Thierer

Research Fellows, Mercatus Center at George Mason University

Excerpted from testimony before the Federal Trade Commission, May 26, 2015

As the debate surrounding the sharing economy moves forward, policymakers must keep in mind that merely because regulations were once justified on the grounds of consumer protection does not mean they accomplished those goals or that they are still needed today.

Markets, competition, reputational systems and ongoing innovation often solve problems better than regulation when they are given a chance to do so. There are two reasons for this. First, market imperfections create powerful profit opportunities for entrepreneurs who are able to find ways to correct them. Second, regulatory solutions too often undermine competition and lock in inefficient business models.

Exempting newcomers from traditional regulations could place incumbents at a disadvantage. Such regulatory asymmetries represent a legitimate policy problem. But the solution is not to discourage new innovations by simply rolling old regulatory regimes onto new technologies and sectors. The better alternative is to level the playing field by "deregulating down" to put everyone on equal footing, not by "regulating up" to achieve parity.

By trying to head off every hypothetical worst-case scenario, preemptive regulations actually discourage many best-case scenarios from ever coming about. For that reason, ex post remedies are often preferable to ex ante regulation. Private insurance, contracts, torts and product liability law, antitrust enforcement and other legal remedies can be utilized here when things go wrong, just as they are used in countless other segments of our economy.

The internet and the information revolution have given rise to new online feedback mechanisms that have made it easier than ever for honesty to be enforced through strong reputational incentives. This has, in turn, alleviated many traditional concerns about informational deficiencies. With the recent growth of the sharing economy, even more robust reputational feedback mechanisms now exist that help consumers solve information problems and secure a greater voice in commercial interactions. These mechanisms have been integrated into the platforms connecting buyers and sellers and have become an essential feature of these sectors.

The internet and real-time reputational feedback mechanisms should force a reevaluation of traditional regulations aimed at addressing perceived market failures based on asymmetric information. Such regulations have typically failed to improve consumer welfare and have undermined innovation and competition. This may explain why, when recently surveyed by PricewaterhouseCoopers, 64 percent of U.S. consumers said that in the sharing economy, peer regulation is more important than government regulation.

UPDATE IN 2020

When 2020 began, it looked as though there would be few limits on growth in the sharing economy. Venture capitalists poured more than $23 billion into a wide variety of sharing-economy companies. Global tourism and travel bookings alone were generating $1.6 trillion in revenue.[69]

Then COVID-19 hit. Suddenly, the freedom that the sharing economy presented to consumers no longer seemed as trustworthy as it did before the pandemic. Within weeks of the pandemic's spread in winter 2020, major names in the sharing economy began to feel the impact of the mind change.

Ride-hailing companies such as Uber and Lyft said their earnings had collapsed. The home-sharing company Airbnb decided to put off an initial public offering, laid off 25 percent of its staff and cut its revenue forecast in half. "While we know Airbnb's business will fully recover, the changes it will undergo are not temporary or short-lived," Brian Chesky, Airbnb's chief executive, wrote in a memo to employees.[70]

Across the travel business, other executives also were wondering whether the fundamentals of their business model have been permanently altered. Prior to the pandemic, the idea of peer-to-peer sharing seemed limitless, especially as major employers embraced the concept of letting their employees use sharing services.

In 2017, a report from the Global Business Travel Association found that half the companies now allowed their employees to use Uber or Lyft, up from 44 percent in mid-2016. It also discovered that 30 percent of policies allow business travelers to book accommodations on Airbnb. Separately, a report from Certify, a business expense-tracking service, found that Airbnb transactions among business travelers had doubled from 2014 to 2017, while Uber had become one of the most-expensed companies in the United States.[71]

However, there were casualties. One of the earliest ride-sharing companies, Sidebar, shut down in 2015, eclipsed by Uber and Lyft.[72]

Meanwhile, federal and local regulators worldwide took aim at the sharing companies, refusing to accept their argument that they offered technology platforms and were not employers. In some instances, Uber was banned in Hungary, Bulgaria, France, Italy, Finland, Germany and The Netherlands.[73]

In May 2020, California's attorney general joined a group of municipalities in suing Uber and Lyft, charging that the companies wrongfully classified their drivers as independent contractors, when a state law said they should be considered employees.[74]

The same month, drivers for Uber and Lyft sued New York State, saying that the state had refused to pay unemployment compensation, or was delaying the payments. The lawsuit said the practice ran counter to the state's practice of protecting drivers who worked for ride-sharing companies.

In December 2019, New York Gov. Andrew Cuomo signed legislation that enhanced benefits available to ride-sharing employees under the Black Car Fund. Drivers were eligible for a variety of protections, including workers' compensation, health and medical resources, paid driver classes, accident assistance and legal assistance.[75]

Amid the pandemic and with increasing action regarding regulation, companies are making short- and long-term adjustments to their operations and policies. Lyft and Uber added "checks" to prioritize the health and safety of both passengers and drivers through the use of face coverings, and also suspended pooled rides in the U.S. and Canada.[76] Airbnb responded by launching an enhanced, five-step cleaning process, though it received flak for its refund policies, as it backed away from a COVID-19 policy that had allowed refunds on bookings placed before Mar. 14, 2020. In a revised refund policy in July 2020, refunds in the event of COVID-19 restrictions resulting from government mandates would not be issued.

The reason, Airbnb said, was that the pandemic and its health consequences "are no longer unforeseen or unexpected. Please remember to carefully review the host's cancellation policy when booking and consider choosing an option that provides flexibility."[77]

—Micheline Maynard

NOTES

Introduction

1. World Bank, "Global Economic Prospects, June 2020," 2020, https://openknowledge.worldbank.org/handle/10986/33748.
2. Gita Gopinath, "Reopening from the Great Lockdown: Uneven and Uncertain Recovery," IMFBlog, Jun. 24, 2020, https://blogs.imf.org/2020/06/24/reopening-from-the-great-lockdown-uneven-and-uncertain-recovery/.
3. Jonathan Cheng, "China's Economy Is Bouncing Back—and Gaining Ground on the U.S. Wall Street Journal, Aug. 24, 2020, https://www.wsj.com/articles/chinas-economy-is-bouncing-backand-gaining-ground-on-the-u-s-11598280917.
4. Dana Mattioli and Sebastian Herrera, "Amazon's Sales Jump as Coronavirus Prompts Surge in Online Shopping," The Wall Street Journal, Apr. 30, 2020, https://www.wsj.com/articles/amazons-sales-jump-as-coronavirus-prompts-surge-in-online-shopping-11588278740.
5. Rishi Iyengar, "Zoom's Revenue Soars 169% As People Flock to Service during Pandemic," CNN Business, Jun. 2, 2020, https://www.cnn.com/2020/06/02/tech/zoom-earnings-coronavirus/index.html.
6. OECD, "COVID-19 and the Retail Sector: Impact and Policy Responses," Jun. 16, 2020, http://www.oecd.org/coronavirus/policy-responses/COVID-19-and-the-retail-sector-impact-and-policy-responses-371d7599/.
7. OECD, "Coronavirus (COVID-19): SME Policy Responses," updated Jul. 15, 2020, http://www.oecd.org/coronavirus/policy-responses/coronavirus-COVID-19-sme-policy-responses-04440101/.
8. Chad Otar, "The Impact of the Coronavirus on Small Business," Forbes, May 29, 2020, https://www.forbes.com/sites/forbesfinancecouncil/2020/05/29/the-impact-of-the-coronavirus-on-small-business/; Goldman Sachs, "US Small Business Owners Face Great Uncertainty; over Half Say They Cannot Operate Beyond Three Months," Mar. 19, 2020, https://www.goldmansachs.com/citizenship/10000-small-businesses/US/no-time-to-waste/.
9. UNCTAD, "Coronavirus Could Cut Global Investment by 40 Percent, New Estimates Show," United Nations Conference on Trade and Development, Mar. 26, 2020, https://unctad.org/en/pages/newsdetails.aspx?OriginalVersionID=2313.
10. Ibid.
11. World Bank, op. cit.
12. WTO, "WTO Contribution to the 2020 HLPF," Sustainable Development Goals, 2020a, https://sustainabledevelopment.un.org/content/documents/26126WTO_HLPF_Input_2020.pdf.
13. Ibid.
14. Ibid.
15. Ibid.
16. Ibid.
17. EU Commission, "Report from the Commission to the Parliament and the Council on Trade and Investment Barriers," 2020, https://trade.ec.europa.eu/doclib/docs/2020/june/tradoc_158789.pdf.
18. Peter Eavis, "These Companies Wanted Tariffs. How Are They Faring Now?" The New York Times, Jul. 10, 2019, https://www.nytimes.com/2019/07/10/business/economy/companies-tariffs-winners.html.
19. U.S. Department of Agriculture, Foreign Agricultural Services, 2020, https://www.fas.usda.gov/regions/china; Yong Xiong and Victoria Cavaliere, "China and the US Ratchet Up Trade War in a Day of Retaliation, CNN Business, Aug. 23, 2019, https://www.cnn.com/2019/08/23/business/china-tariffs-trade-war/index.html.
20. John D. Daniels, Lee Radebaugh, and Daniel J. Sullivan, "International Business: Environments and Operations," 2018, Pearson.
21. Yen Nee Lee, "Coronavirus Pandemic Will Cause a 'Much Bigger Wave' of Protectionism, Says Trade Expert," Apr. 9, 2020, https://www.cnbc.com/2020/04/10/coronavirus-expect-a-lot-more-protectionism-says-trade-expert.html.
22. Gopinath, op. cit.
23. Liza Lin, Stu Woo and Lingling Wei, "China May Retaliate against Nokia and Ericsson If EU Countries Move to Ban Huawei," The Wall Street Journal, Jul. 20, 2020, https://www.wsj.com/articles/china-may-retaliate-against-nokia-and-ericsson-if-eu-countries-move-to-ban-huawei-11595250557.
24. SenateRPC, "The Importance of 5G," Jun. 27, 2019, https://www.rpc.senate.gov/policy-papers/the-importance-of-5g.
25. Statista, "Funding of Artificial Intelligence (AI) Startup Companies Worldwide from 2014 to 2019," 2020, https://www.statista.com/statistics/621468/worldwide-artificial-intelligence-startup-company-funding-by-year/; Kathleen Walch, "Why the Race for AI Dominance Is More Global Than You Think," Forbes, Feb. 9, 2020, https://www.forbes.com/sites/cognitiveworld/2020/02/09/why-the-race-for-ai-dominance-is-more-global-than-you-think/#490e9815121f.
26. WTO, "WTO Report Shows Members Moving to Facilitate Imports Even as Trade Restrictions Remain High," 2020b, https://www.wto.org/english/news_e/news20_e/trdev_24jul20_e.htm.
27. WTO, 2020b, op. cit.

28. Katie Lobosco, "NAFTA Is Officially Gone. Here's What Has and Hasn't Changed," CNN Politics, Jul. 1, 2020, https://www.cnn.com/2020/07/01/politics/usmca-nafta-replacement-trump/index.html.

Chapter 1: Bitcoin

1. Hugh Son, Hannah Levitt and Brian Louis, "Jamie Dimon Slams Bitcoin as a 'Fraud,'" Bloomberg, Sep. 12, 2017, https://tinyurl.com/ycfnwj73.
2. Shawn Langlois and Sally French, "7 Cryptocurrencies to Watch in 2018 if You're on the Hunt for the Next Bitcoin," MarketWatch, Jan. 4, 2018, https://tinyurl.com/y7nsj7jx.
3. Stan Higgins, "From $900 to $20,000: Bitcoin's Historic 2017 Price Run Revisited," Coindesk, Dec. 29, 2017, https://tinyurl.com/y7x5yx4m.
4. Angela Monaghan, "Bitcoin Biggest Bubble in History, Says Economist Who Predicted 2008 Crash," The Guardian, Feb. 2, 2018, https://tinyurl.com/ydxxz7tk.
5. Richard Partington, "RBS Boss Likens Bitcoin to Dante's Inferno As Currency Tops $15,000," The Guardian, Dec. 7, 2017, https://tinyurl.com/y78zb9nr.
6. Kevin Costelloe, "Bitcoin 'Ought to Be Outlawed,' Nobel Prize Winner Stiglitz Says," Bloomberg, Nov. 29, 2017, https://tinyurl.com/yddwsckh.
7. Ivana Kottasová, "Davos: Bitcoin Is Not a Currency," Money-CNN, Jan. 26, 2018, https://tinyurl.com/yddntrth.
8. Berkeley Lovelace Jr., "Buffett on Cryptocurrencies: 'I Can Say Almost with Certainty That They Will Come to a Bad Ending,'" CNBC.com, Jan. 10, 2018, https://tinyurl.com/y78h32v3.
9. Kiran Vaidya, "Origins and Philosophical Ideology Behind Bitcoin," Medium, Nov. 11, 2016, https://tinyurl.com/y7hcjugz.
10. Maria Bustillos, "The Bitcoin Boom," The New Yorker, Apr. 1, 2013, https://tinyurl.com/y9hgplkb.
11. Tim Wu, "The Bitcoin Boom: In Code We Trust," The New York Times, Dec. 18, 2017, https://tinyurl.com/y7qy5asq.
12. Ameer Rosic, "What Is Blockchain Technology? A Step-by-Step Guide for Beginners," Blockgeeks.com, February 2017, https://tinyurl.com/mkmf62o.
13. Marc-David L. Seidel, "Bitcoin Is Making Banks Nervous. Here's Why," Agenda, World Economic Forum, Oct. 6. 2017, https://tinyurl.com/yahl9v6p.
14. Tony Yates, "The Consequences of Allowing a Cryptocurrency Takeover, or Trying to Head One off," Financial Times, Jun. 7, 2017, https://tinyurl.com/yadk7mrs.
15. Rosic, op. cit.
16. Karen Tso and Arjun Kharpal, "Bitcoin Is 'Gambling' and Regulations Are Needed, Canada Central Bank Head Says," CNBC.com, Jan. 25, 2018, https://tinyurl.com/yceb5cmb.
17. Ibid.
18. Ceri Parker, "Robert Shiller: Bitcoin Is Just an 'Interesting Experiment,'" World Economic Forum, Jan. 25, 2018, https://tinyurl.com/y8l948s9.
19. Rosic, op. cit.
20. "What Is Bitcoin Mining?" bitcoinmagazine.com, undated, https://tinyurl.com/y9dq6jge.
21. Ibid.
22. Ryan Browne, "Big Transaction Fees Are a Problem for Bitcoin—But There Could Be a Solution," CNBC.com, Dec. 19, 2017, https://tinyurl.com/y7wvaek5.
23. Ibid.
24. "Number of Bitcoins in Circulation Worldwide from 1st Quarter 2011 to 4th Quarter 2017 (in Millions)," Statista, 2018, https://tinyurl.com/y98zto7o.
25. Jeff John Roberts and Nicolas Rapp, "Nearly 4 Million Bitcoins Lost Forever, New Study Says," Fortune, Nov. 25, 2017, https://tinyurl.com/y8ympsns.
26. David Galland, "5 Industries That Blockchain Will Likely Disrupt by 2020," Forbes, Mar. 29, 2017, https://tinyurl.com/ya28z6du; Mike Miliard, "How Does Blockchain Actually Work for Healthcare?" Healthcare IT News, Apr. 13, 2017, http://tinyurl.com/ybcj4o2f.
27. Ron Miller, "IBM Unveils Blockchain as a Service Based on Open Source Hyperledger Fabric Technology," TechCrunch, Mar. 19, 2017, https://tinyurl.com/jvwcs5g.
28. Galland, op. cit.
29. Bradley Fink, "How to Slip Some Blockchain Exposure into Your Portfolio," Nasdaq, Jun. 9, 2017, https://tinyurl.com/yaapns5z; Jemima Kelly, "Amex Launches Blockchain-Based Business Payments Using Ripple," Reuters, Nov. 16, 2017, https://tinyurl.com/yb6xeb3q; Bloomberg, "Blockchain Is Pumping New Life into Old-School Companies Like IBM and Visa," Fortune, Dec. 26, 2017, http://tinyurl.com/ybz2b2rx.
30. Samuel Gibbs, "WannaCry: Hackers Withdraw £108,000 of Bitcoin Ransom," The Guardian, Aug. 3, 2017, https://tinyurl.com/y879gvcc.
31. Tom Simonite, "What Bitcoin Is, and Why It Matters," MIT Technology Review, May 25, 2011, http://tinyurl.com/yamf4aqg.
32. Ibid.
33. Anthony Cuthbertson, "North Korea Hacking War on Bitcoin Exchanges Is Part of 'Biggest Global Sting,'" Newsweek, Dec. 19, 2017, https://tinyurl.com/y7r9m5ej.
34. "Long Island Woman Indicted for Bank Fraud and Money Laundering to Support Terrorists," press release, U.S. Attorney's Office, Eastern District of New York, Department of Justice, Dec. 14, 2017, https://tinyurl.com/yaw2rm64.
35. Lynnley Browning and Julia Werdigier, "Switzerland to Allow Its Banks to Disclose Hidden Client Accounts," The New York Times, May 29, 2013, http://tinyurl.com/yat3jepj.
36. Saleha Mohsin, "Mnuchin Warns Against Bitcoin Becoming the Next 'Swiss Bank Account,'" Bloomberg, Jan. 12, 2018, https://tinyurl.com/ybfjzyy6.

37. Olga Kharif, "The Criminal Underworld Is Dropping Bitcoin for Another Currency," Bloomberg, Jan. 2, 2018, https://tinyurl.com/ybdxk5bb; Ivana Kottasová, "Bitcoin Is Too Hot for Criminals. They're Using Monero Instead," CNNtech, Jan. 3, 2018, http://tinyurl.com/y8wjv7vn.
38. Andy Greenberg, "Monero, the Drug Dealer's Cryptocurrency of Choice, Is on Fire," Wired, Jan. 25, 2017, https://tinyurl.com/jyt9phj; Shawn Langlois and Sally French, "7 Cryptocurrencies to Watch in 2018 if You're on the Hunt for the Next Bitcoin," MarketWatch, Jan. 4, 2018, http://tinyurl.com/yap8e8ly.
39. Anthony Cuthbertson, "Darkcoin to Rebrand as DASH to Disassociate Itself from Dark Web," International Business Times, Mar. 18, 2015, https://tinyurl.com/y8mtkz2k.
40. Browne, op. cit.
41. "Transactions Speeds: How Do Cryptocurrencies Stack Up to Visa or PayPal?" HowMuch.net, Jan. 10, 2018, https://tinyurl.com/ybtagf9t.
42. Jan Vermeulen, "Bitcoin and Ethereum vs Visa and PayPal—Transactions per Second," My Broadband, Apr. 22, 2017, https://tinyurl.com/ya5wptpp.
43. David Dinkins, "Satoshi's Best Kept Secret: Why Is There a 1 MB Limit to Bitcoin Block Size," CoinTelegraph, Sep. 19, 2017, http://tinyurl.com/y8fh3xt7.
44. Ibid.
45. Laura Shin, "Will This Battle for the Soul of Bitcoin Destroy It?" Forbes, Oct. 23, 2017, https://tinyurl.com/yavumcb3.
46. "How Many Transactions per Second Can Bitcoin Cash Handle?" Coinanalysis, Jan. 3, 2018, https://tinyurl.com/y7nlcvwp.
47. Evelyn Cheng, "Largest US Bitcoin Exchange Added 100,000 Customers in One Day after Futures Announcement," CNBC, Nov. 3, 2017, https://tinyurl.com/ydy8qdbv.
48. Browne, op. cit.
49. Nathaniel Popper, "Coinbase: The Heart of the Bitcoin Frenzy," The New York Times, Dec. 6, 2017, https://tinyurl.com/ybtedn49; Prableen Bajpai, "A Look at the Most Popular Bitcoin Exchanges," Investopedia, http://tinyurl.com/y7qc93bj.
50. "Coinbase Review: Is Coinbase Safe to Buy Cryptocurrency?" CoinCentral.com, Oct. 16, 2017, https://tinyurl.com/ya8dbuvg.
51. Fitz Tepper, "Coinbase Now Lets You Buy and Sell Bitcoin Cash," TechCrunch, Dec. 19, 2017, https://tinyurl.com/yamem9uc.
52. Bajpai, op. cit.
53. Laura Shin, "Bitstamp to Launch Bitcoin Cash Trading," Forbes, Nov. 21, 2017, https://tinyurl.com/yamlonvk.
54. Joe Liebkind, "How Did Ethereum's Price Perform in 2017?" Investopedia, Jan. 2, 2018, https://tinyurl.com/ycyr6yog; "Total Market Capitalization," Coin Market Cap, last accessed Mar. 1, 2018, https://tinyurl.com/hwufgaj; George Kingslay, "2017—Cryptocurrency Year in Review," CoinCodex, https://tinyurl.com/yad8w9lq.
55. Joon Ian Wong, "Here Are the Top 10 Cryptoassets of 2017 (and Bitcoin's 1,000% Rise Doesn't Even Make the List)," Quartz, Jan. 1, 2018, https://tinyurl.com/ya798aml.
56. Brad Tuttle, "Bitcoin Could Hit $100,000 This Year, Says Analyst Who's Been Right Before," Money, Jan. 16, 2018, https://tinyurl.com/y99muvp9; Sissi Cao, "Ethereum Founder Vitalik Buterin: Cryptocurrency Could Drop to Near-Zero Anytime," Observer, Feb., 21, 2018, https://tinyurl.com/yb4k5xgv.
57. Jim Edwards, "One of the Kings of the '90s Dot-Com Bubble Now Faces 20 Years in Prison,' Business Insider, Dec. 6, 2016, https://tinyurl.com/zxbem24.
58. Bernadette Johnson, "10 Tech Companies That Totally Imploded," HowStuffWorks, May 29, 2013, https://tinyurl.com/y964qavy.
59. Steven Russolillo, "Initial Coin Offerings Surge Past $4 Billion—and Regulators Are Worried," The Wall Street Journal, Dec. 14, 2017, https://tinyurl.com/y9d9str4; Mike Orcutt, "2017 Was the Year of the ICO—Now What?" MIT Technology Review, Dec. 28, 2017, https://tinyurl.com/ydyl748h.
60. Cao, op. cit; Claire Brownell, "Vitalik Buterin: The Cryptocurrency Prophet," Financial Post, Jun. 27, 2017, http://tinyurl.com/yctfouds.
61. "Ethereum Blockchain App Platform," Ethereum Project, 2018, https://tinyurl.com/mqak6hd.
62. Prableen Bajpai, "The 6 Most Important Cryptocurrencies Other Than Bitcoin," Investopedia, Dec. 7, 2017, https://tinyurl.com/y8gpgzco.
63. "Ethereum (ETH) Price," CoinDesk, accessed Mar. 1, 2018, http://tinyurl.com/ydh6tqaq.
64. Bajpai, op cit; Arjun Kharpal, "All You Need to Know About the Top 5 Cryptocurrencies," CNBC, Dec. 14, 2017, http://tinyurl.com/ycnvko3m.
65. Coinbase, accessed Mar. 1, 2018, https://tinyurl.com/yd5fw5an.
66. Bernard Marr, "What Is the Difference Between Bitcoin and Ripple?" Forbes, Feb. 28, 2013, http://tinyurl.com/yaq2zthh.
67. Ariella Brown, "10 Things You Need to Know About Ripple," Coindesk, May 17, 2013, https://tinyurl.com/ya9d3d6y.
68. "Ripple (XRP)," CoinGecko, accessed Mar. 1, 2018, https://tinyurl.com/ydh2h9a3.
69. Jeff Kauflin, "Dash Is Up 8,000% in 2017. Is This 'Darkcoin' a Better Version of Bitcoin?' Forbes, Dec. 22, 2017, https://tinyurl.com/ycr85g7c.
70. Kauflin, op cit.
71. David Dinkins, "Arizona State University Partners with Dash to Fund Research, Scholarships," CoinTelegraph, Jan. 19, 2018, http://tinyurl.com/yavkt3wa.
72. Wong, op. cit.
73. "Dash (DASH)," CoinGecko, accessed Mar. 1, 2018, https://tinyurl.com/ydcqxpwb.
74. Bajpai, op. cit.

75. "Monero," Investopedia, undated, https://tinyurl.com/yc7c39ft.
76. "Monero (XMR)," CoinGecko, accessed Mar. 1, 2018, https://tinyurl.com/gq66ocj.
77. Ellie Cambridge, "Monero Price and How to Buy—What Is XMR Worth Today and How Does the Cryptocurrency Compare to Bitcoin?" The Sun, Feb. 12, 2018, https://tinyurl.com/y88usv2c.
78. Olga Kharif, "The Bitcoin Whales: 1,000 People Who Own 40 Percent of the Market," Bloomberg Businessweek, Dec. 8, 2017, https://tinyurl.com/ycuqxnvd.
79. Nathaniel Popper, "How the Winklevoss Twins Found Vindication in a Bitcoin Fortune," The New York Times, Dec. 19, 2017, https://tinyurl.com/ycbdsrhr.
80. Chris Morris, "The Winklevoss Twins Have Lost Nearly $1 Billion in the Bitcoin Meltdown," Fortune, Jan. 18, 2018, https://tinyurl.com/y9yrdpko.
81. Robin Wigglesworth, "Bitcoin ETF providers See New Hope for Approval," Financial Times, Dec. 17, 2017, https://tinyurl.com/yafbc2qb.
82. Eric Schatzker and Saijel Kishan, "Novogratz Halts Hedge Fund, Says Bitcoin May Drop to $8,000," Bloomberg, Dec. 22, 2017, https://tinyurl.com/yd997ak3.
83. "28 Things You Didn't Know You Could Buy with Bitcoin," CNET, Aug. 2, 2016, https://tinyurl.com/yb5p4qlr.
84. Jonas Chokun, "Who Accepts Bitcoins as Payment? List of Companies, Stores, Shops," 99bitcoins.com, Jan. 14. 2018, http://tinyurl.com/zjaybrl.
85. Ben Fox Rubin, "Bitcoin: Big in Investing, but Still Lousy for Buying a Sandwich," CNET, Feb. 15, 2018, https://tinyurl.com/yafqjrpt.
86. Rob Price, "Someone in 2010 Bought 2 Pizzas with 10,000 Bitcoins—Which Today Would Be Worth $100 Million," Business Insider, Nov. 28, 2017, https://tinyurl.com/yay9k4cv.
87. Ryan DeRousseau, "There's a Hidden Bitcoin Tax You Need to Know About," Money magazine, Nov. 2, 2017, https://tinyurl.com/y9wtkslc.
88. Kenneth Rapoza, "Goldman Sachs Caves: Bitcoin Is Money," Forbes, Jan. 10, 2018, https://tinyurl.com/yaz96345.
89. Ibid.
90. Tae Kim, "Jamie Dimon Says He Regrets Calling Bitcoin a Fraud and Believes in the Technology Behind It," CNBC.com, Jan. 9, 2018, https://tinyurl.com/yct8x8om.
91. Alex Lielacher, "Chinese Exchanges Curb Bitcoin Margin Trading," Bitcoin Magazine, Jan. 16, 2017, http://tinyurl.com/jxyzpg8.
92. Zheping Huang, "It's Over: China's Biggest Bitcoin Exchanges Will Halt All Trading Services for Local Customers," Quartz, Sep. 18, 2017, https://tinyurl.com/yc3rbtmf.
93. Chao Deng, "China Quietly Orders Closing of Bitcoin Mining Operations," The Wall Street Journal, Jan. 11, 2018, https://tinyurl.com/y8458l8h.
94. Rosie Perper, "China Is Moving to Eliminate All Cryptocurrency Trading with a Ban on Foreign Exchanges," Business Insider, Feb. 5, 2018, http://tinyurl.com/ycho4vjc.
95. Cynthia Kim, "South Korea to Ban Cryptocurrency Traders from Using Anonymous Bank Accounts," Reuters, Jan. 22, 2018, https://tinyurl.com/y9vok6r2.
96. Sotaro Suzuki, "Young South Koreans Slam Cryptocurrency Trading Crackdown," Nikkei Asian Review, Jan. 13, 2018, http://tinyurl.com/ydbob8z2.
97. Francine McKenna, "Here's How the U.S. and the World Regulate Bitcoin and Other Cryptocurrencies," MarketWatch, Dec. 28, 2017, http://tinyurl.com/y96z2no5.
98. Ibid.
99. "St Moritz Becomes First Swiss Ski Resort to Accept Bitcoin," swissinfo.ch, Dec. 28, 2017, http://tinyurl.com/ycm9k82e.
100. Ralph Atkins, "Switzerland Embraces Cryptocurrency Culture," Financial Times, Jan. 25, 2018, https://tinyurl.com/y7xlu6qt.
101. Rachelle Krygier, "Venezuela Launches the 'Petro,' Its Cryptocurrency," The Washington Post, Feb. 20, 2018, https://tinyurl.com/ydgrgr4g.
102. Adam Samson, "Venezuela Launches Presale of State-Backed 'Petro' Cryptocurrency," Financial Times, Feb. 20, 2018, https://tinyurl.com/y8z9e8dh.
103. "Countries Where Bitcoin Is Welcomed," CryptoCentral, Feb. 13, 2018, http://tinyurl.com/y75z2ymx.
104. Nathaniel Popper, Oleg Matsnev and Ana Vanessa Herrero, "Russia and Venezuela's Plan to Sidestep Sanctions: Virtual Currencies," The New York Times, Jan. 3, 2018, https://tinyurl.com/ycb4ykxn.
105. Akin Oyedele, "Wall Street Analyst Unleashes on Jamie Dimon and Everyone Else Calling Bitcoin a Fraud," Business Insider, Sep. 28, 2017, https://tinyurl.com/yc6e46xd.
106. "Bitcoin," Coindesk, accessed Aug. 10, 2020, https://www.coindesk.com/price/bitcoin.
107. Sebastian Sinclair and Omkar Godbole, "Bitcoin Suddenly Drops $500, After Passing $12K," Coindesk, Aug. 10, 2020, https://www.coindesk.com/bitcoin-closes-on-yearly-high-with-return-to-12k.
108. Shalini Nagarajan, "Young Investors Have Flooded into the Bitcoin Market During the Pandemic, While the Older Generation Can't Get Enough of Gold, a Team of JP Morgan Analysts Said," Business Insider, Aug. 5, 2020, https://markets.businessinsider.com/currencies/news/gold-bitcoin-jpmorgan-older-investors-buy-gold-millennials-prefer-bitcoin-2020-8-1029471716#.
109. Ofir Beigel, "Who Accepts Bitcoins," 99 Bitcoins, Apr. 27, 2020, https://99bitcoins.com/bitcoin/who-accepts/.
110. Ibid.
111. Jesus Fernandez-Villaverde, Daniel Sanches, Linda Schilling and Harald Uhlig, "Central Bank Digital Currency, Central Banking for All?" Federal Reserve of Philadelphia, June 2020, https://doi.org/10.21799/frbp.wp.2020.19.

Chapter 2: Brexit

1. "Global Prospects and Policy Challenges," International Monetary Fund, July 23–24, 2016, http://tinyurl.com/hhxx8mj; Larry Elliott, "IMF Cuts UK Growth Forecasts Following Brexit Vote," The Guardian, Jul. 19, 2016, http://tinyurl.com/hj334v6.
2. Anne Applebaum, "Britain's Decision to Leave the E.U. Is a Warning to America," The Washington Post, Jun. 24, 2016, http://tinyurl.com/zwlmr7k.
3. Joseph Curtis, "British-Born BBC Radio Host Was Branded a N***** and Told to 'Go Home' by a Passing Cyclist Days After Brexit Vote," Daily Mail, Jun. 30, 2016, http://tinyurl.com/hsw33yv.
4. Lizzie Dearden, "Anger Over 'Bregret' As Leave Voters Say They Thought UK Would Stay in EU," The Independent, Jun. 25, 2015, http://tinyurl.com/z827uhy.
5. Ayesha Vardag, "I Voted for Brexit, But Now I Regret the Terrifying Chaos I Have Unleashed," The Telegraph, Jul. 6, 2016, http://tinyurl.com/jgrm3p3.
6. "HM Treasury Analysis: The Long-Term Economic Impact of EU Membership and the Alternatives," HM Government, April 2016, p. 12, http://tinyurl.com/jar59tq.
7. "The Economic Consequences of Brexit: A Taxing Decision," Organisation for Economic Co-operation and Development, April 2016, http://tinyurl.com/gskjrfm.
8. "Inflation Report Q&A," Bank of England, May 12, 2016, http://tinyurl.com/hvgbljw.
9. "Uncertainty Clouds the United Kingdom's Economic Prospects," IMF Survey, International Monetary Fund, Jun. 17, 2016, http://tinyurl.com/hmmdg8h.
10. Ben Glaze and Dan Bloom, "'Brexit' Could Trigger World War Three, Warns David Cameron," Daily Mirror, May 9, 2016, http://tinyurl.com/hjjsv92.
11. Henry Mance, "Britain Has Had Enough of Experts, Says Gove," Financial Times, Jun. 3, 2016, http://tinyurl.com/hd546eo.
12. Ned Simons, "Boris Johnson Claims EU Stops Bananas Being Sold in Bunches of More Than Three. That Is Not True," The Huffington Post, May 17, 2016, http://tinyurl.com/zjovsut.
13. "Euromyths A–Z Index," European Commission, 2016, http://tinyurl.com/owrw7ma.
14. David Rennie, blog post, referenced in "EU Rule on Mumbai Mix? You Could Make It Up, Apparently," Not Saussure, Sep. 27, 2006, http://tinyurl.com/zh74dtr.
15. "The Infamous 'Euro-Sausage' Threatens British Bangers," Euromyths, European Commission, http://tinyurl.com/jdzmxfs.
16. Vincent Moss, "Brit Yoghurt; Exclusive EU Says We Have to Call It Fermented Milk Pudding," Sunday Mirror, Mar. 5, 2006, http://tinyurl.com/h7ut8ox.
17. Katherine Butler, "Size Does Matter for the Euro-Condom," The Independent, Feb. 28, 1996, http://tinyurl.com/zozd7v4.
18. Kate Connolly, "Barmaids Protest As EU Plans Cover-Up in the Beer Gardens," The Telegraph, Aug. 3, 2005, http://tinyurl.com/zmufc99.
19. Nigel Farage, "Immigration Will Be the Defining Issue of This EU Referendum Campaign," The Telegraph, Aug. 21, 2015, http://tinyurl.com/op4fp7d.
20. Heather Stewart and Rowena Mason, "Nigel Farage's Anti-Migrant Poster Reported to Police," The Guardian, Jun. 16, 2016, http://tinyurl.com/jpkxukn.
21. Oliver Hawkins, "Migration Statistics," House of Commons library briefing paper, May 26, 2016, http://tinyurl.com/qb34mbh.
22. "Today," BBC Radio 4, Jun. 20, 2016.
23. Ed Conway, "By Staying in the EU We Can Help to Dismantle It," The Times, Apr. 22, 2016, http://tinyurl.com/h83xh6x.
24. "Euro Area Unemployment Rate at 10.3%," Eurostat, Apr. 4, 2016, http://tinyurl.com/gtxhdow.
25. Ibid.
26. "Slovakian Far Right Party Launches Petition for Referendum on EU Membership," Reuters, Jun. 25, 2016, http://tinyurl.com/zqucyk8.
27. BBC, "EU Referendum: Brexit Sparks Calls for Other EU Votes," Jun. 24, 2016, http://tinyurl.com/gr5xhx2.
28. Jan Dams, Martin Greive and Daniel Friedrich Sturm, "Schäubles Geheimplan für Großbritanniens Zukunft," Die Welt, Jun. 24, 2016, http://tinyurl.com/junq8tc.
29. "IMF Cuts Global Growth Forecasts on Brexit, Warns of Risks to Outlook," International Monetary Fund, Jul. 19, 2016, http://tinyurl.com/jktgup8.
30. "Government Statement on Brexit: Our Historical Responsibility for the EU," Federal Government, Jun. 28, 2016, http://tinyurl.com/zqksclm.
31. James Crisp, "Juncker: Brexit Won't Be the Death of the EU," EurActive, Jun. 16, 2016, http://tinyurl.com/jgx6wcu; Joey Millar, "Desperate Angela Merkel Insists EU Is 'Strong Enough' to Survive Brexit," The Express, Jun. 28, 2016, http://tinyurl.com/z85g4ww.
32. Adam Twardowski, "Poland, Not Brexit, Is the Real Threat to Europe's Unity," The National Interest, Jul. 27, 2016, http://tinyurl.com/zhd8gjo.
33. Nigel Morris, "Nigel Farage to Brexit Ministers: You've Got Five Months to Trigger Article 50," iNews, Jul. 21, 2016, http://tinyurl.com/huzvlka.
34. Jason Douglas and Paul Hannon, "Bank of England Cuts Key Interest Rate to New Low," The Wall Street Journal, Aug. 4, 2016, http://tinyurl.com/h54lan3.
35. "European Union Finances 2015," HM Treasury, December 2015, p. 14, http://tinyurl.com/huhrbl8.
36. "Reality Check: What Would Happen to Funding from EU Post-Brexit?" BBC, Jun. 14, 2016, http://tinyurl.com/h3gyh7m.
37. Henry Mance, "Michael Gove Says Brexit Should Not Start This Year," Financial Times, Jul. 1, 2016, http://tinyurl.com/z95qqhe.

38. "Top 100 EU Rules Cost Britain £33.3bn," Open Europe, Mar. 16, 2015, http://tinyurl.com/jubwhjt.
39. Ralph Buckle, et al., "Brexit: Directions for Britain Outside the EU," Institute of Economic Affairs, 2015, http://tinyurl.com/jkqg4m8.
40. "2016 Article IV Consultation," International Monetary Fund, Jun. 17, 2016, http://tinyurl.com/j59bvqe.
41. Larry Elliott, "IMF Cuts UK Growth Forecasts Following Brexit Vote," The Guardian, Jul. 20, 2016, http://tinyurl.com/hj334v6.
42. "2016 Article IV Consultation," op. cit.
43. Anne-Sophie Brändlin, "Brexit Strategist Daniel Hannan: 'Five Years from Now, Britain Will Be Flourishing,'" Deutsche Welle, Jul. 13, 2016, http://tinyurl.com/hrahsxg.
44. "Watch: Ken Clarke Ridicules Tory Candidates," Sky News, Jul. 7, 2016, http://tinyurl.com/jr9dgs3.
45. Gloria Tyler, "Financial Services: Contribution to the UK Economy," House of Commons Library, Feb. 26, 2015, http://tinyurl.com/gte4cjl.
46. "London: Europe and the World's Financial Centre," City of London, http://tinyurl.com/z6jgeuc.
47. "The Economic and Financial Costs and Benefits of the EU's UK membership," House of Commons Treasury Committee, May 27, 2016, http://tinyurl.com/hzpwbwc.
48. "ECB's Villeroy—Brexit Talks Must Be Quick, City of London at Risk of Losing 'EU Passport,'" Reuters, Jun. 26, 2016, http://tinyurl.com/jxm69j8.
49. Martin Arnold and Laura Noonan, "Banks Begin Moving Some Operations out of Britain," Financial Times, Jun. 26, 2016, http://tinyurl.com/h867bzg.
50. "BCG: Brexit Could See One in Five Banking Jobs Leave London," The Wall Street Journal, Jul. 5, 2016, http://tinyurl.com/jhnhk2h.
51. "Andrew Marr Show," BBC1, May 15, 2016, http://tinyurl.com/h3rpfm6.
52. Peter Kellner, "EU Referendum: 'Remain' on Course for Clear Victory," The Politics Counter, May 20, 2016, http://tinyurl.com/zbk48qc.
53. Matt Singh and James Kanagasooriam, "Polls Apart: An Investigation into the Differences Between Phone and Online Polling for the UK's EU Membership Referendum," Populus, Mar. 2016, http://tinyurl.com/jynbect.
54. Nate Cohn, "Is Traditional Polling Underselling Donald Trump's True Strength," The New York Times, May 17, 2016, http://tinyurl.com/hndhrao.
55. Andrew Hawkins, "Statement: EU Referendum Polls," ComRes, Jun. 24, 2016, http://tinyurl.com/hd8ty3c.
56. "EU Referendum Results," The Electoral Commission, undated, http://tinyurl.com/zthfzg2.
57. "General Election 2015," briefing paper, House of Commons Library, Jul. 28, 2015, http://tinyurl.com/pbzb2ud.
58. Tony Judt, "Postwar: A History of Europe Since 1945," Penguin Press, 2005, p. 17.
59. Robert Neild, "The National Debt in Perspective," Royal Economic Society, Jan. 2013, http://tinyurl.com/8xf9wek.
60. Andrew Moravcsik, "The Choice for Europe: Social Purpose and State Power from Messina to Maastricht," Cornell University Press, 1998, p. 2.
61. House of Commons Official Reports, Jun. 25, 1996, column 240, http://tinyurl.com/gopt9qz.
62. Oliver Wright, "EU Referendum: Boris Johnson Launches Most Personal Attack on David Cameron Yet," The Independent, May 9, 2016, http://tinyurl.com/z2uqjq4.
63. European Union," World Bank, 2016, http://tinyurl.com/z2lozam.
64. "International Migration Outlook 2014," Organisation for Economic Co-operation and Development, Dec. 1, 2014, p. 23, http://tinyurl.com/h98nf38.
65. "International Migration Outlook 2015," Organisation for Economic Co-operation and Development, Sep. 22, 2015, pp. 234, 256, http://tinyurl.com/zvleb5f.
66. "Foreign Population," Statistisches Bundesamt, http://tinyurl.com/jjo9zga.
67. Jon Stone, "Don't Control EU Immigration at the Expense of Losing Single Market Access, Voters Tell Politicians—Poll," The Independent, Jul. 8, 2016, http://tinyurl.com/hv92pal.
68. Jim Armitage and Ben Chu, "Greek Debt Crisis: Goldman Sachs Could Be Sued for Helping Hide Debts When It Joined Euro," The Independent, Jul. 10, 2015, http://tinyurl.com/oxueskd.
69. "Greece," World Bank, http://tinyurl.com/24q6db2; "Euro Area and EU27 Government Deficit at 6.3% and 6.8% of GDP Respectively," news release, World Bank, Apr. 22, 2010, http://tinyurl.com/zecmw89.
70. "Youth Unemployment," Table 1, Eurostat, Jul. 1, 2016, http://tinyurl.com/j733sbc; "Unemployment Rate," Table 2, http://tinyurl.com/zsdxgox.
71. Mark Thompson, "Greece Joining Euro Was a Mistake: Merkel," CNN, Aug. 28, 2013, http://tinyurl.com/zbxv2sp.
72. "EU Referendum Rules Triggering a 2nd EU Referendum," U.K. Government and Parliament, http://tinyurl.com/zmp3xla.
73. Andy McSmith, "And Then There Was One: Theresa May Is the Last Candidate Standing in the Race for PM," The Independent, Jul. 11, 2016, http://tinyurl.com/zsfbnvl.
74. Hamish Macdonell, "Theresa: I'll Save the Union If I'm Elected PM . . . It's Key Priority," Scottish Mail on Sunday, Jul. 10, 2016, http://tinyurl.com/gwvhpvr.
75. Boris Johnson, "I Cannot Stress Too Much That Britain Is Part of Europe—and Always Will Be," The Daily Telegraph, Jun. 26, 2016, http://tinyurl.com/gsskfmz.
76. Alex Barker and Jim Brunsden, "EU Will Not Help Britain out of 'Black Hole,' Belgian Premier Warns," Financial Times, Jul. 8, 2016, http://tinyurl.com/hajb7g3.
77. Lord Ashcroft, "How the United Kingdom Voted on Thursday . . . and Why," Lord Ashcroft Polls, Jun. 24, 2016, http://tinyurl.com/gp725l7.

78. Alan Beattie, "Brexit and the WTO Option: Key Questions About a Looming Challenge," Financial Times, Jul. 12, 2016, http://tinyurl.com/gsgqj28.
79. Michael Nienaber, "Merkel Urges Britain to Quickly Clarify Relationship with EU," Reuters, Jul. 11, 2016, http://tinyurl.com/hewuhne.
80. Alex Barker, "British Exit from EU Could Take 10 Years, Study Says," Financial Times, Jun. 24, 2015, http://tinyurl.com/j4tb6pl.
81. "Post-Brexit Trade Deal with US Could Take 10 Years, Obama Warns," BBC, Apr. 24, 2016, http://tinyurl.com/zwrkq9p.
82. David Davis, "Trade Deals. Tax Cuts. and Taking Time Before Triggering Article 50. A Brexit Economic Strategy for Britain," Conservativehome, Jul. 14, 2016, http://tinyurl.com/z8m58yl.
83. David Davis, "Brexit Strategy: May's New Chief Europe Negotiator David Davis Lays Out Plans to Take Us out of EU," The Sun, Jul. 15, 2016, http://tinyurl.com/jzowdkl.
84. Swati Dhingra, et al., "The Consequences of Brexit for UK Trade and Living Standards," Centre for Economic Performance, Mar. 2016, http://tinyurl.com/jqpgmt4.
85. Ibid.
86. Alan McGuinness, "Brexit Day: Celebration and Regret as Britain Leaves the EU after 47 Years," Sky News, Feb. 1, 2020, https://news.sky.com/story/brexit-day-celebration-and-regret-as-britain-leaves-eu-after-47-years-11923114.
87. "UK and EU Fail to Strike Brexit Talks Deal," BBC News, Dec. 4, 2017, https://www.bbc.com/news/uk-politics-42217735.
88. David Reid and Spira Srivastava, "Scotland's Sturgeon Calls for Fresh Independence Vote after UK Election Landslide," CNBC, Dec. 12, 2019, https://www.cnbc.com/2019/12/13/snp-sturgeon-says-johnson-has-no-mandate-to-take-scotland-out-of-eu.html.
89. "The EU-UK Withdrawal Agreement," European Commission, Oct. 17, 2019, https://ec.europa.eu/info/european-union-and-united-kingdom-forging-new-partnership/eu-uk-withdrawal-agreement_en.
90. Amanda Sloat, "Brexit Endgame: Brexit Nears, Northern Ireland Assembly Reconvenes, and Megxit Distracts," Brookings Institution, Jan. 13, 2020, https://tinyurl.com/yycjxnnq.
91. Amanda Sloat, "Brexit Is Not Immune to Coronavirus," Brookings Institution, Mar. 26, 2020, https://tinyurl.com/yygq9992.
92. Ibid.

Chapter 3: China's Slowdown

1. "China's Factory to the World Is in a Race to Survive," Bloomberg News, Jun. 5, 2016, http://tinyurl.com/zjgat34.
2. Wayne M. Morrison, "China's Economic Rise: History, Trends, Challenges, and Implications for the United States," Congressional Research Service, Oct. 21, 2015, http://tinyurl.com/l87nlln.
3. "225m Reasons for China's Leaders to Worry," The Economist, Jul. 9, 2016, http://tinyurl.com/ze5r577.
4. Andy Rothman, "Cleaning Up China's Debt," Sinology, Matthews Asia, Sep. 9, 2016, http://tinyurl.com/jtuvvkb; "Active Fiscal, Monetary Policies to Boost Economy," China Daily, Nov. 9, 2008, http://tinyurl.com/h57xrle.
5. International Monetary Fund, "People's Republic of China, 2015 Article IV Consultation," Aug. 2015, http://tinyurl.com/zllecwl; "People's Republic of China, 2016 Article IV Consultation," August 2016, http://tinyurl.com/h84g2ry.
6. "China's Hidden Unemployment Rate," Bloomberg News, Jun. 5, 2016, http://tinyurl.com/h5phoxb.
7. Morrison, op. cit.
8. Michael Schuman, "China's Big Debt Worries George Soros. Should It Worry You?" The New York Times, Sep. 7, 2016, http://tinyurl.com/h6gauee; "People's Republic of China, Selected Issues," IMF Country Report No. 16/271, International Monetary Fund, August 2016, http://tinyurl.com/jk3fzp7.
9. Schuman, ibid.
10. Arthur R. Kroeber, "Should We Worry About China's Economy?" Brookings Institution, Feb. 9, 2016, http://tinyurl.com/z58w7pc.
11. Andrew England, "Zambia Bears the Brunt of China's Economic Slowdown," Financial Times, Sep. 9, 2015, http://tinyurl.com/zsb8l6f.
12. Kevin Yao and Meng Meng, "China Expects to Lay Off 1.8 Million Workers in Coal, Steel Sectors," Reuters, Feb. 29, 2016, http://tinyurl.com/zqs3bvx.
13. Nicholas R. Lardy, "Markets over Mao: The Rise of Private Business in China," Peterson Institute for International Economics, 2014, p. 8.
14. International Monetary Fund, "People's Republic of China, 2016 Article IV Consultation," op. cit.
15. Morrison, op. cit.
16. Keith Bradsher, "In Trade Stances toward China, Clinton and Trump Both Signal a Chill," The New York Times, Jun. 29, 2016, http://tinyurl.com/z3uk78l.
17. Eleanor Albert and Beina Xu, "China's Environmental Crisis," Council on Foreign Relations, Jan. 18, 2016, http://tinyurl.com/6496rvc.
18. Herman Wong, "2013 Will Be Remembered as the Year That Deadly, Suffocating Smog Consumed China," Quartz, Dec. 19, 2013, http://tinyurl.com/grwlngk.
19. Justin Sink and Toluse Olorunnipa, "Global Climate Accord Closer to Reality as Obama, Xi Sign On," Bloomberg Politics, Sep. 3, 2016, http://tinyurl.com/hfdjek9.
20. Edward Wong, "Smog So Thick, Beijing Comes to a Standstill," The New York Times, Dec. 8, 2015, http://tinyurl.com/ph983zl.
21. Carol Rasmussen, "Global Is the New Local: Pollution Changes Clouds, Climate Downstream," NASA Jet Propulsion Laboratory, California Institute of Technology, Jan. 26, 2015, http://tinyurl.com/zgyr9hj.

22. Ibid.
23. Eleanor Albert and Beina Xu, "China's Environmental Crisis," Council on Foreign Relations, Jan. 18, 2016, http://tinyurl.com/6496rvc.
24. Ibid.
25. "Linking Air Pollution with Life Expectancy in China," Stanford Center for International Development, Jan. 19, 2016, http://tinyurl.com/jt2l34t.
26. Edward Wong, "China Blocks Web Access to 'Under the Dome' Documentary on Pollution," The New York Times, Mar. 6, 2015, http://tinyurl.com/kfzudrr.
27. Albert and Xu, op. cit.
28. Ibid.
29. Ibid.
30. John Sousanis, "World Vehicle Population Tops 1 Billion Units," WardsAuto, Aug. 15, 2011, http://tinyurl.com/h6jksgy.
31. "China's Idled Wind Farms May Spell Trouble for Renewable Energy," Bloomberg News, Jun. 28, 2016, http://tinyurl.com/jrh8yud.
32. Chris Buckley, "Thousands in Eastern Chinese City Protest Nuclear Waste Project," The New York Times, Aug. 8, 2016, http://tinyurl.com/jhe4ca7.
33. Jake Maxwell Watts, "Xi Threatens 'Lifetime' Consequences for Officials Who Hurt the Environment," Quartz, May 27, 2013, http://tinyurl.com/zjhbzxo.
34. Samantha Page, "No, the Paris Climate Agreement Isn't Binding. Here's Why That Doesn't Matter," ThinkProgress, Dec. 14, 2015, http://tinyurl.com/z6hh4cy.
35. Arthur R. Kroeber, "China's Economy: What Everyone Needs to Know," Oxford University Press, 2016, p. 4.
36. Martin Farrer, "Asian Stock Markets Drop as China Devaluation, Oil and Fed Stoke Fears," The Guardian, Dec. 13, 2015, http://tinyurl.com/zccoyau.
37. Lingling Wei, "China Unveils Economic Blueprint for 2016," The Wall Street Journal, Dec. 21, 2015, http://tinyurl.com/haveocp.
38. John Lyons and Paul Kiernan, "How Brazil's China-Driven Commodities Boom Went Bust," The Wall Street Journal, Aug. 27, 2015, http://tinyurl.com/olyuh5f.
39. "Impact of Chinese Slowdown on U.S. No Longer Negligible," Federal Reserve Bank of Dallas, May 2016, http://tinyurl.com/zu84b2z.
40. Stephen S. Roach, "Global Growth—Still Made in China," Project Syndicate, Aug. 29, 2016, http://tinyurl.com/zs6upez.
41. Ibid.
42. Lyons and Kiernan, op. cit.
43. Michael Pettis, "How Might a China Slowdown Affect the World?" Michael Pettis' China Financial Markets, Dec. 2, 2014, http://tinyurl.com/h3nnsn6.
44. Sue Chang, "China Is Near a Financial Crisis Similar to the U.S. in 2008, Says Soros," MarketWatch, Apr. 21, 2016, http://tinyurl.com/h36xpea.
45. Pettis, op. cit.
46. Ibid.
47. "2016 AmCham China White Paper: American Business in China," American Chamber of Commerce in the People's Republic of China, 2016, http://tinyurl.com/gsh4qrl.
48. Laurie Burkitt, "American Companies Say Doing Business in China Is Getting Tougher," The Wall Street Journal, Jan. 19, 2016, http://tinyurl.com/zdl5paf; Enda Curran, "Made in China Not as Cheap as You Think," Bloomberg News, Mar. 16, 2016, http://tinyurl.com/z5y4qpu.
49. "US Firms Moving Operations out of China: Survey," Agence France-Presse, Jan. 20, 2016, http://tinyurl.com/hx6swpv.
50. Paul Mozur and Mike Isaac, "Uber to Sell to Rival Didi Chuxing and Create New Business in China," The New York Times, Aug. 1, 2016, http://tinyurl.com/hpr5apu.
51. Ibid.
52. Paul Mozur and Jane Perlez, "China Quietly Targets U.S. Tech Companies in Security Reviews," The New York Times, May 16, 2016, http://tinyurl.com/hma4c2x.
53. Noah Smith, "China's Self-Defeating Clampdown on Foreign Companies," BloombergView, May 16, 2016, http://tinyurl.com/hkamgnv.
54. Chris Devonshire-Ellis, "China-ASEAN Wage Comparisons and the 70 Percent Production Capacity Benchmark," China Briefing, Jun. 3, 2014, http://tinyurl.com/qdusm3o.
55. Smith, op. cit.
56. "China Vows Bigger Role for Markets as Party Closes Summit," Bloomberg News, Nov. 12, 2013, http://tinyurl.com/gvgvfl9.
57. "CPC Acknowledges Market's 'Decisive' Role," Xinhua, Nov. 12, 2013, http://tinyurl.com/gnyz5ln.
58. Tania Branigan, "Xi Jinping Vows to Fight 'Tigers' and 'Flies' in Anti-Corruption Drive," The Guardian, Jan. 22, 2013, http://tinyurl.com/zsuo7dj.
59. "Graft Busters Discipline Nearly 300,000 Officials in 2015," Xinhua, Mar. 6, 2016, http://tinyurl.com/hatqdxc.
60. Jeremy Page, "Bo Xilai Found Guilty, Sentenced to Life in Prison," The Wall Street Journal, Sep. 22, 2013, http://tinyurl.com/hh8bkgz; Michael Forsythe, "Zhou Yongkang, Ex-Security Chief in China, Gets Life Sentence for Graft," The New York Times, Jun. 11, 2015, http://tinyurl.com/nnrwgpc.
61. Josh Chin, "Retired Chinese General Sentenced to Life in Prison for Corruption," The Wall Street Journal, Jul. 25, 2016, http://tinyurl.com/hx2fp88.
62. Arthur R. Kroeber, "China's Economy: What Everyone Needs to Know," Oxford University Press, 2016.
63. Susan Ariel Aaronson, "How China Can Reduce Corruption and Save Face," SFGate, May 4, 2012, http://tinyurl.com/jnvuhlu.
64. Edward Wong, "China Admits Building Flaws in Quake," The New York Times, Sep. 4, 2008, http://tinyurl.com/h492el8.
65. Ibid.

66. Willy Wo-lap Lam, "Growing CCDI Power Brings Questions of Politically-Motivated Purge," China Brief, The Jamestown Foundation, Feb. 4, 2015, http://tinyurl.com/jjlvk9k.
67. Simon Denyer, "Grumbling Mounts in China, Even in the Party. Is President Xi Losing His Grip?" The Washington Post, Mar. 29, 2016, http://tinyurl.com/jht6oew.
68. Arthur R. Kroeber, et al., "Without Reform from Beijing, 'The World Will Endure More China Scares,'" Foreign Policy, Jan. 28, 2016, http://tinyurl.com/jeq9l7b.
69. Ibid.
70. Guy de Jonquieres, "The Problematic Politics of China's Economic Reform Plans," International Journal of China Studies, Aug. 2014, pp. 399–412, http://tinyurl.com/gqswlfy.
71. "Escaping the Middle Income Trap," Global Economic Symposium, http://tinyurl.com/hpz388s.
72. de Jonquieres, op. cit.
73. Ibid.
74. Michael Schuman, "Venture Communism: How China Is Building a Start-Up Boom," The New York Times, Sep. 2, 2016, http://tinyurl.com/h8rgje6.
75. Ryan Rutkowski, "A Bright Light on China's Reform Agenda," Matthews Asia Weekly, May 19, 2016, http://tinyurl.com/j9jp2zf.
76. Kroeber, "Without Reform," op. cit.
77. George Magnus, "China's Contradictions Will Catch Up With It," Prospect, May 16, 2016, http://tinyurl.com/jpab2go.
78. Andrew Jacobs, "Chinese Web Censors Struggle With Hong Kong Protest," The New York Times, Sep. 30, 2014, http://tinyurl.com/mh7ncds; Bethany Allen-Ebrahimian, "China's G-20: The Most Censored Day of the Year," Foreign Policy, Sep. 6, 2016, http://tinyurl.com/haqblwm.
79. Magnus, op. cit.
80. Jonathan Spence, "The Search for Modern China," W.W. Norton & Co., 1990, p. 275.
81. Ibid., p. 329.
82. Ibid., p. 336.
83. Ibid., pp. 430–431.
84. Barry Naughton, "The Chinese Economy: Transitions and Growth," MIT Press, 2006, p. 43.
85. Spence, op. cit., p. 434.
86. Ibid., pp. 368–369.
87. Naughton, "The Chinese Economy," op. cit., pp. 47-49.
88. Ibid., p. 49.
89. Spence, op. cit., pp. 368–369.
90. Ibid., p. 438.
91. Naughton, "The Chinese Economy," op. cit., p. 65.
92. Yan Qin and Yunbo Zhou, "Transformation of Property Rights in China," International Review of Business Research Papers, Mar. 2008, pp. 243–248, http://tinyurl.com/zogg7ag.
93. Naughton, "The Chinese Economy," op. cit., p. 61.
94. Ibid.
95. Lardy, op. cit.
96. Naughton, op. cit., p. 60.
97. Lardy, op. cit., p. 12.
98. Naughton, "The Chinese Economy," op. cit., p. 61.
99. Lardy, op. cit., p. 13.
100. Naughton, "The Chinese Economy," op. cit., p. 60.
101. Ibid., pp. 61–62.
102. Ibid., pp. 70–72.
103. Ibid., p. 73.
104. Ibid.
105. Ibid., p. 79.
106. Barry Naughton, "A Political Economy of China's Economic Transition," in "China's Great Economic Transformation," Cambridge University Press, 2010, pp. 97, 98, 104.
107. Morrison, op. cit.
108. Lardy, op. cit., p. 18.
109. Naughton, "A Political Economy," op. cit., p. 104.
110. Edward Tse, "The Rise of Entrepreneurship in China," Forbes.com, Apr. 5, 2016, http://tinyurl.com/jbp3cu7.
111. Naughton, "A Political Economy" op. cit., p. 111.
112. Morrison, op. cit.
113. Naughton, "A Political Economy" op. cit., p. 110.
114. "Timeline: China Milestones Since 1978," Reuters, Dec. 8, 2008, http://tinyurl.com/j5x9g7j.
115. Naughton, "A Political Economy," op. cit., p. 119.
116. Naughton, "The Chinese Economy," op. cit., p 184.
117. Lardy, op. cit., pp. 18, 19.
118. Min Ye, "Diasporas and Foreign Direct Investment in China and India," Cambridge University Press, 2014.
119. Ibid.
120. Ibid.
121. Tse, op. cit.
122. David R. Meyer, "Structural Changes in the Economy of Hong Kong Since 1997," The China Review, Spring 2008, pp. 7–29.
123. Naughton, "A Political Economy," op. cit., p. 112.
124. Peter Wonacott, "China Formally Enters the WTO on Tuesday," The Wall Street Journal, Dec. 11, 2001, http://tinyurl.com/zepnxha.
125. Mo Zhang, "From Public to Private: The Newly Enacted Chinese Property Law and the Protection of Property Rights in China," Berkeley Business Law Journal, September 2008, http://tinyurl.com/jm49bov.
126. Lardy, op. cit., p. 1.
127. "China Overview," The World Bank, Sep. 14, 2016, http://tinyurl.com/kh2o5vp.
128. "Top Trading Partners, July 2016," Foreign Trade, U.S. Census Bureau, http://tinyurl.com/z7yk3o2.
129. "Hillary Clinton's Strategy to 'Make It in America," Hillary for America, http://tinyurl.com/hcnwf5l.
130. "Donald J. Trump's 7 Point Plan to Rebuild the American Economy by Fighting for Free Trade," Donald J. Trump for President Inc., http://tinyurl.com/o2wlack.
131. "China 2030: Building a Modern, Harmonious and Creative Society," International Bank for Reconstruction and

Development/The World Bank and the Development Research Center of the State Council, People's Republic of China, 2013, http://tinyurl.com/87x77h4.
132. Lyons and Kiernan, op. cit.
133. Karl Lester Yap, "China Slowdown to Hurt Export-Heavy Singapore the Most in Southeast Asia," Bloomberg, Jan. 10, 2016, http://tinyurl.com/jcxgj9x; Singapore, The Observatory of Economic Complexity, accessed Sep. 14, 2016, http://tinyurl.com/z4ghpxd.
134. Malcolm Scott, "China's Slowdown Hits Nearby Economies Hardest," Bloomberg, May 30, 2016, http://tinyurl.com/hxflvda.
135. "Exports-Partners," The World Factbook, CIA, http://tinyurl.com/hhajoxk.
136. Scott, op. cit.; Matthew Fulco, "Taiwan Economy Boosted by Turnkey Exports," Taiwan Business Topics, Feb. 17, 2016, http://tinyurl.com/hnsb6mx.
137. Tse, op. cit., p. 2; "China to Encourage Mass Entrepreneurship, Innovation," Xinhua, Mar. 11, 2015, http://tinyurl.com/hcj2qtz.
138. Schuman, "Venture Communism," op. cit.
139. Tse, op. cit., p. 1.
140. Schuman, "Venture Communism," op. cit.
141. Paul Mozur, "China, Not Silicon Valley, Is Cutting Edge in Mobile Tech," The New York Times, Aug. 2, 2016, http://tinyurl.com/zg68c5z.
142. Schuman, "Venture Communism," op. cit.
143. Ibid.
144. Ibid.
145. Daron Acemoglu and James A. Robinson, "Will China Rule the World?" The Huffington Post, May 21, 2012, http://tinyurl.com/bhvtm6v.
146. "Special Topic Paper: China's Household Registration System: Sustained Reform Needed to Protect China's Rural Migrants," Congressional-Executive Commission on China, accessed Sep. 14, 2016, http://tinyurl.com/hufo6vg.
147. Magnus, op. cit.
148. Orville Schell, "Crackdown in China: Worse and Worse," New York Review of Books, Apr. 21, 2016, http://tinyurl.com/jb3wj72.
149. Pettis, op. cit.
150. Magnus, op. cit.
151. China Gross Domestic Product, Federal Reserve of St. Louis, August 2020, https://data.worldbank.org/country/china.
152. Yu Jie, "Xi Enforces Party Control," Chatham House, Dec. 4, 2019, https://www.chathamhouse.org/publications/twt/xi-enforces-party-control.
153. Huileng Tan and Evelyn Chung, "China Says Its Economy Grew 3.2% in the Second Quarter This Year, Rebounding from Coronavirus," CNBC, Jul. 15, 2020, https://www.cnbc.com/2020/07/16/china-economy-beijing-reports-q2-2020-gdp.html.
154. Reuters Staff, "China Smog Rises in April for First Time This Year," Reuters, May 18, 2020, https://www.reuters.com/article/us-china-pollution-idUSKBN22U12S.
155. Charlotte Edmond, "China's Air Pollution Has Overshot Pre-Pandemic Levels as Life Begins to Return to Normal," World Economic Forum, Jul. 7, 2020, https://www.weforum.org/agenda/2020/07/pollution-co2-economy-china/.
156. Soon Chen Kang, "COVID-19 Accelerates Repatriation of Chinese Luxury Goods Spending," S&P Global, Aug. 19, 2020, https://www.spglobal.com/marketintelligence/en/news-insights/latest-news-headlines/covid-19-accelerates-repatriation-of-chinese-luxury-goods-spending-59866013.
157. China Gross Domestic Product, Federal Reserve of St. Louis, August 2020, https://data.worldbank.org/country/china.
158. "A Quick Guide to the U.S.-China Trade War," BBC News, Jan. 16, 2020, https://www.bbc.com/news/business-45899310.
159. Ryan Hass and Abraham Denmark, "More Pain Than Gain: How the U.S.-China Trade War Hurt America," Aug. 7, 2020, https://www.brookings.edu/blog/order-from-chaos/2020/08/07/more-pain-than-gain-how-the-us-china-trade-war-hurt-america/.
160. Cissy Zhou, "China to Buck Global Downturn in 2020," South China Morning Post, Jun. 24, 2020, https://www.scmp.com/economy/global-economy/article/3090420/china-buck-global-economic-downturn-2020-coronavirus.
161. Ibid.

Chapter 4: Commodities Supercycles

1. Amrith Ramkumar and Ira Iosebashvili, "Electric-Vehicle Bulls Shake Up Metals Markets," The Wall Street Journal, Dec. 10, 2017, https://tinyurl.com/y9yvpp2q.
2. "LME Cobalt, LME Official Prices, US$ per tonne," London Metal Exchange, Feb. 2, 2018, https://tinyurl.com/y6uepadl; David George-Cosh, "Miners Look to Cash in on Cobalt Demand," The Wall Street Journal," Jan. 1, 2018, https://tinyurl.com/yaa6ool8; "Lithium Price," Metalary, undated, https://tinyurl.com/ycdahfvd.
3. Ramkumar and Iosebashvili, op. cit.
4. "LME Nickel, LME Official Prices, US$ per Tonne," London Metals Exchange, Feb. 2, 2018, https://tinyurl.com/y8wmq4xr; "LME Copper, LME Official Prices, US$ per Tonne," London Metals Exchange, Jan. 9, 2018, https://tinyurl.com/ybal5rhs; Ramkumar and Iosebashvili, op cit.
5. Ramkumar and Iosebashvili, ibid.
6. "Australia Is the New Frontier for Battery Minerals," The Economist," Nov. 25, 2017, https://tinyurl.com/y85wbvvh.
7. Ramkumar and Iosebashvili, op. cit.
8. Ibid.
9. "2016–2017 Investment Plan Update for the Alternative and Renewable Fuel and Vehicle Technology Program," report,

California Energy Commission, May 2016, https://tinyurl.com/ybnwgzkv.
10. Ramkumar and Iosebashvili, op. cit.
11. Ibid.
12. Ibid.
13. "Australia Is the New Frontier for Battery Minerals," The Economist, op. cit.
14. Ibid.
15. Amrith Ramkumar and Ira Iosebashvili, "Electric-Vehicle Bulls Hoping for Next Commodity Supercycle," The Wall Street Journal, Dec. 11, 2017, http://tinyurl.com/yab57f25.
16. "Exposed: Child Labor Behind Smart Phone and Electric Car Batteries," Amnesty International, Jan. 19, 2016, https://tinyurl.com/hs5ztum.
17. George-Cosh, op. cit.
18. Ramkumar and Iosebashvili, "Electric-Vehicle Bulls Shake Up Metals Markets," op. cit.
19. Eduardo Porter, "Slowdown in China Bruises Economy in Latin America," The New York Times, Dec. 16, 2014, https://tinyurl.com/ydga2k3n; Norimitsu Onishi, "African Economies, and Hopes for New Era, Are Shaken by China," The New York Times, Jan. 25, 2016, https://tinyurl.com/ya9b3uss.
20. Robert D. Kaplan, "The Oil and Gas Sector Is Changing—and So Is Geopolitics," The New York Times, Dec. 28, 2017, https://tinyurl.com/y9qraf3d.
21. David Baily, "In North Dakota, Hard to Tell an Oil Millionaire from Regular Joe," Reuters, Oct. 3, 2012, https://tinyurl.com/y88nx286; Nathan Bomey, "Six of the Eight Top Oil-Producing States Hit Recession," USA Today, Jan. 24, 2017, https://tinyurl.com/y9lpqhba.
22. Mike Nowatzki, "N.D. Legacy Fund Tops $4 Billion in Less Than Six Years," The Bismarck Tribune, Sep. 30, 2016, https://tinyurl.com/y9f9rdew.
23. Michael Hasenstab, "The Lessons from Argentina," The New York Times, Dec. 6, 2016, https://tinyurl.com/yb7ue889.
24. Vladimir Isachenkov and Laura Mills, "Amid Currency Gyrations, Russia Floats Ruble," The Associated Press/Savannah Morning News, Nov. 10, 2014, https://tinyurl.com/ydya4xp2.
25. Jane Kinninmont, "Vision 2030 and Saudi Arabia's Social Contract: Austerity and Transformation," Chatham House, Jul. 20, 2017, https://tinyurl.com/ya7cp3uw.
26. "World Economic Outlook | Seeking Sustainable Growth: Short-Term Recovery, Long-Term Challenges," International Monetary Fund, October 2017, https://tinyurl.com/yct35aby.
27. Dana Mattioli and Dana Cimilluca, "Boeing Tries to Overcome Brazil's Resistance to Embraer Takeover," The Wall Street Journal, Jan. 5, 2018, https://tinyurl.com/y8umc3mm.
28. "World Economic Outlook," op. cit.
29. Meghan L. O'Sullivan, "Windfall: How the New Energy Abundance Upends Global Politics and Strengthens America's Power," Simon & Schuster, 2017.
30. Kaplan, op. cit.
31. "World Economic Outlook," op. cit.
32. "Australia Is the New Frontier for Battery Minerals," The Economist, op. cit.
33. Ibid.
34. Zheping Huang, "260% of GDP: A Quick Look at the Debt Levels That Earned China a Ratings Downgrade," Quartz, May 24, 2017, https://tinyurl.com/y7hgxv2e.
35. "China's Sovereign Wealth Fund Hits 900 Bln USD," Xinhua/China Daily, Oct. 7, 2017, https://tinyurl.com/ycfmk6cx.
36. Ramkumar and Iosebashvili, "Electric-Vehicle Bulls Shake Up Metals Markets," op. cit.
37. Matt Egan, "Oil Prices Turned Negative: Hundreds of US Oil Companies Could Go Bankrupt," CNN Business, Apr. 21, 2020, https://www.cnn.com/2020/04/20/business/oil-price-crash-bankruptcy/index.html.
38. "Electric Vehicle Sales: Facts and Figures," EEI, October 2019, https://www.eei.org/issuesandpolicy/electrictransportation/Documents/FINAL_EV_Sales_Update_Oct2019.pdf.
39. Peter Nagle, "Coronavirus and Commodity Markets: Lessons from History," The World Bank, May 8, 2020, https://blogs.worldbank.org/voices/coronavirus-and-commodity-markets-lessons-history.
40. "Bright Spots in Gold," Citibank, generated Sep. 2, 2020, https://www.citibank.co.uk/personal/outlook2020-commodities.do.
41. Hollie Tomlinson, "Commodities versus Stocks: Which Are Easier to Trade in 2020?" Investment U, Sep. 2, 2020, https://investmentu.com/commodities-vs-stocks/.
42. Jeff Remsburg, "The Next Supercycle Is Here," Investor Place, Aug. 18, 2020, https://investorplace.com/2020/08/the-next-supercycle-is-here/.

Chapter 5: Data Security

1. Tim Johnson, "How the Dark Overlord Is Costing U.S. Clinics Big Time with Ransom Demands," Miami Herald, May 15, 2017, https://tinyurl.com/yataul74.
2. Joseph Cox, "Hackers Threaten Release of Atlanta Professional Athletes' Medical Data," Motherboard, Nov. 16, 2016, https://tinyurl.com/y7k2qr6n.
3. Johnson, op. cit.; "Threat Actor Profile: 'thedarkoverlord'," FireEye, Jun. 20, 2017.
4. "Threat Actor Profile," ibid.
5. Janko Roettgers, "Hackers Confirm Leaking 'Orange Is the New Black' Despite Ransom Payment," Variety, Jun. 20, 2017, http://tinyurl.com/ycmjyz7w.
6. Johnson, op. cit.
7. Ibid.
8. Michael Kan, "A Hacker Wants to Sell 10 Million Patient Records on the Black Market," PCWorld, Jun. 27, 2016, https://tinyurl.com/ybvkrt7z.

9. "Bitcoin (USD) Price," coindesk.com, Sep. 11, 2017, http://tinyurl.com/ybyazcwb.
10. "Threat Actor Profile," op. cit.
11. "Internet Usage Statistics," Internet World Stats, Jun. 30, 2017, https://tinyurl.com/7mswb.
12. Larry Ponemon, "2017 Ponemon Institute Cost of a Data Breach Study," SecurityIntelligence, Jul. 26, 2017, https://tinyurl.com/y8l8jj8s.
13. Steve Morgan, "Hackerpocalypse: A Cybercrime Revelation, 2016 Cybercrime Report," Cybersecurity Ventures, 2016, https://tinyurl.com/y7jxx3zw.
14. "IBM X-Force Finds Historic Number of Records Leaked and Vulnerabilities Disclosed In 2016," IBM X-Force, Mar. 29, 2017, https://tinyurl.com/kh63yjd; Asha McLean, "Leaked Records Up 566 Percent to 4 Billion in 2016: IBM Security," ZDNet, Mar. 30, 2017, https://tinyurl.com/l62oo2w.
15. Tara Siegel Bernard, et al., "Equifax Says Cyberattack May Have Affected 143 Million in the U.S.," The New York Times, Sep. 7, 2017, http://tinyurl.com/yaytbtgf.
16. Ibid.
17. Ibid.
18. Steve Morgan, "Top 5 Industries at Risk of Cyber-Attacks," Forbes, May 13, 2016, https://tinyurl.com/y9g6qdqf; Jessica Davis, "7 Largest Data Breaches of 2015," Healthcare IT News, Dec. 11, 2015, http://tinyurl.com/hvd48m6.
19. Tara Seals, "Healthcare Breaches Spike 63% in 2016," Infosecurity, Dec. 22, 2016, https://tinyurl.com/ybc38wuf.
20. Lily Hay Newman, "Medical Devices Are the Next Security Nightmare," Wired, Mar. 2, 2017, https://tinyurl.com/znulb88; "Fast Facts on US Hospitals," AHA Hospitals Statistics, 2017, https://tinyurl.com/bq4albt.
21. Andrea Peterson, "Yes, Terrorists Could Have Hacked Dick Cheney's Heart," The Washington Post, Oct. 21, 2013, https://tinyurl.com/y787b67y.
22. Casey Harper, "FDA, Industry Fear Wave of Medical-Device Hacks," The Hill, Apr. 10, 2017, https://tinyurl.com/kcsgyq8.
23. Thomas Fox-Brewster, "Medical Devices Hit by Ransomware for the First Time in US Hospitals," Forbes, May 17, 2017, https://tinyurl.com/y9umuhx3.
24. "Code Blue: Why Healthcare Organizations Are Facing More Cyber Attacks, and What They Can Do About It," FireEye, 2015, https://tinyurl.com/yawvgwmw.
25. Michelle Alvarez, "A Magnet for Cybercrime: Financial Services Sector," SecurityIntelligence, Apr. 27, 2017, https://tinyurl.com/ych9tplu.
26. Pierluigi Paganini, "The Total Potential Loss for Financial Services Globally Is Estimated at £8 Billion," Security Affairs, Mar. 6, 2017, https://tinyurl.com/ycxq8xp8.
27. Kim Zetter, "That Insane, $81M Bangladesh Bank Heist? Here's What We Know," Wired, May 17, 2016, https://tinyurl.com/z8qcgh2.
28. Jim Finkle, "Cyber Security Firm: More Evidence North Korea Linked to Bangladesh Heist," Reuters, Apr. 3, 2017, https://tinyurl.com/y9jyaxau.
29. Bill Chappell, "WannaCry Ransomware: What We Know Monday," NPR, May 15, 2017, https://tinyurl.com/lj8tp4l.
30. Thomas Fox-Brewster, "An NSA Cyber Weapon Might Be Behind a Massive Global Ransomware Outbreak," Forbes, May 12, 2017, http://tinyurl.com/y92j6quj.
31. Richard Waters, "Microsoft Issues WannaCry Cyberattack Patch," Financial Times, May 13, 2017, https://tinyurl.com/y8zl5dpl.
32. Ibid.
33. Ibid.
34. Andy Greenberg, "The WannaCry Ransomware Hackers Made Some Real Amateur Mistakes," Wired, May 15, 2017, https://tinyurl.com/ml8d4fc.
35. Choe Sang-Hun, "North Korea Tries to Make Hacking a Profit Center," The New York Times, Jul. 27, 2017, https://tinyurl.com/y8ctpq9z.
36. Cara McGoogan, "WannaCry Cyber Hackers Linked to China Not North Korea, Experts Say," The Telegraph, May 30, 2017, https://tinyurl.com/y82hucm4.
37. Alex Hern, "Ransomware Attack 'Not Designed to Make Money', Researchers Claim," The Guardian, Jun. 28, 2017, https://tinyurl.com/yb9wxkl2.
38. Ibid.; Nicole Perlroth, Mark Scott and Sheera Frenkel, "Cyberattack Hits Ukraine Then Spreads Internationally," The New York Times, Jun. 27, 2017, https://tinyurl.com/ycsyxkwz.
39. Andy Greenberg, "How an Entire Nation Became Russia's Test Lab for Cyberwar," Wired, Jun. 20, 2017, https://tinyurl.com/y9gx5thj.
40. Kimberly Zenz, "Is Russia or North Korea Behind Petya, the Latest Cyberattack?" Newsweek, Jul. 7, 2017, https://tinyurl.com/ybef9wyt.
41. Bruce Schneier, "Who Are the Shadow Brokers?" The Atlantic, May 23, 2017, https://tinyurl.com/yby94oxe.
42. Ibid.
43. "Overview of the General Data Protection Regulation (GDPR)," Information Commissioner's Office, https://tinyurl.com/zqfmm48.
44. Lily Hay Newman, "Taking Stock of Trump's Cybersecurity Executive Order So Far," Wired, Sep. 3, 2017, https://tinyurl.com/yby288b6.
45. Dan Merica, "The Life and Death of Trump's 'Cyber Security Unit' Plan with Putin," CNN.com, Jul. 10, 2017, https://tinyurl.com/y9faxxol.
46. Ibid.
47. "Agencies Issue Advanced Notice of Proposed Rulemaking on Enhanced Cyber Risk Management Standards," press release, Board of Governors of the Federal Reserve System, Oct. 19, 2016, http://tinyurl.com/ybn26g2j.
48. Greg Masters, "New York's New Cybersecurity Requirements Go into Effect Today," SC Media, Mar. 1, 2017, https://tinyurl.com/y8hjnrju.
49. "Governor Cuomo Announces First-in-the-Nation Cybersecurity Regulation Protecting Consumers and Financial

Institutions from Cyber-Attacks to Take Effect March 1," Feb. 16, 2017, https://tinyurl.com/y9ydwoyv.
50. Ibid.
51. "New Medicare Cards," Centers for Medicare & Medicaid Services, page last modified Aug. 22, 2017, http://tinyurl.com/ybrufyxr.
52. "$5.5 Million HIPAA Settlement Shines Light on the Importance of Audit Controls," U.S. Department of Health and Human Services, Feb. 16, 2017, https://tinyurl.com/y9tgkewn.
53. Maggie Miller, "FBI Sees Spike in Cyber Crime Reports During Coronavirus Pandemic," The Hill, Apr. 16, 2020, https://thehill.com/policy/cybersecurity/493198-fbi-sees-spike-in-cyber-crime-reports-during-coronavirus-pandemic.
54. Tyler Sonnemaker, "Google Blocked an Average of 18 Million Daily Malicious Coronavirus Messages to Gmail Users in the Past Week As Hackers Try to Capitalize on Fear and Less Secure Remote-Work Setups. Business Insider, Apr. 17, 2020, https://www.businessinsider.com/google-says-gmail-blocked-18-million-coronavirus-phishing-emails-2020-4.
55. "The World Will Store 200 Zettabytes of Data by 2025," Cybersecurity Ventures, Jun. 9, 2020, https://www.prnewswire.com/news-releases/the-world-will-store-200-zettabytes-of-data-by-2025-301072627.html.
56. Ibid.
57. Patty Tehrani, "Analysis: Will GDPR Report Cards Prompt Easier Implementation?" Bloomberg Law, Aug. 21, 2020, https://news.bloomberglaw.com/bloomberg-law-analysis/analysis-will-gdpr-report-cards-prompt-easier-implementation.
58. Gilad Edelman, "California's Privacy Law Goes into Effect Today. Now What?" Wired, Jan. 1, 2020, https://www.wired.com/story/ccpa-guide-california-privacy-law-takes-effect/.
59. Dimitri Sirota, "Why U.S. Companies Should Know about the CCPA and New York SHIELD Act," Forbes, Sep. 16, 2020, https://www.forbes.com/sites/forbestechcouncil/2020/09/16/why-us-companies-should-know-about-the-ccpa-and-new-york-shield-act/#1526a2b432e1; Laurel Wamsley, "Your Technology Is Tracking You. Take These Steps for Better Online Privacy," NPR, Oct. 13, 2020, https://www.npr.org/2020/10/09/922262686/your-technology-is-tracking-you-take-these-steps-for-better-online-privacy.

Chapter 6: Doing Business with Japan

1. Whill website, undated, accessed Jul. 8, 2015, http://tinyurl.com/oo5pr3t.
2. Hiromi Murakami and Kiyoshi Kurokawa, "Fukushima Crisis Fueling the Third Opening of Japan," The Japan Times, Dec. 1, 2011, http://tinyurl.com/q8kgxt6.
3. "Japan's Third Opening," The Wall Street Journal, Nov. 14, 2011, http://tinyurl.com/o2naqos.
4. Masaaki Iwamoto, "Japan's Record Run of Annual Trade Deficits Is Set to Continue," Bloomberg Business, Apr. 22, 2015, http://tinyurl.com/nvtpgrz.
5. "Japan," Observatory of Economic Complexity, undated, accessed Jul. 10, 2015, http://tinyurl.com/nz9z47q.
6. "Japan," Office of the U.S. Trade Representative, Apr. 29, 2014, http://tinyurl.com/pqton47.
7. Brian Wingfield, "Japan Seen Ending Protectionism, Avoid 'Second-Rate' Role," Bloomberg Business, Jun. 18, 2013, http://tinyurl.com/obbubtl; "Trans-Pacific Partnership," American Automotive Policy Council, undated, accessed Sep. 9, 2015, http://tinyurl.com/pzu4hbx.
8. James McBride and Beina Xu, "Abenomics and the Japanese Economy," Council on Foreign Relations, Mar. 10, 2015, http://tinyurl.com/k8m3akh; Toru Fujioka and Masahiro Hidaka, "Bank of Japan Leaves Monetary Policy Unchanged As Forecast," Bloomberg Business, Aug. 6, 2015, http://tinyurl.com/najd9xv.
9. McBride and Xu, ibid.
10. "Emergency Economic Measures for the Revitalization of the Japanese Economy," Government of Japan, Jan. 11, 2013, http://tinyurl.com/peztlr3.
11. McBride and Xu, op. cit.
12. Jack Detsch, "Can Shinzo Abe Inspire Silicon Valley's Dynamism in Japan?" The Diplomat, May 1, 2015, http://tinyurl.com/q9ssnm6.
13. Julie Makinen, "A Subculture of Entrepreneurship Hatches in Japan," Los Angeles Times, Mar 29, 2015, http://tinyurl.com/ptlmw35.
14. Elise Hu, "A Startup Scene That's Not So Hot," NPR, May 7, 2015, http://tinyurl.com/o54bk45.
15. "Kashiwa-no-ha Smart City," Mitsui Fudosan, undated, accessed Sep. 9, 2015, http://tinyurl.com/m8xgotj.
16. Hiromichi Shinohara, "Co-innovation Challenges," NTT Technical Review, February 2014, http://tinyurl.com/ohyw6cd; NTT Group, undated, accessed Jul. 7, 2015, http://tinyurl.com/odbvjw7.
17. "Farming in Japan: Field Work," The Economist, Apr. 13, 2013, http://tinyurl.com/blcp8jv.
18. Aya Takada, "Japan's Farm Lobby Concedes to Abe's Agriculture Reform Plans," Bloomberg Business, Feb. 9, 2015, http://tinyurl.com/q4m7nmy.
19. "Farming in Japan: Field Work," op. cit.
20. Bernard K. Gordon, "The End Game for the Trans-Pacific Partnership," Georgetown Journal of Asian Affairs, Spring/Summer 2015, http://tinyurl.com/nfoavfj; Steven Greenhouse, "Hilary Clinton's TPP Deal Disapproval is 'a Critical Turning Point,'" The Guardian, Oct. 8, 2015, http://tinyurl.com/o64qpd7.
21. "The Incredible Shrinking Country," The Economist, Mar. 25, 2014, http://tinyurl.com/lbflfgp.
22. McBride and Xu, op. cit.
23. "The Incredible Shrinking Country," op. cit.
24. Rob Goss, "Business Opportunities of an Ageing Population," Japan Today, Nov. 21, 2014, http://tinyurl.com/nzxummm.
25. Toru Fujioka, "Japan's Consumer Prices Rise Fractionally While Spending Drops," Bloomberg, Jul. 30, 2015, http://tinyurl.com/nps3nzh.

26. "About 2MA," in "The Second Machine Age," undated, accessed Jul. 6, 2015, http://tinyurl.com/pbl84y3.
27. Michael Ruessmann, et al., "Industry 4.0: The Future of Productivity and Growth in Manufacturing Industries," BCG Perspectives, Apr. 9, 2015, http://tinyurl.com/ooby274.
28. Erik Brynjolfsson and Andrew McAfee, "The Second Machine Age," http://tinyurl.com/qenbv3t.
29. "Germany Passes Japan to Have World's Lowest Birthrate—Study," BBC, May 29, 2015, http://tinyurl.com/qz5a3o8.
30. Kyodo Jiji, "Japan Population Drops for Third Year Straight; 25% Are Elderly," The Japan Times, Apr. 15, 2014, http://tinyurl.com/pek5jvn.
31. Bruce Stokes, "The Countries That Will Be Most Impacted by Aging Population," Pew Research Center, Feb. 4, 2014, http://tinyurl.com/klj38sv.
32. Takeshi Suezaki, "Immigrants Eyed as a Key to Maintaining Population Level," The Asahi Shimbun, Feb. 25, 2014, http://tinyurl.com/q8zlrv6; Reiji Yoshida, "Japan May Boost Immigrant Numbers," The Japan Times, Mar. 14, 2014, http://tinyurl.com/opbdhuh.
33. Toko Sekiguchi, "Japan Opens Door Wider for Foreign Workers," The Wall Street Journal, Apr. 4, 2014, http://tinyurl.com/pc5nctv.
34. "Seven-Eleven Japan," undated, accessed Jul. 6, 2015, http://tinyurl.com/o2tf7o4.
35. "The Incredible Shrinking Country," op. cit.; "The Incredible Shrinking Country: For the First Time, a Proper Debate Is Starting About Immigration," The Economist, May 31, 2014, http://tinyurl.com/nx5sgfr.
36. Chris Matthews, "Can Immigration Save a Struggling, Disappearing Japan?" Fortune, Nov. 20, 2014, http://tinyurl.com/pt59bl5.
37. "2011 Japan Earthquake-Tsunami Fast Facts," CNN, updated Feb. 13, 2015, http://tinyurl.com/pkoc8na.
38. "Fukushima Accident," World Nuclear Association, undated, accessed Jul. 7, 2015, http://tinyurl.com/oo8dzbm.
39. Mari Iwata, "Japan Sees Key Role for Nuclear Power," The Wall Street Journal, Feb. 25, 2014, http://tinyurl.com/oy5e7wm.
40. Mike Orcutt, "The Numbers Behind Japan's Renewed Embrace of Nuclear," MIT Technology Review, Mar. 11, 2014, http://tinyurl.com/pkp33sk.
41. Iwata, op. cit.
42. Kentaro Hamada and Aaron Sheldrick, "Japan Nuclear Power Outlook Bleak Despite First Reactor Restart," Reuters, Sep. 1, 2015, http://tinyurl.com/ne2p2rk.
43. "Japan Nuclear Update," Nuclear Energy Institute, Sep. 24, 2015, http://tinyurl.com/pz2l3fd.
44. Chisaki Watanabe and Emi Urabe, "Japan's Nuclear Shutdown Tests Shinzo Abe's Green Pledges," Bloomberg, Apr. 8, 2015, http://tinyurl.com/qdmwfdg.
45. Justin McCurry, "Japan Moves Nearer to Restarting Nuclear Reactors After Court Gives Go-ahead," The Guardian, Apr. 22, 2015, http://tinyurl.com/o79uyek.
46. Jeff Kingston, "Japan's Nuclear Village," The Asia-Pacific Journal: Japan Focus, undated, accessed Jul. 7, 2015, http://tinyurl.com/nt5dszl.
47. Watanabe and Emi Urabe, op. cit.
48. "Less of the Same," The Economist, Sep. 30, 2015, http://tinyurl.com/osothsj.
49. "Japan's Abe Battles Doctors' Lobby Over 'Third Arrow' Reform," Reuters, Aug. 24, 2013, http://tinyurl.com/oyfg4ol.
50. McBride and Xu, op. cit.
51. "Japan's Economy: About That Debt," The Economist, Nov. 18, 2015, http://tinyurl.com/luw9ewg.
52. Jessica Menton, "Japan Recession 2014: Why Abenomics Isn't Working," International Business Times, Dec. 8, 2014, http://tinyurl.com/nw9sng6.
53. Ibid.
54. Robin Harding, "Shinzo Abe's Approval Ratings Fall to a New Low," Financial Times, Jun. 15, 2015, http://tinyurl.com/pc3rcqx.
55. Makiko Inoue, "Shinzo Abe of Japan Re-elected as Leader of Ruling Party," The New York Times, Sep. 8, 2015, http://tinyurl.com/p4eutpz.
56. "Nikkei 225," Yahoo Finance, undated, accessed Oct. 6, 2015, http://tinyurl.com/pzm7ojm; "Abenomics Delivers Another Win for Japan Stocks," Fast FT, Jun. 30, 2015, http://tinyurl.com/pr8uc3w.
57. "Japan: The Official Guide," Japan National Tourism Organization, undated, accessed Jun. 30, 2015, http://tinyurl.com/qxce8rz.
58. "The United States and the Opening of Japan," Office of the Historian, U.S. Department of State, undated, accessed Jun. 30, 2015, http://tinyurl.com/otgsxxd.
59. James Huffman, "The Meiji Restoration Era, 1868–1889," About Japan, Apr. 21, 2008, http://tinyurl.com/lf5bctt.
60. "Sino-Japanese War, 1894–1895," Encyclopedia Britannica, undated, accessed Jul. 1, 2015, http://tinyurl.com/osn8ovv.
61. Ibid.
62. "Treaty of Shimonoseki," Encyclopedia Britannica, undated, accessed Jul. 10, 2015, http://tinyurl.com/qbejs52.
63. "The Treaty of Portsmouth and the Russo-Japanese War, 1904–1905," Office of the Historian, U.S. Department of State, undated, accessed Jul. 1, 2015, http://tinyurl.com/osmcj2u.
64. "The Annexation of Korea," The Japan Times, undated, accessed Oct. 5, 2015, http://tinyurl.com/q8qftxy.
65. "Sino-Japanese War, 1894–1895," op. cit.
66. Eric Johnston, "Japan's Gambit in WWI Set Stage for a Dark Future," The Japan Times, Jun. 16, 2014, http://tinyurl.com/oco28v4.
67. "The Mukden Incident of 1931 and the Stimson Doctrine," Office of the Historian, U.S. Department of the State, undated, accessed Jul. 1, 2015, http://tinyurl.com/p74jht4.
68. "Sino-Japanese War, 1937–1945," Encyclopedia Britannica, undated, accessed Oct. 6, 2015, http://tinyurl.com/obp6upg.

69. "Occupation and Reconstruction of Japan 1945–52," Office of the Historian, U.S. Department of State, undated, accessed Jul. 1, 2015, http://tinyurl.com/q7v8mx8.
70. Thayer Watkins, "The Zaibatsu of Japan," undated, accessed Jul. 28, 2015, http://tinyurl.com/nmnz793.
71. Evelyn Iritani, "Remade in Japan," Jun. 2, 1996, Los Angeles Times, http://tinyurl.com/pnw3dkl.
72. Chalmers Johnson, "MITI and the Japanese Miracle: The Growth of Industrial Policy: 1925–1975," 1982, p. 132.
73. Iritani, op. cit.
74. "Mitsubishi A6M Reisen," The Aviation History Online Museum, updated Mar. 25, 2014, http://tinyurl.com/yaldjtc.
75. Kenneth Pyle, "The Making of Modern Japan," 1995, p. 248.
76. "Converting to Meet Civilian Demand and Dealing with Post-War Reforms," 75 Years of Toyota, undated, accessed Jul. 3, 2015, http://tinyurl.com/d7l85kl.
77. "The Keiretsu of Japan," San Jose State University, undated, accessed Oct. 5, 2015, http://tinyurl.com/oce9y3a.
78. Benjamin Reeves, "Drive from the Rising Sun, Why Japan's Car Companies Are Moving Manufacturing Overseas," International Business Times, May 19, 2012, http://tinyurl.com/odnqzyw.
79. Ralph Kisiel, "Gamble in Rural Ohio Pays Off Big," Automotive News, Jun. 8, 2009, http://tinyurl.com/pf9rwaj.
80. "Global Robotics Industry: Record Beats Record!" news release, International Federation of Robotics, Jun. 4, 2014, http://tinyurl.com/nkttcf9.
81. Roger Schreffler, "Auto Industry Leading Market for Japanese Robotics," Aug. 21, 2013, WardsAuto, http://tinyurl.com/p85mvew.
82. "Toyota Is Global Hybrid Leader with Sales of 7 Million," news release, Toyota, Oct. 13, 2014, http://tinyurl.com/odz38fo.
83. Brad Tuttle, "Why This Might Be the Beginning of the End for the Toyota Prius," Money, Jan. 6, 2015, http://tinyurl.com/qz7j94m.
84. Kenneth Pyle, "The Making of Modern Japan," 2nd ed., 1996, http://tinyurl.com/2r8clx.
85. John W. Dower, "The Useful War," in Carol Gluck and Stephen R. Graubard, eds., "Showa: The Japan of Hirohito," 1992, http://tinyurl.com/2r8clx.
86. Watkins, op. cit.
87. Robert J. Cole, "Japanese Buy New York Cachet with Deal for Rockefeller Center," The New York Times, Oct. 31, 1989, http://tinyurl.com/pssdkzo.
88. Doron P. Levin "Grim Outlook of Early 1980's Is Back for U.S. Auto Makers," The New York Times, Dec. 7, 1989, http://tinyurl.com/ptwburf.
89. Eric Johnston, "Lessons from When the Bubble Burst," The Japan Times, Jan. 6, 2009, http://tinyurl.com/qzq2vu4.
90. "Nikkei 225," Yahoo Finance, op. cit.
91. "Thailand Floats the Baht," CNNMoney, Jul. 2, 1997, http://tinyurl.com/pjahowa.
92. "Timeline of the Panic," PBS Frontline, undated, accessed Jul. 1, 2015, http://tinyurl.com/222wzn.
93. "Domestic Product," OECD Data, undated, accessed Sep. 10, 2015, http://tinyurl.com/q2svsly.
94. Chico Harlan, "Shinzo Abe's Comeback as Prime Minister Drives Japan's Turnaround," The Washington Post, Feb. 9, 2014, http://tinyurl.com/nzcrmfk.
95. Daniel Harari, "Japan's Economy: From the 'Lost Decade' to Abenomics," House of Commons Library, Oct. 24, 2013, http://tinyurl.com/qhs7fcw.
96. Hiroko Tabuchi, "Japan Pays Foreign Workers to Go Home," Apr. 22, 2009, The New York Times, http://tinyurl.com/ob2pz3m.
97. Ibid.
98. Toko Sekiguchi, "Japan Opens Door Wider for Foreign Workers," The Wall Street Journal, Apr. 4, 2014, http://tinyurl.com/pc5nctv.
99. Becky Oskin, "Japan Earthquake & Tsunami of 2011: Facts and Information," Live Science, May 7, 2015, http://tinyurl.com/oquyurg.
100. "Greece Government Debt Ratio," Trading Economics, undated, accessed Jul. 13, 2015, http://tinyurl.com/oqr2hwy.
101. "About That Debt," The Economist, Nov. 18, 2014, http://tinyurl.com/luw9ewg.
102. T. Rajamoorthy, "The Origins and Evolution of the Trans-Pacific Partnership," Global Research, Jul. 1, 2013, http://tinyurl.com/q3ocyhr.
103. Faith Aquino, "Japan Becomes 12th Nation to Join TPP Free Trade Talks," Japan Daily Press, Jul. 24, 2013, http://tinyurl.com/q86fo8z.
104. Hiroko Tabuchi, "Japan Moves to Enter Talks on Pacific Trade," The New York Times, Mar. 15, 2013, http://tinyurl.com/bo3uhtl.
105. "The Trans-Pacific Partnership Trade Accord Explained," The New York Times, Oct. 5, 2015, http://tinyurl.com/ood58o7.
106. Krista Hughes, "Trans-Pacific Pact to Reshape Stock Portfolios Alongside Trade Flows," Reuters, Jul. 6, 2015, http://tinyurl.com/qhy7uoo.
107. Bernard K. Gordon, "Trading Up in Asia," Foreign Affairs, July/August 2012, http://tinyurl.com/pr7bc8k.
108. "Japan Balance of Trade," Trading Economics, undated, accessed Aug. 4, 2015, http://tinyurl.com/ph748ue.
109. "Japan Exports," Trading Economics, undated, accessed Aug. 4, 2015, http://tinyurl.com/7pch9zp.
110. Georgina Prodhan, "China to Have Most Robots in World by 2017," Reuters, Feb. 5, 2015, http://tinyurl.com/k5h96q3.
111. Masami Ito, "Learning to Love Robots," The Japan Times, Dec. 27, 2014, http://tinyurl.com/nce3hoc.
112. Ibid.
113. Ibid.
114. Justin McCurry, "Japan's Muscle Suit Makes Light Work of Heavy Lifting," The Guardian, Aug. 12, 2014, http://tinyurl.com/lz8wbxg.
115. "What's Hal?" Cyberdyne, undated, accessed Jul. 8, 2015, http://tinyurl.com/pbbe522.
116. McCurry, op. cit.

117. "Hotel Staffed by Robots Opening in Japan," Japan National Tourism Organization, Jan. 30, 2015, http://tinyurl.com/lbgof2t.
118. Naver Matome, "Why Is Japan Such an Unpopular Tourist Destination?" Japan Today, Jan. 19, 2015, http://tinyurl.com/pcvalas.
119. Stephen Harner, "Abe's Japan Is 'Back' . . . to 'Normal': A Great Tourist Destination; Heading to Fiscal Crack-Up?" Forbes blog, Jan. 20, 2015, http://tinyurl.com/myzvq22.
120. Yoshiaki Nohara, "As Tokyo Shrinks, Olympics May Be Last Blast," Bloomberg, Jul. 8, 2015, http://tinyurl.com/nkoslky.
121. Toko Sekiguchi, "Abe Wants to Get Japan's Women Working," The Wall Street Journal, Sep. 11, 2014, http://tinyurl.com/q2xx9aq.
122. Devin Stewart, "Abenomics Meets Womenomics," Foreign Affairs, Jan. 29, 2015, http://tinyurl.com/ouywwlt.
123. Ibid.
124. David Corbin, "Meet Yoshiaki Ishii, the Government Official Who Can Save Startups in Japan," Tech in Asia, Jul. 30, 2014, http://tinyurl.com/oktkyqh.
125. Makinen, op. cit.
126. Ibid.
127. Wire services, "Japan's Emperor Akihito Abdicates the Throne," DW, Apr. 30, 2019, https://www.dw.com/en/japans-emperor-akihito-abdicates-throne/a-48541557.
128. Kaori Enjoji and James Griffiths, "Japan's Prime Minister Shinzo Abe Resigns for Health Reasons," CNN, Aug. 28, 2020, https://www.cnn.com/2020/08/28/asia/shinzo-abe-japan-resignation-health-intl-hnk/index.html.
129. Kelly Cohen, "Tokyo 2020 Olympics Officially Postponed until 2021," ESPN, Mar. 24, 2020, https://www.espn.com/olympics/story/_/id/28946033/tokyo-olympics-officially-postponed-2021.
130. "Debt to GDP Radio," World Population Review, 2020, https://worldpopulationreview.com/country-rankings/debt-to-gdp-ratio-by-country.
131. Matthew C. Klein, "Shinzo Abe Had Big Ambitions for Japan," Barron's, Sep. 2, 2020, https://www.barrons.com/articles/shinzo-abe-had-big-ambitions-for-japan-here-is-where-abenomics-succeeded-and-failed-51599062403.
132. Kazuhiko Hori, "Japan Gov't to Push Back 30% Target for Women in Leadership Positions by up to 10 Years," The Mainichi, Jun. 26, 2020, https://mainichi.jp/english/articles/20200626/p2a/00m/0fp/014000c.
133. Ayumi Teraoka, "Resolved: Abe's Investment in His Relationship with President Trump Has Advanced Japan's Interests," Center for Strategic and International Studies, Jan. 30, 2020, https://www.csis.org/analysis/resolved-abes-investment-his-relationship-president-trump-has-advanced-japanese-interests.
134. "US Relations with Japan," Bureau of East Asian and Pacific Affairs, Jan. 21, 2020, https://www.state.gov/u-s-relations-with-japan/.
135. "Proclamation on Adjusting Imports of Derivative Aluminum Products and Derivative Steel Products into the United States," The White House, Jan. 24, 2020, https://www.whitehouse.gov/presidential-actions/proclamation-adjusting-imports-derivative-aluminum-articles-derivative-steel-articles-united-states/.
136. Chad P. Brown, "Trump's Steel and Aluminum Tariffs Are Cascading Out of Control," Peterson Institute for International Economics, Feb. 4, 2020, https://www.piie.com/blogs/trade-and-investment-policy-watch/trumps-steel-and-aluminum-tariffs-are-cascading-out-control.
137. Mike Mochizuki and Jiaxiu Han, "Is China Escalating Tensions with Japan in the East China Sea?" The Diplomat, Sep. 16, 2020, https://thediplomat.com/2020/09/is-china-escalating-tensions-with-japan-in-the-east-china-sea/.

Chapter 7: EU at the Crossroads

1. "Bank of America Moves Senior London Bankers to Paris Ahead of Brexit," Reuters, Jun. 26, 2018, https://tinyurl.com/y8nf2tuw.
2. Sarah Graham, "EY Financial Services Brexit Tracker: Firms Forge Ahead with Contingency Plans Despite Transition Agreement," Ernst & Young Global Limited, Jun. 25, 2018, https://tinyurl.com/yayogssw.
3. "World Economic Outlook Update, July 2018," International Monetary Fund, Jul. 16, 2018, https://tinyurl.com/yaccm5b3.
4. Maurice Obstfeld, "The Global Expansion: Still Strong but Less Even, More Fragile, Under Threat," International Monetary Fund, Jul. 16, 2018, https://tinyurl.com/y8yte8ym.
5. "United Kingdom: Staff Concluding Statement of the 2017 Article IV Mission," International Monetary Fund, Dec. 20, 2017, https://tinyurl.com/ybx3xmf4.
6. "United Kingdom GDP Growth Rate," Trading Economics, Jun. 29, 2018, https://tinyurl.com/yad24myr.
7. "Brexit Uncertainty Blamed for UK Slowdown at Start of 2018," The Associated Press, Business Insider, Feb. 5, 2018, https://tinyurl.com/ybyjlsk7.
8. "The UK and EU Agree Terms for Brexit Transition Period," BBC, Mar. 19, 2018, https://tinyurl.com/y8j88ur7.
9. Adam Becket, "Theresa May's Cabinet Agrees to Pay £40 Billion Brexit Divorce Bill," Business Insider, Nov. 21, 2017, https://tinyurl.com/ybzxeq5y.
10. George Parker, "Brexit Chaos Puts Conservatives on the Edge of a Breakdown," Financial Times, Jul. 13, 2018, https://tinyurl.com/ybmetbh3.
11. "EU Rejects Britain's Key Elements of Special Customs Plan after Brexit," Euractiv.com, Jul. 27, 2018, https://tinyurl.com/y82sqpjv.
12. Theresa May, "The Future Relationship Between the United Kingdom and the European Union," UK Government Publications Office, July 2018, https://tinyurl.com/yatln69h.

13. Boris Johnson, "Boris Johnson's Resignation Speech, Full Text," The Spectator, Jul. 18, 2018, https://tinyurl.com/ydeb27bh.
14. Anna Mikhailova, "Brussels Warns EU Countries: Get Ready for a No-Deal Brexit," The Daily Telegraph, July 19, 2018, https://tinyurl.com/y9p7ht2z.
15. Oliver Sachgau and Alex Morales, "BMW Warns of U.K. Pullback if There's No Brexit Deal," Bloomberg, Jun. 25, 2018, https://tinyurl.com/y9bu3asg.
16. Alex Morales, "Airbus Warns U.K. Investment in Danger in No-Deal Brexit," Bloomberg, Jun. 21, 2018, https://tinyurl.com/y8r27lwa.
17. Dan Sabbagh and Peter Walker, "Justine Greening Endorses Second Brexit Referendum," The Guardian, Jul. 16, 2018, https://tinyurl.com/yaslqo8u.
18. Camilla Hodgson, "Soros on Europe: 'Everything That Could Go Wrong Has Gone Wrong,'" Financial Times, May 29, 2018, https://tinyurl.com/y8ymxpxj.
19. Wen Chen, et al., "The Continental Divide? Economic Exposure to Brexit in Regions and Countries on Both Sides of The Channel," Papers in Regional Science, Dec. 20, 2017, https://tinyurl.com/y9977uev.
20. Kumar Lyer, et al., "The 'Red Tape' Cost of Brexit," Oliver Wyman and Clifford Chance, 2018, https://tinyurl.com/ya28m3hd.
21. Lisa O'Carroll, "Dover-Calais 'Facing Economic Catastrophe' Due to Brexit," The Guardian, Jul. 17, 2018, https://tinyurl.com/ybgq7645.
22. Tim Wallace, "EU's TTIP trade deal with the US has collapsed, says Germany," The Daily Telegraph, Aug. 28, 2016, https://tinyurl.com/y6wcwmt6.
23. Silvia Amaro, "US-EU Trade Agreement Lacks Specifics and Fails to Eliminate Issues with China," CNBC.com, Jul. 26, 2018, https://tinyurl.com/y98chyfl.
24. David J. Lynch, Josh Dawsey and Damian Paletta, "Trump Imposes Steel and Aluminum Tariffs on the E.U., Canada and Mexico," The Washington Post, May 31, 2018, https://tinyurl.com/y8ut7zb4.
25. Chad P. Bown, "Europe Is Pushing Back Against Trump's Steel and Aluminum Tariffs. Here's How," The Washington Post, Mar. 9, 2018, https://tinyurl.com/yaj3r5sf.
26. "Trade in Goods with European Union," U.S. Census Bureau, Jul. 18, 2018, https://tinyurl.com/jqfx3dr.
27. "'I Think the European Union Is a Foe,' Trump Says Ahead of Putin Meeting in Helsinki," CBS News, Jul. 15, 2018, https://tinyurl.com/ybrh9cbs; "Speech: Donald Trump Holds a Political Rally in Fargo, North Dakota—June 27, 2018," Factbase, Jun. 27, 2018, https://tinyurl.com/y77f4ama.
28. Jonathan Stearns, "EU Retaliation Against U.S. over Metal Tariffs to Start June 22," Bloomberg, Jun. 20, 2018, https://tinyurl.com/yc9shz2l.
29. "Form 8-K, Harley-Davidson, Inc.," U.S. Securities and Exchange Commission, Jun. 25, 2018, https://tinyurl.com/ydcltaly.
30. Jeff Cox, "Trump Threatens 20% Tariff on All Car Imports from the EU," CNBC.com, Jun. 22, 2018, https://tinyurl.com/y9msn8ur; Konrad Fischer and Sebastian Schaal, "Why American Cars Don't Sell in Germany (Hint: It's Not Tariffs)," Handelsblatt Global, Apr. 30 2018, https://tinyurl.com/y72j9krn.
31. Donald Trump, "Remarks by President Trump in Meeting with Cabinet Members," WhiteHouse.gov, Jul. 18, 2018, https://tinyurl.com/y7o7njl6.
32. Valentina Pop, Vivian Salama and Bob Davis, "U.S., Europeans Agree to Iron Out Trade Differences," The Wall Street Journal, Jul. 25, 2018, https://tinyurl.com/y8baw3sn.
33. "U.S. Trade in Services by Selected Countries and Areas," U.S. Census Bureau, Jul. 20, 2018, https://tinyurl.com/ycv3pzvj.
34. "ifo Expert Felbermayr: USA Is Running Surplus against EU," ifo Institute, Apr. 30, 2018, https://tinyurl.com/y7ovjddx.
35. Alastair Gale and Emre Peker, "Japan, EU Sign Trade Deal: 'We Stand Together against Protectionism,'" The Wall Street Journal, Jul. 17, 2018, https://tinyurl.com/y8wmvdjm.
36. Obstfeld, op. cit.
37. Winston Churchill, "Ein britischer Patriot für Europa," Die Zeit, May 5, 2009, https://tinyurl.com/yat5y4j7.
38. Daniel Politi, "Merkel Wins in Germany but Anti-Immigrant Far-Right Makes Big Gains," Slate.com, Sep. 24, 2017, https://tinyurl.com/ya976j2m.
39. Patrick Wintour, "EU Takes Action against Eastern States for Refusing to Take Refugees," The Guardian, Jun. 13, 2017, https://tinyurl.com/y9tea6fc.
40. Jason Horowitz, "Italy's New Populist and Anti-Establishment Government Is Sworn In," The New York Times, Jun. 1, 2018, https://tinyurl.com/ycdpvwpp.
41. Gaia Pianigiani, Jason Horowitz and Raphael Minder, "Italy's New Populist Government Turns Away Ship with 600 Migrants Aboard," The New York Times, Jun. 11, 2018, https://tinyurl.com/yc7wdz4t.
42. Gabriela Baczynska, "Papering over Cracks, EU Leaders Claim Summit Victory on Migration," Reuters, Jun. 27, 2018, https://tinyurl.com/y7rpsn6n.
43. "EU Leaders Reach Deal on Migration after Marathon Talks," AlJazeera.com, Jun. 29, 2018, https://tinyurl.com/ycvgv6g3.
44. Nicola Slawson, "Austrian President Approves Far-Right Freedom Party Joining Coalition Government," The Guardian, Dec. 16, 2017, https://tinyurl.com/yccjbsl4.
45. David M. Herszenhorn, Florian Eder and Jacopo Barigazzi, "Sebastian Kurz's European Debutante Ball," Politico.com, Jul. 4, 2018, https://tinyurl.com/ycc3elqj.
46. "The Latest: Austrian Leader: EU Budget Not Acceptable," The Associated Press, Chicago Tribune, May 5, 2018, https://tinyurl.com/yaep7f5v.
47. David M. Herszenhorn and Lili Bayer, "Commission Wants Bigger Budget for Smaller EU," Politico.com, May 2, 2018, https://tinyurl.com/y9od732h.

48. Sybille de La Hamaide, "EU Proposes to Cut Farm Subsidies, France Says Unacceptable," Reuters, May 2, 2018, https://tinyurl.com/yac7x7ta.
49. Ibid.; "France Slams Proposed Cut to EU Farm Subsidies," Radio France International English Service, Mar. 5, 2018, https://tinyurl.com/y7u2mo4z.
50. "Macron Says Eastern Europe 'Betrayed' EU, Polish FM Wants Explanation," Radio Poland, Jun. 22, 2017, https://tinyurl.com/ycz2d38j.
51. Anna Martinelli, "Italy, Europe's First Populist Government Is a Reality," La Stampa, Jun. 1, 2018, https://tinyurl.com/y73ltyom; Crispian Balmer, "New Italian Economy Minister Vows to Stay in Euro, Cut Debt Level," Reuters, Jun. 10, 2018, https://tinyurl.com/y6vklzbw.
52. Silvia Dall'Angelo, "Italy and Europe: The Integration Dilemma," Hermes Investment Management, Jul. 5, 2018, https://tinyurl.com/y8jgoseu.
53. Ibid.
54. Jennifer Rankin, "Weakest Eurozone Economies on Long Road to Recovery," The Observer, Sep. 16, 2017, https://tinyurl.com/y9jtygw5.
55. Eshe Nelson, "Five Years Ago Today, Mario Draghi Saved the Euro," Quartz, Jul. 26, 2017, https://tinyurl.com/y7xmo93a.
56. Jan Strupczewski, "EU Leaders See Bigger ESM Role, but Budget, Deposit Insurance on Hold," Reuters, Jun. 29, 2018, https://tinyurl.com/ya83nw9m.
57. Frank Langfitt, "Brexit Day: What to Know When the U.K. Leaves the E.U.," NPR, Jan. 31, 2020, https://www.npr.org/2020/01/31/801289239/brexit-day-what-to-know-when-the-u-k-leaves-the-eu.
58. Silvia Amaro, "Deal over American Lobster Helps to Ease U.S.-E.U. Trade Tensions," CNBC, Aug. 24, 2020, https://www.cnbc.com/2020/08/24/deal-over-american-lobster-helps-to-ease-us-eu-trade-tensions.html.
59. Ibid.
60. Michael Peel and Sam Fleming, "EU to Step Up Pressure over Migrant Returns," Financial Times, Sep. 18, 2020, https://www.ft.com/content/05837dfe-1739-4aae-9a37-aee94f588327.
61. Charlemagne, "Germany Is Doomed to Lead Europe," The Economist, Jun. 25, 2020, https://www.economist.com/europe/2020/06/27/germany-is-doomed-to-lead-europe.

Chapter 8: Fashion Industry

1. Suzanne Bearne, "Not a Far-Fetched Idea: How One Man Built a $1.5bn Fashion Business," BBC, Nov. 7, 2016, http://tinyurl.com/hzbzdrv.
2. Amy Thomson and Matthew Campbell, "Farfetch Tries to Reach a Little Further," Bloomberg, Nov. 12, 2015, http://tinyurl.com/gnf3v2d.
3. Astrid Wendlandt and Pascale Denis, "Farfetch CEO Says IPO on the Horizon Within 2–3 Years," Daily Mail/Reuters, Nov. 7, 2016, http://tinyurl.com/z4zh5jm.
4. "Global Powers of Luxury Goods 2016: Disciplined Innovation," Deloitte, http://tinyurl.com/h22s8sz.
5. "Fast Fashion in 2016: Industry Disruption and Geographic Dominance Part 1," Euromonitor International, November 2016, http://tinyurl.com/jbsm2ot.
6. U.S. Census Bureau Business and Industry Time Series Trend Chart, http://tinyurl.com/j3e4vlb.
7. Ashma Kunde, "New Apparel Research: Part 1—a Focus on Geographies," Euromonitor, Mar. 11, 2013, http://tinyurl.com/h3hylzq.
8. Iryna Sychyk, "Clothing and Footwear to Be Less Important Amid Growing Affluence of Urban Consumers," Euromonitor, Apr. 16, 2016, http://tinyurl.com/zo8o28j.
9. Imran Amed, et al., "The State of Fashion," McKinsey & Company, December 2016, http://tinyurl.com/j4gu5l8.
10. Ibid.
11. Ibid.
12. Phil Wahba, "Ralph Lauren Has a $1.8 Billion Department Store Problem," Fortune, Jun. 8, 2016, http://tinyurl.com/jtzm8qd.
13. "Employees in 24 Countries Say What Attire Is Proper—and What's Not—in the Workplace . . . ," Ipsos Global @dvisory, July 2010, http://tinyurl.com/jxy7ng5.
14. Jacob Gallagher, "Has Fashion Abandoned the Suit?" The Wall Street Journal, Sep. 1, 2016, http://tinyurl.com/hbvnsh8.
15. Christina Binkley, "The New Trend in Office Wear: Comfort," The Wall Street Journal, Sep. 18, 2016, http://tinyurl.com/hfp95ez.
16. James F. Peltz, "Q&A: Why Office Dress Codes Keep Getting More Casual," Los Angeles Times, Jun. 16, 2016, http://tinyurl.com/zlkq3fx.
17. Binkley, op. cit.
18. "We Are What We Wear," Malamalama: The Magazine of the University of Hawaii System, July 2001, http://tinyurl.com/z7l8386.
19. Jill Engledow, "Talk Story: Aloha Friday," Maui No Ka Oi Magazine, March–April 2007, http://tinyurl.com/jen3fdg.
20. "Aloha: Aloha Friday," University of Hawaii Community Colleges, http://tinyurl.com/zt5j3o5.
21. "Casual Wear in the Office: Dressing for Success or Dressing for Stress?" Knowledge@Wharton, University of Pennsylvania, Jun. 7, 2000, http://tinyurl.com/hy3hyt3.
22. Sarah Maloney Hughes, "The Effect of Casual Dress on Performance in the Workplace," Journal for the Human Sciences, http://www.kon.org/urc/maloney.html.
23. Michael W. Kraus and Wendy Berry Mendes, "Sartorial Symbols of Social Class Elicit Class-Consistent Behavior and Physiological Responses: A Dyadic Approach," Journal of Experimental Psychology, December 2014, http://tinyurl.com/jddz8r5.
24. Ray A. Smith, "Why Dressing for Success Leads to Success," The Wall Street Journal, Feb. 21, 2016, http://tinyurl.com/zw6kyeq.

25. Lauren Sherman, "Why Americans Aren't Shopping," Business of Fashion, May 16, 2016, http://tinyurl.com/hhzqjw6.
26. Ibid.
27. Ann C. Foster, "Consumer Expenditures Vary by Age," Bureau of Labor Statistics, December 2015, http://tinyurl.com/gnuugz2.
28. Rod Sides, "2016 Deloitte Holiday Survey: Ringing in the Retail," Oct. 25, 2016, http://tinyurl.com/zvc8j3c.
29. Fflur Roberts, "Luxury Industry Facing Mounting Risks into 2017," Euromonitor, Nov. 21, 2016, http://tinyurl.com/h255sex.
30. Sarah Halzack, "Are Women Ready to Rent Their Work Wear? Rent the Runway Bets Yes," The Washington Post, Mar. 23, 2016, http://tinyurl.com/gl6hy37.
31. "2016 WTM Global Travel Trends Report," Euromonitor, http://tinyurl.com/jtsvryx.
32. Tim Gunn, "Designers Refuse to Make Clothes to Fit American Women. It's a Disgrace," The Washington Post, Sep. 8, 2016, http://tinyurl.com/jlgab9h.
33. Ibid.
34. Robin Givhan, "Yet Another Way Fashion Is Unfair to Plus-Size Women—and One Entrepreneur's Solution," The Washington Post, Jul. 6, 2016, http://tinyurl.com/h64udgh.
35. Robin Givhan, "Michelle Obama Didn't Like to Discuss Her Clothes, but They Spoke Volumes," The Washington Post, Nov. 23, 2016, http://tinyurl.com/j9aesf8.
36. "Fashion: BLS Spotlight on Statistics Fashion," U.S. Bureau of Labor Statistics, June 2012, http://tinyurl.com/hn5r4z9.
37. "Wages and Working Hours in the Textiles, Clothing, Leather and Footwear Industries," International Labour Organization, Sep. 2014, http://tinyurl.com/hr7bycs.
38. Jason Burke and Saad Hammadi, "Bangladesh Textile Factory Fire Leaves More Than 100 Dead," The Guardian, Nov. 25, 2012, http://tinyurl.com/j76jpvs; "Bangladeshi Garment Factory Owners Surrender Over Deadly 2012 Fire," ABC Australia, Feb. 9, 2014, http://tinyurl.com/lapjj3b.
39. "Global Fashion & Luxury Market: Private Equity and Investors Survey 2016," Deloitte, http://tinyurl.com/jmttmxe.
40. Lauretta Roberts, "Browns Unveils New Look, New Website and Innovative Window Campaign," The Industry, Nov. 11, 2016, http://tinyurl.com/jxmtylb.
41. Elizabeth Holmes, "Where Luxury Fashion Is a High Speed, High Volume Business," The Wall Street Journal, Oct. 26, 2016, http://tinyurl.com/zgyl7bt.
42. Wendlandt and Denis, op. cit.
43. "Fashion Graduate Helen Boxall Aiming for a 'Fashion Free' Year to Raise £500 for Oxfam," Rochdale Online, Dec. 12, 2016, http://tinyurl.com/z6nv77b.
44. Donna Ferguson, "Dreaming of a Frugal Christmas? Meet the People Who've Stopped Shopping," The Guardian, Dec. 12, 2016, http://tinyurl.com/jzrd7lu.
45. "The #Haulternative/a Guide for Fashion Lovers," Fashion Revolution, 2016, http://tinyurl.com/zo4myyy.
46. "Global Luxury Goods Trend Report," Euromonitor, April 2016, http://tinyurl.com/j468qeq.
47. Christina Binkley, "The New Trend in Office Wear: Comfort," The Wall Street Journal, Sep. 18, 2016, http://tinyurl.com/hfp95ez.
48. "The Importance of Visible Logos on Handbags is Diminishing, Reports NPD," press release, NPD Group, Oct. 17, 2016, http://tinyurl.com/hcfoxzh.
49. Diane Whitmore Schanzenbach, et al., "Where Does All the Money Go: Shifts in Household Spending over the Past 30 Years," The Hamilton Project/Brookings Institution, pp. 3–4, http://tinyurl.com/gpx6tfc.
50. Scheherazade Daneshkhu and Mark Vandeveld, "Clothes Buying Goes Out of Style in the UK," Financial Times, Sep. 24, 2016, http://tinyurl.com/jqsvdrn.
51. Saabira Chaudhuri, "Birthday at Burberry? Luxury Brands Add Personal Services," The Wall Street Journal, Nov. 30, 2016, http://tinyurl.com/hdrjqna.
52. Khanh T.L. Tran and Kari Hamanaka, "The Hot Trend in Fashion and Retail: Pizza, Pressed Juices and Macarons," Womens' Wear Daily, Dec. 31, 2015, http://tinyurl.com/j49j785.
53. Brittany Talarico, "The Pro Files: Designer Zaid Affas on Dressing the Social Media Generation," People, Nov. 23, 2016, http://tinyurl.com/h8[illegible]pdto.
54. David Yermack, "The Michelle Markup: The First Lady's Impact on Stock Prices of Fashion Companies," Stern School of Business, New York University, Dec. 1, 2011, http://tinyurl.com/zpgn8rz.
55. Ibid.
56. David Yermack, "Vision Statement: How This First Lady Moves Markets," Harvard Business Review, November 2010, http://tinyurl.com/jx2y2qb.
57. "Viva La 1990s!" The Daily Beast, Apr. 28, 2010, http://tinyurl.com/jg3h88x.
58. Aly Weisman, "Here's How Much Celebrities Are Paid to Wear Designer Dresses on the Red Carpet," Business Insider, Jun. 15, 2015, http://tinyurl.com/hfa67vh.
59. "Celebrity Power and Its Influence on Global Consumer Behavior," Euromonitor, March 2014, http://tinyurl.com/hwuwfqf.
60. Karla McCormick, "Celebrity Endorsements: Influence of a Product-Endorser Match on Millennials Attitudes and Purchase Intentions," Journal of Retailing and Consumer Services, September 2016, http://tinyurl.com/jyq6kvx.
61. Ibid.
62. Teri Agins, "Celebrity Fashion Hijackers," Business of Fashion, May 11, 2015, http://tinyurl.com/zub33rb.
63. Kim Bhasin, "How Jessica Simpson Built a Billion Dollar Fashion Empire," Bloomberg, Apr. 6, 2015, http://tinyurl.com/hqebfos.
64. YouTube, http://tinyurl.com/h2pk4w3.
65. Christopher Nickens and George Zeno, "Marilyn in Fashion: The Enduring Influence of Marilyn Monroe," pp. 170–171.

66. Barbara Thau, "Will J.Lo and Mark Anthony Fashion Top the Charts for Kohl's?" AOL Daily Finance, Sep. 15, 2011, http://tinyurl.com/gojxm8e.
67. Hannah Seligson, "What Ivanka Trump Can't Sell," The New York Times, Nov. 7, 2016, http://tinyurl.com/gmw3umu.
68. Melissa Chan, "Ivanka Trump Starts to Separate Herself from Her Fashion Brand," Fortune, Nov. 23, 2016, http://tinyurl.com/zdd6bkm.
69. Bridget Foley, "Designers Weigh in on Dressing Melania Trump," Women's Wear Daily, Nov. 30, 2016, http://tinyurl.com/znw4lbq.
70. Booth Moore, "Top Names in Fashion Shill for . . . 'The Minions'?," Los Angeles Times, Jun. 22, 2015, http://tinyurl.com/zjz88t3.
71. Amed, et al., op. cit.
72. "Wages and Working Hours in the Textile, Clothing, Leather and Footwear Industries," op. cit., pp. 10–11.
73. John Still, "Before the Label: The Crowdfunding Platform That Puts Designers First," The Guardian, Jan. 14, 2015, http://tinyurl.com/gwaqrbd.
74. Amed, et al., op. cit.
75. Ibid.
76. "International Trade Statistics 2015," World Trade Organization, 2015, http://tinyurl.com/q2bmcyf.
77. Corinne Gretler, "LVMH Sales Beat Estimates as Demand Grows for Leather Goods," Bloomberg, Oct. 10, 2016, http://tinyurl.com/zk4jat3.
78. Luigi Dumitrescu and Simona Vinerean, "The Glocal Strategy of Global Brands," Studies in Business and Economics, http://tinyurl.com/jthyfg6.
79. Carsten Keller, et al., "Succeeding in Tomorrow's Global Fashion Market," McKinsey & Company, September 2014, http://tinyurl.com/jophupr.
80. Amed et al., op. cit.
81. "The Global Personal Luxury Goods Market Holds Steady at €249 Billion amid Geopolitical Uncertainty," Bain & Company, Oct. 20, 2016, http://tinyurl.com/zszpntq.
82. Heather Long, "Donald Trump Suits and Ties Are Made in China," CNN Money, Mar. 8, 2016, http://tinyurl.com/jdlk8eu.
83. Jennifer Jacobs, "Trump Taps China Critic Lighthizer for U.S. Trade Representative," Bloomberg, Jan. 2, 2017, http://tinyurl.com/hc67jrf.
84. Sarah Halzack, "Retail and Apparel Industries Take Wait-and-See Approach to Trump's Talk of Tariffs," The Washington Post, Dec. 5, 2016, http://tinyurl.com/z789roa.
85. Nick Carvell, "Meet the Woman Who Made H&M Recycle 100 Million T-Shirts," GQ, Oct. 28, 2016, http://tinyurl.com/jtcvh5m.
86. Marc Bain, "Recycling or Donating Your Unwanted Clothes 'Is Not a Solution' for the Planet, Greenpeace Says," Quartz, Nov. 30, 2016, http://tinyurl.com/z4ucb6m.
87. "Eco Worriers: Global Green Behavior and Market Impact," Euromonitor, http://tinyurl.com/jlkwegd.
88. Alden Wicker, "Fast Fashion Is Creating an Environmental Crisis," Newsweek, Sep. 1, 2016, http://tinyurl.com/hvc6le6.
89. Eric Bellman, "Fast-Fashion Castoffs Fuel Global Recycling Network," The Wall Street Journal, Jun. 26, 2016, http://tinyurl.com/znphk39.
90. "Once Worn, Thrice Shy—British Women's Wardrobe Habits Exposed!" Barnardo's Retail, Jun. 11, 2015, http://tinyurl.com/j4ov69a.
91. American Apparel and Footwear Association report, http://tinyurl.com/pajcpdu.
92. "Eco Worriers," op. cit.
93. Magdalena Kondej, "The New Consumerism in Fashion: Will the Apparel Industry Seize the Circular Economy Opportunity?" Euromonitor, Oct. 28, 2016, http://tinyurl.com/zdk9lmx.
94. Vivian Hendriksz, "55 Fashion Companies Sign 'Milestone' Sustainability Covenant," Fashion United, Jul. 4, 2016, http://tinyurl.com/zkkvb4v.
95. Kim Bhasin, "The Future of Fashion Is Mushroom Leather," Bloomberg Businessweek, Dec. 22, 2016, http://tinyurl.com/jszogbj.
96. Robin Givhan, "Luxury Fashion Brands Are Going Green. But Why Are They Keeping It a Secret?" The Washington Post, Dec. 8, 2015, http://tinyurl.com/hdmdcqx.
97. "The Detox Catwalk 2016: Who's on the Path to Toxic-Free Fashion?" Greenpeace, 2016, http://tinyurl.com/pqbycf7.
98. "Germany-Based SOEX GROUP Invests 5 Million Euros in Building a New Sorting Plant," SOEX GROUP news release, http://tinyurl.com/zb7no4g.
99. Paromita Dey, "Sharjah: German Firm to Build $5.6m Plant in HFZ," Construction Week Online, Jun. 21, 2016, http://tinyurl.com/z5wvp3l.
100. Anka Muhlstein, "The Cut of Coco," New York Review of Books, Oct. 9, 2014, http://tinyurl.com/jouhywc.
101. Lisa Chaney, "Coco Chanel: An Intimate Life," Penguin, 2011.
102. Ibid.
103. "Ensemble," The Museum at the Fashion Institute of Technology, http://tinyurl.com/zta6pfx.
104. Patricia Cunningham, "Reforming Women's Fashion 1850–1920: Politics, Health and Art," Kent State University Press, 2015, p. 37.
105. Manisha Aggarwal-Schifellite, "When American Feminists Were Pilloried for Daring to Wear Bloomers," Atlas Obscura, May 31, 2016, http://tinyurl.com/gksg76a.
106. "Women's Clothing," University of Vermont, http://tinyurl.com/zyqjced.
107. April Calahan, Karen Trivette Cannell and Anna Sui, "Fashion Plates: 150 Years of Style," Yale University Press, 2015, p. 326.
108. Ibid.

109. Lilah Ramzi, "Ten Influential Fashion Designers You've Probably Never Heard Of," Fashionista, May 14, 2013, http://tinyurl.com/zwnuwkc.
110. Chaney, op. cit., p. 203.
111. Isabel Sanchez Vegara, "Top 10 Amazing Facts You Didn't Know about Coco Chanel," The Guardian, Feb. 24, 2016, http://tinyurl.com/jmdrtoy.
112. Muhlstein, op. cit.
113. Jason Chow, "Chanel CEO Maureen Chiquet Leaving Company at End of Month," The Wall Street Journal, Jan. 27, 2016, http://tinyurl.com/hlyww4s.
114. Chaney, op. cit., p. 288.
115. Elaine Woo, "Liz Claiborne, 78, Clothes Designer for Career Women Built Vast Fashion Empire," Los Angeles Times, Jun. 28, 2007, http://tinyurl.com/nveo23.
116. Adam Bernstein, "Liz Claiborne, 78; Fashion Industry Icon," The Washington Post, Jun. 28, 2007, http://tinyurl.com/27dnys.
117. Woo, op. cit.
118. Bernstein, op. cit.
119. Chaney, op. cit.
120. "1955: The 2.55 Bag," Inside Chanel Timeline, http://tinyurl.com/zqeaje2.
121. Amy de Klerk, "The Investment Potential of a Chanel Handbag," Harper's Bazaar, Jun. 15, 2016, http://tinyurl.com/z9stfpb.
122. Katy Steinmetz, "From Horse People to Hillary Clinton: A History of Women Wearing Pants," Time, Jun. 14, 2016, http://tinyurl.com/jve37sy.
123. Mitra Toossi, "A Century of Change: The U.S. Labor Force 1950–2050," Bureau of Labor Statistics Monthly Labor Review, May 2002, Table 4, http://tinyurl.com/zlaezd9.
124. "Remembering Fashion Designer Liz Claiborne: Designer Liz Claiborne Dead at 78," NPR, Jun. 28, 2007, http://tinyurl.com/grtac72.
125. Sylvia Rubin, "Liz Claiborne/1929-2007/Designer's Career Mirrored the Rise of Working Women," San Francisco Chronicle, Jun. 28, 2007, http://tinyurl.com/zz53hjn.
126. Walter Loeb, "J.C. Penney Tramples on Liz Claiborne and Misses a Great Opportunity," Forbes, Mar. 18, 2013, http://tinyurl.com/jtzlbne.
127. Adrianne Pasquarelli, "Diane von Furstenberg, Liz Claiborne: Designer Greats, Different Fates," Crain's New York Business, Nov. 27, 2011, http://tinyurl.com/zomddqj.
128. Cathy Horyn, "Looking Through Mrs. Prada's Eyes," Harper's Bazaar, Aug. 12, 2014, http://tinyurl.com/hbu738r.
129. "Background Miu Miu," Vogue, Nov. 24, 2015, http://tinyurl.com/zlzrop2.
130. Horyn, op. cit.
131. Jo-Ann Furniss, "Miuccia Prada on Being Shy, Working with Her Husband and Her Mad Office with a Helter Skelter," The Telegraph, Aug. 26, 2016, http://tinyurl.com/zcsfrs7.
132. Andrew O'Hagan, "Power of One: Miuccia Prada's Circle of Influence," New York Times Magazine, May 27, 2013, http://tinyurl.com/hw8aavr.
133. "The World's 100 Most Powerful Women," Forbes, http://tinyurl.com/j6hxrek.
134. Andrew Roberts, "Prada Revenue Growth Evaporates as Luxury-Goods Maker Struggles," Bloomberg, Feb. 17, 2016, http://tinyurl.com/hwn426j.
135. "The World's Most Valuable Brands: #80 Chanel," Forbes, May 2016, http://tinyurl.com/j9ed8au.
136. Dana Mattioli, "Liz Claiborne Must Say Adieu to Liz," The Wall Street Journal, Oct. 13, 2011, http://tinyurl.com/joncqp6; "Fifth & Pacific CEO Departs," The Associated Press, Crain's New York Business, Jan. 10, 2014, http://tinyurl.com/j6g4lzj.
137. Patricia Kowsmann, "Fast Fashion: How a Zara Coat Went from Design to Fifth Avenue in 25 Days," The Wall Street Journal, Dec. 6, 2016, http://tinyurl.com/guggzkj.
138. Luisa Zargani, "Miuccia Prada Talks Men's Wear, Revolution and History," Women's Wear Daily, Mar. 23, 2016, http://tinyurl.com/gourfnw.
139. Alanna Petroff, "Amazon Has Quietly Launched 7 In-House Clothing Brands," CNN Money Feb. 24, 2016, http://tinyurl.com/glmu4wo.
140. Marc Bain, "Robots Are Set to Take the Jobs of Millions of Asian Workers in the Coming Years," Quartz, Jul. 8, 2016, http://tinyurl.com/gqyphwz.
141. Ananya Bhattacharya, "We're Getting Closer to Clothing Made Entirely by Robots," Quartz, Oct. 9, 2016, http://tinyurl.com/zyxcyk7.
142. E. Tammy Kim, "Cambodian Garment Workers Rise Up and Face a Crackdown," Al Jazeera America, Mar. 11, 2015, http://tinyurl.com/pfeplxz.
143. Kowsmann, op. cit.
144. Elizabeth Blair, "Slow Fashion Shows Consumers What It's Made Of," NPR, Apr. 24, 2015, http://tinyurl.com/le9zdbo.
145. Elizabeth Paton, "Kylie Jenner and the Year of the Drop," The New York Times, Dec. 14, 2016, http://tinyurl.com/zj4jre2.
146. Lauren Coleman-Lochner, "Kenneth Cole to Shut Down Almost All Brick-and-Mortar Stores," Bloomberg News, Nov. 11, 2016, http://tinyurl.com/jzra5my.
147. Kerry Close, "12 Major Retailers Closing Stores Like Crazy," Time, Jun. 30, 2016, http://tinyurl.com/z39g9np.
148. Nathan Wajsman, Carolina Arias Burgos and Christopher Davies, "The Economic Cost of IPR Infringement in the Clothing, Footwear and Accessories Sector," European Union Intellectual Property Office, June 2015, http://tinyurl.com/hwyq4nw & http://tinyurl.com/zue5psf.
149. Kathy Chu, "Luxury Brands Get Tough with Counterfeiters," The Wall Street Journal China Real Time Report, Aug. 16, 2016, http://tinyurl.com/hoa8lg7.

150. Matt McCue, "These retailers are betting on transgender customers," Fortune, May 21, 2015, http://tinyurl.com/zdz4hlc.
151. Mona Chalabi, "The Countries Where People Are Most Likely to Celebrate Singles Day (and Make Alibaba Richer)," FiveThirtyEight, Nov. 11, 2014, http://tinyurl.com/jk36h33.
152. Christina Binkley, "Trendy Brands Market Gender-Neutral Styles," The Wall Street Journal, Jul. 20, 2016, http://tinyurl.com/hcd7vf8.
153. Denise Dahlhoff and Sarah Wittenborn, "Exploring Cross-Generational Buying Behavior at a Time of Complex Change in the Retail Landscape," NPD Group, http://tinyurl.com/z43f7z6.
154. Noah Berlatsky, "Project Runway's Fashion Aspirations Fall Short (but It's Not Necessarily a Bad Thing)," The Guardian, Jan. 15, 2016, http://tinyurl.com/zj2nra4.
155. Robin Givhan, "Project Runway Hasn't Launched a Real Star, but It Is a lesson in Fashion Today," The Washington Post, Jul. 23, 2014, http://tinyurl.com/zwym22q.
156. Sandra Lopez, "CFDA/ Vogue Fashion Fund Designers Embrace Tech Effect on Fashion," Intel, Nov. 8, 2016, http://tinyurl.com/h86dwbg; Karli Petrovic, "Fashion Futurists Combine Tech and Couture," Intel, Oct. 19, 2016, http://tinyurl.com/hf5aa2c.
157. Marc Bain, "Forget Wearables. In the Future, Your Clothing Will Connect to the Internet," Quartz, Nov. 20, 2016, http://tinyurl.com/hlx2cor.
158. David Meyer, "Exclusive: Internet of Clothing Is Coming through Huge Label Deal," Fortune, Apr. 18, 2016, http://tinyurl.com/gq55o3o.
159. Fflur Roberts, "Harnassing a Global Technological Revolution in Luxury Goods," Euromonitor, Mar. 22, 2016, http://tinyurl.com/jpx7dqd.
160. Elizabeth Paton, "Fashion's Future, Printed to Order," The New York Times, Dec. 5, 2016, http://tinyurl.com/hxnt3xv.
161. Matthew Caines, "HUUB Design Founder on the Importance of Research and Development for SMEs," The Telegraph, Nov. 7, 2016, http://tinyurl.com/h38gtp5.
162. Eric Roston, "Your Summer Clothes Don't Keep You Cool, but This Plastic Fabric Will," Bloomberg News, Sep. 1, 2016, http://tinyurl.com/h5gndyx.
163. Liz Mermin, "Is Your T-Shirt Clean of Slavery? Science Soon May Be Able to Tell," Thomson Reuters, Nov. 28, 2016, http://tinyurl.com/zsevtfw.
164. Sarah Knapton, "'Smart Clothes' of Future Will Auction Themselves on eBay If They Are Not Worn," The Telegraph, Aug. 5, 2016, http://tinyurl.com/jxvmx8n.
165. Meg Miller, "The MIT Lab That's Quietly Pioneering Fashion for Everyone," Fast Company, Aug. 15, 2016, http://tinyurl.com/zlyg483.
166. Meyers, op. cit.
167. Bekah Wright, "From Coffee Grounds to Couture, Food Waste Transforms into Fashion," TakePart, May 23, 2016, http://tinyurl.com/jsswlu9.
168. Charlie Campbell, "The Mixmaster of Fashion," Time, Oct. 6, 2016, http://tinyurl.com/zao2hze.
169. "Consumer Expenditures, 2019" Bureau of Labor Statistics, Sep. 9, 2020, https://www.bls.gov/news.release/cesan.nr0.htm.
170. Sheng Lu, "US-China Tariff War—the Textile and Apparel Hit-List Updated," Sep. 4, 2020, https://www.just-style.com/analysis/us-china-tariff-war-the-textile-and-apparel-hit-list-updated_id136519.aspx.
171. Melissa Twigg, "U.S.-China Trade War Accelerates Apparel Factories' Shift from China to Southeast Asia and Bangkok," South China Morning Post, Nov. 4, 2019, https://www.scmp.com/lifestyle/fashion-beauty/article/3035927/us-china-trade-war-accelerates-apparel-factories-shift.
172. Achim Berg and Imran Amed, "The State of Fashion 2020," McKinsey & Co, September 2019, https://www.mckinsey.com/~/media/mckinsey/industries/retail/our%20insights/the%20state%20of%20fashion%202020%20navigating%20uncertainty/the-state-of-fashion-2020-final.ashx.
173. Chris Remington, "Fashion to Bounce Back with Sustainability Focus," Ecotextile News, Jun. 22, 2020, https://www.ecotextile.com/2020062226232/fashion-retail-news/fashion-to-bounce-back-with-sustainability-focus.html.
174. Saloni Sardana, "China's Retail Sales Rise the First Time This Year in August, as the World's Second Largest Economy Recovers from the Pandemic," Business Insider, Sep. 15, 2020, https://markets.businessinsider.com/news/stocks/china-economy-retail-sales-rise-first-time-industrial-recovery-covid-2020-9-1029588893#.
175. Vogue Business Team, "Fashion Industry Crisis Deepens amid COVID-19 Chaos," Vogue Business, Apr. 6, 2020, https://www.voguebusiness.com/companies/fashion-industry-crisis-deepens-amid-covid-19-chaos.
176. Emily Pandise, "Which Major Retail Companies Have Filed for Bankruptcy Since the Coronavirus Crisis Hit? Here's the List," CNBC, May 18, 2020, https://www.nbcnews.com/business/consumer/which-major-retail-companies-have-filed-bankruptcy-coronavirus-pandemic-hit-n1207866.
177. Luisa Zargani, "Giorgio Armani Writes Open Letter to WWD," Women's Wear Daily, Apr. 3, 2020, https://wwd.com/fashion-news/designer-luxury/giorgio-armani-writes-open-letter-wwd-1203553687/.
178. Chris Remington, "Fashion to Bounce Back with Sustainability Focus," Ecotextile News, Jun. 22, 2020, https://www.ecotextile.com/2020062226232/fashion-retail-news/fashion-to-bounce-back-with-sustainability-focus.html.

Chapter 9: Free Trade

1. "World Economic Outlook," International Monetary Fund, October 2016, http://tinyurl.com/zg9zo8a.
2. Ibid, p. 63.
3. Ibid.

4. Douglas A. Irwin, "Free Trade Under Fire," Fourth Edition, Princeton University Press, 2015.
5. "Report on G20 Trade Measures," World Trade Organization, Jun. 21, 2016, http://tinyurl.com/zokzhgu.
6. Shawn Donnan, "WTO Warns on Rise of Protectionist Measures by G20 Economies," Financial Times, Jun. 21, 2016, http://tinyurl.com/j6a35jh.
7. "The Elephant Chart in the EU Room," Harvard University Press, Jun. 30, 2016, http://tinyurl.com/zlzsbk7.
8. "The Economic Benefits of U.S. Trade," Council of Economic Advisers, Office of the President of the United States, May 2015, http://tinyurl.com/zcxz2bq.
9. Romain Wacziarg and Karen Welch, "Trade Liberalization and Growth: New Evidence," World Bank Economic Review, Vol. 22, Issue 2, May 2008, http://tinyurl.com/hn4rhym.
10. Irwin, op. cit., chapter 2.
11. Joseph Parilla and Mark Muro, "Maladjusted: It's Time to Reimagine Economic 'Adjustment' Programs," Brookings Institution, Jan. 10, 2017, http://tinyurl.com/hswjbr9.
12. Richard Dobbs, et al., "Poorer Than Their Parents? A New Perspective on Income Inequality," McKinsey Global Institute, July 2016, http://tinyurl.com/hb7rrqw.
13. "All Employees: Manufacturing/All Employees: Total Nonfarm Payrolls," Federal Reserve Bank of St. Louis, FRED Economic Data, http://tinyurl.com/h2odmq7.
14. Michael J. Hicks and Srikant Devaraj, "The Myth and the Reality of Manufacturing in America," Ball State University Center for Business and Economic Research, June 2015, http://tinyurl.com/jaj7o8o; "Net Exports of Goods and Services," Federal Reserve Bank of St. Louis, FRED Economic Data, updated Feb. 28, 2017, http://tinyurl.com/h2q6yz9.
15. Susan Houseman and Michael Mandel, "Measuring Globalization: Better Trade Statistics for Better Policy," Upjohn Institute Press, 2015, http://tinyurl.com/zrbdp5c.
16. Jared Bernstein, "Don't Blame the Robots! An Interview on Manufacturing, Automation, and Globalization with Susan Houseman," The Washington Post, Oct. 18, 2016, http://tinyurl.com/z8pm9hc.
17. David Acemoglu, et al., "Import Competition and the Great US Employment Sag of the 2000s," University of Chicago Press, Dec. 18, 2015, http://tinyurl.com/jrshlm9.
18. Josh Bivens, "Using Standard Models to Benchmark the Costs of Globalization for American Workers without a College Degree," Economic Policy Institute, Mar. 22, 2013, http://tinyurl.com/d933d3r.
19. J. Bradford DeLong, "NAFTA and Other Trade Deals Have Not Gutted American Manufacturing—Period," Vox.com, Jan. 24, 2017, http://tinyurl.com/jm2ozld.
20. David H. Autor, David Dorn, and Gordon H. Hanson, "The China Shock: Learning from Labor-Market Adjustment to Large Changes in Trade," Annual Review of Economics, Aug. 8, 2016, http://tinyurl.com/hmw2gb7.
21. "The iPhone Supply Chain," The Gateway, Jan. 8, 2014, http://tinyurl.com/hxmpzgd.
22. Madhur Ja, Samantha Amerasinghe and John Calverley, "Global Supply Chains: New Directions," Standard Chartered, 2015, http://tinyurl.com/jjqz5fn.
23. Christopher Wilson, "Working Together: Economic Ties between the United States and Mexico," Woodrow Wilson International Center for Scholars, Dec. 13, 2011, http://tinyurl.com/hjscqe9.
24. "Donald Trump's Trade Bluster," The Economist, Dec. 10, 2016, http://tinyurl.com/gnodwrw.
25. Kevin O'Marah, "Trump Wins: Supply Chain Implications of Stated Policies," Forbes, Nov. 10, 2016, http://tinyurl.com/hpa4x7g.
26. David H. Autor, David Dorn and Gordon H. Hanson, "The China Shock: Learning from Labor-Market Adjustment to Large Changes in Trade," National Bureau of Economic Research, January 2016, http://tinyurl.com/hmw2gb7.
27. Ibid.
28. Ibid.
29. Mark Wu, "The 'China, Inc.' Challenge to Global Trade Governance," Harvard International Law Journal, Spring 2016, http://tinyurl.com/zdjukbo.
30. Autor, Dorn and Hanson, op. cit.
31. Ibid.
32. Wu, op. cit.
33. Lawrence Summers, "Revoking Trade Deals Will Not Help American Middle Classes," Financial Times, Feb. 5, 2017, http://tinyurl.com/jf3hhx8.
34. "The Future of Factory Asia: A Tightening Grip," The Economist, Mar. 12, 2015, http://tinyurl.com/z9k84jf.
35. Shawn Donnan, "US Trade Chief Seeks to Reshore Supply Chain," Financial Times, Jan. 31, 2017, http://tinyurl.com/jbnjgup.
36. Peter S. Goodman, et al., "Trump's Tough Trade Talk Could Damage American Factories," The New York Times, Dec. 2, 2016, http://tinyurl.com/z8wwx9c.
37. Lucy P. Eldridge and Michael J. Harper, "Effects of Imported Intermediate Inputs on Productivity," BLS Monthly Labor Review, June 2010, http://tinyurl.com/h87tgs6.
38. Peter Navarro and Wilbur Ross, "Scoring the Trump Economic Plan: Trade, Regulatory, & Energy Policy Impacts," Sep. 29, 2016, http://tinyurl.com/j7wsenc.
39. Paul Krugman, "Trump, Trade and Workers," The New York Times, Jul. 4, 2016, http://tinyurl.com/zljhook.
40. Gary Hufbauer and Euijin Jung, "Is Our Trade Deficit a Problem?" Peterson Institute for International Economics, Feb. 2, 2017, http://tinyurl.com/znnwt7b.
41. Navarro and Ross, op. cit.
42. Patti Domm, "Trump Just Signaled the Death of Clinton-Era Strong Dollar Policy," CNBC, Jan. 17, 2017, http://tinyurl.com/hxkex6u; Richard Rubin and Peter Nicholas, "Donald

Trump Warns on House Republican Tax Plan," The Wall Street Journal, Jan. 16, 2017, http://tinyurl.com/h9er6we.
43. Adam Smith, "An Inquiry into the Nature and Causes of the Wealth of Nations," W. Strahan and T. Cadell, 1776.
44. William J. Bernstein, "A Splendid Exchange: How Trade Shaped the World," Grove Press, 2009.
45. Edward Kaplan, "The Fordney-McCumber Tariff of 1922," EH.net Encyclopedia, http://tinyurl.com/zokgnaw.
46. Irwin, op. cit.
47. Ibid.
48. "Bretton Woods-GATT, 1941–1947," U.S. Department of State, Office of the Historian, http://tinyurl.com/h3tc5cn.
49. "Proposals for Expansion of World Trade and Employment," U.S. Department of State, 1945, http://tinyurl.com/j7vscvf.
50. William Bernstein, op. cit.
51. In addition to setting the stage for the General Agreement on Tariffs and Trade (GATT), the Bretton Woods conference created the International Monetary Fund, charged with overseeing a system of fixed exchange rates and financial assistance to nations in financial trouble, and the World Bank, which was to provide financial assistance to war ravaged and poor nations.
52. George Monbiot, "Clearing Up This Mess," The Guardian, Nov. 18 2008, http://tinyurl.com/jsshc43.
53. "U.S. Trade in Goods and Services—Balance of Payments Basis," U.S. Census Bureau, Feb. 7, 2017, http://tinyurl.com/yg2dkg.
54. Irwin, op. cit.
55. Andrew K. Rose, "Do WTO Members Have More Liberal Trade Policy?" National Bureau of Economic Research, November 2002, http://tinyurl.com/h6372ln; Andrew K. Rose, "Do We Really Know That the WTO Increases Trade?" National Bureau of Economic Research, October 2002, http://tinyurl.com/h3ydpc8.
56. "World Economic Outlook," IMF, October 2016, http://tinyurl.com/hf529wv.
57. Jonty Bloom, "The European Coal and Steel Community Turns 60," BBC News, Aug. 10, 2012, http://tinyurl.com/h62pg76.
58. Wolfgang Münchau, "The Eurozone Cannot Escape Political and Fiscal Union," Financial Times, Jun. 5, 2016, http://tinyurl.com/gtqrrrn.
59. Paul Solman, "What Is the Trump Trade Doctrine? His Economic Adviser Explains," The PBS Newshour, Aug. 25, 2016, http://tinyurl.com/jjlqlv6.
60. Shawn Donnan, "Trump's Top Trade Adviser Accuses Germany of Currency Exploitation," Financial Times, Jan. 31, 2017, http://tinyurl.com/gu3vtdt.
61. Irwin, op. cit.
62. John McCormick and Terrence Dopp, "Free-Trade Opposition Unites Political Parties in Bloomberg Poll," Bloomberg News, Mar. 24, 2016, http://tinyurl.com/jgoe8yt.
63. Bruce Stokes, "Republicans, Especially Trump Supporters, See Free Trade Deals as Bad for U.S.," Pew Research Center, Mar. 31, 2016, http://tinyurl.com/hqozsxq.
64. Carrie Dann, "Trump's Rise Jumbles Partisan Views of Free Trade," NBC News, Feb. 26, 2017, http://tinyurl.com/zjwgwyp.
65. Peter Navarro and Wilbur Ross, "Scoring the Trump Economic Plan: Trade, Regulatory, & Energy Policy Impacts," Sep. 29, 2016, http://tinyurl.com/j7wsenc.
66. "National Trade Policy Agenda for 2017," The White House, Mar. 1, 2017, http://tinyurl.com/gvlr7er.
67. Donnan, "US Trade Chief Seeks to Reshore Supply Chain," op. cit.
68. Kate Lyons and Gordon Darroch, "Frexit, Nexit or Oexit? Who Will Be Next to Leave the EU," The Guardian, Jun. 27, 2016, http://tinyurl.com/glamgq4.
69. Steve Liesman, "Trump's Protectionism Biggest Threat to US Economy's Growth, CNBC Fed Survey Respondents Say," CNBC News, Jan. 31 2017, http://tinyurl.com/hq9r8q6.
70. Peter Navarro and Wilbur Ross, "Scoring the Trump Economic Plan: Trade, Regulatory, & Energy Policy Impacts," Sep. 29, 2016, http://tinyurl.com/j7wsenc.
71. Robin Harding, "TPP 'Has No Meaning' without US, Says Shinzo Abe," Financial Times, Nov. 22, 2016, http://tinyurl.com/jb3c3ep.
72. Mireya Solis, "The Containment Fallacy: China and the TPP," Brookings Institution, May 24, 2013, http://tinyurl.com/jdfrmxn; David Pilling, "It Won't Be Easy to Build an 'Anyone but China' Club," Financial Times, May 22, 2013, http://tinyurl.com/zecj74d.
73. Michael Martina, "China Pushes Asia-Pacific Trade Deals as Trump Win Dashes TPP Hopes," Reuters Business News, Nov. 10, 2016, http://tinyurl.com/jgw4u2g.
74. Frida Ghitis, "Why Trump's Rise Is Sending Latin America into China's Arms," World Politics Review, Feb. 2, 2017, http://tinyurl.com/hzz6gzq.
75. "The Future of Global Trade: Armchair Conversation with Ambassador Michael Froman, United States Trade Representative," Center for Strategic and International Studies, Jan. 13, 2016, http://tinyurl.com/z8886lz.
76. John Brinkley, "Trump Hands China a Gift in Dumping Trans-Pacific Partnership," Forbes, Jan 24, 2017, http://tinyurl.com/jhrvndl.
77. Matthew J. Belvedere, "Trump's Point Man on Trade: 'We Envision a More Germany-Style Economy'," CNBC, Jan. 25, 2017, http://tinyurl.com/zxqeppb.
78. Donnan,"US Trade Chief Seeks to Reshore Supply Chain," op. cit.
79. Neil Irwin, "Will Trump Go After NAFTA with Tweezers or a Hammer?" The New York Times, Jan. 25, 2017, http://tinyurl.com/gsfz6j9.
80. Jim Tankersley, "Donald Trump's Trade War Could Kill Millions of U.S. jobs," The Washington Post, Mar. 25, 2016, http://tinyurl.com/gqsggqf.
81. Saurabh Mishra, Susanna Lundstrom and Rahul Anand, "Service Export Sophistication and Economic Growth," The World Bank, March 2011, http://tinyurl.com/hmagoyl.

82. Lydia Saad, "Americans' Vanishing Fear of Foreign Trade," Gallup, Feb. 26, 2020, https://news.gallup.com/poll/286730/americans-vanishing-fear-foreign-trade.aspx.
83. "Trade Falls Steeply in the First Half of 2020," World Trade Organization, Jun. 22, 2020, https://www.wto.org/english/news_e/pres20_e/pr858_e.htm.
84. "President Donald J. Trump's United States-Mexico-Canada Agreement Delivers a Historic Win for American Workers," The White House, Jan. 29, 2020, https://www.whitehouse.gov/briefings-statements/president-donald-j-trumps-united-states-mexico-canada-agreement-delivers-historic-win-american-workers/.
85. "Canada Says It Will Impose Retaliatory Tariffs on U.S. Imports," The Associated Press, Aug. 8, 2020, https://apnews.com/389b0b34b74d93d17766d629ea46d7cb.
86. Jeanne Whalen and Amanda Coletta, "Trump Re-imposes Tariffs on Canadian Aluminum, Prompting Trudeau to Vow Retaliation," The Washington Post, Aug. 7, 2020, https://www.washingtonpost.com/business/2020/08/06/trump-canada-aluminum-tariffs/.
87. Ibid.

Chapter 10: Global Manufacturing

1. Angelique Chrisafis, "Concern on Continent as Heatwave Set to Drive Temperatures Beyond 40C," The Guardian, Jun. 30, 2015, http://tinyurl.com/ouhm8vq.
2. Elisabeth O'Leary, "Zara-Owner Inditex Posts Robust Results but Shares Slip," Reuters, Jun. 10, 2015, http://tinyurl.com/qzbbjkx.
3. Theodore Levitt, "The Globalization of Markets," Harvard Business Review, May 1983, http://tinyurl.com/mtx9gaw.
4. "Jack Smith on Emerging Markets and Changes and Challenges for GM," GM Heritage Center, undated, accessed Sep. 1, 2015, http://tinyurl.com/ngom4oo.
5. "Industries at a Glance; Manufacturing: NAICS 31-33/Workforce Statistics," Bureau of Labor Statistics, August 2015, http://tinyurl.com/c59gkj5.
6. Ian Bremmer, "The New Rules of Globalization," Harvard Business Review, January–February 2014, http://tinyurl.com/n9oxf8q.
7. "Prepared Remarks by President Akio Toyoda on Financial Results for Fiscal Year Ended March 2014," Toyota, May 8, 2014, http://tinyurl.com/nkb5xkq.
8. Leslie T. Chang, "Factory Girls: From Village to City in a Changing China," 2008.
9. Scott Kennedy, "Made in China 2025," Center for Strategic and International Studies, Jun. 1, 2015, http://tinyurl.com/obagfvu.
10. "China Auto Sales Will Tank If Stocks Enter Bear Market," Bloomberg Business, Jul. 31, 2015, http://tinyurl.com/pv3bfwk.
11. "China Average Yearly Wages," TradingEconomics.com, updated Sep. 1, 2015, http://tinyurl.com/pxguvel.
12. Harold L. Sirkin, Michael Zinser and Douglas Hohner, "Made in America, Again," The Boston Consulting Group, August 2011, http://tinyurl.com/notq88j.
13. "Industries at a Glance," op. cit.
14. "The Trans-Pacific Partnership: Four Countries That Don't Comply with U.S. Trade Law," AFL–CIO, 2015, http://tinyurl.com/ohbuorh.
15. Organization for International Investment, undated, accessed Sep. 21, 2015, http://tinyurl.com/nwrdtdx.
16. Chris Murphy, "GE Capital CIO: Outsourcing Went Too Far," InformationWeek, Aug. 5, 2014, http://tinyurl.com/os2epsg.
17. Marc Mancher, "Deloitte's 2014 Global Outsourcing and Insourcing Survey," Deloitte, 2014 http://tinyurl.com/nnju3jk.
18. For background, see Christina Hoag, "Doing Business in Mexico," SAGE Business Researcher, Sep. 14, 2015, http://tinyurl.com/oh48ggk.
19. "2014 Reshoring/Nearshoring Executive Survey and Outlook," AlixPartners, May 2014, http://tinyurl.com/nv8zpfh.
20. "Mexico's Manufacturing Sector Continues to Grow," Stratfor Global Intelligence, Apr. 5, 2015, http://tinyurl.com/npb5dyr.
21. M. Angeles Villarreal, "Mexico's Free Trade Agreements," Congressional Research Service, Summary, Jul. 3, 2012, http://tinyurl.com/nbsanwz.
22. Anthony Harrup, "Mexico's Foreign Direct Investment Falls in 2014," The Wall Street Journal, Feb. 24, 2015, http://tinyurl.com/onclpo8.
23. Ibid.
24. Micheline Maynard, "The Selling of the American Economy: How Foreign Companies Are Remaking the American Dream," 2009, p. 18.
25. Ibid.
26. Ibid., p. 20.
27. "International Yearbook of Industrial Statistics," UNIDO, 2015, p. 7, http://tinyurl.com/nckvycf.
28. "Industries at a Glance," op. cit.
29. Melissa Burden and Michael Martinez, "Expert: UAW Talks Could Bring End to 2-Tier Wage System," The Detroit News, Jun. 23, 2015, http://tinyurl.com/oxebm8q.
30. "Foreign Direct Investment in the United States," Department of Commerce and President's Council of Economic Advisers, October 2013, http://tinyurl.com/ocf4chl.
31. Micheline Maynard, "Orders for Aretha's Hat Still Going Strong," The New York Times, Mar. 12, 2009, http://tinyurl.com/bc2vm4.
32. Marco Breu, et al., "Sustaining Vietnam's Growth: The Productivity Challenge," McKinsey & Company, February 2012, p. 2, http://tinyurl.com/ofox3sb.
33. "Retail in Vietnam, Emerging Market, Emerging Growth," Economist Intelligence Unit, October 2014, http://tinyurl.com/o3gqsnh.
34. Vikas Bajaj, "Bangladesh, With Low Pay, Moves in on China," The New York Times, Jul. 16, 2010, http://tinyurl.com/npb3zst.

35. Hannah Lutz, "China Gets the Lion's Share of Vehicle Production Capacity Investments in 2014," Automotive News, Aug. 7, 2015, http://tinyurl.com/p3zxzct.
36. Biman Mukherji, John Miller and Chuin-Wei Yap, "Why Chinese Steel Exports Are Stirring Protests," The Wall Street Journal, Mar. 15, 2015, http://tinyurl.com/q43xkpr.
37. "Our Suppliers," Apple.com, undated, accessed Sep. 16, 2015, http://tinyurl.com/oqgtavy.
38. Stacey Vanek Smith, "How Much Would an American iPhone Cost?" Marketplace, May 20, 2014, http://tinyurl.com/oc7uq6d.
39. "A Brief History of Container Shipping and Logistics," Marpak Extrusions, Apr. 14, 2014, http://tinyurl.com/pjj6mth.
40. James Kanter, Micheline Maynard and Hiroko Tabuchi, "Toyota Has Pattern of Slow Responses on Safety Issues," The New York Times, Feb. 6, 2010, http://tinyurl.com/nvnwzmk.
41. "Prepared Remarks by President Akio Toyoda on Financial Results for Fiscal Year Ended March 2014," op. cit.
42. "Toyota Executive Julie Hamp Resigns after Drug Scandal," BBC News, Jul. 1, 2015, http://tinyurl.com/q2gofh5.
43. Makiko Kitamura and Yuki Hagiwara, "Toyota's 2009 Global Vehicle Sales Fall 13% as Volkswagen Gains," Bloomberg, Jan. 24, 2010, http://tinyurl.com/pot5lgp.
44. Brian Ross, et al., "Toyota to Pay $1.2 B for Hiding Deadly 'Unintended Acceleration,'" ABC News, Mar. 19, 2014, http://tinyurl.com/jw2x5ke.
45. James R. Healey, "Toyota's New $1B Mexico Plant to Build 2020 Corolla," USA Today, Apr. 15, 2015, http://tinyurl.com/prcxxxh.
46. Ben Rooney, "Lumber Liquidators CEO Resigns," CNN Money, May 21, 2015, http://tinyurl.com/pyqeasy.
47. U.S. Coalition for TPP website, undated, accessed Sep. 16, 2015, http://tinyurl.com/qdudc92.
48. Paul Lewis, "Barack Obama Given 'Fast-Track' Authority over Trade Deal Negotiations," The Guardian, Jun. 24, 2015, http://tinyurl.com/qjhb579.
49. "The Trans-Pacific Partnership," The White House, undated, accessed Sep. 1, 2015, http://tinyurl.com/pvjz4nm.
50. Jason Hidalgo, "Elon Musk Indicates Gigafactory Is First of Many," The Reno Gazette-Journal, May 1, 2015, http://tinyurl.com/pardca8.
51. Felix Richter, "These Are the Top 10 Manufacturing Countries in the World," World Economic Forum, Feb. 25, 2020, https://www.weforum.org/agenda/2020/02/countries-manufacturing-trade-exports-economics/.
52. "Manufacturing Is Now the Lowest Share of U.S. Economy in 72 Years," Bloomberg, Oct. 29, 2019, https://www.industryweek.com/the-economy/article/22028495/manufacturing-is-now-smallest-share-of-us-economy-in-72-years.
53. Jim Tankersley, "Trump's Push to Bring Back Jobs to the U.S. Shows Limited Results," The New York Times, Aug. 13, 2019, https://www.nytimes.com/2019/08/13/business/economy/donald-trump-jobs-created.html.
54. Ibid.
55. "Global Manufacturing Production Drops Sharply Due to Economic Disruptions Caused by COVID-19," United Nations Industrial Development Corporation, Jun. 3, 2020, https://www.unido.org/news/global-manufacturing-production-drops-sharply-due-economic-disruptions-caused-covid-19-unido-report.
56. Gerima Bora, "Covid-19 Has Upended a Key Management Principle—or Has It?" Economic Times of India, Jun. 20, 2020, https://economictimes.indiatimes.com/small-biz/sme-sector/covid-19-has-upended-a-key-management-principle-just-in-time-jit-inventory/articleshow/76477328.cms.
57. Scott Tong, "Just in Time Manufacturing Model Challenged by COVID-19," Marketplace, Feb. 27, 2020, https://www.marketplace.org/2020/02/27/justintime-manufacturing-model-challenged-coronavirus/.
58. "Canada Almost Self-Sufficient in PPE As Canadian Businesses Step Up: PM," Canadian Press, Jun. 26, 2020, https://www.cbc.ca/news/politics/canada-ppe-covid19-1.5628237.

Chapter 11: Global Oil and Gas Industry

1. Russell Gold and Daniel Gilbert, "The U.S. Is Overtaking Russia as Largest Oil-and-Gas Producer," The Wall Street Journal, Oct. 2, 2013, http://tinyurl.com/mu87nuw.
2. Doug Esser, "5 Arrested, Tracks Blocked in Everett Protest of Oil Trains," The Associated Press, Sep. 2, 2014, http://tinyurl.com/kj7f8ba; "Oil Trains," Seattle City Council, Jul. 21, 2014, http://tinyurl.com/nptmvtr; and Phuong Le, "BNSF Data Show Recent Drop in State's Oil Train Traffic," The Associated Press, Jul. 7, 2014, http://tinyurl.com/luoxfma.
3. Sari Horwitz, "Dark Side of the Boom," The Washington Post, Sep. 28, 2014, http://tinyurl.com/nmwvw3b; Matthew Yglesias, "Inflation Doesn't Create Jobs, Jobs Create Inflation," Slate, Jun. 21, 2012, http://tinyurl.com/7vz88ou.
4. Dana Van Wagener, "U.S. Tight Oil Production: Alternative Supply Projections and an Overview of EIA's Analysis of Well-Level Data Aggregated to the County Level," Annual Energy Outlook 2014, U.S. Energy Information Administration, Apr. 7, 2014, http://tinyurl.com/nlyuqbc.
5. "Shale in the United States," U.S. Energy Information Administration, Sep. 4, 2014, http://tinyurl.com/mv53vvv; U.S. Energy Information Administration, "Monthly Natural Gas Production," Oct. 31, 2014, http://tinyurl.com/kkhwp4a.
6. U.S. Energy Information Administration, http://tinyurl.com/l87y7z8.
7. Rabah Arezki and Olivier Blanchard, "Seven Questions about the Recent Oil Price Slump," International Monetary Fund blog, Dec. 22, 2014, http://tinyurl.com/q6rpaua.
8. Daniel Yergin, "The Global Shakeout from Plunging Oil," The Wall Street Journal, Nov. 30, 2014, http://tinyurl.com/poy36te.

9. John Larson and Richard Fullenbaum, "America's New Energy Future," IHS, September 2013, http://tinyurl.com/olnl3xu.
10. Clifford Krauss, "Free Fall in Oil Prices Underscores Shift Away from OPEC," The New York Times, Nov. 29, 2014, http://tinyurl.com/nd8yuqy.
11. Matthew Philips and Asjylyn Loder, "Amid U.S. Oil Boom, Railroads Are Beating Pipelines in Crude Transport," Bloomberg Businessweek, Jun. 13, 2013, http://tinyurl.com/n42e4b6.
12. Joel Kotkin and Tory Gattis, "Houston, Middle-Class Magnet," Dallas Morning News, Aug. 1, 2014, http://tinyurl.com/lz7we3b.
13. U.S. Energy Information Administration, http://tinyurl.com/p5wdckr.
14. Larson and Fullenbaum, op. cit.
15. Daniel Wiessner and Edward McAllister, "New York Bans Fracking After Health Report," Reuters, Dec. 17, 2014, http://tinyurl.com/ldt2pok.
16. Eric de Place, "The Northwest's Pipeline on Rails," Sightline Institute, May 2014, http://tinyurl.com/otnf48j.
17. Ángel González, "Spill's Toll on Oil Output Grows Clearer," The Wall Street Journal, Apr. 20, 2011, http://tinyurl.com/oqbymdp.
18. China's oil consumption doubled in the decade between 1995 and 2005, according to the U.S. Energy Information Administration; for more information, see http://tinyurl.com/nctott8.
19. Alan Greenspan, "Energy Remarks Before the National Petrochemical and Refiners Association Conference, San Antonio," Federal Reserve Board, April 2005, http://tinyurl.com/5wp4t.
20. Ibid; Russell Gold, "ConocoPhillips, BP Plan Pipeline for Alaska Gas," The Wall Street Journal, Apr. 9, 2008, http://tinyurl.com/lpyhpmb.
21. The U.S. imported slightly more than 7.7 million barrels of crude per day on average in 2013, down from a peak of above 10 million in the middle of last decade, according to the U.S. Energy Information Administration; for more information, see http://tinyurl.com/kk4s8aw.
22. Liam Pleven and Russell Gold, "U.S. Nears Milestone: Net Fuel Exporter," The Wall Street Journal, Nov. 30, 2011, http://tinyurl.com/p5v2xah.
23. Christian Berthelsen and Lynn Cook, "U.S. Ruling Loosens Four-Decade Ban on Oil Exports," The Wall Street Journal, Jun. 24, 2014, http://tinyurl.com/n74p7d3; Christian Berthelsen and Lynn Cook, "New Oil Shipment Shows Cracks in U.S. Export Ban," The Wall Street Journal, Nov. 4, 2014, http://tinyurl.com/pgctgdb.
24. Jay Fitzgerald, "2 Costly LNG Terminals Sit Idle," Boston Globe, Jan. 23, 2013, http://tinyurl.com/mamg6gu.
25. Becky Bohrer, "Alaska Governor Unveils New Plan for Gas Pipeline," USA Today, Jan. 10, 2014, http://tinyurl.com/lapd6tc.
26. "The Seven Sisters Still Rule," Time, Sep. 11, 1978, http://tinyurl.com/m2nt97u.
27. Valérie Marcel, "Oil Titans: National Oil Companies in the Middle East," Brookings Institution Press, 2006, http://tinyurl.com/oov9ncv.
28. "Chronology: Big Oil's Years of Merger Mania," Reuters, Jul. 14, 2014, p.11, http://tinyurl.com/673pxt3.
29. Amy Myers Jaffe and Ronald Soligo, "The International Oil Companies," James A. Baker III Institute for Public Policy, Rice University, November 2007, p. 11, http://tinyurl.com/o3jjn8q.
30. Jad Mouawad, "As Oil Giants Lose Influence, Supply Drops," The New York Times, Aug. 18, 2008, http://tinyurl.com/obdb4n4.
31. Chevron annual reports for 1998 and 2013, filed with the Securities and Exchange Commission, http://tinyurl.com/k5b6p8f.
32. Mark Tran, "Shell Fined Over Reserves Scandal," The Guardian, Jul. 29, 2004, http://tinyurl.com/p6zkd8w.
33. Chesapeake Energy Corp. Annual Report for 2013 and for 2003, filed with the Securities and Exchange Commission, http://tinyurl.com/ohjjwfs and http://tinyurl.com/lr8znur.
34. Summary Annual Report 2013, Exxon Mobil, 2013, http://tinyurl.com/q8up9yn; Exxon Mobil Annual Report for 2003, filed with the Securities and Exchange Commission, http://tinyurl.com/plcjkaf.
35. Rupert Hargreaves, "Is It Time to Abandon Big Oil?" Motley Fool, Sep. 5, 2013, http://tinyurl.com/p7hu2va.
36. Jim Polson and Edward Klump, "ConocoPhillips Plans to Split in Two, Mulva to Retire," Bloomberg News, Jul. 14, 2011, http://tinyurl.com/6zvq2uo.
37. "Chevron's 2013 Security Analyst Meeting," Thomson Reuters StreetEvents, Mar. 12, 2013, http://tinyurl.com/p2xpco2.
38. "Exxon Mobil Corporation Analyst Meeting," Exxon Mobil, Mar. 8, 2012, http://tinyurl.com/p2hzpel.
39. Dev Sanyal, "Perspectives on the Challenges Facing Super-Majors," Oxford Energy Seminar, Sep. 19, 2012, http://tinyurl.com/ofszwod.
40. Ángel González, "Expanded Oil Drilling Helps U.S. Wean Itself from Mideast," The Wall Street Journal, Jun. 27, 2012, http://tinyurl.com/nkcf9te.
41. President George W. Bush, "State of the Union Address," Jan. 31, 2006, http://tinyurl.com/ahvcl.
42. Van Wagener, op. cit.
43. González, "Expanded Oil Drilling Helps U.S. Wean Itself from Mideast," op. cit.
44. Steven Mufson, "Plunging Oil Prices Are Doing Obama's Foreign Policy for Him," Wonkblog, The Washington Post, Dec. 16, 2014, http://tinyurl.com/m48rme5.
45. Bruce Jones, "Despite Growing Energy Independence, U.S. Cannot Escape Global Risks," Brookings Institution, May 27, 2014, http://tinyurl.com/mbuklwz.

46. Amy Myers Jaffe, "U.S. Energy Abundance: Exports and the Changing Global Energy Landscape," testimony before House Energy and Commerce Committee's Subcommittee on Energy and Power, May 7, 2013, http://tinyurl.com/mlo7svl.
47. Brian Spegele and Matt Bradley, "Middle East Oil Fuels Fresh China-U.S. Tensions," The Wall Street Journal, Oct. 10, 2013, http://tinyurl.com/pw4qv7t.
48. "U.S. Imports from Venezuela of Crude Oil," U.S. Energy Information Administration, updated Oct. 30, 2014, http://tinyurl.com/m6mpbx4.
49. "U.S. Net Imports from Venezuela of Total Petroleum Products," U.S. Energy Information Administration, updated Oct. 30, 2014, http://tinyurl.com/mrhlvdn; Jose Orozco, "Venezuela's Oil Product Imports from U.S. Surge Ninefold," Bloomberg News, Nov. 29, 2012, http://tinyurl.com/nnchdek.
50. Jerin Matthew, "US Set to Overtake Saudi Arabia in Liquid Petroleum Production," International Business Times, Sep. 30, 2014. http://tinyurl.com/ljjvlay.
51. Gold and Gilbert, "The U.S. Is Overtaking Russia," op. cit.
52. Lananh Nguyen, "U.S. Oil Output to Overtake Saudi Arabia's by 2020," Bloomberg, Nov. 12, 2012, http://tinyurl.com/bokjgf4.
53. "U.S. Net Imports of Total Petroleum Products," U.S. Energy Information Administration, updated Oct. 30, 2014, http://tinyurl.com/3rauffr; Liam Pleven and Russell Gold, "U.S. Nears Milestone: Net Fuel Exporter," The Wall Street Journal, Nov. 30, 2011, http://tinyurl.com/p5v2xah.
54. "U.S. International Trade in Goods and Services, November 2014," U.S. Department of Commerce, Jan. 7, 2015, http://tinyurl.com/nhf36kz.
55. "World Energy Outlook 2013," Executive Summary, International Energy Agency, 2013, http://tinyurl.com/opyab5o.
56. "Title 15: Commerce and Foreign Trade: Crude Oil," Electronic Code of Federal Regulations, http://tinyurl.com/l8558ya.
57. "Long Term Applications Received by DOE/FE to Export," U.S. Department of Energy, Jul. 31, 2014, http://tinyurl.com/pqowgyu.
58. "FERC Approves Cameron LNG Export Project," Federal Energy Regulatory Commission, Jun. 19, 2014, http://tinyurl.com/nuleftm.
59. Mary L. Landrieu, "Importing Energy, Exporting Jobs. Can It Be Reversed?" (opening statement), Senate Committee on Energy and Natural Resources, Mar. 25, 2014, http://tinyurl.com/n44ow4v.
60. "Sen. Murkowski Offers Roadmap for Lifting Ban on Crude Exports," keynote address, IHS CERAWeek energy conference; text available at the website of the Senate Committee on Energy and Natural Resources, Mar. 3, 2014, http://tinyurl.com/qhx7ruf.
61. Ben van Beurden, "Working Together to Build a Lower Carbon, Higher Energy Future," speech at Center on Global Energy Policy at Columbia University, Sep. 2, 2014, http://tinyurl.com/myxvpgr.
62. Alicia Mundy, "Refiners Form Coalition to Fight Exports of Crude Oil," Washington Wire blog, The Wall Street Journal, Mar. 12, 2014, http://tinyurl.com/opnru3m.
63. "Dow Statement on U.S. Department of Energy Cameron LNG Export Decision," Dow Chemical, Feb. 11, 2014. http://tinyurl.com/kllgzh9.
64. Ken Cohen, "Opponents of LNG Exports Miss the Paradigm Shift," Exxon Mobil Perspectives blog, Jan. 11, 2013, http://tinyurl.com/pttlkn7.
65. Daniel Yergin, "The Prize: The Epic Quest for Oil, Money and Power," 2008, p. 8.
66. "Petróleos de Venezuela S.A.," PDVSA, 2005, http://tinyurl.com/mx8m77o.
67. Yergin, op. cit., p. 11.
68. "Development of the Pennsylvania Oil Industry," American Chemical Society, Aug. 26, 2009, http://tinyurl.com/kguxxqu.
69. "Financier's Fortune in Oil Amassed in Industrial Era of 'Rugged Individualism,'" The New York Times, May 24, 1937, http://tinyurl.com/7oqojjj.
70. "Our History," Exxon Mobil, undated, http://tinyurl.com/l25qg5n.
71. "The Model T," The Henry Ford museum, undated, http://tinyurl.com/kk5qoxb.
72. David Wilma, "Gas Station May Have Been Invented in Seattle in 1907," History Link, January 1999, http://tinyurl.com/bnjclu7.
73. Yergin, op. cit., p. 140.
74. Ibid., p. 167.
75. Ibid., pp. 213–220.
76. Ibid., pp. 100, 220–226.
77. Frederick H. Gareau, "The United Nations and Other International Institutions: A Critical Analysis," Burnham Inc. Publishers, 2002, p. 83.
78. "Secrets of History: The C.I.A. in Iran," The New York Times, 2000, http://tinyurl.com/lludzlw.
79. Yergin, op. cit., p. 506.
80. Ibid., p. 596.
81. "Oil Embargo, 1973–1974," U.S. Department of State, Office of the Historian, Oct. 31, 2013, http://tinyurl.com/l9qgtsp; "Les trente glorieuses," France's Economy Ministry, http://tinyurl.com/mk6lbjn.
82. Fernando Coronil, "The Magical State, Nature, Money and Modernity in Venezuela," University of Chicago Press, 1997.
83. Yergin, op. cit., pp. 657-680.
84. Ibid., pp. 647-652, 731.
85. Yegor Gaidar, "The Soviet Collapse, Grain and Oil," American Enterprise Institute, April 2007, http://tinyurl.com/kx6sx5v.
86. Carol Singleton Slade, et al., "The Next Energy Shortage: Big Oil CEOs," Forbes, Mar. 21, 2013, http://tinyurl.com/bufd9n2.
87. "China's Growing Demand for Oil and Its Impact on U.S. Petroleum Markets," Congressional Budget Office, April 2006, http://tinyurl.com/moh87ko.

88. Jaffe and Soligo, op. cit.
89. Russell Gold, "The Boom: How Fracking Ignited the American Energy Revolution and Changed the World," 2014.
90. U.S. Energy Information Administration, Brazil data, http://tinyurl.com/lopdu36.
91. Monte Reel, "Brazil's Road to Energy Independence," The Washington Post, Aug. 20, 2006, http://tinyurl.com/ykjlof.
92. Oswaldo Pedrosa, "Prevention First," presentation by Brazil's National Petroleum Agency, 2002, http://tinyurl.com/kfq264h.
93. Alan Petzet, "First Gulf of Mexico FPSO Receiving Cascade Oil," Oil and Gas Journal, Mar. 2, 2012, http://tinyurl.com/lnecflg.
94. "Cheap at the Price," The Economist, Oct. 26, 2013, http://tinyurl.com/kmqzncb.
95. Brazil and Venezuela data, U.S. Energy Information Administration, http://tinyurl.com/l4mtb9q and http://tinyurl.com/ka2vhfr.
96. World Energy Outlook 2013, International Energy Agency, Nov. 12, 2013, http://tinyurl.com/lxkqcab.
97. Maria Luiza Rabello and Peter Millard, "Brazil Congress Makes Petrobras Sole Pre-Salt Operator," Bloomberg News, Dec. 2, 2010, http://tinyurl.com/paoej8m.
98. "Brazil," U.S. Energy Information Administration, Oct. 1, 2013, http://tinyurl.com/knob5at.
99. Jonathan Watts, "Brazil's Largest Company, Petrobras, Accused of Political Kickbacks," The Guardian, Sep. 17, 2014, http://tinyurl.com/oclk427.
100. Harry R. Weber and Dan Murtaugh, "Brazil Energy Giant Buys $1.24 Billion of Pain in Texas," Bloomberg Businessweek, Jun. 18, 2014, http://tinyurl.com/la3cmly; Peter Millard and Mario Sergio Lima, "Petrobras Debt Crunch Buoys Exxon's Prospects in Brazil: Energy," Bloomberg News, Apr. 12, 2013, http://tinyurl.com/bm8hhy3.
101. "The Perils of Petrobras," The Economist, Nov. 17, 2012, http://tinyurl.com/l59m6o3.
102. International Energy Agency, op. cit.
103. "Cushing, OK Crude Oil Future Contract 1," U.S. Energy Information Administration, http://tinyurl.com/kz3o77b.
104. William Pentland, "Bye, Bye Biofuels: Why U.S. Renewable Fuels Standard Failed," Forbes, Dec. 6, 2013, http://tinyurl.com/ku88uo2.
105. Kevin Bullis, "Obama Turns to Fossil Fuels," MIT Technology Review, Jan. 25, 2012, http://tinyurl.com/lj7ay2u.
106. Daniel Gilbert and Justin Scheck, "BP Is Found Grossly Negligent in Deepwater Horizon Disaster," The Wall Street Journal, Sep. 4, 2014, http://tinyurl.com/mapnoke.
107. U.S. Energy Information Administration, http://tinyurl.com/l87y7z8.
108. Russell Gold, "Back to the Future? Oil Replays 1980s Bust," The Wall Street Journal, Jan. 13, 2015, http://tinyurl.com/ns4pl8p.
109. "Moving Crude Oil by Rail," American Association of Railroads, July 2014, http://tinyurl.com/k9rs3fk.
110. Justin Giovannetti and Kim Mackrael, "Then and Now: A Year Later Lac-Mégantic Continues to Rebuild," The Globe and Mail, Jul. 4, 2014, http://tinyurl.com/k5xny45.
111. "U.S. DOT Announces Comprehensive Proposed Rulemaking for the Safe Transportation of Crude Oil, Flammable Materials," U.S. Department of Transportation, Jul. 23, 2014, http://tinyurl.com/mmpyace.
112. "AAR Responds to U.S. DOT Proposed Rule on Safety of Moving Flammable Liquids by Rail," American Association of Railroads, Jul. 23, 2014, http://tinyurl.com/l7p6nlj.
113. Ryan Parker, "State of Emergency Declared in West Virginia After Train Derails, Explodes," Los Angeles Times, Feb. 16, 2015, http://tinyurl.com/lup5ptf; Brad Plumer, "Another Oil Train Explodes in West Virginia. Here's Why This Keeps Happening," Vox, Feb. 17, 2015, http://tinyurl.com/pxpwq9y.
114. Ángel González, "Oil Trains Crowd Out Grain Shipments to NW Ports," The Seattle Times, Jul. 26, 2014, http://tinyurl.com/m6rypg9.
115. Edward R. Hamberger, "Hamberger: Railroads Able to Invest, Address Service and Capacity Issues, Thanks to Balanced Regulations," testimony before the Senate Committee on Commerce, Science and Transportation, American Association of Railroads, Sep. 10, 2014, http://tinyurl.com/mtozaqp.
116. "TNK-BP: A Troubled History," Reuters/The Telegraph, May 28, 2012, http://tinyurl.com/ck8kdcx; BP Annual Report 2011, p. 49, http://tinyurl.com/oco8nm9.
117. "Rosneft and BP Complete TNK-BP Sale and Purchase Transaction," BP, Mar. 20, 2013, http://tinyurl.com/m7jaw9n.
118. Douglas Busvine, Melissa Akin and Vladimir Soldatkin, "Exxon, Rosneft Unveil $500 Billion Offshore Venture," Reuters, Apr. 18, 2012, http://tinyurl.com/cwkud88.
119. Dan Roberts, "Sweeping New US and EU Sanctions Target Russia's Banks and Oil Companies," The Guardian, Sep. 12, 2014, http://tinyurl.com/nvk8j8t.
120. Stanley Reed and Clifford Krauss, "New Sanctions to Stall Exxon's Arctic Oil Plans," The New York Times, Sep. 12, 2014, http://tinyurl.com/n5phc8w.
121. Olga Tanas and Lyubov Pronina, "Russian Woes Worsen As Recession Looms with Banks in 'Panic,'" Bloomberg News, Dec. 2, 2014, http://tinyurl.com/qg5he2m.
122. Ken Cohen, "Keystone XL and the National Interest," Exxon Mobil Perspectives blog, Mar. 13, 2014, http://tinyurl.com/mqjlten; TransCanada, http://tinyurl.com/kd5upwt.
123. "About the Project," TransCanada, undated, http://tinyurl.com/kd5upwt.
124. Philip Bump, "No Matter What Happens in 2014, the Keystone XL Pipeline Is Still Obama's Decision," The Washington Post, Aug. 14, 2014, http://tinyurl.com/n27rshz; "Oilsands Climate Impacts," Pembina Institute, http://tinyurl.com/3twmur4.
125. Gregory Korte, "Obama Keystone Pipeline Bill 'Has Earned My Veto,'" USAToday, Feb. 25, 2015, http://tinyurl.com/m5o7y4n.

126. "Keystone XL Delay Frustrates Alberta Premier, TransCanada CEO," CBC News, Apr. 18, 2014, http://tinyurl.com/n8dkduf.
127. Yadullah Hussain, "Oil Sands Players Shrug Off Falling Prices, Eye Narrowing Differentials," Financial Post, Sep. 11, 2014, http://tinyurl.com/myx8oap.
128. Robert Tuttle, "Canada's Heavy Oil Nearing $40 Threatens Oil Sands Projects," Bloomberg News, Dec. 11, 2014, http://tinyurl.com/ncsxhmw.
129. Rob Gillies, "Canada OKs Oil Pipeline to Pacific Coast," The Associated Press, Jun. 17, 2014, http://tinyurl.com/l8ps3q3.
130. Jeff Lewis, "Gateway Delay Clouds Industry's Asia Export Push," The Globe and Mail, Sep. 4, 2014, http://tinyurl.com/nstk7fg.
131. Alex Lawler, "Oil Demand Has Peaked in Developed World: IEA," Reuters, Jan. 28, 2010, http://tinyurl.com/jwwxv9v.
132. "Fuel Economy Standards Drive Down Projected Gasoline Use; Diesel Use, Product Exports Rise," Energy Information Administration, Jun. 26, 2014, http://tinyurl.com/lhpep7d.
133. "Global EV Outlook," International Energy Agency, April 2013, http://tinyurl.com/m7nw5dk.
134. Joel Kirkland and Climatewire, "Natural Gas Could Serve as 'Bridge' Fuel to Low-Carbon Future," Scientific American, Jun. 25, 2010, http://tinyurl.com/mf4xb6w.
135. "The Outlook for Energy: A View to 2040," Exxon Mobil, Dec. 9, 2013, http://tinyurl.com/l8knnha.
136. "Are We Entering a Golden Age of Gas?" World Energy Outlook 2011, International Energy Agency, 2011, http://tinyurl.com/kucbtyj.
137. "Technically Recoverable Shale Oil and Shale Gas Resources," U.S. Energy Information Administration, Jun. 10, 2013, http://tinyurl.com/6gjx5ln.
138. "Shale Development in France," Vinson & Elkins' Shale and Fracking Tracker, undated, http://tinyurl.com/o3adqom; Law No. 0162, Jul. 14, 2011, p. 12217, Text No. 2, http://tinyurl.com/3ev768z.
139. Chou Hui Hong, "Water Management Biggest Risk to China Shale Gas, Bernstein Says," Jun. 14, 2013, http://tinyurl.com/kc5mukd.
140. Maciej Onoszko, "Europe Shale Push Shaken by Exxon's Poland Pullout," Reuters, Jun. 18, 2012, http://tinyurl.com/obdxxwa.
141. "Dead-Cow Bounce," The Economist, Aug. 23, 2014, http://tinyurl.com/kns4t6s.
142. Richard Nield, "Algeria Looks to Develop Shale Gas Sector," Al Jazeera, Jul. 28, 2014, http://tinyurl.com/pty3pkj.
143. Isabel Ordonez and Victoria Stilwell, "Exxon Expands Rosneft Alliance to Siberian Shale," The Wall Street Journal, Jun. 15, 2012, http://tinyurl.com/kdb55t7.
144. Melissa Eddy and Stanley Reed, "Germany Leans toward Allowing Fracking," The New York Times, Jun. 5, 2014, http://tinyurl.com/nugwo9k.
145. Stanley Reed, "Britain Proposes Easier Access to Tap Shale Rock Energy," The New York Times, May 23, 2014, http://tinyurl.com/pqprqoy.
146. "Shale Gas—a Global Perspective," KPMG Global Energy Institute, 2011, http://tinyurl.com/ppq475u.
147. Rex Tillerson, "Rex Tillerson: CERAWeek Opening Address," Feb. 13, 2007, http://tinyurl.com/mmtexap.
148. Russell Gold and Tom McGinty, "Energy Boom Puts Wells in America's Backyards," Wall Street Journal, Oct. 25, 2013, http://tinyurl.com/qxqtdbh.
149. A.R. Brandt, et al., "Methane Leaks from North American Natural Gas Systems," Science, Feb. 14, 2014, http://tinyurl.com/lfbaay6; "EPA Needs to Improve Air Emissions Data for the Oil and Natural Gas Production Sector," U.S. Environmental Protection Agency Office of Inspector General, Report No. 13-P-0161, Feb. 20, 2013, http://tinyurl.com/qzvyefh.
150. Mike Soraghan, "Spills Up 18 percent in U.S. in 2013," E&E EnergyWire, May 12, 2014. http://tinyurl.com/k7fu2c4.
151. Gunnar Myhre, et al., "Anthropogenic and Natural Radiative Forcing," in T.F. Stocker, et al., "Climate Change 2013: The Physical Science Basis. Contribution of Working Group I to the Fifth Assessment Report of the Intergovernmental Panel on Climate Change," 2013, p. 714, Cambridge University Press.
152. "U.S. Imports of Crude Oil and Petroleum Products (Thousand Barrels)," U.S. Energy Information Administration, Oct. 30, 2020, https://www.eia.gov/dnav/pet/hist/LeafHandler.ashx?n=PET&s=MTTIMUS1&f=A.
153. "Total Energy Production from Natural Gas 2017," U.S. Energy Information Administration, generated Oct. 2020, https://www.eia.gov/international/rankings/world?pa=287&u=0&f=A&v=none&y=01%2F01%2F2017&ev=false.
154. John Duff, "As Total U.S. Crude Oil Imports Have Fallen, Imports from Canada Have Increased," U.S. Energy Information Administration, Mar. 19, 2020, https://www.eia.gov/todayinenergy/detail.php?id=43196; "U.S. Imports by Country of Origin," U.S. Energy Information Administration, Sep. 30, 2020, https://www.eia.gov/dnav/pet/PET_MOVE_IMPCUS_A2_NUS_EPC0_IM0_MBBL_A.htm.
155. Ibid.
156. Drew Desilver, "Renewable Energy Use Is Growing Fast in the U.S. but Fossil Fuels Still Dominate," Pew Research Center, Jan. 15, 2020, https://www.pewresearch.org/fact-tank/2020/01/15/renewable-energy-is-growing-fast-in-the-u-s-but-fossil-fuels-still-dominate/.
157. "The U.S. Was Energy Independent in 2019 for the First Time Since 1957," Institute for Energy Research, May 11, 2020, https://www.instituteforenergyresearch.org/fossil-fuels/gas-and-oil/the-united-states-was-energy-independent-in-2019-for-the-first-time-since-1957/.
158. Ibid.
159. Chuck Jones, "The Coal Industry Has Lost Almost One Thousand Jobs Since Trump Became President," Forbes, Mar. 7, 2020, https://www.forbes.com/sites/chuckjones/2020/03/07/

the-coal-industry-has-lost-almost-one-thousand-jobs-since-trump-became-president/#2e9033f72e29.

160. Jessica Resnick-Ault and David French, "Bankruptcy Looms over U.S. Energy Industry, from Oil Fields to Pipelines," Reuters, Apr. 23, 2020, https://www.reuters.com/article/us-global-oil-usa-restructuring/bankruptcy-looms-over-u-s-energy-industry-from-oil-fields-to-pipelines-idUSKCN2250FQ.
161. Ambrogio Visconti, "Chesapeake Energy Corporation's Chapter 11 Restructuring," Global Legal Chronicle, Jul. 3, 2020, https://www.globallegalchronicle.com/chesapeake-energy-corporations-chapter-11-restructuring/.
162. Bethany Blankley, "Texas Leads U.S. in Oil and Gas Bankruptcies; Job Losses Are 'a Bloodbath,'" The Center Square, Jun. 12, 2020, https://www.thecentersquare.com/texas/texas-leads-u-s-in-oil-and-gas-bankruptcies-job-losses-are-a-bloodbath/article_d6957a14-accb-11ea-9a66-5f52818d3f8e.html.
163. Erin Cox, "Energy Companies Abandon Long-Delayed Atlantic Coast Pipeline," The Washington Post, Jul. 6, 2020, https://www.washingtonpost.com/local/virginia-politics/atlantic-coast-pipeline-canceled/2020/07/05/da1c0f40-bef5-11ea-b178-bb7b05b94af1_story.html.

Chapter 12: Hong Kong's Economy

1. Barry Naughton, "The Chinese Economy, Transitions and Growth," MIT Press, 2006.
2. Ibid.
3. Simon Cartledge, "A System Apart: Hong Kong's Political Economy from 1997 until Now," Penguin Group, 2017.
4. "GDP (Current US$)," The World Bank, last accessed Dec. 21, 2017, https://tinyurl.com/y99jf4lq.
5. "China GDP," Trading Economics, last accessed Dec. 21, 2017, https://tinyurl.com/y9phdaen.
6. Cartledge, op. cit., p. 13.
7. "Hong Kong GDP Annual Growth Rate," Trading Economics, Nov. 10, 2017, https://tinyurl.com/y7cw3opw.
8. Eric Lam, "Hong Kong's Economy May Soon Be Eclipsed by the Chinese City Next Door," Bloomberg, Sep. 5, 2017, https://tinyurl.com/ybqv5ee2.
9. Cartledge, op. cit., pp. 59-60.
10. Naughton, op. cit.
11. "The Basic Law of the Hong Kong Special Administrative Region of the People's Republic of China," last accessed Dec. 21, 2017, https://tinyurl.com/c8xvap7.
12. Steve Tsang, "A Modern History of Hong Kong: 1841–1997," I.B. Tauris, 2004, p. 60.
13. Ibid.
14. Ibid., p. 177.
15. Ibid., pp. 176-78.
16. "Moody's Downgrades Hong Kong's Rating to Aa2 from Aa1 and Changes Outlook to Stable from Negative," Moody's, May 24, 2017, https://tinyurl.com/ycjgmdlw.
17. Ibid.
18. "Ranking of Container Ports of the World," Government of the Hong Kong S.A.R. Marine Department, last accessed Jan. 2, 2018, https://tinyurl.com/yd2ddcf3.
19. Ibid.; "Summary Statistics on Port Traffic of Hong Kong," Hong Kong Transport and Housing Bureau, November 2017, https://tinyurl.com/ycfsp43g.
20. Greg Knowler, "Latest Volume Tumble at Hong Kong Port Highlights Steady Traffic Decline," JOC.com, Jul. 16, 2016, https://tinyurl.com/ydah7wvp.
21. Paul Mozur, "China, Not Silicon Valley, Is Cutting Edge in Mobile Tech," The New York Times, Aug. 2, 2016, http://tinyurl.com/y76byqum.
22. "HK Off to a Slow Start in Technology Development, Says Yang," EJ Insight, Oct. 3, 2017, https://tinyurl.com/y8fvxqe9.
23. Ann Fang, "How to Boost Hong Kong's Entrepreneurial Culture," The Chinese University of Hong Kong CUHK Business School, last accessed Dec. 21, 2017, https://tinyurl.com/y7sjycs8.
24. Cannix Yau, "Hong Kong Smart City Blueprint Rolled Out amid Scepticism over Pace and Scope," South China Morning Post, Dec. 15, 2017, https://tinyurl.com/y779bma5.
25. Ibid.
26. Stephen Chen, "China to Build Giant Facial Recognition Database to Identify Any Citizen Within Seconds," South China Morning Post, Oct. 12, 2017, https://tinyurl.com/y9y8a6fu.
27. Mark Magnier, "China's Economic Growth in 2015 Is Slowest in 25 Years," The Wall Street Journal, Jan. 19, 2016, https://tinyurl.com/yc35lm44.
28. "Why China's Economy Is Slowing," The Economist, Mar. 11, 2015, https://tinyurl.com/y9ucy5gu.
29. Magnier, op. cit.
30. Ibid.
31. The Economist, op. cit.
32. Ibid.
33. "China's Infrastructure Binge Is Set for a Major Slowdown," Bloomberg, Dec. 2, 2017, https://tinyurl.com/y9zxexvv.
34. "China Government Debt to GDP," Trading Economics, last accessed Dec. 21, 2017, https://tinyurl.com/ydc3xccj.
35. Michael Heath, "China Is Set to Lose Manufacturing Crown," Bloomberg, Apr. 28, 2015, https://tinyurl.com/ycbnngoq.
36. "Hong Kong GDP Annual Growth Rate," Trading Economics, last accessed Jan. 3, 2018, https://tinyurl.com/y7cw3opw.
37. "What's Wrong with HK Today, and Why It Will Change Only over the Dead Bodies of the Civil Service and the Property Tycoons," Hemlock's Musings, undated, https://tinyurl.com/y9vmbtkd.
38. Alice Poon, "Land and the Ruling Class in Hong Kong," Second Edition, Enrich Professional Publishing, 2010.
39. Tsang, op. cit., p. 239.
40. Joyce Ng, "What Exactly Is Hong Kong's Executive Council and Why Does It Matter?" South China Morning Post, Jun. 23, 2017, https://tinyurl.com/yb7bj9kz.

41. Poon, op. cit.
42. "Tax Rates of Salaries Tax & Personal Assessment," Government of the Hong Kong Special Administrative Region, last accessed Dec. 21, 2017, https://tinyurl.com/yd6mbunu.
43. "Tycoons: The Men Who Rule Hong Kong," Time Out Hong Kong, Oct. 4, 2016, https://tinyurl.com/ybyv3z9u.
44. "13th Annual Demographia International Housing Affordability Survey: 2017," Demographia, 2016, https://tinyurl.com/2vj4r8; Alicia Adamczyk, "This Is the Least Affordable City in the World," Money, Jan. 26, 2016, https://tinyurl.com/zqyalds.
45. "UBS Global Real Estate Bubble Index," UBS, Sep. 19, 2016, https://tinyurl.com/y86ffaf2.
46. Peter Guy, "Hong Kong Is in Danger of Losing Its Renowned Entrepreneurial Spirit," South China Morning Post, Dec. 4, 2016, https://tinyurl.com/y98rjgm2.
47. Nikki Sun, "Free-Trade Zone in Shenzhen Lures Hong Kong Entrepreneurs Chasing Their Dream," South China Morning Post, Nov. 30, 2016, https://tinyurl.com/zg43ugg.
48. UBS, op. cit.
49. Lalaine C. Delmendo, "Hong Kong's Red-Hot Property Market," Global Property Report, May 18, 2017, https://tinyurl.com/ycrgysf4.
50. Venus Wu, "Hong Kong Unveils Fresh Property Curbs as Chinese Buyers Rush In," Reuters, Nov. 4, 2016, https://tinyurl.com/y8855hsw.
51. Nisha Gopalan, "Why Chinese Developers Love Hong Kong," Bloomberg, Sep. 13, 2017, https://tinyurl.com/yc2o27k4.
52. Ibid.
53. "Asian Financial Crisis: Causes and Development," Hong Kong Institute of Economics and Business Strategy, 2000, https://tinyurl.com/yd47tnm5.
54. Wolf Richter, "Hong Kong Warns: Its Housing Bubble Is a 'Dangerous Situation,'" Business Insider, Jun. 21, 2017, https://tinyurl.com/y77xnz4c.
55. Moxy Ying, "Hong Kong Property Prices Are Near Their Peak: JPMorgan," Bloomberg, Apr. 9, 2017, https://tinyurl.com/ybxdnd56.
56. Frederik Balfour, "Hong Kong Existing Home Prices Rise to Record, Defying Curbs," Bloomberg, Feb. 24, 2017, https://tinyurl.com/y9h4feln.
57. Ying, op. cit.
58. "Population Estimates," Census and Statistics Department, Government of Hong Kong, last accessed Jan. 2, 2018, https://tinyurl.com/y97g59vq.
59. "Archive of Previous Sales Exercises Since 2007," Hong Kong Housing Authority, last accessed Jan. 2, 2018, https://tinyurl.com/ydgs4b9m.
60. "Number of Applications and Average Waiting Time for Public Rental Housing," Housing Department, the Government of Hong Kong, last accessed Dec. 21, 2017, https://tinyurl.com/ybqfqfcu.
61. "Survey Results of 2016 Annual Earnings and Hours Survey Released," Census and Statistic Department, Government of Hong Kong, Mar 17, 2017, https://tinyurl.com/y7jaby6h.
62. Ibid.
63. Y C Richard Wong, "Understanding Inequality, Poverty and Intergenerational Mobility," Hong Kong Ideas Centre, Mar. 7, 2014, https://tinyurl.com/y7pdulpe.
64. Ibid.
65. Jeffie Lam, "Poverty in Hong Kong Hits Record High, with 1 in 5 People Considered Poor," South China Morning Post, Nov. 17, 2017, https://tinyurl.com/y7amcgaq.
66. "(Policy Address) Affordable Starter Homes for Middle-Class Families," The Standard, Oct. 11, 2017, https://tinyurl.com/ybufzxfe.
67. Suzanne Sataline, "'Hong Kong Is Quite Seriously Divided,'" Foreign Policy, Jun. 18, 2015, https://tinyurl.com/ya2qokqr.
68. Suzanne Sataline, "Beijing Deals Another Blow to Hong Kong's Autonomy," Foreign Policy, Jul. 26, 2017, https://tinyurl.com/y6uhg5wt.
69. Jasmine Siu, "Charges against Hong Kong Occupy Leaders Are 'Prosecution Overkill', Barrister Says," South China Morning Post, Sep. 19, 2017, https://tinyurl.com/ycbgscea.
70. Stuart Lau, "President Xi Jinping Marks 'Red Line' in Warning to Hong Kong on National Sovereignty," South China Morning Post, Jul. 2, 2107, https://tinyurl.com/y8uof657.
71. Keith Bradsher, "Once a Model City, Hong Kong Is in Trouble," The New York Times, Jun. 29, 2017, https://tinyurl.com/y7grxng6.
72. Kimmy Chung, "Number of People Seeking a Fresh Start Outside Hong Kong Hits Three-Year High," South China Morning Post, May 4, 2017, https://tinyurl.com/ybjgxvqx.
73. Lam, op. cit.
74. "Moody's Downgrades China's Rating to A1 from Aa3 and Changes Outlook to Stable from Negative," Moody's Investors Service, May 24, 2017, https://tinyurl.com/yb3swmbs.
75. "Moody's Downgrades Hong Kong's Rating," op. cit.
76. "The Hong Kong Protests Explained in 100 Words and 500 Words," BBC News, Nov. 28, 2019, https://www.bbc.com/news/world-asia-china-49317695.
77. Ibid.
78. Grace Shao, "Hong Kong Just Entered a Recession. Experts Say Economy Will 'Remain Weak' amid Protests, Trade War," CNBC, Nov. 1, 2019, https://www.cnbc.com/2019/11/01/hong-kong-recession-economy-will-remain-weak-amid-protests-trade-war.html.
79. Yen Nee Lee, "Hong Kong Cuts GDP Forecast for 2020 after Economy Contracts 9% On-Year in the Second Quarter," CNBC, Aug. 14, 2020, https://www.cnbc.com/2020/08/14/hong-kong-releases-second-quarter-2020-gdp-data-economic-updates.html.
80. George Wright, "Hong Kong Protest Singers Fear for Their Future, BBC News, Aug. 25, 2020, https://www.bbc.com/news/world-asia-china-53655913.

81. Max Colchester, "Boris Johnson Offers Millions in Hong Kong the Chance to Emigrate to U.K.," The Wall Street Journal, Jul. 3, 2020, https://www.wsj.com/articles/boris-johnson-offers-millions-in-hong-kong-chance-to-emigrate-to-u-k-11593614303.
82. "The President's Executive Order on Hong Kong Normalization," The White House, Jul. 14, 2020, https://www.whitehouse.gov/presidential-actions/presidents-executive-order-hong-kong-normalization/.
83. "Latest Developments," The Government of Hong Kong, Aug. 19, 2020, https://www.hkeconomy.gov.hk/en/situation/development/index.htm.
84. Srinivas Mazumdaru, "China's Actions Risk Hong Kong's Future as Global Financial Center," DW, Aug. 3, 2020, https://www.dw.com/en/chinas-actions-risk-hong-kongs-future-as-global-financial-center/a-54410597.

Chapter 13: Minimum Wage

1. Emily Jane Fox, "The Real Budgets of McDonald's Workers," CNNMoney, Jul. 17, 2013, http://tinyurl.com/o7x59x3.
2. Quoted in Chris Cumming, "McDonald's Budget Backlash Hits Visa, Payroll Cards," American Banker, Jul. 19, 2013, http://tinyurl.com/nmy93yy.
3. Laura Shin, "Why McDonald's Employee Budget Has Everyone Up in Arms," Forbes.com blogs, Jul. 18, 2013, http://tinyurl.com/l9c67eb.
4. "Most See Inequality Growing, but Partisans Differ over Solutions," Pew Research Center for the People & the Press, Jan. 23, 2014, http://tinyurl.com/nnelewd.
5. "Germany to Introduce Minimum Wage," The Local, Nov. 21, 2013, http://tinyurl.com/k6nmb2g.
6. Mark Serwotka, "Strangle Lies and Spin about Our Welfare State," The Huffington Post UK, Jan. 17, 2014, http://tinyurl.com/pksfy3w.
7. "H.R. 1010: Fair Minimum Wage Act of 2013," govtrack.us, http://tinyurl.com/pfq424g; "Joined by Business Leaders and Workers, Sen. Harkin, Rep. Miller Unveil Bill to Raise the Minimum Wage to $10.10," press release, Senate Health, Education, Labor and Pensions Committee, Mar. 5, 2013, http://tinyurl.com/neox37l; Sam Stein, Dave Jamieson and Samantha Lachman, "How Democrats Could Get Outflanked on the Minimum Wage," The Huffington Post, Jan. 13, 2015, http://tinyurl.com/o4j6e8b.
8. Ibid. (Stein, Jamieson and Lachman); Sylvia A. Allegretto and David Cooper, "Twenty-Three Years and Still Waiting for Change," Economic Policy Institute, Jul. 10, 2014, http://tinyurl.com/llta6xv.
9. "Executive Order—Minimum Wage for Contractors," White House, Feb. 12, 2014, http://tinyurl.com/qddw5mt.
10. "UK to See More above-Inflation Rises in Minimum Wage, Says Low Pay Body," Reuters, Mar. 12, 2014, http://tinyurl.com/m399wb6.
11. "Germany's Merkel Agrees to Social Democrats' Demand for a Universal Minimum Wage," Agence-France-Press/The Raw Story, Nov. 21, 2013, http://tinyurl.com/oxyveg6; Matt Tempest, "Merkel Strikes Wage Deal as Price for Government," Independent [Ireland], Nov. 28, 2013, http://tinyurl.com/nm5w3at; Liz Alderman, "Minimum Wage in Europe Offers Ammunition in U.S. Debate," The New York Times, Feb. 13, 2013, http://tinyurl.com/b6oerho; "Germany Approves First-Ever National Minimum Wage," BBC News, Jul. 3, 2014, http://tinyurl.com/o7x7ysj.
12. Ibid, "Germany's Merkel Agrees . . . ."
13. Quoted in ibid.
14. "China Wages Seen Jumping in 2014 amid Shift to Services," Bloomberg News, Jan. 6, 2014, http://tinyurl.com/onl7q87.
15. "Minimum Wages in South Africa," Mywage.co.za, http://tinyurl.com/qzd5y2r.
16. Amogelang Mbatha, "ANC in Talks on Minimum Wage to Distribute Wealth," Mail & Guardian (South Africa), Mar. 10, 2014, http://tinyurl.com/m4yns4a.
17. "Characteristics of Minimum Wage Workers: 2012—Table 1," U.S. Bureau of Labor Statistics, Feb. 26, 2013, http://tinyurl.com/l2529ab.
18. David Cooper, "Raising the Federal Minimum Wage to $10.10 Would Lift Wages for Millions and Provide a Modest Economic Boost," Economic Policy Institute, Dec. 19, 2013, p. 7, http://tinyurl.com/llr5huy.
19. Jeanne Mejeur, "Studies Abound on the Minimum Wage, but the Conclusions Drawn Vary Greatly," State Legislatures Magazine, National Conference of State Legislatures, March 2014, http://tinyurl.com/pft5cy5.
20. Quoted in Joseph Berger, "Fearing a Minimum Wage Increase Will Be Bad for Business," The New York Times, Feb. 19, 2013, http://tinyurl.com/ppyt7w5.
21. Quoted in Steven Greenhouse, "Proposal to Raise Tip Wages Resisted," The New York Times, Jan. 26, 2014, http://tinyurl.com/nqrzm7h.
22. Quoted in Fred Lucas, "Sen. Cruz: Minimum Wage Hike Would Cost Jobs for Young People, Hispanics, African Americans," CNS News, Feb. 13, 2013, http://tinyurl.com/ovauxfe.
23. For background, see Dale Belman and Paul J. Wolfson, "What Does the Minimum Wage Do?" 2014.
24. "National Minimum Wage: Low Pay Commission Report 2014," United Kingdom Low Pay Commission, 2014, p. xiii, http://tinyurl.com/kcl7z53.
25. Quoted in Andrea Thomas and Ulrike Dauer, "German Minimum Wage Plan Gains Backing from Business," The Wall Street Journal, Mar. 28, 2014, http://tinyurl.com/pnxtwrk.
26. "The Effects of a Minimum Wage Increase on Employment and Family Income," Congressional Budget Office, February 2014, p. 9, http://tinyurl.com/jwbua42.
27. John Schmitt, "Why Does the Minimum Wage Have No Discernible Effect on Employment?" Center for Economic and Policy Research, February 2013, http://tinyurl.com/aql662k.

28. Dale Belman and Paul Wolfson, "What Does the Minimum Wage Do?" W.E. Upjohn Institute for Employment Research, 2014.
29. David Neumark and William Wascher, "Employment Effects of Minimum and Subminimum Wages: Panel Data on State Minimum Wage Laws," Industrial and Labor Relations Review, October 1992, http://tinyurl.com/knqkrnd.
30. David Card and Alan B. Krueger, "Minimum Wages and Employment: A Case Study of the Fast-Food Industry in New Jersey and Pennsylvania," The American Economic Review, September 1994, p. 772, http://tinyurl.com/mf8p35q.
31. David Card and Alan B. Krueger, "A Reanalysis of the Effect of the New Jersey Minimum Wage Increase on the Fast Food Industry with Representative Payroll Data," National Bureau of Economic Research, January 1998, http://tinyurl.com/jwfv984.
32. Arindrajit Dube, T. William Lester and Michael Reich, "Minimum Wage Effects across State Borders: Estimates Using Contiguous Counties," The Review of Economics and Statistics, November 2010, p. 945, http://tinyurl.com/2665wg4.
33. Quoted in Schmitt, op. cit.
34. "CBO Report Fuels Debate on Costs and Benefits of Raising the Minimum Wage," PBS NewsHour, Feb. 19, 2014, http://tinyurl.com/ojs9szo.
35. Quoted in ibid.
36. John Schmitt, "Why Does the Minimum Wage Have No Discernible Effect on Employment?" Center for Economic and Policy Research, February 2013, http://tinyurl.com/aql662k.
37. Ibid.
38. Andria Cheng, "Obama's Gap Visit Aside, Most Retailers Say They Will Cut Hiring if Minimum Wage Hiked," MarketWatch, The Wall Street Journal, Mar. 12, 2014, http://tinyurl.com/oo7cgkl.
39. James Hamilton, "New Estimates of the Effects of the Minimum Wage," Econbrowser blog, Dec. 7, 2014, http://tinyurl.com/otwmmlx; Danielle Kurtzleben, "Study: The 2007 Minimum Wage Hike Cost More Than 1 Million Jobs During the Recession," Vox, Dec. 12, 2014, http://tinyurl.com/ovcrr49.
40. "The Complex Economics of America's Minimum Wage," Knowledge at Wharton, Nov. 11, 2013, http://tinyurl.com/odsl4ke.
41. Quoted in "Business Day TV: Minimum Wage," BDLive, Mar. 10, 2014, http://tinyurl.com/njb8ofo.
42. Quoted in Alex Conrad, "Chili's to Install Tablets at Every Table: More Tips but a Cloudier Future for Servers," Forbes, Sep. 17, 2013, http://tinyurl.com/mkmyjpf.
43. Quoted in Rick Aristotle Munarriz, "Welcome to Applebee's. My Name Is Tablet. May I Take Your Order?" Daily Finance, Dec. 12, 2013, http://tinyurl.com/jwbzy74.
44. David Cooper, "Raising the Federal Minimum Wage to $10.10 Would Lift Wages for Millions and Provide a Modest Economic Boost," Economic Policy Institute, Dec. 19, 2013, http://tinyurl.com/obropdo.
45. Cooper, ibid.
46. Rachel West and Michael Reich, "The Effects of Minimum Wages on SNAP Enrollments and Expenditures," Mar. 5, 2014, http://tinyurl.com/o7wdw2e.
47. Barry Ritholtz, "How McDonald's and Walmart Became Welfare Queens," Bloomberg News, Nov. 13, 2013, http://tinyurl.com/k4pqz7w.
48. "The Low-Wage Drag on Our Economy: Wal-Mart's Low Wages and Their Effects on Taxpayers and Economic Growth," U.S. House Committee on Education and the Workforce Democratic Staff, May 2013, http://tinyurl.com/lk24y88.
49. Richard Dickens, Rebecca Riley and David Wilkinson, "Re-examining the Impact of the National Minimum Wage on Earnings, Employment and Hours: The Importance of Recession and Firm Size," Report to the Low Pay Commission, Aug. 9, 2013, http://tinyurl.com/nprolme.
50. Gregory Mankiw, "EITC Is Better Than the Minimum Wage," Greg Mankiw's blog, Dec. 10, 2013, http://tinyurl.com/q8qjt8x.
51. Quoted in Andy Radia, "Ontario Raises Minimum Wage to $11 an Hour, the Highest in the Country," Yahoo!News Canada, Jan. 30, 2014, http://tinyurl.com/q4xqs7y.
52. Kevin A. Hassett and Michael R. Strain, "The Minimum-Wage Debate," Los Angeles Times, Mar. 10, 2013, http://tinyurl.com/nten9e8.
53. Quoted in Stacy Perman, "As Minimum Wages Rise, Businesses Grapple with Consequences," The New York Times, Feb. 5, 2014, http://tinyurl.com/pgdsrno.
54. Ken Jacobs, Dave Graham-Squire and Stephanie Luce, "Living Wage Policies and Big-Box Retail: How a Higher Wage Standard Would Impact Walmart Workers and Shoppers," University of California, Berkeley, Center for Labor Research and Education, April 2011, http://tinyurl.com/4xuqfq5.
55. Wayne F. Cascio, "The High Cost of Low Wages," Harvard Business Review, December 2006, http://tinyurl.com/6b9zanj.
56. Quoted in Thomas and Dauer, op. cit.
57. Daniel Aaronson and Eric French, "How Does a Federal Minimum Wage Hike Affect Aggregate Household Spending?" Chicago Fed Letter, Federal Reserve Bank of Chicago, August 2013, http://tinyurl.com/l6nlnjv.
58. Quoted in "The Complex Economics of America's Minimum Wage," op. cit.
59. Quoted in Karen E. Klein, "Why a Minimum Wage Increase Divides Small Business," Bloomberg Business Week, Aug. 17, 2012, http://tinyurl.com/kuraptr.
60. Quoted in Louisa Peacock, "National Minimum Wage Rise 'Unwelcome' and 'Illogical'," The Telegraph (UK), Apr. 15, 2013, http://tinyurl.com/oq8l2zh.
61. Megan Brockett, "Rural Counties Have Different View of Wage Hike," Capital News Service/Cumberland Times-News, Jan. 27, 2014, www.times-news.com/news/local_news/rural-counties-have-different-view-of-wage-hike/article_80271013-bdd0-577a-92c4-c2a653550470.html.

62. Adam Smith, "Of the Wages of Labour," An Inquiry into the Nature and Causes of the Wealth of Nations, Book 1, Chapter 8, http://tinyurl.com/oyhwf5u.
63. For background, see Jerold Waltman, "The Politics of the Minimum Wage," 2000.
64. For background, see "A Social Laboratory," Glorious Days—Australia 2013, National Museum Australia, http://tinyurl.com/oe43k6l; "Fact Sheet 8: Abolition of the 'White Australia' Policy," Australian Government Department of Immigration and Border Protection, http://tinyurl.com/29y63z.
65. For background, see "A Brief Look Back on 100+ Years of Advocacy," History, National Consumers League, http://www.nclnet.org/history; "Kelley, Florence," Poverty and the Government in America: A Historical Encyclopedia, Volume 1, p. 345.
66. For background, see "Sweatshop," New World Encyclopedia, http://tinyurl.com/3gwkype.
67. Walter Lippmann, "The Campaign against Sweating," The New Republic, Mar. 27, 1915, p. 1, http://tinyurl.com/nppktq8.
68. Clifford F. Thies, "The First Minimum Wage Laws," Cato Journal, Winter 1991, p. 717, http://tinyurl.com/q6m972k.
69. The case is Adkins v. Children's Hospital, 261 U.S. 525 (1923). Text is available at http://tinyurl.com/oqblonl.
70. The 1908 case is Muller v. Oregon, 208 U.S. 412 (1908). Text is available at http://tinyurl.com/on6h2b9.
71. The case is A.L.A. Schechter Poultry Corp. v. United States, 295 U.S. 495 (1935). Text is available at http://tinyurl.com/ppvxosn. For background, see David Kestenbaum, "The Birth of the Minimum Wage in America," Planet Money, NPR, Jan. 17, 2014, http://tinyurl.com/l5asdxv; Jonathan Grossman, "Fair Labor Standards Act of 1938: Maximum Struggle for a Minimum Wage," History, U.S. Department of Labor, http://tinyurl.com/n6o2u69.
72. Text is available at http://tinyurl.com/lx2rz2m.
73. For background, see "Making the Most Out of the Minimum: Statutory Wages, Employment and Poverty," Employment Outlook, Chapter 2, Organisation for Economic Co-operation and Development, 1998, http://tinyurl.com/mjljtus.
74. "History of Federal Minimum Wage Rates under the Fair Labor Standards Act, 1938–2009," Wage and Hour Division, U.S. Department of Labor, http://tinyurl.com/7xe6b8m; "History of Changes to the Minimum Wage Law," Wage and Hour Division, U.S. Department of Labor, http://tinyurl.com/2wadar8.
75. "The Effects of a Minimum-Wage Increase on Employment and Family Income," Congressional Budget Office, February 2014, p. 4, http://tinyurl.com/jwbua42; "Minimum Wage History," Wealth and Poverty, http://tinyurl.com/75zad.
76. Quoted in Rick Wartzman, "How Minimum Wage Lost Its Status as a Tool of Social Progress in the U.S.," The Wall Street Journal, Jul. 19, 2001, http://tinyurl.com/pzw9tml.
77. Jerold L. Waltman, "Minimum Wage Policy in Great Britain and the United States," 2008, p. 2; Polly Toynbee, "This Withering Assault on Farm Workers' Wages Is a Race to the Bottom," The Guardian, Oct. 25, 2012, http://tinyurl.com/py9jtwh.
78. Michael Reich, "Minimum Wages in the United States: Politics, Economics and Econometrics," preliminary draft for Institute for Research on Labor and Employment conference, Oct. 27, 2007, http://tinyurl.com/aa5nect.
79. "State Minimum Wages: 2014–2015 Minimum Wage by State," National Conference of State Legislatures, Dec. 18, 2014, http://tinyurl.com/kxsucwu.
80. Heather Brady, "The Handful of Countries without a Minimum Wage," Slate, Feb. 21, 2013, http://tinyurl.com/a8o9ek6.
81. François Eyraud and Catherine Saget, "The Fundamentals of Minimum Wage Fixing," International Labor Organization, 2005, http://tinyurl.com/lsg7v?6.
82. "Fact Sheet: Final Rule to Implement Executive Order 13658, Establishing a Minimum Wage for Contractors," United States Department of Labor Wage and Hour Division, http://tinyurl.com/nmdcyjs.
83. Mark Landler, "With Eye on Midterms, Obama Pushes Rise in Minimum Wage," The New York Times, Mar. 5, 2014, http://tinyurl.com/np2c5xp.
84. Dave Jamieson, "Lamar Alexander Says the Minimum Wage Should Be Abolished," The Huffington Post, Jun. 25, 2013, http://tinyurl.com/omaxldm.
85. Jana Kasperkevic, "Voters Create Paradox as They Support Higher Minimum Wage but Elect Anti-Union Governors," The Guardian (UK), Nov. 14, 2014, http://tinyurl.com/k4qnya6; Hunter Schwarz, "Voters Don't Seem to View the Minimum Wage as a Partisan, Political Issue," The Washington Post, Nov. 6, 2014, http://tinyurl.com/nbr94ln.
86. Shellie Nelson, "Illinois voters approve Minimum Wage Hike, Millionaire Tax and Birth Control Coverage," WQAD TV, Nov. 5, 2014, http://tinyurl.com/muh3wth.
87. Ray Long and Monique Garcia, "Rauner Says Chicago Minimum Wage Hike Could Make City Less Competitive," Chicago Tribune, Dec. 2, 2014, http://tinyurl.com/kg2bhjy.
88. John O'Connor, "Rauner Reverses Quinn Orders on Taxes, Minimum Wage," The Associated Press, Jan. 16, 2015, http://tinyurl.com/mj9slxj.
89. State Minimum Wages/2014–2015 Minimum Wage by State, National Conference of State Legislatures, Dec. 18, 2014, http://tinyurl.com/kxsuowu.
90. Ibid.
91. Richard Weizel, "Connecticut Gov. Expected to Sign Minimum Wage Hike," Reuters, Mar. 27, 2014, http://tinyurl.com/lyup3gs.
92. Quoted in "Connecticut Is Increasing Minimum Wage to $10.10 an Hour," The Associated Press/The New York Times, Mar. 26, 2014, http://tinyurl.com/lq4xzhw.
93. Megan Brockett, "Rural Counties Have Different View of Wage Hike," Capital News Service/Cumberland Times News, Jan. 27, 2014, http://tinyurl.com/l63wyrs.

94. "Local Living Wage Laws and Coverage," National Employment Law Project, July 2011, http://tinyurl.com/op6sbdh; Mark Oswald, "Minimum Wage in SF Set to Rise 1.3%," Albuquerque Journal, Dec. 28, 2013, http://tinyurl.com/odto55o.
95. "Unemployment Rates for Metropolitan Areas," Bureau of Labor Statistics, Mar. 21, 2014, http://tinyurl.com/2eg49b8.
96. Kim Vallez, "Santa Fe County OKs Minimum Wage Increase," KRQE Radio (Santa Fe), Feb. 26, 2014, http://tinyurl.com/nez2gul; Justin Horwath, "Equalizing the Wage Floor," Santa Fe Reporter, Mar. 30, 2014, www.sfreporter.com/santafe/article-8252-equalizing-the-wage-floor.html.
97. Gregory Wallace, "Seattle Approves $15 Minimum Wage," CNN Money, Jun. 3, 2014, http://money.cnn.com/2014/06/02/news/economy/seattle-minimum-wage.
98. Ben Moonye, "San Francisco Votes in $15 Minimum Wage," CNN Money, Nov. 5, 2014, http://tinyurl.com/q537exv.
99. Jenni Bergal, "Cities Forge Policy Apart from States," Stateline, Jan. 15, 2015, http://tinyurl.com/naqgxte.
100. Quoted in ibid.
101. "Boston Bruins Tri-Blend T-shirt," Shop.NHL.com, http://tinyurl.com/qgydezu.
102. Fred de Sam Lazaro, "Can Garment Factories Pay a Living Wage and Still Compete in a Global Economy?" PBS NewsHour, Feb. 18, 2014, http://tinyurl.com/mrf7qnk.
103. Quoted in Steven Greenhouse, "Factory Defies Sweatshop Label, but Can It Thrive?" The New York Times, Jul. 17, 2010, http://tinyurl.com/ozac56b.
104. Quoted in Kim Bhasin, "Can You Make Clothes without Sweatshop Labor? This Dominican Factory Is Trying," The Huffington Post, Oct. 9, 2014,http://tinyurl.com/q22l6v2.
105. "Code of Conduct for Georgetown University Licensees," Georgetown University Office of Public Affairs, http://tinyurl.com/no3ua9j.
106. Ibid.
107. Jason Hickel, "It's Time for a Global Minimum Wage," Al Jazeera, Jun. 10, 2013, http://tinyurl.com/pjrkcna.
108. Ibid.
109. Stein, Jamieson and Lachman, op. cit.; Alegretto and Cooper, op. cit.
110. Quoted in ibid. (Stein, Jamieson and Lachman).
111. Ibid.
112. Annie Linskey and Kathleen Hunter, "Chance of Wage Rise So Remote Lobbyists Pay Little Heed," Bloomberg Businessweek, Mar. 17, 2014, http://tinyurl.com/pk59flt.
113. U.S. Department of Labor, "Minimum Wage," June 2020, https://www.dol.gov/general/topic/wages/minimumwage.
114. National Conference of State Legislatures, "Minimum Wage by State," Jan. 6, 2020, https://www.ncsl.org/research/labor-and-employment/state-minimum-wage-chart.aspx.
115. Kira Buttrey and Amy Glasmeier, "Two Sides of the Debate about Raising the Minimum Wage," Living Wage Calculator, Jul. 19, 2019, https://livingwage.mit.edu/articles/46-two-sides-of-the-debate-about-raising-the-minimum-wage.
116. Ibid.
117. Nandita Bose, "House Passes Bill to Raise Federal Minimum Wage to $15 an Hour," Reuters, Jul. 18, 2019, https://www.reuters.com/article/us-usa-congress-minimum-wage/house-passes-bill-to-raise-federal-minimum-wage-to-15-an-hour-idUSKCN1UD2DV.
118. Mitch McConnell, Twitter, Jul. 18, 2010, https://twitter.com/senatemajldr/status/1151885990862237697?s=20.
119. Eric Ravenscraft, "What a 'Living Wage' Actually Means," The New York Times, Jun. 5, 2019, https://www.nytimes.com/2019/06/05/smarter-living/what-a-living-wage-actually-means.html.
120. "National Living Wage and National Minimum Wage Rates," Government of the UK, April 2020, https://www.gov.uk/national-minimum-wage-rates.
121. Ella Torres, "Target Raising Minimum Wage to $15, Announces Bonuses for Front-line Workers," ABC News, Jun. 18, 2020, https://abcnews.go.com/Business/target-raising-minimum-wage-15-announces-bonuses-front/story?id=71302114.
122. Retail Council of Canada, "Minimum Wage by Province," Jun. 18, 2020, https://www.retailcouncil.org/resources/quick-facts/minimum-wage-by-province/.
123. Vasundhara Rastogi, "Minimum Wages in ASEAN: How Are They Calculated?" ASEAN Briefing, Jan. 14, 2020, https://www.aseanbriefing.com/news/minimum-wages-in-asean-how-are-they-calculated/.

Chapter 14: Paid Leave

1. Sheryl Sandberg, Facebook post, Feb. 7, 2017, http://tinyurl.com/mntk8z7.
2. Ibid.
3. "DOL Factsheet: Paid Family and Medical Leave," U.S. Department of Labor, June 2015, http://tinyurl.com/md5vm7r.
4. "Forging Ahead or Falling Behind: Paid Family Leave at America's Top Companies," PL+US, Nov. 16, 2016, http://tinyurl.com/mkvcbbk.
5. Danielle Paquette, "When Workers Don't Get Paid Sick Days, Everyone Else Is More Likely to Get Sick," Chicago Tribune, Aug. 26, 2016, http://tinyurl.com/kaf2fu3.
6. Alicia Adamczyk, "These Are the Companies with the Best Parental Leave Policies," Money, Nov. 4, 2015, http://tinyurl.com/jbf8v27.
7. Ibid.; "Join Our Team," Squarespace, undated, http://tinyurl.com/mc5qg86.
8. Jena McGregor, "An 'Unlimited Parental Leave Policy Sounds Great, but Will It Work?" Los Angeles Times, Aug. 16, 2015, http://tinyurl.com/m5nnz7t.
9. Joshua Reeves, "Unlimited Vacation Policy? What You Should Know," The Muse, undated, http://tinyurl.com/jfjlnkm.

10. Minda Zetlin, "The Surprising Benefits of Unlimited Vacation," Inc., June 2016, http://tinyurl.com/m9o7cky.
11. Jena McGregor, "The Catch of Having an Unlimited Vacation Policy," The Washington Post, Aug. 13, 2013, http://tinyurl.com/mj6psj8.
12. Sue Shellenbarger, "Companies Deal with Employees Who Refuse to Take Time Off by Requiring Vacations, Paying Them to Go," The Wall Street Journal, Aug. 12, 2014, http://tinyurl.com/k682q2v.
13. Jonathan Crew, "Why Unlimited Vacation May Sound Better Than It Really Is," Fortune, Mar. 10, 2016, http://tinyurl.com/kd8ofzt.
14. "10 Awesome Companies That Give You Unlimited Vacation," The Muse, undated, http://tinyurl.com/lbhy5cs.
15. Reeves, op. cit.
16. Zetlin, op. cit.
17. "Key Characteristics of Parental Leave Systems," OECD Family Database, Directorate of Employment, Labour and Social Affairs, Mar. 15, 2017, http://tinyurl.com/mclgdbw.
18. John Dodge, "The War for Tech Talent Escalates," Boston Globe, Feb. 19, 2016, http://tinyurl.com/zog2col.
19. "83% of Millennials—Now Largest Group of New Parents—Would Leave Their Job for One with Better Family/Lifestyle Benefits," Care.com, Aug. 10, 2015, http://tinyurl.com/ljep5xb.
20. "Global Generations: A Global Study on Work-Life Challenges Across Generations," Ernst & Young, 2015, http://tinyurl.com/mm8uc5s.
21. Brigit Katz, "Trump Administration May Amend Maternity Leave Plan to Include Men," The New York Times, Feb. 7, 2017, http://tinyurl.com/l6avedx.
22. Frank Newport, "Trump Family Leave, Infrastructure Proposals Widely Popular," Gallup, Apr. 7, 2017, http://tinyurl.com/k47mxwa.
23. Frank Kerbein, "Legislative Memo," Business Council, Feb. 4, 2016, http://tinyurl.com/l2xjop4.
24. "Health Policy Brief: Paid Family and Medical Leave," Health Affairs, Robert Wood Johnson Foundation, Nov. 21, 2016, http://tinyurl.com/n6gb9ff.
25. "The Economic Benefits of Paid Leave: Fact Sheet," Joint Economic Committee, U.S. Congress, Jan. 20, 2015, http://tinyurl.com/nylay7w.
26. Susan Wojcicki, "Paid Maternity Leave Is Good for Business," The Wall Street Journal, Dec. 16, 2014, http://tinyurl.com/k3tdubl.
27. Susan Wojcicki, "Closing the Tech Industry Gender Gap," The Huffington Post, Jan. 27, 2017, http://tinyurl.com/m8jq3tk.
28. Celeste Smith, "Duke Energy to Provide Paid Parental Leave," The Charlotte Observer, Jan. 26, 2017, http://tinyurl.com/kam3wua.
29. Kristen Bellstrom, "EY Comes out Swinging at Other Consulting Firms with New Parental Leave Policy," Fortune, Apr. 13, 2016, http://tinyurl.com/zrn6v3h.
30. "Deloitte Announces 16 Weeks of Fully Paid Family Leave Time for Caregiving," Deloitte, Sep. 8, 2016, http://tinyurl.com/zvway5m.
31. Juliana Menasce Horowitz, et al., "Americans Widely Support Paid Family and Medical Leave, but Differ over Specific Policies," Pew Research Center, Mar. 23, 2017, http://tinyurl.com/m7v6tfy.
32. "Paid Family and Medical Leave: Good for Business," National Partnership for Women & Families, March 2015, http://tinyurl.com/qzhnmxw.
33. "The Economic Benefits of Paid Leave: Fact Sheet," op. cit.
34. "Disability Insurance (DI) and Paid Family Leave (PFL) Weekly Benefit Amounts in Dollar Increments," California Employment Development Department, Jan. 1, 2017, http://tinyurl.com/ktkch8l.
35. Ibid.
36. "DOL Factsheet: Paid Family and Medical Leave," op. cit.
37. Alexia Fernández Campbell, "D.C.'s Battle for Paid Family Leave," The Atlantic, Dec. 19, 2016, http://tinyurl.com/mow4kpx.
38. Sean Sullivan and Robert Costa, "Donald Trump Unveils Child-Care Policy Influenced by Ivanka Trump," The Washington Post, Sep. 13, 2016, http://tinyurl.com/l8qlmgd; "Inside the Candidates' Plans for Paid Leave and Child Care," PBS NewsHour, Sep. 14, 2016, http://tinyurl.com/znprv78.
39. Russell Berman, "A Conservative Push for Paid Family Leave," The Atlantic, Aug. 15, 2016, http://tinyurl.com/kc2x6bc.
40. Bourree Lam, "There's Superficial Agreement in Congress on Paid Family Leave," The Atlantic, Feb. 11, 2017, http://tinyurl.com/lfdk3oc.
41. Tim Wallace and Alicia Parlapiano, "Crowd Scientists Say Women's March in Washington Had 3 Times as Many People as Trump's Inauguration," The New York Times, Jan. 22, 2017, http://tinyurl.com/h9ggezt.
42. Heather Long, "Wait, Did Trump Endorse Paid FAMILY Leave?" CNN Money, Mar. 6, 2017, http://tinyurl.com/ld7pcc5.
43. Ibid.
44. David Weigel, "Democrats Get Ahead of Trump with Family Leave Plan," The Washington Post, Mar. 14, 2017, http://tinyurl.com/n2m5xfs.
45. Jane Farrell and Sarah Jane Glynn, "The FAMILY Act: Facts and Frequently Asked Questions," Center for American Progress, Dec. 12, 2013, http://tinyurl.com/mgofkvv.
46. Claire Zillman, "Kirsten Gillibrand Is Giving Her Paid Family Leave Proposal Its First Trump-Era Test," Fortune, Feb. 7, 2017, http://tinyurl.com/z7xrxfk.
47. "Economic Effects of the Family and Medical Leave Insurance Act," Wharton School, University of Pennsylvania, Sep. 1, 2015, http://tinyurl.com/klbqezh.
48. Neyla Zannia, "SIA Refutes Claims That Employees Are Penalized for Taking Sick Leave," The Online Citizen, Feb. 9, 2017, http://tinyurl.com/m4gd6v3.

49. "Work-Life Imbalance: Expedia's 2016 Vacation Deprivation Study Shows Americans Leave Hundreds of Millions of Paid Vacation Days Unused," Expedia, Nov. 15, 2016, http://tinyurl.com/l38zw76.
50. Ibid.
51. Ibid.
52. "The State of American Vacation: How Vacation Became a Casualty of Our Work Culture," Project: Time Off, 2016, http://tinyurl.com/kqf5tze.
53. Jay L. Zagorsky, "Divergent Trends in US Maternity and Paternity Leave, 1994–2015," American Journal of Public Health, March 2017, http://tinyurl.com/l29spvb.
54. "What Is Paid Family Leave," Paid Family Leave California, undated, http://tinyurl.com/kkbjecv.
55. Zagorsky, op. cit.
56. "TED: The Economics Daily," Bureau of Labor Statistics, U.S. Department of Labor, Nov. 4, 2016, http://tinyurl.com/l8kqcbt.
57. "Access to and Use of Leave—2011 Data from the American Time Use Survey Summary," Bureau of Labor Statistics, U.S. Department of Labor, Aug. 15, 2012, http://tinyurl.com/mwbxgpl.
58. Zagorsky, op. cit.
59. Ibid.
60. David I. Kertzer and Marzio Barbagli, eds., "Family Life in the Long Nineteenth Century, 1789–1913," Yale University Press, 2002, p. 149.
61. Ibid.
62. Ibid.
63. Jessica Deahl, "Countries around the World Beat the U.S. on Paid Parental Leave," NPR, Oct. 6, 2016, http://tinyurl.com/ztdxu4p.
64. "History of the FMLA," National Partnership for Women & Families," undated, http://tinyurl.com/lgf4srg.
65. "Family and Medical Leave Act (FMLA) of 1993," Society for Human Resource Management, http://tinyurl.com/m35xrdp.
66. "Employee Benefits in the United States—March 2016," Bureau of Labor Statistics, U.S. Department of Labor, Jul. 22, 2016, http://tinyurl.com/l9sdon9.
67. "Family and Medical Leave Act," Wage and Hour Division, U.S. Department of Labor, undated, http://tinyurl.com/mu524ez.
68. "State Paid Family Leave Insurance Laws," National Partnership for Women & Families, February 2017, http://tinyurl.com/l7crnbf.
69. "New and Expanded Employer Paid Family and Medical Leave Policies (2015–2017)," National Partnership for Women & Families, 2017, http://tinyurl.com/jnljruc.
70. Christine Sloane, "Maryland Senate Makes History," National Paid Sick Days Coalition, undated, http://tinyurl.com/l5bfjk4.
71. Carrie H. Colla, et al., "Early Effects of the San Francisco Paid Sick Leave Policy," American Journal of Public Health, December 2014, http://tinyurl.com/lp4x2rg.
72. Ibid.
73. "Current Paid Sick Days Laws," National Partnership for Women & Families, Nov. 9, 2016, http://tinyurl.com/mt424nb.
74. "A History of Paid Sick Leave Legislation," TimeForce, undated, http://tinyurl.com/m8eyx4e.
75. "Current Paid Sick Days Laws," op. cit.
76. "H.R. 1516—Healthy Families Act," U.S. Congress, Mar. 13, 2017, http://tinyurl.com/mb9l28m.
77. "Paid Time off Programs and Practices," WorldatWork, June 2016, http://tinyurl.com/zu8en2c.
78. Ibid.
79. Chris Crowley, "World's Best Brewery Offers Paid Leave for Employees with New Puppies," Grub Street, Feb. 17, 2017, http://tinyurl.com/ztb8bjn.
80. "Egypt: Constitutional Court Grants Coptic Christians the Right to Paid Leave for Pilgrimage to Jerusalem," Global Legal Monitor, Law Library of Congress, Feb. 17, 2017, http://tinyurl.com/mbg7p68.
81. Lynn Davidson, "Bid to Stop Stress: Workers Should Be Allowed Spontaneous 'Chill Days' and 52 Weeks Sick Pay Instead of 28, Report Says," Feb. 16, 2017, http://tinyurl.com/hb2fdn6.
82. Ibid.
83. Cynthia Than, "Defending 'Meternity': Why All Women Should Get Paid Leave (Not Just New Moms)," Inc., undated, Apr. 30, 2016, http://tinyurl.com/krrg94o.
84. "The State of American Vacation: How Vacation Became a Casualty of Our Work Culture," Project: Time Off, undated, http://tinyurl.com/kqf5tze.
85. Jessica Leber, "Vacation Policies You'll Envy from Companies You Don't Work For," Fast Company, Mar. 9, 2015, http://tinyurl.com/n5hn3xo.
86. Anders Melin and Ben Steverman, "Vacation Deprivation? Startup Lets Employees Trade Unused Days for Flights and Hotel Stays," Skift, Oct. 11, 2016, http://tinyurl.com/lu9ut53.
87. Justin Held, "Most Appreciated, Most Successful and Most Unique Benefits," International Foundation of Employee Benefit Plans, Sep. 30, 2014, http://tinyurl.com/la2qvdo.
88. Sam Sanders, "Netflix's New, Generous Parental Leave Policy Leaves Some Employees Out," NPR, Aug. 6, 2015, http://tinyurl.com/msf5web.
89. Susan Adams, "Virgin's New Paternity Leave Policy: It's Not Quite as Great as the Hype," Forbes, Jun. 12, 2015, http://tinyurl.com/ko9gbfw.
90. Shannon Murphy, "Netflix: Extend Paid Parental Leave Policy to ALL Employees," Coworker.org, August 2015, http://tinyurl.com/lzsp94m.
91. Shane Ferro, "Netflix Just Made Another Huge Stride on Parental Leave," The Huffington Post, Jan. 16, 2017, http://tinyurl.com/mwbrde8.
92. Gina Hall, "Activists Petition Netflix to Include Hourly Workers in Parental Leave Policy," Silicon Valley Business Journal, Sep. 2, 2015, http://tinyurl.com/mwfn2yx.

93. Emily Peck, "Under Fire, Netflix Defends Lopsided Parental Leave Policy," The Huffington Post, Sep. 2, 2015, http://tinyurl.com/lh9unah.
94. Ibid.
95. Maggie Mertens, "Tech Companies Offer Great Perks, Just Not for Everyone," Refinery29, Aug. 10, 2015, http://tinyurl.com/lozhwno.
96. Anne D'Innocenzio, "Movement Grows to Require Employers to Offer Paid Sick Leave for Workers," U.S. News & World Report, May 19, 2015, http://tinyurl.com/ld2m4p8; Christopher Ingraham, "More Than a Third of American Workers Don't Get Sick Leave, and They're Making the Rest of Us Ill," The Washington Post, Jan. 15, 2015, http://tinyurl.com/lawn84t.
97. "The Cost of Doing Nothing," U.S. Department of Labor, Sep. 4, 2015, http://tinyurl.com/mh68u57.
98. "New and Expanded Paid Family and Medical Leave Policies (2015–2017)," National Partnership for Women & Families, 2017, http://tinyurl.com/jnljruc.
99. Jennifer Ludden, "From Cooks to Accountants: Hilton Extends Paid Parental Leave to All," NPR, Oct. 11, 2016, http://tinyurl.com/ltdtydl.
100. Ibid.
101. Sanders, op. cit.
102. Claire Cain Miller, "Trump Called for Paid Family Leave. Here's Why Few Democrats Clapped," The New York Times, Feb. 5, 2020, https://www.nytimes.com/2020/02/05/upshot/paid-leave-trump.html.
103. Gretchen Livingston and Deja Thomas, "Among 41 Countries, Only U.S. Lacks Parental Leave," Pew Research Center, Dec. 16, 2019, https://www.pewresearch.org/fact-tank/2019/12/16/u-s-lacks-mandated-paid-parental-leave/.
104. Ibid.
105. Emily Cochrane, Claire Cane Miller and Jim Tankersley, "Trump Administration Scales Back Paid Leave in Coronavirus Relief Bill," The New York Times, Apr. 2, 2020, https://www.nytimes.com/2020/04/02/us/politics/coronavirus-paid-leave.html.
106. Suzanne Hultin and Tatiana Follett, "State Family Medical Leave Laws," National Conference of State Legislatures, Sep. 21, 2020, https://www.ncsl.org/research/labor-and-employment/state-family-and-medical-leave-laws.aspx.
107. Brian O'Connell, "COVID-19 Spurs Expanded Paid Leave," Society for Human Resource Management, May 30, 2020, https://www.shrm.org/hr-today/news/all-things-work/pages/covid-19-spurs-expanded-paid-leave.aspx.
108. Kim Willsher, "France Doubles Paid Paternity Leave to 28 Days," Sep. 23, 2020, https://www.theguardian.com/world/2020/sep/23/france-doubles-paid-paternity-leave-to-28-days; "Gender Equality in Sweden," Swedish Institute, last updated Aug. 12, 2020, https://sweden.se/society/gender-equality-in-sweden/; "Employment, Social Affairs & Inclusion," European Commission, https://tinyurl.com/y6skwggz.
109. Noele Illien, "Switzerland Votes to Approve Paternity Leave," The New York Times, Sep. 27, 2020, https://www.nytimes.com/2020/09/27/world/europe/switzerland-paternity-leave.html; Zack Budryk, "Switzerland Votes to Create Nationwide Paternity Leave," The Hill, Sep. 27, 2020, https://tinyurl.com/y4e4x2wg.

Chapter 15: Supply Chains and Protectionism

1. Mark Landler and Jim Tankersley, "Trump Hits China with Stiff Trade Measures," The New York Times, Mar. 22, 2018, https://tinyurl.com/y8jq7vuu.
2. "Boeing Co.," CNN Money, accessed Jun. 18, 2018, https://tinyurl.com/878ezjg.
3. Dominic Gates, "Boeing to Cut Management Layers in Streamlining of Supply Chain" The Seattle Times, Nov. 10, 2017, https://tinyurl.com/ycax9fod.
4. Dhierin Bechai, "Why Boeing Shares Really Dropped," Seeking Alpha, Mar. 15, 2018, https://tinyurl.com/yablfgmk; Bill Chappell, "Trump Hits China with Tariffs on $50 Billion of Goods; China Says It Will Retaliate," NPR, Jun. 15, 2018, http://tinyurl.com/y9298bhr.
5. Boeing Co.," op. cit.; "S&P 500 Index," CNN Money, accessed Jun. 18, 2018, https://tinyurl.com/pnfnv; "Dow Jones INDU Average NDX," CNN Money, accessed Jun. 18, 2018, https://tinyurl.com/qjljw.
6. "The Uruguay Round," The World Trade Organization, undated, accessed Jun. 7, 2018, https://tinyurl.com/zwhwwu2.
7. "Trade and Tariffs: Trade Grows as Tariffs Decline," The World Trade Organization, last updated Aug. 8, 2017, https://tinyurl.com/y8pu7d6q.
8. Ibid.
9. Cristina Constantinescu, Aaditya Mattoo and Michele Ruta, "Does Vertical Specialization Increase Productivity?" The World Bank, February 2017, https://tinyurl.com/y7s6g4yl.
10. Michael Froman, "We Are at the End of the Line on the Doha Round of Trade Talks," Financial Times, Dec. 13, 2015, https://tinyurl.com/yc2xbq4s.
11. Alanna Petroff, "Trump Is Starting a Global Trade War," CNN, Jun. 1, 2018, https://tinyurl.com/yaex2lkx.
12. "The Charlevoix G7 Summit Communique," last modified Jun. 13, 2018, https://tinyurl.com/y94ofkbw.
13. "Global Economic Prospects: The Turning of the Tide?" The World Bank, January 2018, https://tinyurl.com/lnmdtze.
14. Constantinescu, et al., op. cit.
15. Charles Engel, "Equivalence Results for Optimal Pass-Through, Optimal Indexing to Exchange Rates, and Optimal Choice of Currency for Export Pricing," Journal of the European Economic Association, December 2006, https://tinyurl.com/y74k9t86.

16. Sheng Lu, "Four Key Patterns in US Apparel Imports," just-style, Mar. 1, 2018, https://tinyurl.com/y9txzyce; "Korn Ferry Hay Group 2017 Salary Forecast: Wage Increases Slow Globally," Korn Ferry, Dec. 6, 2016, https://tinyurl.com/yamu8ujs.
17. Sheng Lu, ibid.
18. Tom Daly and Muyu Xu, "China April Aluminum, Steel Exports Rise, Defying U.S. Tariffs," Reuters, May 8, 2018, https://tinyurl.com/y783zwmp.
19. Kevin Granville, "Will Trump's Trade Policy Fit into a Can of Beer?" The New York Times, Mar. 2, 2018, https://tinyurl.com/y9n79awt.
20. "Insignificant Impact on Boeing from Aluminum Tariff: JP Morgan," Leeham News and Comment, Mar. 2, 2018, https://tinyurl.com/y93o6qxf.
21. "Reports, Trends & Statistics: Driver Shortage," American Trucking Associations, undated, accessed Jun. 7, 2018, https://tinyurl.com/ydb79bp7.
22. "Reports, Trends & Statistics: Industry Data," American Trucking Associations, undated, accessed Jun. 7, 2018, https://tinyurl.com/z336caf; "New Survey Data Reveals Increases in Driver Compensation," American Trucking Associations, Mar. 27, 2018, https://tinyurl.com/ybofahkz.
23. Mike Wilder, "The Consumer Cost of Washington's 'Win-Win' NAFTA Timeline," Journal of Commerce, May 8, 2018, https://tinyurl.com/ybx8xfc5.
24. Ibid.
25. Damian Paletta, "Trudeau Says NAFTA Talks Broke Down After Pence Made Ultimatum," The Washington Post, May 31, 2018, https://tinyurl.com/y8d6x5or.
26. James Bovenzi, "Automotive Logistics Global 2016: The Automotive Logistics World," Automotive Logistics, Sep. 21, 2016, https://tinyurl.com/y86nyysg.
27. Shay Scott, Ted Stank and Ben Hazen, "A Savvy Guide to the Digital Supply Chain," Global Supply Chain Institute, April 2018, https://tinyurl.com/yb53utfm.
28. Gates, op. cit.
29. "How WHO Is Re-imagining and Fixing the Links in the Supply Chains during COVID-19," World Health Organization, May 7, 2020, https://tinyurl.com/yxefjkem.
30. Ibid.
31. "One-third of Supply Chain Leaders Moved Business Out of China or Plan to by 2023," Managing, Handling & Logistics, Jun. 30, 2020, https://www.mhlnews.com/global-supply-chain/article/21135454/onethird-of-supply-chain-leaders-moved-business-out-of-china-or-plan-to-by-2023.
32. Andy Blatchford, "Bains: Domestic Industry Now Supplying Half of Canada's PPE Needs," Politico, Sep. 30, 2020, https://www.politico.com/news/2020/09/30/navdeep-bains-canada-ppe-424029.
33. "The Post-Covid Economy," Barclay's, Aug. 14, 2020, https://tinyurl.com/y3tsdhkq.

Chapter 16: The Border Economy

1. Kevin Liptak and Dan Merica, "Trump Agrees 'Not to Terminate NAFTA at This Time,'" CNN, Apr. 27, 2017, https://tinyurl.com/myemook.
2. M. Angeles Villarreal and Ian F. Fergusson, "The North American Free Trade Agreement (NAFTA)," Congressional Research Service, Feb. 22, 2017, https://tinyurl.com/khqb46b.
3. Michael J. Boskin, "NAFTA at 20," The Hoover Institution, 2014, p. 128.
4. M. Angeles Villarreal, "U.S.-Mexico Economic Relations: Trends, Issues, and Implications," Congressional Research Service, Apr. 27, 2017, https://tinyurl.com/maf63qd; M. Ayhan Kose, Guy M. Meredith and Christopher M. Towe, "How Has NAFTA Affected the Mexican Economy? Review and Evidence," International Monetary Fund, 2004, https://tinyurl.com/l84u6ga.
5. Villarreal and Fergusson, op. cit.
6. "Mexico—Market Overview," Export.gov, https://tinyurl.com/hrb277g.
7. "World Input-Output Database," Netherlands Organisation for Scientific Research, http://www.wiod.org/database/wiots16; Christopher Wilson and Duncan Wood, "Growing Together: Economic Ties between the United States and Mexico," Wilson Center Mexico Institute, Sep. 26, 2016, https://tinyurl.com/lmy9f3o.
8. "Trade in Goods with Mexico," U.S. Census Bureau, https://www.census.gov/foreign-trade/balance/c2010.html.
9. "OECD Employment Outlook 2015," OECD Publishing, p. 291, https://tinyurl.com/lzt2p7p; "Average Annual Hours Actually Worked per Worker," OECD.Stat, OECD, https://tinyurl.com/kd25gjh.
10. Ibid.
11. Mark Weisbrot, Stephan Lefebvre and Joseph Sammut, "Did NAFTA Help Mexico? An Assessment after 20 Years," Center for Economic and Policy Research, February 2014, https://tinyurl.com/jcbaqa5.
12. Ibid.
13. Luis de la Calle and Luis Rubio, "Mexico: A Middle Class Society: Poor No More, Developed Not Yet," Woodrow Wilson International Center for Scholars, January 2012, https://tinyurl.com/knqveuf.
14. Carrie Kahn, "How NAFTA Helped the Mexican Billionaires' Club," NPR, Dec. 13, 2013, https://tinyurl.com/k9jnj4m.
15. Ibid.
16. Ibid.
17. John Summa, "Mexico's New Super-Billionaires," Multinational Monitor, November 1994, http://tinyurl.com/ms2u553; "Carlos Slim Helu & Family," Forbes, May 17, 2017, http://tinyurl.com/msln6bg.
18. Kahn, op. cit.
19. "'Trump Is Not Terminator, He's a Negotiator,' Carlos Slim Says," Telesur, Jan. 27, 2017, http://tinyurl.com/l98bbx3.

20. Elisabeth Malkin, "Mexico Takes Aim at a Titan in Telecom," The New York Times, May 8, 2011, http://tinyurl.com/lrwv3nm; "Global Internet Geography: Capacity and Traffic Trends," TeleGeography, 2014.
21. "U.S. Relations with Mexico: Fact Sheet," U.S. Department of State, Jan. 25, 2017, https://tinyurl.com/j8yn7ef.
22. Villarreal, "U.S.-Mexico Economic Relations," op. cit.
23. "2016 Top Markets Report Automotive Parts Country Case Study," International Trade Administration, 2016, https://tinyurl.com/nyw33ej.
24. Patti Domm, "Trump Is Mad about 'Made in Mexico' Cars—but This Is Bigger," CNBC, Jan. 3, 2017, https://tinyurl.com/gp2d6gp.
25. David Shepardson, "General Motors Says to Invest Additional $1 Billion in U.S.," Reuters, Jan. 17, 2017, https://tinyurl.com/mtoqx8z.
26. Chris Isidore, "Despite Trump, Ford Moves Ahead with Plans for Mexico Plants," CNN Money, Feb. 17, 2017, https://tinyurl.com/mshydqk.
27. Michael A. Hitt, R. Duane Ireland and Robert E. Hoskisson, "Strategic Management: Competitiveness and Globalization," Cengage Learning, Jan. 1, 2014, p. 345.
28. "Sales of the Leading Imported Beer Brands of the United States in 2016 (in Million U.S. Dollars)," Statista, http://tinyurl.com/kcmub4s.
29. "United States of America," Cemex, https://tinyurl.com/l3jnapq.
30. Jude Webber, "Weak Peso Helps Cemex Deliver Bumper Earnings," Financial Times, Feb. 9, 2017, https://tinyurl.com/lxz7ygx.
31. "Industria Farmacéutica: Situación macroeconónomica," Government of Mexico, 2016, https://tinyurl.com/mj78gl2.
32. Topher McDougal, et al., "The Way of the Gun: Estimating Firearms Traffic across the U.S.-Mexico Border," University of San Diego Trans-Border Institute, March 2013, https://tinyurl.com/nstta7o.
33. "FY 15–16 Foreign Military Sales and Direct Commercial Sales Congressional Notifications for Mexico," http://tinyurl.com/kolypr9.
34. "Putting American Workers First: USCIS Announces Further Measures to Detect H-1B Visa Fraud and Abuse," U.S. Citizenship and Immigration Services, Apr. 3, 2017, https://tinyurl.com/lrnhhv7; Hannah Kuchler, Aliya Ram and Jude Webber, "Trump Visa Crackdown Spurs Tech Moves to Mexico," Financial Times, May 4, 2017, https://tinyurl.com/ms9thac.
35. "Mexico Main Topics Weekly," Notimex, Apr. 26, 2017, http://tinyurl.com/ksytrbb.
36. Doug Palmer and Megan Cassella, "NAFTA 2.0 Is Signed—but It's Far from Finished," Politico, Nov. 30, 2018, https://www.politico.com/story/2018/11/30/usmca-signed-g20-999748.
37. Jen Kirby, "USMCA, Trump's New NAFTA Deal, Explained in 600 Words," Vox, Jul. 1, 2020, https://www.vox.com/2018/10/3/17930092/usmca-mexico-nafta-trump-trade-deal-explained.
38. Andrew Chatzky, James McBride and Mohammed Aly Sergie, "NAFTA and the USMCA: Weighing the Impact of North American Trade," Council on Foreign Relations, Jul. 1, 2020, https://www.cfr.org/backgrounder/naftas-economic-impact.
39. Kirby, op. cit.
40. Noi Mahoney, "Borderlands: FedEx Logistics Expands in El Paso; Stanley Black & Decker Picks Mexico for New Plant," Freightwaves, Sep. 6, 2020, https://www.newsbreak.com/news/2055525160955/borderlands-fedex-logistics-expands-in-el-paso-stanley-black-and-decker-picks-mexico-for-new-plant.
41. Sara B. Potter, "Five Economic Charts to Watch: Canada," Insight, Aug. 13, 2020, https://insight.factset.com/five-economic-charts-to-watch-canada-covid-19-edition; Kelsey Johnson, "Canada Extends COVID-19 International Border Closures, Mandatory Quarantine Order," Reuters, Jul. 1, 2020, https://www.reuters.com/article/us-health-coronavirus-canada/canada-extends-covid-19-international-border-closures-mandatory-quarantine-order-idUSKBN2413AY.
42. Michael Crowley, "Trump Welcomes Mexico's President in Surprisingly Warm Terms," The New York Times, Jul. 8, 2020, https://www.nytimes.com/2020/07/08/us/politics/trump-mexico-president-andres-manuel-lopez-obrador.html.

Chapter 17: The On-Demand Economy

1. Alan Ohnsman, "Honeymoon's Over? GM Cruise Said to Turn to Uber as Lyft Alliance Cools," Forbes, Oct. 18, 2017, http://tinyurl.com/y994f3al; Stephen Edelstein, "Book by Cadillac Car Subscription Service Expands to Los Angeles and Dallas," The Drive, Nov. 13, 2017, http://tinyurl.com/y8m3wx6x.
2. Charles Colby and Kelly Bell, "The On-Demand Economy Is Growing, and Not Just for the Young and Wealthy," Harvard Business Review, Apr. 14 2016, http://tinyurl.com/h9v4bqr.
3. Alan Amling, "My Way Highway—the Future of Delivery in Our New On-Demand Economy," TED.com, Oct. 29, 2015, http://tinyurl.com/ya3ccs5y.
4. Ibid.
5. "How the On-Demand Economy Is Changing the Concept of Luxury," Porsche/Quartz Media, https://tinyurl.com/y83o9elo.
6. Colby and Bell, op. cit.
7. Ibid.
8. "Freelancing in America: 2017," Upwork Global, Oct. 17, 2017, https://tinyurl.com/ybcmfx92.

9. "Worldwide Retail Ecommerce Sales Will Reach $1.915 Trillion This Year," eMarketer, Aug. 22, 2016, http://tinyurl.com/y7n6c4tu.
10. Ayat Shukairy, "Mobile Commerce Statistics and Trends," Invesp, undated, accessed Nov. 6, 2017, http://tinyurl.com/ycltzd64.
11. Cathy Boyle, "Mobile Commerce Trends," eMarketer, Jul. 24, 2014, http://tinyurl.com/y76322ul.
12. Sunil Rajaraman. "The On-Demand Economy Is a Bubble—and It's About to Burst," Quartz Media, Apr. 28, 2017, https://tinyurl.com/y7ummfzl/.
13. Ibid.
14. Farhad Manjoo, "The Uber Model, It Turns Out, Doesn't Translate," The New York Times, Mar. 24, 2016, https://tinyurl.com/y7jskvn7.
15. Sam Shead, "ANALYST: Food Delivery and Valet Parking Startups Are Turning Out to Be 'Donkeys Not Unicorns,'" Business Insider, Mar. 21, 2016, https://tinyurl.com/yaxu4or8.
16. Nathan Resnick, "The On-Demand Economy: What It Is and How It's Changing Business," Business.com, Apr. 26, 2017, https://tinyurl.com/yaqrcb7a.
17. Richard Fry, "Millennials Overtake Baby Boomers as America's Largest Generation," Pew Research Center, Apr. 25, 2016, http://tinyurl.com/hapcwq3.
18. Colby and Bell, op. cit.
19. Lisa Gevelber, "Micro-Moments Now: 3 New Consumer Behaviors Playing Out in Google Search Data," Think with Google, July 2017, https://tinyurl.com/y78acupb.
20. Lisa Gevelber, "Micro-Moments Now: Why Expectations for 'Right Now' Are on the Rise," Think with Google, August 2017, http://tinyurl.com/yafmm7cf.
21. Karl Siebrecht, "Every Company Is an Ecommerce Company," Supply Chain 24/7, Dec. 20, 2017, https://tinyurl.com/y98jxmlo.
22. Kevin O'Marah, "Zara Uses Supply Chain to Win Again," Forbes, Mar. 9, 2016, http://tinyurl.com/y8shltp7.
23. Nelson M. Fraiman, et al., "Zara," Summer 2008, https://tinyurl.com/y6wzhqx4.
24. Maya Kosoff, "Is This the End of the On-Demand Era?" Vanity Fair, Mar. 23, 2016, http://tinyurl.com/y8wtr2hk.
25. Ellen Huet, "What Really Killed Homejoy? It Couldn't Hold on to Its Customers," Forbes, Jul. 23, 2015, http://tinyurl.com/yat2pa7k.
26. Biz Carson, "The 'Uber for Private Jets' Startup Backed by an Uber Cofounder Is Shutting Down," Business Insider, May 6, 2016, http://tinyurl.com/gofv5hh.
27. Sam Shead, "Take Eat Easy Is Shutting Down Its Food Delivery Business As Uber Muscles In," Business Insider, Jul. 26, 2016, http://tinyurl.com/ybdcnwqz; "Local Commerce on an API," OrdrX.com, Apr. 15, 2015, http://tinyurl.com/ychyvkd9.
28. Selina Wang, "Sidecar Squeezed Out by Uber and Lyft, Will Shut Down," Bloomberg, Dec. 29, 2015, http://tinyurl.com/zmnksze; Catherine Clifford, "Carpooling Startup Tripda Runs Out of Gas, to Shut Down," Entrepreneur, Feb. 29, 2016, http://tinyurl.com/yd4lfyf2; "Carpooling Startup Ridejoy Shutting Down," The Wall Street Journal, Dec. 17, 2013, http://tinyurl.com/y9qnlxxo.
29. Kia Kokalitcheva, "Why This Valet Parking Startup Gave Up on Its Uber-Like Service," Fortune, Apr. 11, 2016, http://tinyurl.com/ycxsfdkf.
30. Max Taves, "Is the On-Demand Economy Dying?" CNET, Mar. 20, 2016, http://tinyurl.com/ya5rxly7.
31. "In What Areas Is Occupancy Tax Collection and Remittance by Airbnb Available?" Airbnb, undated, accessed Nov. 20, 2017, http://tinyurl.com/hccwne7.
32. Zach Schiller and Carl Davis, "Taxes and the On-Demand Economy," Institute on Taxation and Economic Policy, Mar. 15, 2017, http://tinyurl.com/ybfmobyj.
33. Rhode Island House Bill 8044, passed Jun. 7, 2016, http://tinyurl.com/yachbhs8.
34. HB 225, "Ride Share Networks; Licensing and Sales Tax Exemption; Repeal Inoperable Provisions," Georgia Legislature, undated, accessed Dec. 4, 2017, http://tinyurl.com/ybuyuzwd.
35. Senate Bill S6340A, New York State Senate, signed Oct. 21, 2016, http://tinyurl.com/yamsladv.
36. Greg Bensinger, "Airbnb Settles New York State Suit, Focusing on City," The Wall Street Journal, Nov. 22, 2016, http://tinyurl.com/yalo7fj7.
37. Liz Alderman, "Uber Dealt Setback After European Court Rules It Is a Taxi Service," The New York Times, Dec. 20, 2017, http://tinyurl.com/y8gcztf5.
38. "McGillis v. Department of Economic Opportunity; and Raiser LLC, d/b/a UBER," 3rd District Court of Appeal—State of Florida, Feb. 1, 2017, http://tinyurl.com/y7hwlhqf.
39. Sarah Kessler, "Pixel & Dimed on (Not) Getting by in the Gig Economy," Fast Company, Mar. 18, 2014, http://tinyurl.com/y7eha6e3.
40. Joint Legislative Audit and Review Commission, "Review of Employee Misclassification in Virginia," June 2012, http://tinyurl.com/ybuwc558.
41. Sarah Kessler, "The Gig Economy Won't Last Long Because It's Being Sued to Death," Fast Company, Feb. 17, 2015, http://tinyurl.com/yabbr7do.
42. Susan Johnston Taylor, "Why These Gig-Economy Startups Hire Salaried Employees Instead of Contractors," Fast Company, May 22, 2017, http://tinyurl.com/kjwsnqb.
43. "Legislation to Test-Drive Portable Benefit Models Introduced in the House and Senate," press release, Office of Sen. Mark Warner, May 25, 2017, http://tinyurl.com/y7zydtzh.
44. Mitch Ratcliffe, "Sizing the Local On-Demand Economy: 2016–2017," BIA/Kelsey, Feb. 1, 2017, http://tinyurl.com/yc8ql6o6.

45. "On-Demand Cools Down: Funding to On-Demand Startups Fell 35% in 2016," CBInsights, Feb. 7, 2017, http://tinyurl.com/ybnhkmph.
46. Mark McDonald, "On-Demand Is in Demand," Accenture, undated, accessed Dec. 1, 2017, http://tinyurl.com/y8bsurjc.
47. Ibid.
48. "The 2017 SAP Hybris Global Consumer Insights Report," SAP, undated, accessed Dec. 26, 2017, http://tinyurl.com/ybnag6zj.
49. "Prime Now," Amazon, undated, accessed Dec. 21, 2017, http://tinyurl.com/mha4zcc.
50. Jeremiah Owyang, "Meet the Resilient Corporations," web-strategist.com, Sep. 15, 2013, http://tinyurl.com/l3qru9o.
51. Dapeng Zhang, "Hyperloop One's Transport Economist Makes the Freight Case," Hyperloop One, Jan. 26, 2017, http://tinyurl.com/y9gqyvc8.
52. Todd Bishop, "Amazon Shelling Out Record Sums for Shipping in Push for Faster Delivery," GeekWire, Oct. 29, 2016, http://tinyurl.com/ycvcvb5y.
53. Pat Conroy, et al., "Consumer Product Trends: Navigating 2020," Deloitte Insights, Jun. 25, 2015, https://tinyurl.com/yd8hgkp4.
54. Rockbridge Associates, "On-Demand Economy Research," May 2019, https://rockresearch.com/on-demand-economy-research/.
55. Sasha Lekach, "Delivery Apps Become Essential for Restaurants to Survive during Pandemic," Mashable, Jul. 21, 2020, https://tinyurl.com/y6l4bm5b.
56. Natasha Lomas, "Europe's Deliveroo and Glovo Switch on Contactless Delivery during COVID-19 Pandemic," Tech Crunch, Mar. 12, 2020, https://techcrunch.com/2020/03/12/europes-deliveroo-and-glovo-switch-on-contactless-delivery-during-covid-19-pandemic/.
57. Sasha Lekach, "Lyft Dips Toes into Food Delivery for First Time," Mashable, Oct. 6, 2020, https://tinyurl.com/y2b6oyxs.
58. Veta Chan, "Grab CEO Anthony Tan Says the Pandemic's Digital Revolution Is 'Permanent'," Fortune, Aug. 13, 2020, https://tinyurl.com/yxweymdu.
59. Yoolim Lee, "Grab Accelerates Expansion of Deliveries across Southeast Asia," Bloomberg, Jun. 4, 2020, https://tinyurl.com/yxwvnypo; Low Zoey, "COVID-19: Grab Cuts 360 Employees in 'Last Organisation-Wide Layoff' This Year," Channel News Asia, Jun. 16, 2020, https://tinyurl.com/yxnrvraz.
60. Medallia Zingle, "COVID-19 & the Future of Commerce," May 2020, https://cdn2.hubspot.net/hubfs/393073/2020%20Consumer%20Report/MedZing2020-Future-Of-Commerce-Report-FNL.pdf.
61. Brian Dumaine, "Amazon Was Built for the Pandemic—and Will Likely Emerge from It Stronger Than Ever," Fortune Magazine, May 18, 2020, https://fortune.com/2020/05/18/amazon-business-jeff-bezos-amzn-sales-revenue-coronavirus-pandemic/.
62. Alina Selyukh, "Walmart Hires Almost a Quarter-Million Workers As Sales Soar," NPR, May 19, 2020, https://www.npr.org/sections/coronavirus-live-updates/2020/05/19/858558844/walmart-hires-almost-a-quarter-million-workers-as-sales-soar.
63. Greg Iacurci, "13 Million Gig Workers Getting Unemployment Benefits, 41% of the Total," CNBC, Jul. 6, 2020, https://www.cnbc.com/2020/07/06/pua-unemployment-benefits-being-paid-to-about-13-million-americans.html.
64. Clayton Rose, "Message to the Campus Community," Bowdoin College, Jun. 22, 2020, https://www.bowdoin.edu/president/writings-and-addresses/messages-to-the-community/2020/june-22.html.

Chapter 18: The Sharing Economy

1. "Every Day in the Sharing Economy, There Are . . . ," Peers, undated, accessed Jul. 15, 2015, http://tinyurl.com/q2czmqn; Ellen Huet, "Uber Says It's Doing 1 Million Rides per Day, 140 Million in Last Year," Forbes, Dec. 17, 2014, http://tinyurl.com/pjyhavq.
2. Scott Austin, Chris Canipe and Sarah Slobin, "The Billion Dollar Startup Club," The Wall Street Journal, updated Jul. 2015, http://tinyurl.com/pbfqsfk.
3. "FTC to Examine Competition, Consumer Protection, and Economic Issues Raised by the Sharing Economy at June Workshop," press release, Federal Trade Commission, Apr. 17, 2015, http://tinyurl.com/ombw5u5.
4. "The Sharing Economy—Sizing the Revenue Opportunity," PricewaterhouseCoopers, undated, accessed Jul. 1, 2015, http://tinyurl.com/oxrhsbm.
5. "Testimony by Alan Mond," House Committee on Small Business, Jan. 15, 2014 http://tinyurl.com/nurboxe.
6. "Written Testimony of Philip Auerswald," House Committee on Small Business, Jan. 15, 2014, http://tinyurl.com/nhu3o2u.
7. Colleen Walsh, "The Big Share: HBS Historian Examines a New Kind of Connectivity," Harvard Gazette, Aug. 5, 2014, http://tinyurl.com/pwcn95b.
8. Boyd Cohen and Jan Kietzmann, "Ride On! Mobility Business Models for the Sharing Economy," Organization & Environment, Aug. 13, 2014, http://tinyurl.com/psqaqlp.
9. Walsh, op. cit.
10. Liz Krueger, "Letter to FTC Regarding the 'Sharing Economy,'" May 28, 2015, http://tinyurl.com/pzrn57o.
11. Brian Chesky, "Who We Are, What We Stand For," Airbnb blog, Oct. 3, 2013, http://tinyurl.com/o8sdzx6.
12. Mark John, "UberPOP Halts Service in France after Clampdown, Protests," Reuters, Jul. 3, 2015, http://tinyurl.com/p6j4aje.
13. Walsh, op. cit.
14. Eric T. Schneiderman, "Airbnb in the City," New York State Office of the Attorney General, Oct. 14, 2014, http://tinyurl.com/m8pqffb.

15. Annie Karni, "De Blasio Administration Files First Lawsuit against Apartments Operating as Illegal Hotels through Sites Like Airbnb," New York Daily News, Oct. 17, 2014, http://tinyurl.com/qguha7n.
16. Mike Isaac and Natasha Singer, "California Says Uber Driver Is Employee, Not a Contractor," The New York Times, Jun. 17, 2015, http://tinyurl.com/qzmxqgl.
17. Frank Shafroth, "The Unforeseen Fiscal Challenges of Uber-Like Services," Government Technology, Mar. 20, 2015, http://tinyurl.com/pmh3mlj.
18. Benjamin Davis, Tony Dutzik and Phineas Baxandall, "Transportation and the New Generation," U.S. PIRG Education Fund and the Frontier Group, April 2012, http://tinyurl.com/764qecl.
19. Shafroth, op. cit.
20. "Staff Memo to the House Committee on Small Business," House of Representatives Committee on Small Business, Jan. 10, 2014, http://tinyurl.com/ovysxfu.
21. Jonathan V. Hall and Alan B. Krueger, "An Analysis of the Labor Market for Uber's Driver-Partners in the United States," Working Paper #587, Princeton University, Jan. 22, 2015, http://tinyurl.com/n5norw8.
22. Sarah Cannon and Lawrence H. Summers, "How Uber and the Sharing Economy Can Win Over Regulators," Harvard Business Review, Oct. 13, 2014, http://tinyurl.com/ntpcweq.
23. Cohen, op. cit.
24. Rachel Botsman and Roo Rogers, "What's Mine Is Yours: The Rise of Collaborative Consumption," 2010, p. 114.
25. Maya Kosoff, "Uber Drivers across the Country Are Protesting Today—Here's Why," Business Insider, Oct. 22, 2014, http://tinyurl.com/ojcwaxx.
26. Ibid.
27. Matthew Feeney, "Level the Playing Field—by Deregulating," Cato Unbound, Feb. 10, 2015, http://tinyurl.com/onphurf.
28. Arun Sundararajan, "Peer-to-Peer Businesses and the Sharing (Collaborative) Economy: Overview, Economic Effects and Regulatory Issues," House Committee on Small Business, Jan. 14, 2014, http://tinyurl.com/pm3r3c5.
29. Feeney, op. cit.
30. James Niccolai, "Uber and Lyft Fail to Convince Judges Their Drivers Are Merely 'Contractors,'" Computerworld, Mar. 12, 2015, http://tinyurl.com/ocwr69j.
31. Isaac and Singer, op. cit.
32. "Topic 762—Independent Contractor vs. Employee," Internal Revenue Service, updated May 27, 2015, http://tinyurl.com/yonzjs.
33. Arun Sundararajan, "A Safety Net Fit for the Sharing Economy," Financial Times, Jun. 22, 2015, http://tinyurl.com/q8w6ude.
34. Yochai Benkler, "Sharing Nicely: On Shareable Goods and the Emergence of Sharing as a Modality of Economic Production," The Yale Law Journal, 2004, Vol. 114, pp. 273-358.
35. Kevin Kelly, "We Are the Web," Wired, August 2005, http://tinyurl.com/p2zdsbw.
36. Ibid.
37. Dustin S. Klein, "Visionary in Obscurity," Smart Business, Jul. 22, 2002, http://tinyurl.com/o42v34t.
38. Nicole Achs Freeling, "The Nerd's Revenge," California CEO, February 2001, http://tinyurl.com/ojfvam8.
39. Zigmund, "Step Back in Time with Pierre Omidyar and Jeff Skoll," The Chatter Newsletter, eBay, 2005, http://tinyurl.com/qaqx4la.
40. Alex Stephany, "The Business of Sharing," New York, 2015, p. 71.
41. Ibid., p. 87.
42. Mimi Whitefield, "Airbnb Cracking the Cuban Market," The Miami Herald, Jul. 5, 2015, http://tinyurl.com/noq6f5u.
43. Stephany, op. cit., p. 73.
44. Chase, op. cit., p. 8.
45. Ibid., p. 9.
46. Ibid., p. 13.
47. "History & Background Information," Freecycle, undated, accessed Jul. 17, 2015, http://tinyurl.com/qjzml3k.
48. "About Zopa," Zopa, undated, accessed Jul. 17, 2015, http://tinyurl.com/25g8bo.
49. "Alternative Financial Services: A Primer," FDIC Quarterly, Apr. 27, 2009, http://tinyurl.com/p643omd.
50. For background, see Robin D. Schatz, "Crowdfunding," SAGE Business Researcher, Feb. 9, 2015, http://tinyurl.com/pk4alyg.
51. Patrick Hoge, "Colorado Becomes the First State to Pass Law Embracing Uber, Lyft et al.," San Francisco Business Times, Jun. 5, 2014, http://tinyurl.com/pee39hf.
52. Alicia Freese, "Fair Share? Officials Struggle to Regulate Vermont's 'Sharing Economy,'" Seven Days, Apr. 8, 2015, http://tinyurl.com/padu6gt.
53. Joseph Rose, "Portland Makes Uber and Lyft Legal—for Now," The Oregonian/OregonLive, Apr. 22, 2015, http://tinyurl.com/ofp2fgx.
54. Brian Heaton, "California Bill Takes Aim at Home-Sharing Websites," Government Technology, May 4, 2015, http://tinyurl.com/ozytgds.
55. John Ribeiro, "Uber Stops Operations in Kansas over New Legislation," PC World, May 6, 2015, http://tinyurl.com/nbkqqup.
56. Sam Sanders, "Santa Monica Cracks Down on Airbnb, Bans 'Vacation Rentals' under a Month," NPR, May 13, 2015, http://tinyurl.com/oqgozky.
57. Joe Fitzgerald Rodriguez, "SFO, SFMTA Ask State for Stricter Regulations of Uber and Lyft," The San Francisco Examiner, May 27, 2015, http://tinyurl.com/od9rnu3.
58. "Governor Signs Bills Giving Green Light to Rideshare Services Uber and Lyft," The Associated Press, The Las Vegas Sun, May 29, 2015, http://tinyurl.com/nheq467.

59. Martyn Williams, "Lyft to Pay $300K, Make Insurance Changes in Settlement with N.Y.," Computerworld, Jun. 18, 2015, http://tinyurl.com/nlxcr68.
60. "The Road Ahead," Uber document submitted to the Portland, Ore., Bureau of Transportation, undated, accessed Jul. 17, 2015, http://tinyurl.com/omrzatv.
61. Don Jergler, "Uber Announces New Policy to Cover Gap," Insurance Journal, Mar. 14, 2014, http://tinyurl.com/pbq2w4t.
62. Brian R. Fitzgerald, "Airbnb: Accidents Can Happen, So Here's $1 Million in Liability Insurance," Digits, The Wall Street Journal, Nov. 20, 2014, http://tinyurl.com/np4t583.
63. Emily Badger, "Airbnb Is About to Start Collecting Hotel Taxes in More Major Cities, Including Washington," The Washington Post, Jan. 29, 2015, http://tinyurl.com/nac6kdd.
64. Elaine S. Povich, "How Governments Are Trying to Tax the Sharing Economy," Governing, Jun. 18, 2014, http://tinyurl.com/o6kgtao.
65. Colleen Walsh, "The Big Share: HBS Historian Examines a New Kind of Connectivity," Harvard Gazette, Aug. 5, 2014, http://tinyurl.com/pzaabz5.
66. Sarah Cannon and Lawrence H. Summers, "How Uber and the Sharing Economy Can Win over Regulators," Harvard Business Review, Oct. 13, 2014, http://tinyurl.com/nb455kt.
67. Robin Chase, "Peers Inc: How People and Platforms Are Inventing the Collaborative Economy and Reinventing Capitalism," 2015, p. 250.
68. Robert Reich, "The Share-the-Scraps Economy," Feb. 2, 2015, http://tinyurl.com/mjyjwyg.
69. Jeff Hong, "Rise of the Sharing Economy and the Future of Travel and Tourism Industry," Journal of Hotel and Business Management, January 2018, https://www.researchgate.net/publication/330493234_Rise_of_the_Sharing_Economy_and_the_Future_of_Travel_and_Tourism_Industry.
70. Kate Conger and Erin Griffith, "The Results Are in for the Sharing Economy. And It's Ugly," The New York Times, May 7, 2020, https://www.nytimes.com/2020/05/07/technology/the-results-are-in-for-the-sharing-economy-they-are-ugly.html.
71. Andrew Sheivachman, "Sharing Economy Goes Mainstream in Business Travel," Skift, Feb. 2, 2017, https://skift.com/2017/02/02/sharing-economy-goes-mainstream-in-business-travel-skift-corporate-travel-innovation-report/.
72. Brian Solomon, "Ride-Share Pioneer Sidecar Shuts Down, Outmuscled by Uber and Lyft," Forbes, Dec. 29, 2015, https://www.forbes.com/sites/briansolomon/2015/12/29/ride-share-pioneer-sidecar-shuts-down-outmuscled-by-uber-and-lyft/#78daeaee29fe.
73. Sam Shead, "Uber's Rocky Road to Growth in Europe: Regulators, Rivals and Riots," Forbes, May 10, 2019, https://www.forbes.com/sites/samshead/2019/05/10/ubers-rocky-road-to-growth-in-europe-regulators-rivals-and-riots/#6e3fe7d15c67.
74. Kate Conger, "California Sues Uber and Lyft, Claiming Workers Are Misclassified," The New York Times, May 5, 2020, https://www.nytimes.com/2020/05/05/technology/california-uber-lyft-lawsuit.html.
75. Kayla Simas, "NY State Will Provide Benefits to Uber, Lyft Drivers," Staten Island Advance, Dec. 21, 2019, https://www.silive.com/news/2019/12/ny-state-will-provide-benefits-to-uber-lyft-drivers.html.
76. Sasha Lekach, "Uber Will Scan Drivers' Faces to Make Sure They're Wearing Masks," MashableIndia, May 14, 2020, https://mashable.com/article/drivers-and-passengers-have-to-wear-mask-in-uber/; Alicia Lee, "Uber and Lyft Suspend Pool Rides in US and Canada to Reduce the Spread of Coronavirus," CNN, Mar. 18, 2020, https://www.cnn.com/2020/03/17/business/coronavirus-uber-pool-trnd/index.html.
77. "Extenuating Circumstances Policy and the Coronavirus (COVID-19)," Airbnb, updated Oct. 1, 2020, https://www.airbnb.com/help/article/2701/extenuating-circumstances-policy-and-the-coronavirus-covid19; Cailey Rizzo, "Airbnb Expands COVID-19 Rules, Requires Guests and Hosts to Wear Face Masks When Meeting," Travel+Leisure, Oct. 8, 2020, https://tinyurl.com/y3zmcn4l.

REFERENCES

Chapter 1: Bitcoin

BOOKS

Narayanan, Arvind, et al., "Bitcoin and Cryptocurrency Technologies: A Comprehensive Introduction," Princeton University Press, 2016.

Professors from Princeton, Stanford and the University of Maryland provide a comprehensive introduction to the revolutionary technologies of digital currency.

ARTICLES

Angel, Jim, "Approving Bitcoin ETFs Will Lead Investors to Slaughter," The Hill, Mar. 7, 2017, https://tinyurl.com/ydgbbkks.

A Georgetown University business professor argues against the approval of bitcoin-based exchange-traded funds (ETFs).

Bustillos, Maria, "The Bitcoin Boom," The New Yorker, Apr. 1, 2013, https://tinyurl.com/y9hgplkb.

In an age of mistrust of institutions, a writer argues that bitcoin is becoming an attractive alternative to banks and fiat currencies.

Cuthbertson, Anthony, "North Korea Hacking War on Bitcoin Exchanges Is Part of 'Biggest Global Sting,'" Newsweek, Dec. 19, 2017, https://tinyurl.com/y7r9m5ej.

Cybersecurity researchers accuse North Korea of stealing bitcoins to offset negative effects of international trade sanctions.

DeRousseau, Ryan, "There's a Hidden Bitcoin Tax You Need to Know About," Money magazine, Nov. 2, 2017, https://tinyurl.com/y9wtkslc.

Many people do not realize that the Internal Revenue Service considers bitcoin property and therefore sales are subject to capital gains taxes, a tax lawyer says.

Galland, David, "5 Industries That Blockchain Will Likely Disrupt by 2020," Forbes, Mar. 29, 2017, https://tinyurl.com/ya28z6du.

A partner in an investment firm writes that the real value of bitcoin may be in the technology behind it and the uses it has for other industries.

Greenberg, Andy, "Monero, the Drug Dealer's Cryptocurrency of Choice, Is on Fire," Wired, Jan. 25, 2018, https://tinyurl.com/jyt9phj.

A journalist writes that as bitcoin is better tracked by the authorities, other cryptocurrencies rise to take its place as the currency of choice of criminals and terrorists.

Kharif, Olga, "The Bitcoin Whales: 1,000 People Who Own 40 Percent of the Market," Bloomberg Businessweek, Dec. 8, 2017, https://tinyurl.com/ycuqxnvd.

One of the biggest dangers of the bitcoin market may be that the assets are very closely held by a handful of investors, many of whom are now billionaires, say market watchers.

McMillan, Robert, "The Inside Story of Mt. Gox, Bitcoin's $460 Million Disaster," Wired, Mar. 3, 2014, https://tinyurl.com/yah84nzn.

Mt. Gox was the biggest bitcoin exchange—until alleged hackers stole 850,000 bitcoins.

Popper, Nathaniel, "How the Winklevoss Twins Found Vindication in a Bitcoin Fortune," The New York Times, Dec. 19, 2017, https://tinyurl.com/ycbdsrhr.

A journalist profiles the brothers, who made a fortune by investing a settlement with Facebook in bitcoin and are now are among the biggest cryptocurrency proponents.

Rosic, Ameer, "What Is Blockchain Technology? A Step-by-Step Guide for Beginners," Blockgeeks .com, February 2017, https://tinyurl.com/mkmf62o.

Blockchain technology is explained for the non-technologist.

Seidel, Marc-David L., "Bitcoin Is Making Banks Nervous. Here's Why," Agenda, World Economic Forum, Oct. 6. 2017, https://tinyurl.com/yahl9v6p.

A professor of entrepreneurship explores why the philosophy behind bitcoin and other cryptocurrencies is such a threat to the financial establishments.

Wu, Tim, "The Bitcoin Boom: In Code We Trust," The New York Times, Dec. 18, 2017, https://tinyurl.com/y7qy5asq.

A Columbia University law professor explains the deep mistrust of institutions and other humans that makes cryptocurrencies' reliance on technology so attractive.

REPORTS AND STUDIES

Nakamoto, Satoshi, "Bitcoin: A Peer-to-Peer Electronic Cash," Satoshi Nakamoto Institute, Oct. 31, 2008, https://tinyurl.com/zbmcts5.

This is the original white paper that started bitcoin and the cryptocurrency boom.

THE NEXT STEP

JASPER PROJECT

Clay, Melanie, "Canada Should Listen to UK Treasury's Questions about Digital Currency Investing," Coinsquare, Feb. 26, 2018, https://tinyurl.com/y7keqsox.

Canada should pay attention to the questions that the United Kingdom is asking about investing in cryptocurrencies, argues a Coinsquare writer.

Ligaya, Armina, "Canadian Securities Exchange to Launch Blockchain-Based Clearing House," The Toronto Star, Feb. 13, 2018, https://tinyurl.com/ydehlrn4.

The Canadian Securities Exchange's plan to create a blockchain-based securities trading platform challenges another initiative called Project Jasper that the TMX Group is developing with the Bank of Canada and Payments Canada.

Wilkins, Carolyn, "Project Jasper: Lessons from Bank of Canada's First Blockchain Project," Coindesk, May 19, 2017, https://tinyurl.com/ybo4v6hq.

The first six months of testing on Project Jasper show that a distributed ledger technology could be used in the private sector, says the senior deputy governor of the Bank of Canada.

SATOSHI NAKAMOTO

Al Ali, Nour, and Chris Kingdon, "Musk: I Am Not Bitcoin's Satoshi Nakamoto," Bloomberg, Nov. 28, 2017, https://tinyurl.com/yancnmfu.

Tech mogul Elon Musk denied that he founded bitcoin after a Medium blog post made a speculative claim to that effect.

Brandom, Russell, "Self-proclaimed Satoshi Craig Wright Is Being Sued for Stealing His Partner's Bitcoin," The Verge, Feb. 26, 2018, https://tinyurl.com/y9lgmxc7.

Craig Wright, who claimed in 2016 that he was the secretive bitcoin founder, is being sued for bitcoin theft by the estate of his deceased former partner in a bitcoin-mining venture.

Wile, Rob, "Bitcoin's Mysterious Creator Appears to Be Sitting on a $5.8 Billion Fortune," Money magazine, Oct. 31, 2017, https://tinyurl.com/y7g4wvsy.

Whoever Satoshi Nakamoto actually is, the mysterious founder of the original virtual currency is sitting on holdings of 980,000 individual bitcoins, according to research by the head of a cryptocurrency firm.

ORGANIZATIONS

American Cryptocurrency Association
www.usacryptoassociation.com/
www.linkedin.com/company/american-cryptocurrency-association/

Association dedicated to bitcoin advocacy and dissemination of bitcoin news.

The Bitcoin Foundation Inc.
1 Ferry Building, Suite 255, San Francisco, CA 94111

https://bitcoinfoundation.org/
llew@bitcoinfoundation.org

Organization dedicated to educating the public and media about the benefits of bitcoin and its technology.

Chamber of Digital Commerce
https://digitalchamber.org/
info@digitalchamber.org
https://www.linkedin.com/company/chamber-of-digital-commerce/

Trade association and political action committee working on behalf of digital commerce and technology innovations, such as blockchain.

DC Blockchain Innovation Center
1133 15th St., N.W., 12th Floor, Washington, DC 20001
1-202-765-3105
https://digitalchamber.org/initiatives/dc-blockchain-center/
hello@dcblockchaincenter.com

Blockchain innovation center created by the Chamber of Digital Commerce.

Global Blockchain Business Council
1440 G St., N.W., 9th floor, Washington, DC 20005
https://www.gbbcouncil.org/
info@gbbcouncil.org

A group that seeks to advance understanding of blockchain technology and promote its adoption.

Wall Street Blockchain Alliance
https://www.wsba.co/
info@wsba.co

Trade association working to guide and promote comprehensive adoption of distributed ledger technology across financial markets.

Chapter 2: Brexit

BOOKS

Connolly, Bernard, "The Rotten Heart of Europe: The Dirty War for Europe's Money," Faber & Faber, 1995.

A senior economist for the European Commission was sacked for writing what became the classic insider exposé about the drawbacks of the common currency.

Hannan, Daniel, "A Doomed Marriage: Why Britain Should Leave the EU," Notting Hill Editions, 2012.

A Conservative member of the European Parliament, who is an articulate and thoughtful opponent of the European Union, argues that the entire edifice should be dismantled.

Judt, Tony, "Postwar: A History of Europe Since 1945," Heinemann, 2005.

A British historian provides a wide-ranging account of postwar Europe that recounts the formation of the European Union in easily comprehensible language.

Young, Hugo, "This Blessed Plot: Britain and Europe from Churchill to Blair," Macmillan, 1998.

A history of Great Britain's relationship with the rest of Europe by a journalist from the generations of Britons who enthused over the EU as a means to bring peace to the continent.

ARTICLES

"Britain's New Prime Minister: May Time," The Economist, Jul. 16, 2016, http://econ.st/29H7wfm.

An analysis of the incoming government's options, summarized as "soft Brexit" or "hard Brexit."

Davis, David, "May's New Chief Europe Negotiator David Davis Lays Out Plans to Take Us Out of EU," The Sun, Jul. 15, 2016, http://tinyurl.com/jzowdkl.

The cabinet minister in charge of Brexit negotiations sets out why he believes the U.K. is in a strong negotiating position.

Johnson, Boris, "I Cannot Stress Too Much That Britain Is Part of Europe—and Always Will Be," The Daily Telegraph, Jun. 26, 2016, http://tinyurl.com/gsskfmz.

The Brexit leader and future foreign secretary asserts that a post-Brexit U.K. could have the advantages of the single market without permitting free movement of labor.

Partington, Richard, and John Glover, "Brexit May Cut Investment Banks' Revenue by $8 Billion, BCG Says," Bloomberg News, Jul. 15, 2016, http://bloom.bg/29zWqdy.

An assessment of Brexit's impact on the global investment banking industry by Boston Consulting Group.

REPORTS AND STUDIES

Dartmouth, William, "Inconvenient Truths about UK Trade and the EU," Institute for Direct Democracy in Europe, 2016, http://tinyurl.com/zog2ghm.

The 10th Earl of Dartmouth, a member of the European Parliament from the U.K. Independence Party, argues that EU regulations harm the British economy; the paper has useful statistical tables.

"The Economic and Financial Costs and Benefits of the EU's UK membership," House of Commons Treasury Committee, May 2016, http://tinyurl.com/hzpwbwc.

A detailed and generally even-handed report—published a month before the vote and therefore one of the best guides to the problems ahead—by a committee consisting of supporters and opponents of Brexit.

"The Economic Consequences of Brexit: A Taxing Decision," Organisation for Economic Co-operation and Development, April 2016, http://tinyurl.com/gskjrfm.

The international body, in which 39 countries that control 80 percent of world trade cooperate in dealing with globalization and related issues, warns that "Brexit would be akin to a tax on GDP, imposing a persistent and rising cost on the economy."

"European Union Finances," Her Majesty's Treasury, 2015, http://tinyurl.com/huhrbl8.

This is the most authoritative source for information on how much the U.K. contributes to the EU budget and how much is returned as a rebate or in regional grants and subsidies.

"HM Treasury Analysis: The Immediate Economic Impact of Leaving the EU," Her Majesty's Government, May 2016, http://tinyurl.com/hxfnjz7.

The U.K. Treasury issues a dire warning about the consequences of Brexit.

"HM Treasury Analysis: The Long-Term Economic Impact of EU Membership and the Alternatives," Her Majesty's Government, April 2016, http://tinyurl.com/jar59tq.

This was the British government's authoritative warning against voting Brexit, with predictions of dire economic consequences.

"Top 100 EU Rules Cost Britain £33.3bn," Open Europe, March 2015, http://tinyurl.com/jubwhjt.

A report by a think tank seeking EU reforms produces the source to which Brexit campaigners refer when arguing that freeing U.K. businesses from EU regulations would produce big dividends. The paper is more factual and carefully argued than some of the statements that have drawn on it.

"Uncertainty Clouds the United Kingdom's Economic Prospects," IMF Survey, International Monetary Fund, Jun. 17, 2016, http://tinyurl.com/hmmdg8h.

The IMF warns that the economic and financial impact of Brexit on the U.K. will be "substantial."

THE NEXT STEP

EUROPEAN MIGRANT CRISIS

Parfitt, Tom, "Theresa May Will Slash EU Migrant Numbers After Brexit, Tory Chairman Vows," Daily Express, Jul. 24, 2016, http://tinyurl.com/ho3zsz7.

New U.K. Prime Minister Theresa May is committed to cutting the number of migrants allowed in Britain after it withdraws from the European Union, Britain's Conservative Party chairman says.

Shackle, Samira, "Brexit Fallout: Anti-Migrant Attacks Surge in the UK," Al Jazeera, Jul. 25, 2016, http://tinyurl.com/gurqfr6.

Hate crimes are up 57 percent since Brexit, and human rights advocates and British immigrants blame anti-immigrant sentiment linked to the Leave campaign's use of scare tactics on migration to gain support.

Szakacs, Gergely, "Hungary's Migrant Referendum Shows Europe's Post-Brexit Challenge," Reuters, Jul. 1, 2016, http://tinyurl.com/huf28sf.

In the wake of the Brexit vote, Hungary's leader Viktor Orban is going toe-to-toe with the EU Commission over its plan to resettle refugees across member states based on quotas.

EU CHANGES

Chazan, David, "Jean-Claude Juncker Admits Brexit Talks Cannot Begin in Months as There Is 'No Deadline' for Britain to Invoke Article 50," The Telegraph, Jul. 25, 2016, http://tinyurl.com/j3tr2y2.

The European Commission president acknowledges Britain's need for time in negotiating its departure from the EU.

McAuley, James, "With Britain's Exit from the European Union, France Sees an Opening," The Washington Post, Jul. 18, 2016, http://tinyurl.com/z4nccew.

The French political mainstream sees Brexit as an opportunity to increase France's influence in Europe.

Taylor, Paul, "EU Authority Fraying in Reaction to Brexit Vote," Reuters, Jul. 5, 2016, http://tinyurl.com/jsf5kp3.

The European Union has begun to face vocal opposition in many member states, with leaders questioning the EU's Brussels-based bureaucracy and its policies.

FREE-TRADE QUESTIONS

"North American Leaders Defend Free Trade amid Brexit, Trump," Chicago Tribune, Jun. 29, 2016, http://tinyurl.com/jtu86bc.

President Obama denounces isolationist politics and the exploitation of immigration fears by pro-Brexit campaigners and GOP presidential nominee Donald J. Trump.

Murphy, Joe, "Brexit: Free Trade with the EU Is Now 'Pie in the Sky,' Theresa May Is Told," Evening Standard, Jul. 21, 2016, http://tinyurl.com/zgcno9d.

Pascal Lamy, former head of the World Trade Organization, calls expectations of a British free-trade deal with Europe unrealistic.

GLOBAL ECONOMY

"Brexit Heightens Uncertainty in Global Economy, Says G20," The Guardian, Jul. 24, 2016, http://tinyurl.com/h7qh6qg.

Finance leaders from the international G-20 forum highlighted the risks Brexit poses to the world economy and advised the U.K. to reduce conflict by remaining close to the EU.

Finch, Gavin, "Banks Face Brexit Bill of $66,000 per U.K. Employee Moved Abroad," Bloomberg, Jul. 25, 2016, http://tinyurl.com/j6y9q8e.

A consulting firm estimates that banks wanting to leave the U.K. to maintain access to the EU will have to spend $66,000 per employee to move them abroad.

Matthews, Chris, "IMF Say Brexit Will Batter the Global Economy,' Fortune, Jul. 20, 2016, http://tinyurl.com/hb5hxuf.

The International Monetary Fund warns of the uncertainty in the U.K. following Brexit and predicts Britain's economy will slow in the coming year.

ORGANIZATIONS

Centre for European Reform
14 Great College St., Westminster, London, SW1P 3RX
+44 (0) 20 7233 1199
https://www.cer.org.uk/contact-us

A think tank "devoted to making the EU work better, and strengthening its role in the world. We are pro-European but not uncritical."

European Commission
Rue de la Loi, 200-1049, Brussels
00800 67 89 10 11
http://europa.eu/contact/write-to-us/index_en.htm

The head offices where staff employed by the European Union are based. For inquiries, it's best to use the Web address.

European Commission (London office)
32 Smith Square, London, SW1P 3EU
+44 20 7973 1992
https://ec.europa.eu/unitedkingdom/about-us/london-office_en

The office that coordinates EU activity in the U.K., and will continue to function until Brexit is complete.

Open Europe
7 Tufton St., London, SW1P 3QN
+44 20 7197 2333
www.openeurope.org.uk

An influential "Euroskeptic" or anti-EU think tank that describes itself as "the go-to source for real-time analysis on breaking European affairs, delivered by our experts as events unfold."

Policy Network
3rd Floor, 11 Tufton St., London, SW1P 3QB
+44 20 7340 2200
www.policy-network.net/

A "center-left," pro-EU think tank whose purpose is to promote and develop social democratic politics across Europe.

U.K. Department for Exiting the European Union
http://tinyurl.com/htgm9ly

A new government department, responsible for handling the Brexit negotiations. Its address and contact numbers will be posted on its website when the department has been set up.

U.K. Department for International Trade
http://tinyurl.com/jav4856

Another new government department responsible for negotiating the trade agreements that the U.K. will sign when it has left the European Union. Its address and contact numbers will be posted on its website when the department is set up.

Chapter 3: China's Slowdown

BOOKS

Hung, Ho-Fung, "The China Boom: Why China Will Not Rule the World," Columbia University Press, 2015.

An associate sociology professor at Johns Hopkins University uses historical, sociological and political analysis to explain how much China depends on the existing economic order and how the interests of Chinese elites maintain those ties.

Kroeber, Arthur R., "China's Economy: What Everyone Needs to Know," Oxford University Press, 2016.

An economics journalist and researcher offers a primer on how China's economy grew and the implications for its slowdown.

Lardy, Nicholas R., "Markets Over Mao: The Rise of Private Business in China," Peterson Institute for International Economics, 2014.

A senior fellow at the Peterson Institute traces the institution and practice of private entrepreneurship in post-Maoist China.

McGregor, Richard, "The Party: The Secret World of China's Communist Rulers," Harper, 2010.

A Financial Times writer deconstructs the secret world that influences China's economy, military and local governments, highlighting the corruption and tension that keep the party from evolving.

Naughton, Barry, "The Chinese Economy: Transition and Growth," MIT Press, 2007.

A classic economic history by the Sokwanlok chair of Chinese international affairs at the University of California, San Diego, explains China's economic experiments, failures and successes from the post-Qing era to the early 2000s.

Osnos, Evan, "Age of Ambition: Chasing Fortune, Truth, and Faith in the New China," Farrar, Straus and Giroux, 2014.

Winner of the Pulitzer Prize and the National Book award, this work by a New Yorker staff writer follows several Chinese citizens as they negotiate a turbulent era of individual attainment amid the Communist Party's quest for control.

Spence, Jonathan D., "The Search for Modern China," 3rd ed.," W.W. Norton and Co., 2012.

A Yale University history professor emeritus outlines China's political, economic, social and cultural past in a dazzling narrative.

ARTICLES

"Back to Business: Special Report, Business in China," The Economist, Sep. 12, 2015, http://tinyurl.com/o4tesht.

The current state of China's entrepreneurs and the private sector is explored.

de Jonquieres, Guy, "The Problematic Politics of China's Economic Reform Plans," International Journal of China Studies, August 2014, pp. 399-412, http://tinyurl.com/gqswlfy.

The scholarly paper provides a thorough overview of the political and economic challenges before President Xi Jingping as he seeks to keep his country socially and financially stable.

"The New Class War: Special Report, Chinese Society," The Economist, Jul. 9, 2016, http://tinyurl.com/gppn5mv.

The rise of China's first large middle class creates opportunities and challenges for the Chinese government.

REPORTS AND STUDIES

"China 2030: Building a Modern, Harmonious, and Creative Society," World Bank and Development Research Center of the State Council, People's Republic of China, 2013, http://tinyurl.com/hza9eta.

A joint report by the World Bank and the Chinese government research body lays out goals for China to become a more stable, wealthier society.

"China's Economic Rise: History, Trends, Challenges, and Implications for the United States," Congressional Research Service, Oct. 21, 2015, http://tinyurl.com/l87nlln.

A report by Congress' nonpartisan research arm describes the history of China's quasi-market system and stunning economic success in the last 30 years.

"China's Environmental Crisis," Council on Foreign Relations, Jan 18, 2016, http://tinyurl.com/6496rvc.

The Council on Foreign Relations provides an introduction to the economic and policy reasons why a massive environmental crisis is engulfing China.

"China-U.S. Trade Issues," Congressional Research Service, Dec. 15, 2015, http://tinyurl.com/jk5g5oz.

A CRS report recounts the politics and current state of trade between the two global giants.

Barton, Dominic, et al., "Mapping China's Middle Class," McKinsey Quarterly, June 2013, http://tinyurl.com/zdlet22.

A business consultancy says that rising prosperity in China's inland cities will fuel consumption.

THE NEXT STEP

DEBT AND ECONOMIC RISKS

Lanman, Scott, "China's Holdings of U.S. Treasuries Fall to Lowest Since '13," Bloomberg, Sep. 16, 2016, http://tinyurl.com/jlygsou.

China's U.S. Treasury holdings fell in July to the lowest level in more than three years.

Magnier, Mark, "Warning Sounded over Chinese Economy," The Wall Street Journal, Sep. 28, 2016, http://tinyurl.com/j7cwjzg.

Despite recent stability, deep-seated problems threaten China's economy as the country heads toward a leadership change in late 2017, according to a survey.

Taylor, David, "China Warned to Rein in Growing Mountain of Debt or Risk Triggering Another Global Financial Crisis," ABC News, Sep. 26, 2016, http://tinyurl.com/zg3ggsa.

The Bank for International Settlements, a Swiss-based international financial organization, cautions that China's ballooning debt is too large and could set off another financial crisis.

CORRUPTION

Blanchard, Ben, "Mayor of China's Tianjin investigated on suspicion of corruption," Reuters, Sep. 10, 2016, http://tinyurl.com/z8svpa3.

The mayor of the major Chinese port city of Tianjin is being investigated on suspicion of corruption.

Chin, Josh, "Retired Chinese General Sentenced to Life in Prison for Corruption," The Wall Street Journal, Jul. 25, 2016, http://tinyurl.com/hx2fp88.

A Chinese military court handed down a life sentence to a retired general, the highest-ranking official to be convicted for corruption.

Martina, Michael, "China Puts New Focus on Illicit Assets in Corruption Fugitive Hunt," Reuters, Sep. 20, 2016, http://tinyurl.com/jboyhg3.

As part of President Xi Jinping's anti-graft campaign, China is accelerating its effort to recover stolen money moved overseas.

ENVIRONMENTAL IMPACT

Harrabin, Roger, "China Embarked on Wind Power Frenzy, Says IEA," BBC, Sep. 20, 2016, http://tinyurl.com/zhg42vj.

Despite China's rapid increase in its wind turbine output, coal-fired power stations are still receiving priority in the power grid, according to the International Energy Agency, an intergovernmental organization.

Hernandez, Javier C., "Chemical Accidents in China Have Killed Nearly 200 This Year, Report Finds," The New York Times, Sep. 21, 2016, http://tinyurl.com/jpme7u6.

Almost 200 people in China have died due to chemical accidents, according to a report by the environmental group Greenpeace, which suggested a relaxed regulatory system was to blame.

Vaughan, Adam, "China Tops WHO List for Deadly Outdoor Air Pollution," The Guardian, Sep. 27, 2016, http://tinyurl.com/z464luo.

The World Health Organization ranked China as the world's deadliest country for outdoor air pollution.

ECONOMIC AND POLITICAL REFORMS

"China Cuts Consumption Tax on Cosmetics to Stir Growth," Reuters, Sep. 30, 2016, http://tinyurl.com/jtumknc.

China's finance ministry will reduce or remove the consumption tax on cosmetic products in an effort to spur more domestic spending.

"China Launches $52.5 Billion Fund to Restructure State Enterprises," Reuters, Sep. 26, 2016, http://tinyurl.com/zr5mdqc.

The $52.5 billion Enterprises Restructuring Fund will be used to improve the competitiveness of inefficient state-owned enterprises.

Wei, Lingling, "China Unveils Economic Blueprint for 2016," The Wall Street Journal, Dec. 21, 2015, http://tinyurl.com/haveocp.

China's 2016 economic blueprint set its sights on improving a sluggish economy and tackling debt.

ORGANIZATIONS

American Chamber of Commerce in the People's Republic of China
The Office Park, Tower AB, 6th Floor, No. 10 Jintongxi Road, Beijing 100020
8610-8519-0800
http://www.amchamchina.org

A trade association for American businesses in China.

Asia Society
725 Park Ave., New York, NY 10021
212-288-6400
http://asiasociety.org

A cultural and educational organization offering lectures and classes on arts, business, culture and policies; has additional locations in Shanghai and Hong Kong.

The Brookings Institution
1775 Massachusetts Ave., N.W., Washington, DC 20036
202-797-6000
https://www.brookings.edu

A nonprofit public policy research organization that has a sister center in Beijing.

Center for Global Economy and Business
Henry Kaufman Management Center, 44 W. Fourth St., New York, NY 10012
212-998-0100
http://www.stern.nyu.edu/experience-stern/about/departments-centers-initiatives/centers-of-research/global-economy-business

The division of the Stern School of Business at New York University promotes faculty research concerning global aspects of modern economies and business. Its China initiative offers specialized information on that country.

Council on Foreign Relations
The Harold Pratt House, 58 E. 68th St., New York, NY 10065
212-434-9400
http://www.cfr.org

A nonpartisan membership organization that conducts research, sponsors discussions and publishes the journal Foreign Affairs.

International Monetary Fund
700 19th St., N.W., Washington, DC 20431
202-623-7000
www.imf.org

A global financial organization that conducts research and publishes extensive data.

RAND Corp.
1776 Main St., Santa Monica, Calif. 90401
310-393-0411
http://www.rand.org

A nonprofit think tank that conducts research and analysis.

World Bank
1818 H St., N.W., Washington, DC 20433
202-473-1000
http://www.worldbank.org/en/country/china

A global financial institution that loans money to developing nations.

Chapter 4: Commodities Supercycles

BOOKS

Mansharamani, Vikram, "Boombustology: Spotting Financial Bubbles Before They Burst," Wiley, 2011.

A financial expert offers a multi-disciplinary approach that relies on economics, politics, psychology and biology to identify and evaluate financial bubbles. The author, writing at the height of the China boom, correctly predicted why it was unsustainable.

O'Sullivan, Meghan L., "Windfall: How the New Energy Abundance Upends Global Politics and Strengthens American Power," Simon & Schuster, 2017.

A Harvard professor of international affairs and former adviser to President George W. Bush explains how the shale oil revolution that produced a worldwide energy glut made the United States more energy self-sufficient, prevented Russia from becoming a petro-superpower, strengthened China's advance across Eurasia and weakened Middle Eastern and Africa oil states.

ARTICLES

"Australia is the New Frontier for Battery Minerals," The Economist, Nov. 25, 2017, https://tinyurl.com/y85wbvvh.

The British newsweekly details the boom in lithium mining in Australia as a result of China's push to manufacture batteries for electric vehicles.

Batovic, Ante, "Five Countries Most Affected by the Oil Price Crash," Global Risk Insights, Feb. 21, 2015, https://tinyurl.com/ybz5hccc.

An analyst with a London-based political risk firm traces the economic and political fallout from the global oil price drop on Venezuela, Nigeria, Iraq, Russia and Iran.

George-Cosh, David, "Miners Look to Cash in on Cobalt Demand," The Wall Street Journal, Jan. 1, 2018, https://tinyurl.com/yaa6ool8.

A journalist reports on new cobalt mining ventures in Canada that seek to satisfy global demand for a socially responsible source of the metal, which now comes primarily from mines in the Democratic Republic of the Congo that use child labor.

Onishi, Norimitsu, "African Economies, and Hopes for New Era, Are Shaken by China," The New York Times, Jan. 25, 2016, https://tinyurl.com/ya9b3uss.

A Johannesburg-based reporter details how China's economic slowdown and the subsequent crash in commodities prices caused economic pain in Africa's commodity-exporting countries.

Porter, Eduardo, "Slowdown in China Bruises Economy in Latin America," The New York Times, Dec. 16, 2014, https://tinyurl.com/ydga2k3n.

A journalist examines how China's economic deceleration has weakened Latin American economies that enjoyed unprecedented growth by exporting soybeans, wheat, copper and other commodities to China.

Ramkumar, Amrith, and Ira Iosebashvili, "Electric-Vehicle Bulls Shake Up Metals Markets," The Wall Street Journal, Dec. 10, 2017, https://tinyurl.com/y9yvpp2q.

Two commodities reporters describe how investors are pushing up prices for a wide variety of metals used to manufacture electric vehicles and their batteries amid growing global enthusiasm for cars fueled by clean, renewable energy.

REPORTS AND STUDIES

"Exposed: Child Labour Behind Smart Phone and Electric Car Batteries," Amnesty International, Jan. 19, 2016, https://tinyurl.com/hs5ztum.

The human rights organization describes widespread use of child labor in cobalt mines in the Democratic Republic of Congo, the source of two-thirds of the world's cobalt.

Spatafora, Nikola, and Irina Tytell, "Commodity Terms of Trade: The History of Booms and Busts," International Monetary Fund, September 2009, https://tinyurl.com/y7abb394.

Two IMF economists provide historical data covering nearly 40 years of booms and busts in the commodity markets in more than 150 countries and compare the most recent commodity-price cycle with its historical precedents.

THE NEXT STEP

CHINA

"China's Economy Set to Slow to 6.5 Percent in 2018 as Government Turns Off Cheap Money: Reuters Poll," Reuters, Jan. 16, 2018, https://tinyurl.com/ycb6q8ae.

Chinese economic growth will slow as the government moves to curb factory pollution and reduce debt, according to a poll of economists.

Duguay, Andrew, "Why the Death of Manufacturing in China Means a Positive Economic Outlook in 2018," Forbes, Jan. 23, 2018, https://tinyurl.com/y9tou4l2.

The decline of low-end manufacturing signals the maturing of China's economy as it transitions to a more consumer-based model and seeks a more diverse and saturated market, says an economist for a research firm.

Huang, Cary, "Why a Cooling in China's Economy Would Be a Good Thing," South China Morning Post, Jan. 27, 2018, https://tinyurl.com/ydxkvz7u.

China's economy, previously reliant on capital investment and exports, is shifting to focus on innovation and private consumption.

ELECTRIC VEHICLES

Frangoul, Anmar, "Electric Vehicles: BP Invests $5 Million in Charging Business FreeWire," CNBC, Jan. 31, 2018, https://tinyurl.com/ya3m97jh.

BP Ventures, a subsidiary of the oil giant, is investing $5 million in a rapid-charging company and plans to introduce charging stations at BP retail sites in the United Kingdom and elsewhere in Europe in 2018.

Nickelsburg, Monica, "Seattle City Light Installs First City-Owned Electric Vehicle Fast-Charging Stations," GeekWire, Jan. 30, 2018, https://tinyurl.com/ybxz9ho8.

Seattle is expanding its electric-vehicle infrastructure to curb the number of gasoline-operated cars and reduce the city's carbon footprint.

Patterson, Scott, "Driven by Electric-Vehicle Demand, Firms Focus on Cobalt," The Wall Street Journal, Jan. 29, 2018, http://tinyurl.com/ydcgsxsm.

Demand for cobalt, a mineral essential to electric-vehicle batteries, has increased exponentially as more car companies turn to such vehicles.

ORGANIZATIONS

BMO Capital Markets
129 Saint-Jacques St., Montreal, QC H2Y 1L6 Canada
1-514-282-5922
www.bmocm.com

A financial services provider with commodities experts who offer commentary and guidance to journalists and scholars

The CME Group, Inc.
20 South Wacker Drive, Chicago, Illinois 60606
1-312-930-1000
www.cmegroup.com

A derivatives marketplace made up of the Chicago Mercantile Exchange, the Chicago Board of Trade, the New York Mercantile Exchange and the Commodities Exchange.

The Heritage Foundation
214 Massachusetts Ave., N.E., Washington, DC 20002-4999
1-202-546-4400
www.heritage.org

Conservative think tank that issues studies, papers and analysis on a wide range of public policy issues, including commodity policy.

London Metals Exchange
10 Finsbury Square, London, United Kingdom, EC2A 1AJ
+44 (0)20 7113 8888
www.lme.com

The world's largest market in options and futures contracts on base and other metals; traces its origins to the opening of London's Royal Exchange in 1571.

Peterson Institute for International Economics
1750 Massachusetts Ave., N.W., Washington, DC 20036-1903
1-202-328-9000
https://piie.com

Think tank that conducts research on how to make globalization more beneficial to all; has published scholarly works on commodity booms and busts.

Shanghai Futures Exchange
500 Pudian Road, Shanghai, 200122, China
+86 (021) 6840 0000
www.shfe.com.cn

A nonprofit, self-regulating corporation that trades in non-ferrous metals, including copper, aluminum, lead, zinc, tin and nickel.

U.S. Commodities Futures Trading Commission
Three Lafayette Centre, 1155 21st St., N.W., Washington, DC 20581

1-202-418-5000
www.cftc.gov

An independent U.S. government agency that regulates commodity futures and options markets.

Chapter 5: Data Security

BOOKS

Payton, Theresa M., and Ted Claypoole, "Privacy in the Age of Big Data: Recognizing Threats, Defending Your Rights, and Protecting Your Family," Rowman & Littlefield Publishers, Inc., 2015.

The book details how citizens can protect their data while online and documents how much information we provide in order to get a coupon or buy an item on line.

Schneier, Bruce, "Data and Goliath: The Hidden Battles to Collect Your Data and Control Your World," W.W. Norton & Company, Inc., 2015.

Schneier, chief technology officer at Resilient Systems Inc. and a fellow at the Berkman Center for Internet and Society at Harvard Law School, writes an overview of privacy and security that documents how private citizens are dissected by both corporations and government through their online data.

ARTICLES

"WannaCry: Ransomware Attacks Show Strong Links to Lazarus group," Symantec, May 22, 2017, http://tinyurl.com/mwn8c4q.

Security experts believe Lazarus is behind the WannaCry ransomware that locked up 300,000 computers in 150 nations in May 2017 and several other cyberattacks, including a raid on the central bank of Bangladesh.

Choe, Sang-Hun, "North Korea Tries to Make Hacking a Profit Center," The New York Times, Jul. 27, 2017, http://tinyurl.com/y8ctpq9z.

North Korea has trained the nation's hackers not only to steal other countries' secrets, but to pursue their cash as well.

Cox, Joseph, "Hackers Threaten Release of Atlanta Professional Athletes' Medical Data," Motherboard, Nov. 16, 2016, http://tinyurl.com/y7k2qr6n.

A journalist looks at The Dark Overlord hacking group's recent attempt to extort money from an orthopedic clinic by threatening to release the stolen medical records of high-profile professional athletes.

Greenberg, Andy, "The WannaCry Ransomware Hackers Made Some Real Amateur Mistakes," Wired, May 15, 2017, http://tinyurl.com/ml8d4fc.

The hackers behind the recent WannaCry malware attack made a number of key errors that helped make the attack a "catastrophic failure" from a ransom perspective.

Hay Newman, Lily, "Medical Devices Are the Next Security Nightmare," Wired, Mar. 2, 2017, http://tinyurl.com/znulb88.

Many pacemakers and other implanted medical devices are vulnerable to cyberattack, offering hackers yet another way to extort money and steal medical information.

Johnson, Tim, "How the Dark Overlord Is Costing U.S. Clinics Big Time with Ransom Demands," Miami Herald, May 15, 2017, http://tinyurl.com/yataul74.

Ransomware attacks by The Dark Overlord hacking group have created havoc at large and small medical facilities across the country.

Masters, Greg, "New York's New Cybersecurity Requirements Go into Effect Today," SC Media, Mar. 1, 2017, http://tinyurl.com/y8hjnrju.

New York's first-in-the-nation cybersecurity requirements mean banking and financial services companies must encrypt non-public data, train workers in cybersecurity and take other steps to protect consumers and themselves.

Merica, Dan, "The Life and Death of Trump's 'Cyber Security Unit' Plan with Putin," CNN, Jul. 10, 2017, http://tinyurl.com/y9faxxol.

The Trump administration retreated from the president's proposal to cooperate with Russian President Vladimir Putin on cybersecurity after the proposal was widely criticized.

Paganini, Pierluigi, "The Total Potential Loss for Financial Services Globally Is Estimated at £8 Billion," Security Affairs, Mar. 6, 2017, http://tinyurl.com/ycxq8xp8.

The latest ThreatMatrix Cybercrime Report says online lending has become a prime target for hackers, and most cybercrime activity originates in developing countries.

Seals, Tara, "Healthcare Breaches Spike 63% in 2016," Infosecurity, Dec. 22, 2016, http://tinyurl.com/ybc38wuf.

Cyberattacks struck 93 health care facilities last year and now present "a direct physical risk" to patients, according to a report from TrapX Labs.

REPORTS AND STUDIES

"2016 Financial Industry Cybersecurity Research Report," Security Scorecard, August 2016, http://tinyurl.com/ya9q7dwe.

The cybersecurity report documents the extent to which the health care and financial services industries are targeted by hackers and the vulnerabilities of both industries.

"Code Blue: Why Healthcare Organizations Are Facing More Cyber Attacks, and What They Can Do about It," FireEye, 2015, http://tinyurl.com/yawvgwmw.

A cybersecurity firm analyzes why the health care industry and the data it collects have become attractive targets for hackers.

"Cybersecurity and Financial Stability: Risks and Resilience," Office of Financial Research, U.S. Treasury Department, Feb. 15, 2017, http://tinyurl.com/y9w277xm.

An independent bureau within the Treasury Department, created in 2010 to assess risks to the nation's financial system, looks at how cyberattacks threaten financial stability and how companies and regulators are dealing with the problem.

"IBM X-Force Threat Intelligence Index 2017," IBM, March 2017, http://tinyurl.com/ya636rj8.

More than four billion hacked records were leaked during "the year of the mega breach" in 2016, and cyberattacks that year "had a discernible impact on real-world events," according to IBM's security services.

"Overview of the General Data Protection Regulation (GDPR)," Information Commissioner's Office, Aug. 17, 2017, http://tinyurl.com/zqfmm48.

An independent British regulatory office analyzes the European Union's new personal data protection law.

THE NEXT STEP

MILITARY INNOVATION

Mehta, Aaron, "Pentagon Tech Advisers Target How the Military Digests Data," Defense News, Apr. 6, 2017, https://tinyurl.com/y9sekshr.

The Pentagon is considering creating a central repository for its vast quantities of military data to remain ahead of the technological curve, after months of research determined that data management is key to innovation.

Popper, Ben, "A Rebuke from the US Army Has DJI Focused on Improving Security," The Verge, Sep. 6, 2017, https://tinyurl.com/y9poss8l.

The world's most successful drone company has come under scrutiny recently over the security and privacy of the millions of photos, videos and flight logs it collects. The Army will continue using the company's equipment only if it passes a security check.

Porche, Isaac, "Reservists and the National Guard Offer Untapped Resources for Cybersecurity," TechCrunch, Apr. 18, 2017, https://tinyurl.com/ybhen6y7.

The U.S. Army Reserves and National Guard have thousands of people with cyber experience who could be trained as information security professionals to better defend national security in cyber terrain, according to research by the RAND Corporation, a California-based think tank.

PRIVATE INDUSTRY

Bendix, Aria, "GOP Firm Exposed U.S. Voters' Personal Data," The Atlantic, Jun. 20, 2017, https://tinyurl.com/ybkcnqh2.

A marketing firm hired by the Republican National Committee accidentally made the personal information of almost every U.S. voter publicly accessible on the Amazon cloud server for two weeks in June, because the firm failed to password-protect the data.

Nakashima, Ellen, "Tech Firm Is Fighting a Federal Demand for Data on Visitors to an Anti-Trump Website," The Washington Post, Aug. 14, 2017, https://tinyurl.com/y8omsblt.

DreamHost, a private tech firm, is fighting a Department of Justice demand for internet data on visitors to a website the firm hosts that coordinated protests against President Trump on Inauguration Day.

Vincent, James, "Ghostery Has Been Bought by the Developer of a Privacy-Focused Browser," The Verge, Feb. 15, 2017, https://tinyurl.com/y9ztbb5s.

Cliqz, a German company that offers a browser focused on privacy protection, has acquired the anti-tracking and ad-blocking plug-in Ghostery to attract more international users, who will benefit from Germany's strict data-protection laws.

ORGANIZATIONS

Center for Insurance Policy and Research, National Association of Insurance Commissioners
444 North Capitol St., N.W., Suite 700, Washington, DC 20001
1-202-471-3990
http://naic.org/cipr_home.htm

Studies cybersecurity issues for the National Association of Insurance Commissioners.

Center for Internet Security
31 Tech Valley Drive, East Greenbush, NY 12061
1-518-266-3460
https://www.cisecurity.org
contact@cisecurity.org

A nonprofit that works to protect public and private companies around the world from the threat of cyberattacks.

Office for Civil Rights, U.S. Department of Health and Human Services
200 Independence Ave., S.W., Washington, DC 20201
1-800-368-1019
https://www.hhs.gov/ocr/index.html
OCRPrivacy@hhs.gov (privacy questions)

The Health and Human Services Department office responsible for monitoring and protecting personal health data.

Office of Financial Research, U.S. Department of the Treasury
717 14th St., N.W., Washington, DC 20220
1-202-622-2000
https://www.financialresearch.gov/

An independent bureau within the Treasury Department that assesses risks to the financial services industry.

Pew Research Center
1615 L St., N.W., Suite 800, Washington, DC 20036
1-202-419-4300
http://www.pewresearch.org/

A research organization that has conducted numerous surveys on public attitudes about cybercrime.

Ponemon Institute
2308 U.S. 31 North, Traverse City, MI 49686
1-231-938-9900
http://www.ponemon.org/

A research organization dedicated to privacy, data protection and information security policy that has done extensive work documenting the cost of data breaches.

Privacy Rights Clearinghouse
3033 5th Ave., Suite 223, San Diego, CA 92103
1-619-298-3396
www.privacyrights.org
www.privacyrights.org/contact/consumers

A nonprofit that monitors invasions of consumer privacy, advocates for privacy rights and maintains a database of significant breaches.

Chapter 6: Doing Business with Japan

BOOKS

Dower, John, "The Useful War," in Carol Gluck and Stephen Graubard, eds., "Showa: The Japan of Hirohito," W.W. Norton, 1992.

A historian examines how World War II affected the Japanese economy and the business world.

Johnson, Chalmers, "MITI and the Japanese Miracle: The Growth of Industrial Policy, 1925–1975," Stanford University Press, 1982.

A specialist in Asian and Japanese policy examines how the auto industry and others gained strength in Japan in the second half of the 20th century via the Ministry of International Trade and Industry (MITI).

Kingston, Jeff, "Contemporary Japan: History, Politics, and Social Change Since the 1980s," Wiley Blackwell, 2nd ed., 2012.

The director of Asian studies at Temple University's Japan campus analyzes that nation's recent history, with updates since the Fukushima disaster and the 2012 election that brought a change in prime minister.

Pyle, Kenneth B., "The Making of Modern Japan," Cengage Learning, 2nd ed., 1995.

A University of Washington history professor, an expert on all things Japanese, describes how Japan became a modern nation; his book includes good details on the roles played by the zaibatsu and the keiretsu.

Saito, William H., "An Unprogrammed Life—Adventures of an Incurable Entrepreneur," Wiley, 2012.

A child prodigy, entrepreneur and current adviser to the Japanese Ministry of Education chronicles his rise in the business world and sheds light on Japan's business culture along the way.

ARTICLES

"About That Debt," The Economist, Nov. 18, 2014, http://tinyurl.com/luw9ewg.

Questions arise about how Japan's debt ratio is calculated and what it actually means.

"The Annexation of Korea," The Japan Times, Aug. 29, 2010, http://tinyurl.com/o72qnad.

The story of how Japan annexed Korea holds lessons for modern-day Japanese, according to an editorial in Japan's oldest English-language newspaper.

Evans, Peter, "Mitsui Fudosan Has a Big Plan for Abroad," The Wall Street Journal, May 16, 2013, http://tinyurl.com/p3bm7y4.

The large Japanese real estate firm is pursuing acquisitions and development deals in the United States and Europe.

"Farming in Japan: Field Work," The Economist, Apr. 13, 2013, http://tinyurl.com/blcp8jv.

The structure of Japan's agriculture sector presents economic and political challenges.

Fingleton, Eamonn, "The Myth of Japan's Failure," The New York Times, Jan. 6, 2012, http://tinyurl.com/npzu2jk.

By some measures, Japan's economy is stronger than many observers admit.

Johnston, Eric, "Lessons from When the Bubble Burst," The Japan Times, Jan. 6, 2009, http://tinyurl.com/qzq2vu4.

Excess spending from 1985 to 1990 preceded the "Lost Decade" of Japan's business history.

Kisiel, Ralph, "Gamble in Rural Ohio Pays Off Big," Automotive News, Jun. 8, 2009, http://tinyurl.com/pf9rwaj.

Despite early detractors, Honda's first auto plant in the United States has become one of the nation's most efficient assembly operations.

Makinen, Julie, "A Subculture of Entrepreneurship Hatches in Japan," Los Angeles Times, Mar. 29, 2015, http://tinyurl.com/ptlmw35.

Business incubators are encouraging entrepreneurship in Japan.

McCurry, Justin, "Japan Moves Nearer to Restarting Nuclear Reactors After Court Gives Go Ahead," The Guardian, Apr. 22, 2015, http://tinyurl.com/o79uyek.

Over numerous legal objections, Japanese courts have approved the reopening of nuclear plants that closed after the 2011 Fukushima disaster.

Murakami, Hiromi, and Kiyoshi Kurokawa, "Fukushima Crisis Fueling the Third Opening of Japan," The Japan Times, Dec. 1, 2011, http://tinyurl.com/q8kgxt6.

Two Japanese academics explore the "third opening"—Japan's willingness to discuss the free-trade agreement that would eventually become known as the Trans-Pacific Partnership.

Schreffler, Roger, "Auto Industry Leading Market for Japanese Robotics," WardsAuto, Aug. 21, 2013, http://tinyurl.com/p85mvew.

Automakers are the biggest buyers of robots, most of which are made in Japan.

Sekiguchi, Toko, "Japan Opens Door Wider for Foreign Workers," The Wall Street Journal, Apr. 4, 2014, http://tinyurl.com/pc5nctv.

New economic policies seem to invite more foreign workers to Japan; memories persist of a 2009 policy to pay foreign workers to leave the country.

Takada, Aya, "Japan's Farm Lobby Concedes to Abe's Agriculture Reform Plans," Bloomberg Business, Feb. 9, 2015, http://tinyurl.com/q4m7nmy.

Prime Minister Shinzo Abe appears to be winning his battle with the powerful farm lobby.

REPORTS AND STUDIES

Kanaya, Akihiro, and David Woo, "The Japanese Banking Crises of the 1990s: Sources and Lessons," International Monetary Fund, January 2000, http://tinyurl.com/m5txk2.

International finance experts review the causes of the Japanese financial meltdown that led to the "Lost Decade," from a banking point of view.

Yoshino, Naoyuki, and Farhad Taghizadeh-Hesary, "Three Arrows of 'Abenomics' and the Structural Reform of Japan: Inflation Targeting Policy of the Central Bank, Fiscal Consolidation, and Growth Strategy," ADB Institute, August 2014, http://tinyurl.com/nbg8va6.

Two economists explain the major components of "Abenomics," Prime Minister Shinzo Abe's plan to invigorate the Japanese economy.

THE NEXT STEP

AGING POPULATION

Moore, Jack, "Two Numbers: Japan Has More Than 60,000 Centenarians, and Tokyo Can't Afford Their Gifts," Newsweek, Sep. 23, 2015, http://tinyurl.com/o9em98j.

The number of Japanese who are at least 100 years old grew to nearly 62,000 in 2014, costing the government $2 million for commemorative gifts that it sends to centenarians.

Nikaido, Yuki, "Japan's Population Decline the Steepest on Record," The Asahi Shimbun, Jul. 2, 2015, http://tinyurl.com/q3cg6qg.

Japan's population declined for the sixth year in a row in 2014, and the number of people age 65 or older accounted for one-fourth of residents for the first time in history.

Nohara, Yoshiaki, "In Japan, the Rise of Machines Solves Labor Shortage," Bloomberg Business, Sep. 13, 2015, http://tinyurl.com/nptgrf2.

The Japanese government is encouraging the country's manufacturing, health care and service industries to use more robots to supplement its aging workforce.

INTERNATIONAL TRADE

Arvinth, Karthick, "Japan's July Trade Deficit Unexpectedly Widens as Exports Slow," International Business Times, Aug. 19, 2015, http://tinyurl.com/qfynadh.

Japanese export growth slowed by nearly 2 percentage points in July while imports fell by 3 percent, creating a $2.2 billion trade deficit.

Chakravorti, Bhaskar, "How Japan's Shortcomings Can Trigger Its Next Burst of Innovation," The Washington Post, Jul. 6, 2015, http://tinyurl.com/q275wyx.

Japan can benefit from the proposed Trans-Pacific Partnership between Pacific Rim countries by investing more in innovation and infrastructure, according to an associate dean of international business and finance at Tufts University.

Soble, Jonathan, "With Ban on Exports Lifted, Japan Arms Makers Cautiously Market Wares Abroad," The New York Times, Jul. 12, 2015, http://tinyurl.com/nscmj2v.

Japanese weapons manufacturers are developing more products to sell to other countries after Prime Minister Shinzo Abe ended a nearly 50-year ban on exporting military equipment.

NUCLEAR POWER

Lavelle, Moira, "Volcano Near Nuclear Plant Raising Concerns in Japan," Public Radio International, Aug. 17, 2015, http://tinyurl.com/noguaw2.

Japan has opened its first nuclear plant since it shut down all reactors in 2011, but critics worry about the potential for another disaster because the reactor is close to an active volcano.

McNeill, David, "Japan's Emissions Have Soared Since Fukushima Nuclear Disaster," The Irish Times, Sep. 21, 2015, http //tinyurl.com/oqys9kt.

Japanese carbon emissions in 2014 rose to their second-highest mark ever, the result of growing dependence on coal-fired power plants for electricity since the Fukushima nuclear disaster in 2011.

Yamaguchi, Mari, "Can Towns Near Japan's Fukushima Nuclear Plant Recover?" The Associated Press, Sep. 9, 2015, http://tinyurl.com/nbvtlz4.

A town heavily affected by radiation that leaked during the Fukushima nuclear plant's 2011 meltdown reopened in September, the first of the evacuated nearby municipalities to do so.

WOMEN IN THE WORKPLACE

Gilman, Azure, "Work Conditions for Japanese Women May Be Affecting Marriage, Birth Rates," Al Jazeera America, Jun. 26, 2015, http://tinyurl.com/pe3tetc.

Poor benefits for working mothers, workplace harassment and low wages deter many Japanese women from having children or marrying, according to experts on Japanese culture.

Kameda, Masaaki, "U.N. Opens Office Dedicated to Women's Empowerment in Tokyo," The Japan Times, Aug. 30, 2015, http://tinyurl.com/nsl6dqk.

The United Nations agency for women's empowerment opened its first Asian office in Tokyo in August, in part to support Prime Minister Shinzo Abe's policies to improve women's workplace rights.

Lewis, Leo, "Number of Japanese Women in Work Reaches Record High," Financial Times, Jul. 31, 2015, http://tinyurl.com/pn8tase.

The number of working women in Japan rose to nearly 28 million in June, the highest ever, representing 43 percent of the country's workforce.

ORGANIZATIONS

Embassy of Japan
2520 Massachusetts Ave., N.W., Washington, DC 20008
202-238-6700
www.us.emb-japan.go.jp/english/html/

Japan's official embassy in Washington, which hosts many social and business-related events.

Foreign Press Center/Japan
6F Nippon Press Center Building, 2-2-1, Uchisaiwaicho, Chiyoda-ku, Tokyo 100-0011, Japan
81-3-3501-5251
http://fpcj.jp/en/

Nonprofit foundation that helps foreign journalists gather news in Japan; also offers fellowships and scholarships.

Japan Association of Corporate Executives
1-4-6, Marunouchi, Chiyoda-ku, Tokyo 100-0005, Japan
81-3-3211-1271
Fax: 81-3-3212-3774
www.doyukai.or.jp/en/opinion/index.html

Group of top Japanese business executives; founded in 1946 to support reconstruction of economy after World War II.

Japan Business Federation
1-3-2 Otemachi, Chiyoda-ku, Tokyo 100-0004, Japan
81-3-6741-0111
www.keidanren.or.jp

Japanese business lobbying association, also known as Nippon Keidanren.

Japan Chamber of Commerce and Industry
New York office: 145 W. 57th St., #6, New York, NY 10019
212-246-8001
http://www.jcci.or.jp/home-e.html

Chamber's New York office made up of large and small businesses throughout Japan.

Japan Commerce Association of Washington, D.C.
1819 L St., N.W., B2, Washington, DC 20036
202-463-3947
Fax: 202-463-3948
www.jcaw.org

Professional organization of Japanese business community members.

Japan International Cooperation Center
Odakyu Dai-ichi Seimei Bldg., 16th Floor, 2-7-1, Nishi-shinjuku, Shinjuku-ku, Tokyo 163-0716
http://sv2.jice.org/e/
81-3-6868-2702
Fax: 81-3-6838-2701

Outreach and coordination agency promoting mutually beneficial relationships between Japan and other nations.

Japan National Tourism Organization
One Grand Central Place, 60 E. 42nd St., Suite 448, New York, NY 10165
212-757-5640
Fax: 212-307-6754
www.jnto.go.jp/eng/

Attached to the Embassy of Japan, the group promotes travel to Japan.

National Association of Japan-America Societies
1819 L St., N.W., Suite 200, Washington, DC 20036
202-429-5545
Fax: 202-429-0027
www.us-japan.org

Private nonprofit organization that offers educational, cultural and business programs about U.S.-Japan relations.

New Energy and Industrial Technology Development Organization (NEDO)
Washington office: 2000 L St., N.W., #605, Washington, DC 20036
202-822-9292
Fax: 202-822-9289
www.nedo.go.jp/english/index.html

Japanese industry, government and academic organization dedicated to international research.

U.S.-Japan Business Council
1615 H St., N.W., Washington, DC 20062-2000
202-659-6000
www.uschamber.com/us-japan-business-council

Business association dedicated to Japanese-American ties.

Chapter 7: EU at the Crossroads

BOOKS

Baldwin, Richard, ed., "Brexit Beckons: Thinking Ahead by Leading Economists," CEPR Press, 2016.

Sixteen leading economists look at Brexit and its financial implications for the United Kingdom and the other countries in the European Union (EU).

Castells, Manuel, et al., eds., "Europe's Crises," Polity, 2018.

Economists, sociologists and political scientists discuss how the EU became embroiled in multiple crises and what can be done to resolve them.

Drozdiak, William, "Fractured Continent: Europe's Crises and the Fate of the West," W.W. Norton & Co., 2017.

A veteran Washington Post foreign correspondent looks at the forces pulling Europe apart in the 21st century.

Piris, Jean-Claude, "The Future of Europe: Towards a Two-Speed EU?" Cambridge University Press, 2012.

A legal scholar who helped draft the EU's structure concludes that the current organization is unworkable and proposes an inner core of countries that move faster toward political and economic union.

ARTICLES

Golod, Vassili, "Austria's Kurz Wants 'Axis of Willing' Against Illegal Migration," Politico.com, Jun. 13, 2018, https://tinyurl.com/y7kpmelu.

While Austria's economy is small by European standards, its young conservative leader is gaining a continent-wide following for his tough approach to migration and European budgets, a journalist writes.

Parker, George, "Brexit Chaos Puts Conservatives on the Edge of a Breakdown," Financial Times, Jul. 14, 2018, https://tinyurl.com/ybmetbh3.

A British journalist provides a comprehensive account of Prime Minister Theresa May's proposals for leaving the European Union and the likely points of friction with officials in Brussels.

Roubini, Nouriel, and Brunello Rosa, "Italy's Slow-Motion Euro Train Wreck," Project Syndicate, Jun. 1, 2018, https://tinyurl.com/ycur2ept.

Two experts offer a detailed analysis of Italy's economic problems and why they are likely to get worse under the new populist government.

REPORTS AND STUDIES

"The Effect of Imports of Steel on the National Security," U.S. Department of Commerce, Jan. 11, 2018, https://tinyurl.com/y8r5wocb.

This commerce department investigation provided the legal basis for President Trump's imposition of tariffs on imported steel and aluminum on the grounds that steel imports posed a national security threat.

"The Future Relationship between the United Kingdom and the European Union," Controller of Her Majesty's Stationery Office, July 2018, https://tinyurl.com/yaxthreg.

In this 98-page plan submitted to Parliament, British Prime Minister Theresa May lays out her compromise vision for Brexit.

"United Kingdom: Staff Concluding Statement of the 2017 Article IV Mission," International Monetary Fund, Dec. 20, 2017, https://tinyurl.com/yc87n86b.

The International Monetary Fund offers the most detailed look at the British economy on the eve of Brexit.

Blair, Tony, "The 'In-Betweener' Solution Is the Worst of All Worlds: Parliament Should Reject It," Tony Blair Institute for Global Change, Jul. 15, 2018, https://tinyurl.com/ybs2rwrk.

The former British prime minister accuses the government of bungling the Brexit process and says it should hold a second referendum on the issue.

THE NEXT STEP

IMMIGRATION IMPACT

"Italy to Block Naval Vessels Carrying Migrants from Docking: Interior Minister Matteo Salvini," Deutsche Welle, Jul. 9, 2018, https://tinyurl.com/y8jpl5aj.

Italy's interior minister has vowed to block naval ships that are on European Union- and NATO-sponsored migrant search-and-rescue missions from docking at Italian ports.

"Migration from EU to UK Lowest for Four Years, ONS Figures Show," BBC, Jul. 16, 2018, https://tinyurl.com/y85jjo62.

Immigration from the European Union to the United Kingdom reached a low in 2017, the first calendar year since the Brexit vote, and a record number of EU citizens left Great Britain, according to the U.K. Office for National Statistics.

Hovet, Jason, and Robert Muller, "Migration Concerns Will Dominate EU Elections Next Year, Czech Leader Says," Reuters, Aug. 1, 2018, https://tinyurl.com/yawkzt8u.

The migration issue will be one of the deciding factors in next year's EU parliamentary elections, and the vote will reveal a rising anti-immigration sentiment, Czech Prime Minister Andrej Babis predicted.

POST-BREXIT TRADE

"Brexit: EU 'Ready to Improve' Irish Border Proposal—Barnier," The Irish Times, Aug. 2, 2018, https://tinyurl.com/y9e53aq8.

The European Union has signaled a willingness to be more flexible in negotiations with the United Kingdom over the post-Brexit border between the Republic of Ireland and Northern Ireland.

"Michel Barnier Questions Theresa May's Brexit White Paper," BBC, Jul. 20, 2018, https://tinyurl.com/y6wde4fv.

Although the United Kingdom's proposed trade plan with Europe is a good start, it still needs work and in its current form could pose a problem for the EU's single market, the EU Brexit negotiator said.

"Post-Brexit Butter and Cheese Restrictions Possible Even with Trade Deal, Report Warns," The Caterer, Jul. 18, 2018, https://tinyurl.com/ycgt6rhw.

The United Kingdom could face post-Brexit shortages in dairy products it imports from the EU, according to a London School of Economics report.

ORGANIZATIONS

Bruegel
Rue de la Charité 33, 1210 Saint-Josse-ten-Noode, Belgium
+32 2 227 4210
www.bruegel.org

Brussels-based think tank specializing in European economic issues.

Department for Exiting the European Union
9 Downing St., London, SW1A 2AS, United Kingdom
+44-7801-404834
https://www.gov.uk/government/organisations/department-for-exiting-the-european-union

British government department negotiating the United Kingdom's exit from the European Union, with a website posting many documents related to proposed Brexit rules.

European Commission
Directorate-General for Communication. European Commission, Brussels, Belgium
+32 2 299 11 11
https://ec.europa.eu/info/about-european-commission/contact_en

Civil servants who carry out the daily business of the European Union, including Brexit, European finance, migration and others issues.

ifo Center for International Economics
Poschingerstraße 5, 81679 Münich, Germany
+49-899-224-1428
https://www.cesifo-group.de/ifoHome/research/Departments/International-Trade.html

Germany's leading research center focusing on international trade.

International Monetary Fund
700 19th St., N.W., Washington, DC 20431
1-202-623-7000
www.imf.org

Global financial group that has detailed analysis of economic trends by region and country.

Organisation of Economic Co-operation and Development
2, rue André Pascal 75775, Paris, France
+33 1 45 24 82 00
www.OECD.org

Intergovernmental organization that tracks economic developments in its 35 developed country members.

Tony Blair Institute for Global Change
50 Broadway, London, SW1H 0BL Britain
+44-2034355612
https://institute.global/

Think tank founded by former British Prime Minister Tony Blair has economic analysis and white papers on British policy.

Chapter 8: Fashion Industry

BOOKS

Agins, Teri, "Hijacking the Runway: How Celebrities Are Stealing the Spotlight from Fashion Designers," Avery, 2014.

A fashion writer explores the growth of celebrity fashion brands and their impact—much of it negative—on the rest of the business.

Callahan, Maureen, "Champagne Supernovas: Marc Jacobs, Alexander McQueen, and the '90s Renegades Who Remade Fashion," Touchstone, 2015.

A journalist explores a "creative brew of art, decadence and genius" at a defining moment in the industry as change blows hard through fashion.

Chaney, Lisa, "Coco Chanel: An Intimate Life," Viking, 2011.

This biography goes beyond the creative business person to profile a woman who feels love, loss and the sting of changing expectations and economic conditions.

Cline, Elizabeth L., "Overdressed: The Shockingly High Cost of Cheap Fashion," Portfolio, 2013.

Fast fashion leads to overfull closets and enormous waste, according to a journalist, who looks at how and why this is happening.

ARTICLES

Bernard, Katherine, "Paris Couture Week Cheat Sheet: A Fashion Dictionary from Atelier to Pret," Vogue, Jul. 9, 2014, http://tinyurl.com/z74pfgz.

This article provides details on some mostly French words of fashion and what they mean today.

Binkley, Christina, "Why Do Women Spend Less on Fashion after 45?" The Wall Street Journal, Apr. 6, 2016, http://tinyurl.com/h7vkgek.

Women in prime earning years, who are often ignored by fashion brands, can find advice and apparel on a new website, Apprécier.com.

Chrisman-Campbell, Kimberly, "A Brief History of Unisex Fashion," The Atlantic, Apr. 14, 2015, http://tinyurl.com/lxk3ume.

From ponchos to jumpsuits to tuxedoes, fashion starting in the 1960s generated styles for his and hers—and theirs.

Daneshkhu, Scheherazada, and Mark Vandevelde, "Clothes Buying Goes Out of Fashion in the UK," The Financial Times, Sep. 24, 2016, http://tinyurl.com/jqsvdrn.

In Great Britain, shoppers are no longer wowed by fashion clothing and sales have slumped.

Givhan, Robin, "Luxury Fashion Brands Are Going Green. But Why Are They Keeping It a Secret?" The Washington Post, Dec. 8, 2015, http://tinyurl.com/jf38a4c.

Gucci, Louis Vuitton and other high-end fashion brands adopt environmental-friendly practices—quietly.

Givhan, Robin, "New York Fashion Exhibit Examines the Influence of Gay Designers," The Washington Post, Sep. 17, 2013, http://tinyurl.com/j7n74bx.

An exhibit in New York City examines the influence and history of gay fashion designers from the 1800s to now.

Gunn, Tim, "Designers Refuse to Make Clothes to Fit American Women. It's a Disgrace," The Washington Post, Sep. 8, 2016, http://tinyurl.com/gpklwba.

The co-host of Project Runway explores the huge hole in fashion: a lack of appealing clothing for larger women.

Holmes, Elizabeth, "Where Luxury Fashion Is a High Speed, High Volume Business," The Wall Street Journal, Oct. 26, 2016, http://tinyurl.com/zgyl7bt.

At Farfetch, speed and efficiency are in fashion at its photo studios.

Kowsmann, Patricia, "Fast Fashion: How a Zara Coat Went from Design to Fifth Avenue in 25 Days," The Wall Street Journal, Dec. 6, 2016, http://tinyurl.com/guggzkj.

An article gives a detailed look at how Zara discovers new fashion ideas and executes them, much faster than its competitors.

Trebay, Guy, "Why Is the Men's Fashion Industry in Such Turmoil?" The New York Times, Apr. 13, 2016, http://tinyurl.com/z6qfwk8.

Top designers are leaving or are being forced out of several men's fashion houses, as suits fall out of favor and men get creative in dressing.

Wicker, Alden, "Fast Fashion Is Creating an Environmental Crisis," Newsweek, Sep. 1, 2016, http://tinyurl.com/hvc6le6.

The rapid rise in fast fashion means a huge glut of used clothing heading into landfills or resold in Eastern Europe or Africa.

Zargani, Luisa, "Miuccia Prada Talks Men's Wear, Revolution and History," Women's Wear Daily, Mar. 23, 2016, http://tinyurl.com/gourfnw.

Prada gives a long interview on fashion's relevance, history and political role.

REPORTS AND STUDIES

"Fashion," U.S. Bureau of Labor Statistics, June 2012, http://tinyurl.com/gsu6jr9.

The government provides an array of data on the global fashion industry, the cities where employment is concentrated and spending on fashion.

"Luxury Goods Worldwide Market Study, Fall–Winter 2016," Bain & Company, 2016, http://tinyurl.com/jtwb525.

The consultancy delivers its annual global report on luxury goods, from cars to travel to clothing and accessories.

"Wages and Working Hours in the Textiles, Clothing, Leather and Footwear Industries," International Labour Organization, September 2014, http://tinyurl.com/hr7bycs.

This international report looks at where textiles and clothing are produced, top export countries and employment and wages.

Amed, Imran, et al., "The State of Fashion," McKinsey & Company, December 2016, http://tinyurl.com/j4gu5l8.

The consulting firm looks at the challenges, trends and growing sectors of fashion, based in part on a survey of fashion executives.

Bennie, Fionna, Ivana Gazibara and Vicky Murray, "Fashion Futures 2015: Global Scenarios for a Sustainable Fashion Industry," Forum on the Future, February 2010, http://tinyurl.com/gr7uvrt.

A report gives four very different future scenarios on fashion, based on different views of socioeconomic trends.

Raustiala, Kal, and Christopher Springman, "The Piracy Paradox: Innovation and Intellectual Property in Fashion Design," Virginia Law Review, December 2006, http://tinyurl.com/zbtutc6.

Unlike science and film, fashion accepts copying and piracy as a way of life; yet it continues to innovate. This paper looks at that paradox.

THE NEXT STEP

EMBRACING DISRUPTION

Cartner-Morley, Jess, "Karl Lagerfeld Electrifies Chanel by Embracing Digital Disruption," The Guardian, Oct. 4, 2016, http://tinyurl.com/zn27ymu.

Chanel's creative director Karl Lagerfeld used the fashion house's Paris fashion week show to make a statement about the fashion industry's relationship with technology, specifically with data centers and servers.

Laws, Nancy, "Can This New Industry Disrupt Fast Fashion?" The Huffington Post, Mar. 2, 2016, http://tinyurl.com/jqb45u8.

A new industry, "Agile Retail," emerging in the fashion world will see companies doing online-only sales, using smart data to predict and target trends and producing and distributing in-house.

Task, Aaron, "How Rebecca Minkoff Keeps Disrupting the Fashion Industry," Fortune, Sep. 6, 2016, http://tinyurl.com/j4kyp9p.

Designer Rebecca Minkoff has used technology to disrupt the fashion industry, including broadcasting her show in virtual reality and introducing a "buy now, wear now" format.

ONLINE BUYING ECONOMY

Chambers, Sam, "Faster than Zara? Boohoo's Online Fashion Fuels 260% Return," Bloomberg, Dec. 28, 2016, http://tinyurl.com/zyyqelm.

Online fast fashion retailer Boohoo.com's shares increased about 260 percent in 2016.

Halzack, Sarah, "Online Shopping Grows Robustly during the Holiday Season," The Washington Post, Jan. 5, 2017, http://tinyurl.com/zzaga2t.

Retailers increased holiday sales by 11 percent in 2016 from the previous year, bringing in $91.7 billion in digital sales.

Wolfe, Nandini, "Shopping for Vintage Fashion: How the Internet Has Transformed It," The Wall Street Journal, Jan. 7, 2017, http://tinyurl.com/hlqprqp.

The vintage fashion industry has found renewed success on e-commerce sites that market directly to secondhand clothing consumers.

SUSTAINABLE BRANDS

Bhasin, Kim, "The Future of Fashion Is Mushroom Leather," Bloomberg Businessweek, Dec. 22, 2016, http://tinyurl.com/jszogbj.

The chief executive of Kering, which owns 16 fashion brands, is on a mission to make his company more sustainable through a set of goals to address the supply chain, the use of new biotechnology and eliminating some toxic chemicals.

Christian, Scott, "Can H&M Really Make Fast Fashion Sustainable?" Esquire, Dec. 20, 2016, http://tinyurl.com/hujr6em.

Fast fashion brand H&M has begun collecting unwanted clothes from its stores to "create a closed loop for textiles" so they can be made into new ones, in the company's latest effort to be more sustainable.

Harilela, Divia, "How Mongolian Cashmere Is Helping Sustainable Fashion," South China Morning Post, Dec. 13, 2016, http://tinyurl.com/hx5levf.

A collaboration between luxury brand Maiyet and four Chinese designers seeks to raise awareness about issues in fashion production through its capsule collections, which use the world's only certified, ethical and environmentally sustainable cashmere yarn.

TRENDING IN 2017

Friedman, Vanessa, "What to Watch for in Fashion in 2017," The New York Times, Jan. 3, 2017, http://tinyurl.com/jhxwvem.

There will be upheaval on the runways, changes in the style of D.C.'s powerful elite and lots of cultural action off the runways, according to a reporter from The New York Times.

Munzenrieder, Kyle, "The '80s Will Be the Biggest Trend of 2017, for Better or Worse," W Magazine, Dec. 13, 2016, http://tinyurl.com/gox4so7.

Two analytical trend forecasts predict that 2017 fashion will be all about 1980s styles, including mules, political T-shirts and ruffles.

Yotka, Steff, "Meet the People, Trends, and Items That Will Rule Fashion in 2017," Vogue, Dec. 28, 2016, http://tinyurl.com/hbu8ebc.

Athluxury will take over athleisure, shades of pink will be hot on the catwalk and phone cases are the new must-have accessory for the New Year, according to Vogue's fashion news editor.

ORGANIZATIONS

American Apparel & Footwear Association
740 6th St., N.W., 3rd and 4th Floors, Washington, DC 20001
202-853-908
https://www.wewear.org/

Trade association for 1,000 brands, providing professional development, best practices and intelligence on global apparel trends.

Clean Clothes Campaign
Postbus 11584 1001 GN, Amsterdam, Netherlands
+31-20-412-27-85
https://cleanclothes.org/about/who-we-are

Researches and campaigns to improve conditions for garment workers by bringing together companies, unions and non-government organizations.

Council of Fashion Designers of America (CFDA)
65 Bleecker, Floor 11, New York, NY 10012
202-302-1821
https://cfda.com/

Influential organization that grants awards, runs a fashion incubator and supports the growth of the American fashion business.

Ethical Fashion Forum
50 Brook Street, London, W1K 5DR
+44-(0)20-3601-8863
http://www.ethicalfashionforum.com/About-the-SOURCE-platform

Gathers best practices and information for ethical choices in fashion sourcing, manufacturing and more.

Fair Wear Foundation
World Fashion Centre, Koningin Wilhelminaplein 13, Amsterdam, Netherlands
+31-(0)20-408-4255
https://www.fairwear.org/

Works with factories, non-government organizations, unions and brands to improve working conditions in apparel factories. Gives a Best Practices award to clothing company at annual conference.

The Fashion Group International
8 W. 40th St., 7th Floor, New York, NY 10018
212-302-5511
http://www.fgi.org/index.php?news=719#

Established in 1930 by prominent women in the fashion business, it focuses on fashion business and careers with chapters in many cities.

The Fashion Jewelry & Accessories Trade Association
25 Sea Grass Way, N. Kingstown, RI 02852
401-667-0520
http://www.fjata.org/

Represents 225 member companies that make, supply and retail jewelry and accessories and "bring science to bear on regulatory issues."

Fashion Revolution
19 Dig St., Ashbourne, Derbyshire, DE6 1GF UK
http://fashionrevolution.org/

Nonprofit organization that seeks to support better fashion jobs and create more sustainable practices.

Chapter 9: Free Trade

BOOKS

Bernstein, William, "A Splendid Exchange: How Trade Shaped the World," Grove Press, 2009.

A financial theorist and historian looks at the long narrative of trade, from ancient Mesopotamia to the WTO Doha round.

Bhagwati, Jagdish, "In Defense of Globalization," Oxford University Press, 2007.

A Columbia University economics professor argues for free trade, detailing how it has the potential to enable prosperity in developing countries by reducing child labor, increasing literacy and supporting the participation of women, among other things.

Fletcher, Ian, "Free Trade Doesn't Work: What Should Replace It and Why," Coalition for a Prosperous America, 2011.

A trade theorist advocates a high (perhaps 30 percent) flat tariff on all U.S. imports of goods and services, saying such a levy would be politics-proof and would trigger a return of capital- and knowledge-intensive industries.

Irwin, Douglas, "Free Trade under Fire," Princeton University Press, 2015.

A Dartmouth College economics professor asks if free trade deserves its poor reputation and concludes that, despite its flaws, trade enables growth and works against poverty.

Mandelbaum, Michael, "The Road to Global Prosperity," Simon & Schuster, 2014.

A professor of foreign policy at the Johns Hopkins School of Advanced International Studies looks at recent worrisome economic developments, yet argues that globalization will continue to be a positive force.

ARTICLES

"CFR's Jagdish Bhagwati Argues against Preferential Trade Agreements in New Book; Recommends Completion of Multilateral Doha Round," Council on Foreign Relations, Jul. 16, 2008, http://tinyurl.com/habkfew.

A Columbia University professor argues that bilateral trade deals make world trade more difficult by creating overlapping and sometimes contradictory agreements.

Appelbaum, Binyamin, "A Little-Noticed Fact about Trade: It's No Longer Rising," The New York Times, Oct. 30, 2016, http://tinyurl.com/j39fwsh.

An economics journalist explains that trade is no longer growing and how that fact affects global economic growth.

Hufbauer, Gary Clyde, and Euijin Jung, "U.S. Bilateral Trade Balances: A New Guide to Trade Policy," Peterson Institute for International Economics, Nov. 15, 2016, http://tinyurl.com/jn83jon.

Two experts at a think tank respond to Trump advisers' assertions that reducing the trade deficit would increase GDP growth.

Rodrik, Dani, "Put Globalization to Work for Democracies," The New York Times, Sep. 17, 2016, http://tinyurl.com/gm5hefz.

A Harvard University economist calls for a more moderate form of trade liberalization, with a balance between national autonomy and economic globalization.

Scheve, Kenneth, and Matthew Slaughter, "A New Deal for Globalization," Foreign Affairs, July/August 2007, http://tinyurl.com/zg3cd7z.

The authors advocate for an open global system that ensures a majority of workers benefit from it, largely through income redistribution.

Slaughter, Matthew, "High-Trade Jobs Pay Higher Wages," The Wall Street Journal, Jan. 20, 2014, http://tinyurl.com/jcp5l23.

A business school dean argues that workers at globally engaged companies earn more than those at purely domestic companies.

Tankersley, Jim, "Donald Trump's Trade War Could Kill Millions of U.S. Jobs," The Washington Post, Mar. 25, 2016, http://tinyurl.com/juky9v9.

A Moody's economic model predicts that a round of retaliatory tariffs could bring recession and job loss.

Verma, Sid, "Barclays Warns 'Politics of Rage' Will Slow Global Growth," Bloomberg News, Oct. 24, 2016, http://tinyurl.com/z2lvzys.

A report discusses the implications of growing opposition to globalization for economies and markets.

REPORTS AND STUDIES

"The Economic Benefits of U.S. Trade," Council of Economic Advisers, Executive Office of the President of the United States, May 2015, http://tinyurl.com/zcxz2bq.

An Obama administration paper argues that trade and globalization since World War II have delivered important benefits for U.S. consumers, workers and businesses.

"Report Urges WTO Members to Resist Protectionism and Get Trade Moving Again," World Trade Organization, July 2016, http://tinyurl.com/zsp5b9j.

The WTO issues a report that finds that protectionist measures are proliferating around the world. It urges member countries to resist such policies and embrace trade as the solution to faster economic growth.

"Trade in 2016 to Grow at Slowest Pace Since the Financial Crisis," World Trade Organization, Sep. 27, 2016, http://tinyurl.com/j5n3uxr.

The WTO looks at the slowing pace of trade growth.

Furman, Jason, "Wal-Mart: A Progressive Success Story," New York University, November 2005, http://tinyurl.com/jlvf32s.

One of President Barack Obama's top economic advisers argues that any harm the retail behemoth has done to workers is outweighed by the price reductions it brings to the entire populace.

Hufbauer, Gary Clyde, and Sean Lowry, "U.S. Tire Tariffs: Saving Few Jobs at High Cost," Peterson Institute for International Economics, April 2012, http://tinyurl.com/hwvxumf.

A study looks at how one punitive tariff saved 1,200 jobs, but at a hefty cost to U.S. car and truck buyers.

THE NEXT STEP

RISE OF NATIONALISM

Chesto, Jon, "GE's Immelt Raises Concern about Nationalist Trade Policies," Boston Globe, Feb. 27, 2017, http://tinyurl.com/go2ba4k.

General Electric CEO Jeff Immelt wrote to his shareholders that he and his company support "multilateralism and free trade," but are prepared for a worldwide pullback from globalization.

Holodny, Elena, "A New Study Shows That Areas in Europe Hit Hardest by Trade Saw a Rise in Support for Nationalist Parties," Business Insider, Feb. 8, 2017, http://tinyurl.com/zsvzohf.

European regions that suffered a stronger shock from Chinese imports were more likely to experience a rise in nationalism and support for far-right political parties, according to an Italian study.

Pazzanese, Christina, "In Europe, Nationalism Rising," Harvard Gazette, Feb. 27, 2017, http://tinyurl.com/jyg6sc5.

Far-right candidates running in upcoming elections in European countries, such as the Netherlands, France and Germany, are encouraged by Donald Trump's presidential victory.

DOMESTIC JOBS

Lee, Don, "Trump's Push for American-Made Could Disrupt NAFTA Supply Chains and Raise Consumer Prices," Los Angeles Times, Feb. 28, 2017, http://tinyurl.com/hdhygup.

President Trump plans to renegotiate the North American Free Trade Agreement (NAFTA) to encourage domestic manufacturing, which could end up raising prices for American consumers.

Light, Larry, "Are Robots or Mexicans to Blame for U.S. Job Losses?" CBS News, Feb. 21, 2017, http://tinyurl.com/hofepae.

The increase in automation and cheap overseas labor are factors in the loss of U.S. manufacturing jobs.

Velazquez, Katarina, "Proposed Mexico Tariff Could Complicate Agriculture Trade," Star-Telegram, Mar. 4, 2017, http://tinyurl.com/jh3m9mj.

President Trump's proposed 20 percent tariff on Mexican imports could lead to a trade war that experts say would result in a loss of income for U.S. agricultural producers.

IMMIGRATION'S EFFECTS

Brewer, Contessa, "Border Towns Feel the Chill from Trump's Tough Talk on Trade and Immigration," CNBC, Mar. 4, 2017, http://tinyurl.com/z5mag2e.

President Trump's calls for a Mexican border tax, renegotiating NAFTA, a border wall and tougher immigration policies are worrying Mexican investors, especially in the produce industry.

Bryan, Bob, "Asked about Trump's Immigration Plans, Janet Yellen Says 'Slowing Immigration Would Slow Economic Growth,'" Markets Insider, Feb. 15, 2017, http://tinyurl.com/hd9wgz6.

Federal Reserve Chair Janet Yellen said during testimony to the Senate Banking Committee that restricting immigration could hurt the economy.

Singh, Shruti, "Cargill at Odds with Trump as It Warns on Trade, Immigration," Bloomberg, Feb. 4, 2017, http://tinyurl.com/hot2gr4.

The CEO of agribusiness giant Cargill, David MacLennan, warns that curbing legal immigration could damage the U.S. economy, cause food shortages and trigger international conflict.

INTERNATIONAL UNCERTAINTY

"EU Awaits 'Solid Outline' of Trump Trade Goals with Europe," The Associated Press, ABC News, Mar. 3, 2017, http://tinyurl.com/jlj3pam.

As the European Union (EU) waits for President Trump to define his trade goals regarding Europe, some of the Continent's leaders are concerned about his "America First" views.

Chrysoloras, Nikos, and Stearns, Jonathan, "The Trump Trade Threat Could Unite the Rest of the World, EU Official Says," Bloomberg, Mar. 4, 2017, http://tinyurl.com/hjmh534.

A European Union official said President Trump's protectionist approach to world trade may result in economic alliances between the EU and Asian, Latin American and Middle Eastern countries.

Donnan, Shawn, "Policy Uncertainty Threatens Trade Growth, Says World Bank," Financial Times, Feb. 21, 2017, http://tinyurl.com/z5n87ms.

A World Bank report, citing a rise in protectionism and threats to global trade agreements, concluded that political uncertainty is slowing trade growth around the world.

ORGANIZATIONS

American Enterprise Institute
1789 Massachusetts Ave., N.W., Washington, DC 20036
202-862-5800
www.aei.org

Think tank that advocates in favor of the free-enterprise system.

Coalition for a Prosperous America
1200 G St., N.W., Washington, DC 20005
202-688-5145
http://www.prosperousamerica.org/

Think tank that promotes an overhaul of U.S. trade policy.

Economic Strategy Institute
1730 Rhode Island Ave., N.W., Suite 414, Washington, DC 20036
202-213-7051
http://www.econstrat.org/

Research organization that favors more transparent and open markets in international trade.

International Monetary Fund
700 19th St., N.W., Washington, DC 20431
202-623-7000
www.imf.org

Institution established by 1944 Bretton Woods conference that works for global monetary cooperation, financial stability and global trade.

International Trade Administration
U.S. Department of Commerce,
1401 Constitution Ave., N.W., Washington, DC 20230
202-482-3809
www.trade.gov

Commerce department office that helps coordinate trade matters and provides studies and data on trade.

Office of the United States Trade Representative
600 17th St., N.W., Washington, DC 20508
202-395-3230
https://ustr.gov

White House agency responsible for coordinating U.S. international trade, commodity and direct investment policy and overseeing negotiations with other nations.

Peterson Institute for International Economics
1750 Massachusetts Ave., N.W., Washington, DC 20036-1903
202-328-9000
https://piie.com

Think tank focused on international economic and trade issues.

U.S. International Trade Commission
500 E St., S.W., Washington, DC 20436
202-205-2000
www.usitc.gov

Federal agency established in 1916 as the U.S. Tariff Commission; gathers and analyzes trade data and provides trade expertise to Congress and the president.

World Trade Organization
Centre William Rappard, Rue de Lausanne 154, CH-1211 Geneva 21, Switzerland
+41 (0)22 739 51 11
www.wto.org

Intergovernmental organization that regulates international trade.

Chapter 10: Global Manufacturing

BOOKS

Isaacson, Walter, "Steve Jobs," Simon & Schuster, 2011.

Best-selling biography of the late Apple CEO discusses his life and influence across seven industries—personal computers, animated movies, music, phones, tablet computing, digital publishing and retail stores.

Martinez, David, "Zara: The Vision and Strategy of Amancio Ortega," Spanish ed., Random House Mondadori, 2012.

Zara, the Spanish clothing and accessories retailer, has made Ortega one of the world's wealthiest and most successful businessmen.

Maynard, Micheline, "The Selling of the American Economy: How Foreign Companies Are Remaking the American Dream," Broadway Books, 2009.

Journalist specializing in automotive industry and the economy explores investments by foreign manufacturers in the United States and the impact on workers, communities, states and regions.

Ohno, Taiichi, "Toyota Production System: Beyond Large-Scale Production," Productivity Press, 1998.

The creator of the much-copied Toyota Production System explains its principles.

Roos, Daniel, James P. Womack and Daniel T. Jones, "The Machine That Changed the World," Harper Perennial, 1991.

Based on a five-year study of the automobile industry by MIT researchers, the book introduced the concept of "lean manufacturing."

Vance, Ashlee, "Elon Musk: Tesla, SpaceX, and the Quest for a Fantastic Future," Ecco, 2015.

A technology writer looks at the life of the entrepreneur whose gigafactory project could be the next wave of global manufacturing, or a disaster.

ARTICLES

Bremmer, Ian, "The New Rules of Globalization," Harvard Business Review, January–February 2014, http://tinyurl.com/o6oq2cj.

Thirty-one years after Theodore Levitt predicted globalization's rise, a political scientist analyzes a "guarded globalization" that is slow moving and selective.

Kazer, William, "China Manufacturing Gauge Hits Two-Year Low," The Wall Street Journal, Aug. 3, 2015, http://tinyurl.com/pq8bn5f.

China's key economic measurement of factory activity slumped to a two-year low in July 2015.

Levitt, Theodore, "The Globalization of Markets," Harvard Business Review, May 1983, http://tinyurl.com/mtx9gaw.

In a classic article, a Harvard University economist predicted the rise of global manufacturing.

Philips, Matthew, "The U.S. South Rises as a Manufacturing Hub," Bloomberg Business, Sep. 4, 2014, http://tinyurl.com/q7wwl2p.

Companies from the United States and abroad continue to invest in Southern states.

"Still Made in China," The Economist, Sep. 12, 2015, http://tinyurl.com/p9d8fxb.

A special report looks at the "Made in China 2025" plan approved by China's State Council to upgrade the nation's factories.

REPORTS AND STUDIES

"C.A.S.E.—Car of the Future: The AlixPartners Global Automotive Outlook 2015," AlixPartners, June 2015, http://tinyurl.com/nsnrkxo.

The growth of automotive production is expected to slow, says a consulting firm.

"Global Manufacturing Outlook 2015," KPMG Consulting, June 2015, http://tinyurl.com/q9w6hf8.

Manufacturers are tightening the supply chain and stressing innovation, according to a management consulting firm.

"Mexico's Manufacturing Sector Continues to Grow," Stratfor Global Intelligence, Apr. 6, 2015, http://tinyurl.com/npb5dyr.

Mexico continues to see solid growth because of its integration with and dependence on the U.S. market, says a global consulting firm.

"Sustaining Employment Growth: The Role of Manufacturing and Structural Change," United Nations Industrial Development Organization, 2013, http://tinyurl.com/o2woudk.

A United Nations agency reviews the status of global manufacturing employment.

THE NEXT STEP

AUTOMOTIVE INDUSTRY

McCarthy, Tom, "Trump's Flawed Policies Would Threaten the Global Economy, Say Analysts," The Guardian, Aug. 26, 2015, http://tinyurl.com/pheun4w.

Republican presidential candidate Donald Trump's proposed 35 percent import tax on cars produced in Mexico would not help bring more manufacturing jobs to the United States, according to a professor of international politics at Tufts University.

Vlasic, Bill, "In Former Hummer Plant in Indiana, Mercedes Turns Out S.U.V.s for China," The New York Times, Aug. 11, 2015, http://tinyurl.com/nw8vx9a.

To produce enough cars to meet Chinese consumers' demand, German car manufacturer Mercedes-Benz reopened a former General Motors factory in Indiana that had closed during the recession.

Young, Angelo, "China's Slowdown Could See Automakers Slowing Factory Construction or Exporting Excess Cars from China," International Business Times, Aug. 31, 2015, http://tinyurl.com/qfu8tu7.

Automakers that recently opened factories in China are weighing whether to cut production or export cars to other countries due to sliding sales amid the Asian nation's economic slowdown.

CHINA'S ECONOMY

Chen, Tim, "3D Printing Can Help Modernise China's Economy: Premier Li Keqiang," South China Morning Post, Aug. 24, 2015, http://tinyurl.com/oqx3xp3.

Chinese Prime Minister Li Keqiang told his nation's top administrative council that the country must use 3-D printing and other new technologies in traditional manufacturing to modernize its economy.

Curran, Enda, "How China's Economy Suffers When It Tries to Cut Pollution," Bloomberg Business, Aug. 3, 2015, http://tinyurl.com/pxwgu64.

Economic data show China's temporary limits on driving and on steel and coal production to reduce smog during international events significantly reduce industrial output.

Spence, Peter, "China Leading World Towards Global Economic Recession, Warns Citi," The Telegraph, Sep. 9, 2015, http://tinyurl.com/qe6znag.

Economic slowdowns in China and other emerging markets could lead to a worldwide recession in 2016–17, according to Citibank's global economics team.

RESHORING AND NEAR-SHORING

Bounds, Andrew, and Tanya Powley, "UK Textiles Eye Reshoring Jobs Boost," Financial Times, Feb. 9, 2015, http://tinyurl.com/of962k5.

The United Kingdom can add 20,000 textiles jobs by 2020 by relying less on labor from Asia and by building factories in underserved areas, according to a report backed by a member of Parliament, clothing manufacturers and the U.K. government.

Carey, Nick, "Wal-Mart Taps Manufacturer Database to Aid U.S. Reshoring Drive," Reuters, Jul. 8, 2015, http://tinyurl.com/nnvc6uk.

The largest U.S. retailer will collaborate with a manufacturing vendor database to help its suppliers source more materials from American firms, part of Walmart's goal to sell $250 billion in domestically made products by 2023.

Woods, Bob, "Is There a Renaissance in US Manufacturing? Numbers Don't Add Up," CNBC, Jun. 10, 2015, http://tinyurl.com/qeoegro.

American companies' promises to bring more jobs to the United States or nearby Mexico will do little to replace the nearly 5 million manufacturing jobs lost since 2000, according to industry experts.

INTERNATIONAL WAGES

Kynge, James, "Mexico Steals a March on China in Car Manufacturing," Financial Times, Apr. 21, 2015, http://tinyurl.com/pgdfrb6.

More auto manufacturers are investing in factories in Mexico instead of China, where automotive wages have climbed by 17 percent since 2009.

McLain, Sean, "Foxconn Seeks Manufacturing Sites in India," The Wall Street Journal, Aug. 4, 2015, http://tinyurl.com/perurf7.

Taiwanese electronics manufacturer Foxconn plans to build factories in India, which has a large labor pool and lower wages than China, where most of the company's facilities now operate.

Timmons, Heather, "The Philippines Factory Fire Shows the Grim Reality behind a Fast-Growth Economy," Quartz, May 18, 2015, http://tinyurl.com/qce5edt.

Economists say for the Philippines to improve domestic consumption and allow for more stable growth in its low-wage manufacturing sector, it must attract better-paying tech manufacturing jobs.

ORGANIZATIONS

Manufacturing Enterprise Solutions Association
107 S. Southgate Drive, Chandler, AZ 85226
480-893-6883
www.mesa.org

Education and training organization that works on global manufacturing topics.

The Manufacturing Institute
733 10th St., N.W., Washington, DC 20001
202-637-3426
www.themanufacturinginstitute.org

U.S. think tank that studies manufacturing topics.

Organization for International Investment
1225 19th St., N.W., Suite 501, Washington, DC 20036
202-659-1903
www.ofii.org

Trade group representing foreign companies investing in the United States.

Society of Manufacturing Engineers
One SME Drive, Dearborn, MI 48128
313-425-3000
www.sme.org

International professional organization serving the manufacturing community.

United Nations Industrial Development Organization
Vienna International Centre
Wagramerstr. 5, P.O. Box 300, A-1400
Vienna, Austria
43-1-26026-0
www.unido.org

United Nations group that tracks international manufacturing data.

U.S.-China Chamber of Commerce
55 W. Monroe St., Suite 630, Chicago, IL 60603
312-368-9911
info@usccc.org

Trade group representing American companies investing in China.

World Trade Organization
Rue de Lausanne 154, 1202
Geneva, Switzerland
41-22-739-51-11
www.wto.org

International body that governs global trade rules.

Chapter 11: Global Oil and Gas Industry

BOOKS

Coronil, Fernando, "The Magical State: Nature, Money and Modernity in Venezuela," University of Chicago Press, 1997.

Coronil, who was a professor of anthropology at the University of Michigan, tells how the discovery of oil shaped Venezuelan society and culture.

Gold, Russell, "The Boom: How Fracking Ignited the American Energy Revolution and Changed the World," Simon & Schuster, 2014.

Gold, a veteran Wall Street Journal energy reporter, recounts the story of hydraulic fracturing and its impact.

Marcel, Valerie, "Oil Titans: National Oil Companies in the Middle East," Brookings Institution Press, 2006.

Marcel, an energy analyst at Chatham House in London and a former professor at the Institut de Sciences Politiques in Paris, describes how the oil industries of Middle Eastern nations unshackled themselves from the Western oil giants.

Yergin, Daniel, "The Prize: The Epic Quest for Oil, Money and Power," Simon & Schuster, 1991, 1992, 2008.

Founder of Cambridge Energy Research Associates, an energy consulting firm recently acquired by IHS, Yergin is considered America's foremost chronicler of the energy industry. "The Prize," the definitive history of the field, won the Pulitzer Prize for nonfiction.

ARTICLES

Gilbert, Daniel, and Justin Scheck, "BP Is Found Grossly Negligent in Deepwater Horizon Disaster," The Wall Street Journal, Sep. 4, 2014, http://tinyurl.com/mapnoke.

BP got handed a big bill for negligence in its massive Gulf of Mexico oil spill.

Gold, Russell, and Daniel Gilbert, "The U.S. Is Overtaking Russia as Largest Oil-and-Gas Producer," The Wall Street Journal, Oct. 2, 2013, http://tinyurl.com/n9s9cy8.

America rose unexpectedly to become the world's top energy producer thanks to hydraulic fracturing.

González, Ángel, "Expanded Oil Drilling Helps U.S. Wean Itself from Mideast," The Wall Street Journal, Jun. 27, 2012, http://tinyurl.com/pl7qukp.

The surge in fracking, coupled with growing imports from Canada, is diminishing the need to import Middle Eastern crude.

Reed, Stanley, "Britain Proposes Easier Access to Tap Shale Rock Energy," The New York Times, May 24, 2014, http://tinyurl.com/nc7ouk6.

The British government seeks to ignite its own hydraulic fracturing industry despite stiff opposition.

Roberts, Dan, "Sweeping New US and EU Sanctions Target Russia's Banks and Oil Companies," The Guardian, Sep. 12, 2014, http://tinyurl.com/nvk8j8t.

The West is adopting a variety of economic measures against Russia in the wake of the Ukraine crisis.

REPORTS AND STUDIES

"Annual Energy Outlook 2014," U.S. Energy Information Administration, May 7, 2014, http://tinyurl.com/365m48b.

In its yearly report, the U.S. government agency in charge of gathering data for policy makers and the public focuses on the factors that shape the nation's energy system over the long term.

"Shale Gas—a Global Perspective," KPMG International, 2011, http://tinyurl.com/ppq475u.

Consulting firm's report estimates the global potential of shale if other countries decide to pursue hydraulic fracturing.

"World Energy Outlook 2013," International Energy Agency, Nov. 12, 2013, http://tinyurl.com/lxkqcab.

Annual report from the IEA, a Paris-based organization of governments of oil-importing countries, projects energy trends by fuel, sector, region and scenario through 2035.

Larson, John, and Richard Fullenbaum, "America's New Energy Future: The Unconventional Oil and Gas Revolution and the Economy—Volume 3: A Manufacturing Renaissance," IHS, September 2013, http://tinyurl.com/mynzvdw.

Energy consulting and analysis firm describes how cheap fuel, especially natural gas, is a boon for petrochemical and other energy-intensive industries, bolstering the U.S. manufacturing sector.

THE NEXT STEP

ENERGY EXPORTS

Cama, Timothy, "Report: Natural Gas Exports Could Hurt Russian State-Owned Company," The Hill, Sep. 22, 2014, http://tinyurl.com/ne379x2.

Researchers at Columbia University predict American competition for natural gas exports to Europe will reduce revenue for Russia's state-owned gas company by 18 percent.

Feng, Bree, "Russia Uses Its Natural Gas to Play the China Card, Again," The New York Times, Sep. 25, 2014, http://tinyurl.com/mytu2u8.

Russia and China are discussing a deal that would authorize a natural gas pipeline from Siberia to western China and would double Russia's gas exports to China.

Snyder, Jim, "Keystone-Oil Export Ban Sought by Senator Backing Pipeline Bill," Bloomberg News, Jan. 13, 2015, http://tinyurl.com/kpa9r65.

Sen. Joe Manchin, D-W. Va., proposed an amendment that would subject oil transported from Alberta via the Keystone XL pipeline to the restrictions of U.S. crude export laws.

MIDDLE EASTERN OIL

El Gamal, Rania, "Facing New Oil Glut, Saudis Avoid 1980s Mistakes to Halt Price Slide," Reuters, Oct. 14, 2014, http://tinyurl.com/mzyyk7l.

Despite a global market similar to the 1980s oil glut, Saudi Arabia plans to maintain its crude oil production levels, rather than cut production, in an effort to retain its market share.

Graeber, Daniel, "EIA: Oil Threats Present, but Subsiding," United Press International, Oct. 8, 2014, http://tinyurl.com/lrgu9or.

Disruptions in global oil production caused by violence in northern Iraq and Libya have mostly subsided since mid-2014, according to a September report from the U.S. Energy Information Administration.

Kantchev, Georgi, "How Low Can Oil Go? And When's It Going Back Up?" The Wall Street Journal, Jan. 19, 2015, http://tinyurl.com/kvhe596.

Experts predict Saudi Arabian oil prices will continue to fall through the first quarter of 2015 due to emerging Russian competition and the current strength of the dollar.

NATURAL GAS

Carrington, Damian, "UK to Allow Fracking Companies to Use "Any Substance" under Homes," The Guardian, Oct. 14, 2014, http://tinyurl.com/oye6a2y.

A proposed law in the United Kingdom would prevent landowners from blocking fracking below their property and would permit companies to use "any substance" to extract natural gas from the earth.

Cama, Timothy, "Obama Sending Mixed Messages on Natural Gas," The Hill, Jan. 18, 2015, http://tinyurl.com/novjcoy.

The president of the American Petroleum Institute argues that proposed regulations on methane gas will raise natural gas production costs and discourage development of a domestic energy supply that has helped to reduce carbon dioxide emissions.

Philips, Matthew, "U.S. Oil Producers May Drill Themselves into Oblivion," Bloomberg Businessweek, Oct. 13, 2014, http://tinyurl.com/qa963aq.

Natural gas companies are drilling more and boosting their oil reserves even as global oil prices continue to fall, which could lead some into bankruptcy.

PETROLEUM INDUSTRY

Crooks, Ed, and Anjili Raval, "US Poised to Become World's Leading Liquid Petroleum Producer," The Financial Times, Sep. 29, 2014, http://tinyurl.com/lnymyyl.

Advances in natural gas extraction have put the United States on track to pass Saudi Arabia as the world's largest producer of liquid petroleum.

Dearen, Jason, "Feds Approve Oil Exploration off US Eastern Coast," The Associated Press, Jul. 19, 2014, http://tinyurl.com/nlhauot.

The Obama administration permitted energy developers to explore offshore drilling in the Atlantic Ocean using blasts of sound that detect oil and gas deposits under the ocean floor.

Gilbert, Daniel, and Justin Scheck, "Big Oil Feels the Need to Get Smaller," The Wall Street Journal, Nov. 3, 2014, http://tinyurl.com/qdp6tsr.

Exxon Mobil, Shell and Chevron are paring back operations as rising production costs squeeze their earnings.

ORGANIZATIONS

American Petroleum Institute
1220 L St., N.W.

Washington, DC 20005-4070
202-682-8000
www.api.org

Trade group for the oil industry that lobbies the public and legislators and propagates guides to best practices for the industry.

Association of American Railroads
425 Third St., S.W.
Washington, DC 20024
202-639-2100
www.aar.org

Lobby for railroad companies; publishes statistics and offers the industry's views on energy transportation.

Canadian Association of Petroleum Producers
2100, 350-7 Ave., S.W.
Calgary, Alberta, Canada T2P 3N9
403-267-1100
www.capp.ca

Trade group for the Canadian oil industry that publishes an array of statistics.

Food and Water Watch
1616 P St., N.W.
Suite 300
Washington, DC 20036
202-683-2500
www.foodandwaterwatch.org

Environmental group that fights hydraulic fracturing.

International Energy Agency
9, rue de la Federation
75739 Paris Cedex 15, France
33-1-4057-6500
www.iea.org

Intergovernmental organization linking oil-consuming countries; publishes international energy statistics.

Organization of the Petroleum Exporting Countries
Helferstorferstrasse 17, A-1010
Vienna, Austria
43-1-2111120
www.opec.org
Intergovernmental organization that unites oil-producing countries in Asia, Africa and Latin America; controls about a third of the global oil market.

U.S. Energy Information Administration
1000 Independence Ave., S.W.
Washington, DC 20585
202-586-8800
www.eia.gov

The energy statistics arm of the U.S. government that gathers and disseminates energy data for the public and policymakers.

Chapter 12: Hong Kong's Economy

BOOKS

Bush, Richard C., "Hong Kong in the Shadow of China: Living with the Leviathan," Brookings Institution Press, 2016.

The director of the Brookings Institution's Center on East Asia Policy Studies examines the roots of Hong Kong's 2014 pro-democracy protest.

Carroll, John M., "A Concise History of Hong Kong," Rowman & Littlefield Publishers, 2007.

An associate professor of history at St. Louis University says Hong Kong is at a crossroads where Chinese, British colonial and global histories collide.

Cartledge, Simon, "A System Apart: Hong Kong's Political Economy from 1997 until Now," Penguin Books, 2017.

A Hong Kong-based editor examines the city's economy, history, politics and policies, and the fiscal and political challenges they created.

Goodstadt, Leo F., "Poverty in the Midst of Affluence: How Hong Kong Mismanaged Its Prosperity," Hong Kong University Press, 2014.

The government's policy leader during the colonial era argues that misguided policies under both British and Chinese leadership created a "new poverty."

ARTICLES

Bland, Ben, "Hong Kong: One Country, Two Economies," Financial Times, Jul. 19, 2016, http://tinyurl.com/y9qgaqa6.

A journalist explores the city's problems 20 years after the handover.

Bradsher, Keith, "Once a Model City, Hong Kong Is in Trouble," The New York Times, Jun. 29, 2017, http://tinyurl.com/y7grxng6.

An Asia-based journalist summarizes the tensions and frustrations that plague Hong Kong's people and policies two decades after China assumed control.

Cheung, Alvin Y.H., "Beijing Is Weakening Hong Kong's Rule of Law. How Far Will It Go?" ChinaFile, May 9, 2017, http://tinyurl.com/ydbnqrjg.

A Hong Kong lawyer, now based in the United States, argues that Hong Kong operates under a "dual state," with one legal system protecting commercial interests and a more restrictive one that governs politically sensitive matters.

Lian, Yi-Zheng, "Red Capital in Hong Kong," The New York Times, Jun. 1, 2017, http://tinyurl.com/yamf9urm.

A former Hong Kong editor says that capital from mainland China now dominates Hong Kong's markets.

REPORTS AND STUDIES

"13th Annual Demographia International Housing Affordability Survey: 2017," Demographia, last accessed Dec. 10, 2017, http://tinyurl.com/2vj4r8.

A report on the world's major housing markets finds Hong Kong the least affordable.

"UBS Global Real Estate Bubble Index 2016," UBS, last accessed Dec. 10, 2017, http://tinyurl.com/y86ffaf2.

A global bank finds that Hong Kong is at risk of a housing bubble, defined as a market that is severely overvalued.

Schenk, Catherine R., "Economic History of Hong Kong," EH.Net Encyclopedia, Mar. 16, 2008, http://tinyurl.com/y777dam5.

An Oxford University professor traces Hong Kong's economic and financial history.

THE NEXT STEP

HOUSING CRISIS

Chen, Laurie, "Crisis Veteran Helps Hong Kong Tackle Acute Housing Shortage, One Renovated Home at a Time," South China Morning Post, Dec. 16, 2017, https://tinyurl.com/y8zyudna.

An experienced Habitat for Humanity worker has started a nonprofit housing project in Hong Kong dedicated to renovating apartments in dilapidated public housing estates.

Kwok, Donny, and James Pomfret, "Between Rampant Inequality and Tensions with China, Hong Kong's New Chief Executive Paints a 'Grave' Picture," Reuters/Business Insider, Oct. 11, 2017, https://tinyurl.com/yddvz2k6.

Hong Kong Chief Executive Carrie Lam pledged to increase land supply and start a subsidized "starter homes" initiative, but also said that the government had no magic fix for the housing crisis.

Mahrotri, Pooja Thakur, "Hong Kong Home Prices Are Unsustainable, $2.6 Billion Fund Says," Bloomberg, Jan. 4, 2018, https://tinyurl.com/y732owgj.

A real estate private equity firm warns that Hong Kong's astronomical housing prices cannot continue and adds the government's "cooling" efforts have done little to improve the situation.

INCOME INEQUALITY

Ewing, Kent, "As Christmas Decorations Highlight Inequality, What Are Hong Kong's Officials Doing about the Poor?" Hong Kong Free Press, Dec. 18, 2017, https://tinyurl.com/yahlvrxt.

Despite a thriving economy and strong fiscal reserves, Hong Kong's government has done little to combat the extreme poverty in the city, asserts a teacher and writer.

Ho, Prudence, and Matthew Campbell, "Life in Hong Kong Is Harder Than Ever—Unless You're a Tycoon," Bloomberg, Jun. 13, 2017, https://tinyurl.com/ya7eadb6.

Economists view Hong Kong as the closest thing to a regulation-free economy, but the laissez-faire approach has led to the biggest income disparity rate in Asia.

Yau, Cannix, and Viola Zhou, "What Hope for the Poorest? Hong Kong Wealth Gap Hits Record High," South China Morning Post, Jun. 9, 2017, https://tinyurl.com/y98rgonk.

Hong Kong's Census and Statistics Department commissioner cites an aging population and an increase in smaller households as contributing factors to the city's extreme income inequality.

ORGANIZATIONS

American Chamber of Commerce in Hong Kong
Bank of America Tower, Room 1904, 12 Harcourt Road, Central, Hong Kong
852-2530-6900
www.amcham.org.hk

A membership organization that promotes American business interests in Hong Kong.

Brookings Institution
1775 Massachusetts Ave., N.W., Washington, DC 20036
1-202-797-6000
www.brookings.edu

A public policy research organization with a sister center in Beijing.

Hong Kong Democratic Foundation
Unit 7, 5/F, Eastern Harbour Centre, 28 Hoi Chak St., Quarry Bay, Hong Kong
852-3104-2767
www.hkdf.org
facebook.com/HongKongDemocraticFoundation/

A think tank that disseminates information on public policy issues, including the democratic development of Hong Kong.

Hong Kong Institute of Economics and Business Strategy
University of Hong Kong, Pokfulam Road, Hong Kong
852-2547-8313
www.hiebs.hku.hk/

A research center that focuses on the study of economic policy and business strategy.

Lau Chor Tak Institute of Global Economics and Finance
Chinese University of Hong Kong, 13/F Cheng Yu Tung Building, 12 Chak Cheung St., Shatin, New Territories, Hong Kong
852-3943-1620
www.igef.cuhk.edu.hk/index.php/en/

A research institute at one of Hong Kong's leading universities that aims to make the Chinese monetary and financial system more transparent.

New York University Center for Global Economy and Business
NYU Stern, Henry Kaufman Management Center, 44 W. Fourth St., New York, NY 10012
1-212-998-0100
www.stern.nyu.edu/experience-stern/about/departments-centers-initiatives/centers-of-research/global-economy-business

A division of the Stern School of Business that promotes faculty research on global aspects of modern economies and business. Its China initiative offers specialized information on that country.

RAND Corp.
1776 Main St., Santa Monica, CA 90401
1-310-393-0411
www.rand.org

A think tank that conducts research and analysis on international affairs and other issues.

Chapter 13: Minimum Wage

BOOKS

Grimshaw, Damian, "Minimum Wages, Pay Equity and Comparative Industrial Relations," Routledge, 2013.

A professor of employment studies at England's University of Manchester examines national differences among European minimum wage-setting systems.

Waltman, Jerold, "Minimum Wage Policy in Great Britain and the United States," Algora Publishing, 2008.

A political science professor at Baylor University, in Waco, Texas, describes the differing histories and policy decisions that underlie minimum wage policy in the United States and Great Britain.

ARTICLES

"Global Minimum Wage," Reuters, undated, accessed Jan. 2, 2015, http://tinyurl.com/p4nmtab.

The news agency presents a collection of reports on minimum wage policies and their effects on workers' lives in countries including China, Brazil, France, Portugal, Bolivia, Hungary, Australia, Greece and Mexico.

"Minimum Wage," Business Day Live (South Africa), Mar. 11, 2014, http://tinyurl.com/njb8ofo.

A South African economist and a trade union official debate a proposal by South Africa's ruling political party to institute a national minimum wage to combat long-standing wage disparities between the country's Black majority and white minority.

Brock, Sam, "Reality Check: Hype or Reality? Numbers behind Wage Hike and Jobs," Bay Area NBC News, Feb. 10, 2014, http://tinyurl.com/lx8oomp.

The minimum wage in San Jose, Calif., rose from $8 to $10 in March 2013, and to $10.15 in January 2014, higher than elsewhere in the state. According to the business-backed Washington, D.C.-based Employment Policies Institute, about two-thirds of local restaurants raised prices and about half reduced employee hours in response. Overall, however, San Jose experienced business growth in the past year, with the number of retail businesses including restaurants registered in the city growing by 19 percent.

DePillis, Lydia, "Why Franchises Are Such a Huge Obstacle to Higher Wages," Wonkblog, The Washington Post, Dec. 6, 2013, http://tinyurl.com/lw297to.

Saddled with pricey requirements imposed by parent companies, local franchise owners may squeeze wages because those are the only costs they can control.

Ton, Zeynep, "A Minimum-Wage Hike Could Help Employers Too," HBR Blog Network, Jan. 28, 2014, http://tinyurl.com/mwqu4td.

An adjunct associate professor of operations management at the Massachusetts Institute of Technology's Sloan School of Management argues that combining higher wages with increased staffing, greater standardization of work processes and several other operational changes produces better business outcomes.

Witte, Griff, "The Minimum Wage Is Set to Rise in Britain. And Conservatives Are All for It," The Washington Post, Jan. 26, 2014, http://tinyurl.com/kdpgkn7.

British Conservatives see a minimum wage increase as a way to trim spending on government benefits as well as a way to reward and encourage work.

REPORTS AND STUDIES

"National Minimum Wage: Low Pay Commission Report 2014," United Kingdom Low Pay Commission, March 2014, http://tinyurl.com/kbqvkgx.

The expert panel that recommends annual minimum wage changes to the government of the United Kingdom describes the research and reasoning that underlie its 2014 recommendation to increase the wage by more than the annual inflation rate.

Bradley, David H., "The Federal Minimum Wage: In Brief," Congressional Research Service, May 30, 2013, http://tinyurl.com/k5eh73q.

An analyst at Congress' nonpartisan research office summarizes the current federal law provisions on the minimum wage, the wage's history in the United States and the main arguments favoring and opposing minimum wage increases.

Eyraud, François, and Catherine Saget, "The Fundamentals of Minimum Wage Fixing," International Labour Organization, 2005, http://tinyurl.com/lsg7vf6.

Analysts for a United Nations agency describe the range of national systems that exist for setting a minimum wage, how the various systems developed and what policy questions are raised as nations contemplate raising their minimum wages.

Sawhill, Isabel, and Quentin Karpilow, "Raising the Minimum Wage and Redesigning the EITC," Brookings Institution Center on Children and Families, Jan. 30, 2014, http://tinyurl.com/n9wbkch.

Economists from the centrist Brookings Institution argue that combining a minimum wage increase to $10.10 with a more effectively targeted Earned Income Tax Credit would be the most effective policy for helping low-income families.

Sherk, James, "Who Earns the Minimum Wage? Suburban Teenagers, Not Single Parents," Heritage Foundation, Feb. 28, 2013, http://tinyurl.com/c86p8zq.

An analyst for a conservative think tank explains that most people who live in poverty are not minimum wage earners, so raising the wage as a means of fighting poverty is ineffective.

THE NEXT STEP

FAST-FOOD WORKERS

Greenhouse, Steven, "$15 Wage in Fast Food Stirs Debate on Effects," The New York Times, Dec. 4, 2013, http://tinyurl.com/l2dxmwx.

In the debate over raising the minimum wage for fast-food workers, one side argues it will reduce employment and increase food prices while the other says it will reduce worker turnover and increase worker productivity.

Semuels, Alana, "More Than Half of U.S. Fast Food Workers on Public Aid, Report Says," Los Angeles Times, Oct. 15, 2013, http://tinyurl.com/peuap3f.

A new report reveals that more than half of U.S. fast-food workers receive some type of public aid, costing the nation $7 billion a year.

Winter, Michael, "Protesters Nationwide Call for $15 Minimum Wage," USA Today, Dec. 4, 2014, http://tinyurl.com/kzwn5aq.

Thousands of low-wage workers protested in 190 U.S. cities in support of a movement that aims to raise the minimum wage for fast-food and retail employees to $15 an hour.

FEDERAL LAWS

Devaney, Tim, "Obama's 'Pen and Phone' Barrage," The Hill, Dec. 28, 2014, http://tinyurl.com/kvn6khh.

President Obama's executive order raised the minimum wage for government-contracted employees from $7.25 to $10.10 per hour.

Morath, Eric, Damian Paletta and Carol E. Lee, "Wage-Rise Report Sees Fewer Jobs, Less Poverty," The Wall Street Journal, Feb. 20, 2014, http://tinyurl.com/kq5lu2u.

A federal minimum wage increase would eliminate about 500,000 jobs by 2016 while also helping nearly 1 million Americans to escape poverty, according to a report by the nonpartisan Congressional Budget Office.

Pfeifer, Stuart, "75 Economists Call for Increase in Federal Minimum Wage," Los Angeles Times, Jan. 14, 2014, http://tinyurl.com/lyzghb6.

Seventy-five economists signed a letter to the White House in support of raising the federal minimum wage to $10.10 per hour by 2016.

JOBS

Kessler, Glenn, "Obama's Claim That There Is 'No Solid Evidence' That Boosting the Minimum Wage Harms Jobs," The Washington Post, Dec. 5, 2013, http://tinyurl.com/q7efjle.

The newspaper's fact-checker says economists remain sharply divided on whether minimum-wage laws hurt employment.

Simon, Jeff, "Raising Minimum Wage Doesn't Affect Employment, in 3 Charts (and 2 McDonald's Meals)," The Washington Post, Jan. 8, 2014, http://tinyurl.com/lhqmlxy.

A reporter says that data show little connection between raising the minimum wage and decreased employment.

Sullivan, Cara, "Minimum Wage Hike Has an Adverse Effect on Jobs for Young Workers," Baltimore Business Journal, Jan. 21, 2015, http://tinyurl.com/mlunjqp.

A task force director for the conservative nonprofit American Legislative Exchange Council says a minimum wage increase in Maryland will lead businesses to cut entry-level positions to reduce costs, which will exacerbate youth unemployment.

STATE LAWS

Connelly, Joel, "States Raise Minimum Wage: Washington Is Tops, but Not for Long," Jan. 2, 2015, SeatllePI.com, http://tinyurl.com/l45njbj.

Minimum wage in Washington, one of several states to hike pay recently, will be $9.47 per hour in 2015. In Seattle, a $15-an-hour minimum will phase in beginning in April.

Cousins, Christopher, "LePage Vetoes Minimum Wage Hike, 20 Other Bills," *Bangor Daily News,* Jul. 8, 2013, http://tinyurl.com/qcy8m8d

Maine Gov. Paul LePage, R, vetoed a bill that would have increased the minimum wage from $7.50 to $9 by 2015, with annual increases tied to inflation.

Johnson, Katie, "Minimum Wage Rising in Much of US," The Boston Globe, Jan. 1, 2015, http://tinyurl.com/k3qc4hk.

Pending minimum wage increases in 20 states will immediately affect more than 3.1 million low-wage earning Americans in 2015.

ORGANIZATIONS

Congressional Budget Office
Ford House Office Building
4th Floor, 2nd and D streets, S.W.
Washington, DC 20515-6925
202-226-2602
www.cbo.gov

Congress' nonpartisan budget-analysis office, which analyzes the effects of legislative proposals on the federal budget and the economy.

Heritage Foundation
214 Massachusetts Ave., N.E.
Washington, DC 20002
202-546-4400
www.heritage.org

Conservative think tank that analyzes economic policies from a free-market perspective.

International Labour Organization
4 route des Morillons
CH-1211 Genève 22
Switzerland
41 22 798 8685
www.ilo.org
United Nations agency governed by government, employer and labor representatives establishes international fair labor standards; provides information and statistics.

Low Pay Commission
8th Floor, Fleetbank House
2-6 Salisbury Square
London EC4Y 8JX
England
44 20 7211 8212

www.gov.uk/government/organisations/low-pay-commission

Expert body established by government of United Kingdom to commission research and make recommendations on wagesetting for low-paid workers.

National Employment Law Program
75 Maiden Lane
Suite 601
New York, NY, 10038
212-285-3025
www.nelp.org

Liberal analysis, information and advocacy group on issues affecting workers.

National Federation of Independent Business
1201 F St., N.W.
Suite 200
Washington, DC 20004
202-554-9000; 615-872-5800
www.nfib.com.

Membership group for small business opposing minimum wage increases.

Organisation for Economic Co-operation and Development
2 rue André Pascal
75775 Paris Cedex 16
France
33 1 4524 8200
www.oecd.org

Membership organization of industrialized nations that provides statistics on national economies, including minimum wage.

UC Berkeley Center for Labor Research and Education
Institute for Research on Labor and Employment
2521 Channing Way #5555
Berkeley, CA 94720
510-642-0323
http://laborcenter.berkeley.edu

University-based center that conducts and disseminates research on labor and employment issues.

Chapter 14: Paid Leave

BOOKS

Boushey, Heather, "Finding Time: The Economics of Work-Life Conflict," Harvard University Press, 2016.

The executive director of the Washington Center for Equitable Growth, a research and grant-making organization, says a changing economy—one in which women work instead of staying home full-time to raise their children—requires employers to provide the resources working mothers need to care for family members.

Gordon, Victoria. "Maternity Leave: Policy and Practice," CRC Press, 2013.

An associate political science professor at Western Kentucky University who has interviewed women who took maternity leave says there is a disconnect between policy and practice.

Sholar, Megan, "Getting Paid While Taking Time: The Women's Movement and the Development of Paid Family Leave Policies in the United States," Temple University Press, 2016.

A Loyola University Chicago instructor explains the development of family leave policies in the United States, and notes that most innovations in family policies have originated at the state level.

ARTICLES

Berman, Russell, "A Conservative Push for Paid Family Leave," The Atlantic, Aug. 15, 2016, http://tinyurl.com/kc2x6bc.

A journalist examines the efforts of Republican politicians, including President Trump, and conservative groups to encourage Congress to pass legislation providing for paid family leave.

Bernard, Tara Siegel, "In Paid Family Leave, U.S. Trails Most of the Globe," The New York Times, Feb. 22, 2013, http://tinyurl.com/krbsulm.

The writer explores why the United States is the only industrialized country without a mandatory paid leave law.

Miller, Claire Cain, "Americans Agree on Paid Leave, but Not on Who Should Pay," The New York Times, Mar. 23, 2017, http://tinyurl.com/mm33z7k.

A journalist questions why the nation has not enacted a mandatory paid leave policy when a majority of citizens on both sides of the political spectrum support it.

Murphy, Robert P., "'Paid Family Leave' Is a Great Way to Hurt Women," Foundation for Economic Education, Jun. 2, 2015, http://tinyurl.com/kqzhyqj.

A Texas Tech University professor argues that paid family leave policies should be voluntary, not mandatory. Businesses, he said, know better than the government how to structure their employee benefits for recruitment and retention purposes, he writes.

Rogers, Megan, "Why New York Businesses Oppose Paid Family Leave Proposal," Albany Business Review, Mar. 25, 2015, http://tinyurl.com/lnaddno.

A journalist summarizes interviews with business leaders who believe small businesses cannot afford overtime costs associated with mandatory paid family leave.

Warner, Judith, and Danielle Corley, "In the Absence of U.S. Action on Paid Leave, Multinationals Make Their Own Policies," Center for American Progress, Nov. 17, 2016, http://tinyurl.com/jwc26tr.

Researchers at a liberal Washington think tank examine a trend among multinational companies to create policies for paid time off that apply to their employees, no matter where in the world they work.

REPORTS AND STUDIES

"Americans Widely Support Paid Family and Medical Leave, but Differ over Specific Policies," Pew Research Center, Mar. 23, 2017, http://tinyurl.com/m7v6tfy.

A nonpartisan "fact tank" finds that most Americans support paid leave but believe that employers, and not the federal or state governments, should pay for it.

"The Economics of Paid and Unpaid Leave," Council of Economic Advisers, June 2014, http://tinyurl.com/mruj93h.

The White House agency dealing with economic policy concludes that businesses would benefit from offering paid family leave to more workers because employees would be more productive on the job and retention of talented workers would increase.

"Employer Costs for Employee Compensation—December 2016," Bureau of Labor Statistics, U.S. Department of Labor, Mar. 17, 2017, http://tinyurl.com/m3y5csc.

In 23 pages of charts, the federal agency reveals the costs of compensation and benefits for private- and public-sector employees. Paid leave, the report notes, accounted for 6.9 percent of private industry compensation.

"Paid Time off Programs and Practices," WorldatWork, September 2016, http://tinyurl.com/zu8en2c.

In a survey of its members, a human resources trade association discovered that 88 percent believe offering some type of paid time-off program is necessary for an organization to be competitive in the labor market.

"Why Paid Family Leave Is Good Business," Boston Consulting Group, Feb. 7, 2017, http://tinyurl.com/krss4gk.

The management consulting firm reviewed the policies of more than 250 companies and interviewed 25 human resource executives at large organizations. The report's conclusion: Employers espouse a strong business case for paid family leave, which they say helps attract and retain qualified employees.

Gitis, Ben, "The Earned Income Leave Benefit: Rethinking Family Leave for Low-Income Workers," American Action Forum, Aug. 15, 2016, http://tinyurl.com/ly5dbue.

The director of labor market policy for a conservative research group breaks with Republican tradition and proposes a paid-leave benefit for workers with annual incomes lower than $28,000.

Ray, Rebecca, Milla Sanes and John Schmitt, "No-Vacation Nation Revisited," Center for Economic and Policy Institute, May 2013, http://tinyurl.com/mcasupx.

This report reviews laws in 21 "rich" countries that require paid vacations and holidays.

Zagorsky, Jay L., "Divergent Trends in US Maternity and Paternity Leave, 1994–2015," American Journal of Public Health, March 2017, http://tinyurl.com/l29spvb.

An economist and research scientist at Ohio State University's Center for Human Resource Research discovers that the number of women who take maternity leave has not grown in 22 years.

THE NEXT STEP

COMPANY POLICIES

Bort, Julie, "Sheryl Sandberg on Tragically Losing Her Husband: 'I'm a Different Person Now,'" Business Insider, Apr. 24, 2017, https://tinyurl.com/mldxk9a.

Facebook COO Sheryl Sandberg, whose husband died unexpectedly two years ago, announced in February that Facebook employees will receive up to 20 days' paid annual leave to mourn an immediate family member's death, and 10 days to mourn for an extended family member.

Kharpal, Arjun, "Tech Firms Are Giving Staff Paid Leave for Political Engagements amid Fear of Immigration Crackdown," CNBC, Apr. 18, 2017, https://tinyurl.com/kj36kfs.

A technology startup company, reacting in part to President Trump's anti-immigration rhetoric, adopted a policy on April 18 that gives employees paid leave for political engagements, including protests.

Lewis, Cora, "Women Ironworkers Will Get Six Months of Paid Maternity Leave," BuzzFeed News, Apr. 17, 2017, https://tinyurl.com/k3kbs2b.

Following the lead of tech companies such as Adobe, Netflix and Spotify, the male-dominated ironworkers union now offers female employees up to six months' maternity leave.

INTERNATIONAL STANDARDS

Bruner, Raisa, "Chinese Workers at Factory for Ivanka Trump's Clothing Maker Earn About $62 a Week: Report," Time, Apr. 25, 2017, https://tinyurl.com/mheo5uf.

The Fair Labor Association watchdog group found that Chinese factory workers who make clothing for Ivanka Trump's brand worked excessive hours for below minimum wage last year and received only five paid leave days per year.

Millington, Alison, "Italy Could Soon Offer Women Three Days of Paid Menstrual Leave Each Month," Business Insider, Mar. 29, 2017, https://tinyurl.com/kq3wgr3.

The lower house of Italy's parliament is considering a proposal that would allow women to take three paid leave days each month for any "painful periods" they experience.

Singhi, Namrata, "Microsoft India Employees to Get Family Caregiver Leave," The Times of India, Apr. 24, 2017, https://tinyurl.com/n3dfr68.

Microsoft India announced that employees who need to care for an immediate family member with a serious health condition will receive four weeks annual paid leave; workers who adopt a child or have a child via surrogacy will receive 26 calendar weeks of paid leave; and paternity leave will increase to six weeks.

LAWSUITS

Blau, Reuven, "JetBlue Hit with Suit for Violating New York Paid Sick Leave Law," New York Daily News, Apr. 1, 2017, https://tinyurl.com/lxtbtot.

New York City's Consumer Affairs Department accuses JetBlue in a lawsuit of using progressive punishments—including possible termination—to discipline employees who called in sick.

Hopkins, Kathleen, "Ocean County Judge Sues, Claims Discrimination," Asbury Park Press, Apr. 25, 2017, https://tinyurl.com/kfkep2v.

A New Jersey Superior Court judge sued his two bosses, saying they tried to force him to resign because he has a 19-year-old son with multiple disabilities.

Salazar, Martin, "Lawsuit Targets Proposed Sick Leave Ordinance," Albuquerque Journal, Apr. 3, 2017, https://tinyurl.com/k8s6ggy.

Businesses and trade associations in Albuquerque, N.M., sued city officials, arguing a proposed sick leave ordinance is unconstitutional and would hurt businesses and the city's economy.

STATE LEGISLATION

Booker, Christopher, and Connie Kargbo, "Can Rhode Island's Paid Family Leave Be a National Model?" PBS NewsHour, Apr. 16, 2017, https://tinyurl.com/l2nqme3.

Rhode Island taxes private-sector employees to finance a program that provides paid leave for part-time and full-time workers, a policy that smaller companies say may hurt productivity.

Dawson, James, "State Lawmakers Considering Family Leave Bills," Delaware Public Media, Apr. 23, 2017, http://tinyurl.com/m2f8mo2.

Delaware lawmakers are studying proposals that would give three months of paid leave to state employees who have worked full-time for at least a year, and an additional six weeks of unpaid leave to mothers who are expecting twins and require hospitalization during pregnancy.

Sagarin, Susan, "D.C. Enacts Paid Family Leave but Lacks Funding for Implementation," Bloomberg BNA, Apr. 17, 2017, http://tinyurl.com/ldekpgz.

The District of Columbia's Universal Paid Leave Act, which entitles employees to 90 percent of their salary while on leave, won approval from a congressional review board in April, but the city may not be able to afford it.

ORGANIZATIONS

The American Action Forum
1747 Pennsylvania Ave., N.W., 5th Floor, Washington, DC 20006
1-202-559-6420
www.americanactionforum.org/

A self-described center-right nonprofit that focuses on domestic policy challenges such as paid leave, health care and tax reform.

Center for American Progress
1333 H St., N.W., Washington, DC 20005
1-202-682-1611
www.americanprogress.org/

An independent, nonpartisan policy institute dedicated to developing new policy ideas in areas such as criminal justice, disability, the economy, education and women.

Center for Economic and Policy Research
1611 Connecticut Ave., N.W., Suite 400, Washington, DC 20009
http://cepr.net/
1-202-293-5380

An organization of economists who promote democratic debate on economic and social issues through professional research and public education.

Center for WorkLife Law
200 McAllister St., San Francisco, CA 94102
1-415-565-4640
http://worklifelaw.org/

Women's leadership organization at the University of California's Hastings College of Law that focuses on jump starting "the stalled gender revolution."

Families & Work Institute
245 5th Ave., #1002, New York, NY 10016
1-212-465-2044

A nonpartisan research organization that studies the changing workforce and workplace, as well as the changing family.

National Partnership for Women and Families
1875 Connecticut Ave., N.W., Suite 650, Washington, DC 20009
1-202-986-2600
www.nationalpartnership.org/

Formerly known as the Women's Legal Defense Fund, this nonpartisan organization promotes fairness in the workplace, reproductive health and rights, access to affordable health care and work-family policies for working parents.

Pew Research Center
1615 L St., N.W., Suite 800, Washington, DC 20036
1-202-419-4300
www.pewresearch.org/

A nonpartisan "fact tank" that conducts public opinion polls and demographic research, and informs the public about issues involving politics, media, technology, religion, global attitudes and demographic trends.

PL+US (Paid Leave For the United States)
2973 16th St., San Francisco, CA 94110
1-415-799-9789
http://paidleave.us/#issue

A new advocacy organization whose mission is to win paid family leave by engaging Americans at the grass-roots level.

Work and Family Researchers Network
c/o the Wharton School, University of Pennsylvania, 3620 Locust Walk, Philadelphia, PA 19104-6302
1-215-898-5605
https://workfamily.sas.upenn.edu/

A membership association of interdisciplinary work and family scholars that oversees an open-access work and family subject matter repository.

WorldatWork
14040 N. Northsight Blvd., Scottsdale, AZ 85260
1-877-951-9191
www.worldatwork.org

A membership organization for human resources professionals that bills itself as "the total rewards association." Its focus is compensation, benefits and work-life effectiveness.

Chapter 15: Supply Chains and Protectionism

BOOKS

Baldwin, Richard E., "The Great Convergence: Information Technology and the New Globalization," Belknap Press of Harvard, 2016.

A trade-policy expert explains how globalization gave companies opportunities to manufacture in low-cost countries, and how companies have combined this geographical freedom with information technology to facilitate the transfer of other functions, such as managerial positions, across the globe.

Bowen, Steven J., "Total Value Optimization: Transforming Your Global Supply Chain into a Competitive Weapon," SDJB LLC, 2017.

A logistics consultant describes how companies can overhaul their transportation and storage operations to improve their supply chains and bottom-line performance.

ARTICLES

"Herfindahl-Hirschman Index," U.S. Department of Justice, last updated Jul. 29, 2015, http://tinyurl.com/y8n3vhs5.

An explanation of how the U.S. government evaluates industries to determine the level of competition and concentration risks in an economic sector.

Lu, Sheng, "Four Key Patterns in US Apparel Imports," just-style, Mar. 1, 2018, http://tinyurl.com/y9txzyce.

A professor from the University of Delaware who studies the global textiles industry explains how the fashion industry has adjusted its supply chains to account for protectionism.

Wilder, Mike, "The Consumer Cost of Washington's 'Win-Win' NAFTA Timeline," Journal of Commerce, May 8, 2018, http://tinyurl.com/ybx8xfc5.

A logistics specialist explains possible motivations for and drawbacks of current U.S. trade policy, even if it succeeds in attracting more investment from companies.

REPORTS AND STUDIES

Constantinescu, Cristina, Aaditya Mattoo and Michele Ruta, "Does Vertical Specialization Increase Productivity?" The World Bank, February 2017, http://tinyurl.com/y7s6g4yl.

Experts explain their methodology to measure the impact of global supply-chain participation on companies worldwide and explain their conclusion that doing so boosts productivity.

Dempsey, Linda Menghetti, "Testimony before the International Trade, Customs and Global Competitiveness Subcommittee of the U.S. Senate Committee on Finance on Market Access Challenges in China," National Association of Manufacturers, Apr. 11, 2018, http://tinyurl.com/ybzmbvmw.

An advocate for manufacturers testifies on the challenges companies face in accessing the Chinese market.

Engel, Charles, "Equivalence Results for Optimal Pass-Through, Optimal Indexing to Exchange Rates, and Optimal Choice of Currency for Export Pricing," Journal of the European Economic Association, December 2006, http://tinyurl.com/y74k9t86.

A University of Wisconsin economist explains how global supply-chain participants typically react to exchange-rate fluctuations, a common variable cost.

"Global Economic Prospects: The Turning of the Tide?" The World Bank, January 2018, http://tinyurl.com/lnmdtze.

World Bank economists address the maturing of supply chains and how this has affected the pace of global growth.

Humphries, Marc, "Rare Earth Elements: The Global Supply Chain," Congressional Research Service, Dec. 16, 2013, http://tinyurl.com/yb323cz2.

A research paper for the U.S. Congress explains the details of an important global supply chain that also serves as a source of raw materials for many other manufacturing supply chains in the global economy.

Shay, Scott, Ted Stank and Ben Hazen, "A SAVVY Guide to the Digital Supply Chain," Global Supply Chain Institute, Apr. 6, 2018, http://tinyurl.com/y78qc7up.

Supply-chain professors at the University of Tennessee explain how moving supply-chain processes from manual to digital can help companies.

Walmsley, Terrie, and Peter Minor, "Reversing NAFTA: A Supply Chain Perspective," ImpactECON, March 2017, http://tinyurl.com/ycw89ubd.

Private-sector economists explain how canceling the North American Free Trade Agreement would reduce GDP, investment and jobs in all three signatory nations: the United States, Canada and Mexico.

THE NEXT STEP

NAFTA RENEGOTIATION

Cattan, Nacha, and Michael McKee, "No NAFTA Better than Bad NAFTA for Mexico's AMLO: Top Aide," Bloomberg, Jun. 5, 2018, https://tinyurl.com/y8aey639.

The front-runner to become Mexico's next president will insist on a trilateral trade agreement with the United States and Canada, rather than separate bilateral accords, if he wins the July election.

Domm, Patti, "US Trade Relations at a Low, as China Set for New Tariffs and amid Fears Trump Will Leave NAFTA," CNBC, Jun. 13, 2018, https://tinyurl.com/ycf9qe9u.

The deteriorating relationship between the United States and Canada continues to threaten the viability of North American Free Trade Agreement renegotiations and could lead to more retaliatory tariffs between the two countries.

Fox, Michelle, "GOP Rep. Kevin Brady: NAFTA allies 'close enough' on talks, should be able to reach deal," CNBC, Jun. 14, 2018, https://tinyurl.com/ybgrbblz.

Renegotiating a NAFTA that promotes growth is vital to the U.S. economy, and discussions should continue despite increasing tensions with Canada and Mexico, says Rep. Kevin Brady, R-Texas, who chairs the House committee that has jurisdiction over trade issues.

STEEL AND ALUMINUM

Ferry, Jeff, "US Steel and Aluminum Tariffs—the Right Move at the Right Time," The Hill, Jun. 2, 2018, https://tinyurl.com/y9b5qamx.

President Trump's steel and aluminum tariffs will protect U.S. national security by halting the decline in domestic production of both metals, says the research director of an organization that favors more restrictive trade policies.

Nienaber, Michael, "EU Will Act against U.S. Tariffs on Steel, Aluminum: Merkel," Reuters, Jun. 10, 2018, https://tinyurl.com/y8787lp7.

German Chancellor Angela Merkel said the European Union will retaliate after the United States imposed steel and aluminum tariffs on the EU.

Timmons, Heather, "Over 146,000 Americans Will Lose Their Jobs Because of Trump's Trade Tariffs," Quartz, May 31, 2018, https://tinyurl.com/ycfaxhef.

Increased prices for U.S. manufacturers that use imported steel will lead to job losses that more than offset the gains in the steel and aluminum industries, an economist has concluded.

ORGANIZATIONS

American Chemistry Council
700 Second St., N.E., Washington, DC 20002
1-202-249-7000
https://www.americanchemistry.com

Trade association representing makers of plastics and other chemical products used in global supply chains.

Global Supply Chain Institute
300 Stokely Management Center, 916 Volunteer Blvd., Knoxville, TN 37996
1-865-974-5061
https://haslam.utk.edu/gsci

A program at the University of Tennessee's Haslam College of Business that publishes academic scholarship and other research focused on supply chains.

Global Trade Alert
Bodanstrasse 8, 9000 St. Gallen, Switzerland
+44 (0)20 7183 8801
https://www.globaltradealert.org
contact@globaltradealert.org

Founded in 2009 by the London-based Centre for Economic Policy Research, this group tracks trade-related policies and trends.

Institute for Supply Management
309 W. Elliot Road, Suite 113, Tempe, AZ 85284
1-480-752-6276
https://www.instituteforsupplymanagement.org

Hosts conferences, conducts training and studies supply-chain trends on behalf of member organizations.

Office of the U.S. Trade Representative
600 17th St., N.W., Washington, DC 20508
1-202-395-3230
https://ustr.gov

The federal office that develops trade and investment policy, advises the president on it and negotiates trade deals with other countries.

Organisation for Economic Co-operation and Development
2 Rue André Pascal, 75775 Paris Cedex 16, France
+33-1-45-24-82-00
FAX: +33-1-45-24-85-00
http://www.oecd.org/

A group of 35 developed countries that studies global economic issues, publishes data and recommends reforms.

The World Bank
1818 H St., N.W., Washington, DC 20433
1-202-473-1000
http://www.worldbank.org

A global organization created to help developing countries end poverty through grants, loans and advisory services for governments.

World Trade Organization
Rue de Lausanne, 154, Case postale, 1211 Geneve 2, Switzerland
+41 (0)22 739 51 11
www.wto.org
enquiries@wto.org

International organization charged with enforcing global trade rules and arbitrating disputes between member nations.

Chapter 16: The Border Economy

BOOKS

Boskin, Michael J., "NAFTA at 20," Hoover Institution Press, 2014.

A Stanford economist brings together presentations from policymakers who helped develop the North American Free Trade Agreement (NAFTA) and academics who have studied it.

ARTICLES

Domm, Patti, "Trump Is Mad about 'Made in Mexico' Cars—but This Is Even Bigger," CNBC, Jan. 3, 2017, http://tinyurl.com/gp2d6gp.

A journalist examines how President Trump's proposed border tax would influence the automobile industry.

Kahn, Carrie, "How NAFTA Helped the Mexican Billionaires' Club," NPR, Dec. 13, 2013, http://tinyurl.com/k9jnj4m.

A journalist looks at how Mexican billionaires increase their fortunes by participating in industries excluded from NAFTA.

REPORTS AND STUDIES

"2016 Top Markets Report, Automotive Parts, Country Case Study," U.S. Department of Commerce, 2016, http://tinyurl.com/nyw33ej.

This report goes into comprehensive detail on how the United States and Mexico work together in the automobile industry.

De la Calle, Luis, and Luis Rubio, "Mexico: A Middle Class Society Poor No More, Developed Not Yet," Woodrow Wilson International Center for Scholars, 2012, http://tinyurl.com/knqveuf.

Two Mexican economists look at how the middle class in their country has fared throughout history and has grown in the last 15 years.

Villarreal, M. Angeles, "Mexico's Free Trade Agreements," Congressional Research Service, 2012, http://tinyurl.com/kr4qrym.

An international trade and finance analyst provides an in-depth look at the history of Mexico's economy and trade decisions.

Villarreal, M. Angeles, and Ian F. Fergusson, "The North American Free Trade Agreement," Congressional Research Service, 2017, http://tinyurl.com/khqb46b.

Two international trade specialists examine the trajectory of NAFTA and its impact on various sectors as well as on the three participating countries' economies.

Weisbrot, Mark, Stephan Lefebvre and Joseph Sammut, "Did NAFTA Help Mexico? An Assessment After 20 Years," Center for Economic and Policy Research, 2014, http://tinyurl.com/jcbaqa5.

Researchers look at how NAFTA has affected Mexico's economy, in particular its unemployment and poverty levels, over the last 20 years.

THE NEXT STEP

EFFECTS ON BUSINESSES

Crow, Kirsten, "In Texas, Companies Await Word on Trump's Border Wall," USA Today, May 19, 2017, http://tinyurl.com/l9s4otc.

Contractors in Texas, which has the largest section of the U.S.-Mexico border, are vying to construct President Trump's proposed border wall. About 20 companies from across the country will advance to the second round to present their prototype plans.

Murphy, Katy, "California Bill Would Blacklist Contractors Involved in U.S.-Mexico Border Wall Project," The Mercury News, Apr. 25, 2017, http://tinyurl.com/lm9lsag.

Two proposed measures in the California Legislature would prevent contractors who want to participate in building a border wall from doing business in the state or receiving state pension investments.

Sherman, Christopher, "Complex World of Border Trade: Cattle Go North, Meat South," ABC News, The Associated Press, May 22, 2017, http://tinyurl.com/me7w2b7.

Business owners and workers in U.S. and Mexican border cities are experiencing store closings and other changes in their interconnected economies that some attribute to fear of the Trump administration.

IMMIGRATION CRACKDOWN

Chardy, Alfonso, "Border Guards Accused of Illegally Turning Away Foreigners Seeking Asylum," Miami Herald, May 21, 2017, http://tinyurl.com/k54n9t5.

Humans Rights First, a human rights organization, alleges in a report that U.S. immigration authorities are blocking asylum seekers from entering the country, in violation of U.S. law and international agreements.

Hesson, Ted, and Seung Min Kim, "Trump's Immigration Crackdown Is Well Underway," Politico, Apr. 28, 2017, http://tinyurl.com/l8u2dmv.

Immigration enforcement numbers in the early months of the Trump administration show a shift from prioritizing undocumented immigrants with criminal records to arresting undocumented immigrants regardless of whether they have criminal records.

Partlow, Joshua, "The 'Trump Effect' Has Slowed Illegal U.S. Border Crossings. But for How Long?" The Washington Post, May 22, 2017, http://tinyurl.com/l7zl6wm.

The number of migrants apprehended at the U.S.-Mexico border decreased by about 40 percent in the first four months of the year. But part of the decline is attributed to Central American migrants sneaking across the border rather than turning themselves in and requesting asylum at the border.

ORGANIZATIONS

Center for International Policy Americas Program
2000 M St., N.W., Suite 720, Washington, DC 20036
1-202-232-3440
011-52-555-324-1201 (Mexico City office)
www.ciponline.org/programs/americas-program

Research center that focuses on public policy and socioeconomics in Mexico.

The Hub for Human Innovation
500 W. Overland Ave., Suite 230, El Paso, TX 79901
1-915-321-3125
http://hubep.org/

Incubator for tech businesses in the El Paso-Ciudad Juarez region.

International Trade Administration
U.S. Department of Commerce, 1401 Constitution Ave., N.W., Washington, DC 20230
www.export.gov
1-800-549-0595 ext.2

Resource for information on foreign industries that participate in the U.S. market.

SAI

Edificio Plaza Reforma, Prolongación Paseo de la Reforma 600-101B, Col. Santa Fe Peña Blanca, C.P. 01210, México D.F.
011-52-55-5985-6618
www.sai.com.mx

Economic research group of former Mexican politicians who worked to develop NAFTA.

Woodrow Wilson International Center for Scholars Mexico Institute
1300 Pennsylvania Ave., N.W., Washington, DC 20004
1-202-691-4000
https://www.wilsoncenter.org/about-21

Research group that examines U.S.-Mexico public policy.

Chapter 17: The On-Demand Economy

BOOKS

Solis, Brian, "X: The Experience When Business Meets Design," Wiley, 2015.

An industry analyst addresses how customers are increasingly expecting meaningful experiences rather than simply a product or service, and how that is changing corporate brands.

Sundararajan, Arun, "The Sharing Economy: The End of Employment and the Rise of Crowd-Based Capitalism," MIT Press, 2017.

A professor of operations and management sciences at New York University explains how crowd-based capitalism might replace the more traditional corporate-centered economic model and the impact that may have on daily life.

ARTICLES

Colby, Charles, and Kelly Bell, "The On-Demand Economy Is Growing, and Not Just for the Young and Wealthy," Harvard Business Review, Apr. 14, 2016, https://tinyurl.com/h9v4bqr.

Two researchers say the on-demand economy is attracting more than 22.4 million consumers annually and generating $57.6 billion in spending.

Gevelber, Lisa, "Micro-Moments Now: 3 New Consumer Behaviors Playing Out in Google Search Data," Google, July 2017, https://tinyurl.com/ydaywmk5.

The search-engine giant provides insight into consumer expectations and behavior based on search data.

Lazar, Michael, "E-commerce Statistics & Technology Trendsetters for 2017," IBM, Mar. 3, 2017, https://tinyurl.com/jfn5ks9.

An analyst concludes that e-commerce has "grown from being an early '90's fascination into giving brick-and-mortar retailers a real run for their money."

Paine, James, "$57 Billion Dollar Opportunity: The State of the On-Demand Economy in 2017," Inc., Jul. 24, 2017, https://tinyurl.com/yb4u8b8v.

A writer predicts the on-demand economy's growth will slow over the next few years.

REPORTS AND STUDIES

Lam, Chungsang Tom, and Meng Liu, "Demand and Consumer Surplus in the On-Demand Economy: The Case of Ride Sharing," SSRN, Jul. 7, 2017, https://tinyurl.com/y6w7grpk.

Two economists from Clemson (Lam) and MIT (Liu) study how economic value is created in ride-sharing platforms based on a review of demand-based pricing, ride sharing and public transportation data in New York City.

Maselli, Ilaria, Karolien Lenaerts and Miroslav Beblavý, "Five Things We Need to Know about the On-Demand Economy," Centre for European Policy Studies, Jan. 8, 2016, https://tinyurl.com/ya9wakly.

A European Union think tank explores what is currently known about the on-demand economy and questions that remain about its future impact, such as how policymakers will approach these new products, services and employers and whether the future global workforce will be primarily self-employed.

Montgomery, Cynthia A., James Weber and Elizabeth Anne Watkins, "The On-Demand Economy," Technical Note 716-405, Harvard Business School, September 2015, https://tinyurl.com/ya8scwcy.

Three Harvard Business School professors describe the on-demand economy and its key players and how the model could upend traditional business and consumer expectations.

Schiller, Zach, and Carl Davis, "Taxes and the On-Demand Economy," Institute on Taxation and Economic Policy, Mar. 15, 2017, https://tinyurl.com/ybfmobyj.

A report by a Washington think tank explores how goods and services provided through the on-demand economy fit into the current U.S. tax system and what changes may be necessary.

Taylor, Terry, "On-Demand Service Platforms," SSRN, Sep. 20, 2017, revised, http://tinyurl.com/y8k2pfmb.

A professor of business administration at the University of California, Berkeley, examines how wait time and the availability of independent contractors affect pricing and wages for on-demand services and products.

THE NEXT STEP

MOBILE APPS

Crook, Jordan, "Favor, the On-Demand Service Focused on Texas, Picks Up $22 million Series B," Tech Crunch, Sep. 7, 2017, https://tinyurl.com/y8jfeq6f.

Favor, a restaurant food delivery app similar to Postmates, shuttered its operations in other states to focus on Texas as it seeks to provide better service in its home territory.

Dahlberg, Nancy, "Need a Fast Fix? Home-Repair App Joins South Florida's On-Demand Economy," Miami Herald, Mar. 15, 2017, https://tinyurl.com/ya6wyvk3.

Home on Demand is an app that promises a cheaper and faster way for people needing home repairs.

Solis, Brian, "Impatience Is a Virtue: How the On-Demand Economy Is Making Mobile Consumers Impatient," Forbes, Nov. 20, 2017, https://tinyurl.com/y9ycgeor.

The increased prevalence of smartphones has created a growing number of impatient consumers seeking instant gratification, says a digital analyst.

RAPID DELIVERY

Dieterle, C. Jarrett, "The Last Frontier: The Online Economy and Alcohol," Forbes, Sep. 21, 2017, https://tinyurl.com/y8rd4kgf.

Amazon Prime and other delivery services are increasingly offering alcohol delivery, but only beer and wine due to strict state restrictions on hard liquor.

Rosenberg, Adam, "Target Acquires Shipt, with Plans to Offer Same-Day Delivery," Mashable, Dec. 14, 2017, https://tinyurl.com/y8j9th3z.

Target announced its $550 million acquisition of Shipt, a subscription-based grocery marketplace, and plans to offer same-day delivery, creating a subscription option similar to Amazon Prime.

Sharma, Rakesh, "Amazon Debuts 'Instant Pickup' on College Campuses," Investopedia, Aug. 15, 2017, https://tinyurl.com/y93s4sm9.

Amazon has introduced a delivery service on five college campuses that it touts as being even faster than Prime Now. After shoppers make a purchase, Amazon employees place it in a nearby locker and text the locker's access code to the customer.

ORGANIZATIONS

Aspen Institute
1 Dupont Circle, N.W., Suite 700, Washington DC 20036
1-202-736-5800
www.aspeninstitute.org
@AspenInstitute

Global think tank that explores best economic practices and promotes open-minded dialogue on current issues.

Brookings Institution
1775 Massachusetts Ave., N.W., Washington, DC 20036
1-202-797-6000
www.brookings.edu

Public policy think tank that conducts research on domestic and global issues.

Catalyst Companies
www.catalystcompanies.co
jko@catalystcompanies.co
@CrowdCompanies

Organization connecting established corporations, startups and leaders in the collaborative economy.

Institute on Taxation and Economic Policy
1616 P St., N.W., Suite 200, Washington, DC 20036
1-202-299-1066
www.itep.org

A nonpartisan research organization that analyzes the impact of tax policy at all levels of government.

JPMorgan Chase & Co. Institute
270 Park Ave., New York, NY 10017
1-212-270-6000
https://www.jpmorganchase.com/corporate/institute/institute.htm
institute@jpmchase.com

A think tank within the global financial institution dedicated to data analysis on current economic trends, both domestic and global.

MIT Initiative on the Digital Economy
Sloan School of Management, Massachusetts Institute of Technology,
245 First St., Room E94-1521, Cambridge, MA 02142
1-617-452-3216
http://ide.mit.edu/

An initiative that looks at how consumers and businesses interact in the digital economy.

National Employment Law Project
75 Maiden Lane, Suite 601, New York, NY 10038
1-212-285-3025
www.nelp.org

An organization promoting policies that support workers' rights and fair access to employment.

Think with Google
1600 Amphitheatre Parkway, Mountain View, CA 94043
1-650-253-0000
www.thinkwithgoogle.com

An arm of the global search engine giant that collects and analyzes real-time data on consumer trends.

Chapter 18: The Sharing Economy

BOOKS

Botsman, Rachel, and Roo Rogers, "What's Mine Is Yours: The Rise of Collaborative Consumption," HarperCollins, New York, 2010.

Botsman, a business consultant, and Rogers, the founder of several sharing-economy companies, trace the roots of the sharing economy and the changes in how people consume goods and services.

Chase, Robin, "Peers Inc: How People and Platforms Are Inventing the Collaborative Economy and Reinventing Capitalism," PublicAffairs, New York, 2015.

Chase, a cofounder of Zipcar, draws on the relatively short history of the sharing economy and explores how it is changing the broader economy.

Stephany, Alex, "The Business of Sharing: Making It in the Sharing Economy," Palgrave Macmillan, New York, 2015.

Stephany, CEO of JustPark, a sharing-economy company in Great Britain, outlines best practices for succeeding in the sharing economy by examining the experiences of his own firm as well as others.

ARTICLES

Asher-Schapiro, Avi, "The Sharing Economy Is Propaganda," Cato Unbound, Feb. 13, 2015, http://tinyurl.com/o2275be.

As part of a multi-author debate on a libertarian website, a journalist who has written about how Uber drivers see their work argues that much of the "sharing economy" is old-fashioned capitalism in disguise.

Badger, Emily, "Airbnb Is About to Start Collecting Hotel Taxes in More Major Cities, Including

Washington," The Washington Post, Jan. 29, 2015, http://tinyurl.com/nac6kdd.

Airbnb agrees to be the tax collector for some cities to ease regulators' concerns about lost revenue.

Benkler, Yochai, "Sharing Nicely: On Shareable Goods and the Emergence of Sharing as a Modality of Economic Production," Yale Law Journal, 2004, pp. 273-358, http://tinyurl.com/nv384q2.

This Harvard law professor's thorough analysis was the first real articulation of the modern sharing economy.

Cannon, Sarah, and Lawrence H. Summers, "How Uber and the Sharing Economy Can Win Over Regulators," Harvard Business Review, Oct. 13, 2014, https://hbr.org/2014/10/how-uber-and-the-sharing-economy-can-win-over-regulators/.

A manager at Google Capital (Cannon) and a former Treasury secretary (Summers) offer detailed advice on how sharing-economy companies can get the best treatment from regulators.

Cohen, Boyd, and Jan Kietzmann, "Ride On! Mobility Business Models for the Sharing Economy," Organization & Environment, Aug. 31, 2014, http://oae.sagepub.com/content/27/3/279.

The authors examine shared transportation business models to find the optimal balance between companies and local governments.

Feeney, Matthew, "Level the Playing Field—by Deregulating," Cato Unbound, Feb. 10, 2015, http://tinyurl.com/onphurf.

A policy analyst at the libertarian Cato Institute argues that new technologies have made much regulation counterproductive.

Kelly, Kevin, "We Are the Web," Wired, August 2005, http://tinyurl.com/p4kjdtj.

Wired magazine's founding executive editor offers a fascinating recounting of the development of the technologies that power the sharing economy.

Shafroth, Frank, "The Unforeseen Fiscal Challenges of Uber-Like Services," Governing, Mar. 20, 2015, http://tinyurl.com/pmh3mlj.

The director of the Center for State and Local Government Leadership at George Mason University illuminates the challenges the sharing economy poses for government.

Sundararajan, Arun, "A Safety Net Fit for the Sharing Economy," Financial Times, Jun. 22, 2015, http://tinyurl.com/qclxwu8.

A professor of information, operations and management sciences at New York University's Stern School of Business argues that benefits such as health coverage, worker's compensation and paid vacations should be available to sharing-economy workers.

REPORTS AND STUDIES

"Alternative Financial Services: A Primer," FDIC Quarterly, Apr. 27, 2009, http://tinyurl.com/p643omd.

Report from the Federal Deposit Insurance Corp. explains how alternative financial services work, including peer-to-peer lending, and how the services interact.

Krueger, Alan B., and Jonathan V. Hall, "An Analysis of the Labor Market for Uber's Driver-Partners in the United States," Working Paper #587, Princeton University, Jan. 22, 2015, http://tinyurl.com/n5norw8.

A Princeton economist (Krueger) and Uber's head of policy analysis (Hall) examine Uber data and find mostly positive effects for communities and employees.

Schneiderman, Eric T., "Airbnb in the City," New York State Office of the Attorney General, Oct. 14, 2014, http://tinyurl.com/m8pqffb.

Report lays out the New York government's case against Airbnb, finding the rental activities supported by the platform frequently violate state laws and harm communities.

THE NEXT STEP

NICHE MARKETS

Goel, Vindu, "Start-ups Clamor to Be the Airbnb of Boats," The New York Times, Jun. 10, 2015, http://tinyurl.com/ndy7hu3.

Boat owners find a niche market in peer-to-peer boat rentals, but face new challenges due to insurance and safety requirements.

Sharam, Andrea, and Lyndall Bryant, "An Uber for Apartments Could Solve Some Common Housing Problems," The Conversation, Jul. 20, 2015, http://tinyurl.com/p2wy2v4.

Two-sided matching markets, commonly used in the sharing economy, could create a housing market that encourages quality and affordability by pairing consumers with developers.

Zhuo, Tx, "5 Lessons Entrepreneurs Can Learn from Niche Marketplaces," Entrepreneur, May 14, 2015, http://tinyurl.com/nj9ltuu.

Successful niche markets employ multiple tools, including partnerships with potential competitors, specialized services and an interest in consumer needs.

REGULATION

Badger, Emily, "Who Millennials Trust, and Don't Trust, Is Driving the New Economy," The Washington Post, Apr. 16, 2015, http://tinyurl.com/p9hjp78.

While trust in individuals has declined over the past 40 years, trust in crowds has increased, allowing for the rise of an industry with fewer regulations, according to a survey by PricewaterhouseCooper.

Peltz, Jennifer, "Cities Keen on 'Sharing Economy' but Concerned about Safety," The Associated Press, Jun. 3, 2015, http://tinyurl.com/pqsok5y.

Officials in U.S. cities support growth in the sharing sector, but question the safety of an unregulated industry, according to a National League of Cities survey.

Popper, Ben, "Uber Can't Be Stopped. So What's Next?" The Verge, Jul. 27, 2015, http://tinyurl.com/ppvl35j.

New York City becomes the latest locale to try to regulate Uber, but fails.

TECHNOLOGY

Bahceli, Yoruk, "Netherlands to Make Room in Rules to Stimulate 'Sharing Economy,'" Reuters, Jul. 20, 2015, http://tinyurl.com/ou9xobv.

Officials in the Netherlands are adapting rules to meet the demands of new services, promising "technology-neutral" regulations that will not discriminate against less-savvy companies.

Howard, Alex, "Open Data, Crowdsourcing, and Sharing Economy Tech Take on New Roles in Disasters," Tech Republic, Aug. 8, 2015, http://tinyurl.com/q56uomg.

Some peer-to-peer companies are attempting to expand services to crisis response, offering "disaster technology" to those seeking information, aid and even housing during emergencies.

Kerr, Dara, "'Sharing Economy' Apps to Boom with Their Lure of Cheap and Easy," CNET, Apr. 14, 2015, http://tinyurl.com/p7alnxb.

User-friendly apps and simple digital transactions help to engage a growing number of customers and entrepreneurs in the sharing economy.

WORKER TREATMENT

Lapowsky, Issie, "A Sharing Economy Star Shuts Down as Labor Issues Simmer," Wired, Jul. 17, 2015, http://tinyurl.com/ovqkeug.

One start-up specializing in home cleaning services closed after failing to supply workers with basic benefits.

Macmillan, Douglas, "Sharing Economy Workers Need 'Safety Net,' U.S. Senator Says," The Wall Street Journal, Jun. 8, 2015, http://tinyurl.com/ngn4xcj.

Sen. Mark Warner, D-Va., is calling for new programs that would protect independent contractors in the United States, providing insurance and other basic employee benefits to freelance workers.

Manjoo, Farhad, "Start-ups Finding the Best Employees Are Actually Employed," The New York Times, Jun. 24, 2015, http://tinyurl.com/q46u73l.

One tech company classifies its workers as employees, not contractors, arguing that valued employees provide better service.

ORGANIZATIONS

Airbnb
888 Brannan St., San Francisco, CA 94103
415-800-5959
www.airbnb.com

Company that provides a platform for peer-to-peer rentals of living spaces.

Cato Institute
1000 Massachusetts Ave., N.W., Washington, DC 20001-5403
202-842 0200
www.cato.org

Libertarian think tank that explores the impact of government policies, including regulation.

Center for Economic and Policy Research
1611 Connecticut Ave., N.W., Suite 400, Washington, DC 20009
202-293-5380
www.cepr.net

Think tank that focuses on the effects of economic policies.

Federal Trade Commission
600 Pennsylvania Ave., N.W., Washington, DC 20580
202-326-2222
www.ftc.gov

The U.S. commission that is charged with preventing business practices considered anti-competitive, deceptive or unfair to consumers.

Lyft
2300 Harrison St., San Francisco, CA 94110-2013
866-292-2713
www.lyft.com

Company that offers on-demand transportation network services.

Mercatus Center, George Mason University
3434 Washington Blvd., 4th Floor, Arlington, VA 22201-4508
703-993-4930
www.mercatus.org

Describes itself as "the world's premier university source for market-oriented ideas—bridging the gap between academic ideas and real-world problems."

Property Casualty Insurers Association of America
8700 W. Bryn Mawr, Suite 1200S, Chicago, IL 60631-3512
847-297-7800
www.pciaa.net

Trade association for property casualty insurers.

Uber
1455 Market St., 4th Floor, San Francisco, CA 94103
877-223-8023
www.uber.com

Company that offers on-demand transportation network services.

E-Business

E-Business

Professor V. P. Gupta

RESEARCHCO BOOK CENTER
NEW DELHI - 110 005

First Published 2006

ISBN : 81-902320-8-8

Published by :

Researchco Book Center
25B/2, New Rohtak Road
(Near Liberty Cinema)
Karol Bagh
New Delhi-110005

Printed at :

Salasar Imaging Systems
New Delhi

TABLE OF CONTENT

1

E-Business Model

Customers

The days of marketers holding consumers captive for 30 seconds in front of a TV screen are quickly coming to a close. The Web is training individuals and organizations to help themselves to information, products, and virtually everything they want at the time and place they desire. Marketers must study consumer and business needs in the online environment and figure out how to meet these needs better than competitors. "The first step is to know who your end customers—and your prospects—are and then to learn as much about them as possible" (Seybold 1998). The next step is to design a marketing mix that provides value. During the process, marketers must figure out which customers are profitable, which to attract, and which to retain. Internet technologies make all of this possible in ways previously thought unimaginable. For example, American Airlines knows a lot about the needs and characteristics of its heaviest users: the frequent flyers. Based on this information, American provides password-protected account information on the Web and special incoming 1-800 telephone numbers to members of its all Advantage club. When a frequent flyer logs onto the Web site to search for flights, American automatically uses the member's closest airport as the trip starting point. For prospects as well as current customers, American provides weekly e-mail notification of specially priced trips to over 1.7 million individuals in its database.

American Airlines identified many social trends and changing values in the United States culture when it designed Internet services for customers and prospects. The following generalizations can be made about individual and business customers at the beginning of the 21st century:

Value is king. Customers and prospects are one click away from competitors if marketing offers do not provide good cost/benefit ratios. Part of value includes exceeding customer expectations when using products or delivering services. As one time-proven marketing adage suggests, "Under-promise and over-deliver."

Price is the most important factor for some customers, but not all. Many will gladly pay a premium to purchase from an online firm with which they have had good experiences or one with a trustworthy brand name. Further, extra services often command premium prices.

Customization adds value. Yahoo! provides custom Web pages for users, and Blue Nile allows customers to create their own diamond rings by combining settings and stones. Because the customization is automated, it comes at a low cost to the consumer.

Speed is everything. Users want to find relevant information and product quickly and receive purchased goods tomorrow. Customers don't want to spend time looking up passwords to enter Web sites or helping firms correct account errors through repeated communication.

Convenience is critical for busy people. They want to shop or pay bills anytime of the day or night, 24/7, and to receive deliveries when convenient for them, not for the firm or package delivery service.

Ease does it. Users have enough problems without having to learn special software or run through elaborate instructions simply to order from a Web site or pay bills online. In the business-to-business market, suppliers can assist businesses with complex installations by providing good customer support.

Personalization makes users feel important, especially when a computer sits between them and the company. Web sites that greet users by name, providing personalized information, Web pages designed for business customers, marketing offers and promotions tailored to user needs, and e-mail addressing specific questions are all ways that marketers personalize in an impersonal computer-networked environment. Furthermore, customers want companies to treat them as if they are important to the firm, especially if they are loyal and place large orders.

One-stop shopping and integrated solutions save people time and make life easier. Microsoft gained a huge following when it integrated word processing, spreadsheet, and presentation software all in one package. Similarly, Yahoo! and other Internet portals attempt to serve all user information and product needs at one site.

Self-service saves time. Customers want to log on, find information, make purchases, track package shipments, check their accounts, and make inquiries anytime, 24/7. Furthermore, they want to do this on a computer via e-mail or the Web, or on a telephone, PalmPilot, or FAX machine. Naturally they want all methods to produce identical information.

E-mail communication to firms deserves answers. Various studies found that up to one-half of all firms do not answer customer e-mails. Of those who do respond, many do not answer in a timely manner. Offering an e-mail address to an individual is like giving a promise.

All of this adds up to one new marketing truth for the information age: The power is now in the hands of the person who holds the mouse. Consumers and business buyers alike have 24/7 instant access to information and products and are literally one click away from doing business with a firm's competitor. This puts a lot of pressure on firms to meet user needs. Naturally, there are many ways to build customer loyalty, and sometimes switching costs are high; however, pre-Internet it was much more difficult to consider competitive offerings on a worldwide basis.

Markets

E-business occurs in five markets:

- **business-to-consumer (B2C),**
- **business-to-business (B2B),**
- **consumer-to-consumer (C2C),**
- **business-to-government (B2G),**
- **government-to-consumer (G2C).**

We focus on the first three in this text. When organizations sell to consumers, this is known as the B2C market, and when firms conduct business with each other they are operating in the B2B market. Sometimes consumers sell to each other in the C2C market. Prior to the Internet, classified advertising was the primary C2C market, but the Net brought widespread C2C activity using auctions. Consumer and business buyers might share similar expectations from the Net; however, their product needs and uses are often quite different. In consumer markets individuals are end users, purchasing products for personal consumption. Businesses and other organizations purchase products for use in the operation of the organization, as components for manufacture into final product, or for resale.

Many e-business activities and most e-commerce transactions occur in the business-to-business market (B2B); however this chapter features the consumer market (B2C or C2C). The reasons are twofold: 1) with the exception of products used in the operation of a business (such as paper clips, consulting services, or software), the ultimate demand for business products is derived from the individual consumer, and 2) the B2B market is better understood through discussion of e-business models in later marketing strategy chapters.

B2B Markets

Before moving on to the consumer market, however, we would like to make a few generalizations about the industrial market. First, over half of all e-commerce occurs in the B2B market. E-commerce B2B activities can include a number of things:

Selling product using electronic networks providing customer relationship management (CRM) functions online coordinating activities in the distribution channel using electronic data interchange (EDI) and just-in-time inventory systems supply chain management (SCM), also known as integrated logistics moving products from supplier to consumer combining with other firms to buy or sell cooperatively simply communicating using e-mail, intranets or extranets.

Many of these activities translate into e-business models and are discussed in later chapters. Second, in addition to the needs business customers share with individual consumers (speed, convenience, and so forth), important are online access to order status, product and price information, product availability, and transparent processes for everything from ordering through billing (Kalakota 1999). Next, as in traditional marketing, the online business market is often segmented by size, geography, **product usage**, and type (e.g., industry). In addition, firms selling in B2B markets segment by level of Internet usage. For example, some small firms do not use the Internet, and some large firms have quite sophisticated technology for e-commerce: Sellers must understand the capabilities of their customers before designing online strategies to reach their markets. Finally, in developing countries with poor technological infrastructures and other barriers to Internet adoption, B2B markets exhibit a higher level of activity and potential than do consumer markets.

There is much greater pressure on companies to adopt the Internet for business in that if a major customer requires that suppliers be capable of doing business over the Net, there is not much choice. GE has said it intends to do all its purchasing over the Net. Ford and GM are combining to create a Web-based purchasing process. Such companies believe that it is possible to reduce their overall costs by as much as 30% by moving many of their business functions on to the Net. No company can remain competitive without following suit.

Forrester Research has forecast that by 2002 as many as 80% of large companies and 45% of small ones will be operating through the Net.

Business-to-Business Models

Introduction:- It is in the business to business domain (B2B) that the real e-commerce revolution is happening - in contrast with business to consumers (B2C) which may follow a more evolutionary path. B2B is the core of the e-market - the most important in economic

terms, with more than 80% of total e-commerce activities. It is the fastest growing and most rapidly evolving area of e-commerce.

Beyond direct impact, B2B e-commerce (hereafter "B2B") has broad indirect effects:-"multiplicator" effects that reach much beyond the total amount of trade. B2B impacts company and market structures. It affects the competitiveness of individual firms - and of entire sectors of the economy. B2B is changing traditional patterns of economic behaviour and shaping a new business culture. Most importantly, B2B – combined with the Euro - represents a powerful catalyst for the Internal Market

For policy makers, B2B is clearly a strategic area – an area that matters. A clear understanding of the B2B revolution is crucial. Fresh challenges are emerging as electronic markets develop. New competitive imbalances may appear between offline and online environment, between new and established players. Based on a full analysis of current developments, enterprise policy should focus on resolutely promoting the positive effects of B2B - while seeking to avoid or reduce potentially negative effects. The main policy challenge is about managing the change towards the digital economy. In that respect, the interests of both "new" and "traditional" businesses should be fully taken into account.

The present paper aims at opening a full debate on the impact of B2B developments on EU enterprise policy. It describes the current "state of play" and analyses "state of the art" developments. It also proposes a policy agenda of key issues to be addressed in order to respond to the B2B challenges.

The HB2B Revolution: The State Of Play

Defining B2B

The first challenge is to define B2B. Multiple definitions of e-commerce exist, none of them fully satisfactory. The same applies to B2B.

A **positive definition is difficul**t. B2B encompasses a complex and fast evolving set of activities carried electronically inside companies and between companies. One certainty: B2B cannot be limited to "electronic transactions" or to "electronic trading". It is also about much broader structural changes - inside companies and in the relations between companies.

A **negative definition** may be easier. B2B can be described as all e-commerce activities that do not address a final individual consumer (B2C) nor public authorities (B2G). This is not only a functional difference. It also entails a major difference in legal regime.

In general, legal regulatory issues are simpler in B2B than in B2C, particularly for cross-border activities. Complex, often contradictory, regulations (e.g. privacy, consumer protection, jurisdiction, commercial communication, and consumption taxes) are hampering the development of global B2C.

In contrast, B2B builds largely on established laws and practices (e.g. private international law, freedom of contract, contractual choice of court, well established and effective arbitration procedures). In B2B, regulatory issues (e.g. electronic contracts) tend to be more straightforward - and less politically sensitive - than when final, individual consumers are involved. However, borders between B2B and B2C are blurring, as many companies engage simultaneously in a number of different activities.

Measuring B2B

According to all estimates, B2B is big - and it is growing fast. However, sizing B2B is fraught with severe measurement problems. There is a lack of official statistics. The US is the only country to have published official figures - and that only for very specific sectors. No official statistics are available as yet in Europe, neither at Member State nor at Community level. Private sector estimates vs. official statistics However, a number of

OECD Member Countries (US, CDN, AUS, DK) are leading the way. These are addressing B2B measurement problems either through ad hoc surveys (Nordic Countries joint e-commerce survey, just published), or by adding specific "new economy" indicators to existing surveys (e.g. small business census in CDN). A model survey including a set of basic "new economy" indicators is being developed by OECD. The aim of such a model survey, to be adopted by all OECD members, is to ensure international comparability, as well as to "catch" the specific added value of B2B. OECD-defined indicators are thus forming the basis of recent Eurostat proposals.

Private sector estimates offer a more variegated picture. Their purpose differs from official data collection - they aim at facilitating strategic decisions by companies, rather than assess long term trends to support policy. Methodologies differ widely (sample surveys, proprietary modeling). So does the choice of indicators.

Assessing the B2B Revolution

If quantitative measurements remain imprecise, qualitative assessment of the B2B revolution are more reliable. Reflecting the shift in investor interest from B2C to B2B, as well as the explosion of new marketplaces, a number of excellent reports from academic institutions and major consultancies, have been published over the past few months. Taken together with earlier assessments of supply chain management and "extended enterprise" phenomena, these reflect complex and accelerating changes in companies and marketplaces. From closed to open markets, from value chain to "value constellation" The Internet a "network of networks" based on open, interoperable protocols – represents a crucial paradigm shift from closed, proprietary networks using proprietary protocols (as in EDI) to open global networks. From being a mere conduit, "the network is becoming the market". In short the evolution is from "basic" e-commerce – with focus on reducing costs, on control, on linear supply chain, and on trading tangibles – to "full" e-commerce – centered on maximizing value, on creative and proactive strategies and on adding value through services and relationships. The B2B landscape is rapidly evolving.

Very few companies or sectors remain unaffected by the Internet and new ways of doing business electronically. Very few, however, are Internet-specific companies – so called "Internet pure plays". Most companies are hybrids. Indeed, moving to new forms of "collaborative" B2B is a challenge for user industries. Integrating pre-existing enterprise applications is a major problem – as was migrating from EDI. Interoperability of technologies and business processes is not always ensured. This is also a challenge for vendors – as "classic" ICT enterprise solutions providers (e.g. Oracle, MySAP) are challenged by "new integrators" (Ariba, Commerce One). Hybridization takes other forms too. Traditional "brick and mortar" companies are aggressively expanding (directly or through filiales) into e-business to become "click 6 and mortar". Conversely, "Internet pure plays" are seeking to root their activities into the concrete world (acquisition of warehouses, setting up of high street stores). Additionally, the emergence of B2B may not mean, of course, the total disappearance of "traditional" commerce. The Silicon Valley saying that "there will be only two types of enterprises, the e-enterprise and the non-enterprise" should be greeted with a grain of caution. For some firms, in some specific areas of activity, it may not make sense to go into e-commerce.

However, it is clear that B2B may rapidly become the norm for European businesses. This does not mean that all sales of all companies will be done over the net - but that various Internet tools and processes will rapidly, and irrevocably, find their way into the business processes, and will be used by a majority of companies.

For many companies, however, this race to "e" may lead to failure. Not only a number of dot.com businesses will fail. Traditional companies, also, will have to prove that their e-business projects can be successfully delivered. From cutting costs to shaping marketplaces.

The real e-commerce revolution goes beyond cost savings. B2B not only reduces time-to-market and improves quality. It speeds up processes, allow better quality of service. In this highly competitive environment, often marked by increased price transparency, better execution is often more important than "first mover" advantage. The edge goes to firms who are able to "execute" better – in particular through more efficient integration of "back end" and "front end" activities. The key phenomenon, however, is the reorganisation of traditional value chains into much more flexible business networks. Competitiveness of a company does not only depend on the efficiency of internal processes, but on the depth and breadth of its network of partners – suppliers, customers, information brokers, etc. Empowered by the Internet, B2B is first and foremost about structural changes – about reinventing companies and marketplaces. Among the fastest growing phenomenon of B2B are electronic marketplaces or e-exchanges.

B2B e-commerce" (IDC). According to Goldman Sachs, SMEs will be the main drivers of B2B (from 17% of global Internet commerce in 1997 to 30% in 2003) – and key users of such marketplaces. This contrasts sharply with former views that SMEs risk being "trapped" in such networks with big companies. Today, the main concern of SMEs is to become an integral part of emerging electronic marketplaces and avoid being locked out. Electronic marketplaces take many different forms, with different drives and different rules. Large players and vendors play a key role. However, there are several common issues that need to be addressed so that SMEs can truly participate in B2B. These include inter alia the establishment of a common system to automate and consolidate the verification process and the provision of efficient and cost-effective conflict resolution and automated credit management services.

B2B: Another It is generally recognized that a number of these exchanges are doomed to fail. Like in the retail "dot.com" environment, causes for failure include the inability to aggregate a critical mass of users - there may be just too many exchanges for the market to support. Another factor is the lack of sustainable business model - a variety of revenue models (advertising, subscriptions, transaction fees) are being tested with more or less success. Moreover, the vast majority of these exchanges are centered on classic, "linear" buy/sell/auction models. There are currently only few examples of advanced collaborative commerce marketplaces. Therefore, it is likely that the "net bubble" will not only burst in the B2C area. In B2B, also, many companies will fail. There will be winners and losers. However, such failures will occur not because the migration to e-business is wrong (as many traditional companies still believe), but because specific business model, strategies and implementation will have failed. Despite such failures, it is clear that e-business will increase substantially. The question is not if but when it will become the norm. E-business will be completely embedded in most enterprise's business processes. The main challenge for enterprise policy is thus to manage the change.

Enterprise Policy Implications

The development of B2B has crucial implications for the EU enterprise policy. It directly impacts a number of key areas, such as competitiveness issues, SME policies and standardization. The EU policy has traditionally focused on removing inhibitors and barriers in order to foster a market-driven process. This has been done, primarily, by guaranteeing fair competition, preventing anti-competitive market developments, and ensuring the right conditions for entrepreneurship to develop. Consensus building (e.g. through standardization, or through the promotion of self-regulation and co-regulation) has also played a key role. In this perspective, a number of new questions and challenges may arise. What will be the impact of B2B on productivity, prices and growth? How to secure a broad participation of SMEs in B2B? What is the role of standardization in shaping open electronic marketplaces? How to develop better synergies between SME policies, research, innovation and standardization to promote the take-up of B2B? How to encourage traditional sectors to embrace fully the new opportunities? These and other questions require consistent enterprise policy responses, based upon a solid analysis of market realities.

Measurement Issues

The challenge of measurement

Measuring B2B is a challenge: The economic impact of B2B on the European economy is still imperfectly understood. Traditional indicators do not "catch" the full consequences of the B2B revolution on individual sectors, and in particular on SMEs. The full impact of new marketplaces remains to be accounted for. A number of indicators have been proposed by Commission services. These still only offer partial responses. The challenge is to assess the full dimensions of the phenomenon - and in particular to track the transition from the industrial to the digital economy.

"Competitiveness indicators" proposed as part of the benchmarking exercise focus on basic measurements such as ITC penetration and Internet connectivity. Such "basic" indicators are important in the take-up phase of e-commerce. However, as experience shows, they tend to "saturate" and lose relevance (in Nordic countries 90 to 95% of firms are already connected to the Internet). Such indicators should be retained – running "in the background", as it were - to track the progress of less advanced Member States or industrial sectors. But different, and more specific, indicators focusing on the impact and intensity of B2B should be introduced as the B2B markets mature. Similarly, "digital economy" indicators, address only part of the equation.

Although e-Europe provides a useful "grille" for benchmarking, the need to fully assess the progress of the digital economy in Europe implies a broader approach. In short, indicators should not be reduced to the ten areas corresponding to e-Europe initiatives.

Comparability, political relevance, statistical feasibility: a need for co-operation In general, broad international comparability is crucial. OECD methodology, which builds on the experience of pioneer EU Member States (e.g. "Nordic Countries Survey"), provides flexible tools specifically focused on the new economy. The approach is to "phase in" different sets of indicators to measure "readiness", then "intensity", as the market matures. Two basic criteria retained are political relevance and statistical feasibility.

OECD guidelines, likely to be adopted by all OECD Member Countries (including EU Member States), will also provide a broader base for international comparison – reflecting the global dimension of the digital economy. For these reasons, we should clearly support the work of OECD – and build on that methodology. In parallel, the role of different Commission services - DG ENTR, DG INFSO, but also DG ECFIN, should be clarified. The interface with Eurostat needs to be streamlined, in particular as concerns the identification of "deliverables" in support of the work of OECD.

Macroeconomic Issues

Macroeconomic estimates: an uncertain picture

This is another crucial area for policy. Goldman Sachs estimates that cost savings in B2B alone will bring a sustained extra economic growth of 0.25% per annum over the next ten years–in an overall effect of 5% of GDP. If this were true, B2B would have a major impact on growth – a fact that that could not be politically ignored. Similarly, the impact of the B2B revolution on job creation and employment is of prime political concern. So far, the analysis is mainly based on the assumption that B2B will lower prices and costs which will stimulate demand, both directly (price elasticity of demand) and indirectly (wealth effects). This is the proposed explanation for the combination of full employment, low inflation and rapid growth experienced in the US (see DoC Report Digital Economy 2000) as well as in some European countries. If the analysis of this paper is correct, B2B may, however, induce in many areas - such as productivity, investments and savings - a “paradigm shift” (in the Schumpeterian sense).

The fundamental economic laws of the “new economy” may not differ from those of the industrial age-in the end, higher productivity will results in higher growth and more jobs. But the dynamics might change, and the short-term effects might differ from the long term perspectives. Thus there are serious doubts that the macroeconomic effect of B2B – i.e. its full impact on productivity, growth, job creation, and inflation - can be reliably assessed and fully validated, at least in the short term. Transmission mechanisms are still far from being fully understood. Past difficulties in assessing a narrower phenomenon, the impact of ICT on productivity (assumed, but never convincingly proved by economists), foretells future difficulties in assessing far more complex e-business processes. In addition, B2B is still at an early stage - so that the macroeconomic impact is difficult to measure. Focusing on structural change It seems reasonable to argue that B2B is part of an economic revolution which will have deep structural effects. Such structural changes are difficult to quantify, but easier to qualify. For enterprise policy, analysis should therefore focus on structura effects. What is the impact of B2B on entrepreneurship? How is the B2B revolution fostering a new generation of risk taking entrepreneurs and start-ups in Europe? How is it challenging the traditional image of SMEs as being “small”, “local” and, by definition almost, “handicapped”?

DG ENTR should concentrate on assessing these structural changes, and provide for analytical documents to feed the policy debate. Delivering what is measurable. On the other hand, and in parallel, macroeconomic analysis should focus of more easily measurable “deliverables” – such as the impact of ICT. This is the basic, “conservative” approach chosen by the US government in its three successive reports on the Digital Economy. In Europe, however, statistics are still fragmented. We are still lacking reliable EU-wide figures on the impact of ICT on productivity and job creation. The objective of the Commission therefore should be to provide a more systematic approach and to prepare for a comprehensive – and ongoing – assessment using a common methodology. The focus should be on statistical feasibility - measuring what is measurable. Decision should also be taken as to the best strategy to follow – to launch of a comprehensive report on the Digital Economy (as the US), or include results in ongoing publications (e.g. EITO reports).

Structural and Sectoral Issues

Providing a better understanding of structural impact of B2B – in particular the impact on industrial and services sectors and services, and in particular SMEs – should be the key mission of DG ENTR. This will build on our unique expertise and knowledge of sectoral developments, as well as on previous work on competitiveness and e-commerce. Analysis and policy definition We have to prepare the Commissioner and hierarchy to react to a rapidly changing environment–and to provide the necessary policy messages (notably through speeches). This is a priority area. In order to "track" ongoing structural changes in sectors, a systematic analysis of sectoral impact of B2B on different industries needs to be carried out. Therefore, further sectoral studies will be launched. In addition, regular briefings on important developments in B2B at sectoral level should be offered. Assessing the needs of traditional sectors Special emphasis should be given to "traditional" sectors. We should assess how B2B impacts "hard industries" and business services - and in particular those sectors under direct responsibility of DG ENTR. Such industries remain the backbone of European competitiveness, even if they need restructuring. We have to understand their fears and, in certain cases, reluctance towards B2B.

Specific obstacles and opportunities should be clearly assessed. In this process, DG ENTR sectors should be actively involved. In fact, every sectoral unit should have an "e-strategy". Coordination should be ensured through the new DG ENTR Working Group on E-commerce and ICT. Ensuring a level playing field between offline and online. Additionally, while focussing on opportunities offered by B2B, special attention should be given to potential distortions between online and offline environments. The main principle should be neutrality between online and offline business. In particular, sectors should be invited to analyse potential legal disadvantages faced by offline businesses in B2B (e.g. potential "double standards" for "e-tailers" and traditional retailers; easy availability of dangerous products from non-EU sources on the Web). If competitive unbalances are shown to exist, these should be removed in the most cost effective and un-bureaucratic manner. E-business should be considered as a powerful catalyst for liberalisation and the simplification of law. On this issue, an internal working document should be prepared. Impact on structural policies: regional development, sustainability The new "location flexibility" of B2B is a powerful factor to encourage a new decentralization of business activities across the EU – and a major contributor to regional development policies. This is also an imperative for the success of the EURO zone as a single currency area – in which the normal prerequisite of labour mobility is not currently met, nor likely to be.

Additionally, the "immaterial services" aspect of B2B may be used to promote more rapid "dematerialization" of growth, in the interest of sustainable development. This is likely to be a priority of the future Swedish presidency. DG ENTR should be prepared to contribute to this policy debate.

SME Policy Issues

B2B: global opportunities, global challenges

E-commerce represents **unprecedented opportunities**. With the "death of distance" and the lowering of barriers of entry to global markets, e-commerce allows SMEs to "punch beyond their weight" – and, in many cases, successfully take on much larger companies. SMEs are therefore ideally placed, in theory at least, to benefit from the e-commerce revolution - not only in terms of cost savings and improved processes, but also of expanding opportunities.

However, obstacles are well documented – high telecommunication costs, limited bandwidth availability, skills gap and training challenges, difficult access to finance, administrative obstacles to creating companies, legal regulatory complexities of cross-border trade, lack of recognized brands, transaction security, etc. Additionally, in many areas, distance still counts. Proximity is an asset, and SMEs remain crucially dependent on the efficiency of logistics. The key challenge is to ensure that SMEs fully grasp the opportunities not only of e-commerce in general but specifically of B2B. At this time, for a number of reasons,B2C seems to be the main horizon for the majority of SMEs, both in the US and in Europe. The challenge is to ensure that SMEs become key players in the "main league" of e-commerce B2B. This is the area where the money is, where legal and regulatory hurdles are less daunting but where fierce commercial competition from global players is at its most intense.

Global competition – the ultimate test for entrepreneurship

At stake is the competitiveness of SMEs. In the B2B environment, only the most competitive companies will succeed. Easier access to global markets is counterbalanced by easier access from global competitors to their home markets. Professionalism, quality of management, excellence of products, strength of brands, reliability of supply are the *condition sine qua non* of success - and of survival. The she have to be promoted as a priority. "Awareness" and "best practice": reassessing the role of public policy In this highly competitive environment, the challenge is no longer to promote "awareness". Most EU entrepreneurs already know about e-commerce – and about B2B. Industry itself (vendors, trade associations, consultants) have done their job. The challenge is to get SMEs started, in practical and real terms – a task which only industry can do. General public campaigns, particularly at EU level, are in general no longer justified (although limited campaigns may still be valuable, in some cases, in less advanced Member States).

Awareness cannot be successfully promoted through piecemeal projects and limited networks. There are already too many. This is why the objective the "Go Digital" campaign, as proposed by e-Europe, should be to build upon the results of completed or ongoing EU projects and to better network with national initiatives. In this context, the role of the Euro Infocentres Network should be valorized. Similarly, public authorities should be prudent in taking up upon themselves to promote "best practices". This should clearly be the main responsibility of industry.

Building entrepreneurship For policy makers, the real challenge is about entrepreneurship. It is to arm – and to "steel" - European SMEs to face the test of global competition. For many companies, taking part in global electronic exchanges is a competitive shock – and a true test of entrepreneurship. Policy makers cannot absorb the shock for companies – but can play a catalyst role to help them do the job in a competitive environment. In this context, the value of proposed "moral suasion" efforts should be carefully assessed. This should not result, in particular, in political claims to offer online services free of charge for SMEs a potentially counterproductive approach in the global competitive environment.

Market Access and Openness Issues

Competition issues A central issue for competition is that of electronic marketplaces. Such e-marketplaces, in their different forms, provide SMEs with new and crucial gateways 14 to "go digital" – and to global markets. They create virtual communities of buyers and sellers – *potentially* on a much broader scale, and with lower access thresholds, than "brick and mortar" equivalents. However, such marketplaces also bear the risk that new business cartels will emerge. The question arises why so many global players have an interest to sharing the same Internet platforms - although each of them could easily establish their own portal to buy and sell.

Potential competition issues may involve controlling pricing to the detriment of competitors. Even if an electronic marketplace is open to all, prices and commissions charged to members as part of their membership could be set at an artificially high level. SMEs in particular may have limited negotiating capacity vis à vis the owners or operators of e-markets – therefore having to accept the membership fees, transaction fees and operating procedures of "market-makers". Others risks may include the possibility of monopolizing an industry's marketplace the "market-maker's" sheer size making it unlikely that rival marketplaces develop to serve as competition. Others may force suppliers to reveal confidential information which will subsequently shared by all platform members.

Competition laws show continued relevance in the fast changing world of B2B. Such laws were enacted to give businesses a level playing field - and in particular to ensure buyers' trust in the marketplace pricing. For example US antitrust laws make it illegal for companies to "rig" bidding, to agree to divide the market, or to fix prices. Already in the US a number of traditional companies have used antitrust laws against an electronic commerce upstart. It may be only a matter of time before similar issues arise in Europe. The key issue is to prepare the Commission to address such emerging challenges. Whereas competition policy issues in the B2B environment are openly discussed in the US the debate has not taken place in Europe. On the other hand, concerns have also been voiced in the EU, as well as in the US, that some of the new marketplaces may be anti-competitive. While Art. 81 and 82 of the Treaty may well prove sufficient, the full impact of the digital economy in the area of competition may need further assessment. DG ENTR needs to be well prepared to participate in – and actively contribute to - this debate. Many of the issues are sector-specific. The expertise of sectoral units will be crucial. DG ENTR needs, as a matter of priority, to invest more resources, notably to monitor market developments in the B2B (but also in B2C) area.

Enterprise policy should play an active role in the "sensibilisation" of sectors on the opportunities and requirements of such marketplaces. This includes the promotion of open, neutral platforms and, more generally, the promotion self-regulation and consensus building. This also implies working closely with industry associations – who should reflect upon their role in shaping open, neutral platforms for e-business. In sectors which are dominated by few players, associations have been traditionally reluctant (and not mandated) to actively participate in such endeavours. However, in many other sectors (e.g. textiles) which are characterized by high fragmentation and many players, notably SME, the need for open, neutral platforms is more evident. . The active promotion of such open platforms is therefore a key tool to familiarize enterprises, and in particular SMEs. Additionally, the credibility of such platforms both in business terms and in technical terms is crucial. Given the "sensitive" nature of information flows (drawings, models, technical specifications, pricing), system security is of paramount importance. A policy initiative should be designed to further promote this approach, possibly as part of the "go digital" initiative.

Openness: the role of standardization In the B2B area, standardization has a key role to play. Combined with the Euro, B2B is a powerful driver towards the realization of the Internal Market. Standardization is needed to deliver the full potential of B2B. This implies ensuring interoperability, and facilitating market access – two fundamental expectations from European businesses that should not be disappointed. European standards organizations should therefore fully seize the opportunities of B2B. Some encouraging examples have already been established by CEN. However, a more pro-active strategy is needed. This requires a further modernization of European standardization. The issue is not only new deliverables (e.g. workshop agreements, instead of formal standards), but also of working methods. More incentives need to be created to attract industry players to participate directly in European standardization. In short, standardization organizations should evolve from technical experts to service providers for consensus building.

To that effect, Commission's funding should be reoriented from direct support of project teams to the establishment of neutral, open platforms. In this area, European standards organisations will position themselves in the commercial environment – in competition with vendors, industry associations. Although they are well placed to offer industry such "consensus-building services", they will no longer be able to claim a monopoly. Additionally, the use of open access to e-business frameworks by SMEs should be a key factor to encourage new job creation – and therefore to meet the Lisbon employment rate targets. Standardization organizations could play an important role in this - e.g. through quality standards for new Internet services. To give the necessary visibility to standardization and to motivate industrial stakeholders to actively participate in consensus building efforts in B2B, a high level conference should be organised.

The role of RTD

There are currently a large number of RTD projects in the area of B2B. Clustering is frequently used to maximise the impact of such projects. The links between RTD projects and standardization should be improved with the view to better exploit the results and to leverage them into the open environment. Similarly, there is a crucial role for innovation policy – to be integrated with both RTD and standardization. RTD projects should result in wider dissemination into the public domain. In parallel, RTD projects should be encouraged to participate in open standardization fora. The selective approach of many RTD projects in the field of B2B platforms can only be justified if they ultimately contribute to openness and fair market access. The objective must be to create a level playing field, not to promote proprietary solutions. Many RTD projects result in further standardization work, but so far no systematic approach to link between them exists. In 1999, a Memorandum of Understanding was signed between former DG III and DG XIII in order better to integrate RTD and standardization policies. This MoU still needs to be fully implemented.

Business to Consumer Models

Business-to-Consumer E-commerce Statistics

Introduction

1. To better inform the Committee on Consumer Policy's work on ensuring effective protection for consumers in the online marketplace, this document provides a quantitative overview of the status of business-to-consumer (B2C) e-commerce. Much of the data referenced is derived from private sources, because statistical offices of Member countries are only beginning to collect such data.

2. This paper begins with a discussion of the methodological challenges involved in quantifying e-commerce activity around the globe. Examples are presented in the following section of different estimates for total B2C e-commerce, as well as estimates of e-commerce distribution by sector / product and by geography. The paper then includes a brief overview of the relationship between access and pricing issues and the potential for e-commerce development. Turning to conclusions, the paper discusses the

expected path of B2C e-commerce sales in the near future and the importance of gathering more data on B2C e-commerce.

Methodological issues

3. Until recently, there has been no internationally-agreed definition of what e-commerce is. It is therefore difficult to compare estimates of its size, breakdown and growth (OECD, 1999a; OECD 2000a). A variety of sources produce estimates, including IT market research firms, investment banks, and increasingly, national statistical offices. Not only are their definitions different, but the methodologies are often not comparable, leading to a wide range of estimates and forecasts. In addition to estimating the value of online purchases, different types of indicators can be used to collect additional information on B2C e-commerce; for example, the number of people who have purchased items online and the frequency of purchases. Although difficult to size, all studies agree on the fact that many facets of this economic activity are growing quite rapidly; a recent study estimates that about 40% of all Internet users have made at least one online purchase (Angus Reid, 2000).

4. Following the Ottawa Ministerial Conference on E-Commerce (October 1998) an Expert Group from the Working Party on Indicators for the Information Society (WPIIS) was established to "compile definitions of electronic commerce which are policy relevant and statistically feasible". In April 2000 a joint WPIE/WPIIS meeting was held and agreement was reached on a provisional framework and follow- up strategy (OECD, 2000a; OECD, 2000b). This framework consists of a set of definitions, a preliminary list of indicators for measurement, and a strategy for developing and refining future work. The framework is intended to assist OECD countries in developing their own statistical programmes for measuring e-commerce and improve international comparability, although it carries no binding obligation on countries to apply the definition or modify existing statistical procedures.

5. Ongoing analytical work at the OECD uses a life-cycle model to highlight three broad phases of e-commerce growth. Each phase can be measured with different sets of indicators which also correspond to different policy concerns for governments (OECD, 2000a; OECD 2000c,). Many of the widely available indicators (from both public and private sources) refer to the "readiness" phase of the cycle. In the OECD framework, however, estimates of e-commerce transactions usually focus on the "intensity" phase, *i.e.* measuring the size and nature of these transactions.

6. When focussing on transactions, the OECD's working definition of an electronic transaction *(transaction)* is a "sale or purchase of goods or services, whether between businesses, households, individuals, governments, and other public or private organisations, conducted over computer-mediated networks" (OECD, 2000b). This definition includes orders placed over a network, regardless of whether or not the payment

and the delivery took place online. Other definitions only include Internet protocol-based networks *(i.e.* excluding Electronic Data Interchange (EDI) or other proprietary systems); others only include orders with online payment. This paper will focus on estimates of the value of these *transactions,* with particular emphasis in differences between countries and product groups.

Total B2C e-commerce

7. Estimates for B2C e-commerce vary widely depending on the source. It is difficult to compare these figures given the differences in methodologies (OECD, 1999b), which result in some cases in estimates that vary by a factor of two.

8. Statistical organisations in some OECD countries have begun to collect data on e-commerce, although the surveys do not necessarily use the same categorization between B2C and B2B. Nonetheless, these surveys do provide insights into online consumer behaviour as they usually distinguish retail from wholesale trade.

9. A more recent study of Canadian Internet shopping (Statistics Canada, 2001) estimates that the value of online orders placed by households reached CAD 417 million in 1999. During that year, 15.3% of all Canadian households used the Internet for some aspect of Internet shopping, either for gathering information, or for placing orders online.

10. The Electronic Commerce Promotion Council of Japan recently estimated that the B2C market in Japan would grow rapidly in the next 4 years, from an estimated size of JPY 824 billion (USD 7.6 billion) in 2000, to around JPY 13.3 trillion (USD 123 billion) in 2005 (ECOM, 2001). However, it should remain far smaller than the B2B market, which is expected to reach JPY 110 trillion (USD 1 trillion) by 2005, against JPY 22 trillion (USD 204 billion) in 2000. According to this study, direct comparison of B2C e-commerce in Japan and the United States, in terms of relative intensity (the ratio of B2C e-commerce to total private sector spending by product segment traded), shows that Japan should reach the 2000 US level by 2003.

11. One of the main factors behind the rapid growth of the Japanese B2C market is the explosion of cellular phone Internet services. This new mobile commerce ("m-commerce") market is currently estimated at some JPY 60 billion (USD 557 million). The rapid growth of m-commerce and the future expansion of broadband networks, such as IMT-2000 (third generation mobile telecommunication technology) are expected to further boost the development of B2C e-commerce. Mobile commerce accounted for less than 7% of the total B2C electronic commerce in 2000, but should grow to reach a share of 18% by 2005

12. Denmark recently published its first official figures on Internet commerce – based on a narrow definition which only includes Internet-based transactions. Statistics Denmark estimates that Internet commerce

reached DKK 12 billion in 2000 (USD 1.5 billion), of which 13% (around DKK 1.5 billion or USD 193 million) was B2C (Statistics Denmark, 2001).

13. In Australia, 10% of all adults, or 1.3 million people, purchased or ordered goods and services for their own private use via the Internet (ABS, 2000). Furthermore, in just the three months prior to November 2000, 13% of Australian adults used the Internet to pay bills or transfer funds, an increase of 5% over the three previous months. While this is a large increase over a short period, it is still low compared to the 49% of Australians who paid bills or transferred funds via the phone, the 66% who used EFTPOS (Electronic Funds Transfer at Point Of Sale) for such transactions and 73% who used ATM facilities during the same period.

Sector / product distribution

14. Growth is occurring unevenly, with different countries and product groups expected to reach different threshold levels. Still, B2C e-commerce remains concentrated in a few product groups: travel/tourism, banking/finance, ICT goods, books, and audio-visual products. Moreover, while these are the most popular product groups, the relative market share among them varies depending on the country. Two main criteria which influence the likelihood that the good will be sold online are its nature (physical vs. digital) and the level of customization. For some goods and services (such as books, music, and financial services) it is already significant and should grow at a faster pace than the total market. Entertainment is the only category for which mobile commerce is already predominant (currently more than 70% of all m-commerce in 2000).

Geographical distribution

15. The United States remains the largest market for B2C e-commerce, currently accounting for more than three-quarters of the world total. As B2C e-commerce develops in Europe, however, its market should reach about one-third of the United States' level within 2 to 3 years.

16. Although e-commerce brings along the promise of borderless trade, online sales continue to take place mostly within the consumer's home country (or region): 80% of European B2C e-commerce takes place within Europe (Boston Consulting Group, 2000), and a recent survey of Canadian online consumers (Angus Reid, 2000) revealed that almost two-thirds had made their most recent purchase at a Canadian Web site, compared to less than one-third a year before. A survey of Australian online shoppers estimates that in late 2000, more than half of all online shoppers purchased or ordered from Australian sites only, compared to less than 40% in February of the same year (ABS, 2000). Price is an important factor for consumers considering online purchases, but other factors such as the quality of service and information, the speed and reliability of delivery, the ease of on-line ordering, and trust towards vendors (payment security,

redress mechanisms), will increasingly determine their propensity to engage in e-commerce (Goldman Sachs, 2001 a and b).

The holiday season 2000

17. United States Online sales, in the United States during the 2000 holiday season doubled compared to the previous year reaching around USD 10 billion (Goldman Sachs, 2001a and b). Mediametrix reports that unique visitors to e-commerce sites increased 21%, from 48.8 million in December 1999 to 59 million in December 2000. Some categories of goods and services have been particularly sensitive to the holiday seasonality, such as books, apparel, toys and video games, and consumer electronics (NRF/Forrester, 2001). For those households already online, there is an increasing trend to do part of their holiday shopping via the Internet. Among the main reasons invoked by consumers for shopping online were their ability to avoid store crowds, to easily compare products and prices, and to have products delivered to home. On the other hand, the ability to return the product directly to the shop was not the main reason for choosing to shop at a physical location, but rather the ability to see and feel the product and to receive it immediately (Goldman Sachs 2001a and b).

In Europe, the Internet is also becoming a significant channel for holiday shopping. The number of retail site visits in most European countries (G7 European, Sweden, Denmark, and Spain) peaked during the month of December (Jupiter/MMXI, 2001).

Beyond online shopping, in Europe the Internet is playing an increasing role in other ways. For example, in the United Kingdom, 90% of users consulted the Internet to help research their purchases this year, even though they did not conduct their holiday shopping online.

Access and pricing

18. The uptake of B2C e-commerce is also constrained by the availability of adequate infrastructure for secure transactions. When considering where the bulk of B2C e-commerce occurs, it is not surprising that data on secure servers show that the infrastructure for conducting e-commerce is unevenly distributed across countries, with Iceland and the United States having almost one server for every 4 000 inhabitants, while around half of the OECD countries have less than 5 servers per 100 000 inhabitants. Although growth of the relative availability of secure servers has been very rapid (on average increasing almost five-fold in one year throughout the OECD region), there are still wide (and growing) disparities.

19. For consumers, the cost of accessing the Internet is also a decisive factor for engaging in e-commerce activities. Differences in Internet penetration (as measured by Internet hosts) are closely linked to the cost of accessing the Internet. While low prices do not guarantee high penetration (as seen for example in Korea), they are an important factor

for more widespread development of the Internet and consequently, of electronic commerce.

20. With B2C e-commerce still accounting for a very small share of all retail trade in OECD countries, usually less than 1%, it is understandable that some public attention has shifted to the B2B e- commerce sphere which accounts for more than four-fifths of all transactions. However, increases in the B2C sphere are still expected and should not be overlooked by policy makers.

21. For example, in the United States, current estimates range from 1.0 to 1.5% of all retail sales, but this figure is expected to continue increasing and reach around 3 to 6% within the next few years. Similarly, in Japan, 4% of household consumption is expected to shift online by 2005 (ECOM, 2001). Data from other OECD countries varies widely with some countries already displaying a relatively high intensity (Sweden, Australia, the United Kingdom, and the Netherlands), while in others, uptake has been slower (Portugal, Spain, and Italy).

22. As governments continue to work to ensure that online consumers are afforded transparent and effective protection, whatever the medium, better data is needed to understand the rapid development of B2C e-commerce. More information not only on the volume of transactions, but also on their nature and on the attitudes and experiences of consumers towards e-commerce is needed.

Indicators for Measuring B2C E-Commerce

A wide range of indicators can be used to measure B2C e-commerce in qualitative and quantitative terms. These can be separated into four broad categories, each one focusing on a different aspect of the process:

- transactions;
- consumers;
- businesses;
- "readiness" indicators.

Transactions

This set of derived indicators focuses on the transaction itself. Usually e-commerce includes all online orders regardless of whether the payment takes places on- or off-line. In addition to the total value of purchases, other aspects of the transaction can be measured such as the type of product/ service purchased, the relative importance of online sales, or the propensity to purchase from foreign sites.

- Total value of transactions (including seasonal purchases).
- Transactions broken down by type of product.
- Sales by product as a percentage of some other indicator (such as

total retail sales, or domestic expenditure).
- Average value of purchases.
- Type of payment and delivery (off/online).
- Source of purchases: domestic or foreign retailer.

Consumers

This set of indicators provides additional information focusing on the consumers.

- Number of online shoppers or online shoppers as a percentage of population/online population.
- Socio-economic differences such as sales by gender or age group.
- Frequency of online purchases.
- Time spent shopping online.
- Technologies used to access e-commerce sites: PCs, mobile phones, personal data assistants (PDAs).
- Attitudinal data: perceived benefits and barriers.

Businesses

These indicators focus on the supply-side of online retailing.

- Number of businesses online/engaged in e-commerce.
- Number of businesses by sector of economic activity or type of product.
- Barriers to adoption.
- Type of retailer: existing retailer recently adopting e-commerce (multi-channel) or newly established, Internet-based retailer ("pure-play").
- Most popular e-commerce sites.
- Industry concentration (market share) by type of product.

An Example of E-commerce Estimation: The Forrester Model

Forrester Research is a US-based IT market research firm which produces e-commerce estimates and forecasts. Its "eCommerce Threshold Model" is an example of how estimates of e-commerce transactions are generated using a combination of supply- and demand-side data. The model covers both B2B (online business trade) and B2C (online private consumption). For each country, an "e-Commerce Potential Index" is calculated to determine when high-growth can be expected. This index reflects the "e-readiness" of each economy in terms of the business environment and the development of its technology infrastructure. The total e-commerce "potential" of each country and sector is thus calculated using both economic data and various measures of technological "readiness". For the B2C part of the model a second set of indicators is compiled and used for each country. It includes:

- "Technographic" data measuring the ownership and usage of PCs, surveys of consumers' attitudes (such as the willingness to shop online or browsing habits).
- Population statistics (including household disposable income).
- Current data on consumption by type of goods; and
- Estimates of potential for online sales (in percentage) and expected timeline for both the high-growth phase and saturation (see Annex Table 1 for the United States).

Finally, a logistic model (or "S-curve") is used to forecast growth for each country and product group based on these parameters. These estimates are complemented by studies of consumer behaviour (based on household surveys) as well as analytical research on IT markets and e-commerce vendors.

E-commerce business models

Developments in computing technology and communication systems, most notablythe Internet, have created many new business opportunities for electronic commerce. New mechanisms for making money have developed. The below overview discusses the most common of these business models.

Since this is a very young field, there are not many reference works available. However, many patents have been granted in this field. When appropriate, a reference to a relevant patent has been included. Please note that this does not mean that that patent covers the technique in question, or even that the patent is a valid one. All it means is that the patent in some way relates to the technique in question.

The Merchant Model

A merchant is a wholesaler or retailer of goods and services. The merchant provides a website with product information and an online ordering mechanism. Users select the products they want to buy and place an order. The product price can be fixed or negotiable. The merchant makes his money the same way as traditional "brick-and-mortar" shops: through the profit margin in the product price. This model is mainly suited for physical goods and services, such as books, computers or a pizza delivery service. The merchant can directly reach end users and sell to them without needing wholesalers or retailers.

Mercantile processes define interaction models between consumers and merchants for on –line commerce. This is necessary because to buy and sell goods, a buyer, seller, and other parties must interact in ways that represent some standard business processes. We, like many others, believe that a common way of doing business over the I –way will be essential to the future growth of e – commerce. A well –established standard process for processing credit card purchases has contributed to the widespread dissemination of credit cards. The war against escalating on –line transaction –processing costs requires new weapons. And designing and implementing new mercantile processes is the most powerful weapon available to wage that war effectively.

The establishment of a common mercantile process (or set of processes) is expected to increase convenience for consumers who won't have to figure out a new business process for every single vendor. The absence of a common process for managing and completing transactions will result in electronic commerce being entangled a in a mesh of bilateral ad hoc mechanisms that are specific to every company doing business on –line.

Before rushing off and developing new mercantile process models, it is prudent to review existing business process models used in the manufacturing and retailing industries. The review would provide the understanding required to determine the features needed in an architectural model designed specifically for electronic commerce. Then, of course, within the scope of such an architecture, we must demonstrate the ability to solve at the problems that the current consumer –oriented business processes require and any new ones we may have identified for the future. The idea behind a general architecture is that it would lead to a set of methods and tools from which specific protocols can be easily implemented.

The broker Brokers or intermediaries create markets by bringing buyers and sellers together and facilitating transactions between them. Those can be **business-to-business (B2B), business-to-consumer (B2C), or Consumer-to-consumer (C2C)** markets. A broker makes money by charging a fee for every facilitated transaction, for instance as a percentage of the price of the transaction. Some special types of brokers are: Group buying - bringing individual potential buyers together in order o buy as a group, which should result in a lower price for each buyer (volume discounts, etc). Classified ads - sellers can advertise their product on a site where buyers can find it. The broker makes money in various ways: the seller pays a placement fee, or the broker receives a portion of the price paid by the buyer. Bounties - the broker offers a reward for finding a person, thing, idea, or other desired, but hard to find item. The broker may list items for a flat fee, or charge a percentage of the reward if the item is successfully found.

The sales representative Sales representatives often work on a commission basis: they sell an item for someone else and get a percentage of the price. On the Web, this model has developed into what is known as affiliate programs or referral fees. Someone creates a website on a particular topic and adds links to products on a merchant site which are related to his topic, so his visitors can buy those. For example, a music reviewer can add a link in a review to an online music store where the CD being reviewed can be ordered. If the reader likes the review, he can following the link and buy the CD. The merchant then pays the reviewer a commission or referral fee to the reviewer for referring to his site (US 6,029,141).

This model is realized as follows. The reviewer registers at the merchant site and receives a unique code. He adds this code to all the links to the merchant site whenever he links to a product at that site. When a reader follows the link, the merchant site sees the code and couples the reader's actions to the code. When the reader buys something the site registers the sale together with the code. Later all sales matching that code can be collected so the percentage can be computed and credit to the reviewer. There are many variations on this theme. A fixed percentage can be paid to all sales resulting from the referral or a high percentage can be given to the actual product to which he linked, possibly with a low percentage on other sales that resulted from the link. This model is used by Amazon, Proxies, CD-Now and others. Some book authors link to their own book this way, making more money to the referral fee than to the royalties they get in. Subscription-based services also sometimes offer a referral fee to anyone who brings in a new subscriber. It is easy and safe to participate in an affiliate model, even for individuals. Anyone who can set up a website can link to a product, and if things go well, make money. If not, then no effort or investment is wasted. This explains the popularity of the model on the World-Wide Web. The advertiser. Advertising-driven sites are currently one of the cornerstones of E-commerce.

The virtual mall. A virtual mall is a site that hosts many merchants, service providers, brokers and other businesses. The virtual mall operator typically charges fee for setting up and maintaining the merchant's "booth", and for including him in the site-wide catalog. Additionally, he may charge a fee for every transaction the merchant performs. Virtual malls can operate within the context of a larger site, such as a portal. The virtual mall can act as an intermediary between individual customers and the business it hosts, for instance by facilitating payment and guaranteeing a full refund if a merchant does not deliver in time. When the virtual mall offers services such as payment facilitation r catalog browsing, it has the ability to create aggregated user profiles on the customers that visit any of the businesses in the mall. This can lead to the development of highly specialized malls (e.g., oriented at kids or sports lovers).

The virtual community. A virtual community is a website which has gathered a group of users with a common interest who work together on the site. Typically, users will share information and make contributions in other ways. Since they have contributed to it themselves, users feel highly loyal to the site and will visit it regularly. This offers possibilities for advertising. Probably the largest virtual community can be found on Slash dot, a Linux-oriented site on which users share interesting news articles and websites (which invariably fail under the load of hundreds of thousands of people visiting it shortly after its URL got posted on Slash dot - this is called "slash dotting").

A specialized type of virtual community is the knowledge network or expert site, where people, layman and expert, share their expertise and experiences. These sites are typically ran like a forum where participants can get questions answered or raise topics for discussion. Long-time participants often meet together in real life. Usenet newsgroups are a good example of such a community. When a knowledge network is devoted to a particular product or company, the active participation of employees of that company is often very much appreciated and can offer a great PR opportunity for the company.

A simple way to monitor a virtual community is to require registration for access to the website, preferably for free. This allows inter-session tracking of users' site usage patterns and thereby generates data of greater potential value in targeted advertising campaigns. Registration can be made more attractive by offering limited access or "teasers" to unregistered users, by offering the option to customize the site after registration, or by allowing only registered users to actively participate in chat or message boards. An infomediary collects, analyzes and sells information on consumers and their buying behavior to other parties who want to reach those consumers. Typically, the infomediary offers the consumers something for free, such as free hardware or free Internet access. The later is especially useful, since it allows the infomediary to control and monitor the user's online activities. After all, the consumer connects through the infomediary's network. The information which the infomediary collects is extremely valuable for marketing purposes. Often the infomediary makes money with an advertising-based model, in which the advertisements are targeted based on the information it collected itself. The infomediary needs to keep track of its users. A simple way to achieve this is to require registration for access to the website, preferably for free. This allows inter-session tracking of users' site usage patterns and thereby generates data of greater potential value in targeted advertising campaigns. Registration can be made more attractive by offering limited access or "teasers" to unregistered users, by offering the option to customize the site after registration, or by allowing only registered users to actively participate in chat or message boards.

The infomediary model is useful in combination with a virtual community model or virtual mall, since those models offer the ability to collect the necessary information.

Collaborative Business Models

The Tool and Die Industry

Many tool and die makers have gone bankrupt during the first years of the new millennia. This study was commissioned to better understand the underlying causes for the demise of these shops, including a benchmarking study comparing selected Japanese (2) and US die shops (4). The results from the benchmarking study are presented in various places in the report. The information presented in the report was derived from the literature, interviews with industry experts, working with different organizations in the industry, the results of the benchmarking study, and CAR's extensive knowledge of the world automotive industry.

Challenges for the Tool and Die Industry Sector

The tool and die (T&D) industry, particularly in Michigan, has always experienced large fluctuations in demand with high and low cycles lasting several years. In Michigan, where nearly 50% of the tool and die industry is automotive related, the cycles are a way of life, and companies have learned to expand and contract over time. These cycles are largely related to the introduction of major vehicle programs in the automobile companies. The questions being asked by T&D companies now is when will the next up-tic begin, will the demand return to full- employment levels, and will the demand support prices that allow T&D companies to make a profit? Two factors contributing to the down turn are overcapacity and foreign

competition. Most T&D manufacturers believe that there is a significant over-capacity in the world and domestic market (by 30% to 50%), with developing countries (mostly in Asia) continuing to build new capacity with the intent of supplying North America.

On the surface, it would appear from the cycles in Figure that all the industry has to do is wait for the next upturn, and business will continue as usual. In fact, when you compare the concerns of T&D companies back in 1975 with those of today, not much has changed. Dominant concerns in 1975 included: foreign competition, increasing productivity (at the T&D shops), over supply, and low profit margins. All these issues are with us today. All these factors continue to put pressure on the industry today. So what has changed? The concern that the downturn is, in fact, a re-structuring of the industry stems from the competitive changes at the automobile OEM level. The T&D industry sector is a microcosm of the automobile industry. International competition is intense with over-capacity, particularly in the major developed countries (North America, Europe and Japan). This has led to falling market share by the principal customers of the domestic T&D industry. A primary mechanism to re-gain market share is to introduce new vehicle models that generate increased sales. The major bottleneck of introducing new programs is funding, which in turns places pressure on lowering tooling costs.

- Shortage of Skilled Help
- Reduced Demand
- Unsupportive Government Policies
- Capacity Increase
- Unfair Competition

State and Federal Involvement

The difficulties experienced by the tool and die industry, particularly in Michigan, have been recognized by state and federal agencies. In addition to commissioning this study, the Michigan Economic Development Corporation (MEDC) has been supporting the industry through several initiatives including support to the Michigan Manufacturing Technology Center (MMTC). The MMTC (www.mmtc.org) provides services to the industry in the form of training and consulting for small manufacturers throughout the state. The MMTC leverages funds from state and federal sources to support the needs of Michigan manufacturers. The federal government recently became actively involved with the tool and die industry when the International Trade Commission (ITC) began an investigation into the competitive conditions vis-à-vis foreign competition. They wish to ascertain whether or not other countries are competing fairly in their pricing of tools and dies to North American customers. The ITC report is expected in October 2002. Representing Michigan's tooling industry to the federal and state government is the Coalition for the Advancement of Michigan Tooling Industries (CAMTI). *"CAMTI's mission is to direct federal and state government attention to the issues facing Michigan's tooling companies and affected communities. It will also advocate for legislative and regulatory initiatives that will advance their interests."* The CAMTI website (www.camti.org) contains information on pending legislation, ITC committee transcripts, and dates of upcoming events that would be of interest to the tooling industry. A report written in spring 2002 by IRN, Inc. for The Right Place Program (a regional economic development organization serving west Michigan) provides an overview of the industry issues and ongoing initiatives. The report, *"A Competitive Assessment of the Die and Mold Building Sector – A West Michigan Perspective,"* provides a summary of issues based on research and broad perspectives gleaned from interviews with tool and die companies and industry experts.

Competitive Observations

A number of benchmarking studies have been conducted showing the cost and lead-time advantages Asian automakers have over the domestic companies. All the major Japanese automakers are recognized as having competitive or superior performance, and have had this advantage for many years. The Japanese companies are known for their efficiency and lean production methods, and better implementation of these practices will undoubtedly improve the competitive performance of North America companies (see section III.B Lean Practices). Lean design and manufacturing practices, along with new technologies in engineering and high-speed milling have greatly increased tool and die production capacity without any increase in labor hours or facility space. This result was largely attributed to implementing lean techniques, focusing on core competencies, and setting up the business as a production-oriented facility, rather than treating each job as a project. There are several key distinctions between the Asian and North American markets that are important to understand. The Japanese customer-supplier model is different, and simply saying North American suppliers are not competitive is incomplete. A key aspect of the Asian relationships is that it evolves over the long-term as a formal partnership, and includes fine-tuning manufacturing and engineering around product expectations. The North American business model has evolved with suppliers competing against each other on every program, and any program could be very different from any past one. Although tools and dies could be taken by a North American supplier and produced by a Japanese source, a Japanese supplier might not be able to generate Honda prices for tools from a domestic company's part design, since their processes are not fined tuned to the domestic company's design standards.

Lean Practices

Most T&D shops outside of Asia do not have close, dedicated, and collaborative relationships with their principal customers. T&D shops tend to be small, independent, and very entrepreneurial, either serving a broad customer base with multiple services, or providing a small niche product. Since the mid-70s, the North American T&D shops have evolved and become more sophisticated. The sophistication extends beyond technology; however technology still plays an important role.

Positive Attributes Negative Attributes

- Effective project management
- "Synchronous" process flow
- Process specialization
- Understanding of costs
- Reduced need for paper (use of math-based tools)
- High machine tool utilization
- Blend of older and newer technology (e.g., machine centers and engineering)
- Effective management of engineering change implementation
- Identification and development of core competencies
- Effective, centralized engineering function
- One or more operators assigned to one machine
- High employee turnover
- Too much time spent in final tooling tryout
- Operators programming or re-programming machine tools when the machines should be running

(i) Project Management – Effective project management has been recognized as one of the most significant developments at today's world-class tool and die shops, because it requires disciplines that instill a standardized managed workflow. The role of tool and die project management is to schedule resources (engineering, machine tools, assembly personnel, tryout presses, etc.) and plan for the timely execution of many tasks (including purchasing parts and outsourcing services). Many companies use software such as Microsoft Project Manager. The key to effective project management is having predictable events that can be planned. Reducing the uncertainty of events, like tryout or the unplanned engineering change is important, as well as having a system that is flexible enough (robust) to adapt to unplanned situations. Two measures of effective project management are efficient use of company resources and reliable prediction of completion dates. A part of project management is to effectively anticipate and manage engineering changes. The system must be able to process engineering changes without significantly deteriorating performance. Decisions about when to implement changes (immediately or batch until later) are key considerations.

(ii) Synchronous Process Flow – Synchronous process flow is consistent with effective project management. The term synchronous is used to suggest production- line style manufacturing for tools and dies. Tools and dies move through the shop in a production line fashion with all resources needed at every point in the process ready for the job when it gets to the downstream operation. Synchronous production requires standardized work, e.g., standardized bill of materials and resource demand at each work center. Certain design and production aspects of construction are standardized so that "bundles" of components are pre-packaged and ready for the tool. This maximizes off-the-shelf supply rather than re-engineering or special ordering parts when needed and, thereby, lowers cost. Although unplanned events, such as machine tool breakdown, engineering change, sick employee, etc., can disrupt synchronous flow, the manufacturing process needs to be designed to be robust to these events, which will occur, even though their frequency and timing is uncertain. production orientation is to begin measuring and managing the shop floor based on throughput of dies. The unit of production measurement is, "dies produced," rather than the more traditional perspective of selling hours of capacity. This significant distinction requires die design/production standardization and will help maximize capacity. For example, one US shop has doubled their capacity in terms of dies produced without increasing their available labor hours. They implemented lean practices that targeted the number of dies produced.

(iii) Process Specialization – Process specialization is also consistent with synchronous flow in that different individuals in the shop become specialists in their job function. This is again analogous to the production line where each operator has a specifically assigned task. The old model with a craftsman toolmaker, which often was the project manager for his/her die, is obsolete. The toolmaker skills, while still very valuable, should be focused toward the engineering and problem solving part of the process. Other individuals should focus on their respective specialties, such as project management (which includes scheduling), engineering design, machining, machine tool programming, setup, tryout, etc.

(iv) Understanding of Costs – Several OEMs indicated that they believe that the T&D shops do not recognize their cost structure, leading to sub-optimal business decisions and non-competitive quotes. A typical approach taken by a shop is to develop an hourly rate for a collection of services and use the rate to quote a job. This rate might, for example, aggregate several costs (including machine tools, computer software, etc.), and assign an hourly rate based on the labor hours involved, irrespective of the capital equipment involved. Suppliers with a broad range of capabilities (e.g., full-service supplier) have a complex cost structure that demands closer scrutiny. The **activity-based costing (ABC) approach** has been recommended for businesses with a complex range of equipment and services. ABC is an

accounting method for allocating overhead charges based on an equipment / space / overhead resource leasing per unit time concept. This also supports lean initiatives, as ABC is much simpler to implement if there are standard work times and the infrastructure is in place to monitor the time of each operation. With ABC, the company can better evaluate the economic viability of certain assets and make better decisions regarding:

- Developing quotes,
- Upgrading capital equipment and technology,
- Expanding capabilities (e.g., into engineering, tooling repair, prototype development, tryout, etc.), and
- Focusing on cost reduction opportunities.

(v) Reduced Paper - The trend toward the paperless factory is prevalent in the T&D business. Few, if any, shops have totally eliminated paper on the shop floor, but all competitive shops have eliminated much of it. State-of-the art today is to have 100% electronic data beginning from process design through cutter path generation, and similarly for all die processes through CNC machining. Various technologies such as SMIRT software (www.smirtware.com) have helped, which allow personnel to interrogate design files or CNC programs directly through a computer. Perhaps more important than eliminating paper itself, the paperless shop floor is indicative of a lean, synchronous shop floor without the need for chronic problem solving.

(vi) Machine Tool Utilization – Overall manufacturing efficiency is heavily correlated with percent of spindle cutting time on the machine tools. Unfortunately, most U. S. T&D shops do not formally measure their machine utilization. Some companies measure machine tool utilization by including setup, run time, etc. Estimated machine times ranged from 60% to 85%. However, "lean" companies rigorously measure their machine utilization emphasizing spindle cutting time. High performing shops strive for spindle cutting time in excess of 90% of machine time (less preventive maintenance). One Japanese shop had an average annual uptime of 87.9% on their 3-D milling machines and 79% on their 2-D milling machines. Factors contributing to a high spindle cutting time include standardized locators for quick load and unload of the work piece/jig, debugged CNC machine programs prior to changeover (e.g., using simulation or other methods for validation), preset tooling, and load/unload pallet automation. Average die changeover times in the US range from 0.5 to 4 hours. In lean shops they range from 18 minutes to 1 hour.

(vii) Technology – Companies need to stay current of the latest manufacturing and engineering technologies as appropriate. This includes the judicious use of such manufacturing technologies as high-speed cutting tools, laser welding, CAD/CAM technology, and engineering design and simulation tools. When effectively applied, machining centers can achieve 24-hour operations with an operator to machine ratio from 1:2 to 1:3. The US companies typically have 1 person per machine and are moving towards 0.5 operators per machine. The lean shops have fewer than 1 per machine and operate some machinery unmanned at night. Engineering design tools are evolving where excellent product feasibility analysis is becoming standard, and spring back prediction is improving. Simulations are extending to manufacturing simulations of dies in the production press, taking into account material handling automation and scrap metal removal. Automakers use this information to maximize production speeds, and they are beginning to expect tool and die suppliers to share in this responsibility.

(viii) Development of Core Competencies – Many tool and die shops actually provide a subset of products and services from a broad range of possible ones, for example:

- Tools
- Dies
- Fixtures
- Patterns (for castings)
- Engineering design (tools and dies)
- Feasibility engineering (product design)
- Tooling tryout
- Prototype development
- Production launch support

Some "full service" suppliers provide many or all of these services along with many more. Although the full service supplier offers many advantages in some circumstances, particularly when fast turnaround is required or when a customer lacks industry knowledge or ability to manage many subtasks, the concern that is raised is whether or not a supplier can be competitive with all these services at the same time. Without specialization, some of these capabilities may come at high costs because of sporadic utilization and experience – a further reason to consider activity based costing analysis so as to determine the cost of non-fully utilized assets. Some suppliers can become more competitive by developing "niche" capabilities from a subset of this list. Although there is a clear need at times for a full service supplier, many world class companies specialize in fewer areas so that they will always be recognized as an industry leader with a few critical capabilities, rather than a generally good supplier of many capabilities. Process specialization includes having strategic suppliers that can execute operations either more efficiently than the primary shop (perhaps with lower labor costs, etc.), or can readily handle simpler operations, like 2-D machining, reserving the more critical operations/ capacity, like 3-D machining, where there may be a competitive advantage at the primary shop.

(ix) Centralized Engineering – It would be difficult today to compete in complex tool and die construction without a major emphasis in a central engineering function. Centralized engineering is consistent with reducing (or eliminating) the craftsmanship approach of tool and die making on the shop floor. Although most auto companies would like to see the need for sophisticated engineering design to decrease and let die sourcing compete as a commodity from labor costs, the intellectual content in tool and die is one of the unique attributes of this product; so developing this capability is important. For example, one Japanese shop has the strategic goal to minimize the assembly function by reducing the number of steel inserts, eliminating cams, and utilizing standard part kits. These latter steps are all a function of the specific die design. Hence, the strategic goal can only be accomplished by having a strong die engineering function.

What the Tool and Die Customers Need to Consider

The domestic auto companies wish to reduce the tooling cost disadvantage they experience with their Asian competition. A significant reduction in costs will require a joint effort between the T&D shops and the auto companies Granted, the T&D shops can more broadly implement cost reduction initiatives that will contribute to reducing total costs as outlined previously, but many opportunities require joint cooperation. The requirements in terms of die standards and die components, quality certifications (ISO and QS standards) and performance requirements including dimensional objectives and the production validation process (such as the production part approval process or PPAP) all contribute to higher costs, leading some to argue their value. Most industry experts do not refute the assertion that the product designs of the domestic automakers are inherently more difficult to produce than those for the Asian auto companies. Consequently, there is less carryover of design and manufacturing knowledge, and the sourcing relationships have not encouraged the development of standardized practices or recognized the "total system cost" in launching a new vehicle. Total system costs in this case include tooling related performance factors such as:

- Capital tooling cost (for all dies, fixtures, assembly tools, etc.)
- Tooling design and engineering
- Tooling tryout and production validation
- Implementation of engineering changes
- Product launch effectiveness (ramp up speed and quality)

Past practices have emphasized reducing tooling costs by focusing on individual tooling quotes (typically by bidding one supplier against another), which likely shifted costs to other areas in the total system. There are several areas of collaborative opportunity (between the auto companies and tool and die shops) where improvements can greatly reduce the total system costs associated with tooling.

Collaborative Product and Process Engineering

Closer communication between product design and the tooling suppliers can significantly reduce complex problems that do not affect the product design features important to the final customer. Tool and die engineers have in-depth knowledge about tooling design that can be brought to bear early in the development process. Closer communication and earlier involvement would allow tooling engineers to identify manufacturing concerns related to part interface features (e.g., flanges) and forming issues that affect die lineup without changing the exterior part appearance. This level of involvement will help offset later engineering changes from process design, and help prevent program delays.

Development of Analytical Design Methods

The auto companies and all major tool and die suppliers have a significant investment in software and technology to support die design. Forming software to analyze feasibility and draw die development is very effective. Many more advances are needed in the rapidly changing field of spring back prediction, particularly given the rapid introduction of new materials (e.g., numerous high strength steel varieties and aluminum), which often have a higher degree of spring back compared to standard mild steels. Most companies, both auto and supplier, consider their knowledge in these fields proprietary and often do little to support co-development. A closer collaboration in developing these analytical methods, and then supporting their use early in the product development process will reduce downstream engineering changes due to product complexities, and accelerate the tool build and tryout process, resulting in higher manufacturing productivity.

Lean Die Standards

There are a number of die construction standards used by the domestic automakers. Some standards are unique to the facility where the tools will be put into production. Many standards are also developed that "over engineer" the dies to compensate for manufacturing negligence, e.g., poor press maintenance or process control discipline such as loading two blanks in the draw die. There are also aspects of the die standards, which differ between auto companies that are not designed to provide anything unique, but help contribute to higher costs. Auto companies and tool and die suppliers have agreed that a coordinated effort could produce substantial savings by re-evaluating the multiple die standards and rationalizing an approach to reduce the number of standards. The number of variations of die components could be reduced, and building dies to the required standards could be simplified. Some of the Asian lean die standards have included:

- Reduced bearing surfaces
- Fewer wear plates
- Using smaller dies as appropriate for the part rather than for the press
- Using fewer die inserts and flame hardening surfaces
- Less finishing on non-show panel dies

Some of the lean die standards require significant internal advancements by the automakers first. For example, lighter dies will require well- maintained presses. "Right-sizing" dies (e.g., making the size of the die match the size of the part rather than a press) requires an internal press replacement / adjustment / maintenance strategy that can be expensive and long-term before implementation.

Functional Build

Numerous studies have been conducted at tooling tryout sources (die shops) and stamping facilities that have shown that very few parts throughout the industry meet all of their initial dimensional specifications set by design. Larger, more complex parts tend to experience this problem more, and the same observation is true for European and Asian auto companies as well. Researchers at the University of Michigan have estimated that 50% of stamped parts at domestic automakers have never passed the production part approval process (PPAP). Further, it has been shown that most of the parts that have not passed PPAP, and therefore are out of specification, still result in assembled bodies that are within specification. This is an indication that the assembly process is insensitive to the incoming part variation, and that many part tolerances are tighter than necessary.

In North America, the conventional process to buyoff dies has required the suppliers to continually rework dies to get the dies as close to design intent as possible. Then when the deadline to ship the dies approaches, engineering evaluates what else must be changed with the time that is left. In effect, the full development time is used in an attempt to create "perfect" parts. Then the process is repeated when the assembly process is validated.

However, studies have shown that 50% of parts are accepted as less than perfect due to deadlines. This imprecise process is deadline driven (forcing many dies to be late) and results in the tooling supplier making many die changes during tryout to create a perfect part that will not necessarily improve the final quality of the assembly.

The functional build process acknowledges that stamped parts do not have to be dimensionally "perfect," yet can still assemble into an acceptable assembly. A development process that recognizes this early during tryout does not wait until time runs out to make the final buyoff decisions. Instead it creates assemblies during the pre-launch phase to evaluate whether parts result in acceptable assemblies, even if they are not within specification. These pre- launch assemblies are usually built on special functional build fixtures, since the production assembly tooling is often not yet available. Hence, there is a two phase approval process. First, the parts are checked to determine whether they are close enough to specifications (often 2x or 3x the specified tolerance) that they will result in a good assembly. If not, then the dies are reworked. Then the functional build assembly is evaluated to determine whether the assembly is close enough that it will result in an acceptable assembly in production.

If the functional evaluation assemblies indicate a potential problem, then a decision must be made between the following options:

- Rework the die of the part that is not within specification
- Rework the die of the mating part (that may or may not be within specification)
- Adjust the assembly tooling

Traditionally, option A would be the only choice possible, since the part is not within specification. Functional build argues to do that which is most expedient in terms of time and cost. Often this is option C. In this manner, only those features that affect the assembly quality are reworked, even if other features do not meet specification. Generally, there are rigorous and statistically based acceptance criteria to ensure a justifiable level of risk. Since either strategy (conventional or functional build) ultimately relies on evaluating the build-up of the assembly instead of the individual parts, both are considered a form of functional build. However, the conventional strategy is called 11th hour functional build, and the former strategy just functional build or pure functional build. The 11th hour functional build process suggests that when die makers meet their timing deadlines (which they almost always do because achieving Cpk is so difficult), then they revert to functional build in a desperate attempt to get things to work at the factory.

The strategy to implement functional build has been pursued to some extent by all of the domestic auto companies, but with limited success. The major barriers to its successful implementation tend to be more organizational than technical. The tooling suppliers, in general, strongly support implementation of functional build. Regardless of whether the execution is controlled by the auto companies or by the tooling suppliers, substantial lead time and quality savings could accrue if it were more widely practiced.

The Collaborative Business Model

Objective

The objective of the collaborative business model approach is to provide a more competitive selection of tools, dies, and related services than any single tool and die supplier could offer individually. Through collaboration, the capabilities of the suppliers will continue to improve, perhaps evolving such that certain suppliers will develop specialty areas of expertise where they will become recognized as world leaders. The intent of the collaborative model is to encourage long-term relationships between a range of suppliers (with both overlapping as well as unique capabilities) and their customers. The principal benefits of the collaborative approach are:

• It is consistent with recent trends by the domestic automakers to outsource large "chunks" of the body structure; an approach already used when dealing with foreign tooling sources. A coalition of collaborating companies can manage the full range of products and services for a new vehicle including project management, engineering, prototype development, tooling construction and tryout, and launch support. A tooling coalition can be designed to manage the volume of work associated with an entire body structure or substructure.

• The collaborative model supports the total systems approach, thus avoiding shifting costs and problems from one part of the process to another.

• It promotes the development of niche specialties by suppliers. There are many small shops with narrow, but deep knowledge on various aspects of tool construction. These small suppliers have difficulty competing on large programs where broad capabilities are needed. These niche shops can better compete in their technical area if they are a part of a larger coalition of companies.

• It better supports the implementation of functional build. The nature of functional build is to identify the lowest-cost solution to quickly fix problems. Many times the best solution is in another area of the process (e.g., change a simple part to correct a difficult problem in a complex part).

The size of the domestic tool and die supply base is likely to continue to contract as the worldwide capacity continues to increase from new shops in developing countries and significant productivity gains at existing shops. The collaborative coalition model provides a mechanism where the most capable shops have a better chance of competing. A competitive domestic tool and die supply base will enhance the competitive position of the domestic auto companies, which is the key to sustaining the domestic business. Since the collaborative business model advocates a total systems approach for engineering, construction, and customer support for new tooling programs, the performance metrics should be adjusted to recognize this broader perspective. The old metrics were heavily skewed toward initial tooling cost, which is still understandably important. However, companies operating under a collaborative approach should be evaluated for additional performance measures such as:

• **Total tooling cost achievement relative to budget**. The total tooling cost should include costs due to engineering changes since the collaborative approach should help reduce the number of required changes and manage how they get implemented.

• **Percent of parts that pass production validation (PPAP) according to schedule** (100% goal).

• **Launch rate**, particularly for measures about body quality, such as time required to achieve six-sigma quality for the body-in-white. Two levels for the collaborative business model are presented below.

The first level, Tool and Die Coalition, combines the resources of several tool and die shops and builds a collaborative model amongst the shops along with their customers. The second model is the Integrator Coalition. The integrator approach further broadens the scope from the tool and die shops to include complementary businesses, such as product engineering and assembly weld tools.

Description of Tool and Die Coalition

The range of products and services offered by tool and die shops is widely variable. Most shops offer a basic range of capabilities including prototype development, prototype fabrication, die design engineering, die construction and assembly, and preliminary tryout. On one end of the spectrum there are shops specializing in one or more of these activities; and on the other end exist "full service shops" offering all these capabilities and sometimes more. The scope of capabilities of the tool and die collaborative business model exceeds what is typically offered today, even by a single full service company. For example, providing program management to support the development of multiple tooling projects across several suppliers. Another critical activity is early product design support, especially checking for product feasibility issues and identifying part design alternatives that do not affect part appearance in the body, but improve manufacturability, can be very important to reduce costs and head off future engineering changes. Additional services at the end of the tool making process include support for functional build evaluation and process launch support at the customer's facility. Shows this range of possible supplier services from which a customer may choose for a given program.

- Prototype
- Die design & engineering (CAD/CAE)
- Programming (CAM)
- Patterns & castings
- Machining
- Construction/Assembly
- Tryout and Buyoff

BASIC

- Program management
- Product design support
- Functional build
- Launch support

EXPANDED

- Program management
- Product design support
- Functional build
- Launch support

The expanded capabilities that are not typically handled by full service shops are coordinated program management responsibility and functional build. Coordinated program management extends the shops' reach both upstream and downstream from tooling construction, and can often include services and tools from other tool shops. Program management improves communication and scheduling coordination. Modular functional build (FB) involves sourcing groups of components and allowing the supplier to make tryout rework decisions based on how well the panels fit together (rather than making independent, isolated decisions panel by panel). The value of these services increases as the coalition responsibility increases to multiple modules, and the coalition approach expands the breadth of the group to handle multiple subassemblies on a program.

- Coordinated management
- Product design
- Modular FB

Basic Coalition Integrated

- BIW FB (weld tool coordination)
- GD&T
- Simultaneous weld tool and stamping launch support
- Prototypes & dies
- Tier 2 (via Coalition)
  - Small tools
  - Special
  - R&D

Die Engineering & Construction

The basic tool and die supplier. The basic supplier provides dies and generally out sources other related activities. The expanded, collaborative supplier provides dies, but also provides coordinated management, early product design, and executes modular functional build. The highest level of collaboration extends the tool and die supplier into body- in-white functional build (beyond just the modular level), gets involved with product design (geometric dimensioning and tolerances), and provides simultaneous launch support for assembly processes and stamping. These capabilities are not resident at the tool and die shops, but require an approach involving additional expertise as described in the integrator model. Very few, if any, single suppliers have the capacity to offer the expanded range of products and services for a major portion of a vehicle body. However, a coalition of tool and die shops can be formed that, in aggregate, does have the capability and capacity to handle large sections (if not an entire) vehicle.

Selected T&D Shops Tool & Die Coalition FB Tryout OEM Operating Committee List of T&D Shops

The schematic in shows one possible collaborative model to support a broad range of products and services for a major vehicle program. Although a coalition might assemble the multiple organizations into a coalition before bidding on a project, the customer (OEM in this case) may wish to select the specific suppliers they wish to have included or excluded based on their past experiences or other motivations. The coalition has to allow for the flexible entry and exit of T&D suppliers. Figure 11 shows a candidate list of loosely aligned suppliers outside of the dotted box. From this list, the customer chooses the specific suppliers to include in the program. The coalition may also include a functional build tryout group that evaluates panel buyoff decisions affecting everyone in the coalition. This may be part of or separate from the coalition, depending upon the customer's wishes. The "operating committee" serves as the principal interface with the customer, i.e., the single point of contact. This is viewed as one of the great advantages to the customer, as the customer no longer has to manage multiple T&D shops with multiple points of contact; the management function is handled by the operating committee. Generally, the organization of the operating committee would include a senior program manager that integrates program schedule information from the supplier shops, and coordinates activities across the group of companies. The senior program manager may also be involved in negotiating engineering changes that affect dies at the various shops. Another potential member of the operating committee is an independent monitor that helps to facilitate the coalition, monitor it for competitiveness (including benchmarking the competition), and provide a mechanism for recommending system improvements both to the customer and to the tool and die shops.

Integrator Coalition

The integrator coalition model expands on the tooling coalition model to include other complementary functions, and offers the highest collaborative capabilities. These activities are often associated with Japanese techniques that focus more attention on the manufacturability of the part designs and assessing the manufacturing process capability during the development process, rather than relying on initial engineering assumptions. The three key activities that the integrator model is intended to address are:

Body-in-white functional build.

The coalition model described above addressed the functional build benefit of evaluating parts at the subassembly or module level. For example, the coalition would be able to make decisions regarding changing a door inner panel, door outer panel, or reinforcement to guarantee an acceptable door assembly. A higher level of functional build can be achieved through the integration of modules. For example, the integrated coalition would be able to make decisions regarding changing a door assembly (and all its associated parts), body side, or the assembly process to guarantee that a door fits correctly the body side opening. The integrator model would be involved in a program pre-launch phase further "upstream" in the development process than tool and die shops normally participate. A product development process (timing and schedule of events) can be designed to include body- in-white functional build with significant improvements in lead-time, quality, and cost avoidance by eliminating unnecessary tooling rework often performed early in the process "just in case" it could cause a problem later downstream.

Product design

The traditional North American design approach assigns numerous dimensional requirements to reduce the risk that a part meeting those requirements will fail. The extension of this approach is to tighten these requirements (reduce the tolerances) to further reduce the risk. Unfortunately, as the requirements increase, the manufacturing cost and lead-time for the associated tooling also increases. Incorporating more manufacturing understanding into the product design phase (i.e., with T&D shop and assembly tooling process knowledge) would improve the manufacturability of the tooling and reducing cost and lead-time without any sacrifice in product quality.

Simultaneous tool and die and assembly tooling process validation.

Just as applying functional build at the module level reduces overall tool and die costs, incorporating the assembly tooling into the decision process further reduces cost and lead-time. Although it is feasible to validate the dies first and then move on to validate the assembly tools, the process would be faster and lower-cost (avoiding die rework) if the two processes were validated together.

Tool and die shops would need to team with other industry partners to assemble the collaborative integrator business model. An engineering company with product design capability and knowledge of product launch issues and management is needed. This company would likely be assigned as the lead organization for a program, helping to manage the tooling suppliers (dies and assembly weld tools). The tool and die shops would collaborate using the tool and die collaboration model described earlier. Another coalition of companies would include one or more assembly tool shops. Similar to the tool and die coalition, the assembly tool shops would likely form a partnership or coalition to provide the tooling for the body shop.

Implementation Issues of the Collaborative Model

There are a number of implementation steps to the collaborative business model, some with many possible solutions. The list below, although far from exhaustive, identifies some of the key issues in assembling the collaborative model.

Tool and Die Collaboration

Building trust and open communication between companies, who are otherwise industry competitors, is difficult and requires the involvement of a neutral third party. The coalition of companies needs to agree on a common mission, vision and operating principles. Further, the coalition needs to develop a business plan that outlines current capabilities, needed capabilities and growth areas, research and development, marketing, etc.

Operational Decision Making

Many sensitive business decisions are required including ownership structure, governance, staffing, and membership (the process of how companies are allowed to join). The bidding process when multiple coalition companies desire the same piece of work needs to be managed within anti-trust regulations.

Internal Sourcing

The process of sourcing tools and services within the coalition is critically important to be fair, avoid anti-trust guidelines, and still promote the development of niche players (recognizing that some companies are superior to others in some areas.) Ideally, certain suppliers would be identified as the preferred supplier because of their technical capability, but this is difficult and can violate anti- trust laws. One approach is to use an independent facilitator that can help identify appropriate sourcing, perhaps using customer input. A heuristic (formula) that achieves the desired result fairly (strives for the lowest cost while maintaining a profitable coalition enterprise) is one approach.

Anti-Trust

Companies have to be concerned about sharing cost and pricing information with companies that are otherwise competitors. The coalition can demonstrate that their collective businesses offer a competitive product that justifies the collaboration, but the communication of certain information must be managed. Individual companies still retain the right to intellectual property in their field of services.

Finance (internal and external)

Internal financing decisions and identifying the control and flow of capital is important. Many shops would prefer to have a purchase order directly with the customer. But this would result in multiple purchase orders and tend to weaken the single-point-of-contact management. A mechanism is needed that allows for coalition- level decision making when a decision is best for the whole, but perhaps not for an individual company. One such possibility is a central pool of funds to support cost and revenue sharing. Lastly, most companies have their own external financing relationships, but the coalition might consider developing a coalition-specific source for capital.

Recent Experiences with the Collaborative Model

The Center for Automotive Research (CAR) at Altarum has been working on the collaborative model for the past year. Many of the observations in this report were developed through experiences gained in developing the model in close cooperation with several die shops and with the input of the domestic OEMs. CAR was chosen as the independent facilitator because of its knowledge of the industry, its reputation in the industry, and its access to OEM management for seeking guidance.

The coalition calls itself the US Tooling Coalition (USTC), and the member companies are:

- American Tooling Center
- Atlas Tool, Inc.
- Autodie International
- Hercules
- QMC Die Tech.
- Riviera Tool Company
- Ronart Industries, Inc.
- Sekely Industries
- Thunder Bay

Besides the comments made in previous sections, the basic necessary elements for creating a collaborative organization were present amongst this group from the beginning. First, the die shops had already communicated with one another prior to approaching CAR for help in forming the coalition. Hence, they had the understanding that cooperation was necessary for survival, and the desire to cooperate. Second, with the addition of CAR to the group, the intellectual capital necessary for the coalition to work, functional build, digital technologies, lean manufacturing, tooling know-how, etc fell into place. Third, the coalition concept was consistent with the customers' business direction of working with fewer companies and developing the so-called tier 0.5: engineering through turn-key startup (launch support). Lastly, the coalition was able to identify the initiatives necessary to reduce costs and make the coalition cost competitive. Once the coalition had developed a workable plan, several other companies, such as product engineering and assembly tooling suppliers, approached the USTC indicating that they were willing and eager to work with the coalition in preparing competitive bids to the OEMs. CAR's primary role has been to act as a neutral, independent participant, helping to create a dialog between competitors, technology partners, and their customers.

Through interviews with the OEMs and the die shops, CAR identified several critical areas for improvement, including communication between the customers and the suppliers, antagonistic relationships that had developed, in part, due to the poor communication, and cost reduction opportunities. Another major responsibility for CAR was the creation of the quote to a customer. The reason was the sensitive nature of individual shop quotes used to create the coalition quote revealing the cost structure of the companies. Hence, CAR was the neutral entity to collect the various cost information and develop a heuristic on how the overall coalition quote would be established, and how the various dies would be distributed amongst the various coalition members. The process did raise concerns over the members' varied pricing strategies, and the heuristic was adjusted several times to accommodate those differences. The response by the OEMs has been varied, but generally positive. One of the OEMs is very supportive, entertaining a coalition bid on a vehicle program, and working with the coalition on developing a program of long term cost reduction initiatives. Another OEM is very interested in the coalition concept, especially if the coalition can demonstrate immediate cost reductions, as opposed to long term cost reductions.

They are also willing to consider the broader integrator coalition approach. The third OEM is supportive of any new strategic concepts and has shared various experiences and suggested new business opportunities it would be willing to entertain, if presented by the coalition. Hence, each OEM sees the benefits of the coalition and is willing to enter into a collaborative relationship, albeit of a varied nature, to reduce costs. This is an indication that the coalition can provide the lower tooling cost of the Asian model, while maintaining the flexibility of US model, namely the ability to work with the different engineering and business systems of the US OEMs.

There are still challenges remaining. For example, it takes extra time and effort to coordinate and balance the multiple priorities of the coalition. This becomes especially critical near the submission deadline of a quote, because the OEM can add or change demands on the format and content of the quote. Under such tight time restrictions it becomes difficult to communicate with everyone and obtain a consensus decision. The ultimate question will be: was it worth it? In the coalitions view, there are not many other options. The business climate is changing, and the industry is consolidating. Customers expect a lower-cost supply chain, which can only occur through cooperation both up and down the supply chain as well as across the supply chain. In other words, suppliers must cooperate with their customers, suppliers, and competitors. The impact of this effort will be long term and will change the way automobiles are built.

Conclusions and Recommendations

The current economic problems facing the tool and die industry are significant, and are considered to be different from previous economic downturns, because there is a fundamental change in the manner in which the automotive industry operates. Some of the causes of the downturn are overcapacity, foreign competition, lower demand for dies, technology improvements, and an increased demand for a greater variety of services. These factors are permanent and not going to disappear; hence the restructuring of the industry. Benchmark data shows the foreign competition can make dies at one-third the cost in approximately one-half the time. These differences can be attributed to three basic reasons: lean operations, simpler part designs from their customers, and closer supplier-customer relationships. This latter factor is particularly important as it drives, in part, the simpler part designs, and because it enables both parties to identify system level cost reduction opportunities, such as functional build. There are three basic recommendations: T&D shops must adopt lean practices, T&D shops must form strategic partnerships / coalitions between T&D shops as well as their customers, and government must support the industry during this transition period.

Adopting Lean Practices

It is imperative that T&D shops adopt lean practices. These practices have been shown to result in lower cost and improved manufacturing performance. The benchmark data clearly shows lower time and cost in manufacturing, assembly, and tryout, which are all manufacturing functions, as opposed to die design and castings. Further, the data show greater efficiencies in machine utilization, fewer labor hours per machine, and shorter machine setup times. Lastly, the data show that the lean shops have not only synchronous production, but also the infrastructure and internal metrics that enable further identification of bottlenecks and cost reduction opportunities. This is driven by a measure of production capacity other than number of labor hours, namely: number of dies produced. Other related initiatives include adoption of ABC accounting, improving CAD/CAM systems to move towards the paperless T&D shop, investing in high speed milling machines to eliminate bench work, standardizing workflow, standardizing common parts, and prepackaging parts in quantities and types needed to assemble a single die. Although these are specific suggestions, each T&D shop should conduct an analysis to determine the most cost effective method to transition to a lean manufacturing system. Within Michigan, the state funded Michigan Manufacturing Technology Center offers numerous training classes and implementation support for lean.

Creating Collaborative Relationships

A significant opportunity exists for the domestic tool and die (and related industry sectors, such as product engineering and assembly tool companies) if they can pool their resources and work to the competitive benefit of their principal customers – the auto companies. The current competitive bid process is antagonistic, short-term and non-collaborative. The complexities in launching a new vehicle require collaboration between the customer and the many suppliers providing products and services that all interact with each other. The bidding process and physical demands expected of the suppliers to support their customers are not compatible. The collaborative model outlined in this study is an attempt to overcome this incongruence.

There are many challenges in the development and implementation of the collaborative model. The facilitation effort to bring many suppliers together is significant. One of the keys to keeping the effort together is finding a customer (e.g., automotive OEM or Tier One) that is willing to entertain the concept. Of course the customer's fear is that they will experience higher costs without competitive bidding, so attention to cost is critical. This places a significant burden on achieving success with the coalition quickly – beginning with the first job. The lead-time and costs to develop a basic operating structure for the coalition, negotiating and marketing the coalition with potential customers, and identifying appropriate member companies is a significant undertaking. Support from industry (both customers and suppliers) and government organizations would greatly increase the likelihood of success. For example, the following actions will help the collaborative model develop and succeed:

Tool and Die and Related Industry Companies

Entertain cooperating together and pursuing joint initiatives to improve individual and industry competitiveness. This requires consideration of core competencies and the movement toward niche specialization. The coalition approach allows one to offer a greater range of services to the customer, as well as the opportunity to practice functional build at the modular or BIW level; a practice that the benchmark data clearly showed reduced tryout time and cost. The coalition approach also requires a progressive mindset to look beyond lean manufacturing techniques into innovative ways to increase customer value through adding, subtracting, or changing processes and technologies on a continual basis. Simply adapting once will not suffice.

A mindset of continuous improvement in both everyday business and the collaborative model will be essential to become a state-of-the art T&D shop. Meanwhile, being able to maintain other parts of the business separate from the coalition initiatives to protect the business from anti-trust concerns will also be paramount. The collaborative efforts may drive major shifts in the business, but they cannot drive competitive interactions outside of the collaborative context.

Automotive OEMs and Tier One Customers

Entertain the coalition as a viable option – perhaps allowing it to compete against other competitive options and recognize that the potential of the collaborative model will increase in its competitive performance over time. Provide direction to the coalition in terms of cost reducing initiatives that are priority to the customer. Make the internal organizational changes required to support a collaborative model. Along those same lines, recognizing that the most powerful cost saving and quality-improvement activities require collaboration between the OEM and the suppliers. For example, the benchmark data showed a significant cost reduction from more efficient die standards and the right sizing of dies, which both require stronger communication between the customer and the supplier. Therefore, allowing the coalition access to critical resources (personnel, design, facilities) to enable true implementation of cost saving initiatives is a crucial step. Tool and die suppliers equipped with in-depth knowledge about their tools can be invaluable to the customer experiencing integration issues related to other parts of the vehicle assembly.

Government Support

Financial and intellectual support is required to move the collaboration development forward. A more in-depth model needs to be developed to serve as a framework to guide companies in forming collaborative relationships. Academic and research & development organizations can work together to refine the collaborative relationships, and facilitation is needed to negotiate operating issues between organizations. It is also likely that the coalition model could be generalized for use in other industries. Local, state, and federal economic development organizations can assist in the implementation and adaptation of the coalition model to fit specific group needs. In addition, state and federal institutions could provide financial support in the form of

- Investment tax credits and faster depreciation schedules to enable T&D shops to keep pace with the changes in technology,
- Change laws to allow coalitions to purchase group healthcare coverage,
- Provide more funds for the education and adoption of lean manufacturing methods,
- Provide funds to help the initiation of coalitions and support coalition cost reduction initiatives. Ultimately, without government support, current market forces and social and organizational obstacles to collaboration will drive the industry overseas.

2

E-Business Architecture

Web Architecture and CGI

Current Web Architecture

The following sections describe the basic two-tier architecture of the web in which static web pages (documents) are transferred from information servers to browser clients world-wide, extensions that permit three-tiered architectures where content pages can be constructed dynamically and where programs as well as data can be transferred, other information transfer protocols, and related standards.

Basic Web Architecture

The basic web architecture is two-tiered and characterized by a web client that displays information content and a web server that transfers information to the client. This architecture depends on three key standards: HTML for encoding document content, URLs for naming remote information objects in a global namespace, and HTTP for staging the transfer.

Hyper Text Markup Language (HTML)

The common representation language for hypertext documents on the Web. HTML had a first public release as HTML 0.0 in 1990, was Internet draft HTML 1.0 in 1993, and HTML 2.0 in 1994. The September 22 1995 draft of the HTML 2.0 specification has been approved as a standard by the IETF Application Area HTML Working Group. HTML 3.0 and Netscape HTML are competing next generations of HTML 2.0. Proposed features in HTML 3.0 include: forms, style sheets, mathematical markup, and text flow around figures. For more detailed information, see the HTML Reference Manual.

HTML is an application of the Standard Generalized Markup Language (SGML ISO-8879), an international standard approved in 1986, which specifies a formal meta-language for defining document markup systems. An SGML Document Type Definition (DTD) specifies valid tag names and element attributes. HTML consists of embedded content separated by hierarchical case sensitive start and end tag names which may contain embedded element attributes in the start tag. These attributes may be required, optional, or empty. In addition, documents can be inter or intra linked by establishing source and target anchor points. Many HTML documents are the result of manual authoring or word processing HTML converters, but now several WYSIWYG editors support HTML styles see listing at W3C and the Internet Tools Survey section on Authoring HTML.

HTML files are viewed using a WWW client browser (software), the primary user interface to the Web. HTML allows for embedding of images, sounds, video streams, form fields and simple text formatting. References, called hyperlinks, to other objects are embedded using URLs (see below). When an object is selected by a hyperlink, the browser takes an action based on the URL's type, e.g., retrieve a file, connect to another Web site and display a HTML file stored there, or launch an application such as an E-mail or newsgroup reader.

Universal Resource Identifier (URI)

An IETF addressing protocol for objects in the WWW ("if it's out there, we can point at it"). There are two types of URIs, Universal Resource Names (URN) and the Universal Resource Locators (URL). The current IETF URI spec is here and the URL spec is here. URLs are location dependent and contain four distinct parts: the protocol type, the machine name, the directory path and the file name. There are several kinds of URLs: file URLs, FTP URLs, Gopher URLs, News URLs, and HTTP URLs. URLs may be relative to a directory or offsets into a document.

Hyper Text Transfer Protocol (HTTP)

An application-level network protocol for the WWW. Tim Berners-Lee, father of the Web, describes it as a "generic stateless object-oriented protocol." Stateless means neither the client nor the server store information about the state of the other side of an ongoing connection. Statelessness is a scalability property but is not necessarily efficient since HTTP sets up a new connection for each request, which is not desirable for situations requiring sessions or transactions. In HTTP, commands (request methods) can be associated with particular types of network objects (files, documents, network services). Commands are provided for establishing a TCP/IP connection to a WWW server, sending a request to the server (containing a method to be applied to a specific network object identified by the object's identifier, and the HTTP protocol version, followed by information encoded in a header style), returning a response from the server to the client (consisting of three parts: a status line, a response header, and response data), and closing the connection. HTTP supports dynamic data representation through client-server negotiation. The requesting client specifies it can accept certain MIME content types (more on this below) and the server responds with one of these. All WWW clients can handle text/plain and text/html. HTTP/1.0 Internet Draft 05 (the seventh release of HTTP/1.0) is targeted as an Internet Informational RFC.

Web Architecture Extensibility

This basic web architecture is fast evolving to serve a wider variety of needs beyond static document access and browsing. The Common Gateway Interface (CGI) extends the architecture to three-tiers by adding a backend server that provides services to the Web server on behalf of the Web client, permitting dynamic composition of web pages. Helpers/plug-ins and Java/JavaScript provide other interesting Web architecture extensions.

Common Gateway Interface(CGI)

CGI is a standard for interfacing external programs with Web servers. The server hands client requests encoded in URLs to the appropriate registered CGI program, which executes and returns results encoded as MIME messages back to the server. CGI's openness avoids the need to extend HTTP. The most common CGI applications handle HTML <FORM> and <ISINDEX> commands. CGI programs are executable programs that run on the Web server. They can be written in any scripting language (interpreted) or programming language (must be compiled first) available to be executed on a Web server, including C, C++, Fortran, PERL, TCL, Unix shells, Visual Basic, Apple script, and others. Security precautions typically require that CGI programs be run from a specified directory (e.g., /cgi-bin) under control of the webmaster (Web system administrator), that is, they must be registered with the system. Arguments to CGI programs are transmitted from client to server via environment variables encoded in URLs. The CGI program typically returns HTML pages that it constructs on the fly. Some problems with CGI are:

- The CGI interface requires the server to execute a program
- The CGI interface does not provide a way to share data and communications resources so if a program must access an external resource, it must open and close that resource. It is difficult to construct transactional interactions using CGI.
- The current version is CGI/1.1. W3C and others are experimenting with next generation object-oriented APIs based on OMG IDL; Netscape provides Netscape Server API (NSAPI) and Progress Software and Microsoft provide Internet Server API (ISAPI).

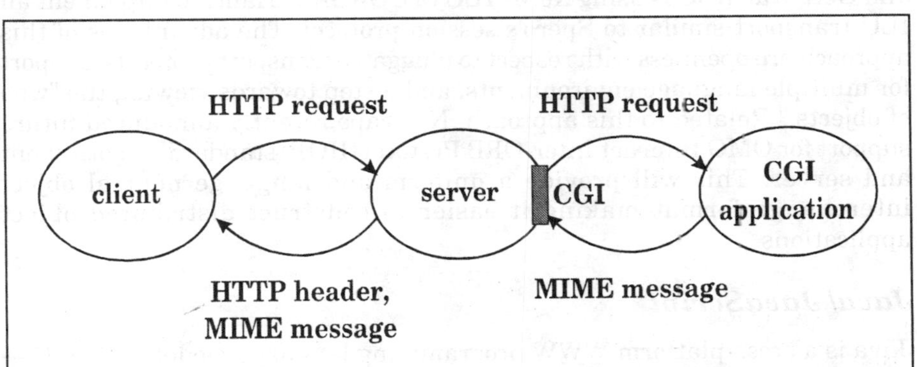

Figure 1: a backend CGI program provides services to the WWW server on behalf of the client.

Helpers/Plug-ins

When a client browser retrieves a file, it launches an installed helper application or plug-in to process the file based on the file's MIME-type (see below). For example, it may launch a Postscript or Acrobat reader, or MPEG or QuickTime player. A helper application runs external to the browser while a plug-in runs within the browser. For information on how to create new Netscape Navigator plug-ins, see The Plug-in Developer's Guide.

Common Client Gateway (CCI)

this gateway allows a third-party application to remotely control the Web browser client. Netscape Client APIs 2.0 (NCAPIs) depends on platform specific native methods of inter process communication (IPC). They plan to support DDE and OLE2 for Windows clients, X properties for UNIX clients, and Apple Events for Macintosh clients.

Extensions to HTTP

W3C and IETF Application Area HTTP Working Group are working together on current and future versions of HTTP. The HTTP-NG project is assessing two implementation approaches to HTTP "replacements":

Spero's approach

allows many requests per connection, the requests can be asynchronous and the server can respond in any order, allowing several transfers in parallel. A "session layer" divides the connection into numerous channels. Control messages (GET requests, meta information) are returned in a control channel; each object is returned in its own channel.

W3C approach

Jim Gettys at W3C is using Xerox ILU (a CORBA variant) to implement an ILU transport similar to Spero's session protocol. The advantages of this approach are openness with respect to pluggable transport protocols, support for multiple language environments, and a step towards viewing the "web of objects." Related to this approach, Netscape recently announced future support for OMG Internet Inter-ORB Protocol (IIOP) standard on both client and server. This will provide a uniform and language neutral object interchange format making it easier to construct distributed object applications.

Java/ JavaScript

Java is a cross-platform WWW programming language modeled after C++ from Sun Microsystems. Java programs embedded in HTML documents are called applets and are specified using <APPLET> tags. The HTML for an applet contains a code attribute that specifies the URL of the compiled applet file. Applets are compiled to a platform-independent bytecode which can be safely downloaded and executed by the Java interpreter embedded into the Web browser. Browsers that support Java are said to be Java-enabled. If performance is critical, a Java applet can be compiled to native machine language on the fly. Such a compiler is known as a Just-In-Time(JIT) compiler. JavaScript is a scripting language designed for creating dynamic, interactive Web applications that link together objects and resources on both clients and servers. A client JavaScript can recognize and respond to user events such as mouse clicks, form input, and page navigation, and query the state or alter the performance of an applet or plug-in. A server JavaScript script can exhibit behavior similar to common gateway interface (CGI) programs. JavaScript scripts are embedded in HTML documents using <SCRIPT> tags. Similar to Java applets, JavaScript scripts are directly interpreted within the client's browser and are therefore platform-independent. For a comparison of Java and JavaScript, see here.

The Java Language Specification can be found here, a Java tutorial here, the Java Virtual Machine (interpreter) here, the Java Developer's Kit (JDK) here, and Java FAQs here. A comprehensive Java page of resources can be found at JPL. The JavaScript Language Specification can be found here, a JavaScript tutorial here, and the JavaScript FAQs here.

The IETF Security Area Web Transaction Security (WTS) Working Group is working on security services for WWW. As chartered, it has produced Internet-drafts of a Requirements for Web Transaction Security and a Secure HyperText Transfer Protocol specification plus Security Extensions For HTML.

Other Transfer Protocols

The Web also uses other HTTP-related protocols for transferring and representing information, including: Transmission Control Protocol/Internet Protocol (TCP/IP) - the fundamental protocol that provides for the reliable delivery of streams of data from one host to another. An introduction to TCP/IP is here. File Transfer Protocol (FTP) - a common method of moving files between two Internet sites. It is based on TCP/IP. Gopher - a distributed document search and retrieval protocol (IETF RFC 1436) for obtaining files or information from hierarchical menus in the Gopher information-retrieval system. Internet Inter-ORB Protocol (IIOP) - an inter-ORB protocol for communication between objects and applications. It is based on the Common Object Request Broker Architecture (CORBA) specification.

Multipurpose Internet Mail Extensions (MIME)

The protocol for multimedia email and a building block of HTTP. The first packet of information received by a client identifies the type of file the server has sent, e.g., binary, audio, video, movie, formatted word-processor documents, graphics, spreadsheets, etc.. The extensions to the SMTP format allow it to carry multiple types of data. When multimedia files are sent using the MIME standard they are encoded into non-readable text. The Web browser maintains a list of pairs of MIME-Types and helper applications for handling each type.

Network News Transfer Protocol (NNTP)

The protocol used to connect to Usenet discussion groups.

Secure Socket Layer (SSL)

A security protocol developed by Netscape for sending and receiving encrypted information. It is based on encryption technology developed by RSA, Inc..

Simple Mail Transfer Protocol (SMTP)

A protocol for transferring electronic mail from one host to another.

Simple Network Management Protocol (SNMP)

A protocol that allows a network administrator to monitor network devices over the network. Z39.50 - a protocol that governs the formats and procedures by which two computers interact with one another. It is used to search several databases of the same type, and is session oriented and tasteful.

Other Open Standards

The Web also builds on additional open standards: GIF, JPEG, and XBM image formats.

Virtual Reality Modeling Language (VRML)

A proposed standard language for describing multi-participant interactive simulations within the WWW.

Hyper Media Management Protocol (HMMP)

A protocol to access and manipulate components of the Hypermedia Management Schema (HMMS), a data representation formalism (schema) for representing managed objects. HMMS and HMMP are major components of the Web-Based Enterprise Management standards effort to integrate existing standards, such as SNMP/UDP, HTML/HTTP and DMI/RPC into a browser-managed architecture.

Real Time Streaming Protocol (RTSP)

A recently proposed communication protocol for control and delivery of video and audio in real-time. Proxy and SOCKS firewall protocols.

S-HTTP security protocol

A more complete list of standards can be found at Netscape and the World Wide Web Consortium. A complete list of Internet Engineering Task Force (IETF) standard RFCs can be found here.

This research is sponsored by the Defense Advanced Research Projects Agency and managed by the U.S. Army Research Laboratory under contract DAAL01-95-C-0112. The views and conclusions contained in this document are those of the authors and should not be interpreted as necessarily representing the official policies, either expressed or implied of the Defense Advanced Research Projects Agency, U.S. Army Research Laboratory, or the United States Government.

When designing distributed applications for enterprise information systems you have to decide how to distribute application functionality or responsibility between distributed processing contexts in order to optimize the usage of components and resources involved. This distribution of functionality carries with it a large number of ramifications. It will affect the way your projects are managed, and how your applications are structured and built. Also, the implementation of this simple idea can prove to be quite challenging. Our patterns are divided into three sections reflecting these areas of concerns:

Architectural patterns:

Three-tier distribution architecture discusses partitioning application functionality into three tiers: front-end clients, domain or application servers, and a storage and DB-server. Four Layer Architecture addresses how the objects in your system as a whole can be organized to best separate concerns and prepare you for distribution and reuse.

Organizational Patterns

Phase-in tiers shows how systems using a four-layer architecture can be built initially for a two-tier architecture, and then moved to a three-tier architecture over time.

Trim client demonstrates how the objects in a four layer architecture can be best distributed into the tiers of a two or three tier architecture.

Implementation Patterns

Specialized Application Servers guides the process of dividing the middle layer into several application servers.

Abstract Database Interface makes the application portable to different database platforms. ORB Proxy for Database Object deals with the integration of the often incompatible worlds of object brokers and object databases.

Automatic Object Locks liberates developers from the tedious and error-prone work of manually locking and unlocking database objects. Shared DB Connections applies to the cases where it is necessary to have more simultaneous users than the number of connections the database servers will accept.

Thread-Based Concurrency Management shows how concurrency control can be implemented in application servers when database locks can no longer be used to synchronize the clients.

Three-Tier Distribution Architecture

You have to design applications for distributed enterprise information systems where usually some desktop components will access or modify shared resources, mostly located within a non-active database. Problem How can you partition application functionality or responsibility between distributed processing contexts best in order to optimize the usage of components and resources involved? Forces You can locate most of the application code on a client. The client has access to a database server that is shared with all other clients using the vendor-supplied API. Even if this architecture is very simple and easy to build, this leads to the so called fat-client problem, addressed by most of the following forces. When putting most or all application code on the clients, they (the clients) have to request or download all the data they need to fulfill their business tasks. This is sometimes too inefficient.

The network becomes overloaded when many clients request a great amount of data (or objects). Also if a client do not has the chance to delegate the processing of the requested data to another client, application performance or response time depends heavily on the power/efficiency of the system supporting this client. If you rely on a vendor specific server API, you can estimate the effort to integrate that kind of server. On the other hand you will become too inflexible or fix at all, because it restricts you to a specific set of services the server places to the clients' disposal. If you are trying to prevent getting "locked into" a specific vendor once you build on top of their proprietary API, you can't use the built-in features of your database server dealing with concurrency control, transactional behavior and recovery directly. So you have to ensure consistency and availability of your application system on your own. Using existing interfaces is constraining, but defining your own interfaces takes effort and is error prone.

Distributing the application code between clients and servers makes it more flexible and scaleable, but the larger the number of parts, the more complex a system seems, and the more failure points exist. Therefore the system becomes more difficult to maintain, too. If your clients interact using a (non-active) database server, automatic change propagation is unsupported, or at best supported by highly vendor specific database triggers mechanisms. This may require continuous checking (polling) of the server to detect changes, resulting in extra network load. Depending of the polling time-frame some clients become inconsistent with the database for a while or may be affected by network traffic problems.

Partition your application functionality or responsibility into three tiers:

• Front-end clients, domain servers (also known as application servers), and a storage and DB-server.

• This results in the so-called three-tier distribution architecture.

The front-end clients tier consists of components unique to every user including application specific logic and the user interface. These single user systems handle the mass of user interaction and task specific local operations originated by the user.

The domain server tier, supported by a multi-user environment, holds the shared parts of application and business logic. This tier needs services like transactions, concurrency control and security. Because most of the data/information requested by the applications are accessed via this layer, data intensive computing operations should be executed here whenever possible. Domain servers are responsible for coordinating transactions and accessing legacy systems. Within this tier parts may cooperate via intra-tier communication.

The task of the storage- and DB-server tier is to manage persistency of certain data/information and to execute the database transactions. An optional storage server may be responsible for special mapping, e.g. the mapping between objects from the application and tables of a RDBMS or between object-ids within the execution space and object-ids within an ODBMS.

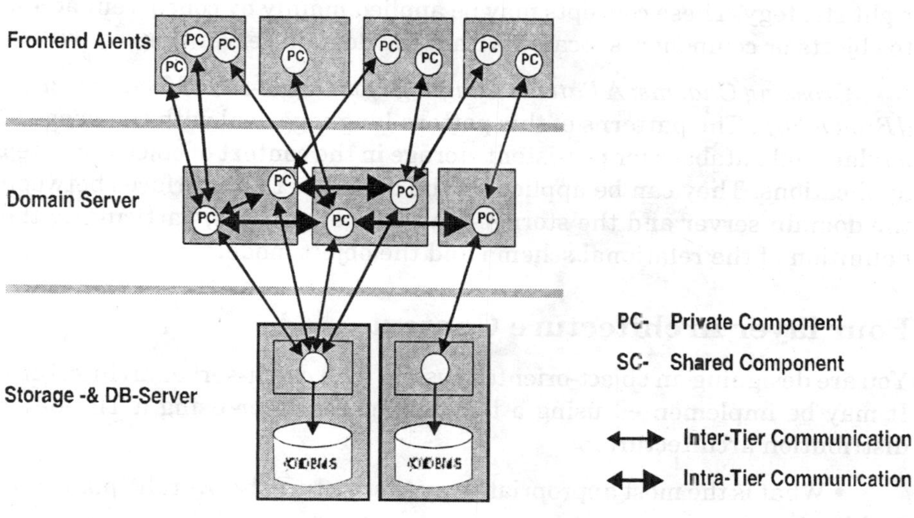

Figure 2: Three-tier distribution architecture

Application processing, located on domain server systems, is separated from both the user interface and the database server. Activities unique to a particular user can be executed local/private. Centralized data can be accessed without moving it completely to the front-end clients. The possibility of information preprocessing on domain servers helps reduce network traffic to clients and therefore increases performance.

Most of the application code is isolated from user specific interaction and interfaces. All application logic common to some users/applications is maintained in one (single/shared) location. So application code/logic can be changed in the middle tier without affecting front ends and database server. The interface between front-ends and domain servers can be designed by the programmer as needed because the programmer doesn't have to fit a vendor supplied API. Domain servers provide good possibilities for integrating legacy systems, because the interfaces and bridges to such systems are concentrated and managed in one location for all applications needing access. Consequences Even if there are many benefits and advantages of a three-tier distribution architecture, the more freedom and increased flexibility leave the developers with more responsibilities. They have to design interfaces between front-end clients and domain servers and to ensure application consistency and availability themselves. Nevertheless one possibility to overcome these obstacles is the consequent use of industry standards like CORBA and CORBA services from the Object Management Group.

Related Patterns

Selecting Locking Designs for Parallel Programs. If you have to deal with locking and concurrency control, these patterns will help you choosing the right strategy. These concepts may be applied mainly by concurrent access to objects or components located within the domain server tier.

Crossing Chasms: A Pattern Language for Object-RDBMS Integration ([Brown 96]). The patterns of this pattern language deal with the usage of a relational database for persistent storage in the context of object-oriented applications. They can be applied on the design of the interfaces between the domain server and the storage- and DB-server tiers, particularly the definition of the relational schema and the object model.

Four layer Architecture Context

You are designing an object-oriented system for a client-server architecture. It may be implemented using a two-tier approach, or using a Three-tier distribution architecture.

• What is the most appropriate way to structure the overall application architecture?

• What is the best way to group your objects together?

When designing the software architecture in a client-server system, you must come up with a way to divide the labor among team members. Your architecture must also be simple enough to be easily explainable to new team members, so they can understand where their work fits. In looking for an application architecture, many developers have looked to the MVC architecture. However, MVC is not the be-all and end-all of object design. While a proper architecture should address the concerns addressed by MVC, and may trace its descent from MVC, modern software systems must also address issues not covered by classic MVC.

MVC promoted reuse by factoring out the UI widgetry away from the domain objects. Modern class libraries derived from MVC have also discovered yet another set of potentially useful and reusable abstractions in separating out the aspect of mediating between views and adapting views to domain models into another set of classes.

However, this still does not address the connection of the domain to the outside world (i.e., object persistency mechanisms, network protocols, etc.). A complete architecture for client-server systems must address these issues as well.

Factor your application classes into four layers in the following way (Figure 2: Four Layer Architecture):

The View layer.

This is the layer where the physical window and widget objects live. It may also contain Controller classes as in classical MVC. Any new user interface widgets developed for this application are put in this layer. In most cases today this layer is completely generated by a window-builder tool.

The Application Model layer

This layer mediates between the various user interface components on a GUI screen and translates the messages that they understand into messages understood by the objects in the domain model. It is responsible for the flow of the application and controls navigation from window to window. This layer is often partially generated by a window-builder and partially coded by the developer.

The Domain Model layer

This is the layer where most objects found in an OO analysis and design will reside. To a great extent, the objects in this layer can be application-independent. Examples of the types of objects found in this layer may be Orders, Employees, Sensors, or whatever is appropriate to the problem domain.

The Infrastructure layer

This is where the objects that represent connections to entities outside the application (specifically those outside the object world) reside. Examples of objects in this layer would include SQLTables, 3270Terminals, SerialPorts, SQLBrokers and the like.

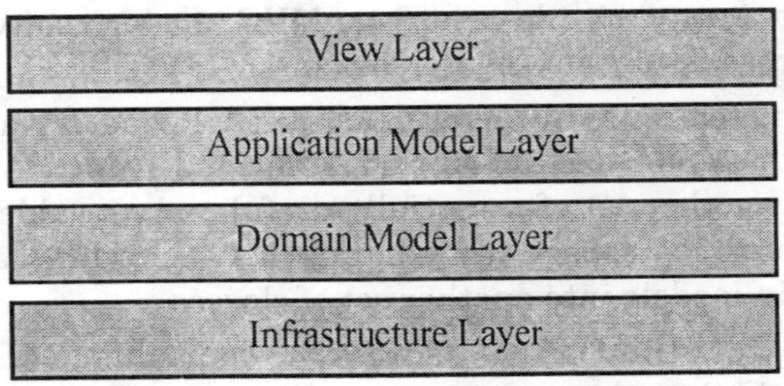

Figure 3: Four Layer Architecture

This choice of layers can have many beneficial effects on your application if it is applied in the proper way. First, since the architecture is so simple, it is easy to explain to team members and so demonstrate where each object's role fits into the "big picture".

If a designer is very strict about clearly defining where objects fit within the layers, and the interfaces between the layers, then the potential for reuse of many objects in the system can be greatly increased. A common problem with many object designs is that they are too tightly constrained to the limits of the particular application being built. Many novice designers tend to put too much of the logic of an application in the Application Model layer. In this case, there are few, if any, domain objects that are potentially available for reuse in other applications.

Another benefit of this layering is that it makes it easy to divide work along layer boundaries. demonstrates how a "layered and sectioned architecture" can be made the basis of a source code control system. It is easy to assign different teams or individuals to the work of coding the layers in a four-layer architectures, since the interfaces are identified and understood well in advance of coding.

Finally, a four-layer architecture makes it possible to code the bulk of your system (in the domain model and application model layers) to be independent of the choice of persistence mechanism and windowing system.

Organizational Patterns

You must come up with a solution that supports both your current and planned network architecture, and yet leverages your investment in object technology to produce results quickly.

You need to best utilize existing and new computing and network resources. You would like to move to a client-server set of solutions as quickly as possible, but there is no way that everything can be replaced at once. The cost of a total redevelopment effort is prohibitive, and your staff could not complete the effort in a reasonable length of time.

A good approach is to begin all development on the client (sometimes resulting in a prototype "fat client") and then push the code from the bottom two layers of a four layer architecture onto a server as development progresses. In this way you can add tiers over time, starting with a two-tiered system (i.e., a "fat client") and moving to a three-tiered system later.

Using distributed object technology does not preclude using either relational or OODBMS technology as appropriate for object persistence on the server(s) in any of the upper tiers. In fact, one common solution is to utilize an ODBMS for object persistence between tiers one and two, and an RDBMS for persistence between tiers two and three.

Trim Client discusses how to distribute behavior between client and server. Four Layer Architecture discusses how to distribute behavior among the layers of a software architecture. Three-tier distribution architecture gives the rationale for going to a three-tier architecture.

Correctly distributing behavior in a client-server system is a difficult task. When PC's were first introduced to major companies, they were most often used as terminal emulator front-ends to existing mainframe programs. These so-called "thin" clients did not take advantage of the capabilities or processing power of the new PC clients, and could not allow for complex user interaction to occur on the client side.

In a response to this, the first generation of client-server systems often overloaded the client by placing all of the domain and display logic on the client. These so-called "fat" clients were often characterized by being big, slow, and inefficient at utilizing machine resources (network traffic, CPU horsepower, etc.). In a response to this, the "thin" client model is back in vogue. This time the client consists of a Web browser that accesses dynamically generated HTML pages from a central host. This "Web 3270" approach has the same problems as the original terminal-emulator approach in that all of the processing takes place on the server end, and complex user interaction is not allowed.

The price of memory, hard-drive space and processor speed come down almost daily. However, it is apparent that the requirements placed on these resources by modern software is expanding at an even faster rate. It is not uncommon to see large-scale client-server programs that take up 15 or more megabytes of memory by themselves. At the same time, these same advances that make client machines more powerful are also making multiprocessor servers more cost-effective. However, most current client-server systems do not take full advantage of this processing power, as the server is most often used only as a data or file server.

This solution minimizes the amount of processing that must be done on a Client, and can reduce its need for memory and computational power. Note that once a system is broken up this way it does not require that the top two layer be implemented in the same language as the bottom two layers. A heterogeneous system will work if some type of object-to-object communication is provided. It would be perfectly acceptable to write the top two layers in Java, and the bottom two in C++ or Smalltalk, or have the entire system written from top to bottom in one language. So long as an object communication technology like CORBA or SOM can be used to provide intra-machine message passing, there should not be any restrictions put on the choice of language or platform.

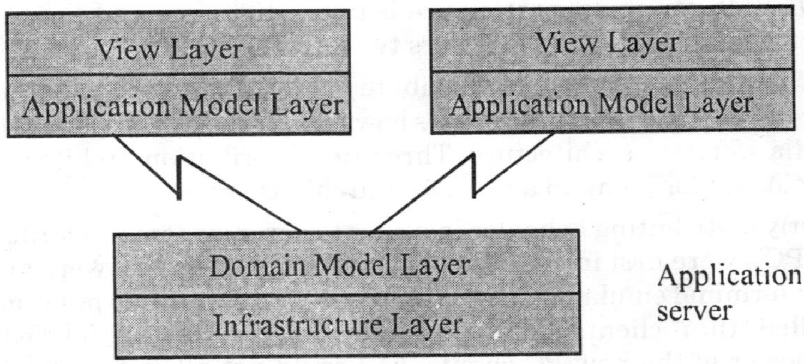

Figure 4: Distributed layers

Four-layer architecture demonstrates why systems should have clear layer boundaries and how that helps make systems more manageable. Three-tier distribution architecture discusses the choices that go into building your system as three tiers of computation.

Distribution Patterns

Moving some of the application classes to a separate server reduces dependencies, and can allow a part of the application to be upgraded without affecting the other parts. However, it also reduces performance because of the remote procedure calls (RPCs) that now become necessary. Therefore, we must take care to partition the application so that as few RPCs as possible are necessary.

The analysis and design phases will produce a large object model, also called the Business Object Model (BOM). In a large application, the BOM covers several different lines of business and business processes.

Group objects from the BOM which are tightly coupled and have high cohesion into application servers. Typically, these groups will represent lines of business or business processes. If your notation uses class categories (as in [Booch 91], [Booch 93]), these can provide good starting points. Some classes need to be in several application servers for performance reasons; do this as little as possible in order to minimize dependencies.

Abstract Database Interface

Application objects are usually stored in an object-oriented database. Sometimes, however, the customer dictates a database platform; in that case the database is usually relational.

As also noted in [Wikman] all object databases have significantly different programming interfaces. Even if a standard exists [ODMG 93] this standard is somewhat incomplete, and every implementer fails to support some parts of it. This means in practice that an application written for a specific object database is not portable to other databases.

A common solution to this problem is to place code specific to the database platform in a limited subset of methods of the classes in which this code is used. Although this approach controls the location of the code that later must be changed, it does not scale very well. In a large application there can be thousands of classes; the task of porting to a different database can soon become overwhelming even if only a few methods of each class must be changed.

Define a standard interface against the database, and implement this interface for the specific database required by each project; see the pattern Interface to Control Modules in and the use of separate interface and implementation objects. If separate interface and implementation objects are used, the switching between different implementations corresponds to the BRIDGE pattern.

Applet/ Servlet

ntroduction

The previous chapter described the client-side CBR design using a Java applet, which provides a platform for creating applications that are accessible via Internet. However, this applet requires connectivity to a data source (case base or database) on the web server, while the security model used by browsers to run Java applets restricts their network connections. Generally, all applet viewers including web browsers have a Security Manager object that checks for applet security violations and imposes the following restrictions to applets:

- An applet cannot load libraries or define native methods;
- An applet cannot ordinarily read or write files on the host that is executing it unless it is specifically granted a policy file and the appropriate read or write access permission;

• An applet cannot make network connections except to the host that it came from;

• An applet cannot read certain system properties.

A solution to the problem of connecting an applet to a data source is to run an application on the server and the application can read and write data, and that is attached with a database. This approach is called the "Server-Side Solution". Currently, there are several kind of server-side applications, such as Common Gateway Interface (CGI), Active Server Pages (ASP), Internet Server Application Programming Interface (ISAPI). Currently, Java servlets provide a new and powerful method of developing server-side solutions.

Java servlets are a key component of server-side Java development. A servlet is small, pluggable extension to a server that can enhance the server's functionality with safety, portability, and flexibility. Servlets can be used to extend the functionality of any Java-enabled server, and provide a more powerful and efficient alternative to Common Gateway Interface (CGI) scripts which is a traditionally popular method.

Servlet vs. CGI

The Common Gateway Interface (CGI) is a method for permitting web pages to communicate with programs on a web server and to create dynamic contents [Felton, 1997]. With CGI, the client sends the web server requests and the server passes them to an external program. After the program processes requests, the client gets the output. Figure shows how CGI works.

Figure 5 How a CGI request is processed

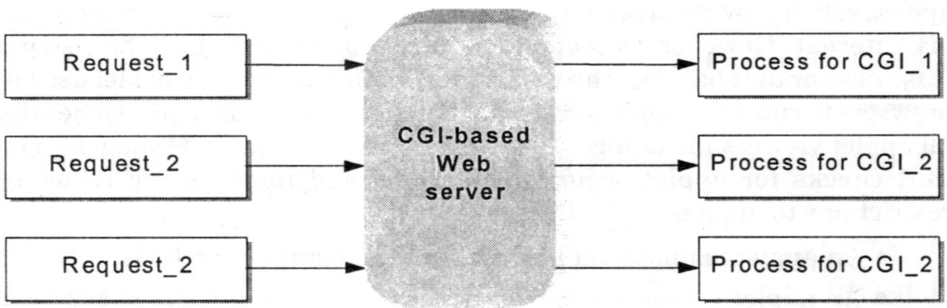

Figure 6 How CGI handles multiple requests [Hunter & Grawford, 1998]

When a client sends a request to the web server, the server must create a child process to run the CGI program. Since creating a process for each request requires time and server resources, the number of the requests that a server can handle is limited. Another disadvantage with CGI is that a CGI program cannot interact with the web server during its execution because it is running in a separate process.

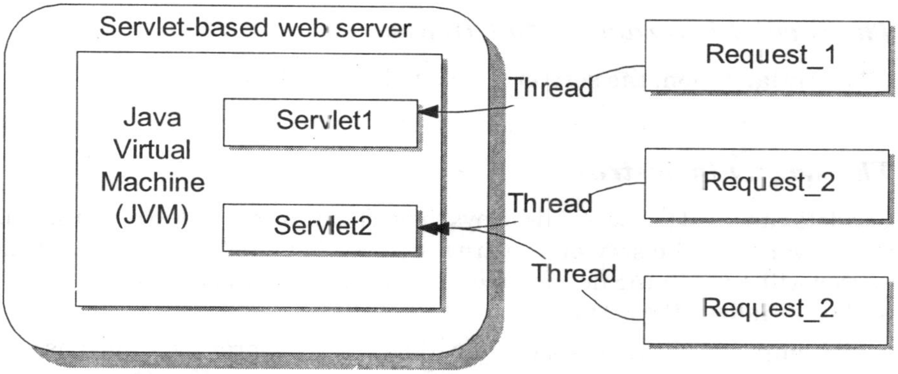

Figure 7 How Java servlet handles multiple requests

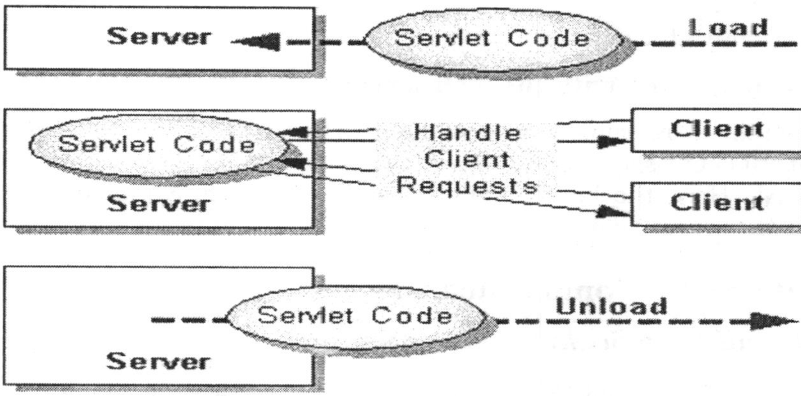

Figure 8 How a server and a servlet work together

Unlike CGI, servlets are all handled efficiently by separate threads within the web server process. They can therefore interact very closely with the server to do things that are not possible with CGI scripts. Figure work together as following steps:

A server loads and initializes the servlet.

When a server loads a servlet, the server runs the servlet's init method. Initialization completes before client requests are handled and before the servlet is destroyed. The server calls the init method once, when the server loads the servlet, and will not call the init method again unless the server is reloading the servlet.

The servlet interacts with Clients.

After initialization, the servlet is able to handle client requests.

The servlet is destroyed.

Servlets run until the server destroys them. When a server destroys a servlet, the server runs the servlet's destroy method. The method is run once; the server will not run the destroy method again until after the server reloads and reinitializes the servlet.

Compared with other dynamic web content approaches, such as CGI, ASP, ISAPI and Server-side JavaScript, servlets offer the following advantages [Hunter & Grawford, 1998]:

- Powerful to implement a number of tasks by using the core Java APIs;
- Excellent portability;
- Safety;
- Highly efficient;

Highly integrated with the web server.

Based on the above considerations, the Java Servlet technique was used to implement client-server communication and server-side I/O operation in I-NaCoDAE. Here, the JavaServerTM Web Development Kit (JSWDK) was used as the server-side servlet engine.

Client-Server Communication

HTTP and Raw Socket Connections

Before Java servlets and JDK 1.1, there were two methods to handle applet-server communication:

- HTTP connection to a CGI program on server side
- Raw socket connection to a non-HTTP server

These two methods have some disadvantages. The first method is slow. Since the applet and the CGI program cannot communicate interactively, they have to set a channel for each request and response. In addition, every time a request is sent to the CGI program the CGI program has to launch and initialize itself. Finally, the first method is not flexible to transfer data since it usually requires requests to be performed as an array of name/ value pairs.

For the second method, the problems include: 1) It does not work if the applets run behind firewalls; 2) The non-HTTP server cannot be easily connected to by a browser; and 3) It may require the development of a custom protocol.

The advent of Java servlets and Java object serialization permits a new approach for applet-server communications. As mentioned above, Java servlets have many advantages over CGI and are replacing CGI programs, improving the performance of HTTP-based applet-server communication. Java object serialization allows applets and servlets to communicate by exchanging Java objects that make the data transfer much easier and more flexible. This chapter describes the Java object serialization technique to transfer data between servlets and applets.

HTTP Servlet

HTTP is a stateless client/server protocol that accepts requests and delivers requests that can be of several methods, such as GET, POST, PUT, HEAD, DELETE, TRACE and OPTIONS. Usually, the GET method and the POST method are used frequently. The GET method is used to get information while the POST method is designed for posting information.

Usually, an HTTP servlet overrides the doGet method to handle GET requests and the doPost method to handle POST requests while a generic servlet overrides service method to handle requests. Figure 5 shows how an HTTP servlet handles GET, POST and PUT requests.

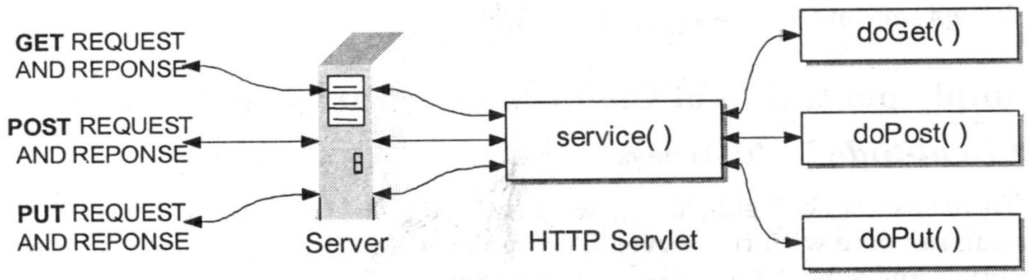

Fig. 9 : How an HTTP servlet handles GET, POST and PUT requests.

3Tier Architecture

To achieve the goal specified by the thesis, the client-server communication should implement the following processes:

- The client sends requests to the server;
- The server handles requests and loads the data from database or case base;

- The server sends data to the client;
- The client gets data and handles the data;
- The client sends back data to the server to save.

According to those methods, the application can be divided into 3 tiers: the UI layer (browser/applet), the service layer (server/servlet), and the database layer (case base/database).

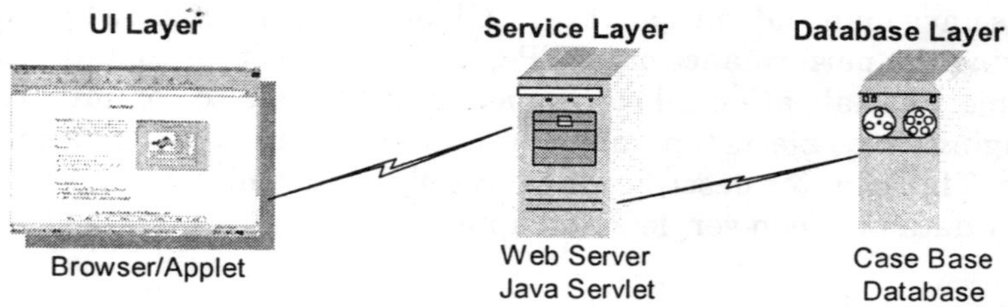

Fig. 10: 3-tier architecture

The first tier consists of the browser and its embedded Applet that gets the case library from the web server and interacts with users. The second layer consists of the web server and servlets. On the one hand, servlets read data from and write to the server. On the other hand, a servlet can harness the power of JDBC to access a relational database to query and retrieve information.

The third layer stores the case base and the relational database. In the JDK 1.1 and Java 2, a JDBC API can be used to allow servlets to connect to the relational database. In addition, a general Java Servlet API allows servlets to access case base files.

Implementation of Client-Server Communication

Client-Side Data Access

To access server-side data, we need a mechanism for the applet to communicate with the server. The applet has to get information from the server and send information to the server.

Use FTP to transfer data from the server.

This method corresponds to Step 5 in the modified 3-tier application interaction. It has the advantage of high speed for data transfer. The traditional 3-tier application interaction does not include this process. Using this method, the applet has to specify a URL where the data source is located:

```
//
// Specify a URL to get retrieve the information from the server
//
Try {
```

```
 FileURL = new URL(getCodeBase(), fileName);
}
catch (MalformedURLException excep) {
 JOptionPane.showMessageDialog(this, "Cannot open the file.",
         "Bad URL", JOptionPane.INFORMATION_MESSAGE);
}
```

Then, the applet can open the file and its byte data stream. InputStreamReader reads data from the stream and transfers the data into character data stream which can be stored in a buffer. If the applet needs data, it can read the information from the buffer. The idea can be illustrated as:

```
//
// Open the file and get data from the opened stream
//
try {
   String str = null;
                     br      =      new      BufferedReader(new
InputStreamReader(fileURL.openStream()));
   while ((str = br.readLine()) != null) {
  // handle the string
  // ......
 }
   br.close();
}
catch(IOException ioe)
{
   WBInfoDialog("File Lost", "Have not found the file, please " +
"contact the administrator!", JOptionPane.ERROR_MESSAGE);
   return;
}
```

Use an HTTP connection to obtain the data.

Since servlets support the HTTP/CGI interface, the applet can communicate with the servlet over HTTP connections. What the applet needs is to open an URL connection. Once the connection is made, the applet can get do input/output operation with the server-side servlet.

To get data from the server, the applet should specify a URL to access a servlet and send a GET request to the servlet. Once the connection has been opened, then the applet can read the output stream sent from the servlet and handle the data accordingly. The following sample code shows us how to proceed:

```
//
// Get input stream from a servlet using HTTP connections
//
try {
// specify a URL connection and pass the file name to the servlet
```

```
   String Location = "http://localhost:8080/servlet/" +
               "CBR_ReadWriteServlet?+FileName="+ fileName;
   URL url = new URL(Location);

   // Open a connection to the servlet specified by url
   URLConnection con = url.openConnection();
   con.setDoInput(true);
   con.setUseCaches(false);
   con.setDefaultUseCaches(false);

  // get the input stream sent from the servlet
          DataInputStream inData = new DataInputStream
(con.getInputStream());
   String str = inData.readUTF();
   // Handle the string here
}
catch (Exception e) {
   e.printStackTrace( );
}
```

Server-Side Data Access

Server-side data access consists of the following steps

" The servlet sends data to the applet;

" The servlet reads data from the applet or writes data to the server.

To accomplish these goals, the servlet can use the service method that is invoked to handle requests made to the servlet. Simply speaking, the steps include:

The servlet sets the content type for the response stream

```
  response.setContentType ("application/octet-stream");
```

The servlet gets the data sent from Applets

```
  DataInputStream inData = new DataInputStream (req.getInputStream());
  // Read UTF format Unicode string
  String str = inData.readUTF();
```

The servlet writes the string to the server

```
  FileWriter CBRFileWriter = new FileWriter (DestFileName, true);
  PrintWriter CBRPrintWriter = new PrintWriter(CBRFileWriter);
  CBRPrintWriter.write(str);
  CBRFileWriter.close();
```

The servlet sends the data to the applet

```
response.setContentLength(buf.length);
ServletOutputStream servletOut = response.getOutputStream();
servletOut.write(buf);
servletOut.close();
```

Through the above steps, the servlet not only can read a data stream sent from an applet and write a data stream to the server, but also can send a data stream to the applet.

Client-Server Communication via Object Serialization

To fully load a case library, we can create a case library class that encapsulates all the information about the case, question and action descriptions. The information can be sent as a Java object using Java Object Serialization technique. Further, the object (information) can be serialized over an HTTP output stream and loaded from a input stream. Figure 7 illustrates the object transaction between the applet and the servlet.

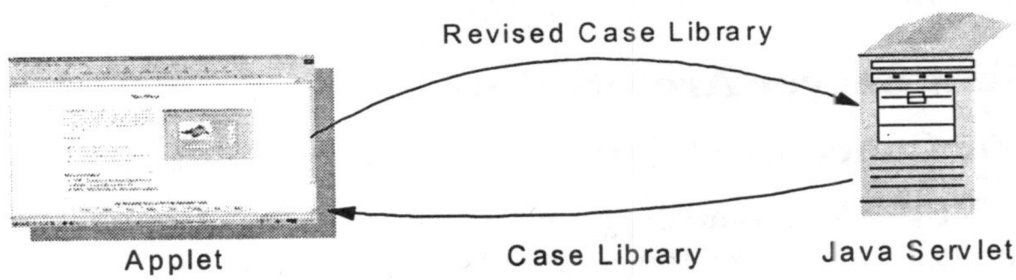

Figure 11: The object transaction between the applet and the server

To serialize a Java object, the case library class must implement the java.io.Serializable interface. The custom class for case library can be created as follows:

```
class case_lib implements java.io.Serialize
{
  // declaration of constructors and the methods
}
```

Usually, to serialize an object to an output stream, we should create an ObjectOutputStream first, then use writeObject method to serialize the object. The mechanism looks like this:

```
Output = new ObjectOutputStream(connection.getOutputStream());
Output.writeObject(new case_lib( ));
Output.flush( );
Output.close();
```

To deserialize/read an object from an object stream, the applet has to get input stream and call readObject method to read the object from the input stream. Moreover, the applet need cast the object to the class case_Lib. The example code is illustrated as follows:

```
Input = new ObjectInputStream(connection.getInputStream());
class_lib inputData = (case_lib) Input.readObject( );
Input.close( );
```

To send an object from the applet to the servlet, the applet opens an connection to the servlet and sends a POST request. After this, the applet creates a FileOutputStream for the data file and an ObjectOutputStream with the specified FileOutputStream. The last steps are writes the object to the stream and close the stream.

To send an object from the servlet to the applet, the servlet responses the appet with the HttpResponse parameter and creates an ObjectOutputStream to the applet. After this, an case library is serialized and passed to the waiting applet with a call

ObjectOutputStream(response.getOutputStream()).writeObject(case_library).

Client Server Architecture

Basic Concepts of Client/server Architecture

CLIENT/SERVER concepts have roots in early computer systems, so it is useful to briefly review the history of modern computing. Early computers (mainframes) were typically in a "glass room," with special power and air conditioning, and attended to by a priesthood of system programmers.

Users typically shared a pool of "dumb" terminals and had to rely on centralized printing and storage resources. In this environment, the mainframe did all the processing, and users had no local computing horsepower.

In the late 1970s and early 1980s, smaller systems (minicomputers) were developed that required less power and air conditioning. Individual business unit owners wanted their own systems, more suited to their needs. Once a substantial number of applications were developed on these computers, inevitably other departments wanted access to them.

Somewhat concurrently, Apple, IBM and others developed the personal computer. Initially it seemed to have little application beyond that of the hobbyist. However, as powerful, shrink-wrapped applications were developed, and arcane operating systems such as MS-DOS were replaced by more user-friendly systems (e.g., Macintosh, Windows), users began to want to use PCs in the corporate computing environment.

This allowed for a new army of computer users who cared little and understood even less about computer "systems." All they wanted was the latest software applications at their fingertips, but they needed the backup and redundant architecture that previously resided only in the glass room.

Concurrently, systems that were more scalable were introduced using common chip sets and operating systems, with features such as redundant power and multiple processors. They were far more powerful than "personal" computers although they were based largely on the same architecture but they were considerably smaller and less costly than mainframes or even minicomputers.

One last piece of technology was needed to make client/server architecture a reality. In the late 1970s, Xerox developed the standards and technology that we know today as Ethernet. This provided a standard means of linking together computers from different manufacturers and formed the basis for modern local area networks (LANs) and wide area networks (WANs).

A strong business need for decentralized computing horsepower standard, powerful computers with user-friendly interfaces mature, shrink-wrapped user applications with widespread acceptance inexpensive, modular systems designed with enterprise-class architecture, such as power and network redundancy and .file archiving network protocols to link them together.

Definition of Client and Server

A client is an individual user's computer or a user application that does a certain amount of processing on its own. It also sends and receives requests to and from one or more servers for other processing and/or data.

A server consists of one or more computers that receive and process requests from one or more client machines. A server is typically designed with some redundancy in power, network, computing and file storage. However, a machine with dual processors is not necessarily a server. An individual workstation can function as a server.

Sometimes the term "server" or "client" may refer to the software rather than the computer. Thus, a "mail client" may refer to the mail software that resides on a client machine, rather than the machine itself.

The Evolution of Clients and Servers

The earliest versions of client/server were merely shared files; when a user needed a file, it was copied from the server to the local machine. When finished, it was returned to the server. It was necessary to develop certain rules to handle conflict and synchronization issues. So as client/server systems evolved, they contained built-in synchronization and sharing engines. Client/server also embodies the concepts of user accounts and sharing of resources the system must separate and keep track of different users' files and applications during a user session, then free up those resources for another user session.

As client/server applications evolved, the functionality of the application was separated logically into two parts: the processes requiring the majority of the computing horsepower were put on the server, and the user interface and less processor-intensive processes were put on the client.

Client/Server Examples

A common client/server example is a print server. Most people have probably noticed a temporary lockup or slowdown when a document is printed on a stand-alone PC, especially if the document is complex. One can attach a printer to a PC and then share it with other users across the network. However, if everyone on the network simultaneously prints to that shared printer, it would likely lock up or even crash. Therefore, many times a machine is dedicated solely to handle printing - a print server. It "serves" print requests to all users, and off-loads this task from local machines. Another example is a mail server which functions much like a post office, receiving mail centrally and delivering individual messages to individual clients.

In a small organization, a single server machine may serve more than one function, if the functions are simple enough. One or more applications may reside on a single server machine, with the server being divided into different "logical" partitions. In a large corporate environment, there may be many servers for separate tasks.

There is typically a primary domain controller (PDC), which authenticates users and controls access and log in to the computer system itself. There may be a mail server, which processes e-mail. There may also be a file server typically containing large disk drives and individual user directories to store user files in a uniform way. And there may be separate application servers for accounting, billing, customer care, Web, e-commerce, database, transaction, manufacturing, inventory, etc. They are typically linked together using integration software (frequently called middleware) so that one can access many server applications from a single (client) machine, through a common interface, typically a browser.

Although client/server in its simplest form is two-tier (server and client), there are newer, more powerful architectures that are three-tier (where application logic lives in the middle-tier and it is separated from the data and user interface) or even n-tier (where there are several middle-tier components within a single business transaction) in nature. Sometimes client/server is referred to as distributed computing; they have the same basic concepts.

Advantages

There are many advantages to client/server architecture including that subsystems can be optimized for a particular set of applications. Systems can grow modularly, as different applications grow. Then more powerful subsystems can be installed without wasting resources on other applications. "Forklift upgrades," where an entire system is replaced, are theoretically kept to a minimum.

With most of the crucial applications and data residing on centralized machines, or clusters of machines, systems can be engineered to high standards of reliability and availability.

Client/server architecture has become the dominant structure for corporate computing in both small and large organizations. It combines the best concepts of centralized, robust infrastructure with decentralized capability and control - in other words, it gives both IT managers and end users what they want and need. If implemented properly, client/server architecture achieves the best balance between complexity, cost and ease of use, with excellent scalability and reliability.

A network architecture in which each computer or process on the network is either a client or a server. Servers are powerful computers or processes dedicated to managing disk drives (file servers), printers (print servers), or network traffic (network servers). Clients are PCs or workstations on which users run applications. Clients rely on servers for resources, such as files, devices, and even processing power. Another type of network architecture is known as a peer-to-peer architecture because each node has equivalent responsibilities. Both client/server and peer-to-peer architectures are widely used, and each has unique advantages and disadvantages. Client-server architectures are sometimes called two-tier architectures. Client/Server Software Architectures--An Overview Software Technology Roadmap What's New Background & Overview Technology Descriptions Defining Software Technology Categories Template for Technology Descriptions Taxonomies Glossary & Indexes Feedback & Participation Software Engineering Information Repository (SEIR).

Client/Server Software Architectures--Status Advanced Purpose and Origin

The term client/server was first used in the 1980s in reference to personal computers (PCs) on a network. The actual client/server model started gaining acceptance in the late 1980s. The client/server software architecture is a versatile, message-based and modular infrastructure that is intended to improve usability, flexibility, interoperability, and scalability as compared to centralized, mainframe, time sharing computing. A client is defined as a requester of services and a server is defined as the provider of services. A single machine can be both a client and a server depending on the software configuration. For details on client/server software architectures see Schussel and Edelstein. This technology description provides a summary of some common client/server architectures and, for completeness, also summarizes mainframe and file sharing architectures. Detailed descriptions for many of the individual architectures are provided elsewhere in the document. Technical Detail Mainframe architecture (not a client/server architecture). With mainframe software architectures all intelligence is within the central host computer. Users interact with the host through a terminal that captures keystrokes and sends that information to the host. Mainframe software architectures are not tied to a hardware platform. User interaction can be done using PCs and UNIX workstations. A limitation of mainframe software architectures is that they do not easily support graphical user interfaces (see Graphical User Interface Builders) or access to multiple databases from geographically dispersed sites. In the last few years, mainframes have found a new use as a server in distributed client/server architectures (see client/Server Software Architectures). File sharing architecture (not a client/server architecture). The original PC networks were based on file sharing architectures, where the server downloads files from the shared location to the desktop environment. The requested user job is then run (including logic and data) in the desktop environment. File sharing architectures work if shared usage is low, update contention is low, and the volume of data to be transferred is low. In the 1990s, PC LAN (local area network) computing changed because the capacity of the file sharing was strained as the number of online user grew (it can only satisfy about 12 users simultaneously) and graphical user interfaces (GUIs) became popular (making mainframe and terminal displays appear out of date). PCs are now being used in client/server architectures.

Client/server architecture, as a result of the limitations of file sharing architectures, the client/server architecture emerged. This approach introduced a database server to replace the file server. Using relational database management system (DBMS), user queries could be answered directly. The client/server architecture reduced network traffic by providing a query response rather than total file transfer. It improves multi-user updating through a GUI front end to a shared database. In client/server architectures, Remote Procedure Calls (RPCs) or standard query language (SQL) statements are typically used to communicate between the client and server. The remainder of this write-up provides examples of client/server architectures. Two tier architectures. With two tier client/server architectures (see Two Tier Software Architectures), the user system interface is usually located in the user's desktop environment and the database management services are usually in a server that is a more powerful machine that services many clients. Processing management is split between the user system interface environment and the database management server environment. The database management server provides stored procedures and triggers. There are a number of software vendors that provide tools to simplify development of applications for the two-tier client/server architecture. The two-tier client/server architecture is a good solution for distributed computing when work groups are defined as a dozen to 100 people interacting on a LAN simultaneously. It does have a number of limitations. When the number of users exceeds 100, performance begins to deteriorate.

This limitation is a result of the server maintaining a connection via "keep-alive" messages with each client, even when no work is being done. A second limitation of the two tier architecture is that implementation of processing management services using vendor proprietary database procedures restricts flexibility and choice of DBMS for applications. Finally, current implementations of the two tier architecture provide limited flexibility in moving (repartitioning) program functionality from one server to another without manually regenerating procedural code.

Three tier architectures.

The three tier architecture (see Three Tier Software Architectures) (also referred to as the multi-tier architecture) emerged to overcome the limitations of the two tier architecture. In the three tier architecture, a middle tier was added between the user system interface client environment and the database management server environment. There are a variety of ways of implementing this middle tier, such as transaction processing monitors, message servers, or application servers. The middle tier can perform queuing, application execution, and database staging. For example, if the middle tier provides queuing, the client can deliver its request to the middle layer and disengage because the middle tier will access the data and return the answer to the client. In addition the middle layer adds scheduling and prioritization for work in progress.

The three tier client/server architecture has been shown to improve performance for groups with a large number of users (in the thousands) and improves flexibility when compared to the two tier approach. Flexibility in partitioning can be a simple as "dragging and dropping" application code modules onto different computers in some three tier architectures. A limitation with three tier architectures is that the development environment is reportedly more difficult to use than the visually-oriented development of two tier applications. Recently, mainframes have found a new use as servers in three tier architectures (see Mainframe Server Software Architectures).

Three tier architecture with transaction processing monitor technology. The most basic type of three tier architecture has a middle layer consisting of Transaction Processing (TP) monitor technology (see Transaction Processing Monitor Technology). The TP monitor technology is a type of message queuing, transaction scheduling, and prioritization service where the client connects to the TP monitor (middle tier) instead of the database server. The transaction is accepted by the monitor, which queues it and then takes responsibility for managing it to completion, thus freeing up the client. When the capability is provided by third party middleware vendors it is referred to as "TP Heavy" because it can service thousands of users. When it is embedded in the DBMS (and could be considered a two tier architecture), it is referred to as "TP Lite" because experience has shown performance degradation when over 100 clients are connected. TP monitor technology also provides the ability to update multiple different DBMSs in a single transaction connectivity to a variety of data sources including flat files, non-relational DBMS, and the mainframe the ability to attach priorities to transactions robust security. Using a three tier client/server architecture with TP monitor technology results in an environment that is considerably more scalable than a two tier architecture with direct client to server connection. For systems with thousands of users, TP monitor technology (not embedded in the DBMS) has been reported as one of the most effective solutions. A limitation to TP monitor technology is that the implementation code is usually written in a lower level language (such as COBOL), and not yet widely available in the popular visual toolsets.

Three tier with message server. Messaging is another way to implement three tier architectures. Messages are prioritized and processed asynchronously. Messages consist of headers that contain priority information, and the address and identification number. The message server connects to the relational DBMS and other data sources. The difference between TP monitor technology and message server is that the message server architecture focuses on intelligent messages, whereas the TP Monitor environment has the intelligence in the monitor, and treats transactions as dumb data packets. Messaging systems are good solutions for wireless infrastructures.

Three tier with an application server. The three tier application server architecture allocates the main body of an application to run on a shared host rather than in the user system interface client environment. The application server does not drive the GUIs; rather it shares business logic, computations, and a data retrieval engine. Advantages are that with less software on the client there is less security to worry about, applications are more scalable, and support and installation costs are less on a single server than maintaining each on a desktop client. The application server design should be used when security, scalability, and cost are major considerations. Three tier with an ORB architecture. Currently industry is working on developing standards to improve interoperability and determine what the common Object Request Broker (ORB) will be. Developing client/server systems using technologies that support distributed objects holds great promise, as these technologies support interoperability across languages and platforms, as well as enhancing maintainability and adaptability of the system.

There are currently two prominent distributed object technologies: Common Object Request Broker Architecture (CORBA) COM/DCOM (see Component Object Model (COM), DCOM, and Related Capabilities). Industry is working on standards to improve interoperability between CORBA and COM/DCOM. The Object Management Group (OMG) has developed a mapping between CORBA and COM/DCOM that is supported by several products. Distributed/collaborative enterprise architecture. The distributed/collaborative enterprise architecture emerged in 1993 (see

Distributed/Collaborative Enterprise Architectures). This software architecture is based on Object Request Broker (ORB) technology, but goes further than the Common Object Request Broker Architecture (CORBA) by using shared, reusable business models (not just objects) on an enterprise-wide scale. The benefit of this architectural approach is that standardized business object models and distributed object computing are combined to give an organization flexibility to improve effectiveness organizationally, operationally, and technologically. An enterprise is defined here as a system comprised of multiple business systems or subsystems. Distributed/collaborative enterprise architectures are limited by a lack of commercially available object orientation analysis and design method oops that focus on applications. Usage Considerations Client/server architectures are being used throughout industry and the military. They provide a versatile infrastructure that supports insertion of new technology more readily than earlier software designs.

Maturity

Client/server software architectures have been in use since the late 1980s. See individual technology descriptions for more detail.

Costs and Limitations

There a number of tradeoffs that must be made to select the appropriate client/server architecture. These include business strategic planning, and potential growth on the number of users, cost, and the homogeneity of the current and future computational environment. Dependencies If a distributed object approach is employed, then the CORBA and/or COM/DCOM technologies should be considered (see Common Object Request Broker Architecture and Component Object Model (COM), DCOM, and Related Capabilities). Alternatives Alternatives to client/server architectures would be mainframe or file sharing architectures. Complementary Technologies Complementary technologies for client/server architectures are computer-aided software engineering (CASE) tools because they facilitate client/server architectural development, and open systems (see COTS and Open Systems--An Overview) because they facilitate the development of architectures that improve scalability and flexibility.

Component Based Architecture

Introduction

Purpose

Industry's shift to **Component-Based Architectures (CBA),** a new enterprise architecture (EA) process for delivering applications, has fueled a tremendous amount of interest in the media over the past few years. With the search for the silver bullet that solves the continuing problems of integrating enterprise solutions as fervent as ever, IT organizations everywhere have jumped on the CBA bandwagon in hopes that it might finally ease the IT planning burden. As one might guess, it is not that simple. The purpose of this white paper is to provide a context for the rise of CBA, sort through the major issues, and provide guidance to the government business and technical managers so that sound business decisions can be made with respect to this key technology approach.

Scope of Paper

This paper briefly provides background on component-based architectures, discusses the business drivers that led to the rise of CBA, outlines the challenges and enablers of CBA, and provides some guidance on implementing CBA in government organizations. These issues will be touched at a high level. This paper is not meant as a comprehensive discussion of the various component technologies and the details of the processes that should be in place in order to build these systems with component-based architectures. The authors recommend the reader see the references provided below for further information on these topics.

Audience

This paper is intended as a vehicle to provide guidance on the implementation of component-based architectures to upper- and mid-level government executives with overall responsibility for the management of IT services with their organization. It is not intended to provide detailed insights to technologists or architects looking for a specific methodology for engaging this new architecture paradigm.

Succeeding with Component-based Architectures

Background

Component-Based Architectures represents a major shift in the IT industry from the traditional software development paradigm. Evolved from object management approaches, the component model enables a "plug and play", solution integration alternative to the custom-development oriented, "design, code, and test" development methodology. As the IT industry has transformed around this new computing model, it is incumbent on government IT organizations to transform their solution development life cycle processes to gain the promised benefits: shorter time to market, lower risk, modular and adaptive systems.

A software component in today's world is any piece of pre-written code that defines interfaces and can be called to provide the functionality that the component encapsulates. Components are typically packaged in "industry standard" ways so that they can be called from multiple languages, or from multiple environments.

Growth in component development and integration has been fueled over the past decade by a number of factors including a desire by organizations to achieve greater levels of reuse, the availability and popularity of component-based technologies, and increasing pressure to reduce time-to-market. These factors have combined to create a vibrant market in third party components that can be reused by organizations building applications for themselves and others.

For the most part, however, these components have generally been fairly fine grained in nature and/or highly specialized, such as GUI widgets or scientific libraries, and have been developed by outside organizations. Developers incorporate such components based on their knowledge of the component market or the components that come bundled with whatever integrated development environment (IDE) they happen to use. Comparatively little reuse of internally developed code has been seen within development organizations other than by developers using snippets of code they themselves had previously written for another project. Reuse of this type often introduces issues arising from version management, or lack thereof, of these snippets. Logic changes in the original code base are rarely propagated to the descendents, thereby allowing bugs to live on for some period of time.

At the other end of the spectrum, reuse has been sought in the form of full COTS applications. SAP, People Soft, Seibel, and Oracle, among others, provide high-end business applications designed to support large portions of an organization's information needs. The approach to implementation of these packages differs significantly from that of fine-grained reuse discussed above. Generally, system integrators or integration teams have been responsible for these installations and have typically had a difficult time customizing them and creating seamless communication between them and other existing business applications.

CBA in the Context of the EA Lifecycle

Building an application architecture from components requires that the overall architecture be divided into "modules" of software with very well defined interfaces and that it be implemented using a compatible set of technologies to ensure interoperability. Identifying the appropriate decomposition is difficult at best and is confused further by the fact that problems can often be solved in a variety of ways. The goal is a solution that minimizes the impact of likely changes in the architecture and aligns with the direction of the organization while providing the best ROI.

The EA lifecycle is concerned with precisely these issues across the enterprise. Typically focused at the coarse grain level, EA looks at the overall business processes and the data, applications, and technology infrastructures that support them. For example, the context in which a COTS package will fit is defined at this level. But even further, this same business modeling activity can also be used to identify opportunities for finer-grained component reuse as the information needs of various organizations are analyzed. Often similar information needs surface across organizations and can be delivered in very similar ways.

In fact, history has shown that information technology evolves at a much greater rate than other factors that affect enterprise architecture. Business processes change, by comparison, more slowly and the information requirements even more slowly. From this we infer that investment in understanding the business and its information needs will pay dividends for a longer period than focusing on the technologies, which are likely to change in a relatively short period. For this reason, detailed analysis and documentation of the business architecture of an enterprise is built into the majority of EA frameworks including the FEAF, the TEAF, and the C4ISR Framework, and should be included in the process of defining and building a CBA.

Business Drivers and Benefits

In recent years the necessary ingredients have become available to enable the vision of CBA. With the market acceptance of two of the leading enablers, the Java 2 Platform, Enterprise Edition (J2EE) and the ".NET" platform, standards-based technical platforms that support reusable components are becoming the norm. This is giving organizations the confidence to build the architectures needed to consume components from internal and external sources. These standards are also opening the door for independent software suppliers to provision components for public consumption. To broker the supply and demand for components, marketplaces, such as Component Source and Flash line, have emerged to meet the demand for application components.

The result is that organizations are now architecting their systems to consume components. Based on the architecture, they can determine how to acquire the components they need - purchase them from the marketplace, build them internally, harvest them from legacy applications, or commission their development by outside providers. Purchasing commercial components is much less expensive than building the functionality internally. Assembling components into applications takes less time than building systems from scratch. And, because publicly available components have been tested under real world conditions, the quality of the systems developed using the CBA approach is improved as well. This section discusses some of the main drivers for adopting CBA and the benefits from this approach.

Adaptable & Flexible Infrastructure

Substantial benefits of CBA are derived from the establishment of a common and interoperable information infrastructure upon which application components and services can be built. This results in an adaptive and resilient architecture that enables faster time to market of new capabilities together with a lower cost of operation. These lower costs are realized by eliminating the need for each program to develop its own set of infrastructure services, thereby reducing stove pipes while enhancing information sharing and interoperability.

By architecting an application as a set of layered components that expose services to higher layers and uses services of lower layers, the CBA approach creates applications that are inherently easier to understand and maintain. Further, by encapsulating functionality, the "plug-and-play" nature of components makes it easier to replace functionality as business requirements change: unplug the old capability and plug in a new one.

This encapsulation also helps prevent application architecture degradation. Over time as systems are modified to reflect changing requirements, the architecture typically deteriorates. What may have started out as a straightforward and clean design becomes a tangled web. CBA minimizes this effect by providing a structure in which components can be replaced to upgrade the functionality without significantly affecting the rest of the system.

Further, the CBA approach creates an adaptable infrastructure (e.g., using Web Services and enterprise application integration EAI) that facilitates the introduction of new channels for access and delivery. For example, wireless access, voice response/synthesis, system to system access (using XML), portals, and a multitude of other access methods are enabled. Architecting the user interface of an application (the presentation) as a separate layer from the control logic and the business functionality, allows new channels of access to be introduced without impacting the core functionality of the system. An ancillary benefit is that the potential life of the application is extended, further increasing the ROI of the system.

Consistent Application of Policy and Guidance

Government agencies are also finding that they operate based on business rules that are similar if not identical to those used by other agencies. Unfortunately, these similarities are not identified until too late in the process. Again, due to the lack of mature enterprise architecture processes, these rules are often implemented multiple times in slightly different forms, frustrating efforts to reuse the capabilities, integrate the systems in which they live, or more importantly apply the rules consistently across the enterprise. These almost parallel efforts drain critical resources in many ways including duplication of initial cost of development, ongoing system maintenance of multiple versions, and system integration.

Recognizing these issues, organizations are striving to establish enterprise architecture processes that will identify potential areas where capabilities can be shared and are establishing solution development life cycle (SDLC) processes to support component development and reuse.

Time to Market/Mission Fulfillment

Building a major application from scratch takes considerable funding and time, and also presents significant risks. Capabilities can be delivered more quickly through assembly of components than by building all of the functionality from scratch. Even in cases where components do not (yet) exist to meet all the functional requirements of an organization, development of the new components can be commissioned and proceed in parallel - again reducing the time to market.

In addition to the initial application development, CBA significantly aids the modification and enhancement of systems. In many cases, a component can simply be unplugged and replaced with a new component that meets the new requirements. Where coding changes are required, the modularity of the system makes it much easier to understand the logic and make changes to the appropriate components, again reducing time to market.

The improved time to market translates into being able to provide better system support for the agency's mission and to respond to changes in legislation, regulations, and executive orders. The result is better service to the citizens.

Lifecycle Cost and Risk Mitigation

In today's budget-constrained environment, CBA offers a practical way to reduce system lifecycle costs and implementation risks. Cost savings result not only from the ability to reuse components within a CBA, but also from reduced integration effort. The savings associated with reuse can be significant: even components that need to be modified slightly for a given application typically cost only 20% of what it would cost to develop the same component from scratch.

Most of these savings arise not from the reuse of the software per se, but from leveraging all of the requirements analysis, design, and testing effort expended to create it. Similarly, by working within the established framework of a CBA, the integration costs and risks are lower than with an ad hoc set of interface conventions created by each project.

Finally, we note that using proven components within a proven framework not only reduces costs, but also eliminates unknowns that drive technical, cost, and schedule risk. In this manner, risk and cost is more tightly confined to the new components being developed.

Interoperability and Information Sharing

One of the greatest challenges facing large, multi-discipline organizations is the failure of target systems to interoperate and effectively share critical information. Leading organizations around the world (governments, standards groups, technology suppliers and integrators) have struggled to achieve interoperability and information sharing goals. This struggle is evidenced by the number of government interoperability initiatives and the plethora of standards organizations created to address shortcomings. Recent evidence from well funded research efforts indicates that these interoperability and information sharing problems are not technology or standards problems, but problems associated with poor IT planning and EA processes. As it turns out, the interoperability and information sharing deficiencies that enterprise users are experiencing can, in fact, be avoided if the IT value chain and business stake holders can develop better "blueprints" that document key interfaces and information sources. Today's technologies, or building materials, are quite capable and can enable a high degree of integration and information sharing. The key is not in picking "the best technology" but having viable "blueprints" that translate business needs into technical solutions.

Thanks to a comprehensive study commissioned by the Department of Defense in 2000 (Dep Sec Def: Electronic Commerce Coalition Working Group), and an analysis of related industry studies, we find the answers to interoperability challenges to be within reach but not easy to attain. Root cause analysis of the problem indicates that the problems are in EA documentation methods and governance models.

Business process owners and CxOs must identify interoperability and information sharing needs up front. Analysis of these needs must be performed at the enterprise level - above the individual project level. Implementation approaches, systems interfaces, and integration points must be defined. Establishing a common and interoperable information infrastructure is a critical success factor that is hard to achieve with the current government funding models. The output of IT planning and EA processes must be modified to support component-based architecture and leverage a common library of components and specifications/interfaces.

IT Value Chain and Business Stakeholder Alignment

Getting stakeholders to come to agreement is often half the battle when it comes to building large systems. Agreement provides the foundation for marshalling resources and making the hard decisions that will inevitably come over the course of the project. But reaching consensus is not always easy.

The starting point for reaching agreement among stakeholders begins with a common understanding of the system to be developed and the process by which it is developed. The first provides the what, the second provides the how. CBA helps in both these dimensions.

From an IT value chain perspective, CBA forces clear specification of interfaces which enables suppliers and customers to agree on exactly what a component must do. Service Level Agreements (SLAs) and other agreements can be written around this agreed upon functionality.

From a Business stakeholder perspective, interface specification means clear agreement on responsibilities of systems that support different business units. Further, reuse of components across the enterprise means common application of business rules. Business units that push component reuse are generally better aligned operationally as well.

CBA Implementation Challenges

In light of the significant business drivers and benefits to CBA, one might wonder why the industry is not further down the road. The answer is that there remain significant cultural and process impediments to the adoption of CBA and these impediments combine to create a significant barrier to organizations trying to implement a CBA program. The following sections describe each of these impediments in more detail.

Cultural and Bureaucratic Impediments

Software development has historically been an industry of creation rather than one of manufacturing. The flexibility of the medium allows developers to realize virtually anything they can imagine. Higher education institutions value experimentation and research over "engineering" when it comes to computer science and so students making the transition to employees bring with them the predisposition to create rather than reuse. Further, creating a new and innovative solution is more appealing than "brushing off" a dusty, old component and plugging it into a brand new application.

Over time the habits of developing from scratch have become engrained in the culture and bureaucracy of organizations. Only with a top-down and bottom up assault will the change occur. Executives must commit both the time and money to the change process. Training, tools, and incentives must be committed in order to make headway. Similarly, higher education institutions must provide a more reasonable balance between research and engineering so that the workforce is replenished with skilled engineers. Unfortunately, all this takes time. Organizations must make the commitment and be in the game for the long haul.

EA, SDLC and Asset Management Process Challenges

Agencies face significant process-oriented challenges to implementing CBA. These can be grouped into three major areas: Enterprise architecture process challenges, SDLC challenges, and asset management challenges.

Early Federal enterprise architecture processes do not include the steps necessary to create a component architecture. Although the FEAF and C4ISR Framework embrace component reuse as one of the eight principles, the process for implementing this guideline and for leveraging reusable components is lacking. As a result, agencies are on their own to create such a process, if they intend to create a component architecture.

Likewise, the primary systems development methodology in use by the Federal government is a waterfall process, although to some extent object-oriented approaches are in use and some functional requirements are met by purchasing commercial packages. These SDLC processes, in general, do not incorporate the necessary steps to create a component architecture or to assemble and implement systems from components.

The processes and infrastructure are also missing in the Federal government to manage software assets produced by a component-based approach. The lack of a Federal component repository that can be easily searched for Federal off-the-shelf components is a major inhibitor to the adoption of CBA. If developers cannot easily locate relevant components, they typically build the (redundant) functionality themselves.

Legacy Technologies and Architecture

Unfortunately, the vast majority of legacy applications are stove-piped systems that do not lend themselves to interoperability with newer component technologies nor facilitate the establishment of a common "plug and play" infrastructure. Even though current implementation initiatives are leveraging COTS and component technologies, monolithic and isolated legacy applications present a significant impediment to the successful adoption and incorporation of CBA into the IT landscape. Evidence of these challenges has been noted in three separate study efforts: ICH sponsored ECCWG Software Quality and Interoperability WG (in partnership with IAC, AFCEA and NDIA), SEI's COTS initiative, and AF Scientific Advisory Board's April 2000 report on Challenges of Integrating Commercial Items into AF mission systems. The evidence points to failures in the architecture process and not in the viability of the technologies. These patterns of failure result from the inability of the EA process to adequately model the business and to adopt a set of interoperable solutions.

Stakeholders require the legacy systems in order to run their businesses and are unable to give them up until replacements are fielded. In the transition to a component-based architecture, stable legacy assets can often be wrapped with component facades to obtain a suite of services at a cost lower than for new development. During the transition, the new and legacy technologies will coexist and must be managed.

Skills Mix

Further complicating the issue, a new set of skills is required to realize reuse in general and CBA in particular. As discussed later in the document, the emphasis of the development process shifts to business modeling, process and application factoring, architecture, COTS evaluation, integration and testing. Architecture skills, the skills needed to produce the "blueprints" and "building codes" for systems, are lacking in most agencies. Organizations are currently focused on where, in their view, the "rubber meets the road" - coding. Particular attention is paid to implementation technologies to the detriment of other skills such as requirements, design and integration. Even more "mature" organizations, while focused more closely on the entire SDLC process, typically do not place the appropriate amount of emphasis on the skills needed for reuse and CBA.

In the new paradigm, coding skills are giving way to component integration skills, although user interface coding is still required, along with development of the "glue code" that ties all of the pieces together. The change in the skills mix does not mean that the overall staffing level should be decreased, rather that the staff is able to produce more and higher quality products.

Budget and Funding Structure

CBA by design emphasizes shared capabilities that can be used by many applications. As stated above, however, this requires analysis and design across the organizations and applications that might reuse the components. Federal budgets and funding, on the other hand, are structured along the concept of a single application or mission. This disconnect makes it difficult to fund construction of the common infrastructure or common components that will eventually benefit multiple applications. The problem is evident within individual agencies, but is even more severe in a cross-agency context. Cross-cutting efforts such as the eGov initiatives, however, are beginning to pave the way for the kinds of cooperative efforts that will be essential to realizing the benefit of CBA.

Licensing and Intellectual Property

One of the key prerequisites for the successful implementation of CBA is that the architects selecting components for inclusion into an application architecture be confident of the performance of the components. This level of confidence goes well beyond technical performance to include such factors as quality (is the component "certified" and will the performance of the component degrade over time?), maintainability (who will fix it if there is a problem?), support (is there help desk support available to help sort things out?), warranty (will someone fix or replace it if something is wrong, and for how long?), and prospects for the continued existence of the "owner" of a component (what if the company goes out of business?).

From the component architect or developer's perspective, issues such as property rights and licensing are important, as well. For example, if a Federal contractor develops a component using their own technology, who owns it? If it is public domain, how can they be compensated for reusing it elsewhere? If component development is federally funded but contains proprietary components, how is it distributed for reuse? Web Services adds another dimension: Service Level Agreements (SLAs) to define availability, response, performance, etc. characteristics. Who do you negotiate the SLA with? Assessing all these factors brings us to the concept of intellectual property (IP) and licensing issues.

Software component licenses address many of these factors. However, there are still significant issues, particularly for large-grained, enterprise components. Commercially available components come with license agreements that spell out the terms discussed above and define who and under what circumstances the component can be used (e.g., single CPU, single site, department-wide, agency-wide, Federal government-wide, etc.).

Government produced components (GOTS) have other issues as well. First of all, the issue of ownership has to be resolved. Public domain components are "owned" by all, and, therefore, by no one. How is the confidence level of the architect assessing the component to be established? Sharing non-commercial components across organizational boundaries (including states, local governments, educational institutions, etc.) may require exercising intellectual property release processes that currently may be lengthy or cumbersome. Agencies may need to refine their contract language and intellectual property release processes before the full benefit of CBA can be realized. Agencies will have to assume a role of responsibility for components they have created and released.

A common approach to describing, managing and licensing components is needed across government. Architects searching for components need to know where the component comes from, who maintains it and how they can use it. If there is no license agreement that spells these things out, another mechanism must be developed.

Key Enablers

The road to effective CBA is long and as described above, riddled with potholes. Recent advances in the market have filled in some of these holes. Taking advantage of these enablers, described in more detail below, will smooth the road to adoption tremendously.

Component Technologies

With the market acceptance of component technologies such as Common Object Request Broker Architecture (CORBA), Common Object Model (COM), the Java 2 Platform, Enterprise Edition (J2EE), and the ".NET" platform, as well as EAI technologies such as Message Oriented Middleware (MOM), XML, and Web Services, standards-based technical platforms that support reusable, interoperable components are becoming the norm. This is giving organizations the confidence to build the architectures needed to consume components from internal and external sources. These standards are also opening the door for independent software suppliers to provision components for public consumption.

Commercially Available Components

Along with the new component technologies has come a wealth of commercially available components. Go online and search for software components and you will find a broad array of components of all sizes available from a variety of sources. Each year, we find a greater percent of the business model being supported by both large and fine grain COTS (and GOTS) components. The question is no longer if or when, but HOW one will apply this new paradigm.

The richness of the market includes all kinds of components: GUI components, mathematical components, supply chain components, workflow components, infrastructure components and many more are available for purchase. Some component solutions are offered as bundled sets either as part of an application server such as WebSphere™ and WebLogic™, or as add-ons. Finding the right component is a different matter but the fact remains that there is a rich market waiting to be tapped.

Standards and Best Practices

Since the mid-90s, commercial best practices, along with a rich, standards driven market, have supported and evolved the CBA process and the underlying technologies. Leading IT organizations in finance, telecom, manufacturing and distribution have adopted this approach and have demonstrated patterns of success. Best practices captured from Delta, Air Products, GM, and Bank of America have identified a set of factors required to transform the SDLC process.

It is the lack of a common technical infrastructure that inhibited widespread adoption of CBA during the 90s, even though the component paradigm was in use by some organizations. One of the main reasons organizations have embraced CBA and supporting component technologies such as J2EE, .NET, and Web Services is the wealth of deployment environments available in the market and the wealth of services they offer. Due to industry-accepted interoperability standards, it matters less what component technology is chosen than that the standards are complied with. Modern application servers offer sophisticated transaction management, integration with TP Monitors, relational database management systems, systems management consoles, directory services, and email servers, as well as both horizontal and vertical scaling. Further, the relatively close adherence of these products to industry or de facto standards provides a level of risk reduction that was not available in the past.

Along with the standards come best practices. These practices are derived from years of experience in solving the problems currently facing the Federal agencies and are often presented as patterns. Business patterns, interoperability patterns, lower-level design patterns, and even coding idioms have been available for many years in published forms such as Martin Fowler's Analysis Patterns or in the Rational Unified Process(RUP). They can be exploited to provide a jump-start for adopting CBA.

BRM as the Starting Point for Service Oriented Architecture

Initially published by the Federal Enterprise Architecture - Program Management Office (FEA-PMO) in 2002, the Business Reference Model defines business functions and sub-functions and relates these to the agencies that perform them. This high level business model is meant to provide the foundation for common understanding of business processes across the Federal government in a service oriented manner. It provides input to the EA lifecycle that enables each agency to define an enterprise architecture as mandated by Clinger-Cohen based on a common business model. As such, it represents a significant step forward in reaching a common understanding as to how services are provided to citizens across the Federal government. Agencies that perform the same function can either share system support or can be reorganized to factor out the common function and thereby operate more efficiently. When coupled with a Service Oriented Architecture (SOA), agencies can directly trace component development to agency mission fulfillment.

CBA Critical Success Factors

The move to component-based architecture has many benefits and rewards for those agencies that successfully transform their organizations and processes to enable this paradigm shift. Successful transition can only be achieved, however, by paying close attention to the factors described in the following sections.

Service Oriented Architecture

The shift to a services-oriented mindset is one of the most important, yet most difficult, factors in succeeding with CBA. It affects virtually all aspects of IT from business analysis to funding and procurement, as well as network architectures. Breaking the silo, isolated functionality way of thinking about applications is critical in adopting CBA. In fact, a services-based approach is most likely the only way to achieve the systems flexibility and adaptability required by government agencies. The manner in which the services approach is implemented is subject to some variation; however, the basic services approach is a fundamental requirement.

Industry experience and best practices lead us to three ingredients of the service-based approach: components (CBA), layered architectures, and architecting for interoperability. Implementing a services approach through a component-based architecture represents the most practical means of achieving the goals of IT. Components offer consistent ways of providing functionality that can be reused by implementing it in multiple, different applications or by invoking the functionality from a single location (as in web services).

For understandability and ease of use, the component architecture should be structured in layers. This layered approach provides a separation of purpose and allows developers to specialize their skill sets, so that each developer does not have to be an expert at everything. At a minimum, the layers should include: presentation, workflow, business, common, infrastructure, and operating system. The presentation layer manages the user's interface with the system; the workflow layer controls the interaction of the clients and the services; the business layer provides services specific to the business application, the common services layer provides business functionality that is common to multiple business areas (such as currency conversion in financial applications); infrastructure level services include those necessary for the application to function properly (such as error/exception handling, audit trails, etc); and, operating system services include low level activities such as secure access to system resources and monitoring system performance.

The component architecture must also be designed for interoperability. Functionality should be consistent and non-redundant ("normalized") through a series of architecture templates. It is not necessary that components reside on the same technical platforms; they must simply adhere to the common standards and be able to operate as "good citizens" within the ecosystem.

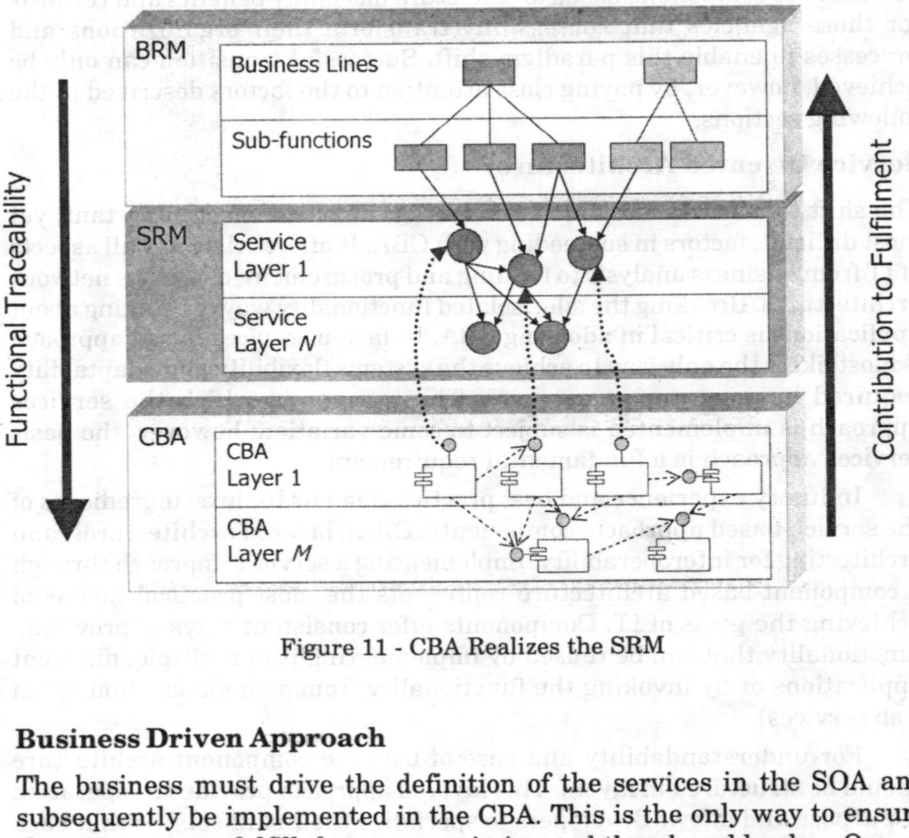

Figure 11 - CBA Realizes the SRM

Business Driven Approach

The business must drive the definition of the services in the SOA and subsequently be implemented in the CBA. This is the only way to ensure that components fulfill the agency mission and thereby add value. Once a business driven approach is established, justification of IT related initiatives becomes much clearer due to the direct trace ability from the business need to the components.

The starting point for this approach is the capture and definition of a business modeling. As discussed above, Agencies should use the BRM as input to their efforts so as to facilitate commonality across the Federal government. The process must go further and define the details of the strategies of the organization, the business drivers and the details of the processes that fulfill those needs. In doing so, activities and artifacts are identified and defined as part of a glossary of terms. These business entities or artifacts are used throughout an organization during the execution of one or more processes. At each step in a business process a worker changes an entity slightly or creates new entities from existing entities. By creating a layered architecture, components that manage the life cycle of business entities can be reused in many applications throughout the organization. Further, since these "business components" are implemented once and shared by all the applications, the organization reduces the risk that different business rules will be enforced in different parts of the organization. The same holds true for other aspects of the architecture, such as presentation logic and data management logic.

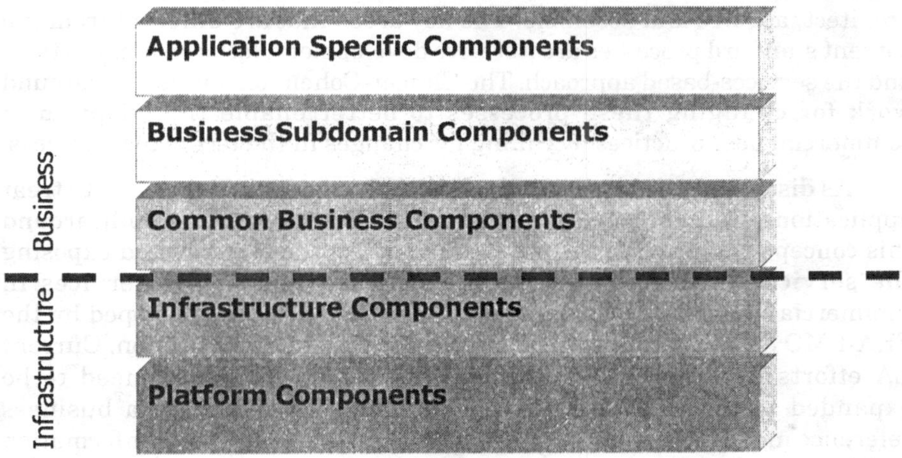

Figure 12 - Component Layering

Organizational Transformation

Another critical success factor in the adoption of CBA is a fundamental transformation of the way in which organizations carry out the IT process. Industry has sought to institute new processes that better align stakeholder views of the IT value chain. This desire to transform and mature the process to a more engineered and component assembly process such as that found in the manufacturing and construction industries, has been driven by the demand for more adaptable and flexible systems. The era of monolithic applications controlled by a centralized IT organization has given way to a decentralized framework in which the IT and business organizations partner to accomplish the overall mission.

The organizational transformation includes several aspects process, structure, and approach. The approach to building applications that support the business mission must evolve to a services-oriented way of thinking.

This involves both the business and IT sides because of the close collaboration required between the two. Applications must be viewed as collections of services grouped together for development or usage convenience. The organizational processes must be altered to reflect the services approach and to encourage the reuse of existing services or components. The organization must be properly structured to facilitate this collaboration and the modified processes required.

Revised Solution Development Lifecycle Process

A critical success factor in establishing adaptive systems that can evolve with both changing requirements and emerging technologies is the adoption of a new software development life cycle that integrates CBA. The IT process must change from a software design, code and test approach to one of architect, acquire and assemble. The key areas that are different from the current standard processes are iterative development, focus on architecture, and the services-based approach. The Clinger-Cohen Act has laid the ground work for changing these processes to better enable the adoption of commercial best practices by calling for changes in the technology process.

As discussed above, the fundamental change in the process is to treat applications as collections of services. The process must be built around this concept and provide the means of defining the services and exposing the services in legacy systems, as well as locating the services in commercially available components. The SDLC process developed by the FEA-PMO SAWG represents a constructive step in this direction. Current EA efforts like the C4ISR Framework (DOD), and FEAF need to be expanded to incorporate a component mind set including a business reference model, validated component frameworks, interfaces/information sharing opportunities, and component "building-codes." Government and industry should collaborate in establishing these building code specifications based not on standards alone but taking into account emerging technology innovations and implementation/testing advances.

The second area for major process redesign is in the area of architecture. In CBA, architectures are developed at several levels. At the highest level, the Enterprise Architecture is created to align all of the business and IT drivers. At the next level, the Application Architecture is created to distribute the normalized services (i.e., non-redundant functionality) across applications. The applications consume components (or the services from them) and a Component Architecture is created that defines the structure of components and how they relate to each other.

The third area of process change is from a sequential (ako, waterfall) process to an iterative process. This concept applies at virtually all levels of the SDLC. For example, at the architecture level, the Application and Component Architectures are developed in conjunction with the search for and assessment of off-the-shelf (COTS and GOTS) components: existing components are factored into the architecture so that they can be taken advantage of. At the development level, the process of producing the application is separated from the process of producing the basic functionality (the "twin track" approach). The application is developed by consuming available components and is incrementally improved as enhanced components become available. The overall development process evolves into an acquire, assemble and test process.

Effective Software Asset Management

One of the key success factors in implementing CBA is the ease of locating, understanding, and using components. What is needed is a mechanism for sharing, selecting and managing components and associated COTS products. This is typically accomplished by establishing an industrial strength component repository. A component repository is an application, with an associated database, designed to manage the inventory of components (and other software artifacts) available to developers. If developers have a difficult time finding a relevant component and testing it against their requirements, they simply build the functionality themselves.

Some progress has been made in providing shared information on COTS solution templates and component specification data. Upon completion of a DoD Wide study on how to implement Clinger-Cohen relative to COTS and E-Business (ECCWG), a joint government/industry initiative was established to better enable the mapping of common e-business needs to COTS solutions. This collaborative effort resulted in the formation of the Interoperability Clearinghouse (ICHnet.org), which established a number of architecture enablers including; Solution Architecture knowledge repository, series of architecture templates, and a formal COTS evaluation and selection methodology.

In recent years, a marketplace for components has emerged to broker the demand and supply of components. Companies such as Component Source and Flash line provide websites where developers and organizations can go to search for application components that meet their needs and purchase components on the spot. These companies and others offer their software as a repository or catalog that can be licensed for managing an organization's internal inventory of components. In addition, these applications are able to assist in managing the purchase and license arrangements for acquired components.

State governments have taken this approach in establishing the National Software Component Exchange (NSCE) under the auspices of the National Association of State CIOs (NASCIO). The NSCE consists of three layers: a commercial catalog of components for purchase, a national state government catalog of components available to state governments, and a state specific catalog where the components owned (acquired or developed) by a state reside. A developer can search the entire catalog for desired components and the results will be presented in order of: (1) the state already owns it, (2) there is a state-oriented component available, and (3) commercial components that can be purchased.

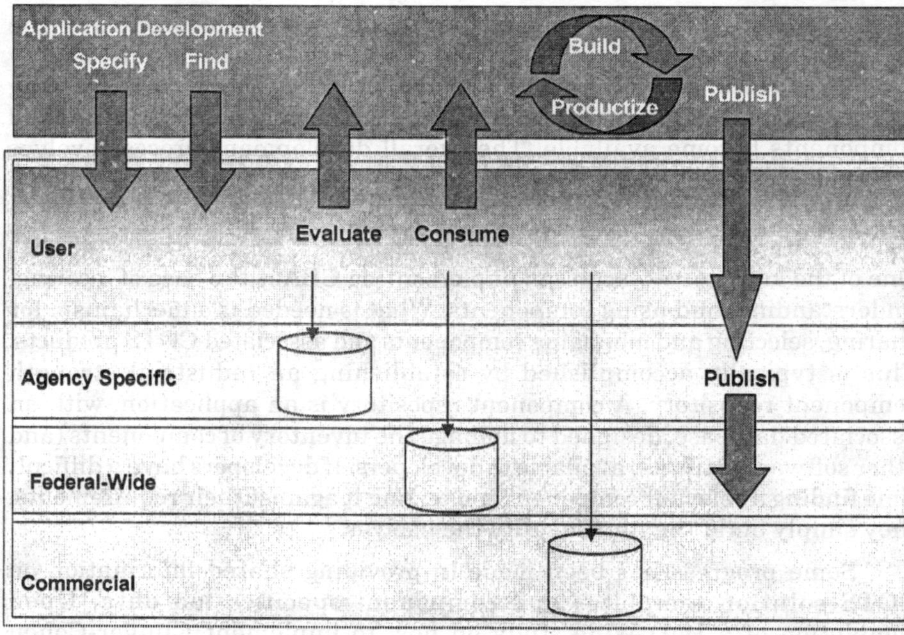

Figure 13 - Government Component Repository Needs

Establish CBA Solution Center

CBA is a relatively new approach in the solutions development lifecycle, particularly for Federal government agencies. Early realization of the benefits from CBA requires that it be adopted rapidly by the agencies - on a small scale at first and rolling it out to major programs as the successes from the initial efforts are demonstrated. As with any new technology or approach, initial efforts will provide experience that leads to best practices and patterns that will be of use to subsequent efforts. A concerted, centralized effort is required to collect these results and share them with other interested parties.

A central function should be established that is responsible for coordinating the acquisition, testing, and certifying of components for use by the agencies. One of the major IT redundancies in the Federal government is the evaluation of COTS/GOTS products - many agencies perform the same evaluation for the same products. Even though each agency's requirements may be somewhat different, there is often a core set of functionality that is common. Allowing the evaluation of products for the common functionality to be centrally performed would benefit the agencies and improve the consistency of COTS evaluations. Another aspect of this centralized evaluation function should be the testing and certification of components. Because certification benefits all agencies, its cost should not have to be borne by the first agency to acquire a particular component.

One of the inhibitors to adopting components and sharing information is the consensus hurdle: It is difficult to get agencies to agree on common definitions, requirements, products, etc. Therefore, a neutral party should facilitate reaching consensus on the many areas necessary for successful adoption of CBA. Rather than attempting to achieve a global consensus, it should be developed among a few motivated agencies and the results provided to other agencies to adopt as they are able. This would not be a static solution. The definitions, specifications, and other artifacts would evolve over time to incorporate a broader perspective.

Recommendations for OMB:

OMB should establish a CBA Solution Center. The CBA Solution Center should consist of three groups:

Process Center of Excellence - This group would focus on improving the CBA/SDLC process. Its role would be to collect, organize, and communicate CBA best practices, lessons learned, business process patterns, and other artifacts that can aid agencies as they launch CBA initiatives. In particular, the Process Center of Excellence would maintain and evolve the reference models and the linkages between them. This "knowledge management" function would most likely require automated support.

Component Integration Lab - The primary role of this organization would be to define COTS/GOTS evaluation process and perform evaluations for COTS/GOTS components with respect to common requirements. It would develop or commission the development of common components, particularly in the early phases, to jump start the adoption process and encourage agencies to consume components rather than (re)build the functionality they provide. An important role this group would play is in the certifying of components. A testing function is necessary and certification that the components perform as advertised is critical to instilling the confidence in the component for an application.

Collaboration Forum - This group facilitates establishment of consensus among agencies on business processes and data. The results of this collaboration will provide input into the SRM and the DRM: common processes and data definitions. As mentioned above, we recommend that OMB not attempt to bring all interested parties together and hope for the best, but rather bring together a few motivated agencies with specific needs to derive an initial set of process, data and service definitions that other agencies can adopt as they evolve their EAs and architect applications. Again, start small and grow from success to success.

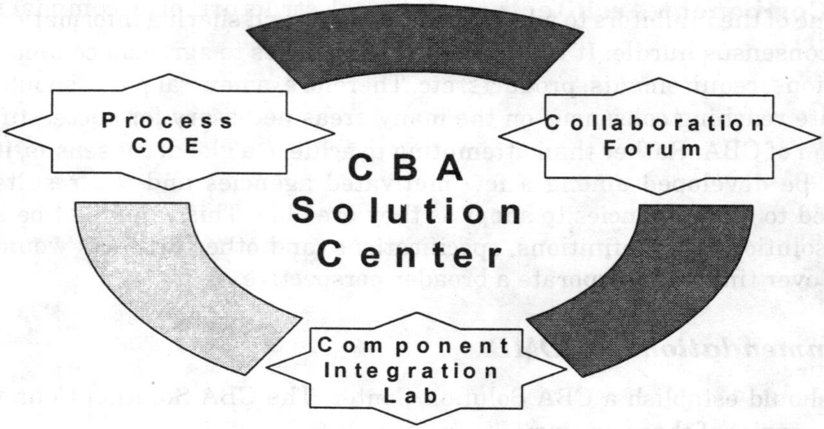

Figure 14 - Proposed CBA Solution Center

Recommendations for Agencies: The Federal agencies should contribute some of their most business-knowledgeable staff (on a detail basis) to participate in the definition of common services, processes and data. They should adopt and share best practices, business process patterns, common services and other products with the CBA Solution Center to facilitate their efforts.

The following are frequently used terms related to components and architecture

Architecture: Representation of the structure of a system that describes the constituents of the system and how they interact with each other.

Application Architecture: Representation of an application and its parts, their inter-relationships and functions.

Application Family Architecture: Representation of a related group of applications, their inter-relationships and functions. Uses the standards and policies defined in the Enterprise Architecture to ensure consistency and interoperability across all components and applications.

Business Component: Component that offers business related services - applying business rules and accessing business data.

Business Logic Component: These components are those that offer small grained business logic that have a large degree of reuse throughout the organization. They include interfaces for services such as currency exchange, remarks, code tables, customer, and address.

Component: Independently deployable unit of software that exposes its functionality through a set of services accessed via well-defined interfaces. A component is based on a component standard and is described by a specification and has an implementation. Components can be assembled to create applications or larger-grained components.

Component Architecture: Internal structure of a component described in terms of partitioning and relationships between individual internal units.

Component-Based Architecture: An architecture process that enables the design of enterprise solutions using pre-manufactured components. The focus of the architecture may be a specific project or the entire enterprise. This architecture provides a plan of what needs to be built and an overview of what has been built already.

Component Repository: Application designed to store component specifications and implementations. Provides facilities to efficiently search for and retrieve components for evaluation against desired component specifications.

Enterprise Architecture: The meta-architecture of an organization, or the sum of all architectures within an organization.

Enterprise Component: A large-grain business component. Typically consume smaller-grained components. Examples include Customer Management, Case Tracking, etc.

Infrastructure Component: A software component that provides application functionality not related to business functionality, such as error/message handling, audit trails, or security.

Interface: Mechanism by which a component describes what it does and provides access to its services. Important because it represents the "contract" between the supplier of services and the consumer of the services.

Notional Component: Set of services packaged into a component, derived from requirements definition. A "desired" component - prior to implementation.

Reuse: Any use of a preexisting software artifact (component, specification, etc.) in a context different from that in which it was created.

Service: Discrete unit of functionality that can be requested (provided a set of pre-conditions is met), performs one or more operations (typically applying business rules and accessing a database), and returns a set of results to the requester. Completion of a service always leaves business and data integrity intact.

Service Oriented Architecture: Representation of a system in which the functionality is provided as a set of services that are called by other parts of the system.

Web Service: Functionality provided by a service, which is exposed using the Internet (XML, TCP/IP) as the transport mechanism. Can be internally provided as part of a suite of services or can be offered by external organizations.

Wrapping: Creation of an interface around legacy functionality (code) that exposes the functionality as services via interfaces that conform to a component specification.

3

E-Procurement System

E-Auctions

The group operates in a highly competitive marketplace with frequent consolidations and restructuring, the group recently divested its brewing and pubs interests. Consequently they need to effectively source to meet the changing requirements of the different businesses, yet leveraging the total spend.

Working with CSC

Whitbread have outsourced the management of its information services to CSC and have begun to jointly explore opportunities that exploit new technology. Part of this process included the e-Auction opportunity, which explored the potential of e-Commerce. This would look to increase the effectiveness of competitively sourcing non-strategic commodities, improving the capability of the central sourcing group.

An integrated solution was developed after the objectives; critical success factors and evaluation criteria were defined. The key to success of the project was the integration of e-Auctions with the existing sourcing process.

E-Auctions represents a new way of working and sometimes there is apprehension on behalf of the buyers and sellers, with regard to the impact it will have on future relationships. CSC overcame this with careful communication and training, which reassured both parties as to the reason for the change and the advantages that it would bring.

The system provides an easy and efficient way to participate in e-Commerce, with limited business and capital risk. The applications require very little integration with other software, although access to the Internet and security has to be assessed. The application is capable of running several different types of auctions, with the solution being tailored to the business requirements.

The Whitbread Solution

For the solution, CSC chose BT Ignite with proven Commerce One Auction software. The application was tailored to provide a simple reverse auction in which only pre-selected suppliers participate. The auctions are completed in hours with the supplier having full visibility of all bids placed, with the actual bidder remaining anonymous. The definition of roles and the issue of individual ID's and passwords maintain system security. The final decision to award the contract is made after the auction.

CSC helped Whitbread design and develop the process and provided skills transfer to the procurement team. The joint team also validated and tested the application and piloted the first few auctions. After each auction, a review was undertaken and process enhancements made, leaving Whitbread with a robust process and a successful introduction to e-Commerce.

Business Benefits

Cutting negotiation lead-times from months to hours Achieving market prices for commodities, which on average resulted in savings of 15% Enhanced Whitbread's ability to source from other suppliers, hence reinvigorating the supplier relationship Provided Whitbread with an insight into how e-Technology can be leveraged to enhance their business. "E-Auctions are set to make a major impact on the way companies conduct their purchasing. Competitive tendering for supply contracts on-line and in real time is faster, more efficient and can generate significant operational efficiencies for both supplier and purchaser," says Steve Apted, Procurement Development Manager, Whitbread.

An Integrated Approach

Having clearly defined and agreed the project objectives, critical success factors and evaluation criteria, an integrated solution was developed addressing the process, people and application issues. Working with CSC, Whitbread has achieved savings of over 15% for a number of commodities, developed an effective integrated sourcing process and reduced the negotiation lead-time by two thirds using online reverse auctions. This e-enabled process will allow Central Whitbread procurement to maintain its leading edge sourcing capability and achieve targeted savings of £10m over three years.

Benefits Delivered

- Cutting negotiation lead-times from months to hours
- Achieving market prices for commodities, which on average resulted in savings of 15%
- Enhancing Whitbread's ability to source from other suppliers, hence reinvigorating the supplier relationships
- Providing Whitbread with an insight into how e-technology can be leveraged to enhance their business

The process

Key to the success of the project was the integration of e-Auctions with the existing sourcing process. The e-Auction replaces the negotiation process in a conventional sourcing process. A new process had to be defined and developed. This included augmenting the existing commodity selection criteria, the set up of auction parameters, training of buyers and suppliers, the set up and management of the auction event and evaluation of the results.

The people

E-Auctions represent a new way of working and inevitably buyers and suppliers are apprehensive about the impact on existing and future relationships. This is overcome with careful communication and training to ensure the reasons for change and the advantages for both parties are clearly understood.

The Application

E-Auctions provide an easy introduction to participating in e-commerce with limited business or capital risk and potentially high rewards. The applications require little or no integration with other software, however access to the internet and security have to be evaluated. The leading applications are capable of running several different types of auctions and the solution has to be tailored to suit the business requirements.

The Whitbread Solution

For the Whitbread solution CSC chose BT Ignite, with proven Commerce One Auction software. This provided an established solution with leading edge auction functionality and a commercial arrangement that allowed unlimited usage for a set period. The application was tailored to provide a simple reverse auction in which only pre selected suppliers participate. The simple solution, with limited parameters to set, enabled Whitbread buyers to be self sufficient in the Auction set-up, following some initial training.

The auctions are completed in hours with the supplier having full visibility of all the bids placed, but the actual bidder remaining anonymous. The definition of roles and the issue of individual ID's and passwords maintain system security. CSC helped Whitbread design and develop the processes and trained the procurement team. The joint team also validated and tested the application and piloted the first few auctions. Following each event a post auction review was undertaken and process enhancements made – leaving Whitbread with a robust process and successful introduction to e-commerce.

Steve Apted summarizes: "Whitbread is to review all its purchasing for its suitability for e-Auctions after making savings of over 15% in auctions carried out so far. Targeted savings of £10m have been identified. E-Auctions is a prime example of how retailers can work with technology companies like CSC to pioneer the application of leading edge technologies and IT management systems in a business environment."

E-auctions were one of the big disappointments of the dot com boom. But the three companies profiled here demonstrate growing confidence in the re-emergence of the electronic market place. Meeting Zone has set itself to support online trading with services and training, pitching its conference call services to corporate and home users. It believes that a careful business strategy and ease-of-use is why it will succeed where others have failed. Our smallest Acorn yet is an Olympic Games memorabilia website, created and supported by Mike Pagomenos. It has proved so successful that he is considering expanding the service to other areas, such as tennis.

Coubertin.com believes that having a clear niche and a strong sense of the customer will be the recipe for success. At the other end of the e-auction scale are big businesses looking for easy savings. E-auctions have the potential to reset the balance of forces in the market, weighing it in favor of the buyer. E-Three works for buyers and sellers to make sure that both sides can win. It is clear from the demise of so many dotcoms that there is a world of pain for those who err over their business models and technology choices. E-Three's co-founder James Anthony believes it is better to not shrink away from telling the customer where the pain is. Experience is also key to success. Over the years, many Acorn founders have made a network of business contacts with the larger corporations with which they once competed. It is the vital experience that can be brought to their businesses now that will prevent a repeat of the e-market place failures of previous years. Each is, or soon will be, in the black - another good reason to hear their stories.

E-Three

The key to e-auctions is to ensure a win-win for both sellers and buyers, but it's not an easy balance to pull off. Sellers may feel that online auctions depress their margins and allow large corporate buyers to drive down prices, while bumping up the conditions they need to fulfill. It is a serious danger that was recognized by the co-founders of an Acorn aimed at helping both sellers and buyers. Jenny Draper and James Anthony set up e-Three in November 2002, blending Draper's operational skills with Anthony's strategic skills. With two other full-time employees, e-Three offers training and services in the growing market for e-auctions. Buyers have taken well to the technology: it has helped them cut prices by 15 per cent. It is not surprising then that the use of e-auctions is growing at 75 per cent a year. But buyers, unless they are careful, will kill off the re-emerging market. Buyers are making life a misery for sellers, sometimes by using unethical practices. Unusually for an e-auction services company, e-Three offers services for both sides: without informed sellers, the e-auction market will stall. Sales teams will increasingly be exposed to e-auctions and they need to know how they can strike the right bargain. "E-auctions are a tool to collect information on quality and services as well as price," said Anthony. E-Three links its work for sellers and buyers with a code of ethics, Integrity Code for E-auctions, launched in November. Anthony and Draper have split their services for buyers and sellers into three layers. The first is a £600-a-day training session separately run for sellers and buyers. The second is a £5,000 to £8,000 e-auction preparation event lasting three days. The third layer is a full service to enable the buyer or seller to become an e-auction-enabled enterprise, hence the name of the company, e-Three. First year trading will generate a turnover of about £250,000, says Anthony. The second year target is £1.5m. The founders have used their own funds to start the company. "We are not in a hurry to dilute our shareholding," said Anthony.

Anthony and Draper have already been approached to set up e-Three in the US. They plan to sign a service deal with US affiliates early in 2004 and will also expand into continental Europe. Within a year they expect to have 10 full-time employees to supplement the affiliates they currently use. E-auctions can be run successfully for the sale and purchase of items from £5,000 to £500m, they say. Both sellers and buyers can benefit by slashing the buying-cycle time by 50 per cent. Sellers can gain an advantage by using e-Three's services to emphasis the quality and service of the product they are selling. One e-Three client on the seller side - Office Angels, a temp agency - was able to retain three customers that it was in danger of losing, and at a reasonable price. "It is difficult to establish the return on investment for e-Three services. But it can be thousands to one. Sellers are winning business at a higher price than before because of our services," said Anthony. One problem e-Three faces is moving from the simple sale of a £600-a-day training course to the larger consulting services deals. "We want to get embedded into clients in the long term to handle new staff coming in who need training and to help manage e-auctions," said Draper.

But to get embedded, e-Three must market to the right targets. "We ploughed about £12,000 into a direct marketing call centre campaign. We got two successes. It wasn't worth it. We have now switched marketing strategy," said Draper. The majority of people did not like being cold-called on such a subject. E-Three will use advertising to create a higher profile. Anthony and Draper are also working on a book outlining their approach which will be finished in early February. They could use an e-auction to find the best publisher.

Meetingzone

The founders of MeetingZone, Tim Duffy and Steve Gandy, were bored with the corporate lives they were leading. So, after getting together in a coffee shop in London, they came up with a plan for a conference-calling service based on internet technologies. By May 2002, they had raised £2.1m of finance: a third from board members, a third from venture firm Springboard, and a third from 'high-value' individuals. They put the technology together in eight weeks and Meeting Zone went operational in September 2002.

The advantage they had over their longer-established competition was that, the big names were caught in a whirlwind of financial difficulties with the collapse of the telecom's market. "They were milking the business and were focused on survival. We thought if we could create the best platform and the most ruthless business processes we could out-gun them from scratch," said Duffy. New customers can be using the conference call services within 30 seconds of hitting the MeetingZone site, they claim. The average call links 4.5 people for 45 minutes at about £20. Other services which supplement the audio, which accounts for 90 per cent of revenue, include web conferencing and a service called Glance where you can view another user's PC. MeetingZone's technology is in three layers. The hardware is the bridging of telecom switches, which link up to 400 people on the same call. The back end is an XML-based billing system. The front end is the website which handles presales to billing using Microsoft's .Net. Billing is the key. "The largest customers don't trust the billing of their conference call suppliers. It's inaccurate and it's late. So we invested heavily in the billing system," said Gandy. They bought the MetraNet package from MIT spin-off Metratech, which also lists MeetingZone's competitors, BT Conferencing and MCI. As a result, MeetingZone turnover is growing at an average of 20 per cent each month in a market growing at 40 per cent a year. But it has some way to catch up with the established players: BT Conferencing alone captured £12m of new business in one quarter this year. But this fast growth has allowed MeetingZone to grow to 13 people: seven in the office at Oxford and six in sales. The focus for the sales efforts are IT directors, financial directors, office managers and personal assistants. Some customers use MeetingZone to brief the managers of their retail branches, others for investor-relations calls. MeetingZone also sells its services in bulk, providing the conference call services for telcos such as Telstra.

E-Tender

Introduction

In accordance with the Law on Public Tenders (LPT) information on all current tender announcements and procedures is maintained in a database. A software product for electronic tendering called *e-Tender*, was developed to facilitate the implementation of LPT requirements. *E-Tender* may be used to enhance the transparency of the defence planning and budgeting processes seen here as a major prerequisite for transparency of a country's defence policy.

The supply and demand of goods and services are the foundation of the market economy. The market is the place where the goods and services are exchanged and their prices are set. Prices depend on the degrees of supply and demand and, thus, free market is a good regulative mechanism for large-scale realization of goods and services. Of course, for that mechanism to work effectively, it is necessary that supply is bigger than demand. This requirement, however, does not apply to some goods and services. In some cases supply is very small to satisfy the demand and does not provide for formation of market prices. For those goods and services the mechanism of an *auction* is worked out. Auction (or *tender*) is used to determine the best price that the buyers are willing to pay, as at the same time an equal chance is given to all participants. Tenders are implemented if the participants give more than is due.

Two types of tenders could be distinguished depending on the bidding procedure – overt and covert. Traditionally, overt tender is implemented as all participants meet at assigned time, in a hall, for bidding about chosen item by raising hand and saying price proposals. Everyone watches the bidding and can participate in it by offering higher price than all other participants. A tender ends when there is no more offers for bidding. That method has been proved during the years as sufficiently honorable and effective; new times, however, place new challenges. In the era of global economic developments, the trade does not recognize any geographic boundaries. People from different regions compete in a unified market, a market that has a global meaning. The conduct of traditional tenders involves traveling of a great number of participants from different geographic regions. Because of that, new forms for conducting public tenders are sought – forms suitable to overcome geographic boundaries.

Due to advances in information technology, many human activities have acquired new dimensions. Today, it is almost unimaginable to live without computers at all levels, as well as with no Internet in the sphere of global communications. There are some solutions for carrying out public tenders, as participants in several geographic points are connected through teleconference. Other solutions are based on building up a tender moment. Such solutions have many advantages, as well as some disadvantages. One drawback is the impossibility to assess the chances for success in bidding, because the number of participants is not known. That sort of tenders lasts a few days in order to allow maximum number of participants to take part in the bid. Another disadvantage is the ambiguity of the bidding process when a participant is not connected to the system virtual space by using Internet technologies, allowing users to log on for bidding in suitable.

This article offers a solution for realizing overt tenders by using Internet technologies for instant messaging. Main privilege of the solution is the relative simplicity, which means that anybody can use the tool on his or her personal computer. Furthermore, a list of all participants in the bid is maintained, thus allowing everyone to estimate their chances for success in the tender. If the bidding has already started, new participants are not allowed to take part. Last but not the least, at any time every participant receives any price announced by other participants.

E-Tender allows effective tender implementation in a few hours. The solution is directed to organisations that have wide geographic audience with similar interests.

Analysis of contemporary information technologies and their application

XML technology for representing documents

The rapid advance of Internet technologies, connecting large variety of computers in a global network, brought to fruition new methods for representing and processing information, which should be universal enough for using on different type of computer systems. The World Wide Web Consortium (W3C), an organization determining directions of WWW development, makes an important contribution. For example, a standard Hyper Text Markup Language (HTML) for representation of correlated information got a great popularity. It was developed in the beginning of the 1990's and continues to evolve. Despite the considerable achievements, HTML has its own restrictions. Because of this, its main application is to represent logically related text documents. Predicting the necessity of ways for universal representation of other types of documents, W3C initiated the development of technology similar to HTML, but much more universal. The first version of the *Extensible Markup Language (XML)* was published in February 1998. Version 4.01 was launched in 1999.

Main directions of the elaboration are following:

- Easy usage of XML in the Internet environment. Any user should be able to view a XML document as easy as HTML one. Practically, that could be achieved when XML documents' browsers become as accessible and widespread as HTML file browsers are at the moment.

- XML should maintain a large range of applications. The initial focus will be on exchange of structured documents in Internet environment, and it should not restrict the application.

- XML should be compatible with the *Standard Generalized Markup Language (SGML),* a standard introduced in late 1960's. Many organizations have large archives in that format. For this reason XML shall be created pragmatically to provide for interoperability with existing standards while, concurrently solving the challenge of sharing structured information via Internet.

- It should be easy to develop programmes that process XML documents. For example, a computer science graduate should be able to compose a program for processing XML documents approximately in two weeks.

- Also, the number of optional XML elements should be restricted to the maximum extent possible. Such elements surely cause problems of the compatibility when users start to exchange documents and sometimes even cause serious obstructions and misunderstanding.

- XML documents should be understandable and precise enough. In this way, if a user does not have an appropriate XML browser and receives XML document, he should be able to view it, in a chosen text editor, in order to obtain an idea about its content.

• XML specification design should be created as soon as possible. The standardization process is well known with its continuity.

· It should be easy to create XML documents. Indisputably, improved tools for creation of XML content will appear, but no immediate availability is to be expected. Therefore, in the initial period, it should be possible to create XML documents by already known tools such as text editors, simple commands of PERL interpreter, etc.

• XML record conciseness does not have a particular value. There are SGML attributes, which allow writing of SGML documents to be minimized. XML technology will not maintain this feature. The maintenance of these attributes would make difficult the realization of XML programme-analyser (or person who creates it). Many recent text editors give an opportunity for defining short key combinations about defined phrases, in order to be used in the writing.

So, everybody could compose his or her own XML document representing random information using uniquely requested elements. The question is how to explain to users what each element we have used means, in order to give them the possibility to read or write document with the same structure. Another approach is to create the application that deals with documents, following a defined structure. But how that application could recognize necessary elements if each author uses his own names? For that purpose SGML is designed as a language for declaring element types in the document - Document Type Declaration (DTD). The types declared by this language (DTD) are elements, element attributes and objects.

After creating the declaration of XML document, we can disseminate it, mentioning that this XML document has a structure described in already created declaration. So, all recipients of the document will know about the structure used and, in their turn, will be able to create their own documents. In that sense, the DTD declaration facilitates the practical application of XML in data representation. Moreover, the DTD has an additional advantage - using it, each author or recipient of document could check its validity. There are XML analysers for verifying the document validity based on the DTD description. Implementing XML analysers the user could be sure that the documents, which he or she communicates, adhere to the previously defined structure.

Peer-to-peer communication

Main function of the communication network is to deliver information from à transmitter to a receiver. To that purpose, all network devices have unique identifiers and the necessary communication protocols. The communication will be fully effective when the sender knows what information any recipient is interested in, and also when the recipient tells it to the sender. In such model of communication the source of information generally is called SERVER and the receiver - CLIENT. Therefore, that sort of communication is called *client-server*. Characteristic of the model is that the server has a certain number of resources, which are ready to be given to its clients. Clients in turn initiate the communication by sending requests to the server for specific information. The server waits for the client's requests and sends the requested information, if it is available, or sends a message describing where the requested information eventually could be found. In this mode, the client who sends a request initiates the communication. It is received by the server, which composes a response and sends it back to the client. In this way the communication cycle ends. The process is depicted on Figure 1.)

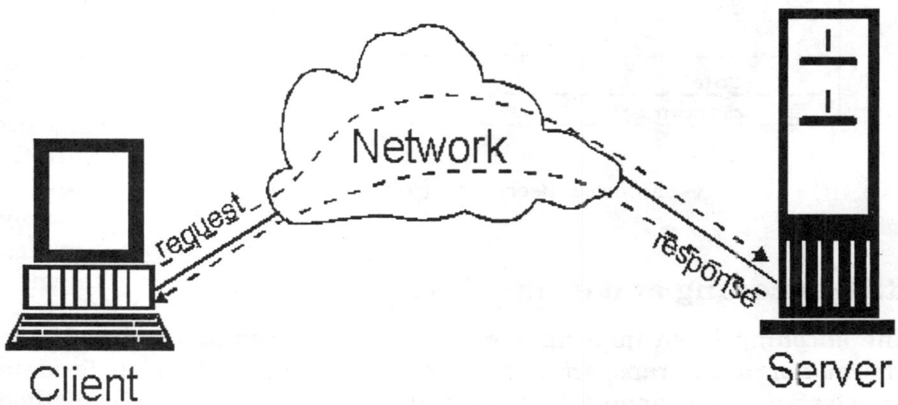

Figure 1: Client-server information exchange.

Serving as a transmitter, the station simultaneously sends and receives information. Or there could be a transmitter that may send information that has not been explicitly requested. In this case the communication is equal in value, or the so-called peer-to-peer communication. In this mode any transmitter sends information to defined receivers, without the need to have a defined request. It is sufficient that receivers should notify the transmitter that they want to receive defined information when it is accessible. At the same time, any receiver could be a transmitter to other receivers. In this mode of communication any receiver establishes initial connection with some transmitters. After connecting, the two sides could exchange information independently of each other, not needing an additional agreement. Simultaneously, both stations play roles of transmitter and receiver. Both transmitter and receiver could terminate the connection (Figure 2). Such scheme of communication is used in systems with distributed structure. Examples for such systems are distributed.net and some applications for file exchange such as Napster and Gnutella.

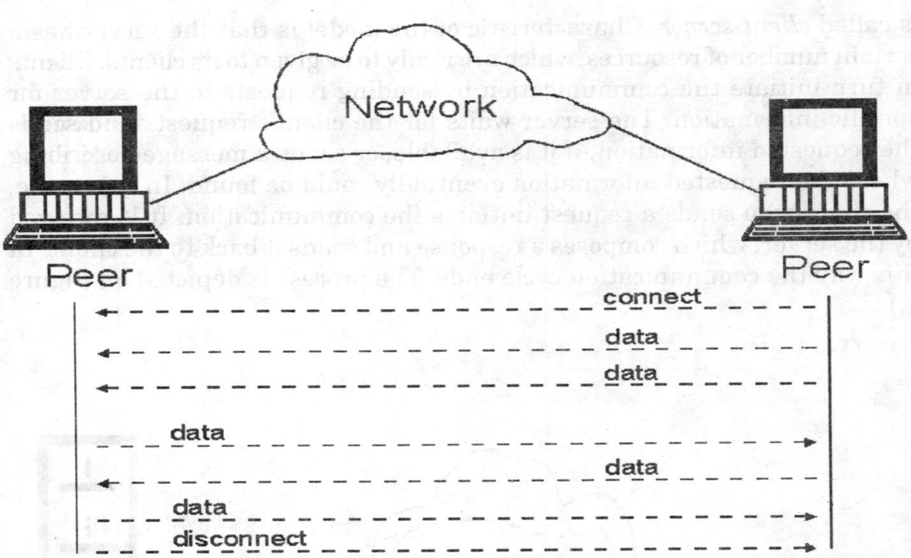

Figure 2: Peer-to-peer communication

RSA encoding and e-signature

The encoding is an important way for keeping confidentiality of the information in its transportation by using unprotected channels for data transferring. Many approaches for encoding exist, for instance the method of RSA Security, Inc. has achieved considerable popularity. The main advantage of this method is the use of pair of keys (public and private) for encoding and decoding. There is a difference between this method, where the private key could be used for decoding and other methods using only one key for both operations. Using public key only specific information could be encoded. In this case, any recipient could disseminate his own public key, but he must keep reliably the private one. Nevertheless, this is easier than delivering a key from the sender to the receiver without compromising it.

The public key is expressed by the two numbers *(e, n)*, the private one - by *(d, n),* where *e, d* and *n* are positive whole numbers. The message, which will be encoded, is expressed as a sequence of whole positive numbers less than *n* and marked with m_i. The encoding the message results in a sequence of numbers c_i less than *n*:

$$ci = m_i^e \bmod n$$

that represents the encoded massage. Obviously, in the encoding process only the public key (numbers *e* and *n*) is used. After receiving the encoded message we it is decoded as follows:

$$mi = c_i^d \bmod n$$

Decoding can be performed if the numbers *d Hn*, which represent the private key of the receiver, are known. Thus, only the owner of the private key can decode. The algorithm for composing private and public keys is of considerable importance for the security of information exchange. In order to calculate *n*, two sufficiently large prime numbers, *p* and *q*, are needed. After such numbers are found, *n* is calculated as follows:

$$n = p \quad q$$

The components of the private key d are defined through the following procedure. A whole number, which is mutually prime with the multiplication *(p-1) ´ (q-1)*, is chosen so that
The greatest common divisor (GCD) of [d, (p-1) ´ (q-1)] = 1

The public key component e is chosen using a whole number that is multipliable conversely of d by module *(p-1) ´ (q-1)*.
(e ´ d) mod *((p-1) ´ (q-1))* = 1

Despite that n is publicly known, it is not easy to find out *p ? q* and, therefore, the private key component *d*. It is difficult to find *d* because *n* is a very high number and can not be expanded into prime factors. This fact, along with the availability of two independent keys, provides for good protection of this algorithm against compromising the encoded information.

E-signature becomes more widespread in electronic communication means by analogy with a personal signature. Any formal document, which is sent electronically, needs an e-signature to prove its authenticity. E-signature requires only one person to put it - the author of the signature, and all concerned persons should be able to perform identification and verification.

Two ways for electronic signing are commonly accepted. In the first approach, the author "signs" a notice, encoding it by his private key implementing the scheme described above. Afterwards, the encoded notice is sent to respective recipients, who in their turn decode it by using the sender's public key. If decoding is successful, the recipient can be sure that the notice really is from the already mentioned sender. However, if the recipient does not possess the sender's public key, he will not be able to read it.

In the second approach the notice, without any changes, is delivered to all recipients, and the signature is added at its end. Generally, a control sum for the original notice is calculated applying an algorithm set in advance. A feature of these algorithms is that the control sum changes when any change in the notice occurs. Thus, it is guaranteed that the control sum will be different if there is an attempt to modify the notice. As a result, according to the described algorithm, the control sum is encoded applying the author's private key and after that it is added to the original notice. Alternatively, it is possible to send the encoded control sum independently of the notice. This is the so-called "detached signature."

The control of such signature is performed in a similar manner. The control sum of the document is decoded by the author's public key, and it is calculated again by using the same algorithm. Finally, both control sums are compared, and if they coincide we could be sure that the document is in the form signed by the author. Advantage of this approach is that the information in the notice is accessible to the readers, even if they are not able to verify the sender's signature. It is also interesting to note, that e-signature does not provide protection of transmitted information, due to the use of author's public key for decoding, which is widely accessible by definition. Therefore, in the most cases the notice and signature of the definite recipient could be encoded by his own public key.

Jabber technology for instant messaging

The main application of Jabber technology is an information exchange about presence and instant messaging. The Jabber instant messaging (IM) system is distinguished from other similar systems by the following key features:

- Jabber is designed on the basis of XML;
- Jabber uses distributed network of servers;
- The Jabber protocol specification and code are opened;
- The Jabber architecture is modular and extensible.

Jabber has been designed as a model of the widely popular messaging system on the Internet, namely e-mail. Similar to e-mail systems, Jabber is built up on distributed network of servers that use common communication protocol, to which specialized clients connect to receive messages as well as to send messages. Unlike traditional e-mail, Jabber delivers messages in real time because the Jabber server knows when a particular user is online. This knowledge of availability is called "presence" and it has key meaning for the development of instant messaging.

In contrast to other instant messaging solutions, Jabber communication always passes through the server. All messages and data from one client to another must go through the server. Despite the important role of the server, the communication model remains peer-to-peer. Any client is free to communicate directly to another client, but that is not recommended because it depends on (and introduces) specifics of the realization.

In the Jabber architecture model, every user has a local server, which receives information directed at him or her, and different servers transfer messages and presence information among themselves. So the client's application is simplified and the server takes care of transferring and processing information. Each server functions independently of the others and maintains its own user list and the necessary information. Also any Jabber server can talk to any other Jabber server that is accessible via the Internet. These features are shown graphically on Figure 3.

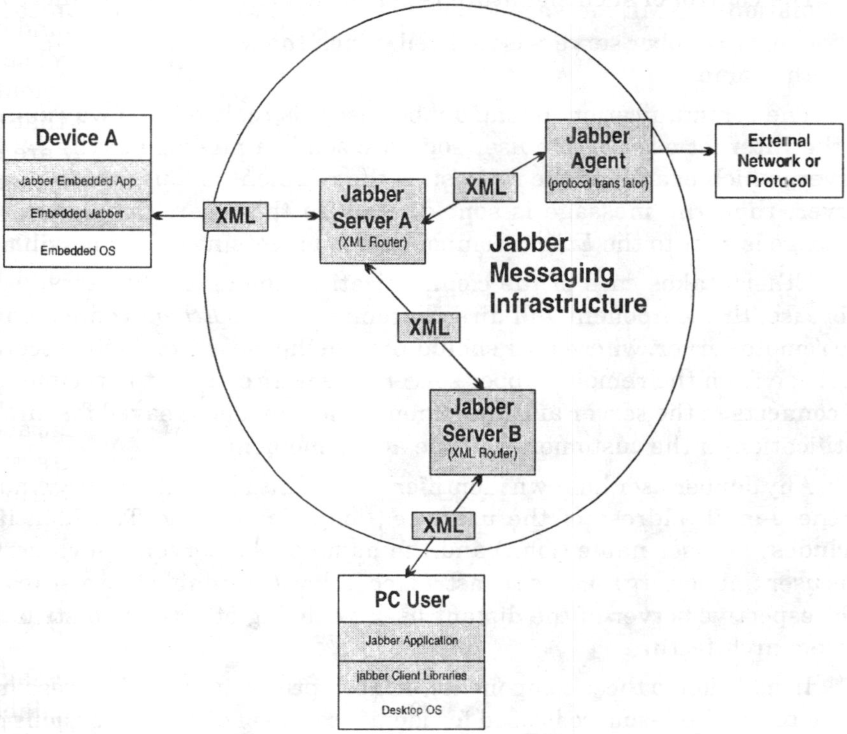

Figure 3: Jabber Architecture Model

The Jabber server is the main component in the instant messaging architecture. It performs two primary roles:

- Watching for client requests and communicating directly with client applications;
- Communicating with other Jabber servers.

The Jabber server has a modular architecture. It consists of several main modules providing respectively the following functionality: user authentication; data storage (user information, offline messages etc.); delivering messages, etc. Additional functionality can be easily added to the server. Thus, the so called "*transports*" or *protocol translators* could be added easily. With their help, a Jabber server communicates with any non-Jabber messaging.

The XML technology takes main place in Jabber's realization. It supports architecture design that is fundamentally extensible and able to use almost any structured data. The communication among architecture's components is realized by the help of *XML Streams*. Any user program creates a XML stream. Through it, the program sends and receives information in XML message form. In a similar way, the communication between two Jabber servers is realized. When the work ends, XML stream does the same.

The communication among Jabber users is realized in a way similar to the Internet e-mail. The user software sends a message to the Jabber server, which examines the request. If the recipient is a user of the same server, then the message is sent directly to this user. Otherwise, the message is sent to the *Etherx* component for processing and transmitting.

Etherx takes care of the communication among Jabber servers. In this case, the component will directly connect to the *Etherx* component of the remote server, whose user should receive the message. So the received message from the remote Jabber server is sent directly to the recipient, if he connects to the server at this moment. The message is saved for further notification, if the customer is offline at the moment.

Any Jabber user has own identifier (JID). This identifier is very similar to the e-mail address of the user, i.e., john@jabber.org. The identifier includes the user name (john) and the name of the server, which serves this user (jabber.org). JID, so constructed, allows any Jabber server to find the respective server of the distant user, realising effectively distributed system architecture.

In addition to these components, JID comprises the so-called "resource" of the user. The resource is used for identification of different sessions of a user, allowing him or her to connect to the system simultaneously from several different applications. The resource is added to the identifier, as it is written after the server name, separated by a slash for example:

john@jabber.org/Work
john@jabber.org/Home

Another important architecture feature is the maintenance of "*presence.*" This is information that shows when a user of a server is in a condition to receive instant messages. Any Jabber client is "at the disposal" when connected to the system and "absent" in the rest of the time. The main idea of the presence is to inform any customer if his interlocutors are also online and could communicate. This feature is realized as any user "*subscribes*" for other clients' presence. This system for subscription allows any user to permit the system to inform some users about his presence and to forbid this for other users. The Jabber server maintains a list with these subscriptions for any user. This list is called *roster*. It is saved on the server automatically, so the information about interlocutors is always available for users independently of the computer and user software. The Jabber server maintains the presence automatically when other users allow or forbid enquiries for a subscription. Additional information about user distribution in groups and their nicknames is saved in the roster. The user provides this information, and the roster serves for facilitation.

Architecture of the e-tendering system

The basis of any Internet application is the operational system that provides for communication in this environment. The general view of the e-Tender system's architecture is represented on Figure 4. Obviously, it does not cover the issues of the centralized server and the number of user computers. The components, building the business logic and database, are realized on a workstation. The architecture includes Jabber server and a database.

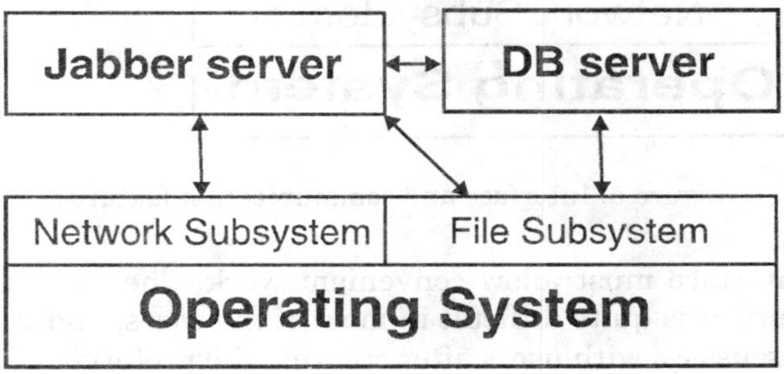

Figure 4: General of e-Tender system architecture.

The Jabber component accomplishes following functions:

- Watches for incoming user requests, that are received from clients by the network subsystem;
- Verifies JID and password, presented by the client, and permits or forbids the access of the user to the system;
- Generates messages about presence of users and sends them to the network subsystem for transfer to clients;
- Receives messages from users and processes them in accordance with the business logic, and generates needed messages about results;
- Exchanges operational information with the database;
- Processes saved messages about offline users, operating on the file subsystem;
- Processes lists of friends and user preferences, operating on the file subsystem.

The database component accomplishes the following functions:

- Operating on the file subsystem, it saves and indexes operational information on a permanent storage device;
- Executes orders for access to and changing of operational information, received from the Jabber component.

The client software runs on user computers. The main role of the client software is to provide the user interface to the system. The system architecture includes user interface component and communication component, represented on Figure 5.

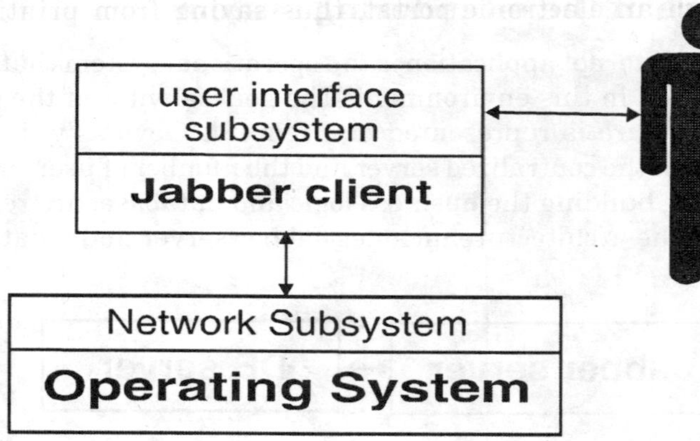

Figure 5: Interface and communication features.

The user interface must allow convenient work. The accomplishment of this requirement is quite difficult in most of the cases, and it necessitates thorough discussion with users after creating the prototype of the product. Therefore, the interface implementation needs to be separated as a component, thus allowing easy interface modification without a program breach. The communication component connects to the server, encodes and sends messages, already received from the interface, and decodes and verifies replies, which are received from the server. The exchanged messages contain information about the user presence, messages between users (chat), announcements of offered price, as well as office messages (start and end of tender, access to the list of user friends, etc.).

Data base architecture

The application has to keep operational information about users, tender goods and announcements. The tender implementation is connected to the bidding of different users for any article. Therefore, the announcements must contain information about the buyer of the article and additional requirements in accordance with the Law on Public Tenders (LPT). The intention is to use relational model for data storage allowing designers to achieve the best results in presenting of this type of information.

Business logic definition

The business logic is defined to a great degree by the necessity to realize a public tender where sellers participate from different geographic regions. Traditional variants of public tender implementation are not applicable to this requirement. Therefore, integrating advanced Internet technologies, we propose an alternative that preserves to a large extent the conventional model of tender while allowing for participation of remotely situated subjects, e.g., companies.

Economically, the implementation allows large savings from rent of proper premises and for publicity. In the electronic variant, publicity is realized through an electronic portal, thus saving from printing and distribution of advertising materials. The expenditure for computer equipment is also smaller than spending to rent an auction auditorium, proper for implementing auction activities. Last but not least, buyers are able to participate without the necessity to leave their work places or homes. Of course, such solution is directed at clients that have the knowledge for using computers and the Internet. The organizers must know the technologies used in order to respond adequately to potential problems and inquiries of consumers.

The traditional model of the public tender is used as foundation of the business logic. Information about required goods is published in advance on the virtual site of the organizer (called also host). Data about the server of the organizer, date and place of the tender are also published on it. All participants, that are interested, are invited to send needed documents in order to create their user profiles in the system. The organizer verifies all received applications and creates respective user profiles. All approved users receive messages, where their personal data for registration in the system (user name and password) is documented. The users in turn obtain software necessary to connect to the system at the announced time. The host (or user with delegated rights) will greet all clients and will give them explanations, if that is necessary. This is realized by sending instant messages to tender participants.

When the host decides that all of interested clients are online, he or she starts the tender session. The system turns into "acceptance" mode for proposals and, at the same time, suspends new user registrations. Any participant receives a list of all client names, included in the tender session, and instant information about announcements of the rest of the participants. In this regard the electronic variant aspires to maximum resemblance with the traditional one. If there is no sufficient interest on the part of clients, the host may decide to suspend the bidding. So the client, that has announced the best price, receives the right of buying. The system automatically names the winner and his announced price. With this, the tender session about this article ends and the system turns again into "registration" module for users. Thus other users are given an opportunity to be online for the next tender session. At this time the host chooses the next article, which is offered on the tender and fixes a time in order to answer new questions. After of all tender sessions are closed, users that have received rights to buy are invited to connect to the organizers by phone or e-mail in order to clarify means of payment and delivery.

The system will maintain functions of instant communication among users, exchange of data and opinions. The aim is to make the tender a means for informal meeting of clients, as in the classic variant of the auction.

The successful realization of a public web site for electronic submission of documents facilitates the achievement of the following objectives:

- public access and transparency of tenders;

• confidentiality of any company information provided and proposals made by the prospective contractors;

• possibility to ask for the opinion of "independent" experts and, thus, to expand the database for analysis and selection of a company that is appropriate for the realization of a particular project.

Another main advantage is the possibility to create a database of all companies that "successfully" execute orders and those, where project implementation is problematic. The software realization of such e-tender would also create excellent opportunities for accelerating the accomplishment of "express" requests, for example, procurement of perishable products. In addition, all those interested would be able to check what are the criteria for choosing a contractor, as well as whether criteria and procedure are in line with the Law on Public Tenders. As a whole, this problem is related to the recently widely discussed problem of the e-Government.

Reverse Auctions

Type of Reverse Auction

Hosted Reverse Auction

(Contractor provides products and services necessary to conduct auction on behalf of ordering agency). The minimum estimated dollar value of the products and/or services auctioned through the hosted reverse auction application is $500,000. The $500,000 minimum estimated order limit is exclusive of the reverse auction Enabler fee.

Dollar Value Ranges Scale - Based on the following estimated dollar value ranges of the products and/or services auctioned through the hosted reverse auction event, the contractor shall propose a fixed fee for each of the dollar values ranges listed below. The fixed fee will be the amount paid to the contractor for each auction event.

Desktop Reverse Auction

(Contractor provides software license, help desk, and web-based tutorial training) There is NO minimum estimated product and/or services auctioned through the Desktop Application.

• Monthly Subscription Fee - A monthly subscription fee for an unlimited number of auctions per month per user (individual person) using the contractor provided desk top software or access to contractor's software. Note: Fee includes help desk support (9 AM - 9 PM EST), and web-based tutorial training in the software program and in the software license agreement.

• Yearly Subscription Fee - A yearly subscription fee for an unlimited number of auctions per year per user (individual person) using the contractor provided desktop software or access to contractor's software. Note: Fee includes help desk support (9 AM - 9 PM EST), and web-based tutorial training in the software program and in the software license agreement.

Reverse Auction e-Procurement: A Suppliers Viewpoint

The increasing trends towards globalization and increased competitiveness across markets have meant that most businesses are looking to increase efficiency. Increasing efficiency by addressing workforce levels and streamlining internal operations has been a favorite of many organisations. Businesses (Minahan & Degnan, 2000: p.3) are now looking at the supply chain and procurement to provide additional efficiencies. Strategically (Minahan & Degnan, 2000: p.3) a superior supply chain increasing business responsiveness and competitive advantage. Anderson and Lee [HREF7] see the supply chain as crucial to organisations:

"The winners in the internet enabled supply chain competition will be those companies that discard the traditional rules of doing business while working collaboratively with customers and supply chain partners to create the future".

Integrating supply chains can yield substantial benefits for enterprises, from a 20-30% reduction in bottom line goods and services costs (Smock, 2001) to a 35% increase in market share (Copacino & Byrnes, 2001). This paper looks at the use of online reverse auctions and uses the case study methodology with an analysis from the viewpoint of a supplier company.

e-Procurement Research Framework

Organisations have been selling products and services to each other as long as recorded history. Organisations spend (Minahan & Degnan, 2001, p.3) over US$20 trillion on external goods and services and the supply chain is now the focus in cost reduction and efficiency increase. The Internet age has coined new terminology describing many existing business processes. Diba (Diba, 2000) refers to the need for using newer terms for old processes. B2B is the accepted term for describing a whole range of procurement type functions.

Many research organisations predict massive growth in the B2B market. Bowles sees the global B2B market growing to US$968 million in 2002 and then US$1551 million in 2004. Whilst these predictions should be accepted with caution there does seem to be a "sea change" in how procurement is operating in organisations. B2B promises (McGarvey, 2000) to drive costs down and streamline procurement operations.

Electronic commerce has increasingly adopted a wider and wider definition and can be defined as any application of information and communication technology to enable business functions. This could include phone, fax, edi-networks and the Internet. This broad definition covers the use of information technologies within the procurement function. Another definition is:

"any electronic communication that facilitates the exchange of goods, services or other assets between suppliers and buyers."

Hemond-Wilson, classified B2B as including sell-side (e-catalogues), e-marketplaces, trading partner agreements and buy-side (e-procurement). Another definition moves closer to the business process of procurement and defines e-Procurement as:

"The use of electronic technologies to streamline and enable procurement activities of an organisation."

Minhan has a definition that interchanges e-sourcing and e-Procurement:

e-Procurement is the process of utilizing Web-based technologies to support the identification, evaluation, negotiation, and configuration of optimal groupings of trading partners into a supply chain network, which can then respond to changing market demands with greater efficiency."

Activities that could be applied to the e-Procurement process include: advertising tenders; electronic submission of tenders; electronic ordering; internet sourcing via third-parties; electronic mail between buyers & sellers; electronic mail in contract management; research into supplier markets and integration of procurement within the financial and inventory systems.

E-Procurement Implementation Model

David Wyld developed an e-Procurement implementation model that looked at the E-Procurement process from drivers through impact to imperatives. The model is presented below.

E-procurement Model

Drivers		
Impacts	**Imperatives**	
Fast pace of tech innovation	Shift of power from suppliers to buyers	Internal linkage between supply chain & portal
Economic Globalisation		Develop online supplier qualification
Rapid growth of eBus portal sector	Market makers increasing competition	Leverage suppliers into e-portal marketplaces
Large orgs become market makers		Develop vertical markets to force B2B and lower costs
Vertical trading communities	New product & services requirements	Build strategic alliances e-comm players

The model above demonstrates some changes that are affecting the e-procurement value chain. Organisations on the buying and selling side will need to address these challenges to capture both the tactical cost control and more strategic market developments. The Aberdeen report divides procurement and e-Procurement technologies into three categories:

- Indirect Procurement- non-production goods & services - office supplies, printing, advertising and casual labour.
- Direct procurement/Supply chain- organisation & management of raw materials, parts and assemblies.
- Sourcing- identification, evaluation, negotiation of products and supplies for both the indirect and direct supply chain.

Most e-Procurement solutions addressing the three categories above strive to achieve the following benefits (Minahan & Degnan, 2001, p.5):

Table 1. e-Procurement Benefits by category (Minahan & Degnan, 2001: p5)

Indirect	**Direct**	**Sourcing**
Price reduction	Visibility of customer demand	Unit cost reduction
Improved contract compliance	Visibility of supply chain capacity	Enhanced decision making
Shortened cycle times	Accuracy of production capacity	Improved market intelligence
Reduced admin costs	Reduced inv/op costs	
Enhanced inventory management	Shortened proc cycle times	

The Auction Economy

In the late 1990's the Internet was being used increasingly for bidding in auction based sales. O'Malley (1998) saw the Web being "a giant bidding war" and Queree (2000) commented that online auctions were becoming mainstream business models. The auction model was settling into the B2B marketplace and also being developed for various e-Government applications. Wyld (2001, p.7) saw the auction model being used in procurement, disposition of used assets and internal management. Batsone (1999) asked the question whether the price of everything is negotiable. At the heart of the auction economy is the concept of pricing and more directly dynamic pricing. Dynamic pricing simply means that a good or service is priced according to what the market determines. The Web introduces a real-time perspective to dynamic pricing. Wyld (2001, p.12) presents a dynamic pricing model developed from Open site.

Table 2. Dynamic Pricing Categories

many	Auction(1s:Mb)		Exchange(Mb:Ms)
Buyers	Haggle(1b:1s)	**Sellers**	Bidding(1b:Ms)
one	one		many

At the heart of the auction model and dynamic pricing is the concept of personal price elasticity. Customers will determine the price depending upon the price/value trade-off. No longer is the supply/demand model determining price, a more complicated customer centric price/value trade-off determines pricing. Airlines use this principle when they have multiple price points for the one product. There are several differing auction formats used in online auctions (Wyld, 2001, pp.17). English, Yankee, Dutch, Sealed bid, Vickrey and the reverse auction are some formats used. The reverse format is the basis for this paper. Other formats include the Vickrey where the winner is the highest bidder and the winning price is determined by the second highest bidder. The Yankee auction allows for multi-item bidding with the winner being determined firstly by price, secondly by quantity and then by time bid. Free markets promote the ability of their auction format to decrease services prices by 16-18% and goods by 2-3%. These cost reductions are very attractive to buyer markets [HREF8] but it is unrealistic to expect repeated annual reductions of 20% per year. The auction format is not perfect, problems such as collusion and "winners curse" do present problems for buyers and sellers. The other pitfall of the online auction is the ability of the auction to connect buyers and sellers and therefore destroy the role of the traditional intermediary. Bowles (2000) sees this as a driving force in the development of B2B e-Marketplaces, where the e-Marketplace is replacing the function of the traditional "middleman".

Reverse Auction Process

The reverse auction process involves intensive work on behalf of the buyer and market maker to structure the bidding process and prepare suppliers for qualification. The process is represented below.

Table 3. Reverse Auction Format

1. Make Market (specs)	2. Identify Suppliers
3. Pre-Award Review	4. Approved Suppliers Listing
5. Identify Specific Terms & Conditions	6. Invite Suppliers
7. Set Up Auction	8. Conduct Auction
9. Contract Write-up	

Wyld (2001, pp.26-28) lists some 60 B2B exchanges or e-marketplaces globally. Some of these including Covisint (Automotives), Chemwatch (Chemicals) and Neoforma (Medical Goods) use an auction format [HREF8] to develop pricing. Globally Ariba Inc., Freemarkets Inc., iPlanet, and Commerce. One among others are leading vendors in e-Procurement applications. In Australia Freemakets.com is the leading vendor in online auctions. In June 2000, Mayne Nickless (Gettler, 2000), a diversified organisation with major interests in health-care and logistics, signed a three-year deal with Freemarkets.com to manage procurement and operate an online auction. Freemarkets [HREF5] have also operated procurement operations for gas, aviation fuel and casual labour.

Methodology

Case study research methodology was used as the paper presents an exploratory look at implications of reverse online auctions. Yin(1994, p. 35) emphasises the importance of asking "what" when analyzing information systems. Yin goes further and emphasises the need to study contemporary phenomena within real life contexts. Walsham (2000, p.204) supports case study methodology and sees a need for a move away from traditional information systems research methods such as survey toward more interpretative case studies, ethnographies and action research projects. Several works have used case studies (Chan, 2001; Lee, 1989; Benbasat et al., 1987) in presenting information systems case-study research. Cavaye (1995) used case study research to analyze inter-organizational systems and the complexity of information systems. The data collection process included examination of existing documentation, content analysis of email, interview of actors and direct observations. The auction event was analyzed from the supplier organisation viewpoint with particular emphasis on the participants and outcomes of the event. In April 2001 AusBuyer commissioned Auction.Com to make a market for the logistics component of their manufacturing activities. The market was broken down into 19 channels both state and nationally based. AusSupplier received notification that a contract that it had partially carried out for three years was to be auctioned on the Internet. AusSupplier started a six-month exploration into online auctions and B2B procurement. Considerable time and financial resources were expended in firstly learning and then secondly participating in the reverse online auction. The three participants in the auction event were AusSupplier, Auction.Com and AusBuyer.

Auction Case Study

AusSupplier is a micro-business with 2 full time and 5 part time consultants. It is an "infomediary" or in older language a "middleman". AusSupplier turns over $AUD 10 million and has a small client base. The role of the "infomediary" is to win a contract for packing and exporting commodities into the Asian marketplace. AusSupplier wins a contract from a large manufacturer and then negotiates transport and shipping rates. The commodity that was to be auctioned was worth about $AUD1.6 million/year and AusSupplier was responsible for about 20% of the contract. A major transport company was responsible for the other 80%. Auction.Com is a multi-national market leading e-Commerce company specializing in e-Procurement and auctions. They have about 1000 employees worldwide and operate with about 140 large multi-national clients. They have conducted about $US21 billion in auctions resulting in savings of about $US 6 billion. It is obvious when looking at Auction.Com and AusSupplier the difference in size, technology and more importantly the chasm in understanding e-Business. The Australian manufacturer (AusBuyer) was the Australian arm of a global organisation based in US. The global organisation was undergoing financial strain due to the poor commodities market worldwide. In order to reduce costs AusBuyer turned to Auction.Com to conduct an auction event. Once again we see a major difference between the globally based Auction.Com and AusBuyer and the micro-business AusSupplier. The auction event was an Australia wide procurement exercise focussing on logistics & transport. The entire procurement operation of AusBuyer was placed in 19 lots with each lot undergoing a 1.5 hour auction. For AusSupplier the auction event went through 5 stages; market-made(client), pre-qualification(supplier), pre-auction planning(supplier), auction-strategy(supplier) and post-auction(client).

Market Made

Shortly after the initial notification AusSupplier undertook research into the reverse auction process, then received a CD containing Web based bidding software and documentation from the manufacturer. This documentation consisted of over 50 files including tender documents, quote spreadsheets, specifications and information. It was updated 4 times before the final auction. Initially the deluge of information was overwhelming.

"I have spent hours retrieving, printing, reading and just trying to make sense of the process." Managing Director

At this stage considerable effort was expended in determining if AusSupplier could participate in more than one channel. It was felt that other channels, including some interstate, could be attempted but a more conservative approach was adopted due to uncertainty in the process.

Pre-Qualification

This is the stage where Auction.Com and AusBuyer weed out non-performing suppliers but try to ensure an adequate number of bidders to create the auction dynamic. AusSupplier had no idea how many other companies had pre-qualified, it only learnt of the number at the auction event. Pre-qualification also introduces some financial parameters for the event. Auction.Com set the switching cost at $AUD1.3million, that is, the price when AusBuyer would consider awarding the contract away from the existing supplier. Market research by AusSupplier showed the existing contract was worth $AUD1.6million. The difference between the switching and existing contract price was about 18%. This figure is very important as much of the advertising material by Auction.Com quotes savings of 18%. AusSupplier again expended considerable resources at this stage; two site visits, 4 sub-contractor meetings, 200 phone calls, 45 emails out, 15 emails in, 30 hours of managing director time and 20 hours of consultants time. The bill for participating in the reverse auction was climbing. Summarising the financial details thus far:

1. AusSuppliers market entry price $AUD 2 million
2. Existing contract price. $AUD 1.6 million
3. Reserve(Switching) price $AUD 1.3 million

The high AusSuppliers market entry price was formulated on the basis of entry into an unknown scenario. It was formulated on the rate of moving the commodity by the tonnages quoted by AusBuyer with a margin built in. At this stage it became apparent that the auction format was introducing an element of incredulity to the quoting process.

"We are flying in the dark, some cowboy could underbid us and have no real idea of what is involved in the job...." Managing Director.

For AusSupplier this new foray into B2B was daunting, no idea of how many others bidders, no idea of their market entry point and only one Auction.Com tutorial on a simulated auction to guide them.

Auction Strategy

Being pre-qualified and waiting for the auction became quite stressful. What strategy should be adopted? What would happen if the power failed, or the ISP went down? What would be the lowest position AusSupplier would take in the auction, would they be swept up in the auction dynamic? Who would press the buttons, would they hold their nerve. Auction.Com conducted a training session from their Asian headquarters and AusSupplier soon mastered the auction interface. They had three strategies for the auction, entry, middle and end-strategy. The entry-strategy was to come in at our high pre-qualification bid after about 3 minutes and then watch the market develop. The middle-strategy was to maintain control on the screen and drive the bids down in a controlled manner. It is important to understand that in the auction event you only see bids and do not know where they come from. The only strategy for the end was to be in the end game and if AusSupplier did not win they wanted to be under the switching cost at the end. This would show AusBuyer that AusSupplier was a serious bidder. AusSupplier had seen sample auction events where the end game was frantic.

The Auction Event

The auction was delayed a week and with a late flurry of updates and clarifications AusSupplier waited until 10.33 to press the bid accept button.

In 5 seconds the early and middle strategies were destroyed. There were three other bidders and one bidder came in right on the switching price. This was felt to be a ploy to scare off other bidders, it was felt that this was the existing contractor.

Middle Game, after about half an hour another bidder entered and soon started to drive down. AusSuppliers strategy was to drive down to the reserve price.

End Game, at this stage it is fair to say that the phones were put on hold. As the scheduled auction time elapsed the bidding intensified. A bid in the last minute extends the auction by one minute. There were three bidders left. The original button presser passed to the managing director when the low position previously agreed upon was passed. The auction entered the phase that Auction.Com call the auction dynamic, the dynamic that drives the price down. The reserve was driven down $90000 in 7 minutes. The number of bids in the last 7 minutes tripled all bids in the previous 1.5 hours. The managing director started to lose some semblance of control as he did not want to lose to the other bidders. The agreed low margin of 12% was reduced to 5%. AusSupplier did not win the auction, they were in the game at the end and drove the market down to inflict some pain on the other bidders.

Post Auction

After the auction AusSupplier were told they would have to wait 5 weeks for the result, it came much earlier. AusSupplier lost the 20% of the contract they had at the start. The managing director took about two weeks to get over losing to the competition. There are several issues that need to be discussed concerning the reverse auction.

Analysis

A six-month process costing thousands of dollars, resulted in the loss of an existing part contract. This was not a desirable outcome. The winner was a transport company that bypassed the "infomediary" in winning the contract. AusBuyer received a 20% reduction in their logistics in one channel. In another channel where only one supplier pre-qualified the existing contract price was inflated by 5%. In this case the auction dynamic was missing and therefore no savings were made. For the supplier there are many issues to consider. Firstly, the web auction format is able to link buyers and suppliers directly thereby cutting out any middle operators. Traditional suppliers will need to engage the e-Markeplace channel to access the growing number of organisations moving towards e-Sourcing. Secondly, the cost to participate is considerable when we consider the size of the participating supplier. Australia has a high proportion of small and micro-business, will the nature and scope of reverse auction suit the current Australian business landscape? Thirdly, the whole issue of driving costs down at the possible expense of contract servicing is crucial. This is demonstrated when we see the auction format not favoured in Asian markets where service is considered paramount. Finally the ability of the auction to drive dynamic pricing produces an ethical dilemma. Wyld (2001, p. 18) refers to the auction principle where there is always another group willing to lower your bid. Do we want business run only on the bottom line? AusSupplier had prided itself on providing a service second to none. Any glitches in the previous contract like variability of supply of the commodity or problems in logistics or shipping never presented a problem. In this case AusBuyer was under pressure to drive down prices due to the global marketplace, but will there be a price to pay if the contract lapses and a premium needs to be paid to bring in another supplier to complete the contract. This scenario occurred three year prior to the online auction being adopted. Much of the literature comments on the popularity of reverse auctions for private industry to drive pricing whereas government use it to source suppliers based on other criteria. For the client who received the 20% reduction in costs all is rosy. Questions remain about the service quality they will receive, whether contracts are adhered to and what sort of supplier relationship they enjoy in the contract period. Verga (2001) reported the importance of the need to maintain a strong relationship between buyers and sellers in Dell Computers move to e-Sourcing. Oracle supply chain manager referred to the need to look after suppliers:

"*..no point in driving your suppliers out of business. You would be out of business yourself*".

Discussion

Wyld describes three main implications of the use of online reverse auctions; merging of online and regular business, cultural and attitudinal change and technological change. The merging of regular and online business has the potential to propel B2B e-commerce into every organisation. Verga (2001) emphasizes the difficulty for suppliers who have perfected the "regular" supply chain and the undeniable imperative that they must move online or be obliterated. Wyld saw this as leveraging suppliers into the market space. AusSupplier's first foray into the online procurement world heralded the need to create a new type of relationship management. Dynamic pricing will be the driving vision (Hof, 2000) and suppliers will need to carve out their business relationships around this reality.

The reverse auction changes the buyer-supplier relationship from one of negotiation often in a one-on-one situation into a more dynamic and removed dialogue. Time frames are collapsed and the art and culture of traditional business negotiation is pancaked into a dialogue with a web auction application. Tapscott (2000) referred to the elevation of price as the single criteria for winning reverse auctions as being flawed. He felt the price only model will be replaced by a more mature model, where quality, customer service, credit terms and shipping reliability were often as important as price. AusSupplier realize only too well the importance of other factors in contract adherence but must obey the absolute nature of dynamic pricing. Technology in the form of "bots" (Bayers, 2000) may provide the answer to the price only dilemma. It is conceivable that smart "bots" will allow buyers and sellers to bid on a range of variables not just on price alone.

Images

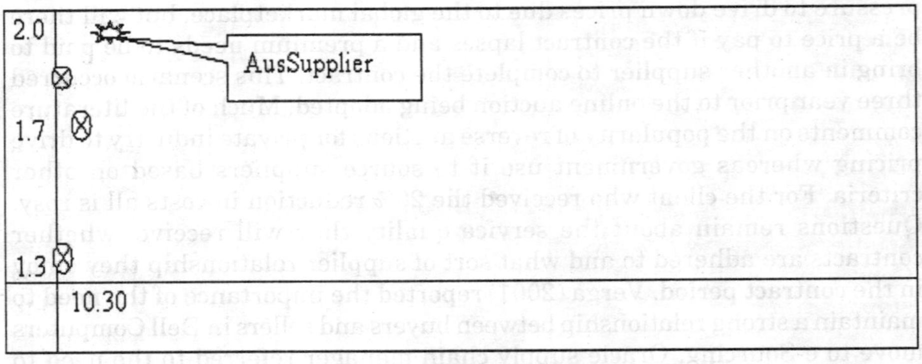

Figure 2 Start of Auction

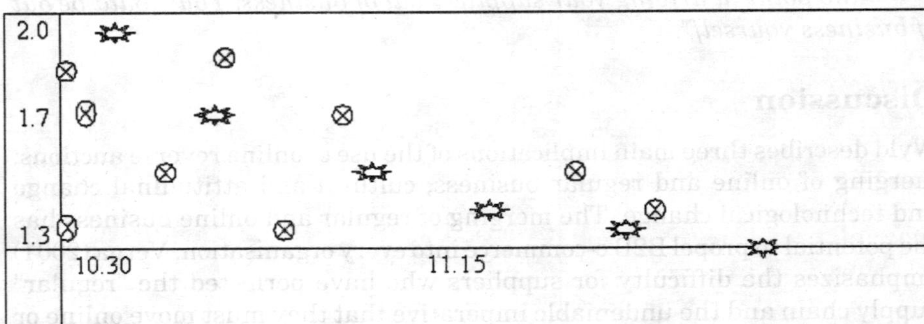

Figure 3 One Hour into the Auction

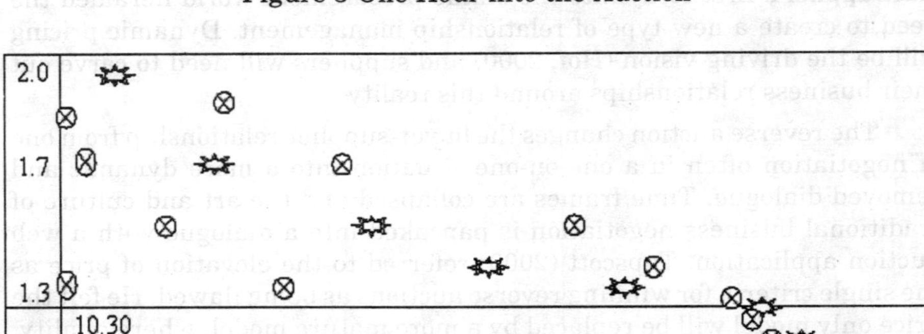

Figure 4 All Over

4

E- Customer Relationship Management

Call Centre

The CALL Centre (Communication Aids for Language and Learning) provides specialist expertise in technology for children who have speech, communication and/or writing difficulties, in schools across Scotland.

Aims and Background

The CALL Centre is a small unit within the Department of Educational Studies, in the Faculty of Education, The University of Edinburgh. The Centre is co-located with the Scottish Sensory Centre, offering a rich one-stop resource. CALL is both a Service and a Research Unit. Service activity is limited by the amount of staff time available, but is open to anyone in Scotland concerned with communication difficulties, particularly in a learning context. New technology has much to offer people with physical, communication or sensory difficulties. Computers and computer-based aids have become smaller, cheaper and more practical and can be readily adapted to provide disabled people with access to communication, education, recreation and employment. Communication systems with synthesized or digitized voice offer a means of communication for those who cannot speak; switches and other devices can be used by people with physical disabilities as an alternative to a standard computer keyboard; enlarged displays or voice feedback offer computer access to those with visual impairments; specialized software helps people with writing or spelling difficulties. 'Low-technology' systems such as picture or symbol books can be valuable too.

However, the wide range of possibilities means that choosing and using these technologies with particular individuals can be complex and sometimes daunting. The CALL Centre addresses these problems and works to help people with disabilities (and their careers and professional helpers) get the most from this new technology.

The geographical remit

Since the core funding for the CALL Centre comes from the Scottish Executive Education Department (SEED), most of our work, particularly with regard to assessments and loans, is concentrated in Scotland. Other organisations, particularly the ACE Centre, ACCESS Centres and Communication Aids Centres perform a similar role in England and Wales. Nevertheless, we will endeavor to respond on a limited scale to general enquiries and questions on CALL Centre research from throughout the United Kingdom, and overseas.

The CALL Centre funded

Core funding is provided by the Scottish Executive Education Department (SEED). Additional funding has come from the Scottish Executive Health Department, Community Care Division, and from service level agreements with local authorities and schools in Scotland (in 2001, CALL has nine small scale assessment and training service contracts) and with the University of Edinburgh Disability Office. Research and development project work over the years has been enhanced by funding support from a number of agencies, including the European Union, Nuffield Foundation, Department of Employment, Gatsby Charitable Trust and others.

Call Services

Information & Advice Service

CALL provides information and advice in response to enquiries on communication technology for people with disabilities. In addition to resources available from this website, CALL maintains an open-access Resource Library of books, journals, video and multimedia materials.

The aim of the CALL Information/Enquiry service is to provide information and advice on technological aids for communication and learning to professionals, careers and disabled people themselves.

CALL will answer both general enquiries and requests for help and information relating to specific communication disabled individuals. CALL also offers direct access to parents and professionals by telephone, letter, email and personal contact. Information available includes books, videos, information sheets, software, educational applications, and resources contained in this website. CALL also has an open-access Resource Library of specialist books, journals, video and multimedia materials.

Ever needed to know, for example:

- What different voice output aids are available and what each does best?
- Where to buy a specific piece of software?
- Where to get a reading list on a specific AAC/micro technology/ Special Educational Needs topic?
- Where to borrow a switch from?
- Further information on scan and switch word-processors?
- Who is the most appropriate person locally to yourself to contact on AAC matters?
- How to connect a voice output device to a printer or a computer?
- Which version of the Spell master range is most appropriate to your needs?

Communication aids, computers, various special interfaces and switches etc. are held in the Centre, but we do not encourage people to come in just to have a general 'look around' at these items. These items tend to be so complex that just 'looking' at them is usually not helpful. CALL staff are not always available to explain and demonstrate equipment. Also this is 'working equipment' and is generally in transit between assessments, loans etc. rather than being laid out in a display as such.

If a group or team wish for further information about specific equipment (say, the range of different voice output aids) you may wish to ask about setting up an in-service session. For information about forthcoming courses and events.

Assessment & Support Service

CALL offers a free assessment and support service for a small number of children with communication, physical, sensory and learning needs who might benefit from information and communication technology.

CALL's Assessment & Support Service aims to give additional support to practitioners by assessing, jointly with their own local teams, people with complex needs who might benefit from technology.

We try for a flexible approach - for example, joint assessments with other specialist agencies (e.g. KEYCOMM); support at the implementation stage, or transition to next stage of technology; 'distant' assessments involving video material and discussion with staff teams, rather than direct contact with the child - as opposed to a traditional 'medical model' of 'one-off' assessment sessions.

Loan Bank

CALL offers loans of specialist equipment for communication and learning to allow for extended assessment and evaluation of a device or system before purchase. Technical support is available.

CALL offers loans specialist equipment for communication and learning to individuals with disabilities throughout Scotland. Loans of equipment are made to allow for extended assessment at home, school or work, and to enable people to evaluate a device or system.

Loans are generally for two months, but it is possible to negotiate an extension provided that another person does not require equipment.

Loans are made to individual users, usually through professions in schools, health care or social work services. Loans are for evaluation and trial use by a named individual and not to supplement school or centre equipment stocks.

Sometimes borrowers know exactly what they want as a detailed assessment has already been done. Otherwise contact your local educational psychologist or speech and language therapist to arrange an assessment. The first step is through the Head teacher or, for adults, through the contact social worker or occupational therapist. If in double, please contact the CALL Centre for discussion and advice.

Loans are free but we ask borrowers to pay delivery charges. These costs can be avoided if borrowers collect and return equipment themselves. Borrowers are responsible for equipment while it is on loan: they may choose to arrange insurance or to be responsible for full replacement costs in case of theft or accident.

CALL sends out a newsletter, *New in CALL,* twice a year which provides information about new acquisitions. It often contains brief reviews of equipment and software available to meet a particular need.

It is not practical to produce a detailed catalogue. You may, however, ask for a listing of specific parts of the inventory, e.g. 'switches' or 'early learning software for the Macintosh'.

All the equipment in the Loan Bank are listed in an on-line database. Click the link below to browse the database - you can search for a particular item to read a brief description about it or to see whether it is currently available for loan. Where details of a supplier are given, this usually represents the source from which CALL purchased the item. The same item can often be purchased from other suppliers.

Training & Staff Development CALL offers a range of training and staff development opportunities relevant to people working with children and adults with communication or curriculum access difficulties. Contact CALL for a list of forthcoming events or to arrange training to meet your own particular requirements.

On-Site In-Service Training and CPD

We realize that for many of you a visit to Edinburgh for a CALL Centre based course is not possible. Any of our courses can be delivered 'on site' whether for a school, centre or authority. Last year we delivered 27 courses on site, the majority of which were tailored for staff in individual schools. Although most of these courses were ones from the course programme, some schools requested training not already specified and had the course created to their specific requirements. As we now have a number of laptops we can bring them to you for the training or you can organize it in your own computer suite. Full day courses are offered anywhere in Scotland. Half day and twilight courses can be arranged for places within reasonable traveling distance of the Central belt, or under separate arrangements for a block of time.

Due to the huge popularity of our in-service and on-site training, we have significantly increased the number and variety of courses on offer. You can choose from our list of onsite courses, choose one of our inhouse courses to be delivered with you, or specify your own requirements. The school or authority would be responsible for organizing participants, releasing staff and arranging cover as necessary, providing catering etc.

The standard charges for Inset courses delivered on site in schools, day centres or local authorities are listed here, with reduced rates for schools or local authorities that have Partnership Agreements (PA) with CALL. These charges are for a small group and, usually, one CALL tutor. Charges for large groups requiring more CALL tutors are by arrangement contact us to discuss your requirements. Contact us if you need to know if your Local Authority has an PA with CALL, or if you want to know how you can arrange one. Discounts may apply for a block of ten or more training days.

Service activity is limited by the amount of staff time available, but is open to anyone in Scotland concerned with communication difficulties, particularly in a learning context. For Scottish users, by and large our services are free, although there are a few special situations where charges may be made. These are outlined below.

The Complete Call Center Business Performance Series

Call center measurement Best Practices Benchmarking Reports

Benchmarking your call center performance Lessons learned from more than 200 companies in call center management and technology. Includes contact center model, best practices, performance metrics and improvement initiatives.

Call Center Measurement Toolkit

Easy-to-use guidelines and worksheets for assessing and benchmarking call center performance, with complete guides on how to establish the right measures.

Call center operations and management

Motivating Agents Toolkit

A comprehensive guide specifically designed to increase productivity and motivate agents. This first ever guide contains assessments and easy to follow steps that allow you to take control of the process.

Quality Monitoring Toolkit

A complete guide to implementing or improving a quality monitoring (call monitoring) program and integrating it into operations with the Quality Monitoring Lifecycle and a research-based scorecard.

Call Center Planning and Design Toolkit

A blueprint for creating a call center strategy, planning and design; an excellent resource for new contact center start-ups, existing call center improvement and future planning; includes detailed templates and planning roadmaps.

Controlling the Cost of Call Center Operations Toolkit

A systematic approach to expense reduction; over 50 initiatives to cut costs, including short-term quick-hits, mid-term tactics and long-term strategies; checklists, worksheets and framework roadmap.

Train your call center **Call Center Training Toolkit** The definitive guide for creating a training program for your call center, providing a methodology and guidelines for developing a call center training curriculum and organization.

Outsourcing Toolkit

An in-depth guide for making outsourcing decisions, conducting a needs assessment, identifying and selecting an outsourcing partner, and establishing a service level agreement. Outsource your entire call center operations or specific functions Monitor calls and improve agent productivity Optimize periodicity and agent retention Plan a new contact center.

The *Best Practices in Call Center Management and Operations* study provides a comprehensive view of the changing environment in the call center. Find out what is working (and what is not working) as call center managers strive to reduce costs and improve service quality. The report includes:

The *Call Center Best Practices Report - Special Technology Edition* shares lessons learned about the most effective technology changes and their effect on customer satisfaction and call center efficiency. 124 call centers from diverse industry areas participated in the technology study.

- . Top five changes with the most impact on cost efficiency and customer satisfaction.
- . Most important changes planned for the next 12 to 18 months.
- How to develop excellent CSR knowledge, skills and abilities.
- A quality monitoring scorecard that has been developed from the collective input of more than 500 call centers.
- . Strategies for supervisors to improve their performance. Discover the advantages and disadvantages to the most commonly used technology applications:
- . Email
- . Contact management systems
- . Voice response systems
- . Web-enabled call centers
- . CTI
- . Knowledge-based applications
- . Technology improvement initiatives

The report also includes the top technology areas targeted for change in the next 12-18 months.

The Threshold Model

- Enables you to create a customized plan for motivation, retention and productivity
- Drives the methods of motivation in your call center
- Illustrates what you should do first to motivate and inspire your agents, and when to take various steps in the process
- Provides you with the "hard numbers" to prove which job factors are most important and problematic in your call center

The Threshold Model

Physical environment and facilities Basic knowledge to perform job Competitive pay and benefits Personal aspiration and ambition Culture and teams Leadership style and Supervisor Incentives and rewards Career advancement and growth Tools, equipment and work station Desired job factors Required job factors.

This toolkit has been specifically designed to help call center managers and supervisors:

- Increase productivity
- Motivate agents
- Reduce turnover

When it comes to call center incentive and motivation programs, one size does *not* fit all. Prosci's *Motivating Call Center Agents Toolkit* will help you discover what really works to inspire and motivate *your* call center agents. The motivation process roadmap and a set of in-depth assessments will help you to evaluate the current state of your call center, prioritize your greatest opportunities for improvement and integrate a plan that aligns with your call center strategy to create a truly motivating call center environment.

In the Call Center Measurement Toolkit, you will find

• In-depth templates, graphs and guidelines to help you understand the definitions of each call center measurement explanations of different industry perspectives on each area of call center management methods to accurately benchmark your results against industry data recommendations and ideas you can act on immediately to initiate improvement projects tips for improving your call center benchmarking results formulas for determining when you have made accurate and valid comparisons.

Call Center Measurement Toolkit

Prosci's *Call Center Measurement Toolkit* is an indispensable tool that will teach you how to assess and improve the performance of your call center. By providing common definitions of terms and a complete overview of performance measures for contact centers, the toolkit will promote your understanding of the functions and procedures that will enhance your call center performance and boost its efficiency.

Measurement areas in the toolkit

- Abandon rate
- Availability
- Agent utilization
- Average speed of answer (ASA)
- Contact volume
- Costs
- Customer satisfaction
- Handle time
- One call resolution rate
- Quality monitoring
- Schedule adherence
- Service level
- Span of control
- Turnover rate

Call Center Quality Monitoring Toolkit

How to monitor and ensure quality customer experiences Toolkit contents:

- Quality monitoring methods
- Agent perception
- QM lifecycle
- Monitoring contacts
- Agent feedback
- Training and coaching
- Survey criteria
- Implementation checklists

This toolkit has been designed to help call center managers and supervisors:

- Create the best possible quality monitoring program.
- Integrate quality monitoring with hiring and training programs.
- Use industry-proven criteria for scoring agents.
- Learn the dos and don'ts of providing feedback to employees.
- Select the best quality monitoring process for your call center. Walk-around

Basic Sophisticated

This toolkit will help you:

- Build a quality monitoring program that agents will support.
- Create a complete monitoring process with integrated feedback loops to agents, supervisors, training and hiring.
- Develop a quality monitoring scorecard that is not only useful to your agents but also improves your levels of customer service.

Worksheets

Prosci's *Quality Monitoring Toolkit* is the most complete guide available for quality monitoring. Whether you are just starting a new program for monitoring contacts, or need to overhaul your current call monitoring program, this toolkit provides definitive guidelines and templates for both phone and multi-media contact monitoring. Using research data from more than 250 call centers.

Call Center Planning and Design Toolkit *Planning Roadmap*

- Guides you through the key activities for creating a world-class call center.
- Planning roadmaps enable you to quickly identify required elements for your call center. The planning roadmap and the master planning guide include:
- Getting Started
- Business Strategy
- Processes
- Technology
- Human Resources
- Facilities

Master Planning Guide

The Master Planning Guide is the answer to the question "Where do I start?" Planning tables and checklists will help you identify and keep track of the multitude of activities that must be done. Master planning guides for strategy, process, technology, HR and facilities provide you with checklists and project management control.

This toolkit is ideal if you...

- Are starting a completely new call center
- Are consolidating call centers
- Want to upgrade to a world-class contact center from your existing call center
- Are taking over call center implementation
- Are managing a portion of a new call center implementation
- Have one call center and need to open an additional location
- Are looking for a better understanding of the components of an effective call center

The *Call Center Planning and Design Toolkit* is your guide for creating a world-class contact center. Developed in collaboration with industry leaders in the call center field, Vanguard Communications, the *Call Center Planning and Design Toolkit* is the definitive guide for creating the best possible contact center for your organization.

The toolkit provides:

- A planning checklist and design guidelines for successfully setting up a new call center or redesigning your existing call center
- The approach and tools to help you create a contact center strategy and manage the implementation effectively

Controlling the Cost of Call Center Operations

Controlling the Cost of Call Center Operations provides a systematic approach to reducing your costs. With this toolkit, you will critically examine multiple channels for reducing expenses. The outcome is a set of identified and prioritized cost saving initiatives that are most suited for your situation.

This toolkit is ideal if you...

- Need to reduce the cost of your call center operations
- Are under pressure to deliver the same level of service with fewer resources
- Are faced with increasing costs in your call center
- Need to manage peak calling periods or seasons without 'breaking the bank'
- Could benefit from over 50 initiatives to lower your costs In the toolkit you receive a master roadmap diagram that shows the framework for cost reduction initiatives including:
- **Content overview:** Reducing the handle time Reducing the cost of resources Reducing the volume of contacts Cost control worksheets Three types of cost control initiatives Prioritization worksheet Topic look-up lowering **handle time** (e.g., talk time plus after-call work time for a phone call) reducing **resource costs** for handling contacts (fully loaded cost per unit time – e.g. cost per minute) decreasing total **volume of contacts** (volume of inbound contacts for all media)

Strategies and plans for call center training development

The *Call Center Training Toolkit* is the definitive guide for creating a training program for your call center. The toolkit provides a methodology and guidelines for developing a call center training curriculum and organization that considers efficiency, effectiveness, quality, quantity, time and cost of training. For call centers with existing training groups, this toolkit provides a format for evaluating the strategy, needs, content, and delivery methodology for your training program. The toolkit includes checklists, guidelines and templates to make sure that you are on the right track.

Call Center Outsourcing

Strategies and plans for successful call center outsourcing

The *Call Center Outsourcing Toolkit* is designed for use by organizations that are considering or have already made a decision to outsource call handling. The toolkit provides an in-depth and easy-to-follow process for selecting a qualified outsourcing partner and then managing a **win-win relationship.** This toolkit guides you through a logical process beginning with the outsourcing **decision** and ending with a **service level agreement**. Key document templates included are: needs assessment, request for proposal, and service level agreement.

Partner Relationship Management

Partner Relationship Management (PRM) is a business strategy for developing and improving relations between companies and their suppliers-channel partners. There are many CRM providers that have incorporated PRM features in their software applications. PRM can be also considered a component of customer relationship management (CRM) that serves the relationships of channel partnerships.

P R M: A Critical e-Business Strategy for a Multi-Channel World

Businesses have always had a love/hate relationship with channels and channel partners. Sure, partners are needed to reach target markets and add services that customers want. However, independent channel businesses (brokers, resellers, integrators, dealers, etc.) can't be managed like a direct sales force, and loyalty can be difficult to maintain as some partners flit from one vendor to another looking for the best deal. And there's always the issue of cost. Middlemen have to earn a profit and sometimes the margin dollar can only be stretched so far while providing a competitive price to the ultimate end customer.

So it has naturally been tempting for companies to look at eCommerce as a new channel that could essentially replace current distribution partners. If a customer could just deal directly with the manufacturer, they could get exactly what they want and at a lower cost and companies would be spared the difficulties of managing fickle, demanding channel partners.

However, the reality is that eCommerce and indirect channel sales are not mutually exclusive. Cisco Systems, the well known network hardware provider, leverages the Internet aggressively and yet continues to rely on channel partners for more than 75% of its business. Investment firm Charles Schwab & Co. has cleverly melded its strength in traditional "brick and mortar" operations with forays into online trading. Microsoft Corp. has remained steadfast in its support of channel partners, while investing heavily in Web-based tools to help them be even more successful. And even Dell Computer Corp., a leader of the eDirect hype, reportedly does 15% of its business through channel partners.

Partner Relationship Management

Customer Relationship Management (CRM) is not just software to manage customer relationships. Effective CRM requires a customer-centric business strategy not something a software package can do for you. And this strategy will almost certainly mean that the organization, culture, and work processes will change, sometimes dramatically. CRM technology is the enabler, not the driver. Have you ever heard of a business automating its way to a new business strategy.

PRM is not just software, either. Rather, it's a business strategy to optimize the value of partner relationships and, like CRM, application software can play a crucial enabling role. In fact, in complex channels it's hard to separate web-based applications from effective PRM these days. But think about it, if a manufacturer has an incoherent channel strategy and chaotic relations with its partners, what good will new Internet applications do? Automated chaos is still chaos.

Another key point is that the most important word in PRM is the middle one – *relationship*. Good relationships are valuable to both parties. Effective PRM means delivering value to partners to help them be successful, not just manipulating them to sell more products or micro-managing their sales activities. Of course, helping partners makes good business sense because successful partners are more likely to be loyal.

Expanding Market for PRM

CRM and eCommerce software solutions have primarily been concerned with *direct* relationships. Until last year, it wasn't easy to find any packaged applications or Internet services for channel partners. This began to change late in1998 as software start-ups emerged to serve this nascent market. Early PRM vendors included Partner ware Inc., Channel Wave Software, Inc., Webridge, Inc. and Allegis Corp. These vendors aimed to apply the concepts of relationship management in fresh new applications designed specifically for indirect sales channels. Nearly two years later, their early vision is being validated by a rapidly growing market opportunity and entry of many other vendors hoping to capitalize on PRM.

As multi-channel or "click and mortar" strategies gain momentum, it's clear that indirect channels remain a vital element in most industries. Despite changes in the role of channel partners, which has shifted to services and more complex sales, channels still account for roughly half of all global commerce.

Analyst firms forecast the market for PRM software and services to reach approximately $1 billion by 2002, and IDC recently forecasted it to reach $2 billion by 2003. Unfortunately there's no standard definition of PRM yet, but if you consider that the CRM market will exceed $5 billion in 2000, it's not inconceivable that PRM technology will be a significant percentage of this figure in a couple of years.

PRM Provide

According to an online survey that my firm conducted during a two-week period in August, the most desired features in a PRM solution are opportunity/lead management and integration with other enterprise (CRM/ERP) applications. The survey netted about 200 responses from channel managers, channel partners, software vendors and consultants in the IT, telecom, financial services and manufacturing industries.

The majority of responses were from channel managers in the IT industry and reflects their interest in sales and marketing as well as channel management. Previous research focused solely on channel partners revealed more of an interest in sales/marketing content (not just leads) and tools to make selling and service processes more effective. Clearly it's important for any company considering a PRM system to carefully assess the needs of both channel managers and partners, because the system must offer value to both parties.

PRM Technology Leaders

In the last 18 months a wide variety of companies have entered the PRM space, some using that term, and many not. The situation for competitors in the PRM market now is much like those of runners in a marathon at the five-mile mark: If you're not near the lead pack it's difficult to catch up, but there are still 21 miles to go. Here are some categories of vendors competing for a share of the PRM market.

Full-function PRM vendors provide a range of applications to support the partner relationship lifecycle, such as partner profiling, lead management, targeted Web-based and e-mail communications, promotion/program management, incentive funds management, literature fulfillment, eCommerce, and training. Allegis, Channel Wave and Partner ware have all earned a strong reputation in the high tech market and remain very focused on PRM. North Systems (formerly Ten North) has focused on smaller manufacturers with independent reps, starting with a basic content management solution and then expanding into lead management. Intelic Software Solutions specializes in the semiconductor market. Foundation Network has established itself in the European market, which appears poised to grow rapidly in 2001 and beyond.

ECommerce vendors started with applications designed for channels, supporting purchasing processes from partner to vendor, customer to partner, or both. These vendors have added more PRM functionality over time and increasingly compete with full-function PRM vendors. Click Commerce, Inc., for example, has been selling large dealer extranets for years in automotive and "rust belt" industries. InfoNow Corp., one of the sleepers in the PRM market, has an excellent roster of customers and many elements of a full PRM solution, but little PRM mind share. Comergent Technologies, Inc. offers an innovative solution for distributed eCommerce, a difficult problem to solve for multi-tier channels.

Content management vendors focus on the organization and distribution of Web-based content to help channel partners sell more effectively. On Demand Inc. staked out this segment with a robust channel portal packaged with other Internet-based services. Promptu Inc.'s e-Marketing application has been applied successfully in channel extranets and offers features that large enterprises could find valuable. Portal and personalization vendors such as Conjoin, Inc., BroadVision, Inc., Vignette

Corp., Eprise Corp., CoVia Technologies, Inc. and many others could be deployed for channel extranets, but as yet are not focused on PRM.

CRM vendors have not ignored the PRM opportunity. Market leaders such as Siebel Systems, Inc., Pivotal Corp., Interact Commerce Corp. (formerly SalesLogix), and Onyx Software Corp. have all introduced PRM modules to expand their CRM product lines. To handle service and support processes, Web-based customer service vendors like Kana Communications, Inc., Right Now Technologies, Inc. and others could be used very effectively with partners. While in some cases the functionality offered is not as rich as the dedicated PRM solutions, CRM vendors offer an easier-to-integrate and potentially less costly solution that will appeal to buyers looking for a CRM/PRM solution from a single vendor.

Marketplace vendors also have a role in PRM, since it's possible to have effective channel relationships via a many-to-many marketplace, not just in a vendor-centric extranet environment. VARStreet.com is becoming a force in the IT industry by offering a full range of eBusiness services, valuable to both channel partners and manufacturers. Companies looking for a platform to build on could consider Bowstreet or Radnet Inc.

PRM Market Trends

New entrants. There are plenty of unsolved problems in the channel space and no lack of new companies that think they will solve these problems better than the current players. Some new companies to watch include ChannelAutomation.com, Channel Logic Data Corp., and Elantix Corp. You can also expect more CRM and e-Business vendors to jump into the PRM market looking for growth opportunities.

More functionality. Current vendors will continue to broaden their range of functionality. In particular, marketing and service functionality will be expanded either through in-house development or partnerships with e-Marketing and e-Service vendors.

Vertical focus. It's doubtful that PRM solutions will translate from one industry to another without major rework. So specialized vertical solutions will proliferate, such as ChannelPoint, Inc. in the insurance industry. CRM vendors could use existing vertical applications to enter the PRM market.

Alliances. Time pressures will motivate vendors to partner aggressively to fill voids in product lines or to leverage marketing resources. Integrators will increasingly be part of PRM vendors' strategies for expanding their market reach.

Mergers and acquisitions. As with any growing market, it's almost certain that larger CRM or e-Business vendors will acquire some of the smaller PRM players. This could be an effective strategy for vendors currently not offering any PRM functionality, since playing catch-up will be risky and expensive.

European expansion. Europe relies heavily on distributors and channel partners of many kinds. The market for CRM technology is growing rapidly and PRM will follow this trend. Both CRM and PRM vendors will seek to penetrate this market in 2001 and position for high growth in 2002 and beyond.

Strategies for Success with PRM

In the process of interviewing 35 managers of PRM projects, my consulting firm learned how projects were managed, what worked, what didn't, and some words of advice. By analyzing interview findings, the research team was able to draw some conclusions about the critical issues that *every* business executive should consider before embarking on a PRM project. Consider this the emerging set of best practices for PRM.

PRM Best Practices

Business executive formally sponsors the project, provides direction on the specific business goals to be accomplished, and resolves critical issues. Project team performs a thorough analysis of short- and long-term requirements, soliciting input from all key stakeholders, but especially channel partners. Project team selects solution partner(s) based on the strength of the technology and commitment to services and support. Project manager staffs the team with competent and committed professionals, with expertise in all critical functional and technical areas. Project team implements a pilot or prototype first, then rolls out applications and user groups in phases.

The best practices shown in the table reaffirm that successful IT projects need executive leadership, thorough planning, effective staffing, and a realistic implementation approach. And, yes, good technology backed by solution providers who act as partners not just vendors.

Act Now for Competitive Advantage

PRM is a leading-edge, but no longer bleeding-edge, strategy and technology. To gain a competitive edge companies must determine the key needs of their channel partners and then select and implement the most appropriate PRM application. My advice for any business that relies on indirect sales channels is to quickly assess their short- and long-term needs and then act aggressively. Because PRM is a critical e-Business strategy in this increasingly multi-channel world.

E-Service Management

Process management technology has recently been employed not only within businesses but also in provision of E-services over the Internet. Urgent requests and critical messages in these systems (referred to as alerts) should be delivered and handled timely. In particular, humans are often involved in critical conditions. Presently, most E-service systems cannot address these requirements, and alerts are often handled in an ad-hoc manner. In this paper, we propose a sophisticated alert management system for effective e-service integration under urgent constraints. We develop a model for specifying alerts, in which alerts are associated with service requests and a set of parameters are captured for their routing. The alert monitor matches the service provider to receive an alert, based on the alert specification. We then propose a routing mechanism that is initiated when the alert message is not acknowledged or serviced within the deadline, so that the alert can be forwarded to other suitable services if necessary. Monitoring is especially essential to ensure timeliness and availability of services, otherwise suitable exceptions should be raised and handled. We outline our implementation framework of an Alert Management System (AMS) with includes Web Services for B2B interactions, together with multiple-platform support for human users. We demonstrate our approach with an example medical house-call AMS.

The wide-spread of Internet connectivity and Web Services gradually changes the way in accessing and use information. Organizations are shifting towards an interoperation paradigm in which quality and timely services are essential. Awareness, accessibility, and responsiveness are the key relationships among organizations in society. In this paper, we looked into the problem efficiently conveying alerts to the right service provider at the right time using Web Services and mobile devices, for E-service provision under urgency constraints. We have proposed a framework of an alert management system that supports both human and E-service providers. This framework introduces a flexible alert conceptual model that allows users to specify tasks, alerts, roles, and their inter-relations. We have also presented our AMS architecture with an implementation outline with Web Services and described the alert monitoring and routing mechanisms involved. The problem of finding the right service provider to send an alert is non-trivial and application dependent, but our approach provides administrators with a guideline to systematically define strategies to address this problem. We have further proposed a matching algorithm based on our alert conceptual model that can be customized based on the application requirements. Moreover, we present an alert monitoring algorithm that monitors the alerts and raises their urgency accordingly while at the same time executes the action that corresponds to the according urgency level. As such, an effective AMS can be built and it can be reused by plugging into systems that require sophisticated alert support. We have demonstrated the applicability of the AMS in a medical house-call system, which need to manage timely services from both human professionals and E-service providers. With this approach, E-service grids can gradually be built up among a group of E-service providers.

Introduction

Recent advances in Internet technologies have created a global platform for organizations and individuals to communicate among one another, carry out various commercial activities, and provide value-added services. E-services refer to these services provided over the Internet. In the current highly competitive and dynamic digital economy, E-services need to response actively and timely to customers' needs. For example in a B2C scenario, when a product recommendation portal finds a suitable product for a customer, the customer should be alerted promptly with the search results because second-hand items and clearance stock might be sold out quickly. Similarly, business-to-business (B2B) interactions may also have such requirements. Timely communication of accurate information is a key success factor for the provision of quality E-services. In particular, for E-services with stringent urgency requirements, such as healthcare and security applications, E-service providers must response actively and very timely to requestors' needs as this may be crucial to success or failure.

There are several issues to be considered in this problem. The alert model should include various alert types and parameters that qualify the E-service provider to receive an alert. Apart from service suitability, application specific considerations like costs, waiting time, service time, etc., may also be important. In addition, routing, monitoring, and logging the alerts are also mandatory functionalities, in order to shift the burden of these communications from the manual work to an automated system. To take advantage of the connected Internet environment, we propose an alert management system (AMS to address the problem of urgent support to E-services.

The AMS aims to minimize delays by providing a monitoring system. This paper generalizes and extends our previous work on workflow modeling [6], process integration [4], and contract enforcement [5]. The contributions of this paper are as follows: (i) a conceptual model for specifying alerts based on the requirements of cross-organizational processes and a set of routing parameters; (ii) a practical architecture for the AMS based on contemporary Web Services for B2B interactions, together with multiple-platform support for human users; (iii) an algorithm for matching service providers to alert requirements; (iv) a mechanism for (re-)routing alerts and increasing their urgency when alerts are not acknowledged or processed within deadline; and (v) demonstrate the applicability.

Motivating Example and Related Work

In Hong Kong, there are some medical corporations providing on-call service called "House Call". Patients can call the medical corporations and request a doctor consultation at their home. When the call center of the medical corporation receives a call from a patient (either electronically or by phone), they will arrange a doctor to perform the consultation immediately or to make an appointment for the consultation in patient's requested time. The call center should find a doctor with the required specialties (if any) from a list of off-duty doctors first, then from a list of on-duty doctors, and lastly, from a list of doctors from medical partners. In some cases, the system may also need to find a nurse to assist doctors to carry out the consultation. When the required personnel are found, the patient will be confirmed. At the same time, the patient's medical records may be required to send from hospitals and other clinics to the doctor's mobile device. After the consultation is finished, the doctor submits a medical report for the consultation. Lastly, the patient or his/her insurance company is charged for the consultation.

Before automation, manual procedures have many problems in providing such services. Call receivers and administration staff of the call center require a lot of knowledge and experience in order to handle it correctly and timely. There is a strong need for systematically handling it by capturing their knowledge and experience should be captured by an E-service system. In particular, the process is error prone and there are many possible exceptional cases, such as, failure of finding suitable personnel, absence and lateness of the personnel, etc.

The call center is also a bottle neck part in the whole E-service process. It is difficult to receive too many requests at the same time manually. If it is automated as E-services, user can request house call via the Internet through different devices. Besides through a browser on a PC, users may call through other mobile devices. On the other hand, patients with long-term sickness can also call via pre-programmed devices with a simple interface (such as just an electronic button). In the manual system, service personnel can only receive alert message by phone or pager. The new system allows them to receive from or reply to the system via different channels, such as, Short Message Service (SMS), email, fax, Personal Digital Assistance (PDA), I seek you (ICQ), etc. Costly and inefficient manual calls and retry calls can be mostly eliminated and therefore this brings a great benefit to the medical corporation.

Communication with medical partners and hospitals is a time-consuming process in the existing system. If their systems are also computerized in such a way, they can form a service grid with a common interface, streamlining E-service provision among partners. In this paper, we shall concentrate on our new proposals of alert mechanisms, while other details on inter-organizational process interoperations can be found in our earlier work [4][5][8].

In the context of workflow management systems (WFMS), we have recently proposed to separate user alerts from user sessions with the WFMS to improve the flexibility in our ME-ADOME system [2]. Online users are alerted through ICQ, with the task summary and reply

URL as the message content. If the user is not online or does not reply within a pre-defined period, the WFMS will send the alert by email. At the same time, another alert may be sent via SMS to the user's mobile phone. Whatever the alert channel has been, the user need not connect to WFMS on the same device, or even on the same platform. For example, after receiving a SMS alert, the user may use his handset to connect to the

WFMS via Wireless Application Protocol (WAP), or he/she may reply with an SMS message. Alternatively, the user may find a PC with Internet connection or use his/her PDA to connect to the WFMS. To our knowledge, there has been no other WFMS employing this approach. So far, there has been no detailed study on the linkage between alerts and workflows, neither in medical applications or e-services.

Point out that information technology (IT) is important to healthcare and the estimated IT expenditure on healthcare in 2002 is 21.6 billions in the United States. New healthcare applications supporting IT-based strategy are required for meeting competitive challenges.

Report that one of the major issues that mobile technologies can help in hospitals is communication and reach ability management. Communications that include the patient, the message sender, and the urgency are useful. Preliminarily identify the need for event monitors, and describe some of the requirements of such monitors, such as, tracking medical events, looking for clinically important situations, and sending messages to the providers. Further categorize messages as alerts, results, and replies. The limitation of their approach is that they only focus on alerts that can be handled by 2-way pagers.

Argue that the problem of figuring out to whom the message should be sent is a difficult one. They only suggested some ad hoc solutions, e.g., sending a message to whoever has recently examined the patient electronic record. In summary, the study of alerts even in healthcare informatics, which involves life critical application, is still preliminary. This also motivates us to conduct an in-depth study on alerts for further applications in these areas.

Alert Conceptual Model

E-Service Application Logic (J2EE/WFMS/...) Alerts (AMS) Events / Exceptions (Web Services)

Alerts capture urgency requirements of a task, as required by some E-service application logic (which can be capture in any type of software implementations). An alert can either be (i) asynchronously received by external events or exceptions, typically incoming E-service requests, or (ii) synchronously generated by internal E-service application logics. It should also be noted that exceptions are subclasses of events [6]. However, different from general events, alerts have much more specific attributes, in particular, urgency and service requirements. Different from exceptions, they need not relate to abnormal behaviors. Alerts received or generated have to be handled by the AMS by requesting services from either

(i) Internal information systems,
(ii) Human service provider, or
(iii) External E-service providers. As such, the AMS also handles inter-organizational interactions.

Our alert conceptual model consists of two parts, the process and the alerts model. This is because besides an alert itself, we must also consider the requirements of the tasks associated with the alert. The process model describes a process that abstracts the procedures of an organization. As an extension to existing process models such as [23], our process model abstracts information regarding roles and their schedules of persons or E-service providers possessing these roles. A preliminary version of our process model in the context of WFMS is available in [6]. We further incorporate alerts and their routing in this paper.

The Process Model

In an organization, some of its tasks have to be performed by another organization via E-services. We call them communication tasks. Besides the task name and description, the requirements for performing each of them has to be specified as well. We call such requirements service-provider roles. Communication tasks generate alerts that are routed to matching service provider(s), which can be human or electronic (E-service provider). This task has to be carried out by a service provider playing the required role that reflects the requestor's requirement. Sometimes, an alert might need to be sent to several service providers (e.g., doctors, or medical partners) with the similar capabilities.

The Alerts

During the execution of an urgent process, an alert has to be sent to the matched service provider(s) that are available for service. Besides identification information, an alert has an urgency level and a response flag that indicates whether it has to be acknowledged by a deadline. The urgency of the alert U could be a function of time. Normally when not acknowledged, the AMS increases alert urgency with time, as further explained in the next section. Although traditionally alerts are small messages, we generalize the concept of alert to include any additional information are urgent, important, or that can better justify the request. For example, an audio file or an image could describe the injured patient better than text. Note that there can be one or more alerts associated to a communication task. Association models the relationship between a task and a set of alerts, i.e., a task will trigger at least one alert. Response is user reply of a alert sent by the AMS. If the alert message is set response flag to be true, it means reply from the receiver of the alert is a must. After receiving an alert, the service provider has to check it with its local policies and respond accordingly. On the other hand, the AMS needs to deal with those alerts that are not acknowledged by the deadline. From reported practice, we observe that as long as an alert is not acknowledged, the service provider assigned to handle the alert may change. As a result, the AMS can revise the matching between the alert and the service provider. In addition, as the time passes without any acknowledgement, the urgency of the alert should increase as well. Thus, this may in turn change the service provider to be requested. In our model, we propose a flexible approach, in which a strategy can be defined by the administrator. Each service provider has either communicated to all interested parties a list of the service descriptions that it provides and/or it allows for a search on the provided web services for example where the alert description tries to match the existing services and/or has published the services though a broker.

E-Marketing

Marketing is the process of planning and executing the conception, distribution, promotion, and pricing of ideas, goods, and services to create exchanges that satisfy individual and organizational objectives. In plain English, this means that marketers plan marketing mixes to meet the needs of customers and marketing organizations, and then carry out those plans.

E-marketing affects traditional marketing in two ways. First, it increases efficiency in traditional marketing functions. Second, the technology of e-marketing transforms many marketing strategies. The transformation results in new business models that add **customer value** and/or increase company profitability. These models will be highlighted shortly.

The Big Picture

Easy, inexpensive, and quick access to digital information transforms economies, governments, societies, and businesses. Digital information enhances economies through more efficient markets, more jobs, information access, communication globalization, lower barriers to foreign trade and investment, and more. In the United States alone, the Internet generated $300 billion for the economy (5-8% of GDP), and 200 dot-com companies went public in 1999. With approximately 266 million users connected to the Internet worldwide and 122 million of those in the United States, many other economies are feeling the positive impact as well especially highly industrialized nations. However, the picture is not entirely rosy. Societies change as global communities based on interests form, and worldwide information access slowly decreases cultural and language differences. Some say that the existence of a truly global village will have the effect of removing cultural differences and that this is not good thing. Furthermore, easy computer networking means that work and home boundaries are dissipating, which makes working more convenient. However, this may encourage more workaholics and less time with family. Finally there is the digital divide. This is the idea that Internet adoption occurs when folks have enough money to buy a computer, the literacy to read what is on Web pages, and the education to be motivated to do it. Internet critics are justifiably concerned that class divisions will grow, making things worse for less fortunate citizens and even entire emerging countries. Governments are working to solve some of these problems; however, they have other important worries. Notably, how to collect taxes and import tariffs when transactions happen in cyberspace in a borderless world?

The digital environment enhances business practices other than marketing and logistics in many ways that are astounding. As you read the following, recall one new rule for the digital economy: interdisciplinary focus. Disciplines must work together with marketing and MIS/CIS using computer networks to share and apply knowledge for increased profitability.

Financial managers distribute shareholder information online, file required government and SEC statements, and invent new ways to value risk, return, and capital investments in dot-com firms that have high sales and few profits.

Human resources folks use the Net for electronic recruiting, training, and sometimes manage corporate knowledge and workflow through corporate Web **portals**.

Production and operation managers can adjust manufacturing to reflect the Internet's ability to give immediate sales feedback. This results in just-in-time inventory and "building to order."

Strategists at the top use the firm's knowledge to build and maintain a competitive edge. Digital tools allow them easy access to data from their desktops on demand and give them results of the firm's strategies on-the-fly.

A Tangled Web We Weave

The Internet has introduced a tremendous amount of new terminology. Some of the least understood terminology concerns the computer networks that form the Internet. An understanding of some of the more salient networks helps to present the big picture

Internet—The global network of interconnected networks. This includes millions of corporate, government, organizational, and private networks as well as e-mail, newsgroups, and the Web.

Web—The portion of the Internet that supports a graphical user interface for hypertext navigation with a browser such as Netscape or Internet Explorer. The Web is what most people think about when they think of the Internet.

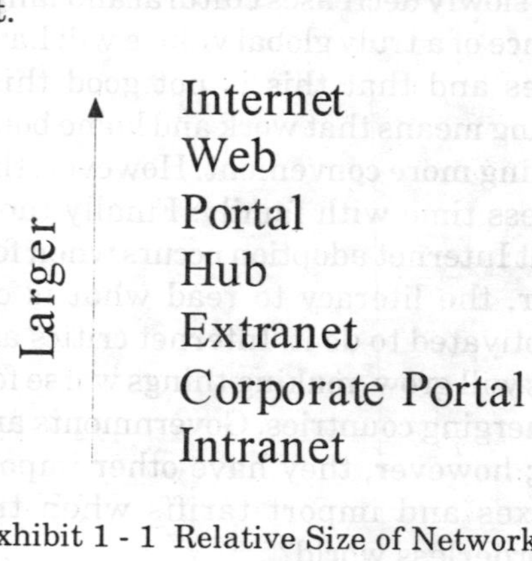

Exhibit 1 - 1 Relative Size of Networks

Intranet—A network that runs internally in a corporation but that uses Internet standards such as HTML and browsers. Thus, an intranet is like a mini-Internet but only for internal corporate consumption.

Extranet—An intranet to which value chain partners have admission for strategic reasons. The access is normally only partial.

Corporate Portal—A second-generation intranet. The goal of a corporate portal is to merge all of the employees' information and communication needs into a single interface. Thus, corporate portals access internal documents, data warehouses, groupware, e-mail, and calendars, in addition to the Web. Plum tree was a pioneer in the development of portals. See a demo of its system at demo .plum tree .com.

Portal—A point of entry to the Internet. Many portals such as Yahoo!, Lycos, and Excite were originally just search engines. What makes them portals is that they now provide many services in addition to searching. In other words, they are destinations for news, games, maps, shopping, and so forth in addition to being jump off points to content provided by others.

Hub—Hubs usually refer to the business-to-business market. They are online markets created in specific industries. Buyers and sellers visit the hub to do business. For example, Chemdex is a hub geared to the laboratory supplies industry.

We are now entering the second generation of e-business, or as *The Industry Standard* recently called it, "the end of the beginning." This is a time when marketers must return to their traditional roots and rely on well-grounded strategy. They must take the new rules and new tools and apply sound marketing practices. According to the Gartner Group, there will be a dot-com shakeout from 2000-2003, with much industry consolidation (Exhibit 1 - 2). Some firms such as Levi-Strauss have already stopped selling online because it both was not efficient and created channel conflict. Other firms are merging, and the strong firms are eating the small ones. This is typical in a maturing market environment. Gartner Group predicts that after the crash a "true" e-business model will emerge, and by 2008 the "e" will be dropped, making electronic business just part of the way things are done. Sounds right, although the cycle timing is uncertain.

An example of a firm that has already gone through this cycle is Charles Schwab, who allowed e.Schwab.com to cannibalize the larger **brick-and-mortar** firm in 1998. Dubbed "eat your own DNA" by Jack Welch at General Electric, Schwab astutely pitted the online and offline business models against each other and allowed the most profitable methods to win. e.Schwab lowered prices, incorporated successful e-marketing strategies, and accounts and assets grew rapidly during 1999. Many e-tailers are incorporating second-generation practices as well. *The Wall Street Journal* reported in April 2000 that 38% of Web retailers are profitable, and 72% of catalog companies with online storefronts are in the black. Sound strategy practiced by these e-tailers include appropriate scale, good service, quick speed, and low costs.

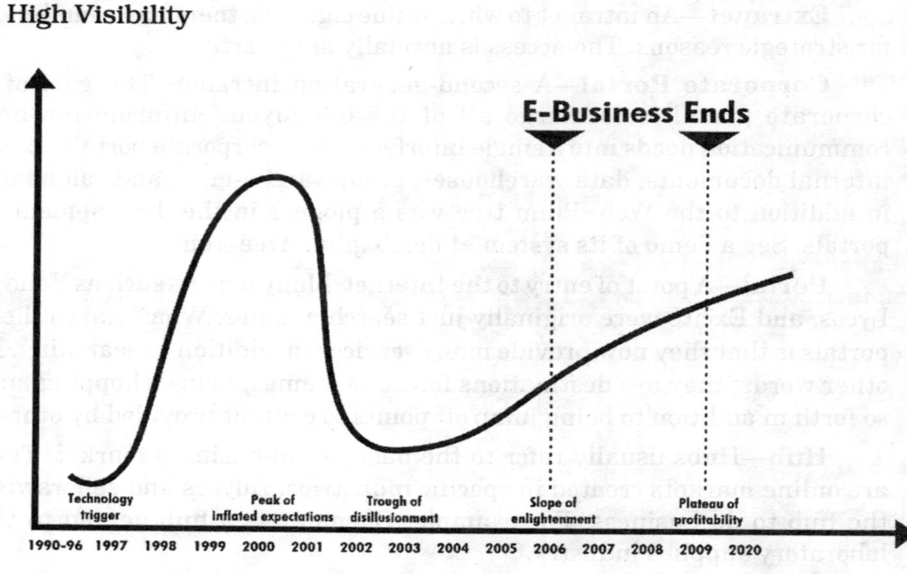

Exhibit 1 - 2 Entering the Second Generation of E-Business
Source: Adapted from the Gartner Group.

New Rules for E-Marketing

Some marketing principles never change. Customers trust good brands, firms compete using well-crafted marketing mix strategies, and lines like "where's the beef?" and "it's the real thing" linger in our minds forever. Regardless, organizations are scrambling to understand the **digital economy** and what it means for business strategies. Marketers want to know which of their time-tested concepts need modification. This textbook attempts to answer these questions through careful examination of **e-business** strategies in light of proven marketing practices. We begin by outlining fundamental changes at the beginning of the twenty-first century based on the earth-shattering move from "atoms to bits." Nicolas Negro Ponte coined this term to represent the shift from physical products to digital products and processes:

for example, from print media delivered in paper form at the newsstand to digital information delivered via a Web site over computer networks. Some call this the change from marketplace to market space. Whatever it is called, it means that text, graphics, audio, and video can be sent from firms to stakeholders and back again like magic over the Internet. And it has marketers scratching their heads in wonder.

Power shift from sellers to buyers

This may be the most fundamental change of all. The days of marketers holding consumers captive for 30 seconds in front of a screen are quickly coming to a close. It started with channel surfing and the remote control, and it is ending with control of the mouse. Both individual and business buyers are more demanding than ever because they are just one click away from a plethora of global competitors, all vying for their business. In this environment, buyer attention is the scarce commodity and customer relationship capital a valued asset.

Increasing velocity

Change in the digital economy is lightning fast: "He who hesitates gets smoked. There's almost no incentive to be conservative," according to J. William Gurley, Benchmark Capital. In the transparent environment of the Web competitors know instantly what the others are doing, and imitation is easy. For example, one day there was eBay, and the next day Amazon.com and a number of other firms offered **online auctions.**

Death of distance

Geographic location is no longer a factor when collaborating with business partners, supply chain firms, or customers, or just chatting with friends. The Internet made place unimportant because people can meet inexpensively in cyberspace regardless of whether or not they ever meet face-to-face. This phenomenon allows many buyers and sellers to bypass traditional intermediaries.

Global reach

The Internet created a borderless global economy where marketers can reach an incredibly larger number of people than with traditional media. This creates challenges as well as opportunities for firms who want to distribute products worldwide and provide post purchase service.

Time compression

Thanks to the Internet, time is not a factor in communication between firms and their stakeholders. Online stores can run on automatic pilot 24/7, and people can communicate asynchronously as their schedules permit. Times zones disappear for managers needing to collaborate with business partners halfway across the world.

Knowledge management is key

Marketers have better information *on* their customers and better information *for* them. In the digital world, customer information is easy and inexpensive to gather, cheap to store, and fruitful to mine Marketing managers can track the results of their strategies as they are implemented, receiving play-by-play reports. Organizations build huge databases of information, but turning them into knowledge that guides future strategy is a difficult challenge. Corporate information can also be delivered to clients much more quickly. Clients will either now pay for this information because they value its timeliness or see it as a significant benefit provided by a supplier.

Market deconstruction

Mohanbir Sawhney first noted that in the absence of time and space constraints, traditional product bundling no longer holds. This is especially true when physical products can be separated from the information with which they are associated. For example, traditional consumers might visit an individual car dealer for automobiles, financing, and repair services. In the digital economy, consumers can also visit auto metamediaries such as Edmunds.com and find information on all brands and makes of cars, auto financing and insurance, and gain referral to dealers with the best prices. Then they can search the Net for auto ratings by the media and individual consumers. Further, they can perform each function at a different time and at a different Web site. This structural transformation of markets opens the possibility for unlimited combinations of products and services worldwide.

Interoperability

One of the most significant developments of the Web is the movement toward open standards for software design. Open standards exist in the public domain and are sanctioned by international bodies. Designing for open standards creates systems that will work well together. Such systems are said to be interoperable. The advantages are tremendous. Firms can purchase best of breed systems in each functional area with some assurance that the systems will smoothly integrate.

Interdisciplinary focus

There was a shift from hierarchical to matrix organizations that predates the Web. What's new is the need for the marketing and MIS disciplines to work together very closely. Marketers have to understand technology capabilities in order to harness their power. The result is that when a consumer orders from a Web site, the firm will be able to fulfill the order properly, replenish its supply from the manufacturer, and provide online customer support, all without dropping the ball. Doing this right saves costs and retains customers. For these reasons, marketers must understand the technologies that drive e-marketing in order to be successful. Marketers do not have to personally develop the technologies; however, they need to know enough to hire suppliers and to explain their needs succinctly to IT professionals. The marriage of marketing and MIS is witnessed by the number of students who now pursue double majors utilizing this powerful combination.

Intellectual capital rules

Imagination, creativity, and entrepreneurship are more important resources than is financial capital. As we enter the twenty-first century in the United States, there is an abundance of money chasing energetic folks with hot ideas. Intangible assets such as intellectual capital and enterprise knowledge draw investors much more quickly than do tangible assets such as physical plants and warehouses. Of course, it takes marketing savvy to turn intellectual capital into profits.

Now that we've outlined 10 fundamental changes in the digital economy, it is important to restate that some things don't change: Treat customers and partners with care, create a sustainable competitive advantage, and follow time-proven marketing processes.

E-Marketing Communication

These models include many ways that firms communicate about products to business customers and individual consumers. MarCom models create awareness of products, prices, and distribution locations, build brands, and create positive images about products and firms. They also help marketers build long-term customer relationships. They do all this through promotion mix elements of advertising, sales promotion, direct marketing, and public relations; however, e-marketing applications are often quite different from traditional uses of these tools.

Online Advertising Model

Firms purchase advertising space on Web sites owned by other firms. It is important to draw a distinction between online advertising and **content publishing** because many confuse the two, thinking that a firm's own Web site is advertising. Advertising has a particular meaning in marketing: when a firm pays for space somewhere else. In so doing they are trying to reach users and communicate about products or promotional offers. Although many of the traditional advertising procedures apply in e-marketing, there are many unique opportunities and challenges online. For example, firms can purchase advertising within the e-mail sent by other firms such as List bot . com.

Online Sales Promotion Model

One of the most interesting twists on traditional marketing is the ability of firms to sample digital products online. Music CDs, software, research reports and, indeed, book chapters: These are all products that allow customers to see a little bit in hopes that they will buy the rest. In addition, online coupons and other sales promotion techniques save costs for e-marketers while communicating about products with customers.

Content Publishing Model

This is the model used by every firm that has a Web site. Also called brochureware, this involves firms displaying information about their product offerings on the Web site to Net users. Content refers to any text, graphics, audio, or video online that informs or persuades. The content publishing model is meant to move prospects closer to buying but does not involve transactions. Content publishing is sometimes directed to stakeholders other than the target market: for example, the media, stockholders, or employees.

E-Mail Model

There are three types of e-mail to interest marketers. The first concerns e-mail to target promotions to specific users. The targeting can be very sophisticated—for example, targeting users when they are most receptive to a promotional offering based on data mining of past purchase patterns. The second form of e-mail is the reverse channel: from the user to the firm. Users need to receive a prompt and thoughtful response to their inquiries. Amazon.com thinks this function so important to the development of customer relationships that they place some of their most talented employees in customer service. The third form of e-mail is from consumer to consumer. This is the modern-day equivalent of word of mouth. Consumer-to-consumer e-mail supports viral marketing campaigns-e.g., have your friend open an account with us and you receive $20.

Relationship Management

Because of its ability to communicate one-to-one with individual users, the Internet has changed customer relationship management (CRM) practices substantially. Online FAQs, automatic e-mail responders, customized Web pages, FAX-on-demand, and supply chains that are integrated with CRM functions are all ways that e-marketing can help build long-term customer relationships

Community Building Model

As previously mentioned in the content sponsorship model, many firms build Web sites to draw communities of special interest users. In this model, firms invite users to chat and post e-mail on their Web sites with the purpose of drawing potential customers to the site. Firms often gather e-mail lists of like-minded users from these communities for future e-mail marketing campaigns. When marketers build community with users they are creating social bonds that enhance customer relationships.

Business Intelligence Systems

B.I.S. Business Intelligence Systems is an IT company that specializes in the field of financial management software adapted to the needs of international development projects as well as internationally acting consulting companies.

As a member of the GFA Group, a leader in this sector for more than 20 years, B.I.S. provides software solutions that combine financial control with flexible business processes. We are channel partners of Systems Union, which is one of the leading software providers in the areas of finance, controlling and stock management.

The democratization of business intelligence from data repositories to collaboration platforms: The need for competitive analysis and other high-level information has spread throughout the organization.

There was a time when if you wanted a report that analyzed information from a variety of sources a marketing database, a sales forecast and a customer database, for example you were one of a chosen few in an organization who could have access to that bit of business intelligence. To actually get the information you needed, however, and to share it with colleagues was difficult at best.

For example, a marketing manager at a bank might look at customer information that was stored in a number of databases checking, savings, credit cards and loans when trying to determine which customers were the most profitable to pursue for a new product or service. Prior to business intelligence systems, that marketing manager would have had to enlist programmers to develop software to gather and analyze all of the information. The rest of the knowledge workers at the bank were relegated to using spreadsheets and other crude methods of data comparison.

"We've really graduated from the spreadsheet," says Dave Henry, VP of product marketing for Agent. "Today's organizations need to respond much more quickly to market conditions. That means putting more information in the hands of more people in a organization. It's not just an issue of getting information to a few data analysts who are going to interact with the data warehouse."

According to Henry, the democratization of business intelligence is part of a larger trend of using business intelligence to collaborate among departments within an organization as well as with trading partners and others outside of the company. "What we're seeing emerging is business intelligence Web services. After you've done all the analysis, you want to share it with other people," Henry says. "Take a manufacturing setting, for example. There are several people in an extended supply chain who need access to information that is being developed within the company. With Web-based business intelligence, it is easier for people from multiple companies to share information." Traditional business intelligence systems haven't been appropriate for collaboration. Henry says, but "now you can have a chart or a graph that is updated every hour. Everyone in the supply chain can collaborate looking at the up-to-date metrics for immediate business activity monitoring."

Data standardization and data integrity are especially important for accurate business analysis, so a number of safeguards have been built into many business intelligence systems. "We've added some data standardization tools to ensure data quality and make sure that there are no missing values or incorrect data getting into the data warehouse," says Henry.

As the trend toward standardization takes hold, BI is becoming a true Web-based technology, according to Neil Patil, senior director of product marketing for Brio. "As we deliver business intelligence to the mainstream, the Web is the platform of choice. This is no longer a technology that is locked in by the financial analysts and IT guys. It is for executives as well as people on the front lines," he says.

As more people in an organization use BI, the need grows for pre-packaged metrics. "We're seeing more and more companies asking for standard packages that look at key performance indicators," Patil says. "They need to get metrics that might relate to the sales pipeline or supply chain or fulfillment."

That trend has also led to more personalization of business intelligence systems as well as modules tailored toward specific job functions, such as sales or marketing. Patil says, "If you're in sales, the system knows your profile and which business metrics relate to your business functions."

As more people in an organization use business intelligence tools, it becomes more important that those tools be adept at Melding together data from a variety of sources, according to Louise Wannier, president and CEO of Enfish.

"It is not just enough to pull together financial data, marketing data and information from the Web, a business intelligence system needs to be able to pull that information together in a fashion that is relevant to the user," she says.

Wannier gives the example of a salesperson preparing to call on a new client. He or she might want to pull in information from an internal database, a report that a colleague wrote, information from the potential client's Web site as well as the latest news items written about the company. "They need that information in front of them on one screen in an easily understood format. They not only need the document, the system has to point them to the right section of the document," Wannier says.

Business intelligence tools are evolving from repositories of data to platforms for collaboration. "Whereas before information that had been produced by a workgroup was stored on the company intranet, it would never be found unless the person who was doing some business intelligence work knew where to look," says Wannier. "Now, that information is distributed and available to everyone."

The collaborative nature of new business intelligence systems means extending availability beyond the organization, according to Donald MacCormick, global product communication director for Crystal Decisions. "It is important to be able to share this information with selected partners outside of the organization," he says. "Companies are finding that they need to deliver these capabilities to their partners, customers and suppliers."

Business intelligence systems also need to be flexible to meet the needs of various users and departments. MacCormick says, "You might have one person who wants a report on the top 10 customers, another one is looking at analyzing phone bill costs." Key to the success of any business intelligence systems is scalability. "Over the past few years, there has been significant change in the amount of data and the number of people who will have access to that data for business intelligence purposes," says MacCormick. "You're getting this information out to thousands of people, instead of a select group of people, so you really do need to scale up quickly and efficiently."

Data Mining Models

Introduction

The point of data visualization is to let the user understand what is going on. Since data mining usually involves extracting "hidden" information from a database, this understanding process can get somewhat complicated. In most standard database operations nearly everything the user sees is something that they knew existed in the database already. A report showing the breakdown of sales by product and region is straightforward for the user to understand because they intuitively know that this kind of information already exists in the database. If the company sells different products in different regions of the county, there is no problem translating a display of this information into a relevant understanding of the business process.

Data mining, on the other hand, extracts information from a database that the user did not already know about. Useful relationships between variables that are non-intuitive are the jewels that data mining hopes to locate. Since the user does not know beforehand what the data mining process has discovered, it is a much bigger leap to take the output of the system and translate it into an actionable solution to a business problem. Since there are usually many ways to graphically represent a model, the visualizations that are used should be chosen to maximize the value to the viewer. This requires that we understand the viewer's needs and design the visualization with that end-user in mind. If we assume that the viewer is an expert in the subject area but not data modeling, we must translate the model into a more natural representation for them. For this purpose we suggest the use of orienteering principles as a template for our visualizations.

Orienteering

Orienteering is typically accomplished by two chief approaches: maps and landmarks. Imagine yourself set down in an unknown city with instructions to find a given hotel. The usual method is to obtain a map showing the large-scale areas of the city. Once the "hotel district" is located we will then walk along looking for landmarks such as street names until we arrive at our location. If the landmarks do not match the map, we will re-consult the map and even replace one map with another. If the landmarks do not appear correct then usually one will backtrack, try a short side journey, or ask for further landmarks from people on the street. The degree to which we will follow the landmark chain or trust the map depends upon the match between the landmarks and the map. It will be reinforced by unexpected matches (happening along a unique landmark for which we were not looking), by finding the landmark by two different routes and by noting that variations are small. Additionally, our experience with cities and maps and the urgency of our journey will affect our confidence as well.

The combination of a global coordinate system (the map analogy) and the local coordinate system (the landmarks) must fit together and must instill confidence as the journey is traversed. The concept of a manifold is relevant in that the global coordinates must be realizable, as a combination of local coordinate systems is some sense. To grow trust in the user we should:

- Show that nearby paths (small distances in the model) do not lead to widely different ends
- Show, on demand, the effect that different perspectives (change of variables or inclusion probabilities) have on model structure
- Make dynamic changes in coloring, shading, edge definition and viewpoint (dynamic dithering)
- Sprinkle known relationships (landmarks) throughout the model landscape.
- Allow interaction that provides more detail and answers queries on demand.

The **advantages** of this manifold approach include the ability to explore it in some optimal way (such as projection pursuit), the ability to reduce the models to a independent coordinate set, and the ability to measure model adequacy in a more natural manner.

Why Visualize a Data Mining Model?

The driving forces behind visualizing data mining models can be broken down into two key areas: Understanding and Trust. Understanding is undoubtedly the most fundamental motivation behind visualizing the model. Although the simplest way to deal with a data mining model is to leave the output in the form of a black box, the user will not necessarily gain an understanding of the underlying behavior in which they are interested. If they take the black box model and score a database, they can get a list of customers to target. There's not much for the user to do other than sit back and watch the envelopes go out. This can be a very effective approach. Mailing costs can often be reduced by an order of magnitude without significantly reducing the response rate.

The more interesting way to use a data mining model is to get the user to actually understand what is going on so that they can take action directly. Visualizing a model should allow a user to discuss and explain the logic behind the model with colleagues, customers, and other users. Getting buy-in on the logic or rationale is part of building the users' trust in the results. For example, if the user is responsible for ordering a print advertising campaign, understanding customer demographics is critical. Decisions about where to put advertising dollars are a direct result of understanding data mining models of customer behavior. There's no automated way to do this. It's all in the marketing manager's head. Unless the output of the data mining system can be understood qualitatively, it won't be of any use. In addition, the model needs to be understood so that the actions that are taken as a result can be justified to others.

Understanding means more than just comprehension; it also involves context. If the user can understand what has been discovered in the context of their business issues, they will trust it and put it into use. There are two parts to this problem: 1) visualization of the data mining output in a meaningful way, and 2) allowing the user to interact with the visualization so that simple questions can be answered. Creative solutions to the first part have recently been incorporated into a number of commercial data mining products. Graphing lift, response, and (probably most importantly) financial indicators (e.g., profit, cost, ROI) give the user a sense of context that can quickly ground the results in reality. After that, simple representations of the data mining results allow the user to see the data mining results. Graphically displaying a decision tree (CART, CHAID, and C4.5) can significantly change that way in which the data mining software is used. Some algorithms can pose more problems than others (e.g., neural networks) can but novel solutions are starting to appear.

It is the second part that has yet to be addressed fully. Interaction is, for many users, the Holy Grail of visualization in data mining. Manipulation of the data and viewing the results dynamically allows the user to get a feel for the dynamics and test whether something really counter-intuitive is going on. The interactivity helps achieve this and the easier this is to do the better. Seeing a decision tree is nice, but what they really want to do is drag-and-drop the best segments onto a map of the United States in order to see if there are sales regions that are neglected. The number of "what if" questions that can be asked is endless: How do the most likely customers break down by gender? What is the average balance for the predicted defaulters? What are the characteristics of mail order responders? The interaction will continue until the user understands what is going on with their customers. Users also often desire drill through so that they can see the actual data behind a model (or some piece of the model), although it is probably more a matter of perceptions rather than actual usefulness. Finally, integrating with other decision support tools (e.g., OLAP) will let users view the data mining results in a manner that they are already using for the purpose of understanding customer behavior. By incorporating interaction into the process, a user will be able to connect the data mining results with his or her customers.

Trusting the Model

Attributing the appropriate amount of trust to data mining models is essential to using them wisely. Good quantitative measures of "trust" must ultimately reflect the probability that the model's predictions would match future test targets. However, due to the exploratory and large-scale nature of most data mining tasks, fully articulating all of the probabilistic factors to do so would seem to be generally intractable. Thus, instead of focusing on trying to boil "trust" down to one probabilistic quantity, it is typically most useful to visualize along many dimensions some of the key factors that contribute to trust (and distrust) in ones models. Furthermore, since, as with any scientific model, one ultimately can only disprove a model, visualizing the limitations of the model is of prime importance. Indeed, one might best view the overall goal of "visualizing trust" as that of understanding the limitations of the model, as opposed to understanding the model itself.

Since data mining relies heavily on training data, it is important to understand the limitations that given data sets put on future application of the resulting model. One class of standard visualization tools involves probability density estimation and clustering over the training data. Especially interesting would be regions of state space that are uncommon in the training data yet do not violate known domain constraints. One would tend to trust a model less if it acts more confident when presented with uncommon data as future inputs. For time-series data, visualizing indicators of non-stationary is also important.

Assessing Trust in a Model

Assessing model trustworthiness is typically much more straight-forward than the holy grail of model understanding per se essentially because the former is largely deconstructive while the latter is constructive. For example, without a deep understanding of a given model, one can still use general domain knowledge to detect that it violates expected qualitative principles. A well-known example is that one would be concerned if ones model employed a (presumably spurious) statistic correlation between shoe size and IQ. Of course, there are still very significant challenges in declaring such knowledge as completely and consistently as possible.

Domain knowledge is also critical for outlier detection needed to clean data and avoid classic problems such as a juvenile crime committed by a 80-year-old "child". If a data mining model were build using the data in Figure 1, it is possible that outliers (most likely caused by incorrect data entry) will skew the resulting model (especially the zero-year-old children, which are more reasonable than eighty-year-old children). The common role of visualization here is mostly in terms of annotating model structures with domain knowledge that they violate.

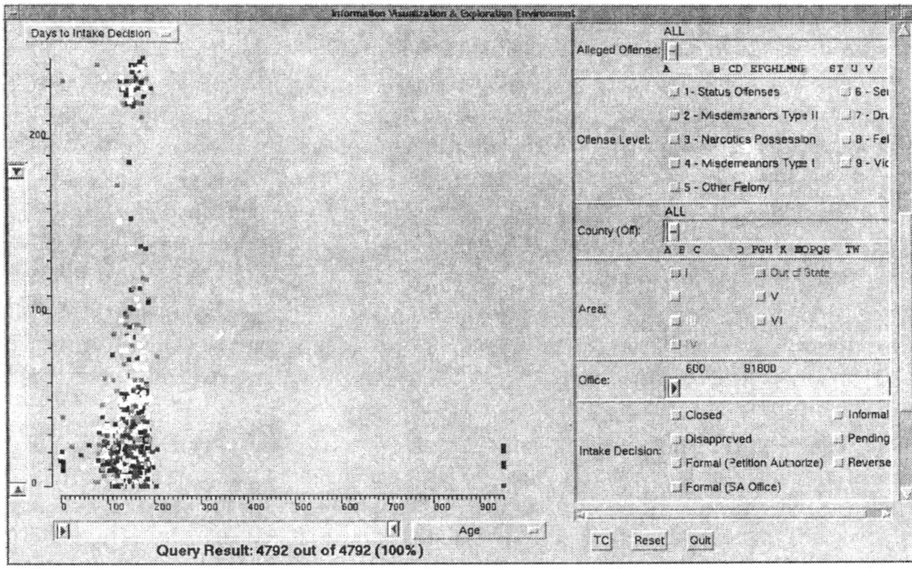

Figure 1: Age (in months) vs. Days to Intake Decision for juvenile crime offenders, Maryland Department of Juvenile Services. Note the 80-year-old children on the right side of the graph.

Not all assessments of trust are negative in nature, however. In particular, one can also increase ones trust in a model if other reasonable models seem worse. In this sense, assessing trust is also closely related to model comparison. In particular, it is very useful to understand the sensitivity of model predictions and quality to changes in parameters and/or structure of the given model. There are many ways to visualize such sensitivity, often in terms of local and global (conditional) probability densities with special interest in determining whether multiple modes of high probability exist for some parameters and combinations. Such relative measures of trust can be considerably less demanding to formulate than attempts at more absolute measures, but do place special demands on the visualization engine, which must support quick and non-disorientating navigation through neighboring regions in model space.

Statistical summaries of all sorts are also common and useful for gathering insights for assessing model trust. Pair wise scatter-plots and low-dimensional density estimates are especially common. Summaries can be particularly useful for comparing relative trust of two models, by allowing analysis to focus on subsets of features for which their interrelationships differ most significantly between two models.

It is often useful to combine summaries with interactive ability to drill-through to the actual data. Many forms of visual summary actually display multiple scales of data along the raw to abstract continuum, making visual drill-through a natural recursive operation.

For example, compressing millions of samples into a time-series strip chart that is only 1000 pixels wide allows one to quickly see the global highest and lowest points across the entire time range, as well as the local high and low points occurring within each horizontal pixel.

Most useful are models that qualify their own trustworthiness to some degree, such as in quantifying the expected variance in the error of their predictions.

In practice, such models tend to be relatively rare. Heavy emphasis on expected case rather than worst case performance is generally not all that inappropriate, since one is typically ultimately interested in concepts such as expected cumulative payoff.

There are important classes of tasks, such as novelty detection (e.g. fraud detection), for which quantified variance is essential. Standard techniques are learning confidence intervals (e.g. error bars for neural networks) and general probability density estimation. A promising recent approach [2], called bounds estimation, attempts to find a balance between the complexity of general probability density estimation and the simplicity of the mean estimation plus variance estimation approach to error bars.

Finally, it is important, though rather rare in practice to date, to consider many transformations of the data during visual exploration of model sensitivities. For example, a model that robustly predicts well the internal pressure of some engineering device should probably also be able to do well predicting related quantities, such as its derivative, its power spectrum, and other relevant quantities (such as nearby or redundant pressures). Checking for such internal consistency is perhaps ultimately one of the most important ways to judge the trustworthiness of a model, beyond standard cross validation error. Automated and interactive means of exploring and visualizing the space (and degrees) of inconsistencies a model entails seems to be a particularly important direction for future research on assessing model trustworthiness.

Understanding the Model

A model that can be understood is a model that can be trusted. While statistical methods build some trust in a model by assessing its accuracy, they cannot assess the model's semantic validity its applicability to the real world.

A data mining algorithm that uses a human-understandable model can be checked easily by domain experts, providing much needed semantic validity to the model. Unfortunately, users are often forced to trade off accuracy of a model for understandability.

Advanced visualization techniques can greatly expand the range of models that can be understood by domain experts, thereby easing the accuracy/understandability trade-off. Three components are essential for understanding a model: representation, interaction, and integration. Representation refers to the visual form in which the model appears. A good representation displays the model in terms of visual components that are already familiar to the user. Interaction refers to the ability to see the model in action in real time, to let the user play with the model as if it were a machine. Integration refers to the ability to display relationships between the model and alternate views of the data on which it is based. Integration provides the user context.

The rest of this section will focus on understanding classification models. Specifically, we will examine three models built using Silicon Graphic's MineSet: decision tree, simple Bayesian, and decision table classifiers [3]. Each of these tools provides a unique form of understanding based on representation, interaction, and integration.

The graphical representation should be simple enough to be easily understood, but complete enough to reveal all the information present in the model. This is a difficult balance since simplicity usually trades off against completeness. Three-dimensional visualizations have the potential to show far more information than two-dimensional visualizations while retaining their simplicity. Navigation in such a scene lets one focus on an element of interest while keeping the rest of the structure in context. It is critical, however, that the user be able to navigate through a three-dimensional visualization in real time. An image of a three-dimensional scene is merely a two-dimensional projection and is usually more difficult to understand than a scene built in two dimensions.

Even with three dimensions, many models still contain far too much information to display simply. In these cases the visualization must simplify the representation as it is displayed. The MineSet decision tree and decision table visualizers use the principle of hierarchical simplification to present a large amount of information to the user. Decision trees are easy to understand but can become overwhelmingly large when automatically induced. The SGI MineSet Tree Visualizers uses a detail-hiding approach to simplify the visualization. In figure 2, only the first few levels of the tree are initially displayed, despite the fact that the tree is extensive. The user can gain a basic understanding of the tree by following the branches of these levels. Additional levels of detail are revealed only when the user navigates to a deeper level, providing more information only as needed.

Using decision tables as a model representation generates a simple but large model. A full decision table theoretically contains the entire dataset, which may be very large. Therefore simplification is essential. The MineSet decision table arranges the model into levels based on the importance of each feature in the table. The data is automatically aggregated to provide a summary using only the most important features. When the user desires more information, he can drill down as many levels as needed to answer his question. The visualization automatically changes

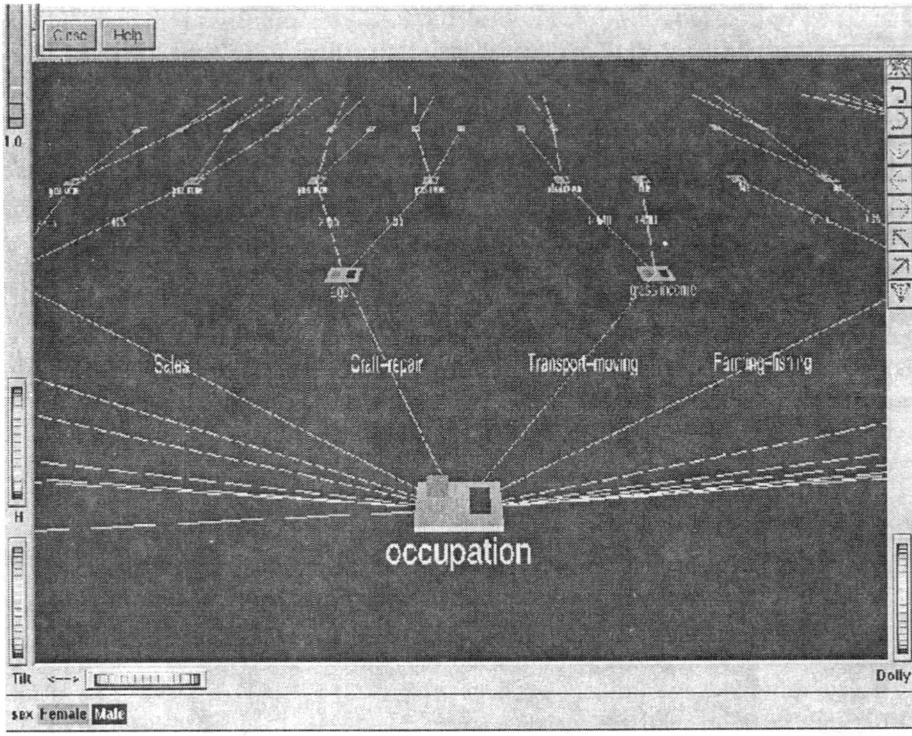

Figure 2: The MineSet Tree Visualizer shows only the portion of the model close to the viewer.

the aggregation of the data to display the desired level of detail. In figure 3, a decision table shows the well-known correlation between head shape and body shape in the monk dataset. It also shows that the classification is ambiguous in cases where head shape does not equal body shape. For these cases, the user can drill down to see that the attribute jacket color determines the class.

While a good representation can greatly aid the user's understanding, in many cases the model contains too much information to provide a representation that is both complete and understandable. In these cases we exploit the brain's ability to reason about cause and effect and let the user interact with the more complex model. Interaction can be thought of as "understanding by doing" as opposed to "understanding by seeing".

Common forms of interaction are interactive classification, interactive model building, drill-up, drill-down, animation, searching, filtering, and level-of-detail manipulation. The fundamental techniques of searching, filtering, drill-up, and drill-down, make the task of finding information hidden within a complex model easier. However, they do not help overall understanding much. More extensive techniques (interactive classification,

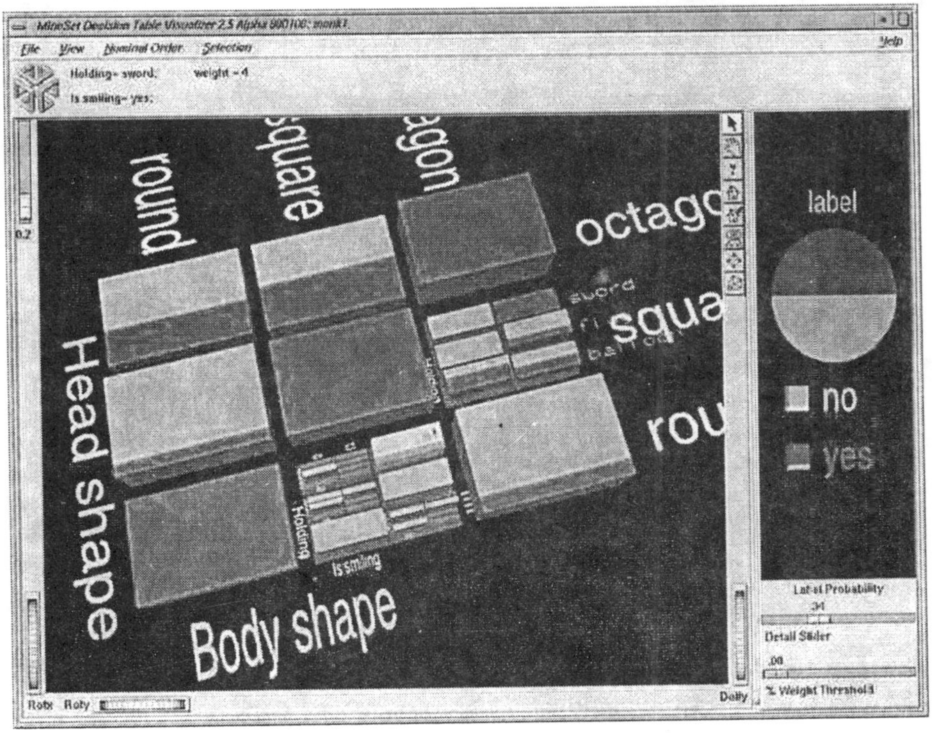

Figure 3: The MineSet Decision Table Visualizer shows additional pairs of attributes as the user drills down into the model.

interactive model building) are required to help the user understand a model which is too complicated to show with a static image or table. These advanced methods aid understanding by visually showing the answer to a user query while maintaining a simplified representation of the model for context.

The MineSet Evidence Visualizer allows the user to interact with a simple Bayesian classifier (Figure 4). Even simple Bayesian models are based on multiplying arrays of probabilities that are difficult to understand by themselves. However, by allowing the user to select values for features and see the effects, the visualization provides cause-and-effect insight into the operation of the classifier.

The user can play with the model to understand exactly how much each feature affects the classification and ultimately decide to accept or reject the result. In the example in the figure, the user selects the value of "working class" to be "self-employed-incorporated," and the value of "education" to be "professional-school". The pie chart on the right displays the expected distribution of incomes for people with these characteristics.

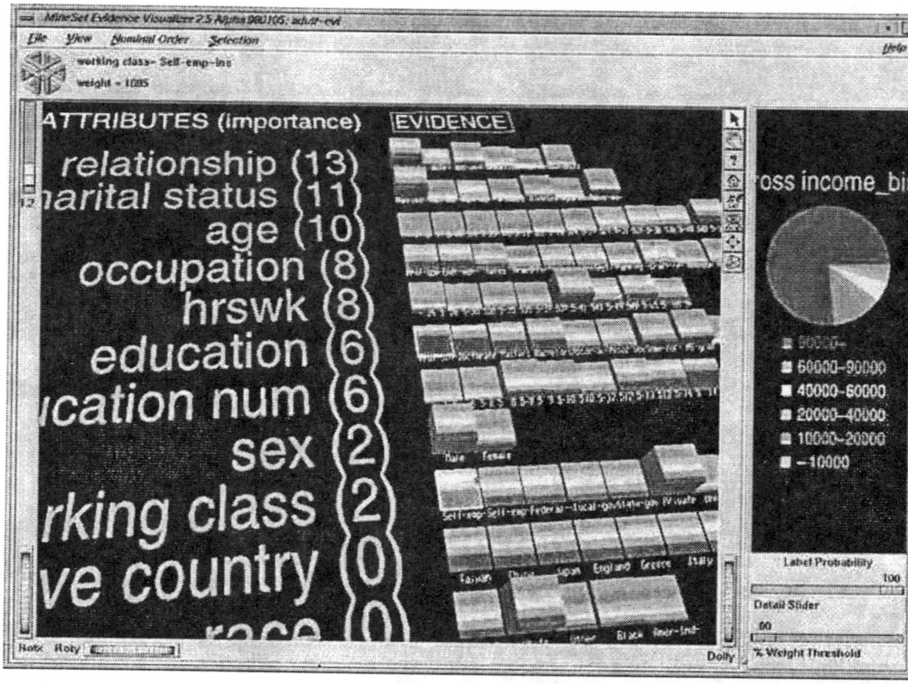

Figure 4: Specific attribute values are selected in the Evidence Visualizer in order to predict income for people with those characteristics.

Beyond interactive classification, interactively guiding the model-building process provides additional control and understanding to the user. Angoss [4] provides a decision tree tool that gives the user full control over when and how the tree is built. The user may suggest splits, perform pruning, or manually construct sections of the tree. This facility can boost understanding greatly. Figure 5a shows a decision tree split on a car's brand attribute. While the default behavior of the tree is to form a separate branch on the tree for each categorical value, a better approach is often to group similar values together and produces only a few branches. The result shown in figure 5b is easier to understand and can sometimes give better accuracy. Interactive models allow the user to make changes like this as the situation warrants.

Interactive techniques and simplified representations can produce models that can be understood within their own context. However, for a user to truly understand a model, he must understand how the model relates to the data from which it was derived. For this goal, tool integration is essential.

Few tools on the market today use integration techniques. The techniques that are used come in three forms: drill-through, brushing, and coordinated visualizations. Drill-through refers to the ability to select a

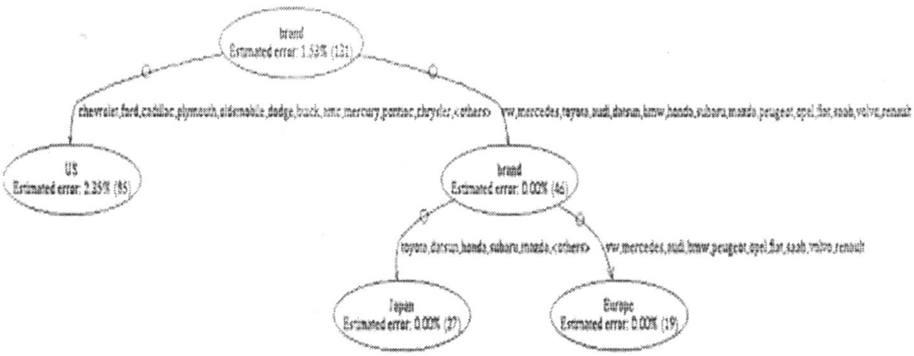

Figures 5a and 5b: A decision tree having branches for every value of the brand attribute (top), and a decision tree which groups values of brand to produce a simpler structure (bottom).

piece of a model and gain access to the original data upon which that piece of the model was derived. For example, the decision tree visualizer allows selection and drill-through on individual branches of the tree. This will provide access to the original data that was used to construct those branches, leaving out the data represented by other parts of the tree. Brushing refers to the ability to select pieces of a model and have the selections appear in an alternate representation. Coordinated visualizations generalize both techniques by showing multiple representations of the same model, combined with representations of the original data. Interactive actions that affect the model also affect the other visualizations. All three of these techniques help the user understand how the model relates to the original data. This provides an external context for the model and helps establish semantic validity.

As data mining becomes more extensive in industry and as the number of automated techniques employed increases, there is a natural tendency for models to become increasingly complex. In order to prevent these models from becoming mysterious oracles, whose dictates must be accepted on faith, it is essential to develop more sophisticated visualization techniques to keep pace with the increasing model complexity. Otherwise there is a danger that we will make decisions without understanding the reasoning behind them.

Comparing Different Models using Visualization

Model comparison requires the creation of an appropriate metric for the space of models under consideration. To visualize the model comparison, these metrics must be interpretable by a human observer through his or her visual system. The first step is to create a mapping from input to output of the modeling process. The second step is to map this process to the human visual space.

Different Meanings of the Word "Model"

It is important to recognize that the word "model" can have several levels of meaning. Common usage often associates the word model with the data modeling process. For example, we might talk of applying a neural network model to a particular problem. In this case, the word model refers to the generic type of model known as a neural network. Another use of the word model is associated with the end result of the modeling process. In the neural network example, the model could be the specific set of weights, topology, and node types that produces an output given a set of inputs. In still another use, the word model refers to the input-output mapping associated with a "black-box." Such a mapping necessarily places emphasis on careful identification of the input and output spaces.

Comparing Models as Input-Output Mappings

The input-output approach to model comparison simply considers the mapping from a defined input space to a defined output space. For example, we might consider a specific 1-gigabyte database with twenty-five variables (columns). The input space is simply the Cartesian product of the database's twenty-five variables. Any actions inside the model, such as creation of new variables, are hidden in the "black-box" and are not interpreted. At the end of the modeling process, an output is generated. This output could be a number, a prioritized list or even a set of rules about the system. The crucial issue is that we can define the output space in some consistent manner to derive an input to output mapping.

It is the space generated by the mappings that is of primary importance to the model comparison. For most applications the mapping space will be well defined once the input and output spaces are well defined. For example, two classifiers could be described by a set of input/output pairs, such as (obs1, class a), (obs2, class b), etc. The comparison metric could then be defined on these pairs as a count of the number differing, or GINI indices, or classification cost, etc. The resulting set of pairs could be visualized by simple plotting of points on a two-dimensional graph. The two model could be indexed by coloring or symbol codes. Or one could focus on the difference between each model directly and plot this. This approach should prove adequate so long as we restrict attention to a well-defined input-output structure.

Comparing Models as Algorithms

In the view of a model as static algorithm, again there seems to be a reasonable way to approach the model comparison problem. For example, a neural network model and an adaptive nonlinear regression model might be compared. These models would be expressed as a series of algorithmic steps. Each model's algorithm could then be analyzed by standard methods for measurement of algorithmic performance such as complexity, the finite word length and the stability of the algorithm. The investigator could also include measures on the physical implementation of the algorithm such as computation time, or computation size. Using these metrics the visualization could take the form of bar charts across the metrics. Again, different models could be encoded by color or symbol, and a graph of only difference between the two models on each metric could be provided. Each comparison would be for a static snapshot but certainly dynamic behavior could be exploited through a series of snapshots, i.e. a motion picture.

Comparing Models as Processes

The view of the model as a process is the most ill defined and therefore most intractable of the three views, but this should not minimize its importance. Indeed its sheer complexity might make it the most important view for the application of visualization. It is precisely in this arena that we encounter the subject area expert for whom these systems should offer the most benefit (such as confidence and trust).

The modeling process includes everything in and around the modeling activity, such as the methods, the users, the database, the support resources, and constraints such as knowledge, time and analysis implementation. Clearly this scope is too large for us to consider. Let us narrow our scope by assuming that the model comparison is being applied for one user on one database over a short time period. This implies that user differences, database differences, and knowledge difference can be neglected. We are left with analysis methods and implementation issues. For most subject area experts the implementation and the analysis are not separable, and so we will make the additional assumption that this issue can be ignored as well. With these simplifying assumptions we are essentially defining model comparison to be the comparison of modeling method and implementation simultaneously.

Imagine two models that are available in some concrete implemented form. These could be different general methods such as neural networks versus tree-based classifiers, or they could be different levels of sophistication within a class of models such as CART versus CHAID tree-structures. Remember that we are now focusing only on the modeling process, and not its input/output or algorithmic structure. It seems that reasonable metrics can be defined in this situation. For example, the running time could be such a metric, or the interpretability of instructions, or the number of tuning parameters that must be chosen by the user at run-time. The key here is that these metrics must be tailored to the user who is the target of the application. Thus, whereas the input-output view focused on these the spaces, and the algorithmic view focused on the properties of the algorithm independently of the user, now we must focus in great detail on the user's needs and perceptions.

Once a set of metrics is chosen, we appear to be in a similar situation to that described under the algorithmic comparison. We should be able to show the distances between models in each of the defined metrics in a bar chart or other standard display. Color or symbol coding can be used to show the results from each model on the same chart as well.

There will be many possible metrics for the model-building process, at least one per user. Since it is unlikely we can choose a set of "one-size-fits-all" metrics, it is more useful to establish properties of good metrics and create methods to establish them in novel situations. The metrics chosen by a academic researcher would likely be very different from those chosen business user. Some properties that good metrics for the modeling process should be:

- That they are expressed in direct risk/benefit to user.
- That they evaluate their sensitivity to model input and assumptions.
- That they can be audited (open to questioning at any point).
- That they are dynamic.
- That they can be summarized in the sense of an overall map.
- That they allow reference to landmarks and markers.

Some aspects of the visualization process will take on added importance. One such aspect is the sequential behavior of the modeling process. For example, it is common to plot frequently the updated fit between the data and the model predictions as a neural network learns. A human being will probably give more trust to a method which mimics his or her own learning behavior (i.e., a learning curve which starts with a few isolated details, then grows quickly to broad generalizations and then makes only incremental gains after that in the typical "S" shape). Unstable behavior or large swings should count against the modeling process.

Another aspect of importance should a visual track of the sensitivity of the modeling process to small changes in the data and modeling process parameters. For example, one might make several random starts with different random weights in a neural network model. These should be plotted versus one another showing their convergence patterns, again perhaps against a theoretical S-shaped convergence.

The model must also be auditable, meaning that inquiries may be made at any reasonable place in the modeling process. For a neural network we should be able to interrupt it and examine individual weights at any step in the modeling process. Likewise for a tree-based model we should be able to see sub trees at will. Ideally there could be several scales in which this interruption could occur.

Since most humans operate on a system of local and global coordinates it will be important to be able to supplement the visualizations with markers and a general map structure.

For example, even though the direct comparison is between two neural nets with different structures, it would be good to have the same distances plotted for another method with which the user is familiar (like discriminate analysis) even if that method is inadequate. If the same model could be used on a known input, the user could establish trust with the new results. It might also be useful to have simultaneously a detailed and a summarized model displayed. For example, the full tree-based classifier might have twenty-five branches, but the summarized tree might show the broad limbs only. And if the output is a rule it might be useful to drive (through logical manipulation) other results or statements of results as a test of reasonableness.

5

Public Key Infrastructure And Digital Signature

Data Encryption Standard (DES)

The Data Encryption Standard (DES) specifies a FIPS approved cryptographic algorithm as required by FIPS 140-1. This publication provides a complete description of a mathematical algorithm for encrypting (enciphering) and decrypting (deciphering) binary coded information. Encrypting data converts it to an unintelligible form called cipher. Decrypting cipher converts the data back to its original form called plaintext. The algorithm described in this standard specifies both enciphering and deciphering operations which are based on a binary number called a key.

A key consists of 64 binary digits ("O"s or "1"s) of which 56 bits are randomly generated and used directly by the algorithm. The other 8 bits, which are not used by the algorithm, are used for error detection. The 8 error detecting bits are set to make the parity of each 8-bit byte of the key odd, i.e., there is an odd number of "1"s in each 8-bit byte1. Authorized users of encrypted computer data must have the key that was used to encipher the data in order to decrypt it. The encryption algorithm specified in this standard is commonly known among those using the standard. The unique key chosen for use in a particular application makes the results of encrypting data using the algorithm unique. Selection of a different key causes the cipher that is produced for any given set of inputs to be different. The cryptographic security of the data depends on the security provided for the key used to encipher and decipher the data.

Data can be recovered from cipher only by using exactly the same key used to encipher it. Unauthorized recipients of the cipher who know the algorithm but do not have the correct key cannot derive the original data algorithmically. However, anyone who does have the key and the algorithm can easily decipher the cipher and obtain the original data. A standard algorithm based on a secure key thus provides a basis for exchanging encrypted computer data by issuing the key used to encipher it to those authorized to have the data.

Data that is considered sensitive by the responsible authority, data that has a high value, or data that represents a high value should be cryptographically protected if it is vulnerable to unauthorized disclosure or undetected modification during transmission or while in storage. A risk analysis should be performed under the direction of a responsible authority to determine potential threats. The costs of providing cryptographic protection using this standard as well as alternative methods of providing this protection and their respective costs should be projected. A responsible authority then should make a decision, based on these analyses, whether or not to use cryptographic protection and this standard.

This standard may be used by Federal departments and agencies when the following conditions apply:

1. An authorized official or manager responsible for data security or the security of any computer system decides that cryptographic protection is required; and

2. The data is not classified according to the National Security Act of 1947, as amended, or the Atomic Energy Act of 1954, as amended. Federal agencies or departments which use cryptographic devices for protecting data classified according to either of these acts can use those devices for protecting unclassified data in lieu of the standard.

Applications. Data encryption (cryptography) is utilized in various applications and environments. The specific utilization of encryption and the implementation of the DES will be based on many factors particular to the computer system and its associated components. In general, cryptography is used to protect data while it is being communicated between two points or while it is stored in a medium vulnerable to physical theft. Communication security provides protection to data by enciphering it at the transmitting point and deciphering it at the receiving point. File security provides protection to data by enciphering it when it is recorded on a storage medium and deciphering it when it is read back from the storage medium. In the first case, the key must be available at the transmitter and receiver simultaneously during communication. In the second case, the key must be maintained and accessible for the duration of the storage period. FIPS 171 provides approved methods for managing the keys used by the algorithm specified in this standard.

Implementations. Cryptographic modules which implement this standard shall conform to the requirements of FIPS 140-1. The algorithm specified in this standard may be implemented in software, firmware, hardware, or any combination thereof. The specific implementation may depend on several factors such as the application, the environment, the technology used, etc. Implementations which may comply with this standard include electronic devices (e.g., VLSI chip packages), micro-processors using Read Only Memory (ROM), Programmable Read Only Memory (PROM), or Electronically Erasable Read Only Memory (EEROM), and mainframe computers using Random Access Memory (RAM).

When the algorithm is implemented in software or firmware, the processor on which the algorithm runs must be specified as part of the validation process. Implementations of the algorithm which are tested and validated by NIST will be considered as complying with the standard. Note that FIPS 140-1 places additional requirements on cryptographic modules for Government use.

Information about devices that have been validated and procedures for testing and validating equipment for conformance with this standard and FIPS 140-1 are available from the National Institute of Standards and Technology, Computer Systems Laboratory, Gaithersburg, MD 20899.

Export Control. Cryptographic devices and technical data regarding them are subject to Federal Government export controls as specified in Title 22, Code of Federal Regulations, Parts 120 through 128. Some exports of cryptographic modules implementing this standard and technical data regarding them must comply with these Federal regulations and be licensed by the U.S. Department of State. Other exports of cryptographic modules implementing this standard and technical data regarding them fall under the licensing authority of the Bureau of Export Administration of the U.S. Department of Commerce. The Department of Commerce is responsible for licensing cryptographic devices used for authentication, access control, proprietary software, automatic teller machines (ATMs), and certain devices used in other equipment and software. For advice concerning which agency has licensing authority for a particular cryptographic device, please contact the respective agencies.

Patents. Cryptographic devices implementing this standard may be covered by U.S. and foreign patents issued to the International Business Machines Corporation. However, IBM has granted nonexclusive, royalty-free licenses under the patents to make, use and sell apparatus which complies with the standard. The terms, conditions and scope of the licenses are set out in notices published in the May 13, 1975 and August 31, 1976 issues of the Official Gazette of the United States Patent and Trademark Office (934 O.G. 452 and 949 O.G. 1717).

Alternative Modes of Using the DES. FIPS PUB 81, DES Modes of Operation, describes four different modes for using the algorithm described in this standard. These four modes are called the Electronic Codebook (ECB) mode, the Cipher Block Chaining (CBC) mode, the Cipher Feedback (CFB) mode, and the Output Feedback (OFB) mode. ECB is a direct application of the DES algorithm to encrypt and decrypt data; CBC is an enhanced mode of ECB which chains together blocks of cipher text; CFB uses previously generated cipher text as input to the DES to generate pseudorandom outputs which are combined with the plaintext to produce cipher, thereby chaining together the resulting cipher; OFB is identical to CFB except that the previous output of the DES is used as input in OFB while the previous cipher is used as input in CFB. OFB does not chain the cipher.

Qualifications. The cryptographic algorithm specified in this standard transforms a 64-bit binary value into a unique 64-bit binary value based on a 56-bit variable. If the complete 64-bit input is used (i.e., none of the input bits should be predetermined from block to block) and if the 56-bit variable is randomly chosen, no technique other than trying all possible keys using known input and output for the DES will guarantee finding the chosen key. As there are over 70,000,000,000,000,000 (seventy quadrillion) possible keys of 56 bits, the feasibility of deriving a particular key in this way is extremely unlikely in typical threat environments. Moreover, if the key is changed frequently, the risk of this event is greatly diminished. However, users should be aware that it is theoretically possible to derive the key in fewer trials (with a correspondingly lower probability of success depending on the number of keys tried) and should be cautioned to change the key as often as practical. Users must change the key and provide it a high level of protection in order to minimize the potential risks of its unauthorized computation or acquisition. The feasibility of computing the correct key may change with advances in technology.

The Data Encryption Standard (DES) shall consist of the following Data Encryption Algorithm to be implemented in special purpose electronic devices. These devices shall be designed in such a way that they may be used in a computer system or network to provide cryptographic protection to binary coded data. The method of implementation will depend on the application and environment. The devices shall be implemented in such a way that they may be tested and validated as accurately performing the transformations specified in the following algorithm.

Data Encryption Algoritham

The algorithm is designed to encipher and decipher blocks of data consisting of 64 bits under control of a 64-bit key. Deciphering must be accomplished by using the same key as for enciphering, but with the schedule of addressing the key bits altered so that the deciphering process is the reverse of the enciphering process. A block to be enciphered is subjected to an initial permutation IP, then to a complex key-dependent computation and finally to a permutation which is the inverse of the initial permutation IP-1. The key-dependent computation can be simply defined in terms of a function f, called the cipher function, and a function KS, called the key schedule. A description of the computation is given first, along with details as to how the algorithm is used for encipherment. Next, the use of the algorithm for decipherment is described. Finally, a definition of the cipher function f is given in terms of primitive functions which are called the selection functions Si and the permutation function P. The following notation is convenient: Given two blocks L and R of bits, LR denotes the block consisting of the bits of L followed by the bits of R. Since concatenation is associative, B1B2...B8, for example, denotes the block consisting of the bits of B1 followed by the bits of B2...followed by the bits of B8.

The Federal Information Processing Standards Publication Series of the National Bureau of Standards (NBS) is the official publication relating to standards, guidelines, and documents adopted and promulgated under the provisions of Public Law 89-306 (Brooks Act) and under Part 6 of Title 15, Code of Federal Regulations. These legislative and executive mandates have given the Secretary of Commerce important responsibilities for improving the utilization and management of computers and automatic data processing in the Federal Government. To carry out the Secretary's responsibilities, the NBS, through its Institute for Computer Sciences and Technology, provides leadership, technical guidance, and coordination of Government efforts in the development of standards, guidelines and documents in these areas.

The selective application of technological and related procedural safeguards is an important responsibility of every Federal organization in providing adequate security to its electronic data systems. This publication specifies a cryptographic algorithm which may be used by Federal organizations to protect sensitive data. Protection of data during transmission or while in storage may be necessary to maintain the confidentiality and integrity of the information represented by the data. The algorithm uniquely defines the mathematical steps required to transform data into a cryptographic cipher and also to transform the cipher back to the original form. The Data Encryption Standard is being made available for use by Federal agencies within the context of a total security program consisting of physical security procedures, good information management practices, and computer system/network access controls. This revision supersedes FIPS 46-1 in its entirety.

A widely adopted implementation of secret key cryptography is **Data Encryption Standard** (DES). The actual software to perform DES is readily available at no cost to anyone who has access to the Internet. DES was introduced in 1975 by IBM the National Security Agency (NSA). DES has been extensively researched and studied over the last twenty years and is definitely the most well –known and widely used cryptosystem in the world. DES is a secret –keys, symmetric cryptosystem: When used for communication, both sender and receive must know the same secret key, which is used both to encrypt and decrypt the message. DES can also be used for single –user encryption, for example, to store files on a hard disk in encrypted form. In a multi-user environment, however, secure –key distribution becomes difficult; public –key cryptography, discussed in the next subsection, was developed to solve this problem.

DES has withstood the test of time. Despite the fact that its algorithm is well known, it is impossible to break the cypher without using tremendous amounts of computing power. A new technique for improving the security of DES is triple encryption (Triple DES), that is, encrypting each message block using three different keys in succession. Triple DES, thought to be equivalent to doubting the key size of DES, to 112 bits, should prevent decryption by a third party capable of single –key exhaustive search [MH81]. Of course, using triple –encryption takes there times as long as single –encryption DES. If you uses DES three times on the same message with different secret keys, it is virtually impossible to break it using existing algorithms. Over the past few years several new, faster symmetric algorithms have been developed, but DES remains the most frequently used.

RSA Cryptosystem

RSA is a cipher algorithm. It is an asymmetric algorithm and plays a key role in public key cryptography. It is widely used in electronic commerce protocols. The algorithm was described in 1977 by Ron Rivest, Adi Shamir and Len Adleman who were all at MIT at the time; the letters RSA are the initials of their surnames. Clifford Cocks, a British mathematician working for GCHQ, described an equivalent system in an internal document in 1973. His discovery, however, was not revealed until 1997 due to its top-secret classification.

The security of the RSA system relies on the difficulty of factoring very large numbers; were such factorization to be quick, cryptanalysis of RSA messages would be quick as well. New fast algorithms in this field could render the RSA algorithm insecure. A working quantum computer implementing Shor's algorithm could factor render RSA insecure though fast factorization. However, this is generally considered not a problem in the short term. At the moment, just as for all ciphers, inadequately long RSA keys are vulnerable to a brute force search approach. The likely effect of an improvement in factoring technique will be to increase the size of adequately long RSA keys. As of 2004, there is no known method of attack which is feasible against the basic algorithm, and sufficiently long RSA keys make brute force attacks infeasible—that is, effectively impossible.

The algorithm was patented by MIT in 1983 in the United States of America. The patent expired 21 September 2000. Since the algorithm had been published prior to patent application, patent filing regulations in much of the rest of the world precluded patents elsewhere. Had Cocks' work been publicly known, a patent in the US would not have been possible either.

RSA can also be used to sign a message. Suppose Alice wishes to send a signed message to Bob. She produces a hash value of the message, encrypts it with her secret key, and attaches it as a "signature" to the message. This signature can only be decrypted with her public key. When Bob receives the signed message, he decrypts the signature with Alice's public key, and compares the resulting hash value with the message's actual hash value. If the two agree, he knows that the author of the message was in possession of Alice's secret key, and that the message has not been tampered with since.

Background

RSA is a public-key cryptosystem developed by MIT professors: Ronald L. Rivest, Adi Shamir, and Leonard M. Adleman in 1977 in an effort to help ensure internet security. Simply put, a cryptosystem is an algorithm that can convert input data into something unrecognizable (encryption), and convert the unrecognizable data back to its original form (decryption).

In a public-key cryptosystem, the sender encrypts a message with a private key. The sender's public key is posted (usually in a table). The recipient looks up the sender's public key and uses it and her/his own private key to unlock the message. Private and public keys are associated by a function. In the RSA cryptosystem, the private and public keys are linked by the factorization of prime numbers.

How the Algorithm Works

The challenge of public-key cryptography is developing a system in which it is impossible to determine the private key. This is accomplished through the use of a one-way function. With a one-way function, it is relatively easy to compute a result given some input values. However, it is extremely difficult, nearly impossible, to determine the original values if you start with the result. In mathematical terms, given x, computing f(x) is easy, but given f(x), computing x is nearly impossible.

The one-way function used in RSA is multiplication of prime numbers. It is easy to multiply two big prime numbers, but for most very large primes, it is extremely time-consuming to factor them. Public-key cryptography uses this function by building a cryptosystem, which uses two large primes to build the private key and the product of those primes to build the public key.

Here's a scenario that shows how the algorithm works. The two people involved in transmitting the message are Alice and Bob.

Step 1. Alice picks two available primes (p1 and p2). Public and private keys will be generated by computer. She records the public key containing the exponent value, E and the product of the primes, N. Alice also records the private key, D, but she keeps this private.

Step 2. Alice gives E and N to Bob (the recipient), or Bob looks up Alice's public key in a table.

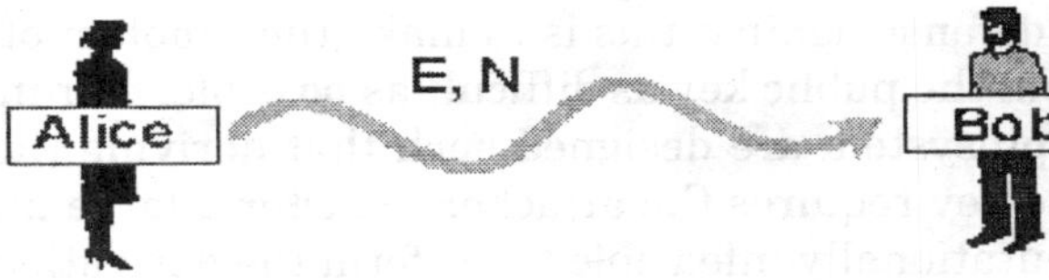

Step 3. Bob encrypts a message using E and N, and send it to Alice. Alice decrypts the message using D and N.

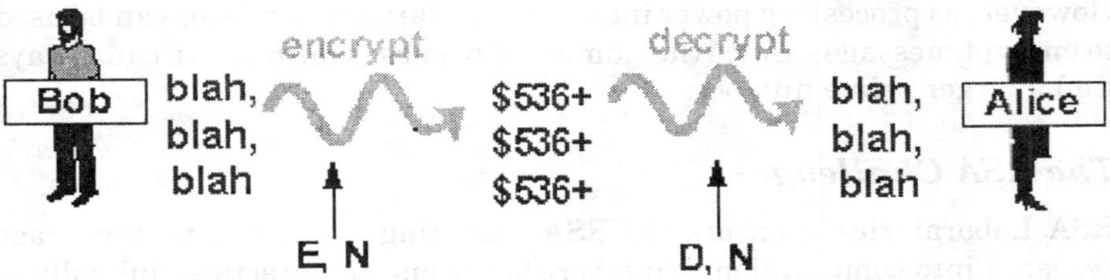

The size of the RSA key typically refers to size of N. The two primes, p1 and p2 , should be of roughly equal length; this makes the modulus harder to factor than if one of primes is much smaller then the other. For example, given a 1024-bit modulus, the primes should have lengths of 512 bits. The best size of the RSA modulus depends on your security needs. As a general guideline, 768 bits for personal use, 1024 for corporate use and 2048 for vital information are recommended lengths.

So why not use the largest modulus possible for all transactions? Well, the greater the modulus, the slower the RSA operations. As an extra measure of security, most indvidual user keys have an expiration key; therefore, keys can be regualrly changed to ensure security.

Prime Factorization

An integer greater than 1 (one) is a prime number if its only positive factors are 1 and itself. The first six primes are 2, 3, 5, 7, 11 and 13. The Fundamental Theorem of Arithmetic proves that the primes are the building blocks of the positive integers: Every positive integer is a unique product of prime numbers (except for the order of the factors).

For example, here is the prime factorization of 665, where 5, 19, and 7 are all prime numbers.

How RSA Can Be Cracked

In a public-key cryptosystem, the private key is always linked mathematically to the public key. Therefore, it is always possible to attack a public-key system by deriving the private key from the public key. Typically, the defense against this is to make the problem of deriving the private key from the public key as difficult as possible. For instance, some public-key cryptosystem are designed such that deriving the private key from the public key requires the attacker to factor a large number, it this case it is computationally infeasible to perform the derivation. This is the idea behind the RSA public-key cryptosystem.

So, the RSA cryptosystem can be cracked theoretically, but it would take a long time and a lot of processing power to factor the numbers in order to derive the private key from the public key. Some people argue that as processing power increases, RSA is at greater risk for being cracked. However, as processing power increases, the larger the primes can be used to encrypt messages. Since the number of primes is infinite, we can always find a larger prime number.

The RSA Challenge

RSA Laboratories sponsors the RSA Factoring Challenge to encourage research into computational number theory and the practical difficulty of factoring large integers. The contest is based on two "challenge lists" of numbers. The first list, the "RSA List,"

Contains numbers representative of those used in the RSA cryptosystem. The second list, the "Partition List," contains what mathematicians define as "partition numbers." The shortest number in each list is 100 decimal digits long (well within the current state of the art). The RSA List contains numbers up to 500 digits in length, while the Partition List contains arbitrarily large numbers. The challenge is to factor the numbers on these lists The RSA List contains numbers of the kind we believe to be the hardest to factor; the numbers on this list should be particularly challenging. These are the kind of numbers used in devising secure RSA cryptosystems.

The Partition List contains numbers that are more-or-less "random"; some of these numbers (even very large ones) may be quite easy to factor, although others may be quite difficult. Although RSA Data Security views the RSA List as the primary and most interesting challenge list, the Partition List challenge is also provided in order to encourage work on factoring in general as well as on factoring numbers of cryptographic interest.

One number on the RSA list was factored with the help of 800 computers that crunched number for eight months. For a chance at winning a piece of RSA 's $1,750 annual award.

Mixing RSA and DES

RSA allows two important functions not provided by DES: secure key exchange without prior exchange of keys, and digital signatures. For encrypting messages, RSA and DES are usually combined as follows first the message is encrypted with a random DES key, then, before being sent over an insecure communications channel, the DES key is encrypted with RSA. Together, the DES –encrypted message and the RSA –encrypted DES key are sent. This protocol is known as an RSA digital envelope.

Why not just use RSA to encrypt the whole message and not use DES at all? Although RSA may be fine for small message, DES (or another cipher) is preferable for larger messages due to its greater speed. In some situations, RSA is not necessary and DES –key agreement can take place (the two parties meeting in private). Also, RSA is usually not necessary in a single user environment; for example, if you want to keep your personal files encrypted, just do so with DES using, say, a password as the DES key.

RSA, and public key cryptography in general, is best suited for a multi-user environment. Also, any system in which digital signature are desired needs RSA or some other public key system.

Public-key and Private-key cryptography

In 1976, Whitfield Diffie and Martin Hellman introduced the concept of **public key** cryptography, a system in which the sender and recipient never exchange secret keys. In their system, each person gets a pair of keys: a public key and a private key. The public key is published, while the private key is kept secret. All communications involve only public keys, and no private key is ever transmitted. Public keys are associated with their users in an authenticated manner (i.e., in a trusted directory). Anyone can send a confidential message by just using public information, but the message can only be decrypted with a private key. The private key to unlock the data is the sole possession of the recipient.

A cryptographic system that uses two keys — a public key known to everyone and a private or secret key known only to the recipient of the message. When John wants to send a secure message to Jane, he uses Jane's public key to encrypt the message. Jane then uses her private key to decrypt it.

An important element to the public key system is that the public and private keys are related in such a way that only the public key can be used to encrypt messages and only the corresponding private key can be used to decrypt them. Moreover, it is virtually impossible to deduce the private key if you know the public key.

Public-key systems, such as Pretty Good Privacy (PGP), are becoming popular for transmitting information via the Internet. They are extremely secure and relatively simple to use. The only difficulty with public-key systems is that you need to know the recipient's public key to encrypt a message for him or her. What's needed, therefore, is a global registry of public keys, which is one of the promises of the new LDAP technology.

Public-key encryption

Public-key encryption uses a key pair made up of a private key and a public key. The public key component can be published (hence the name) without revealing anything about the private key component. Data encrypted with a public key can only be decrypted with the recipient's private key. The reverse is also true: data encrypted with the private key can only be decrypted with the public key. Since anyone could be in possession of your public key, this is not a great approach for hiding information, but it's perfect for digital signatures. If someone successfully decrypts a message using your public key, they are assured of two things: you encrypted the message (or at least the holder of your private key did), and the message hasn't been tampered with since it was encrypted (else the decryption would fail).

Since public-key encryption is slow compared with symmetric encryption, its use is usually limited to digital signatures and the sharing of symmetric keys.

Public-key infrastructure (PKI)

Public-key infrastructure (PKI) is the name for a system of cryptographic algorithms — software and infrastructure used in the implementation of security services, such as confidentiality, identification, authorization, and non-repudiation. At the core of PKI is the use of public-key certificates.

The **private key** is linked to the public key mathematically. Some cryptosystems link the private and public keys based on complex hash functions or properties of elliptic curves (see ECC). In the RSA cryptosystem, the private and public keys are linked by the factorization of prime numbers. See the next section for a fuller discussion of RSA.

Illustration of Public Key Encryption

Alice wants to send a secret message to Bob:

- Alice looks up Bob's public key in a directory, uses it to encrypt the message and sends it off.
- Bob then uses his private key to decrypt the message and read it.

No one listening in can decrypt the message. Anyone can send an encrypted message to Bob, but only Bob can read it (because only Bob knows Bob's private key).

Illustration of Public Key Digital Signatures

Digital signatures is like encryption in reverse. In essence, the recipient looks up the public key of the sender and uses it to determine the authenticity of the sender and integrity of the data transmitted.

- To sign a message, Alice does a computation using her private key and the message itself. The output is a digital signature and is attached to the message.
- To verify the signature, Bob does a computation using the message, the purported signature, and Alice's public key. If the result is correct according to a prescribed mathematical relation, the signature is genuine; otherwise, the signature is fraudulent, or someone may have tampered with the message.

A more powerful form of cryptography involves the use of public keys. Public –key techniques involve a pair of keys; a private key and a public key associated with each user. Information encrypted by the private key can be decrypted only using the corresponding public key. The private key is used to decrypt information at the receiver and is not kept secret. Since only the bona fide author of an encrypted message has knowledge of the private key, a successful decryption using the corresponding public key verifies the identity of the author and ensures message integrity.

Public keys can be maintained in some central repository and retrieved to decode or encode information. Public key techniques alleviate the problem of distribution of keys. Let's.examine how this process works.

Each party to a public key pairing receives a pair of keys, the public key and the private key. when A wishes to send a message to B, A looks up B's public key in a directory, A then uses the public key to encrypt the message and mail it to B. B uses the secret private key to decrypt the message and read it. Anyone can send an encrypted message to B but only B can read it. Unless, a third party, say C, has access to B's private key, it is impossible to decrypt the message sent by A. This ensures confidentiality.

This "fingerprint" is attached to the original message and further encrypted with the signer A's private key. The result of the second encryption is then sent to B, who then first decrypts the document using A's public key. B checks whether the message has been tampered with or is coming from a third party C, posing as A. To verify the signature, B does some further computation involving he original document, the purported signature, and A's public key. If the results of the computation generate a matching "fingerprint" of the signature may be fraudulent or the message altered, and they are discarded. This method is the basis for secure e – commerce, variations of which are being explored by several companies.

Clearly, one **advantage** of public key cryptography is that on one can figure out the private key from the corresponding public key. hence, the key management problems is mostly confined to the management of private keys. The need for sender and receiver to share secret information over public channels is completely eliminated: All transactions involve only public keys, and no private key is ever transmitted or shared. The secret key never leaves the user's PC. Thus a sender can send a confidential message merely by using public information and that message can be decrypted only with a private key in the sole possession of the intended recipient.

Furthermore, public key cryptography can be used for sender authentication, knows as digital signatures. Here's how authentication is achieved using public –key cryptography: A, to digitally sign a documents, puts his private key and the document together and performs a computation on the composite (key + document) to generate a unique number called the digital signature. For instance, when an electronic document, such as an order form with a credit card number, is run through the method, the output is a unique "fingerprint" of the document.

Several implementations of these popular encryption techniques are currently employed. In public key encryption, the RSA implementation dominates and is considered very secure, but using it for overseas traffic conflicts with the U.S. government' s position on export of munitions technology of military importance. Clearly, the government has not reckoned with the Internet and tans border data flow.

Certificates

A certificate, sometimes known as an X.509 certificate or public-key certificate, is a file that binds a public key (from an asymmetric key pair) to an identity (usually a person, computer, or corporate entity). These certificates contain the public key in question in addition to information that can uniquely identify the subject of the certificate (e.g. name, organization, location), the validity period of the certificate (think of it as an enforceable freshness date), the issuer (certification authority), and details regarding the issuance of the certificate, such as the digital signature of the issuer.

Certificate authorities

Certificate authorities (CAs) are trusted organizations that offer certificate creation, issuance, and revocation services. There are basically two classifications of CA: subordinate CAs, whose own signing certificate has, in turn, been signed by another CA; and root CAs, which have issued and signed their own signing certificate.

Trust

One of the key requirements behind the motivation for PKI is the notion of distributed trust. For instance, how do I, the user, trust the assertion that the Web site to which I am about to submit my credit card information does indeed belong to the company it claims to? A solution to this problem lies with the use of certificates.

If, in the course of loading the Web site in question, the site's server first sends its public-key certificate to me for inspection, it could then encrypt all subsequent data it sent to me using the private key corresponding to the public key in its certificate. I could use the server's certificate to verify that the Web page information loaded did indeed come from the certificate's owner, since only that certificate's public key could decrypt the data originally encrypted with the server's private key.

However, we still have the problem of identity. Although I now know that the data I'm receiving did indeed originate from the server that sent me the certificate, I know nothing at all about that server, except that it's sending me encrypted data. One possible solution to this problem would be to drive to the vendor's offices, satisfy myself that the business is legit, and personally meet with a corporate representative, who would give me the company's server certificate file right then and there. I could then take that file home and add it to a collection of certificates I trust, since I have personally verified its provenance. This solution doesn't scale very well, however.

Therefore, in order for a PKI to be at all useful, trust solutions must accommodate hundreds, thousands, or potentially millions of certificates, but should do so in a way that does not require the user to personally vet each and every one. The PKI approach to this problem is through transitive trust relationships.

Transitive trust works as follows. Let's say there are two individuals, Alice and Bob, who know and trust one another. Further, Bob has a friend, unknown to Alice, named Cassandra, whom he trusts.

This is how CAs are used in PKI. Rather than having to make explicit trust decisions regarding every certificate that one encounters, one can trust just a few CAs. Then, if a certificate you encounter has been issued (or signed) by one of your trusted CAs, you can trust that certificate transitively. This is how PKI can scale.

Although most CAs will create for you a keypair along with its signed public-key certificate, you can create your own keypairs and (self-signed) certificates. Let's walk through the steps necessary to request that a trusted CA sign your certificate.

Keys and certificates generated by these examples will be usable by any application that recognizes such standards as RSA, DSA, and X.509. And even though we will limit our usage scenarios to Apache's Tomcat servlet container, you can use these techniques with other Web service applications via their respective configuration frameworks.

Two readily available tools for key/certificate management are OpenSSL, a library of cryptographic functionality which includes a command line tool for performing specific functions; and Keytool, a key and certificate management utility that comes with Sun's Java Development Kit (JDK).

OpenSSL

Although the OpenSSL distribution includes other functions, such as an SSL/TLS implementation, we will only touch on its keypair/certificate generation and management tools here.The following command will generate an RSA private key, from which a public key can be derived:

```
openssl genrsa -out private_key.pem 2048
```

If you wish to protect your private key with a password generally a good idea use either the -des, des3, or -idea switch, depending on which password encryption algorithm you wish to use. The size of the key (in bits) here is 2,048, which is the current generally accepted minimum for RSA key sizes.

If you wish to generate a DSA keypair, there are two steps to follow. First, create a DSA parameter file:

```
openssl dsaparam -out dsa_param.pem 2048
```

Once this step is complete, you can generate the actual DSA key:

```
openssl gendsa -out private_key.pem dsa_param.pem
```

As with the RSA example above, if you wish to protect your private key with a password, use either the des, des3, or idea switch.

Both of the above examples use PEM as their output format, which wraps Base64 ASN.1 DER data with ASCII headers. In order to convert PEM files to PKCS#12 format (for use with Tomcat or many Web browsers), use the following command:

```
openssl pkcs12 -export -in pem_formatted_file -out pkcs12-formatted-file
```

We're not done yet, however. We still need a public-key certificate to go with our corresponding private key. We'll start by creating our own self-signed X.509 certificate:

```
openssl req -new -x509 -key private_key.pem -out certificate.der
```

This command interactively asks the user for information about the entity for which the certificate is being generated (e.g., a Web server or a user), all of which is used to identify the subject of the public-key certificate; that is, to bind the entity to a public key.

If you're generating the certificate for test purposes, this may suffice. However, for most real applications, it's necessary for the certificate to be signed by a trusted CA. The details behind this process vary by CA, but most will ask for and accept a certificate signing request (CSR).

Notice that this command differs from the last one only by the omission of the x509 switch (which self-signs the certificate). The output from this command a CSR can now be sent to a CA via whatever method it requires.

Once the CA has been satisified as to the identity of the subject (and again, these steps will vary from CA to CA), the CA will issue a signed certificate.

The private key and public-key certificate combination can now be used for PKI-enabled applications, e.g., to enable SSL connections with your Tomcat servlet container, as we'll see in a moment.

Digital Signatures

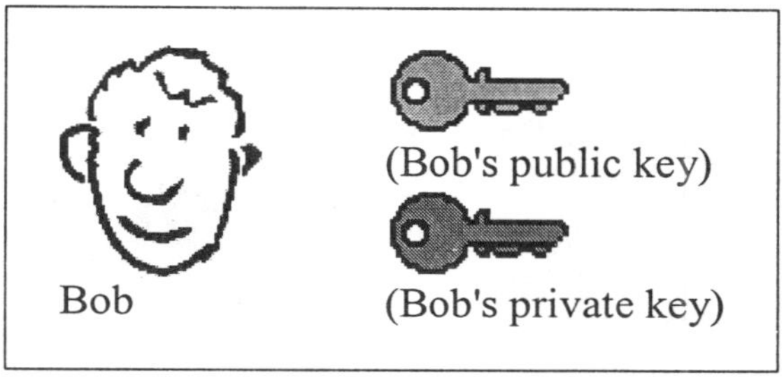

Bob has been given two keys. One of Bob's keys is called a Public Key, the other is called a Private Key.

Bob's Public key is available to anyone who needs it, but he keeps his Private Key to himself. Keys are used to encrypt information. Encrypting information means "scrambling it up", so that only a person with the appropriate key can make it readable again. Either one of Bob's two keys can encrypt data, and the other key can decrypt that data. Susan (shown below) can encrypt a message using Bob's Public Key. Bob uses his Private Key to decrypt the message. Any of Bob's coworkers might have access to the message Susan encrypted, but without Bob's Private Key, the data is worthless.

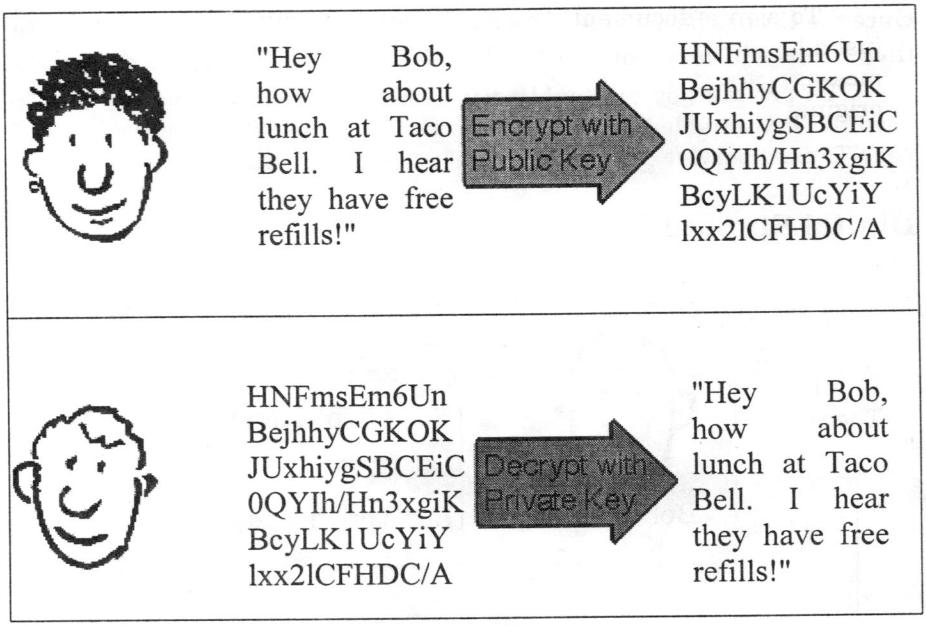

With his private key and the right software, Bob can put digital signatures on documents and other data. A digital signature is a "stamp" Bob places on the data which is unique to Bob, and is very difficult to forge. In addition, the signature assures that any changes made to the data that has been signed can not go undetected.

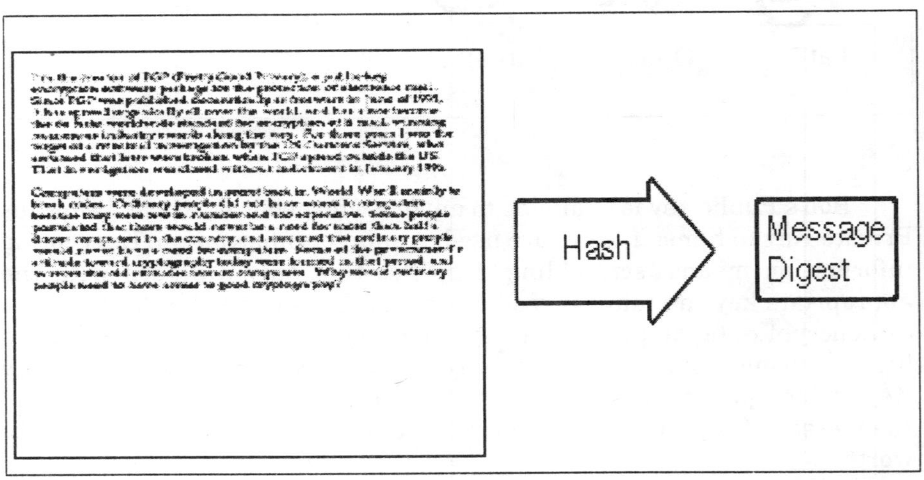

To sign a document, Bob's software will crunch down the data into just a few lines by a process called "hashing". These few lines are called a message digest. (It is not possible to change a message digest back into the original data from which it was created.)

Bob's software then encrypts the message digest with his private key. The result is the digital signature.

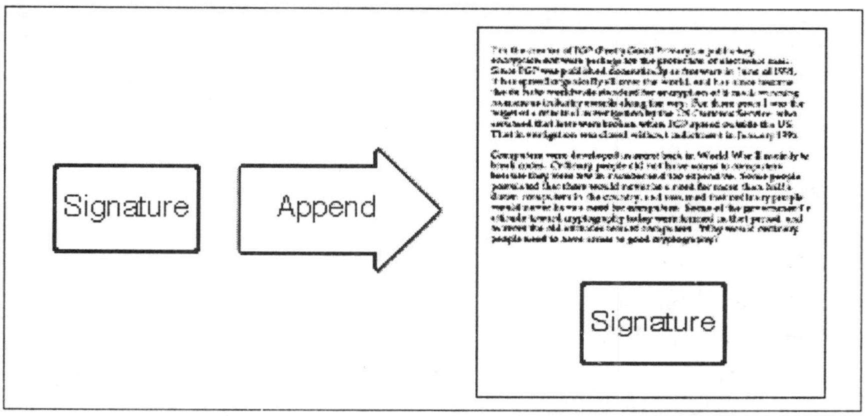

Finally, Bob's software appends the digital signature to document. All of the data that was hashed has been signed.

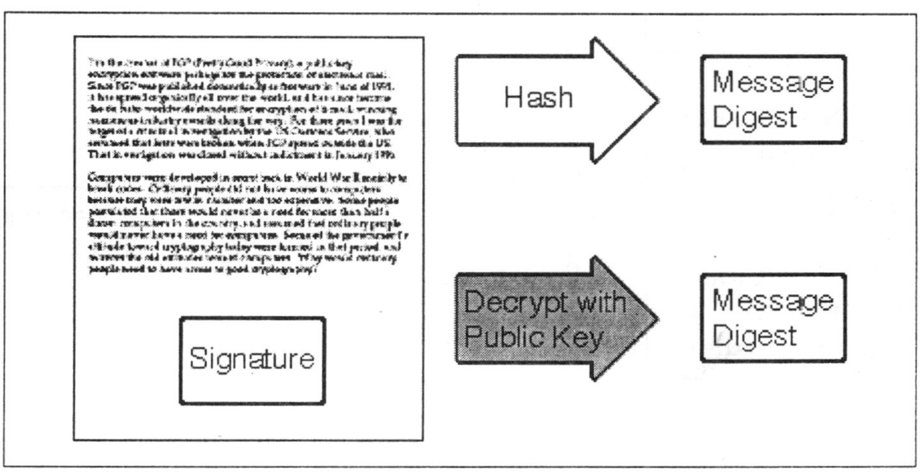

Bob now passes the document on to Pat.

First, Pat's software decrypts the signature (using Bob's public key) changing it back into a message digest. If this worked, then it proves that Bob signed the document, because only Bob has his private key. Pat's software then hashes the document data into a message digest. If the message digest is the same as the message digest created when the signature was decrypted, then Pat knows that the signed data has not been changed.

Plot complication...

Doug (our disgruntled employee) wishes to deceive Pat. Doug makes sure that Pat receives a signed message and a public key that appears to belong to Bob. Unbeknownst to Pat, Doug deceitfully sent a key pair he created using Bob's name. Short of receiving Bob's public key from him in person, how can Pat be sure that Bob's public key is authentic?

It just so happens that Susan works at the company's certificate authority center. Susan can create a digital certificate for Bob simply by signing Bob's public key as well as some information about Bob.

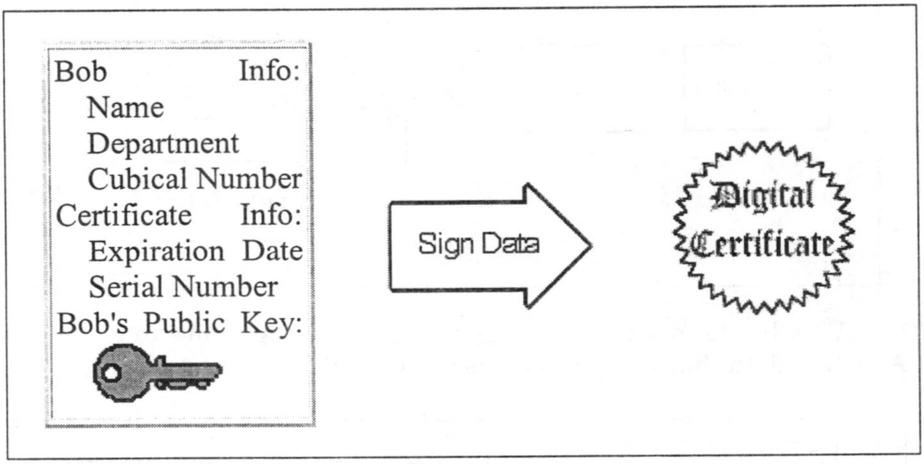

Now Bob's co-workers can check Bob's trusted certificate to make sure that his public key truly belongs to him. In fact, no one at Bob's company accepts a signature for which there does not exist a certificate generated by Susan. This gives Susan the power to revoke signatures if private keys are compromised, or no longer needed. There are even more widely accepted certificate authorities that certify Susan.

Let's say that Bob sends a signed document to Pat. To verify the signature on the document, Pat's software first uses Susan's (the certificate authority's) public key to check the signature on Bob's certificate. Successful de-encryption of the certificate proves that Susan created it. After the certificate is de-encrypted, Pat's software can check if Bob is in good standing with the certificate authority and that all of the certificate information concerning Bob's identity has not been altered.

Pat's software then takes Bob's public key from the certificate and uses it to check Bob's signature. If Bob's public key de-encrypts the signature successfully, then Pat is assured that the signature was created using Bob's private key, for Susan has certified the matching public key. And of course, if the signature is valid, then we know that Doug didn't try to change the signed content.

Explanation: This Standard specifies a Digital Signature Algorithm (DSA) appropriate for applications requiring a digital rather than written signature. The DSA digital signature is a pair of large numbers represented in a computer as strings of binary digits. The digital signature is computed using a set of rules (i.e., the DSA) and a set of parameters such that the identity of the signatory and integrity of the data can be verified. The DSA provides the capability to generate and verify signatures. Signature generation makes use of a private key to generate a digital signature. Signature verification makes use of a public key which corresponds to, but is not the same as, the private key. Each user possesses a private and public key pair. Public keys are assumed to be known to the public in general. Private keys are never shared. Anyone can verify the signature of a user by employing that user's public key. Signature generation can be performed only by the possessor of the user's private key.

A **hash function** is used in the signature generation process to obtain a condensed version of data, called a message digest. The message digest is then input to the DSA to generate the digital signature. The digital signature is sent to the intended verifier along with the signed data (often called the message). The verifier of the message and signature verifies the signature by using the sender's public key. The same hash function must also be used in the verification process. The hash function is specified in a separate standard, the Secure Hash Standard (SHS), FIPS 180. Similar procedures may be used to generate and verify signatures for stored as well as transmitted data.

Applicability: This standard is applicable to all Federal departments and agencies for the protection of unclassified information that is not subject to section 2315 of Title 10, United States Code, or section 3502(2) of Title 44, United States Code. This standard shall be used in designing and implementing public-key based signature systems which Federal departments and agencies operate or which are operated for them under contract. Adoption and use of this standard is available to private and commercial organizations.

Applications: The DSA authenticates the integrity of the signed data and the identity of the signatory. The DSA may also be used in proving to a third party that data was actually signed by the generator of the signature. The DSA is intended for use in electronic mail, electronic funds transfer, electronic data interchange, software distribution, data storage, and other applications which require data integrity assurance and data origin authentication.

Implementations: The DSA may be implemented in software, firmware, hardware, or any combination thereof. NIST is developing a validation program to test implementations for conformance to this standard. Information about the planned validation program can be obtained from the National Institute of Standards and Technology, Computer Systems Laboratory, Attn: DSS Validation, Gaithersburg, MD 20899.

Export Control: Implementations of this standard are subject to Federal Government export controls as specified in Title 15, Code of Federal Regulations, Parts 768 through 799. Exporters are advised to contact the Department of Commerce, Bureau of Export Administration for more information.

Patents: The Department of Commerce is not aware of any patents that would be infringed by this standard.

Implementation Schedule: This standard becomes effective December 1, 1994. Specifications: Federal Information Processing Standard (FIPS186) Digital Signature Standard (DSS).

Waiver Procedure: Under certain exceptional circumstances, the heads of Federal departments and agencies may approve waivers to Federal Information Processing Standards (FIPS). The head of such agency may re delegate such authority only to a senior official designated pursuant to section 3506(b) of Title 44, United States Code. Waiver shall be granted only when:

- Compliance with a standard would adversely affect the accomplishment of the mission of an operator of a Federal computer system; or
- Compliance with a standard would cause a major adverse financial impact on the operator which is not offset by Government-wide savings.

Agency heads may act upon a written waiver request containing the information detailed above. Agency heads may also act without a written waiver request when they determine that conditions for meeting the standard cannot be met. Agency heads may approve waivers only by a written decision which explains the basis on which the agency head made with required finding(s).

In addition, notice of each waiver granted and each delegation of authority to approve waivers shall be sent promptly to the Committee on Government Operations of the House of Representatives and the Committee on Government Affairs of the Senate and shall be published promptly in the Federal Register.

When the determination on a waiver applies to the procurement of equipment and/or services, a notice of the waiver determination must be published in the Commerce Business Daily as a part of the notice of solicitation for offers of an acquisition or, if the waiver determination is made after that notice is published, by amendment to such notice.

In the case of business transactions, authentication refers to the use of digital signatures, which play a function for digital documents similar to that played by handwritten signatures for printed documents: The signature is an unforgivable piece of data asserting that a named person wrote or otherwise agreed to the document to which the signature is attached.

Unlike encryption, digital signatures are a recent development, the need for which has arisen with the proliferation of electronic commerce. The recipient, as well as a third party, can verify that the document did indeed originate from the person whose signatures is attached and that the document has not been altered since it was signed.

A secure digital signature system thus consists of two parts: a method of signing a document such that forgery is infeasible, and a method of verifying that a signature was actually generated by whomever it represents. Furthermore, secure digital signatures cannot be repudiated; that is, the signer of a document cannot later disown it by claiming it was forged.

Digital Signature Standard (DSS)

The Digital Signature Standard specifies a Digital Signature Algorithm (DSA) as part of the U.S. government's Capstone project. It was selected to be the digital authentication standard of the U.S. government; whether the government should in fact adopt it as the official standard is still under debate. The Internal Revenue Service pushed for DSS because all its efforts to conduct electronic commerce under Tax System Modernization depend on the ability to send signatures over networks electronically. For a detailed description of DES.

DSS has been controversial in the computer industry, which had hoped the government would choose the RSA algorithm as the official standard since RSA has become the most widely used authentication algorithm. The DSS is also controversial, because vendors seeking to use DSS face lawsuits from Public Key Partners Inc., which alleges the government infringed on its patentee public –key encryption methods.

Criticism of DSS has focused on a few main issues: It lacks key exchange capability; the underlying cryptosystem is too recent and has been subject to too little scrutiny for users to be confident of its strength; verification of signatures with DSS is too slow; the existence of a second authentication standard will cause hardship to computer hardware and software vendors, who have already standardized on RSA; and the process by which DSS was chosen in too secretive and arbitrary. In the DSS system, signature generation is faster than signature verification, whereas in the RSA system, signature verification is faster than signature generation. NIST claims that it is an advantage of DSS that singing is faster, but many people in cryptography think that it is preferable for verification to be the faster operation.

The most serious criticism of DSS involve security. DSS was originally proposed with a fixed 512 –bit key size, but after much criticism that this is not secure enough, NIST revised DSS to allow key sizes up to 1024 bits. More critical, however, is the fact that DSS has not been around long enough to withstand repeated attempts to break it; although the algorithm is old, the particular form of the algorithm used in DSS was first proposed for cryptographic use in 1989 by Schnorr and has not receive much public study.

In general, any new cryptosystem could harbor serious flaws that the discovered only after years of scrutiny by cryptographers. DES and RSA have withstood over fifteen years of vigorous examination. In the absence of mathematical proofs of security, anything builds confidence in a cryptosystem like sustained attempts to crack it. Although DSS may well turn out to be a strong cryptosystem, its relatively short history will leave doubts for years to come. Some researchers warned about the existence of "trapdoor" primes in DSS, which could enable a key to be broken. These trapdoor primes are rare and rare avoidable if proper key generation procedures are followed.

Introduction

This publication prescribes the Digital Signature Algorithm (DSA) for digital signature generation and verification.

General

When a message is received, the recipient may desire to verify that the message has not been altered in transit. Furthermore, the recipient may wish to be certain of the originator's identity. Both of these services can be provided by the DSA. A digital signature is an electronic analogue of a written signature in that the digital signature can be used in proving to the recipient or a third party that the message was, in fact, signed by the originator. Digital

signatures may also be generated for stored data and programs so that the integrity of the data and programs may be verified at any later time.

Use of the DSA Algorithm

The DSA is used by a signatory to generate a digital signature on data and by a verifier to verify the authenticity of the signature. Each signatory has a public and private key. The private key is used in the signature generation process and the public key is used in the signature verification process. For both signature generation and verification, the data which is referred to as a message, M, is reduced by means of the Secure Hash Algorithm (SHA) specified in FIPS YY. An adversary, who does not know the private key of the signatory, cannot generate the correct signature of the signatory. In other words, signatures cannot be forged. However, by using the signatory's public key, anyone can verify a correctly signed message.

A means of associating public and private key pairs to the corresponding users is required. That is, there must be a binding of a user's identity and the user's public key. This binding may be certified by a mutually trusted party. For example, a certifying authority could sign credentials containing a user's public key and identity to form a certificate. Systems for certifying credentials and distributing certificates are beyond the scope of this standard. NIST intends to publish separate document(s) on certifying credentials and distributing certificates.

DSA Parameters

The DSA makes use of the following parameters:

1. p = a prime modulus, where $2L-1 < p < 2L$ for $512 = < L = <1024$ and L a multiple of 64

2. q = a prime divisor of $p - 1$, where $2159 < q < 2160$

3. $g = h(p-1)/q \bmod p$, where h is any integer with $1 < h < p - 1$ such that $h(p-1)/q \bmod p > 1$

(g has order q mod p)

4. x = a randomly or pseudo randomly generated integer with $0 < x < q$

5. $y = gx \bmod p$

6. k = a randomly or pseudo randomly generated integer with $0 < k < q$

The integers p, q, and g can be public and can be common to a group of users. A user's private and public keys are x and y, respectively. They are normally fixed for a period of time. Parameters x and k are used for signature generation only, and must be kept secret. Parameter k must be regenerated for each signature.

Parameters p and q shall be generated as specified in Appendix 2, or using other FIPS approved security methods. Parameters x and k shall be generated or using other FIPS approved security methods.

Signature Generation

The signature of a message M is the pair of numbers r and s computed according to the equations below:

- $r = (gk \bmod p) \bmod q$ and
- $s = (k-1(SHA(M) + xr)) \bmod q$.

In the above, k-1 is the multiplicative inverse of k, mod q; i.e., (k-1 k) mod q = 1 and $0 < k-1 < q$. The value of SHA(M) is a 160-bit string output by the Secure Hash Algorithm specified in FIPS 180. For use in computing s, this string must be converted to an integer.

As an option, one may wish to check if r = 0 or s = 0. If either r = 0 or s = 0, a new value of k should be generated and the signature should be recalculated (it is extremely unlikely that r = 0 or s = 0 if signatures are generated properly). The signature is transmitted along with the message to the verifier.

Signature Verification

Prior to verifying the signature in a signed message, p, q and g plus the sender's public key and identity are made available to the verifier in an authenticated manner.

Let M', r' and s' be the received versions of M, r, and s, respectively, and let y be the public key of the signatory. To verifier first checks to see that 0 < r' < q and 0 < s' < q; if either condition is violated the signature shall be rejected. If these two conditions are satisfied, the verifier computes

- w = (s')-1 mod q
- u1 = ((SHA(M')w) mod q
- u2 = ((r')w) mod q
- v = (((g)ul (y)u2) mod p) mod q.

If v = r', then the signature is verified and the verifier can have high confidence that the received message was sent by the party holding the secret key x corresponding to y. For a proof that v = r' when M' = M, r' = r, and s' =s,

If v does not equal r', then the message may have been modified, the message may have been incorrectly signed by the signatory, or the message may have been signed by an impostor. The message should be considered invalid.

Digital Certificates

A certificate is a data package that completely identifies an entity, and is issued by a Certification Authority (CA) only after that authority has verified the entity's identity. The data package includes the public key that belongs to the entity. When the sender of a message signs the message with its private key, the recipient of the message can use the sender's public key (retrieved from the certificate either sent with the message or available elsewhere on the network) to verify that the sender is legitimate.

X.509 Certificates

The X.509 protocol defines the following structure for public-key certificates:

Version
Serial Number
Signature Algorithm
Issuer Name
Period of Validity • Not Before Date • Not After Date
Subject Name
Subject's Public Key • Algorithm • Public Key
Extensions
Signature

The version field identifies the certificate format. The serial number is unique within the CA. The Signature Algorithm identifies the algorithm used to sign the certificate. Issuer is the name of the CA. The period of validity is a pair of dates; the certificate is valid during the time period between the two. Subject is the name of the user to whom the certificate is issued. The subject's public key field includes the algorithm name and the public key itself. The last field is the CA's signature.

Certification Hierarchy

In order for digital certificates to be effective, the users of the network must have a high level of trust in the certificate. But what happens if someone doesn't trust the CA perhaps the person has never heard of the CA before. This problem is addressed in the certifying process by something called the hierarchy of trust.

The concept of hierarchy of trust is simply that the process must begin with some certifying authority that everyone agrees is trustworthy. This ultimate authority is called the root authority. The root authority then can certify other CAs below it, who can then certify CAs below them, etc. This is illustrated on the following diagram:

When someone receives a certificate that has been issued by a first or second tier CA, he or she can verify that the CA that signed the certificate

Hierarchy of Trust

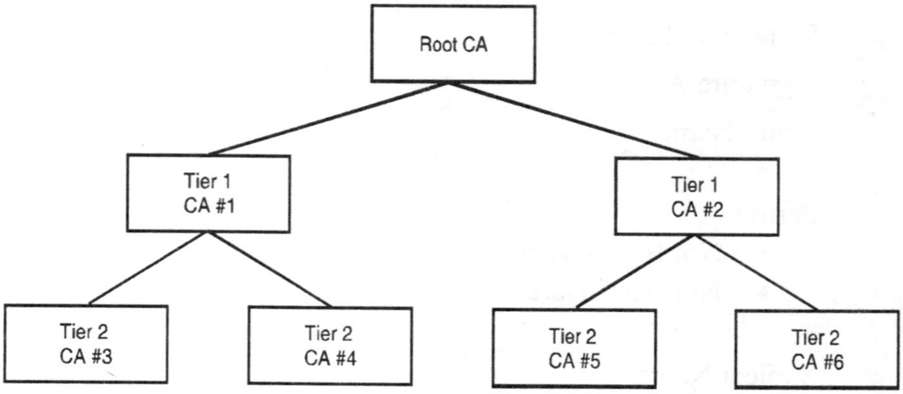

has been certified by a CA at the tier above it and that, in turn, that CA has been certified by the one above it, and so on until a chain of trust exists between the lower level CA (or a user certificate) and the root CA. For example, in the preceding diagram, it can be verified that CA #4 was certified by CA #1 and that CA #1 was certified by the root CA. This means that when a certificate from a lower-level CA is passed along with the encrypted message, all of the certificates in its chain of trust up to the root should be passed along with it.

Certificate Requests

A certificate request is a signed data package that contains a person's information such as name, email address, company name etc, and his/her public key. A certificate request is generated by a person wishing to obtain a certificate from the CA. Certificate requests are signed by the person's private key to prevent tampering with during transmission.

When the CA receives a certificate request it extracts a person's name and public key information and performs a certain procedure aimed at verifying that the public key really belongs to the person whose name is included in the certificate request. If the verification process is successful, the CA issues the certificate and sends it to the requestor.

Certificate Revocation Lists

Certificates can also be revoked, either because the user's key has been compromised, the CA's key has been compromised, or because the CA no longer wants to certify the user. Each CA maintains a list of all revoked but not expired certificates. When Alice receives a new certificate she should check to see if it has been revoked. She can check a database of revoked keys on the network or locally cached list or revoked certificates.

Multipurpose Internet Mail Extensions (MIME)

Introduction

Since its publication in 1982, RFC 822 has defined the standard format of textual mail messages on the Internet. Its success has been such that the RFC 822 format has been adopted, wholly or partially, well beyond the confines of the Internet and the Internet SMTP transport defined by RFC 821. As the format has seen wider use, a number of limitations have proven increasingly restrictive for the user community.

RFC 822 was intended to specify a format for text messages. As such, non-text messages, such as multimedia messages that might include audio or images, are simply not mentioned. Even in the case of text, however, RFC 822 is inadequate for the needs of mail users whose languages require the use of character sets richer than US-ASCII. Since RFC 822 does not specify mechanisms for mail containing audio, video, Asian language text, or even text in most European languages, additional specifications are needed.

One of the notable limitations of RFC 821/822 based mail systems is the fact that they limit the contents of electronic mail messages to relatively short lines of 7bit US-ASCII. This forces users to convert any non-textual data that they may wish to send into seven-bit bytes representable as printable US-ASCII characters before invoking a local mail UA (User Agent, a program with which human users send and receive mail). The limitations of RFC 822 mail become even more apparent as gateways are designed to allow for the exchange of mail messages between RFC 822 hosts and X.400 hosts. X.400 specifies mechanisms for the inclusion of non-textual material within electronic mail messages.

The current standards for the mapping of X.400 messages to RFC 822 messages specify either that X.400 non-textual material must be converted to (not encoded in) IA5Text format, or that they must be discarded, notifying the RFC 822 user that discarding has occurred. This is clearly undesirable, as information that a user may wish to receive is lost. Even though a user agent may not have the capability of dealing with the non-textual material, the user might have some mechanism external to the UA that can extract useful information from the material. Moreover, it does not allow for the fact that the message may eventually be gate wayed back into an X.400 message handling system (i.e., the X.400 message is "tunneled" through Internet mail), where the non-textual information would definitely become useful again.

This document describes several mechanisms that combine to solve most of these problems without introducing any serious incompatibilities with the existing world of RFC 822 mail. In particular, it describes

- A MIME-Version header field, which uses a version number to declare a message to be conformant with MIME and allows mail processing agents to distinguish between such messages and those generated by older or non-conformant software, which are presumed to lack such a field.

• A Content-Type header field, generalized from RFC 1049, which can be used to specify the media type and subtype of data in the body of a message and to fully specify the native representation (canonical form) of such data.

• A Content-Transfer-Encoding header field, which can be used to specify both the encoding transformation that was applied to the body and the domain of the result. Encoding transformations other than the identity transformation are usually applied to data in order to allow it to pass through mail transport mechanisms which may have data or character set limitations.

• Two additional header fields that can be used to further describe the data in a body, the Content-ID and Content-Description header fields.

All of the header fields defined in this document are subject to the general syntactic rules for header fields specified in RFC 822. In particular, all of these header fields except for Content-Disposition can include RFC 822 comments, which have no semantic content and should be ignored during MIME processing.

Finally, to specify and promote interoperability, RFC 2049 provides a basic applicability statement for a subset of the above mechanisms that defines a minimal level of "conformance" with this document.

HISTORICAL NOTE: Several of the mechanisms described in this set of documents may seem somewhat strange or even baroque at first reading. It is important to note that compatibility with existing standards AND robustness across existing practice were two of the highest priorities of the working group that developed this set of documents. In particular, compatibility was always favored over elegance. Please refer to the current edition of the "Internet Official Protocol Standards" for the standardization state and status of this protocol. RFC 822 and STD 3, RFC 1123 also provide essential background for MIME since no conforming implementation of MIME can violate them. In addition, several other informational RFC documents will be of interest to the MIME implementer, in particular RFC 1344, RFC 1345, and RFC 1524.

Definitions, Conventions, and Generic BNF Grammar

Although the mechanisms specified in this set of documents are all described in prose, most are also described formally in the augmented BNF notation of RFC 822. Implementers will need to be familiar with this notation in order to understand this set of documents, and are referred to RFC 822 for a complete explanation of the augmented BNF notation.

Some of the augmented BNF in this set of documents makes named references to syntax rules defined in RFC 822. A complete formal grammar, then, is obtained by combining the collected grammar appendices in each document in this set with the BNF of RFC 822 plus the modifications to RFC 822 defined in RFC 1123.

All numeric and octet values are given in decimal notation in this set of documents. All media type values, subtype values, and parameter names as defined are case-insensitive. However, parameter values are case-sensitive unless otherwise specified for the specific parameter.

CRLF

The term CRLF, in this set of documents, refers to the sequence of octets corresponding to the two US-ASCII characters CR (decimal value13) and LF (decimal value 10) which, taken together, in this order, denote a line break in RFC 822 mail.

Character Set

The term "character set" is used in MIME to refer to a method of converting a sequence of octets into a sequence of characters. Note that unconditional and unambiguous conversion in the other direction is not required, in that not all characters may be representable by a given character set and a character set may provide more than one sequence of octets to represent a particular sequence of characters.

This definition is intended to allow various kinds of character encoding, from simple single-table mappings such as US-ASCII to complex table switching methods such as those that use ISO 2022's techniques, to be used as character sets. However, the definition associated with a MIME character set name must fully specify the mapping to be performed. In particular, use of external profiling information to determine the exact mapping is not permitted.

Message

The term "message", when not further qualified, means either a (complete or "top-level") RFC 822 message being transferred on a network, or a message encapsulated in a body of type "message/rfc822" or "message/partial".

Entity

The term "entity", refers specifically to the MIME-defined header fields and contents of either a message or one of the parts in the body of a multipart entity. The specification of such entities is the essence of MIME. Since the contents of an entity are often called the "body", it makes sense to speak about the body of an entity. Any sort of field may be present in the header of an entity, but only those fields whose names begin with "content-" actually have any MIME-related meaning. Note that this does NOT imply they have no meaning at all an entity that is also a message has non MIME header fields whose meanings are defined by RFC 822.

Body Part

The term "body part" refers to an entity inside of a multipart entity.

Body

The term "body", when not further qualified, means the body of an entity, that is, the body of either a message or of a body part.

7bit Data

"7bit data" refers to data that is all represented as relatively short lines with 998 octets or less between CRLF line separation sequences. No octets with decimal values greater than 127 are allowed and neither are NULs (octets with decimal value 0). CR (decimal value 13) and LF (decimal value 10) octets only occur as part of CRLF line separation sequences.

8bit Data

"8bit data" refers to data that is all represented as relatively short lines with 998 octets or less between CRLF line separation sequences [RFC-821]), but octets with decimal values greater than 127 may be used. As with "7bit data" CR and LF octets only occur as part of CRLF line separation sequences and no NULs are allowed.

Binary Data

"Binary data" refers to data where any sequence of octets whatsoever is allowed.

Lines

"Lines" are defined as sequences of octets separated by a CRLF sequences. This is consistent with both RFC 821 and RFC 822. "Lines" only refers to a unit of data in a message, which may or may not correspond to something that is actually displayed by a user agent.

MIME Header Fields

MIME defines a number of new RFC 822 header fields that are used to describe the content of a MIME entity. These header fields occur in at least two contexts:

- As part of a regular RFC 822 message header.
- In a MIME body part header within a multipart construct.

The formal definition of these header fields is as follows:

```
Entity-headers := [ content CRLF ]
                  [ encoding CRLF ]
                  [ id CRLF ]
                  [ description CRLF ]
                  *( MIME-extension-field CRLF )

MIME-message-headers := entity-headers
                  fields
                  version CRLF
                  ; The ordering of the header
```

; fields implied by this BNF
; definition should be ignored.

MIME-part-headers := entity-headers
[fields]
; Any field not beginning with
; "content-" can have no defined
; meaning and may be ignored.
; The ordering of the header
; fields implied by this BNF
; definition should be ignored.

MIME-Version Header Field

Since RFC 822 was published in 1982, there has really been only one format standard for Internet messages, and there has been little perceived need to declare the format standard in use. This document is an independent specification that complements RFC 822. Although the extensions in this document have been defined in such a way as to be compatible with RFC 822, there are still circumstances in which it might be desirable for a mail-processing agent to know whether a message was composed with the new standard in mind.

Therefore, this document defines a new header field, "MIME-Version", which is to be used to declare the version of the Internet message body format standard in use.

Messages composed in accordance with this document MUST include such a header field, with the following verbatim text:

MIME-Version: 1.0

The presence of this header field is an assertion that the message has been composed in compliance with this document. Since it is possible that a future document might extend the message format standard again, a formal BNF is given for the content of the MIME-Version field:

version := "MIME-Version" ":" 1*DIGIT "." 1*DIGIT

Thus, future format specifiers, which might replace or extend "1.0", are constrained to be two integer fields, separated by a period. If a message is received with a MIME-version value other than "1.0", it cannot be assumed to conform with this document.

Note that the MIME-Version header field is required at the top level of a message. It is not required for each body part of a multipart entity. It is required for the embedded headers of a body of type "message/rfc822" or "message/partial" if and only if the embedded message is itself claimed to be MIME-conformant. It is not possible to fully specify how a mail reader that conforms with MIME as defined in this document should treat a message that might arrive in the future with some value of MIME-Version other than "1.0".

It is also worth noting that version control for specific media types is not accomplished using the MIME-Version mechanism. In particular, some formats (such as application/postscript) have version numbering conventions that are internal to the media format. Where such conventions exist, MIME does nothing to supersede them. Where no such conventions exist, a MIME media type might use a "version" parameter in the content-type field if necessary.

NOTE TO IMPLEMENTORS: When checking MIME-Version values any RFC 822 comment strings that are present must be ignored. In particular, the following four MIME-Version fields are equivalent:

- MIME-Version: 1.0
- MIME-Version: 1.0 (produced by MetaSend Vx.x)
- MIME-Version: (produced by MetaSend Vx.x) 1.0
- MIME-Version: 1.(produced by MetaSend Vx.x)0

In the absence of a MIME-Version field, a receiving mail user agent (whether conforming to MIME requirements or not) may optionally choose to interpret the body of the message according to local conventions. Many such conventions are currently in use and it should be noted that in practice non-MIME messages can contain just about anything.

It is impossible to be certain that a non-MIME mail message is actually plain text in the US-ASCII character set since it might well be a message that, using some set of nonstandard local conventions that predate MIME, includes text in another character set or non textual data presented in a manner that cannot be automatically recognized (e.g., a uuencoded compressed UNIX tar file).

Content-Type Header Field

The purpose of the Content-Type field is to describe the data contained in the body fully enough that the receiving user agent can pick an appropriate agent or mechanism to present the data to the user, or otherwise deal with the data in an appropriate manner. The value in this field is called a media type.

The Content-Type header field specifies the nature of the data in the body of an entity by giving media type and subtype identifiers, and by providing auxiliary information that may be required for certain media types. After the media type and subtype names, the remainder of the header field is simply a set of parameters, specified in an attribute=value notation. The ordering of parameters is not significant.

The top-level media type is used to declare the general type of data, while the subtype specifies a specific format for that type of data. Thus, a media type of "image/xyz" is enough to tell a user agent that the data is an image, even if the user agent has no knowledge of the specific image format "xyz". Such information can be used, for example, to decide whether or not to show a user the raw data from an unrecognized subtype such an action might be reasonable for unrecognized subtypes of text, but not for unrecognized subtypes of image or audio. For this reason, registered subtypes of text, image, audio, and video should not contain embedded information that is really of a different type. Such compound formats should be represented using the "multipart" or "application" types.

Parameters are modifiers of the media subtype, and as such do not fundamentally affect the nature of the content. The set of meaningful parameters depends on the media type and subtype. Most parameters are associated with a single specific subtype. However, a given top-level media type may define parameters which are applicable to any subtype of that type. Parameters may be required by their defining content type or subtype or they may be optional. MIME implementations must ignore any parameters whose names they do not recognize.

An initial set of seven top-level media types is defined in RFC 2046. Five of these are discrete types whose content is essentially opaque as far as MIME processing is concerned. The remaining two are composite types whose contents require additional handling by MIME processors.

This set of top-level media types is intended to be substantially complete. It is expected that additions to the larger set of supported types can generally be accomplished by the creation of new subtypes of these initial types. In the future, more top-level types may be defined only by a standards-track extension to this standard.

If another top-level type is to be used for any reason, it must be given a name starting with "X-" to indicate its non-standard status and to avoid a potential conflict with a future official name.

Syntax of the Content-Type Header Field

-00In the Augmented BNF notation of RFC 822, a Content-Type header field value is defined as follows:

content := "Content-Type" ":" type "/" subtype
*(";" parameter)
; Matching of media type and subtype
; is ALWAYS case-insensitive.
type := discrete-type / composite-type
discrete-type := "text" / "image" / "audio" / "video" /
"application" / extension-token
composite-type := "message" / "multipart" / extension-token
extension-token := ietf-token / x-token
ietf-token := <An extension token defined by a
standards-track RFC and registered
with IANA.>
x-token := <The two characters "X-" or "x-" followed, with
no intervening white space, by any token>
subtype := extension-token / iana-token

```
iana-token := <A publicly-defined extension token. Tokens
        of this form must be registered with IANA
        as specified in RFC 2048.>
parameter := attribute "=" value
attribute := token
        ; Matching of attributes
        ; is ALWAYS case-insensitive.
value := token / quoted-string
token := 1*<any (US-ASCII) CHAR except SPACE, CTLs,
        or tspecials>
tspecials := "(" / ")" / "<" / ">" / "@" /
        "," / ";" / ":" / "\" / <">
        "/" / "[" / "]" / "?" / "="
        ; Must be in quoted-string,
        ; to use within parameter values
```

Content-Type Defaults

Default RFC 822 messages without a MIME Content-Type header are taken by this protocol to be plain text in the US-ASCII character set, which can be explicitly specified as:

Content-type: text/plain; charset=us-ascii

This default is assumed if no Content-Type header field is specified. It is also recommend that this default be assumed when a syntactically invalid Content-Type header field is encountered. In the presence of a MIME-Version header field and the absence of any Content-Type header field, a receiving User Agent can also assume that plain US-ASCII text was the sender's intent. Plain US-ASCII text may still be assumed in the absence of a MIME Version or the presence of an syntactically invalid Content-Type header field, but the sender's intent might have been otherwise.

Content-Transfer-Encoding Header Field

Many media types which could be usefully transported via email are represented, in their "natural" format, as 8bit character or binary data. Such data cannot be transmitted over some transfer protocols.

For example, RFC 821 (SMTP) restricts mail messages to 7bit US-ASCII data with lines no longer than 1000 characters including any trailing CRLF line separator.

It is necessary, therefore, to define a standard mechanism for encoding such data into a 7bit short line format. Proper labelling of unencoded material in less restrictive formats for direct use over less restrictive transports is also desirable. This document specifies that such encoding will be indicated by a new "Content-Transfer-Encoding" header field. This field has not been defined by any previous standard.

Content-Transfer-Encoding Syntax

The Content-Transfer-Encoding field's value is a single token specifying the type of encoding, as enumerated below. Formally:

```
encoding := "Content-Transfer-Encoding" ":" mechanism
mechanism := "7bit" / "8bit" / "binary" /
        "quoted-printable" / "base64" /
        ietf-token / x-token
```

Content-Transfer-Encoding Semantics

This single Content-Transfer-Encoding token actually provides two pieces of information. It specifies what sort of encoding transformation the body was subjected to and hence what decoding operation must be used to restore it to its original form, and it specifies what the domain of the result is.

The transformation part of any Content-Transfer-Encoding specifies, either explicitly or implicitly, a single, well-defined decoding algorithm, which for any sequence of encoded octets either transforms it to the original sequence of octets which was encoded, or shows that it is illegal as an encoded sequence. Content-Transfer-Encoding transformations never depend on any additional external profile information for proper operation. Note that while decoders must produce a single, well-defined output for a valid encoding no such restrictions exist for encoders: Encoding a given sequence of octets to different, equivalent encoded sequences is perfectly legal.

Three transformations are currently defined: identity, the "quoted-printable" encoding, and the "base64" encoding. The domains are "binary", "8bit" and "7bit".

The Content-Transfer-Encoding values "7bit", "8bit", and "binary" all mean that the identity (i.e. NO) encoding transformation has been performed. As such, they serve simply as indicators of the domain of the body data, and provide useful information about the sort of encoding that might be needed for transmission in a given transport system.

Mail transport for unencoded 8bit data is defined in RFC 1652. As of the initial publication of this document, there are no standardized Internet mail transports for which it is legitimate to include unencoded binary data in mail bodies. Thus there are no circumstances in which the "binary" Content-Transfer-Encoding is actually valid in Internet mail. However, in the event that binary mail transport becomes a reality in Internet mail, or when MIME is used in conjunction with any other binary-capable mail transport mechanism, binary bodies must be labelled as such using this mechanism.

New Content-Transfer-Encodings

Implementors may, if necessary, define private Content-Transfer- Encoding values, but must use an x-token, which is a name prefixed by "X-", to indicate its non-standard status, e.g., "Content-Transfer-Encoding:x-my-new-encoding". Additional standardized Content-Transfer -Encoding values must be specified by a standards-track RFC. The requirements such specifications must meet are given in RFC 2048. As such, all content-transfer-encoding namespace except that beginning with "X-" is explicitly reserved to the IETF for future use.

Unlike media types and subtypes, the creation of new Content-Transfer-Encoding values is STRONGLY discouraged, as it seems likely to hinder interoperability with little potential benefit

Interpretation and Use

If a Content-Transfer-Encoding header field appears as part of a message header, it applies to the entire body of that message. If a Content-Transfer-Encoding header field appears as part of an entity's headers, it applies only to the body of that entity. If an entity is of type "multipart" the Content-Transfer-Encoding is not permitted to have any value other than "7bit", "8bit" or "binary". Even more severe restrictions apply to some subtypes of the "message" type. It should be noted that most media types are defined in terms of octets rather than bits, so that the mechanisms described here are mechanisms for encoding arbitrary octet streams, not bit streams. If a bit stream is to be encoded via one of these mechanisms, it must first be converted to an 8bit byte stream using the network standard bit order ("big-endian"), in which the earlier bits in a stream become the higher-order bits in a 8bit byte. A bit stream not ending at an 8bit boundary must be padded with zeroes. RFC 2046 provides a mechanism for noting the addition of such padding in the case of the application/octet-stream media type, which has a "padding" parameter.

The encoding mechanisms defined here explicitly encode all data in US-ASCII. Thus, for example, suppose an entity has header fields such as:

Content-Type: text/plain; charset=ISO-8859-1

Content-transfer-encoding: base64

This must be interpreted to mean that the body is a base64 US-ASCII encoding of data that was originally in ISO-8859-1, and will be in that character set again after decoding. Certain Content-Transfer-Encoding values may only be used on certain media types. In particular, it is EXPRESSLY FORBIDDEN to use any encoding other than "7bit", "8bit", or "binary" with any composite media type, i.e. one that recursively includes other Content-Type fields. Currently the only composite media types are "multipart" and "message". All encoding that are desired for bodies of type multipart or message must be done at the innermost level, by encoding the actual body that needs to be encoded.

It should also be noted that, by definition, if a composite entity has a transfer-encoding value such as "7bit", but one of the enclosed entities has a less restrictive value such as "8bit", then either the outer "7bit" labeling is in error, because 8bit data are included, or the inner "8bit" labeling placed an unnecessarily high demand on the transport system because the actual included data were actually 7bit-safe.

Translating Encodings

The quoted-printable and base64 encodings are designed so that conversion between them is possible. The only issue that arises in such a conversion is the handling of hard line breaks in quoted-printable encoding output. When converting from quoted-printable to base64 a hard line break in the quoted-printable form represents a CRLF sequence in the canonical form of the data. It must therefore be converted to a corresponding encoded CRLF in the base64 form of the data. Similarly, a CRLF sequence in the canonical form of the data obtained after base64 decoding must be converted to a quoted-printable hard line break, but ONLY when converting text data.

Canonical Encoding Model

There was some confusion, in the previous versions of this RFC, regarding the model for when email data was to be converted to canonical form and encoded, and in particular how this process would affect the treatment of CRLFs, given that the representation of new lines varies greatly from system to system, and the relationship between content-transfer-encodings and character sets. A canonical model for encoding is presented in RFC 2049 for this reason.

Quoted-Printable Content-Transfer-Encoding

The Quoted-Printable encoding is intended to represent data that largely consists of octets that correspond to printable characters in the US-ASCII character set. It encodes the data in such a way that the resulting octets are unlikely to be modified by mail transport. If the data being encoded are mostly US-ASCII text, the encoded form of the data remains largely recognizable by humans. A body which is entirely US-ASCII may also be encoded in Quoted-Printable to ensure the integrity of the data should the message pass through a character-translating, and/or line-wrapping gateway.

In this encoding, octets are to be represented as determined by the following rules:

(1) (General 8bit representation) Any octet, except a CR or LF that is part of a CRLF line break of the canonical (standard) form of the data being encoded, may be represented by an "=" followed by a two digit hexadecimal representation of the octet's value. The digits of the hexadecimal alphabet, for this purpose, are "0123456789ABCDEF". Uppercase letters must be used; lowercase letters are not allowed. Thus, for example, the decimal value 12 (US-ASCII form feed) can be represented by "=0C", and the decimal value 61 (US-ASCII EQUAL SIGN) can be represented by "=3D". This rule must be followed except when the following rules allow an alternative encoding.

(2) (Literal representation) Octets with decimal values of 33 through 60 inclusive, and 62 through 126, inclusive, MAY be represented as the US-ASCII characters which correspond to those octets (EXCLAMATION POINT through LESS THAN, and GREATER THAN through TILDE, respectively).

(3) (White Space) Octets with values of 9 and 32 MAY be represented as US-ASCII TAB (HT) and SPACE characters, respectively, but MUST NOT be so represented at the end of an encoded line. Any TAB (HT) or SPACE characters on an encoded line MUST thus be followed on that line by a printable character. In particular, an "=" at the end of an encoded line, indicating a soft line break (see rule #5) may follow one or more TAB (HT) or SPACE characters. It follows that an octet with decimal value 9 or 32 appearing at the end of an encoded line must be represented according to Rule #1. This rule is necessary because some MTAs (Message Transport Agents, programs which transport messages from one user to another, or perform a portion of such transfers) are known to pad lines of text with SPACEs, and others are known to remove "white space" characters from the end of a line. Therefore, when decoding a Quoted-Printable body, any trailing white space on a line must be deleted, as it will necessarily have been added by intermediate transport agents.

(4) (Line Breaks) A line break in a text body, represented as a CRLF sequence in the text canonical form, must be represented by a (RFC 822) line break, which is also a CRLF sequence, in the Quoted-Printable encoding. Since the canonical representation of media types other than text do not generally include the representation of line breaks as CRLF sequences, no hard line breaks (i.e. line breaks that are intended to be meaningful and to be displayed to the user) can occur in the quoted-printable encoding of such types. Sequences like "=0D", "=0A", "=0A=0D" and "=0D=0A" will routinely appear in non-text data represented in quoted-printable.

Content-ID Header Field

In constructing a high-level user agent, it may be desirable to allow one body to make reference to another. Accordingly, bodies may be labelled using the "Content-ID" header field, which is syntactically identical to the "Message-ID" header field:

id := "Content-ID" ":" msg-id

Like the Message-ID values, Content-ID values must be generated to be world-unique.

The Content-ID value may be used for uniquely identifying MIME entities in several contexts, particularly for caching data referenced by the message/external-body mechanism. Although the Content-ID header is generally optional, its use is MANDATORY in implementations, which generate data of the optional MIME media type "message/external-body". That is, each message/external-body entity must have a Content-ID field to permit caching of such data. It is also worth noting that the Content-ID value has special semantics in the case of the multipart/alternative media type. This is explained in the section of RFC 2046 dealing with multipart/ alternative.

Content-Description Header Field

The ability to associate some descriptive information with a given body is often desirable. For example, it may be useful to mark an "image" body as "a picture of the Space Shuttle Endeavor." Such text may be placed in the Content-Description header field. This header field is always optional.

description := "Content-Description" ":" *text

The description is presumed to be given in the US-ASCII character set, although the mechanism specified in RFC 2047 may be used for non-US-ASCII Content-Description values.

Additional MIME Header Fields

Future documents may elect to define additional MIME header fields for various purposes. Any new header field that further describes the content of a message should begin with the string "Content-" to allow such fields which appear in a message header to be distinguished from ordinary RFC 822 message header fields.

MIME-extension-field := <Any RFC 822 header field which begins with the string "Content-">

6

Internet Security and Firewall Systems

IP Sec protocol

Introduction

This memo specifies the base architecture for IP Sec compliant systems. The goal of the architecture is to provide various security services for traffic at the IP layer, in both the IPv4 and IPv6 environments. This document describes the goals of such systems, their components and how they fit together with each other and into the IP environment. It also describes the security services offered by the IP Sec protocols, and how these services can be employed in the IP environment. This document does not address all aspects of IP Sec architecture. Subsequent documents will address additional architectural details of a more advanced nature, e.g., use of IP Sec in NAT environments and more complete support for IP multicast. The following fundamental components of the IP Sec security architecture are discussed in terms of their underlying, required functionality. Additional RFCs define the protocols in (a), (c), and (d).

- Security Protocols - Authentication Header (AH) and Encapsulating Security Payload (ESP)
- Security Associations - what they are and how they work, how they are managed, associated processing
- Key Management - manual and automatic (The Internet Key Exchange (IKE))
- Algorithms for authentication and encryption

This document is not an overall Security Architecture for the Internet; it addresses security only at the IP layer, provided through the use of a combination of cryptographic and protocol security mechanisms.

The target audience for this document includes implementers of this IP security technology and others interested in gaining a general background understanding of this system. In particular, prospective users of this technology (end users or system administrators) are part of the target audience. A glossary is provided as an appendix to help fill in gaps in background/vocabulary. This document assumes that the reader is familiar with the Internet Protocol, related networking technology, and general security terms and concepts.

Design Objectives

Goals/Objectives/Requirements/Problem Description

IP Sec is designed to provide interoperable, high quality, cryptographically-based security for IPv4 and IPv6. The set of security services offered includes access control, connectionless integrity, data origin authentication, protection against replays (a form of partial sequence integrity), confidentiality (encryption), and limited traffic flow confidentiality. These services are provided at the IP layer, offering protection for IP and/or upper layer protocols. These objectives are met through the use of two traffic security protocols, the Authentication Header (AH) and the Encapsulating Security Payload (ESP), and through the use of cryptographic key management procedures and protocols. The set of IP Sec protocols employed in any context, and the ways in which they are employed, will be determined by the security and system requirements of users, applications, and/or sites/organizations.

When these mechanisms are correctly implemented and deployed, they ought not to adversely affect users, hosts, and other Internet components that do not employ these security mechanisms for protection of their traffic. These mechanisms also are designed to be algorithm-independent. This modularity permits selection of different sets of algorithms without affecting the other parts of the implementation. For example, different user communities may select different sets of algorithms (creating cliques) if required.

A standard set of default algorithms is specified to facilitate interoperability in the global Internet. The use of these algorithms, in conjunction with IP Sec traffic protection and key management protocols, is intended to permit system and application developers to deploy high quality, Internet layer, cryptographic security technology.

Caveats and Assumptions

The suite of IP Sec protocols and associated default algorithms are designed to provide high quality security for Internet traffic. However, the security offered by use of these protocols ultimately depends on the quality of the their implementation, which is outside the scope of this set of standards. Moreover, the security of a computer system or network is a function of many factors, including personnel, physical, procedural, compromising emanations, and computer security practices. Thus IP Sec is only one part of an overall system security architecture.

Finally, the security afforded by the use of IP Sec is critically dependent on many aspects of the operating environment in which the IP Sec implementation executes. For example, defects in OS security, poor quality of random number sources, sloppy system management protocols and practices, etc. can all degrade the security provided by IP Sec. As above, none of these environmental attributes are within the scope of this or other IP Sec standards.

System Overview

This section provides a high level description of how IP Sec works, the components of the system, and how they fit together to provide the security services noted above. The goal of this description is to enable the reader to "picture" the overall process/system, see how it fits into the IP environment, and to provide context for later sections of this document, which describe each of the components in more detail.

An IP Sec implementation operates in a host or a security gateway environment, affording protection to IP traffic. The protection offered is based on requirements defined by a Security Policy Database (SPD) established and maintained by a user or system administrator, or by an application operating within constraints established by either of the above. In general, packets are selected for one of three processing modes based on IP and transport layer header information (Selectors, Section 4.4.2) matched against entries in the database (SPD). Each packet is either afforded IP Sec security services, discarded, or allowed to bypass IP Sec, based on the applicable database policies identified by the Selectors.

IP Sec Does

IP Sec provides security services at the IP layer by enabling a system to select required security protocols, determine the algorithm(s) to use for the service(s), and put in place any cryptographic keys required to provide the requested services. IP Sec can be used to protect one or more "paths" between a pair of hosts, between a pair of security gateways, or between a security gateway and a host. (The term "security gateway" is used throughout the IP Sec documents to refer to an intermediate system that implements IP Sec protocols. For example, a router or a firewall implementing IP Sec is a security gateway.)

The set of security services that IP Sec can provide includes access control, connectionless integrity, data origin authentication, rejection of replayed packets (a form of partial sequence integrity), confidentiality (encryption), and limited traffic flow confidentiality. Because these services are provided at the IP layer, they can be used by any higher layer protocol, e.g., TCP, UDP, ICMP, BGP, etc.

The IP Sec DOI also supports negotiation of IP compression [SMPT98], motivated in part by the observation that when encryption is employed within IP Sec, it prevents effective compression by lower protocol layers.

How IP Sec Works

IP Sec uses two protocols to provide traffic security — Authentication Header (AH) and Encapsulating Security Payload (ESP). Both protocols are described in more detail in their respective RFCs

- The IP Authentication Header (AH) provides connectionless integrity, data origin authentication, and an optional anti-replay service.

• The Encapsulating Security Payload (ESP) protocol may provide confidentiality (encryption), and limited traffic flow confidentiality. It also may provide connectionless integrity, data origin authentication, and an anti-replay service. (One or the other set of these security services must be applied whenever ESP is invoked.)

• Both AH and ESP are vehicles for access control, based on the distribution of cryptographic keys and the management of traffic flows relative to these security protocols.

These protocols may be applied alone or in combination with each other to provide a desired set of security services in IPv4 and IPv6. Each protocol supports two modes of use: transport mode and tunnel mode. In transport mode the protocols provide protection primarily for upper layer protocols; in tunnel mode, the protocols are applied to tunneled IP packets.

IP Sec allows the user (or system administrator) to control the granularity at which a security service is offered. For example, one can create a single encrypted tunnel to carry all the traffic between two security gateways or a separate encrypted tunnel can be created for each TCP connection between each pair of hosts communicating across these gateways. IP Sec management must incorporate facilities for specifying:

- which security services to use and in what combinations
- the granularity at which a given security protection should be applied
- the algorithms used to effect cryptographic-based security

Because these security services use shared secret values (cryptographic keys), IP Sec relies on a separate set of mechanisms for putting these keys in place. (The keys are used for authentication/integrity and encryption services.) This document requires support for both manual and automatic distribution of keys.

Where IP Sec May Be Implemented

There are several ways in which IP Sec may be implemented in a host or in conjunction with a router or firewall (to create a security gateway). Several common examples are provided below:

• Integration of IP Sec into the native IP implementation. This requires access to the IP source code and is applicable to both hosts and security gateways.

• "Bump-in-the-stack" (BITS) implementations, where IP Sec is implemented "underneath" an existing implementation of an IP protocol stack, between the native IP and the local network drivers. Source code access for the IP stack is not required in this context, making this implementation approach appropriate for use with legacy systems. This approach, when it is adopted, is usually employed in hosts.

• The use of an outboard crypto processor is a common design feature of network security systems used by the military, and of some commercial systems as well. It is sometimes referred to as a "Bump-in-the-wire" (BITW) implementation. Such implementations may be designed to serve either a host or a gateway (or both). Usually the BITW device is IP addressable. When supporting a single host, it may be quite analogous to a BITS implementation, but in supporting a router or firewall, it must operate like a security gateway.

Security Associations

This section defines Security Association management requirements for all IPv6 implementations and for those IPv4 implementations that implement AH, ESP, or both. The concept of a "Security Association" (SA) is fundamental to IP Sec. Both AH and ESP make use of SAs and a major function of IKE is the establishment and maintenance of Security Associations. All implementations of AH or ESP MUST support the concept of a Security Association as described below. The remainder of this section describes various aspects of Security Association management, defining required characteristics for SA policy management, traffic processing, and SA management techniques.

Definition and Scope

A Security Association (SA) is a simplex "connection" that affords security services to the traffic carried by it. Security services are afforded to an SA by the use of AH, or ESP, but not both. If both AH and ESP protection is applied to a traffic stream, then two (or more) SAs are created to afford protection to the traffic stream. To secure typical, bi-directional communication between two hosts, or between two security gateways, two Security Associations (one in each direction) are required.

A security association is uniquely identified by a triple consisting of a Security Parameter Index (SPI), an IP Destination Address, and a security protocol (AH or ESP) identifier. In principle, the Destination Address may be a unicast address, an IP broadcast address, or a multicast group address. However, IP Sec SA management mechanisms currently are defined only for unicast SAs. Hence, in the discussions that follow, SAs will be described in the context of point-to-point communication, even though the concept is applicable in the point-to-multipoint case as well.

As noted above, two types of SAs are defined: transport mode and tunnel mode. A transport mode SA is a security association between two hosts. In IPv4, a transport mode security protocol header appears immediately after the IP header and any options, and before any higher layer protocols (e.g., TCP or UDP). In IPv6, the security protocol header appears after the base IP header and extensions, but may appear before or after destination options, and before higher layer protocols. In the case of ESP, a transport mode SA provides security services only for these higher layer protocols, not for the IP header or any extension headers preceding the ESP header. In the case of AH, the protection is also extended to selected portions of the IP header, selected portions of extension headers, and selected options (contained in the IPv4 header, IPv6 Hop-by-Hop extension header, or IPv6 Destination extension headers). For more details on the coverage afforded by AH, see the AH specification.

A tunnel mode SA is essentially an SA applied to an IP tunnel. Whenever either end of a security association is a security gateway, the SA MUST be tunnel mode. Thus an SA between two security gateways is always a tunnel mode SA, as is an SA between a host and a security gateway. Note that for the case where traffic is destined for a security gateway, e.g., SNMP commands, the security gateway is acting as a host and transport mode is allowed. But in that case, the security gateway is not acting as a gateway, i.e., not transiting traffic. Two hosts MAY establish a tunnel mode SA between themselves. The requirement for any (transit traffic) SA involving a security gateway to be a tunnel SA arises due to the need to avoid potential problems with regard to fragmentation and reassembly of IP Sec packets, and in circumstances where multiple paths (e.g., via different security gateways) exist to the same destination behind the security gateways.

For a tunnel mode SA, there is an "outer" IP header that specifies the IP Sec processing destination, plus an "inner" IP header that specifies the (apparently) ultimate destination for the packet. The security protocol header appears after the outer IP header, and before the inner IP header. If AH is employed in tunnel mode, portions of the outer IP header are afforded protection (as above), as well as all of the tunneled IP packet (i.e., all of the inner IP header is protected, as well as higher layer protocols). If ESP is employed, the protection is afforded only to the tunneled packet, not to the outer header.

Security Association Functionality

The set of security services offered by an SA depends on the security protocol selected, the SA mode, the endpoints of the SA, and on the election of optional services within the protocol. For example, AH provides data origin authentication and connectionless integrity for IP data grams (hereafter referred to as just "authentication"). The "precision" of the authentication service is a function of the granularity of the security association with which AH is employed.

AH also offers an anti-replay (partial sequence integrity) service at the discretion of the receiver, to help counter denial of service attacks. AH is an appropriate protocol to employ when confidentiality is not required (or is not permitted, e.g , due to government restrictions on use of encryption). AH also provides authentication for selected portions of the IP header, which may be necessary in some contexts. For example, if the integrity of an IPv4 option or IPv6 extension header must be protected en route between sender and receiver, AH can provide this service (except for the non-predictable but mutable parts of the IP header.)

ESP optionally provides confidentiality for traffic. (The strength of the confidentiality service depends in part, on the encryption algorithm employed.) ESP also may optionally provide authentication (as defined above). If authentication is negotiated for an ESP SA, the receiver also may elect to enforce an anti-replay service with the same features as the AH anti-replay service. The scope of the authentication offered by ESP is narrower than for AH, i.e., the IP header(s) "outside" the ESP header is(are) not protected. If only the upper layer protocols need to be authenticated, then ESP authentication is an appropriate choice and is more space efficient than use of AH encapsulating ESP. Note that although both confidentiality and authentication are optional, they cannot both be omitted. At least one of them MUST be selected.

Combining Security Associations

The IP **data grams** transmitted over an individual SA are afforded protection by exactly one security protocol, either AH or ESP, but not both. Sometimes a security policy may call for a combination of services for a particular traffic flow that is not achievable with a single SA. In such instances it will be necessary to employ multiple SAs to implement the required security policy. The term "security association bundle" or "SA bundle" is applied to a sequence of SAs through which traffic must be processed to satisfy a security policy.

The order of the sequence is defined by the policy. (Note that the SAs that comprise a bundle may terminate at different endpoints. For example, one SA may extend between a mobile host and a security gateway and a second, nested SA may extend to a host behind the gateway.)

Security Association Databases

Many of the details associated with processing IP traffic in an IP Sec implementation are largely a local matter, not subject to standardization. However, some external aspects of the processing must be standardized, to ensure interoperability and to provide a minimum management capability that is essential for productive use of IP Sec. This section describes a general model for processing IP traffic relative to security associations, in support of these interoperability and functionality goals. The model described below is nominal; compliant implementations need not match details of this model as presented, but the external behavior of such implementations must be map able to the externally observable characteristics of this model.

There are two nominal databases in this model: the Security Policy Database and the Security Association Database. The former specifies the policies that determine the disposition of all IP traffic inbound or outbound from a host, security gateway, or BITS or BITW IP Sec implementation. The latter database contains parameters that are associated with each (active) security association. This section also defines the concept of a Selector, a set of IP and upper layer protocol field values that is used by the Security Policy Database to map traffic to a policy, i.e., an SA (or SA bundle).

Each interface for which IP Sec is enabled requires nominally separate inbound vs. outbound databases (SAD and SPD), because of the directionality of many of the fields that are used as selectors. Typically there is just one such interface, for a host or security gateway (SG). Note that an SG would always have at least 2 interfaces, but the "internal" one to the corporate net, usually would not have IP Sec enabled and so only one pair of SADs and one pair of SPDs would be needed. On the other hand, if a host had multiple interfaces or an SG had multiple external interfaces, it might be necessary to have separate SAD and SPD pairs for each interface.

The Security Policy Database (SPD)

A security association is a management construct used to enforce a security policy in the IP Sec environment. Thus an essential element of SA processing is an underlying Security Policy Database (SPD) that specifies what services are to be offered to IP data grams and in what fashion. The form of the database and its interface are outside the scope of this specification. However, this section does specify certain minimum management functionality that must be provided, to allow a user or system administrator to control how IP Sec is applied to traffic transmitted or received by a host or transiting a security gateway.

The SPD must be consulted during the processing of all traffic (Inbound and Outbound), including non-IP Sec traffic. In order to support this, the SPD requires distinct entries for inbound and outbound traffic. One can think of this as separate SPDs (inbound vs. outbound). In addition, a nominally separate SPD must be provided for each IP Sec-enabled interface.

An SPD must discriminate among traffic that is afforded IP Sec protection and traffic that is allowed to bypass IP Sec. This applies to the IP Sec protection to be applied by a sender and to the IP Sec protection that must be present at the receiver. For any outbound or inbound data gram, three processing choices are possible: discard, bypass IP Sec, or apply IP Sec. The first choice refers to traffic that is not allowed to exit the host, traverse the security gateway, or be delivered to an application at all. The second choice refers to traffic that is allowed to pass without additional IP Sec protection. The third choice refers to traffic that is afforded IP Sec protection, and for such traffic the SPD must specify the security services to be provided, protocols to be employed, algorithms to be used, etc.

For every IP Sec implementation, there MUST be an administrative interface that allows a user or system administrator to manage the SPD. Specifically, every inbound or outbound packet is subject to processing by IP Sec and the SPD must specify what action will be taken in each case. Thus the administrative interface must allow the user (or system administrator) to specify the security processing to be applied to any packet entering or exiting the system, on a packet by packet basis. The management interface for the SPD MUST allow creation of entries consistent with the selectors defined in Section 4.4.2, and MUST support (total) ordering of these entries. It is expected that through the use of wildcards in various selector fields, and because all packets on a single UDP or TCP connection will tend to match a single SPD entry, this requirement will not impose an unreasonably detailed level of SPD specification. The selectors are analogous to what are found in a stateless firewall or filtering router and which are currently manageable this way.

In host systems, applications MAY be allowed to select what security processing is to be applied to the traffic they generate and consume. Means of signaling such requests to the IP Sec implementation are outside the scope of this standard. However, the system administrator MUST be able to specify whether or not a user or application can override (default) system policies. Note that application specified policies may satisfy system requirements, so that the system may not need to do additional IP Sec processing beyond that needed to meet an application's requirements. The form of the management interface is not specified by this document and may differ for hosts vs. security gateways, and within hosts the interface may differ for socket-based vs. BITS implementations. However, this document does specify a standard set of SPD elements that all IP Sec implementations MUST support.

The SPD contains an ordered list of policy entries. Each policy entry is keyed by one or more selectors that define the set of IP traffic encompassed by this policy entry. These define the granularity of policies or SAs. Each entry includes an indication of whether traffic matching this policy will be bypassed, discarded, or subject to IP Sec processing. If IP Sec processing is to be applied, the entry includes an SA (or SA bundle) specification, listing the IP Sec protocols, modes, and algorithms to be employed, including any nesting requirements.

Selectors

An SA (or SA bundle) may be fine-grained or coarse-grained, depending on the selectors used to define the set of traffic for the SA. For example, all traffic between two hosts may be carried via a single SA, and afforded a uniform set of security services. Alternatively, traffic between a pair of hosts might be spread over multiple SAs, depending on the applications being used (as defined by the Next Protocol and Port fields), with different security services offered by different SAs. Similarly, all traffic between a pair of security gateways could be carried on a single SA, or one SA could be assigned for each communicating host pair. The following selector parameters must be supported for SA management to facilitate control of SA granularity. Note that in the case of receipt of a packet with an ESP header, e.g., at an encapsulating security gateway or BITW implementation, the transport layer protocol, source/destination ports, and Name (if present) may be "OPAQUE", i.e., inaccessible because of encryption or fragmentation. Note also that both Source and Destination addresses should either be IPv4 or IPv6.

The IP Sec implementation context determines how selectors are used. For example, a host implementation integrated into the stack may make use of a socket interface. When a new connection is established the SPD can be consulted and an SA (or SA bundle) bound to the socket. Thus traffic sent via that socket need not result in additional lookups to the SPD/SAD. In contrast, a BITS, BITW, or security gateway implementation needs to look at each packet and perform an SPD/SAD lookup based on the selectors. The allowable values for the selector fields differ between the traffic flow, the security association, and the security policy.

Security Association Database (SAD)

In each IP Sec implementation there is a nominal Security Association Database, in which each entry defines the parameters associated with one SA. Each SA has an entry in the SAD. For outbound processing, entries are pointed to by entries in the SPD. Note that if an SPD entry does not currently point to an SA that is appropriate for the packet, the implementation creates an appropriate SA (or SA Bundle) and links the SPD entry to the SAD entry. For inbound processing, each entry in the SAD is indexed by a destination IP address, IP Sec protocol type, and SPI. The following parameters are associated with each entry in the SAD. This description does not purport to be a MIB, but only a specification of the minimal data items required to support an SA in an IP Sec implementation.

For inbound processing: The following packet fields are used to look up the SA in the SAD:

- Outer Header's Destination IP address: the IPv4 or IPv6 Destination address.
- IP Sec Protocol: AH or ESP, used as an index for SA lookup in this database. Specifies the IP Sec protocol to be applied to the traffic on this SA.
- SPI: the 32-bit value used to distinguish among different SAs terminating at the same destination and using the same IP Sec protocol.

The following SAD fields are used in doing IP Sec processing:

- Sequence Number Counter: a 32-bit value used to generate the Sequence Number field in AH or ESP headers.
- Sequence Counter Overflow: a flag indicating whether overflow of the Sequence Number Counter should generate an auditable event and prevent transmission of additional packets on the SA.
- Anti-Replay Window: a 32-bit counter and a bit-map (or equivalent) used to determine whether an inbound AH or ESP packet is a replay.
- AH Authentication algorithm, keys, etc.
- ESP Encryption algorithm, keys, IV mode, IV, etc.
- ESP authentication algorithm, keys, etc. If the authentication service is not selected, this field will be null.

• Lifetime of this Security Association: a time interval after which an SA must be replaced with a new SA (and new SPI) or terminated, plus an indication of which of these actions should occur. This may be expressed as a time or byte count, or a simultaneous use of both, the first lifetime to expire taking precedence. A compliant implementation MUST support both types of lifetimes, and must support a simultaneous use of both. If time is employed, and if IKE employs X.509 certificates for SA establishment, the SA lifetime must be constrained by the validity intervals of the certificates, and the Next Issue Date of the CRLs used in the IKE exchange for the SA. Both initiator and responder are responsible for constraining SA lifetime in this fashion.

• IP Sec protocol mode: tunnel, transport or wildcard. Indicates which mode of AH or ESP is applied to traffic on this SA. Note that if this field is "wildcard" at the sending end of the SA, then the application has to specify the mode to the IP Sec implementation. This use of wildcard allows the same SA to be used for either tunnel or transport mode traffic on a per packet basis, e.g., by different sockets. The receiver does not need to know the mode in order to properly process the packet's IP Sec headers.

• Path MTU: any observed path MTU and aging variables.

SA and Key Management

IP Sec mandates support for both manual and automated SA and cryptographic key management. The IP Sec protocols, AH and ESP, are largely independent of the associated SA management techniques, although the techniques involved do affect some of the security services offered by the protocols. For example, the optional anti replay services available for AH and ESP require automated SA management. Moreover, the granularity of key distribution employed with IP Sec determines the granularity of authentication provided. In general, data origin authentication in AH and ESP is limited by the extent to which secrets used with the authentication algorithm (or with a key management protocol that creates such secrets) are shared among multiple possible sources. The following text describes the minimum requirements for both types of SA management.

Manual Techniques

The simplest form of management is manual management, in which a person manually configures each system with keying material and security association management data relevant to secure communication with other systems. Manual techniques are practical in small, static environments but they do not scale well. For example, a company could create a Virtual Private Network (VPN) using IP Sec in security gateways at several sites. If the number of sites is small, and since all the sites come under the purview of a single administrative domain, this is likely to be a feasible context for manual management techniques. In this case, the security gateway might selectively protect traffic to and from other sites within the organization using a manually configured key, while not protecting traffic for other destinations.

It also might be appropriate when only selected communications need to be secured. A similar argument might apply to use of IP Sec entirely within an organization for a small number of hosts and/or gateways. Manual management techniques often employ statically configured, symmetric keys, though other options also exist.

Automated SA and Key Management

Widespread deployment and use of IP Sec requires an Internet-standard, scalable, automated, SA management protocol. Such support is required to facilitate use of the anti-replay features of AH and ESP, and to accommodate on-demand creation of SAs, e.g., for user- and session-oriented keying. (Note that the notion of "rekeying" an SA actually implies creation of a new SA with a new SPI, a process that generally implies use of an automated SA/key management protocol.)

When an automated SA/key management protocol is employed, the output from this protocol may be used to generate multiple keys, e.g., for a single ESP SA. This may arise because:

- The encryption algorithm uses multiple keys (e.g., triple DES)
- The authentication algorithm uses multiple keys
- Both encryption and authentication algorithms are employed

The Key Management System may provide a separate string of bits for each key or it may generate one string of bits from which all of them are extracted. If a single string of bits is provided, care needs to be taken to ensure that the parts of the system that map the string of bits to the required keys do so in the same fashion at both ends of the SA. To ensure that the IP Sec implementations at each end of the SA use the same bits for the same keys, and irrespective of which part of the system divides the string of bits into individual keys, the encryption key(s) MUST be taken from the first (leftmost, high order) bits and the authentication key(s) MUST be taken from the remaining bits. The number of bits for each key is defined in the relevant algorithm specification RFC. In the case of multiple encryption keys or multiple authentication keys, the specification for the algorithm must specify the order in which they are to be selected from a single string of bits provided to the algorithm.

Locating a Security Gateway

This section discusses issues relating to how a host learns about the existence of relevant security gateways and once a host has contacted these security gateways, how it knows that these are the correct security gateways. The details of where the required information is stored is a local matter. Consider a situation in which a remote host (H1) is using the Internet to gain access to a server or other machine (H2) and there is a security gateway (SG2), e.g., a firewall, through which H1's traffic must pass. An example of this situation would be a mobile host (Road Warrior) crossing the Internet to the home organization's firewall (SG2). This situation raises several issues:

- How does H1 know/learn about the existence of the security gateway SG2?
- How does it authenticate SG2, and once it has authenticated SG2, how does it confirm that SG2 has been authorized to represent H2?
- How does SG2 authenticate H1 and verify that H1 is authorized to contact H2?
- How does H1 know/learn about backup gateways which provide alternate paths to H2?

To address these problems, a host or security gateway MUST have an administrative interface that allows the user/administrator to configure the address of a security gateway for any sets of destination addresses that require its use. This includes the ability to configure:

- The requisite information for locating and authenticating the security gateway and verifying its authorization to represent the destination host.
- The requisite information for locating and authenticating any backup gateways and verifying their authorization to represent the destination host.

It is assumed that the SPD is also configured with policy information that covers any other IP Sec requirements for the path to the security gateway and the destination host.

This document does not address the issue of how to automate the discovery/ verification of security gateways.

Security Associations and Multicast

The receiver-orientation of the Security Association implies that, in the case of unicast traffic, the destination system will normally select the SPI value. By having the destination select the SPI value, there is no potential for manually configured Security Associations to conflict with automatically configured (e.g., via a key management protocol) Security Associations or for Security. Associations from multiple sources to conflict with each other. For multicast traffic, there are multiple destination systems per multicast group. So some system or person will need to coordinate among all multicast groups to select an SPI or SPIs on behalf of each multicast group and then communicate the group's IP Sec information to all of the legitimate members of that multicast group via mechanisms not defined here.

IP Traffic Processing

"The Security Policy Database (SPD)", the SPD must be consulted during the processing of all traffic (INBOUND and OUTBOUND), including non-IP Sec traffic. If no policy is found in the SPD that matches the packet (for either inbound or outbound traffic), the packet MUST be discarded.

Outbound IP Traffic Processing

Selecting and Using an SA or SA Bundle

In a security gateway or BITW implementation (and in many BITS implementations), each outbound packet is compared against the SPD to determine what processing is required for the packet. If the packet is to be discarded, this is an auditable event. If the traffic is allowed to bypass IP Sec processing, the packet continues through "normal" processing for the environment in which the IP Sec processing is taking place. If IP Sec processing is required, the packet is either mapped to an existing SA (or SA bundle), or a new SA (or SA bundle) is created for the packet. Since a packet's selectors might match multiple policies or multiple extant SAs and since the SPD is ordered, but the SAD is not, IP Sec MUST:

- Match the packet's selector fields against the outbound policies in the SPD to locate the first appropriate policy, which will point to zero or more SA bundles in the SAD.
- Match the packet's selector fields against those in the SA bundles found in (1) to locate the first SA bundle that matches. If no SAs were found or none match, create an appropriate SA bundle and link the SPD entry to the SAD entry. If no key management entity is found, drop the packet.
- Use the SA bundle found/created in (2) to do the required IP Sec processing, e.g., authenticate and encrypt.

In a host IP Sec implementation based on sockets, the SPD will be consulted whenever a new socket is created, to determine what, if any, IP Sec processing will be applied to the traffic that will flow on that socket.

Header Construction for Tunnel Mode

This section describes the handling of the inner and outer IP headers, extension headers, and options for AH and ESP tunnels. This includes how to construct the encapsulating (outer) IP header, how to handle fields in the inner IP header, and what other actions should be taken. The general idea is modeled after the one used in RFC 2003, "IP Encapsulation with IP":

- The outer IP header Source Address and Destination Address identify the "endpoints" of the tunnel (the encapsulator and decapsulator). The inner IP header Source Address and Destination Addresses identify the original sender and recipient of the data gram.
- The inner IP header is not changed except to decrement the TTL as noted below, and remains unchanged during its delivery to the tunnel exit point.
- No change to IP options or extension headers in the inner header occurs during delivery of the encapsulated data gram through the tunnel.
- If need be, other protocol headers such as the IP Authentication header may be inserted between the outer IP header and the inner IP header.

Processing Inbound IP Traffic

Prior to performing AH or ESP processing, any IP fragments are reassembled. Each inbound IP data gram to which IP Sec processing will be applied is identified by the appearance of the AH or ESP values in the IP Next Protocol field (or of AH or ESP as an extension header in the IPv6 context).

Selecting and Using an SA or SA Bundle

Mapping the IP data gram to the appropriate SA is simplified because of the presence of the SPI in the AH or ESP header. Note that the selector checks are made on the inner headers not the outer (tunnel) headers. The steps followed are:

- Use the packet's destination address (outer IP header), IP Sec protocol, and SPI to look up the SA in the SAD. If the SA lookup fails, drop the packet and log/report the error.
- Use the SA found in (1) to do the IP Sec processing, e.g., authenticate and decrypt. This step includes matching the packet's (Inner Header if tunneled) selectors to the selectors in the SA. Local policy determines the specificity of the SA selectors (single value, list, range, wildcard). In general, a packet's source address MUST match the SA selector value. However, an ICMP packet received on a tunnel mode SA may have a source address other than that bound to the SA and thus such packets should be permitted as exceptions to this check. For an ICMP packet, the selectors from the enclosed problem packet (the source and destination addresses and ports should be swapped) should be checked against the selectors for the SA. Note that some or all of these selectors may be inaccessible because of limitations on how many bits of the problem packet the ICMP packet is allowed to carry or due to encryption.
- Find an incoming policy in the SPD that matches the packet. This could be done, for example, by use of back pointers from the SAs to the SPD or by matching the packet's selectors (Inner Header if tunneled) against those of the policy entries in the SPD.
- Check whether the required IP Sec processing has been applied, i.e. verify that the SA's found in (1) and (2) match the kind and order of SAs required by the policy found in (3).

At the end of these steps, pass the resulting packet to the Transport Layer or forward the packet. Note that any IP Sec headers processed in these steps may have been removed, but that this information, i.e., what SAs were used and the order of their application, may be needed for subsequent IP Sec or firewall processing.

ICMP Processing (relevant to IP Sec)

The focus of this section is on the handling of ICMP error messages. Other ICMP traffic, e.g., Echo/Reply, should be treated like other traffic and can be protected on an end-to-end basis using SAs in the usual fashion.

An ICMP error message protected by AH or ESP and generated by a router SHOULD be processed and forwarded in a tunnel mode SA. Local policy determines whether or not it is subjected to source address checks by the router at the destination end of the tunnel. Note that if the router at the originating end of the tunnel is forwarding an ICMP error message from another router, the source address check would fail. An ICMP message protected by AH or ESP and generated by a router MUST NOT be forwarded on a transport mode SA (unless the SA has been established to the router acting as a host, e.g., a Telnet connection used to manage a router). An ICMP message generated by a host SHOULD be checked against the source IP address selectors bound to the SA in which the message arrives. Note that even if the source of an ICMP error message is authenticated, the returned IP header could be invalid. Accordingly, the selector values in the IP header SHOULD also be checked to be sure that they are consistent with the selectors for the SA over which the ICMP message was received.

Auditing

All systems that implement IP Sec will implement auditing. For the most part, the granularity of auditing is a local matter. However, several auditable events are identified in the AH and ESP specifications and for each of these events a minimum set of information that SHOULD be included in an audit log is defined. Additional information also MAY be included in the audit log for each of these events, and additional events, not explicitly called out in this specification, also MAY result in audit log entries. There is no requirement for the receiver to transmit any message to the purported transmitter in response to the detection of an auditable event, because of the potential to induce denial of service via such action.

Use in Systems Supporting Information Flow Security

Information of various sensitivity levels may be carried over a single network. Information labels (e.g. Unclassified, Company Proprietary, Secret) are often employed to distinguish such information. The use of labels facilitates segregation of information, in support of information flow security models, e.g. the Bell-LaPadula model. Such models, and corresponding supporting technology, are designed to prevent the unauthorized flow of sensitive information, even in the face of Trojan Horse attacks. Conventional, discretionary access control (DAC) mechanisms, e.g. based on access control lists, generally are not sufficient to support such policies, and thus facilities such as the SPD do not suffice in such environments.

In the military context, technology that supports such models is often referred to as multi-level security (MLS). Computers and networks often are designated "multi-level secure" if they support the separation of labeled data in conjunction with information flow security policies. Although such technology is more broadly applicable than just military applications, this document uses the acronym "MLS" to designate the technology, consistent with much extant literature.

IP Sec mechanisms can easily support MLS networking. MLS networking requires the use of strong Mandatory Access Controls (MAC), which unprivileged users or unprivileged processes are incapable of controlling or violating. This section pertains only to the use of these IP security mechanisms in MLS (information flow security policy) environments. Nothing in this section applies to systems not claiming to provide MLS.

Performance Issues

The use of IP Sec imposes computational performance costs on the hosts or security gateways that implement these protocols. These costs are associated with the memory needed for IP Sec code and data structures, and the computation of integrity check values, encryption and decryption, and added per-packet handling. The per-packet computational costs will be manifested by increased latency and, possibly, reduced throughout. Use of SA/key management protocols, especially ones that employ public key cryptography, also adds computational performance costs to use of IP Sec. These per association computational costs will be manifested in terms of increased latency in association establishment. For many hosts, it is anticipated that software-based cryptography will not appreciably reduce throughput, but hardware may be required for security gateways (since they represent aggregation points), and for some hosts.

The use of IP Sec also imposes bandwidth utilization costs on transmission, switching, and routing components of the Internet infrastructure, components not implementing IP Sec. This is due to the increase in the packet size resulting from the addition of AH and/or ESP headers, AH and ESP tunneling (which adds a second IP header), and the increased packet traffic associated with key management protocols. It is anticipated that, in most instances, this increased bandwidth demand will not noticeably affect the Internet infrastructure. However, in some instances, the effects may be significant, e.g., transmission of ESP encrypted traffic over a dialup link that otherwise would have compressed the traffic.

Conformance Requirements

All IPv4 systems that claim to implement IP Sec MUST comply with all requirements of the Security Architecture document. All IPv6 systems MUST comply with all requirements of the Security Architecture document.

Security Considerations

The focus of this document is security; hence security considerations permeate this specification.

Differences from RFC 1825

This architecture document differs substantially from RFC 1825 in detail and in organization, but the fundamental notions are unchanged. This document provides considerable additional detail in terms of compliance specifications. It introduces the SPD and SAD, and the notion of SA selectors.

It is aligned with the new versions of AH and ESP, which also differ from their predecessors. Specific requirements for supported combinations of AH and ESP are newly added, as are details of PMTU management.

S-HTTP

An extension to the HTTP protocol to support sending data securely over the World Wide Web. Not all Web browsers and servers support S-HTTP. Another technology for transmitting secure communications over the World Wide Web Secure Sockets Layer (SSL) — is more prevalent. However, SSL and S-HTTP have very different designs and goals so it is possible to use the two protocols together. Whereas SSL is designed to establish a secure connection between two computers, S-HTTP is designed to send individual messages securely. Both protocols have been submitted to the Internet Engineering Task Force (IETF) for approval as a standard. S-HTTP was developed by Enterprise Integration Technologies (EIT), which was acquired by Verifone, Inc. in 1995.

This memo describes a syntax for securing messages sent using the Hypertext Transfer Protocol (HTTP), which forms the basis for the World Wide Web. **Secure HTTP (S-HTTP)** provides independently applicable security services for transaction confidentiality, authenticity/integrity and non-reputability of origin. The protocol emphasizes maximum flexibility in choice of key management mechanisms, security policies and cryptographic algorithms by supporting option negotiation between parties for each transaction.

Introduction

The World Wide Web (WWW) is a distributed hypermedia system which has gained widespread acceptance among Internet users. Although WWW browsers support other, preexisting Internet application protocols, the native and primary protocol used between WWW clients and servers is the Hyper Text Transfer Protocol (HTTP). The ease of use of the Web has prompted widespread interest in its employment as a client/server architecture for many applications. Many such applications require the client and server to be able to authenticate each other and exchange sensitive information confidentially. The original HTTP specification had only modest support for the cryptographic mechanisms appropriate for such transactions.

Secure HTTP (S-HTTP) provides secure communication mechanisms between an HTTP client-server pair in order to enable spontaneous commercial transactions for a wide range of applications. Our design intent is to provide a flexible protocol that supports multiple orthogonal operation modes, key management mechanisms, trust models, cryptographic algorithms and encapsulation formats through option negotiation between parties for each transaction.

Summary of Features

Secure HTTP is a secure message-oriented communications protocol designed for use in conjunction with HTTP. It is designed to coexist with HTTP's messaging model and to be easily integrated with HTTP applications. Consequently, it mimics much of HTTP's style and syntax.

Secure HTTP provides a variety of security mechanisms to HTTP clients and servers, providing the security service options appropriate to the wide range of potential end uses possible for the World-Wide Web. The protocol provides symmetric capabilities to both client and server (in that equal treatment is given to both requests and replies, as well as for the preferences of both parties) while preserving the transaction model and implementation characteristics of HTTP.

Several cryptographic message format standards may be incorporated into S-HTTP clients and servers, particularly, but in principle not limited to, and S-HTTP supports interoperation among a variety of implementations, and is compatible with HTTP.

S-HTTP aware clients can communicate with S-HTTP oblivious servers and vice versa, although such transactions obviously would not use S-HTTP security features. S-HTTP does not require client-side public key certificates (or public keys), as it supports symmetric key-only operation modes. This is significant because it means that spontaneous private transactions can occur without requiring individual users to have an established public key. While S-HTTP is able to take advantage of ubiquitous certification infrastructures, its deployment does not require it.

S-HTTP supports end-to-end secure transactions, in contrast with the original HTTP authorization mechanisms which require the client to attempt access and be denied before the security mechanism is employed. Clients may be "primed" to initiate a secure transaction (typically using information supplied in message headers); this may be used to support encryption of fill-out forms, for example. With S-HTTP, no sensitive data need ever be sent over the network in the clear.

S-HTTP provides full flexibility of cryptographic algorithms, modes and parameters. Option negotiation is used to allow clients and servers to agree on transaction modes cryptographic algorithms (RSA vs. DSA for signing, DES vs. RC2 for encrypting, etc.); and certificate selection (please sign with your "Block buster Video certificate").

S-HTTP attempts to avoid presuming a particular trust model, although its designers admit to a conscious effort to facilitate multiply rooted hierarchical trust, and anticipate that principals may have many public key certificates.

Changes

This document describes S-HTTP/1.2. It differs from the previous draft in coalescing all option negotiation headers onto a single header line and in replacing PEM with MOSS. Also, the relationship between S-HTTP and HTTP has been clarified.

Processing Model

Message Preparation

The creation of an S-HTTP message can be thought of as a function with three inputs:

• The clear text message. This is either an HTTP message or some other data object.

• The receiver's cryptographic preferences and keying material. This is either explicitly specified by the receiver or subject to some default set of preferences.

• The sender's cryptographic preferences and keying material.

• This input to the function can be thought of as implicit since it exists only in the memory of the sender.

In order to create an S-HTTP message, then, the sender integrates the sender's preferences with the receiver's preferences. The result of this is a list of cryptographic enhancements to be applied and keying material to be used to apply them. This may require some user intervention. For instance, there might be multiple keys available to sign the message. Using this data, the sender applies the enhancements to the message clear text to create the S-HTTP message.

The processing steps required to transform the clear text message into the S-HTTP. The processing steps required to merge the sender's and receiver's preferences.

Message Recovery

The recovery of an S-HTTP message can be thought of as a function of four distinct inputs:

• The S-HTTP message.

• The receiver's stated cryptographic preferences and keying material. The receiver has the opportunity to remember what cryptographic preferences it provided in order for this document to be de referenced.

• The receiver's current cryptographic preferences and keying material.

• The sender's previously stated cryptographic options.

• The sender may have stated that he would perform certain cryptographic operations in this message.

In order to recover an S-HTTP message, the receiver needs to read the headers to discover which cryptographic transformations were performed on the message, then remove the transformations using some combination of the sender's and receiver's keying material, while taking note of which enhancements were applied. The receiver may also choose to verify that the applied enhancements match both the enhancements that the sender said he would apply and that the receiver requested as well as the current preferences to see if the S-HTTP message was appropriately transformed. This process may require interaction with the user to verify that the enhancements are acceptable to the user.

Modes of Operation

Message protection may be provided on three orthogonal axes: signature, authentication, and encryption. Any message may be signed, authenticated, encrypted, or any combination of these (including no protection).

Multiple key management mechanisms are supported, including password-style manually shared secrets, public-key key exchange and Kerberos ticket distribution. In particular, provision has been made for prearranged (in an earlier transaction or out of

band) symmetric session keys in order to send confidential messages to those who have no public key pair. Additionally, a challenge-response ("nonce") mechanism is provided to allow parties to assure themselves of transaction freshness.

Signature

If the digital signature enhancement is applied, an appropriate certificate may either be attached to the message (possibly along with a certificate chain) or the sender may expect the recipient to obtain the required certificate (chain) independently.

Key Exchange and Encryption

In support of bulk encryption, S-HTTP defines two key transfer mechanisms, one using public-key enveloped key exchange and another with externally arranged keys. In the former case, the symmetric-key cryptosystem parameter is passed encrypted under the receiver's public key.

In the latter mode, we encrypt the content using a prearranged session key, with key identification information specified on one of the header lines. Keys may also be extracted from Kerberos tickets.

Message Integrity and Sender Authentication

Secure HTTP provides a means to verify message integrity and sender authenticity for a message via the computation of a Message Authentication Code (MAC), computed as a keyed hash over the document using a shared secret which could potentially have been arranged in a number of ways, e.g.: manual arrangement or Kerberos. This technique requires neither the use of public key cryptography nor encryption.

This mechanism is also useful for cases where it is appropriate to allow parties to identify each other reliably in a transaction without providing (third-party) non reputability for the transactions themselves. The provision of this mechanism is motivated by our bias that the action of "signing" a transaction should be explicit and conscious for the user, whereas many authentication needs (i.e. access control) can be met with a lighter-weight mechanism that retains the scalability advantages of public-key cryptography for key exchange.

Freshness

The protocol provides a simple challenge-response mechanism, allowing both parties to insure the freshness of transmissions. Additionally, the integrity protection provided to HTTP headers permits implementations to consider the Date: header allowable in HTTP messages as a freshness indicator, where appropriate (although this requires implementations to make allowances for maximum clock skew between parties, which we choose not to specify).

Implementation Options

In order to encourage widespread adoption of secure documents for the World-Wide Web in the face of the broad scope of application requirements, variability of user sophistication, and disparate implementation constraints, Secure HTTP deliberately caters to a variety of implementation options. See Section 8 for implementation recommendations and requirements.

Message Format

Secure HTTP syntax deliberately mimics HTTP syntax in an effort to ease integration with systems that already process HTTP. In addition, certain HTTP headers are promoted to be Secure HTTP headers because they provide useful functionality that has security implications.

A Secure HTTP message consists of a request or status line (as in HTTP) followed by a series of RFC-822 style headers followed by encapsulated content. Once the content has been recovered, it should either be another Secure HTTP message, an HTTP message, or simple data.

For the purposes of compatibility with existing HTTP implementations, we distinguish S-HTTP transaction requests and replies with a distinct protocol designator.

The Request Line

The S-HTTP request line format is similar to that of HTTP. However, all S-HTTP request use the method method, 'Secure'. All S-HTTP requests (using this version of the protocol) should read:

Secure * Secure-HTTP/1.2

All case variations should be accepted. The asterisk shown here is a placeholder and should be ignored by servers; proxy-aware clients should substitute the URL (and must provide at least the host + port portion) of the request when communicating via proxy, as is the current HTTP convention; proxies should remove the appropriate amount of this information to minimize the threat of traffic analysis.

The Status Line

For server responses, the first line should be:

Secure-HTTP/1.2 200 OK

whether the request succeeded or failed. This prevents analysis of success or failure for any request, which the correct recipient can determine from the encapsulated data. All case variations should be accepted.

Secure HTTP Header Lines

The header lines described in this section go in the header of a Secure HTTP message. All except 'Content-Type' and 'Content-Privacy Domain' are optional. The message body shall be separated from the header block by two successive CRLFs.

All data and fields in header lines should be treated as case insensitive unless otherwise specified. Linear white space should be used only as a token separator unless otherwise quoted. Long header lines may be line folded in the style of [RFC-822].

This document refers to the header block following the S-HTTP request/response line and preceding the successive CRLFs collectively as "S-HTTP headers".

Content

The content of the message is largely dependent upon the values of the Content Privacy-Domain and Content-Transfer-Encoding fields.

For a PKCS-7 message, with '8BIT' Content-Transfer-Encoding, the content should simply be the PKCS-7 message itself.

If the Content-Transfer-Encoding is 'BASE64', the content should be preceded by a line that reads:

——BEGIN PRIVACY-ENHANCED MESSAGE——

and followed by a line that reads

——END PRIVACY-ENHANCED MESSAGE——

with the content simply being the base-64 representation of original content. If the inner (protected) content is itself a PKCS-7 message, then the Content Type of the outer content should be set appropriately; else, the Content Type should be represented as 'Data'.

If the Content-Privacy-Domain is MOSS, the content should consist of a MOSS Security Multipart as described in RFC1847. It is expected that once the privacy enhancements have been removed, the resulting (possibly protected) contents will be a normal HTTP request. Alternately, the content may be another Secure-HTTP message, in which case privacy enhancements should be unwrapped until clear content is obtained or privacy enhancements can no longer be removed.

Encapsulation Format Options

Content-Privacy-Domain: PKCS-7

Content-Privacy-Domain 'PKCS-7' follows the form of the PKCS-7 standard.

Message protection may proceed on two orthogonal axes: signature and encryption. Any message may be either signed, encrypted, both, or neither. Note that the 'auth' protection mode of S-HTTP is provided independently of PKCS-7 coding via the MAC-Info header of section 2.3.6 since PKCS-7 does not support a 'Key Digested Data' type, although it does support a 'Digested Data' type.

Signature

This enhancement uses the 'Signed Data' (or 'Signed And Enveloped Data') type of PKCS-7. When digital signatures are used, an appropriate certificate may either be attached to the message (possibly along with a certificate chain) as specified in PKCS-7 or the sender may expect the recipient to obtain its certificate (and/or chain)

independently. Note that an explicitly allowed instance of this is a certificate signed with the private component corresponding to the public component being attested to. This shall be referred to as a self-signed certificate. What, if any, weight to give to such a certificate is a purely local matter. In either case, a purely signed message is precisely PKCS-7 compliant.

Encryption

Encryption normal, public key

This enhancement is performed precisely as enveloping (using either 'Enveloped Data' or 'Signed And Enveloped Data' types) under PKCS-7. A message encrypted in this fashion, signed or otherwise, is PKCS-7 compliant.

Encryption prearranged key

This uses the 'Encrypted Data' type of PKCS-7. In this mode, we encrypt the content using a DEK encrypted under cover of a prearranged session key with key identification information specified on one of the header lines. The IV is in the Encrypted Content Info type of the Encrypted Data element. To generate signed, encrypted data, it is necessary to generate the 'Signed Data' production and then encrypt it.

Content-Privacy-Domain: MOSS

The body of the message should be a MIME compliant message with content type that matches the Content-Type line in the S-HTTP headers. Encrypted messages should use multipart/encrypted. Signed messages should use multipart/signed. However, since multipart/signed does not convey keying material, is acceptable to use multipart/ mixed where the first part is application/ moss key-data and the second part is multipart/mixed in order to convey certificates for use in verifying the signature. Implementation Note: When both encryption and signature are applied by the same agent, signature should in general be applied before encryption.

Imported HTTP headers

Overview

Some HTTP facilities, particularly those involved with caching and proxies, require special consideration when S-HTTP processing has been applied. Secure HTTP makes special accommodation for these features by copying the relevant HTTP header lines into Secure HTTP header syntax as well.

The behavior of these headers is intended to be in line with HTTP practice. This text is largely paraphrased from HTTP/1.0.

Connection: Keep-Alive

The 'Connection: Keep-Alive' header is designed to permit persistent connections between client/proxy and proxy/server pairs. A client or proxy which desires persistent connections should send the header 'Connection: Keep-Alive'. A server which agrees should respond with 'Connection: Keep-Alive'.

The persistent connection ends when either side closes the connection or after the receipt of a response which lacks the "keep-alive" key word. The server may close the connection immediately after responding to a request without a "keep-alive" keyword. A client can tell if the connection will be closed by looking for a "keep-alive" in the response.

Proxies and gateways should remove the Keep-Alive header, though, of course, they may optionally regenerate it if they desire a persistent connection with the next hop. HTTP clients not using gateways and desiring a persistent connection with the server should not use this mechanism, but rather should use whatever mechanisms HTTP provides.

If-Modified-Since

This may be used by the proxy to indicate that the document may be in its cache and that it is prepared to serve the document to the current requestor. Servers receiving this header and deciding not to resend the document should respond using the 320 response code. This header should only be placed in S-HTTP headers by proxies. Clients wanting to use If-Modified-Since should place it in the HTTP headers of the inner content.

Content-MD5

Servers may generate a Content-MD5 header to enable proxies to detect when valid cache hits have occurred. Note that the Content-MD5 header provides the possibility of traffic analysis. Servers using this should bear that risk in mind.

Cryptographic Parameters

Options Headers

Every S-HTTP request is preconditioned by the negotiation options provided by the potential receiver. The two primary locations for these options are

- In the headers of an HTTP Request/Response.
- In the HTML which contains the anchor being de referenced.

There are two kinds of cryptographic options which may be provided: Negotiation options, convey a potential message recipient's cryptographic preferences. Keying options, provide keying material which may be of use to the sender when enhancing a message.

Binding cryptographic options to anchors using HTML extensions HTML is the topic of the companion document draft-ietf-wts-shtml-01.txt and will not be treated here.

Negotiation Options

Both parties are able to express their requirements and preferences regarding what cryptographic enhancements they will permit/require the other party to provide. The appropriate option choices depend on implementation capabilities and the requirements of particular applications.

A negotiation header is a sequence of specifications each conforming to a four-part schema detailing:

• Property — the option being negotiated, such as bulk encryption algorithm.

• Value — the value being discussed for the property, such as DES-CBC

• Direction — the direction which is to be affected, namely: during reception or origination (from the perspective of the originator).

• Strength — strength of preference, namely: required, optional, refused

Non-Negotiation Headers

There are a number of options that are used to communicate or identify the potential recipient's keying material.

Encryption-Identity

This header identifies a potential principal for whom the message described by these options could be encrypted; Note that this explicitly permits return encryption under (say) public key without the other agent signing first (or under a different key than that of the signature). Or, in the Kerberos case, provides information as the agent's Kerberos identity. The syntax of the Encryption-Identity line is:

Encryption-Identity: <name-class>,<key-sel>,<name-arg>
<name-class> := 'DN-1485' | MOSS name forms

The name-class is an ASCII string representing the domain within which the name is to be interpreted, in the spirit of the new MOSS drafts. In addition to the MOSS name forms of RFC1848, we add the DN-1485 name form to represent a more convenient form of distinguished name.

Certificate-Info

In order to permit public key operations on DNS specified by Encryption-Identity headers without explicit certificate fetches by the receiver, the sender may include certification information in the Certificate-Info option. The format of this option is:

Certificate-Info: <Cert-Fmt>','<Cert-Group>
<Cert-Fmt> should be the type of <Cert-Group> being presented.

Defined values are 'PEM' and 'PKCS-7'. PKCS-7 certificate groups are provided as a base-64 encoded PKCS-7 Signed Data message containing sequences of certificates with or without the Signer Info field. A PEM format certificate group is a list of comma-separated base64-encoded PEM certificates. Multiple Certificate-Info lines may be defined.

Key-Assign

This option serves to indicate that the agent wishes to bind a key to a symbolic name for (presumably) later reference. The general syntax of the key-assign header is:

Key-Assign:<Method>,<Key-name>,<Lifetime>,<Ciphers>;
<Method-args>

<Key-name> := <string>

<Lifetime> := 'this' | 'reply' | "

<Method> :='inband' | 'krb-'<kv>

<Ciphers> := 'null' | <Cipher>+

<Cipher> := "Header cipher from section 3.2.4.7"

<kv> := '4' | '5'

Key-Name is the symbolic name to which this key is to be bound. Ciphers is a list of cipher for which this key is potentially applicable. The keyword 'null' should be used to indicate that it is inappropriate for use with ANY cipher. This is potentially useful for exchanging keys for MAC computation.

Lifetime is a representation of the longest period of time during which the recipient of this message can expect the sender to accept that key. 'this' indicates that it is likely to be valid only for reading this transmission. 'reply' indicates that it is useful for a reply to this message. If a Key-Assign with the reply lifetime appears in a CRYPTOPTS block, it indicates that it is good for at least one (but perhaps only one) dereference of this anchor. An unspecified lifetime implies that this key may be reused for an indefinite number of transactions.

This header line may appear either in an unencapsulated header or in an encapsulated message, though when an uncovered key is being directly assigned, it may only appear in an encrypted encapsulated content. Assigning to a key that already exists causes that key to be overwritten.

Keys defined by this header are referred to elsewhere in this specification as Key-IDs, which have the syntax:

<Key-ID> := <method>':'<key-name>

Key-Assign may also be used as a header line in the S-HTTP headers if the data it is carrying does not need to be secured itself, e.g. with Kerberos.

Inband Key Assignment

This refers to the direct assignment of an uncovered key to a symbolic name. Method-

args should be just the desired session key encoded in hexadecimal as in:

Key-Assign: inband,akey,reply,DES-ECB;0123456789abcdef

Short keys should be derived from long keys by reading bits from left to right.

Kerberos Key Assignment

This permits the binding of the shared secret derived from a Kerberos ticket/ authenticator pair to a symbolic key name. In this case, method-args should be the ticket/authenticator pair (each base 64 encoded), comma separated. For example:

Key-Assign: krb-4,akerbkey,reply,DES-ECB;<krb-ticket>,<krb-auth>

Grouping Headers With SHTTP-Cryptopts

In order for servers to bind a group of headers to an HTML anchor, it is possible to combine a number of headers on a single S-HTTP Crypt opts header line. The names of the anchors to which these headers apply is indicated with a 'scope' parameter.

SHTTP-Cryptopts

This option provides a set of cryptopts and a list of references to which it applies. (For HTML, these references would be named using the NAME tag). The names are provided in the scope attribute as a comma separated list and separated from the next header line by a semicolon.

SSL

Short for **Secure Sockets Layer (SSL),** a protocol developed by Netscape for transmitting private documents via the Internet. SSL works by using a private key to encrypt data that's transferred over the SSL connection. Both Netscape Navigator and Internet Explorer support SSL, and many Web sites use the protocol to obtain confidential user information, such as credit card numbers. By convention, URLs that require an SSL connection start with https: instead of http.

Another protocol for transmitting data securely over the World Wide Web is Secure HTTP (S-HTTP). Whereas SSL creates a secure connection between a client and a server, over which any amount of data can be sent securely, S-HTTP is designed to transmit individual messages securely. SSL and S-HTTP, therefore, can be seen as complementary rather than competing technologies. Both protocols have been approved by the Internet Engineering Task Force (IETF) as a standard.

SSL (Secure Sockets Layer) home white papers special reports events web casts books / training vender view subscribe stores tore it Seminars Executive Forums Web casts IT Education and Training IT Certifications Certification Practice Tests Classroom Learning Online Learning On-site Training Self-Paced Training the Bookstore Shopping Cart Free e-mail newsletters Print subscriptions

RESEARCH CENTERS

- Applications
- Careers
- Convergence
- Data Center
- LANs
- Net/Systems Mgmt.
- NOS
- Outsourcing
- Routers/Switches
- Security
- Service Providers
- Small / Med. Business
- Storage
- WAN Services
- Web/e-commerce
- Wireless/Mobile

SITE RESOURCES

- Daily News
- Newsletters
- This Week in NW
- Tests/Reviews

- Buyer's Guides
- Opinion
- Forums
- Special Issues
- How to/Primers
- Case Studies
- Encyclopedia
- IT Briefings

SSL (Secure Sockets Layer)

Although originally developed by Netscape as a way of ensuring the security of e-comm transactions, SSL is developing into a low-cost alternative to virtual private networks:

Browser-based SSL alternatives require little or no software on remote PCs, and in most cases any PC with a browser can be used to make the secure connection, as long as the user can authenticate to a central server. And SSL firewall ports that the traffic uses are generally left open, so firewall reconfiguring is usually unnecessary. The idea is that SSL's simplicity translates into an easier installation and long-term cost savings because of simpler ongoing support.

The SSL standard is not a single protocol, but rather a set of accepted data transfer routines that are designed to protect the integrity of transmitted messages. SSL relies on certificates digital identification cards and keys. Certificates include the name of the certificate authority that issued the certificate, the name of the entity to which the certificate was issued, the entity's public key, and time stamps that indicate the certificate's expiration date. Two types of keys are used as ciphers to encrypt and decrypt data. Private keys are issued to entities and are never given out. Public keys are given out freely. Both keys are necessary for authentication routines. Data encrypted with the public key cannot be decrypted with the same key: The private key must be used.

IP Spoofing

Criminals have long employed the tactic of masking their true identity, from disguises to aliases to caller-id blocking. It should come as no surprise then, that criminals who conduct their nefarious activities on networks and computers should employ such techniques. IP spoofing is one of the most common forms of on-line camouflage. In **IP Spoofing**, an attacker gains unauthorized access to a computer or a network by making it appear that a malicious message has come from a trusted machine by “spoofing” the IP address of that machine. In this article, we will examine the concepts of IP spoofing: why it is possible, how it works, what it is used for and how to defend against it.

History

The concept of IP spoofing, was initially discussed in academic circles in the 1980's. While known about for sometime, it was primarily theoretical until Robert Morris, whose son wrote the first Internet Worm, discovered a security weakness in the TCP protocol known as sequence prediction. Stephen Bellovin discussed the problem in-depth in Security Problems in the TCP/IP Protocol Suite, a paper that addressed design problems with the TCP/IP protocol suite. Another infamous attack, Kevin Mitnick's Christmas Day crack of Tsutomu Shimomura's machine, employed the IP spoofing and TCP sequence prediction techniques. While the popularity of such cracks has decreased due to the demise of the services they exploited, spoofing can still be used and needs to be addressed by all security administrators. Technical Discussion To completely understand how these attacks can take place, one must examine the structure of the TCP/IP protocol suite. A basic understanding of these headers and network exchanges is crucial to the process. Internet Protocol – IP Internet protocol (IP) is a network protocol operating at layer 3 (network) of the OSI model. It is a connectionless model, meaning there is no information regarding transaction state, which is used to route packets on a network. Additionally, there is no method in place to ensure that a packet is properly delivered to the destination.

Examining the IP header, we can see that the first 12 bytes (or the top 3 rows of the header) contain various information about the packet. The next 8 bytes (the next 2 rows), however, contains the source and destination IP addresses. Using one of several tools, an attacker can easily modify these addresses – specifically the “source address” field. It's important to note that each data gram is sent independent of all others due to the stateless nature of IP. Keep this fact in mind as we examine TCP in the next section. Transmission Control Protocol – TCP IP can be thought of as a routing wrapper for layer 4 (transport), which contains the Transmission Control Protocol (TCP). Unlike IP, TCP uses a connection-oriented design. This means that the participants in a TCP session must first build a connection via the 3-way handshake (SYN-SYN/ACK-ACK) - then update one another on progress - via sequences and acknowledgements. This “conversation” ensures data reliability, since the sender receives an OK from the recipient after each packet exchange. As you can see above, a TCP header is very different from an IP header. We are concerned with the first 12 bytes of the TCP packet, which contain port and sequencing information. Much like an IP data gram, TCP packets can be manipulated using software. The source and destination ports normally depend on the network application in use (for example, HTTP via port 80). What's important for our understanding of spoofing are the sequence and acknowledgement numbers. The data contained in these fields ensures packet delivery by determining whether or not a packet needs to be resent. The sequence number is the number of the first byte in the current packet, which is relevant to the data stream. The acknowledgement number, in turn, contains the value of the next expected sequence number in the stream. This relationship confirms, on both ends, that the proper packets were received. It’s quite different than IP, since transaction state is closely monitored. Consequences of the TCP/IP Design Now that we have an overview of the TCP/IP formats, let's examine the consequences. Obviously, it's very easy to mask a source address by manipulating an IP header. This technique is used for obvious reasons and is employed in several of the attacks discussed below. Another consequence, specific to TCP, is sequence number prediction, which can lead to session hijacking or host impersonating. This method builds on IP spoofing, since a session, albeit a false one, is built. We will examine the ramifications of this in the attacks discussed below.

Spoofing Attacks

There are a few variations on the types of attacks that successfully employ IP spoofing. Although some are relatively dated, others are very pertinent to current security concerns. Non-Blind Spoofing This type of attack takes place when the attacker is on the same subnet as the victim. The sequence and acknowledgement numbers can be sniffed, eliminating the potential difficulty of calculating them accurately. The biggest threat of spoofing in this instance would be session hijacking. This is accomplished by corrupting the data stream of an established connection, then re-establishing it based on correct sequence and acknowledgement numbers with the attack machine. Using this technique, an attacker could effectively bypass any authentication measures taken place to build the connection. Blind Spoofing This is a more sophisticated attack, because the sequence and acknowledgement numbers are unreachable. In order to circumvent this, several packets are sent to the target machine in order to sample sequence numbers. While not the case today, machines in the past used basic techniques for generating sequence numbers. It was relatively easy to discover the exact formula by studying packets and TCP sessions. Today, most OSs implement random sequence number generation, making it difficult to predict them accurately. If, however, the sequence number was compromised, data could be sent to the target. Several years ago, many machines used host-based authentication services.

A properly crafted attack could add the requisite data to a system (i.e. a new user account), blindly, enabling full access for the attacker who was impersonating a trusted host. Man In the Middle Attack Both types of spoofing are forms of a common security violation known as a man in the middle (MITM) attack. In these attacks, a malicious party intercepts a legitimate communication between two friendly parties. The malicious host then controls the flow of communication and can eliminate or alter the information sent by one of the original participants without the knowledge of either the original sender or the recipient. In this way, an attacker can fool a victim into disclosing confidential information by “spoofing” the identity of the original sender, who is presumably trusted by the recipient. Denial of Service Attack IP spoofing is almost always used in what is currently one of the most difficult attacks to defend against – denial of service attacks, or DoS. Since crackers are concerned only with consuming bandwidth and resources, they need not worry about properly completing handshakes and transactions. Rather, they wish to flood the victim with as many packets as possible in a short mount of time. In order to prolong the effectiveness of the attack, they spoof source IP addresses to make tracing and stopping the DoS as difficult as possible. When multiple compromised hosts are participating in the attack, all sending spoofed traffic, it is very challenging to quickly block tariff Misconceptions of IP Spoofing

While some of the attacks described above are a bit outdated, such as session hijacking for host-based authentication services, IP spoofing is still prevalent in network scanning and probes, as well as denial of service floods. However, the technique does not allow for anonymous Internet access, which is a common misconception for those unfamiliar with the practice. Any sort of spoofing beyond simple floods is relatively advanced and used in very specific instances such as evasion and connection hijacking. Defending Against Spoofing. There are a few precautions that can be taken to limit IP spoofing risks on your network, such as: Filtering at the Router - Implementing ingress and egress filtering on your border routers is a great place to start your spoofing defense. You will need to implement an ACL (access control list) that blocks private IP addresses on your downstream interface. Additionally, this interface should not accept addresses with your internal range as the source, as this is a common spoofing technique used to circumvent firewalls. On the upstream interface, you should restrict source addresses outside of your valid range, which will prevent someone on your network from sending spoofed traffic to the Internet. Encryption and Authentication - Implementing encryption and authentication will also reduce spoofing threats. Both of these features are included in Ipv6, which will eliminate current spoofing threats. Additionally, you should eliminate all host-based authentication measures, which are sometimes common for machines on the same subnet. Ensure that the proper authentication measures are in place and carried out over a secure (encrypted) channel.

Conclusion

IP Spoofing is a problem without an easy solution, since it’s inherent to the design of the TCP/IP suite. Understanding how and why spoofing attacks are used, combined with a few simple prevention methods, can help protect your network from these malicious cloaking and cracking techniques. Matt Tanase is President of Qaddisin. He and his company provide nationwide security consulting services. Additionally, he produces

The Security Blog, a daily weblog dedicated to network security. Relevant Links Session Hijacking Demonstration and Notes Dave Dittrich Closing the Floodgates: DDoS Mitigation Techniques Matt Tanase, Security Focus

Firewall

Overview

With the explosive growth of the Internet and of private intranets, the firewall has emerged as the security system of choice. The usefulness of firewalls has been limited, however, by their inability to work in hybrid network environments that employ multiple protocols and multiple platforms, and by the difficulties of managing the security system. Net Road Fire WALL from Ukiah Software, Inc., is the only integrated security platform that supports both NetWare and Windows NT server operating systems as well as both TCP/IP and IPX clients. Net Road Fire WALL is two products in one: an IP-IP firewall (with Network Address Translation) and an IPX/IP gateway. And, since it's a multi-level firewall, it provides the best defense against many types of security attacks from the network layer to the application layer. This set of capabilities makes Fire WALL the perfect security solution for heterogeneous network environments and can also provide a clear path for those who want to migrate from IPX to TCP/IP or even from NetWare to Windows NT. Net Road Fire WALL is also the only firewall that integrates with Novell Directory Services (NDS), enabling both network and security management to be handled from a single point. With support for the LDAP standard, the product will soon be able to integrate with other directory services as well. This is a formidable strength of the product, simplifying the management of the firewall (or multiple firewalls) and ensuring more efficient, lower cost management of the network security system. The robust design of the Ukiah security platform will enable it to evolve over the long term, providing users with a high level of network security even as they migrate to new protocols, new platforms and new applications.

The Market Need

The growth of the Internet has spawned a burgeoning network security industry. As corporations and other organizations connect their networks to the public Internet, the risks of endangering information assets have risen dramatically. Not a day or a week passes without the popular press commenting on the latest episode of Internet-related fraud, information corruption, or other incidents that dramatically underscore the darker side of the communications revolution. Computer and communications security, a topic once the exclusive province of obscure firms catering mainly to the government defense and intelligence agencies and to financial services companies, has become mainstream almost overnight. It is difficult to determine just how extensive the security problem is. Not only are security problems difficult to quantify various studies have shown that the majority of Fortune 1000 companies have experienced network security breaches and that less than 10 percent are detected but, most companies will not publicly admit if they have had security breaches. Some estimates place the cost of computer crime at up to $8 billion a year. The concern for network security has led to a need for more sophisticated security systems than most organizations have needed until now. Once, these organizations were content with the security provided by their network operating systems, network directory services, routers, and gateways. These are no longer sufficient to resist the attacks of legions of determined Internet hackers, to say nothing of attacks from an organization's own employees. Today, firewalls are almost universally acknowledged to be at the heart of good network security. A firewall is a security mechanism for controlling access between a private, trusted network and an untrusted outside network (which might be the public Internet or some other part of the corporate network within the intranet). Yet firewalls are not all created alike. They differ greatly in their architecture, the platforms they run on, their security capabilities, and their ability to support mixed protocol networks. In particular, consider the mixed protocol network: TCP/IP is not, contrary to popular belief, the only protocol still left standing - millions of IPX clients still need to get secure access to the Internet without going through the dreaded "forklift upgrade" to a whole new protocol stack. Rumors of the death of NetWare are similarly exaggerated - NT is gaining fast and will continue to do so, but there are in excess of three million NetWare servers (and 55 million NetWare clients) that are not going away anytime soon. Mixed networks at both the protocol and operating system platform level will be around for years to come - and need secure, seamless access to the Internet and its rich information resources. It is this need that Ukiah's Net Road Fire WALL is designed to address.

Today's Solutions for Connecting Mixed Networks to the Internet

Various alternatives to providing security in mixed protocol networks do exist, but all represent only a fraction of the total required solution: IPX/IP gateways provide Internet connectivity for IPX clients, but the security is very basic. Application security, for example, is generally based only on TCP ports - some products also support ICMP or UDP port-based filtering. The security focus with most of these gateway products is on controlling outbound access, not on dealing with the more serious problem of inbound network access. More importantly, these gateways do nothing to provide security for IP clients. Filtering bridges or packet-level filtering by routers are partial solutions, but they also have major security limitations (see section on Types of Firewalls), and don't support Internet services for IPX clients. IP firewalls can provide great security (as long as they provide capabilities up to and including an application level gateway), but they only support IP clients not IPX. Dual-protocol stack clients can be implemented to get around the IP-only nature of the Internet and of IP firewalls, but this is complex to implement and manage and is likely to be a nightmare for network administrators. There is only one product on the market which provides a true firewall today running on NetWare: Net Road Fire WALL. And there is only one product on any platform - NetWare, Windows NT or other that provides both an integrated IP firewall and an IPX/IP gateway: once again, Net Road Fire WALL. No other product family offers integrated firewall support for both IP and IPX clients, and also offers this firewall on both NetWare and Windows NT servers.

Firewall Primer

Definitions of Firewall: A security mechanism for controlling access between a private trusted network and an untrusted outside network (which might be the public Internet or some other part of the corporate network within an intranet). It is comprised of software running on general purpose or specialized hardware. Protocol gateway: A protocol translation mechanism for connecting (for example) an IPX network to an IP network (public or private). The term 'gateway' is also sometimes used to refer to circuit-level and application-level firewalls - see section on 'Types of Firewalls' but these are not protocol gateways. Network address translation (NAT): With the growing shortage of IP addresses, it has become increasingly difficult for organizations to obtain all the registered IP addresses they need. A network address translator solves this problem by dynamically converting between a re-usable pool of dynamically assigned registered IP addresses and the internal IP addresses used in an organization's intranet. This not only alleviates the IP address crunch, it also eliminates the need to renumber when an organization changes Internet service providers (ISPs). Some firewalls can provide NAT. Transparent proxy: A transparent proxy provides the ability to use an application process running on a firewall without explicitly requiring the client to specify that proxy. In other words, the client perceives that it is still speaking to the router gateway. This makes it considerably easier to install a firewall without having to reconfigure every client in a TCP/IP environment. The major types of networks in terms of their security classification are as follows:

Trusted network: Users on this network are, by default, deemed to be trustworthy. Users may be physically on a common network, or linked together via a virtual private network (VPN).

DMZ: The 'Demilitarized Zone' lies outside the perimeter defenses provided by the firewall but contains systems that are owned by a private organization. Common examples would be Web servers and anonymous ftp servers providing information to Internet users. Untrusted network: These are outside networks of various kinds, among the many thousands of networks connected to the Internet, or even untrusted networks that may be part of other departments or divisions within an organization.

Types of Firewalls

Firewalls typically provide one of three different levels of security

a. packet filtering,
b. circuit-level gateway
c. application gateway
d. some combination of these.

a. Packet filtering: This firewall delivers the most basic form of firewall security and is also a standard feature of routers. Packet filters inspect the header of each incoming and outgoing packet for user-defined content, such as an IP address or a specific bit pattern, but do not validate or track the state of sessions. These firewalls can also filter at the application port level — for example, ftp generally uses port 21. However, since any packet with the right IP address can pass through the filter once the port is enabled, there is a security hole for other applications or sessions addressed to the same port. Packet filtering is the least secure form of firewall but the cheapest.

b. Circuit-level gateway: This is a firewall that validates TCP and, in some products, User Data gram Protocol (UDP) sessions before opening a connection or circuit through the firewall. The state of the session is monitored, and traffic is only allowed while the session is still open. This is more secure than packet filtering but allows any kind of data through the firewall while the session is open, creating a security hole. This is better than packet filtering but still falls short of total security. And if this gateway doesn't support UDP, it can't support native UDP traffic such as domain name service (DNS) and SNMP.

c. Application-level gateway: Considered to be the 'high-end' firewall choice, application- level gateways run an application process (sometimes termed a 'proxy') on the firewall for each application that is supported. By understanding the application content of the traffic flowing through the firewall, a high degree of control can be applied. For example, a given user can have the right to use a certain application, such as ftp, but only for some commands (such as "get") and not for others (such as "put"). Or application traffic down to the level of specific file types can be controlled, allowing .doc files to be transferred through the gateway, but not xls files, which might contain company financial data. These firewalls can also provide highly detailed logging of traffic and security events. In addition, application firewalls can use NAT to mask the real IP address on a node on the internal network and thus make it invisible to the outside.

State full inspection: This firewall is essentially a hybrid that has elements of all of the above firewalls, but lacks the full application layer inspection capabilities of an application level gateway. An example of such a firewall is one whose traffic inspection engine is based on a generalized scripting language. The engine executes inspection rules written in this language. Its principal advantage over an application gateway is that, while it trades off some security robustness, it can provide greater simplicity in terms of adding firewall support for new applications. The most secure form of firewall is a 'multi-level firewall' - one which combines the capabilities of a packet filter, a circuit level gateway and an application level gateway to provide defense in depth. Security attacks can come at any level. For example, some kinds of attacks are best prevented at the application level (such as an illegal file write operation to a corporate server using FTP) while others are best prevented at the packet level (such as IP spoofing) - clearly, the combination of multiple levels of security is stronger than any one of them used alone. The only way to have both formidable security and support for multi-protocol networks with IP and IPX clients is to go a step further to a new category of firewall - one that integrates both a multi-level IP firewall and an IPX/IP gateway. This is exactly the Net Road Fire WALL approach. Security Policy Firewalls provide a means of enforcing security policies that define acceptable uses of applications and acceptable access to information - both inbound and outbound. Since all network communications between a trusted network and all other types of network must pass through the firewall in a well-designed network, the firewall is uniquely well positioned to play the role of network traffic cop. The user organization's access rules on the inbound side might cover defining acceptable access to specific servers or other host by time of day, by type of application, and/or by type of file. On the outbound side, policy might also prevent users from accessing specific Web sites or even specific pages within a Web site. The source of a communication, its destination, and the specific application it may use might all be included in a security policy. Inbound or outbound communications that fall outside of the parameters of the policy are considered security violations, and a multi-level firewall can and should be configured to detect and prevent them.

However sophisticated the hardware and software that provides a network's security perimeter, network security can only be as good as the organization's security policy and the people who must implement it including end users and network administrators alike. Since people are the weak link in any security system, ease of use and ease of management are essential to providing a security system that will not be abandoned because it is too hard to use or too expensive to manage. For Inquiring Minds Who Want to Know More Firewalls and Internet Security: Repelling the Wily Hacker. Bill Cheswick and Steve Bellovin. Addison-Wesley,1994. Building Internet Firewalls.

D.Brent Chapman and Elizabeth Zwicky. O'Reilly & Associates, 1995. Web Server Technology. Nancy Yeager and Robert McGrath. Morgan Kaufman Publishers, 1996. 'The World Wide Web Security FAQ.' Lincoln D. Stein

(www-genome.wi.mit.edu/WWW/faqs/www-security-faq.html).

Key Features and Benefits of NetRoad FireWALL:

Breadth of Application Support: No application-level firewall product matches Firewall's breadth of client support and application support. For IPX nodes, FireWALL supports the full range of TCP and UDP applications.

For IP nodes, it supports any TCP/IP client stack and the TCP and UDP applications that use them. This allows the broadest possible range of application and platform support, including new applications — such as Winsock 2.0-based applications as they are deployed. Breadth of Server Support: NetWare 4.x, Intranet Ware and Windows NT. Breadth of Client OS Support: For IPX clients: Windows 3.x, Windows95, Windows NT. For IP clients: any client, regardless of operating system, that supports a TCP/IP stack (including Novell's, Microsoft's etc.).Ease of Management: Integration with NDS at multiple levels: This provides a single point of administration for the network and its security system. The FireWALL administration utility is an NWADMIN snap-in - so one tool does it all. All configuration information can be stored in the NDS database. Password control is administered and enforced through NDS, including the support of one time passwords (S/Key) and of 'intruder detection' to prevent password guessing attacks. All logs, including security event logs and connection log information, can be stored through NDS. Names, groups, and access control policies are defined in one place - ending the multi-console,.multi-database management nightmare. Flexible alarming mechanisms: Alarming is user configurable, so that the administrator can define event severity and the associated alarming method, including pager notification, e-mail, on-screen messages, SNMP traps, and log entries. Audit mechanisms: FireWALL allows extensive logging of both usage and security statistics (real-time and historical).Transparent proxies: These allow Internet access without having to re-configure each and every client to specify the firewall as the gateway instead of the router.

Spoofing

The most common form of spoofing is 'IP spoofing', whereby an attacker obtains a legitimate IP address, which normally resides somewhere on a trusted network, and uses that address to penetrate network defenses. NetRoad FireWALL filters out such attacks through low-level filtering that can identify if the source of the traffic is not where it should be; e.g., an IP address that should be resident on a trusted network is originating from an outside network. Another form of spoofing is DNS spoofing, whereby an attacker obtains access to a system that is the name server for a network. The attacker then sets up a name that maps from the address of his system to the name of a host defined within the victim's '.rhosts' file. The attacker can then use rlogin to access the victim's system. NetRoad FireWALL prevents these attacks using a technique called 'double reverse lookup'.

Password Attacks

Passwords can be illegitimately obtained by attackers in many different ways. For example, attackers use packet sniffers, guess passwords through the use of so-called dictionary attacks, or simply read the yellow Post-It note affixed to the victim's computer monitor. NetRoad FireWALL protects against some of these attacks though not the problem of the Post-It note on the monitor - by implementing the CHAP, notably the S/Key scheme (both the MD4 and MD5 versions), which controls outside access to a target system through the use of an ever-changing password. NetRoad FireWALL also provides intruder detection to prevent brute-force password guessing attempts. This can be implemented through NetRoad Fire WALL's integration with NDS, which allows it to detect and prevent repeated failed password attempts. At the same time, NDS enforces password aging, to still further reinforce security. Denial of Service Denial of service attacks have gained great prominence recently as a result of several ISPs experiencing crippling hacker attacks that shut down service for extended periods. The mode of attack is generally referred to as a 'syn' attack, which overloads the buffers of the target system by generating massive numbers of connection requests which effectively lock out legitimate connection requests by anyone else. Operating system and protocol stack vendors have moved rapidly to incorporate protection against such attacks into their products - as Microsoft has done with its TCP/IP stack. NetRoad FireWALL also provides the ability to detect such attacks and generate a critical alarm, and will soon also provide the ability to actually shut off the attack before the system fails.

Evolution of the Firewall Industry

In today's world, most businesses, regardless of size, believe that access to the Internet is imperative if they are going to compete effectively. Even though the benefits of connecting to the Internet are considerable, so are the risks. When a business connects its private network to the Internet, it is not just providing its employees access to external information and Internet services; it is also providing external users with a means to access the company's own private information. Horror stories abound in the media regarding companies that have had proprietary information stolen, modified, or otherwise compromised by attackers who gained access via the Internet. For this reason, any business that has ever contemplated connecting to the Internet has been forced to deal with the issue of network security.

In response to these risks, a whole industry has formed during the last several years to meet the needs of businesses wanting to take advantage of the benefits of being connected to the Internet while still maintaining the confidentiality, integrity, and availability of their own private information and network resources. This industry revolves around firewall technology.

A firewall provides a single point of defense between two networks—it protects one network from the other. Usually, a firewall protects the company's private network from the public or shared networks to which it is connected. A firewall can be as simple as a router that filters packets or as complex as a multi-computer, multi-router solution that combines packet filtering and application-level proxy services.

Firewall technology is a young but quickly maturing industry. The first generation of firewall architectures has been around almost as long as routers, first appearing around 1985 and coming out of Cisco's IOS software division. These firewalls are called packet filter firewalls. However, the first paper describing the screening process used by packet filter firewalls did not appear until 1988, when Jeff Mogul from Digital Equipment Corporation published his studies.

During the 1989-1990 timeframe, Dave Presotto and Howard Trickey of AT&T Bell Laboratories pioneered the second generation of firewall architectures with their research in circuit relays, which are also known as circuit level firewalls. They also implemented the first working model of the third generation of firewall architectures, known as application layer firewalls. However, they neither published any papers describing this architecture nor released a product based upon their work.

As is often the case in research and development, the third generation of firewall architectures was independently researched and developed by several people across the United States during the late 1980's and early 1990's. Publications by Gene Spafford of Purdue University, Bill Cheswick of AT&T Bell Laboratories, and Marcus Ranum describing application layer firewalls first appeared during 1990 and 1991. Marcus Ranum's work received the most attention in 1991 and took the form of bastion hosts running proxy services. Ranum's work quickly evolved into the first commercial product—Digital Equipment Corporation's SEAL product.

Around 1991, Bill Cheswick and Steve Bellovin began researching dynamic packet filtering and went so far as to help develop an internal product at Bell Laboratories based upon this architecture; however, this product was never released. In 1992, Bob Braden and Annette DeSchon at USC's Information Sciences Institute began independently researching dynamic packet filter firewalls for a system that they called "Visas." Check Point Software released the first commercial product based on this fourth generation architecture in 1994.

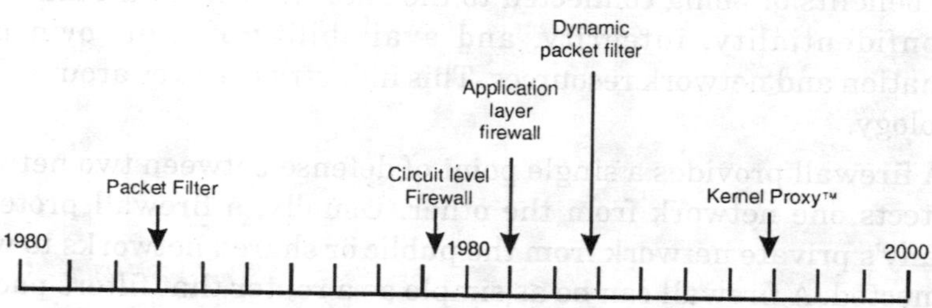

Figure :6.1 Time Line of Firewall Architectures

During 1996, Scott Wiegel, Chief Scientist at Global Internet Software Group, Inc., began laying out the plans for the fifth generation firewall architecture, the Kernel Proxy architecture. Cisco Centri Firewall, released in 1997, is the first commercial product based on this architecture. While the Kernel Proxy architecture is not discussed in this chapter, it is thoroughly discussed in later chapters of this guide.

The next section describes how to establish perimeter networks, which allow you to focus your security solution at defined points within your network. The concepts presented within this section are important for planning your network so that you place your firewall server correctly within your network. Specifically, we define what it means to establish a security perimeter and the differences among trusted, untrusted, and unknown networks.

If you are familiar with the concepts and terminology used to describe security perimeters, packet filters, and proxy servers, you can skip the remainder of this chapter and proceed to the next. However, in the remaining sections of this chapter, we establish terminology and concepts important to understanding the revolutionary advancements in network security provided by Cisco Centri Firewall, as well as how to position Cisco Centri Firewall within your network.

Establishing a Security Perimeter

When you define a network security policy, you must define procedures to safeguard your network and its contents and users against loss and damage. From this perspective, a network security policy plays a role in enforcing the overall security policy defined by an organization. A network security policy focuses on controlling the network traffic and usage. It identifies a network's resources and threats, defines network use and responsibilities, and details action plans for when the security policy is violated. When you deploy a network security policy, you want it to be strategically enforced at defensible boundaries within your network. These strategic boundaries are called *perimeter networks*.

Perimeter Networks

To establish your collection of perimeter networks, you must designate the networks of computers that you wish to protect and define the network security mechanisms that protect them. To have a successful network security perimeter, the firewall server must be the gateway for *all* communications between trusted networks and untrusted and unknown networks. Each network can contain multiple perimeter networks within it. When describing how perimeter networks are positioned relative to each other, we observe three types of perimeter networks: the outermost perimeter, internal perimeters, and the innermost perimeter.

Figure 6-2 depicts the relationship among the various perimeters. Note that the multiple internal perimeters are relative to a particular asset, such as the "internal perimeter that is just inside the firewall server."

The *outermost perimeter network* identifies the separation point between the assets that you control and the assets that you do not control—usually, this point is the router that you use to separate your network from your Internet service provider's network. *Internal perimeter networks*

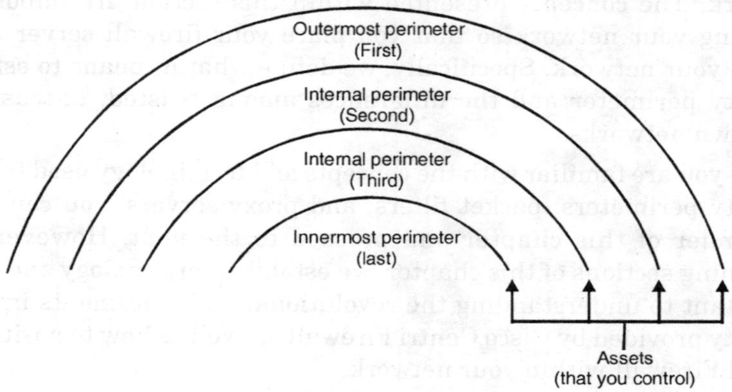

Figure 6-2: Perimeter Networks

represent additional boundaries where you have other security mechanisms in place, such as intranet firewalls and filtering routers.

Figure 6-3 depicts two perimeter networks (an outermost perimeter network and an internal perimeter network) defined by the placement of the internal and external routers and the firewall server.

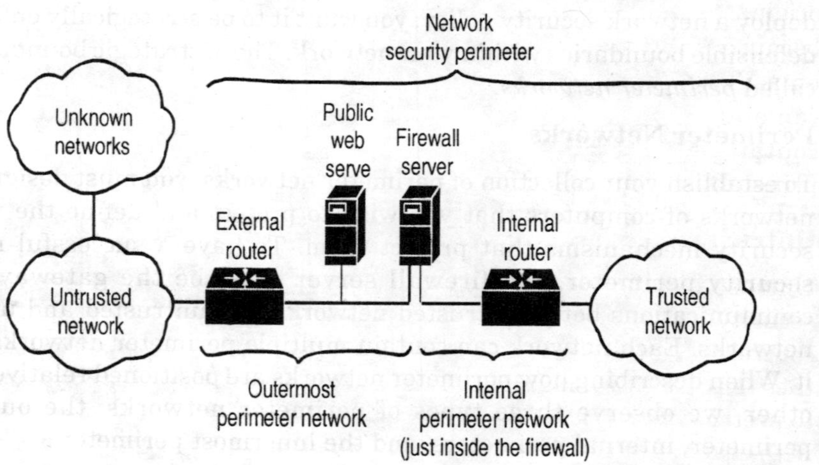

Figure 6-3: Network Security Perimeter

From the perspective of users on an external network, the firewall server represents all accessible computers on the trusted network. It defines the point of focus, or choke point, through which all communications between the two networks must pass.

The outermost perimeter network is the most insecure area of your network infrastructure. Normally, this area is reserved for routers, firewall servers, and public Internet servers, such as HTTP, FTP, and Gopher servers. This area of the network is the easiest area to gain access to, and therefore, it is the most frequently attacked, usually in an attempt to gain access to the internal networks. Sensitive company information that is for internal use only should *not* be placed on the outermost perimeter network. Following this precaution helps avoid having your sensitive information stolen or damaged.

Trusted Networks

Trusted networks are the networks inside your network security perimeter. These networks are the ones that you are trying to protect. Often, you or someone in your organization administers the computers that compose these networks, and your organization controls their security measures. Usually, trusted networks are within the security perimeter. When you set up the firewall server, you explicitly identify the type of networks that are attached to the firewall server through network adapter cards. After the initial configuration, the trusted networks include the firewall server and all networks behind it.

One exception to this general rule is the inclusion of *virtual private networks* (VPNs). These networks are trusted networks that transmit data across an untrusted network infrastructure. For the purposes of our discussion, the network packets that originate on a VPN are considered to originate from within your internal perimeter network. This origin is logical because of how VPNs are established. For communications that originate on a VPN, security mechanisms must exist by which the firewall server can authenticate the origin, data integrity, and other security principles contained within the network traffic according to the same security principles enforced on your trusted networks.

Untrusted Networks

Untrusted networks are the networks that are known to be outside of your security perimeter. They are untrusted because they are outside of your control. You have no control over the administration or security policies for these sites. They are the private, shared networks from which you are trying to protect your network. However, you still need and want to communicate with these networks even though they are untrusted. When you set up the firewall server, you explicitly identify the untrusted networks from which that firewall can accept requests. Untrusted networks are outside of the security perimeter and external to the firewall server.

Unknown Networks

Unknown networks are those networks that are neither trusted nor untrusted. They are unknown quantities to the firewall because you cannot explicitly tell the firewall server that this network is a trusted or an untrusted network. Unknown networks exist outside of your security perimeter. (By default, all non-trusted networks are considered unknown networks, and the firewall applies the security policy that is applied to *The Internet* node in the user interface, which represents all unknown networks. However, you can identify unknown networks below *The Internet* node and apply more specialized policies to those untrusted networks.

Table 6: Summarizes the relationships among the network designations and common networks:

Relationships Among Network Designation and Network Configurations Common Networks	**Network Designation**	**Description**
Innermost Perimeter Network	Trusted	Protects innermost assets behind other perimeter networks.
Internal Perimeter Network	Trusted and behind the firewall	A perimeter network that exists behind the firewall.
Outermost Perimeter Network	Trusted but likely to be attacked	The perimeter network between the outermost router and the firewall server. The network area that is exposed to external networks and is most likely to be attacked because it is accessible.
Known External Networks	Untrusted	Required access by trusted users.
Unknown External Networks	Unknown	Not aware of their existence.

Four Generations of Firewall Architectures

A firewall is a network gateway that enforces security rules on the conversion of peer-to-peer communications. Essentially, a firewall creates a boundary between two or more networks. A firewall is usually configured as a bastion host or a dual-homed bastion host. It evaluates each network packet against a network security policy, which is a collection of security rules, conventions, and procedures governing communications into and out of a network. Usually, IP traffic forwarding is disabled on the firewall to ensure that all traffic between the internal network and external networks passes through the firewall server, thereby allowing the firewall to inspect all network packets that traverse the network boundary.

Most firewall technologies provide different capabilities for auditing communication events. Usually, the firewalls generate audit records detailing the cause and circumstances surrounding the triggering of audit events. As firewall technology improves, firewalls inspect additional network packet information, use more sophisticated inspection algorithms, maintain more state information, and inspect the network packets at more network layers. As such, more mature firewall technology provides more detailed audit records, or summary information, about the network packets that are allowed through or prevented from traversing the firewall. By analyzing such audit records, administrators can often detect network security policy problems, such as attempts to break in or misconfiguration of the firewall's network security policy enforcement features. As a general rule, more detailed and descriptive audit record information yields better monitoring capabilities in a firewall product.

Packet Filters

A ***packet filter firewall*** is a first-generation firewall technology that analyzes network traffic at the transport protocol layer. Each IP network packet is examined to see if it matches one of a set of rules defining what data flows are allowed. These rules identify whether communication is allowed based upon information contained within the internet and transport layer headers and the direction in which the packet is headed.

Packet filters typically enable you to manipulate (that is, permit or prohibit) the transfer of data based on the following controls:

- the physical network interface that the packet arrives on
- the address the data is (supposedly) coming from (source IP address)
- the address the data is going to (destination IP address)
- the type of transport layer (TCP, UDP, ICMP)
- the transport layer source port
- the transport layer destination port

Figure 6-4 depicts the network packet evaluation process used by a packet filter firewall.

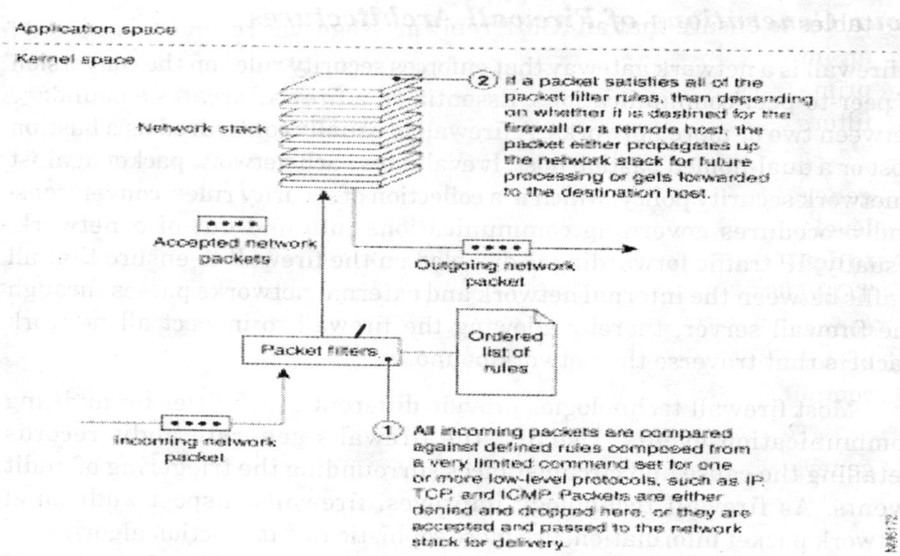

Figure 6-4: Simple Packet Filter Architecture

Packet filters generally do not understand the application layer protocols used in the communication packets. Instead, they work by applying a rule set that is maintained in the TCP/IP kernel. This rule set contains an associated action that will be applied to any packets matching the criteria mentioned above.

The action taken may take on one of two values: "deny" or "permit" the network packet. Two lists, the *deny list* and the *permit list*, are maintained in the kernel. For a network packet to be routed to its proper destination, it must first pass a check of both the deny and permit lists. That is, it must not be expressly denied, and it must be expressly permitted. Some packet filters that are incorporated into router hardware implement a different policy. In these types of packet filters, the packet must be expressly denied or else it is permitted. In order for you to understand the filtering rules, you must consider the security stance utilized by the routing hardware.

Packet filters typically implement command sets that allow the checking of the source and destination *port* numbers on the TCP and UDP transport layer protocols. This check determines whether an applicable permit or deny rule exists for that specific port and protocol combination. Due to the fact that the ICMP protocol layer does not utilize port numbers for its communications protocol, it is difficult for packet filters to apply any security policy to this form of network traffic. In order to apply an effective security policy to ICMP, the packet filter must maintain state tables to ensure that an ICMP reply message was recently requested from an internal host. This ability to track communications state is one of the primary differences between simple packet filters and dynamic packet filters.

Because packet filters are implemented in the network layer, they generally do not understand how to process state information in the high-level protocols, such as FTP. The more sophisticated packet filters are able to detect IP, TCP, UDP, and ICMP. Using a packet filter that includes the TCP/UDP port filtering capability, you can permit certain types of connections to be made to specific computers while prohibiting other types of connections to those computers and similar connections to other computers.

The complete network packet inspection adheres to the following general algorithm:

- If no matching rule is found, then drop the network packet.
- If a matching rule is found that permits the communication, then allow peer-to-peer communication.
- If a matching rule is found that denies the communication, then drop the network packet.

Because this type of firewall does not inspect the network packet's application layer data and does not track the state of connections, this solution is the least secure of the firewall technologies. It allows access *through* the firewall with a minimal amount of scrutiny. In other words, if the checks succeed, the network packet is allowed to be routed through the firewall as defined by the rules in the firewall's routing table. However, because it does less processing than the other technologies, it is the fastest firewall technology available and is often implemented in hardware solutions, such as IP routers.

Packet filter firewalls often readdress network packets so that outgoing traffic appears to have originated from a different host rather than an internal host. The process of readdressing network packets is called *network address translation*. Network address translation hides the topology and addressing schemes of trusted networks from untrusted networks.

Firewalls based on the packet filtering technologies have the following advantages:

- Packet filters are generally faster than other firewall technologies because they perform fewer evaluations. Also, they can easily be implemented as hardware solutions.
- A single rule can help protect an entire network by prohibiting connections between specific Internet sources and internal computers.

- Packet filters do not require client computers to be specifically configured; the packet filters do all of the work.
- In conjunction with network address translation, you can use packet filter firewalls to shield internal IP addresses from external users.

Firewalls based on the packet filtering technologies have the following disadvantages:

- Packet filters do not understand application layer protocols. They cannot restrict access to protocol subsets for even the most basic services, such as the PUT or GET commands in FTP. For this reason, they are less secure than application layer and circuit level firewalls.
- Packet filters are stateless in that they do not keep information about a session or application-derived information.
- Packet filters have very limited abilities to manipulate information within a packet.
- Packet filters do not offer value-added features, such as HTTP object caching, URL filtering, and authentication because they do not understand the protocols being used and cannot discern one from another.
- Packet filters cannot restrict what information is passed from internal computers to services on the firewall server. Packet filters only restrict what information can go *to* it. Thus, intruders can potentially access the services on the firewall server.
- Packet filters have little or no audit event generation and alerting mechanisms.
- Because of the complexity of supporting most non-trivial network services, it can be difficult to test "accept" and "deny" rules.

Circuit Level Firewalls

A ***circuit level firewall*** is a second-generation firewall technology that validates the fact that a packet is either a connection request or a data packet belonging to a connection, or virtual circuit, between two peer transport layers. To validate a session, a circuit level firewall examines each connection setup to ensure that it follows a legitimate handshake for the transport layer protocol being used (the only widely used transport protocol that uses a handshake is TCP). In addition, data packets are not forwarded until the handshake is complete. The firewall maintains a table of valid connections and lets network packets containing data pass through when network packet information matches an entry in the virtual circuit table. Once a connection is terminated, its table entry is removed, and that virtual circuit between the two peer transport layers is closed.

Figure 6-5 depicts the network packet evaluation process used by a circuit level firewall.

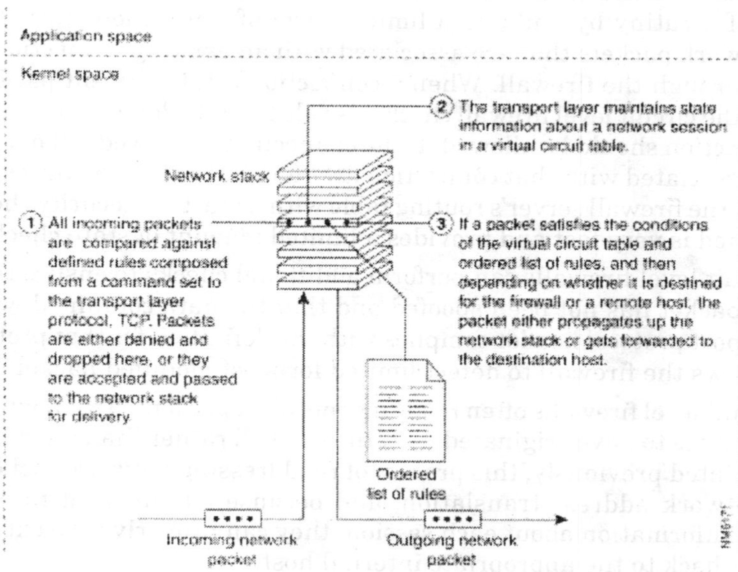

Figure 6-5 : Circuit Level Firewall Architecture

When a connection is set up, the circuit level firewall typically stores the following information about the connection:

- A unique session identifier for the connection, which is used for tracking purposes
- The state of the connection: *handshake*, *established*, or *closing*
- The sequencing information
- The source IP address, which is the address from which the data is being delivered
- The destination IP address, which is the address to which the data is being delivered
- The physical network interface through with the packet arrives
- The physical network interface through which the packet goes out

Using this information, the circuit level firewall checks the header information contained within each network packet to determine whether the transmitting computer has permission to send data to the receiving computer and whether the receiving computer has permission to receive that data.

Circuit level firewalls have only limited understanding of the protocols used in the network packets. They can only detect one transport layer protocol, TCP. Like packet filters, circuit level firewalls work by applying a rule set that is maintained in the TCP/IP kernel.

Circuit level firewalls allow access *through* the firewall with a minimal amount of scrutiny by building a limited form of connection state. Only those network packets that are associated with an existing connection are allowed through the firewall. When a connection establishment packet is received, the circuit level firewall checks its rule bases to determine whether that connection should be allowed. If the connection is allowed, all network packets associated with that connection are routed through the firewall as defined in the firewall server's routing table with no further security checks. This method is very fast and provides a limited amount of state checking.

Circuit level firewalls can perform additional checks to ensure that a network packet has not been spoofed and that the data contained within the transport protocol header complies with the definition for that protocol, which allows the firewall to detect limited forms of modified packet data.

Circuit level firewalls often readdress network packets so that outgoing traffic appears to have originated from the firewall rather than an internal host. As stated previously, this process of readdressing network packets is called network address translation, and because circuit level firewalls maintain information about each session, they can properly map external responses back to the appropriate internal host.

To summarize, circuit level firewalls have the following advantages:

- Circuit level firewalls are generally faster than application layer firewalls because they perform fewer evaluations.
- A circuit level firewall can help protect an entire network by prohibiting connections between specific Internet sources and internal computers.
- In conjunction with network address translation, you can use circuit level firewalls to shield internal IP addresses from external users.

Circuit level firewalls have the following disadvantages:

- Circuit level firewalls cannot restrict access to protocol subsets other than TCP.
- Circuit level firewalls cannot perform strict security checks on a higher-level protocol should the need arise.
- Circuit level firewalls have limited audit event generation abilities but can typically tie a network data packet to an application layer protocol by building limited forms of session state.
- Circuit level firewalls do not offer value-added features, such as HTTP object caching, URL filtering, and authentication because they do not understand the protocols being used and cannot discern one from another.

Application Layer Firewalls

An ***application layer firewall*** is a third-generation firewall technology that evaluates network packets for valid data at the application layer before allowing a connection. It examines the data in all network packets at the application layer and maintains complete connection state and sequencing information. In addition, an application layer firewall can validate other security items that only appear within the application layer data, such as user passwords and service requests.

Most application layer firewalls include specialized application software and proxy services. *Proxy services* are special-purpose programs that manage traffic through a firewall for a specific service, such as HTTP or FTP. Proxy services are specific to the protocol that they are designed to forward, and they can provide increased access control, careful detailed checks for valid data, and generate audit records about the traffic that they transfer.

Figure 6-6 depicts the network packet evaluation process used by a application layer firewall.

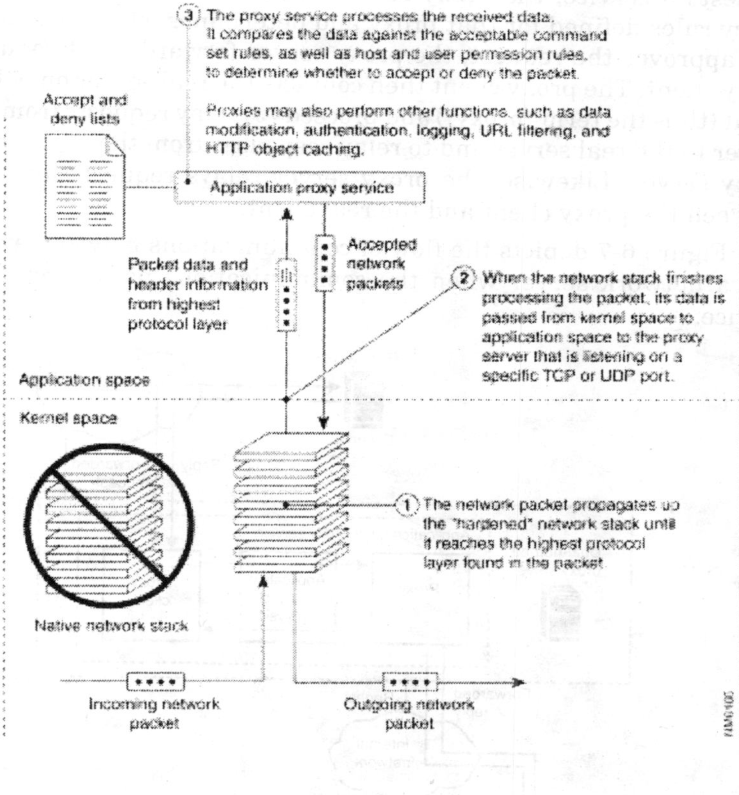

Figure 6-6: Application Layer Firewall Architecture

Each application proxy requires two components that are typically implemented as a single executable: a proxy server and a proxy client. A *proxy server* acts as the end server for all connection requests originated on a trusted network by a real client. That is, all communication between internal users and the Internet passes through the proxy server rather than allowing users to communicate directly with other servers on the Internet.

An internal user, or client, sends a request to the proxy server for connecting to an external service, such as FTP or Telnet. The proxy server evaluates the request and decides to permit or deny the request based on a set of rules that are managed for the individual network service. Proxy servers understand the protocol of the service that they are evaluating, and therefore, they only allow those packets through that comply with the protocol definitions. They also enable additional benefits, such as detailed audit records of session information, user authentication, and caching.

A *proxy client* is part of a user application that talks to the real server on the external network on behalf of the real client. When a real client requests a service, the proxy server evaluates that request against the policy rules defined for that proxy and determines whether to approve it. If it approves the request, the proxy server forwards that request to the proxy client. The proxy client then contacts the real server on behalf of the client (thus the term "proxy") and proceeds to relay requests from the proxy server to the real server and to relay responses from the real server to the proxy server. Likewise, the proxy server relays requests and responses between the proxy client and the real client.

Figure 6-7 depicts the flow of communications between a real client and a network server when the communications pass through a proxy service.

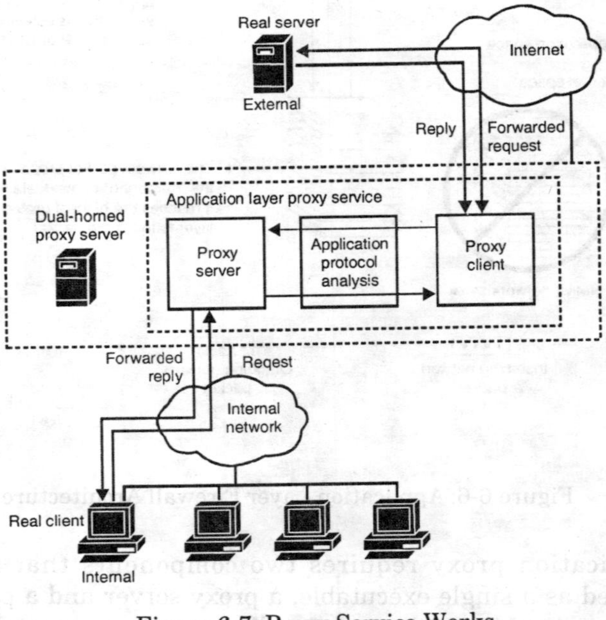

Figure 6-7: Proxy Service Works

Proxy services never allow direct connections, and they force all network packets to be examined and filtered for suitability. Instead of communicating directly with the real service, a user communicates to the proxy server (because the user's default gateway is set to point to the proxy server on the firewall). The same is true from the perspective of the real service communicating with a user. The proxies handle all communications between the user and a real service.

A proxy service sits transparently between a user on the internal network and the real service on the external network. That is, from the user's perspective, that user is dealing directly with the real service. From the real service's perspective, it is dealing directly with a user on the proxy server (instead of the user's real computer).

Proxy services are implemented on top of the firewall host's network stack and operate only in the application space of the operating system. Consequently, each packet must pass through the low-level protocols in the kernel before being passed up the stack to application space for a thorough inspection of the packet headers and packet data by the proxies. Then, the packet must travel back down to the kernel, and then back down the stack for distribution. Because each packet in a session is subject to this process, proxy services are notoriously slow.

Like circuit level firewalls, application layer firewalls can perform additional checks to ensure that a network packet has not been spoofed, and they often perform network address translation.

To summarize, proxy services have several key advantages:

- Proxy services understand and enforce high-level protocols, such as HTTP and FTP.
- Proxy services maintain information about the communications passing through the firewall server. They provide partial communication-derived sate information, full application-derived state information, and partial session information.
- Proxy services can be used to deny access to certain network services, while permitting access to others.
- Proxy services are also capable of processing and manipulating packet data.
- Proxy services do not allow direct communications between external servers and internal computers, so the names of internal computers do not have to be made known to external computers. In other words, proxy services shield internal IP addresses from the external world.
- By providing transparency, proxies provide users with the appearance that they are communicating directly with external servers.
- Proxy services can route internal services, as well as external-to-internal requests, elsewhere (for example, they can route services to an HTTP server on another computer).

- Proxy services can provide value-added features, such as HTTP object caching, URL filtering, and user authentication.
- Proxy services are good at generating audit records, allowing administrators to monitor attempts to violate the firewall's security policies.

Proxy services also have some disadvantages. These disadvantages include the following:

- Proxy services require you to replace the native network stack on the firewall server.
- Because the proxy servers listen on the same port as network servers, you cannot run network servers on the firewall server.
- Proxy services introduce performance delays. Inbound data has to be processed twice, by the application and by its proxy (for example, the Internet e-mail application talks to the proxy e-mail agent, which in-turn talks to a LAN e-mail application).
- Generally, a new proxy must be written for each protocol that you want to pass through the firewall, and therefore, the number of available network services and their scalability is limited. Usually a lag of six months or more exists from when the application is available and when its proxy is available, meaning users must wait for mission-critical applications to be available to them.
- Application level firewalls cannot provide proxies for UDP, RPC, and other services from common protocol families.
- Proxy services often require modifications to clients or client procedures, thus adding a task to the configuration process.
- Proxy services are vulnerable to operating-system and application-level bugs. Most packet filter firewalls do not rely extensively on operating system support mechanisms; however, they do generally rely on device drivers, etc. Most application layer firewalls require extensive support from the operating system to operate correctly, such as support from NDIS, TCP/IP, WinSock, Win32, and the standard C library. If a security relevant bug appears in any of these libraries, it can have undesirable effects on the security of the firewall server.
- Application layer firewalls overlook network packet information that is contained in lower layers. If the network stack is not performing correctly (which is complex to validate), then some of the information used to perform security checks that application layer firewalls request using standard calls from operating system libraries could return incorrect information. An example call that is often utilized by application layer firewalls is the **getpeeraddress**() call.
- Proxies may require additional passwords or other validation procedures that introduce delays and frustrate users.

Dynamic Packet Filters

A dynamic packet filter firewall is a fourth-generation firewall technology that allows modification of the security rule base on the fly. This type of technology is most useful for providing limited support for the UDP transport protocol. The UDP transport protocol is typically used for limited information requests and queries in application layer protocol exchanges.

This firewall accomplishes its functional requirements by associating all UDP packets that cross the security perimeter with a virtual connection. If a response packet is generated and sent back to the original requester, then a virtual connection is established and the packet is allowed to traverse the firewall server. The information associated with a virtual connection is typically remembered for a short period of time, and if no response packet is received within this time period, the virtual connection is invalidated.

Figure 6-8 depicts the network packet evaluation process used by a dynamic packet filter firewall.

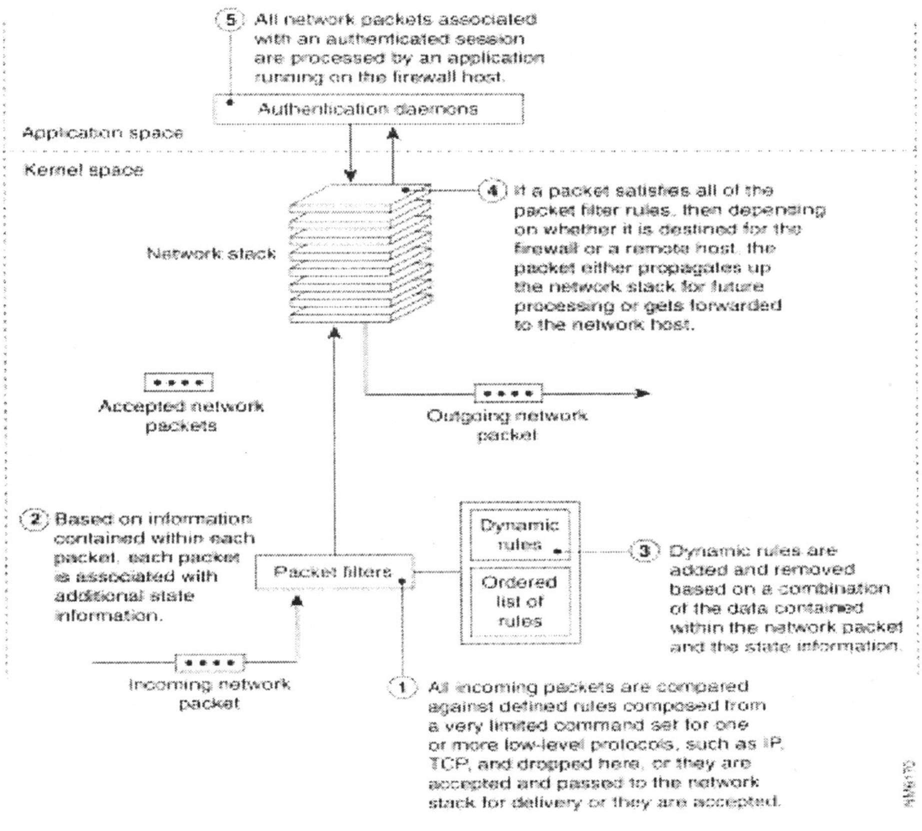

Figure 6-8: Dynamic Packet Filter Architecture

Dynamic packet filter firewalls have the same advantages and disadvantages associated with first-generation packet filter firewalls with one notable exception: the advantage of not allowing unsolicited UDP packets onto your internal network. As long as a UDP request packet originated on your internal network and is delivered to an untrusted host, the firewall server allows what appears to be a response packet to be delivered to the originating host. The response packet that is allowed back must contain a destination address that matches the original source address, a transport layer destination port that matches the original source port, and the same transport layer protocol type. This feature is useful for allowing application layer protocols, such as the Domain Name System (DNS), to operate across your security perimeter. An internal DNS server must originate requests to other DNS servers running on the Internet to retrieve address information for unknown hosts. DNS servers may make these requests using a TCP connection or UDP virtual connection. A dynamic packet filter firewall may also be used to provide support for a limited subset of the ICMP transport protocol. ICMP is often used to test network connectivity by sending a pair of network packets between two cooperating hosts. Because the firewall server can allow a response to cross the firewall at the request of an internal host, the internal host is able to deduce that a host exists on an untrusted network

7

E-Payment Systems

Set Protocols

Packet Hound Default Rule Set: Protocols & Applications

Packet Hound Network Applications Management

Out of the box, Packet Hound can be set to monitor, manage, block, throttle, or shape the following protocols and applications:

FILE SHARING APPLICATIONS: Applications that allow users to share files across the Internet.

- **AresXfer.** File-sharing application.
- **AresServer.** Web server program for the Ares file sharing application.
- **AudioGalaxyLogin.** AudioGalaxy is a real-time file-sharing system for sharing MP3s; it uses a Web-based interface and a local client that controls sharing and downloading.
- **AudioGalaxySearch.** This setting allows you to manage file searches on AudioGalaxy.
- **AudioGalaxyDownloadReq.** This setting allows you to manage download requests on AudioGalaxy.
- **AudioGalaxyStream.** This setting allows you to manage download requests on AudioGalaxy.
- **AudioGalaxyWeb.** This setting allows you to manage access to the AudioGalaxy web sites.
- **BitTorrent.** BitTorrent is a tool for copying and sharing files. Files clients download are automatically copied onto the client's machine and are made available for peer-to-peer sharing.
- **BlubsterXfer.** A peer-to-peer file sharing application for MP3 files.
- **DirectConnectHub.** Matches initial hub connection message.
- **DirectConnectXfer.** A host-based synthesizer/sampler streaming tool.
- **EDonkey (including OverNet).** Peer-to-peer file-sharing application.
- **EDonkeyXfer.** Peer-to-peer file-sharing application.

• **FiletopiaXfer.** Filetopia is a free communications software that includes: instant messaging, chat, file sharing system with a search engine, online friends list and message boards.

• **FreeNet.** A distributed, encrypted file sharing system used to anonymously share files. FreeNet nodes store encrypted pieces of files that are indexed by keys. As a result of its design, FreeNet can be used to anonymously and confidentially store and retrieve data, thus avoiding content filters and government limitations.

• **FurtherNetClient.** A peer to peer file sharing system.

• **Gnutella.** Gnutella is a file-sharing application that allows users to exchange any type of files by connecting them to a "daisy-chain" of other machines. PacketHound also manages these other applications that are based on the

• **GnutellaSearch**. A log-only rule that records the file search terms used in Gnutella Query messages on the network.

• **GnutellaSearchHit.** A log-only rule records the name of each file, IP address, and port number of the server that provides the file in Gnutella QueryHit messages.

• **Gnutella2UDP.** A UPD-only rule that matches UDP packets with Gnutella2 data that would not be matched by the Gnutella rules.

• **Gnutella Web.** Gnutella Web allows users to trade files on the Gnutella network through a Web browser.

• **GnutellaXfer.** GnutellaXfer matches file transfers between many Gnutella clients, including Bearshare, LimeWire, Gnotella, Gnutella, Gnucleus, and Morpheus.

• **IRC-DCC-Send.** Direct chat (DCC) file transfers on Internet Relay Chat (IRC).

• **iTunes.** A pay-per-song music download service. CAUTION: The signature matches after the user pays for the song.

• **KaZaA (including Morpheus).** KaZaA is a file-sharing service where users can trade audio, video, images, and other documents through a "daisy chain" connection.

• **KaZaAXfer.** Blocks attempts to transfer files using the KaZaA protocol.

• **Napster.** Napster is a central-server based file-sharing application that allows users to exchange MP3 music files.

• **Napster Xfer.** This setting allows you to manage all Napster uploads, downloads, and hot list transfers.

• **SoulSeekLogin.** File-sharing application known for exchange of rare music files.

• **SoulSeekXfer.** Manages all SoulSeek transfers.

• **Twister.** A free Internet program to find and download MP3 and other music files.

INSTANT MESSAGING. Applications that allow users to send and receive messages in real time

- **AIMLogin.** America Online Instant Messenger (AIM) is an instant message and file-transfer application that allows users to chat and share files. This setting allows you to manage user logins to AIM.
- **AIMMsg.** This setting allows you to manage incoming and outgoing AIM messages.
- **AIMXfer.** This setting allows you to manage AOL Instant Messenger file transfers.
- **ICQLogin.** ICQ is an instant messenger and file transfer service that allows you to manage user logins to ICQ.
- **ICQMsg.** This feature allows you to manage incoming and outgoing ICQ messages.
- **IRCLogin.** Matches logins to the Internet Relay Chat (IRC) protocol. IRC provides chat rooms, but is often used to share files in violation of copyright laws. Intruders will often set up IRC servers on compromised computers to assist their sharing of files.
- **MSNMessengerLogin.** MSN Messenger is an instant messaging service provided by the Microsoft Network. This feature allows you to block your users from logging into MSN Messenger.
- **MSNMessengerXfer.** This feature allows you to block users from transferring files through MSN Messenger.
- **YahooMsgrLogin.** Yahoo Messenger is an instant messaging service. This feature allows you to block your users from logging into Yahoo Messenger.
- **YahooMsgrMsg.** This setting allows you to block Yahoo messages and file transfers.

File/Printer/OS.

- **LPR.** LPR is a BSD UNIX printing protocol that supports printing to network and local printers. It also acts as a print server. LPR uses port 515.
- **Microsoft-DS.** Microsoft-DS is a file sharing application that allows users to share files through port 445.
- **NetBIOS-SSN.** NetBIOS-SSN is a Microsoft File Sharing application that uses port 139.
- **NFS.** A Network File System (NFS) provides remote access to shared file systems across networks, allowing them to be accessed as if they were local.

MULTI-MEDIA. Applications that allow users to stream audio and video to their desktops.

• **RealMedia 1, 2, and Multi Rate.** RealAudio and RealVideo are streaming formats that many sites use to transfer audio and video; Real Networks use two different protocols, and we've included both separately for your convenience. To block *all* RealMedia, you must block both of these protocols.

• **ShoutCast.** ShoutCast is a streaming media format that many sites use to transfer audio.

• **WindowsMedia.** Windows Streaming Media is a streaming format that many sites use to transfer audio and video.

HTTP PROTOCOLS. Protocols that use the HTTP protocol to transfer files.

• **HTTP.** HTTP (Hyper Text Transfer Protocol) is the underlying protocol of the World Wide Web.

• **HTTP-ACTIVEX.** ActiveX controls are objects inserted into a Web page or other applications to reuse packaged programming functionality; because these controls execute on a user's computer, they may be a security and/or virus risk. This setting manages user attempts to transfer ActiveX controls through the HTTP protocol.

• **HTTP-AVI.** Microsoft video format file transfers over HTTP.

• **HTTP-EXE.** HTTP-EXE manages user attempts to transfer executable files through the HTTP protocol. Because these files execute on a user's computer, they may be a security and/or virus risk.

• **HTTP-Audio-MPEG.** HTTP-Audio-MPEG manages user attempts to transfer MPEG audio files through the HTTP protocol.

• **HTTP-Video-MPEG.** HTTP-Video-MPEG manages user attempts to transfer MPEG video files through the HTTP protocol.

• **HTTP-QuickTime.** Manages user attempts to transfer Quick Time files through the HTTP protocol.

• **HTTP-RAR.** RAR-format archive files transferred over HTTP.

• **HTTPS.** HTTPS is a secure connection for the HTTP protocol; it uses port 443.

• **HTTP-SHOCKWAVE-FLASH.** Shockwave allows users to view interactive Web content like games, business presentations, entertainment and advertisements from a Web browser. This setting manages user attempts to transfer Shockwave through the HTTP protocol.

• **HTTP-Zip.** HTTP-Zip manages user attempts to transfer Zip files through the HTTP protocol. Because these files execute on a user's computer, they may be a security and/or virus risk.

ADS/SPYWARE. Spyware is often installed as part of other software. Though it cannot be completely blocked, you can use the spyware rules to identify where spyware has been installed on your network. However, you can block the downloading of programs like BonziBuddy by blocking access to the web site. Create an HTTP rule, add the web site to a List, and set the rule to block.

- **BonziBuddy.** Spyware program that gathers information about user activity and transmits this information to ad services and define which pop-ups appear on your system.
- **ClickSpring.** Ad service that identifies traffic, tracks browsing habits and creates specialized pop-ups.
- **DoubleClick.** An ad service that supplies a majority of the Web's banner ads and also gathers information from user activity.
- **Gator.** An ad server that displays pop-up ads based on browsing habits.
- **GroksterSpy.** Spyware included with the download of Grokster and other software that reports user information to an ad service.
- **Hotbar.** Hotbar is a browser and email add-on and contains skins to go over your browser toolbar. Hotbar then monitors the websites that you visit and adds these topics to your toolbar. The email toolbar allows users to download graphics form Hotbar to add to their emails.
- **RealDownloadAds.** Ads associated with the RealDownload program. Web site: http://www.real.com/download/
- **RVPopup.** Ad content from the RV popup program, often included with other downloaded software.
- **SaveNow.** An affiliate program that tracks browsing habits and promotes special offers.
- **ShopAtHome.** Tracks browsing habits and promotes sponsor sites.
- **SmartPops.** Tracks browsing habits and displays pop-up ads based on sites recorded for the user.
- **VX2.** VX2 covers very small background software applications that facilitate targeted advertising from VX2.cc.
- **WebHancer.** Ad service that identifies traffic, tracks browsing habits and creates specialized pop-ups.

Vulnerabilies

- **HTTP-CodeRed.** Code Red is a worm that propagates over HTTP and invades Windows systems running

Microsoft's ISS web server. After it infects a server, it attempts to infect other servers.

- **HTTP-CodeRed II.** Code Red II is a worm-like Code Red that propagates over HTTP and invades Windows systems running Microsoft's ISS web server. After it infects a server, it attempts to infect other servers. It is more virulent than Code Red because it does a better job of selecting target IP addresses. Code Red II also inserts backdoors into the system to enable future system compromises.

• **HTTP-IDA.** File extension used by the Microsoft Index Server ISAPI Extension. The CodeRed and CodeRed II worms exploited a vulnerability in the code that handles request for index server lookups. This rule could be used to block future attacks on this vulnerability.

• **WakeOnLan.** A UDP packet that can start a machine on the network that has been shut down.

MAIL PROTOCOLS. Protocols used to transfer e-mail.

• **IMAP.** IMAP (Interim Mail Access Protocol) is a mail protocol that uses port 143.

• **IMAPS.** IMAPS allows users to access their mail through a secure SSL connection; it uses port 993.

• **POP.** POP (Post Office Protocol) is a mail protocol that uses port 109/110.

• **POP3S.** POP3S allows remote users to access their mail through a secure SSL connection; it uses port 995.

• **SMTP.** SMTP (Simple Mail Transfer Protocol) is a mail protocol that uses port 25.

WEB-BASED MAIL. E-mail programs using standard HTTP.

• **AOLWebmail.** Web access for AOL mail.

• **Hotmail.** An e-mail program that provides e-mail access from any computer connected to the Internet.

• **YahooMail.** Another e-mail program providing access to e-mail from the Internet.

FTP. File transfer protocol.

• **CVS-PServer.** Concurrent Versions System (CVS) is an open-source change management system. This rulematches the protocol used to access files on the CVS server.

• **CVSup.** Concurrent Version System Update (CVSup) is a high-performance protocol used to mirror changes in a file on the CVS server. This rule matches the protocol used by the client to access the server.

• **FTPActive.** This setting allows you to block FTP active file transfers on Port 20.

• **FTPControl.** This setting allows you to block the FTP control port (port 21).

• **FTPPassive.** This setting allows you to block passive FTP file transfers.

HTTP INFORMATION.

• **HTTP_Hosts.** This rule matches host names in HTTP requests with host names in a list that you create. If a hostname in the list begins with a period (.), it is considered a domain name and all hosts in that domain will match.

• **HTTP_Servers.** This rule enables the ability to capture data for the Web Monitor capability in TrendReporter and logs URLs and hosts in the URL Log. This rule, like LogUnmatched, does not match connections. It is used for data collection only, not for blocking or allowing. When adding this rule, some options in the Rule Properties window are unavailable. It is recommended that you place this rule near the top of the list so it captures information from all HTTP data.

• **HTTP_URLs.** This rule matches URLs in HTTP requests with URLs in a list that you create.

REMOTE LOGIN.

• **CitrixICA.** Matches Citrix's Independent Computing Architecture (ICA) protocol, which is used for remote access to computers running Microsoft Windows applications.

• **GotoMyPCShare.** Application that allows remote access to a user's computer.

• **RLogin.** RLogin (Remote Login Protocol) allows users to log into the network remotely using port 513.

• **REXEC.** Allows remote execution of commands on UNIX hosts, or any other system with the REXEC interface.

• **RSH.** RSH (Remote Shell Protocol) allows users to execute shell commands remotely using port 514.

• **SSH.** A secure shell protocol that provides connectivity, encryption, and authentication for servers using port 22.

• **Telnet.** Telnet Remote Terminal Protocol allows users to login to other systems remotely. Telnet uses port 23.

• **VNC.** Virtual Network Computing (VNC) is a remote display system allowing users to remotely view a desktop from anywhere on the Internet. VNC uses port 5190.

• **WindowsTerminalServer.** Remote connections using Windows Terminal Server.

• **XWindows.** Graphical user interface primarily for UNIX similar to Microsoft Windows.

DISTRIBUTED COMPUTING. These programs allow organizations to use your computer when it is idle.

• **BOINC.** SETIatHome's new distributed computation protocol.

• **SETIATHOME.** Downloads radio telescope information, process it, and sends it to the Search for Extraterrestrial Intelligence at Home project.

• **GOOGLECOMPUTE.** Sponsored by Google Toolbar, uses idle computer time from the Google Compute project.

Worm Mitigation. The Palisade support team often adds new signatures to our web site for you to download. Many of these effect worms that may compromise your system. Check the signature page at http://www.palisadesys.com/support/ downloads/ packethound/ sigupdates.shtml for the most recently added signatures. Your Palisade web site user name and password is required.

Information Services.

AOL-TCP. Manages use of the AOL information service over the internet.

Compuserve-TCP. Manages use of the Compuserve information service over the internet.

OTHER. Standard TCP/IP protocols and others you may wish to manage.

- **DNS Query.** Manage activity on the domain name server (DNS).
- **Finger.** Finger User Information Protocol is a UNIX command used to gather information about other Internet users.
- **Gopher.** Gopher is a system that pre-dates the World Wide Web for organizing and displaying files on Internet servers. Gopher uses port 70.
- **IDENT.** UNIX-based protocol that looks up real user names when a user attempts to login to a server.
- **NetBIOS-SendMulti.** Multi-packet NetBIOS user messages.
- **NNTP.** NNTP (Network News Transfer Protocol) is a news service that transmits information through port 119.
- **Port.** The Port setting allows users to specify a block of a specific TCP/IP port.
- **Socks4/5.** Protocol that provides access to network services through a SOCKS proxy server. This may be used to hide a user's identity and evade network management systems like PacketHound.
- **SSL.** Used to assist system administrators in determining how much encrypted traffic is running (aside from HTTPS and POP3S)

SPECIAL RULES

- **Custom.** This setting allows you to enter your own Custom Match String for a protocol that you've identified and wish to manage. This is recommended only for advanced users.
- **EthernetAddresses.** This rule matches packets that have a source or destination Ethernet address that is in a user-created list.
- **Everything.** This setting allows you to block, monitor, or ignore any connection by any of the protocols managed by PacketHound.
- **LogUnmatched.** The LogUnmatched rule allows you to log all connections that do not match defined protocols.

E-Check

Electronic checks are another form of electronic tokens. They are designed to accommodate the many individuals and entities that might prefer to pay on credit or through some mechanism other than cash. In the model shown in Fig. Buyers must register with a third –party account server before they are bale to write electronic checks. The account server also acts as a billing service. The registration procedure can vary depending on the particular account server and may require a credit card or a bank account to back the checks.

Once registered, a buyer can then contact sellers of goods and services. To complete a transaction, the buyer sends a check to the seller for a certain amount of money. These checks may be sent using e –mail or other transport methods. When deposited, the check authorizes the transfer of account balances from the account against which the check was drawn to the account to which the check was deposited.

The e–check method was deliberately created to work in much the same way as a conventional paper check. An account holder will issue an electronic document that contains the name of the payer, the name of the financial institution, the payer's account number, the name of the payee and the paper check, an e –check will bear the digital equivalent of a signature: a computed number that authenticates the check as coming from the owner of the account. And, again like a paper check, an e –check will need to be endorsed by the payee, using another electronic signature, before the check can be paid. Properly singed and endorsed checks can be electronically exchanged between financial institutions through electronic clearinghouses, with the institutions using these endorsed checks as tender to settle accounts.

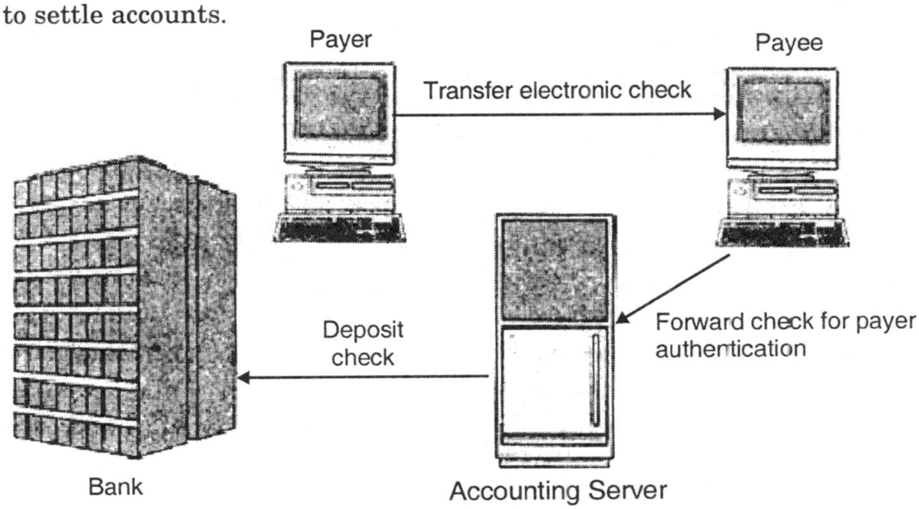

Figure Payment transaction sequence in an electronic check system

The specifics of the technology work in the following manner. On receiving the check, the seller presents server verifies the digital signature on the check using the Kerberos authentication scheme. In the language of Kerberos, an electronic check is a specialized kind of "ticket" created by the Kerberos system. A user's digital "signature" is used to create one ticket – a check –which the seller's digital "endorsement" transforms endorses add successive layers of information onto the tickets, precisely as a large number of banks may wind up stamping the back of a check along its journey through the system.

Electronic checks have the following advantages:

- They work in the same way as traditional checks, thus simplifying customer education.

- Electronic checks are well suited for clearing micro payments; their use of conventional cryptography makes it much faster than systems based on public –key cryptography (e –cash).

- Electronic checks create float and the availability of float is an important requirement for commerce. The third –party accounting server can make money by charging the buyer or seller a transaction fee or a flat rate fee, or it can act as a bank and provide deposit accounts and make money on the deposit account pool.

- Financial risk is assumed by the accounting server and may result in easier acceptance. Reliability and scalability are provided by using multiple accounting servers. There can be an inter account server protocol to allow buyer and seller to "belong" to different domains, regions, or countries.

A prototype electronic check system called " **Net Cheque"** was developed at Information Science Institute by Clifford Neumann [MN93]. Net Cheque will include software for writing and depositing checks independent of other applications and an application programming interface that will allow common functions to be called automatically when integrated with other programs. ISI is expected to make available "accounting server" software that will allow organizations to set up their own in –house, on line "banks," which would accept paper checks or credit card payments in exchange for crediting a customer's Net Cheque account. Such accounting servers will enable large organizations to pay bills and settle accounts with Net Cheque written with their own banks, in effect integrating their own internal accounting systems with the external financial hierarchy.

The interesting implication of Net Cheque is that it can be used as a resources management tool inside organizations could be given an account and allowed to use various resources and be billed for it. Thus organizations will able to manage resources more effectively using accounting mechanisms. This will become important in the future as corporate networks become more congested and such qualities of e –cash as anonymity are not major requirements.

An eCheck is an electronic version of a paper check. It uses the same legal and business protocols associated with traditional paper checks it can be used in any transactions where paper checks are used today yet it capitalizes on the speed and processing efficiencies of all-electronic payments. The technology used to standardize the implementation of eChecks was developed by the Financial Services. Technology Consortium (FSTC), whose eCheck project is currently being used by the United States Treasury in a two-year pilot program. eChecks are based on the Financial Services Markup Language (FSML, the markup language developed to allow eCheck technology into the marketplace. The FSTC's eCheck technology takes the basic, and nearly ubiquitous, concept and applies it to a markup-language-based document, thereby recognizing the need for basic signing, co-signing, and countersigning or notarizing. eChecks also utilize several different state-of-the-art security techniques including authentication, public key infrastructure, and certificate authority in order to ensure the integrity of each electronic transaction. The path an eCheck takes looks something like this: the payer writes the eCheck on a computer, signs it, and e-mails it over the Internet. The payee receives it, verifies signatures, endorses it, writes a deposit slip, and signs it. The endorsed check is then sent by e-mail to the payees bank for deposit. Bank personnel verify signatures, credit the deposit, and then clear and settle the endorsed eCheck by sending it on to the payer's bank, where signatures are once again verified and the amount of the eCheck is debited from the payer's account. The cryptographic certificates used with an eCheck enable a check payee to determine the validity of the signatures. Initially, these certificates are actually transmitted with the eCheck, but alternative models where the transmission, or possibly even issuance, of the certificate is not required are currently in the making.

eCheck technology also allows digital signatures to be applied to document blocks, rather than to the entire document. This allows parts of a document to be separated from the original, without compromising the integrity of the digital signature. At eCheck 2004 you will learn how your organization can adopt and benefit from eCheck solutions. Areas to be covered include:

Practical Information:

- What you need to know to determine
- your best mix of eCheck applications.
- What is Check 21? How does/can it apply to my organization?
- What are the costs, benefits, legal and implementation ramifications?
- How to scale ARC solutions that are appropriate for your business.
- ARC & Check 21: It not an either/or proposition.

- What is commercially reasonable authentication and how do I ensure the security of my business online payment applications?

Origination Best Practices: Ongoing and proposed steps to manage unauthorized return entries, mitigate risk and instill best practices on the ACH Network. How to maximize control and benefits with web-based eCheck platforms. Winning fraud detection, prevention and risk management techniques. The latest market trends, consumer research, pilot results, implementation approaches and more! Whether you are a biller collecting remittances for services rendered to customers, a government body collecting tax payments and other fees from citizens, a retailer selling products to buyers online or in your store, or a financial institution providing eCheck services to your corporate customers, eCheck 2004 will provide the education you need and allow you to make the right contacts to help you make the decisions that are right for your business. Enterprises that are collecting payments from customers and citizens are realizing the value of and turning to eCheck solutions to expedite their accounts receivable at increasingly rapid rates. eCheck solutions can encompass debits made to an individual demand deposit account for bills or purchases when payment is initiated over the Internet or via telephone, or result from the conversion of a paper check into an electronic debit at the point-of-sale or at a lockbox, to name just a few of the more prevalent examples.

eCheck 2004 will cover a comprehensive range of topics and approaches, including ACH-based applications (ARC, POP, WEB, TEL and RCK), card-based debit options, image-based solutions and Check 21. You will gain valuable insights for evaluating and selecting from among these options, and choosing the bank and/or service providers that are right for your A/R shop, and for your customers. You will also learn about market trends and customer research, implementation approaches, and the best practices for ensuring that you are operating in compliance with payment rules and regulations.

E-Cash

Electronic cash (E-Cash)

Electronic cash (E–Cash) is a new concept in on –line payment systems because it combines computerized convenience with security and privacy that improve on paper cash. Its versatility opens up a host of new markets and applications. E–Cash presents some interesting characteristics that should make it an attractive alternative for payment over the Internet.

E-Cash focuses on replacing cash as the principal payment vehicle in consumer oriented electronic payments. Although it may be surprising to some, cash is still the most prevalent consumer payment instrument even after thirty years of continuous developments in electronic payment systems. Cash remains the dominant form of payment for three reasons: (1) lack of trust in the banking system, (2) inefficient clearing and settlement of non-cash transactions, and (3) negative real interest rates paid on bank deposits.

These reasons seem like issues seen primarily in developing countries. Not true. Even in the most industrialized countries, the ratio of notes and coins in circulation per capita is quite large and is estimated to range from $446 to $2748. consider the situation in two of the most industrialized nations in world: the United States and the United Kingdom. In the United States, there supposedly was about $300 billion of notes and coins in circulation in 1992. Interestingly, this number is not shrinking but growing at approximately 8 percent per year. Deposits by check are growing by only 6 percent per year. It has been reported that in the United Kingdom about a quarter of all "spontaneous" payments over 100 pounds sterling are still made with cash. For payments under five pounds sterling, the percentage is 98 percent.

The predominance of cash indicates an opportunity for innovative business practice that revamps the purchasing process where consumers are heavy users of cash. To really displace cash, the electronic payment systems need to have some qualities of cash that current credit and debit cards lack. For example, cash in negotiable, meaning it can be given or traded to some one else. Cash is legal tender, meaning the payee is obligated to take it. Cash is a bearer instrument, meaning that possession is prima facie proof of ownership. Also, cash places no risk on the part of the acceptor that the medium of exchange may be not be good.

Now compare cash to credit and debit cards. First, they can't be given away because, technically, they are identification cards owned by the issuer and restricted to one user. Credit and debit cards are not legal tender, given that merchants have the right to refuse to accept them. Nor are credit and debit cards bearer instruments; their usage requires an account relationship and authorization system. Similarly, checks require either personal knowledge of the payer or a check guarantee system. Hence, to really create a novel electronic payment method, we need to do more than recreate the convenience that is offered by credit and debit cards. We need to develop e –cash that has some of the properties of cash.

Properties of E-Cash

Of the many ways that exist for implementing an e –cash system, all must incorporate a few common features. Specifically, e –cash must have the following four properties: monetary value, interoperability, irretrievability, and security.

E–cash must have a monetary value; it must be backed by either cash(currency), bank authorized credit, or a bank –certified cashier's check. When E–cash created by one bank is accepted by others, reconciliation must occur without any problems. Stated another way, e –cash without proper bank certification carriers the risk that when deposited, it might be returned for insufficient funds.

E–cash must be interoperable –that is, exchangeable as payment for other e–cash, paper cash, goods or services, lines of credit, deposits in banking accounts, bank notes or obligations, electronic benefits transfers, and the like. Most e–cash proposals use a single bank [MN93]. In practice, multiple banks are required with an international clearinghouse that handles the exchangeability issues because all customers are not going to be using the same bank or even be in the same country.

E-cash must be storable and retrievable. Remote storage and retrieval (e.g., from a telephone or personal communications device) would allow users to exchange e –cash (e.g., withdraw from and deposit into banking accounts) from home or office or while traveling. The cash would be stored on a remote computer's memory, in smart cards, or in other easily transported standard or special purpose devices. Because it might be easy to create counterfeit cash that is stored in a computer, it might be preferable to store cash on a dedicated device that cannot be altered. This device should have a suitable interface to facilitate personal authentication using passwords or other means and a display so that the user can view the card's contents. One example of a device that can store e–cash is the Mondex card a pocket sized electronic wallet.

E–Cash should not be easy to copy or tamper with while being exchanged; this includes preventing or detecting duplication and double spending. Counterfeiting poses a particular problem, since a counterfeiter may, in the Internet environment, be anywhere in the world and consequently be difficult to catch without appropriate international agreements. Detection is essential in order to audit whether prevention is working. Then there is the tricky issue of double spending. For instance, you could use your e–cash simultaneously to buy something in Japan, India, and England. Preventing double–spending from occurring is extremely difficult if multiple banks are involved in the transaction. For this reason, most systems rely on post–fact detection and punishment.

E-Case in Action

Electronic cash is based on cryptographic systems called "digital signatures". This method involves a pair of numeric keys (very large integers or numbers) that work in tandem: one for locking (or encoding) and the other for unlocking (or decoding). Messages encoded with one numeric key can only be decoded with the other numeric key and none other. The encoding key is kept private and the decoding key is made public.

By supplying all customers (buyers and sellers) with its public key, a bank enables customers to decode any message (or currency) encoded with the bank's private key. If decoding by a customer yields a recognizable message, the customer can be fairly confident that only the bank could have encoded it. These digital signatures are as secure as the mathematics involved and have proved over the past two decades to be more resistant to forgery than handwritten signatures. Before e–cash can be used to buy products or services it must be procured from a currency server.

Purchase of E–Cash from Currency Server (or bank)

The purchase of e –cash from an on –line currency server (or bank) involves two steps: (1) establishment of an account and (2) maintaining enough money in the account to back the purchase. Some customers might prefer to purchase e –cash with paper currency, either to maintain anonymity or because they don't have a bank account.

Currently, in most e –cash trials all customers must have an account with a central on line bank. This is overly restrictive for international use and multi currency transactions, for customers should be able to access, e –cash must be available in multiple currencies backed by several banks. A service provider in one country could then accept tokens of various currencies from users in many different countries, redeem them with their issuers, and have the funds transferred back to banks in the local country. A possible solution is to use an association of digital banks similar to organizations like VISA to serve as a clearinghouse for many credit card issuing banks, and finally, consumers use the E-Cash software on the computer to generate a random number, which serves as the "note." In exchange for money debited from the customer's account, the bank uses its private key to digitally sign the note for the amount requested and transmits the note back to the customer. The network currency server, in effect, is issuing a "bank note," with a serial number and a dollar amount. By digitally signing it, the bank is committing itself to back that note with its face value in real dollars.

This method of note generation is very secure, as neither the customer (payer) nor the merchant (payee) can counterfeit the bank's digital signature (analogous to the watermark in paper currency). Payer and payee can verify that the payment is valid, since each knows the bank's public key. The bank is protected against forgery, the payee against the bank's refusal to honor a legitimate note, and the user against false accusations and invasion of privacy.

How does this process work in practice? In the case of Digit Cash, every person using e–cash has an E-Cash account at a digital bank (First Digital Bank) on he Internet. Using that account, people can withdraw and deposit e –cash. When an e –cash withdrawal is made, the PC of the e–cash user calculates how many digital coins of what denominations are needed to withdraw the requested amount. Next, random serial numbers for those coins will be generated and the blinding (random number) factor will be included. The result of these calculations will be sent to the digital bank. The bank will encode the blinded numbers with its secret key (digital signature) and at the same time debit the account of the client for the user and finally the user will take out the blinding factor that he or she introduced earlier. The serial numbers plus their signatures are now digital coins; the bank guarantees their value.

Electronic cash can be completely anonymous. Anonymity allows freedom of usage to buy illegal products such as drugs or pornographic material or to buy legal product and services. This is accomplished in the following manner. When the e –cash software generates a note, it masks the original number or "blinds" the note using a random number and transmits it to a bank. The "blinding" carried out by the customer's software makes it impossible for anyone to link payment to payer. Even the bank can't connect the signing with the payment, since the customer's original not number anonymous, untraceable currency. What makes it even more interesting is that users can prove unequivocally that they did or did not make a particular payment. This allows the bank to sign the "note" without ever actually knowing how the issued currency will be used.

For those readers who are mathematically inclined, the protocol behind blind signatures is presented.

- The customer's software chooses a blinding factor R, independently and uniformly at random and presents the bank with (XR) E and (mod PO), where X is the note number to be signed and E is the bank's public key.
- The bank signs it: (XRE) D = RXD (mod PQ). D is the bank's private key.
- On receiving the currency, the customer divides out the blinding factor (RXD)/R XD = (mod PQ).
- The customer stores XD, the signed note that is used to pay for the purchase of products or services. Since R is random, the bank cannot determine X and thus cannot connect the signing with the subsequent payment.
- While blinding works in theory, it remains to be seen how it will be used in the real business world.

Using the Digital Currency

Once the tokens are purchased, the e–cash software on the customer's PC stores digital money undersigned by a bank. The user can spend the digital money at any shop accepting e–cash, without having to open an account there first or having to transmit credit card numbers. As soon as the customer wants to make a payment, the software collects the necessary amount from the stored tokens.

Two types of transactions are possible: bilateral and trilateral. Typically, transactions involving cash are bilateral or two party (buyer and seller) transactions, whereby the merchant checks the veracity of the note's digital signature by using the bank's public key. If satisfied with the payment, the merchant stores the digital currency on his machine and deposits it later in the bank to redeem the face value of the note.

Transactions involving financial instruments other than cash are usually trilateral or three party (buyer, seller, and bank) transactions, whereby the "notes" are sent to the merchant, who immediately sends them directly to the digital bank. The bank verifier the validity of these "notes" and that they have not been spent before. The account of the merchant is credited. In this case, every "note" can be used only once.

In many business situations, the bilateral transaction is not feasible because of the potential for double spending, which is equivalent to bouncing a check. Double spending becomes possible because it is very easy to make copies of the e –cash, forcing banks and merchants to take extra precautions.

To uncover double spending, banks must compare the note passed to it by the merchant against a database of spent notes. Just as paper currency is identified with a unique serial number, digital cash can also be protected. The ability to detect double spending has to involve some form of registration so that all "notes" issued globally can be uniquely identified. However, this method of matching notes with a central registry has problems in the online world. For most systems, which handle high volumes of micro payments, this method would simply be too expensive. In addition, the problem of double spending means that banks have to carry added overhead because of the constant checking and auditing logs.

Double spending would not be a major problem if the need for anonymity were relaxed. In such situations, when the consumer is issued a bank note, it is issued to that person's unique license. When he or she gives it to somebody else, it is transferred specifically to that other person's license. Each time the money changes hands, the old owner adds a tiny bit of information to the bank note based on the bank note's serial number

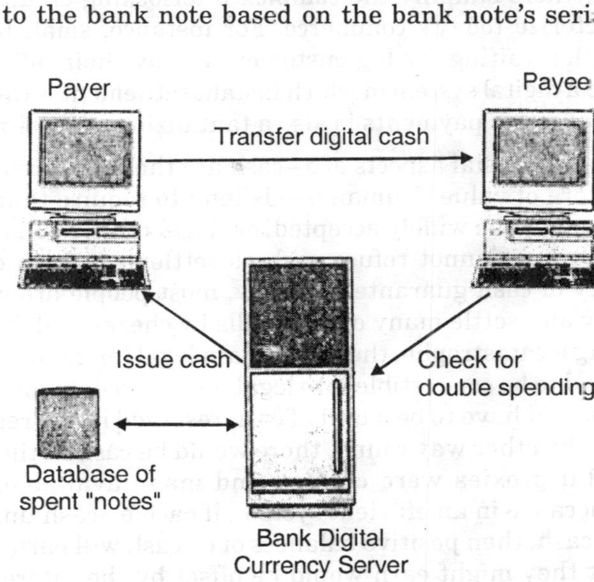

Figure Detection of double spending

and his or her able to use the two bank notes to determine who the cheater is. Even if the bank notes pass through many different people's hands, whoever cheated will get caught, and none of the other people will ever have to know.

The downside is that the banks can tell precisely what your buying habits are since it can check the numbers on the e –cash and the various merchant accounts that are being credited. Many people would feel uncomfortable letting others know this personal information.

One drawback of E–cash is its inability to be easily divided into smaller amounts. It is often necessary to get small denomination change in business transactions. A number of variations have been developed for dealing with the "change" problem. For the bank to issue users with enough separate electronic "coins" of various denominations would be cumbersome in communication and storage. So would a method that required payees to return extra change. To sidestep such costs, customers are issued a single number called an "open check" that contains multiple denomination values sufficient for transactions up to a prescribed limit. At payment time, the e –cash software on the client's computer would create a note of the transaction value from the "open check".

Business Issue and E-Cash

Electronic cash fulfills two main functions: as a medium of exchange and as a store of value. Digital money is a perfect medium of exchange. By moving monetary claims quickly and by effecting instant settlement of transactions, e –cash may help simplify the complex interlocking credit and liabilities that characterize today's commerce. For instance, small businesses that spend months waiting for big customers to pay their bills would benefit hugely from a digital system in which instant settlement is the norm. Instant settlement of micro payments is also a tantalizing proposition.

The controversial aspects of e –cash are those that relate to the other role, as a store of value. Human needs tend to require that money take a tangible form and be widely accepted, or "legal tender". In most countries, a creditor by law cannot refuse cash as settlement for a debt. With the acceptability of cash guaranteed by law, most people are willing to bank their money and settle many of their bills by checks and debits, confident that, barring a catastrophe, they can obtain legal tender (cash) on demand. If e –cash had to be convertible into legal tender on demand, then for every unit there would have to be a unit of cash reserved in the real economy: or, to look at it the other way round, there would be cash in the real world for which digital proxies were created and made available. This creates problems, because in an efficient system, if each e –cash unit represents a unit of real cash, then positive balances of e –cash will earn no interest; for the interest they might earn would be offset by the interest foregone on the real cash that is backing them.

The enormous currency fluctuations in international finance pose another problem. On the Internet, the buyer could be in Mexico and the seller in the United States. How do you check that the party in Mexico is giving a valid electronic currency that has suitable backing? Even if it were valid today, what would happen if a sudden devaluation occurs such as the one in December 1994 where the peso was devalued 30 percent overnight. Who holds the liability, the buyer or the seller? These are not technological issues but business issues that must be addressed for large – scale bilateral transactions to occur. Unless, we have one central bank offering one type of electronic currency, it is very difficult to see e –cash being very prominent except in narrow application domains.

From a banker's point of view, e–cash would be a mixed blessing. Because they could not create new money via lending in the digital world, banks would see electronic money as unproductive. They might charge for converting it, or take a transaction fee for issuing it, but on-line competition would surely make this a low –profit affair. In the short term, banks would probably make less from this new business than they would lose from the drift of customers away from traditional services.

It seems unlikely that e–cash would be allowed to realize its potential for bypassing the transaction costs of the foreign exchange market. If you pay yen for e–cash in Osaka and buy something form a merchant based in New York who cashes them for francs, a currency conversion has taken place. That, however, is an activity toward which most governments feel highly defensive; and if e–cash started to bypass regulated foreign exchange markets by developing its own gray market for settlement, then governments might be provoked into trying to clamp down on it. Because of these obstacles, e–cash in its early forms may be denominated in single currencies and exchanged at conventional market rates.

Operational Risk and E-Cash

Operational risk associated with e –cash can be mitigated by imposing constraints; such as limits on (1) the time over which a given electronic money is valid, (2) how much can be stored on and transferred by electronic money, (3) the number of exchanges that can take place before a money needs to be red posited with a bank or financial institution, and (4) the number of such transactions that can be made during a given period of time.

These constraints introduce a whole new set of implementation issues. For example, time limits could be set beyond which the electronic money would expire and become worthless. The customer would have to redeem or exchange the money prior to the expiration deadline. For this feature to work, electronic money would have to be time–stamped, and time would have to be synchronized across the network to some–degree of precision.

The objective of imposing constraints is to limit the issuer's liability. A maximum upper limit could be imposed on the value that could be assigned to any single transaction or that could be transferred to the same vendor within a given period of time. Since the user's computer could be programmed to execute small transactions continuously at a high rate over the network, a strategy of reporting transactions over a certain amount would be ineffective for law enforcement.

However, a well–designed system could enforce a policy involving both transaction size and value with time. For example, an "anonymous coin purse" feature might be capable of receiving or spending no more than $500 in and twenty four hour period. Alternatively, the "rate ceiling" for the next twenty four hours could be made dependent on the rate of use or on the number of exchanges that could be permitted before any electronic money would have to be re deposited in a bank or financial institution and reissued.

Finally, exchange could also be restricted to a class of services or goods (e.g., electronic benefits could be used only for food, clothing, shelter, or educational purposes). The exchange process should allow payment to be withheld from the seller upon the buyer's instructions until the goods, or services are delivered within a specified time in the future. Conversely, it should allow delivery to be withheld upon the seller's instructions until payment is received.

Legal Issue and E-Cash

Electronic cash will force bankers and regulators to make choices that will shape the form of lawful commercial activity related to electronic commerce. As a result of the very features that make it so attractive to many, cash has occupied an unstable and uncomfortable place within the existing taxation and law enforcement systems.

Anonymous and virtually untraceable, cash transactions today occupy a place in a kind of underground economy. This underground economy is generally confide to relatively small –scale transactions because paper money in large quantities is cumbersome to use an manipulate – organized crime being the obvious exception. As long as the transactions are small in monetary value, they are tolerated by the government as an unfortunate but largely insignificant by product of the modern commercial state. As transactions get larger the government becomes more suspicious and enlists the aid of the banks, through the various currency reporting laws, in reporting large disbursements of cash so that additional oversight can be ordered.

Consider the impact of e–cash on taxation. Transaction –based taxes (e.g., sales taxes) account for a significant portion on state and local government revenue. But if e –cash really is made to function the way that paper money does, payments we would never think of making in cash to buy a new car, say, or as the down payment on a house could be made in this new form of currency because there would be no problem of bulk and no risk of robbery. The threat to the government's revenue flow is very real one, and officials in government are starting to take cognizance of this development and to prepare their responses.

To prevent an underground economy, the government through law may prevent a truly anonymous and untraceable e–cash system from developing. But that raises its own problems because the vision of "Big Brother" rears its ugly head. Just as powerful encryption schemes permit the design of untraceable e –cash systems, so, too, do powerful electronic record –keeping tools permit the design of traceable systems – systems in which all financial transactions are duly recorded in some database, allowing those with access to know more about an individual than anyone could know today.

Anything that makes cash substantially easier to use in a broader range of transactions holds the potential to expand this underground economy to proportion posing ever more serious threats to the existing legal order. Under the most ambitious visions of e –cash, we would see a new form of currency that could be freely passed off from one computer to another with no record, yet incapable of being forged. A consumer could draw such e –cash electronically from his or her bank. The bank would have a record of that transaction, just as a withdrawn or checks is record now. But after that, the encrypted e –cash file could be handed off without the knowledge of anyone but he parties to the transaction.

However, as the politics and business play out, the technology is forcing legal as issues to be reconsidered. The question e –cash poses is not, "Should the law take notice of this development?" but rather, "How can it not?" By impacting revenue –raising capabilities, e –cash cannot escape government scrutiny and regulation; but it is going to take some serious thinking to design a regulatory scheme that balance personal privacy, speed of execution, and case of use.

Without a functioning system, what the government will do remains a mystery. Moreover, it is not even clear yet that the market as a whole will adopt an anonymous e –cash standard. For now, we are mainly watching and trying to educate ourselves about the likely path of the transition to electronic cash.

Micro Payment System

ntroduction

Micro-payment systems have been proposed for small and frequent payment such as data base query, software, and e-news. Because the overhead cost for card company is higher than price of goods, and the processing time related to public key computation is required too much, most of the previous systems exclude public key computation or admit the minimal computational overhead for efficiency. Several protocols that use computationally secure one-way hash function were proposed in [4, 5, 7, 8]. Stern and Vaudenay's system [12]used MAC (Message Authentication Code) and an unkeyed one-way hash function instead of using public key cryptography and adopted tamper resistant devices for both customer and merchant sides. MilliCent used "scrips", and hash functions extensively. MicroMint [8]used k-way hash function collision to make money. Micro-payment system is considered to be proper for areas where efficiency is the most critical factor. Even if a customer loses his e-cash, it is not critical to him due to the small amount. The e-cash of a customer, computational cost is too big to gain a profit from the attack. Although damage by system errors or attacks is trivial, customers do not want to lose his money, or goods. To solve these problems, protocols in [1, 2, 10, 13, 14]were proposed to satisfy atomicity. From the security point of view, micro-payment system is mainly concerned about preventing or detecting from double spending and forgery.

We propose a new micro-payment system, in which a customer generates and maintains only one hash chain for every vendor. Since Pay Word requires to use each hash chain for each vendor, the customer has to maintain all indices after dealing with vendors. To solve this problem, we use a receipt which includes a signature of vendor. The customer uses this signature for different vendors to enable them to verify whether the start index of payment is correct or not. Moreover, we design each phase of protocol to guarantee atomicity.

Related works

Basic Architecture of Micro-payment

Basically, a micro-payment system is composed of three entities, i.e., customer, vendor, and broker.

- Customer : does business with vendors by using micro-payment system.
- Vendor : offers customers goods and deposits e-cash through a broker.
- Broker : issues e-cash, validates customers, and manages accounts of customers and vendors.

Basic Requirements

Efficiency

- Minimizing of public key computation: We do not use public key computation at all or use as few as possible to reduce high cost of public key computation.
- Off-Line Verification: A broker doesn't carry on on-line verification due to limitation of the bandwidth of communication line during the transaction.
- Minimum usage of message: The number of messages among entities, especially between customers and vendors, should be kept lower during transaction.
- Minimum usage of memory space: Permanent variables should be used as few as possible.

Security

• Double spending prevention or detection : If the same e-cash is used more than once, then it should be detected.

• Un forge ability : Only publishers who have a authority should be able to issue e-cash.

Atomicity

In addition to basic requirements, atomicity is also of another importance in serving a complete payment system. If network crashes in the middle of payment protocol, some disputes such as loss of money, repudiation, and no procurement of goods even after a complete payment will happen. Under a network model where customers purchase electronic goods and receive its service, Tygar [13]introduced the problem of atomicity in electronic transactions and defined three classes of atomicity; money atomic, goods atomic, and certified delivery.

• Money atomicity : The transfer of funds from one entity to another should be done without creation and loss of money.

• Goods atomicity : With the money atomic, it should be ensured that customers will receive goods if and only if the money is transferred.

• Certified delivery : Including goods and money atomic, both customers and vendors should be able to prove exactly what was delivered. If there is a dispute, this evidence can be shown to a judge to prove exactly what goods were delivered.

Pay Word

This system employs the cryptographic properties of digital signature and hash chain. Principal entities consist of customer, broker and vendor. Customers open an account with a broker. The broker issues a digitally signed certificate, which authorizes the customer to make Pay Word chain and assures vendors that the customer's Pay Words are redeemable.

Problems of Pay Word system

Pay Word has several problems as follows:

• A customer should keep a different hash chain according to each vendor. Hence, in the customer's side, she must compute expensive public key operations as many as the number of vendors that she wants to transact.

• A customer should preserve all of last indices that she used to deal with vendors.

• This system doesn't present the complete steps of business to sale goods.

• When a customer sends the index with respect to goods' price to a vendor, the vendor issues no receipt on it. Due to absence of verification of receiving, it occurs the loss of money.

• A customer can make payment exceeding her credit limit.

In order to address these problems, we propose a new payment protocol in which we make use of only one hash chain with respect to a number of transactions. The new protocol assures atomicity as well.

Analysis of Our Proposed System

Atomicity

Money atomicity

Money atomicity is preserved by:

- Only after a customer pays for goods, the customer can receive the key used for the decryption for goods, and the receipt. Therefore, loss of the money can be prevented.
- In the negotiation phase between a customer and a vendor, the predetermined time limit is established over money from the beginning of transaction to the deposit. Therefore, the available period of money can be established.
- Since a broker certifies information on the length of money, a customer can create money at her own discretion.

Goods atomicity

Goods atomicity is guaranteed only when money atomicity is guaranteed for a customer who receives the goods that has been already paid. In the case of the proposed system, if a customer doesn't pay for the ordered goods, she can't obtain the key for the decryption. Therefore, she can't get the decrypted goods. On the other hand, although a customer has already completed payment for goods, a customer cannot get the key for the decryption until the predetermine time limit is over. Then, the customer processes as following ways:

- The customer sends the index value (w i, i) of payment to the vendor, the random number r C used for the transaction, certification C V of the vendor, the value of predetermined time limit t to the broker, and requests for the confirmation of whether the deposition into the vendor's account is completed.
- If the deposition is completed, the broker sends the index value, and the random number to the vendor in order to request for the customer to send the value of receipt for the transaction. If the vendor refuses, the broker terminates the account with the vendor, registers a blacklist, and considers legal action.
- If the deposition has not yet completed, notify the customer that the transaction with the vendor was cancelled.

Security Issues

Double spending detection

Our system makes use of a unique hash chain to each vendor so that it has the following advantages:

• When a customer uses an identical index to a different vendor once more, a broker is able to detect double spending since he verifies the customer's certificate transferred from the vendor to be paid redemption. For the purpose of preserving this property, the broker should keep both the root value and the length information in the certificate that is issued to the customer.

• In case that the previously used index range is reused in a different vendor, for instance, a customer used index range from i to j to kth vendor, and he paid from i to j to arbitrary (k + 1)th vendor once more. As the same way above, the broker can detect two indices which were spent in k and (k + 1)th vendors identically. Broker is able to keep blacklist of the double spenders. The broker also has a flexibility on a term of "validity" according to the length of hash chain and the credit of customer when she issues a certificate.

Overspending prevention

The length of hash chain is sent to a broker and included in the certificate so that a vendor can verify the excess of the limit by identifying a customer's certificate.

Forgery preventing

An unused hash chain value cannot be inferred from a used one. If malicious vendors conspired each other, they could know unused hash values. But, the right redemption will not occur since a broker can verify double spending when it requested.

Efficiency

In Pay Word, it doesn't provide a complete protocol for electronic commerce so that the loss of money happens and atomicity is not assured. On the contrary, our proposed system presents a complete protocol to deal with digital goods. This expansion makes transaction steps and the length of message increase slightly. But, in customers' side, they utilize only one unique hash chain to a number of vendors. Thus, it is not necessary for customers to select a new hash chain to do a business with a different vendor. Furthermore, since the remaining hash index can be used with the signature of previous vendor, all what customers do is to handle the index of one hash chain.

Previous Micro Payment Schemes

Software-only electronic payment systems (which are the only ones we will discuss from now on) can be secure if they are fully on-line, so that the issuer participates in each transaction . However, that is precisely what is not acceptable in micro payments, since the computational and communication requirements this imposes are excessive when a purchase costs a fraction of a penny. Therefore, many micro payment schemes have been proposed, Pay Word, Net-Card, Pedersen's proposal, and Pay Tree which are off-line. In all these systems, to make purchases from vendors, a customer must receive a digital certificate from a bank or some other financial intermediary. The deficiency in these systems is that they either expose the issuer of the certificate to large losses or else they limit the user's flexibility. Issuer losses arise when the user spends up to her total limit at each of, say, 10,000 vendors. (This is a disadvantage of Pay Word, Net Card, Pay Tree, and Pedersen's scheme.). Such losses can be prevented if the customer needs to obtain a separate certificate for each vendor she intends to deal with (as in Millicent), but these certificates must then sum up to no more than the customer's bank account balance. Similarly, Micro-iKP ([HSW96]), a protocol that is an adaptation of *iKP* to micro payments, prevents overspending by freezing in the customer's account the maximal amount that the customer can spend with a given vendor. Both of these solutions might be unacceptably restrictive when a customer might want to deal with any of thousands of online vendors and not know beforehand how much she might spend with each.

Smart Card

Introduction

The **smart card,** an intelligent token, is a credit card sized plastic card embedded with an integrated circuit chip. It provides not only memory capacity, but computational capability as well. The self-containment of smart card makes it resistant to attack as it does not need to depend upon potentially vulnerable external resources. Because of this characteristic, smart cards are often used in different applications which require strong security protection and authentication.

For examples, smart card can act as an identification card which is used to prove the identity of the card holder. It also can be a medical card which stores the medical history of a person. Furthermore, the smart card can be used as a credit/debit bank card which allows off-line transactions. All of these applications require sensitive data to be stored in the card, such as biometrics information of the card owner, personal medical history, and cryptographic keys for authentication, etc.

In the near future, the traditional magnetic strip card will be replaced and integrated together into a single card by using the multi-application smart card, which is known as an electronic purse or wallet in the smart card industry. The smart card is becoming more and more significant and will play an important role in our daily life. It will be used to carry a lot of sensitive and critical data about the consumers ever more than before when compared with the magnetic strip card. Therefore, there are many arguments and issues about whether or not the smart card is secure and safe enough to store that information. This has always been a source of controversy.

This paper discusses the security of the smart card in three different aspects. Firstly, we will have a look of the physical structure of a smart card, and how it protects the data through the card's life cycle. Secondly, we will examine how the data is protected through logical controls over the files in the card. Thirdly, we will discuss how the smart card can provide a secure and authenticated environment for applications through procedural operation and mechanism. At last, before we conclude whether the smart card is secure or not, some of the available techniques of attacking the smart card will be reviewed.

Physical Structure and Life Cycle

This section discusses the physical structure of a smart card and examines the components of a smart card. It will also discuss all the phases of a card's life cycle, and explores how the micro controller handles and transfers data securely from the card manufacturer to the application supplier and then to the bearer. As a result, we can determine how the data or information stored on the card can be protected.

Physical Structure

The physical structure of a smart card is specified by the International Standards Organization (ISO) 7810, 7816/1 and 7816/2. Generally it is made up of three elements. The plastic card is the most basic one and has the dimensions of 85.60mm x 53.98mm x 0.80mm. A printed circuit and an integrated circuit chip are embedded on the card. Figure 1 shows an overview of the physical structure of a smart card.

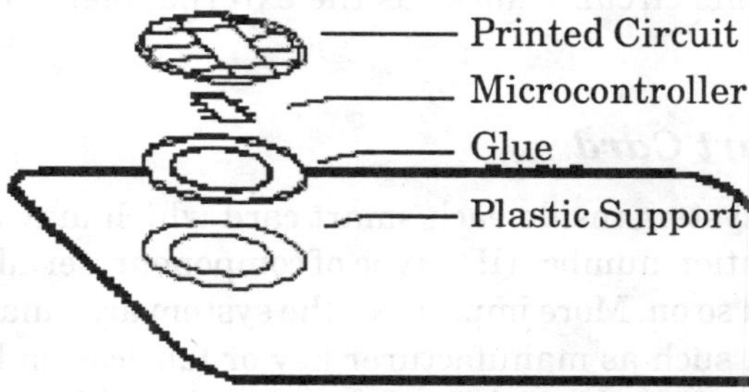

Figure 1: Physical structure of a smart card (Source: Philips DX smart card reference manual, 1995)

The printed circuit conforms to ISO standard 7816/3 which provides five connection points for power and data. It is hermetically fixed in the recess provided on the card and is burned onto the circuit chip, filled with a conductive material, and sealed with contacts protruding. The printed circuit protects the circuit chip from mechanical stress and static electricity. Communication with the chip is accomplished through contacts that overlay the printed circuit.

The capability of a smart card is defined by its integrated circuit chip. Typically, an integrated circuit chip consists of a microprocessor, read only memory (ROM), non static random access memory (RAM) and electrically erasable programmable read only memory (EEPROM) which will retain its state when the power is removed. The current circuit chip is made from silicon which is not flexible and particularly easy to break. Therefore, in order to avoid breakage when the card is bent, the chip is restricted to only a few millimeters in size. Furthermore, the physical interface which allows data exchange between the integrated circuit chip and the card acceptor device (CAD) is limited to 9600 bits per second. The communication line is a bi-directional serial transmission line which conforms to ISO standard 7816/3. All the data exchanges are under the control of the central processing unit in the integrated circuit chip. Card commands and input data are sent to the chip which responses with status words and output data upon the receipt of these commands and data. Information is sent in half duplex mode, which means transmission of data is in one direction at a time. This protocol together with the restriction of the bit rate prevent massive data attack on the card.

In general, the size, the thickness and bend requirements for the smart card are designed to protect the card from being spoiled physically. However, this also limits the memory and processing resources that may be placed on the card. As a result, the smart card always has to incorporate with other external peripherals to operate. For example, it may require a device to provide and supply user input and output, time and date information, power and so on. These limitations may degrade the security of the smart card in some circumstances as the external elements are un trusted and precarious.

Life Cycle of a Smart Card

There is an operating system inside each smart card which may contain a manufacturer identification number (ID), type of component, serial number, profile information, and so on. More important, the system area may contain different security keys, such as manufacturer key or fabrication key (KF), and personalization key (KP). All of this information should be kept secret and not be revealed by others.

Hence, from the manufacturer to the application provider, then the card holder, the production of a smart card is divided into different phases. Limitation on transfer and access of data is incremental at different phases in order to protect different areas in the smart card. There are five main phases for a typical smart card life cycle. We will discuss each of them below.

Fabrication Phase

This phase is carried out by the chip manufacturers. The silicon integrated circuit chip is created and tested in this phase. A fabrication key (KF) is added to protect the chip from fraudulent modification until it is assembled into the plastic card support. The KF of each chip is unique and is derived from a master manufacturer key. Other fabrication data will be written to the circuit chip at the end of this phase. Then the chip is ready to deliver to the card manufacturer with the protection of the key KF.

Pre-personalization Phase

This phase is carried out by the card suppliers. In this phase, the chip will be mounted on the plastic card which may have the logo of the application provider printed on it. The connection between the chip and the printed circuit will be made, and the whole unit can be tested. For added security and to allow secure delivery of the card to the card issuer, the fabrication key will be replaced by a personalisation key (KP). After that, a personalisation lock V_{PER} will be written to prevent further modification of the KP. In addition, physical memory access instructions will be disabled. Access of the card can be done only by using logical memory addressing. This preserves the system and fabrication areas being accessed or modified.

Personalisation Phase

This phase is conducted by the card issuers. It completes the creation of logical data structures. Data files contents and application data are written to the card. Information of card holder identity, PIN, and unblocking PIN will be stored as well. At the end, a utilisation lock V_{UTIL} will be written to indicate the card is in the utilisation phase.

Utilisation Phase

This is the phase for the normal use of the card by the card holder. The application system, logical file access controls, and others are activated. Access of information on the card will be limited by the security policies set by the application. This will be discussed in detail in the next section.

End-of-Life Phase (Invalidation Phase)

There are two ways to move the card into this phase. One is initiated by the application which writes the invalidation lock to an individual file or the master file. All the operations including writing and updating will be disabled by the operating system. Only read instructions may remain active for analysis purposes. The another way to put the card into this phase is that, when the control system irreversibly blocks access because both the PIN and unblocking PIN are blocked, then all the operations will be blocked including reads.

Finally, table 1 summarizes the conditions and memory accesses of a smart card during the various phases which are mentioned above.

Areas/Phases	Fabrication	Pre-personalisation	Personalisation	Utilisation	End-of-Life
Access mode	Physical addressing		Logical addressing		
System	Not accessible				
Fabrication (keys)	Write KF	Write KP	Not accessible		
Fabrication (data)	Read, write, erase	Read	Read		
Directory	Read, write, erase		According to logical file access conditions		
Data	Read, write, erase		According to logical file access conditions		
Optional code	Read, write, erase		Not accessible		

Table 1: Phases and access rights of smart card's life cycle
(Source: Philips DX smart card reference manual, 1995)

Logical Structure and Access Controls

After a smart card is issued to the consumer by the application provider, the protection of the card will be controlled by the application operating system mainly. Physical addressing mode of accessing data is no longer available. Access of data has to be done through the logical file structure on the card. This section will discuss how the operating system accomplishes the security protection of the data stored on the card by examining the logical file structure and the corresponding access controls of a smart card.

Logical File Structure

In general, in terms of data storage, a smart card can be viewed as a disk drive where files are organised in a hierarchical form through directories. Similar to MS-DOS, there is one master file (MF) which is like the root directory. Under the root, we can have different files which are called elementary files (EFs). We can also have various subdirectories called dedicated files (DFs). Under each subdirectory will be elementary files again. The main difference of a smart card file structure and a MS-DOS file structure is that dedicated files can also contain data. Figure 2 shows logical view of a smart card file structure.

In smart card terminology, the root or master file (MF), besides the header part which consists of itself, the body part contains the headers of all of the dedicated files and elementary files which contain the MF in

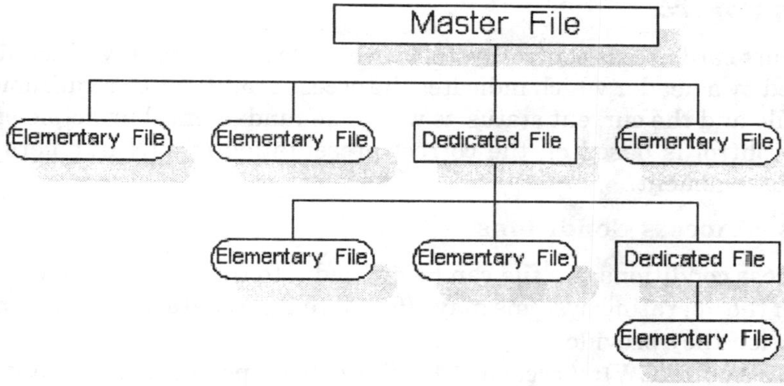

Figure 2: Logical file structure of smart card

their parental hierarchy. The dedicated file (DF) is a functional grouping of files consisting of itself and all the files which are immediate childs of the DF. The elementary file (EF) simply consists of its header and the body which stores the data.

The ways that the data is managed within a file differ and are dependent on different operating systems. Some of them may manage the data simply by offset and length, while the others may organise data in fixed or variable lengths of records such as Global System for Mobile Communication (GSM) system. In any cases, the file must be selected before performing any operations. This is equivalent to opening a file.

The logical access and selection mechanisms are activated after the power is supplied to the card while the master file is selected automatically. The selection operation allows movement around the tree. It can be descending by selecting an EF or a DF, or it can be ascending by selecting a MF or DF. Horizontal movement can be done by selecting an EF from another EF as well.

After the success of selection, the header of the file can be retrieved, which stores the information about the file such as identification number, description, types, size, and so on. Particularly, it stores the attribute of the file which states the access conditions and current status. Access of the data in the file depends on whether those conditions can be fulfilled or not. This will be described in the following section.

In short, the file structure of the smart card operating system is similar to other common operating systems such as MS-DOS and UNIX. However, in order to provide greater security control, the attribute of each file is enhanced by adding accessing conditions and file status fields in the file header. Moreover, file lock is also provided to prevent the file being accessed. These security mechanisms and algorithms provide a logical protection of the smart card.

Access Control

The smart card access control system covers file access mainly. Each file is attached by a header which indicates the access conditions or requirements of the file and the current status as well. The fundamental principle of the access control is based on the correct presentation of PIN numbers and their management.

Levels of Access Conditions

The access conditions of a file can be defined into the following five levels. Some of the operating systems may offer more than these depending on the application they provide.

Always (ALW): Access of the file can be performed without any restriction.

Card holder verification 1 (CHV1): Access can only be possible when valid CHV1 value is presented.

Card holder verification 2 (CHV2): Access can only be possible when valid CHV2 value is presented.

Administrative (ADM): Allocation of these levels and the respective requirements for their fulfillment are the responsibility of the appropriate administrative authority.

Never (NEV): Access of the file is forbidden.

Those condition levels are not hierarchical. For instance, correct presentation of CHV2 does not mean that access of file is allowed, which requires presentation of CHV1. During the operation, corresponding requirements have to be fulfilled before the selection of the file. For example, correct CHV1 value has to be presented if it is the access condition of a file.

PIN Presentations

The PINs are normally stored in separate elementary files, EF_{CHV1} and EF_{CHV2} for example. Use of the access conditions on those files can prevent the PINs from being changed. The PIN can be changed by issuing the change PIN instruction together with the new and old PIN. However, for most of the smart card operating systems, the corresponding PIN will be invalidated or blocked when a fixed number of invalid PINs are presented consecutively. The number of times will vary with different systems.

At this moment, all the files require that PIN will be blocked and unaccessible. Unblocking has to be carried out with the knowledge of the correct PIN and a specific unblocking PIN stored in the card. Still, if an invalid unblocking PIN is presented consecutively and up to a particular number of times, the unblocking PIN will be blocked as well. Then both of the PIN and the unblocking PIN will be invalidated and are no longer to be restored. This is called an irreversible blockage. Some of the systems may even invalidate the whole card in order to prevent further attacks.

PIN Management

To achieve the protection and blockage of the PINs mentioned above, two counters have to be implemented for each of the card holder verification numbers (CHVs). The counters are composed in such a way that any possible errors in writing or erasing will be avoided, which could adversely affect the access control on the card. There are three states in the management of the PIN which are described below.

PIN has been presented: Files or functions which have PIN presentation as a pre-requisite or condition can be carried out. Every time the PIN is presented correctly, the PIN counter will be reset to the maximum number of tries, three for example.

PIN has not been presented or was presented incorrectly: The PIN counter will be decremented by one after each incorrect PIN was presented. All the operations or instructions which require PIN presentation will be invalidated. If the PIN counter reaches zero, then the PIN will be blocked.

PIN is blocked: In this state, all the operations require PIN presentation and even the PIN presentation instruction itself is blocked. Unblock PIN instruction has to be carried out. If correct unblocking PIN is presented, the PIN counter will be reset to the maximum number of tries and backed to the first state. However, if invalid unblocking PIN is presented, the unblock PIN counter will be decremented by one and when this counter reaches zero, the PIN can never be unblocked again.

Summing up the file structure and access control the smart card provided, data stored on the card can be protected either individually by setting access conditions in the header of each file or hierarchically by grouping files together under a single dedicated file (DF) with access conditions set on it. Furthermore, the irreversible blockage gives maximum protection to the card so that enormous intrusions are impossible.

Procedural Protection

Because of the on-board computing power of the smart card, it is possible to achieve off-line transactions and verifications. For instance, a smart card and a card acceptor device (CAD) can identify each other by using the mutual active authentication method. Moreover, data and codes stored on the card are encrypted by the chip manufacturer by using computational scrambling encryption, which makes the circuit chip almost impossible to be forged. All of these features together with the protected access control are discussed in the previous section.

Today, smart cards are being used in different areas becuase they can be used together with other technologies, such as asymmetric cryptographic algorithms and biometrics identification, to provide highly assured and trusted applications. This section discusses three particular areas where demonstrated how different systems can make use of the smart card to enhance their securities.

Identification of Documents

Traditional document based identifications, such as identification card, licenses, passport/visa, and so on, are always considered unreliable. All of them are easy to be forged and copied. Particularly with today's technologies, high quality Colour photocopies, printers, and scanners are easily accessed and owned, as a result high quality fraudulent documents can be produced easily. This makes the inspection of documents more and more difficult. The smart card probably is the best solution to solve this problem. Printed information and photographs can be digitized and stored into the card. By setting up the access condition and password on files, only authorised persons or authorities, such as government departments, are allowed to access the information. Moreover, together with the biometrics technology, biometrics information of the card holder can be placed on the card, so that the smart card can corporate with biometrics scanner to identify or verify whether the card is owned by the card holder or not. This significantly improves the reliability of the document the smart card carries.

The operation procedures could be similar to the traditional paper based identification system. However, instead of verifying the documents by observation of an inspection officer, a card acceptor device will be used. The device which contains the authorised code and PIN can unlock the file and retrieve the owner's information for verification. In the case when biometrics is used, the user can be authenticated by placing the required portion of his/her body onto a biometrics reader, the data collected by the reader can be used to compare with the one in the card.

Nowadays, many organisations or governments in different countries already have research on this issues. For example, many airlines intend to develop their electronic tickets by using smart cards which co-operate with the baggage handling system in some airports. The smart card typically stores the passenger's flight details such as name, seat number, flight number, baggage details and so on. This helps to verify correct passenger checked-in and identify the owner of baggage in case of lost or unclaimed baggage's. More importantly the system may help to identify criminals and terrorists.

Authentication in Kerberos

In an open distributed computing environment (DCE), a workstation cannot be trusted to identify its users because the workstation may not be located in a well controlled environment and may be far away from the central server. A user can be an intruder who may try to attack the system or pretend to be someone else to extract information from the system which he/she is not entitled to. In order to protect a system from being attacked by remote network hosts, a certain kind of authentication must be taken into account.

Kerberos is one of the systems which provides trusted third-party authentication services to authenticate users on a distributed network environment. Basically, when a user or client requests an access to a particular service from the server, he/she has to obtain a ticket or credential from the Kerberos authentication server (AS). The user then presents that credential to the ticket granting server (TGS) and obtains a service ticket. Hence, the user can request for service by submitting the service ticket to the desired server. Figure 3 shows this authentication protocol

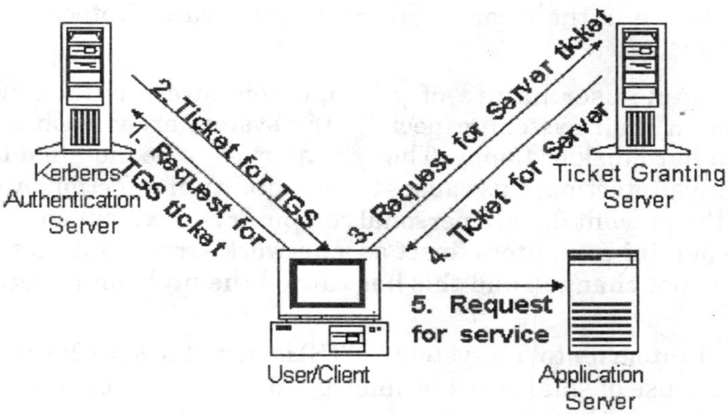

Figure 3: Kerberos authentication protocol (source: Jennifer & Clifford & Jeffrey, 1988)

Having this protocol, the server can be assured offering services to the correct client who is entitled to have access. This is because Kerberos assumed that only the correct user can use the credential as others do not have the password to decrypt it. And also because of this, a user can actually request the credential of others. That is, the user is not authenticated at the beginning stage.

In this way, an attacker can obtain the credential of another user, and perform off-line attack by using a password guessing approach as the ticket is sealed by password only. This security weakness of Kerberos is pointed out by Mark and Gary (1995) in one of their papers "Integrating Smart Card Into Authentication Systems".

In their report, they proposed to integrate the smart card into the Kerberos system to overcome this problem. Six different schemes are proposed. The whole idea is to enhance the security of Kerberos authentication by authenticating the user directly at the beginning and before the granting of the initial ticket, so that one user cannot have the ticket of another. And, "the use of smart card requires user logging into the system not only recall a password, but also to be in possession of a token".

The details of those six proposed schemes to integrate smart card into the Kerberos are not discussed here as it is not the concern in this paper. In conclusion, the model mentioned here demonstrated how smart card technology can secure a system procedurally.

Access Control On Operating System

Access control is one of the important usage of the smart card technology. It is also the motivation behind the development of smart card. In this section, we discuss how to control the access of an operating system in a personal computer by using the smart card. The original idea is come from Paul and Lance in their paper "BITS: A Smart card Protected Operating System, 1994".

The single-user nature of personal computers is lack of security protection on their system, especially the system areas such as the boot sector of a hard disk or floppy. They are allowed to be modified by anyone without any protection, this causes the possibility of infection by computer virus. In the present days, a personal computer is powerful enough to take the place of mini-computers to act as a network server, but its single-user nature has not changed and this has caused the problem to become more serious.

A boot integrity token system (BITS) is introduced by Paul and Lance which make use of smart card technology to protect the operating system. The basic idea is that the host computer is booted actually from a smart card or it requires critical information from the card to complete the boot sequence. So that even if an attacker can gain physical access to the hardware, it is impossible to guarantee system integrity.

The smart card is configured to require user authentication prior to the data access. During system startup, two authentications have to be performed before the completion of boot sequence. At first, the user is authenticated to the smart card by means of a password. And then the host authenticates the card by reading the shared secret from the card. After both of them are matched, host reads boot section information from the smart card and completes the boot sequence. Then the PC operates as normal.

The smart card can also store the checksum of critical data and executable programs. It is effective against virus by validating files integrity rather than scan for known virus signatures. In general, the use of smart card here enhanced the security of the computer by utilizing the inherent secure storage and processing capabilities.

Attacks on Smart Card

As discussed in all above, the smart card seems to be a superior tool for enhancing system security and provides a place for secure storage. One of the security features provided by most of the smart card operating systems, which is not mentioned in this paper, is the cryptographic facilities. They provide encryption and decryption of data for the card; some of them can even be used to generate cryptographic keys.

The secret of the cryptographic algorithm, the keys stored, and the access control inside the smart card become the targets of attackers. Nowadays many companies and cryptographers claim to be able to break the smart card and its micro controller. Some of them perform logical non-invasive attacks, some of them attack the card physically while others just prove their success by mathematical theorems.

We will review the first two briefly and examine how the attacks are achieved. For the third one, since their attacks are theoretical and relate to a lot of complicated mathematical calculations and formulas which are outside the scope of this paper, it is not discussed here.

Logical Attacks

As all the key material of a smart card is stored in the electrically erasable programmable read only memory (EEPROM), and due to the fact that EEPROM write operations can be affected by unusual voltages and temperatures, information can be trapped by raising or dropping the supplied voltage to the micro controller. In the report of "Tamper Resistance - A Cautionary Note" by Ross and Markus (1996), several examples of attacking the smart card micro controller by adjusting the voltage are provided.

For example, a widely known attack of PIC16C84 micro controller is that the security bit of the controller can be clear with erasing the memory by raising the voltage VCC to VPP - 0.5V. An attack on DS5000 security processor is another example. A short voltage drop can release the security lock without erasing the secret data sometimes. Low voltage can facilitate other attacks as well, such as an analogue random generator used to create cryptographic keys will produce an output of almost all 1's when the supply voltage is lowered slightly.

For these reasons, some security processors implemented sensors which will cause an alarm when there is any environmental changes. However, these kinds of sensors always causes false alarm due to the occurrence of fluctuations when the card is powered up and the circuit is stabilising. Therefore this scheme is not commonly used.

Physical Attacks

Invasive physical attacks are typical. Before this kind of attack can be performed, the circuit chip has to be removed from the plastic card. This can be done by simply using a sharp knife to cut away the plastic behind the chip module until the epoxy resin becomes visible. And then the resin can be dissolved by adding a few drops of fuming nitric acid (>98% HNO_3).

The acid and resin can be washed away by shaking the card in acetone until the silicon surface is fully exposed. Ultimately the chip can be examined and attacked directly.

At Cavendish laboratory in Cambridge, a technique is developed for reverse engineering the circuit chips. The layout and function of the chip can be identified using that technique. Then another technique developed by IBM can be used to observe the operation of the chip. As a result its secret can be fully revealed.

Besides this, there are many different ways to perform physical attacks. For instance, erasing the security lock bit by focusing UV light on the EPROM, probing the operation of the circuit by using micro probing needles, or using laser cutter microscopes to explore the chip, and so on. However, these kinds of attacks are only available for well funded laboratories as the costs associated are considerably high.

Electronic Fund Transfer

Research into electronic payment systems for consumers can be traced back to the 1940s, and the first applications credit cards appeared soon after. In the early 1970s, the emerging electronic payment technology was labeled **electronic funds transfer (EFT)**. EFT is defined as "any transfer of funds initiated through an electronic terminal, telephonic instrument, or computer or magnetic tape so as to order, instruct, or authorize a financial institution to debit or credit an account." EFT unitizes computer and telecommunication components both to supply and to transfer money or financial assets. Transfer is information –based and intangible. Thus EFT stands in marked contrast to conventional money and payment modes that rely on physical delivery of cash or checks (or other paper orders to pay) by truck, train, or airplane.

Work on **EFT** can be segmented into three broad categories:

1. Banking and financial payments
    - Large –scale or wholesale payments (e.g., bank –to – bank transfer)
    - Small –scale or retail payments (e.g., automated teller machines and cash
    - dispensers)
    - Home banking (e.g., bill payment)

2. Retailing payments
    - Credit cards (e.g., VISA or MasterCard)
    - Private label credit /debit cards (e.g., J.C.Penney Card)
    - Charge cards (e.g., American Express)]

3. On –line electronic commerce payments
   - Token –based payment systems
     - Electronic cash (e.g., DigiCash)
     - Electronic checks (e.g., NetCheque)
     - Smart cards or debit cards (e.g., Mondex Electronic Currency Card)
   - Credit card –based payment systems
     - Encrypted credit cards (e.g., World Wide Web form –based encryption)
     - Third –party authorization numbers (e.g., First Virtual)
     - Large –scale payments between banks and business, widely recognized as the pioneering efforts in electronic commerce that involve the extensive use of EDI of transferring payment information.

Electronic Fund Transfer (EFT)

An electronic fund transfer is a transfer of funds initiated through an electronic terminal, telephone, computer, or magnetic tape that instructs a financial institution to either credit or debit a consumer's asset account.

Examples of EFT services may include:

- .Automated teller machine (ATM) transfers
- .Direct deposits or withdrawals of funds
- .Transfers initiated by telephone
- .Point-of-sale (POS) terminal transfers
- .Transfers resulting from debit card transactions

The **Electronic Fund Transfer Act** (EFTA) provides a basic framework establishing the rights, liabilities, and responsibilities of participants in electronic fund transfer (EFT) systems. The Federal Reserve Board's Regulation E provides protection of the rights of consumers in their dealings with these systems.

NOTE: Certain electronic fund transfers, such as any wire transfer of funds for a consumer through the Federal Reserve Communications System or other similar network that is used primarily for transfers between financial institutions or between businesses, are not covered by the EFTA. Refer to Section 205.3(c) of Regulation E for a complete listing of exempt transactions.

Electronic Terminal

An electronic device, other than a telephone operated by a consumer, through which a consumer may initiate an electronic fund transfer. The term includes, but is not limited to, point-of-sale terminals, automated teller machines, and cash dispensing machines.

Preauthorized Electronic Fund Transfer

An electronic fund transfer authorized in advance to recur at substantially regular intervals.

Unauthorized EFT

An electronic fund transfer from a consumer's account initiated by a person other than the consumer without actual authority to initiate the transfer and from which the consumer receives no benefit. The term does not include any electronic fund transfer (1) initiated by a person who was furnished with the access device to the consumer's account by the consumer, unless the consumer has notified the financial institution involved that transfers by that person are no longer authorized, (2) initiated with fraudulent intent by the consumer or any person acting in concert with the consumer, or (3) that is initiated by the financial institution or its employee.

8

E-Markets

Web Advertising

You have probably noticed that across the Web, two different things are happening right now:

• More and more sites are asking you to pay a fee to subscribe to all or part of the Web site.

• Advertising is becoming more and more "in your face." There are now pop-up ads, ads that play music and sound tracks, ads that swim across the screen, and so on.

The second trend is true of nearly all-commercial Web sites. There are many new forms of Web advertising, and they are more and more obvious. Many Web users have questions about all of these new ad types. For example:

• Why do Web sites have so many ads now?

• Why do Web sites allow pop-up ads that open new windows? (Many people hate closing them all.)

• Why do Web sites allow these floating ads that cover the content so I cannot read it?

• How can I make all these ads go away?

• In this article, we will look at all the different forms of Web advertising in use today, as well as the economics that are driving them, so that you can have a much better understanding of how Web advertising works. Whether you are a casual surfer or someone running your own Web site, you will find this article to be a real eye-opener.

• The HowStuffWorks Ad-Free Server has zero ads throughout. The user can also customize the view with the CUSTOMIZE! button to, for example, remove the sidebars or the graphics within the article. You can get HowStuffWorks ad-free for just $1 per month.

With web advertising some believe in time tested strategies and others believe that keeping up with every single theory out there is worth while. We here at Smart ads really believe in a little from side A, and a little from side B.

When the Web first started being a "commercial endeavor" around 1997 or so, thousands of new sites were born and billions of dollars in venture capital flowed into them. The sites divided into two broad categories:

- E-commerce sites - E-commerce sites sell things. E-commerce sites make their money from the products they sell, just like a brick-and-mortar store does.
- Content sites - Content sites create or collect content (words, pictures, video, etc.) for readers to look at. Content Web sites make their money primarily from advertising, like TV stations, radio stations and newspapers.

In the beginning, “advertising” on the Internet meant “banner ads” — the 468x60-pixel ads you see at the top of almost all Web pages today (including this one). In 1998 or so, banner advertising was a lucrative business. Popular sites like Yahoo could charge $30, $50, even $100 per thousand impressions to run banner ads on their pages. These advertising rates provided fuel for much of the venture capital boom on the Web. The idea was that sites could start up and increase their page impressions to make easy money from banner ads. If a site could generate 100 million page impressions per month, it could make $3 million per month with banner ad rates at $30 per thousand impressions.

At some point, advertisers came to the conclusion that banner ads were not as effective as full-page magazine ads or 30-second TV commercials. At the same time, there was an incredible glut of advertising space — thousands of sites had a million or more page impressions available per month, and companies like Double Click began collecting these sites into massive pools of banner-ad inventory. The economic principle of “supply and demand” works the same way on the Web as it does everywhere else, so the rates paid for banner advertising began to plummet.

Banner Ads

A company buys advertising for one of two reasons:

- Branding
- Direct sales

Branding refers to the process of impressing a company name or a product name onto society’s collective brain. Let’s say you have come up with a new brand of soda, or you are opening a new restaurant, or you are selling a new widget. You want to get the product’s name (and sometimes the product’s features and benefits) firmly planted in people’s heads. This is branding.

Branding happens with both new and existing products. When you see a billboard that says nothing but “Coke” on it, or you see a NASCAR car that says “Tide” on the hood, or you see a feel-good ad on TV about a car company or an oil company but there’s no mention of a product, that is branding. The advertiser does not necessarily expect you to do anything today. On the other hand, a direct sales ad is an ad that is trying to get you to do something today, right now, as you look at the ad. The advertiser wants you to:

- Click on the ad
- Call an 800 number
- Drive immediately to the store

What branding advertisers came to feel about banner ads is that banner ads are not the most effective vehicle for branding. Relative to a magazine ad or a TV ad, banner ads are small and easily ignored.

What direct sales advertisers came to feel about banner ads is that the response rate for banner ads is low. For most banner ads, the industry average seems to hover between two and five clicks per 1,000 impressions of the ad. That is, if a banner ad appears on 1,000 Web pages, between two and five people will click on the ad to learn more.

Those five clicks per thousand impressions don't have much value to most advertisers. The reason is because those five clicks will not all generate sales. Out of 100 clicks, perhaps one person will actually do the desired thing (buy something, download something, etc.).

Example. Let's say that a publisher wants people to buy a book, and hopes to increase sales of the book through advertising. The publisher has budgeted $3.00 per copy of the book to spend on advertising. If the publisher is paying $30 per 1,000 impressions for banner ads and purchases 100,000 impressions for $3,000, here is what happens:

- The banner ad appears 100,000 times.
- Let's say the response rate is five clicks per 1,000 impressions, so 500 people click on the ad during the time the 100,000 total impressions are running.
- If two percent of those 500 people actually purchase the book, that results in 10 purchases.
- The publisher had to pay ($3,000/10) $300 for each book purchased through that ad.
- Obviously, paying $300 to sell one book is not a good economic model for a publisher, especially since the budget is $3.00 per book. For this type of advertising to work for the publisher, the publisher would need to pay 30 cents per 1,000 impressions, rather than 30 dollars.

So banner ad rates began to decline. Today, if you shop around, you can buy banner ads from thousands of Web sites or brokers for 50 cents or so per thousand impressions — which is pretty much exactly what they are worth to a person who is trying to sell something with banner ads using a direct sales model.

It is possible for some Web sites to charge more than 50 cents per 1,000 impressions. For example, the top 100 or so Web sites can charge a premium because of their size. There is also a process called targeting. For example, if you want to sell a GPS, you can advertise on the HowStuffWorks GPS article and get a targeted audience for your ad, which will typically increase the click-through and response rate for the ad. Yahoo and many search engines target their banner ads to the search words people type in, and they charge more for these targeted ads. But for most other Web sites, there is very little money to be made from banner ads.

In order to charge more than 50 cents per thousand impressions, Web sites have to offer ads that either:

- Have a lot more branding power
- Get a much higher click-through rate
- Therefore, you find many different advertising formats and experi ments on the Web today.

Sidebar Ads

A sidebar ad (also known as a skyscraper ad) is similar to a banner ad, but it is vertically oriented rather than horizontally. Because it is vertical, the height of a sidebar ad can often reach 600 pixels or more, and sidebars are generally 120 pixels wide.

A sidebar ad has more impact than a banner ad for at least two reasons:

A tall sidebar ad is two to three times larger than a banner ad.

You cannot scroll a sidebar ad off the screen like you can a banner ad. With a banner ad, you can scroll just 60 pixels down and the ad is gone. With a sidebar ad, the ad is with you much longer. Because of this increased impact, sidebar ads have higher branding power and a higher click-through rate. A typical sidebar ad has a click-through rate of 1 percent (10 clicks per 1,000 impressions), or about two to three times that of a banner ad. Advertisers will typically pay $1.00 to $1.50 per 1,000 run-of-site impressions for sidebar ad placement. Advertisers pay more for targeted sidebar ads, just like they do with targeted banner ads.

Varied Shapes and Sizes

Banner ads and sidebar ads have standard sizes, but in the last year or two people have tried all different sizes and placements. Here are three examples:

The orange ad in the upper right is 250x250 pixels. Ads this size or larger can be found within the text of articles in some cases. They act like magazine ads that break up the text to get more attention.

Pop-up and pop-under ads annoy many users because they clutter up the desktop and take time to close. However, they are much more effective than banner ads. Whereas a banner ad might get two to five clicks per 1,000 impressions, a pop-up ad might average 30 clicks. Therefore, advertisers are willing to pay more for pop-up and pop-under ads. Typically, a pop-up ad will pay the Web site four to 10 times more than a banner ad. That is why you see so many pop-up ads on the Web today.

In the **traditional marketplace**, every operation, apart from the exchange of physical goods and services, is based on information: offers, brokerage, negotiations, orders, contracts, payments, documents, receipts and the resolution of disputes. Similar to traditional commerce, the electronic marketplace should facilitate the establishment of relationships between potential sellers and buyers. Sellers and buyers should be able to negotiate the terms and conditions of transactions, such as the goods and services that are being offered – which may be dependent on the profile of the buyer, the applicable laws or regulations, the price, the means of payment, the mode of delivery and guarantees, etc. The negotiation may be concluded with an explicit contract, signed electronically. The parties should be able to dispute the transaction both before/after its conclusion. The viability of electronic commerce (e-commerce) requires that trust be restored. Buyers must be able to identify sellers securely and obtain assurance that they are established and accredited legitimately. Buyers might only trust sellers that are accredited by a particular payment system provider or a particular consumer organization. The integrity of the transaction must be preserved – buyers need to be confident that they will receive the goods or the service that they actually ordered in return for their payment and sellers must be sure that they will be paid for the goods or the service delivered.

Privacy is receiving increasing attention. In most cases, confidentiality will be required regarding communications, the existence of transactions or their specific details – price, conditions, date and identity of the parties, etc. The recovery of transactions and the resolution of disputes must also be guaranteed in order to provide the parties with genuine recourse should equipment or network failures occur or if they are confronted by dishonest practices on the part of their business partner.

Agent -based Market places

Many companies are engaged in the development of systems and services for e-commerce including cataloguing, ordering, payments, and logistics systems and services. Current approaches to the development of e-commerce usually involve an existing market actor, such as a communications gateway and connection service provider, offering customers a set of facilities that will support their participation as buyers and sellers in an e-marketplace. The sorts of facilities offered include catalogue services, transaction management and settlement systems. Clients of the facility provision are thereby equipped to play the roles of consumers and suppliers in a market. In volatile complex markets, automated systems based on agents should be implemented to handle interactions and knowledge about the market and customer requirements.

During the preliminary phase in business interactions publicity and dissemination agents add value for suppliers by organizing and distributing market offers in the form of catalogues and advertisements. On the customer side, needs are interpreted by information gathering and decision-making agents in the light of the market information that they access. This results in the selection of a specified market offering. Customer behavior is also interpreted as a demand to guide the future strategies of suppliers. The information retrieval business area includes the majority of services that are available currently on the Internet, where the users are looking for all kinds of information on any subjects: weather reports, stock options and financial data, cultural or scientific information, shareware and audio or video clips, etc.

It should be noted that such a generic definition includes all types of information from simple textual information to multimedia streams. The service provision chain can be simple or complex depending on the number of intervening actors. As with traditional commerce, different sectors can be distinguished between: production, packaging, marketing, retailing, distribution (well-defined as the network can be used for these purposes), and infrastructure.

Business Briefing: Global Infose Curity 2002

Information changes quickly and depends on the user's individual demands. This is why the parties that provide a 'classical' information brokerage service (paper-based publisher) either concentrate on special thematic areas with contents that are capable of achieving a constant price over a longer period or bundle their information from different areas in order to reach a wider audience by producing new products periodically (daily, weekly and monthly, etc.) Therefore, an important component of e-commerce is the retailer-active virtual catalogue service that may be a World Wide Web (WWW)-based application, providing the company with a new channel to market, sell and support products and services over an open network environment such as the Internet. From the customer's point of view, it offers an alternative means of finding out what product or service is available currently in a given market, who the suppliers of that product or service are, and where and how to get such a product or service. e-Catalogues can be integrated seamlessly with other functions of the company and its business partners. The catalogue may support capabilities for browsing only, Boolean, Wide Area Information Service (WAIS), fuzzy or product-specific. It could support cross-searching of multiple product databases and provide an online ordering capability. It may support secured payment mechanisms. It may allow online testing and direct downloading of a product.

Feedback mechanisms may be provided by the catalogue through e-mail, real time chatting, voice-mail, live video or discussion forums. It may be unrestricted or require registration, authentication or any other pre-arrangement in order to use it. On account of these possible characteristics, e-catalogues can be viewed as an interactive channel that links together a company with its suppliers, business partners and consumers. They may be used to create brand awareness, market a product or service, test-run a product, generate sales or sales leads and provide after-sales support. During the contracting and transactions (brokering) phase purchasing agents interpret the specifications of need and generate orders which refer to catalogued or advertised items. They also proffer payments. The models considered so far have been concerned with the market information phase of brokerage, which is preceded by the issuing of market offers. An offer, which may be the subject of brokering, is not simply the specification of a product, but is the offer to supply that product as well. For the offer to be well-formed, it must include information concerning availability, the means of delivery and the acceptable means of payment. In addition, several conditions should apply as follows:

- Tradability – that which is offered must be tradable legally by the offered.
- Specifiability – that which is offered must be described appropriately.
- Availability – it must be possible to deliver what has been offered.
- Suitability – the purchaser must be qualified to own or use what is offered.
- Pay ability – the purchaser or the credit provider must pay.

The market for information and content has been seen as one of the most important potential developments in network-based commerce because the means of advertising and the means of delivery is the network itself. On the supply side, publishing enterprises, the developers and authors of content and, in some cases, the subjects of content must be distinguished between. When the subject of a transaction is a registration to use a service, a complex set of rights and obligations is generated for the service-providing enterprise. The offer of service is generated by a marketing agent for advertising and publicity, cataloguing and explanation, regulatory and business objectives in an interaction where the concept of a service is user-oriented and defines capability, quality and cost. Each registration that is sold generates an obligation to provide contractual arrangements, resource assignment and credit control at some time or over some period. The response to these obligations in the service-providing enterprise is reflected in the structure of its service management systems and also in the structure of the human organization that operates it. The specification of quality and availability in a service relationship may range from a best effort, as is the case in Internet service provision, to strict requirements on availability and quality associated with the universal provision of an emergency voice service.

Online Market Research

Market research is an important tool for any organization seeking a commercial opportunity, particularly for small firms looking to grow their business. From discovering a gap in the market to ensuring customer satisfaction and planning effective marketing campaigns, research can provide the market intelligence needed to encourage success, enhance competitiveness and maximize profits. An increasingly popular way to undertake market research is to conduct surveys via the internet. The continuing growth in on-line technology has had a positive impact on market research, offering clients a fast and cost effective method for researchers to reach their target audiences.

Currently, on-line research is an area of the industry that is still in its infancy - internet surveys represent less than five per cent of the value of research conducted in the UK. However, it is a market which is steadily growing and has already proved highly effective in certain instances; most specifically with conducting research into websites.

According to Richard Windle, spokesperson for The Market Research Society, "Internet research offers many opportunities, most of which are currently unexplored. This is an exciting time for companies to consider the possibility of on-line surveys and a definite growth area for the future.

Advantages

There are a number of benefits to commissioning market research on-line, including:

- The fact that large numbers of respondents can be surveyed at one time
- International boundaries no longer need to be an obstacle to research - worldwide

surveys can be conducted at the click of a button

- It can be an inexpensive way to conduct large surveys - it is possible to get thousands of responses for just a few thousand pounds
- Pre-screened panels. Most large agencies have access panels which provide an easily accessible, reliable respondent base which can respond promptly to on-line questionnaires
- It allows for a very rapid turnaround – research can be undertaken and results received
- with in a few days.

For a business which needs to gain a general view from a large cross-section of the population, and in as short a time as possible, there is no doubt that on-line research offers a viable benefit.

Commissioning an on-line survey

As with any other form of market research, there are certain guidelines which companies are advised to follow when commissioning on-line research. Three key considerations are:

• Provide the researcher with a detailed brief. It is essential that both parties understand exactly what you are hoping to achieve from the survey to avoid confusion and disappointment later on

• Focus on the important issues. Is getting your results quickly more important than gaining in depth information? Decide what is most important to you

• Make certain that the researcher has the necessary resources to interview a representative sample. This is essential for achieving accurate results. There is a concern that internet surveys could allow for greater levels of deception from respondents. Pre-screened access panels greatly reduce this risk and allow agencies fast access to a representative audience

A word of warning

Despite its convenience, electronic research should not be undertaken lightly, nor should it be regarded as a substitute for traditional research methods. On-line research has limitations which need to be considered from the outset. It may be that, in some instances, these outweigh the benefits. These include:

• DIY surveys (where the clients put the questions directly to the respondent without a researcher as an intermediary) compromise objectivity of questioning and impartial interpretation.

• The fact that the internet is a limited medium from which to draw a truly representative sample. Research conducted via internet surveys can only target internet users and, more specifically, it can only target internet users who are prepared to answer on-line questionnaires – currently still a small percentage of the population

• While suitable for quantitative surveys, currently electronic surveys provide partial accurate qualitative information as on-line focus groups are difficult to run and stimulate limited true group debate

• Electronic research is still relatively uncharted territory. There is limited guidance governing the practice of internet research, although The Market Research Society has drafted some guidelines

These considerations are not intended to denigrate the valuable role electronic research has to play in today's fast-paced business environment. If a business opts for an on-line survey then the research should be undertaken with the same degree of responsibility that would accompany a more traditional method of market research. For instance, the respondent interface must be designed with social expertise and sensitivity to the technology users; the questions should be meticulously planned to minimize misinterpretation; and care should be taken that the right audience is targeted.

Combining research techniques

Although the potential for higher speed and lower costs involved in on-line research make it an attractive method for interviewing a large sample of people, care should be taken that over reliance on electronic interfaces does not allow your business to lose its human touch. With online research, possibly more than with any other variety, there is a strong need for creativity. Grafting old ways onto new technologies will not assist the development of on-line research and will result in the internet losing its value to businesses as a research tool. Companies looking to take advantage of the benefits that new technology allows must ensure that they are pushing for the highest professional standards and constantly challenging the norm. Potentially, the most valuable use of on-line research is in conjunction with a more traditional form of market research, whether it be quantitative or qualitative. Completing a questionnaire on the internet could be offered as an alternative to a telephone or postal questionnaire. Alternatively, a business can conduct a broad-brush electronic survey, and follow up the outcome with more targeted, personal interviews. One result of the advent of on-line research is clear – market research is now accessible to most businesses and provides them with yet another route for seeking the opinions of their customers.

Richard Windle concluded, "Internet surveys are one of the most exciting new techniques to be introduced into the market research mix in recent years. How they will progress is uncharted territory. Currently, on-line research rarely replaces traditional techniques, but in many instances it can be considered a useful component of a research project."

Online market research

The importance of online methods has increased significantly in recent years within the spectrum of methodological approaches for market and organizational research.

In many cases, these methods offer advantages in terms of time, organizational expenditure and cost-effectiveness. For a range of content queries, they have already become the 'method of choice'. Online methods open up a multitude of - sometimes totally new - approaches and research options. Even so, psychonomics applies the same strict quality standards for online methods as for 'offline' methods.

Online research poses high demands in terms of implementation and application of the study objectives that have been set, which is, among other things, due to the fact that this type of research relies on technology-based access routes to the internet or to intranets. Some of the tasks in this context are, for example, the qualified selection of samples, the specific choice of online tools, a stable technological implementation, as well as determining the relationship to other research methods and their respective results.

Psychonomics has many years of solid experience and highly qualified staff specializing in online methods for market and organizational research. Our particular strength lies in methodologically linking 'online' and 'offline' together.

In the following, you will find a summary of methods we frequently use. We develop further methodological approaches and their specific details as part of the project, based on the concrete objectives and framework factors of our clients and guided by principles of cost-effectiveness.

In-depth advice on methodological approaches for our clients is part of the basic service we provide with every online research project:

- method-based consulting for online market research
- online feedback system
- usability tests
- website tests
- online focus groups
- interviews in the online access panel
- online interviews

Method-based consulting for online market research

Research methods via internet or intranet have gained an independent significance for psychonomics over the past few years. With the diverse and new possible fields of application of the Internet as a research medium there are, however, also risks and possible failures. Hastily put-together online questionnaires or self-selected random tests are hardly likely to build a confident basis for making sound decisions based on the results. For psychonomics the same quality standards apply for online and offline market research (link to the ADM online guidelines).

We advise our customers on all questions and options regarding online methods. If requested, our online specialists provide in-house training for market research and marketing departments.

Qualitative or quantitative

On the Internet too, the choice of a research method should be dependent on the questions relevant to an individual project.

Are you interested in a broad analysis of possible opinions and views on a particular question ("psychological representativity")? Do you want weak points and pitfalls in your online offer to be made visible in a detailed way? In these cases, we could help you using qualitative research approaches.

Do you require known cohesions and chains of cause and effect to be underpinned by statistical procedures? Do you need standardized comparison values ("benchmarks") for evaluation of your interview results in comparison with competitors? Then quantitative methods of online research are suitable for you.

For qualitative as well as quantitative methods of online market research, psychonomics has solid experience and highly qualified employees available.

For recruitment there are no central lists available on the Internet. Often, participants in online interviews are thus invited on to your homepage using advertising banners. This can however lead to distortion of the results through self-selection, because experience has shown that people with a high interest in the subject of the interview in random tests are overly represented in this form of recruitment. We would be glad to explain some possible methodological counter-measures for random test selections (e.g. x-th visit methods, interview on our online access panel) in order to guarantee optimal random test quality on the Internet as well.

Online market research useful

Market research about the Internet can, but does not necessarily also have to take place on the Internet. Traditional offline methods (e. g. interviews in a test studio) can be also used for analysis of related questions and cohesions.

We use offline methods in Internet market research, amongst others

Within the framework of website evaluation, for example as a part of qualitative usability tests or biotic interviews, for qualitative research about general Internet related topics (e.g. acceptance of new product ideas, use of new technologies)

Online surveys that are conducted entirely over the Internet (e. g. online focus groups or online interviews) are especially useful

- If you want to organize a survey especially quickly
- If the target group in which you are interested is difficult to recruit offline (e. g. users of a specific Internet site)
- If a media break is to be avoided when dealing with Internet-specific questions
- If a high value is to be placed on creating an interview situation that is especially close to reality.

Online feedback system

Gaining users of your company's Internet offer and then retaining them in the long-term is an important marketing task for many of today's companies. In order to incite users to visit the company's website, it is a good idea to install interactive feedback systems, amongst other things. Besides the general goal of "traffic" generation on the company's homepage (maybe even as part of a widespread PR campaign) such systems offer further advantages: increase of the "fun factor" without drifting too far from the general content of the website. The online offer remains in harmony with the rest.

Interactive feedback systems can also be used for personalizing the Internet presence, for example, by referring the individual customer types who have completed the online questionnaire to different pages (e.g. price-conscious users to a page with special offers, etc.) As a so-called "by-product", information on the psychological profile of the website users is thus also generated.

Exp: of an entertainment offering that additionally generates concrete market research results ("infotainment") is the implementation of empirically developed customer typologies in an Internet interview. For this purpose an online questionnaire is programmed which contains questions that have proven to be especially selective in segmenting customers. Following the interview the corresponding customer type is calculated automatically and a corresponding feedback text is generated for the user. Psychonomics has the necessary tools available in order to transform offline typologies into an online offer within a relatively short time.

Qualitative development of psychological market segments and/or customer typologies (e. g. within the framework of depth interviews or group discussions), Statistical underpinning of types and identification of specially selective items via a quantitative survey. Programming of an online questionnaire, either as Java or HTML/PHP3-version, if requested, adjustment to the website layout of the customer. The customer puts a link onto his/her own Internet site that links to the page with the online questionnaire. Interested participants go to this if needed, password protected–Internet page and can fill in their answers to the questions online after the interview, the input data is collected in an online database. A psychological report for their particular type is calculated and then presented to the interviewees interactively.

Depending on customer type, the participants will then be referred on to different pages (e. g. price-sensitive users to a page with special offers) customers can get information about intermediate results online usability tests.

The psychonomics Usability Test is a procedure which we use to check the functionality and psychological quality markers of Internet offers. Here, the central question is to what extent the online offer to be evaluated fulfils defined usability targets effectively and efficiently. psychonomics differentiates here between two central usability dimensions:

• "Usability" in the narrower sense covers the aspect of technical-navigational functionality, for example the absence of programming failures and/or smooth user handling within the online offer.

• By "likeability" we understand the psychological incentive value of the offer. Here, the aspects of information, design and harmony (congruence, consistency) are of prime importance.

The core idea behind the psychonomics Usability test is creating a test situation which is everyday and close to real experience: The participants test and evaluate the offer as far as possible in their own familiar surfing surroundings (which means ideally at their own PC) and are not influenced by the interviewer or other users, because weaknesses in the offer often show up only when the user is denied the opportunity to ask questions or receive external support.

Usability tests are basically suitable for all questions with regard to Internet offers, and cover a wide spectrum of procedures. We would gladly advise you on which quantitative or qualitative procedures are most suitable for your particular goals. The exact time when the test is to be carried out is especially important:

- Do you need to test a completely new offer thoroughly before the start? You should run a qualitative pre-study in that case.
- Do you plan on restructuring and re launching an existing website? Again, we would recommend a combination of qualitative and quantitative analysis.
- Does your existing offer merely need a facelift? In this case, a purely quantitative survey may be sufficient.

Psychonomics' usability tests deal with navigational functionality as well as the concrete experiences and motivations of the individual online user. Within the framework of comprehensive usability engineering, we will gladly advise you throughout the whole process of conception, development, analysis and implementation of your existing or planned Internet offers.

Preparation of measuring tools and target sizes in close consultation with the client

Agreement of testing procedures and thorough methodological consulting recruitment in line with the agreed target group criteria when recruiting offline, psychonomics works onsite using its own panel. For non-local interviews we work together with local recruitment offices and test studios.

In addition, we offer the use of the psychonomics online panel, especially if you need to recruit users of specific online offers (e. g. competitors' websites) carrying out of usability tests. The budget required for a company's web presence, if it wants to leave more than just its business card behind on the Internet, can quickly climb into the 6-digit-plus area. Despite this, many Internet presences do not live up to the user's quality demands: there are often serious flaws in the navigation, you do not find your way around, get frustrated and quit. But the search for information and opportunities for interaction can also end in dissatisfaction for many users. Or the website may not be able to get across what the company's core competencies are. Thus, the website does not live up to its aims and just gets used a stepping-stone to competitors' sites – because on the Internet these are just one click away.

A new core competency on the Internet therefore has to be a high level of acceptance and user-friendliness for each website. This should be checked directly from the users' point of view. Various studies have shown, for example that shortcomings on a website will drastically minimize sales opportunities.

But even without direct sales via Internet a defective Internet presence leads to communication barriers and in the end also damages the company image due to negative experiences the user has gained there.

psychonomics supports you in consistently analyzing and controlling your Internet presence and web offers in a user-oriented way. To do this, we draw on our solid experience and methodological know-how in the area of website testing.

psychonomics offers you two different forms of website tests:

• As a standardized and benchmark-orientated website testing tool: sitecockpit

• As individual solution: company-specific developed website tests

The aim of both procedures is to optimize your websites in a user and customer-focused way.

• Which questions are suitable for website tests?

• How does the website as a whole affect the user?

• How does the user judge the way s/he is dealt with?

• How are the information and services offered perceived?

• Where are the concrete strengths and weaknesses compared to your competitors?

• Does the Internet presence fit the image of the company?

• Will the desired targets be reached?

• Where are the starting points for optimizing and further developing the website?

Standardized and scientifically based: sitecockpit

In order to check usability and acceptance of Internet presences in a standardized way, psychonomics has developed sitecockpit, a methodologically reliable website testing tool with differentiated content. sitecockpit shows up important deficiencies and weak points versus important competitors, but it also points out strengths so that the concrete need for action can be derived from it in a differentiated way. sitecockpit guarantees internal sector and overlapping sector comparisons – according to the motto "learn from the best". Furthermore, special add-on modules can be added for different sectors and website types if required.

Advantages of website tests using sitecockpit

Standardized and scientifically based tool

Testing directly from users' point of view: how does the user – and not the expert or designer perceive the website?

Benchmarking on the basis of a comparison database (sector-specific or overlapping)

Testing of design, functionality and psychological effect of your website

Differentiated measurement of targets, dimensions and concrete qualities:

• Results for agencies and decision-makers

• Online reporting

• Pointers for action: The results point out strengths and weaknesses in a targeted way and offer concrete starting points for optimization

For specialized issues: Website tests specifically developed for your company

For very specialized questions about acceptance and usability, psychonomics develops individualized website testing tools for its clients. If you are, for instance, planning

an ongoing evaluation process for your web presence or you want to follow up individual questions regarding user-friendliness or user behaviour, we recommend using a testing tool that is tailored specifically for your company's needs.

Advantages of website tests specifically developed for companies

Together with you we discuss starting point, questions and aims
We advise you on the most suitable testing tool and relevant methodology
We carry out the testing of your website:

• Interview on your website via "x-th visit" method

• Online studio tests

• Online access panel interview of special target groups

• You receive the results in the form of an online reporting system

If requested, we generate a management summary with action recommendations and present the results to your company

Online focus groups represent an innovative and efficient possibility in terms of organising group discussions on the Internet. Instead of meeting in test studios, participants of online focus groups meet in a virtual test studio. Specially trained psychologists act as online moderators. The test persons can participate in the discussion directly from their own PC. The online discussion process is recorded and can be evaluated directly after the end of the interview.

Advantages of online focus groups

• Can be carried out rapidly and independently of location

• Automatic logging

• Reaching of specific target groups that are difficult to recruit offline

• Evaluation of online offers in real situations

We expect socially approved response behavior to be reduced on the Internet due to the anticipated anonymity of the medium. Through the possibility of passing on multimedia material (images, animation, etc.) online focus groups take on a more "creative" and therefore specially motivating character. Spatial separation of the participants allows for the presentation of stimulus material to isolated members of the group at first as a test.

Online interviews are suitable for the following topics:

Interviewing members of existing online communities

Evaluation of online offers in the form of a brief highlighting of specific strengths and weaknesses image and brand positioning on the Internet customer satisfaction, customer behavior and customer loyalty on the Internet market potentials and product innovations on the Internet joint interviews of participants with very different regional origins (e.g. within the framework of international expert groups).

We recruit participants in accordance with the agreed target group criteria. For recruiting online focus groups we offer you for example the use of our online panel. The discussion is recorded automatically and is made available to you right after the end of the discussion as a text file, if requested, individual protocols can be created and carefully evaluated for each discussion that has taken place within the framework of a study the results will be summarized in a chart report and presented to our customer

Interviews in the online access panel

Before online interviews and/or online focus groups are conducted on the Internet there is often the question of how Internet users can be recruited. In contrast to phone books or postal address lists there is still no central register of e-mail addresses on the Internet that could be used for the selection of online random tests. As a short-cut, we can use centrally maintained pools of interview-willing Internet users ("Online-Access-Panels"). Similar to traditional offline panels, the panel lists are available for ad hoc interviews as well as for longitudinal interviews.

Advantages of online panel interviews

Through the prior determination of core background variables ("master data") it is possible to select targeted samples from the address pool. The master data can thus be passed on as additional information for the interview or used for quotas and/or weighting of the sample.

Interviews in the panel also have the advantage that the participants can be invited directly to attend individual interviews after registration. Distortions due to self-selection (e. g. participation due to individual interest in the interview topic) can be minimized in this way.

Multiple participation in surveys can be controlled for panel surveys. Since only a certain number of panellists are invited for interviews the field time is also normally reduced compared to the purely "click-me" surveys.

Within the framework of various cooperative partnerships psychonomics is currently able to draw on two different online access panels:

ePanel: approx. 19,000 online-recruited interview-willing Internet users in Germany and approx. 30,000 e-mail addresses worldwide. The ePanel is continuously expanded and to include offline-recruited test persons.

imafo-panel: Address pool with exclusively offline-recruited Internet users in Germany. In parallel to offline-recruiting, an online-recruited panel is currently being set up.

Both panels are suitable for recruitment of different survey types:

The ePanel is especially suitable for ad hoc interviews, experimental designs (e. g. testing logos or names) and for recruitment of online focus groups. Selection of representative random test samples is not possible since the panel registration has no default random selection. In the ePanel experienced online users are overly represented due to online registration.

These disadvantages are avoided in the imafo-panel. Basis of registration here is a representative offline sample. The imafo-panel aims to create a representative illustration of Internet users. Via the offline-recruiting it is guaranteed that people with less user experience stand the same chance of getting into the panel as experienced "heavy users". The imafo-panel is run by imafo GmbH, a subsidiary of psychonomics AG.

Offline recruiting of panellists (with imafo-panel) and/or registration of interview-willing Internet users via an online form (with ePanel). Sample-screening according to pre-set data. Recruiting in the online-panel is especially suitable for online interviews and online focus groups, but also for recruitment of special target groups for biotic interviews or usability tests. Sending of invitation e-mails to panellists that fulfill the screening requirements. Depending on complexity and topic, the participants are incentives by a lottery system.

In the invitation e-mail the panelists will find a link that will refer them to the Internet page with the online questionnaire. During the recruitment for online focus groups or offline methods, the link refers to a page where the panellist can sign up for participation at a certain date.

Slowed reflux, non-participation or the indication of data of dubious quality will be registered for every panellist. This way, interviewees with low participation motivation or who raise suspicion of wilful fraud will be directly excluded from later interviews.

Online interviews

The significance of online research is growing steadily. For 2005 the share of online market research in total market research is estimated at approx. 30%. Even though prognoses should always be considered in a thorough and critical way, the increasingly widespread acceptance of Internet-based forms of enquiry is clear. Online methods are not suitable for every question, but in many cases they can deliver efficient and reliable results. Psychologies advises and supports you in carrying out sound research.

Advantages of online interviews

- Quick and easy allocation of questionnaires; low costs for questionnaire distribution and data surveys
- Data are immediately available as coded dataset
- Reaching specific target groups that are difficult to recruit offline
- Evaluation of online offers in a realistic situation
- Possibility of using multimedia in the interview tool
- Possibility of direct online feedback for the interviewees
- Possibility of passing on background data quickly
- Client can get information on interview reflux and intermediate results online
- Comparatively easy carrying out and implementation of international studies
- Possibility of adaptive testing via programmed filter settings

Online interviews are for example suitable for the following topics:

- Website tests, evaluation of online offers
- Online experiments in order to test various versions and/or requirements (e.g. logo or name test, acceptance tests)
- Image and brand positioning
- Online feedback systems
- Customer satisfaction, customer behavior and customer loyalty
- Concept tests
- Employee interviews (also on the intranet)
- Advertising effectiveness research
- General studies on user behavior
- Surveys on general topics as long as the target group can be reached especially effectively on the Internet

We recruit the participants in line with the agreed target group criteria

During recruitment various forms of making contact are possible, e.g.: "xth visitor method," which means every xth time someone accesses your homepage (or leaves your homepage) a pop-up window opens with an invitation for an interview, or existing address lists, e.g. customer files, recruiting from our online panels, and in individual cases even a "click-me interview" can be of use; this is a link on your homepage which links to the online interview)

Market Making

Market maker

A brokerage or bank that maintains a firm bid and ask price in a given security by standing ready, willing, and able to buy or sell at publicly quoted prices (called making a market). These firms display bid and offer prices for specific numbers of specific securities, and if these prices are met, they will immediately buy for or sell from their own accounts. Market makers are very important for maintaining liquidity and efficiency for the particular securities that they make markets in. At most firms, there is a strict separation of the market-making side and the brokerage side, since otherwise there might be an incentive for brokers to recommend securities simply because the firm makes a market in that security.

You probably take for granted that you can buy or sell a stock at a moment's notice. Place an order with your broker, and within seconds, it is executed. Have you ever stopped to wonder how this is possible? Whenever an investment is bought or sold, there must be someone on the other end of the transaction. If you wanted to buy 1,000 shares of Disney, you must find a willing seller, and visa versa. It's very unlikely you are always going to find someone who is interested in buying or selling the exact number of shares of the same company at the exact same time.

A **market maker** is a bank or brokerage company that stands ready every second of the trading day with a firm ask and bid price. This is good for you, because when you place an order to sell your thousand shares of Disney, the market maker will actually purchase the stock from you, even if he doesn't have a seller lined up. In doing so, they are literally "making a market" for the stock.

Market Makers must be compensated for the risk they take; what if he buys your shares in IBM then IBM's stock price begins to fall before a willing buyer has purchased the shares? To prevent this, the market maker maintains a spread on each stock he covers. Using our previous example, the market maker may purchase your shares of IBM from you for $100 each (the ask price) and then offer to sell them to a buyer at $100.05 (bid). The difference between the ask and bid price is only $.05, but by trading millions of shares a day, he's managed to pocket a significant chunk of change to offset his risk.

A market maker's expected average costs increase with the size (absolute value) of his inventory position; the cost of financing inventory increases with its size. Further, in the case where the market maker faces increasing marginal financing cost, expected average costs increase with security price volatility. These costs, in equilibrium, must be covered out of the bid/ask spread. Consequently, the bid/ask spread varies directly with security price volatility and with the size of the market maker's trading inventory position. Since an increasingly turbulent asset market is characterized by imbalance of trading demand and supply and by increasing price volatility, this model suggests that (and provides an explanation why) such a market is likely to be accompanied by a deterioration in market liquidity.

When making application for listing, issuers must appoint an intermediary institution among the Market members as market maker and notify the ISE. The market maker is responsible for providing fair, organized and effective operation of the Market for the depositary receipt. The market maker encourages the constitution of a liquid and continuous market through quoting bids and asks for the relevant stock during the whole trading session.

General responsibilities of a market maker are:

- Keeping accurate and update accounts and data regarding the Market transactions,
- Employing fully-trained trading floor personnel and supervising the operational effectiveness and professionalism of those on the trading floor as well as taking all the necessary measures in order to promote such qualities,
- Providing necessary collateral in compliance with the ISE regulations.

Operational responsibilities of a market maker are:

- To make transactions on its own account and behalf,
- To give bid and ask quotations on a continuous basis,
- To maintain price continuity at an adequate depth,
- To minimize bid and ask order imbalances,
- To minimize price changes across transactions and maximize trade volume,
- To establish an orderly and fair market.

Appointment of a Market Maker

It is the issuer and market maker's choice to enter into contractual relationships, since the Market Regulations do not require a written market making agreement between them. However, the issuer must notify the ISE in writing that an intermediary institution among the Market members has been appointed as market maker for the depositary receipt.

Introduction: Market Makers and Market Liquidity

Liquidity in a financial market:- the ability to absorb smoothly the flow of buying and selling orders comes from two principal sources: from the depth of buyers and sellers in the market and from the actions of market makers (specialists on the organized exchanges). The market makers' business is acting as intermediaries: buying from public sellers and selling to public buyers. The market maker provides market liquidity immediacy services and makes his profit from the difference between buying and selling (bid and ask) prices. One simple measure of the liquidity of a financial market at any moment is the bid/ask spread. Liquid markets will be characterized by a narrow spread, illiquid markets by a wide spread. This description applies both cross sectionally and over time. Reduced liquidity is signaled by a broadening of the bid/ask spread.

In actual markets, the behavior of the bid/ask spread varies with market conditions. Increasingly turbulent markets are accompanied by significant expansion of the bid/ask spread. In this paper we develop a simple model of market maker pricing that gives an elementary explanation of the variation in market liquidity with variation in market conditions. It derives the market maker's bid/ask spread as the result of the market maker's optimizing behavior. The bid/ask spread is the price of the market-maker's services. The market maker is characterized as a monopolistic competitor, a profit maximizer subject to an (average) zero-profit condition due to the threat of entry. The market maker borrows capital on a perfect (or slightly imperfect) capital market; he faces constant (or increasing) marginal interest rates as his debt position increases.

The principal results of this model then are that the bid/ask spread is an increasing function of two variables: the size of the market maker's net long or short position and (in the case of increasing marginal cost) market price volatility. Both of these variables increase the market maker's average cost of making a market. Hence they are priced in the bid/ask spread.

A distinctive element of the treatment presented here is the simplicity of the market maker's problem. He acts primarily as a reseller of a good subject to the risk of price variability. We purposefully ignore the issues of differential information (informed versus uninformed traders) not because we regard them as unimportant but rather that they may be independent of the volume and volatility considerations (particularly for the market as a whole) that the present study emphasizes. We suppose the market maker to be risk neutral; he needs no attitude toward risk to determine a bid/ask spread. We consider two cases, first where the capital market is default risk averse and second where the capital market is default risk neutral. In both cases, the bigger the inventory of the market maker, then the higher will be the average capital cost, and the wider will be the bid/ask spread. In the second case, where the capital market is risk averse, the market maker faces an increasing interest rate to finance inventory as his exposure to market risk increases. Therefore, increasing price risk also increases the market maker's average cost, and that cost is priced in the bid/ask spread. The model hence provides a particularly simple explanation for declining market liquidity during periods of large price movements and trading imbalances.

This essay differs from these papers as our market makers neither target a desired inventory position nor receive utility from the value of their inventories. The market makers in our model can always liquidate their long positions at the market bid price (or close out their short positions at the market ask price). Inventory enters their choices of bid/ask spreads mainly because the costs of carrying the inventory need to be covered by the revenues from making the market under the equilibrium condition of expected zero profit.

It is common in the literature to characterize the market maker as setting a bid and an ask price in level terms. The treatment here simplifies the bid/ask spread decision to choosing a percentage of the prevailing asset price.

Modeling the Market Maker

We consider the market maker for a single security whose price at date t is denoted Pt. The evolution of price over time is exogenous. The market maker sets a symmetric proportional spread St at date t representing his price markup for the ask price and the markdown for the bid price. At date t, he faces a (long, buying) demand volume V *l* t and a (short, selling) supply volume V s t . The market presents the market-maker with demand for securities V *l* t , that the market-maker provides. The market presents the market maker with supplies of the security V s t that the market maker purchases. The market maker's position (net holding) of the security may be positive or negative. At the start of date t, we denote the position as Nt. The market maker's position in the security evolves over time. At t+1, 2 By focusing on both bid and ask prices, the study tries to solve two problems in one shot: one is the determination of security price, and the other is the determination of the price of the market maker's service – the bid/ask spread. Our model, by using the percentage bid/ask spread, separates the two issues and focuses only on the latter, which allows us to simplify the model greatly and thus gain useful insight on the role of inventory.

Intelligent Market-Making in Artificial Financial Markets

The Problem: Market-makers serve important functions in financial markets, providing liquidity to the markets and immediacy to the execution of trades. We are designing algorithms for automated market-making in different market conditions such as competitive vs. monopolistic dealer markets and studying outcomes in terms of indicators of market quality such as the bid–ask spread.

Motivation: Progress in machine learning techniques has led to the development of various techniques well suited to online estimation and rapid aggregation of information. Theoretical models of market-making have led to price-setting equations for which solutions cannot be achieved in practice, whereas empirical work on algorithms for market-making has so far focused on sets of heuristics and rules that lack theoretical justification. We are developing algorithms that are theoretically justified by results in finance, and at the same time exiles enough to be easily extended by incorporating modules for dealing with considerations like portfolio risk and competition from other market-makers.

Previous Work: Previous research at CBCL on market-making has focused on heuristics that use the limit-order book to set prices and on reinforcement learning for market-making in very simple environments. Our work draws heavily on the market-microstructure literature, especially the price competition between market-makers. Some simulations of the NASDAQ stock market have been setting equations derived by Glosten and Milgrom under conditions of information asymmetry and perfect carried out, but none of them have focused on market-maker behavior or on adaptive agents.

Approach: We are developing a market model loosely based on standard models of informed traders who trade based on their perception of the true or fundamental value of a stock, and uninformed or liquidity traders who add noise to the market. Under these conditions of information asymmetry, the market-maker attempts to track the fundamental value of the stock by maintaining an online probability density estimate based on the orders it receives. In addition, the market-making algorithm can be extended by controlling inventory and increasing or decreasing the spread in response to competition. Results indicate that the algorithms are very successful in tracking the true value, making profit while maintaining a small bid-ask spread and also respond as expected to market conditions (by, for example, increasing the spread in more volatile market conditions) in the stylized market models we consider [5]. See figure 1 for results on tracking of the fundamental value using our density estimation technique and examples of profits obtained in different market conditions.

Impact: This research will provide insight into the dynamics of financial markets with liquidity provided by the presence of market makers. Also, simulating markets with electronic market makers allows one to determine the effects of various structural and regulation changes to markets without the expense of experimenting in a real market. This research is also an important application of machine learning techniques like nonparametric density estimation and online estimation. The fact that we can set prices by approximately solving equations for which closed form solutions may not exist demonstrates that computational methods have important applicability in both theoretical and practical financial market domains.

Market making is an important institutional activity in financial markets. However, there is a wide gap between the theoretical work on optimal market making and how market makers actually set prices and execute orders in practice. Over the last few years, computational methods to bridge the gap between theory and practice have become more popular, and we hope that simulations of markets will yield insights into the behavior of real markets and their connection to simpler, stylized models.

Future Work: We are working on several extensions to the market-making algorithm based on machine learning. For example, we are trying to add modules for predicting price jumps and for raising and lowering the spread in response to competition in an automated manner. In addition, we are interested in extending our model of market-making to richer, more complex market models.

8

Cyber Law

Introduction

The Information Technology Act, 2000 was enacted by the Indian Parliament in June, 2000. It was notified for implementation in October, 2000 with the issuance of Rules under the Act. The purpose of the Act is to promote the use of digital signatures for the growth of E-Commerce and E-Governance. It provides legal recognition to electronic records, and puts digital signatures at par with handwritten signatures. The Act defines the legal and administrative framework for the creation of Public Key Infrastructure (PKI) in the country to generate trust in electronic environment. To help establish PKI in the country and ensure interoperability among all Certifying Authorities, technical standards have been framed in Rules and Regulations under the Act. Electronic authentication of individuals, businesses and other entities, as also secure communication of messages over the Internet and any open networks are the aims of the PKI. The Controller of Certifying Authorities (CCA) has been appointed by the Central Government under section 17 of the Act for purposes of the IT Act. The Office of the CCA came into existence on November 1, 2000. It aims at promoting the growth of E-Commerce and E-Governance through the wide use of digital signatures.

The CCA has to license Certifying Authorities (CAs) and exercise supervision over their activities. It is required to certify the public keys of the CAs, as also lay down the standards to be maintained by the CAs, and perform several other functions under section 18 of the Act to regulate the functioning of CAs in the country. It is also required to issue licences to CAs by signing/certifying their public keys, i.e. signing their Digital Signature Certificates more commonly known as Public Key Certificates (PKCs). The Certification Practice Statement (CPS) of the Controller of Certifying Authorities has been prepared to address the issues related to the licensing process and other relevant topics such as certificate policy, issuance and cancellation of licences, security control and operational policy & procedures and other matters relevant to obligations and responsibilities of the CCA and CAs in accordance with the IT Act, Rules and Regulations.

This CPS uses certain expressions. These are given below. Their definitions are as given in **the IT Act, Rules and Regulations:**

Licensed Certifying Authority (CA): means a person or organization who has been granted a Licence to issue Digital Signature Certificates under Section 24 of the IT Act, 2000.

Information Technology Act, 2000 (IT Act, 2000): means the Act to provide legal recognition for transactions carried out by means of electronic data interchange and other means of electronic communication, commonly referred to as "electronic commerce" which involve the use of alternatives to paper based methods of communication and storage of information, to facilitate electronic filing of documents with the Government agencies.

National Repository of Digital Certificates (NRDC): means the repository of all Digital Signature Certificates issued under the IT Act, 2000.

Root Certifying Authority of India (RCAI) is the Root CA operated by the CCA that certifies the public keys of all CAs in India.

Certification Practice Statement (CPS): means the statement issued by a Certifying Authority to specify the practices that the Certifying Authority employs in issuing Digital Signature Certificates, in accordance with the Guideline No. 1(6)/2001-CCA dated July 9, 2001.

Controller: means the Controller of Certifying Authorities appointed under sub-section (1) of section 17 of the IT Act, 2000.

Office of Controller of Certifying Authorities (CCA): means the Office of the Controller appointed under section 17(1) of the IT Act, 2000.

Cyber Appellate Tribunal: means the Cyber Regulation Appellate Tribunal established under sub-section (1) of section 48 of IT Act, 2000.

Digital Signature: means authentication of any electronic record by a subscriber by means of an electronic method or procedure in accordance with the provisions of section 3 of the IT Act, 2000.

Digital Signature Certificate (DSC): means a Digital Signature Certificate issued under sub-section (4) of section 35 of the IT Act, 2000.

Licence: means a Licence granted to a Certifying Authority under section 24 of the IT Act, 2000.

Overview

This CPS provides information that describes the practices employed by the Controller of Certifying Authorities in operating the RCAI and NRDC services.

The RCAI is responsible for:

- Issue of Licence by means of an X.509 certificate
- Digitally signing the public key of the Licensed CA
- Generating CRLs for the licences issued

The NRDC is responsible for:

- Publishing digital signature certificates and CRLs issued by the RCAI
- Publishing digital signature certificates and CRLs of subscribers issued by all Licensed CAs

The CCA issues Licences to Certifying Authorities under section 24 of the IT Act, after duly processing their applications as provided for under the Act. This process includes examining the application and accompanying documents as provided for in sections 21 to 24 of the IT Act, and all the Rules and Regulations there under; approving the CPS; auditing the physical and technical infrastructure of the applicants through a panel of auditors maintained by the CCA. The CCA can suspend or revoke Licences in accordance with the provisions of sections 25 and 26 of the IT Act. The CCA also approves changes in the CPS, if any, of the CAs. CCA also receives the periodic audit reports from all the Licensed CAs, and proposes action as provided for under section 18 of the IT Act and Rule 31 of the Rules under the Act. The CCA operates the RCAI under section 18(b) and NRDC under section 20 of the IT Act.

The structure of this CPS is based on the Internet X.509 PKI Certificate Policy and Certificate Practice Framework (RFC 2529) circulated by the CCA as part of its Guidelines issued on 9 July, 2001 vide No. 1(6)/2001-CCA. This CPS covers the practices followed by the CCA for the procedures related to the Licence/certificate application, issuance, use, validation, suspension, revocation and their expiry, as well as the operational maintenance of the RCAI and NRDC. This CPS is referred to as the "Root Certifying Authority of India CPS". All documents issued by the CCA including the CPS.

This CPS is subject to a regular review process that strives to take into consideration developments in international PKI standardization initiatives, development in technology and information security, as well as other relevant issues.

Identification

This document is the Certification Practice Statement of the Root Certifying Authority of India. RCAI has assigned following OID to this document.

RCAI will also issue OIDs to licensed CAs. The CAs will then choose to assign OIDs for different purposes under this scheme.

Joint – ISO – ITU-T Assigned Country Code : India	2.16.356
CCA	100
CPS	2

Community and Applicability

The CCA PKI community comprises all the Licensed CAs and their subscribers. The Licensed CAs are issued certificates digitally signed by the RCAI of the CCA and hence specifically this CPS shall apply to all the Licensed CAs. At the apex level, the Department of Information Technology and the CCA are also members of this PKI community. CCA, through its RCAI and NRDC, is at the hub of trust in electronic environment.

Ministry of Communications and Information Technology

The Ministry of Communications and Information Technology is the ministry of the Government of India under whose administrative control the office of the CCA functions. This ministry is responsible for policy on E-Commerce and E-Governance, as also on the IT Act in particular and cyber laws in general. It is also responsible for certain practices and procedures, and standards under the IT Act.

Controller of Certifying Authorities

The CCA regulates the CAs in the country under various sections of the IT Act. It discharges its responsibilities in the PKI regime in the country. Towards this end, it operates the RCAI and NRDC. The following acts are performed by the CCA:

- It follows procedures and norms laid down under the Act to issue a licence to a CA.
- It operates the RCAI to certify the public keys of CAs by digitally signing them thereby making available their licences in the electronic world for verification by any user.
- It operates the NRDC containing all the PKCs and CRLs issued by all the CAs in the country.
- It ensures that alternate mechanisms are put in place for a CA whose certificate/licence has been revoked by it.
- It maintains a Panel of Auditors.
- It arranges audit for first time CA Applicant.
- It receives periodic audit report from CAs.
- It provides date and time stamping for all the certificates issued by it.
- It maintains database of CAs.
- It receives disclosure record of all CAs.
- It assigns unique OIDs to all entities in the PKI regime in the country.
- It organizes other digital signature certification related practices.

The CCA has constituted the following forums as advisory groups to advise it on PKI matters:

CA Technology Forum

Advisory forum of CA technology providers to advise the CCA on technology standards and other related issues of PKI
Advising on inter-operability issues for a successful PKI in the country

CA's Council

Discussions with the CAs operating in the country to resolve issues of concern to the CAs and users so as to ensure widespread use of digital signatures in the country.

DS User Forum

Discussions with the digital signature users at large to study their problems and difficulties concerning PKI and other implementation issues.
Formulate response for resolving them with CAs.

Legal Advisory Forum

Advise the CCA on legal issues concerned with the implementation of the IT Act, and any other issues such as the modifications of the Act so as to improve the PKI framework for facilitating the growth of E-Commerce and E-Governance.

Auditor's Panel

Discussions with the Auditor's Panel on a regular basis to maintain and augment audit standards to continuously improve the effectiveness of CAs.

RCAI

The CCA has established the RCAI under section 18(b) of the IT Act to digitally sign the public keys of CAs in the country. It operates RCAI as per the standards laid down under the Act. The requirements fulfilled by the RCAI include the following:

- The licence issued to the CA is digitally signed by the CCA.
- All public keys corresponding to the signing private keys of a CA are digitally signed by the CCA.
- That these keys are signed by the CCA can be verified by a relying party through the CCA's website or CA's own website.

The RCAI is operated using Smart Trust software. The authorized CCA personnel access the Administrator Workbench to initiate and perform Root CA functions. Where necessary, this CPS distinguishes the different users and roles accessing the Smart Trust software for Root CA functions. Where this distinction is not required, the term Root CA is used to refer to the total CA entity, including the software and its operations.

The RCAI root certificate is the highest level of certification in India. It is used to sign the public keys of the Licensed CAs in India. The RCAI root certificate is a self-signed certificate.

National Repository : NRDC

The CCA's repositories are as follows:

- National Repository of Digital Certificate
- Certificate Suspension and Revocation List

In accordance with Section 20 of the IT Act, all certificates and CRLs issued by all the licence CAs are contained in the NRDC. This also contains the certificates and CRLs issued by the CCA through its RCAI. Relying parties can verify the CA's public keys from the NRDC.

Licensed Certifying Authorities

A Certifying Authority (CA) can operate in the country after being duly licensed by the CCA as per provisions of the IT Act. It provides services to its subscribers and relying parties as per its CPS which is approved by the CCA as part of the licensing procedure. The licence of a CA can be suspended or revoked by the CCA as provided under section 25 of the IT Act. During the period of suspension, the said CA cannot operate as a CA.

A CA provides the following services:

- Identification and authentication
- Certificate issuance
- Certificate suspension and revocation
- Certificate renewal
- Notification of certificate-related information
- Display of all these on its website
- Time-stamping

In addition, the CA communicates to the CCA the following information as required under the IT Act:

- Any changes in its CPS
- Certificates issued by it to its subscribers
- CRLs issued by it
- Compromise of its private key under section 34 of IT Act
- Disclosure record under section 34 of the IT Act
- Periodic audit reports under Rule 31

End entities

The End entities of RCAI would be the Licensed CAs in India. However, the subscribers and relying parties who use the certificates issued by a CA need to be assured that the CA is licensed by the CCA. Relying Parties trust and use the certificates issued by a CA who has been licensed by the CCA. They should be able to verify the licence through an indicator to that effect in the PKCs issued by a CA. By viewing the PKC using any standard application, the relying party should be able to verify the CA Distinguished

Name and its public key as appearing in the Certificate as having been certified by the CCA.

Applicability

This CPS is applicable to all certificates issued by RCAI. The practices described in this CPS apply to the issuance and use of certificates and Certificate Revocation Lists (CRLs) for Licensed CAs within India.

Contact Details

Specification administration organization

The organization administering this CPS is the Controller of Certifying Authorities.

General Provisions

CCA Obligations

CCA obligations

RCAI shall

- Operate as an offline Root.
- Issue Licence in the form of a certificate to the CAs.
- Revoke licence on a valid request and update CRL within a maximum of 6 hours of the revocation.
- Issue and publish digital signature certificates for all keys used by Licenced CA and CRLs
- Provide accurate Information
- CA Licence information
- Suspension or revocation of a CA Licence
- Cancellation of a CA Licence
- Transfer or merger of a CA
- Suspension or revocation of a PKC
- Conduct signing operations only on working days. No signing operations will be carried out on Saturday, Sunday or public holidays.
- Shall neither send nor receive any encrypted communication.

The National Repository Obligations

The NRDC shall Ensure operation of 7 days a week, 24 hours a day access to the NRDC. Planned exceptions to the 24x7x365 availability will be notified on CCA's web site. These are:

- Monthly emergency power off tests
- Yearly business continuity test

CCA provides access to the NRDC, enabling subscribers and the relying parties to search CA's and end-users certificates, suspension and revocation list of certificates through information and communication networks.

CCA also maintains a separate directory which gives information on the licensed CAs and the revocation list i.e. the Authority Revocation List (ARL). The mechanisms for NRDC access include:

- X.500 Directory Server System that is accessible through the Lightweight Directory Access Protocol (LDAPV3)
- Availability of the information through the website of the CCA – cca.gov.in.
- Access control mechanisms when needed to protect repository information as described in later sections

Measures on Vulnerability of Private Key

CCA revokes its self-signed certificate when CCA recognizes that its private key has been compromised. It then creates a new key pair for signing, issues its self-signed certificate, and issues signed certificates for all the CAs using its new signing private key. CCA notifies this to all the CAs so as to enable them to guarantee the safety and trustworthiness in the management under this CPS.

CCA, when informed of the compromise or vulnerability of the private key of a CA, revokes the certificate issued to the CA and immediately notifies this through its ARL so as to enable everybody to be aware of the event under this CPS.

Licensed CA Obligations

A CA that has been issued a Licence by the CCA under the IT Act, 2000, to act as a CA, shall comply with the terms and conditions of the Licence set forth in the Regulations. The Licensed CA shall ensure compliance with its approved CPS.

Providing and Notifying Accurate Information

A Licensed CA has to notify its subscribers and the relying parties about the information as given below which can affect the trustworthiness or validity of a certificate in order to enable anybody confirm whether it is as per the provisions of the IT Act:

- CA Licence
- CPS of the CA, including changes
- Certificate suspension and revocation practice of CA
- Cancellation of CA Licence
- Transfer or merger of CA with another entity
- Information on a subscribers certificate
- Certificate suspension and revocation practice of a subscriber
- Disclosure record as required under Section 34 of IT Act, 2000
- Other certification practice related information.

Protecting Private Key

The Licensed CA must create its own key pair in a secure way using a trustworthy Hardware Security Module as stipulated in Regulations. It will manage its private key securely in accordance with the procedures mandated under the Act, Rules and Regulations. When creating a subscriber's key pair, on subscriber's request, a CA must create it in a secure way using a trustworthy software or hardware and distribute the private key securely to the subscriber. Upon request by a subscriber, a CA shall make available software for generation of his key pair at subscriber's end. (No trace of the private key would be available in Hardware or software of CA. The private key of the subscriber would not be known to the CA at any time).

Using a Certified Private Key

A CA shall use only those private keys in its operations, the public keys corresponding to which have been certified by the CCA.

Compromise of Private Key

As soon as a CA realizes that any of its private keys has been compromised, it shall immediately report the matter to the CCA, revoke the certificates issued with that key and update its CRL. It will suspend its self-signed certificate corresponding to that key pair. It shall securely generate another key pair, and get the public key certified by the CCA.

Subscriber Obligations

Subscribers who receive certificates from licensed CAs shall be required to comply with the requirements set forth in sections 40 to 42 of the IT Act, and the Rules there under.

Relying Party Obligations

This CPS does not specify what steps a relying party should take to determine whether to rely upon a certificate. The CCA, however, has mandated that the CAs shall make available their digital signature certificates that have been signed by the CCA for access by any relying party. They will also make available the tools necessary for performing the trust path creation, certificate mappings, for validation of their public keys with the help of public key of CCA by the relying parties. The CCA shall also enable PKCs of CAs that have been signed by it for access by any subscribers and relying parties.

In general, a Relying party has to understand the purpose of a certificate, its validity period, utilization range, use and trustworthiness prior to using the same. It has to ascertain from the CRLs that the certificate has not been revoked.

Liability

CA Liability

The Government of India disclaims any liability that may arise from use of any certificate issued by the CCA, or by the CCA's decision to revoke a certificate issued by it. In no event will the CCA or the Government of India be liable for any losses, including direct or indirect, incidental, consequential, special, or punitive damages, arising out of or relating to any certificate issued by the CCA.

The CCA, however, guarantees that the contents given below relevant to the Licence/certificate issued by it are correct.

The contents in the issued certificate are correct.

The certificate is issued under the IT Act.

The matters about suspension and revocation of certificate are correct.

The CCA has no responsibility for any delays or damages due to force majeure such as warfare or a natural disaster or reasons beyond provisions of the IT Act, the rule and regulations.

Financial responsibility

The CCA disclaims all liability due to the use of any certificates issued by the CCA which certify public keys of CAs.

Indemnification by relying parties

No Stipulation

Fiduciary Relationships

The CCA is not the agent, fiduciary, trustee or any other representative of any of the Licensed CAs and must not be represented by the Licensed CAs in that form. Licensed CAs have no authority to bind the CCA, by contract or otherwise of any obligation or financial implication.

Administrative processes

No Stipulation.

Interpretation and Enforcement

Governing Law

The Certification Practice Statement, relationship between CCA and Licensed CA and any other parties will be interpreted in accordance with the IT Act, 2000 and the relevant rules and regulations.

Dispute Resolution procedures

The CCA is competent under the IT Act, clause 18(l), to resolve any dispute between CAs and subscribers. However, Cyber Appellate Tribunal, under the IT Act, is the competent court to mediate a dispute arising out of any order of the CCA.

The CCA can mediate between CAs and subscribers directly or through an arbitrator. For this purpose he can request any information or materials from both the parties which are in order as per their CPS, and the provisions of the IT Act. It will be the endeavour of the CCA to facilitate the resolution of conflicts between CAs and subscribers that may arise as a result of the use of certificates.

Fees

Certificate Issuance or renewal fees

Certificate Issuance

CCA charges a fee of twenty five thousand rupees for issuance of a Licence/ certificate as per notified rules, regulations and guidelines. In case more than one public key is certified then the fees will be per PKC.

Certificate Renewal

An application for renewal of a Licence shall be in such form as may be prescribed by the Central Government and available on web site of CCA and shall be made not less than forty-five days before the date of expiry of the period of validity of the Licence. In case more than one public key is certified then the fees will be per PKC. CCA charges a fee of five thousand rupees for renewal of a licence/certificate as per notified rules, regulations, and guidelines.

Certificate Access Fee

CCA makes no charge to the relying party reading and confirming certificate

Revocation or status information access fees

CCA makes no charge to the relying party accessing the suspension and revocation list of certificates.

Fees for other services such as policy information

CCA can charge for printed documents, CD-ROMs etc., if required under the provisions of the IT Act.

Refund policy

Not Applicable

Publication and Repository

Publication of information on services offered by CCA

The CCA publishes following information to the repository and/or on its website. The repository is referred to as NRDC

- Digital self-signed CCA certificate of RCAI
- Digital Certificates of all Licensed CAs and of all the public keys used by them

• Digital Certificates of all subscribers

• Practices being followed in issuing / renewing / revoking / suspending the digital certificates

• List of invalid digital certificates (commonly known as Certificate Revocation Lists [CRLs])

Frequency of publication

Issued Certificates

The RCAI shall publish all certificates in the NRDC within one working day of the completion of the issuance of the certificate.

Revoked Certificates

The RCAI shall add revoked certificates originally certified by CCA to the relevant CRL on a daily/weekly basis on the completion of the revocation process.

Access controls

All users will be able to read the information published in the NRDC. Access controls declining write, modify or any other capability other than read shall be defined and managed by the RCAI.

Repositories

The CCA shall maintain NRDC containing

- Digital signature certificates of Licensed CAs
- ARL's of licensed CAs.
- Digital signature certificates of end entities of Licensed CAs
- CRLs of end entities of licensed CAs.

Compliance audit

Audit logs of all transactions are maintained to provide an audit trail of all actions, transaction and processes. Audit logs are monitored by the CCA as per procedures detailed in the Operations Manual.

Frequency of entity compliance audit

The CCA shall conduct, half yearly audit of the Security Policy, physical security and planning of its operation; a quarterly audit of its repository.

Topics covered by audit

The CCA shall get its operations audited annually by an auditor and such audit shall include inter–alia:

- security policy and planning;
- physical security;
- technology evaluation;
- Certifying Authority's services administration;
- relevant Certification Practice Statement;

- compliance to relevant Certification Practice Statement;
- contracts/agreements;
- regulations prescribed by the CCA;

Policy requirements of Certifying Authorities Rules, 2000.

Actions taken as a result of deficiency

The CCA shall immediately take appropriate action on the deficiencies pointed out by the audit so as to secure the operations of RCAI and NRDC.

Confidentiality

The CCA collects information about the CAs as part of the application. These data are processed in a way that ensures protection of their private information. All information other than what is published in their licence and digital signature certificate, and in CRL is kept in confidence.

Types of information to be kept confidential

The following information shall be confidential namely:

- CA licence application, whether approved or rejected;
- CA licence application information collected from the CA or elsewhere as part of the registration and verification process but not included in the Digital Signature Certificate information;

Types of information not considered confidential

Information included in public certificates and CRLs of Licensed CAs issued by the RCAI is not considered confidential.

Disclosure of certificate revocation/suspension information

When a certificate is revoked/suspended, a reason code shall be included in the CRL entry for the action. This reason code is not considered confidential and may be shared with all other users and relying parties. However, no other details concerning the revocation are disclosed.

Release to law enforcement officials

Confidential Information shall only be released by the CCA to courts and law enforcement agencies in accordance with applicable legal requirements.

Release as part of civil discovery

No Stipulation

Disclosure upon owner's request

The information related to the CA's certificate would be disclosed by the CCA to a third party, only when required by the CA, with a signed request.

Other information release circumstances

No Stipulation

Intellectual Property Rights

No right or interest in any intellectual property rights are granted to any Licensed CA or any relying party. All rights in intellectual property are reserved . Any content copied from this document should include reference to this source.

Intellectual property rights on the items listed below belong to the CCA according to the Copyright Act and other related regulations:

- Software and hardware developed by CCA
- Certification Practice Statement of CCA
- Name of CCA
- Corporate Name
- Internet Domain Name
- Key pairs created by CCA

Identification and Authentication

Initial Registration

All CA applicants shall fill the 'Form for Application for grant of Licence to be a Certifying Authority' as described in Information Technology (Certifying Authority) Rules, 2000 - Schedule I, supported by such documents and information as required by CCA.

Types of names

Each CA Applicant must have a clearly distinguishable and unique X.501 Distinguished Name (DN) in the certificate subject Name field and in accordance with PKIX Part 1(RFC 2459). Each CA Applicant may use an alternative name via the Subject Alternate Name field, which must also be in accordance with PKIX Part 1. The DN must be in the form of a X.501 printable String and must not be blank. It should have the following structure :-

c=in, o=India PKI, ou=<Licensed CA>

Need for names to be meaningful

The Subject name contained in a Licence CA certificate MUST be meaningful in the sense that the CCA is provided with proper evidence of the association existing between the name and the entity to which it belongs.

Rules for interpreting various name forms

The naming convention used by CCA to identify certificate holders uniquely is ISO/IEC 9595 (X.500) Distinguished Name (DN).

Uniqueness of names

The CCA shall ensure that the set of names is unambiguous. The CCA shall reject a Licence application in the case where the name cannot sufficiently distinguish the Applicant from an existing Licensed CA's

Distinguished Name. The name shall conform to X.500 standards for name uniqueness.

Name claim dispute resolution procedure

The CCA may, by reasonable endeavors, resolve disputes that may arise over the allocation of names and in its discretion may reject, change, re-issue or revoke certificates in relation to any Distinguished Name.

Recognition, authentication and role of trademarks

No Stipulation

Method to prove possession of private key

To establish that the applicants possess valid functioning key pairs, CCA would require applicants to submit a Certificate Signing Request (CSR) in accordance with the PKCS#10 standard. The signing key pair of the Licensed CA shall be stored in FIPS 140-1 level 3 or higher level device. An independent verification shall be performed as a part of the auditing process.

Authentication of organization identity

The documents ensure the authentication of organization identity.

Authentication of individual identity

The documents ensure the authentication of individual identity.

Routine Rekey

Not Applicable

Rekey after Revocation

Not Applicable.

Revocation Request

The authority to revoke the RCAI root certificate rests with the Controller of Certifying Authorities. Licensed CAs shall designate an authority, who can request the revocation of its Licence. The Controller of Certifying Authorities also can authorize the revocation of a Licensed CA under section 25 of the IT Act, 2000.

Operational Requirements

Certificate Application

An application for a certificate is made by filling out the application form as given in Schedule I of the Rules of the IT Act. The form and relevant information can be obtained directly from the office of the CCA or downloaded from the web site of the CCA .

Certificate Application Submission

All applications are to be submitted, in triplicate, physically to the office of the CCA .

As part of the application for grant of Licence, the date by which the applicant will be ready to start the audit will be indicated. The application will be deemed to have been received on this date for processing purposes.

Information required as part of an Application

Each application for issue of a licence to become a CA must be accompanied by documents and information as stipulated in the Guidelines for submission to operate as a CA. In addition to the documents listed in Rule 10, the following documents, among others, may also be furnished.

- Certified true copies of the company's incorporation, articles of association etc.
- Original business profile report with certification from Registrar of Companies.
- Audited accounts for the past 3 years (if applicable).
- The CA's Certification Practice Statement (CPS) as laid down in Annexure I to these Guidelines.
- Technical specifications of the CA system and CA security policies, standards and infrastructure available/proposed and locations of facilities.
- Information Technology and Security Policy proposed to be followed by the CA in its operations under Rule 19.
- Statement addressing the manner in which the CA shall comply with the requirements stipulated in the IT Act, Rules and Regulations.
- Organizational chart and details of all trusted personnel.

Date by which the applicant will be ready for audit to start. The application shall be deemed to have been received on this date for processing purposes. Date by which commencement of CA operations is proposed. Operations can only commence after due compliance with Rule 20. An undertaking by the applicant that they will make payment to the Auditor appointed by the CCA at the rate to be prescribed by the CCA.

Processing of an Application

On receipt of an application, the application and supporting documents/ information will be examined in the office of the CCA with regard to the financial parameters as well as in respect of the information supplied by the applicant in the CPS and other documents.

The financial parameters will be examined by the office of the CCA for compliance with all relevant stipulations in the IT Act.

The remaining information, on successful completion of desk evaluation of legal, regulatory, technical & infrastructure requirements in the office of the CCA, will be handed over for auditing to one of the Auditors empanelled for this purpose by the office of the CCA. Audit will be carried out by the Auditor within the ambit of the Terms & Conditions stipulated by the CCA. The applicant will be informed about the Auditor deputed to carry out the audit. The audit report has to be submitted by the Auditor within 21 Days. Based on the audit report, the results of the financial evaluation, and on the applicant's meeting all technical, financial, infrastructure, legal and regulatory requirement, the CCA will decide whether a Licence is to be issued to the applicant or not. Any shortcomings in conformance as indicated by the Auditor, will be notified to the applicant who will be expected to correct the same and report to the CCA. If the non-conformance is major, then a fresh audit evaluation may be scheduled at a mutually agreed time.

Certificate Issuance

Licence Issuance

On successful completion of evaluation of the application for grant of Licence with respect to qualification, expertise, manpower, financial resources other infrastructure facilities and legal and regulatory requirements, the CCA will commence the process of issuance of Licence.

Paper Licence

Each Licence issued will be accompanied by a certificate digitally signed by the CCA. One of the public keys included for certification will be identified as the primary public key to be certified. The certificate issued by the CCA along with the Licence will contain this public key. The remaining public keys will also be certified through certificates digitally signed by the CCA.

Certificate Issuance

CCA issues the certificate after checking the following criteria, in the case of each of the above public keys.

- A certificate request is generated by the applicant in PKCS # 10 format and submitted to the CCA. The CCA establishes that the public key corresponds to a functioning key pair
- The CCA establishes the uniqueness of the public key being certified.
- The CCA establishes the uniqueness of the DN submitted by the applicant.
- The certificate request is used by the CCA to generate the certificate.
- The certificate is physically handed over to the applicant.
- All certificates issued are published in the National Repository and are accessible through the web site of the CCA.

Validity period: All Licences are valid from the date & time of issue for a period of five years, and will not be, in any case, later than the expiry date of the CCA's Root certificate.

Information in Licence

The paper licence issued by the CCA includes the following :

- Licence serial no.
- Name of the CA
- Address
- Date of issue
- Valid until
- Public Key

The format for the licence serial no. is as follows:

YYYYXXXXD	DMMYYNNNMMMMZZZ		(24 characters)
YYYY	Year of issuance		(serialized based on order of
XXXX	Serial Number allotted to CA		receipt of application)
DDMMYY	Valid until date		(DD)/ month (MM)/ year (YY)
NNN	000	-	Primary Licence
	001, 002 etc.	-	Incremented for each key submitted by the CA for certification. This will be indicated by the CA in it's application.
MMMM	0000	-	in case of fresh licence
	yyyy	-	year of renewal
ZZZ	Reserved for future use		

The digital signature certificate(s) issued by the CCA corresponding to the above licence and other public keys submitted by the CA contain the following information :

- Version
- Serial Number
- Signature Algorithm used by the CCA to sign the certificate
- Issuer (CCA's) DN
- Validity
- Subject information including CA's DN
- Public key of the CA
- Signature of CCA
- Extensions

Validity Period of a Certificate

The licence is valid for a period of five years from the date of its issue. The licence is not transferable.

Certificate Acceptance

The certificate issued by the CCA to the CA applicant will be deemed to have been accepted on its receipt by the CA applicant.

Certificate Suspension and Revocation

The Controller of Certifying Authorities can order, or an Authorized Signatory of the Licensed CA can request, that a certificate be revoked when any of the information it contains is known or suspected to be inaccurate, or when the private key associated with the certificate is compromised or suspected to have been compromised, or in the interests of national security as per the provision under section 25 and 26 of the IT Act, 2000.

Suspension of certificates issued by CCA always precedes revocation but revocation shall follow only under the specific procedures described in this section. All suspension and revocation requests are required to be valid. Such validity shall be determined by their compliance or non-compliance with the procedures of this CPS, which include references to the authority of the person who may make a request.

The CCA may revoke a certificate when it considers revocation necessary or expedient.

Circumstances for Suspension & revocation

Licences can be revoked or suspended by the CCA under Rule 14. The CCA shall revoke a certificate if the CCA has reasons to believe that the CA :

- made a statement in, or in relation to, the application for the issue or renewal of the licence, which is incorrect or false in material particulars;
- failed to comply with the terms and conditions subject to which the licence was granted;
- failed to maintain the standards specified under clause (b) of sub-section (2) of section 20;
- contravened any provisions of the IT Act, Rule, Regulation or orders made there under,
- the private key corresponding to the public key in the certificate has been lost, disclosed without authorization, stolen or compromised in any way.
- the security, trustworthiness or integrity of the CA's PKI is materially affected due to the CA's activities.
- the licence does not meet material obligations of its agreements with CCA, those of any applicable CPS;

there has been an improper or faulty issuance of a certificate due to:

- A material prerequisite to the issuance of the Certificate not being satisfied;

• A material fact in the Certificate is known, or reasonably believed, to be false.

• the licences is bankrupt, being wound-up or is making arrangements or compositions with its creditors;

• the CA does not possess sufficient financial resources to maintain its provision of certification services;

Any other material circumstance that requires investigation to ensure the security, integrity or trustworthiness of the CA's PKI. An investigation into the need for suspension will take place by which the following is carried out:

• Validate the need for suspension and obtaining authorization for the suspension

• On completion of investigation into need for suspension, either certificate is suspended or reinstated with certificate status as valid.

• On suspension of a certificate.

• The reason for the suspension is recorded.

• A CRL (Certificate Revocation List) is immediately generated and published on the Root CA Directory and the NR.

• The CA to which the certificate refers publishes in a prominent manner a suspension notice on its Web Site and its Certification Revocation List distribution point.

• CA to which the certificate refers, notifies its End Users of the suspension.

A notice containing the Certificate details and the date and time of suspension is issued to the subscriber. Pending completion of any inquiry ordered by the CCA, no CA whose certificate has been suspended will issue any certificates during this suspension. The suspension of certificates issued by the CCA Root may occur immediately if the suspension has been requested by the authorized signatory of the licensed CA or after an investigation has taken place.

Who can request suspension

The CCA shall action suspension request from an Authorized signatory of the Licensed CA. The CCA, on his own, can also initiate suspension of a certificate.

Procedure for suspension request

When a suspension or revocation is requested by an authorized signatory of a CA, the suspension or revocation request may be submitted through:

• a digitally signed suspension or request verifiable with the public key contained in the certificate to which the request refers to and performance of an off-line request

• a certificate suspension or request physically delivered to CCA by an appropriately authorized person

Limits on suspension period

Certificates issued by the RCAI of the CCA can remain suspended for a maximum period of ten working days. Upon termination or prior to termination of suspension, CCA will determine whether it should be revoked or reinstated as valid. If on completion of the inquiry, any of the above is established beyond doubt then the certificate may be revoked by the CCA. Revocation of the certificate of a CA can happen for a number of reasons.

- When a CA applies for a certificate revocation
- When the CCA recognizes that a certificate of a CA was issued in an illegal manner.
- When the CCA recognizes the dissolution of a CA
- When the CCA recognizes that a private key of a CA is lost, damaged, stolen or compromised

Who can request revocation

Revocation request from the following parties can be accepted :

- An Authorized signatory of the Licensed CA
- Controller of Certifying Authorities

Procedure for revocation request

When a revocation is requested by any entity external to the CCA, the revocation request may be submitted through:

- A digitally signed revocation request through the communication of compromise of private key by a CA to the CCA verifiable with the public key contained in the certificate to which the request refers to and performance of an off-line request in accordance with procedures designed by CCA for such purpose.
- A certificate suspension or revocation request physically delivered to CCA by an appropriately authorized person.

In processing a revocation request, the Root CA will:

- Revoke the certificate on the Root CA, record the reason for the revocation, and maintain relevant documentation.
- Generate immediately a CRL (Certificate Revocation List) from the Root CA
- Withdraw the certificate from the CCA Web site and place a prominent revocation notice on its place.
- Issue a notice containing the Certificate details and the date and time of revocation to the certificate subscriber.
- Notify the CA that its certificate has been revoked under the provisions of the IT Act.
- Publish the revocation on the National Repository.

Revocation request grace period

Revocation requests shall be processed within one working day of having a definitive decision by the CCA to revoke the certificate in accordance with CCA's operational procedures.

CRL issuance frequency

The CCA shall update the CRL within one working day after a valid revocation request is processed and at least every month, even if no changes to the CRL have been made.

CRL checking requirements

A relying party may check the CCA's CRL for determining the CA's certificate status before relying on any certificate issued by the CA.

On-line revocation/status checking availability

The CCA shall provide on-line certificate status checking through publication in NRDC.

Other forms of revocation advertisements available

On suspension and/or revocation of a certificate issued by the RCAI, the CCA will issue advertisement in at least two national newspapers and one vernacular newspaper in the region where the Licensed CA is established.

Checking requirements for other forms of revocation advertisements

No Stipulation

Special requirements regarding key compromise

The CCA is to be notified immediately by a CA in case of a key compromise.

Security Audit Procedures

Types of event recorded

The minimum audit records of RCAI to be kept include:

- System start-up and shutdown;
- RCAI's application start-up and shutdown;
- Attempts to create, remove, set passwords or change the system privileges of the CA Master Officer, CA Officer, or CA Administrator;
- Changes to keys of the RCAI or any of his other details;
- Changes to Digital Signature Certificate creation policies, e.g. validity period;
- Login and logoff attempts;
- Unauthorized attempts at network access to the RCAI's system;
- Unauthorized attempts to access system files;
- Generation of keys;
- Creation and revocation of Digital Signature Certificates;

Failed read-and-write operations on the Digital Signature Certificate or Certificate Revocation List (CRL) directory.

Records of the following application transactions shall be maintained:

- Registration;
- Certification;
- Publication;
- Suspension; and
- Revocation.

Records and log files shall be reviewed regularly for these activities.

To facilitate decision-making, all agreements and correspondence relating to services provided by RCAI are collected and consolidated at a single location.

Certificate application records, including records relating to rejected applications;

Certificate generation requests, whether or not Certificate generation was successful;

Certificate issuance, suspension and revocation records, including CRLs;

Audit records, including security-related events;

Frequency of processing log

The CCA's audit logs are regularly reviewed by its personnel and all significant events are detailed in an audit log summary. Such reviews verify that the log has not been tampered with, and then briefly inspect all log entries, with a more thorough investigation of any alerts or irregularities in the logs. Action taken following these reviews are documented.

Retention period for audit log

The CCA retains its audit logs onsite for at least twelve months and subsequently retains them in the manner described in the Information Technology Security Guidelines as given in Schedule-II of IT (CA) Rules, 2000.

Protection of audit log

The electronic audit log system includes mechanisms to protect the log files from unauthorized viewing, modification, and deletion. Manual audit information will be protected from unauthorized viewing, modification and destruction.

Audit log backup procedures

CCA uses highly secure systems to maintain the integrity of its electronic audit logs over time and has established a series of security procedures regarding their storage, access and backup.

Audit collection system

The CCA audit collection system is a combination of automated and manual processes. The system is maintained through access control mechanisms and role separations with regard to the software and hardware and through confidential documented operational procedures known and followed by CCA personnel. The control measures of both the automated and the manual processes are audited in accordance with of this CPS.

Notification to event-causing subject

Operations personnel notify the security administrator when a process or action causes a critical security event or discrepancy.

Vulnerability assessments

Events in the audit process are logged, in part, to monitor system vulnerabilities. The RCAI ensures that a vulnerability assessment is performed, reviewed and revised, if necessary, following an examination of these monitored events. A full risk assessment has been completed for the CCA Root CA operations and will be performed at a minimum annually.

Records Archival

Types of event recorded

All significant events are recorded including new officer creation, incident reports, daily events, changes to the environment or system, CCTV recording of CA operations.

All events concerning the operation of CCA Root CA certification services are recorded.

Transactions that meet exception criteria are completely and accurately highlighted and reviewed by personnel independent of those that initiate the transaction.

Adequate audit trails are captured and certain information needed to determine sensitive events and pattern analysis that would indicate possible fraudulent use of the system (e.g. repeated unsuccessful logons, access attempts over a series of days) are analyzed. This information includes such information as who, what, when, where, and any special information such as: Success or failure of the event, Use of authentication keys, where applicable, Automated or manual procedures are used to monitor and promptly report all significant security events, such as accesses, which are out-of-pattern relative to time, volume, frequency, type of information asset, and redundancy. Other areas of analysis include:

- Significant computer system events (e.g. configuration updates, system crashes),
- Security profile changes,
- Actions taken by computer operations,
- system administrators, systems , programmers, and/or security administrators.
- Digital Signature Certificates stored and generated by the RCAI are recorded.

Retention period for archive

All CCA Root CA records concerning the operation of its certification services are archived and are retained for a period of ten (10) years.

Computer system access records shall be kept for a minimum of two years, in either hard copy or electronic form. Records, which are of legal nature and necessary for any legal or regulation requirement or investigation by a law enforcement agency, shall be retained as per provisions of the IT Act.

Protection of archive

All information pertaining to the CCA's operation, CA's application, verification, identification, authentication and CA's agreement to Terms and Conditions of the licence shall be stored within the country. Archive backup procedures. A second copy of all information retained or backed up by CCA shall be stored at a location within the country duly protected either by physical security alone, or a combination of physical and cryptographic protection. The secondary site shall have adequate protection from environmental threats such as temperature, humidity and magnetism. Such a disaster recovery site is under planning.

Requirements for time-stamping of records

The time source GPS clock for the CCA Root CA is independently verified periodically and all electronic automated Root CA records are associated with the time and date of their occurrence. The real time clock of the computer system shall be set accurately to ensure the accuracy of audit logs, which may be required for investigations or as evidence in legal or disciplinary cases. The real time clock of the computer or communications device is set to Indian Standard Time (IST). Further, there is a procedure in place that checks and corrects drift in the real time clock.

Archive collection system

Only authorized and authenticated staff are allowed to handle archive material.

Procedures to obtain and verify archive information

The CCA verifies the integrity of the backups once every six months. Information stored off-site is also periodically verified for data integrity. This is done at least once every six months.

Key changeover

The lifetime of RCAI signing keys is set to five years. On key rollover, a new public key will be made available via the web and through the NRDC.

A Licensed CA may only apply to renew its key within three months prior to the expiration of its Licence, provided the previous certificate has not been revoked. Automated key changeover for Licensed CAs is not permitted.

Compromise and Disaster Recovery

Computing resources, software, and/or data are corrupted

The CCA has established business continuity procedures that outline the steps to be taken in the event of the corruption or loss of computing and networking resources, nominated website, repository, software and/or data.

Entity public key is revoked

In the event of the RCAI private signature key being revoked, the CCA shall revoke and re-issue all certificates in use at that instant.

Entity key is compromised

In the event of the RCAI private signature key being revoked, the CCA shall revoke and re-issue all certificates in use at that instant.

Secure facility after a natural or other type of disaster

In the event of a natural or other type of disaster the operation of RCAI and NRDC will be re-established on an independent disaster recovery site, using the backup data taken on a daily basis from the primary CA site. The recovery time for bringing up the secondary site is targeted to be better than 48 hours. The disaster recovery site is under planning.

CA Termination

In the event of change in government policies, and/or Acts, as a result of which if the CCA is terminated, the CCA shall:

Provide no less than 6 months notice to all current Licensed CA of its intent to cease operations, Ensure the secure preservation and maintenance of all relevant databases, archives, records and documents with an independent custodian and/or designated government body. The CCA archives will be retained in the manner. Provide access to National Repository maintained by the CCA, for a maximum period of 12 months following cessation of services. Revoke all valid certificates at the end of the notice period. Ensure availability and access to relevant CRLs for a period of 12 months following cessation of operations.

Physical, Procedural and Personnel Security Controls

The technical and physical infrastructure of the Root Facility (RF), established for the operation of the Root Certifying Authority of India (RCAI), and the National Repository of Digital Certificates (NRDC) is fully secured in accordance with the requirements laid down under the IT Act.

Physical controls

Site Location and Construction

The Root CA of India (RCAI) operations are being conducted from the Root Facility of CCA. The National Repository (NR) and its operations are conducted from Jawaharlal Nehru Stadium, New Delhi.

Physical access

Physical access to RF for performing RCAI operations is controlled and restricted to the authorized individuals only.
Entry to the working area (WA), anteroom (AR) and the SR are registered in the log register. Entry to the WA is done using an access control system. The log register and access control audit trail files are reviewed regularly.

The 6-tier security for RCAI

Six-tier security has been implemented at the RF.

- Tier 1 – The security of the building where the RF is located, forms the first level of security.
- Tier 2 – Entry to the WA is after entering details to a log register and proper physical verification by the security guard at the entrance. This is the second tier of Security.
- Tier 3 – Entry to the WA is through a proximity access control system. This forms the third tier of security.
- Tier 4 – Entry to SR is through AR. The entry to AR is restricted by twin doors and proximity access control system. This forms the fourth tier of security.
- Tier 5 – The entry to SR is restricted by twin doors and a combination of proximity and biometric access control system. This is the fifth-tier of security.
- Tier 6 – A fire resistant safe is placed inside the SR. This forms the sixth-tier of security.

By-pass or deactivation

The By-pass or deactivation of normal physical security arrangements are authorized and documented.

Trespass detection and alarm system

Access to the site is controlled through proximity cards. In addition, a biometric access system is used for access to the SR, of the authorized personnel.

Vibration sensors along with motion sensing and alert devices have been installed to ensure that no unauthorized personnel can gain access to the SR. In the case of a forceful entry, alert gets activated and is sounded at the designated place.

Sensing and preventive measures for RF.

The RF is monitored using appropriate equipment for surveillance based on various sensors. The sensors installed are:

- Motion sensors
- Vibration sensors
- Smoke sensors

These sensors are connected to an alarm system. On security breach the alarm gets activated. The security guard in the RF and the Chief Security Officer (CSO) take the suitable escalation procedures.

DVR (Digital Video Recorder) system

The RF is constantly monitored using a CCTV system to detect any unusual activities.

HSM and smart card storage at the SR

The Hardware Security Module (HSM) is installed in one of the server in SR. The smart cards in the SR are protected by the tier-6 of security.

At RF, it is ensured that:

Access to RF is restricted to authorized personnel.
The RF is provided with physical security round the clock.

Emergency planning for RF

Following measures are in position to attend to any emergency situation at the RF:

Provisions have been made to provide access to the security guards in case of emergency.

Fire extinguishers are placed at RF to overcome fire hazards. In case of any untoward incident or emergency the designated AC(Tech) will be informed by Security officer and guard. Officers, staff and security guards are given adequate training and routine mock drills are conducted to ensure their readiness.

Power supply and air conditioning

Continuous power supply has been ensured by suitable deployment of UPS and DG set.

Emergency lights are also placed in RF. The air conditioning system installed in the RF is equipped with temperature and humidity control.

Natural disaster protection

Necessary precautions have been taken to protect and prevent the impact of natural disasters such as flood, earthquake etc.

Water exposures

The RF is well protected from potential water related threats.

Fire prevention and protection

Fire alarm system has been installed to handle any emergent situation arising out of fire.

Media storage

Storage media are protected from environment threats such as temperature, humidity and magnetic field. Any media, which is to be transported to National Repository (NR), is done so in secured and tamper proof manner.

Waste disposal

Sensitive documents and materials are shredded before disposal. Media used to collect or transmit sensitive information are rendered unreadable before disposal. HSM and related devices are physically destroyed or zero zed in accordance with the manufacturers' guidance prior to disposal. Other waste is disposed off in accordance with the CCA's normal waste disposal requirements.

Off-site backup for SR

Routine backups of the system data, audit log data, and other sensitive information are performed and stored in a secure place at the CCA's office.

Procedural controls

Trusted roles

The following roles have been identified in connection with RCAI operations at SR:

- Coordinator
- System Administrator
- System Operator
- Auditor

At least two persons are required to perform each critical and routine task in the RCAI operation. DC (T) authorizes all the activities of RCAI operation. For each session DC (T) designates an AC (T) as a coordinator. The AC (T) in turn assigns the roles to various officers

All the officers designated to perform various roles have been issued proximity cards and granted access to specific locations. They are also issued electronic tokens for the session by the coordinator to perform specific functions.

Personnel Controls

Background, qualifications, experience, and clearance requirements

The background, qualifications, and experience of the technical personnel are verified as per the rules and regulations.

Employees Verification/Investigation

CCA has followed appropriate government procedures for appropriate investigation of all personnel

Training Requirements

CCA has provided comprehensive training to all the technical personnel performing duties, in the following areas:

Relevant aspects of the IT Security Policy and Security Guidelines framed in IT (CA) Rules, 2000;

- RCAI related software /hardware training
- RCAI related duties they are expected to perform
- Disaster recovery and continuity procedures.

Re-training frequency and requirements

Refresher training of technical personnel is conducted as and when required, and CCA reviews these requirements on a regular basis.

Sanctions for unauthorized actions

In the event of actual or suspected unauthorized actions by a person performing duties with respect to RCAI operation, access to RF is denied to him/her, with immediate effect. Further actions will be initiated as per government procedures/rules.

Contracting personnel requirements

No contractor is allowed access to RCAI system.

Documentation supplied to personnel

Officers/staff operating SR have been provided with comprehensive user manuals detailing the procedure of certificate creation, update, renewal, suspension, and revocation, and software functionality etc.
Compliance with Security Service Regulations
Office of CCA observes and adheres strictly to 'Security Service Regulations' for the security measures, which are not shown in the Certification Practice Statement.

Technical Security Controls

Key Pair Generation and Installation

Key Pair Generation

Key pair for the CCA is generated in a hardware security module (HSM) which is FIPS 140-1 level 4 certified. Licensed CAs generate their key pairs in a HSM certified to meet the requirements of FIPS 140-1 level 3 certified at minimum.

Private Key Delivery to Entity

Not applicable.

Public Key Delivery from CA (applicant) to CCA

CAs' Public keys are delivered to the CCA as a PKCS#10 certificate request. The signature on the PKCS#10 request is verified to confirm that the CA is in possession of the private key associated with each public key delivered. A certificate is then signed by the CCA and issued to the CA.

Root CA Public Key Delivery to Users

The self-signed Certificate of the CCA is available to End-Users for Certificate validation purposes. The certificate hash (thumbprint) and the Root CA certificate are available on the web site of each licensed CA as well as CCA's Web site (cca.gov.in). Relying parties must confirm the validity of their copy of the CCA certificate using this thumbprint. The CCA Digital signature certificate, along with this CPS and other documentation such as the IT Act, Rules and Regulations are available on CD from the office of the CCA or on CCA's website cca.gov.in. This certificate shall also be made available by each CA and sub-CA on its website to enable verification by relying parties.

Key Sizes

The modulus of the CCA Root CA and the keys of CCA are all 2048 bits in length and use the RSA algorithm. The hash algorithm used by the CCA for signing is SHA-1.

Public Key Parameters Checking

Not Applicable

Parameter Quality Checking

Not Applicable

Hardware/Software Key Generation

Keys are generated in a hardware security module that complies with FIPS 140-1 Level 4.

Key Usage Purposes

The key of the CCA will be used for:

- The issuance of certificates to the Certification Authorities that have been Licensed.
- Issuance of Certificate Revocation Lists

Private Key Protection

Standards for Cryptographic Module

The cryptographic module used by the CCA is certified to FIPS 140-1 level 4.

Private Key (n out of m) Multi-person Control

The private key stored on the HSM does not leave the HSM for any purpose whatsoever. Whenever the private key on the HSM is to be used for signing, three levels (?) of authorizations (based on smart cards and PINs) will be invoked. The first will be at the 'Crypto-Officer' level specifically for activating the HSM. The second two will be at the 'Security Officer' level of the Certificate Issuing System (CIS). All three authorizations are required, thus establishing 3-out-of-3 control.

Private Key Backup

CCA's Private Key is backed up only for disaster recovery purposes. This backup is also done under the same multi person control as in the case of the original key. During key generation, the HSM is configured to generate 3 sets of smart cards, containing backup keys. The first 2 sets are housed in the Strong Room containing the CIS and the backup system, while the 3rd set will be placed in the Disaster Recovery site.

Private Key Archival

The Root Private Key will not be archived.

Private Key Entry into Cryptographic Module

Private key for the CCA is generated in Hardware Security Modules as described in CPS. The HSM is sensitive to motion, tilting and temperature. To ensure that the private key does not get destroyed, it is ensured that the HSM is maintained within the limits set for the above three parameters.

Method of Activating Private Key

CCA Private key activation requires entry and validation of a PIN/pass phrase compliant with specified security parameters. CCA's private key for signing can only be activated by authorization at three levels of trusted persons. Two Security officers at the level of the CIS.

One Crypto officer at the HSM level. All the above authorizations will be through smart cards and associated PINs.

Method of Deactivating Private Key

The CCA Private key is deactivated after each use by manually shutting down the system.

Method of Destroying Private Key

The CCA Private key in the HSM may be destroyed by returning the HSM to its factory initialized state. Smart Cards and other cryptographic tokens used by the CCA will be physically destroyed prior to disposal. The HSM can be destroyed through motion, tilting or temperature changes outside preset limits. Other than this, destroying the lithium battery on the HSM, will also destroy the private key from the HSM.

Other Aspects of Key Pair Management

Public Key Archival

All public keys of the CCA will be archived.

Usage Periods for the Public and Private Key

The Root key pair of the CCA and certificate will expire after 15 years from the moment of their generation.

Activation Data

Activation Data Generation and Installation

Not applicable

Activation Data Protection

Not applicable.

Computer Security Controls

Specific Computer Security Technical Requirements

CCA has established and documented all computer security technical controls implemented for the Root CA as specified in IT Security Guidelines of IT (CA) Rules, 2000.

Life Cycle Technical Controls

System Development Controls

Not Applicable

Security management controls

Security management controls are enforced by rigid separation of operator roles.

- Security Officer
- Registration Officer
- System Administrator

Network Security Controls

The CCA's Root is maintained and operated off-line and is not networked with any external components. The National Repository Service is maintained on-line and uses firewalls and other mechanisms for connections to un trusted networks including the Internet. These connections are further secured by using intrusion detection systems where applicable. The configuration and access control to these network security devices is strictly controlled and limited to authorized personnel only.

Cryptographic Module Engineering Controls

The cryptographic module used by the CCA is certified to FIPS 140-1 level 4.

Certificate, Certificate Suspension and Revocation List Profile

Certificate Profile

Version number(s)

CCA issues certificates in conformance with X.509 version 3 and RFC 2459.

Certificate Extensions

Certificate Extension used are

- Key Usage Marked critical
- Basic Constraints with a path Len Constraint of '0' marked critical
- Policy Constraint marked critical
- Alternate Identity marked critical

Algorithm object Identifiers

Certificates shall be signed using the RSA algorithm

Name Forms

CCA shall populate the name constraint field in the certificates with directory names.

Name Constraints

RCAI does not support anonymous names. Names must be meaningful and must be associated with the subscriber. Names are constrained to be unique Distinguished Names (DN)

Certificate policy object Identifier

All certificates issued in accordance with this Certification Practice statement shall reference the OID for this policy

Usage of Policy Object Identifier

The Policy Constraint is marked critical to ensure that all certificate holders and relying parties are aware of the requirement to conform with this CPS.

Policy qualifiers syntax and semantics

None in the present version.

Processing semantics for the critical certificate policy extension

None in the present version.

Certificate Format

An issued certificate shall contain:

- The identify of the Licensed CA
- Copy of the public key of the Licensed CA
- Unique distinguished name
- Validity period of no longer than five years from the date of issue
- Unique certificate serial number
- Digital signature of RCAI
- For future use.

CRL Profile / Certificate Suspension and Revocation List Profile

Version number(s)

The CCA issues CRLs in conformance with X.509 Ver. 2 CRLs.

CRL and CRL entry extensions

None

Specification Administration

Specification change procedures

CCA will periodically review the CPS in light of policy and/or infrastructure technology change. The CPS will be revised if required. The revision-related record of the Certification Practice Statement will be maintained and will include the following:

- Latest Version of the Certification Practice Statement with version no.
- Revised contents with changes highlighted
- Revision record of the Certification Practice Statement
- Previous versions of the Certification Practice Statement

Publication and notification policies

The revised Certification Practice Statement will be made available by the CCA to the user community through publication on CCA's website. CCA also notifies the CAs about the revised Certification Practice Statement. The revised Certification Practice Statement is in force from the date and time of publication on CCA's website.

CPS approval procedures

Items that can change without notification

Editorial, typographical corrections or changes to the contact details shall be made to this Certification Practice Statement without notification.

Changes with notification

The CCA shall give a minimum of 45 days notice to the certificate holders of any substantial changes made to the certification practice statement.

Changes to items, which in the judgment of the CCA will not materially impact a substantial majority of certificate holders may be changed on a minimum 30 days notice. While changes required by law, or those in the judgment of the CCA required to be implemented for the benefit of certificate holders may be made with a reasonable notice period.